PENGUIN BOOKS

A WORLD ON FIRE

'It rolls along with the ragged grandeur of one of Ulysses S. Grant's infantry battalions. If you've an appetite for serious history, you'll be in hog-heaven' Sam Leith, *Spectator*

'If Amanda Foreman, author of the best-selling biography *Georgiana, Duchess Of Devonshire*, set out to enhance her academic reputation, she has succeeded . . . Foreman draws deeply on a wide-range of contemporary letters, memoirs and sketches to produce graphic and haunting descriptions of the carnage of battle' Christopher Hudson, *Daily Mail*

'A passionate and trenchant analysis of the complex and much misunderstood British involvement in the American civil war' *Economist*, Books of the Year

'Marvellous . . . What is most impressive of all is Foreman's ability to keep her multi-faceted narrative and her vast array of characters under control. There are so many fascinating aspects to this story and Foreman does justice to them all. Humble individuals are portrayed with as much care as leading figures, enriching anecdotal evidence is afforded as much attention as the explanation of complex historical forces. *A World on Fire* is a staggering achievement' Christopher Silvester, *Daily Express*

'*A World on Fire* is remarkable above all for putting a human face on one of the most brutal conflicts in history. Foreman's book reminds us – if we currently needed reminding – that though united by language and shared heritage, there is much that separates Britons and Americans' Mark Bostridge, *The Times Literary Supplement*

'This book of nearly 1,000 pages is as comprehensive as any single study can be . . . The key players in the conflict are meticulously analysed, not only for their ideas, motivations and strategies, but also for their personalities and appearance. There is much that is new in this epic book. Foreman's archive-rich evocation of this civil war is an eloquent testimony to her powers as an historian and storyteller' Joanna Bourke, *The Times*

ABOUT THE AUTHOR

AMANDA FOREMAN

A World On Fire

An Epic History of
Two Nations Divided

PENGUIN BOOKS

PENGUIN BOOKS

Published by the Penguin Group
Penguin Books Ltd, 80 Strand, London WC2R ORL, England
Penguin Group (USA) Inc., 375 Hudson Street, New York, New York 10014, USA
Penguin Group (Canada), 90 Eglinton Avenue East, Suite 700, Toronto, Ontario,
Canada M4P 2Y3 (a division of Pearson Penguin Canada Inc.)
Penguin Ireland, 25 St Stephen's Green, Dublin 2, Ireland (a division of Penguin Books Ltd)
Penguin Group (Australia), 250 Camberwell Road, Camberwell,
Victoria 3124, Australia (a division of Pearson Australia Group Pty Ltd)
Penguin Books India Pvt Ltd, 11 Community Centre,
Panchsheel Park, New Delhi – 110 017, India
Penguin Group (NZ), 67 Apollo Drive, Rosedale, Auckland 0632, New Zealand
(a division of Pearson New Zealand Ltd)
Penguin Books (South Africa) (Pty) Ltd, 24 Sturdee Avenue,
Rosebank, Johannesburg 2196, South Africa

Penguin Books Ltd, Registered Offices: 80 Strand, London WC2R ORL, England

www.penguin.com

First published by Allen Lane 2010
Published in Penguin Books 2011
1

Copyright © Amanda Foreman, 2010

or t...   ...al,

A CIP catalogue record for this book is available from the British Library

ISBN: 978-0-141-04058-5

www.greenpenguin.co.uk

For the children

Contents

Contents

PART I
Cotton is King

PART II
Fire All around Them

PART III
If Only We Are Spared

CONTENTS

List of Illustrations

xi

List of Plates

ENDPAPERS

List of Maps

Introduction

Some years ago, while researching the life of Georgiana, Duchess of Devonshire, I learned that her great-nephew, later the 8th Duke of Devonshire, had spent Christmas Day 1862 making eggnog for the Confederate cavalry officers of General Robert E. Lee's army. 'I hope Freddy [his younger brother, Lord Frederick Cavendish] won't groan much over my rebel sympathies, but I can't help them,' he wrote to his father three days later. 'The people here are so much more earnest about the [war] than the North seems to be.'

I was aware that the American Civil War had sharply polarized public opinion in Britain (my original doctoral thesis had examined attitudes to race and colour in pre-Victorian England), but it was still a shock to discover that the heir to the greatest Liberal peerage in England thought the slave-holding South had the moral advantage over the anti-slavery North. Understanding how the Confederacy had managed to achieve this ascendency, not only with the Duke but also with people who might generally be considered as belonging to the 'progressive' classes in Britain – journalists, writers, university students, actors, social reformers and even the clergy – became one of the driving obsessions behind this book.

My original intention was to write a history of the British volunteers who fought in the Civil War. I had assumed that by examining their reasons for joining the Union or Confederate armies, I would gain an insight into the forces that had shaped public opinion. But once I began, the book refused to stay within its intended confines, especially as it became clear that these volunteers were part of an Anglo-American world that was far greater and more complex than I had ever imagined. It gradually became a biography of a relationship or, more accurately, of the many relationships that together formed the British-American experience during the Civil War.

The war began on 12 April 1861, when Confederate troops fired on the Federal garrison at Fort Sumter in Charleston, South Carolina. The ensuing four-year struggle would lead to the freedom of four million slaves and cost the lives of more than 620,000 soldiers and 50,000 civilians. President Abraham Lincoln responded to the attack on Fort Sumter by calling for 75,000 volunteer soldiers and declaring a blockade of Southern ports. Across the Atlantic, however, Lord Palmerston's Liberal government was chiefly concerned with ensuring that Britain did not become embroiled in the conflict. There was too much at stake: the livelihoods of 900,000 workers depended on Southern cotton, while British investors held $444 million of US stocks and securities. On 13 May, reflecting a rare moment of unanimity between Parliament, the press and the public, Queen Victoria issued a proclamation of neutrality which recognized that a state of war existed between the Union and the Confederacy, and forbade British subjects from taking part. But this well-meaning act had precisely the opposite effect of what was intended. Both sides accused Britain of favouring the other: the North threatened to invade Canada in retaliation, the South used every legal loophole to build its warships in British dockyards, and Britons ignored the injunction against interfering to volunteer in their thousands in the Union and Confederate armies. Twice in four years Britain and the North were on the brink of war; the first time, in December 1861, British troops were already halfway to Canada by the time the two governments backed down.

Biography is a subset of history, and yet it stands independently, too. The most obvious difference is that biographers delve deeply into individual lives and the influences that shaped them, whereas for historians it is the sum of individual experiences that is important. In *A World On Fire* I have tried to combine both approaches. I decided from the beginning to treat each of the significant figures, and many of the lesser ones, as though he or she was the principal subject of the book, so that I could understand the antecedents of their motives and decisions during the Civil War. This not only added several years to the project, but also created the problem of how to construct a single narrative out of competing points of view, within a timeframe that encompassed multiple simultaneous events. The challenge seemed insurmountable until one day I remembered how years before I had seen Trevor Nunn's 1980 production of *Nicholas Nickleby*, an extraordinary 'theatre-in-the-round' which brought together a vast panoply of characters through a combination of three-dimensional staging, shifting scenes and running narratives that created an all-enveloping experience for the audience. This memory became my guide and inspiration, and I set about writing a history-in-the-round in the hope of being able to immerse the reader inside the British-American world of the Civil War. I was fortunate that many areas of this world had already been researched by Brian Jenkins, Howard Jones, R. J. M. Blackett, Charles Hubbard, D. P. Crook, Frank Merli, Warren F. Spencer, Norman Ferris and others. My debt to their pioneering work cannot be overstated, though any omissions or errors in this book are mine alone.

I am deeply grateful to Eve and Michael Williams-Jones, Hugh Dubrulle, Jonathan Foreman, Brian Jenkins, James McPherson, Christopher Mason, Michael Musick, Fredric Smoler and Richard Snow for their help and criticisms of early versions of *A World On Fire*. The book took twelve years to complete and I owe heartfelt thanks to Andrew Wylie, Sarah Chalfant and Jeffrey Posternak of The Wylie Agency for their loyalty during all that time. True to the spirit of the book, *A World On Fire* was simultaneously edited by Susanna Porter at Random House in New York and Stuart Proffitt at Allen Lane in London: it has been a profoundly rewarding and intellectually satisfying process to work with them both. Over the years I have benefited enormously from the help and guidance provided by librarians and archivists all over the world, and they are thanked by name in the acknowledgments section. My family have been a tremendous support to me, but there is one person who, above all, made this book possible, and that is my husband, Jonathan; the centre of *my* world.

Dramatis Personae

Diplomats, Commissioners and Agents

Charles Francis Adams (1807–86) UNION – Minister at the US legation in London 1861–68; son of President John Quincy Adams; grandson of President John Adams; married Abigail Brooks and had six children including John Quincy, Charles Francis Jr., Louise, Henry, Mary and Brooks.

Charles Francis Adams Jr. (1835–1915) UNION – Captain in the 1st Massachusetts Cavalry; later Colonel of the 5th Massachusetts (Colored) Cavalry; son of Charles Francis Adams.

Henry Adams (1838–1918) UNION – Author, journalist and historian; private secretary at the US legation in London to his father, Charles Francis Adams.

Edward Anderson (1813–82) CONFEDERATE – Purchasing agent for the Confederate navy in England, 1861.

William H. Aspinwall (1807–75) UNION – Northern shipowner, sent to England to prevent the Confederacy from purchasing ships.

August Belmont (1813–90) UNION – New York financier and US agent for the Rothschilds.

John Bigelow (1817–1911) UNION – US Consul in Paris, 1861–4; Minister at the US legation in Paris, 1865–6.

Irvine Bulloch (1842–98) CONFEDERATE – Youngest officer on the CSS *Alabama*; half-brother of James Dunwoody Bulloch.

James Dunwoody Bulloch (1823–1901) CONFEDERATE – Chief Confederate secret service agent in England and architect of the Confederate naval acquisition programme in Europe.

Clement Claiborne Clay (1789–1866) CONFEDERATE – US Senator from Alabama, 1853–61; Confederate Senator from Alabama, 1862–4; Confederate Commissioner in Canada, 1864–5.

George Mifflin Dallas (1792–1864) UNION – Minister at the US legation in London, 1856–61.

William Lewis Dayton (1807–64) UNION – Minister at the US legation in Paris, 1861–4.

Edwin De Leon (1818–91) CONFEDERATE – US Consul in Cairo 1853–61; Confederate propagandist in England and France, 1862–4.

Thomas Haines Dudley (1819–93) UNION – US Consul in Liverpool, England, 1861–5; co-head of the US secret service with Freeman H. Morse.

Ambrose Dudley Mann (1801–89) CONFEDERATE – US Assistant Secretary of State, 1853–5; Confederate Commissioner to Belgium, 1861–5.

William Maxwell Evarts (1818–1901) UNION – New York lawyer, sent to England to liaise with Crown prosecution lawyers in the *Alexandria* trial in 1863.

John Murray Forbes (1813–98) UNION – Influential businessman; sent to England to prevent the Confederacy from purchasing ships.

Rose O'Neal Greenhow (1817–64) CONFEDERATE – Washington society leader and Confederate spy.

James Holcombe (1820–73) CONFEDERATE – Confederate Commissioner in Canada, 1864; former law professor at the University of Virginia.

Henry Hotze (1833–87) CONFEDERATE – Confederate propagandist, sent to England in 1862; editor of the pro-Southern *Index*.

Caleb Huse (1831–1905) CONFEDERATE – Purchasing agent for the Confederate army in England.

Colin McRae (1813–77) CONFEDERATE – Confederacy's chief financial agent in Europe, 1863–5.

James Murray Mason (1798–1871) CONFEDERATE – Senator from Virginia, 1847–61; Confederate Commissioner in Britain, 1861–5; with Slidell, one of the two subjects of the *Trent* affair.

Benjamin Moran (1820–86) UNION – Assistant Secretary at the US legation in London, 1857–64, and Secretary, 1864–74.

Freeman Harlow Morse (1807–91) UNION – US Consul in London, 1861–9; co-head with Thomas Haines Dudley of the US secret service.

John Lothrop Motley (1814–77) UNION – Historian; US Minister to the Austrian Empire, 1861–7.

Pierre Adolphe Rost (1797–1868) CONFEDERATE – Confederate Commissioner to France, 1861, and subsequently to Spain, 1862–5.

Henry Shelton Sanford (1823–91) UNION – US Minister at the US legation in Brussels; set up US secret service in operations in England and then in Belgium, 1862–5.

John Slidell (1793–1871) CONFEDERATE – Confederate Commissioner to France; captured, with Mason, aboard the *Trent*.

Jacob Thompson (1810–85) CONFEDERATE – Colonel in Confederate army; head of clandestine operations in Canada.

Norman Walker (1831–1913) CONFEDERATE – Major in Confederate army; shipping agent in Bermuda; husband of Georgiana Walker.

Thurlow Weed (1797–1882) UNION – Adviser to Seward; unofficial envoy to France with Archbishop Hughes, Bishop McIlvaine and General Winfield Scott, 1861.

Charles Wilson (1818–78) UNION – Illinois newspaper editor; Secretary to the US legation in London, 1861–4.

William Lowndes Yancey (1814–63) CONFEDERATE – Confederate Commissioner to Britain and France, 1861–5.

Military

Nathaniel Prentice Banks (1816–94) UNION – Commander of the Department of the Gulf, 1862–4.

Braxton Bragg (1817–76) CONFEDERATE – Principal Confederate commander in the Western theatre of the war; commander of the Department of Western Florida and the Army of Pensacola, 1861; commander of the Army of Mississippi and the Army of Tennessee, 1862–3; chief military adviser to Jefferson Davis, 1864–5.

John Yates Beall (1835–65) CONFEDERATE – Confederate privateer.

Pierre Gustave Toutant Beauregard (1818–93) CONFEDERATE – First prominent general of the Confederacy, 1861–5; hero of Fort Sumter and First Battle of Bull Run; commander in the defence of Charleston.

Ambrose Everett Burnside (1824–81) UNION – Brigadier General and commander of the Army of the Potomac, 1861–3; commander of the Department of the Ohio, 1863–4; his prodigious whiskers allegedly inspired the word 'sideburns'.

Benjamin Franklin Butler (1818–93) UNION – Commander of Fort Monroe, 1861; administrator of the occupation of New Orleans; commander of the Department of Virginia and North Carolina, 1863, later designated the Army of the James, 1864.

Josiah Gorgas (1818–83) CONFEDERATE – Chief of the Confederate Ordnance Bureau.

Ulysses S. Grant (1822–85) UNION – Commander of the Army of the Tennessee, 1862–3 and the Military Division of the Mississippi, 1863–4; commanding general of the US army, 1864–9. Known as 'Unconditional Surrender Grant' because of the terms he offered to the defeated Confederates at Fort Donelson.

Henry Wager Halleck (1815–72) UNION – Commander of the Department of the Missouri, 1861–2, and the Department of the Mississippi, 1862; general-in-chief of all Union armies, 1862–4; chief of staff, 1864–5; known as 'Old Brains' for his treatise on military theory.

John William Headley (1841–1930) CONFEDERATE – Captain in General John Hunt Morgan's brigade; participated in the plot to bomb New York in 1864.

Thomas Henry Hines (1838–98) CONFEDERATE – Spy sent to Canada, via Chicago, to recruit propagandists and fighters for the South.

James Longstreet (1821–1904) CONFEDERATE – Commander of the Department of Virginia and North Carolina, 1863; commander of the Department of East Tennessee, 1863–4; principal subordinate to General Lee, who called him 'Old War Horse'. Also known as 'Old Pete'.

Thomas Jonathan 'Stonewall' Jackson (1824–63) CONFEDERATE – Leader of the 1862 Valley Campaign; commander of the Army of Northern Virginia under Robert E. Lee, 1862–3; nicknamed 'Stonewall' after the First Battle of Manassas.

Albert Sidney Johnston (1803–62) CONFEDERATE – Commander of the Western Department, 1861; led the Army of the Mississippi to defend Confederate lines from the Mississippi river to Kentucky and the Allegheny Mountains.

Joseph Eggleston Johnston (1807–91) CONFEDERATE – Commander of the Army of the Shenandoah, 1861; commander of the Army of the Potomac (later rechristened the Army of Northern Virginia), 1862; commander of the Department of the West, which gave him control over the Army of the Tennessee and the Department of Mississippi and East Louisiana.

Fitzhugh Lee (1835–1905) CONFEDERATE – Rose from lieutenant colonel to major-general of the 1st Virginia Cavalry, 1861–5; nephew of Robert E. Lee.

Robert Edward Lee (1807–70) CONFEDERATE – Commander of the Army of Northern Virginia, 1862–5; general-in-chief of Confederate forces, 1865.

George Brinton McClellan (1826–85) UNION – Commander of the Department of the Ohio, 1861; commander of the Department of the Potomac, July 1861–November 1862; general-in-chief of the Union army, November 1861–March 1862.

Irvin McDowell (1818–85) UNION – Commander of the Army of Northeastern Virginia, 1861; commander of the Army of the Potomac, 1861–2.

George Gordon Meade (1815–72) UNION – Commander of the Army of the Potomac, 1863–5; defeated General Lee at the Battle of Gettysburg; nicknamed 'The Old Snapping Turtle' for his hair-trigger temper.

George Washington Morgan (1820–93) UNION – Commander of the 7th Division of the Army of the Ohio, 1862–3; commander of the 3rd Division of the Union army's 13th Corps, 1863.

John Hunt Morgan (1825–64) CONFEDERATE – Colonel and brigadier general, 2nd Kentucky Cavalry Regiment, 1862–4; commander of the Trans-Allegheny Department, 1864; known for instigating 'Morgan's raid'.

John Singleton Mosby (1833–1916) CONFEDERATE – Commanded the 43rd Battalion, 1st Virginia Cavalry (known as the Partisan Rangers), 1863–5; nicknamed the 'Gray Ghost'.

John Pope (1822–92) UNION – Commander of the District of North and Central Missouri, 1861–1862; commander of the Army of the Mississippi, 1862; commander of the Army of Virginia, 1862.

Winfield Scott (1786–1866) UNION – Commanding general of the US army, 1841–61.

Phillip Henry Sheridan (1831–88) UNION – Commander of the 3rd Division, 14th Corps, Army of the Cumberland, 1862–3; commander of the 2nd Division, 4th Corps, Army of the Cumberland, 1863–4; commander of the Army of the Shenandoah, 1864–5.

William Tecumseh Sherman (1820–91) UNION – Brigadier general of the Army of the Tennessee, 1862; commander of the Department of the Tennessee, 1863–4; commander of the Military Division of the Mississippi, 1864–5.

James Ewell Brown ('Jeb') Stuart (1833–64) CONFEDERATE – Commander of the 1st Virginia Cavalry Regiment, 1861; commander of the Virginia Cavalry Brigade, 1861–2; commander of the Virginia Cavalry Division, 1862–3; commander of the Virginia Cavalry Corps, 1863–4.

Politicians

Judah Philip Benjamin (1811–84) CONFEDERATE – The second Jewish Senator in US history; Confederate Attorney General, 1861; Secretary of War, 1861–2; and Secretary of State, 1862–5.

John Cabell Breckinridge (1821–75) CONFEDERATE – Confederate Secretary of War, 1865.

Salmon Portland Chase (1808–73) UNION – US Secretary of the Treasury, 1861–4.

Jefferson Davis (1808–89) CONFEDERATE – President of the Confederate States, 1861–5.

John Adams Dix (1798–1879) UNION – Military governor of New York.

Edward Everett (1794–1865) – US Secretary of State, 1852–3; US Senator from

Massachusetts, 1853–4; celebrated educator and orator, famous for his two-hour speech before Lincoln's Gettysburg Address.

Abraham Lincoln (1809–65) UNION – First Republican President of the United States, 1861–5.

Stephen Russell Mallory (1813–73) CONFEDERATE – Confederate Secretary of the Navy, 1861–5.

James Alexander Seddon (1815–80) CONFEDERATE – Confederate Secretary of War, 1862–5.

Frederick William Seward (1830–1915) UNION – US Assistant Secretary of State, 1861–9 and 1877–9; son of William H. Seward.

William Henry Seward (1801–72) UNION – US Secretary of State, 1861–9.

Edwin Stanton (1814–69) UNION – US Secretary of War, 1862–5.

Charles Sumner (1811–74) UNION – US Senator from Massachusetts, 1851–74.

George Alfred Trenholm (1807–76) CONFEDERATE – Confederate Secretary of the Treasury 1864–5; founder of Fraser, Trenholm and Co.

Robert Augustus Toombs (1810–85) CONFEDERATE – Confederate Secretary of State, February–July 1861.

Clement Laird Vallandigham (1820–71) UNION – US House of Representatives, 3rd District Ohio, 1858–63; head of the Copperhead anti-war movement.

LeRoy Pope Walker (1817–84) CONFEDERATE – Confederate Secretary of War, February–September 1861.

Gideon Welles (1802–78) UNION – US Secretary of the Navy, 1861–9.

Pro-Northern Supporters

Edwin Thomas Booth (1833–93) – Actor; brother of John Wilkes Booth.

Frederick Douglass (1818–95) – Former slave; social reformer and abolition campaigner.

Horace Greeley (1811–72) – Editor of the *New York Herald*.

Sarah Parker Remond (1826–94) – Campaigner for abolition.

George Templeton Strong (1820–75) – Lawyer, co-founder and treasurer of the US Sanitary Commission.

Pro-Southern Supporters

Belle Boyd (1844–1900) – Confederate spy.

Mary Boykin Chesnut (1823–86) – South Carolinian diarist.

William Wilkins Glenn (1824–76) – Maryland journalist; conduit for British travellers entering the South.

John B. Jones (1810–66) – Virginian diarist; clerk in the War Department, Richmond, Virginia.

Charles Kuhn Prioleau (1827–87) – Head of Fraser, Trenholm and Co., Liverpool, England.

John R. Thompson (1828–73) – Poet, editor of the *Southern Literary Messenger*, 1847–59; contributor to the *Index*.

At Sea

David Glasgow Farragut (1801–70) UNION – Admiral on the USS *Hartford*, 1862–6.

John Newland Maffitt (1819–86) CONFEDERATE – Captain of the CSS *Florida*.

Matthew Fontaine Maury (1806–73) CONFEDERATE – Oceanographer; Confederate purchasing agent in Britain.

William Lewis Maury (1813–78) CONFEDERATE – Commander of the CSS *Georgia*.

James Morris Morgan (1845–1928) CONFEDERATE – Lieutenant on the CSS *Georgia*.

David Dixon Porter (1813–91) UNION – Commander of the USS *Powhatan*; rear admiral of the Mississippi River Squadron.

Raphael Semmes (1809–77) CONFEDERATE – Commander of the CSS *Sumter*, 1861–2; Captain of the CSS *Alabama*, 1862–4.

Charles Wilkes (1798–1877) UNION – Captain of USS *San Jacinto*; instigator of the *Trent* affair.

John Ancrum Winslow (1811–73) UNION – Captain of the USS *Kearsarge*; sank the CSS *Alabama*.

BRITISH

Diplomats

Sir Edward Mortimer Archibald (1810–94) –British Consul at New York, 1857–71.

Robert Bunch – British Consul at Charleston, South Carolina, 1853–64.

Joseph Hume Burnley – Secretary of the British legation, Washington.

Richard Bickerton Pemell Lyons, 2nd Lord Lyons (1817–87) – Minister at the British legation, Washington, 1859–65.

Edward Baldwin Malet (1837–1908) – Attaché at the British legation, Washington, 1862–4.

Charles Stanley Monck, 4th Viscount Monck (1819–94) – Governor General of Canada, 1867–9.

William Mure (1813–64) – British Consul at New Orleans, Louisiana, 1843–57.

Francis Napier, 10th Lord Napier (1819–98) – Minister at the British legation, Washington, 1857–9.

Arthur H. Seymour – Third Secretary of the British legation, Washington.

George Sheffield – Attaché at the British legation, Washington, 1859–64.

William Stuart (1824–96) – Secretary of the British legation, Washington, 1861–4.

Henry Wellesley, 1st Earl Cowley (1804–84) – British Ambassador to France, 1852–67.

Journalists

John Chandler Bancroft Davis (1822–1907) – Pro-Northern correspondent, *The Times*, 1861.

Samuel Phillips Day – Pro-Southern British correspondent, *Morning Herald*, 1861.

John Thadeus Delane (1817–79) – Editor of *The Times*, 1841–77.

Edward James Stephen Dicey (1832–1911) – Pro-Northern contributor, *Spectator*.

The Hon. Francis Charles Lawley (1825–1901) – Pro-Southern contributor, *The Times*.

Charles Mackay (1814–89) – Pro-Southern New York correspondent, *The Times*, 1862–5.

Harriet Martineau (1802–76) – Writer, social theorist and contributor to the *Edinburgh Review* and the *Daily News*, 1852–68.

Mowbray Morris (1819–74) – Managing editor of *The Times*.

William Howard Russell (1820–1907) – Celebrated war reporter for *The Times*.

George Augustus Henry Sala (1828–95) – Novelist, pro-Southern contributor, *Daily Telegraph*; ghost writer for several pro-Southern memoirs.

Tom Taylor (1817–80) – Journalist and contributor to *Punch*, playwright, author of *Our American Cousin*, 1858.

Frank Vizetelly (1830–83) – War artist and correspondent, *Illustrated London News*.

Observers

Thomas Conolly (1823–76) – Member of Parliament for the County of Donegal.

Griffith Evans (1835–1935) – Veterinarian officer, Royal Artillery, British army.

Arthur James Lyon Fremantle (1835–1901) – Lieutenant colonel, British army; member of Her Majesty's Coldstream Regiment of Foot Guards; observer of the Battle of Gettysburg and the New York Draft Riots, April–July 1863.

Spencer Compton Cavendish, 8th Duke of Devonshire, Marquess of Hartington (1833–1908) – Civil Lord of the Admiralty, 1863; British Under-Secretary for War, 1863–6.

George Alfred Lawrence (1827–76) – British lawyer and novelist; author of *Guy Livingstone*, 1857.

Edward Fitzgerald Turton Ross (1835–?) – Captain, Austrian Hussars; Confederate propagandist and observer, 1863–4.

Lord Edward Percy St Maur (1841–65) – Captain, volunteer cavalry, British army; diplomat.

Edward Lyulph Stanley, 4th Baron Sheffield, 4th Baron Stanley of Alderly, and 3rd Baron Eddisbury (1839–1925) – British peer and Member of Parliament for Oldham, 1880–85.

Leslie Stephen (1832–1904) – Author, literary critic and editor of the *Dictionary of National Biography*, 1885–91.

Henry Yates Thompson (1838–1928) – Owner of the *Pall Mall Gazette*, 1878–92; observer of the Second Battle of Chattanooga, 1863.

Garnet Wolseley, 1st Viscount Wolseley (1833–1913) – Field marshal, British army; special service officer sent to Canada following the *Trent* affair, 1861; Pro-Southern observer, 1862–5.

Politicians

George John Douglas Campbell, 8th Duke of Argyll (1823–1900) LIBERAL – Lord Privy Seal, 1853–5, 1859–66, and 1880–81; Postmaster General, 1855–8.

John Bright (1811–89) LIBERAL – Manufacturer; Liberal Member of Parliament, and co-founder, with Richard Cobden MP, of the Anti-Corn Law League, 1836.

George William Frederick Villiers, 4th Earl of Clarendon (1800–1870) LIBERAL – Secretary of State for Foreign Affairs, 1853–8, 1865–6, and 1868–70.

Richard Cobden (1804–65) LIBERAL – Businessman, Liberal Member of Parliament, and co-founder, with John Bright, of the Anti-Corn Law League, 1836; he and John Bright were known derisively in the House of Commons as 'Members for the United States'.

Edward Smith Geoffrey Smith-Stanley, 14th Earl of Derby (1799–1869) CONSERVATIVE – Prime Minister, February–December 1852, 1858–9 and 1866–8.

Benjamin Disraeli, 1st Earl of Beaconsfield (1804–81) CONSERVATIVE – Leader of the Opposition in the House of Commons, 1851–2, 1852–8, 1859–66; Chancellor of the Exchequer, 1852, 1858–9, 1866–8; Prime Minister, 1868, 1874–80.

William Edward Forster (1818–86) LIBERAL – Industrialist; Member of Parliament for Bradford, Yorkshire, 1861–85.

William Ewart Gladstone (1809–98) LIBERAL – Chancellor of the Exchequer, 1852–5, 1859–66; Prime Minister, 1868–74, 1880–85.

William Henry Gregory (1817–92) CONSERVATIVE – Pro-Southern Member of Parliament for Dublin City, 1842–7, and County Galway, 1857–72.

Edmund Hammond, 1st and Last Baron Hammond of Kirkella (1802–90) LIBERAL – Permanent Under-Secretary of Foreign Affairs, 1854–73.

John Laird (1805–74) CONSERVATIVE – Pro-Southern Member of Parliament for Birkenhead, 1861–74; founder of John Laird, Sons and Co.

Sir Austen Henry Layard (1817–1894) LIBERAL – Under-Secretary of State for Foreign Affairs, January–February 1852, 1861–6.

Sir George Cornewall Lewis, 2nd Baronet (1806–1863) LIBERAL – Chancellor of the Exchequer, 1855–8; Home Secretary, 1859–61; Secretary of State for War, 1861–3.

William Schaw Lindsay (1816–77) LIBERAL – Pro-Southern, Scottish shipping magnate; founder and owner of W. S. Lindsay and Co., 1849–64; Member of Parliament for Tynemouth and North Shields, 1854–9; Member of Parliament for Sunderland, 1859–65.

Richard Monckton Milnes, 1st Baron Houghton (1809–85) CONSERVATIVE – Poet; Member of Parliament for Pontefract, 1837–63; pro-Northern supporter.

Henry Pelham-Clinton, 5th Duke of Newcastle (1811–1864) LIBERAL – Secretary of State for War and the Colonies, 1852–4; Secretary of State for War, 1854–5; Secretary of State for the Colonies, 1859–64.

Roundell Palmer, 1st Earl of Selborne (1812–95) LIBERAL – Pro-Northern Solicitor General, 1861–3; Attorney General, 1863–6; Lord Chancellor, 1872–4 and 1880–85.

Henry John Temple, 3rd Viscount Palmerston, known as Lord Palmerston (1784–1865) LIBERAL – Secretary of State for Foreign Affairs, 1830–34, 1835–41 and 1846–51; Home Secretary, 1852–5; Prime Minister, 1855–8 and 1859–65.

John Arthur Roebuck (1802–79) LIBERAL – Member of Parliament for Bath, 1832–7 and 1841–7; Member of Parliament for Sheffield, 1849–68 and 1874–9; pro-Southern.

John Russell, 1st Earl Russell (1792–1878) LIBERAL – Secretary of State for Foreign Affairs, 1852–3 and 1859–65; Leader of the Opposition, February–December 1852 and 1866–8; Prime Minister, 1846–52 and 1865–6.

Edward Adolphus Seymour (later St Maur), 12th Duke of Somerset (1804/5–85)

LIBERAL – First Commissioner of Woods and Forests, 1849–51; First Commissioner of Works, 1851–52; First Lord of the Admiralty, 1859–66.

Pro-Northern Supporters

Elizabeth Blackwell (1821–1910) – British-born doctor; the first woman to earn a medical degree in the United States; first woman to be placed on the British Medical Register; founder of the New York Infirmary for Indigent Women and Children, 1857.

John Elliott Cairnes (1823–75) – Irish economist; Whatley Professor, Trinity College, Dublin, 1856–61; Professor of Jurisprudence and Political Economy at Queen's College Galway, 1859–70; author of *The Slave Power*, 1862.

Lord Frederick Charles Cavendish (1836–82) – Progressive politician; private secretary to Lord Granville, 1859–64; private secretary to Prime Minister Gladstone, 1872–73.

Thomas Hughes (1822–96) – Author of *Tom Brown's Schooldays*, 1857.

Fanny Kemble (1809–93) – Actress; author of *Journal of a Residence on a Georgian Plantation in 1838–1839*, 1863.

Peter Sinclair – Social reformer; author of *Freedom or Slavery in the United States: Being Fact and Testimonies for the Consideration of the British People*, 1863.

Goldwin Smith (1823–1910) – British-Canadian historian and journalist; Regius Professor of Modern History at Oxford University, 1858–66.

Harriet Sutherland-Leveson-Gower, Duchess of Sutherland (1806–68) – Granddaughter of Georgiana, Duchess of Devonshire; a champion of the American anti-slavery movement.

Pro-Southern Supporters

Mary Sophia Hill (1819–1902) – Sister of Sam Hill, 6th Louisiana Volunteers; regimental nurse in the 6th Louisiana Volunteers; Federal prisoner of war, 1864.

Thomas Kershaw – British peace campaigner on behalf of the South.

James Spence (1816–1905) – Author of *The American Union*, 1862; Liverpool businessman; pro-Southern propagandist and lobbyist.

Francis William Tremlett (1821–1913) – Vicar of St Peter's Church, Belsize Park; unofficial chaplain to the Confederate navy in England.

Edward Montagu Stuart Granville Montagu-Stuart-Wortley-Mackenzie, 3rd Baron Wharncliffe (1827–99) – President of the Manchester Southern Independence Association.

The War at Sea

Sir William Nathan Wrighte Hewett (1834–88) – Commander of the HMS *Rinaldo*, 1861–2, and the HMS *Basilisk*, 1865–9; commander of the ill-fated *Condor*, 1864.

The Hon. Augustus Charles Hobart-Hampden (1822–86) – Under the pseudonym

'Captain Roberts' commanded the blockade-runners *Don* and *Falcon* during the Civil War.

Sir Alexander Milne, 1st Baronet (1806–96) – Royal Navy commander-in-chief, North America and West Indies, 1860–64; First Naval Lord, 1866–8 and 1872–6.

Thomas Taylor (1841–?) – Supercargo on the blockade-runners *Banshee, Will o' the Wisp, Wild Dayrell, Stormy Petrel* and *Wild Rover*; author of *Running the Blockade*, 1896.

Volunteers

Bennet Graham Burley [also spelled Burleigh] (*c.* 1844–1914) CONFEDERATE – Scottish volunteer, Confederate navy; Federal prisoner of war, 1864; went on to become a notable war correspondent.

Charles Culverwell (1837–1919) UNION – Actor (stage name: Charles Wyndham); brigade surgeon in the Union army, 1862–4.

Leonard Douglas Hay Currie (1832–1907) UNION – Assistant adjutant general to Brigadier General W. F. Smith; colonel in the 133rd New York Infantry Volunteers.

Francis Warrington Dawson [né Austin John Reeks] (1840–89) CONFEDERATE – Common sailor, CSS *Nashville*, 1861; master's mate, CSS *Louisiana*, 1862; 1st lieutenant of artillery in the 'Purcell Artillery' battalion, under the command of Captain William 'Willy' Johnson Pegram.

John Fitzroy De Courcy, 31st Baron Kingsale (1821–90) UNION – Stipendiary magistrate of San Juan, Vancouver Island; colonel of the 16th Ohio Volunteer Infantry.

Frederick Farr (1844–64) UNION – Private, Company F, 7th Maine Infantry, 1863–4.

Henry Wemyss Feilden (1838–1921) CONFEDERATE – Private, 42nd (Royal Highland) Regiment of the Foot (also known as the Black Watch), 1857–60; assistant adjutant general in Charleston, Confederate army.

George St Leger Grenfell (1808–68) CONFEDERATE – Assistant inspector general of the corps of cavalry of the Army of the Tennessee, 1862; assistant inspector general of the corps of cavalry of the Army of Northern Virginia, 1863.

George Henry Herbert UNION – Lieutenant, 9th New York Volunteer Infantry ('Hawkins' Zouaves').

Henry George Hore (d. 1887) UNION – Aide-de-camp to Major-General Sedgwick.

James Horrocks UNION – Private, 5th Battery New Jersey Volunteers.

Robert Moffat Livingstone (1846–64) UNION – 3rd New Hampshire Infantry; son of the explorer Dr David Livingstone.

Henry Ronald Douglas MacIver (1841–1907) CONFEDERATE – Lieutenant, variously as aide to Generals 'Stonewall' Jackson, Jeb Stuart and Edmund Kirby-Smith.

Charles Mayo (1837–1877) UNION – Staff surgeon-major and medical inspector of the 13th Army Corps.

Robert Neve (1831–79) UNION – 5th Kentucky Volunteers.

James Pendlebury (1841–97) UNION – Private, 69th New York Infantry.

Alfred Rubery CONFEDERATE – Would-be privateer.

Llewellyn Traherne Bassett Saunderson (1841–1913) CONFEDERATE – Staff officer to General Fitzhugh Lee.

Henry Morton Stanley [né John Rowlands] (1841–1904) CONFEDERATE – and Union 'Dixie Grays', Company E, 6th Arkansas Regiment of Volunteers, Confederate army.

William Watson (1826–?) CONFEDERATE – Scottish businessman living in Louisiana; enlisted in the Confederate army in 1861 with the 3rd Louisiana Infantry; author of *Life in the Confederate Army*.

Ebenezer Wells UNION – Wagon master, 79th New York Highlanders.

Stephen Winthrop (1839–79) CONFEDERATE – Staff officer to General Alexander.

Sir Percy Wyndham (1833–79) UNION – Colonel of 1st New Jersey Cavaliers.

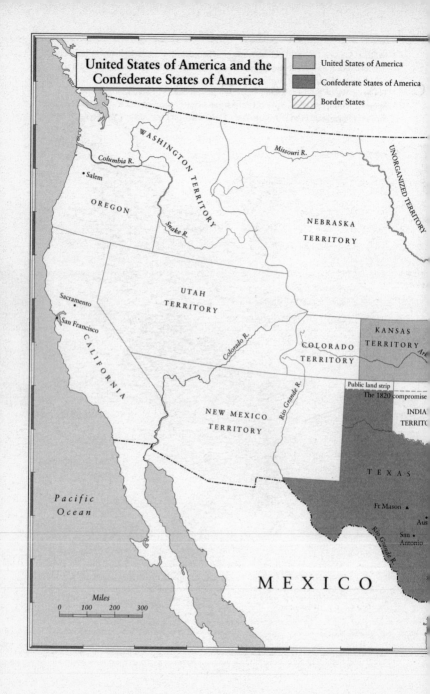

United States of America and the Confederate States of America

United States of America
Confederate States of America
Border States

WASHINGTON TERRITORY

Columbia R.

• Salem

OREGON

Snake R.

Missouri R.

UNORGANIZED TERRITORY

NEBRASKA TERRITORY

Sacramento •

• San Francisco

C A L I F O R N I A

UTAH TERRITORY

Colorado R.

KANSAS TERRITORY

Ark

COLORADO TERRITORY

Public land strip

The 1820 compromise

INDIA TERRITO

NEW MEXICO TERRITORY

Rio Grande R.

T E X A S

Ft Mason ▲

Aus

Pacific Ocean

San Antonio

Rio Grande R.

M E X I C O

Miles
0   100   200   300

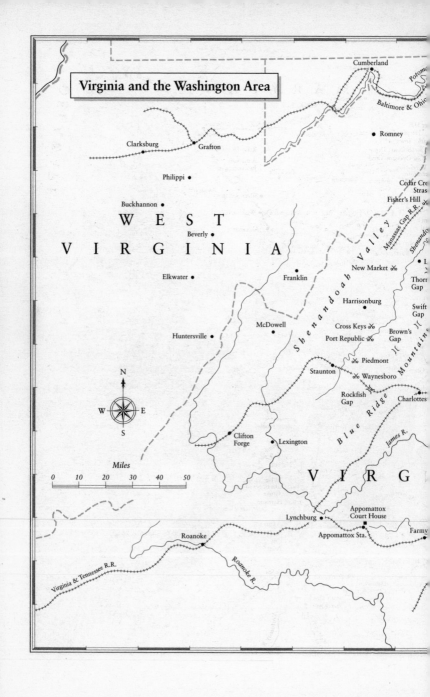

Virginia and the Washington Area

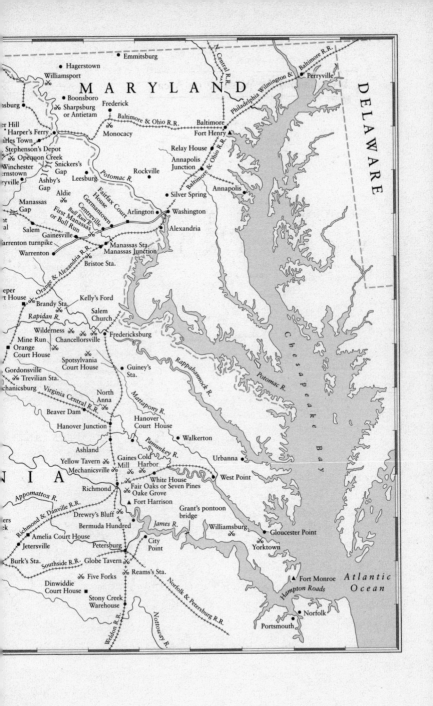

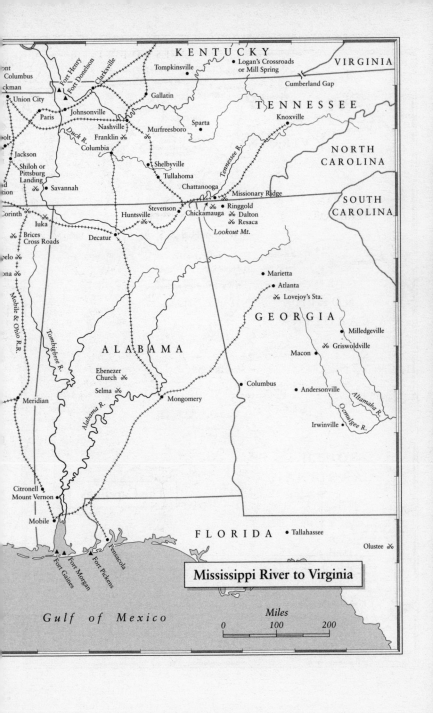

Mississippi River to Virginia

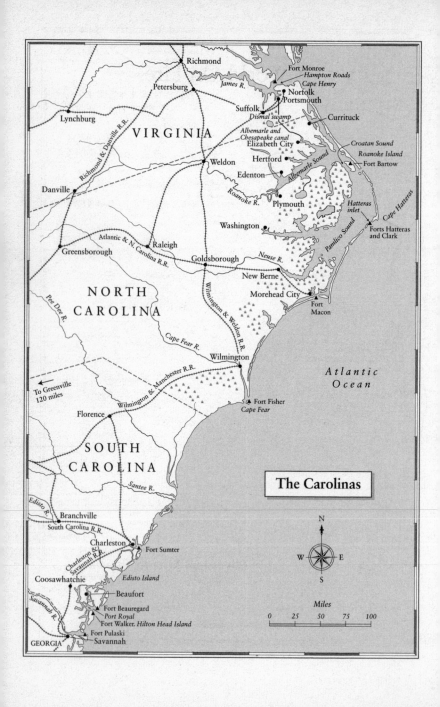

The Carolinas

A World On Fire

Prologue

Washington society adored the Napiers. From the moment they had arrived at the British legation in 1857, Lord Napier was hailed as the friendliest and most sensible diplomat ever to set foot in the capital. For her part, Lady Napier soon won her own following as a hostess of unparalleled warmth and grace. 'Her cozy at-homes were remarkable for their informality,' recalled a Southerner after the war. Their presence was considered essential at any fashionable gathering. The legation was neutral territory and 'one met there the talented and distinguished; heard good music, listened to the flow of wholesome wit; and enjoyed delectable repasts ... A feeling of universal regret spread over the capital when it became known [in 1859] that the Napiers were to return to England.'[1]

Senator William Henry Seward of New York, Lord Napier's closest friend in Washington and the heir apparent to the Republican leadership, invited a small group of Senators to join him in organizing a farewell ball. The committee had hoped to control the number of guests by charging $10 per head,* but the heady combination of popularity and power resulted in no fewer than 1,800 subscriptions for the gala. Only one venue other than the White House could accommodate so large a gathering, Willard's Hotel on the corner of E and 14th Streets. The *New York Times* joked that a ticket to the Napier ball was harder to come by than a front-row seat at the current Broadway hit comedy *Our American Cousin*, by the British playwright Tom Taylor.[2]

---

* The equivalent to $1,700 in today's money.

On 17 February 1859, the grand ballroom at Willard's was specially decorated with an Anglo-American theme. Flags and mirrors lined the walls and two large portraits, one of George Washington, the other of Queen Victoria, hung majestically from the ceiling. A representation of St George and the Dragon, made out of sand, covered the floor. It was, however, the lavish banquet that created the most excitement. The chef had fashioned the Napiers' coat of arms out of spun sugar, as well as 'dolphins in a sea of rock candy, and ices in every form, from a pair of turtle doves to a pillared temple'.[3]

The Napiers made their appearance at 9.45 p.m. to the strains of 'God Save the Queen', and were greeted with loud cheers and applause. Their evening dress was decidedly old-fashioned according to American tastes. Boldly resisting the trend among men for black evening attire, Lord Napier wore a royal blue jacket over a white waistcoat. Lady Napier's dress was also characteristically idiosyncratic; rather than trying to compete with her wealthy friends, she had chosen to wear a white silk gown decorated with tulle and edged in black lace. 'You did not hear ladies say of her, as of so many others: "What a splendid dress – how much did it cost!"' commented the *New York Times*'s reporter. 'When will women learn that to beauty and perfection of attire, cost is but a small essential?' The gallant journalist was clearly ignorant of the sartorial revolution that had taken place during the previous year. On the inside, every woman of means was wearing one of W. S. Thompson's new steel crinoline cages; on the outside, they were experimenting with the new range of colours made possible by the invention of synthetic dye. (Even Queen Victoria was not immune to the changes in fashion and had worn mauve to the wedding of her eldest daughter, Princess Victoria, to Prince Frederick of Prussia in January 1858.) Lady Napier's elegant but austere dress reflected none of these developments and yet still managed to cause a sensation, not only on account of its simple design but also because amid the unavoidable clash of magentas and fuchsias the pure white cast all other colours in the shade.

The enmity that had begun to poison social life in Washington went into suspension during the ball. The crush was so great that dancing had to take place in relays, the guests jamming the bars and corridors while they waited their turn to enter the ballroom. Decorated veterans from the Mexican War chatted sociably with bankers from New York, and the broad vowels of Mississippi intermingled with the clipped tones of Massachusetts. The reigning queens of society made a rare collective appearance: Mrs John

Slidell and Mrs Rose Greenhow rotated around one another like brilliant stars, their orbits passing close by but never quite touching. It was said by Mrs Greenhow's rivals that she had adorned the British legation in much the way that Lord Nelson's mistress, Lady Hamilton, had adorned his ship.[4]

Among the few who were missing from the ball was President Buchanan, who remained at home with a head cold; and William Lowndes Yancey of Alabama, who was also indisposed – this was, perhaps, fortunate since his booming voice could overpower a brass band, particularly when warming to his twin obsessions of slavery now, and slavery for ever. Charles Francis Adams, the Congressman-elect from Massachusetts, had also stayed away, despite his family's long association with British–American diplomacy.* Adams despised small talk, hardly drank, and never danced, and not even the disappointment of his wife, Abigail, could overcome his reluctance to attend.

One of the highlights of the evening came when Lord Frederick Cavendish, second son of the 7th Duke of Devonshire, and the Hon. Evelyn Ashley, step-grandson of the former Prime Minister, Viscount Palmerston, walked onto the dance floor. There were frissons among the debutantes as the two bachelors repaid many debts of hospitality accrued during their tour of America by dancing into the small hours of the morning. However, it was only in retrospect that the Napier ball became famous, not for its exalted guests or its lavish banquet, but as the last time Northerners and Southerners socialized together before the war.

Lord Napier's replacement as the senior British diplomat in America, Lord Lyons, arrived in Washington at the beginning of April 1859. Even by English standards, 42-year-old Richard Bickerton Pemell Lyons was an eccentric character. Any display of emotion – including his own – made him uncomfortable. Women and servants tended to suffer from an excess of it in his opinion, which made him dread close contact with either. He was reluctant to look people in the eye and knew the shoes and stockings of his servants far better than their faces. Though not a killjoy, Lyons had never developed a taste for alcohol and smoking

---

* Charles Francis Adams's grandfather, John Adams (the second President of the United States), and father, John Quincy Adams (the sixth President), had both served as Ministers Plenipotentiary to the Court of St James's, 1785–8 and 1815–17, respectively.

The Napier ball at Willard's Hotel, Washington DC, 17 February 1859

made him ill; this was less of a handicap in Europe, where his witty and erudite conversation made him a favourite of hostesses.[5] But in Washington, his lack of interest in cigars and whisky simply accentuated his strangeness. Napier did his best for Lyons during the short time they overlapped at the legation. With Congress in recess and mass departures from Washington already under way, he rushed to introduce Lyons to potential allies in the Senate before they scattered to their home States. But William Seward left Washington in April to spend a couple of weeks with his family before embarking on an extended tour of Europe. Seward's early departure prevented Napier from fostering any meaningful understanding between his friend and his successor.

'Lord Napier has exerted himself very much to assist me in every way,' wrote Lyons gratefully in mid-April, 'and has done all that was possible to start me well both socially and politically'.[6] Privately, he was relieved that his education in the complexities and nuances of American politics had begun during the quiet season. Lyons had never previously heard of the term 'Mason–Dixon line', yet every person he met described himself as either living above or below this boundary. Napier explained that it was the cultural as well as geographical divide between the North and South.* Although America was one country, Lyons would discover that it was two distinct regions, whose ties were straining over the question of slavery. Above all else, warned Napier, a British Minister must not become embroiled or be thought to take sides in this fractious debate.

Napier used the term 'Minister' because there were no Ambassadors or embassies in Washington. In the mid-nineteenth century there were only three British embassies abroad: Paris, Vienna and Constantinople. The rest of the world had to make do with second-tier 'legations', which functioned in the same way, only with less pomp and a smaller budget. These were headed by a representative with the long-winded title of 'British Envoy Extraordinary and Minister Plenipotentiary', or 'Minister' for short. Naturally, there was a hierarchy; the British Minister to the United States ranked lower than his colleagues in Russia and Spain, but above those in Greece, Denmark and Bavaria. Languishing below the legations were general consulates, which were reserved for countries of unproven stability in places like South America.[7]

The British legation was the largest and most important of the diplomatic missions in Washington. With the exception of the French legation, the other twenty-one were insignificant establishments. The nine Latin American Ministers were too impoverished to receive visitors; the Austrian legation consisted of one Minister living in a hotel, and the Italian Minister loathed the capital so much that he lived in New York.[8] The burdens placed on the British Minister were also greater than those faced by his foreign counterparts. Lyons was not only the conduit between London and Washington but also Her Majesty's guardian over the rights and interests of the 2.5 million British expatriates living in America.[9]

The tumultuous history between the two countries made every British Minister a soft target for American politicians. Lyons was sent to Washington with the same set of instructions and warnings that had accompanied each of his predecessors. He was to improve relations between the two countries; and he must be prepared to accept that the

---

* The line was originally drawn in 1767 by two British astronomers, Charles Mason and Jeremy Dixon, who had been commissioned to settle a border dispute between Maryland and Pennsylvania. But by the mid-nineteenth century the 'Mason–Dixon line' had come to mean the separation between the Northern State of Pennsylvania and the Southern State of Maryland, and all the States above and below the 39th parallel.

kindness bestowed on him in private would be matched by untrammelled hostility in public, and to expect a regular whipping from the
White House and Congress.[10]

Lyons was used to loneliness. 'A trained diplomatist is reserved while
appearing open,' wrote a nineteenth-century journalist; 'one who has the
air of telling you everything, and yet tells you nothing; who seems to go
with you all the way, yet advances never an inch beyond the line he has
drawn for himself.'[11] This described Lyons perfectly. He was tactful and
discreet to the point of parody; outside his work he had few interests
that could not be met by a comfortable chair and a warm fire. Many
years later the Paris police compiled an intelligence report on Lyons
which consisted of one line: 'On ne lui connait pas de vice' (he has no
known vices).[12] His most regular female correspondents were his two
sisters, particularly his youngest and favourite, Minna, who was married
to the Duke of Norfolk. Lyons's horror of 'scenes' made him so reticent
that for years he put up with the same breakfast every morning rather
than risk upsetting his valet with a request for something different.[13]

Lyons had hesitated to accept the Washington post for fear that he
might prove to be a disappointment. Though the eldest of four children,
he had always suffered in comparison to his younger brother Edmund.
Richard was portly, non-athletic and incapable of stepping onto a boat
without being sick. In contrast, Edmund was charismatic, adventurous
and loved the sea, like their father, the 1st Lord Lyons. The latter had
forged a successful double career in the Royal Navy and the Foreign
office, which led to him becoming a rear admiral in 1851 and receiving
a peerage in 1856.

Richard Lyons had entered the diplomatic service in 1839 after grad-
uating from Oxford with a fourth-class degree and no other prospects.
For five years he worked as an unpaid attaché for his father, who was
serving as the British Minister in Athens. In his sixth year, he was promoted to paid attaché, but there he remained long after his father moved
on to more interesting posts. For thirteen years Richard worked quietly
and efficiently, hoping that the Foreign Office would take notice of him.
Finally, he could no longer bear his life at the conflict-riven legation nor
put up with the humiliation of being the oldest attaché in the service, and
in 1852 he announced his intention to resign. His protest resulted in a
rapid transfer to Dresden, though with the same rank.

By 1857 Lyons was serving in the Florence legation, though still only ranked twenty-fourth out of the twenty-six Secretaries in the service. This was a significant improvement in his fortunes yet one which his father thought long overdue. Admiral Lyons's beloved Edmund had been killed in 1855, in the waning months of the Crimean War, while carrying out his father's order to attack the batteries of Sebastopol. The Admiral's health declined rapidly after Edmund's death, but during his last years he continued to exert himself on Richard's behalf, arguing his merits to former colleagues.[14] His efforts were vindicated after Lyons surprised himself and others with his elegant resolution of a dispute between the Neapolitans and the Sardinians before it escalated into an international controversy. Overnight he became the Foreign Office's preferred man for difficult situations. Admiral Lyons died in November 1858, a few days after learning of his son's promotion to the Washington legation.

Lord Lyons would have arrived in Washington much sooner had not the settlement of the will detained him in England until mid-February 1859. There was a further delay caused by the Foreign Office's parsimonious attitude to travel; Lyons had to cross the Atlantic on an inferior ship that burned through its coal halfway through the voyage. The crossing took a stomach-churning six weeks to complete, instead of the usual ten days, a torture for a man who was terrified of water.[15]

Lyons's doubts about his fitness for his new post were shared by President James Buchanan, who resented the implication that Washington ranked next to Florence in importance, especially since 80 per cent of Britain's cotton supply came from America. The textile industry was one of the most important in Britain, and the cotton trade translated into a business worth $600 million a year, providing employment and financial security in England for more than 5 million men and women. This alone, believed Buchanan, merited a 'first-rate man whose character is known to this country'.[16] Lord Lyons's courtesy call to the American legation in London before he sailed had unwittingly confirmed the US administration's suspicion that the British Foreign Office was sending a nonentity. 'Sensible', 'unobtrusive' and 'short' were the legation's chief impressions of Lyons.[17]

Buchanan's misgivings about the quality of his new British Minister were mild compared to Lord Lyons's judgement of his new place of residence. Washington was not a city at all, in his opinion. 'It is in fact little more than a large village,' he wrote to Lord Malmesbury, the Conservative Foreign Secretary, a month after he arrived, 'and when Congress is not sitting it is a deserted village.'[18] The original political and strategic reasons for building the nation's capital by the Potomac river had been obsolete for decades. The War of 1812 between Britain and America had demonstrated that the city could be invaded just as easily as New York. The Potomac had seemed to promise a thriving water trade, but the river proved too shallow for modern transports. Washington had been the geographical centre when the Union was only thirteen States; the country's expansion to thirty-three now placed it on the periphery.

Washington lacked the literary salons, studios, universities and conservatories that distinguished the capitals of Europe. The theatres relied on touring productions from New York; the shops were small and under-stocked. There was no commercial or manufacturing district such as one found in the new industrial cities, though the levels of violence, drunkenness and corruption were not dissimilar. There were few cultural amenities save for the Smithsonian Institution, which had been established in 1846 with a bequest from the British scientist James Smithson. (Strangely, Smithson had never even visited the United States, let alone Washington.) The majority of the permanent residents were civil servants, lawyers or saloonkeepers. When Charles Dickens travelled to the capital in 1842 he thought the city had 'Magnificent Intentions' but little else. It had 'spacious avenues, that begin in nothing and lead to nowhere', and 'streets, [a] mile long, that only want houses, roads, and inhabitants'.[19]

Fifteen years later, these intentions remained unfulfilled. 'Most members of Congress live in hotels or furnished lodgings,' wrote an English tourist. 'In consequence, there is no style about the mode of living ... The whole place looks run up in a night, like the cardboard cities which Potemkin erected.'[20] The boundaries of Washington were still ragged and ill-defined. A disagreement between the government and a local landowner had stranded the unfinished Capitol on top of a steep hill at the edge of town, facing the wrong way. Washington's smart district lay two miles in the opposite direction, across marshland and noisome swamps which were breeding grounds for malaria in the summer. Elsewhere, the roads were still dirt tracks that frequently ended in a pile of rubble, or were interrupted by pasture. A pedestrian was in danger not only from one of the city's unregulated hackney cabs, but also from being run over by wandering livestock. 'On nine days out of every ten, the climate of Washington is simply detestable,' complained a British journalist. 'When it rains, the streets are sloughs of liquid mud ... in a couple of hours from the time the rain ceases, the same streets are enveloped in clouds of dust.'[21]

The real political centre of the city was Willard's Hotel. Just a five-minute walk from the White House, this was where the 'wire pullers', the information seekers (and sellers), and those looking for employment seized the opportunity to mix with the temporary occupants of the Capitol. Here, on an average day, 2,500 people passed through its doors. 'Heavy persons, whom you have never seen before, with moist hands, eyes luminous with intoxicating beverages, break through the crowd and wildly shake your hand,' observed an anonymous journalist. 'They convict you of having met them before somewhere. You say you have been there, whereupon you are instantly saddled with an acquaintance who grasps your hand fifty times a day, and whom you heartily wish at the – antipodes.'[22] The regulars downed cocktails in one of its many saloons or puffed themselves hoarse in the cigar bar, rendering real tourists appalled. 'The tumult,' complained one English traveller, 'the miscellaneous nature of the company, the heated, muggy rooms,' the revolting globs of tobacco spit on every surface, 'despite a most liberal provision of spittoons', made it 'by no means agreeable to a European'.[23]

The arrival of President Lincoln at Willard's Hotel, 23 February 1861

The British legation was established in Rush House at 1710 H Street, only a block from Lafayette Square, where the White House, the State Department and many of Washington's grandest mansions were clustered. Rush House was large enough to accommodate the Chancery, the business end of the legation, and was sufficiently imposing to impart an air of consequence to diplomatic functions. Lord Lyons's arrival created a stir similar to the excitement described by Jane Austen after the leasing of Netherfield Hall. 'The gossips at once set about predicting that the newcomer would capitulate to the charms of some American woman, and speculation was already rife as to who would be the probable bride,' wrote Mrs Clay, the wife of Senator Clay of Alabama.[24]

It was soon discovered, however, that Lyons, with his little round face and droopy eyes, was neither a Mr Bingley nor a Mr Darcy. Mrs Clay received a 'formidable card to the first Senatorial dinner given by the newly arrived diplomat', and decided this was her chance to collar him for a Southern belle. 'I soon became emboldened to the point of suggesting to him the possibility of some lovely American consenting to become "Lyonised." His Lordship's prompt rejoinder and quizzical look quite abashed me, and brought me swiftly to the conclusion that I would best let this old lion alone.'[25] Lyons had quoted *Tristram Shandy* at Mrs Clay, but his arcane reference to Uncle Toby's habit of sleeping 'slantindicularly' not only passed over her head but made her wonder whether the new Minister was quite sane.

Mrs Clay's encounter with Lyons confirmed the general impression in Washington that he had replaced the Napiers but would never supplant them in the capital's affections. Varina Davis, the wife of Senator Jefferson Davis of Mississippi, wrote that people thought Lyons 'very taciturn and very stupid'.[26] Lord Napier gave his final speech in the United States on 15 April 1859. 'I can never forget or requite the incessant kindness ... offered to me by the American people,' he told an emotional audience at Astor House in New York. The following day, the press commented on the coincidence that Britain's two most popular exports should make their farewells to America on the same night. The 15th marked the last performance of Tom Taylor's comedy *Our American Cousin*. It had run for 140 nights, a feat never before achieved in the history of American theatre.

Lord Napier's popularity had proved to be his undoing at the Foreign Office. 'Napier is much too frank and too yielding to the Yankees,' the then Prime Minister, Lord Derby, had complained, 'and they take advantage of him in every way.'[27] Napier's friendship with Senator Seward was considered symptomatic of his mistaken priorities. The Foreign Office was not interested in having a Minister who understood the Americans' point of view. The choice of Lord Lyons to replace the adored Lord Napier, a decision that seemed incomprehensible to Washington, made perfect sense to London. Lyons's views of America were generally in keeping with those of the Foreign Office: he was well-disposed to its people but thought that democracy made the government weak and handed too much power to the violent and ignorant elements of society. If he were to feel concern over whether or not the Americans liked him, his superiors in London were confident it would be sublimated by his renowned sense of duty.

Lord Lyons soon realized that Napier had not been exaggerating when he described America as the 'Castle Dangerous' of British diplomacy. His first request to the Foreign Office was for more staff; 'considering . . . the very great importance of not giving offence and the extreme readiness of people here to take it, I think that few ministers abroad have so much need of a private secretary's help as I have.'[28] Already, it was apparent to him that the taking and giving of offence had become a reflexive habit in Anglo-American relations since the separation of 1775–83. For prudence's sake he had decided to 'gratify their vanity by treating them in matters of form as [a] great people . . . as if they were really a considerable military power'.[29] But Lyons had made an error in assuming that he only needed to practise a little flattery to assuage America's suspicions about Britain. Relations between the two countries had been bent and twisted by eighty-three years of wars, disputes and reconciliations. 'I HATE England,' the American novelist Nathaniel Hawthorne had recently written from his consular post in Liverpool, 'though I love some Englishmen, and like them generally.'[30]

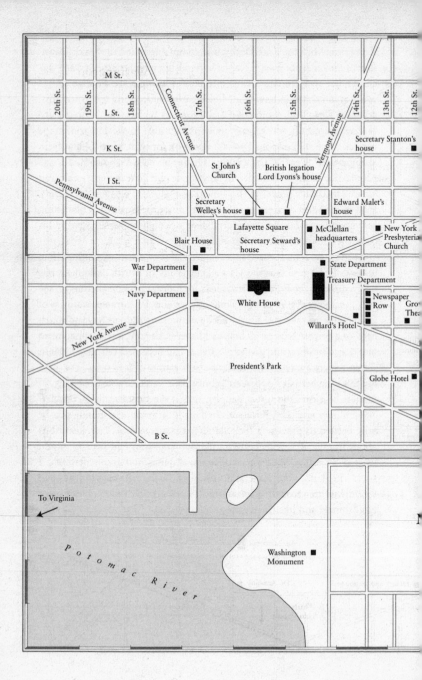

PART ONE
Cotton is King

I

The Uneasy Cousins

Britain and America – Divisions over slavery – Lord Palmerston –
Uncle Tom's Cabin *and the Stafford House Address – Charles*
Dickens's disappointment – The caning of Charles Sumner

In the seventy-five years after the War of Independence, the British
approach to dealing with the Americans had boiled down to one simple
tactic, to be 'very civil, very firm, and to go our own way'.[1] During the
late 1850s the prevailing view in London was that Washington could not
be trusted. 'These Yankees are most disagreeable Fellows to have to do
anything about any American Question,' the Prime Minister Lord Palmerston had complained in 1857 to Lord Clarendon, his Foreign Secretary,
fourteen months before Lord Lyons's arrival in America. 'They are on the
Spot, strong . . . totally unscrupulous and dishonest and determined somehow or other to carry their Point.'[2] It went without saying that the Foreign
Office expected Lyons to be on guard against any American chicanery.

One of the legacies of the War of 1812 was a British fear that the
United States might try to annex British North America (as Canada was
then known), and a conviction among Americans that they should never
stop trying. It was neither forgiven nor forgotten in England that precious ships and men had to be diverted from the desperate war against
Napoleon Bonaparte in order to defend Canada from three invasion
attempts by the United States between 1812 and 1814. London regarded
the burning of Washington and the White House by British soldiers in
August 1814 as a well-deserved retribution for the sacking of York
(later Toronto) by American troops.

Lyons soon discovered, as had each of his predecessors, that the War
of 1812 had not only an entirely different meaning in the United States,

but also a different outcome. In American histories, Britain had provoked the war by her arrogant and unreasonable behaviour; first by
blockading all ports under Napoleonic rule, thereby stifling American
trade, and second by boarding American ships in search of deserters
from the Royal Navy. The practice of 'impressing' American sailors into
the navy was considered beyond the pale, especially when it took place
off the coast of Virginia.*[3] Despite furious protests from Washington,
the number of American citizens wrongly impressed had steadily increased
over the years, and by 1812 the tally had reached over 6,000. But when
the US Congress declared war on 8 June 1812 it was to stop a practice
that had finally been disavowed by the English; two days earlier, in London, the British government had agreed to stop impressment – too late
to effect the outcome of the debates in Washington.

The peace treaty signed by Britain and America in 1814, the Treaty
of Ghent, was based on the assumption that the war had been a draw
since no territory was lost or gained by either side. However, news of
the treaty had not yet reached the British and American armies facing
one another in New Orleans and a battle took place on 26 January.
Though a small engagement compared to the great battles unfolding
in Europe, it was a decisive American victory. General Andrew Jackson's force of 4,000 men defeated a British expedition almost three
times the size. The fact that the battle occurred after peace had been
agreed was brushed aside in the telling. Two great American myths were
born: Andrew Jackson *won* the war, and had not only put the British in
their place, but also thrashed the army which defeated Napoleon.

The failure of the United States to conquer Canada during the war
had come as a great surprise to many Americans. The former President,
Thomas Jefferson, had written to a colleague in August 1812: 'The
acquisition of Canada this year, as far as the neighborhood of Quebec,
will be a mere matter of marching, and will give us experience for the
attack of Halifax the next, and the final expulsion of England from the
American continent.'[4] Over the next few decades, politicians often
expressed their desire to expel England from the 'American continent'.
When small, local rebellions broke out in Quebec and Toronto in 1837,

---

* The term impressment meant the legal conscription of a British civilian, usually a sailor,
into the Royal Navy. The practice had been going on since the 1600s. It was rare for 'land-
lubbers' to be impressed but in time of war all kinds of injustices took place, and for the
most part the authorities pretended not to notice.

it came as no surprise to the British to learn that President Martin Van Buren had ostentatiously invoked international law and declared US neutrality, or that American sympathizers were providing arms and volunteers to the Rebels. By announcing 'neutrality', Van Buren elevated the uprising of a few hundred Canadians to the standard applied to an international war, giving hope to Americans who believed that a Canada free from British 'shackles' would want to join the Union.[5]

That the original thirteen States would increase in number over the years had never been in doubt; but whether these new States would allow slavery or not was a question which troubled Americans from the beginning. When the first Constitutional Convention met in Philadelphia in 1787, five of the thirteen* – Massachusetts, Pennsylvania, New Hampshire, Rhode Island and Connecticut – had abolished slavery, and eight – New York, New Jersey, Delaware, Maryland, Virginia, North Carolina, South Carolina and Georgia – had not. But there had been slaves in America since 1619 – one year before the arrival of the *Mayflower* – and at the time of Independence one in five of the 4 million ex-colonists were black. The Constitutional Convention agreed on a compromise, the first of many which would be tried until the Civil War. Slavery was left alone but the slave trade was given a twenty-one-year time limit. After 1808, the importation of slaves was to be banned.

The invention in 1793 of Eli Whitney's cotton gin (which separated the tough cotton fibres from their seeds, saving many hours of manual labour), however, meant that slavery not only continued but even flourished in the Southern States. The demand for cotton from England's textile mills was apparently inexhaustible and within two years of Whitney's gin arriving in the South shipments of cotton across the Atlantic had risen from roughly 130,000 pounds a year to more than 1.5 million. The rise of cotton over rice, tobacco or corn as the primary Southern crop coincided with the government's acquisition of the Louisiana territories from the French in 1803. The United States doubled in size as a result of the Louisiana Purchase, opening up to development and potential statehood more than 820,000 square miles, from the Gulf of Mexico to the Canadian border. Instead of dying out, as some of the

---

* Although slavery was abolished in Vermont in 1777, the former colony attempted to go it alone for the first fourteen years after Independence, only joining the Union in 1791.

original framers of the Constitution had hoped, slavery was spreading north and west.

By 1819 the thirteen States had become twenty-two, and were evenly split between free and slave States. But in 1819 the territory of Missouri applied to join the Union and the balance was suddenly upset. Missouri straddled the parallel established by the Mason–Dixon line; both the Northern and Southern States claimed her as one of their own. Both feared what would happen to the balance of power in the Senate, where each State sent two Senators regardless of size or population. By now, the two regions were developing separate though intertwined economies. The Northern States were hurtling towards industrialization, building factories, constructing cities and developing financial institutions; the Southern States kept to their agricultural base, received fewer immigrants and developed an alternative financial system based on the buying and selling of slaves and cotton.* The majority of Northerners could read and write; in the South, the literacy rate was less than half. The growing political, economic and cultural differences between the North and South could not be easily reconciled. Finally, in 1820 Congress agreed to the 'Missouri Compromise', which admitted the State of Missouri to the Union with slavery allowed. As a balance, however, Maine was admitted as a free State, and the future growth of slavery was confined to new States south of the Missouri border. The Southern States suddenly became deeply interested in the expansion of the United States into Mexico and Central America.

Britain could not help becoming entangled in these territorial disputes. In 1823 President James Monroe announced the 'Monroe Doctrine', which essentially claimed US hegemony over the Americas and called for the Old World to stay on its side of the Atlantic and allow the New World to develop without interference. Since Britain had possessions and interests in both continents, this was neither desirable for her nor possible.† After a decade as Foreign Secretary, from 1830 to 1841, Lord Palmerston had become thoroughly exasperated by the

---

* Southerners referred to slavery (and by extension the cotton economy) as the 'peculiar institution', not because it was strange but because the mode of life was particular to the South and nowhere else.

† For the first half of the nineteenth century, the 'Monroe Doctrine', when it was observed at all, was enforced by Britain's Royal Navy since it was in her interest to prevent other Great Powers from interfering with the balance of power in South America.

continuous bickering between the two countries over Canada's borders. 'It never answers to give way [to the Americans],' he wrote in January 1841, 'because they always keep pushing on their own encroachments as far as they are permitted to do so; and what we dignify by the names of moderation and conciliation, they naturally enough call fear.'[6] Palmerston followed his own advice in the case of a British subject named Alexander McLeod who was being held in a New York prison on the charge of murder. McLeod had been arrested in November 1840 after he drunkenly boasted in a New York bar of killing an American sympathizer who had been on his way to take part in the Canadian revolts of 1837. Palmerston informed Washington that McLeod's execution 'would produce war; war immediate and frightful in its character'.[7] Hints from William H. Seward, then the Governor of New York, that he would pardon McLeod once the public outcry had petered out had no effect on Palmerston's determination to go to war unless the prisoner was released. Fortunately, a jury acquitted McLeod since there was no evidence against him except his own bibulous lies.[8]

Palmerston's approach to American issues was a reflection of his general attitude to foreign policy: that Britain's interests should never be sacrificed to satisfy her friends or appease her enemies. His unapologetic nationalism made him widely disliked in Europe. According to legend, a Frenchman once complimented him saying, 'If I were not a Frenchman, I should wish to be an Englishman.' To which Palmerston replied, 'If I were not an Englishman, I should wish to be an Englishman.' The Prussians complained, 'Hat der Teufel einen Sohn, / So ist er sicher Palmerston' ('If the Devil has a son, surely he must be Palmerston'). Palmerston's willingness to use the Royal Navy, which was the largest in the world, at the slightest provocation earned him the sobriquet 'Lord Pumicestone' among his detractors. It was also noticed that Palmerston only ever employed his gunboat diplomacy against smaller nations such as Greece, while his manner towards the other Great Powers of Europe (France, Austria, Prussia and Russia) was far more conciliatory.

Palmerston's attitudes had been formed when wigs and rouge were worn by men as well as women. He had personally witnessed the first wave of violent revolutions in Europe as a child when his parents joined the retinue of friends and relations escorting Georgiana, Duchess of Devonshire, through France. The family's brief but terrifying experience at the hands of a citizens' committee in Paris left Palmerston with only tepid faith in the ability of the lower orders to make rational decisions. During the first half of his political career, Palmerston was better known for his womanizing (which won him his initial nickname of 'Lord Cupid') than for his work at the War Office, where he toiled diligently for twenty years at the mid-level post of Secretary at War. But, apart from his enjoyment of female company – the more the better – Palmerston was in every other way a serious politician whose capacity for long hours and hard work almost incited a rebellion among the clerks when he became Foreign Secretary in 1830. It was a shame, Florence Nightingale remarked after she came to know the real Palmerston, that people accepted his jocular, almost flippant manner at face value since 'he was so much more in earnest than he appeared'. Once his slumbering humanitarian instincts were aroused by a particular cause he could act with unbounded zeal. The abolition of the slave trade became a lifelong obsession as Palmerston painstakingly tried to create an impregnable web of international treaties which would allow the navy the right to search suspected slave ships in any part of the world.

One of the driving forces behind Palmerston's enmity towards the United States was its refusal to agree to a slave-trade treaty. To his mind, the Acts abolishing the slave trade in 1807, and then slavery throughout the British Empire in 1833, had joined such other events as the Glorious Revolution and Waterloo in the pantheon of great moments in the nation's history. For many Britons, the eradication of slavery around the globe was not simply an ideal but an inescapable moral duty, since no other country had the navy or the wealth to see it through. At the beginning of 1841 Palmerston had almost concluded the Quintuple Treaty which would allow the navy to search the merchant ships of the Great Powers. 'If we succeed,' Palmerston told the House of Commons on 15 April 1841, 'we shall have enlisted in this league . . . every state in Christendom which has a flag that sails on the ocean, with the single exception of the United States of North America.'[9] The Quintuple Treaty was signed but without the signature of the United States. As a consequence, the slave trade continued exclusively under the American flag. The one concession Britain did obtain – and this was not on account of Palmerston's efforts, as he was out of government between 1841 and 1846 – was the formation of joint patrols with the US navy off the West African coast.

Whether Palmerston was Foreign Secretary or not, however, made no difference to the constant wrangling or the relentless expansion of the Union over the lands of Native Americans as well as British-held territories. Three years later, in 1844, the Presidential candidate for the Democratic Party, James Polk, ran on a platform that all Britain's Oregon territories right up to Russian America should be annexed by the United States. 'The only way to treat John Bull is to look in him the eye,' Polk wrote in his diary. 'If Congress falters or hesitates in their course, John Bull will immediately become arrogant and more grasping in his demands.'*[10] Polk's claim for all the land as far as what is now southern Alaska resulted in the popular slogan 'Fifty-Four Forty or Fight!' (meaning that the new boundary line should be drawn along the 54° 40' parallel). But the expected fight never occurred; Texas joined the Union as a slave State in 1845, and a year later President Polk declared war on Mexico, a far less dangerous opponent. The Foreign Secretary Lord Aberdeen, who shied away from gunboat diplomacy, was willing to negotiate and the Oregon Treaty was signed in June 1846, giving all of present-day Washington, Oregon and Idaho to the United States.[11] Victory in the Mexican–American War in 1848 resulted in the United States acquiring a further 600 million acres, most of them below the Mason–Dixon line.† There were now thirty States in the Union, once again in an even split between slave and free.

In 1848 the discovery of gold in California led to a rush of settlers – more than 80,000 of them in a matter of months – and the urgent need to accept the newly acquired territory as the 31st State so that law and order could be imposed. But the Southern States would not agree to the addition (since the Californians were demanding to be admitted as a free State) until they had secured a series of concessions. The most bitterly contested was the Fugitive Slave Act of 1850, which allowed 'owners' to pursue and recapture their escaped 'property' in whatever State he or she happened to be hiding. Graphic newspaper reports of families torn apart, and blacks dragged in chains back to their erstwhile masters, raised an outcry in the North. Several Northern States passed personal liberty

* 'John Bull' was the personification of Great Britain, just as 'Brother Jonathan' was the personification of the United States. Both were eighteenth-century terms that were still widely used in the mid-nineteenth century, although 'Uncle Sam' and 'Columbia' were gaining popularity in the US as American alternatives.
† The actual Mason–Dixon line was only 23 miles long, but its existence became a metaphor to describe the cultural differences between the North and South.

laws to try to circumvent the Act; in some towns there was violent resistance to the Federal agents who arrived in search of fugitive slaves; and
the 'underground railroad' with its vast network of safe houses from
Louisiana to the Canadian border received many more volunteers.

The domestic upheaval and political turbulence during 1850 was one of
the reasons why the United States' pavilion at the Great Exhibition in
London in 1851 displayed so few objects compared to those of other
nations. The suspicion among Americans that Britain had put on the
exhibition simply to show off its status as the richest country in the
world also diminished enthusiasm for taking part. Yet even with a fraction of the exhibits presented by the Great Powers, the American pavilion
still won 5 out of the 170 Council medals (admittedly, France won 56);
and the American photography contingent, led by Mathew Brady, won
first, second and third prize.* The great number of American tourists
and businessmen who visited the exhibition brought more contact
between the citizens of the two countries than at any other time during
the century. Britons now realized the extent to which the United States
had developed separately from the mother country. Americans not only
had different accents and wore different fashions; their choice of words
and phrases sounded quite foreign. They talked about 'fixing things'
and 'running for office'. They said 'I guess' instead of 'I suppose', and
'let's skedaddle' instead of 'shall we go'. They employed adjectives such
as 'reliable', 'lengthy' and 'talented'; and called conmen 'shysters', an
epithet entirely new to English ears.[12] It was their strange and different
mannerisms that inspired Tom Taylor to write *Our American Cousin*.

Taylor also wrote the popular stage version of the novel *Uncle Tom's
Cabin* by Harriet Beecher Stowe, which appeared in 1852. The English
took to heart the story of the saintly slave whose goodness and humanity upstage a succession of masters until his murder by the evil Simon
Legree. In 1852, the first year of publication, the book sold a million
copies in Britain – compared to 300,000 in the United States.[13] Every
respectable household owned a copy. *Uncle Tom's Cabin* was allegedly
the first novel Lord Palmerston had read in thirty years, and whether it
was the effects of the long abstinence or the allure of the book, he read

---

* Several objects, including the Singer sewing machine and the Colt .45-caliber single-action
army revolver, were subsequently sent on a successful tour around Britain.

it from cover to cover three times.[14] The grisly portrayal of slavery in *Uncle Tom's Cabin* articulated what the British had long suspected was the truth, despite the South's self-depiction as an agrarian paradise of courtly manners, charming plantations and contented slaves. Few Britons had ever seen how slaves really lived, unlike the celebrated British actress Fanny Kemble, whose marriage to Pierce Butler, a southern slave-owner, fell apart after they moved to his Georgian plantation in 1838. They divorced acrimoniously in 1849, with Butler holding Fanny's daughters hostage until they turned 21.

The publication of *Uncle Tom's Cabin* led to a renaissance of anti-slavery clubs in Britain after they had tottered along in a state of earnest torpor since 1833. The public agitated for Britain 'to do something'. In November 1852 Harriet, Duchess of Sutherland, and the Earl of Shaftesbury drafted a petition to 'the Women of the United States of America', urging them to 'raise your voices' against slavery. More than half a million British women signed their names to the public letter, which was known as the Stafford House Address. Predictably, the American response was one of outrage.[15] Julia Tyler, the wife of ex-President John Tyler, led the barrage of sarcastic replies to 'The Duchess of Sutherland and the Ladies of England'. Britain's labour conditions, rigid class structure and lack of opportunity for self-betterment all came under attack. But it could not be denied that Britain possessed the moral high ground on the issue of slavery. American abolitionists who visited England were amazed to discover that British blacks enjoyed the same rights as their white peers. 'We found none of that prejudice against color in England which is so inveterate among the American people,' Elizabeth Cady Stanton had written about her honeymoon in Britain during the summer of 1840. 'At my first dinner in England I found myself beside a gentleman from Jamaica, as black as the ace of spades.'[16] Similarly, a former slave, the author Harriet Jacobs, recalled how her self-esteem had changed after visiting England. 'For the first time in my life,' she wrote, 'I was in a place where I was treated according to my deportment, without reference to my complexion. I felt as if a great millstone had been lifted from my breast.'[17]

The Stafford House Address had been doomed to fail no matter how good and sincere its intentions. The Anglophobia which was so often articulated in Congress was no more than a reflection of public opinion. Alexis de Tocqueville commented in *Democracy in America* in 1835 that he had never encountered a hatred more poisonous than that which Americans felt for England.[18] There were notable exceptions, of course. In the early 1840s the American Minister in London told a wildly receptive audience that 'the roots of our history run into the soil of England ... For every purpose but that of political jurisdiction we are one people.'[19] But there had existed a deep-rooted prejudice since the War of Independence. The influx of a million Irish refugees during the potato famine merely added more venom to the mix. 'Why', wrote a nineteenth-century American journalist, 'does America hate England?' He answered: 'Americans believe that England dreads their growing power, and is envious of their prosperity. They detest and hate England accordingly. They have "licked" her twice and can "lick" her again.'[20]

Tocqueville attributed the hostility to fifty years of self-congratulatory propaganda. He thought Americans were convinced that their country was a beacon of light to the world; 'that they are the only religious, enlightened, and free people ... hence they conceive a high opinion of their superiority and are not very remote from believing themselves to be a distinct species of mankind'. The more the English scoffed at this view, the more furious and resentful Americans became towards Britain. The most memorable attack on American exceptionalism was Sydney Smith's scornful comparison between the two cultures in 1820. 'Who reads an American book?' wrote the celebrated wit, author and Canon of St Paul's in the *Edinburgh Review*:

> Or goes to an American play? Or looks at an American picture or statue? What does the world yet owe to American physicians or surgeons? Who drinks out of American glasses? Or eats from American plates? Or wears American coats or gowns? Or sleeps in American blankets? Finally, under which of the old tyrannical governments of Europe is every sixth man a slave whom his fellow-creatures may buy and sell and torture?[21]

A decade later, Fanny Trollope, the novelist and mother of Anthony Trollope, rekindled the impression that all Britons looked down their noses at the former colonists with her book *Domestic Manners of the Americans*. Mrs Trollope had spent a brief and unhappy period in Ohio in the late 1820s, trying to build a commercial business, which had ended with the family becoming bankrupt and homeless. The book was not meant to be a serious study of America but a piece of entertainment

LIFE IN AN AMERICAN HOTEL?

Punch's view of American manners, 1856

to help solve their financial difficulties. While not condemning all Americans in all areas of life, she portrayed the majority as too vulgar, violent and vainglorious to be really likeable. Her view of America inspired hundreds of English imitators, further souring cultural relations between the two countries.

Other British writers sneered that the self-styled 'superior' United States was militarily weak, politically corrupt and financially unsound.[22] America's markets were prone to panics; its people preached equality but practised 'mobocracy'. English travellers who saw American democracy in action either condemned it outright, or praised it half-heartedly as an evolving system. The greatest blow to American pride came from Charles Dickens. Until his visit to the country in 1842, Americans had considered the world's best-selling novelist to be almost an adopted son. His humble beginnings and liberal politics had fostered their assumption that the United States would be far more preferable to him than class-ridden England. Dickens had indeed wanted to admire America during his triumphant lecture tour. 'Still it is of no use,' he wrote dolefully to a friend during the tour. 'I *am* disappointed. This is not the republic I came to see; this is not the republic of my imagination.' He warmed to the friendliness and generosity of its people, and he admired the emphasis on education and public philanthropy. But he found American society as a whole utterly intolerant of dissenting views. 'Freedom of opinion! Where is it?' he asked rhetorically after being warned not to discuss the slave mutiny on board the *Creole* outside of abolitionist circles, even though the subject was dominating British–American relations.* If American democracy was simply a vehicle for majority rule, then, asserted Dickens, 'I infinitely prefer a liberal monarchy.'[23] He gave vent to his disenchantment in *American Notes*, which was published in 1842, and *Martin Chuzzlewit*, which followed the year after.

The great influx of immigrants into the country after 1846 accelerated the rise of the harsh, strident politics which Dickens so deplored. In 1840 there had been 17 million people living in America; by 1850 there were 23 million, an increase of 35 per cent. The altered political landscape, where ethnic identity and class affiliation translated into thousands of votes, demanded a new breed of politician – the kind exemplified by William Henry Seward, who was elected to one of the two New York Senate seats in 1849. While Governor he had behaved with shameless opportunism, courting the State's large Irish vote with vitriolic diatribes against England. The annexation of Canada was a constant theme in his speeches.[24] Though not a bigot himself, Seward was an expert at appealing to popular prejudices to shore up his power base. Once he realized that the Democratic and Whig parties were frag-menting into Northern and Southern, pro-slavery and anti-slavery factions, he abandoned the Whigs and became a Republican.† He subtly

* In November 1841 the journey of the *Creole* from Virginia to Louisiana was interrupted when the slaves on board mutinied and took the ship to Nassau in the Bahamas. The British authorities refused to hand over the mutineers or return the slaves.
† Despite fronting four Presidents, the Whig Party survived for less than twenty-five years and was more a collection of factions than a cohesive national party. By the time of its demise in the early 1850s, several new parties were forming, including the anti-immigrant Know-Nothing Party, so-called because, when questioned about their affiliation, its members were instructed to say 'I know nothing.'

repositioned himself, raising his anti-slavery rhetoric and emphasizing his protectionist credentials, which infuriated the free-trade South but endeared him to States that feared competition from European goods.

There were two different Sewards, according to his friend, Henry Adams: the 'political and the personal'. But over time they had become so entwined 'that no one could tell which was the mask and which the features'. 'I am an enigma, even to myself,' Seward once quipped.[25] With his soft, husky voice and confiding manner, he exuded the air of a man who knew the foibles of humanity but did not sit over them in judgement. 'You are at your ease with him at once,' recorded an English admirer. 'There is a frankness and bonhomie ... In our English phrase, Mr Seward is good company. A good cigar, a good glass of wine, and a good story, even if it is a little risqué, are the pleasures which he obviously enjoys keenly.' His opposition to slavery was never in doubt, but his preference for pragmatism over principles meant that sometimes his ends became lost in the means. Shortly after his election to the Senate, Seward explained that one consideration governed all his political actions: 'My duty is to promote the welfare, interest, and happiness of the people of the United States.' But whether this view was a goal or a cover remained the subject of debate. His wife Frances became increasingly disillusioned by her husband's ability to temporize. Once a woman of strong political views, her confidence had been crushed by prolonged exposure to Seward's ego. She preferred to live her life in quiet seclusion in New York, pleading ill health, while Seward lived in Washington. It was almost as if Frances represented some part of his conscience; safely left at home but still accessible by post.

Seward had become a leader of the nascent Republican Party in the Senate when Senator Stephen Douglas, a Democrat from Illinois, proposed a bill in 1854 to admit two new territories, Kansas and Nebraska, into the Union. However, the provisions included a bombshell. The two territories would decide for themselves whether to be free or slave States. Douglas had proposed breaking the 1820 Missouri Compromise because it was the only way he could achieve his real aim of obtaining Southern support for a transcontinental railroad. But the result was catastrophic for the residents of Kansas. In theory, majority rule was going to decide the issue. In practice, pro- and anti-slavery settlers began to slaughter one another in a vicious little war. 'Border Ruffians' based in Missouri charged over the border to join forces with Kansas slave-owners, while New England abolitionists shipped caseloads of rifles to their western brethren. The rival factions each proclaimed their own legislatures. Throughout 1855 American newspapers referred to 'Bleeding Kansas'.

Seward tried to find common ground with the Southern Senators as a means to ending the violence in Kansas without endangering the Union. But the North and South each regarded the fate of Kansas as the key to slavery's future. There could be no compromise. In the spring of 1856 President Franklin Pierce gave his full support to a bill proposed by Senator Douglas to repeal the Missouri Compromise ban on slavery in territories north of the 36° 30' parallel, which included Kansas. Seward responded on behalf of the Republican Party with a bill to admit her as a free State. The Senate leader of the Free Soil Party,* Charles Sumner, showed Seward the speech he was preparing to deliver on 19 May. Entitled 'The Crime against Kansas', the speech was a devastating indictment of the South, her institutions and the characters of her most prominent politicians. Although Seward personally disliked Sumner, considering him to be far too priggish for a politician, he shuddered at his folly. He tried in vain to persuade him to at least remove the personal attacks. Sumner refused. After initially hailing Seward as a fellow soldier in the battle against slavery, the aristocratic Bostonian had come to regard him with disdain. According to a mutual friend, 'The two men would have disliked each other by instinct had they lived in different planets.'[26] Seward had brawled and clawed his way from New York to national prominence; by contrast, Sumner was a seventh-generation American; a Harvard man who spoke four languages and was an acknowledged authority in jurisprudence.

The 40-year-old Sumner had never held office before he took his Senate seat in 1851. Unlike Seward, who knew the inside of every backroom between Buffalo and Brooklyn, Sumner had deliberately eschewed politics. Seward had only been abroad once, in 1833, and had returned with his prejudices against Britain confirmed. By contrast, Sumner had become something of a sensation when he visited England in 1838, prompting the essayist and historian Thomas Carlyle, who opposed abolition, to dub him sarcastically 'Popularity Sumner'. Although he lacked a sense of

---

* The East Coast-based Free Soilers, whose slogan was 'Free soil, free speech, free labor, and free men', initially competed with the Republican Party, which was born in the Midwest in 1854 and also opposed slavery, and then became absorbed by its newer rival.

humour – a fatal disability for most foreigners in Britain – Sumner exuded a charismatic earnestness combined with obvious brilliance. He knew more dukes and earls than most Englishmen, let alone any other American. But the most important friend he made during this time was Harriet, Duchess of Sutherland, whose views on abolition and social reform coincided with his own. After he returned to America, they maintained their friendship. She saw him as he wished to see himself: a proud and tireless advocate of society's victims.

Sumner's lack of experience or even understanding of basic political realities proved to be his undoing. In contrast to Seward, he was incapable of modulating his speeches to suit political expediencies. Sumner abhorred compromise; 'from the beginning of our history,' he explained, 'the country has been afflicted with compromise. It is by compromise that human rights have been abandoned.' Sumner was prepared to make a last, defiant stand against the forces of accommodation, and did so at every opportunity. On 19 May 1856 he began in the Senate a two-day marathon of invective. Congress had just learned that the border town of Lawrence, Kansas – which had held out against slavery – was surrounded by a thousand Border Ruffians. The tension in the chamber added force to words which needed no extra help. Sumner was already a mesmerizing orator; his speeches were emotional to the point of being histrionic. Between damning the South to hell, he accused Senator Andrew Butler of South Carolina of being so attached to the idea of slavery that he was like an adulterer obsessed with his harlot. Then he scored some gratuitous blows by making fun of Butler's infirmities. He also insulted Senator Stephen Douglas, who responded, 'That damn fool will get himself killed by some other damned fool.'

Two days later, while Sumner was sitting at his desk in the near-empty Senate chamber, one of Butler's cousins, Congressman Preston Brooks, silently approached him from behind. After speaking a few words, Brooks raised his arm and smashed his heavy cane on Sumner's head. Blinded by blood and in shock, Sumner struggled to get his long legs out from under his desk. He finally managed to stand up while Brooks continued to beat him with increasing ferocity. According to horrified observers, Sumner tried to stagger away, only to be grabbed by Brooks, who held his lapel with one hand while raining down blows with the other. By his own counting, he struck Sumner about thirty times before his cane splintered. His mission completed, Brooks calmly walked away unmolested. Within a few minutes he was strolling down Pennsylvania Avenue as if nothing had happened.[27]

The House of Representatives failed to muster enough votes to expel Brooks and, although he immediately resigned his seat, South Carolinians expressed their views by promptly re-electing him. To Southerners, infuriated by the constant moral and political tirades aimed at them by Northern abolitionists, Brooks was a hero. They had long felt beleaguered by the persistence of Northern attempts to curtail slavery. For many, Brooks had acted out their greatest fantasy against the abolitionists. Thousands of canes arrived at his house, some with gold or silver tips and one which bore the words, 'Hit Him Again'.

Abolitionists, on the other hand, regarded Sumner's savage beating as a call to action. The terrible scene on the chamber floor, described in lurid detail by every newspaper, also served to unite the North. Rather than worrying about the activities of immigrants, or black preachers, or Freemasons, Northerners could finally agree on a common enemy. The Republican Party was overwhelmed with new members. But for Sumner, his martyrdom came at a terrible price. Even after his wounds healed, the psychological scars proved to be far more intractable. On 7 March 1857 the frail patient was gently conveyed onto a steamer bound for England. It was the beginning of three years of self-imposed exile. By his own estimation his political career and possibly his life were concluded. Still, Sumner was not just popular abroad, he was now a bona fide hero. His English friends welcomed him as though he were a wounded general returning from war. Later some would claim that his assault marked the beginning of the Civil War.[28]

The Duchess of Sutherland insisted that the wounded warrior recuperate at Stafford House. After his caning she had redoubled her efforts to rouse English sympathy against Southern slavery. One of her most successful events was a public reading of *Uncle Tom's Cabin* by the black American performer Mary Webb. The scene at Stafford House 'would have caused considerable astonishment to any gentleman of the Southern States of America', reported the *Illustrated London News*. 'A large audience was gathered together in that hall ... to listen to a lady of colour giving dramatic readings ... our Southerner would have been confounded and disgusted at the sight of what he would call a "tarnation nigger" being listened to with the most respectful attention by no inconsiderable number of the aristocracy of England.'[29]

Among the new friends Sumner made during his stay at Stafford House were the Duchess of Sutherland's daughter, Elizabeth, and her husband, the Duke of Argyll. For the Argylls it was the perfect meeting of minds. 'He was a tall, good-looking man,' recalled the Duke in his memoirs, 'very erect in attitude, with a genial smile and a very intellectual expression ... I always found his conversation full of charm, not only from his devotion to one great cause, but from his wide and cultivated interest in literature and in art.'[30] Like Sumner, the 33-year-old Duke was a striking figure, whose flaming red hair – which he wore shoulder length – and theatrical dress were considered emblematic of his idiosyncratic politics. His views were always logical and well thought out, and yet strangely angular, so that on any given subject it defied prediction whether they coincided with those of his own party or with those of the opposition. This, combined with his caustic and often dogmatic style of debating, meant that Argyll carried weight in politics but would never inspire a following. Both he and Sumner would always be forces in their own right, and also their own greatest impediments to power. For the future of British–American relations, however, the relationship between Argyll and Sumner would prove to be one of the most important friendships of the Civil War.

2

On the Best of Terms

The Dred Scott case – William Seward visits London – The Liber-
als come to power – John Brown's raid – The Prince of Wales
tours America

Seward was delighted when many Southern newspapers suggested that he ought to be next in line for a caning. With Sumner recuperating in Europe, Seward hoped to appeal to radical anti-slavery voters in the Republican Party. His chance to shine came just two days after Sumner set sail, and the Democrat James Buchanan was sworn in as President. On 6 March 1857 the Supreme Court handed down its opinion on the notorious Dred Scott case. Scott was a former slave who had been taken by his late master from Missouri, where slavery was legal, to Illinois, which had abolished slavery in 1818, and then to the free territory of Wisconsin. Scott had sued for his freedom but the Southern-dominated court decided that the Federal government had no right to decide on matters pertaining to slavery in any part of the United States, whether free or unfree.

The court's decision wrecked the thirty-seven-year-old Missouri Compromise, which had ensured that as more territories joined the Union there would always be an even balance between the slave and free-soil States. Worse still, the court declared that black people were not citizens, and were 'so far inferior that they had no rights which the white man was bound to respect'. Blacks were no more entitled to citizenship than horses or sheep; they could not vote, own a passport, or apply to the courts. Seward denounced the Dred Scott decision at every opportunity, accusing President Buchanan and Chief Justice Taney of having colluded over the ruling. Northern public opinion supported Seward's attacks since it was widely believed above the Mason–Dixon

36

line that there was a slave-power conspiracy afoot to spread slavery throughout the United States.

In the autumn of 1857, six months after the Dred Scott ruling, the collapse of the largest insurance company in the country sparked a catastrophic economic crisis throughout the North. During the financial panic that followed, prices on the New York Stock Exchange plunged by 45 per cent, hundreds of banks failed, railroads went bankrupt, factories closed, and overnight there was mass unemployment running into hundreds of thousands. The panic of 1857 spread to Britain, too – where investors held, among other securities, £80 million worth of railroad stocks and bonds.[1] Only the Southern cotton-growing States escaped the panic largely unscathed, apparently vindicating the superiority of a slave system over the factory-based economy of the North. In a speech to the Senate on 4 March 1858, Senator James Hammond of South Carolina boasted that Southern cotton exports had saved the economy from total collapse during the 1857 panic, and for this reason had the right to dictate terms to the whole of the United States. 'Cotton is King ... What would happen if no cotton was furnished for three years? ... England would topple headlong and carry the whole civilized world with her, save the South.' Hammond and the other Southern Senators fiercely resisted subsequent attempts by the Northern States to protect their domestic industrial base by imposing high tariffs on foreign imports.

Seward's language became increasingly violent whenever he discussed the differences between the two sections of the country. By the end of 1858 he was arguing that the Dred Scott case should mark the end of all Northern concessions to the South. During a speech on 25 October 1858, in Rochester, New York, he declared that the South had started 'an irrepressible conflict' with the North: 'the United States must ... become either entirely a slave-holding nation or entirely a free-labour nation.' A week earlier, while debating his Democratic opponent in the contest for one of Illinois's two seats in the United States Senate, the Republican candidate, a lawyer from Springfield had made a similar-sounding statement: that 'a house divided against itself cannot stand'.* The lawyer, Abraham Lincoln, lost the election but his speech won him

---

* From the outset Abraham Lincoln promoted himself as representing the middle ground. He believed that whites were superior to blacks, but this did not give one human being the right to deprive another of his liberty. 'As God made us separate, we can leave one another alone, and do one another much good thereby.'

national acclaim. Whereas Lincoln sounded as though he were giving a warning, Seward seemed to be laying down a challenge.[2] Seward later claimed that 'irrepressible' was not the same as 'unavoidable', but the damage could not be undone. The press dubbed him 'irrepressible conflict Seward', fostering the sense that he was a divisive rather than a unifying figure, and voiding three years of careful positioning by Seward to be perceived as the moderate alternative to Charles Sumner.

Seward's friend and political manager, Thurlow Weed, advised him to take a long trip abroad in the hope that the public would forget the unfortunate phrase. The Presidential election would not be until November 1860, which was two years away. There was still sufficient time for Seward to repair his reputation. Weed was confident that the British would have no idea that anything was amiss with Seward's Presidential aspirations and would treat him with the respect afforded to the next leader of the Americans.

Seward's arrival in England on 20 May 1859 coincided with a recent improvement in Anglo-American relations. English outrage over US support for the Russians during the Crimean War of 1854–6[*] had become less acute after the Indian Mutiny of 1857–8, when the Americans were firmly behind the British army rather than the mutinous sepoys. Closer to home, Lord Napier's popularity in Washington had overcome some of the bad feelings on both sides of the Atlantic after his unlucky predecessor, John Crampton, was expelled by the US government for participating in a secret scheme to recruit American volunteers to fight on the British side in the Crimean War. The perennial flashpoints between Britain and America – the right of the Royal Navy to search American ships suspected of transporting slaves from Africa or the Caribbean, and the jostling over boundaries and territorial control in British North America and Central America – had threatened to ignite in 1858 but were contained by successful diplomacy in some instances, and plain reluctance to go from words to something worse in others.[4] In his second annual address to Congress in December 1858, President Buchanan stressed the importance of peaceful relations between the two countries: 'Any serious interruption of the commerce between the United States

---

* The English were furious that US sympathy for the Russians had extended to military aid, in the form of a steamship built for the Russian government by a private firm, as well as practical help from American doctors and engineers who volunteered their services.[3]

and Great Britain would be equally injurious to both. In fact, no two nations have ever existed on the face of the earth which could do each other so much good or so much harm.'

When the two navies did meet at sea, on 29 July 1858, it was to perform the heroic manoeuvre of linking together the first transatlantic telegraph cable. An underwater cable had been laid in 1851 between Dover and Calais, but the raging storms of the Atlantic had twice defeated the combined efforts of British and American engineers. This time, the cable held strong as the HMS *Agamemnon* and the USS *Niagara* sailed towards their respective destinations flying specially designed flags that incorporated the stars of 'Old Glory' with the stripes of the Union Jack. On 16 August 1858 the line was opened with the message: 'Glory to God in the highest; on earth, peace and goodwill to men.' Queen Victoria followed with a cable of congratulations to President Buchanan and the people of the United States. Both countries celebrated in a 'Festival of Connection', New York held a special candlelight parade, newspapers printed special editions, the streets were decorated with special flags, and shops displayed commemorative posters and ribbons.[5] Cyrus Field, the American investor behind the venture, was hailed as a genius and visionary. But the telegraph only worked for a month and the disintegrating connection was destroyed in a clumsy repair attempt by one of the English engineers. The Atlantic cable would remain a dream for another eight years.

The Central America disputes were still under negotiation, however, when Seward arrived in London on 20 May 1859. The city had grown larger, noisier and more frantic since Seward's previous visit in his youth. Its population had increased from 900,000 to more than 3 million. Horse-drawn omnibuses, carriages, wagons and pedestrians bumped and jostled each other on some of the most congested streets in the world; a thousand vehicles an hour crossed over London Bridge.[6] Nor was London the same dirty, unregulated city of a generation before. The Great Stink of 1858 (a mini heatwave 'cooked' the raw sewage in the Thames, sending noxious fumes through the capital) had forced city planners to begin an ambitious sewerage and water system for the capital. The squares and parks were just as Seward remembered, but these green spaces were now dwarfed by a new set of landmarks. The Gothic architecture of the rebuilt Houses of Parliament – after the great fire of 1834 – seemed especially foreign to him compared to the neoclassical government buildings of Washington. This was a bold, even arrogant, London that dared other cities to emulate its style.

As Weed predicted, Seward's arrival was eagerly anticipated by the denizens of Fleet Street and Westminster, who assumed that he was visiting England to cement his relationship with the country's leaders ahead of his election to the Presidency. That it might be curiosity rather than admiration behind the scramble to make the acquaintance of the great Anglophobe never seemed to occur to Seward. He peppered his letters to his wife Frances with exclamations of excitement that so many famous figures wished to meet him. The morning after his first London ball, he boasted that he had 'conversed with royalties and nobles infinitum'. There were 'Princesses and Princes, and Dukes and Duchesses of the royal party, Indian Princes, and all the Diplomatic Corps. It was a thorough jam – like the Napier ball.'[7]

Seward owed his initial entrée into London society to the Napiers, who took great pains to introduce him to their friends and relations. By the time the Season was in full swing, he was on nodding terms with every senior politician and fashionable hostess in London. Lord Napier also prepared Seward for his presentation to the Queen, sending him to his own tailor, shoemaker and hatter. But as memorable as the occasion was for the unabashed republican, Seward was more star-struck by his visit to Stafford House to meet the Duke and Duchess of Sutherland. 'The Duchess is the most accomplished lady in England. I could not tell you how kind and gracious she was to me,' he wrote to his wife. 'She detained me after the party had left, and we had a long, and most agreeable tete-a-tete.' Believing Seward's abolitionism to be sincere, the Duchess ordered her relations to show him the same hospitality: her daughter and son-in-law, the Duke and Duchess of Argyll, her brother, the Earl of Carlisle, and her cousin, the Duke of Devonshire, dutifully opened their houses to Seward, the last being anxious to repay him for the courtesy shown to his son, Lord Frederick Cavendish. By the beginning of June, Seward was able to reel off the names and titles of society figures as though they had been his friends for years: 'I dined with the Earl of Carlisle, and a large party of nobles and statesmen of the Liberal class. It would be tedious to recount [all] their names,' he wrote to Frances in early June; 'Lord Granville, Lord and Lady Shaftsbury [sic], Lord and Lady Palmerston, Lord John Russell, Mr. and Mrs. Gladstone, Mr. Delane, editor of the Times, and others. It was a most agreeable party.'[8]

The polite conversations around the table were merely a façade; behind the scenes, intense political negotiations were taking place. Seward had arrived in London at an extraordinary moment in British politics. The liberal factions in Parliament were coming together to oust Lord Derby's Conservative government. Lord John Russell and Viscount Palmerston had reached a cordial understanding to form a new political party. Since Palmerston was on what could loosely be termed the 'right' of liberal politics and Russell on the 'left', between them they would be able to form a broad coalition.

On 6 June 1859, 274 MPs assembled in the ballroom of Willis's Rooms in St James's and declared themselves the 'Liberal Party'. Lord Palmerston and Lord John Russell shook hands, demonstrating forgiveness of all previous acts of treachery and rivalry towards one another during their previous stints as Prime Minister, agreeing to become the party's joint leaders. (It was noted that the 75-year-old Palmerston sprung onto the dais while the 69-year-old Russell had to be helped up the steps.) Four days later, on 10 June, the Liberals voted en masse in a motion of no confidence against Lord Derby's Ministry, winning by a majority of thirteen votes. The Queen, who disliked both Russell and Palmerston, was annoyed with 'those two terrible old men', as she called them. After considerable prevarication she chose Palmerston as her new Prime Minister, much to Russell's disappointment. Russell became Foreign Secretary, a post that played to his weaknesses rather than his strengths.

Nothing had quite gone Russell's way since he gained iconic status as the young man who ushered through the Great Reform Bill of 1832. The achievement had been all the more remarkable considering his lifelong poor health and nervous disposition, which had turned him into something of a self-absorbed eccentric.* Many of his ailments could be traced back to the fact he had been born more than two months premature and his survival was almost without precedent in the nineteenth century. Throughout his life, Russell would be blessed and cursed in equal measure. He enjoyed close relations with his family, particularly his older brother, the Duke of Bedford, and yet was never comfortable in society.

---

* According to a well-known anecdote, Russell was chatting to the Duchess of Inverness at a party one winter evening, when he suddenly stood up, went over to the far corner, and began a conversation with the Duchess of Sutherland. A short time later, one of his friends asked him what an earth had happened. He had been sitting too close to the fire, Russell explained. 'I hope', the friend remarked, 'that you told the Duchess of Inverness why you abandoned her.' After a pause he replied, 'No, but I did tell the Duchess of Sutherland.'

Both of his marriages were reasonably happy; on the other hand, the second Lady John never pretended that her love was of the romantic kind. Nor was she capable of providing the support and help that Palmerston received from his wife. Unlike Lady John, who never entertained if she could help it, Lady Palmerston used all the means in her power to assist her husband. They had been lovers for many years until the death of her husband, Lord Cowper, enabled them to marry. During their long political partnership, she had developed her own skills and insights into human nature. According to one diplomat, a morning call on her 'was more instructive than studying the newspapers'.[9] Lady Palmerston was adept at converting enemies and newspaper editors into political allies; her most important conquest being John Delane, editor of *The Times*.

Russell was one of the most cultured politicians of his generation, but 'Little Johnny', as he was called on account of his diminutive stature, was desperately shy and stiff to the point of rudeness, while also being overly sensitive and demanding of others. Consequently, he was a dreadful manager of men, incapable of fulfilling the most basic requirements of leadership.[10] Although not exactly devious, he could be slippery with his colleagues, who accused him of withholding information and of acting without consultation or in contrary to agreed plans. Sydney Smith once said of him, 'It is impossible to sleep soundly while Lord John has command of the watch.'

With all these talents and handicaps, Russell was driven by a lofty idealism for genuine political and social reform; but the failures of his career had been catastrophic, not least his inability to come to grips with the Irish Potato Famine in the 1840s. Russell ought to have retired from politics after the fall of his administration in 1852, as one of his biographers noted, 'with his two and a half dozen bottles of Australian wine* and his Colt's revolving firearm from the Great Exhibition'. Then he would have been remembered as a great but flawed leader.[11]

The new Liberal Cabinet had fifteen members, a substantial number by the standards of the day, and included a broad cross-section of views and personalities, from the flamboyant and combative Duke of Argyll (Lord Privy Seal) to the intellectual and moderately inclined Sir George Cornewall Lewis (Home Secretary).† The most surprising inclusion was William Gladstone as Chancellor of the Exchequer. Once hailed as the

---

* Small quantities of Australian wine were exhibited at the Great Exhibition of 1851.
† Lewis's sardonic humour is best remembered in his quip: 'Life would be tolerable were it not for its amusements.'

'rising hope of those stern unbending Tories', Gladstone had initially refused to show any interest in joining the Liberal Party, staying away from Willis's, and voting with the Conservative government on 10th June. What brought him into the fold was a case of mutual need. Gladstone could not bear the thought of four more years in the wilderness after his celebrated turn as Chancellor from 1852 to 1855 and, despite a personal antipathy towards him, Palmerston needed Gladstone's reputation and proven abilities as Chancellor to give weight to his administration. Gladstone was by far the best orator in the House of Commons, which made him a hazard outside government. Moreover, there was one topic on which they both agreed: neither wanted Russell to succeed in enacting further political reform. It was not the most promising of partnerships. Gladstone always joked that he never attended a Cabinet meeting without a letter of resignation in his pocket, while Palmerston liked to claim that he kept the fires stoked for just such an event.*

In the matters of faith and the Church of England, Gladstone had few competitors. His rather ostentatious moral rectitude once led the Radical MP Henry Labouchere to complain that he did not object to Gladstone's always having the ace of trumps up his sleeve, only to his pretence that God had put it there. If Seward was an enigma, Gladstone was a man of complex contradictions. In contrast to Palmerston and Russell, whose political principles remained consistent, Gladstone's could and did change. He had begun his career as hostile to the abolition of slavery and cool on political reform. But the man who once said, 'I am a firm believer in the aristocratic principle – the rule of the best. I am an out-and-out inegalitarian', would develop a zeal for both causes during the 1860s, later becoming known as the 'The People's William'.

Seward was conscious that there was no place for a man like him in British society, a professional politician with neither land nor personal wealth to sustain him. 'I would not be an aristocrat here,' he mused. 'I could not be a plebeian.'[13] He had received more kindness and respect

---

* On hearing the news that Gladstone had joined the government, Charles Sumner claimed with his customary humility that he always knew Mr Gladstone would join the Liberals. 'Mr Gladstone's fame seems constantly ascending,' he wrote to the Duchess of Argyll. 'When I first met him at Clifton, at a time when he was out of office and much abused, I predicted what has taken place, though I hardly thought it would come so soon.'[12]

from the English than he had ever expected and never again would he feel abashed by Charles Sumner's casual references to his aristocratic friends. But his success in London had been rather more mixed than Sumner's.

Seward had failed to impress the Assistant Secretary at the American legation. Benjamin Moran had worked at the legation since 1853, starting as a temporary clerk and gradually moving up the ranks to Assistant Secretary in 1857. His wife died a few months after his promotion, leaving him to grieve in the basement of the legation, where, surrounded by mildewed records, broken lamps and rusting trunks, he diligently copied out dispatches and reviewed documents. When the occasion arose, he also issued passports and performed minor services for American citizens. Moran was sympathetic to those who came begging for help, but his manner was a repellent combination of the insinuating and the supercilious. Although he could never understand why, every Minister he served took pains to keep him in the basement and away from social functions. His diary became his best friend, a silent confidant with whom he could share his prejudices and disappointments. Moran yearned to be a popular man about town, a desire so entirely out of keeping with his manner and humble Pennsylvanian origins that, if known, it would have provoked hoots of laughter. Yet he persisted in believing it an attainable goal, despite the cruel neglect of his superiors.

Moran was prepared to give Seward the benefit of the doubt at their first meeting on 21 May 1859. 'He is a much smaller man than I thought him,' wrote Moran with a thrill of pleasure. His head, he noticed, was only a 'little larger than mine' and he had 'a pleasing manner'.[14] His opinion altered when Seward ignored him at the next occasion. 'I met Seward at Fenton's [hotel] last night,' recorded Moran on 23 June, adding bitterly, 'and found his head turned with the attention he has received from England's aristocracy.'[15] Moran was consoled that his political heroes in Parliament, the Radical MPs Richard Cobden and John Bright, had shown little interest in cultivating Seward.[16] Known somewhat derisively as the 'Members for the United States' (Bright's portrait hung in the American legation), their friendship with Charles Sumner was well known and Moran had expected the same with Seward. Cobden and Bright were generally spoken of in the same breath even though they did not always agree with one another. Cobden was the quieter, the more intellectual and the better liked of the two. Bright, his one-time protégé, was a brilliant orator whose passion for denouncing the sins of the aristocracy made him a hero among the working classes. Both MPs were exponents of the so-called Manchester School of politics: they believed in democracy, low taxation, universal education, no government regulation, no military expenditure unless in self-defence, and free trade. America had already achieved many of these goals, which in their view rendered its other faults far more excusable than any of the 'great crimes' committed by Britain. Lord Palmerston angrily attacked the pair for being traitors and haters of all things English for whom 'everything that was hostile to England was right'.[17]

Seward was unaware that Richard Cobden thought him a 'light weight' who 'wrote too much, and thought too little'.[18] Seward had also disappointed Harriet Martineau, whose reputation as a woman of letters, social reformer, and commentator was almost as great in America as it was in England. Her study of the United States in 1837, *Society in America* – written after a 10,000-mile trek across the country which took two years – was considered by Americans to be one of the least obnoxious ever written by an English writer. Seward had travelled to her home in the Lake District to pay court. 'Miss Martineau ... applied her ear trumpet; and we talked right on, an hour and a half, chiefly, of course, about the great American question.' Seward was honest about the difficulty of forcing abolition on the country, perhaps too honest: 'I gave her my own more practical views, and spoke, of course, hopefully ... She betrayed, or rather confessed, an opinion, that I was a politician, rather than an abolitionist of her school.' But Harriet Martineau's actual objection was not over his abolition principles per se but his lack of principles in general. She thought he was cynical and self-aggrandizing, especially after he revealed that he had supported the complaints against the Royal Navy's pursuit of suspected slave traders because 'the more noise there is about war, the less probable war becomes; he always makes the utmost possible noise at the earliest moment', wrote Miss Martineau. 'In truth I was aghast. "You see," said he, "I am very candid."'[19]

Lord Palmerston himself went even further in his condemnation of Seward. The American was a 'vapouring, blustering, ignorant Man', whose overbearing egotism made him a danger to Anglo-American relations.[20] Palmerston had accepted his first ministerial post when Seward was 7 years old and by 1859 he had served as Secretary at War, Foreign Secretary (three times), Home Secretary and Prime Minister. He had been in politics long enough to recognize a fellow bluffer and opportunist. But having observed Seward's evident pleasure with his reception in England, Palmerston hoped that the good experience would translate into better diplomacy in the future.*

Seward was still abroad when the radical abolitionist John Brown led a raiding party of sixteen whites and five blacks in an attack on the Federal armoury at Harpers Ferry in Virginia on 16 October 1859. The raid was meant to be the catalyst for a slave uprising. But rather than sparking a Santo Domingo-style revolution, the attempt ended in a bloody stand-off against a company of US Marines directed by Colonel Robert E. Lee. Brown was hanged for treason on 2 December. The public's hysterical reaction to the raid, particularly in the South, frightened many abolitionists. The former slave and abolition campaigner Frederick Douglass, fearing arrest because of his known friendship with John Bright, gathered his family and fled to England.

Soon after his arrival Douglass was invited to give a lecture in Paris. The visit required a passport but Benjamin Moran at the legation refused to give him one, in accordance with the Dred Scott decision. Douglass felt it was beneath his dignity to protest and called upon the French embassy instead, which issued a passport without demur. In a separate incident on 21 November, Moran also shooed away Sarah Parker Remond, a black abolitionist from Boston who had become a popular public speaker since her arrival in England the previous February.[21] In his diary he claimed he would have issued a passport if she had sent the request by post, but Moran could not bear to be challenged, especially by a social inferior. Remond 'was so impudent', he recorded, 'that I had to order her out of the house.'[22]

The following week, on 28 November 1859, Moran foiled Remond's

---

* Shortly after Seward departed, a report arrived from China that the US Navy Commodore in command of the American Squadron had come to the aid of the Royal Navy during a fierce battle to capture the Taku Forts in north-eastern China. The US Commodore explained his decision to join the fight by declaring: 'blood is thicker than water.' This unexpected display of Anglo-American solidarity lent a rosy glow to Seward's visit. If the traditional enmity between the two navies could be overcome, then anything was possible – even a friendly White House under a Republican administration.

attempt to gain a passport using a third party. This, he thought, was the end of the matter until he read about her 'unjust' treatment in the newspapers. The *Morning Star*, which represented the views of Richard Cobden and John Bright, took the lead and attacked the legation for three days running. 'This has fallen like a bomb-shell among the family,' recorded Moran, referring to the Minister, George Dallas. Notwithstanding his Quakerism, Dallas was incensed at having his character impugned over a spat with a 'negress', and talked wildly of teaching the English a lesson by closing down the legation.[23] He wrote an angry letter to Remond, who replied by reminding him that it was her taxes that paid his salary.[24] To the British, the passport episode portrayed the United States as a racist and morally backward country whose treatment of non-whites was reprehensible. 'You may read the facts,' wrote Remond in the Quaker journal the *British Friend*, 'but no words can express the mental suffering we are obliged to bear because we happen to have a dark complexion. No language can give one an idea of the spirit of prejudice which exists in the States.'[25]

Charles Sumner returned to Washington in time for the opening of Congress on 5 December 1859. By staying in Italy throughout May and June, the wounded Senator had spared himself the spectacle of Seward being welcomed in London as though he were already the next President. Sumner had changed during his time abroad. He had always been prone to bombast and fanaticism, and had always abhorred compromise; after his caning on the floor of the House, these qualities were joined by a lack of restraint that made him vain and capricious.

Washington was much worse, Sumner complained to his friends in Europe.[26] He was not only more unpopular than ever in the South, but was also blamed in many quarters for inspiring John Brown's raid. The atmosphere in Washington was growing poisonous as Southerners sought to implicate leading Republicans in the supposed conspiracy behind the raid. Senator James Murray Mason was elected head of a Select Committee with powers to call witnesses to testify before Congress. One such witness was Seward, who received a summons as soon as he returned to America on 28 December. He kept his cool while Mason, whose seat was next to his in the Senate, harangued him for being the moral, though not actual, instigator of the action. Again and again, Seward's unfortunate phrase 'irrepressible conflict' was hurled back in his face. Democratic newspapers denounced him as the 'arch agitator who is responsible for this insurrection'. One Virginia newspaper even went so far as to put a price of $50,000 on his head; the Governor of Virginia urged the South to demand Seward's exclusion from the Presidency.[27]

The hysteria created by the raid led to Louisiana and South Carolina calling in December for the imprisonment of free Negro sailors while their ships were docked at port. 'There are plans for the re-enslavement of all the emancipated Negroes, and for purging the South of all Whites suspected of abolition tendencies, and what not,' Lord Lyons informed the Foreign Office.[28] But the Minister was ready to fight 'the Lynch Law Assassins', as he called them, and ordered the British Consuls in the South to insist on 'decent treatment for Coloured British Subjects', even if it meant defying local opinion.

Mason's Select Committee found no evidence of Republican connivance in John Brown's raid.[29] This did not lessen Southern suspicions, however. 'Our social lines were now strictly drawn between North and South,' recalled Mrs Roger Pryor, the Southern memoirist. 'Names were dropped from visiting lists, occasions avoided on which we might expect to meet members of the party antagonistic to our own.'[30] The few attempts to revive the old Washington life ended in failure. Shortly after Seward testified to the Committee, he went to a large dinner party given by the Southern society hostess Mrs Rose Greenhow. His protégé, the newly elected Representative for Massachusetts, Charles Francis Adams, was also present, with his wife, Abigail. 'An unfortunate allusion was made to some circumstances connected with the affair at Harpers Ferry, when Mrs. Adams launched out into a panegyric on John Brown,' wrote Mrs Greenhow, 'calling him that "holy saint and martyr," turning her glance full upon me at the time – to which I replied, in a clear and audible voice – for it may be supposed that this conversation silenced all other – "I have no sympathy for John Brown: he was a traitor, and met a traitor's doom."'[31] The rest of the company remained mute, including Charles Francis Adams, who was too mortified to put together a coherent sentence. He had expressly refrained from speaking about the raid in order to begin his Congressional career 'perfectly unencumbered'.[32] Seward was the first to recover. He 'aided me with great skill in directing [the conversation] into a new channel', Mrs Greenhow continued.

'A few days after I encountered Mr. Seward, and he approached me, saying, "I have just been writing to our friend Lady Napier, and have told her that in all Washington you were the only person who had the independence to give a mixed dinner party".' Mrs Greenhow had not given the dinner party for the reasons Seward supposed. 'Perhaps,' she wrote, 'had he fathomed my real object, he would not have been so grateful to me for the social countenance. At this early day I saw foreshadowed what was to follow, and I desired to obtain a thorough insight into the plans and schemes of those who were destined to become the prominent actors in the fearful drama, in order that I might turn it to the advantage of my country when the hour for action arrived.'[33]

Abigail Adams's career as a Washington hostess was stillborn as a result of her faux pas at the dinner. She had never wholeheartedly embraced the idea anyway; it was Seward and Henry Adams, her third son, who had pushed her into the role. Henry had written to her from Germany, where he was studying, 'Be ambitious, Mrs A. You're young yet! I wish you could make your "salons" the first in Washington . . . not on my own account, but as a family joint-stock affair.' Papa needed her, Henry argued: 'His weak point is just where you can fill it; he doesn't like the bother and fuss of entertaining and managing people who can't be reasoned with, and he won't take the trouble to acquire strength and influence that won't fall into his mouth.'[34]

Henry's assessment of his father's social limitations was harsh but accurate. At 53, Charles Francis Adams was a curious figure of a man; he managed to convey the impression of being not quite formed, that there were still untapped reserves of potential, while simultaneously appearing old and disillusioned with the world. Being the son and grandson of American Presidents had both defined and yet robbed him of ambition. He sought neither power nor attention. Small by American standards, he cultivated a professorial appearance, accentuated by a receding hairline that ended in fluffy wisps just above his ears. His face was kind, but it seemed more like a mask than a canvas for displaying emotion. It was as if at a young age Adams had entered internal exile and found the place congenial.

Adams's unsettled early life had no doubt impressed upon him a sense of being different from others. In 1815, after six years in Russia, his father became the American Minister to the Court of St James's, having helped negotiate peace with England. But for 8-year-old Charles it meant being transplanted from cosmopolitan St Petersburg to a small country house in the village of Ealing, several miles to the west of London, which his father preferred to living in the city. It also meant leaving a friendly nation to go to one that had been, until a few months earlier, America's enemy.

It was the Adams legacy, however, rather than any particular childhood event that cast the longest shadow over Charles's life. His father constantly invoked the family name as a form of praise and chastisement; if one of his children performed well he was simply doing what was expected of an Adams, if he failed the shame would follow him into the afterlife.[35] The treatment crushed his elder brother, but in Charles it created a morbid sense of duty. When they returned to Boston, Charles followed a well-trodden path, entering law then politics, the occupations of an Adams, and taking up the family crusade to see slavery abolished.

Charles Francis Adams loathed the noisy, public side of politics. He admired Sumner and Seward precisely because they possessed the drive and bravado he lacked. He could never emulate Seward's theatrical embrace of working-class voters, and public speaking made him miserable. He also lacked Sumner's charisma and conversational ease. Adams was no more likely to frequent Willard's Hotel than was Lyons. His greatest pleasures were the quiet concentration of historical research and the inner satisfaction of rock collecting. John Quincy Adams, who had become President at the age of 58 – beating his own father by four years – would not have been impressed to learn that at 51 his son had only just managed to reach the House.[36]

The price Adams paid for this determination to remain above, or at least away from, the fray was his failure to be considered for a place on any of the prestigious committees in Congress. Indeed he was so reticent that the winter of 1860 passed by without his making his maiden speech. He did not even attempt to cultivate Lord Lyons, despite a family history that gave him a far greater claim to the Minister's notice than Sumner, who stopped by the legation at every opportunity.

Lyons appreciated Sumner's visits. The Senator happily shared with him the sort of insider political gossip that diplomats are required to know but find it hardest to obtain. Although Lyons was one of the only

Washington figures whose standing had not been affected by the widening social chasm between the North and South, he was still as friendless as the day he had arrived in the city. Ironically, his inability to make social inroads made it easier for President Buchanan to confide in him. On 5 April 1860 Lyons bumped into Buchanan while taking his constitutional around Lafayette Square. The President looked harassed and careworn. He felt helpless, he told Lyons, against the forces that were driving the country apart. The only realm in which he hoped to make a positive contribution was that of Anglo-American relations; here he still considered himself master of his own house. 'He began by repeating an observation he often makes to me,' reported Lyons after their meeting, 'that it has been his great ambition to be able to say at the end of his Administration that he had left no question with Great Britain unsettled; that for the first time since the Revolution "the docket was clear".' Yet even in this, Buchanan feared that events were conspiring against him.

Ten months earlier, in June 1859, a domestic pig on the island of San Juan Island in the Strait of Juan De Fuca had wandered from its enclosure into the potato patch of a neighbouring farm. The patch belonged to Lyman Cutlar, one of twenty-five Americans living on the rugged, tree-lined island. Cutlar was tired of having his potatoes raided by the pig and he settled the matter for good with a bullet. The pig's owners happened to be British. They demanded compensation, and when Cutlar refused they took their case to the Governor of British Columbia. Unfortunately, it was unclear where the exact boundary lay between the territory of Washington and the province of British Columbia. The arrival in July of a company from the 9th US Infantry under Captain George Pickett appeared to settle the question, but then the Governor countered by dispatching a magistrate, Major John Fitzroy De Courcy, to the island. The Major was a decorated veteran of the Crimean War, and fighting rather than diplomacy was his forte. He did not bother to hold a parley with Pickett, instead ordering him to leave the island or face arrest. Pickett refused and requested several hundred reinforcements. The Governor sent several warships to reinforce De Courcy's authority. Pickett's men dug in, the ships manoeuvred into position.

Alarmed that the two nations could stumble into war over a dead pig, Lord Lyons and Secretary of State Lewis Cass immediately ordered the withdrawal of their respective troops. But the actual details surrounding the dispute were more difficult to resolve. Neither nation was willing to concede its right to the island. The best that Lyons and Cass could achieve was a compromise whereby both countries would maintain a small company of soldiers on the island until the question was resolved.[37] President Buchanan confessed to Lyons that he could not see any way to end the matter. 'The People of the West Coast were becoming very excited,' he told Lyons, 'and he really did not know what to do. He concluded by begging me to set my wits to work to devise some plan of coming to an amicable settlement.' Lyons promised to try, though privately he doubted that anything he suggested would be acceptable to the inhabitants of the West Coast.[38]

Lyons was still considering the problem when the Democratic Party convened in Charleston on 23 April 1859. A total of 630 delegates from around the country descended on the city to select the party's Presidential candidate for the election in November. The Southerners who openly advocated secession from the United States, known as the 'Fire-eaters', were determined to force the slavery debate into the open. William Yancey of Alabama had sufficiently recovered from the illness that had kept him from Lord Napier's farewell ball to lead the way with his brilliant oratory. The Fire-eaters wanted the party to endorse a platform guaranteeing Federal protection of slavery in all States and territories, including any new acquisitions such as Cuba or Honduras. But most Northern members of the party wanted to maintain the status quo. Yancey ostentatiously led a walkout of fifty delegates from the cotton States after the Northern majority voted down the pro-slavery platform. The Convention ended in disarray, without a Presidential nominee being selected.

It was obvious to all that the Fire-eaters were blackmailing the party with the threat of a split unless their platform was adopted. The Southern Democrats in the Senate pleaded with Yancey and the others not to turn the election into a three-horse race. The Democrats' turmoil had naturally boosted the morale of the Republican Party by the time its delegates gathered in Chicago in mid-May to choose their Presidential candidate. Seward was so certain of victory that he departed for his home town of Auburn in upstate New York with his farewell speech to the Senate already prepared. But once the balloting began his supporters realized they had made a tactical mistake in allowing the Convention to take place in Illinois, Abraham Lincoln's State, instead of in New York.

Seward's campaign was outmanoeuvred at every turn. Lincoln's supporters successfully portrayed their candidate as an American success
story. Lincoln was 'honest Abe', the humble 'rail-splitter' turned prominent lawyer, whose moderate views on slavery would do more to unite
the country than Seward's radical rhetoric. Seward's campaign manager,
Thurlow Weed, spent too much time doing deals and not enough on
assuaging the fears of the doubters. After a blazing start, Seward's camp
began to lose supporters and by the third ballot Lincoln had emerged as
the clear winner.

Seward was crushed. He had refrained from running for the Presidency in 1856 on Thurlow Weed's advice. Now he looked back and saw
it as his squandered opportunity. His loss to Lincoln seemed inexplicable
to anyone who had not attended the Convention. 'Seward went away
from Washington a few days ago feeling perfectly certain of being named
as the Candidate of the Republicans,' Lyons reported on 22 May 1860.
'I never heard Lincoln even mentioned by the heads of the Party here.'
Lyons could provide only scant details: 'he is, I understand, a rough
farmer who began life as a farm labourer and got on by a talent for stump
speaking. Little more is known of him.'[39] Charles Sumner sent a letter of
commiseration to Seward expressing his shock at the surprise result,
although he wrote to the Duchess of Argyll that, 'while in England,
I always expressed a doubt whether Seward could be nominated'.[40]

The British government was pondering the meaning of Seward's defeat
for Anglo-American relations when President Buchanan issued an invitation for the Prince of Wales to tour the United States.* The President had
heard that Queen Victoria was sending the 18-year-old Prince Edward to
Canada, in fulfilment of a long-standing request from the Canadians for
a royal visit. Buchanan suggested that the Prince's trip could be extended
by a further six weeks to include a stay at the White House.

Although the Queen was initially doubtful whether her son was up
to the job, Prince Albert and the Cabinet realized that Britain had been

---

* The biggest Anglo-American controversy in the early months of 1860 had been the bare-
knuckle prize fight between the Englishman Tom Sayers and the American John Heenan on
17 April. Billed as the world's first international boxing contest, the match dragged on for
thirty-seven rounds until Heenan's supporters broke into the ring. The contest was declared
a draw, which led to the claim by furious supporters of Sayers that he had been robbed of
his victory.

presented with a rare opportunity to improve the transatlantic relationship. Lyons, having been awarded the daunting task of deciding the Prince's itinerary, was delighted to have something other than the island of San Juan to discuss with Buchanan. Together with the Queen and the Foreign Office, Lyons devised an arrangement whereby the Prince would travel to the United States in an unofficial capacity, as if on holiday, though accompanied by himself and the Duke of Newcastle at all times. There were to be no official deputations, delegations or ceremonies. This, Lyons hoped, would dampen any attempts by Irish agitators to whip up local Anglophobia. Furthermore, in a nod to republican sentiment, the Prince would use the least of all his titles, Baron Renfrew, allowing him to be treated as an ordinary British subject while 'incognito'. Except for a passing visit to Virginia, Lyons simply left the South off the Prince's itinerary.

Naturally, in all the cities on the Prince's route, the request for 'Baron Renfrew' to be treated as a private citizen was ignored. Almost every inhabitant of Detroit was at the docks when the royal party clambered off the ferry *Windsor* on 20 September 1860. The same was true at the train station in Chicago. Bertie, as his family called him, was taken aback by the enthusiasm that greeted his arrival. The Americans seemed to like him even more than the Canadians did. At every stop there were parades, fireworks, banquets, triumphant tours, and thousands upon thousands of cheering spectators. For a young man who was used to being treated as a great disappointment by his parents, this was an experience beyond fantasy.

By the time the royal entourage arrived at Washington in early October, Bertie had become an enthusiastic admirer of America; he even thought the unfinished capital was a fine place to visit. He spent a night at the White House, where President Buchanan and his niece, Miss Harriet Lane, made an exception for the young Prince by allowing card games after dinner (although no dancing).[41] After being shown Congress, Washington's Monument, the Treasury and a score of other public buildings, he informed his parents, 'We might easily take some hints for our own buildings, which are so very bad.'[42]

From Washington, Lyons accompanied him to Mount Vernon, George Washington's estate on the banks of the Potomac river, 16 miles from Washington, where the Prince planted a tree at Washington's Tomb. The Minister was just beginning to congratulate himself upon a splendid piece of organization when the visit threatened to unravel during the trip to Richmond, Virginia. The locals were furious because the Prince's hosts had cancelled a large slave auction, and a hostile crowd gathered outside his hotel. Lyons managed to avoid a public confrontation, but that afternoon he and Newcastle encountered a second embarrassment when they discovered en route that the royal party was being taken to visit a slave plantation. Only with great difficulty did they convince their hosts that a tour of the Mayor's office would be much more pleasurable.[43]

When 'Baron Renfrew' arrived in New York on 11 October, his guardians were beginning to fear that the good-natured Prince's appetite for orphanages and parades had run its course. But Bertie absolutely loved New York. Some 300,000 people (out of a population of 800,000) lined the streets, climbing on rooftops, trees, carriages, and even hanging from street lamps to watch his carriage proceed up Broadway to his hotel. They cheered, threw flowers and waved banners which said 'Welcome, Victoria's Royal Son'. 'I never dreamed we would be received as we were,' he wrote.[44]

The Prince had never imagined such comforts, either. The Fifth Avenue Hotel was the newest and grandest addition to New York's already magnificent accommodations. Built in 1859 on the 'edge' of town on 24th Street and Madison Square, the marble-clad, six-storey building had the latest conveniences, including en suite bathrooms, communication tubes which allowed a guest to speak his request to room service, central heating and, most exciting of all, a 'perpendicular railway intersecting each floor'. The American ideal of luxury was different from the European. The ornaments and objets d'art often taken for granted in English or French houses were missing but 'the rooms are so light and lofty; the passages are so well warmed; the doors slide backward in their grooves so easily and yet so tightly; the chairs are so luxurious; the beds are so elastic, and the linen so clean, and, let me add, the living so excellent,' he wrote, 'that I would never wish for better quarters . . . All the domestic arrangements (to use a fine word for gas, hot water, and other comforts) are wonderfully perfect.'[45]

For one night the Prince was allowed to sample life as it was lived by New York's gilded 'Four Hundred'. On 12 October 1860 the entire entourage, including Lyons, travelled in a parade of open carriages to a grand ball at the Academy of Music on 14th Street organized by New York's most distinguished citizen, Peter Cooper. Four thousand guests bribed, blackmailed or otherwise insinuated their way into the most coveted social event of the decade. The danger of the Prince inadvertently starting a stampede was so great that the entrances to the supper rooms were guarded by prominent citizens, who admitted fifty guests at a time.[46] Even so, the ballroom floor partially collapsed beneath the dancers' weight and carpenters had to be called in during dinner. Bertie danced until five in the morning. Four hours later he was dressed and dutifully touring P. T. Barnum's American Museum, where he saw the 'Feejee Mermaid' and shook hands with Tom Thumb.

Grand torchlight parade of the New York firemen in honour of the Prince of Wales, passing the Fifth Avenue Hotel, 13 October 1860

That night 5,000 men from the City Fire Brigade marched in a torch-light procession past his hotel. Each company let off fireworks as it went under the Prince's balcony. 'This is all for me! All for me!' he exclaimed.[47] He was exhausted, like the rest of his entourage, but also elated. The warmth of the American reception made it difficult to imagine that there had ever been open hostility between the two countries. Even the much-anticipated protests from Irish immigrants had been confined to a single incident, when the Irish-dominated 69th Regiment of the New York State

Militia refused to march in the parade up Broadway.[48] Leaving New York with great regret, the Prince travelled to Albany on 15 October 1860, for a grand dinner given by the Governor of the State, Edwin Morgan.

Seward also attended Morgan's dinner. The past few months had been turbulent for him. Seward's return to Washington following the Convention was one of the most humiliating episodes in his life. He told his wife that the house felt 'sad and mournful' and that he missed the Napiers, whose engravings on the wall seemed 'like pictures of the dead'.[49] Seward could not decide which was worse, the complacent sympathy of Sumner, or the exaggerated politeness of Mason and the other Senate Democrats.[50] The demeanour of both demonstrated that they considered his political career effectively at an end. Only the Adamses, wrote Seward, were as 'generous, kind, faithful as ever'. Adams took him to task with uncharacteristic force after he learned that Seward was contemplating his retirement from politics. Neither Adams nor Weed thought Lincoln capable of winning the election without Seward, let alone running the country. Thurlow Weed had met with Lincoln after the Convention and offered his services for the upcoming campaign. His conversation had convinced him that if Lincoln were elected, which was beginning to look quite possible, the newcomer would never be a match for Seward; Lincoln might be President in name, but the real power would reside with Seward.

Weed's optimism about Seward's role stemmed from the Democrats' recent split into two camps. The Northern and Southern factions had decided to field their own candidates, Stephen Douglas for the North and John Breckinridge for the South, almost guaranteeing the defeat of both in favour of the Republicans. By early August Weed had managed to drag Seward out of his despondency and into a sufficiently robust frame of mind to contemplate a tour through northern and western States on Lincoln's behalf. Seward had to put up a brave front and conduct himself as a loyal party man; any other action would have given Lincoln an excuse to leave him out of his Cabinet. Seward knew that Weed was right, but its wisdom did not make the effort any less painful.[51] The Republican message that Seward carried to the Northern States contained something for everyone: no expansion of slavery, a protective tariff for American industries, a homestead law giving away undeveloped Federal land, and government aid to construct a transcontinental railroad.

Seward decided that he could not face the next leg of his tour unless he had sufficient company to keep him distracted. He set off in September with a large retinue which included a reluctant but loyal Adams and his 25-year-old son, Charles Francis Jr.; the president of the New York City police board, General James Nye (and Nye's daughter); his biographer, George Baker; and his daughter Fanny. But, even surrounded by friends and family, Seward had to wrestle with his emotions. The signs of his inner struggle were evident in the copious cigars and glasses of brandy that he consumed during the long train journeys. Charles Francis Jr. never saw Seward visibly drunk, but sometimes sufficiently inebriated to lose control, 'and set his tongue going with dangerous volubility'. Throughout the north-western States thousands of people flocked to hear Seward speak. The public adulation heightened Seward's already febrile emotions; his speeches became coarser and more strident. In Michigan on 4 September he marred a strong anti-slavery speech with racist asides about the feebleness of the African race. In Minnesota on 22 September he declared that Canada was destined to become part of the United States.

Seward no doubt believed that it was more important to reach out to undecided voters with his populist message than to concern himself with the effect of his pronouncements in far-off places. The Prince of Wales's tour of Canada was in mid-swing when Seward made his speech about its future as a United States territory. The poor timing prompted the Canadian and British press to give his speech much greater attention and credence than it merited. When he sauntered into Governor Morgan's house on the night of the dinner for the Prince, Seward was apparently unaware of the huge offence he had caused. The occasion was already a difficult one for Seward; he had often discussed the idea of a royal visit with Lord Napier. But Seward had rarely visited the legation after Napier's departure, and had not bothered to cultivate Lyons; he felt more comfortable talking to the Duke of Newcastle, who gratifyingly remembered him from his visit to England. Seward started well, until the same urge to drink and talk crept over him. By the end of the meal the Duke was reeling from the encounter. 'He fairly told me he should make use of insults to England to secure his own position in the States, and that I must not suppose he meant war. On the contrary he did not wish war with England and he was confident we should never go to war with the States – we dared not and could not afford it,' the Duke reported later to the Governor-General of Canada.

Outraged by Seward's effrontery, Newcastle did not mince his words in reply: 'I then told him there was no fear of war except from a policy as he indicated, and that if he carried it out and touched our honour, he would, some fine morning, find he had embroiled his country in a disastrous conflict at the moment when he fancied he was bullying all before him.'[52] Seward never gave another thought to the conversation. With the election less than a month away, all his energy was directed towards the campaign in New York.

The royal party went to Boston for more banquets, balls and celebrations, and finally to Maine for a last hurrah. 'During his last day [in America] I was with the party & parted with him on the pier,' wrote Charles Sumner to his friend Evelyn Denison, Speaker of the House of Commons. 'At every station on the railway there was an immense crowd, headed by the local authorities, while our national flags were blended together. I remarked to Dr Acland [Radcliffe Librarian at Oxford] that it seemed as if a young heir long absent was returning to take possession. "It is more than that," said he affected almost to tears.'[53]

Sumner believed that the two countries had arrived at a turning point in their relations. The Prince was 'carrying home an unwritten Treaty of Alliance and Amity between two great nations'.[54] A similar feeling was evident in England. After reading his New York correspondent's reports, Mowbray Morris, managing editor of *The Times*, wrote that the royal tour 'will do a great deal of good here. It will convince persons who know nothing of Americans except by very bad specimens, that Brother Jonathan really has brotherly feelings towards John Bull.'[55]

It was only later, when Lyons could reflect on the tour from the comfort of his Washington drawing room, that he realized its 'wonderful success'. 'I have now had time to talk quietly about it with men whose opinion is worth having,' he wrote, 'and also to compare newspapers of various shades of politics.'[56] He had seen nothing to make him wince, or even complain. During this period of political uncertainty, the American press had found in the ever-obliging Prince of Wales the one subject that did not stir controversy. Even the Anglophobic *New York Herald* announced that 'henceforth the giant leaders of Liberty in the Old World and in the New are united in impulse and in aim for the perpetuation of Freedom and the elevation of man'.[57]

But six weeks after the Prince had sailed away to the strains of 'God Save the Queen', Lyons confided to the Duke of Newcastle that all their exertions might have been for naught. 'It is difficult to believe that I am in the same country which appeared so prosperous, so contented, and one may say, so calm when we travelled through it,' he wrote. 'The change is very great even since I wrote to you on the 29th October. Our friends are apparently going ahead on the road to ruin with their characteristic speed and energy.'[58]

3

'The Cards are in our Hands!'

Seven States secede – 'Slaveownia' – Seward rises to the occasion –
Bluster – Adams is offended – William Howard Russell at the White
House – The April Fool's Day memorandum – The Confederate
Cabinet – The fall of Fort Sumter – Lincoln declares a blockade –
Southern confidence

'It seems impossible that the South can be mad enough to dissolve the Union,' Lyons wrote to the Foreign Secretary, Lord John Russell, after Lincoln was elected President on 6 November 1860. Yet South Carolina had already announced it would be holding a special convention to decide whether to secede, sending the price of shares tumbling at the New York Stock Exchange. The financial markets suffered another blow when a merchant vessel departed from Charleston, South Carolina, on 17 November, with only the State flag flying from its mast. President Buchanan pleaded in vain with his pro-slavery Cabinet to agree on a united response.

Lord Lyons cursed the little pig from San Juan Island and its penchant for Farmer Cutlar's potatoes. He wished he had been able to settle San Juan's boundary dispute during the Prince of Wales's visit. With the secession crisis gathering momentum, and Buchanan's growing feebleness with his colleagues, he doubted whether the issue would be resolved before Lincoln's inauguration. Lyons suspected that the Republicans would be far less inclined than the Democrats to agree on a compromise. He had noticed that the Republican Party as a whole – not just Seward – tended to pander to anti-British sentiment as a way of showing that its abolition platform was independent of foreign opinion. It was important not to give the Republicans a reason to complain, Lyons wrote to Lord John Russell, and he suggested that the government refrain from making any public statements about the current political turmoil in America.

Lord John Russell received Lyons's letter on 18 December, the same day the South Carolina convention began its debate on the question of secession. The Cabinet had become increasingly concerned by the South's reaction to Lincoln's victory. Palmerston thought it meant a second American Revolution was at hand. 'There is no saying what attitude we may have to assume,' he wrote with concern to the Duke of Somerset, 'not for the purpose of interfering in their quarrels, but to hold our own and to protect our Fellow subjects and their interests.'[1] Lyons's insistence that Britain stand aloof seemed eminently sensible. 'I quite agree with Lord John Russell and Lord Lyons,' Palmerston stated in a memorandum for the Cabinet. 'Nothing would be more inadvisable than for us to interfere in the Dispute.'[2] The law officers of the Crown assured Russell that the South Carolina ship flying its State flag could dock at Liverpool without any fuss. Customs officials there would treat the questionable flag as though it were a bit of holiday 'bunting', beneath anyone's notice and certainly not a matter for official comment.[3]

The imperative to stay out of America's troubles was one of the few issues that united Palmerston's fractious Cabinet. The other was Giuseppe Garibaldi's campaign to unite Italy. Here, too, the Cabinet had agreed in July that the best course was to remain neutral and allow Garibaldi to fail or succeed on his own. Since setting out in the spring of 1860 to lead the Sicilian revolution against the Bourbon monarchy, Garibaldi had inspired hundreds of British volunteers to join his Brigade. Dozens of officers had taken a leave of absence from the army in order to don the famous red shirt. Two ships from the navy's Mediterranean Squadron were almost emptied as sailors left en masse to form their own battery; even the Duke of Somerset, Palmerston's First Lord of the Admiralty, could not dissuade one of his own sons from running away to join the English Battalion. The willingness of so many volunteers to help the Italians left the army and navy chiefs with little doubt that they would have a problem on their hands if war erupted in America, where both sides spoke English and the ties of friends and family were even stronger.

'We have the worst possible news from home,' the Assistant Secretary of the American legation, Benjamin Moran, wrote in his diary. A few days later he stood with the American Minister, George Dallas, in front of a wall map of the United States, speculating with him as to which of the Southern States would go.⁴ 'The American Union is defunct,' pronounced Moran after the next diplomatic bag revealed that on 20 December 1860 South Carolina had voted to secede.

Moran was relieved by the reaction of the British press to what it called the 'cotton states'.⁵ *The Times* scoffed at the idea of secession: 'South Carolina has as much right to secede from . . . the United States as Lancashire from England.'⁶ But *The Economist* was less sympathetic, calling South Carolina's secession poetic justice since Americans were always boasting about their perfect democracy. The *Illustrated London News* was the worst, in Moran's opinion, since it asked 'our American

MONKEY UNCOMMON UP, MASSA!

Punch tells the Southern planters that the days of slavery
are numbered, December 1860

63

Cousins' to let the cotton States go in order to avoid making the same mistake as Austria, which almost bankrupted itself resisting the Italians' desire for independence.[7] Yet most newspapers followed the line of *The Times*. Words such as 'sharp', 'ignoble' and 'unprincipled' were frequently used to describe South Carolina. *Punch* suggested that the seceding States could name their new country 'Slaveownia'.[8]

The boastful rhetoric of Southern politicians was also attacked in the press. Senator Louis Wigfall of Texas came in for particular censure for his arrogant speech to the Senate on 6 December 1860. The South would be able to dictate her own terms to the world, he declared, because 'Cotton is King . . . Cotton waves his sceptre not only over thirty-three States, but over the island of Great Britain.' Queen Victoria herself, Wigfall roared, must 'bend the knee in fealty and acknowledge allegiance to that monarch'. The South could turn off the supply of cotton and cripple England in a single week. The Cabinet feared Wigfall could be right and agreed with Palmerston 'that no time should be lost in securing a supply of cotton from other quarters than America'.[9]

The South owed more than $200 million to the North, with most of the debt concentrated in New York, a city whose commercial ties with the cotton States were so close that some banks accepted slaves as collateral. The financial community was sent into a panic by the readiness of Southern businesses to use South Carolina's self-declared independence as an excuse to repudiate their debts. The *New York Post* denounced the practice as treachery, declaring, 'The city of New York belongs almost as much to the South as to the North.' The victims of the financial crisis were not only New Yorkers. In Britain, investors had almost $400 million in US stocks, bonds and securities; Benjamin Moran lost most of his savings in a matter of weeks. But the impact went deeper and wider in New York, and included victims such as Dr Elizabeth Blackwell, whose hard-won funds for her women's medical college simply evaporated. Mayor Fernando Wood was so anxious about the state of the financial markets that he briefly entertained a proposal for New York to secede from the Union and become a 'free city'.

In late December, with Lincoln still in Illinois going through appointment lists, and President Buchanan having retreated to his bedroom in the White House, Seward took the leading role in guiding the North's response to the seceding States. Thurlow Weed's prediction that Lincoln would 'share' power – and the escalating crisis – had persuaded Seward to put aside his hurt pride and agree to become Secretary of State.[10] His self-belief and ambition returned in full force once the decision was made: 'I have advised Mr L that I will not decline [the post],' Seward wrote to his wife, Frances, on 28 December. 'It is inevitable. I will try to save freedom and my country.'[11]

The Senate had appointed the 'Committee of Thirteen', and the House of Representatives the 'Committee of Thirty-three', to address Southern grievances. Seward not only dominated the Senate Committee but also made sure that his supporters – particularly Charles Francis Adams – were among the Thirty-three. Their work became all the more urgent after news reached Washington that the Southern states were seizing Federal arsenals and forts. Seward's strategy was to conciliate and delay for as long as possible. The South had been threatening to secede for years; he was convinced that if the hotheads could be contained, the moderates would gradually reassert control. He talked with such confidence that young Henry Adams felt he was in the presence of greatness.[12] But to Charles Sumner, Seward's willingness to guarantee the institution of slavery in order to save the Union was an insupportable betrayal of abolition principles. Sumner cornered Henry's brother, Charles Francis Adams Jr., when he visited the Senate and ranted at him like a 'crazy man', blaming 'the compromisers, meaning Seward and my father'.[13] As far as Sumner was concerned, his friendship with Adams was irreparably broken.

Seward ignored Sumner's ravings, confident that his conciliation plan would work given sufficient time. But in early January two delegations from the New York business community were told by Southern leaders in Washington that a movement had started which could not be stopped. Mississippi voted to secede on 9 January; Florida on the 10th. Alabama, Georgia and Louisiana followed in quick succession; their Senators left Washington and went to Montgomery, Alabama, where a special convention was due to begin on 4 February. Texas followed on 1 February 1861, the seventh State to secede from the Union. On the morning of the 3rd, Seward paid a surprise call on Lord Lyons, to reassure him that the South would be back in the fold in less than three months. Lyons had been wondering for several weeks when either the old or the new administration would remember the existence of the diplomatic community. He did not discount the value of being able to talk privately with the incoming Secretary of State, but everything else about the interview made Lyons dread his future relationship with Seward. He sent two reports of the meeting to Lord John Russell. In the official dispatch, which would be printed for public consumption in the parliamentary 'blue books', he gave a bland description that only hinted at the threats and preposterous claims Seward had levelled at him. Seward has, wrote Lyons with classic understatement, 'unbounded confidence in his own skill in managing the American people'.

In the dispatch marked 'private and confidential', however, Lyons admitted that he had been horrified by Seward's mix of cynicism and *naïveté*. The Secretary of State had tried to persuade him that there was enough Federal patronage at his disposal to bribe the South back into the Union. As far as Seward was concerned, there was no need to discuss the international ramifications of the conflict because none existed. As long as there was no bloodshed, he told Lyons, the seceding States would eventually change their minds. Seward also repeated to him a recent conversation with the Minister for Bremen (one of the smaller states of the German Confederation), 'no doubt for my instruction'. The hapless diplomat had complained about the Republican Party's election promise to place tariffs on foreign imports, saying that such a move would turn Europe against America at the moment when she most needed friends. Seward claimed to have replied that nothing would give him more pleasure since he would then have the perfect excuse for an international quarrel 'and South Carolina and the seceding States would soon join in'. 'I am afraid', concluded Lyons, 'that he takes no other view of Foreign Relations, than as safe levers to work with upon public opinion here.'[14]

A few days later, Lyons heard that Seward was trying to pass a message to him and the French Minister that they should ignore anything he might say about either Britain or France since underneath he had 'the kindest motives towards the two countries'. Lyons thought that Seward's visit to Britain the previous summer had given him not only a handful of fond memories but also the dangerous misconception 'that England will never go to war with the United States' and therefore 'could be safely played with without any risk'.[15] Lord John Russell advised Lyons to be blunt with Seward: he should understand that England's 'forbearance sprung from a consciousness of strength, and not from the timidity of weakness'.[16]

On 8 February 1861 Henry Adams wrote to his brother that Seward was in high spirits 'and chuckles himself hoarse with his stories. He says it's all right. We shall keep the border states . . . the storm is weathered.' The next day in Montgomery, Alabama, the Provisional Congress of the Confederate States of America elected Senator Jefferson Davis – one of Seward's closest Washington friends before the crisis – as Provisional President. William Lowndes Yancey, the voice of secession, proclaimed memorably 'that the man and the hour have met'. Davis was inaugurated on 18 February. A future general in the Confederate army informed his wife that 'the firm conviction here is that Great Britain, France and Russia will acknowledge us at once in the family of nations'.[17] Davis placed so much confidence in the power of cotton that he appointed Yancey, who had never been abroad, to lead the Confederate diplomatic mission to Europe.

Seward was still offering deals to Southern negotiators, even though Confederate troops were threatening the tiny Federal garrison at Fort Sumter in Charleston, when Lincoln arrived in Washington on 23 February. Everything about the new President proclaimed his rusticity. The two years he had spent in Congress during the late 1840s appeared to have left him in the same unpolished state as when he first entered. During Seward's initial conversation with him, Lincoln admitted with startling candour that he had no idea about international relations, saying, 'I shall have to depend upon you for taking care of these matters of foreign affairs, of which I know so little, and with which I reckon you are familiar.' More extraordinarily still, Lincoln showed Seward his inaugural address and invited him to give his comments.[18] Less than a week before Lincoln's arrival, Seward had insisted to the Bremen Minister that the Presidency was a matter of luck – rather like the monarchy – no one took the office-holder seriously. 'The actual direction of public affairs belongs to the leader of the ruling party here.'[19] Seward was obviously referring to himself, as though he was expecting Lincoln to settle meekly into his role as the ceremonial leader of the country, leaving him in charge.

No matter how hard Seward argued and cajoled, however, Lincoln would not be swayed from his notion that he alone had the right to select the members of his Cabinet. Nor did he accept Seward's contention that the US should abandon Fort Sumter rather than take a stand against Southern threats. Seward dared not reveal his promises to the Southern negotiators that Fort Sumter would not be reinforced. While

Seward struggled to assert his will over Lincoln, the Northern Republicans in the Senate took advantage of the missing Southern politicians, who were free traders to a man, to pass the Morrill Tariff on 27 February. The protectionist bill placed high import duties on most imported manufacturing goods; since 40 per cent of Britain's export trade went to the United States, the effect of the tariff on Britain would be devastating. Its impact on international relations ought to have been of the highest priority to the State Department.*

Seward was bitterly disappointed by Lincoln's refusal to alter his appointments for the Cabinet. His dismay was not palliated by the fact that the six other members were either neutral towards the President or former rivals, and equally suspicious of each other. Three – Caleb Smith (Interior), Edward Bates (Attorney General) and Simon Cameron (War) – were cool towards him. But the others, Salmon Chase (Treasury), Gideon Welles (Navy) and Montgomery Blair (Postmaster General), were outright enemies.[20] Seward tendered his resignation on 2 March. Lincoln calmly offered him the American legation in Britain as an alternative. He already had a second choice for Secretary of State: William L. Dayton, the Attorney General of New Jersey. 'I cannot afford to let Seward take the first trick,' Lincoln explained to his private secretary. Furious at being outsmarted by the novice leader, Seward conceded defeat before Dayton could be alerted to his good fortune. He withdrew his resignation on 4 March, and the unsuspecting Dayton was put down for London. But having lost the battle to keep some of his greatest enemies out of the Cabinet, Seward became even more determined that no one should interfere with his conciliation strategy and all through March he feverishly schemed and manoeuvred behind Lincoln's back.

Among the diplomatic community in Washington, the main topic of conversation was whether the North would employ any commercial sanctions against countries doing business with the South. Lyons agreed with Lord John Russell that Britain's commercial interests were paramount but he also thought that it would be a calamity if the North forced the 'maritime Powers of Europe to interfere' to protect their cotton

---

* The taxation on foreign goods depended on the economic interests of various Northern States; sugar, raw wool, iron, flaxseed, hides, beef, pork, grain, hemp, coal, lead, copper and zinc all received protection from outside competition – as did dried, pickled and salted fish.

supply since, in his view, the 'stain of slavery' made the South 'loath-some to the civilized world'.[21]

On 20 March Seward made another of his unscheduled visits to Lyons, this time to sound out the Minister's opinion on how the British would react if the North 'interrupted' the South's commerce. Realizing this meant a blockade of Southern ports, Lyons attempted a little bluster of his own and threatened point-blank that, if the North recklessly deprived Britain of cotton, she would fight back and 'the most simple, if not the only way, would be to recognize the Southern Confederacy'. Recognition, in legal terms, meant granting the South the status of a sovereign country. The North would not only then suffer a psychological blow, but might also find itself facing a united Europe which was prepared to protect the supply of cotton at the point of a gun.

Lyons was unaware that he had committed a grave error. He had given the impression to Seward, who thought that Lyons was too unimaginative to be bluffing, that Britain was looking for an excuse to recognize the South. Seward pretended that he agreed with Lyons's position, a tactic he often employed when he wanted to buy time. According to Seward's political philosophy, a frightened enemy was better than an untrustworthy friend. When he left the legation, it was to think about how to keep Britain at bay rather than how to help her avoid a disruption to her cotton industry.

The following day Lyons gave a formal dinner that included Seward and the senior members of the diplomatic corps. Though Washington had not taken to the Minister, it welcomed his copious champagne and French chef. The dinner itself passed without incident, but by the time the guests had moved to the drawing room, Seward was lubricated and loquacious. His gravelly voice suddenly rose above the gentle hum, causing Lyons to stop his conversation and turn around. He saw that Seward was having a heated discussion with the French and Russian Ministers. Seward impatiently motioned him to join them.

'When I came up,' Lyons reported, 'I found him asking M. Mercier [the French Minister] to give him a copy of his instructions to the French Consuls in the Southern States.' Unsure whether Seward was mad or just grossly ignorant, the Frenchman retreated behind a veil of diplomatic coyness, assuring him that the instructions contained nothing more than an exhortation to protect French commerce while observing strict neutrality. Seward then repeated the demand to Lyons, who employed the same device. This was tantamount to poking a rhinoceros. Seward lost control of himself; according to witnesses, he accused Lyons of threatening him with Britain's acknowledgement of the South. 'Such recognition will mean war!' he is said to have shouted. 'The whole world will be engulfed and revolution will be the harvest.'[22] Lyons avoided being too specific in his own report, merely saying that Seward had become 'more and more violent and noisy' so he had turned away, taking 'a natural opportunity, as host, to speak to some of the ladies in the room'.[23]

The French Minister, Henri Mercier, was a large, hearty figure who did not cave easily. He was sufficiently irritated by Seward's badgering to suggest to Lyons that they obtain discretionary power from their governments to recognize the South whenever they saw fit. Lyons was appalled by the idea and persuaded Mercier that it would put them in considerable personal danger from Northern and Southern extremists. He proposed a different plan – that they keep to a unified policy at all times. Seward would be less ready to pick a quarrel if it meant engaging America in a battle of two against one, and he would never be able to use one country as his tool against the other. Mercier agreed. A few days later, Lyons heard that there had been a 'stormy sitting of the Cabinet' on the day of his dinner and assumed this had been the reason for Seward's outburst.

In only three weeks Seward had changed from being the self-appointed 'ruler' to the odd man out in Lincoln's Cabinet. He tried to maintain his old mastery while struggling to find a place in the new order. His ability to dictate to Lincoln had come down to thwarting Charles Sumner's bid to become the Minister to Great Britain. Seward managed to persuade Lincoln that Charles Francis Adams should have the post. William Dayton was once again moved around the chessboard of patronage and given the Paris legation, despite being unable to speak French. It was a pyrrhic victory for Seward, however, since by staying in Washington Sumner became the new chairman of the Senate Committee on Foreign Relations. The post would give him great power and leverage against Seward, if he could change Lincoln's impression of him as a pompous know-it-all. 'Sumner', Lincoln allegedly said after their initial meeting in late February, 'is my idea of a Bishop.'[24]

Adams was no longer sure he wanted to be a Minister when the telegram announcing his appointment arrived in Massachusetts. 'The

President had seemed so intent on the nomination of Dayton, that the news finally came on us like a thunderbolt,' recalled Charles Francis Jr. 'My mother at once fell into tears and deep agitation; foreseeing all sorts of evil consequences, and absolutely refusing to be comforted; while my father looked dismayed. The younger members of the household were astonished and confounded.' Mrs Adams was surprised, continued Charles Francis Jr.,

> when presently every one she met, instead of avoiding a painful subject or commiserating her, offered her congratulations or expressions of envy. So she cheered up amazingly. As to my father, he had then lived so long in the atmosphere of Boston, that I really think the great opportunity of his life when suddenly thrust upon him caused a sincere feeling of consternation. He really felt that he was being called on to make a great personal and political sacrifice.[25]

Adams's poor opinion of Lincoln had increased after the inauguration ball when the President did not even pretend to recognize him. He travelled to Washington to accept his appointment in a state of deep pessimism. Breakfast with Seward on 28 March made him feel worse: 'he spoke of my appointment as his victory,' complained Adams indignantly, 'whilst he made a species of apology for the selection of Mr Wilson which seemed to me a little lame.' Charles Wilson was to have the important post of legation Secretary as compensation for missing out on the plum job of heading the Chicago Post Office, a position with a high salary and little responsibility.[26] Seward admitted that the Illinois newspaper editor could hardly be less qualified or suited to work under Adams, but Lincoln had insisted on the move as a quid pro quo for changing Dayton.

Seward accompanied Adams to the White House for his interview with Lincoln. Adams was shocked by the 'ravenous crowd' of office-seekers who milled around the building, blocking stairs and corridors.[27] Inside Lincoln's office they found the President in deep conversation with a Congressman over other potential candidates to head the much-discussed Chicago Post Office job. When Adams began to express his gratitude for the appointment to London, Lincoln hurriedly cut him short, saying it was all Seward's doing. He then turned his back on Adams in order to engage Seward and the Congressman in further discussion on 'the Chicago case'. Adams waited, uncertain whether the conversation was over, until a gesture from Seward indicated he had been dismissed.[28]

Adams was insulted. 'Such was his fashion of receiving and dismissing the incumbent of one of the two highest posts in the foreign service of the country!' he complained in his diary. Nor had he been invited to attend the first state dinner of the White House, taking place that night, a gross slight considering that Seward was bringing as his guest William Howard Russell of *The Times*, who had arrived in Washington shortly after Lincoln's inauguration.

The 40-year-old war correspondent William Howard Russell, known to his friends as Billy, was the most famous journalist in the world. His honest and searing reports from the Crimean War had made a heroine of Florence Nightingale as they had rocked the Aberdeen government.

Russell was the ideal choice to represent *The Times* in the United States. Over-eating and drinking were his chief vices – especially drinking, which had grown worse as his wife, Mary, became increasingly frail and dependent on him. Their four older children were in boarding school, but Russell had left her nursing their four-month-old son, Colin, who seemed as weak and poorly as his mother. After saying goodbye, 'I went to the station in a storm of pain', Russell wrote in his diary, feeling guilty that the night before he had been enjoying himself at the Garrick Club, where the novelist William Makepeace Thackeray proposed a toast in his honour.[29]

The qualities which made Russell an unsatisfactory husband to Mary were precisely those which John Thadeus Delane, the editor of *The Times*, hoped would endear him to the Americans. Russell was at his happiest in company; over dinner his round face and bright blue eyes would come alive as he amused his listeners with witty observations and stories. He could converse easily with anyone, which Delane knew was a vital prerequisite for success in democratic America.

Although *The Times*'s circulation was small by US standards, hardly more than 65,000, the paper's influence was felt around the globe. Unlike its newer rivals, such as the *Daily Telegraph* and the *Daily News*, *The Times*, which was founded in 1785, had the financial resources to provide the latest news from distant countries. There were many who resented its power. 'What an absurd position we are in, so completely dictated to and domineered by one newspaper,' complained the MP

Richard Cobden, who was nevertheless grateful when, in April 1859, a fellow passenger on a Mississippi steamboat, Senator Jefferson Davis, had offered to share his copy with him.

William Howard Russell soon discovered that celebrity in America had its drawbacks. A drunken night at the Astor Hotel with the Friendly Society of St Patrick made the front pages. Apparently – since he could not remember the evening's events – Russell had made a rousing speech in favour of the Union. He confessed in his diary, 'O Lord, why did I do it?' When Delane learned of the episode, he asked him the same question. English writers had a poor reputation in the South for coming 'with their three p's: pen – paper – prejudices'.[30] Russell had jeopardized the paper's credibility and his own, which was not as high in America as he assumed.[31] 'I should imagine that you must be very perplexed in England,' a British immigrant in New York remarked to his relatives. 'The idea is somewhat amusing to us here that Mr Russell should be sent over specially to report on American politics, as we are perfectly confidant [sic] no novice could possibly be acquainted with the ins and outs, schemes, shifts and knaveries of this glorious disunion.'[32]

During his journey to Washington in March, Russell had shared a railway carriage with Henry Sanford, the new American Minister to Belgium. They talked at great length – Russell had no idea that he was conversing with the future head of the US secret service in Europe. Sanford, on the other hand, grasped Russell's usefulness to the North and invited him to dine with Seward and his friends that evening. Seward dominated the dinner with his jokes and confidential anecdotes, giving Russell the opportunity to study him at length. He liked the way Seward's eyes twinkled when he talked, although he suspected it was from self-importance rather than kindliness. Seward strutted as though he was 'bursting with the importance of state mysteries, and with the dignity of directing the foreign policy of the greatest country – as all Americans think – in the world'.[33]

The following day Seward showed him around his kingdom, a plain brick building which housed the State Department. There were usually a hundred people scattered throughout its offices, but a recent purging of Southern sympathizers made the place seem almost devoid of activity. Seward's own office was surprisingly modest in Russell's view, merely a 'comfortable apartment surrounded with book shelves and ornamented with a few engravings'. Also in evidence was his liking for cigars.[34] In the afternoon Seward introduced him to Lincoln. The President may have been new to the role of national leader, but he was an old hand at flattering men's vanities. 'Mr Russell,' he said, 'I am very glad to make your acquaintance, and to see you in this country. The London *Times* is one of the greatest powers in the world – in fact, I don't know anything which has more power – except perhaps the Mississippi. I am glad to know you as its minister.'

Russell was 'agreeably impressed with his shrewdness, humour, and natural sagacity'. But it was impossible for him to overlook the sheer ungainliness of the President. Lincoln was a 'tall, lank, lean man', he wrote, 'considerably over six feet in height, with stooping shoulders, long pendulous arms, terminating in hands of extraordinary dimensions' which were only exceeded by his enormous feet. 'He was dressed in an ill-fitting wrinkled suit of black, which put one in mind of an undertaker's uniform at a funeral.' His ears were wide and flapping, his mouth unnaturally wide, his eyebrows preternaturally shaggy. Yet all was mitigated for Russell by the look of kindness in his eyes.[35]

The state dinner from which Charles Francis Adams had been excluded was fascinating to Russell for the view it provided of Lincoln's relationship with his new Cabinet. The formality of the occasion did not deter some of them from continuing their arguments with the President over the dispensing of patronage. Russell observed that the difference between Lincoln and politicians 'bred in courts, accustomed to the world' was that they used sophisticated subterfuge to escape awkward situations, whereas the President told shaggy-dog stories. But the effect was the same: Lincoln disarmed his enemies without causing offence. As for the Secretaries, they all seemed like men of ordinary or average ability, with the exception of Salmon Chase, the Secretary of the Treasury, who 'struck me as one of the most intelligent and distinguished persons in the whole assemblage'. Mrs Lincoln caught Russell's attention for other reasons. She was not as ludicrous as the Washington gossips had led him to believe, but her energetic fanning and over-use of the word 'sir' were a decided distraction.

Russell returned to his rooms at Willard's after the dinner, unaware that Lincoln had asked the Cabinet to remain behind for an emergency meeting. Fort Sumter had become the flashpoint in the tense relations between the North and South; the decision whether to abandon it or fight to preserve Federal control could no longer wait. The Cabinet deliberations continued the next day. Seward tried every expedient to prevent Lincoln from forcing a decision: he had practically promised Southern negotiators that the President would sacrifice the fort in return for peace and loyalty to the Union. Seward saw dishonour facing him if his double-dealing became known, and his efforts to prevent troops from being sent became ever more serpentine.

Seward was conspicuously absent when William Howard Russell visited the White House again, on 31 March, for a near-deserted reception given by Mrs Lincoln. Nor did he attend Lord Lyons's dinner that evening, which gave Charles Sumner the field to himself. The other missing person was Charles Francis Adams, who ought to have paid his respects at the British legation after accepting his post but had hurried home to Massachusetts instead. 'My visit has changed my feelings much,' he wrote. 'For my part I see nothing but incompetency in the head. The man is not equal to the hour.' Like William Howard Russell, he dismissed the rest of the Cabinet as 'a motley mixture, consisting of one statesman, one politician, two jobbers, one intriguer, and two respectable old gentlemen'.[36] Adams was determined to avoid inconveniencing himself or his family any more than was necessary. Although the last of the Southern diplomatic envoys had already left for London, Adams could not see why he should chase after them. He was going to arrange his affairs, pack in an orderly fashion and, most important of all, attend his oldest son's wedding in Massachusetts. Decades later his son Charles Francis Jr. severely criticized his father for being so petulant:

> Every stage of our action was thus marked by extreme deliberation; and the Confederate Commissioners took full advantage of the fact. There can, I think, be no question that my brother John's marriage on the 29th of April 1861, led to grave international complications. It is creditable to neither Seward nor my father that the latter was allowed to dawdle away weeks of precious time because of such a trifle. It was much as if a general had permitted some social engagement to keep him away from his headquarters on the eve of a great battle.[37]

Adams's casual neglect of Lord Lyons was another serious mistake. Lyons would have been able to give him valuable insights and directions in his dealings with the British government, among them that the British genuinely desired to keep aloof. He might even have discovered, as Russell did, that Lyons was 'strong for the Union'. The information might have been helpful to Seward as well, whose paranoia was increasing by the day. A few days in Seward's company had allowed Russell to see through the bonhomie to the ambiguities of his character. Initially he had found him to be slightly absurd; but the more Seward insisted that there was no imminent Civil War, and that neither England nor France was allowed to refer to it as such, the more Russell inclined to Lyons's opinion that Seward was either a deluded narcissist or a desperate bully, and possibly both.

Seward was tormented by his declining political influence, telling his wife that he felt like 'a chief reduced to a subordinate position, and surrounded with a guard to see that I do not do too much for my country, lest some advantage may revert to my own fame'.[38] He made one last effort to reassert his authority and composed a memorandum entitled 'Thoughts for the President's Consideration', which was delivered to Lincoln's office on 1 April. It is often called the 'April Fool's Day memorandum', and in it Seward argued that a foreign war was the only salvation for the Union. What possessed him to make such a bizarre proposal has puzzled historians ever since.[39] Seward criticized the administration, meaning Lincoln, for being 'without a policy, either domestic or foreign'. As a remedy, Seward proposed to reunite the country by creating a foreign threat – in his words, to 'change the question before the Public from one upon Slavery . . . to one of Patriotism or Union'.[40]

Seward concluded his letter with the statement: 'Whatever policy we adopt, there must be an energetic prosecution of it. Either the President must do it himself . . . or devolve it on some member of his Cabinet . . . It is not in my especial province, but I neither seek to evade nor assume responsibility.' This was sheer flummery. Seward was making a last grab for power. He had forewarned Henry Raymond, the editor of the *New York Times*, and shown him the memorandum so that a positive story would accompany the sudden change in policy.[41] As it transpired, Raymond had nothing to report. Lincoln shrugged off Seward's attempt to coerce him with magnificent indifference. The proud Secretary of State was gradually being corralled into his own corner. Once the Cabinet decided upon a relief expedition to Fort Sumter, the only concession Seward was able to wrest from Lincoln was that the South Carolina authorities be forewarned. It was not much, but it would save him from appearing to have deliberately and recklessly misled the Southern negotiators about the President's intentions.

By 6 April the time for deals and machinations had drawn to a close. A relief fleet bearing provisions for the hungry defenders of Fort Sumter was making its way towards Charleston. The expectation in Washington was that its appearance would almost certainly provoke violence. William Howard Russell sent a note to Seward, asking him for a definite answer regarding the truth about a relief expedition. He was rewarded with an invitation to dine on 8 April. The evening began with a foursome of whist beside the fire. As the game progressed Seward became more vehement in his pronouncements about the government's intentions. Suddenly, he put down his cards and ordered his son to fetch his portfolio from the office. His daughter-in-law understood the hint and left the room. When they were alone, Seward handed Russell a cigar and removed a paper from the portfolio. It was, he told Russell, the dispatch he was about to send to Charles Francis Adams.

Seward proceeded to read the dispatch aloud, 'slowly and with marked emphasis', almost as though he was declaiming a speech in front of a large audience. 'It struck me', wrote Russell in wonderment,

> that the tone of the paper was hostile, that there was an undercurrent of menace through it, and that it contained insinuations that Great Britain would interfere to split up the Republic, if she could, and was pleased at the prospect of the dangers which threatened it. At all the stronger passages Mr Seward raised his voice, and made a pause at their conclusion as if to challenge remark or approval.[42]

Russell did not know what to make of such a performance. Ignorant of Seward's conversations with Lyons, he was baffled why Seward should want to turn a potential ally into an enemy.

The following day, 9 April, Davis's Confederate Cabinet agreed to attack Fort Sumter before the Federal relief fleet could arrive. In Washington, Russell scouted in vain for information, sloshing through the rain from one Department to the next. He wanted to investigate conditions in the South before one or both sides imposed travel restrictions across the lines, but at the same time he was loath to leave the capital in case he missed something of importance. Finally, on the 12th, he bought a train ticket for Charleston. As he paid a final round of calls to his new acquaintances he received strong hints that something was about to happen. In fact, the first Confederate gun had fired on Fort Sumter at 4.30 in the morning.

Lord Lyons was keen to hear from Russell during his travels and invited him to rely on the consulates for his postal needs. The offer soon proved to be indispensable to Russell. He had noticed a certain ugliness creeping into the public mood as he progressed further south. Virginia was relatively calm but in North Carolina, he wrote, 'the wave of the secession tide struck us in full career'.[43] A 'Vigilance Committee' in Wilmington demanded to know his sympathies and refused to let him telegraph his copy to New York. At subsequent train stops Russell observed drunken posses brandishing their guns.

He reached Charleston on 16 April 1861, two days after the Federal garrison had surrendered to the elaborately named Confederate general Pierre Gustave Toutant Beauregard. The boisterous celebrations on the city's streets reminded him of Paris during the last revolution there. Russell did not pretend to understand the South but 'one thing is for certain', he asserted to Lyons, 'nothing on earth will induce the people to return to the Union'.[44] Russell was surprised when the British Consul in Charleston, Robert Bunch, revealed that a mere quarter of the Southern population owned all 3.5 million slaves. Even if slavery were abolished tomorrow, calculated Russell, fewer than 300,000 whites would be affected out of a population of 5.5 million. Yet every conversation demonstrated a support for slavery and independence that was inextricably entwined with a hatred of the North.

Robert Bunch had been the Consul in Charleston since 1853 and was regarded by many as a permanent fixture in Southern society. He gave a dinner for Russell on 18 April that was singular in the brutal honesty with which the guests predicted Britain's swift humiliation by the South if she did not immediately recognize the Confederate government. Only the day before, Virginia had provisionally voted to join the Confederacy, raising the number of seceded States from seven to eight. Arkansas, North Carolina and Tennessee looked certain to follow. Bunch's Southern guests were exultant. 'It was scarcely agreeable to my host or myself', wrote Russell, to be told that England owed allegiance to the 'cotton kingdom'. 'Why, Sir,' sneered one of the guests. 'We have only to shut off your supply of cotton for a few weeks, and we can create a revolution in Great Britain. There are four millions of your people depending on us for their bread ... No, sir, we know that England must recognise us.' Russell and Bunch maintained a polite silence as all the Southern guests present voiced their agreement.[45]

Two days later, the Charleston papers reported that a local shipping company was starting its own direct line to Europe. Almost as an aside, the papers noted that Jefferson Davis had invited civilian ships to apply for 'letters of marque',* and that Abraham Lincoln had declared a blockade of Southern ports. When Russell questioned a businessman about the wisdom of launching a shipping line in the midst of a blockade, he was told, '"If those miserable Yankees try to blockade us and keep you from your cotton, you'll just send their ships to the bottom and acknowledge us. That will be before autumn, I think." It was in vain I assured him he would be disappointed.'[46]

The Cabinet in Washington had argued furiously over whether to blockade the South. Lincoln's decision in April to call for 75,000 volunteers had been universally approved, but the blockade issue thrust Seward squarely into a challenge against his foe, Gideon Welles, the Secretary of the Navy. Welles and his supporters in the Cabinet wanted Southern ports closed by Federal mandate rather than blockaded by the US navy. He pointed out that a 'blockade' was bound by a set of legal definitions and practices. First and foremost, a country could not blockade itself. A blockade was a weapon of war between two sovereign countries, or 'belligerents' in technical terms. By formally blockading the South, the North would in effect be granting it belligerent status, which would be extremely useful to the Confederacy. The quasi-recognition of its existence conferred on the South the power to raise foreign loans and purchase supplies from neutral nations. Its navy would have the right of search and seizure on the high seas. It would also be able to enlist foreign volunteers in countries that had not declared neutrality. These would be no mere trifles.

Welles argued that Europe would almost certainly go the next step and recognize the existence of the Confederacy. Nevertheless, it was Seward who prevailed, although whether he truly understood the difference between a blockade and a port closure, or why it mattered in international law, remains open to conjecture.[47] In addition to declaring

---

* A letter of marque was a government licence, allowing a civilian ship to attack the merchant shipping of the enemy in time of war. Ships that carried such letters were called privateers – to distinguish them from pirates. Davis had resorted to this old-fashioned method of sea warfare because it would be many months before the Confederacy had its own navy.

a blockade, Lincoln announced that captured privateers would be treated as pirates and executed.[48]

Lord Lyons sided with Seward, not about the execution of Southern privateers, but about the blockade, since it would force the North to abide by the Declaration of Paris of 1856.* He soon realized, however, that the Secretary of State had no interest in knowing the Paris rules, let alone following them. Seward ignored or failed to carry out even the most basic responsibilities demanded by the Declaration.[49] Neither the US Ministers abroad nor the diplomatic community in Washington was given advance warning. When Seward finally sent an official notice to the foreign Ministers on 27 April, Lyons was dismayed by the vagueness of the document. It appeared to have been written on the fly, without addressing a single question as to how and when the blockade would be enforced.

Lyons had never quite given up hope that Britain might support the North, either actively or surreptitiously; it was part of the reason he was working so hard to hold the French in check. Henri Mercier had revealed that France was prepared to ignore the blockade if Britain agreed to the same policy. Having known Mercier since their Dresden days, when they used to partner each other in whist, Lyons thought it was typical of him to devise a plan so fraught with danger. He also disagreed with Mercier's alternative, which was for Britain and France to respect the blockade until the beginning of the cotton season in September. This would be giving the South 'a moral encouragement scarcely consistent with neutrality', he reprimanded Mercier. Furthermore, it might 'entail utter ruin upon the [Northern] Administration and their supporters'.[50]

Lyons could not go any further than this with Mercier; Seward's behaviour had made it impossible. 'I confess I can see no better policy for us than a strict impartiality for the present,' he wrote sadly to Lord John Russell on 6 May:

> The sympathies of an Englishman are naturally inclined towards the North – but I am afraid we should find that anything like a quasi alliance

* The treaty had been drawn up and signed by the seven Great Powers of Europe – Austria, France, Great Britain, the Ottoman Empire, Prussia, Russia and Sardinia – after the Crimean War in order to establish a set of international laws governing both blockades and privateering. Ironically, America had not signed the treaty because President Pierce refused to relinquish the right to use licensed privateers.

with the men in office here, would place us in a position which would soon
become untenable ... my feeling against Slavery might lead me to desire to
co-operate with them. But I conceive all chance of this to be gone for ever.[51]

Seward's earlier messages to ignore his public statements made Lyons
fairly certain that the current display of aggression was for the benefit
of the Northern public. It perplexed him that a man of Seward's intelligence could not see the danger he was courting.[52] With an army of
16,000 men and a navy of 9,000, the United States was a military midget
compared to any of the Great Powers. If Seward does not 'pick a quarrel
with us', wrote Lyons to Lord John Russell, it will not be because 'of the
insanity which doing so at this crisis ... would seem to indicate'. Seward
clearly had no intention of 'conciliating the European Powers or at all
events of not forcing them into hostility'.[53] Charles Francis Adams Jr.
later admitted that his family had worshipped a false god. Seward was
not the grand strategist or great statesman they had believed him to be.
Seward had 'found himself fairly beyond his depth; and he plunged! The
foreign-war panacea took possession of him; and he yielded to it. The
fact is, as I now see him, Seward was an able, a specious and adroit, and
a very versatile man; but he escaped being really great. He made a parade of philosophy, and by it I was very effectually deceived.'[54]

President Jefferson Davis declared an official state of war on 6 May, the
same day that Lyons decided Britain could not risk making common
cause with the North. William Howard Russell saw the bill lying on
Davis's desk when he arrived to interview him for *The Times*. Davis
proudly informed Russell that more than 400,000 volunteers had
answered his call to arms, far more than they needed or could equip.
'He asked me if I thought it was supposed in England there would be
war between the two States,' wrote Russell. 'I answered, that I was under
the impression the public thought there would be no actual hostilities.
"And yet you see we are driven to take up arms for the defence of our
rights and liberties",' Davis had replied.[55]

   Russell had witnessed for himself the Southern version of liberty.
During a break in his journey to Montgomery, a slave girl, hardly more
than 10 years old, had begged him to take her away from 'the missus'.
She promised to serve him faithfully in return, since 'she could wash and
sew very well'.[56] The incident helped Russell to clarify his feelings about

the South. At first glance, its ruling class was just like the English aristocracy. 'They travel and read, love field sports, racing, shooting, hunting, and fishing, are bold horsemen, and good shots,' he admitted. But behind the façade was not an enlightened society founded on the ideals of ancient Rome but 'a modern Sparta – an aristocracy resting on helotry, and with nothing else to rest upon . . . Their whole system rests on slavery, and as such they defend it.'[57]

Montgomery, Alabama, was dreary and hot. 'I have rarely seen a more dull, lifeless place,' he wrote. 'It looks like a small Russian town in the interior.'[58] The ubiquitous slave auctions filled him with disgust. He was also unnerved by the discovery that he was the only white man in the city who was not carrying a loaded revolver. His interview with Davis had been a strange anti-climax. Both men were aware that the meeting could have far-reaching consequences. This was Davis's first, and perhaps only, opportunity to speak directly to Great Britain. Thousands of miles away, there was an audience waiting to meet the man who could hold Britain's textile industry to ransom should he so choose. Yet Davis was too proud to make a grand statement or appeal. 'He proceeded to speak on general matters,' wrote Russell, 'adverting to the Crimean War and the Indian Mutiny.' Apart from asking the journalist whether 'England [thought] there would be war between the two States', Davis hardly mentioned the crisis at all. Their conversation was so ordinary that Russell padded out his report for The Times with a description of Davis's appearance. The former Secretary of War under President Pierce was, 'about fifty-five years of age', wrote Russell, 'his features are regular and well-defined . . . the face is thin and marked on cheek and brow with many wrinkles, and is rather careworn and haggard. One eye is apparently blind, the other is dark, piercing and intelligent.'[59] Russell avoided mention of Davis's tic or his demeanour, which, though gentlemanly, was cold.[60]

Russell was equally disappointed with the Confederate Secretary of War, Leroy Walker, and the Secretary of State, Robert Toombs. The former spat and chewed while talking mostly nonsense, not being a military man; the latter seemed earnest but dim. 'Seward had told me', Russell wrote, 'that but for Jefferson Davis the secession plot could never have been carried out. No other man of the part had the brain, or the courage and dexterity . . .' Consul Bunch had said something similar to him during his stay in Charleston. In a frank appraisal protected by diplomatic seal, Bunch had commended Davis for his statesmanlike qualities but dismissed the rest of the Confederate Cabinet as 'the dead level of mediocrity'.[61] Having now made their acquaintance, Russell agreed.

The one Confederate Cabinet member who did make a forcible impression on Russell was Judah Benjamin. Russell disliked Jews in general, but he could not help warming to Benjamin, describing him as 'the most open, frank, and cordial of the Confederates whom I have yet met'.[62] Benjamin, he learned, was not a native Southerner. He had been born in the Caribbean on the island of St Croix, which technically made him a British subject. His family moved to the South when Benjamin was a baby, eventually settling in Charleston when he was 11 years old. Benjamin's undeniable brilliance propelled him to Yale Law School when he was only 14; something else – the cause has never been discovered – led to his expulsion. Russell noted in his diary that Benjamin was: 'clever keen & well yes! What keen and clever men sometimes are', referring, perhaps, to a certain ambiguity about Benjamin's sexuality.[63] Women enjoyed his company (although not his wife, Natalie, who had moved to Paris with their daughter in 1847); he could banter with them for an entire evening in English or French on any subject they pleased. But behind his perpetual smile there was a mysterious veil which none could penetrate.

Though he was only Attorney General, Benjamin had already made himself indispensable to Davis. There was so little for him to do at the newly formed Department of Justice that Benjamin could devote most of his energies to whatever appealed. For the time being, he was acting as the President's grand vizier. He shielded Davis from the place-hunters and took on the burden of sorting through many of the tedious but necessary details of government. 'When in doubt', recorded a visitor, all strangers were referred to 'Mr Judah P. Benjamin, the "Poo Bah" of the Confederate Government'.[64]

In contrast to his inarticulate colleagues, Benjamin immediately engaged Russell in an intelligent debate. Referring to the blockade and the legality of letters of marque, Russell asked, 'Suppose, Mr Attorney-General, England, or any of the great powers which decreed the abolition of privateering, refuse to recognise your flags?' What if, he added, 'England, for example, declared your privateers were pirates?' In that case, replied Benjamin, 'it would be nothing more or less than a declaration of war against us, and we must meet it as best we can'. He did not seem too downcast at the possibility. It was obvious to Russell that Benjamin was thinking about next season's cotton crop. Benjamin confirmed his suspicion by saying with a smile, 'All this coyness about acknowledging a slave power will come right at last ... we are quite easy in our minds on this point at present.'[65]

Many years later, when Benjamin was an exile in London, Russell bumped into him at a dinner party. They walked home together, reminiscing about the war. Russell reminded him of their meeting in Montgomery, and how he had been so certain that the British and French would intervene as soon as their cotton stocks were low. 'Ah, yes,' Benjamin replied, 'I admit I was mistaken! I did not believe that your government would allow such misery to your operatives, such loss to your manufacturers, or that the people themselves would have borne it.'[66]

Benjamin was too discreet to say that when the Confederate Cabinet held its first meeting his had been the lone voice in favour of making preparations for a severe war. The Secretary of War, Leroy Walker, remembered the meeting with shame: 'At that time, I, like everybody else, believed there would be no war. In fact, I had gone about the state ... promising to wipe up with my pocket-handkerchief all the blood that would be shed,' he recalled despairingly:

> there was only one man there who had any sense, and that man was Benjamin. Mr Benjamin proposed that the Government purchase as much cotton as it could hold, at least 100,000 bales, and ship it at once to England ... For, said Benjamin, we are entering on a contest that must be long and costly. All the rest of us fairly ridiculed the idea of a serious war. Well, you know what happened.[67]

Benjamin allowed himself to be swayed by his colleagues' optimism. Europe would end the blockade by the following October, he explained genially to Russell, 'when the Mississippi is floating cotton by the thousands of bales, and all our wharfs are full'.[68] Shortly after Russell left Montgomery for Mobile, Alabama, the Provisional Confederate Congress voted to prohibit all trade with the North, in order to prevent cotton from being shipped via Northern ports. 'The cards are in our hands!' proclaimed the editors of the *Charleston Mercury*, obviously unfazed by the doubts expressed by Russell when he visited their offices, 'and we intend to play them out to the bankruptcy of every cotton factory in Great Britain and France or the acknowledgement of our independence'.[69]

4

Expectations are Dashed

Where is Adams? – Debate in the Commons – The neutrality
proclamation – First interview with Lord John Russell – Seward's
horseplay – The power of Uncle Tom

A poem in *Punch*, on 30 March 1861, neatly expressed Britain's cotton
dilemma:

> Though with the North we sympathize,
> It must not be forgotten,
> That with the South we've stronger ties,
> Which are composed of cotton.

William Howard Russell's revelation that the South hoped to exploit
these ties, along with his poignant descriptions of slave life, provoked
outrage in England when his reports started to appear in April. But the
North gained less support than Southerners had feared since, in his inaugural address on 4 March 1861, Lincoln had promised not to interfere
with slavery. The Morrill Tariff, with its rampant protectionism and
whiff of anti-British bias, was an even greater gift to the Confederacy.[1]

At the US legation, Benjamin Moran read the angry protests against
the new tariff and took it to mean that the country as a whole had turned
against the North. But George Dallas, the outgoing American Minister,
whose existence was barely acknowledged by Seward, was much more
sanguine about the hostile opinion expressed in newspapers. Britain
'cannot be expected to appreciate the weakness, discredit, complications,
and dangers which we instinctively and justly ascribe to disunion,' he
told Seward on 9 April. 'English opinion tends rather, I apprehend, to the
theory that a peaceful separation may work beneficially for both groups

of States and not injuriously affect the rest of the world.'[2] He had obviously heard this said by many different people: even Thackeray had written to an American friend, asking: 'In what way will it benefit the North to be recoupled to the South?' After all, at this time, England had not wanted 'the Colonies' to go their own way, 'and aren't both better for the Separation?'[3]

Nor did Dallas believe there was anything to be feared from the British government. Lord John Russell had rebuffed Seward's demand for a promise never to have any dealings with the South or its representatives, but 'His lordship assured me with great earnestness that there was not the slightest disposition in the British government to grasp at any advantage,' Dallas reported to Seward.[4] Far from looking for an advantage, the Cabinet was approaching a state of panic over American affairs. Russell was shocked that six weeks after Lincoln's inauguration there was still no replacement for the now irrelevant Dallas, and was mystified as to what could be delaying the arrival of Charles Francis Adams at such a perilous moment in his country's history.

Benjamin Moran thought Dallas's benign view of the British made him either an idiot or a crypto Southern sympathizer. Dallas was certainly neither, but the knowledge that he was soon to go home may have made him apathetic when he should have been wooing potential Northern allies in Parliament. Moran also knew of at least one MP who was collaborating with the nascent Southern lobby in England. William Gregory, the MP for Galway, had given notice in the House of Commons that he was going to propose recognition of the Confederacy on 1 May. Moran thought the move had been prompted by Gregory's friend Robert Campbell, the American Consul at the London consulate.*

Campbell was a genial though strident secessionist from North Carolina who had supplied Gregory with letters of introduction for his tour of the United States in 1859. In Washington, Gregory had stayed in a boarding house popular with Southern Senators; their 'fire-eating talk' of independence, interspersed with liberal amounts of whisky, had swept the MP into their ranks. Privately, he thought their humanity had been dulled by slavery, but Gregory accepted his new friends' claim that emancipation was morally and economically impossible.[5]

---

* The US consulate in London was a separate entity from the legation in the nineteenth century, and dealt primarily with matters arising from shipping and trade.

Moran was furious with Dallas for failing to curb the pro-Southern activities of Consuls who had not yet been replaced by Republican appointees, but he dared not speak out when his own future seemed so uncertain. He remained in suspense until confirmation of his reappointment arrived on the 15th. Moran's other fear – that he was the only loyal American official left in Britain – seemed a certainty after he caught one of the new Southern envoys, Ambrose Dudley Mann, sneaking into the legation to see Dallas.

The arrival of the Confederate envoys was not unexpected. Their identities had been public knowledge for several weeks. Consul Bunch wrote from Charleston to warn the Foreign Office that they were three of the rankest amateurs ever to have been sent on so sensitive a diplomatic mission. He attributed President Davis's selection of such men to Southern arrogance and the belief that the Confederacy did not need proper advocates when cotton could do the talking. Dudley Mann had served as the US Minister to Switzerland, but Bunch dismissed him as 'a mere trading politician, possessing no originality of mind and no special merit of any description'. The second envoy, William Lowndes Yancey, had never been anything but a rabble-rouser. His campaign to reopen the slave trade, not to mention his support for expeditions against British territories in Central America, made him a peculiar choice to send to England. Bunch was particularly disdainful of Yancey: 'He is impulsive, erratic and hot-headed; a rabid secessionist.' Bunch could not see a single reason for the appointment of the third envoy, Pierre Rost, apart from his friendship with Jefferson Davis's family and his proficiency in Creole-French.[6]

Moran despised Dallas's excuse that Dudley Mann was an old and valued friend, until he too was forced to choose between loyalty and patriotism. A few days after Dudley Mann visited the legation, Moran received a letter from a friend in London who asked him for the Confederate envoy's address. The friend, Edwin De Leon, until recently the US Consul in Egypt, had invited him to his wedding two years earlier, but Moran was appalled at his request and wrote sorrowfully 'I would do anything in reason for him, but could not find it in my conscience to assist treason'.[7]

Forcing a debate in the House of Commons had become William Gregory's mission, and he would not be thwarted. Palmerston pulled the pro-Confederate MP aside in the Commons on 26 April and demanded to know why he saw fit to place the government in such an awkward position. He reminded Gregory that the speeches would be reprinted in Union and Confederate newspapers, and that both sides would end up being 'offended by what is said against them, and will care but little for what is said for them; and that all Americans will say that the British Parliament has no business to meddle with American affairs'. He reported to Lord John Russell that Gregory 'admitted the truth of much I said, but said he had pledged himself to Mr Mann, the Southern envoy ... Perhaps your talking to Gregory, either privately or in the House, might induce him to put his motion off.'[8] Russell was anxious about being pushed to make a public statement ahead of events. George Dallas had shown that he was as ignorant of the situation as the Foreign Office. During his last interview with Russell on 1 May, he had insisted that a blockade was not under consideration since there was no mention of the fact in the latest State Department instructions: it had to be a fabrication of the New York press. But Russell discovered the next day from Lord Lyons's dispatches that the idea was very much under consideration.

The day after Palmerston's confrontation with Gregory, the government learned that the Confederates had captured Fort Sumter. The initial newspaper reports were brief, but it appeared as though the South had won an easy victory. (The Thompson family in Belfast became the envy of the neighbourhood after they received a long account of the battle from their son, a Federal private in the Sumter garrison.[9]) 'We cut a sorry enough figure indeed,' complained Moran as he read through the dailies. 'Everybody is laughing at us.' Many papers described the news as 'a calamity', and 'a subject of regret, and indeed of grief', but Moran's attention was held by the *Illustrated London News*, which printed a pious editorial in favour of peace and 'no coercive measures' next to an announcement that Frank Vizetelly, the paper's star artist, war reporter and brother of the editor, was taking the next steamer to New York.[10] The tutting and clucking in the British press about the demise of the democratic experiment and the sorry state of 'our American cousins' also grated on Moran's nerves. *The Economist* recalled Britain's futile reaction to the American Declaration of Independence and advised the North to settle the dispute with grace; to continue fighting now, its editor Walter Bagehot scolded, would be 'vindictive, bloody and fruitless'.[11] The conservative *Saturday Review* could not resist

A FAMILY QUARREL.

Punch depicts the North and South as a mismatched couple

making a dig at Seward, who, 'though he cannot keep the Federal fort at Charleston, has several times announced his intention of annexing Canada'.[12]

Lord John Russell had still not spoken to William Gregory when the Southern Commissioners, Yancey and Rost, finally reached London on 29 April, a week after Dudley Mann. Unaccustomed to foreign travel, they had passed two miserable days in Southampton and had arrived in the capital feeling bewildered and frightened. Rather than pausing for a moment to consider the best way of contacting the Confederate community, they sent a telegram to the legation addressed to Ambrose Dudley Mann. 'The unblushing impudence of these scoundrels,' ranted Moran, 'to send their message to the US Legation for one of their fellow traitors.'[13] The timing and announcement of their arrival was fortunate for Lord John Russell since it gave him a bargaining chip with Gregory, who agreed to postpone his motion to 7 June in return for a Foreign Office meeting with the Southerners on 3 May.

Russell was not making a great concession, since it was standard Foreign Office practice to receive representatives from breakaway countries. These meetings never carried official weight, nor were the emissaries accorded diplomatic rank. Russell assumed that Dallas had lived in England long enough to know this, and that Charles Francis Adams could have it explained to him when he eventually arrived. Russell was more disturbed by the thought of Confederate privateers roaming the seas, and, at his request, the Admiralty was already taking precautionary measures to reinforce the North Atlantic Squadron. The prospect of encountering lawless privateers so frightened Dallas that he booked passage for his wife and three daughters for 1 May, hoping they would be home before transatlantic travel became impossible.

Russell's satisfaction over his dealings with Gregory lasted only twenty-four hours. On 2 May he received a run of telegrams: the first announced that Lincoln had decided on a blockade rather than port closures; the next, that Virginia, that mainstay of the American Revolution, had seceded, depriving the North of the large weapons arsenal at Harpers Ferry; and finally, that Maryland had erupted in violence, leaving eleven people dead in Baltimore during street fighting between Federal troops and Southern protesters.* 'This is the first bloodshed and God knows where it will end,' Moran wrote in his diary. It surprised and comforted him when several Englishmen called at the legation, vainly asking to join the Federal army. But the reaction of Russell's predecessor at the Foreign Office, Lord Clarendon, showed that old resentments had a habit of reviving: 'For my own part if we could be sure of getting raw cotton from them, I should not care how many Northerners were clawed at by the Southerners & vice versa!'[14]

When Russell went to the House of Commons that evening, he was bombarded with questions from MPs, not a few of whom shared Clarendon's view. He could give little enlightenment, but to those who expressed a desire for the government to intervene he warned against such a reckless

---

* It took ten days for a newspaper report in New York to be reprinted in *The Times*. There was a slightly quicker diplomatic route: if Lord Lyons needed to send an urgent message, he could send a telegram to Halifax, Nova Scotia, where it would be taken by steamer to Liverpool and telegraphed to London; this could cut the delay to eight or, in good weather, seven days.

move. 'Nothing but the imperative duty of protecting British interests, in case they should be attacked, justified the Government in at all interfering,' he told the House. 'We have not been involved in any way in that contest. For God's sake, let us if possible keep out of it.'[15] He delivered a similar message to the Southern envoys when they arrived for their interview on Friday, 3 May. Gregory had warned them about Russell's notorious shyness but they had not expected the frigid politeness with which they were received. Russell caught them off guard by declaring he had 'little to say'. William Yancey stumbled through a speech about the Constitution, Liberty and States' rights. He insisted the slave trade would not be revived, which Russell disbelieved, threw in a warning about cotton, which Russell ignored, and finally asked for immediate recognition, which Russell refused. The envoys returned to their lodgings at 40 Albemarle Street thoroughly disheartened.

Lord John Russell spent the weekend of 4 and 5 May carefully analysing the choices open to the British government. He hoped that anti-slavery would become the overriding cause of the war, but feared that the North would throw it over without hesitation if the Union could thus be saved. He was also torn between despising the South for its dependency on slavery and admiring its spirited bid for independence. Above all, he agreed with Lord Lyons that to give preferential treatment to the North would be unwise and possibly dangerous with Seward at the helm. Accepting the legality of the blockade, which would require a declaration of official neutrality, struck him as the wisest course, he told his colleagues, especially in light of Seward's evident keenness to manufacture a reason for declaring war.

The Cabinet was not enthusiastic about adopting a policy that was so dangerous to the country's cotton industry. Palmerston agreed with the proposal, though he felt it was a heavy price for staying out of the conflict. 'The South fight for independence; what do the North fight for,' asked the Home Secretary, Sir George Cornewall Lewis, 'except to gratify passion or pride?'[16] William Gladstone was privately even more outspoken for the South and compared Jefferson Davis to General Garibaldi. When his friend Harriet, Duchess of Sutherland, heard about this, she was outraged and demanded to know how he could 'think the Southern states most in the right – I did not hear you say; I don't believe it'.[17] Nor did she accept his explanation that the wishes of minorities ought to be respected.[18] Only the Duke of Argyll, her favourite son-in-law, wholeheartedly supported Russell. He abhorred revolutionary move-ments on principle; moreover, his friendship with Charles Sumner had given him an insight into American politics. He rightly understood that the Union had to be safeguarded since the South would never abolish slavery on its own.

In declaring neutrality, Russell was convinced he had chosen the best alternative; he had consulted the law officers of the Crown, as he always did when in doubt, and in their opinion the crisis in America was not a minor insurgency but a genuine state of war. The blockade could and should be recognized, they told him, and so should the right of the South to employ privateers. Russell endured some aggressive question-ing in Parliament when he announced the government's decision on 6 May. He was also pressured by Gregory into seeing the Confederate envoys for a second time, on the grounds that the Northern blockade had not been confirmed at the first meeting. Russell suspected they would try to make more of the neutrality announcement than the gov-ernment intended. Their exultant demeanour on 9 May showed that his instincts had been correct.[19] The envoys were unaware, however, that even as they pressed their arguments on him, the law officers were com-posing an additional proviso to Britain's declaration of neutrality which would make it illegal for a British subject to volunteer for either side in the war. Russell had meant it when he said, 'for God's sake, let us if possible keep out of it.'

Yancey, Rost and Dudley Mann were dumbfounded when they read the 'Queen's Proclamation of Neutrality' in *The Times* on 14 May. A close examination of the wording showed that Russell had taken away many of the advantages that belligerent status had initially seemed to give to the Confederacy. He had invoked the rarely used 1819 Foreign Enlist-ment Act, under which British subjects were forbidden to volunteer for a foreign cause or encourage others to do so.[20] The Act also prohibited the selling or arming of warships to either belligerent; those who disobeyed the proclamation would be prosecuted, and the offending items confiscat-ed.[21] The more populous, industrial North would be able to overcome these obstacles on its own, but not the smaller, agrarian South.

The Southern envoys realized that their two interviews with Russell had failed to make the slightest impression on him. Yancey ascribed their failure to Russell's prejudice against the 'peculiar institution', as Southerners euphemistically called slavery: 'We are satisfied that the public mind here is entirely opposed to the Government of the Confederate States of America on the question of slavery,' he reported to Robert Toombs, the Confederate Secretary of State. 'All that we can do at present is to affect public opinion in as unobtrusive a manner, as well as we can.'[22]

Charles Francis Adams also read the neutrality proclamation in *The Times* on 14 May. He had arrived in London the night before, having endured the worst sea crossing of his life. Henry, Mary and Brooks had, like their father, been prostrate with seasickness. Abigail, his wife, had stayed below deck for a different reason: Cassius Clay of Kentucky, Lincoln's appointee to the US legation in Russia, had embarrassed them by sauntering around the boat like a *Punch* caricature of the boorish American, with three pistols at his belt and a toothpick between his teeth.

Adams knew nothing of what had passed between Seward and Lyons. But even if he had known, his outrage at the British government's decision to act without waiting for his arrival and consulting him first would have been the same. 'Charles Francis Adams naturally looked on all British Ministers as enemies,' acknowledged Henry Adams in his autobiography; 'the only public occupation of all Adamses for a hundred and fifty years at least, in their brief intervals of quarrelling with State Street, had been to quarrel with Downing Street, and the British Government.'[23]

That first morning Adams was ready to confront Lord John Russell and asked George Dallas, who arrived at the hotel after breakfast, to escort him to Russell's house. To his dismay, the Foreign Secretary was not at home; a footman informed them that the family had been called suddenly to Woburn Abbey. Russell's brother, the Duke of Bedford, had collapsed and was not expected to recover. Forced to delay his confrontation for a few days, Adams turned his attention to the family's living situation. London had changed so much that he barely recognized it from the memories of his childhood. The city seemed ostentatious and gaudy; 'shops fail in taste in everything here,' he wrote.[24] His disapproval of English exhibitionism did not blind him to the fact that Dallas's residence was far too modest for its purpose; the family would have to remain at the hotel until something grander was found. He was also irritated with Dallas for having neglected to renew the legation's lease, which was ending in five days' time.[25] Adams responded to these twin challenges with stoicism, but Abigail's fragile courage deserted her. Benjamin Moran was called to the hotel to reassure her that the Adamses would not be made social pariahs. Unconvinced, she insisted that he help give the family lessons in social etiquette. 'Altogether I feel pretty sick and tired of the whole thing,' Henry Adams complained to Charles Francis Jr.[26]

Adams's first invitation was from an MP named William Forster. Dallas's enquiries about him revealed that Forster belonged to the Liberal Party and had been an MP for all of three months. Like John Bright, Forster was a Quaker from a northern mill town, in his case Bradford, whose wealth came from manufacturing. But there the similarities ended. Bright was not interested in small acts or minor details; in Anthony Trollope's damning judgement, 'It was his business to inveigh against evils, and perhaps there is no easier business.'[27] Forster was a modest and sincere man who sought neither power nor popularity. These attributes inclined the House to be gentle towards the newcomer. His maiden speech on the slave trade had been listened to without interruption (although afterwards he was informed by a fellow MP that in London one said la-*ment*-able, not *la*-ment-able).

Forster's father had twice visited the United States to preach against slavery, in some places risking his life to be heard. Forster senior's experiences had provided his son with an unsentimental attitude to the South's desire for secession. 'A Mr Gregory, MP, for Galway, who lately travelled in the South,' Forster wrote to a friend in America, 'has returned well humbugged by the Southerners.' Gregory was talking all sorts of nonsense without anyone daring to challenge him: 'I wish it had fallen into the hands of a member of more experience to stand up for the North and the Union; but I must do what I can.'[28] Forster decided his first step should be to organize a meeting of pro-Northern MPs.

Adams accepted Forster's invitation even though the date was set for 16 May, the day of his presentation at Court. When he arrived at Forster's house, he was disconcerted to discover that there were only seven people at the meeting, three of whom were American. Neither John Bright nor Richard Cobden had bothered to come. Cassius Clay and the historian John Lothrop Motley were the other Americans. Forster introduced the first two MPs so quickly that Adams missed their names. But the third, Richard Monckton Milnes, impressed Adams at once. 'One might discuss long whether, at that moment, Milnes or Forster were the more valuable ally, since they were influences of different kinds,' recalled Henry Adams:

Monckton Milnes was a social power in London ... who knew himself to
be the first wit in London, and a maker of men – of a great many men. A
word from him went far. An invitation to his breakfast-table went farther ...
William E. Forster stood in a different class. Forster had nothing whatever
to do with May Fair. Except in being a Yorkshireman he was quite the
opposite of Milnes. He had at that time no social or political position;
he never had a vestige of Milnes's wit or variety; he was a tall, rough, ungainly figure ... Pure gold, without a trace of base metal; honest, unselfish,
practical.[29]

'I found them all very tolerably informed and strongly inclined to the
anti-Slavery side,' Adams wrote in his diary. However, Milnes declared
he had come 'mainly for the abominable selfishness of the South in
breaking up a great country'; Adams could not decide whether that was
English irony or a genuine statement.[30] John Motley informed the meeting that he had received a letter from the Duke of Argyll, who insisted
that the government had no alternative but to declare neutrality. 'When
the American colonies revolted from England we attempted to treat
their privateers as pirates, but we very soon found this would be out of
the question,' the Duke wrote; 'the rules affecting and defining the rights
and duties of belligerents are the only rules which prevent war from
becoming massacre and murder.'[31]

Cassius Clay refused to be persuaded of England's good intentions.
He was already tired of the country, with its rude servants and hotels
which claimed not to have his reservation. Adams was also dubious,
though he might have felt less wretched about the small number of MPs
around the table had he known that the Southern envoys were in no
better position. Gregory had managed to introduce Yancey to two MPs,
John Laird, owner of one of the largest shipbuilding firms in the country, and William Schaw Lindsay, a self-made shipping magnate. Both
professed interest in helping the South achieve independence, but only
on the understanding that slavery would eventually be abolished.

Adams went home after the meeting to change for his presentation at
Court. This was not the time, he told Moran, 'for indulging oddities of
any kind', nor for wearing clothes which made them look like servants
caught on the wrong side of the green baize door.[32] The plain black uniform mandated by the State Department was to be put away; under his
tenure, the legation would attend royal functions in the usual brocade

and breeches of the diplomatic corps. Dallas and Adams arrived at
Buckingham Palace twenty-five minutes early, giving Adams the chance
to study the paintings in the Great Saloon while he steadied his nerves.
'I reasoned with myself with severity,' he wrote in his diary.[33] Queen
Victoria received him with a few gracious words and then asked with
polite lack of interest whether he had ever been to England before.
Keeping his composure, Adams replied that he had, when young.

George Dallas and his son left for Southampton immediately after
Charles Francis Adams's presentation. Adams wrote in his diary: 'from
this time I take the burden on my shoulders.'[34] He was justifiably uneasy
about his staff; the legation Secretary, Charles Wilson, displayed a lingering disappointment at being denied the Chicago Post Office. Benjamin
Moran's open hostility towards Dallas was also an ill omen. 'I part with the
whole lot with joy,' Moran crowed when the two Dallases set sail. He
felt they had taken him for granted, never asking about his late wife
during her illness, nor bothering to include him at legation dinners. His
job was all he had and he clung to it with ferocious desperation. Moran
did not know that retaining him at the legation had been Henry Adams's
idea or that he was the one who arranged it with the State Department.[35] From the moment Moran set eyes on Henry he regarded him as
a rival, even though the young Adams was only his father's private
secretary with no official standing at the legation.

Adams received his first dispatch from Seward on 17 May. Its tone and
the peremptory demands of the British government worried him, but he
obeyed Seward's orders and requested an interview with Lord John Russell, who had returned to London following the death of the Duke of
Bedford. Russell replied with an offer of lunch that day if Adams was
prepared to come to his house, Pembroke Lodge, in Richmond Park. In
his haste, Adams arrived at the house before his message of acceptance,
which caused Russell to greet him with more reserve than he had
intended. Both men were momentarily struck by the physical similarities
between them. Their small stature, coupled with their bald crowns,
meant that from the back they could be taken for twins. Since neither
had the least facility for small talk the meeting quickly escalated into an
acrimonious debate about the neutrality proclamation. Each thought the
other was rude and arrogant, and each set out to prove his superior
knowledge of diplomatic history. They continued arguing after the bell

rang for lunch. However, by the end of the meal their animosity had given way to a grudging respect. Russell showed his goodwill by inviting him for a stroll around the grounds. 'I like Adams very much,' he wrote a few weeks later, 'though we did not understand one another at first.'[36]

When he reflected on the interview, Adams thought he had acquitted himself reasonably well, but he was less positive about the state of relations between the two countries.[37] He never imagined the sense of emergency he had created in Lord John Russell. During the closing days of May the Cabinet spent many hours trying to divine Seward's real purpose. The Duke of Newcastle's conversation with him the previous October was again analysed. It was recalled how Napoleon had always reacted to failure with aggression; was Seward of the same mould, they wondered? If the South became independent, would he try to deflect public anger by attacking Canada? The question became not whether but how many regiments should be sent to reinforce the Canadian border. The Duke of Argyll agreed to warn Charles Sumner about the effect of Seward's threatening behaviour. 'Mr. Seward knows Europe less well than you do,' Argyll explained in his letter of 4 June; 'he may be disposed to do high-handed and offensive things which would necessarily lead to bad blood, and perhaps finally to rupture.'[38]

'The great question of all is the American,' Lord John Russell wrote to Lord Cowley, the British Ambassador in Paris, 'and that grows darker and darker every day. I do not expect that Lyons will be sent away, but it is possible. Seward and Co. may attempt to revive their waning popularity by a quarrel with Great Britain, but if we avoid all offence, I do not see how they can do it.'[39] Since Russell was blind to his remarkable ability to make speeches that offended all parties, his confidence was perhaps misplaced. The Cabinet had made a decision on privateering which it hoped would soothe Northern irritation over the belligerency issue: they had stretched the meaning of neutrality as far as it could go by closing British ports in every part of the globe to privateers and their captures. Since the North had no need of privateers, the new prohibition only affected the South and its ability to wage war at sea.

However, the South was picking up backhanded support from politicians who were keen to rub John Bright's nose in the apparent failure of democracy. 'We are now witnessing the bursting of the great republican bubble which had so often been held up to us as a model on which to recast our own English Constitution,' Sir John Ramsden MP proclaimed

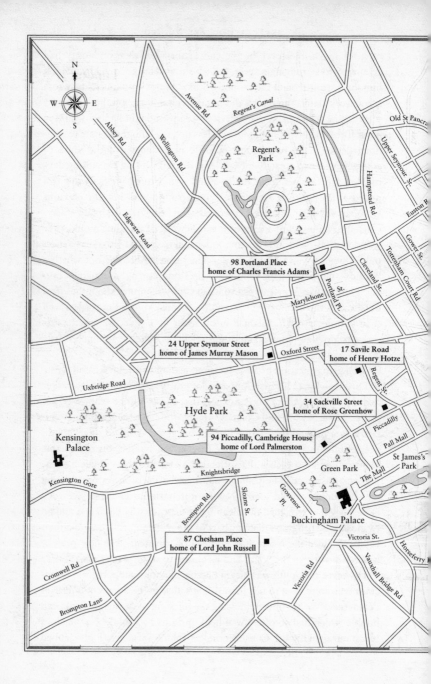

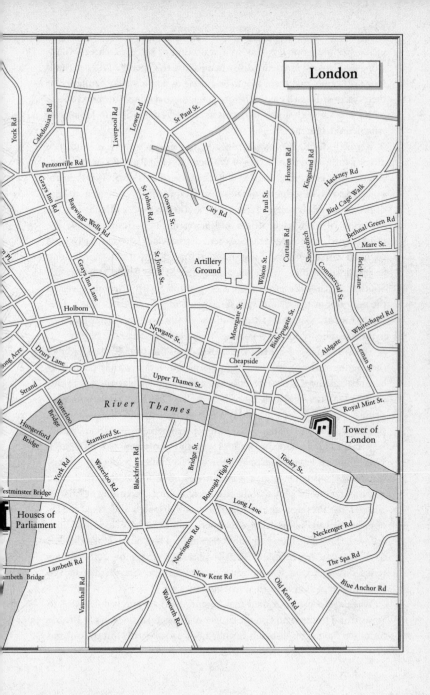

in the Commons on 27 May to a scattering of sarcastic cheers. Gladstone and Russell hurriedly disowned Ramsden's speech. 'I do not think
it just or seemly that there should be among us anything like exultation at
their discord,' Russell chided, before going on to diminish the good effects
of his speech with some unnecessary observations on the failings of
American democracy.[40]

Reports of the Commons debate reached an American audience
already infuriated by excerpts of William Howard Russell's candid trav-
elogues that had found their way back across the Atlantic. Northerners
objected to his description of racism, and especially his honest appraisal
of pro-Southern feeling in New York. Southerners were offended by his
depiction of them as heartless and arrogant. ('Charleston people are
thin skinned,' commented the Southern diarist Mary Chesnut, 'I expected
so much worse.'[41]) Seward was incensed for a different reason. All along
he had insisted there was a silent majority of pro-Union voters in the
South, but Russell's letters from Georgia and South Carolina revealed
the very opposite. Seward was sure they had influenced Britain's decision to award belligerent rights to the South and was determined to
make Russell pay for his reporting when he returned to the North.

Seward had also learned from Dallas that Lord John Russell had met
the Southern envoys. Whether his subsequent reaction was driven by fear
or embarrassment, it was nevertheless a gross miscalculation with regard
to his own standing with Lincoln as well as his future relations with
Britain. He composed on 21 May 1861 an insolent and threatening dispatch for Adams to read to Lord John Russell, which stated there would
be war if England had any dealings with the Confederacy or its envoys.
This infamous letter came to be known by its number in the sequence of
dispatches: Dispatch No. 10. Lincoln was no more inclined to declare
war on England in May than he had been in April. According to Charles
Sumner, the President showed him Seward's dispatch and asked for his
opinion. Seward's blunder was Sumner's opportunity to ingratiate himself with the White House. Sumner encouraged Lincoln to make changes
to the document. The more offensive phrases were removed, the threats
toned down. Adams was no longer ordered to present the dispatch to
Russell; it was simply for his own guidance.

Washington gossip related that Sumner paid an unscheduled visit to
Seward and lectured him on the danger of misusing his powers.[42] Already
furious at having his dispatch amended, Seward allegedly lost control and

kicked his desk, shouting, 'God damn them, I'll give them hell,' referring
to Britain and France. 'I'm no more afraid of them than I am of Robert
Toombs [the Confederate Secretary of State].' It was a delicious victory,
made sweeter for Sumner when he recounted the interview to Lincoln.
'You must watch him and overrule him,' he urged the President.

Seward asserted his independence by reversing some of Lincoln's
changes before the dispatch was sent. He also preserved the original
document in the State Department's files so that when the annual compilation was published, it was his letter rather than the amended dispatch
that appeared.[43] But he could not erase the perception among the diplomatic community in Washington that Charles Sumner was the more
reasonable and better statesman of the two.[44] All the foreign Ministers
heard the gossip about Dispatch No. 10, including Lyons, who was able
to give Lord John Russell a fair indication of its contents before the letter
reached London. Seward accused Britain of deliberately ruining his plan
to quarantine the South by encouraging the Confederates to believe that
full recognition was imminent. Britain had acted precipitately and maliciously in declaring neutrality, he argued, since the President had only
announced his intention to declare a blockade.

Seward was ignoring such inconvenient facts as the four British merchant ships that were seized by Federal navy blockaders when they tried
to sail from Southern ports.[45] He was also discounting the desire of neutral
countries to have their legal rights as neutrals acknowledged. Earlier in the
month, the State Department had been misinformed about a Canadian
steamer named the *Peerless*, which was alleged to have been purchased by
the Confederacy. In fact, it was Federal agents who had bought the ship,
but this had not been communicated to Seward. Seward threatened to
send the US navy into Canadian waters to seize the *Peerless* unless Britain
voluntarily handed over the vessel. 'I said', Lyons informed Lord John
Russell, 'that even if the *Peerless* should in fact be sold to the Seceded
States, she could never cause the United States anything like the inconvenience which would follow a deliberate violation of neutral rights.'[46]

The longer Seward reflected on the belligerency issue the more he
portrayed himself, and by extension the North, as the victim of British
machinations. His language towards Lord Lyons was so coarse that the
Minister sought to avoid social occasions where they might meet. Seward
was using his relationship with the New York press to whip up public
excitement against Britain; he even went so far as to write an anonymous

attack on Lyons for the *Daily Herald*.[47] 'I shall do my best not to be a discredit to you,' Lyons promised Russell after a group of Senators demanded his expulsion, 'but I am on very dangerous ground.'[48]

The French had yet to announce neutrality officially, although Seward was aware that France and Britain had agreed to work in tandem on American issues. It suited him to claim that England had acted alone and precipitately. He refused to receive Lyons and Mercier together or to acknowledge that there was an official understanding between the two countries. Mercier did not mind since he was rushing ahead with schemes to end the blockade, which required extreme tact and patience on Lyons's part to discourage.

'Every imaginable accusation of hostility to the United States is brought against Her Majesty's Government,' Lyons reported to the Foreign Office. Seward's propaganda campaign had succeeded in convincing the entire country that Britain had wronged the North. 'Disappointment and exasperation are universal and deep,' wrote a New York lawyer in his diary. 'The feeling of cordiality toward England – of brotherhood, almost of loyalty, which grew out of the Prince's visit last fall (how long ago that seems!) – is utterly extinguished.'[49] Lyons's advice to London was to be firm, conciliatory, stay abreast with France, and 'manifest a readiness on our part for war [though] the possibility of our being forced into hostilities is so painful a subject that I shrink from contemplating it'. Nevertheless, on 10 June Lyons telegraphed in cipher to Rear Admiral Sir Alexander Milne, the commander of the North Atlantic Squadron, to be ready for the following signal: 'Could you forward a letter for me to Antigua?' Milne sent a notice to his officers: 'Be on your guard and prepared. States may declare war suddenly.'[50]

Charles Francis Adams first heard of the government's anxiety about Seward on 1 June, during a dinner party at Lord Palmerston's house. Lady Palmerston had chosen the guest list with care, inviting people who were known friends of the North, such as Richard Monckton Milnes. Hoping this would have put Adams at his ease, after dinner Lord Palmerston spoke to him about Seward's behaviour. 'He intimated', recorded Adams, 'that his ways of doing things towards Lord Lyons had been ungracious and unpleasant.' This was the first time Adams had heard of the tensions in Washington. It seemed unbelievable and he almost told Palmerston that it had to be a misunderstanding. After reflecting on the conversation the following morning, Adams decided that Seward's brusque manner was probably the cause and resolved to warn his friend to be more circumspect.[51]

On 7 June Dudley Mann went to the Commons to observe William Gregory make his motion for recognition. Moran was also sitting in the Strangers' Gallery and noticed with glee that Dudley Mann 'scowled awfully', as speakers from both sides of the House criticized Gregory for his unseemly haste. At length the scolding became unbearable and Gregory withdrew his motion. Adams was writing his report of the debate when Dispatch No. 10 arrived at the legation. 'I scarcely know how to understand Mr Seward,' he wrote in disbelief. 'The rest of the government may be demented for all that I know, but he surely is calm and wise.' Henry Adams was less forgiving. 'A despatch arrived yesterday from Seward,' he informed his brother on 11 June, 'so arrogant in tone and so extraordinary and unparalleled in its demands that it leaves no doubt in my mind that our Government wishes to face a war with all Europe . . . I urged papa this morning, as the only man who could by any chance stop the thing, to make an energetic effort . . .'[52]

Adams was still angry and embarrassed that the neutrality proclamation had been issued on the day of his arrival. He considered Russell's explanation to be spurious and self-serving. Nor did he accept Mr Forster's contention that 'GB had done all they could to aid us'. Cunard had offered to lease twenty steamships to the Federal navy, which would have doubled its force of working steamers, until the Foreign Enlistment Act made such transactions illegal. But it was difficult for Adams to take the moral high ground when Seward seemed so intent on giving it away.

During an interview with Russell on 12 June, Adams rephrased much of Seward's dispatch and 'softened as well as I could the sharp edges'. He also threw in a question about the *Great Eastern*, which had departed for Canada the week before with more than 2,000 troops on board.[53] Russell answered bluntly that it was due to Seward's threats to seize a British vessel in Canadian waters; more regiments were on their way, he added. This was 'another curse of Seward's horseplay', Adams recorded in irritation.[54] He could easily imagine how news of the reinforcements would be received in Washington, and consoled himself with the fact that he had not yet signed the lease for his house: Henry Adams thought they would all be home in two months.

The expectation of his recall lent an unreal cast to the London season;

Charles Francis Adams attended the first Drawing Room of the season feeling more like an observer than a participant. In his diary he admitted that, as far as aristocracies went, the English managed theirs tolerably well but the system remained deficient. 'My feelings, as you know, have never been partial to the English,' he wrote to a friend.[55] He resented the relatively low status awarded to him by the rules of English society. The American legation in London had none of the social and political importance enjoyed by its British counterpart in Washington, and the fact that he was the third Adams to represent America counted but little among families whose record of diplomatic service went back two or three hundred years. The feeling that 'he was there to be put aside' was magnified by the English reluctance to speak to strangers. 'No effort is made here to extend acquaintances,' Adams complained after the family went to a ball only to spend the entire evening in a lonely cluster.[56] Yet he knew this had not been the experience of Charles Sumner, or of John Motley and he wondered whether Sumner was poisoning his English friends against him and Seward.[57]

But those who did try to be friendly to Adams were often put off by his stiff manner. Five Cabinet members gave dinners in his honour during June; only one, the Duke of Argyll, was prepared to repeat the experiment. 'I have not yet been to a single entertainment where there was any conversation that I should care to remember,' Adams complained to Charles Francis Jr.[58] The Argylls were able to look past Adams's reserve since they regarded him more as a cause than a person. Adams unbent a little once he experienced the difference between a normal London dinner and the informal, lively gatherings at Stafford House. 'The Duke and Duchess', he recorded in his diary, 'have the simplest and most engaging manners of any of the nobility I have yet seen.'[59]

Even Americans could find Adams difficult to approach. 'He said he was very glad to see me,' recorded a visiting diplomat, 'in a tone which no doubt was intended for kindness. It was certainly courteous. But there was a lack of warmth and stiffness about it which ... made me feel as though the temperature of the room had dropped several degrees.'[60] Adams was incapable of producing charm on demand, a serious handicap for a diplomat. 'My own wish', he wrote in his diary, 'is to be silent when I have nothing to say, and not to be compelled to make conversation on topics which do not interest me.'[61] Lord and Lady Macclesfield went out of their way to welcome the new Minister, only to be met with suspicion. 'I am at a loss to know the cause of their civility to us,' he wrote, adding, 'It is always irksome to me, who have the same cold manners [as the English] to attempt to make acquaintances, so that I hardly know how I shall get on.'[62] Yancey sneered in his report to the Confederate Secretary of State that, 'in his diplomatic and social relations, Mr. Adams is considered a blunderer', though the same could be said of him.

Adams would have welcomed any excuse to stay at home. 'We are invited everywhere, and dine out almost every day, but this brings us no nearer [to belonging],' he admitted to Charles Francis Jr.[63] Henry Adams yearned to cut a dash among the fashionable young men, like any 23-year-old, but, as an 'American who neither hunted nor raced, neither shot nor fished nor gambled, and was not marriageable', there was no obvious circle for him to join. Nor did he have school or university ties to ease his entry. Tagging along to events with his father made him feel like a burden. 'Every young diplomat,' he wrote, 'and most of the old ones, felt awkward in an English house from a certainty that they were not precisely wanted there, and a possibility that they might be told so.'[64] Henry's introduction to the season began with a dance given by the Duchess of Somerset, where he was forced into a Scottish reel with the daughter of the new Turkish Ambassador. He could not remember a more excruciating twenty minutes.

Adams was too busy to notice his son's unhappiness. Seward showed more restraint in his subsequent dispatches, but he continued to insist on a retraction of the neutrality proclamation.[65] The Queen's Advocate, Sir John Harding, claimed that his sympathies lay with the North but, recorded Adams, when 'I tried to explain to him the nature of my objection which is much misunderstood here, he defended it with the usual argument'.[66] The British attitude in general dismayed him. 'People do not quite understand Americans or their politics,' he wrote to Charles Francis Jr. He had heard that Richard Cobden thought separating from the South would be good for the North.[67] John Bright had come out strongly for 'strict neutrality'.[68] 'They think this a hasty quarrel,' complained Adams. 'They do not comprehend the connection which slavery has with it, because we do not at once preach emancipation. Hence they go to the other extreme and argue that it is not an element of the struggle.'[69]

Adams was himself guilty of mischaracterization. The English reaction was far more complicated than he allowed. The celebrated novelist Mrs Gaskell, an ardent admirer of the United States, confessed to being 'thoroughly puzzled by what is now going on in America'. 'I don't mind your thinking me dense or ignorant,' she wrote candidly to the future president of Harvard, Charles Eliot Norton. 'But I should have thought (I feel as if I were dancing among eggs) that separating yourselves from the South was like getting rid of a diseased member.' She added: 'and you know I live in S. Lancashire where all personal and commercial intimacies are with the South. Everyone looks and feels sad (– oh so sad) about this war. It would do Americans good to see how warm the English heart is towards them.'[70]

Charles Darwin, whose *Origin of Species* had been published in 1859, highlighted another aspect that troubled the English. 'Some few, and I am one of them, even wish to God', he wrote to the American botanist Asa Gray, 'that the North would proclaim a crusade against slavery.'[71] A leading abolitionist, Richard Webb, voiced a similar complaint from Ireland: 'Neither Lincoln nor Seward has yet spoken an antislavery syllable since they took office.'[72] Seward had specifically instructed all US Ministers and Consuls to avoid mentioning the word in connection with the Union. The deliberate omission was a grievous miscalculation. Seward had sacrificed the North's trump card in Britain, hoping it would appease the South. Instead, he had provided ammunition to his critics who accused the North of hypocrisy. *The Economist* had already stated that 'The great majority of the people in the Northern States detest the coloured population even more than do the Southern whites'.[73] At the beginning of June, Moran's nemesis, Sarah Parker Remond, gave credence to the charge in an article about her family's persecution as free blacks in New England. Though she included a plea for England to support the North, it sounded absurd against the backdrop of her harrowing experiences of racism.[74]

Yet for all the finger-pointing and public criticism of the North, the Southern envoys failed to make the slightest change to Britain's policy. 'We are satisfied that the Government is sincere in its desire to be strictly neutral in the contest,' Yancey repeated in his next letter to Secretary Toombs, 'and will not countenance any violation of its neutrality.'[75] Writing to a close friend in the South, Yancey admitted that the mission was not turning out the way he had envisioned: 'In the first place, important as cotton is, it is not King in Europe.' Furthermore, he added, 'The anti-Slavery sentiment is universal. *Uncle Tom's Cabin* has been read and believed.'[76]

5

The Rebel Yell

William Howard Russell in New Orleans – Sam and Mary Sophia Hill volunteer – Elizabeth Blackwell inspires the US Sanitary Commission – 'On to Richmond' – Battle of Bull Run – Not a fight but a stampede

'There is on the part of the South an enormously exaggerated idea of its own strength,' William Howard Russell wrote to Lord Lyons from New Orleans on 21 May 1861.[1] The city was celebrating secession with parades and fireworks as though the war was already won. All the public buildings and many private houses were flying the new Confederate flag.* There were no doubts here about the power of cotton. It was 'not alone king but czar', remarked the *Times* journalist after he was told for the dozenth time that the shipping season just past had been the most profitable in the city's history.[2]

Russell was not enamoured with the Deep South. The unceasing battle against mosquitoes, the crude sanitation and the greasy food that typified Southern cuisine made him consume more alcohol than his liver could tolerate. 'Too much talk, smoke & brandy & water', was becoming a frequent complaint in his diary.[3] The South's erratic postal service was also a source of torment. It had taken a month for a plaintive letter from his wife, Mary, to reach him. He knew she would assume he had not bothered to reply. 'God comfort her,' he wrote sadly in his diary on 25 May, 'and make me worthy of her.'[4]

William Mure, the British Consul in New Orleans, rescued Russell

---

* The Confederate flag changed several times; for the moment it sported nine stars in a circle inside a blue square, next to three bars of red and white.

from many hours of lonely reflection by inviting him to stay at his house. The extensive commercial ties between New Orleans and Liverpool were reflected in the social prominence of the British Consulate; Mure's generosity gave Russell the best possible introduction to the South's biggest and wealthiest city. New Orleans was the fourth largest port in the world and a commercial juggernaut compared to Richmond in Virginia, which had been chosen as the Confederacy's new capital. Known as the Crescent City because of the way it curled around a deep bend of the Mississippi river, New Orleans was the epicentre of the slave trade and the gateway not only for the majority of the South's cotton crop, but also for its tobacco and sugar. As business opportunities came and went, so too did many of New Orleans' foreign immigrants. The 1860 census had revealed that barely more than half the population of 168,000 had been born in the South.[5] Russell grasped at once how an outsider like Judah Benjamin could find opportunities here that were denied him elsewhere in the Confederacy.[6]

New Orleans had belonged to Spain first, and then France, until the Louisiana Purchase of 1803 made it part of the United States. The original French and Spanish settlers called themselves Creoles, and their descendants still lived in the sixty-six blocks downtown known as the Vieux Carré, or the French Quarter. Here, they built their houses in the Caribbean style with inner courtyards, pastel-coloured façades and ornate balconies that allowed the occupants to see and be seen from the street. The English-speaking newcomers had congregated uptown, on the other side of the canal that ran through the city, in the so-called Garden District. They pointedly built their houses in the Greek Revival style, using red brick instead of plaster, and planted lush gardens that screened the buildings from the street.

New Orleans' French culture was reflected in the number of volunteer regiments with names such as Chasseur, Lafayette and Beauregard in the title. Russell noticed that the foreign immigrants tended to cluster together; hence there was the Irish Brigade, the Garibaldi Legion and the European Brigade.* Russell was especially taken with the Dickens-inspired 'Pickwick Rifles', though the name itself suggested that Mure had not been entirely successful in persuading Britons to adhere to the Foreign Enlistment Act.[7]

---

* At the beginning of the war, a Confederate infantry regiment generally consisted of 1,100 officers and men divided into 10 companies.

It was not the willing recruits that concerned Mure, however, but rather those who were forced to volunteer whether they wanted to or not.[8] King Cotton ruled with a brutal hand in New Orleans. British subjects were being marched to recruiting posts by self-appointed vigilantes, 'not in twos or threes, but in tens and twenties', the Consul told Russell. One woman had complained to him that her husband was held hostage and beaten for three days until he agreed to enlist; his face was so badly disfigured when they brought him home that she failed to recognize him. Dissent was treated in the same harsh manner. 'Every stranger is watched, every word is noted,' Russell wrote in one of his dispatches to *The Times*. People who stated 'their belief that the Northerners will be successful are sent to prison for six months'.[9]

Throughout the Confederacy intense pressure was being exerted on the 233,000 foreign residents to prove their loyalty to the South. For William Watson, a Scotsman working as a mechanic in Baton Rouge, failure to follow his friends into the Pelican Rifles of the 3rd Louisiana Infantry would have been unthinkable. 'I would never take up arms to maintain or enforce slavery,' he wrote in his memoirs. But Watson's friends told him he would be fighting for independence, a cause so worthy that he could not remain aloof 'without injury' to his honour.[10] A Welsh immigrant in Texas joined for similar reasons: 'every man and child that can carry a gun is a soldier in the South,' he explained to his family.[11]

In Arkansas, another Welsh immigrant, 20-year-old Henry Morton Stanley (who would later achieve fame by 'finding' Dr Livingstone in Africa), was shamed into enlisting in the Dixie Grays of the 6th Arkansas Infantry by a neighbour who sent him the Southern equivalent of a white feather. He received a parcel, 'which I half-suspected, as the address was written in a feminine hand, to be a token of some lady's regard', he wrote. 'But, on opening it, I discovered it to be a chemise and petticoat, such as a Negro lady's-maid might wear. I hastily hid it from view, and retired to the back room, that my burning cheeks might not betray me.'[12]

Even without the threat of ostracism or harassment, there were other, more prosaic forces bearing down on the British expatriate and immigrant community. The blockade was not only hurting the city financially, it was also an impediment to those who wished to leave the South. Many unemployed Britons were trapped in New Orleans: 'nothing remains for them but to enlist,' admitted Russell.[13] Two Anglo-Irish siblings from

England, Mary Sophia Hill and her twin brother Sam, were among the early victims of the blockade. The merchant families who sent their daughters to Mary's seminary in the Garden District were suddenly unable to pay the fees. Six weeks after the blockade began there was not a single pupil left in the school.

Mary and Sam were an eccentric pair. She was tight-lipped, fussy and prone to shrillness; he was quiet, absent-minded and passive. Despite having trained as a civil engineer under Isambard Kingdom Brunel, he had never been able to withstand the rigours of an occupation, and over the years his dependence on her had become absolute. The siblings had arrived in New Orleans in 1850 so Sam could take up yet another new position. His inevitable failure gave Mary the idea that they should start a school together. She would teach English, French and music; Sam, if he were able, could teach mathematics.

'In my eyes,' wrote Mary, 'the only blot I ever saw in the sunny South was slavery; but as a stranger, an alien, I had no right to meddle.'[14] But her sympathy for the South did not extend to Sam volunteering. 'I was, and still am, and ever will be, a British subject,' she wrote in her diary.[15] Nevertheless, her brother had joined the Irish Brigade after a furious argument over the failure of the seminary. Mary woke up one morning in early June to discover he had packed his bags and disappeared. She had seen the placards calling for Irishmen to join the 6th Louisiana Volunteers, as the Irish Brigade was officially designated, but never once did she think that her introverted and clumsy brother might heed the call. Nor dared she imagine how the Irish Catholic volunteers would treat a Protestant whose loyalty was not to Ireland but to the Crown.

> I tried all I could to get him free [Mary recalled]; went to Mr. Muir [*sic*], who was then Consul, to see what he could do, but with no good result. It nearly broke my heart to see my only brother and only near male relative leave me and leave the flag we were born under for a stranger, and perhaps get killed for his folly; so I concluded I would follow him to Virginia to care for him where I knew he would sadly want a woman's care, and that I would, whenever needed, care for the wounded, the sick and the distressed. Miss Nightingale God bless her taught us, women of the British flag, this lesson of humanity.[16]

Sam's regiment was in need of a nurse and Colonel Isaac Seymour was willing to overlook the fact Mary was unmarried, since he doubted that the 42-year-old spinster would interest the men. 'So,' she recorded, 'having no particular ties; being as the law has it, a femme sole, I made up my mind to this humane calling.' Two weeks later Mary jotted in her diary: 'My brother quite miserable at the step he has taken. I am so glad I made up my mind to look after him.'[17]

Mary Sophia Hill would have found it much more difficult to become a nurse in the North. There was no shortage of women wanting to help. The Infirmary founded by Dr Elizabeth Blackwell, the first woman to qualify as a doctor in the United States, was deluged with nursing applicants after the Federal surrender of Fort Sumter.* She was cross that the same society ladies who had previously claimed to be scandalized by the Infirmary were now begging to be admitted for training.[18] But she soon realized there would never be a better opportunity to attract support for her medical college. With the aid of Henry Bellows, the charismatic pastor of All Souls Unitarian Church, she invited 'the women of New York' to attend a mass meeting at the Cooper Institute. They expected large numbers but not the 4,000 who crammed into the hall.

The result of this historic event was the creation of the Women's Central Association of Relief. Elizabeth envisioned it as a kind of civilian central command that would direct the various relief efforts on the home front, from the training of nurses to the distribution of woollen socks. The WCAR would work side by side with the army, ensuring that the needs of soldiers were met as quickly as possible. The Revd Bellows and a delegation of doctors went to Washington to seek government approval for the plan. But during the thirteen-hour train journey they conceived a different idea: a national organization modelled on the British Sanitary Commission, which had been formed in response to Florence Nightingale's exposure of army hospital conditions during the

---

* Elizabeth Blackwell (1821–1910) was not only the first woman to earn a medical degree in the United States, but also the first female doctor to be placed on the British General Medical Council's register. Born in England and having lived and studied in both countries, she was the quintessential British-American, though 'I look upon England as my home, and must always do so', she wrote to her best friend, the feminist writer Barbara Bodichon, in 1860. Dr Blackwell had been unable to raise sufficient funds to start a medical school for women in London, but since 1853 she had been running the New York Infirmary for Indigent Women and Children where her aim was to train women to become doctors in the course of serving the poor. The novelist George Eliot met Elizabeth Blackwell in 1859, recording in her diary: 'Esteemable for the courage and perseverance she has shown . . . but very repulsive and schoolmistress-like in manner.'

Crimean War. Bellows suggested they call it the United States Sanitary Aid Commission.[19]

The Army Medical Bureau resented any interference or infringement on its domain and tried to block the Commission from receiving official sanction. President Lincoln shared the Bureau's doubts over the wisdom of allowing philanthropists and women to interfere with the work of professionals.[20] Yet on 18 June he reluctantly signed the United States Sanitary Commission into existence, remarking as he did so that it would probably be a 'fifth wheel to the coach'. The Commission was awarded an office in the Treasury building along with a table and some chairs. Still fighting a rearguard action, the army medical chiefs succeeded in limiting its operations to the new volunteer regiments. The 16,000 regulars that made up the standing army would be kept safe from the civilians.

Elizabeth Blackwell's name did not appear in any literature put out by the Sanitary Commission. Although she had been the initial force behind the volunteer movement, neither she nor the Infirmary was invited to participate. 'We shall do much good but you will probably not see our names,' Elizabeth wrote to her best friend Barbara Bodichon on 6 June:

> We would have accepted a place on the health commission which our asso-
> ciation is endeavouring to establish in Washington and which the government
> will probably appoint – but the Doctors would not permit us to come for-
> ward. In the hospital committee, which you will see referred to in the report,
> they declined to allow OUR little hospital to be represented – and they refused
> to have anything to do with the nurse education plan if the 'Miss Blackwells
> were going to engineer the matter'. Of course as it is essential to open these
> hospitals to nurses, we kept in the background, had there been any power to
> support us, we would have found our true place, but there was none.[21]

Elizabeth and her sister Emily accepted their exclusion gracefully. Elizabeth became chairman of the WCAR's nurse registration committee, and together the two sisters began to interview and select those who showed the most promise. Each candidate received a month's training at the Infirmary, followed by a further month's practical experience at Bellevue or New York Hospital.

Dr Blackwell had no doubt that her nurses would prove themselves in the field, as long as the well-meaning but catastrophically inept Dorothea Dix was prevented from ruining the enterprise. The 59-year-old veteran campaigner for the mentally ill had arrived at Washington in early May to offer herself as superintendent of army nurses. A lack of candidates had given her the position by default. Miss Dix was a 'meddler general' without peer, complained Elizabeth; 'For it really amounts to that, she being without system, or any practical knowledge of the business.'[22] She soon confirmed Elizabeth's fears: erratic, disorganized and quarrelsome, Dorothea Dix was a positive hindrance to the scheme. Most applicants were turned away on ludicrous grounds, such as being too pretty or too recently widowed, but Elizabeth's trained nurses she dared not refuse.[23]

'If the Doctors would only do the part they have chosen and educate that material, we should have a capital band of nurses,' Elizabeth wrote to Barbara Bodichon in June.[24] She hoped they would accept the field hospital designs sent over by Florence Nightingale, but feared that the same chauvinism and anti-British prejudice which had led to her exclusion from the Sanitary Commission might also extend to anything originating from Miss Nightingale.[25] There was nothing to be gained from being associated with England since the neutrality proclamation. 'To be scolded now whenever I enter a friend's house with "well what do you say to England's behaviour . . ." is a great irritation to me,' complained Elizabeth. 'I have been deeply chagrined by the tone our papers have been taking towards England.'[26]

The Anglophobia encouraged by Seward was growing in strength. The *New York Herald* was the worst offender. Its Scottish editor, James Gordon Bennett, had no qualms about printing incendiary articles if they whetted public appetite for more. The *Herald* had toned down its anti-war rhetoric after a mob tried to burn down the building, but attacking England remained a popular alternative. New York had transformed from the ambivalent, even apathetic, city described by William Howard Russell in *The Times* into a noisy carnival of war. The shops along Broadway had become recruiting offices; posters and handbills advertising new regiments covered the city.

'The outbreak of the Civil War has given me a great addition of new and extraordinary duties, in the incessant applications for protection, and advice, etc.,' wrote the British Consul in New York, Edward Archibald.[28] He was rising to the challenge with valiant enthusiasm. A career diplomat for almost thirty years, Archibald was a devoted family man who spent his Sunday afternoons visiting sick and needy Britons. Since taking up his post in 1857, he had diligently collected statistics, written reports, resolved commercial disputes, found lost relatives, sent home destitute Britons and performed all the myriad duties, both practical and pastoral, that were a Consul's lot in a busy city like New York. Until Archibald shocked his superiors by denouncing the rebellion in an official dispatch, the Foreign Office had considered him their most reliable Consul in the United States.[29]

Forced volunteering was not solely a Southern phenomenon and the greatest call on Archibald's time was the plight of Britons who had been imprisoned or punished for their refusal to join a regiment.[30] His task was made more difficult by those who had joined willingly but had changed their minds and were looking for an excuse to escape.[31] Despite Archibald's efforts to publicize the Foreign Enlistment Act, Britons were volunteering in droves.* The slightest hint of a conflict between the North and Britain had also encouraged thousands of Irish immigrants to join the war effort.

The language employed by Irish recruiters was so explicit that Archibald warned the Foreign Office to prepare for a new threat. Posters urged their fellow Irishmen to train in America in order to fight the British oppressors back home. At least three regiments in New York were filled with Irish recruits, the majority of whom were avowed Fenians. Michael Corcoran, the Colonel of the famous 69th Infantry Regiment – the regiment that had refused to parade in honour of the Prince of Wales – was also the commander of the Fenian movement's military wing.[32] Another well-known Irish revolutionary in the 69th was Thomas Meagher, whose stature among the New York Irish community was almost godlike since his escape from a penal colony in Tasmania where he had been banished for sedition.[33] (Meagher's friend and fellow escapee, John Mitchell, had thrown in his lot with the South.)

A large number of British immigrants volunteered out of idealism but equally there were many, like 25-year-old George Henry Herbert, who joined to stave off destitution after the company that had recruited

---

* The 19-year-old Thomas Beach was working for a British bank in Paris when the war began. 'Friends and associations, many of them American, were leaving on every hand for the seat of war,' he wrote. As a lark, Beach decided to go along with a group of friends who were sailing for New York. They all joined the same regiment: 'Regarding the whole proceeding more in the light of a good joke than anything else, [I called] myself Henri Le Caron.' (Under this name, during the 1870s Le Caron became one of the most notorious and successful spies in the British Secret Service.)[27]

him from England went bankrupt. He had been unemployed since Christmas and he was down to his last pair of socks. They were holding up well: 'There is only one hole in the heel of one of them,' he had written cheerfully to his mother, but he could no longer continue without work. Such was the clamour for new recruits that even a man as short and overweight as Herbert could join a popular regiment like the 9th New York Volunteers, better known as Hawkins' Zouaves.* Unlike the majority of the new volunteers, who enlisted for ninety days, Herbert signed up for two years and in return was awarded the rank of 1st Sergeant. He was grateful for any sort of position but harboured secret hopes of becoming an officer: 'I study as much as I can,' he wrote to his mother, 'and do not despair of getting a commission sometime or other.'34 Herbert's hope of promotion would depend on his popularity with the men, since the volunteer regiments were allowed to elect their own officers.

'There is a British Regiment gotten up here,' one English immigrant, Edward Best, told his Aunt Sophie in Somerset. 'It seems to be very popular and I trust will carry its flag through this affair with credit to our dear old country.'35 Consul Archibald, however, was embarrassed when the recruiters for the British Volunteers opened their office in the same building as the consulate.36 He sent a letter to the main newspapers denying any involvement, though this provoked the press to label him a Southern sympathizer.

The British Volunteers started off well and could be seen training each morning in the drill room at the Astor Riding School.37 But the regiment soon became a magnet for anti-British hostility, as did a regiment in Massachusetts that called itself the British Rifle Club.38 'It is not right that British residents should be taunted and twitted without cause,' complained the *Albion*, a weekly journal for the British community in New York.39 The British Volunteers lost its appeal to recruits after one

---

* The original Zouaves were an elite North African corps in the French army, whose uniform of white leggings, baggy blue trousers, magenta jacket and bright red fez made them unmistakable on the battlefield. A Chicago lawyer named Elmer Ellsworth had started the American craze for Zouave regiments in 1859. He formed his own outfit, trained the men in the complicated drills and swordplay of a Zouave regiment, and took them on a nineteen-city tour of America. Colonel Hawkins had seen a demonstration by Ellsworth's Zouaves the previous summer, which was all the encouragement he needed to organize a New York version. His small company of Zouaves was among the first to be granted permission to recruit a full regiment, hence its designation as the 9th New York Volunteer Infantry.

of the captains was accused of being a Confederate agent, a charge that was repeated in the press even after the unfortunate captain was exonerated.

By mid-June the British Volunteers' difficulties became insurmountable and they merged with an Irish regiment to become the 36th New York Volunteers. There were frequent fights and stabbings in the new outfit between the English and Irish factions, and mealtimes could be explosive. The violence encouraged many of the former British volunteers to join the 79th New York Highlanders, which in contrast to the Irish 69th had provided the Prince of Wales's honour guard during his visit in 1860. It was safe to be called Scots, Irish or Welsh, but not British or English, noted Mr Archibald.

A young Englishman named Ebenezer Wells had joined the 79th Highlanders when he arrived in New York in 1860, in order to have something to do at the weekends. 'When the Civil War broke out, the regiment volunteered for the war,' he wrote in his memoirs. 'I was buglar [sic] and being away from parental restraint thought it would be a splendid excursion.'[40] The men were thrilled when they received their orders in early June. 'It was a beautiful Sunday when we marched down Broadway amidst deafening applause,' wrote Wells. The crowds adored their tartan uniform, especially the officers' kilts. Nothing about the occasion hinted at the hardships ahead. Their knapsacks were packed with every conceivable delicacy, as though they were on a Sunday outing. But, Wells added ruefully, if they had known what lay in store for them, 'how depressed instead of elated would our spirits have been'.[41]

Ebenezer Wells experienced his first brush with violence as the regiment passed through Baltimore. He was ambushed by a stone-throwing mob and lost his cap and blanket before being rescued by members of his company. The 79th Highlanders were tired and hungry when they finally reached Washington on 4 June. The sweltering city had become a vast military camp. Rows of white tents and parked artillery occupied the green fields around the half-built Capitol. Long trains of covered wagons filled the dusty thoroughfares.[42] At night the city resonated with wild shouts and hoots, and thunderous fireworks were answered with rounds of gunfire.

The Highlanders were allocated temporary quarters at Georgetown University. The 69th had only recently vacated the premises and their detritus still littered the grounds. The campus was eerily silent, all but fifty of the student body having volunteered to fight for the South. The men were nervous. The Confederate army, under the command of the hero of Fort Sumter, General Beauregard, was only 17 miles to the west. 'We lay every night with our muskets by our sides, ready cocked, and one finger on the trigger,' wrote one of the recruits from the old British Volunteers. 'It is a tough life, I can tell you.'[43] His sentiment was widely shared in camps around the city. No regiment was so experienced or so confident that its men did not live in fear of an ambush or a surprise raid. The roar of the bullfrog, the screech of the night owl, 'every rustle of the wind among the trees', wrote the newly arrived war reporter and artist Frank Vizetelly, 'every sound that breaks the stillness of the night, is taken for the advance of the Secessionists'.[44]

Vizetelly had accompanied the 2nd New York Regiment to their camp on the border between Washington and Virginia. The sounds of the forest did not frighten him; the 30-year-old Vizetelly had spent the past ten years in the midst of battles and revolutions all over Europe. He had never known any other life than journalism. His father and grandfather were both well-known printers and engravers on Fleet Street. His

Attack on the pickets of the Garibaldi Guard on the East Branch of the Potomac, by Frank Vizetelly

three brothers were also in the trade; Henry, the second oldest, was one of the founders of the *Illustrated London News*, which was the first weekly newspaper to illustrate its articles with eyewitness drawings. Vizetelly's fame in England rested on his pictures of Garibaldi's Sicily campaign. Dispatched by Henry to provide sketches of the fighting, Frank Vizetelly had abandoned any pretence at objectivity and allied himself with Garibaldi. It was not in his nature to be impartial: his drawings were not only skilful depictions of a moment or tableau but moving narratives that engaged the emotions of the viewer. His images demanded a reaction, not unlike Vizetelly himself, whose craving to be the centre of attention was insatiable. 'He was a big, florid, red-bearded Bohemian,' recalled an admirer, 'who could and would do anything to entertain a circle.'[45] Whether sitting round a campfire, or dining in an officers' mess, he would transfix his listeners with vivid stories, replete with voices and accents, or lead them in boisterous singalongs that lasted until the small hours.

William Howard Russell envied Vizetelly in just one respect: he was unmarried and could travel wherever he pleased without upsetting his family. Otherwise he pitied him. Vizetelly constantly teetered between depression and mania, and when not distracted by the thrill of danger he became self-destructive and reckless. Vizetelly partially understood his limitations and chose to live rough with the 2nd New York Volunteers, even though the camp was infested with rattlesnakes and 'myriads of bloodthirsty mosquitoes', rather than lounge in the saloon at Willard's.[46] Sometimes he visited the camp of the Garibaldi Guard to swap stories with the handful of genuine veterans in the regiment (the Colonel was a Hungarian conman and most of the volunteers were not Italian but adventurers from the four corners of the globe). On one of the few occasions Vizetelly did go to the capital, he received an invitation to dinner from Seward. He arrived expecting to regale his host with stories about the American volunteers he had encountered among Garibaldi's Red Shirts, but Seward was only interested in the tenor of his sympathies and whether he was planning to visit the South like that villain William Howard Russell. 'I disclaimed any idea of so doing,' reported Vizetelly.[47]

Once Seward took against a person it was rare for him to change his mind. Russell had sensed at their first meeting that he could be a dangerous enemy. During his return journey he read enough of the Northern press to warn him of the reception awaiting his arrival in Washington. But 'I can't help it', he wrote on 22 June to his fellow *Times* correspondent in New York, J. C. Bancroft Davis, 'I must write as I feel and see . . . I would not retract a line or a word of my first letters . . .' He hoped that Northern newspapers would reprint his *Times* reports from the South, which would show that he was not a Rebel sympathizer.[48]

Russell arrived in Washington on 3 July 1861. This time he stayed away from Willard's and found lodgings in a private house on Pennsylvania Avenue. He regretted the decision as soon as he unlocked the door to his room and caught the stench of the privy beneath the window. Once he had changed his clothes, Russell called on Lord Lyons to give him a report on the South, glad that he had an excuse to escape his lodgings if only for a few hours. The legation was almost as dark as his bedroom since Lyons had ordered the gas lamps to be kept unlit in order to avoid adding unnecessary heat. 'I was sorry to observe he looked rather careworn and pale,' Russell wrote afterwards.[49] One of the attachés whispered to Russell as he was leaving that 'the condition of things with Lord Lyons and Seward had been very bad, so much so Lord L would not go near State Dept. for fear of being insulted by the tone and manner of little S'.[50] Ever since the neutrality proclamation had become known, Seward had been threatening and plotting to force a reversal of the South's belligerent status. Lyons was constantly on the watch against Seward's stratagems to weaken Britain's leadership, and Mercier's attempts to sabotage the blockade. Try as he might, Lyons could not make Seward understand that Europe was only respecting the blockade out of deference to Britain. Russell returned to his lodgings feeling depressed by Seward's misguided behaviour towards Lord Lyons. There was no other foreign Minister in Washington, Russell wrote in his diary, 'who watches with so much interest the march of events as Lord Lyons, or who feels as much sympathy, perhaps, in the Federal Government'.[51]

'Sumner makes it appear he saved the whole concern from going smash,' Russell wrote after he bumped into him on the street and had to stand for an hour in the blistering heat while Sumner gleefully enlarged on 'the dirty little mountebankism of my weeny friend in office'.[52] Russell was not sure whether to believe him until he called on Seward the following day and was subjected to another of his tirades. The Secretary of State informed Russell that if he wished to go anywhere near the army, his passport would have to be countersigned by Lord Lyons, himself, and General-in-Chief Winfield Scott. He ended the interview with a lecture on the impropriety of Britain granting belligerent status to the Confederates: 'If any European Power provokes a war, we shall not shrink from it. A contest between Great Britain and the United States would wrap the world in fire, and at the end it would not be the United States which would have to lament the results of the conflict.' Russell tried to appear serene during this outburst, but as he listened to Seward's monologue he could not help seeing the funny side. There they were, 'in his modest little room within the sound of the evening's guns, in a capital menaced by [Confederate] forces', and yet Seward was threatening 'war with a Power which could have blotted out the paper blockade of the Southern forts and coast in a few hours'.[53]

'Seward is losing ground in Washington and New York very fast,' Charles Francis Adams Jr. reported to his father on 2 July. 'Sumner has been here fiercely denouncing him for designing, as he asserts, to force the country into a foreign war.'[54] It was true that Seward had not calculated on Sumner's relentless plotting against him or that he would try to set himself up as a rival Secretary of State from the Senate, but both William Howard Russell and Adams Jr. had been misled by Sumner. Far from being humiliated, Seward was re-emerging in triumphant form, as the crush at his parties attested. June had been a month of consolidation and reconciliation between the President and his wayward Secretary; Lincoln had won Seward's support through a combination of firmness and magnanimity in victory. Displaying more statesmanship than his detractors would admit, Seward recognized that Lincoln possessed the skills required in a President 'but he needs constant and assiduous cooperation'.[55]

The alteration in Seward's attitude towards Lincoln was accompanied by a realization that neither bribery nor the lure of fighting Britain would make the Southern States return to the Union. The change in Seward could be discerned in early July after Gideon Welles engineered a bill through Congress that gave Lincoln the authority to close Southern ports by decree. The foreign Ministers in Washington warned Seward that Europe would ignore any attempt by the North to impose legal restrictions on ports it did not physically control. If he genuinely sought a foreign war, all Seward had to do was demand compliance with fictitious port closures and the Great Powers would revolt. Seward believed them and persuaded Lincoln to say nothing publicly about the bill.

A few days later, on 19 July, Seward paid a private visit to the legation. He 'proceeded, with some hesitation,' reported Lord Lyons, 'and with an injunction to me to be secret', swearing 'that he had used strong language in his earlier communications to Foreign Powers ... from the necessity of making them clearly understand the state of Public Feeling here'. He added that his only motive had been to prevent disunion, not begin a foreign war. 'I was not altogether unprepared for the change in Mr Seward's tone,' Lyons admitted; he had heard from the French legation that Seward had made a similar speech to Mercier a few hours earlier. He thought the real question was whether the change was temporary or permanent – and that would depend on the Federal army's progress in Virginia.[56]

The decision to send the army into battle, rather than wait until the civilian recruits had been trained into soldiers, had been taken by the Cabinet on 29 June. The military advisers at the meeting had argued against the idea; General Scott had already presented Lincoln with a strategy, derisively called the 'Anaconda Plan' by critics, which aimed to minimize the bloodshed on American soil by trapping the South behind its own borders and slowly applying pressure. But Northern newspapers were demanding a battle. Horace Greeley's New York *Tribune* had started running the same banner headline every day: 'Forward to Richmond! Forward to Richmond! The Rebel Congress cannot be allowed to meet there on 20 of July!' which incited newspapers in other States to follow suit.[57] Lincoln explained to Scott that it would be politically impossible to delay a fight, and even if it were not, there was the problem of the 75,000 volunteers whose ninety days were about to expire.

General Winfield Scott had fought in every American war since 1812 and was a revered national figure, although some of the younger officers in the army referred to him as 'Old Fuss and Feathers'. He was too old and infirm to lead the troops himself, so the command of the new Federal army at Washington went to Irvin McDowell, a young officer on his staff, whose drive and intelligence had already marked him out as a future general. But McDowell had not been Scott's first choice; he had originally offered the position to Colonel Robert E. Lee, who lived in Arlington, just across the Potomac river from Washington. But Lee declined, deciding that his loyalty belonged to Virginia and therefore the South.

McDowell was energetic but he had never actually commanded an army, nor was Scott convinced that he would remain calm under pressure. He had sufficient experience, however, to know that the 35,000 would-be soldiers currently camping in the woods around Washington were more of a danger to themselves than to the Confederacy. His objections were dismissed by Lincoln, who told him: 'You are green, it is true, but they are green, also, you are all green alike.' McDowell diligently executed Lincoln's order and devised a plan that he thought would answer the country's wish for a quick and dramatic victory. He would march his men into Virginia to Manassas, where a Confederate army of 22,000 soldiers was stationed under the command of General Beauregard. Manassas was a small crossroads some 25 miles west of Washington; though hardly more than a hamlet, its railroad junction linked two important railroads going west and south into Virginia. If McDowell could smash the Confederate army blocking the way, the North would have an open route into northern Virginia, and from there it would indeed be 'forward to Richmond'.

William Howard Russell liked McDowell, whose manner, despite some personal peculiarities (Russell had never met a teetotal glutton before), he found to be engagingly frank and honest. When Russell bumped into him on 16 July at Washington Station, McDowell admitted that he was there looking for two missing batteries of artillery. The army had started its march towards Manassas that morning and already there was utter chaos at his headquarters. Even 'the worst-served English general has always a young fellow or two about him', thought Russell pityingly as the forlorn figure walked up and down the platform, poking his head into each train carriage. He was almost tempted to accept McDowell's offer to travel with him on the train but decided it was impractical without his bags or a servant.

Over the next four days, the Federal army picnicked and pillaged its way from Washington to Manassas, leaving a trail of burning houses, discarded army kit and stragglers that stretched for many miles. Although small by European standards, McDowell's army was the largest ever assembled in America's short history. He had organized it as

best he could into five divisions with a total of thirteen brigades.*
Almost all the commanders were officers from the regular army, which
gave McDowell confidence that at least he would have men who knew
how to give and receive orders. The commander of the 3rd Brigade was
Colonel William T. Sherman, who would become the greatest Union general after Ulysses S. Grant. Sherman had asked for the 79th New York
Highlanders and the 69th New York Irish because of the large number
of European veterans in their ranks, but his hope that they would display more professional behaviour than some of the other regiments was
dashed from the outset. The Highlanders had refused to leave their
camp, because they had been given Model 1816 smoothbore muskets
instead of the modern Springfield rifles.† Colonel James Cameron restored order by promising that every man would receive his own rifle as
soon as possible, and since the Colonel's brother was the Secretary of
War, the men decided they could believe him.[58] The situation was worse
at the camp of the 69th, where Captain Thomas Meagher, the Irish
'Prince of New York', almost started a mutiny by arguing that their
ninety days were up and that they should all be allowed to go home.
Colonel Corcoran eventually managed to persuade the men to stay until
after the anticipated battle.

The army's destination was Centreville, a pretty town whose tree-
lined streets promised the relief of shade to the dusty and parched
soldiers. The Federal troops arrived in such a state of disarray and
exhaustion that McDowell spent an entire day trying to reshuffle the
various disorganized parts into some semblance of order; more regiments announced they were leaving since their ninety days had expired.[59]
The Confederate army was massed along an 8-mile line a little further
to the south behind a narrow, winding stream called Bull Run. Over the
previous two days, General Beauregard had been receiving reinforcements from General Joseph E. Johnston's army in the Shenandoah
Valley. According to McDowell's plan, this second army was supposed
to be engaged by General Patterson in a diversionary battle so that the
Confederates at Manassas would remain outnumbered. But Johnston

---

* A regiment was officially composed of 1,000 officers and men divided into 10 companies;
a brigade generally consisted of four to six regiments; and a division normally had three or
four brigades. In theory, a division contained 12,000 men.
† The effective range of a smoothbore was about 100 yards, compared to the more deadly
and accurate 1861 Springfield, which had a range of 300 yards.

had eluded his attackers and was, at this moment, piling his men onto trains for Manassas.

Generals Beauregard and McDowell had been classmates at West Point. They had studied the same military classics, learned the same tactics and admired the same generals. Beauregard's recent success at Fort Sumter had unleashed his Napoleonic tendencies to an unfortunate degree and given him visions of a great victory. Now, not only was his numerical disadvantage being rectified, but he had been prepared in advance for McDowell's attack with the help of spies in Washington. Rose Greenhow, the alluring pro-Southern society hostess, had stayed behind in Washington with the express purpose of sending information to the Confederacy. She had been supplied with a cipher key for writing in code and had organized her own spy ring of pretty young women who charmed their way past Union guards to deliver messages, sewn inside their petticoats, to a Confederate contact in Virginia. The most important of Rose's sources was Senator Henry Wilson of Massachusetts, chairman of the Military Affairs Committee, who swore, 'You well know that I do love you – and will sacrifice anything', which may explain how a copy of McDowell's route ended up in her possession.[60] Rose also knew the date of McDowell's departure and when he proposed to attack.[61]

Although Jefferson Davis was not tied down by the Federal law which limited the service of State militias to a mere ninety days, Beauregard was hampered by other problems, including a severe shortage of arms and equipment. The 6th Louisiana Volunteers, Sam Hill's regiment, had arrived at Manassas Junction with only their personal rifles and home-made uniforms. 'The men badly off for clothes', wrote Mary Sophia Hill in her diary. When Sam ripped his uniform she had to repair it with red flannel. 'Just imagine a patch of this behind and on your knees!' she complained.[62] Sam had been unable to master the most basic skills of soldiering, but his commanding officer turned down Mary's plea to assign him to a non-military function. The hard truth was that Sam fulfilled a function already, if only by being there to stop a bullet destined for someone else.

In Washington, Russell realized he had made a costly mistake by turning down McDowell's offer at the station. He had failed to engage a servant and there was not a horse or any kind of transport left in the city; what the army had not requisitioned had been hired by civilians

who wanted to watch the spectacle. On Saturday, 20 July, Russell heard
from Federal officers in the city that McDowell's attack would take place
the next morning. His search for transport became frantic; Russell revis-
ited one of the larger livery stables and begged the owner to rent him his
last remaining carriage. He paid the exorbitant price demanded and
rushed to General Scott's headquarters to have his pass countersigned.
'But the aide-de-camp shook his head, and I began to suspect from his
manner and from that of his comrades that my visit to the army was not
regarded with much favour.'63 Russell would not be able to leave until
the morning.

> I returned to my lodgings [he wrote], laid out an old pair of Indian boots,
> cords, a Himalayan suit, an old felt hat, a flask, revolver and belt. My mind
> had been so much occupied with the coming event that I slept uneasily, and
> once or twice I started up, fancying I was called. The moon shone in through
> the mosquito curtains of my bed, and just ere day-break I was aroused by
> some noise in the adjoining room, and looking out, in a half dreamy state,
> imagined I saw General McDowell standing at the table ... so distinctly
> that I woke up with the words, 'General, is that you?'64

By the time Russell was fully awake on the 21st, McDowell's army
had already marched into position and was awaiting orders. The two
opposing generals had formed precisely the same plan: to trick the
enemy with a feint against one side, while mounting the real attack on
the other. McDowell moved first and his initiative appeared to bring
rewards. Vizetelly placed himself rather precariously in a field and made
sketches of the Federal regiments charging into their Confederate opponents. Both sides displayed unexpected courage and determination in
their first introduction to warfare. It was the Confederates who wavered
and were gradually pushed back; they ran towards the crest of a rise
known as Henry House Hill, after the little white farmhouse that overlooked the ridge.

Confident that McDowell was on the verge of driving the Confederates off the field, Vizetelly galloped back to Centreville to give his first
sketches to a waiting courier. A journalist for the *New York Times* also
left and returned to Washington to write a report on McDowell's victory. On the way back to the fighting, Vizetelly bumped into a hot and
perspiring Russell, who was accompanied by Frederick Warre, one of the
more adventurous attachés from the legation. The driver of their gig had

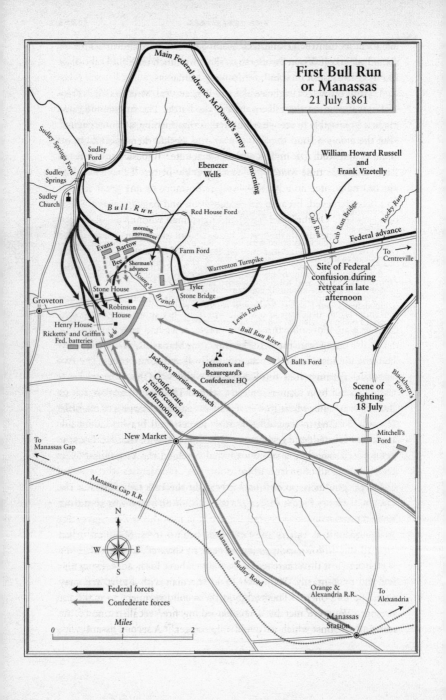

First Bull Run
or Manassas
21 July 1861

Main Federal advance McDowell's army – morning

Sudley Springs Ford

Sudley Ford

Sudley Springs

Sudley Church

Ebenezer Wells

William Howard Russell and Frank Vizetelly

Bull Run

Red House Ford

Cub Run Bridge

Cub Run

Rocky Run

Federal advance

To Centreville

morning movement

Evans

Bartow

Bee

Sherman's advance

Farm Ford

Stone House

Young's Branch

Warrenton Turnpike

Tyler

Stone Bridge

Site of Federal confusion during retreat in late afternoon

Groveton

Robinson House

Henry House

Ricketts' and Griffin's Fed. batteries

Lewis Ford

Bull Run River

Ball's Ford

Blackburn's Ford

Jackson's morning approach

Johnston's and Beauregard's Confederate HQ

Scene of fighting 18 July

Confederate reinforcements in afternoon

To Manassas Gap

New Market

Mitchell's Ford

Manassas Gap R.R.

N
W   E
S

Manassas - Sudley Road

Manassas - Sudley Road

Orange & Alexandria R.R.

To Alexandria

Federal forces

Confederate forces

Manassas Station

Miles
0   1   2

left them at Centreville and they were wandering around in search of something to eat. Vizetelly offered to share his lunch with them and they found a shady spot on a hill overlooking Manassas.

A large crowd of sightseers, including several Senators and their wives, was also on the hill to observe the battle. The smoke and haze made it impossible to see what was actually happening, although whenever there was a loud explosion a woman beside them would shout, 'That is splendid. Oh my! Is not that first-rate? I guess we will be in Richmond this time tomorrow.' Russell knew better: 'I was well convinced', he wrote, 'no advance of any importance or any great success had been achieved, because the ammunition and baggage wagons had never moved.' On the other hand, an Englishman whom Russell did not recognize 'came up flushed and heated from the plain', saying that the Federals were behaving 'most gallantly'.[65] His announcement that the Confederates were retreating provoked 'guttural "hochs" from the Deutschland folk and loud "hurroos" from the Irish'.[66]

Russell's instincts were correct. McDowell was no longer leading but reacting; when urgently asked for orders by his subordinates he told them to wait. 'For some three hours previous, we had seen long lines of dense dust rising from the roads leaving from Manassas,' wrote Vizetelly. The dust clouds were in fact the last of the Confederate brigades arriving off the trains from the Shenandoah Valley.[67] One of these fresh regiments, led by a former professor named Thomas J. Jackson, ran to Henry House Hill, where the Confederate stand was starting to crumble. There, according to legend, Jackson's firmness and bravery under fire inspired a Confederate general to rally his troops with the cry: 'Look at Jackson standing like a stone wall! Rally behind the Virginians!'[68] So began the legend of Stonewall Jackson.

The sudden increase of firepower caught the Federal soldiers at the bottom of Henry House Hill by surprise. While Sherman was preparing his regiments to make a charge, some of the men threw themselves flat on the ground as others sought refuge behind trees. Sherman urged them to stay in formation. It was useless, he shouted, to duck after the explosions. Just then there was a loud bang above his head, causing him to duck involuntarily. 'Well, boys,' said Sherman with a grin, 'you may dodge the big ones.'[69] The 79th was the second regiment to make the attempt. 'We were met by a terrible raking fire,' recalled one of the survivors, 'against which we could only stagger.'[70] A second assault with the same result convinced the survivors that it was time to retreat. By the time the Highlanders had reached the safety of the river they had suffered 198 casualties, including their colonel and half the regiment's officers.

The field was littered with bodies when Sherman ordered the 69th to make their charge. By now it was late afternoon and many Union soldiers had reached the end of their strength. Sensing his enemies' exhaustion, in one of his few sensible decisions that day, General Beauregard ordered the Confederates to make a countercharge. The Rebels surged forward, letting out wild, whooping screams as they ran. The 'Rebel yell', as it later became known, froze the Union soldiers in their tracks. Just as Colonel Corcoran shouted to his men to rally to the flag, two other Federal regiments on the hill smashed into them, pursued by the Confederate cavalry.

The sudden urge to flee spread to other parts of McDowell's army. Russell had ridden down to the turnpike bridge and was about to cross it when he saw a mob running towards him. The Union retreat had turned into a mass rout. 'The crowd from the front continually increased,' he wrote; 'the heat, the uproar, and the dust were beyond description. I got up out of the road and into a cornfield, through which men were hastily walking or running, their faces streaming with perspiration, and generally without arms.'[71] Vizetelly was riding to Centreville to hand over another set of drawings to a waiting courier when he was forced off the road by a roaring cavalcade of horses and wagons. He looked behind and saw a dense cloud, thick and impenetrable like an explosion, hurtling towards him. He quickly turned his horse around and galloped ahead to avoid being trampled. Soldiers and spectators became tangled in a bloody struggle to escape.

Ebenezer Wells was not far behind. 'I had been detached into the transportation department, having volunteered for such, and was on my way to the front,' he wrote:

> when an officer met me and ordered me to turn back saying the troops were retreating, I answered I dare not accept any orders but from Headquarters, as I had ammunition. He drew his revolver threatening to shoot me if I disobeyed . . . I went on but soon found it was too true. The Army was on the retreat, and after having had a view of some of the renowned Southern Black Horse Cavalry I turned and joined in the run. And it was

indeed a run, some never stopped until they reached New York. We lost more men then by desertion than all the rest of the war put together.[72]

The stampede from Bull Run, by Frank Vizetelly

Russell also became part of the flight. 'What occurred at the hill I cannot say,' he wrote, 'but all the road from Centreville for miles presented such a sight as can only be witnessed in the track of the runaways of an utterly demoralised army.' He asked one soldier why he was running. '"I am not afraid of you," replied the ruffian, levelling his piece at me and pulling the trigger. It was not loaded or the cap was not on, for the gun did not go off.'[73] Shaken, Russell concentrated on surviving the ride home. It was almost midnight when he reached his lodgings. Lightning played about the sky. Russell shut the door and sat down at his desk, intending to write his report before daybreak. A messenger arrived from Lord Lyons, who had become alarmed after Warre returned to Washington without him. Russell scribbled a quick note in reply. But after a few minutes of writing, his pen slipped and he slumped in his chair. 'I awoke from a deep sleep this morning, about six o'clock,' he wrote.

The rain was falling in torrents and beat with a dull, thudding sound on the leads outside my window; but louder than all, came a strange sound, as if of the thread of men, a confused tramp and splashing, and a murmuring of voices. I got up and ran to the front room . . . I saw a steady stream of men covered with mud, soaked through with rain, who were pouring irregularly, without any semblance of order up Pennsylvania Avenue towards the Capitol.[74]

Russell stayed at his desk all day, occasionally pausing to watch McDowell's dejected army stumble past his window. Hundreds of prisoners, including Colonel Corcoran of the 69th, remained at Manassas. Mary Sophia Hill caught a glimpse of them whenever she ran between hospital tents. She had been working without a rest since the morning of the battle. 'They have not half the supplies,' she wrote. 'I tore down all the window blinds, and rolled them into bandages.' She cleaned, bandaged, fed and comforted scores of wounded soldiers, all of whom reminded her of Sam. Some of the men begged for water, others pleaded with her to remove bullets from their shattered limbs. 'I heard and saw it all,' she recorded, 'war in its grandeur and war in its meanness.'[75] Only later did she learn that Sam's regiment never actually fired a shot.

6

War by Other Means

*McClellan takes charge – Prince Napoleon at the White House –
Sanford's spies – Desperate for arms – The British join up – The
raging storm*

Frank Vizetelly diplomatically skimmed over the Federal rout in his dispatch for the *Illustrated London News*; William Howard Russell could describe little else, since it was the only part of the battle he had actually witnessed. Knowing how dreadful it would sound, he was careful not to condemn the soldiers for the mistakes of their leaders. 'The men were overworked,' Russell explained in his report, 'kept out for 12 or 14 hours in the sun exposed to long-range fire, badly officered, and of deficient regimental organization.' The army's lack of experience, he added, made an orderly retreat all but impossible.[1]

Russell also blamed the generals for the subsequent mayhem in the capital; Washington was held hostage for two days by drunken soldiers roaming the city. 'The Secretary of War knows not what to do, Mr Lincoln is equally helpless,' Russell recorded. 'There is no provost guard, no patrol, no authority visible in the streets.'[2] He wondered why the Confederates did not simply march in and take the city while it lay helpless and disorganized. The French Minister agreed with him. 'Ever since I first met M. Mercier,' wrote Russell, 'he has expressed his conviction that the North never can succeed in conquering the South, or even restoring the Union.' Mercier wondered if the South had lost more men in the Battle of Bull Run than it was publicly admitting. Nothing else, he thought, could explain the Confederacy's failure to exploit the chaos of the Federal army.

Rose Greenhow sent messages to General Beauregard, urging him to strike while the city was undefended: 'Come on! Why do you not come?'

she pleaded.[3] Beauregard stayed because his forces were almost as disorganized as the defeated Federals. The problem of supplies was as acute as ever, his men were exhausted and he knew that McDowell's army had not been destroyed at Manassas (as the Confederates called the battle*) – it had simply run away. But Southern public opinion agreed with Rose Greenhow; newspapers voiced anger towards Beauregard for not finishing the task, but also expressed overweening confidence, even exultation, in the superiority of the Confederate army. The light number of casualties at Manassas contributed to the belief that the war would soon be over with little cost to the South.[4]

In the North, the expressions of shame and horror were also accompanied by calls for better leadership. Lincoln responded decisively. Less than twenty-four hours after the Battle of Bull Run he dismissed Irvin McDowell and ordered his replacement, General George McClellan, to come at once to Washington; he also asked Congress for a million additional soldiers. Lincoln used the intervening time until McClellan's arrival to write a private memorandum setting out his thoughts for the next phase of the war. The defeated army would be renamed the Army of the Potomac, the other Northern armies in the field would also be reorganized and the army chiefs would be assigned a clear set of objectives. He even added a list of what the objectives should be, starting with the capture of Manassas, followed by Virginia and Tennessee.[5]

General McClellan arrived in Washington on 26 July; by then most of the army had staggered back to camp, although it was still an unruly rabble. Two regiments were in outright rebellion and more could follow, unless McClellan imposed his authority quickly. The 79th Highlanders was one of the regiments in mutiny; it was not the lack of rifles which upset the men but the appointment of a new colonel without their consent. McClellan sent in trustworthy regiments to put down both rebellions and the 79th was marched in shame through Washington under armed guard.[6] He hung the regiment's colours in his office as a warning to others.

The 35-year-old McClellan possessed a flair for organization and within a few weeks the changes to the Army of the Potomac were so

---

* The Union and Confederacy often gave different names to their battles. The Confederates generally preferred the name of the nearest town, the Federals the nearest river or landmark.

noticeable that the press was hailing him as America's answer to Napoleon Bonaparte. He was treated with almost reverential deference by the Cabinet and greeted with lusty cheers whenever he rode into the camps. McClellan reacted to the adulation with the calm acceptance of a man whose life had hitherto been blessed by an unbroken train of good fortune. He came from a wealthy Philadelphian family; in addition to good looks, intelligence and physical prowess, he could boast an adoring wife and a wide circle of friends.

William Howard Russell was not altogether surprised by the General's meteoric rise. Russell had met McClellan in the Crimea, when the latter had been sent as a military observer by the US army, and he thought him a rather overconfident young man. He did not know if McClellan had outgrown his youthful arrogance, but he noticed that his riding style had not changed; the General 'is stumpy and with an ungraceful seat on horseback', he noted in his diary.[7]

McClellan's lack of horsemanship did not prevent him from becoming the star attraction when a real Prince Napoleon and his entourage arrived in Washington on 2 August. Prince Joseph Charles Bonaparte – 'Plon-Plon' in certain circles – was a cousin of Napoleon III (who himself was Napoleon Bonaparte's nephew). He had fled from France to avoid a duel, although this was not known in the North. No one had informed the administration that Plon-Plon was coming, which led to an unintended snub when the French Minister accompanied the Prince to the White House. The doorbell was rung, the knocker pulled and yet the front door remained closed. The royal party waited impatiently to be let in until 'an employee, who happened to be passing by, took care of this duty', recalled an aide.

The Prince had his revenge on Lincoln by not uttering a word after the initial introduction. The President and Seward, who was also present, were both overcome with confusion. Lincoln bought some time by inviting the Prince to sit down, which required the fetching and repositioning of several chairs. 'But once these new positions were acquired,' wrote the aide, 'the two parties sat opposite each other ... the Prince, impatient because he had had to wait, took a cruel pleasure in remaining silent. Finally, the President took the risk of speaking.' He tried to ask the Prince about his father, but mistakenly referred to a childless uncle. 'This incident made him lose his confidence still further.' Mercier stepped in with a comment about the weather in general, and then about the rain of a few days previously. Lincoln resorted to another round of handshaking that took up just enough time to allow the party to be shown to the door without undue haste.[8]

Lord Lyons took advantage of the temporary *froideur* between France and America to give a dinner in the Prince's honour. Seward, Charles Sumner and General McClellan were all invited, but not William Howard Russell, to the latter's disgust.[9] Lyons had intended the event to be a grand demonstration of the Anglo-French alliance, and, though he admired Russell, he considered the dinner far too important to include a mere journalist. The next morning Lyons wrote proudly to his sister that 'it went off very well', despite the appalling heat, 'as it was not hotter in my dining room than everywhere else'.[10] The French had unwittingly scored a blow for England in the battle of wits between Lyons and Seward. McClellan had glowed with pleasure under the flattery lavished on him by the Prince's military aides. Sumner, too, had been the recipient of extravagant compliments. But to Seward they displayed a Gallic aloofness that was noticeable and embarrassing. The French considered him uncultured, unpolished and profoundly non-intellectual. Seward 'does not speak any language but English', wrote one of the aides contemptuously, 'and knows Europe very little, though he customarily declares in a comically emphatic way that he has travelled throughout Europe for several years'.[11]

Seward was not amused when Prince Napoleon requested a pass to visit the Confederate headquarters. He pretended at first not to understand his hints and forced him to make a direct application. The French party, once again accompanied by Mercier, travelled to General Beauregard's headquarters, where they listened with great respect to the Confederate version of Bull Run.[12] As word spread through the camps of the Prince's arrival, French volunteers, including some who had fought in Garibaldi's army, stopped by to pay their respects. 'Such strange and romantic personalities!' recorded the French aide, surprised that even members of the French aristocracy were coming across the Atlantic to fight for the Confederacy. Beauregard had appointed as his assistant inspector general Lieutenant Colonel Prince Camille de Polignac, whose father, Jules de Polignac, had served as Prime Minister under Charles X, and whose grandmother, Yolande, had made the family rich and powerful through her notorious friendship with Marie-Antoinette.[13]

The Prince returned to Washington unconvinced by the South's arguments or its military confidence, although his aides, he confessed with a laugh to Lord Lyons, 'seemed to think that they would rather command the Southern soldiers'. Mercier escorted the Prince and his party to New York on 11 August before anyone in Washington could discover their views. As they were leaving, a report reached the French legation that Seward had ordered the arrest of Charles James Faulkner, the former American Minister to France and a citizen of Virginia, on suspicion of treason. Faulkner had been popular in France and his detention sealed the party's dislike of the Secretary of State.

Faulkner's arrest was not the only diplomatic upset of that week. On 16 August Lyons was called to the State Department by Seward, who informed him, with a gleam in his eye, that Mr Robert Mure, a naturalized American of Scottish birth, had been arrested in New York as he was about to sail for Liverpool. Mure had been caught with treasonable correspondence hidden inside a diplomatic bag he was carrying from the British consulate in Charleston. So began a long-drawn-out affair that caused Lyons many sleepless nights. Seward continually pestered him with alleged crimes committed by British subjects who were said to be in cahoots with the Rebels. Lyons suspected that much of Seward's professed outrage was bluster, but he could not deny there was an element of truth to his claims about some of the British Consuls. One or two were highly partisan – especially Consul Bernal in Maryland.[14]

An investigation by Lyons revealed that Consul Bunch in Charleston was not one of the alleged Southern sympathizers. Bunch had entrusted his diplomatic pouch to Robert Mure, who was heading to England via New York, because the Northern blockade prevented its going directly by sea from South Carolina and the Southern ban on 'commercial intercourse' meant there was no post between the States. It was Mure who made the egregious error of allowing the bag to be contaminated with private letters and documents. Seward had been waiting for one of the British Consuls to make a slip and was amply rewarded by the contents of this bag. He graciously allowed the sealed dispatches to be sent to London unopened, the rest he passed on to the press. Not surprisingly, many of the letters contained vitriolic comments about the North.[15]

There was a fresh outcry for Lyons's expulsion that almost made him wish for his own removal. 'I am getting a longing for home which it will be difficult to gratify,' he confided to his sister on 23 August, 'for I don't see how can I well get out of the scrape of happening to be the Minister here just now ... I don't believe the Americans mean to quarrel with us and I would rather not be removed in consequence of making some blunder – and I see no other means of getting away.'[16] William Howard Russell dined at the legation that evening and was shocked by the sadness emanating from Lyons. 'My Lord not at all well looking', he wrote, 'worn and sickly and very nervous and fidgeting'.

Russell felt guilty because he suspected that his own actions had contributed to Lyons's difficulties. The first copy of his Bull Run report in *The Times* arrived in New York on 18 August. Within forty-eight hours nearly every newspaper in the North carried front-page denunciations of Russell. He was branded a liar and Confederate sympathizer. One newspaper claimed he was never at Bull Run; another, that he had incited the panic himself.[17] The *New York Times* derisively called him 'Bull Run Russell'. He received hate mail and death threats; shop-owners would not serve him; the Lincolns ignored his greeting when their carriage passed by. Seward received a mass petition from Philadelphia demanding Russell's expulsion. Sherman and other senior officers assured him that his description of the rout was perfectly fair, but the feeling among the lower ranks was implacably hostile. A German soldier levelled his gun at Russell, shouting: 'Pull Run Russell! You shall never write Pull's Runs again!' Somewhat recklessly, Russell rode up to the man and challenged him. Although the soldier later claimed it was a 'choake', 'as his rifle was capped and loaded and on full cock, with his finger on the trigger, I did not quite see the fun of it', Russell wrote. General McDowell commiserated with him, saying, 'he was very much rejoiced to find that I was as much abused as he had been'.[18]

From Beauregard's headquarters in Virginia, Samuel Phillips Day, the English correspondent for the London *Morning Herald* and the *Morning Chronicle*, brought more ire on Russell by sending an inflammatory letter to the *New York Times* about Northern cowardice at Bull Run.[19] The day after the letter was printed a young English officer named Henry Ronald MacIver called at Russell's lodgings, asking if he knew how to find Mr Day. MacIver bored Russell with stories of his military adventures in India and Italy until he realized that the journalist had no intention of helping him, at which point he left rather crossly. A few days later, Russell heard that MacIver had been caught trying to sneak across the lines into Virginia; he assured Lord Lyons that this was one arrest the legation could ignore.

'I feel it is my doom to be the best abused man in America on both sides,' Russell lamented to the *Times*'s New York correspondent, J. C. Bancroft Davis. Southern newspapers were being almost as vicious about him as those in the North. 'He prefers to attribute our victory at Bull Run to Yankee cowardice rather than to Southern courage,' complained the diarist Mary Chesnut.[20] In Richmond, Samuel Phillips Day was forced to deny that he had anything to do with *The Times*. Russell was furious with Delane for ignoring his request to preface the Bull Run report with others from American papers.[21] But the opportunity to embarrass John Bright, who had finally announced his support for the North, was too great for Delane to resist; he not only printed Russell's report without any additional commentary, but mischievously also placed the account next to a bombastic editorial from the *New York Herald* about the retribution coming to Europe once the war was won.[22]

Since Frank Vizetelly's last dispatch in the *Illustrated London News* had been so laudatory about Northern recruits, the contrast between his suggestion of an easy victory and Russell's description of the Federal collapse was stunning. Prince Albert's private secretary, General Charles Grey, whose views were typical of a certain kind of crusty conservative, celebrated Bull Run as a victory for England. 'I confess I cannot help being pleased with the course things are taking in America,' he wrote to his brother, Earl Grey, 'because I think it will before long put an end to the fighting and leave the world in a much safer state.'[23] General Grey thought a divided America would be too busy quarrelling with itself to bother with Britain. The Federal army's collapse on the battlefield also appeared to vindicate those who claimed that the North was fighting the war out of vanity whereas the South was fighting for independence.[24]

The image of the rout was so powerful that no British bank was now prepared to invest in Union bonds. August Belmont, the American agent for the Rothschilds, was unable to convince his own employers, let alone any of their rivals. Bull Run also overshadowed the North's subsequent successes in the following months. In late August, when the Union gained control of Cape Hatteras, North Carolina's main route to the Atlantic, the victory was largely ignored by the British press. George

Henry Herbert's family were among the few who followed the campaign. Herbert's regiment, the 9th New York Volunteers, was part of an amphibious attack on the two Confederate forts guarding the inlet. The Rebels were shelled out of their position, leaving Herbert and the invaders to face the poisonous snakes, toads, ticks and mosquitoes that inhabited the 40-mile-long sandbank.[25] Until recently, he had been the target of much mockery from his comrades, but their experiences were bringing the men together.[26] 'I have now quite a love for my profession,' he told his family.[27]

In London, the occupants of the US legation had their suspicions confirmed by the North's vilification in some newspapers. 'I cannot conceal from myself the fact that as a whole the English are pleased with our misfortunes,' Charles Francis Adams confided miserably to a friend. 'There never was any real good will towards us . . . Of course, you will keep these views to yourself. It is not advisable in these days for Ministers abroad to be quoted.'[28] It was just as well he was unaware of Palmerston's quip that Bull Run should be renamed 'Yankees Run'.

Adams had finally settled in his new life when William Howard Russell's report of the battle appeared in *The Times*. The legation had moved into new premises in Portland Place, the archives had been unpacked and a new cataloguing system put in place. Defeat robbed these improvements of their lustre. Benjamin Moran sulked in the basement and Adams's doubts about his mission returned; recalling Seward's threatening dispatches with embarrassment, Adams wrote in his diary, 'we deserve it all'.[29] Harriet Martineau continued to write supportive articles in the *Daily News* and *Morning Star* but she too had decided that Seward was the most dangerous politician she had ever encountered: 'Seward in the Cabinet is enough to ruin everything,' she complained to a friend.[30] She blamed him for having allowed the passage of the Morrill Tariff, since the bill was practically 'inviting the world to support the Confederate cause'.[31] The Rothschilds' agent, August Belmont, agreed; during his unsuccessful visit to England to drum up interest in Union bonds he was repeatedly asked to justify the attack on British trade. Palmerston told him at a private meeting shortly after Bull Run: 'We do not like slavery, but we want cotton, and we dislike very much your Morrill tariff.'[32] Even the pro-Northern *Spectator* appeared to have lost patience, complaining on 15 June, 'The Americans are, for the moment, transported beyond the influence of common sense. With all of England sympathising, more or less heartily, with the North, they persist in regarding her as an enemy, and seem positively anxious to change an ally . . . into an open and dangerous foe.'

The 18th of August was Adams's fifty-fourth birthday. That evening he was despondent. 'My career in life is drawing on to its close,' he wrote in his diary, seeing no future for himself or his country. Yet the situation in Britain was not as desperate as he believed. Immediately after the Battle of Bull Run, Vizetelly's *Illustrated London News* had sternly reminded readers 'that the victory of the South places its cause in no better position in English eyes'.[33] In Liverpool, the authorities ordered Southern ships to haul down the Confederate flags that suddenly appeared after the battle. But the most significant development by far was the rejection of the Southern envoys' request on 7 August for a formal interview with Lord Russell.* Undeterred, the Confederates sent him a 39-page letter, outlining the reasons why the South had attained the right to recognition. Russell's reply was short and pointed. 'Her Majesty', he replied on 24 August, 'has, by her royal proclamation, declared her intention to preserve a strict neutrality between the contending parties in that war.'[34]

Russell's rebuff brought the relations between the Confederate diplomats to a new low. They had been arguing among themselves for some time and after this latest blow their disagreements became increasingly personal. Not only were they isolated in England, but weeks would go by while they waited for instructions from Richmond. 'Our sources of information are the New York and Baltimore papers,' the envoys complained to the Confederate Secretary of State.[35] Left to their own devices, Yancey became the odd man out as Rost and Dudley Mann turned to Edwin De Leon, the former US Consul in Egypt, whose arrival in London had caused Benjamin Moran so much heartache. De Leon was a journalist by training and had originally intended to plant a few articles in the press before going home. But he soon realized that Dudley Mann needed his help; Yancey had to be controlled. 'He was not a winning or persuasive man,' wrote De Leon, 'but a bold, antagonistic and somewhat dogmatical one; abrupt in manner, regardless of the elegancies and small courtesies of life, a refined man in feeling, but not deportment.'[36]

Dudley Mann and De Leon tried to keep Yancey distracted while

---

* Lord John Russell became Earl Russell in July and moved to the House of Lords.

they negotiated a secret deal with Paul Julius de Reuter's Telegraph Agency. Shortly before Bull Run, Reuter had personally approached both the legation and the Southerners for the exclusive right to distribute their official reports from America. Benjamin Moran had indignantly rebuffed him, but the Southerners knew there was great potential in the deal since many English and European newspapers relied on Reuter's telegrams for their American news.[37] Benjamin Moran soon rued his mistake; Reuter 'is against us', he grumbled in his diary. 'He systematically prostitutes the monopoly he holds to depreciate the Union ... there is no way to remedy the business but by buying the fellow up. This I would not do.'[38] The sudden alteration from a pro-Northern to a pro-Southern tone made the US Consul in Leith wonder if the Scottish editors had been bribed. They 'exaggerate as might be expected all the little mistakes of our Northern Army into a mountain', he protested. 'No sheet in South Carolina could serve them better.'[39]

William Yancey was also resentful of the patronizing way he was treated by the four purchasing agents who were buying arms for the South.[40] It was his friendship with John Laird MP, Yancey liked to point out, which had opened the door to the largest shipbuilding firm in Liverpool. In many ways, the Confederate Cabinet regarded weaponry as of greater importance than diplomacy.[41] Before the war, the North had manufactured 97 per cent of the country's weapons.[42] The Confederacy had declared its independence with a mere 160,000 firearms and limited means of manufacturing any more. Only one factory in the entire South, the Tredegar Ironworks in Richmond, was capable of producing artillery. There was not enough time for the chief of the Ordnance Bureau, Major Josiah Gorgas, to develop the iron mines, erect the foundries and build the factories required to equip a modern army. The soft-spoken Confederate Secretary of the Navy, Stephen Mallory, found his department in an equally deprived state. The Confederate Navy had no warships and only two naval dockyards, in Norfolk, Virginia, and Pensacola, Florida. Its 300 officers were on shore leave until Mallory could provide them with vessels. From the outset, Mallory accepted that he could not construct an entire navy; the best he could hope for, and perhaps all he really needed, was a few raiders to attack Northern merchant ships, and a small fleet of ironclad warships to attack the Federal blockade.[43]

The two agents selected by Gorgas and Mallory to run the international war effort were a far cry from the amateurs in charge of

Southern diplomacy. Caleb Huse, the purchasing agent for the army, and James Dunwoody Bulloch, whom Mallory assigned to acquire ships for the navy, were men of the highest integrity and resourcefulness. Both had family and business connections in the North, but it was to the Confederacy's immeasurable good fortune that their hearts belonged to the South. Major Huse was an artillery officer who had spent six months in Europe, courtesy of the US army, studying the armaments industry.[44] The 40-year-old Bulloch was a former naval officer who had been working for a Northern mail company at the start of the war. He had not seen his native Georgia for ten years, but, he wrote, 'my heart and my head were with the South'.[45] He was about to sail his mail ship out of New Orleans when the guns at Fort Sumter began firing. In the face of bitter Southern opposition, Bulloch scrupulously insisted on returning the vessel to its rightful owners in New York. Only then did he offer his services to the Confederacy.

When Huse had arrived in England in April, he discovered that Northern agents had almost stripped the country of surplus arms. They were paying cash in advance, as though part of their mission was to prevent guns from reaching the Confederacy. Huse had come with limited funds; Edwin De Leon lent him $10,000 of his own money but it was not nearly enough to outbid the Federal agents.[46] Huse was rescued by Charles Prioleau, the director of the merchant-shipping firm Fraser, Trenholm and Co. in Liverpool, who agreed to advance him the payments for his weapons. Prioleau was from Charleston, a fact he proudly advertised by fixing the 'Bonnie Blue' star of South Carolina above his front door. Moreover, his firm was the British arm of a large Charleston firm called John Fraser and Co. There was already an agreement in place between the Confederacy and Fraser, Trenholm for the company to act as the South's financial agents in Europe. But Prioleau was going much further by giving credit to Huse without a guarantee in place. He did the same for James Bulloch when the naval agent arrived the following month in a similar condition.

Bulloch had no difficulty finding Fraser, Trenholm's Liverpool headquarters, which took up an entire three-storey building near the docks.[47] Although he used the precaution of entering via the back door, Bulloch was spotted by Federal spies. The Union report compiled on him had provided an extremely detailed description of his features: he was a 'very dark, sallow man with black hair and eyes, whiskers down each cheek but shaved clean off his chin and ... about 5'8" high'.[48] For the first few days Bulloch continued to creep about the city until he read in the local newspapers the precise details of his mission. The information was all there, from the number of ships he was seeking, to his means of paying for them. It was, Bulloch wrote in astonishment, 'as if the particulars had been furnished direct from the Treasury Department or from the pages of my instructions'.[49]

The man behind the exposure was the flamboyant American diplomat Henry Sanford, who had introduced William Howard Russell to Seward in March. Shortly thereafter, he had left Washington to take up the post of Minister to Belgium. Sanford inspired contradictory reactions in people. Charles Sumner was one of his most loyal supporters; Charles Francis Adams had loathed him from the moment they met. Sanford was not awed by the Adams name; he was wealthy and well connected, had studied abroad, could speak several languages and although only 38 had served in numerous legations, including St Petersburg and Paris. In his own mind he was an ingenious sophisticate, a ladies' man and a puppeteer. To others, such as Lincoln's Secretary of the Navy, Gideon Welles, Sanford might have been tolerable were it not for his insatiable desire 'to be busy and fussy, to show pomp and power'.[50]

Seward had diverted Sanford to Paris to serve as the interim Minister until William Dayton could settle his affairs at home. But he expected Sanford to perform many roles and to travel widely. At one time, Seward entertained serious hopes that Garibaldi would agree to lead the Union war effort, since he had briefly lived in the United States during his exile in the 1850s, and one of Sanford's tasks was to persuade Garibaldi to accept Seward's offer. (Garibaldi told Sanford he was not interested unless abolition became the main objective of the war, and he was made supreme commander of all US forces.) Sanford's most important mission was to counteract Confederate activity in Europe 'by all proper means'.[51] Sanford took these words literally and from the moment he arrived in Europe focused his formidable energy on creating a surveillance network that stretched from London to Belgium. He wanted every Rebel to have at least one Federal operative dogging his footsteps.[52]

Sanford knew even before Huse and Bulloch that two more Confederate agents were on their way. One of them, navy Lieutenant James North, had orders to buy or order two armoured warships. The other, Major Edward Anderson, would be working with Caleb Huse.[53] They landed at Liverpool on 25 June, by which time Sanford had hired a private detective with a murky reputation named Ignatius Pollaky. Sanford told Seward that Pollaky operated his own agency and 'knows his business'. Together they were going to destroy the Confederate network from the inside. 'How it will be done,' wrote Sanford on 4 July, 'whether through a pretty mistress or a spying landlord is nobody's business; . . . but I lay . . . stress on getting . . . full accounts of their operations here . . . I go on the doctrine that in war as in love everything is fair that will lead to success.'[54] Letters and telegrams could be copied, messages intercepted, informants bribed, or perhaps the odd accident might befall an unlucky Confederate agent. One of Sanford's ideas involved paying postmen £1 a week to reveal the frequency and origins of all the letters received by the Confederates.[55]

An English arms manufacturer tipped off the Confederates to the fact that they were under surveillance. 'My attention was brought to these people by Mr Isaacs who came over to my quarters one morning and asked me if I knew I was being watched,' wrote Edward Anderson. 'Come with me to your window then, said he, and I will point out to you a shadow that never loses sight of you – at the same time directing my notice to a rough looking fellow standing across the street on the corner.' Anderson immediately went down and tried to embarrass the detective by asking for street directions, which he gave rather awkwardly.

> He was a plain, countrified looking man, roughly clad and by no means
> bearing about him the appearance of a detective officer. Subsequently, when
> I came to know him better I was impressed with the effect produced by
> dress, for when I met my man on the following day, he was accoutred in a
> neat suit of black clothing like a gentleman, and on subsequent occasions
> in different costumes . . . Sometimes with moustache and whiskers and
> again clean shaved. I never failed however to recognize my shadow. Assist-
> ing him were one or two others.[56]

On another occasion, while returning on the night train from Paris, Anderson shared a carriage with one his shadows. 'We had some little talk together,' he recorded in his diary, 'but neither of us learned much of the other.'[57] He was not alone in having such face-to-face encounters. Suspicious figures seemed to loiter in every doorway. 'They have agents employed for no other purpose,' commented Caleb Huse.[58] Sanford intended to keep all the Confederates under surveillance but he realized that James Bulloch had to be the chief target. 'He is the most dangerous man the South have here and fully up to his business,' he told Seward. 'I am disbursing at the rate of £150 a month on this one man which will give you an idea of the importance I attach to his movements.' He hoped that Bulloch might try to slip off to the Continent, where it would be relatively easy to have him arrested for failing to carry the proper documentation. 'Of course, no one official would appear in the matter,' he assured Seward.[59] Sanford was less concerned about Lieutenant North, whose contribution to the Southern war effort puzzled the detectives. North appeared to be working on his own, but what he was doing, apart from costing Sanford money in espionage expenses, remained a mystery. He seemed to spend a great deal of time moping and, from the look of his intercepted mail, complaining.

Sanford's fears about Bulloch had been prescient. The Confederate agent knew that the real threat to his operations was not from the spies (who were irritating) but from the legal obstacles created by the Foreign Enlistment Act. Before he set about any naval business, Bulloch obtained expert legal opinion on what the Act allowed and disallowed, hoping to uncover any loopholes. To his surprise, he discovered it would be relatively easy to circumvent the rules: the Act forbade a belligerent nation from outfitting or equipping warlike vessels in British waters, but there was nothing to prevent the construction of a ship with an unusual design. A vessel could be built with gun ports, for example, but it could not leave with any guns on board; it could have a magazine to store gunpowder, but would not be allowed to set sail with the powder present.

Bulloch went to work as soon as he received his legal advice. Within a few weeks he had made two contracts, one for a gunboat and the other for a top-of-the-line warship with copper-plated bunkers and enough storage space to hold a year's worth of spare parts. For the first, Bulloch used an intermediary to hide the involvement of the Confederacy and invented some Italian owners who were expecting delivery in eight months' time.[60] To give authenticity to the Italian claim, the vessel was called the *Oreto* for the time being. But the other ship did not require the same subterfuge since it was being built by Laird and Sons, the Liverpool company owned by Yancey's friend, John Laird. With a nod and a wink, Lairds accepted the explanation that the modifications were innocent. This vessel, project number 290 on Lairds' books, was going to cost a staggering £47,500, to be paid in five instalments.[61]

With the first part of his mission now fulfilled, Bulloch turned his attention to helping Caleb Huse buy munitions. The victory at Bull Run lent urgency to their mission. 'We want arms,' implored LeRoy Walker, the Confederate Secretary of War, 'and must have them if they are to be had ... the enemy is daily augmenting his supplies.'[62] By the end of August, the agents had amassed so considerable a quantity of supplies that their most pressing problem was the threat of discovery by the authorities.[63] Now the Confederates found themselves stymied by the neutrality proclamation. Bulloch was unable to persuade any shipping owner to break the blockade. Finally, after much negotiation, Bulloch and Anderson made a deal with Fraser, Trenholm to rent space on the *Bermuda*, one of the company's fastest steamers, which was docked at Hartlepool on the east coast and already slated for use during the cotton season, when the blockade would be tested in earnest.

Henry Sanford knew about the *Bermuda* and had a plan that involved the Federal navy pouncing on her as soon as she reached the open sea, 'no matter what her papers'. 'We can discuss the matter with the English afterwards,' he asserted confidently.[64] Seward ignored his suggestion, and Lord Russell turned down Charles Francis Adams's request to detain the *Bermuda* since the Minister was unable to show that she was anything other than a private ship on a private commercial venture. The officials in Hartlepool had observed her loading, and even noted that arms and ammunition were being 'packed to resemble earthenware'.[65] But there was no legal reason for her detention and the vessel sailed away on 22 August, despite everyone concerned knowing her real purpose and destination.

Fraser, Trenholm and Co. had great hopes for the *Bermuda*. Every Southerner, not to mention every British merchant with a half-decent cargo ship, believed that the blockade was a fiction. Latest estimates put the entire US navy blockading fleet at forty-two steamships. The Southern coastline extended over 3,500 miles, from the tip of Virginia to the banks of the Rio Grande in Texas, and included hundreds of ports, bays and inlets. Almost 200 navigable rivers fed into the sea; many harbours had several entrances and numerous channels for hiding ships. Much of the South lay behind an enormous sandbar that acted like a double coastline, allowing ships to sail from port to port without ever having to go out into open sea. When these considerations were added to the poor condition of the US navy, it seemed incomprehensible to

Southerners that any country, let alone Britain, would accept that the blockade met the main legal requirement for its international recognition, namely that it was real and being enforced on a daily basis. They were hoping that the Royal Navy would sweep away the miserable little wooden ships stifling the South's commerce, and declare the ports once again open to the world.

Ordered by the Foreign Office to keep a record of blockade activity, the British Consuls responded by saying there really wasn't any. Phrases such as 'totally inefficient' and 'totally ineffective' appeared with regularity.[66] Yet the picture conveyed by the statistics was misleading. The South was not one vast open harbour, ready to receive and distribute all the goods that Europe cared to ship. If that had been the case, New York would have never been so vital a trade partner. Only ten Southern ports were deep enough for transatlantic shipping; and just five of those (Charleston, Mobile, New Orleans, Savannah and Wilmington) were adequately provided with road and rail links.[67] The US navy merely needed to be well placed rather than omnipresent. The Union Blockade Board, instituted by the Secretary of the Navy in June, was already at work analysing the Confederacy's strategic weaknesses.

Two days after the departure of the *Bermuda*, Anthony Trollope and his wife, Rose, set sail for Boston. They arrived on 5 September, after a brief stop in Halifax, beating the *Bermuda* to America by two weeks. Trollope had long wanted to visit the United States in order to write a travel book. It would be a break from writing fiction and perhaps, he hoped, might even put an end to the notoriety attached to the Trollope name. His mother had intended to be funny rather than offensive in her *Domestic Manners of the Americans*, but the book had caused such damage to Anglo-American relations that Trollope had often thought, 'If I could do anything to mitigate the soreness, if I could in any small degree add to the good feeling which should exist between two nations which ought to love each other so well . . . I should.'[68]

Boston literary circles welcomed the Trollopes with a warmth that belied the harsh statements against Britain in the press. The only sharpness they encountered was directed at Rose; people often asked her if she regretted writing *Domestic Manners*, to which she patiently replied that she was not her mother-in-law. Trollope had the occasional argument over Britain's neutrality. Bostonians, in common with the rest of the North, believed that England's greed for cotton was the real reason it had granted belligerency to the South.

But no one abused Trollope with the freedom or viciousness with which Washingtonians insulted William Howard Russell. Every obstruction was now thrown in Russell's way. Although General McClellan was unfailingly polite to him, and never turned down his request for a pass, Russell found that the guards and sentries took a mean delight in turning him away. He did not know when his punishment would end, and while it continued he was useless as a war correspondent. Frank Vizetelly had no such impediments and was able to witness the rehabilitation of the 79th Highlanders when he visited them on 11 September. Among them, Ebenezer Wells had been promoted to wagon master, a change that increased the young man's chances of survival but kept him on the move all day long. During one gruelling marathon, his raw and bloody feet swelled out of their boots. 'After cutting my boots here and there,' he wrote, 'I was obliged to throw them away and marched the last six miles on a stony road, nearly barefoot.'[69] The 79th Highlanders were now deemed trustworthy enough to participate in a reconnaissance mission on a Confederate outpost near Lewinsville, a small town less than 13 miles from Washington.

Vizetelly sketched the aftermath as McClellan greeted the returning soldiers with a dip of his hat. The artist was delighted to have something to occupy himself with for a couple of days; the endless training was driving him mad.[70] Russell was also bored. 'Time passes away in expectation of some onward movement, or desperate attack, or important strategical movements; and night comes to reassemble a few friends, Americans and English, at my rooms or elsewhere, to talk over the disappointed hopes of the day, to speculate on the future, to chide each dull delay, and to part with a hope that tomorrow would be more lively than to-day,' he wrote in his diary on 11 September. General McClellan would probably spend all winter pummelling his volunteer army into shape, a prospect Russell found extremely disheartening. 'I like the man,' he wrote in his diary. 'But I do not think he is equal to his occasion or his place.'[71] 'In truth,' he added, 'life is becoming exceedingly monotonous and uninteresting ... But for the hospitability of Lord Lyons to the English residents, the place would be nearly insufferable.'[72]

'The only thing that makes me stick out here', Russell wrote to Delane on 13 September, 'is the determination not to show a white feather for these fellows.' He refused to follow the suggestion of Mowbray Morris, the managing editor of *The Times*, to seek safety in the British legation. The quickest way to stop the death threats and petitions against him, Russell told Delane, would be to tone down the anti-Northern bias in the newspaper: 'I don't want to ask you to sacrifice the policy of *The Times* to me, but I would like you if possible not to sacrifice me.'[73] He warned Delane that his penchant for quoting the demagogic *New York Herald* as though it were the chief mouthpiece of the Union would eventually rebound on *The Times*, but the editor denied he was baiting the Americans. It was, Delane wrote back, 'simply that we don't mean to be bullied by a so-called Power that can scarcely defend its capital against its fellow-citizens'.[74]

Delane's sarcastic reply to Russell showed how little attention he was paying to the journalist's reports. By the beginning of October, McClellan had equipped and trained more than 100,000 soldiers who, even if he felt they were not yet ready to be deployed, would never drop their arms and stampede off the battlefield as they had done at Bull Run.[75] The humiliation suffered in July had made the North determined to defeat not only the South but also her perceived allies. The treatment of blockade-runners became harsher. When Edward Archibald, the British Consul in New York, went to Fort Lafayette to check on the welfare of a crew from a captured blockade-runner, he found thirty men squeezed into a small, airless cell with barely enough headroom to stand. A bucket in the corner was the only lavatory, a small basin on a table their only access to water. Archibald took down their statements by the light from the doorway 'using my hat for a desk. The men had lost everything except for the clothes on their backs and these were filthy and infested.' The prisoners were so dejected that he arranged for new clothing to be sent to them at his own expense.[76] The international treaty governing the application of blockades forbade the sentencing or imprisonment of foreign blockade-runners; they could be held for questioning only. But the timing of their release was at the discretion of the authorities. It could take just three days or, if Archibald lodged a complaint, as long as five months.[77]

Bull Run also made Northern politicians more realistic about the challenges ahead. Seward quietly reserved his nationalism for his dispatches and began to encourage foreign officers to volunteer for the

Union, knowing that the army would benefit from their experience.[78] His open-door policy caused problems for the US legation in London, where would-be volunteers were constantly calling on Adams, expecting to be given a commission and free passage to America.[79] But Seward was unrepentant; he would rather keep them 'on the Northern side', he told William Howard Russell, 'lest some really good man should get among the rebels'.[80]

The *New York Times* began to carry frequent reports of a major or colonel, late of the British army, 'who has tendered his services [to] the President'.[81] Major-General Charles Havelock, the brother of the more famous Havelock of India, discovered that this was not always the best way, however. When Lincoln appointed him to McClellan's staff the General retaliated for the encroachment on his authority by refusing to acknowledge Havelock's presence. Leonard Douglas Hay Currie, Captain of the 19th Regiment of Foot and a distinguished veteran of the Indian and Crimean wars, had more success by applying to the Governor of New York. 'Thinking I might be of use,' he explained, 'I was glad when an opportunity was offered me to place my services at the disposal of the government.'[82] He was sent to Brigadier General W. F. 'Baldy' Smith, who immediately made him assistant adjutant general.

Seward was responsible for recruiting one of the least likely British volunteers to appear in Washington: Major John Fitzroy De Courcy, the British Magistrate in San Juan during the 'Pig War'. De Courcy lived for soldiering, and rather than moulder on the island during the ongoing stalemate, he wrote to Seward to ask if he could lead a regiment. Amazed and delighted by the irony, Seward invited him to Washington. Frances and Fanny Seward were disappointed to have the brusque soldier thrust upon them during their brief visit to the capital. Fanny, Seward's 18-year-old daughter, complained that De Courcy's presence spoiled her last evening with her father. She might have forgiven him had he been handsome, but De Courcy's face reminded her of a rocky beach and he suffered from 'an imperfection in one of his eyes'. It was typical of Seward to sacrifice the needs of his family for a moment of transient importance; but he did follow through on his promise to De Courcy, who was made a colonel of the 16th Ohio Volunteers.

The hostility with which Britain was regarded in the North meant that none of the British volunteers received as much attention as the

Reconnaissance made by General Stoneman, accompanied by the Comte de
Paris and the Duc de Chartres, by Frank Vizetelly

Comte de Paris, the Bourbon pretender to the French throne, and his
brother the Duc de Chartres. The arrival of another set of French royalty
(albeit the exiled kind whose only hope of gaining military experience
was to go to America) was hailed as proof of the excellent relations
between the two countries. Seward waived the rules so that they would
not have to take the US oath of allegiance. The Comte entered the army
as plain 'Captain Paris' and his brother as 'Captain Charters'. Their
uncle, the Prince de Joinville, who had accompanied his nephews on the
journey in order to place his son in the US Naval Academy, politely
turned down the offer of a command in the navy.

Lord Lyons ignored the spectacle of Seward paying assiduous attention
to the former British Magistrate of San Juan. Of all the provocations he
had endured since August, the welcome given to De Courcy was among
the least troubling. Seward 'is at present very wild with Lord Lyons',
William Howard Russell remarked to Delane in September, after the
Secretary of State had embarrassed Lyons by leaking to the press a portion

of their correspondence – selectively edited to make the Minister appear arrogant and Seward patriotic.

The letters in question concerned the arrests of British subjects on charges of sedition. Seward's power over Lyons had increased dramatically during the summer; every case of forcible enlistment and underage volunteering went through his office, and now, since Lincoln had suspended the writ of habeas corpus for a large section of the North, Seward had gained the additional power to detain indefinitely all persons suspected of treason. 'I am afraid that he takes a personal pleasure in spying and arresting,' Lyons wrote to Lord Russell in a rare outburst after Seward harangued him for an hour before casually taking out his pen and signing the release of a British prisoner.*[83]

Lyons was relieved that the arrests for sedition were not solely confined to British subjects, though they made up almost 15 per cent of the suspects in prison.[84] No one was exempt, he informed the Foreign Office. Lyons had heard from his friend the English actress Fanny Kemble (who remained tied to the United States because of her daughters), that her former husband had been arrested in Philadelphia and incarcerated without trial at Fort Lafayette in New York. The family was discovering, as had Lyons, that 'it is vain to resort to the Courts of law for redress'.[85] Rose Greenhow was also arrested during one of Seward's sweeps of Rebel sympathizers in Washington; in deference to her status in Washington she was placed under house arrest rather than carted off to prison in a blaze of publicity.

Russell watched as the military authorities hounded Samuel Phillips Day out of Washington when the English journalist came through the lines on 1 October. Edmund Monson, Lord Lyons's private secretary, told Day that the offensive letters he had been sending to the *New York Times* put him beyond the help of the legation. Day sailed for home on 12 October on the *Young America*, already planning his revenge on the North. Russell envied him. 'Could it not be possible to arrange for me to go home for a month?' he begged Delane two days later. He missed

* Seward's bullying of Lyons on the subject of political arrests played into the hands of his critics. A story spread through Washington and into the history books that he boasted to Lyons: 'My Lord, I can touch a bell on my right hand, and order the arrest of a citizen of Ohio. I can touch the bell again, and order the arrest of a citizen of New York. Can the Queen of England, in her dominions, do as much?' Seward's 'little bell' became famous throughout both North and South.

his family, but even if he wanted to stay, 'It is impossible to express one's opinion freely. The press and the politicians would desire nothing better than to hunt me out of this country.'[86]

Seward 'will probably play out the play and send me my passports', Lyons wrote to Lord Russell two weeks later. 'If he is in his present mood, he will be glad to find a pretext for performing other half-violent acts of the same kind.' But, he added despondently, 'this cannot go on forever'. Some incident would push the war of words into a war of arms; Lyons could feel the crackling animosity in the air. William Howard Russell could sense it too. A fury and desire to punish England was evident in the press, in politics, in the army and among ordinary citizens. 'The storm may blow over,' he wrote to Delane; 'now it rages furiously.'[87]

7

'It Takes Two to Make a Quarrel'

An unlikely friendship – The Fingal *escapes – The success of Confederate propaganda – Seward rues his mistake – Appointment of Mason and Slidell – Capture of the* Trent

The departure of Samuel Phillips Day on the *Young America* from New York in the middle of October coincided with the escape of the *Theodora* out of Charleston. The cargo on board the swift blockade-runner was not cotton, but the successors to Pierre Rost and William Yancey. Frustrated by their failure to secure diplomatic recognition after the victory at Manassas, Jefferson Davis had selected two of the South's most prominent and experienced politicians, Senators James Mason and John Slidell, to be the new Confederate Commissioners in Europe. Slidell was to go to Paris, Mason was to remain in London and Dudley Mann would be transferred to Brussels.

In place of the broad suggestions given to the original Commissioners, Mason carried with him a long and detailed set of instructions on how to approach the British government. In particular, the Confederate Cabinet ordered him to ram home the illegality of the blockade under the Declaration of Paris, in the hope this would encourage Britain to force the reopening of Southern ports. Without its own fleet, the Confederacy remained incapable of lifting the blockade; so far just one cruiser had been launched, a converted passenger ship renamed the CSS *Sumter*, whose limited capabilities made it effective only as a raider against merchant ships.

The chronic shortages caused by the blockade were forcing whole regiments to sit idle for want of arms and munitions. Even before the departure of Mason and Slidell, Davis had sent an agent to England, his instructions hidden for safe keeping inside the sole of his boot, imploring Caleb Huse to 'send forward supplies as rapidly and as securely as possible ... You will not allow yourself to be governed by the political agents of the Government, but act upon your own responsibility.'[1] Davis's exhortation had already been anticipated; frustrated by the slow pace of shipments, Edward Anderson and James Bulloch had pooled their funds and bought their own steamship, the *Fingal*.

The challenge for the Confederates lay in keeping the identity of the *Fingal* from Henry Sanford's spies; otherwise the US navy would have no difficulty in tracking and capturing the cargo before it reached Savannah. They were helped by one of Anderson's most important suppliers, who had a relative in the Foreign Office. 'Money will accomplish anything in England,' wrote Anderson. 'The bait took, and every night before I retired to bed I was thoroughly advised of all [Charles Francis Adams's] operations for the day.'[2] He was counting on the mole to give sufficient warning if the *Fingal* was discovered.

Anderson frequently passed Federal agents in the street, but he had learned to tell the difference between those who were genuine arms purchasers like himself, and those whose real business was to keep a watch on his movements. 'My friend McGuire is indefatigable in his attentions towards me,' he observed. 'His instructions must be very stringent for he posts himself opposite the very door of the Hotel.' Ignatius Pollaky, Sanford's detective, insisted that he had a 'fix upon every agent of the rebellion', but still the name and location of the *Fingal* remained a mystery.[3] Sanford had been successfully intercepting the Confederates' telegrams until clerks at the Liverpool telegraph office became suspicious and uncovered the operation. The blunder enabled the Confederates to lodge an official complaint with the authorities. Reports appeared in the press, accusing the legation of setting up an illegal 'system of political espionage and terrorism' in Britain.[4] Charles Francis Adams was mortified to be blamed for Sanford's handiwork. The spying 'has been productive of great evil', raged Moran in his diary. 'Not one farthing of good has it done us.'[5]

Adams had never imagined that his post would be so troublesome and difficult. 'Indeed the position of a minister at this Court is far more important and responsible than I had supposed,' he admitted in his diary.[6] It disturbed him that Seward would stoop to playing dirty tricks against his opponents. 'Early training in the school of New York State politics' had blunted some of his finer qualities, Adams thought. '[This] shows itself in a somewhat brusque and ungracious manner towards the representatives of foreign nations ... [and] in a rather indiscriminate appliance of means to an end.' Adams did not desire to be a part of Seward's schemes, but equally he resented learning about them in the press.

A suspicion that Seward's behaviour was the real reason behind Lord Russell's invitation to him to stay at Abergeldie Castle in Scotland made Adams extremely reluctant to accept. He had no wish to travel a thousand miles in order to be grilled about his wayward chief, especially since his confidence in Seward had declined over the summer. Benjamin Moran was delighted to have the opportunity to act as the Minister's conscience. 'I have advised him to go, and he probably will,' he wrote complacently in his diary on 21 September. Two days later Adams reluctantly boarded the train for the overnight journey to Aberdeen.

Although Seward's threats of war had died down since Bull Run, the substitution of high rhetoric for low-level harassment had made the British Cabinet nervous about his intentions. Knowing that Adams shared his dislike of ceremony, Russell had asked him to his private retreat in Scotland in the hope that the informal setting would enable them to be frank towards one another; it had worked with John Lothrop Motley, who had visited earlier in the month before taking up his new post at the US legation in Vienna. Russell deliberately avoided any searching interviews or prolonged conversations of the type Adams dreaded. Their 'desultory' talks ebbed and flowed around family meals and bracing country walks along the wooded banks of the River Dee.

Russell's campaign to charm Adams was a complete success. 'He was for the first time', recorded Adams, 'easy, friendly, I might almost call it genial ... I liked him better the nearer I saw him.' Some of the misunderstandings and fears from the summer, which had seemed so intractable before, simply melted away. 'The result of this protracted interview was decidedly advantageous,' wrote Adams. 'In the first place we tacitly grew into more confidence in one another.'[7]

Refreshed by his initiation into the pleasures of alfresco tea with Scotch eggs and boiled peat water, Adams's good mood lasted until his return to the legation on 27 September where he found a scene of perfect chaos. Benjamin Moran was losing his temper at an unruly crowd of would-be volunteers and passport seekers while the Secretary, Charles Wilson, who, if not drunk, was only recently sober, sat hunched behind his desk reading the newspapers. Only after the legation had been cleared and the latest surveillance reports retrieved from the piles of rubbish in Wilson's corner did Adams learn that no progress at all had been made in finding Bulloch's secret cargo ship. He was about to give up on the project when a stranger came to the legation on 1 October, offering to sell information about the Rebels. Much as it offended Adams's sensibilities to pay him, he realized it was their best chance to thwart the Confederates. 'The truth is,' he wrote in his diary, 'of late they have been too cunning for us.'[8]

Ten days later, the Confederates' mole in the Foreign Office sent word that Adams knew the name and the location of the *Fingal*. Anderson and Bulloch went down to Holyhead in Wales on 15 October, but were too late to prevent a customs officer from boarding the *Fingal*, his pen and notebook in hand. Bulloch was aghast: 'I thought of the rifles and sabres in the hold, and the ill-armed pickets on the Potomac waiting and longing for them.'[9] The two men took a desperate risk. Anderson tricked the officer into leaving the steamer. Then, instead of sailing into dock as promised, Bulloch ordered the *Fingal* to weigh anchor and 'we cracked on all the steam her boilers would bear'. They expected to be fired upon or chased by a customs ship but nothing happened. 'It was half past eight o'clock before we got fairly out to sea beyond the reach of batteries and pursuit,' wrote Anderson. 'How my heart lightened as I looked at the blue water again and found myself on board a good staunch ship once more.'[10]

Shortly after the *Fingal*'s escape the legation heard that the *Bermuda* had arrived at Savannah. 'Wilson pretends to disbelieve it,' complained Moran on 17 October. 'But I fear it is fact.' Otherwise, he thought, there would not be so many advertisements in *The Times* for investors to buy shares in blockade-running ships. 'John Bull would violate every law of honor and every principle of justice if he can secure his own ends thereby,' Moran declared.[11] The same criticism was being levelled, with equal rancour, by the British government against Seward.

'Mr Seward appears to have deemed it advisable to get up a little excitement about the European Powers again,' was how Lord Lyons wryly characterized the situation to Lord Russell on 22 October.[12] William Howard Russell was not constrained like Lyons by the language of diplomacy. Seward was up to 'his usual tricks', he noted in a letter to J. C. Bancroft Davis. 'He is determined to resort to his favourite panacea of making the severed States reunited by a war with England.'[13] Neither Lyons nor William Howard Russell thought it was a coincidence that Seward's latest salvoes against England had started when public confidence in the Lincoln administration was wavering. 'A victory would do much to set things straight,' Lyons had written privately to Lord Russell in September, 'but some of the illusions with which the war was begun are gone forever. The appearance of unanimity in the North has completely vanished.'[14] Lyons was referring to the political controversy started by US General John C. Fremont in the border State of Missouri, who in August had announced the emancipation of all slaves in the State belonging to Confederate sympathizers. His impetuous act not only threatened to tear the army apart, with some regiments appearing ready to resign or desert en masse rather than fight for the Negro, but also gave the strongest possible incentive to Missouri and the other slave-owning border States to join forces with the Confederacy.

Lincoln was already considering the removal of Fremont from his post when General McClellan suffered his first significant defeat. It was only a small engagement between two brigades at a place called Ball's Bluff, 40 miles upriver from Washington, but the high number of Federal soldiers killed and wounded shook Lincoln's confidence in his new military commander. The possibility that the South might grow from eleven to thirteen or fourteen States could tip the scales against the North. The next day, 22 October, Lincoln announced to the Cabinet that he was repudiating both Fremont and his emancipation declaration. He was prepared to lose the support of the radical abolitionists in his own party but not that of Kentucky, Missouri and Maryland, which would make 'the job on our hands', Lincoln confessed, 'too large for us'.[15]

Lord Lyons had at first paid little attention to Seward's rather obvious attempts to distract attention from the government's woes.[16] He was too busy trying to prevent the Secretary of State from undermining the Anglo-French alliance. Seward had begun to woo Emperor Napoleon III in the delusion that France was the friendlier of the two nations.*[17]

---

* Lyons suspected that Seward and Mercier had only a vague idea of what the other was saying, and although he faithfully reported all that Mercier told him, Lyons warned Russell not to take his words too literally. 'Your Lordship will not fail to recollect that the conversation, which was carried on in English, was repeated to me by M. Mercier in French, and that it took place between a Frenchman not very familiar with English, and an American having little or no knowledge of French.'[18]

When Mercier, the French Minister, warned him that his government was losing patience with the blockade, Seward hinted that if the Emperor withdrew his recognition of Southern belligerency, the North would do everything in its power to ensure a steady supply of cotton. Rather than being grateful for this show of favouritism, the French saw it as further proof that the North was heading for defeat. Mercier regarded Southern independence as a fait accompli and was trying to persuade Lyons that it was in everybody's interest for the Powers to recognize the Confederacy. Logic must prevail over sentiment, Mercier patiently but persistently argued. Lyons refused to be drawn in: 'I take, perhaps, a more hopeful view than M. Mercier does of the Military prospects of the North,' he explained to Lord Russell.[19]

However, Lyons could not ignore Seward's declaration on 26 October that the North was 'expelling' Consul Bunch from Charleston (where it had no effective jurisdiction) for holding talks with the Confederacy about privateering. The staff at the British legation was furious that Seward made no reference to the French Consul, who had also taken part in the negotiations. Lyons maintained a stony silence during his interview with Seward, knowing that it would annoy the Secretary of State to be denied a reaction. 'Mr Bunch has merely been selected as a safer object of attack than the British or French Government,' he reported angrily to Lord Russell after the meeting.[20] It was not the transparency of Seward's motives that worried Lyons but his failure to realize the impact of his words and deeds on the international stage. 'He always tries violence in language first,' observed Lyons, 'and then runs the risk of pledging himself and the nation to violent courses, if he be taken at once at his word.'[21]

When Lord Russell heard the news about Consul Bunch he realized that his efforts with Adams were unlikely to have the slightest effect on Seward's behaviour. 'It is the business of Seward to feed the mob with sacrifices every day,' he wrote to Lord Palmerston, 'and we happen to be the most grateful food he can offer.' As long as there were no actions accompanying the Secretary of State's words, Russell thought the safest course was to pay no attention to him, since Seward was a 'singular mixture of the bully and coward'.[22] Palmerston agreed, although he wished that more regiments had been sent to Canada as a warning to Seward against becoming too cocky. But the Cabinet's anxieties were dismissed by the new Secretary of War, Sir George Cornewall Lewis, who told them not to be fooled by Seward's charade of aggression: 'the Washington government is violent and unscrupulous,' he wrote, 'but it is not insane.'[23]

Throughout the country, however, the effect of Seward's threats, which he ensured were known to the press, was to swing public opinion dramatically away from the North. The mills had already moved to short time in order to preserve their dwindling cotton stocks. *Reynolds's Newspaper*, a popular weekly aimed at the working classes, blamed the Northern blockade rather than the Southern cotton embargo for the looming crisis. 'England must break the Blockade,' cried an editorial in early autumn, 'Or Her Millions must starve.'[24] Henry Adams was trying without success to plant favourable articles in the press. 'I hope that you will see in some of the London newspapers if not my writing, at least

KING COTTON BOUND;
Or, The Modern Prometheus.

Punch acknowledges the threat posed by the Union blockade to 'King Cotton'

my hand,' he wrote in confidence to his brother, Charles Francis Jr. 'They need it, confound 'em.'[25] Benjamin Moran was convinced that the Confederates were either feeding Reuter with false information or encouraging him to slant his news. 'That he is under the influence of the rebels is too clear to be the subject of doubt,' he fulminated in his diary. Only after the news service turned a recent Federal victory into a defeat was Moran able to persuade Charles Francis Adams to deliver a friendly warning to Reuter.[26]

Henry Adams complained to Charles Francis Jr. that their father would not engage in any form of journalism or public speaking. Although Adams received many more invitations than his Confederate rivals, he invariably turned them down. While Adams agreed to attend the Lord Mayor's dinner on 9 November on the assurance that he would not be called upon to speak, William Yancey eagerly accepted an invitation to the less coveted Fishmongers' Company because there was a chance that he might.[27] The departing Confederate Commissioners had been working hard, they informed Richmond, to cultivate anyone 'likely to bring to bear a favorable influence on the British cabinet'.[28] But the greatest Southern propaganda coup had nothing to do with the envoys' efforts: in September a book entitled *The American Union*, which defended the South's claim to independence, became a surprise best-seller. The author was a Liverpool businessman named James Spence, whose travels in America had persuaded him that, while slavery was doomed, the cultural and economic differences between the North and South would never be overcome. In his opinion, it was politically and morally unfeasible for two such distinct entities to remain united.

The great strength of *The American Union* was its sober style and earnest attempt to discuss the merits of secession. Although Northern sympathizers disagreed with Spence's arguments they had to admit that the book was too well written to dismiss. 'It is studiously suited to the English taste,' explained the abolitionist Richard Webb, 'being moderate in tone, lucid in style, and free from personalities.'[29] Moreover, the subject matter – independence – appealed to English sensibilities. 'I believe Englishmen instinctively sympathize with rebels,' the American Vice-Consul Henry Wilding commented to his former superior, Nathaniel Hawthorne. So long as 'the rebellion be not against England'.[30] 'Why do the Southern agents have it all their own way?' grumbled Charles Francis Jr., when he heard about the success of *The American Union* and other polemics. 'Our agents abroad apparently confine their efforts to cabinets and officials and leave public opinion and the press to take care of themselves.'[31]

Henry Adams assured his brother that the situation in England was worse than he could imagine, even 'our own friends fail to support us'. Lincoln's rejection of General Fremont and his emancipation proclamation had played into the Confederates' hands; without the slavery issue the North was simply a large country fighting a rebellion in its nether regions. 'Look at the Southerners here,' Henry wrote indignantly on 25 October. 'Every man is inspired by the idea of independence and liberty while we are in a false position.'[32] *The Times* seemed to take a malicious pleasure in repeating as often as it could the hoary claim that the war was a contest between one side fighting for 'empire' and the other 'for independence'.[33] The only politician who was prepared to attack Delane's crafty misrepresentation of the conflict was the Duke of Argyll, who delivered a ringing defence of the Union at his annual estate dinner on 2 November. 'I do not care whether we look at it from the Northern or from the Southern point of view,' the *Illustrated London News* reported him as saying. 'Gentlemen, I think we ought to admit, in fairness to the Americans, that there are some things worth fighting for, and that national existence is one of these.'[34]

The public in both countries would have been shocked had they known Seward's real thoughts about the state of Anglo-American relations. Although the Secretary of State was always talking as though he were locked in a life-or-death struggle with Britain, he knew that there was no desire in London for conflict with the North. Even if he discounted Lyons's protestations and Adams's dispatches, John Motley, whose opinion Seward trusted, had been giving him verbatim reports of his conversations with persons of note in England, including Lord Russell, Prince Albert and the Queen. Motley's letters contained 'a most cheering account of the real sentiment of honest sympathy existing in the best Class of English Society towards us', exclaimed the President's private secretary, John Hay, who was present when Seward read out sections to Lincoln.[35]

The truth was, Seward cared little for what foreign governments thought about the war, so long as they obeyed his directive to regard it as a minor insurrection and not a fully fledged rebellion. He worried even less about foreign sentiment and persistently ignored the warnings from his Consuls and Henry Sanford that the North was squandering its goodwill abroad.[36] 'Foreign sympathy ... never did and never can create or maintain any state,' Seward wrote flippantly to John Bigelow, the new American Consul in Paris.[37] But once he learned that the new Confederate Commissioners were to be Senators Mason and Slidell, Seward started to feel anxious about the North's representation in Europe. John Bright's complaint about the Morrill Tariff having 'done immense harm to the friendly feeling which ought to exist here towards you', and Motley's observation of the 'very great change in English public sympathy since the passing of the Morrill Tariff', suddenly became the talk of the State Department.[38]

William Howard Russell had disregarded rumours that Seward was looking for emissaries to send to Europe until he bumped into him on 4 November and learned that the stories were true. 'He begged of me to come and dine with him tomorrow,' Russell recorded in his diary, 'to meet Mr Everett who is here as one of a secret commission.'[39] But having embraced the need for special agents abroad, Seward discovered that it was no easy task to find the right men. The august Edward Everett, a former Secretary of State, Minister to Britain, Governor of and Senator for Massachusetts and the greatest orator of his generation, changed his mind two days later. Several other candidates showed a similar reluctance. Finally Seward was able to enlist four suitable representatives: General Winfield Scott, who had been forced to retire from the army; John Hughes, the Roman Catholic Archbishop of New York, who would battle with Slidell for the sympathy of the French; the Episcopal Bishop of Ohio, Charles McIlvaine, who was to woo the Anglican clergy; and his own old political partner, Thurlow Weed, whom Seward knew would be more than a match for James Mason. William Howard Russell could see why Seward admired Weed as a political lobbyist, although he doubted that the skill would serve him as well in a foreign environment. 'Thurlow is a crafty old fellow,' he wrote to the *Times* correspondent in New York, 'but he will be of small weight among the polished politicians of France or England.'[40] Weed, Archbishop Hughes and General Scott sailed together on 8 November from New York. Weed was angered by a newspaper report that exposed the nature of their mission. He was sure that Charles Sumner had either written it or told the writer what to say in order to embarrass Seward. Weed had seen him the day before and noticed that he had a 'hang-dog look'. But they had only Seward to blame for the pandemonium on the docks. All persons wishing to depart from New York, including foreigners, were suddenly required to have their passport countersigned by the Secretary of State. Among those worst affected were British travellers passing through New York on ship connections to other ports. Consul Archibald's office was filled with stranded families seeking his help. Some of them would have to wait another month for the next boat to their destination. Even a British army officer who was en route from Canada to his regiment in Nassau was forcibly detained at the quayside. Archibald begged Lyons to make Seward appoint a civil servant with signatory powers, so at least the process might be done in New York.[41] Archibald assumed that the purpose of all this was to annoy England.[42] He was not alone in thinking so; Anthony Trollope accused Seward of having 'resolved to make every Englishman in America feel himself in some way punished because England had not assisted the North'.[43]

The real reason lay with Mason and Slidell. Initial reports claimed that they had managed to sail out of Charleston on board the CSS *Nashville*, another converted steamship like the *Sumter*. The Secretary of the Navy, Gideon Welles, had immediately dispatched several warships to run her down before she reached Europe, but the only ship which spotted the *Nashville*, the USS *Connecticut*, lost sight of her in the pursuit. Then Seward received a different report: the Confederates had travelled by way of Cuba and were going to dock in New York in early November.[44] No longer sure what to believe, the passport fiasco was an attempt by Seward to save the administration from the embarrassment of the Confederates escaping in full view.

The *Nashville* was not carrying the Commissioners, although her mission was no less dangerous to the North. The Confederate Secretary of the Navy, Stephen Mallory, had ordered her to England to be fitted as a warship. The *Nashville* had reached St George's Harbour in Bermuda when the *Fingal* arrived on 2 November, carrying Edward Anderson and James Bulloch. The two ships anchored only a few hundred yards from each other. 'The *Nashville* ran up the Confederate flag as we stood in,' recorded Anderson, '& I supposed had been sent out by Mr Mallory for the express purpose of communicating with us, but how to learn this was the question.' Their disguise was working a little too well. 'To all intents and purposes we were an English merchant steamer,' he recorded.

'We were sporting the British flag, had an English captain and crew, and desired above all things to keep our movements secret. To send a boat to the *Nashville* direct would be to betray ourselves.' It was a ridiculous situation. The ships rocked gently side by side, neither daring to make the first move. Anderson grew impatient. 'Taking a spyglass from one of the quarter masters I affected to be admiring the surrounding objects until by degrees my vision turned upon the *Nashville*. Her officers were on deck scrutinizing us.' He ordered coded signals to be raised but it soon became clear that they meant nothing to the *Nashville*. Finally, one of the *Fingal*'s officers rowed over on the pretext of asking for a casket of fresh water, and was recognized by a former crewmate.

The captain of the *Nashville* turned out to be a former naval colleague of Anderson's named Robert Pegram. That night, as they swapped news and experiences, Pegram warned Anderson and Bulloch to banish any thoughts of an easy entry into Savannah: if his encounter with the *Connecticut* was anything to go by, they would be chased all the way from the outer banks. Five days later, on 7 November, the *Fingal* set sail for the South during a tropical storm; after five nights of hurricane-force wind the weather calmed and the Confederates were glad to realize they were only 140 miles from Savannah. 'The night closed in upon us bright and clear, with the moon shining sweetly down upon us,' wrote Anderson. 'Everyone was on the alert.' The moment of reckoning had come. It was not long before they caught sight of a Federal sail ship bobbing on the water. 'The silence of the dead was preserved on board our vessel,' Anderson continued. 'In my anxiety as I stood beside the helmsman, I could hear the throbbing of my heart.' As dawn approached the heavy night dew condensed into a thick, wet fog. Suddenly, one of the caged cockerels began its morning crow. A dozen hands reached frantically into the coop. The creature was strangled and thrown overboard. A second cockerel awoke, and then a third, forcing the crew to pitch the whole cage into the sea. It was too late for secrecy now. The *Fingal* raced towards the harbour, somehow managing to elude the steam frigate that guarded the entrance. At last, wrote Anderson on 12 November, 'everything had come about just as I had dreamed of'.[45] Thousands lined the quayside to cheer the *Fingal*'s entry into Savannah.[46]

Anderson and Bulloch's arrival in Richmond, however, was overshadowed by the Federal capture of Port Royal in South Carolina on 7 November.

The South had lost the only good harbour between Charleston and Savannah, while the North gained a second base on the Confederate coast which could provide fuel and supplies to the blockading fleets. The battle had brought together the largest US battle fleet ever assembled up to that time. Seventy-seven vessels carrying 12,000 troops had set sail on 1 November from the recently captured Cape Hatteras. Ebenezer Wells and the reinstated 79th were among the three regiments on board the USS *Vanderbilt*.

The expedition began smoothly enough, but by nightfall the wind had picked up and the flotilla began to lose cohesion. The next day a fierce gale assaulted the Union convoy. A supply ship went down with all hands; another jettisoned its guns in a frantic attempt to stay afloat. On the *Vanderbilt* the terrified soldiers and animals howled in unison. As the storm continued to rage the horses were driven into such a frenzy that a dozen were able to struggle free and went careering about the ship. Unable to capture or subdue them, Wells was forced to kill the animals by slitting their throats. Their blood spilled out across deck and down through every crack and crevice, traumatizing the already shattered soldiers. When the battered fleet reassembled outside the sandbank off Port Royal on 7 November, the 79th Highlanders were too sick and exhausted by their journey, recorded Wells, to care whether they were in the South or in hell.

The uplifting sight of artillery shells smashing through the Confederate defences brought the soldiers back to life. 'We took them on completely by surprise,' recorded Wells. In less than a day the two forts guarding the entrance to the port were bombarded into submission. The Federals followed up their victory by sweeping inland and seizing the town of Beaufort. 'The soldiers and inhabitants all left in a hurry so much so that when we landed some of us had the satisfaction of sitting down to unfinished breakfasts and finishing them,' Wells wrote. Afterwards he and his friends made a thorough inspection of the empty plantations, riding around in the owners' carriages and generally helping themselves to anything of interest.[47]

Southerners, observed Anderson, 'were frightened to death by the capture of Port Royal' and looking for someone to blame.[48] At the Confederate War Department, he learned that President Davis was considered in some quarters to be the main culprit because of his constant meddling and countermanding of orders. Leroy Walker had resigned as Secretary of War in September and the new Secretary, Judah P. Benjamin, had no qualification for the post other than his loyalty to Davis.

In Benjamin's defence, he had inherited a badly organized and unhappy department. Boredom and disease were sapping the strength of the Confederate armies. Sam Hill's regiment, the 6th Louisiana Volunteers, was losing half a dozen men a month.[49] 'Our hospital tents are full of sick; I am always busy,' wrote Mary Sophia Hill from their camp in Northern Virginia, after yet another healthy young man died from typhus. One of her charges asked for a letter to be written to his mother in England, giving 'an account of his death, and his reason for joining the Southern army'. It was done as he requested, although she thought the letter contained little to comfort the young man's mother. Some of Mary Sophia's friends urged her to leave the camp for her own safety. 'But I will risk it,' she wrote on 13 November. 'I am determined to keep my brother in view, and I have no other means of protection.'[50] Sam was always losing something, whether it was his blanket one day, his belt and cartridge-box the next. He had no idea how to forage for himself and remained dependent on the food parcels sent to Mary by their friends in New Orleans.

The Southern press demanded to know why the troops were so poorly supplied. 'We are credibly informed', expostulated the Richmond *Examiner*, 'that there has not been a day within the past two months when full rations were served to the army. There has been great and almost constant want of candles and soap; sometimes and for the past ten days allegedly no sugar or rice.'[51] Judah Benjamin was valiantly trying to reorganize the sclerotic relationship between the army and the commissary, but neither department was willing to compromise or take responsibility for mistakes. Yet he was also guilty of shortsightedness, as Edward Anderson discovered when he tried to interest him and Mallory in running a joint operation to improve the flow of supplies from England. Believing that Mason and Slidell would soon be in Europe, Benjamin thought there was no need to take action against a blockade that would not be around for much longer. Mallory also regarded the blockade as merely a stumbling block rather than a threat to the South's existence. 'Mallory met my suggestions with evident discourtesy,' Anderson recorded, 'and yet he knew nothing whatever of the details of my arrangements.'[52] Benjamin failed to understand the importance of Anderson and his ideas, and although the agent begged to be sent back to London, he allowed Anderson to be reassigned to General Robert E. Lee's staff. Anderson spent the rest of the war commanding the forts and batteries around Savannah, his expertise and brilliance wasted.

James Bulloch fared somewhat better than Anderson, suggesting to Mallory they use the *Fingal* to ship cotton to England and take the profits to pay for supplies brought back on the return journey. But once the *Fingal* was loaded with cotton and made ready to go, Bulloch realized that she was too slow to outrun the blockading fleet. Rather than allowing him to transfer the cargo to a faster vessel, Mallory lost confidence in the idea and ordered Bulloch to return to London on a civilian blockade-runner. Like Benjamin, Mallory decided that the shipping business was a distraction from far more pressing matters; the privateering scheme had failed to attract many volunteers and for the moment all he had was the *Sumter* and the *Nashville*, neither of which would stand up against a real navy vessel. On reflection, Mallory thought it was just as well that the new Confederate Commissioners had travelled on a private vessel rather than the easily identifiable *Nashville*.

The three US warships dispatched by Secretary Welles had searched in vain for the missing Confederates. One of the vessels, the USS *James Adger*, limped into Southampton on 2 November after being damaged in a storm off the coast of Ireland. The vessel's unexpected arrival led Henry Sanford to consider using it against a Confederate cargo ship called the *Gladiator* which was about to set sail from a London dockyard. His plan was complicated and probably illegal; Sanford thought that if he could bribe the *Gladiator*'s pilot to steer the ship into a mudbank on the Thames, the *James Adger* could seize the cargo and the crew and steam away before the authorities had time to react.

Sanford hurried round to the legation to share his idea, expecting some resistance from Adams but not the furious tirade that greeted him. Adams interrupted Sanford in mid-flow to reveal that his spy system was being shut down. 'Whilst he was quietly sitting on the other side of the channel without any responsibility for the acts of the worthless people whom he was employing,' Adams told him, 'the odium of their dirty conduct was inevitably fastened upon me.' But no more: he had obtained Seward's agreement that from now on Sanford would have to confine his activities to Belgium, where he belonged. Shocked and bewildered, Sanford first protested, then pleaded and finally tried bargaining with Adams, but the Minister cut him off by rising from his chair. Mortified, Sanford followed suit, saying 'good-bye' with as much dignity as he could muster; 'but', wrote Adams, 'I imagine he will never forgive me.'[53] Benjamin Moran had always envied Sanford, and his humiliation felt like justice served: 'One million of dollars were placed at this man's disposal for Gov't purposes and it has been greatly squandered to our injury,' Moran wrote in his diary. 'With one half of what he threw away in odious espionage I could have bought the British Press ... every newspaper writer in London can be purchased, from those of *The Times* down ... I do not mean to say that each would openly take cash; but each will take a consideration suitable to his taste.'[54]

Adams was still uncertain whether Sanford had left for good when a polite summons arrived from Lord Palmerston on 12 November. Regardless of its tone, the request for an immediate meeting suggested trouble. Adams was filled with trepidation as he made his way to Cambridge House at 94 Piccadilly through another London fog. He had never been there during the day, but the yellow gloom that shrouded the city made the difference seem slight. Flaming pyres only partially illuminated the forecourt. Inside, old-fashioned gaslights threw off as much smoke as light.* Palmerston was waiting for him in a library that was untenably dark by American standards. He was alone, and 'at once opened on the subject then evidently weighing on his mind': the government knew the true purpose of the *James Adger*.[55] For a moment Adams thought that Sanford had carried out his plan, but as Palmerston talked it became clear that his concern had nothing to do with the *Gladiator*.

The government, he said, had learned that the North was hunting for the Confederate Commissioners, Mason and Slidell, though its latest information on the duo was sketchy and contradictory. The Foreign Office could not be certain, but their reports suggested that the Confederates were travelling on a British mail ship, and that the *James Adger* had been sent to intercept her. Palmerston was less concerned about the *James Adger*'s right to seize the Rebels – although he did consult the law officers on the question – than the obvious threat such an act posed to national honour, since an attack on a British ship could not pass unchallenged. The Confederates could send an entire fleet of commissioners to

---

* Cambridge House, wrote Sir George Trevelyan memorably, was 'Past the wall which screens the mansion, hallowed by a mighty shade, / Where the cards were cut and shuffled when the game of State was played'.

England, he informed Adams gravely, without its having the slightest effect on the government's actions. The North would do better to leave all British ships alone. Offended by Palmerston's assumption that the United States would stoop to waylaying British mail packets, Adams explained rather huffily that the *James Adger* had been chasing a Rebel cruiser called the *Nashville*. Having failed to find her, the captain was waiting for the departure of the *Gladiator*, which, he laboured the point, was laden with arms and munitions for the South. Palmerston refused to be drawn in and responded with the candid assertion that the North might eventually crush Southern resistance, 'but that would not be restoring the Union'.

After the meeting, Adams's relief that it had nothing to do with San-ford was tempered by his indignation at Palmerston's accusations. A week later, on the 21st, the *James Adger*'s prey, the *Nashville*, sailed into Southampton with a Confederate flag flying from its mast. Although the Confederate Commissioners were not on board, there were thirty prisoners from an American clipper called the *Harvey Birch*, which the *Nashville* had captured and burned in the English Channel. Lord Russell promptly sent orders that she was not to receive any military supplies or fittings. Her arrival was embarrassing and obviously provocative to the North; Charles Francis Adams demanded the arrest of Captain Pegram on the charge of piracy. Pegram responded with a letter to *The Times* pointing out that he was a regularly commissioned officer of the Confed-erate navy and therefore not a pirate. The locals in Southampton preferred Adams's version and treated Pegram like a swashbuckling hero.

Russell naturally refused Adams's request, since the *Nashville* was a regular ship of war belonging to a recognized belligerent, but he did agree to keep her under surveillance in case the Confederates attempted to smuggle guns on board.[56] The torrent of correspondence between the legation and Whitehall was now so great that Henry Adams and the two Secretaries were overwhelmed by the drudgery of copying and archiving each and every letter. Benjamin Moran's tirades and twitter-ings made life in the office almost intolerable for Henry, who struggled 'to resist complete nervous depression' resulting from the prolonged exposure.[57] On the morning of the 27th, the subject of Moran's ire was Lord Russell's latest response, which he characterized as unforgivably 'hostile'. The embittered secretary cursed Russell and Palmerston 'for playing into the hands of the rebels'. The Prime Minister had hated

America since the War of 1812, contended Moran, and 'has deliberately determined to force us into war'.[58] He believed it was only a matter of time before Palmerston found some pretext or other to unleash his designs.

The moment came sooner than Moran expected. At precisely half past twelve, a messenger called with another telegram from Consul Britton in Southampton. This time it was not about the *Nashville*. A ship from St Thomas had arrived, bearing the astonishing news that Mason and Slidell had been captured off the coast of Cuba. They had been travelling on the *Trent*, a British mail packet bound for St Thomas, when the USS *San Jacinto* under Captain Charles Wilkes forcibly stopped the vessel and took the Commissioners prisoner. The jaded occupants of the legation began cheering, even though, Henry Adams admitted, they knew it meant 'not merely diplomatic rupture – but a declaration of war'. His opinion was echoed around the country. 'Have these Yankees then gone completely crazy to carry out this mad coup with the Confederate Commissioners?' Friedrich Engels asked Karl Marx, whose prodigious journalistic output from his home in Manchester included weekly articles about the Civil War. 'To take political prisoners by force, on a foreign ship, is the clearest casus belli there can be. The fellows must be sheer fools to land themselves in war with England.'[59]

Charles Francis Adams was not at the legation to hear the news. He had accepted an invitation from Richard Monckton Milnes to join a large house party at Fryston Hall in Yorkshire. Neither Charles Francis nor Abigail had experienced life in a grand country house before; Fryston's 'somewhat ancient' decoration and total lack of modern conveniences confirmed their prejudices about the superiority of New England to Olde England. The wet weather forced the guests to huddle together in Milnes's library, whose relatively efficient fireplace made it also double as the breakfast room. By the 27th, the guests had become restless. Unable to stand the confinement any longer, the group, which included the MP William Forster, the novelist Elizabeth Gaskell and Austen Henry Layard, the excavator of the ancient city of Nineveh (who had recently put away his tools to become Lord Russell's Under-Secretary for Foreign Affairs), accepted Milnes's invitation to brave the rain for a visit to the ruins of Pomfret Castle.

A messenger bearing Moran's telegram from London tracked Adams down at the ruins. The Minister would always remember standing in the persistent drizzle, making polite conversation with his fellow guests, while in his hand he clutched the news about the *Trent.* 'We had a very dark and muddy walk home,' he recorded. William Forster accompanied him but Adams did not reveal the contents, Forster told his wife, until 'as we got in, Adams said, in his cool, quiet way "I have got stirring news"'. Forster continued: 'I think he is as much grieved as I am, and does not think a hundred Masons and Slidells would be worth the effect on us.' Dinner that evening was a torturous affair. No one knew what to say, and Forster's attempts to make conversation were so ham-fisted that Adams could not help commenting in his diary: 'He is no courtier.'[60] In the end, it was left to a local manufacturer, who had been invited to make up the numbers, to fill the void, which he did at great length in a diatribe addressed solely to Adams on the iniquities of the Morrill Tariff.

The next morning Layard and Forster went to London immediately after breakfast. Adams thought it best to travel by a different train and left at noon. Milnes and his wife were so warm and earnest at the parting that Adams felt rather emotional; it seemed at that moment as though no one in England had ever been so kind to him. He arrived at the legation in the evening to find Henry, Moran and Wilson overexcited and making inappropriate comments to a crowd of visitors. A note from Lord Russell was waiting on Adams's desk. The hour was late, he realized with a tinge of relief; the meeting would have to wait until tomorrow, giving him a little more time to prepare.

'There was a shade more of gravity visible in his manner, but no ill will,' Adams wrote after the interview on the 29th. He had decided to be frank with the Foreign Secretary. 'Not a word had been whispered to me about such a project,' he confessed. This seemed to reassure Russell, who then asked whether the *James Adger* had received orders respecting British vessels. Adams replied no, not as far as he knew. There was nothing more to be said by either man. 'The conference lasted perhaps ten minutes,' Adams recorded. He could not imagine Seward being as civil in similar circumstances. But he was under no illusions that Russell's politeness signified an unwillingness to retaliate. During the carriage journey home, Adams wondered if this had been his final visit to the Foreign Office: 'On the whole, I scarcely remember a day of greater strain in my life.'[61] The press, he saw, was urging the government to stand up for British rights, even including liberal papers like the *Manchester*

Guardian, which accused the American government of testing 'the truth of the adage that it takes two to make a quarrel'.[62]

Lord Russell described his conversation with Adams at a hastily called Cabinet meeting on Friday, 29 November. Every member was present except for the Duke of Argyll, who was on holiday in France. Palmerston was bristling with pugnacious indignation. He had spent the past few days calculating ship distances and totting up troop numbers. Whether Captain Wilkes's act had been premeditated or not, Palmerston had decided it was time 'to read a lesson to the United States which will not soon be forgotten'.[63]

8

The Lion Roars Back

Captain Wilkes – Northern glee – Britain prepares for war –
Prince Albert's intervention – Waiting for an answer – Seward's
dilemma – Lord Lyons takes a risk – Peace and goodwill on
Christmas Day

'A cold, raw day', William Howard Russell noted in his diary on 16 November 1861. 'As I was writing,' he continued, 'a small friend of mine, who appears like a stormy petrel in moments of great storm, fluttered into my room, and having chirped out something about a "jolly row," – "Seizure of Mason and Slidell," – "British flag insulted," and the like, vanished.' Russell hastily grabbed his coat and followed him outside where he bumped into the French Minister, M. Mercier, coming from the direction of the British legation. 'And then, indeed, I learned there was no doubt about the fact that [on 8 November] Captain Charles Wilkes, of the US steamer *San Jacinto*, had forcibly boarded the *Trent*, a British mail steamer, off the Bahamas, and had taken Messrs. Mason, Slidell, [and their secretaries] Eustis, and Macfarland from on board by armed force, in defiance of the protests of the captain and naval officer in charge of the mails.'[1]

The press was jubilant over the capture. 'Rightly or wrongly, the American people at large look upon it as a direct insult to the British flag,' wrote Lord Lyons.[2] But the opportunity to humiliate England was not the only reason behind the public's excitement. Mason and Slidell had been needling the North from the Senate floor for many years and their banishment to Fort Warren in Boston harbour was deemed a fitting punishment.* The

---

* It may have disappointed Northerners to know that the prisoners ate far better and had larger rooms than the regulars at Willard's.

New York Times's first editorial on the affair called for Wilkes to be honoured with a medal or a public holiday. The Philadelphia *Sunday Transcript* went further and committed the country to war, reminding its readers that American soldiers had routed 'the best of British troops' in 1812, and would do so again. 'In a word, while the British government has been playing the villain, we have been playing the fool,' the paper declared. 'Let her now do something beyond drivelling – let her fight. If she has a particle of pluck . . . if she is not as cowardly as she is treacherous – she will meet the American people on land and on the sea, as they long to meet her, once again, not only to lower the red banner of St George . . . but to consolidate Canada with the union . . .'³

LOOK OUT FOR SQUALLS.

<small>Jack Bull. "YOU DO WHAT'S RIGHT, MY SON, OR I'LL BLOW YOU OUT OF THE WATER."</small>

Punch sends a British warning to the US, December 1861

What was not clear to Russell, however, was whether Captain Wilkes had acted on his own or in accordance with secret government instructions. His visits to the State and Navy Departments on 18 November were inconclusive since the former was not prepared to comment, and the latter had obviously been taken by surprise.[4] No one at the Navy Department had a good word to say in Wilkes's defence. Although a renowned cartographer, he had the reputation of being a bully and a braggart.[5] The command of the *San Jacinto* had been given to him with great reluctance; 'he has a superabundance of self-esteem and a deficiency of judgment,' warned an official in August. 'He will give us trouble.'[6] Since his appointment, Wilkes had been trawling the oceans, in defiance of his actual orders, on a personal hunting expedition of Confederate ships. It was sheer luck that he stumbled onto the Confederate Commissioners, and it was pure Wilkes, his colleagues told Russell, to decide that a search and seizure of the two men on a neutral ship would be legal under international law.

At the legation, Russell encountered Lord Lyons politely fending off questions from a group of foreign Ministers who had come ostensibly to offer their support, but really to ascertain England's probable response. This, Lyons made clear, would have to come from London. He explained to William Howard Russell that his overriding concern was to prevent anything coming from himself or the legation that might help the warmongers. The staff had been given orders not to discuss the *Trent* with anyone, although Russell could see from the look on their faces that they thought war was inevitable.

The following day Russell prepared his letter to *The Times*. 'I rarely sat down to write under a sense of greater responsibility,' he admitted in his diary.[7] Russell assumed that his report would be 'the first account of the seizure of the Southern Commissioners which will reach England' and the thought of how the public would react to the news filled him with foreboding. He was no longer just describing the attack on the *Trent*, but also the North's exultation and the US government's silence, which he feared would be as provocative to the English as Wilkes's original act. Without excusing the Lincoln administration, Russell tried to explain the pressures placed upon it by democracy: 'There is a popular passion and vengeance to be gratified by the capturing and punishment of Mr Mason and Mr Slidell,' he wrote, 'and I believe the Government will retain them at all risk because it dare not give them up.'[8]

Russell was only partially correct about the administration. Public opinion naturally played a roll in its deliberations, but from the start virtually all the Cabinet were adamantly opposed to releasing the Commissioners. Lincoln allegedly complained to a journalist on 16 November about the embarrassment Wilkes had caused the country. 'I fear the traitors will prove to be white elephants,' he reportedly said; 'we must stick to American principles concerning the rights of neutrals. We fought Great Britain for insisting, by theory and practice, on the right to do precisely what Captain Wilkes has done.'⁹ If true, Lincoln would have been the only Cabinet member, apart from Montgomery Blair, the Postmaster General, to accept that Wilkes had violated international law, and the only member to realize the grave threat to America's moral reputation if the government supported him. The United States had fought the War of 1812 in part to defend its broad interpretation of 'neutral rights'. It had protected the slave trade, allowing it to flourish, and had expelled the British Minister, John Crampton, in 1856, risking a third Anglo-American war, for his perceived violation of these rights. The United States would be inviting the censure and mockery of the entire world if the government suddenly repudiated a fundamental principle of American foreign policy because it was no longer expedient to maintain.

Regardless of how Lincoln originally understood the issue, within twenty-four hours of hearing the news he had joined the celebrations. He wrote about the seizure with exclamation marks to Edward Everett, the former American Minister in London; and to General McClellan, who came to deliver a warning from the Prince de Joinville that England would demand an apology, Lincoln replied categorically that the Commissioners were not going to be released. The Cabinet, excepting Montgomery Blair, behaved shamefully. The worst offender was the Attorney General, Edward Bates, who gave ill-judged, but also incorrect, legal advice to his colleagues. 'Some timid persons are alarmed, lest Great Britain should take offence at the violation of her Flag,' he wrote in his diary. 'There is no danger on that score. The law of Nations is clear upon the point, and I have no doubt that, with a little time for examination, I could find it so settled by English authorities.'¹⁰

General McClellan also called on Seward to give him de Joinville's warning, but the Secretary of State did not want to hear bad news – especially from McClellan, whom he disliked. He resented having his expertise questioned and told the General that his information about England was based on ignorance. 'I said I thought I was right,' recorded McClellan; 'he again contradicted me & I told him that the future would prove the correctness of my story.' McClellan left, inwardly cursing that 'so weak and cowardly a thing should now control our foreign relations'.[11] Seward's unfounded optimism that Britain would not dare make a protest thoroughly depressed Lord Lyons. 'I am so worn out with the never ending labour of keeping things smooth,' Lyons wrote to Lord Russell on 22 November. He had heard about Seward's reaction and was beginning to wonder whether the policy of keeping quiet was 'leading these people to believe that they may go all lengths with us with impunity'. 'I am sometimes half tempted to wish that the worst may have come already,' he confessed. 'However I do not allow this feeling to influence my conduct and I have done nothing which can in the least interfere with any course which you may take concerning the affair of the "*Trent*".'[12]

There was apparently limited discussion of the *Trent* affair at the Cabinet meeting on 24 November. Lincoln agreed that they would wait to hear Britain's response before the government publicly committed itself on the legality of the seizure. No one remarked on the South's euphoric reaction to the capture or questioned why its press was so quick to agree that the British had been given a studied blow. President Jefferson Davis had laid particular stress on the insult in a speech to the Confederate Congress on 18 November. 'These gentlemen were as much under the jurisdiction of the British Government upon that ship and beneath its flag as if they had been on its soil,' he said. Wilkes's act was no different from a kidnapping on Piccadilly.[13]

After the Cabinet meeting Seward realized that it would be impossible to keep Charles Francis Adams in limbo for two or three more weeks. He composed a dispatch on 27 November saying as little as possible about the affair except to admit that Wilkes had acted without orders. The administration was waiting for Britain's reaction, he informed Adams. That night, the apotheosis of Wilkes continued. The Governor of Massachusetts spoke at a public banquet in his honour, praising him for giving 'illustrious service' to the war and for humbling the 'British lion' to boot. Gideon Welles ignored Lincoln's injunction to wait and published a letter of congratulation to Wilkes, which, fortunately, mentioned that the Captain had acted on his own initiative.

When Congress reconvened on 2 December, Lincoln did not specifically refer to Wilkes in his speech, but the House of Representatives passed a vote of thanks and awarded him a gold medal. In Boston, Anthony Trollope was forced to pronounce on the subject, though he felt there was more farce than force to the affair. 'Who ever before heard of giving a man glory for achievements so little glorious?' he asked. Trollope was amused when people quoted obscure legal authorities at him in order to justify the *Trent* affair. '"Wheaton is quite clear about it," one young girl said to me. It was the first I had ever heard of Wheaton, and so far was obliged to knock under,' he wrote. 'All the world, ladies and lawyers, expressed the utmost confidence in the justice of the seizure.' Yet, Trollope added, 'it was clear that all the world was in a state of the profoundest nervous anxiety on the subject'.[14] As the countdown began for the arrival of newspapers from London, the press began to change its tone as editorials asked – what if the British lion roared back?

The 'Lion' had been roaring since 27 November. On Palmerston's orders the Secretary of State for the Colonies, the Duke of Newcastle, advised the Governor General of Canada to prepare for war: 'Such an insult to our flag can only be atoned by the restoration of the men who were seized,' he wrote, 'and with Mr Seward at the helm of the United States, and the mob and the Press manning the vessel, it is too probable that this atonement may be refused.' His opinion was shared in both Houses; peace, argued Lord Clarendon (who had been Foreign Secretary in the 1850s), was not 'worth the price of national honour'.[15]

Although the Crown's law officers were unanimous that the seizure was unlawful, at a meeting on 29 November the Cabinet was unable to agree on the proper measure of response to the Americans. If it was too strong, argued Gladstone, the Lincoln administration would be denied a graceful exit. Too weak, countered Palmerston, it would send a false impression of Britain's intentions. They resolved to leave the drafting of the letter to Russell. He was to state the facts of the case, and demand the restoration of the Commissioners along with an apology for the outrage. Failure to do so within seven days of receiving the letter would mean the immediate departure of Lord Lyons to Canada and war between the two nations.

When the Cabinet reconvened the following day, nobody had a positive comment about Russell's resulting draft, which was clumsy and overly obsessed with national honour. The three main principles at stake (the rights of neutral countries in time of war, the right to free movement on neutral ships, and the protection of diplomatic correspondence) were not made clear at all.[16] But the more the Cabinet tried to amend the letter, the more defensive Russell became until finally they agreed that Lord Lyons should receive two letters. The first would outline the case; the second would contain the threat that the United States had seven days to comply with Britain's demand. The temporary truce collapsed immediately as they now had not just one but two letters over which to fight. Gladstone incensed Palmerston with his musings on whether the law was entirely on their side.*[17] Finally there came a point when further discussion was useless and, even though no one was satisfied, the drafts were sent to the Queen and Prince Albert for their approval.

The Prince lay mortally ill with typhoid fever when the letters arrived at Windsor Castle on 30 November. He had been kept informed of the Cabinet's discussions and had rightly feared that the official response would be pompous and aggressive. In the last of the Prince's many services to his adopted country, he roused himself from his bed and composed a memorandum (though he could hardly hold a pen in his hand) on what the letter ought to say. There should be 'the expression of a hope', he wrote,

> that the American captain did not act under instructions, or, if he did, that he misapprehended them – that the United States Government must be fully aware that the British Government could not allow its flag to be insulted, and the security of her mail communications to be placed in jeopardy; and Her Majesty's Government are unwilling to believe that the United States Government intended wantonly to put an insult upon this country.

---

* Gladstone was posturing for effect; Wilkes had clearly violated international law by 1. Taking the Confederates off the ship; 2. Acting as his own court of law in determining that the Confederates could be taken, instead of going to a prize court, which alone had the authority to make such a ruling. The prize court would have set the *Trent* and the Confederates free, since human beings cannot be kidnapped willy-nilly off the high seas. Wilkes's argument, that the Confederates were a living, breathing dispatch, which made them in legal terms 'contraband of war', would have been laughed out of court. But likelihood is that Wilkes would have precipitated a crisis even if he had sailed to a prize court, because Britain would have demanded an apology from the United States for stopping a British mail ship without cause, and the apology would have become the sticking point.

Gone were the peremptory demands and in their place were merely polite statements of expectation.*[18]

Russell conceded that the changes were necessary, but even so he doubted that they would temper Seward's reaction or produce an apology.[19] He therefore composed a third letter to Lyons, describing how the demands should be presented. Russell wanted him to be tactful but unequivocal; the release of the prisoners would negate the need for atonement, but no words or species of apology would appease Britain's anger if the prisoners were retained.[20] With any luck Seward would realize that retreat was preferable to war, but it would be up to Lyons to make the Secretary of State understand that there could be no amateur dramatics, no clever little feints or attempts at bargaining. Only a straightforward answer would do.

The Postmaster General, Lord Stanley, was keeping his wife informed of the Cabinet's deliberations. 'The accounts from America', he wrote on 2 December, had confirmed their fears; Northern public opinion could be summed up as 'great exaltation at the insult to England, great satisfaction at the capture of Mason and Slidell and the deification of Capt. Wilkes'.[21] The next day Captain Conway Seymour boarded the Boston-bound *Europa* with the Cabinet's letters. Lord Stanley chafed when he realized how long it would be until they received a reply: 'It cannot get to [Lord Lyons] in less than 12 days & another 12 days to return will be the earliest we can get any intelligence of its reception.'[22] As soon as the messenger left, however, Russell began to suffer misgivings about the plan. 'I cannot imagine their giving a plain yes or no to our demands,' he wrote. 'I think they will try to hook in France, and if that is, as I hope, impossible, to get Russia to support them.'[23] At the bottom of Russell's anxiety was the sense that his actions had been misunderstood by the Americans and that he was being wrongly blamed for reasons he still could not understand. 'Not a word had been spoken, not a deed done by him but what showed the friendliest feeling,' Lady Russell wrote loyally about her husband's dealing with the North.[24]

Palmerston thought that the United States would not even bother with negotiation. The 'masses', he categorically stated, will 'make it impossible for Lincoln and Seward to grant our demands; and we must therefore

---

* Years later, Queen Victoria wrote on the memorandum: 'This draft was the last the Beloved Prince ever wrote.'

look forward to war as the probable result'. George Cornewall Lewis, the Secretary of War, complained that they were doing France's dirty work, which was rather ungrateful of him considering Napoleon had promised his support. 'It is quite certain that the French Govt wish for war between England and America,' wrote Lewis. 'The blockade of the South would be raised, and they would get the cotton which they want.'[25]

Late on 3 December, Russell and Palmerston called another Cabinet meeting; the Treasury had received an alarming report that a Federal agent had bought up the country's entire saltpetre reserves – about 4.5 million pounds. Most of it was due to be shipped the following day. The Cabinet agreed to an immediate export ban; lacking sufficient mines of their own, the Federals would be hard pressed to manufacture gunpowder without this precious commodity.[26] The Admiralty issued a worldwide alert to every station. Admiral Milne's instructions to ready his squadron reached him in Bermuda, where he replied: 'The ships' companies are in a high state of excitement for war, they are certainly all for the South. I hear the Lower Decks today are decorated with the Confederate colours.'[27]

The next day, the 4th, Stanley scribbled to his wife: 'I write from the Cabinet where it has been decided to issue another order in Council, prohibiting the exportation of arms & munitions of war, in addition to the former order prohibiting the exportation of saltpetre. I fear that the prospects of a satisfactory & amicable settlement are small.'[28] One or two of his colleagues had protested against the ban, fearing that it would ruin Britain's arms trade, but Stanley was entirely with Palmerston and Russell. 'If we are to be at war it is as well not to let them have improved rifles to shoot us with.'[29] 'If this goes on,' added Stanley, 'a Brigade of Guards will go out, one Battalion out of each Regiment.' His younger son, Jonny, would be among the first to go.

The Cabinet agreed to form a six-member war committee. Military experts were called in and at the War Office strategic plans drawn up during previous periods of tension were taken out for revision. Maine was to be the first target, with simultaneous actions by the navy to blockade Boston, New Bedford, Newport, Long Island, New York and the Delaware river. If necessary, some of these ports would be bombarded into submission. 'War has no doubt its honours and its evils,' Admiral Milne reminded the Secretary of State for the Navy, who deprecated such wanton destruction, 'but to make war felt it must be carried out against the Enemy with energy, and every place made to feel what war really is.'[30]

The strategic difficulties were indeed formidable. The Canadian border was more than 1,500 miles long, thinly fortified and connected by the most basic roads and waterways. It would require a minimum of 10,000 regular troops and 100,000 militia volunteers to repel an invasion.[31] Moreover, as *The Times* had pointed out, 'We can sweep the Federal fleet from the seas, we can blockade the Atlantic cities; but we cannot garrison and hold 350,000 square miles of country.' If the Americans chose to attack Montreal or Quebec they would face a paltry British force of less than 5,000. Canada's only real defences were snow and bad weather.[32] Their best option was to launch the first strike and capture Maine. 'Do not be surprised if you hear of us all being made prisoners of war before the end of February,' one of the departing officers wrote pessimistically.

> If the Yankees are worth their salt, they will at once make peace with the South and pour 100,000 men into Canada where they can easily compensate themselves for their losses of the Confederate states, and England be perfectly unable to prevent it. Unless the British Government at once make up their minds to fitting out an expedition which can start (as soon as war is declared) to seize Portland, and open up the railway communication from there to Quebec, I cannot see how we are to maintain our position in Canada this winter.[33]

Lord Stanley went down to Southampton to see off his son. Lady Stanley was too distraught and remained in London. The navy did not have eighteen troop ships on hand to transport the 11,000 soldiers who were going to Canada in the first wave. Jonny's vessel, the *Adriatic*, had been purchased from an American shipping firm and refitted in such haste that the US flag could still be seen on the paddle box. As the *Adriatic* passed the *Nashville* on Southampton Water, the Guards band started to play 'I'm Off to Charleston'. This cheeky act of bravado elicited a few half-hearted cheers from relatives who had gathered on the banks to wave farewell.[34] 'It will be very cold in Canada and I am afraid Jonny will feel it,' Stanley wrote to his wife.[35] Their son was sailing at a dangerous time. Ice was beginning to close Canada's navigable rivers and monster storms would soon lash her seas.[36]

'The all engrossing question is will America be foolish enough to go to War with us,' wrote James Garnett, the owner of a large mill in Clitheroe in Lancashire. 'Many people think it will.'[37] Yancey and Dudley Mann fervently hoped so. They had not wasted any time in presenting Lord Russell with a letter protesting the seizure of Mason and Slidell, and had followed up two days later, on 29 November, with a list of ships that had slipped through the blockade since April. Here was proof, they had argued, that the Northern blockade was ineffective and therefore not binding on neutral countries. Russell's cold response on 7 December left them temporarily crushed until they reflected on the thousands of British soldiers who were leaving for North America. This was a case, they decided, of actions speaking louder than words.

Charles Francis Adams was both furious and humiliated that his know-ledge of the *Trent* affair was no better than what a reader could glean from *The Times*. 'Mr Seward's ways are not those of diplomacy,' he wrote crossly on 9 December. 'Here have I been nearly three weeks without positively knowing whether the act of the officer was directed by the govt or not.'[38] Henry Adams was equally indignant. 'What Seward means is more than I can guess,' he told his brother Charles Francis Jr. 'But if he means war also, or to run as close as he can without touching, then I say that Mr Seward is the greatest Criminal we've had yet.' The seizure had undone all his father's hard work. 'We have friends here still, but very few. Bright dined with us last night, and is with us, but is evi-dently hopeless of seeing anything good ... my friends of the *Spectator* sent up to me in a dreadful state and asked me to come down to see them, which I did, and they complained bitterly of the position we are now in.'[39]

Henry was not exaggerating the difficulties confronting Northern supporters. William Forster lamented to his wife that his efforts for peace resembled 'the struggles of a drowning man'.[40] John Bright was at first too nervous to speak about the *Trent* affair, explaining apologeti-cally to Adams that since his opposition to the Crimean War he had lost his appetite for being a national hate-figure. Given Bright's violent rhetoric, Adams rather hoped that this was true. Unfortunately, Bright overcame his fears and made a speech in Rochdale on 4 December that blasted the country for not being sufficiently pro-Union. This was too

much even for the *Spectator*, which accused Bright of being prepared
to sacrifice any principle if it did not sit well with America.[41] Harriet
Martineau was one of the few English writers who could write with
authority since she was personally acquainted with Captain Wilkes, and
even she was very careful in her choice of words. Wilkes was not, she
stressed in her articles for the *Daily News*, an Anglophobe or a warmonger, 'but he lacks judgement and knowledge'.[42]

Benjamin Moran realized the extent of the feeling against the North
when he chanced to look out of the window of his taxi and saw that the
American owners of the Adelphi Theatre had added the Confederate
flag next to the usual Stars and Stripes. 'The sight of this base emblem
of slavery, treason and piracy made me ill with rage . . .' he wrote in his
diary.[43] The Confederates and their supporters were also putting up
posters in railway stations and distributing Rebel banners to street
hawkers; hackney cabs were given miniature Union Jacks crossed with
the Confederate flag.[44] Moran heard that such overt displays of Confederate sympathy were even more prevalent in Liverpool. The new Consul,
Thomas Haines Dudley, reported that Southern exiles living in the city
were gleefully capitalizing on the *Trent* incident.

Although Moran longed to have an American representative in the
country who would not be afraid to engage with the press, he regarded
Thurlow Weed's arrival on 2 December as a mixed blessing. 'This morning's *Times* contains a letter from Thurlow Weed defending Mr Seward,'
wrote Moran in mid-December. 'The letter is strong in some things, but
weak in others and *The Times* assails its vulnerable points with its usual
malignity.'[45] Until the *Trent* affair, Weed had been in France, working
with Henry Sanford on schemes to influence European opinion.

Seward's idea to send the four emissaries 'seems to me of no value',
Charles Francis Adams had written frankly to Edward Everett. But
Weed disagreed; when he arrived at the US legation on 6 December his
first reaction was that he should have come earlier. There was a general air
of disarray about the place. The misfits in the basement made him wonder
how business was done, while upstairs Charles Francis Adams was in an
alarming state: bewildered and angered by Seward's silence, paranoid
about England's intentions, and mentally more than halfway home.[46]

Weed immediately sent out letters and left his cards in all the great
houses of London. The relative ease with which he connected with

'intelligent and influential English friends of the North' led him to suspect that Adams had not tried very hard to penetrate society. Weed was
able to arrange an interview with Lord Russell and had a perfectly sensible, albeit non-committal, conversation with him. Although he did not
say it in so many words, Weed was appalled that Adams had allowed
Seward to become so thoroughly feared and hated.[47] 'You have been
infernally abused, and are wholly misunderstood here,' he told Seward.
Everyone he met believed that the Secretary of State was determined to
have a war. This was true even of Seward's friends. Lady Napier unhappily related to Weed a remark Seward had made just before their
departure from Washington. 'On some occasion', wrote Weed, 'you
talked about the incoming Administration going to war with England;
that subsequently when alone with you, she asked, "Why do you talk
about war with England?" and that you replied seriously, "that it was
the best thing that could happen for America".'[48] More damning still,
The Times printed the story of his 'joke' to the Duke of Newcastle
during the Prince of Wales's tour of America in 1860 that when he
became President he would manufacture a quarrel with England.[49]

It was already midnight on 10 December when Thurlow Weed sat at
his desk to compose one of the most serious letters he had ever written
to his friend. 'I have finally got Lord [*sic*] Newcastle's own version of
what was said to him,' he wrote; 'whatever you DID say – WAS said.
This, with the allusions to Canada ... is regarded as evidence of your
determined enmity to England, and even the Friends you made here –
many of whom I have met – are carried away by this idea. And
consequently War, unless you avert it, is inevitable. I pray that I am not
mistaken in the hope that you comprehend the disastrous effects of such
a war.'[50]

The days passed and still there was no word from Washington. Nothing, however, worried Weed so much as his friend's silence. He sent a
letter to Lincoln, imploring him to 'turn the other cheek'; Adams sent yet
another letter to Seward.[51] On 14 December, *Punch* published a cartoon,
entitled 'Waiting for an Answer', which showed Britannia ready to fire
the cannon. At the Foreign Office, Russell continued to fret over whether
they had made the right decision. Their dispatch to Lyons left no room
to manoeuvre if Seward prevaricated or refused point-blank. But 'I
do not think', wrote Russell, 'the country would approve an immediate

declaration of war.' A 'peace meeting' at Exeter Hall in the Strand had
attracted 4,000 people. Russell asked Palmerston if they should give the
United States a second chance, should the worst happen, so long as
Seward's letter was a 'reasoning, and not a blunt answer'.[52]

On Monday, 16 December, London was plastered with black-
bordered announcements of Prince Albert's death. He had died at eleven
o'clock on Saturday night. Moran knew about the Prince's alteration of
the Cabinet dispatch to Lord Lyons, and, though he feared his action
could be misinterpreted, he went defiantly to Buckingham Palace and
signed his name in the condolence book; for good measure he added
'Mr and Mrs Adams' next to his own. Late that same night, a messenger

WAITING FOR AN ANSWER.

Britannia ready to fire, *Punch*, 1862

arrived with a dispatch from the State Department. The letter was short, too short considering the nature of the crisis, but it did contain Seward's admission that Wilkes had acted 'without any instructions' as well as the remark that the American government hoped that London would 'consider the subject in a friendly temper'. Adams thought this 'was not discouraging' but hardly a clear endorsement for peace. He wondered whether it was even worth showing to Russell. Alarmed by this untimely display of diffidence, Moran and Wilson pleaded with Adams to go to the Foreign Office. Troop ships were continuing to depart for Canada and time was running out.

The British Lion had turned tail, or so Washington thought during the first week of December. Baron Mercier's execrable English created such confusion that Lincoln came away from their conversation believing that the Minister had given him good news about England, that Britain's law officers saw nothing wrong in the Commissioners' seizure. 'There would probably be no trouble about it,' Lincoln cheerfully asserted to his friend, Senator Orville Browning, after the meeting.[53] Lincoln was also being misled by Charles Sumner, whose straightforward and sensible position on the *Trent* had become infected by his craving for popularity. At the beginning of the crisis, Sumner had assured the Duchess of Argyll that he would do everything in his power to resolve 'any ill-feeling between our two countries'.[54] But after he saw Lincoln on 1 December and realized that the President had no desire to release the prisoners, he abandoned his original position and suggested that they turn over the case to international arbitration. The plan protected America's pride and salvaged Sumner's, who had not been consulted or included in any of the Cabinet discussions about Captain Wilkes. Sumner had no hesitation about blaming Seward: 'The special cause of the English feeling is aggravated by the idea on their part that Seward wishes war, they say – "very well – then we will not wait",' he told a friend in New York. 'If the [British] Govt & the people could be thoroughly satisfied of the real good will of this Administration, a great impediment to Peace would be removed.' That impediment, of course, was Seward.[55]

The arrival of the British newspapers on Friday, 13 December brought an abrupt end to all the speculation and celebrations that had been allowed to proliferate unchecked since 16 November. The angry leaders and articles demanding reparation left no doubt as to how the British regarded Wilkes's act. On Monday morning in New York there were rowdy scenes at the Stock Exchange as investors dumped their bonds and rushed to buy commodities such as gold, saltpetre and gunpowder. A run on the banks suspended all business, including the payment of a loan to the Treasury that Secretary Chase had been expecting in mid-December. The New York offices of Barings and the Rothschilds closed their doors and Rothschilds transferred their American holdings to France to safeguard them from confiscation by the US government.[56]

Dr Elizabeth Blackwell took a brief rest from her teaching duties at the New York Infirmary to explain to her friends in London that it was all a terrible mistake. 'Indeed, I have never before had cause for so much gloom,' she wrote. 'The *Trent* affair was no intentional insult to the English flag – on the contrary . . . the whole thing is marked more by the ILL-BREEDING of Americans and a reckless ignoring of consequences than by . . . deliberate insults which England attributes to her.' Her friends and relatives were keenly divided on the issue. 'With part of our own family furiously American and part as furiously English – disapproving as we do of the conduct of both countries – it is a terrible trial of feeling,' she admitted.[57]

In Washington, Seward was aghast, having received over the weekend the first of Adams's reports regarding the *Trent*. A plaintive letter had also come from the Duchess of Sutherland, begging him to stay true to his ideals: 'I do not know if you will recollect me; but I think so. I liked much having known you. Your feeling toward England seemed so friendly. Your aspirations, your earnestness against slavery were so great, I rejoiced in hearing you speak,' she wrote.[58] The letters so shook him that he ran across the street to the White House. He burst in on Lincoln, who was entertaining a few friends, to announce that Britain was preparing for war. 'I don't believe England has done so foolish a thing,' declared Orville Browning, one of the Senators present. After Seward had read out Adams's dispatch, their incredulity turned to outrage. Browning jumped up and urged Lincoln to 'fight to the death'.[59]

More newspapers arrived on the 16th, with reports that Britain was backing up her demands with thousands of 'crack troops'. Perhaps almost as disturbing for Seward was the discovery that Sumner and Lincoln had been discussing the *Trent* affair behind his back. Seward realized he had three choices: to press for war, to follow Sumner's lead and support arbitration, or to argue for the correct but unpopular course demanded by England. Seward hated all three alternatives. That night he went to the Portuguese Minister's ball looking dishevelled and bloodshot. He further ruined his attempt to appear relaxed by swearing and speaking loudly. Towards the end of the evening Seward unsteadily approached a group of guests, which included William Howard Russell and the Prince de Joinville, and began boasting of what would happen to Britain if she forced the United States into war. 'We will wrap the whole world in flames!' he exclaimed. 'No power so remote that she will not feel the fire of our battle and be burned by our conflagration.'[60]

William Howard Russell assumed that Seward had made up his mind to fight, even though a guest at the ball had scoffed that the Secretary of State 'always talks that way when he means to break down'. Russell's letters from home showed that war was a foregone conclusion over there; The Times was already making arrangements for him to report from Canada. The following night, however, Russell went to Seward's house for dinner and was greeted by the Secretary of State as if the previous day had never happened. Seward smoothly assured him 'that everything consistent with US honour would be done' to assuage Britain's feelings.[61] Russell silently disagreed with Seward's prediction; he thought the public would never stand for it and neither would Congress.[62] From his military contacts, Russell heard that the army's commanders were confident they would 'whip' the British, which he found rather amusing, having recently spent an evening with Captain Leonard Currie, the English Assistant Adjutant General to General Smith, who told him 'amusing stories of utter want of subordination, mutiny in refusing to go on guard or on duty, etc.'[63]

Seward's dinner was in full swing when the *Europa* sailed into Boston harbour. Quietly and unobtrusively, Captain Conway Seymour boarded the Washington train for the last stage of his journey. He had only been travelling for a few hours when the train came to a shuddering halt in the dark countryside. Hearing that the repairs would not take place until the morning, Seymour commandeered a horse and rode all night to Baltimore, where he succeeded in chartering a special train to Washington. Finally, a little before midnight on Wednesday, 18 December, the white-faced and exhausted Queen's messenger climbed the steps of Lord Lyons's house.

The following day, at three o'clock in the afternoon, Lyons presented himself at Seward's office. (In one of those strange quirks of timing, on the other side of the Atlantic Charles Francis Adams had his meeting with Lord Russell on the same day, at the same hour.) Everything, it seemed to him, depended upon his delivery. He had to persuade the Secretary of State to bring his games to an end, without provoking him into making some last desperate attempt at bravado. Lord Russell was confident in his Minister, but his namesake, William Howard Russell, shuddered to think that peace depended on the shyest man in North America. 'Lord Lyons is a very odd sort of man,' he wrote to the editor of *The Times* on 20 December, 'and not quite the person to deal with this crisis tho' he is most diligent, clear headed and straight viewed. He is nervous and afraid of responsibility – and he has no personal influence in Washington because he never goes into American society tho' he gives dinners very frequently.'[64]

Lyons was nervous, but he carried himself with surprising aplomb. Seward let him speak without interruption and then asked to know the truth: what would happen if the government refused or requested further discussion? 'I told him that my instructions were positive and left me no discretion,' reported Lyons. Seward looked straight at him and begged for more time; he would never be able to bring round the Cabinet let alone the country in only seven days. Lyons believed him and agreed to return in two days, at which point the clock would be started. He went home feeling that his mission was already lost; he sincerely doubted that two, ten or twenty days would make a difference. Rear Admiral Milne was sent a coded telegraph instructing him to be ready to transport the legation staff to Canada.

When Lyons returned to Seward on Saturday, 21 December, he met with a plea for a couple days more. Ordinarily Lyons never disobeyed orders, but he knew that Seward was in a corner. Lyons had received an assurance from Mercier that France's letter in support of Britain would be arriving any day. If Seward did not succeed in convincing the Cabinet, the United States would be fighting an Anglo-French alliance in the North and the Confederacy in the South. A new appointment was set for Monday the 23rd at 10 a.m., but this had to be the final meeting, he told Seward. The official protest would be presented on Monday, and would give the United States seven days to respond. That afternoon, Lincoln told Senator Browning that Seward had asked Lyons to read the demands to him in two days' time. The President had 'an inkling of what they were', reported Browning, unaware that Lincoln knew exactly what they were since Seward had been keeping him informed from the beginning. After Seward's first meeting with Lyons, Lincoln had approached the editor of the *Philadelphia Press* for his help in 'preparing the American people for the release of Mason and Slidell'.[65] But Lincoln was being pulled in different directions; Sumner had also come by the White House to show him letters from John Bright and others that supported arbitration. Frustrated by his three-way conversation with Lyons, Lincoln asked Sumner why he could not speak to the Minister himself. 'If I could see Lord Lyons, I could show him in five minutes that I am heartily for peace,' he said.[66] But Sumner would not allow it, saying without justification that a meeting between the President and a Minister would be a breach of protocol. Sumner went further and not only extracted a promise from Lincoln to show him any correspondence before it was sent to Lord Lyons, but also set him up to defy Seward.

On the 23rd Lord Lyons went to the State Department for the third time, wondering if the meeting with Seward would be their last together. There was little for them to say to one another after he presented Lord Russell's letter; but Lyons could not help feeling sorry for Seward. He knew that the Secretary of State was carrying an immense burden. Lyons had tried to make the situation easier for him by granting the extra time; if the transatlantic cable had still been working, he would not have had the discretion but, as it was, Lyons had boldly made the decision in his belief that Seward would do his utmost to prevent a war. 'You will perhaps be surprised to find Mr Seward on the side of peace,' Lyons explained to Lord Russell. But 'ten months of office have dispelled many of his illusions ... he no longer believes ... in the ease with which the United States could crush rebellion with one hand, and chastise Europe with the other'. Lyons was optimistic that Seward had learned his lesson and would never again regard relations with England as 'safe playthings to be used for the amusement of the American People'.[67]

Seward persuaded Lincoln to call a Cabinet meeting for 10 a.m. on Christmas Day. The Secretary of State began by passing around copies of Lord Russell's 'seven-days' letter. As he talked, however, it became clear that the Cabinet remained opposed to releasing the Confederate Commissioners.[68] Sumner, who was also present, spoke after Seward; he had come armed with letters from England. John Bright's was particularly eloquent about the aristocratic mob screaming for war. Sumner outlined to the Cabinet what he had previously told Lincoln: since capitulation was politically impossible, an offer to go to arbitration was the government's only option. Otherwise Britain and probably France would break the blockade. The ironclad ships of the Royal Navy would smash the wooden US fleet, the North would in turn be blockaded and its ports destroyed. The Confederacy, in the meantime, would sign a free-trade agreement with England 'making the whole North American continent a manufacturing dependency of England'.[69]

Sumner was still speaking when the door opened and a messenger brought in the official French response to the crisis. The dispatch unambiguously denounced Wilkes's act as a violation of international law. For a second, Seward was crestfallen until he realized that his case had just been made for him. Edward Bates, the Attorney General, was the first to see that Sumner's proposal for arbitration was hardly less dangerous than retaining the Commissioners. Bates recorded in his diary:

> I . . . urged that to go to war with England is to abandon all hope of suppressing the rebellion . . . The maritime superiority of Britain would sweep us from the Southern waters. Our trade would be utterly ruined and our treasury bankrupt. In short . . . we MUST NOT have war with England. There was great reluctance on the part of some of the members of the cabinet – and even the President himself – to acknowledge these obvious truths.[70]

The situation was too galling, objected Salmon P. Chase, despite the fact that (or possibly because) the country was facing bankruptcy unless he could raise another loan. The markets had reacted almost as badly to the notion of arbitration as they had to that of the prisoners arriving in Fort Warren. Banks were nearly at the bottom of their specie reserves, government bonds were plummeting again and gold was running high.[71]

The meeting adjourned at 2 p.m. with an agreement to reconvene the following day. Before he left, Lincoln turned to Seward and asked him to summarize his arguments on paper. The President would do the same for Sumner's arbitration idea, and they would debate the two positions in the morning. Seward wrote all night; Lincoln made a half-hearted attempt before accepting that it was useless to delay the inevitable.

When Senator Browning anxiously questioned him after dinner, Lincoln reassured him that there was not going to be a war with England.

By morning, Seward had drafted a 26-page response to Lord Russell, which in effect dismissed the entire imbroglio as a consequence of Wilkes's forgetting to take the *San Jacinto* to a prize court for adjudication. He hoped it answered all the Cabinet's objections but he was too tired to judge. He left his house on Lafayette Square early and paid a surprise visit on Chase. If the Secretary of the Treasury could be persuaded, he thought, the others would follow his line. In fact, Chase, like Lincoln, had already begun to come round to Seward's way of thinking. Seward showed him the letter and explained why his idea was so much better than Sumner's. Rather than risk war by insisting on arbitration, they should pack the Commissioners off to London and claim it as a victory for American neutral rights.[72] Chase consoled himself with the thought that, if that happened, revenge on England would only be postponed.

Emotions were running high in the Senate. A last-ditch attempt by Senator Hale to force a resolution against releasing the Rebel Commissioners prevented Sumner from attending the meeting on the 26th. His absence allowed Seward to explain his letter to a far less critical audience. Seward kept expecting Lincoln to offer his alternative, but the President said nothing, and after comparatively little discussion, the Cabinet approved Seward's proposal. He could hardly believe the sudden change of opinion. When the others had filed out Seward turned to Lincoln and asked him why he had not made the case for arbitration. Because 'I could not make an argument that would satisfy my own mind', the President replied.[73]

The Cabinet had agreed to say nothing of the matter until Lyons received Seward's letter the following morning, the 27th. That night, Sumner was in an ebullient mood when he attended a dinner given by William Howard Russell. After some diversionary talk about Prince Albert's death, the discussion turned exclusively to the *Trent*. Even at this late stage, Russell told the group, he had not heard a single voice in favour of giving up the Southerners; the government would never be able to pull off something so unpopular. But Sumner corrected him. There was no need for the administration to do anything so drastic, he insisted. 'At the very utmost,' he declared, 'the *Trent* affair can only be a matter for mediation.' Russell assumed that he was hearing the official line since Sumner was in 'intimate rapport with the President'.[74]

The next day Russell was reading the Washington newspapers, which were still insisting that the Rebels would never be given up, when he received a note from one of the secretaries at the legation. 'What a collapse!' he wrote, a trifle disappointed that it was back to business as usual. Sumner's surprise was even greater. Not twenty-four hours ago the President had been adamantly opposed to any such settlement. Sumner had already accepted Seward's invitation to dinner that night. Crying off now would only call attention to his defeat.

Among the guests at Seward's was Anthony Trollope, who was oblivious to the drama unfolding in front of him.[75] Charles Sumner was unusually quiet and left the talking to Senator Crittenden, who made disparaging comments about Florence Nightingale to Trollope, no doubt unaware that the woman whose reputation he was rubbishing had recently donated her sanitation reports and hospital plans to the War Department.[76] Seward played the genial host to the hilt; after dinner, he invited the four Senators at the table to accompany him to his study. He bade them all sit down while he took out the dispatches from London and Paris. To these he added his 26-page reply to Lord Russell, his dispatch to Charles Francis Adams and his response to the French Foreign Minister. Sumner and the others then had to sit in silence while Seward read out every line.[77]

A week later, on 1 January 1862, the two Confederate Commissioners and their secretaries sailed for England on board the warship HMS *Rinaldo*. '[The Americans] are horribly out of humour,' Lyons wrote to Lord Russell on 31 December. He did not think this was the end of the story but, for now, they could put their faith in Seward. 'For he must do his best to maintain peace, or he will have made the sacrifice ... in vain.'[78] Seward had triumphed, but only just and only for the moment. His reply to Russell, which Seward had composed with his domestic audience firmly in mind, failed as a legal document or as a new elaboration of US foreign policy, but it successfully appealed to North American readers, especially the part where he claimed that because of the *Trent* case Britain would again never attempt to impress American sailors (a practice last used in 1812).

Sumner tried to diminish Seward's victory by claiming that the President had preferred arbitration, but the need for a quick decision had forced him into a hasty act.[79] There was, perhaps, some consolation to him in the vitriolic and bitter speeches that enlivened Congress during the first week of January. On the 9th Sumner gave a long speech in the Senate that was meant to explain and justify the government's decision. All the press, most of the Cabinet, nearly every Senator and all the foreign Ministers – except Lord Lyons – went to hear the performance. The Senator had dressed for the occasion. Afterwards, he was remembered as much for his olive-green gloves and tailored suit as for what he said. It was notoriously hard to follow Sumner. 'He works his adjectives so hard', a journalist once commented, 'that if they ever catch him alone, they will murder him.'[80] He spoke for three and a half hours, flatly contradicting many of the arguments Seward had employed in his dispatch to Lord Russell.

The public's response exceeded all Sumner's expectations. There were tributes and editorials in the press. People who usually avoided him because of his abolition politics were eager to shake his hand.[81] Sumner's previous criticisms of Seward's reckless diplomacy were repeated and turned into the reason for Britain's 'over-reaction'. The remarkable courage and patriotism Seward had displayed in forcing the Cabinet to make an unpopular decision were brushed aside.

Lord Lyons knew what it was like to have one's intentions maligned and efforts discounted, and he was among the few people in Washington who secretly applauded Seward for his bravery. The shy Minister did not know it, but he too had gained an admirer on account of his behaviour during the crisis. As 'one who witnessed the difficulties of Lord Lyons's position here, and how his pathway was strewn with broken glass', wrote Adam Gurowski, the State Department's chief translator, '[I] must feel for him the highest and most sincere consideration ... During the whole *Trent* affair, Lord Lyons's conduct was discreet, delicate, and generous ... a mind soured by human meanness is soothingly impressioned by such true nobleness in a diplomat and an Englishman.'[82]

"UP A TREE."
Colonel Bull and the Yankee 'Coon.
'Coon. "AIR YOU IN ARNEST, COLONEL?"
Colonel Bull. "I AM."
'Coon. "DON'T FIRE—I'LL **COME DOWN.**"

Punch crows after the Union backs down, January 1862

1. Richard Bickerton Pemell Lyons, 2nd Lord Lyons (1817–87). Lyons arrived at the British legation in the spring of 1859 and stayed until December 1864, when he returned to England, having worked himself to exhaustion.

2. The British legation at Rush House, 1710 H Street, Washington.

3. The US Capitol, Washington. Charles Dickens visited the capital in 1842 and thought the city had 'Magnificent Intentions', with 'streets [a] mile long, that only want houses, roads, and inhabitants'. Fifteen years later, these intentions remained unfulfilled. A disagreement between the US Federal government and a local landowner had stranded the unfinished Capitol building on top of a steep hill at the edge of town, facing the wrong way. The dome was finally completed on 2 December 1863.

4. President Lincoln's inauguration in front of the incomplete Capitol on 4 March 1861. In his inauguration speech, Lincoln tried to reassure the Southern States about his intentions towards slavery, but by then it was too late to stem the tide of secession: the war began six weeks later.

5. The US Senate. Here, on 22 May 1856, Congressman Preston Brooks of South Carolina ambushed Senator Charles Sumner, who was sitting at his desk reading, and beat him with his cane. By Brooks's own account, he struck Sumner thirty times before the cane splintered.

6. President Abraham Lincoln (1809–65). Lincoln's physical appearance astonished people. The British journalist William Howard Russell was introduced to him at around the time this photograph was taken in 1861: 'There entered, with a shambling, loose, irregular, almost unsteady gait, a tall, lank, lean man, considerably over six feet in height, with stooping shoulders, long pendulous arms, terminating in hands of extraordinary dimensions which, however, were far exceeded in proportion by his feet. He was dressed in an ill-fitting wrinkled suit of black, which put one in mind of an undertaker's uniform at a funeral.' By the end of the war, the world saw past Lincoln's appearance to his humanity and magnanimity towards his foes.

7. William Seward (1801–72), US Secretary of State, Lincoln's rival for power before the war, but who became his greatest ally during it. Seward's frequent statements that Canada would one day belong to the United States, coupled with his unscrupulous playing to American Anglophobia, made him the most detested US politician in Britain.

8. London, view of the Royal Exchange. In 1861 Britain was the richest nation on earth. A trading country par excellence, its exports in the 1860s counted for a quarter of the world's manufactured goods.

9. Cambridge House, Piccadilly, where Prime Minister Lord Palmerston lived from 1855 to 1865. Sir George Trevelyan wrote of it: 'Past the wall which screens the mansion / Hallowed by a mighty shade / Where the cards were cut and shuffled / When the game of State was played.'

10. The chamber of the House of Commons. The pro-Northern faction of MPs led by William Forster and John Bright successfully prevented all attempts by pro-Southern MPs to persuade the House to vote in favour of recognizing Southern independence.

11. Lord John Russell, 1st Earl Russell (1792–1878), Foreign Secretary. A cultured and intellectual man but an abrasive politician, Russell held thirteen political offices during his long career in politics, and was twice Prime Minister. He and Palmerston were referred to by Queen Victoria as 'those two dreadful old men'.

12. Henry John Temple, 3rd Viscount Palmerston (1784–1865), Prime Minister, popularly known as 'Lord Cupid' when young and 'Pam' when an elder statesman. His dislike of the United States went back to the War of 1812, when he was Secretary at War, and was exacerbated by America's protection of the slave trade. Palmerston's brinkmanship was successful during the *Trent* crisis of 1861, but his bluff was called three years later by the Germans.

13. Charles Sumner (1811–74), Senator for Massachusetts. Until the Civil War, he was the most revered US politician in Britain on account of his unflinching campaigns to abolish slavery and win equal rights for blacks.

14. Frederick Douglass (1818–95), writer, orator and the leading abolitionist in America. Douglass campaigned in Britain several times, and in 1859 briefly fled to London to avoid persecution after the radical abolitionist John Brown tried to start a slave uprising by raiding the armoury at Harpers Ferry, Virginia.

15. Gideon Welles (1802–78), US Secretary of the Navy. Nicknamed 'Father Neptune' by Lincoln because of his flowing beard, Welles was a lawyer and journalist with no maritime experience before his appointment. His loathing of William Seward, the Secretary of State, interfered with their ability to work together.

16. Salmon P. Chase (1803–73), US Secretary of the Treasury. An effective Treasurer who established a national banking system and paper currency – the greenback – he was also a schemer who tried to engineer the dismissal of William Seward in 1862, and the removal of President Lincoln from the Republican ticket in 1864.

17. General George McClellan (1826–85), commander of the US Army of the Potomac, 1861–2. He was removed by President Lincoln after the Battle of Antietam for being overly passive and cautious.

18. The 69th New York Irish Regiment, the 'Fighting 69th', one of five Irish-dominated regiments which made up the Irish Brigade of the Union Army of the Potomac. The regiment suffered disproportionate losses in the Battle of Fredericksburg.

19. US General William Sherman (1820–91). Sherman began the war in command of a single brigade (which included the 'Fighting 69th'), but he so distinguished himself that General Grant gave him control over all the Union armies west of Virginia. Sherman implemented a policy of 'total war' against the South during his march from Atlanta to Savannah, Georgia, in 1864.

20. William Howard Russell (1820–1907). 'Russell of the Crimea' was the most famous journalist in the world when he arrived in the North to cover the Civil War. His unbiased reports for *The Times* were considered insufficiently favourable by the North and in 1862 he was harassed into leaving the country.

21. Edward Dicey (1832–1911), pro-Northern English journalist for the *Spectator*. He published an account of his travels after his return home.

22. The Hon. Francis Lawley (1825–1901), pro-Southern British journalist for *The Times*. The war gave Lawley a second chance to redeem himself after his gambling debts forced him into exile. He became so enamoured with the South that he willingly misrepresented events to show the Confederacy in a better light.

23. Frank Vizetelly (1830–83), British war artist and pro-Southern correspondent for the *Illustrated London News*. 'He was a big, florid, red-bearded Bohemian,' recalled an admirer, 'who could and would do anything to entertain a circle.'

9

The War Moves to England

Hard times in Lancashire – Burnside captures Roanoke Island –
The sorrows of Lincoln – A victory at last – Mason and Slidell arrive
in Europe – Dawson joins the Nashville *– Southern propaganda –*
The debate in Parliament

'We are beginning the New Year under very poor prospects,' recorded a cotton spinner named John Ward from Clitheroe on 1 January 1862. Twenty-seven thousand workers in Lancashire had been fired and another 160,000 were, like him, surviving on short time. Families on his street were selling their furniture to buy food. 'A war with America' would be the final straw, wrote Ward, 'as we will get no cotton ... Every one is anxious for the arrival of the next mail, which is expected every day.'[1]

In Liverpool, crowds gathered each morning on the quayside, waiting for America's response. The arrival of the *Africa* on 2 January caused brief excitement, but she carried only newspapers in her hold. Reuter came to see Charles Francis Adams on Monday the 6th, to ask if the Minister would be so kind as to alert him the minute there was news. 'He little imagines how entirely my government keeps me without information,' Adams wrote angrily.[2] Two days later, it was Reuter who did Adams the kindness; his office had received an early telegram announcing the Commissioners' release. Weed came an hour later to confirm that it was all over the City. Adams's relief was tempered by his vexation at being the last to know.

Benjamin Moran rushed to St James's, the club of the diplomatic corps on Charles Street, and probably the only club in London which would have him. For once he was the centre of attention as two dozen minor diplomats and Secretaries 'sprang to their feet as if electrified', he

NAUGHTY JONATHAN.

Mrs Britannia. "THERE, JOHN! HE SAYS HE IS VERY SORRY, AND THAT HE DIDN'T MEAN TO DO IT—SO YOU CAN PUT THIS BACK INTO THE PICKLE-TUB."

Punch depicts the US as a recalcitrant child in need of a whipping

wrote. Several even shook his hand before running off to the telegraph office. 'In a few minutes messages were flashing over the wires to all the Courts of Europe.' In the West End theatres, evening performances were already under way, but as soon as the curtains fell on the first act the news was announced, causing audiences to rise spontaneously and cheer.[3] Within the Cabinet, however, reactions were rather more mixed: 'The Admiralty is flat and dull, now there is to be no war,' the Duke of Somerset wrote sarcastically to his son, Lord Edward St Maur.[4]

More than £2 million had been spent in the scramble to get ships and troops to America. It would be some time before the soldiers came home. Jonny Stanley wrote to his parents from Montreal to say that he was safe although lonely. The infinite forests and frozen lakes of Canada were 'very dull, and the people, however socially inclined, thoroughly different in manners and ways of thinking'.[5] The troops had so little to do that a sizeable number would slip away over the winter months, only to reappear on the other side of the American border as Northern volunteers.[6]

The press assumed that relations between the two countries would quickly return to normal. The *Illustrated London News* congratulated England for having dealt with the crisis so adroitly. 'We are therefore clear of all blame in the whole transaction,' it opined on 11 January, 'and legally, morally, and even sentimentally, we have shown ourselves friends to the Americans.'[7] This was not the view of 20 million Americans. Huddled in his frozen headquarters in northern Virginia, US General Meade wrote to his wife that 'if ever this domestic war of ours is settled, it will require but the slightest pretext to bring about a war with England'.[8] A Congressman from Illinois swore before the House that he had 'never shared in the traditional hostility of many of my countrymen against England. But I now here publicly avow and record my inextinguishable hatred of that Government. I mean to cherish it while I live and to bequeath it as a legacy to my children when I die.' From Paris, Seward's unofficial emissary, Archbishop Hughes, exhorted him to remember that the 'awful war between England and America must come sooner or later, – and in preparing for it, even now, there is not a moment to be lost'.[9]

Charles Francis Adams had neither the clarity of anger nor the cushion of complacency to comfort him. The news about the *Trent* had been followed by a letter from Charles Francis Jr. informing his family he had joined the 1st Massachusetts Cavalry. The unexpected blow made ordinary business seem 'utterly without interest', wrote Adams.[10] The upset to the family was not enough, however, to divert attention from an embarrassing gaffe by Henry Adams. On 10 January *The Times* revealed that 'Mr H. Adams', the younger son and private secretary of the American Minister, had published a mildly insulting article about English society for the American press. Henry had never intended to acknowledge 'A Visit to Manchester' as his own, and so he had vented some of his frustrations about his social isolation in London society, pointedly remarking that 'in Manchester, I am told, it is still the fashion for the hosts to see that the guests enjoy themselves. In London the guests shift for themselves . . . one is regaled with thimbles full of ice-cream and hard seed cakes.' Charles Francis Jr. had accidentally left Henry's name on the manuscript when he sent it to the editor of the *Boston Courier*.[11] Until then, Henry had been enjoying great success as the *New York Times*'s anonymous London correspondent. 'The Chief', as Henry called his father, gave his son a sharp dressing down; so sharp that Henry briefly considered self-exile on the Continent.[12] He was teased without mercy by Benjamin Moran, who repeated ad nauseam that 'it is not every boy of 25 who can in 6 mos. residence here extort a leader from *The Times*'.[13]

When he visited the Foreign Office on 11 January for his first meeting since the *Trent* crisis, Adams hoped that Lord Russell had not seen the *Times* article about his son. There was no cause for concern: Russell could be curiously obtuse about what he read in the papers. (Lady Russell had a far better understanding of the power of the press than her husband; she thought the American public had been goaded beyond endurance by the 'sneering, exulting tone' in English newspapers after Bull Run.[14]) The two men passed the first half of the interview congratulating one another on preserving the peace, after which it was down to business again. Russell's current concern was the risk to peace posed by Union and Confederate cruisers. The CSS *Sumter* had recently arrived at Cadiz, having destroyed a number of US merchant ships along the way. The government expected a confrontation with a US navy ship, but would not tolerate a free-for-all in British waters, which in Palmerston's words would be a 'scandal and inconvenience'. In Southampton, the disruption to ordinary business had risen to unsupportable levels; the crews of the CSS *Nashville* and the USS *Tuscarora* – which had been pursuing the *Nashville* since December – were fighting each other in the streets.[15] Adams was caught by surprise, having not given a thought to either vessel during the past few weeks. It was back to the old state of affairs, he realized.

Life for all the occupants of the legation was slowly returning to normal. People had stopped inviting them, Henry told Charles Francis Jr., 'on the just supposition that we wouldn't care to go into society'. The drought ended with a dinner at the Argylls' on 17 January. The evening passed far more enjoyably than the US Minister expected; Gladstone sat next to him and showed genuine interest in his views. The guest on his other side praised him for 'my conduct during the difficulties'. But Adams's enjoyment was curtailed when the conversation turned to Seward and his now infamous quip to the Duke of Newcastle. 'I feel my solitude in London much more than I do at home,' he wrote in his diary a short time later. 'The people are singularly repulsive. With a very considerable number of acquaintances, I know not a single one whose society I should miss one moment.'[16]

Adams did not know the true state of affairs in Washington, and Seward did not wish to enlighten him. The *Trent* was only one of many crises that threatened the administration during the winter of 1862. Criticism of the government's lack of progress was growing ever louder, with Lincoln receiving the largest share of the blame. The border States had not been secured and the vast Army of the Potomac encamped around Washington had yet to do anything other than drill. Its leader, General McClellan, remained bedridden with typhoid. The War Department was riddled with incompetence and corruption and the Treasury had run out of gold, leaving Secretary Chase with no alternative but to print more money. On the night of 10 January, Seward received a summons to the White House. There he found Chase, Assistant Secretary of War Peter Watson, and two generals gathered in a solemn huddle around the President. They had to act now, Lincoln told them, and find a way to produce victories or face the possibility 'of our being two nations'.[17] Frustrated by the generals' objections, Lincoln decided he would issue a Presidential Order for all naval and military forces to begin any advance on 22 February, regardless of obstacles or delays.

The President's frustration presented an opportunity for Seward to strengthen their relationship at a time when his own allies were deserting him in droves. 'There is a formidable clique organized against Mr. Seward,' the Attorney General noted in his diary on 2 February. 'I do not think I heard a good word spoken of Mr. Seward as a Minister even by one of his own party,' observed Trollope of his time in Washington. 'He seemed to have no friend, no one who trusted him.'[18] Frank Blair, the powerful Congressman from Missouri, complained to colleagues that Seward was 'selfish, ambitious and incompetent' and apparently more concerned with fighting England than the South.[19] Another Senator attacked him for being 'a low, vulgar, vain demagogue'.[20]

Seward gave loyal service to Lincoln; while Mary Lincoln seemed incapable of fulfilling the role of confidante, the former contender for the White House found that he could adapt to the role with ease. Seward could not solve the President's military problems, but he was able to smooth the way for the Secretary of War's departure on 14 January 1862, and the appointment of Edwin Stanton. The new Secretary was arrogant and devious but, in contrast to Cameron, was efficient and would attack the Department's problems with energy. The amiable but useless Cameron chose to spend his forced retirement in Russia, where he replaced the equally useless Cassius Clay as Minister.

Simultaneously with Cameron's removal, some flicker of life appeared in the North's military machine. On 14 January the English volunteer George Henry Herbert learned that the 'Zou-Zous' – as members of the 9th New York Infantry (Hawkins' Zouaves) were affectionately called – were going to evacuate from Hatteras Inlet. Despite the monotony of drilling and digging at Camp Wool, Herbert had never felt so content with his life. 'Since I wrote to you I have received my promotion. I am now 2nd Lieutenant,' he informed his mother. He promised to send a photograph of himself in his new officer's uniform in his next letter in case it was his last. 'Our boys here are in high glee, we are going to leave Hatteras in a day or two,' he explained. 'We are part of an expedition under the command of General Burnside. It consists of somewhere about an hundred vessels of all sorts, containing a land force of as near as I can learn, about 10,000 men of all arms. Its destination is unknown. The rumour is New Orleans. I fervently hope so.'[21]

The rumours were unfounded. Thirteen thousand men were leaving Cape Hatteras, heading up the North Carolina sounds to the mysterious Roanoke Island, a forlorn stretch of grass and swamp between the mainland and the Outer Banks. Its first inhabitants, Sir Walter Raleigh's ill-fated colonists, had survived in the New World for less than four years before they mysteriously disappeared. Three hundred years later the island seemed as untamed as ever. Its chief importance was strategic: whoever owned Roanoke held the key to Richmond's back door.[22]

General Ambrose Burnside (whose name and prodigious whiskers allegedly inspired the word 'sideburns') had convinced General McClellan that he could lead a combined amphibious force in light-draft and flat-bottomed boats that would have no trouble navigating the shallow waters in the sound. The Confederate garrison guarding Roanoke was small, and unlikely to withstand a sustained assault. Burnside was so confident that he gave permission for journalists to accompany the expedition. Russell heard the news from his sickbed in a hotel in New York. He was worn down by the unrelenting campaign of abuse against him: 'there is a sort of weakness and languor over me that I never experienced before,' he told Delane. Frank Vizetelly would go and report for both of them.[23]

Vizetelly, so deep in debt that even Russell would no longer lend him money, was overjoyed at the prospect of escaping Washington. He joined Burnside's flotilla on 10 January with nothing except a small bag containing a change of clothes and his pencils. 'Woe is me!' he wrote after several days of crashing seas and hurricane winds. One night, a thunderous wave hit the boat with such force that he was catapulted from his bed against the cabin door, which burst open, depositing him with a thud in eight inches of briny water. He decided this would be his first and last amphibious expedition.[24]

The USS *Picket* leading the ships of the Burnside expedition over the Hatteras Bar in North Carolina, by Frank Vizetelly

The first phase of the attack was easily accomplished and the southern half of Roanoke was captured on 7 February without Herbert or his friends firing a shot. 'Day broke cold, damp, and miserable,' Vizetelly wrote on the 8th. 'After a drink of water and a biscuit for each man, the Federal force prepared to advance into the interior.'[25] Cannonfire alerted Herbert that it would soon be his regiment's turn to leave the makeshift camp. 'Near the centre of the island it is very narrow and at the narrowest point a battery was erected,' he explained to his mother. 'The road is in fact nothing but a cow path through fine woods and a thick growth of underbrush.'[26]

The men had to march along the track two by two in order to allow room for the stretcher-bearers carrying the wounded back to the ships. 'I remember after that', commented a private in the regiment, 'a sort of sickening sensation as if I was going to a slaughter-house to be butchered.'[27]

'At last we came in front of the battery,' wrote Herbert. The order came to charge and they plunged into the knee-deep swamp that surrounded the Confederate position. Vizetelly watched as they hurled themselves up the slope towards the battery. The men behaved, he continued, 'in the most brilliant manner, dashing through the swamp and over the stumps of the pine-clearing, and into the battery, which the Confederates were hastily leaving'. When they reached the top they discovered that the Rebels had fled. The 9th took up the chase for four miles, and finally cornered the defenders at the northern tip of the island, in their own camp.

Herbert was delighted to hear that a journalist from the *Illustrated London News* was with them, and asked his mother to look out for his reports. A total of 264 Federals and 143 Confederates had been killed in the attack; later, he would consider such casualty numbers remarkably small, but for now he thought he had survived a great battle. Vizetelly admitted to being impressed. 'I will not attempt to prophesy a triumph for the Federalists,' he told readers at home; 'but, seeing the improved condition in the morale of the Union forces, and feeling somewhat competent to give an opinion, I am inclined to believe that these first successes are not to be their last. I have watched the Northern army almost from its first appearance in the field. I have seen it a stripling . . . I now see it arrived at man's estate.'[28]

News of Burnside's success on Roanoke Island reached Washington while the city was still under the rosy glow of Mary Lincoln's triumphant White House ball, held on 5 February. The capital celebrated even harder when it learned that a great victory had been won in Tennessee. US General Ulysses S. Grant had captured Fort Henry on the 6th and Fort Donelson on the 15th, giving him control of Tennessee's two main rivers, the Cumberland and the Tennessee. An important water highway had been opened for the North, which ran from the north of Kentucky all the way down to Mississippi and Alabama.

Lyons wished in his heart he could escape while there was relative calm. 'I don't expect to be ever free here from troubles,' he wrote.[29] There would always be another incident. 'I have no doubt that for me personally this would be the moment to give up this place. I can never keep

The 9th New York Volunteers (Hawkins' Zouaves) and the 21st Massachusetts in a
bayonet charge on the Confederate fieldworks on Roanoke Island, by Frank Vizetelly

things in as good a state as they are,' he confided to his sister two days
after the ball. 'However, I cannot propose this to the Government, especially after the GCB – and of course feel bound to stay as long as they
wish to keep me.'[30] Lyons was referring to the Order of the Bath, which
Lord Russell had arranged to be bestowed upon him for his handling of
the *Trent* crisis. When he had learned of the honour, Lyons had written
to Russell with characteristic humility that he had done nothing 'brilliant
or striking'; 'the only merit which I can attribute to myself is that of having laboured sedulously, though quietly and unobtrusively ... to carry
out honestly your orders and wishes'.[31] He also commended his staff for
their exemplary behaviour during the crisis – although he would not
have been able to say the same for them now. Since the resolution of the
affair, the attachés and Secretaries had been living up to their nickname
of 'the Bold Buccaneers'. Two of the more literary members of the group
had decided to put on a play, and persuaded Lyons to allow them to perform it at the legation.

The attachés' youth and high spirits insulated them from the subdued atmosphere that pervaded Washington after the sudden death of Lincoln's middle son, Willie, on 20 February. The precocious 11-year-old, who had reigned as the undisputed favourite of the family, was suspected to have died of typhoid fever. Mary Lincoln withdrew into her own private agony of grief, leaving her devastated husband with the burden of caring for their other boy still at home, 7-year-old Tad, who was battling the same illness that had killed his brother. The *Spectator*'s correspondent, Edward Dicey, was introduced to Lincoln not long after Willie's funeral and noted the 'depression about his face, which, I am told by those who see him daily, was habitual to him, even before the recent death of his child'. During their short interview Lincoln earnestly interrogated him about English public opinion. 'Like all Americans', commented Dicey, he 'was unable to comprehend the causes which have alienated the sympathies of the mother country'. *[32]

The same question about England's sympathies was being asked in the South. 'Seward has cowered beneath the roar of the British Lion,' bemoaned John B. Jones, a clerk in the Confederate War Department. 'Now we must depend upon our own strong arms and stout hearts for defense.'[33] Even the shrewd and unflappable diarist Mary Chesnut had given in to her optimism during the *Trent* affair. For a brief moment she had shared the belief so prevalent in the South that the Royal Navy would appear off the coast and blow the blockade to smithereens. Now she wondered if the British were laughing at them, 'scornful and scoffing ... on our miseries'.[34] Despite the brouhaha over their release, she feared that Commissioners Slidell and Mason were chasing a chimera. 'Lord Lyons has gone against us. Lord Derby and Louis Napoleon are silent in our hour of need,' she wrote. The loss of Roanoke and the forts in Tennessee caused uproar in Richmond. Someone had to bear the blame for these dreadful and unexpected defeats and who better than the Confederate Secretary of War, Judah Benjamin? 'Mr Davis's pet

---

* Dicey never realized how much his references to the 'mother country' alienated Americans. His innocent, if tongue-in-cheek, comparison of New York with London caused great irritation. 'Everything around and about me looked so like the Old Country,' he wrote. Landing on the docks, 'Irish porters seized upon my luggage as they would have done at the Tower steps in London. Street newsboys pestered me with second editions of English-printed newspapers. An Old-fashioned English hackney coach carried me to my destination, through dull, English-looking streets, with English names; and the driver cheated me at the end of my fare, with genuine London exorbitance.'

Jew', as his critics called him, was accused of having sacrificed Roanoke Island by refusing to send reinforcements. Benjamin's stint at the War Department had been hampered from the start by his lack of rapport with the military and this latest crisis would make his position untenable. However, the truth in the case of Roanoke, which out of loyalty he never revealed, was that there were neither weapons nor men to spare.[35] Two or three arms shipments a month from England were not enough to maintain one army, let alone several across hundreds of miles.

The freedom experienced by the four Confederates on board HMS *Rinaldo* as she crossed the Atlantic in early January was far worse than the dull confinement endured at Fort Warren. Just to walk on the icy deck was to risk death. Huge icicles dangled above their heads. Any person not wearing a safety rope was liable to slip or be blown out to sea. Before the journey's end, many of the sailors had suffered frostbite. 'If you have no news of "Rinaldo" I fear she is lost – horrible to think of,' William Howard Russell wrote to Delane on 16 January. Horrible but somehow not unexpected, considering the appalling misfortunes that had already blighted the Southerners' mission.[36]

'Mr Slidell', declared a Northern journal, 'is the ideal of a man who would think it a privilege to get into a scrape himself, if he could only involve his host and patron too.' Mr Mason, on the other hand, was 'more of a bull-dog, ready to fasten on friends and foes alike'.[37] Yet, until the *Trent* affair, there had been nothing in their previous histories to suggest that either James Mason or John Slidell were the type of men whose fate would move armies. They so neatly fitted into Southern stereotypes as to be walking caricatures of a Virginia aristocrat and Louisiana politician. Mason had been brought up amid elegant surroundings and liveried servants, and could trace his family back to the English Civil War, where one of his Cavalier ancestors commanded a regiment at the Battle of Worcester. Slidell, on the other hand, was the son of a moderately successful New York candle-maker who had fled the city after a scandal involving a pistol fight and reinvented himself as a successful lawyer in New Orleans.[38] Slidell had few hatreds but one of them was for New Yorkers who refused to forget his humble beginnings.[39] He was happier in New Orleans, where he could lift his finger and see his puppets raise their hands.

William Howard Russell had met both men and found them tolerable.

Mason was tall, heavy-set and crowned with a bouffant that was once leonine but had started to recede into a mohawk. His bright blue eyes and ruddy cheeks made him appear kindly, but out of his small, thin mouth came the most unashamedly racist and pro-slavery statements Russell had ever heard. His proudest achievement up to this point had been the drafting of the 1850 Fugitive Slave Act, which denied escaped slaves any place of sanctuary in the United States. Mr Mason, Russell informed readers of *The Times* on 10 December, 'is a man of considerable belief in himself; he is a proud, well-bred, not unambitious gentleman, whose position gave him the right to expect high office', though, as would become apparent, not necessarily the talent. His ten years as chairman of the Senate Foreign Relations Committee had left no discernible trace of experience on him. Mary Chesnut considered him to be one of the bigger imbeciles among her acquaintances: 'My wildest imagination will not picture Mr. Mason as a diplomat,' she had written after hearing of his appointment. 'He will say "chaw" for "chew", and he will call himself "Jeems", and he will wear a dress coat to breakfast. Over here, whatever a Mason does is right in his own eyes. He is above law.' Mary knew the English horror of tobacco chewing too. 'I don't care how he pronounces the nasty thing but he will do it,' she wrote. 'In England a man must expectorate like a gentleman if he expectorates at all.'[40] This last observation was certainly true, and would count against Mason almost as much as his passionate belief in slavery.*

By contrast, 'Mr Slidell', Russell wrote in his diary, 'is to the South something greater than Mr Thurlow Weed has been to his party in the North.' Like Mason, he was tall and well built, but feline rather than bluff, with 'fine thin features, [and] a cold keen grey eye'.[42] His French was excellent, thanks to his Creole wife, as was his taste in wine. His suave manner was the antithesis of Mason's chomping heartiness. 'He is not a speaker of note, nor a ready stump orator, nor an able writer, but he is an excellent judge of mankind, adroit, persevering, and subtle, full of device, and fond of intrigue . . . what is called here a "wire-puller".'[43]

---

* Benjamin Moran took enormous delight in recording the effect of Mason's tobacco habit: 'Mr Mason was the unfittest man they could have sent here, and has proved an ignominious failure. His antecedents were bad, his associates were questionable, and his manners vulgar. Even Bear Ellice couldn't endorse his coarseness, much as he supported his cause, and had to rebuke him hypothetically for spitting tobacco on his drawing room carpets in Scotland. Mr Mason spirted his tobacco juice about there liberally . . .'[41]

He could destroy a man or make him, as he did Judah Benjamin, who owed his entire political career to Slidell's connections. If the attainment of power was a belief, then Slidell was a practising zealot. On all other questions he was agnostic. Slidell's urge to politic was so great, wrote Russell, that if he were shut up in a dungeon he 'would conspire with the mice against the cat rather than not conspire at all'.[44]

The Confederates arrived in England on 29 January to an absence of fanfare. The press, including *The Times*, had warned the country against turning them into heroes; the Confederate Commissioners were representatives of a government that was waging an undeclared war against Britain's cotton industry. Mason asked his friend the MP William Gregory, whom he had not seen since Gregory's visit to Washington in 1859, whether British resentment about the cotton embargo was the reason for the 'harsh' treatment meted out to the *Nashville* and Captain Pegram, who had been forbidden to make any military alterations to his ship or stay longer once his repairs were completed. Gregory told him that, on the contrary, this was in accordance with the neutrality proclamation.

The *Nashville* set sail from Southampton on 3 February, cheered on by thousands of well-wishers. (William Yancey's departure, on the same day but in a different ship, went unremarked.) With her Confederate flags and black-painted hull, the ship managed to look warlike and dashing at the same time. The HMS *Shannon* – with ports open and steam up – stood guard between the *Nashville* and *Tuscarora*. There could be no engagement between the warring vessels in British waters. Much to Captain Craven's chagrin, the *Tuscarora* would have to wait twenty-four hours before she could begin her pursuit of the *Nashville*.*

Unbeknown to Captain Robert B. Pegram, a young man called Francis Dawson had joined the crew under false pretenses as its fifty-first member. Pegram had thought he was dealing with a boy of 16 or 17 when Dawson first asked to come on board. He offered him a position 'as a sailor before the mast', meaning the lowest rank of seaman, and assumed that this would be the last he saw of him. Dawson secretly boarded the ship with the help of one of the master's mates. But he was no teenage runaway; he was in fact a 21-year-old who had failed to break into the theatre as a playwright and was looking for a new occupation. His real

---

* Under the Declaration of Paris, when two belligerent ships arrived at a neutral port, their departure had to be separated by twenty-four hours to forestall the risk of a battle in the neutral country's waters.

name was Austin Reeks; his father had ruined the family through one idiotic financial speculation after the other, leaving his mother dependent on the charity of relatives. A widowed aunt who paid for Austin's education was the inspiration for his new name: Francis Warrington Dawson. Mrs Dawson's late husband, William Dawson, had been an officer in the Indian army. The change of identity and leap into an adventure was not untypical behaviour for Austin. He had never wanted to be himself, living in poverty with a father who made him ashamed and a mother he pitied. 'My idea simply was to go to the South, do my duty there as well as I might, and return home to England,' Dawson wrote in his reminiscences. One of his great strengths was that he believed his own stories and once he had claimed that he was motivated to fight for the South by idealism it became true.

He needed every shred of his sense of duty to survive his difficult initiation into life at sea. On his second day, Dawson's trunk was broken open and his belongings stolen. The old sea-hands disliked the interloper who spoke fine English and said his rosary at night. They resented even more his obvious rapport with the ship's officers, and punished him with the worst jobs. After nearly three weeks of hazing from the crew, Dawson decided that his life was 'truly a hard one. I could not have borne it but that I know how judicious is the step I have taken ... Time does not in the least reconcile me to the men in the forecastle! More and more do I detest and loathe them.' But once Captain Pegram discovered Dawson's presence he took pity on him and gave orders for his bunk to be moved to the upper deck. He soon felt an avuncular concern for the impetuous youth and was overheard saying that he would do something for Dawson once they reached home. Dawson hoped so. 'I am told that I may make a fortune in the South if I chose,' he wrote his mother. 'God grant that I may for your sakes.'[45]

Dawson was part of a small but growing number of potential recruits who were trying to reach the South in spite of the blockade. 'There may be some whose experience in the field or for drill may be useful,' Mason wrote to Richmond after several ex-officers called at the new headquarters of the Confederate commission at 109 Piccadilly. 'Will you please advise me what I am to say to such applicants.'[46] While he waited, Mason was careful to be encouraging without committing himself or the Commission to anything illegal under the Foreign Enlistment Act. The British authorities' punctiliousness over the *Nashville* had shown him that there would be no leniency as far as the law was concerned. Slidell could afford to be less fastidious. Soon after his arrival in Paris, he received a visit from a tall, leather-faced Englishman in his mid-fifties, who declared his intention of joining the Confederate army. Impressed by the man's soldierly past and bearing, Slidell agreed to supply him with letters of introduction. In late spring the Knoxville *Register* announced that an English volunteer, Colonel George St Leger Grenfell, had arrived in Charleston, South Carolina on board the blockade-runner *Nelly*.[47]

William Gregory was pleased to learn that Richmond had instructed Mason to challenge Britain's observance of the blockade; safeguarding the country's economy would be taken much more seriously by MPs than independence for slave-owners. The Commissioner had come armed with statistics that proved it was a blockade on paper only. True, the records stopped at the end of October, but they nevertheless showed that more than 600 vessels had succeeded in getting through since April. The first step was to bring Mason together with Lord Russell. Gregory helped Mason draft a note, asking for an *unofficial* interview. 'This is I think', Gregory wrote, 'the most dignified course to pursue, and I have asked advice on the subject.' He reminded Mason to use the correct form: 'The Right Hon. Earl Russell, Foreign Office. I should not address your letter to his private house.'[48] While they were waiting for Russell's reply, James Spence, the author of *The American Union*, introduced himself to the group. The Liverpudlian businessman had realized that there were social and financial opportunities to be gained from befriending the nascent South; in a bid to prove his usefulness, Spence offered to help Mason to prepare for his meeting with Lord Russell.

Russell had no wish to see Mason. 'What a fuss we have had about these two men,' he exclaimed.[49] He had heard that William Gregory and William Schaw Lindsay had decided to force a debate on the blockade after the opening of Parliament on 6 February. Russell already had a fair idea of the number of ships getting through from the diligent reports of the local Consuls, but he baulked at challenging its legality. There was no telling when Great Britain might find herself in the similar position of mounting a feeble blockade.[50] At the meeting on 10 February Russell resorted to his usual method with the Confederates and forced Mason to do most of the talking. Mason noticed that the Foreign Secretary 'took very little part in the conversation' and felt that he had been played throughout the interview. 'On the whole,' wrote Mason bitterly, 'it was manifest enough that his personal sympathies were not with us, and his policy inaction.'[51] This was true. 'At all events, I am heart and soul a neutral,' Russell wrote to Lord Lyons just before the meeting.[52]

The Confederate lobby's obstinacy exasperated Palmerston and Russell. Both were highly sensitive as to how it would appear to the North if Parliament debated whether or not to disregard its blockade. Coming so soon after the *Trent* crisis, it would add credence to the charge that Britain was simply looking for an excuse to turn on the United States. No one in the Cabinet believed that the war could last for much longer. Why irritate either side, was the general consensus, when all they had to do was wait for perhaps only three more months? The Lord Chancellor, Lord Westbury, expressed himself in his customary splenetic way: 'I am greatly opposed to any violent interference . . . Let them tear one another to pieces . . .'[53] To try to forestall a debate, Russell invited James Spence to attend a meeting at the Foreign Office, since it was known that he was held in high esteem by the Confederates. Spence was delighted with his newfound importance. He listened gravely as Russell explained why he should use his influence to stop the Confederates from forcing a vote. As soon as the interview was over, Spence hurried to the commission headquarters on Piccadilly to urge the group to redouble its efforts.

Charles Francis Adams had heard that the Confederates' political friends were pushing the blockade question. He wrote to Seward on 7 February, urgently requesting any facts and statistics he could pass on to the North's supporters in Parliament. It was embarrassing personally and diplomatically, he hinted, for the State Department to leave him so ill-informed. Adams had become reconciled to Thurlow Weed's presence, 'but my patience is gradually oozing out of me at this extraordinary practice of running me down with my own colleagues', he wrote in his diary. 'Mr Seward was not brought up in the school of refined delicacy of feeling or he would not have continued these inflictions.'

What they needed, Weed told Seward, was a host of unofficial representatives whose sole purpose was to shape public opinion. Adams was a good man but useless for anything other than strict diplomacy. 'We may want the good-will of England before our troubles are over, and it can be had on easy terms,' he wrote. 'I believe now that nine tenths of the English People would rejoice to see us successful.'[54] But this was hinged on precarious foundations. It was no good Seward arguing that slavery was de facto abolished in the small areas of the South held by the Federal army. He would have to say publicly that this was a war for abolition.[55] Could not Seward help them a little, he asked, by at least granting passports to free blacks? It would help counter the claim that the North was just as racist as the South and hypocritical as well.[56]

For the upcoming debate in Parliament, Weed and Adams looked to William Forster rather than John Bright to outmanoeuvre William Gregory and the small but growing Confederate lobby. 'On the whole Mr Forster has been our firmest and most judicious friend,' Adams admitted privately. 'We owe to his tact and talent even more than we do to the more showy interference of Messrs Cobden and Bright.'[57] The latter seemed to relish his powers of alienation. On 17 February Bright made a blistering speech in the Commons against aristocratic support-ers of slavery, which struck his listeners as ludicrous considering Lord Shaftesbury was leading a national campaign to reunite a fugitive slave named Anderson with his wife and children. One MP commented after-wards, 'I don't think the people of England like [Bright] and his policy better than they do his friends the Yankees.'[58]

'We are miserably prepared to meet and answer objections,' Weed grumbled to Seward on 20 February. 'Members of Parliament beset me for materials, and I cannot get anything official. I have picked what could be found of the Newspapers.'[59] Although still chastened by his recent exposure in the press, Henry Adams discreetly tried to aid his father by pushing Frederick Seward, Seward's son, to send over any reports that could be of use. 'The truth is, we want light here,' Henry told him. 'Our friends have got to be stuffed with statistics and crammed with facts ... The Southerners will parade a great number of vessels which have run it. Our side must show an equal or greater number either captured, or chased, and must have at hand any evidence ...' Otherwise, he warned, the Confederates would argue that the fourth provision of the Declaration of Paris was not being met – that the block-ade actually exist and be effective – and therefore was illegal.[60]

As the day of the debate approached, Adams noticed a rise in news-paper articles that were sympathetic to the South. He blamed the 'unscrupulous and desperate emissaries' who were prepared to spread any number of lies – even that slavery in the South would be abolished after independence – for a credulous British public.[61] The 'emissaries' were actually one agent, Henry Hotze, a journalist from Mobile, Alabama, who had been appointed by the Confederate State Department to liaise between the commission and the press. Hotze had arrived in England on the same day as Mason and Slidell, but had not travelled with them. Although he was only 27 years old, Hotze exuded the confidence of someone twice his age. He was fluent in French and German, having spent his childhood in Switzerland. His charm and powers of conversation were still legendary in Brussels, where he had served as the Secretary of the American legation during the late 1850s.[62]

The mission to England had been Hotze's own idea. During the autumn he had spent a few weeks in London on behalf of the War Department, checking on the progress of arms shipments. This was long enough to convince him that the South needed to 'educate' the English press, and that he was the person to do it. Although Hotze despised Mason and abhorred his tobacco habit, he accepted that he was dependent on Mason's contacts until he could make his own.[63] Mason had no idea of Hotze's feelings towards him and during their first weeks in London he invited the journalist to accompany him everywhere he went. In this way Hotze forged many useful acquaintances and learned a great deal in a short amount of time.

On 23 February Hotze gleefully informed the Confederate State Department that his attempts to cultivate the press had succeeded far beyond his initial expectations. After only three weeks in London he had placed his first editorial in an English newspaper – a feat Henry Adams had failed to achieve in nearly twelve months. Furthermore, the newspaper was the *Morning Post*, Lord Palmerston's own mouthpiece. 'With this I have acquired the secret of the "open sesame" of the others I may need,' he wrote from his new lodgings in Savile Row. He had expected weeks, if not months, of disappointment. 'Although this success is due to an accidental combination of fortunate circumstances which I could not have concerted . . . it has nevertheless greatly encouraged me.'[64]

In the days running up to the debate, Hotze and James Spence helped several of the Southern supporters with their speeches. Meanwhile the American legation was still frantically putting together a rebuttal of the Confederates' statistics. Benjamin Moran spent every waking hour with William Forster, coaching him on his answers, hoping that Forster's debating skills were more polished than his manners. Moran was flabbergasted to discover that the MP was married, and his wife 'a nice and ladylike person'.[65]

On Friday, 7 March the combatants assembled in the public galleries of the Commons to watch their proxies fight. The Confederates appeared confident despite the news in yesterday's papers of the Federals' double victories at Roanoke and Forts Henry and Donelson. The House was more crowded than normal for a Friday evening and from his vantage point in the Diplomatic Gallery, Moran noticed there were a large number of Cabinet ministers present. William Gregory's pro-Southern speech was in his usual ebullient style. Every cheer from the House brought a smile to the Confederates and a wince to the legation. His claim that Britain was supporting an illegal blockade to the detriment of her own workers appeared to strike home with many members. After he sat down, a large number left for dinner, evidently having decided there was no need to listen to any more speeches in support of the motion. Forster was well into his speech when the House refilled. 'We watched closely', recorded Mason, 'as Forster went on with his exposé, and reduced the tables down almost to nil.' To his surprise, Forster's speech received an even more favourable reception than Gregory's. Palmerston appeared to be listening intently and Gladstone had actually turned around to watch Forster.

After Forster sat down, however, the Federal and Confederate observers realized that the Ministry had merely been biding its time while it waited for the supporters of both sides to declare themselves. Sir Roundell Palmer now rose to speak on behalf of the government. A thin, pale man with an unfortunate lisp and squeaky voice, Palmer was no one's choice as a debater, but as the Solicitor-General he was more qualified than anyone else present to speak on the legality of the blockade. Palmer's shyness had always made him seem devoid of emotion – 'Bloodless', his critics called him. Tonight, though, unmistakable moral outrage against the South and all that it represented ran through his speech. The government would remain neutral, he declared, because 'honour, generosity and justice' demanded it 'and because it was the only course consistent with the Divine law, that we should do to others as we would wish others to do to ourselves'. Years later, at the end of a long and illustrious career, he remembered the debate with pride. 'The speech ... gained me more applause than, perhaps, any other which I ever made.'[66]

There were more speakers – Thurlow Weed had primed at least twenty to speak on the North's behalf – but it was obvious to all except Mason that the Confederates had lost the debate. When Gregory rose for the second time it was to withdraw his motion. Weed was immediately surrounded by a dozen MPs who came over to shake his hand, while only a couple sauntered over to commiserate with Mason.[67]

The following morning, Adams tucked in to a celebratory breakfast at the legation with Weed, Bright, Forster and several other supporters. Adams admitted to the group that he had ceased to worry about the debate once he learned of the Federal victories. 'Mr. Gregory', he announced, 'could not have selected a more difficult moment for himself as the current of opinion is setting much the other way. Nothing shines so dazzling to the military eye of Europe as success.'[68] Adams was allowing his cynicism too much rein. Moreover, if such success could sway political opinion so could a cotton famine. Though it had not happened yet, Mason informed the State Department on 11 March that supplies 'were now very low', and the cotton workers were dependent on charity 'to keep them from actual starvation'.[69] The cause of the South in England, he assured them, was by no means lost.

OVER THE WAY.

Mr. Bull. "OH! IF YOU TWO LIKE FIGHTING BETTER THAN BUSINESS, I SHALL DEAL AT THE OTHER SHOP."

Punch's John Bull knows there is an alternative supply of cotton

The First Blow against Slavery

Ambiguous attitudes – Consul Dudley vs. James Bulloch in Liverpool – Henry Adams is embarrassed – Rise of the ironclads – Farewell to Russell – A brilliant manoeuvre

Not once during the blockade debate had any of the speakers referred to slavery. The issue was an embarrassment to both sides. Northern supporters were not allowed to claim that the war was to end slavery, and Southern supporters naturally could not say, as John Stuart Mill had so trenchantly put it in an essay published shortly before the debate, that the South was fighting for the right 'of burning human creatures alive'.*[1] Nor would they, since every Confederate sympathizer in Britain assumed that the South would abolish the 'peculiar institution' as soon as its economy could sustain free labour.

A speech by Gladstone to an audience in Manchester in April 1862 – many of whom were being financially drained by the war – revealed the extent to which ambiguity over the slavery question benefited the South and damaged the North. Gladstone asked the question that was deeply troubling his listeners: were they suffering for nothing? There was, 'no doubt', he declared, 'if we could say that this was a contest of slavery and freedom, there is not a man within the length and breadth of this

---

* William Yancey arrived back in New Orleans thoroughly disheartened by his mission. Cotton was a false god, he announced to the crowd that had gathered to greet him. The Queen was in favour of the North, and Lord Palmerston was not interested in aiding the South. 'Gladstone we can manage, but the feeling against slavery in England is so strong that no public man there dares extend a hand to help us. We have got to fight the Washington Government alone'.[2]

DIVORCE À VINCULO.

Mrs. Carolina Asserts her Right to "Larrup" her Nigger.

Punch reminds the British that the South is fighting to keep its slaves

room, there is, perhaps, hardly a man in all England, who would for a moment hesitate upon the side he should take'.[3]

The Duke of Argyll berated Gladstone for allowing himself to be blinded by fashionable opinion. 'That this war is having a powerful, a daily increasing effect on the hold of slavery over opinion in America is, in my judgment, a fact so evident ... that I cannot understand its being in question,' he wrote impatiently.[4] But Gladstone felt vindicated for expressing his doubts after he received a letter from a Liberian diplomat named Edward Wilmot Blyden, who declared that he was 'very glad of the position which England maintains with reference to the war ... Both sections of the country are negro-hating and negro-crushing.'[5]

Seward's interdiction against calling the conflict a war for abolition was so strict that Adams was placed in the invidious position of having to turn away supporters of the Northern cause who wanted to help. When a deputation from the British and Foreign Anti-Slavery Society visited the legation in April, 'expressing interest and sympathy with our cause', he could only say a few platitudes about voluntary emancipation after the war.[6] This 'was not much to their liking', according to Benjamin Moran.[7] It was not enough for Adams to echo John Stuart Mill, that one set of people were fighting for independence in order to keep another in bondage; his listeners wanted him to promise abolition.

Although the slavery question was a persistent stumbling block for both sides in their bid to win public support in Britain, there was nothing to prevent them from waging unrestrained and barely concealed war on every other front. 'Both the Northern and Southern parties have chosen to make this country a kind of supplemental fighting ground,' railed the *Liverpool Mercury* on 10 April 1862. 'Their respective agents here have been extremely active in their efforts to promote their own cause, as well as to discover and thwart the plans of their opponents. Each party has a place here which may be styled its headquarters; each party has in its service a number of agents, scouts and spies . . .'

James Bulloch, the Confederate navy's purchasing agent and architect of its overseas fleet, had returned to England on 10 March aboard one of Fraser, Trenholm's commercial vessels. He had been expecting to hear that the *Oreto* – one of the two raiders commissioned the previous year – was already launched. Instead, he found the vessel bobbing uselessly in Liverpool harbour, in plain view of the world. He quickly went about looking for a captain and crew who could sail it out of port before the authorities became suspicious of the empty but martial-looking ship in their midst.

Bulloch was too late. Federal agents had known about the *Oreto* for several weeks and were already trying to have her seized for contravening the Foreign Enlistment Act. His new adversary, now that Henry Sanford had been forced to confine his operations to continental Europe, was Consul Thomas Haines Dudley, the dour but intrepid Quaker from New Jersey. As a young lawyer he had actively fought against slavery, taking extraordinary risks such as disguising himself as a slave trader, complete with whip and pistols, and travelling to the South to rescue a free black family who had been kidnapped and forced into slavery. But, at the age of 36, Dudley narrowly survived a ferryboat fire that killed more than thirty people, leaving him with permanent physical and mental scars. After his recovery he concentrated on politics; Lincoln had owed him a sinecure for his help in securing the Republican nomination, and had offered him either the legation in Japan or the lower position of Consul in Liverpool. Dudley had chosen Liverpool because he thought the doctors would be better in England. Yet he did not intend to ride out his appointment like Charles Wilson at the legation in London.[8] His experience on the ferryboat had left him determined to live the rest of his life with force and conviction.

Dudley's personal appearance pleased no less a critic than Benjamin Moran, who thought him 'as intelligent as he looks'.[9] Tall and wavy-haired, with a sad-looking face that was framed by a neatly trimmed beard, he seemed unthreatening to Moran; but Moran was not on the receiving end of Dudley's surveillance operations. Within six months of his arrival at the Liverpool consulate, Dudley had created a new intelligence network that far outstripped Sanford's effort. The team consisted of himself, his Vice-Consul Henry Wilding, the London Consul Freeman H. Morse, and a large number of operatives under the direction of Matthew Maguire, Pollaky's more reliable replacement. It was expensive to find spies who were both effective and trustworthy, but this was one area where Seward was so far prepared to be generous.[10]

Dudley was able to insert his men only around the fringes of Confederate society, but it was enough to penetrate their defences. One operative gained hold of the list of Confederate agents in Britain, another obtained proof that the suspicious ship with the capacity to carry sixteen guns in Liverpool was definitely one of Bulloch's raiders.[11] Charles Francis Adams forwarded Dudley's report to Lord Russell, and the government began quietly conducting its own investigation.[12] By the middle of March, Dudley believed that he had all the information he needed to lodge a protest with the city's customs officials. He could also prove that the *Oreto* was not destined for the Italian navy, as Millers claimed.

Bulloch was aware of Thomas Dudley's scrutiny, however, and already had a strategy, based on the legal advice given to him last year, to thwart his attempts to have the vessel seized. An English captain and crew would sail the ship out of Liverpool with not a single military component on board; once in neutral waters, the *Oreto* would rendezvous with a cargo vessel to receive her guns and supplies. Caleb Huse was put in charge of procuring the arms shipment. The timing could hardly have been worse for him. His funds had run out and he was forced to borrow small sums from friends in Liverpool – £200 here and £1,000 there – to cobble together the cargo, all the while being 'watched by the agents of the United States wherever I may go', as he complained to Major Josiah Gorgas of the Confederate Ordnance Bureau.[13]

When the Liverpool authorities inspected the *Oreto* at Dudley's request they found nothing that actually contravened the Foreign Enlistment Act, even though it was unusual for a merchant ship to have gun ports. They refused to impound her until Dudley could produce more concrete evidence. Bulloch was lucky, but it would only be a matter of time before something or someone incriminated them and the ship's clearance would be revoked. On 22 March, a chill, misty morning, the *Oreto* was slowly guided out of the harbour, ostensibly to test her engines. On board there was a small party with female guests to give credence that the vessel was simply going on a Saturday outing. But, as soon as she left the harbour, the passengers clambered down into the pilot boat and the *Oreto* steamed out to sea. From now on she would be known under her new name, the CSS *Florida*.

Bulloch had taken a gamble by sending off the *Florida* without arms or a proper crew. Although the Captain, James Duguid, knew the truth since he was William Miller's son-in-law, the rest of the English crew had been told they were bound for Palermo. Bulloch was relying on John Low, a Scotsman who had emigrated to the South in his early twenties, to protect his investment. Low was travelling on the *Florida* as a passenger, though in reality he had command of the vessel. His orders were to have the *Florida* delivered to Nassau, Bahamas, where he was to hand the ship over to Lieutenant John N. Maffitt (whom Bulloch knew well and believed was resourceful enough to know what to do with her) or, in his absence, any Confederate officer.

Thomas Dudley was convinced that the Liverpool customs officers had dragged their feet during the investigation into the *Florida*. A report in late March that the US navy had captured Captain Pegram and the *Nashville* off the coast of North Carolina cheered the Federals a little but did not lessen their sense of grievance against the British authorities, whom they suspected of ill-concealed bias towards the South. Adams went to see Russell on 25 March to protest against England's laxity over

Confederate violations of the Foreign Enlistment Act. Russell listened sympathetically until Adams's indignation took on such a strident tone that he undermined his case. 'Adams has made one of his periodical blistering communications about our countenancing the South,' reported an internal Foreign Office communiqué after the meeting.[14]

Russell found the Minister's charge of bias especially unfair after the government's concessions to the North, not least its propping up the shaky legal foundations of the blockade.[15] Their relations deteriorated further after Adams complied with Seward's instruction to remonstrate once more against Britain's declaration of belligerency. This was not some 'local riot' of twelve months' duration, expostulated Russell. Furthermore, he complained, when it came to blockade violations why was Britain always being made out to be the villain, when other nations were following the same practice?[16]

Ironically, while Adams was accusing Russell of being insincere, the French Emperor was playing a multiple hand between his own ministers and the rival American camps. Much to the annoyance of everyone except the Confederates, Napoleon held several private interviews in April with the shipping magnate William Schaw Lindsay MP. He had played a significant role during Anglo-French negotiations of the 1860 trade treaty and was easily able to gain an audience with the Emperor without exciting the suspicion of the British embassy. Napoleon said everything Lindsay wished to hear.[17] John Slidell's spirits soared when Lindsay reported back to him. 'This is entirely confidential,' he wrote to James Mason in London, 'but you can say to Lord Campbell, Mr Gregory etc. that I now have positive and authentic evidence that France only waits the assent of England for recognition and other more cogent measures.'[18] Russell was so annoyed by Lindsay's interference that he refused to meet him when the MP returned to England. The Confederates were elated, however, by the news from France; Consul Morse reported to Seward that the 'Rebels here confidently predict two or three great southern victories and the recognition of the Confederate States before the adjournment of Parliament'.[19]

The commencement of Parliament had brought with it the resumption of Lady Palmerston's 'At Homes'. Neither James Mason nor Henry Hotze was on the guest list, but Benjamin Moran was able to finagle an invitation for himself, Charles Wilson and Henry Adams. He was one of the first guests to arrive at Cambridge House on 22 March and spent the early part of the evening gawping at his surroundings. The 'drawing rooms are not so large as one might expect', he pronounced, but they were brilliantly lit for the occasion and as more people entered they 'began to assume an animated and even gorgeous appearance'.[20] Too shy to speak to strangers, he hovered in corners and by tables. Henry Adams, on the other hand, arrived determined to make this his entry into society. He longed to be friends with 'Counts and Barons and numberless untitled but high-placed characters'.[21] Henry just hoped that the 'unfortunate notoriety' caused by his caustic comments on English high society in 'A Visit to Manchester' had been forgotten in the intervening three months. At the foot of the lofty staircase he gave his name to the footman, only to hear it called up as 'Mr Handrew Adams'. He corrected him and the footman shouted loudly, 'Mr Hantony Hadams'. 'With some temper', Henry corrected him again, and this time the footman called out, 'Mr Halexander Hadams'. Henry accepted defeat and 'under this name made [my] bow for the last time to Lord Palmerston who certainly knew no better'.[22] After this painful event he decided it was not worth trying to storm the social ramparts of 94 Piccadilly.

'I have no doubt that if I were to stay here another year, I should become extremely fond of the place and the life,' Henry mused to his brother, Charles Francis Jr., on 11 April. But for now he had a 'greediness for revenge'. He approved of the Chief's 'putting on the diplomatic screws'. England should not be allowed to wriggle out of her responsibility for aiding the Confederates. At least the *Nashville* 'has been taken or destroyed', he wrote. Moreover, it turned out that the *Harvey Birch*, which CS Captain Pegram had triumphantly claimed as his first capture, belonged to Confederate sympathizers. Writing on the same day, Bulloch warned the Confederate Secretary of the Navy, Stephen Mallory, that Pegram's mistake had caused them considerable embarrassment. Indiscriminate attacks on Northern ships were perhaps not the best method of waging war.[23]

Despite Charles Francis Adams's complaints to Russell, Bulloch knew better than anyone the truth about the government's intentions. It 'seems to be more determined than ever to preserve its neutrality', he wrote in disappointment; 'the chances of getting a vessel to sea in anything like fighting condition are next to impossible'. The fate of his prize cruiser under construction, Lairds' No. 290, now preoccupied him. He had her moved to a private 'graying dock' where she would be masted and coppered out of sight of prying eyes. But with the *Nashville* captured and the *Florida* sailing off on a blind adventure, defenceless and without a real crew, Bulloch was beginning to wonder whether they were pursuing the right course of action. His anxiety was, for the moment, misplaced. Three days later, on 14 April, Benjamin Moran recorded in shock: 'It seems as though the *Nashville* was not captured at Beaufort, N.C., but escaped. This is one of the most mortifying events of the war to us. Our naval officers on the sea-board have covered themselves with disgrace.'[24]

'I cannot say that my value as a sailor had increased materially during the voyage,' wrote Francis Dawson after the *Nashville* arrived at Morehead City, North Carolina, on 28 February. He was so relieved to be on dry land that it hardly mattered to him that he was homeless and friendless. Captain Pegram departed for Richmond as soon as they docked, bearing boxes of much-needed supplies, including stamps and banknote paper. Dawson was left to find his own lodgings. 'I had determined to take my discharge from the *Nashville*, and decide, by tossing-up, which one of the various companies named in the newspaper I should join.' Pegram, however, made good on his promise. 'I also wish to call specially your attention to the sacrifices made by Mr Frank Dawson,' he wrote to Stephen Mallory in early March. The 'young Englishman' had 'left family, friends, and every tie to espouse our cause', and, 'not to be put off by any difficulties thrown in his way, insisted upon serving under our flag, performing ... the most menial duties of an ordinary seaman'.[25] On the strength of his recommendation, Dawson was appointed master's mate, the lowest officer rank in the navy. Pegram personally gave him the news, 'one furious cold morning', while Dawson was 'scraping the fore-yard, wet through with the falling sleet and intensely uncomfortable'.[26]

Dawson's orders were to report for duty at the Norfolk shipyard in Virginia. This was the same destination as Pegram, who was going to take command of a ship that was still in dry dock. 'To crown my satisfaction,' Dawson recorded, 'Captain Pegram told me that he intended to make a visit to his family, in Sussex County, Virginia, and would be glad if I should accompany him, and remain with him until it was necessary to go to Norfolk.' They left Morehead on 10 March and took the train

The Confederate steamer *Nashville*, having run the blockade, arrives at
Beaufort, North Carolina

up to Virginia. The young man was fascinated by the alien landscape
that rolled past his window; there were no neat hedgerows and green
pastures filled with sheep, only mile after mile of scrub and woodland.
Dawson's short stay at the Pegrams' plantation exceeded his wildest
expectations. The family adored him and local worthies hailed him as a

foreign knight come to their rescue. Dawson was already a convert to the Southern cause; all the attention he received gave him personal as well as fanciful reasons to embrace the Confederacy. 'You may rest assured', he wrote earnestly to his mother, 'that while one of her children has power to wield a sword or pull a trigger, the South will never desist from her struggle against the Northern oppressor.'[27]

On the day of his departure, news reached the plantation of the CSS *Merrimac*'s encounter with the USS *Monitor*. The ships were the result of a frantic race between the North and South to construct the first American ironclads. The Confederates won, by twenty-four hours, when they launched the *Merrimac* (renamed the CSS *virginia*) on 8 March 1862. The vessel was an old US warship that had been burned by Union sailors when they abandoned the Norfolk Navy Yard in Virginia the previous summer. Since then the *Merrimac* had been completely remodelled except for her engines, which the Confederates had not had time to repair. Engineers literally 'clad' the *Merrimac* in iron plates and added a ram to the stem of the ship. Long and squat, she looked more like an iron champagne bottle or a turtle than a ship. Her speed was terrible but the armour plating made her invincible. When the *Merrimac* slowly steamed into Hampton Roads to confront the Federal blockading fleet, nothing like her had ever been seen before. Hampton Roads is a wide body of water where three large rivers converge before flowing into Chesapeake Bay and out into the Atlantic. The Union navy had been in control of the bay and Hampton Roads for almost a year. Stephen Mallory knew that it was vital for the Confederacy that he take them back, and as the wooden Union gunboats fired ineffectively at the *Merrimac*'s hull, it seemed as though he would.

There was cheering in Richmond and hysteria in Washington after the battle. Lincoln called a special Cabinet meeting where the new Secretary of War, Edwin Stanton, made a spectacle of himself, ranting that every city on the eastern seaboard would now be laid waste. The Secretary of the Navy, Gideon Welles, was unfazed. The newly clad and outfitted *Monitor* was already on its way to Hampton Roads, and he expected a more favourable outcome than the previous day's rout. The equally strange-looking Federal vessel, described by some as a 'tin-can on a shingle' (the tin-can being a revolving turret that could fire in any direction), could not sink the *Merrimac* but was powerful enough to pin her down. After four hours of point-blank firing, both ships withdrew, damaged but not inoperable. The possibility that the *Merrimac* might yet force its way to Washington had almost as powerful an effect on Edwin Stanton as the first Hampton Roads bombardment. To stop the Confederate monster, he wanted the main water-channels to Washington blocked with sunken ships.

Lord Lyons was fascinated by reports of the encounter between the two ironclads. 'This is, I suppose,' he wrote to Lord Russell, 'the severest test to which the system of coating vessels in iron armour has yet been exposed.' The officers of Rear Admiral Milne's North Atlantic Squadron were equally agog. The ironclad warships in the British and French navies had, for obvious reasons, never been tested in the same way. Milne's entire fleet would have gladly assembled to watch another encounter, but the coveted task was awarded to Commander William N. W. Hewett of HMS *Rinaldo*, who was told to loiter near Fortress Monroe (at the entrance of Chesapeake Bay) 'in order to obtain as much information as possible'.[28] Newspapers in the North and South were hailing the battle as a revolution in naval warfare, not to mention proof that America would one day rule the oceans.[29] Francis Dawson saw the *Merrimac* when he reported to the Norfolk Navy Yard. He noticed something that Commander Hewett had been too far away to see: that the vessel's armour plating was actually railroad tracks rolled flat.

Lyons was frustrated that he had no eyewitness reports of the battle to pass on to the Admiralty. None of the British journalists he relied upon for news had been present; increasingly of late, their applications for military passes were being turned down by the War Department. The worst affected was William Howard Russell. He had returned from a two-month sojourn in Canada on 1 March, having failed to persuade *The Times* to release him from his contract. 'I am writing to you, my dear Morris, as a friend,' he pleaded with the managing editor of the paper, Mowbray Morris. Russell listed all the reasons – family, financial, even life and death itself. 'I have not met a man in Canada who has not declared to me he never thought I should have left the United States alive ... if you could see what I have had to bear in railway trains and in the street you would at least give me the credit of no common devotion.'[30]

Russell's fears were soon confirmed. It was useless to remain in Washington, he told Morris, because no one would speak to him. 'They are determined, I hear, to throw every impediment in my way,' he wrote.

McClellan is never to be seen by me, his staff are all surly ... the officers I know are fearful of being attacked in the press if they are pointed out for any civility to me. Therefore I never get any intelligence of what is going to be done and secrecy on all points is so well kept I don't hear of any event coming off, and so cannot get a chance of describing it.[31]

His friends were sympathetic but there was nothing they could do to reduce the prejudice against him.

The small band of British journalists in Washington had increased by two with the arrival of Edward Dicey of the *Spectator* and, recently, a freelance writer named Francis Lawley. They were liable to suffer the same penalty as Russell if they travelled together, but neither was as keen to see action as Russell: a little excursion to General Louis Blenker's camp and back was sufficient war reporting for them. Blenker was a German exile from the Revolution of 1848, whose division 'was filled with black sheep of every nation under the sun', wrote Dicey. 'The word of command had to be given in four languages, and the officers were foreigners almost without exception.'[32] Francis Lawley was rather grateful for the opportunity to take things easy for a time. He had joined Anthony Trollope for part of his tour of the Midwest after Rose Trollope went home to England. Lawley and Trollope were friends and distant cousins, a tie that played an increasingly important role as the journey became more challenging. Neither was accustomed to travelling rough, and both thought the other was a ninny over the hardships they endured. After 120 miles on a provincial railroad, Lawley declared that an Englishman did not know discomfort until he had experienced a crowded American carriage, going 15 miles an hour across flat nothingness for an entire day.

At 36, Lawley was still young enough to retain the air of a man of promise. But by this stage in his life he had already taken that promise and squandered it several times over, until it seemed to his friends and family that it would never be fulfilled. He was the youngest son of the 1st Baron Wenlock. Success had come to him easily. He was a Fellow of All Souls College (the academic citadel of Oxford) at 23 and an MP at 27. Six months later, in 1852, he achieved an even greater coup when the then Chancellor of the Exchequer, William Gladstone, made him his private secretary. In 1853 his name was put forward for Governor-General of South Australia. To those who did not know him, it seemed as though he was leading a charmed existence. Only those closest to him knew his terrible secret. Lawley was a gambling addict.[33] Ironically the governorship, which he had only accepted to escape his racing debts, proved to be his undoing. The Colonial Secretary objected to sending an unreformed gambler to govern the South Australians. This unexpected rejection led to some unsavoury revelations. Since Lawley had already resigned his seat in Parliament, believing the post was his, he was suddenly faced with loss of his reputation, his career and his only source of income. He fled England to escape his creditors.

Lawley made a new life for himself, of sorts, as a freelance writer in New York. He admired the energy and optimism of Americans, telling his close friend and fellow gambler William Gregory, 'this nation is destined to be greater than the greatest'.[34] When the war started, Lawley was able to increase his income slightly by writing articles for English newspapers. He was not sure it was gentlemen's work. 'It is hard', he confessed to his family, 'to write and enter into very minute details without trenching upon information gained in the familiarity of private conversation, and to this I have an intolerable aversion.' He was fortunate that the *Daily Telegraph* took a relaxed attitude to the objectivity of its foreign reports. Lawley was resolutely pro-Northern and had no intention of touring the South: 'I can do better as a correspondent in the North,' he wrote, 'seeing it only and writing from a one-sided view, than if I saw both sides and was embarrassed thereby.'[35]

Washington suited Lawley very well. His travels with Trollope had trained him to be less delicate about the presence of mud, and his chronic shortage of funds made him just like everyone else. The 'Buccaneers' at the legation welcomed him at once and he was given a role in their production of a burlesque opera called 'Bombastes Furioso'. A large part of the English community in Washington was in the play. William Howard Russell reported to Mowbray Morris that it 'was a complete success at the legation and Shiny William, as I call Seward, complimented me immensely'.[36] This was an impolitic admission for one who was seeking his recall on compassionate grounds. 'It is your business to report the military proceedings of the Federal Army,' complained Morris, 'and so I repeat: Go to the Front or come home.'[37]

Russell felt that neither Delane nor Morris understood his position or else they would not keep insisting that he go where he was barred from entering. Russell could not help worrying that he had made a mistake in returning to Washington. Vizetelly had decided to go out west, and the idea no longer seemed so hare-brained; a significant battle had taken place on 7 March at Pea Ridge, near the Arkansas–Missouri border. President Jefferson Davis had sent a new general, Earl Van Dorn, to take over the disorganized forces in the region. This much Van Dorn achieved. The little general with a large ego boasted to his wife that he would take his army all the way north to the city of St Louis in Missouri. His plan was simple: a Union army of only 11,000 men, under US General Samuel R. Curtis, controlled the passage from north-west Arkansas into Missouri; Van Dorn would divide his own army into two forces, surround the Federals front and back, and then pounce in a surprise attack.

William Watson, the Scotsman who had joined the 3rd Louisiana Infantry in New Orleans the previous summer, was at first relieved by Van Dorn's arrival, but he soon developed misgivings over whether the new general understood the limitations posed by territory or was aware of the real condition of the army. Their supplies were already low when he gave the order for every man to be ready to march with ten days' rations in his haversack. But Union sympathizers had sent word to General Curtis of the Confederates' approach: Curtis was waiting for them.

The Battle of Pea Ridge, Arkansas, began on 7 March as the fog lifted from the trees to reveal a grey winter morning. Watson and his fellow soldiers had been marching through frost and snow with little sleep and no food for almost seventy-two hours. 'Cold, hungry, and fatigued we moved sullenly along,' he wrote, 'some of the lads almost sleeping on their feet.' They thought they had marched to the rear of the Federal forces only to discover 'that they were also in our rear, and they had the advantage of being in a strong position'. Watson's regiment had stumbled into the centre of the waiting Federals; when the firing died down, the 3rd's officers were all either dead or missing, except for one remaining lieutenant. Fortunately, the sun was beginning to set and the soldiers who had survived were able to creep away under the cover of darkness. The following morning, a Federal counterattack broke the Confederates' line and the Rebels fled the battlefield, Van Dorn first. Watson and his fellow soldiers were left to fend for themselves. It was a 90-mile march to the nearest Confederate stronghold, a trek through rattlesnake-infested country, without food or maps. Seven days later Watson staggered into the border town of Van Buren, 400 miles from Van Dorn's stated destination of St Louis. In retrospect, Watson admitted, 'I never got what the Americans would call the "hang" of this battle . . . It was a mass of mixed up confusion from beginning to end.'[38] Nevertheless, the outcome was clear; the Confederates had suffered 2,000 casualties, the Federals 1,384, and US General Curtis's victory ensured that the key border state of Missouri would stay in Northern hands.

The Federal victory out West made General McClellan's failure to commit the Army of the Potomac in a major battle look all the more inexplicable. Lincoln had tolerated the General's arrogance (though he did not know that McClellan referred to him as 'the gorilla') and shown leniency when the army did not advance into Virginia on 22 February as directed. But his patience was now at an end. Lincoln ordered McClellan to have the Army of the Potomac in motion no later than 18 March. Russell could hardly believe that something was finally going to happen after almost eight months of anticipation. He visited McClellan's headquarters and asked permission to accompany the march. McClellan agreed, with the usual proviso that Russell first obtain the necessary pass from the War Department. As Russell was busily writing his letters, reports began to filter through of a general retreat by the Confederate army. CS General Joseph E. Johnston had also heard of McClellan's order to move south and had concluded that his own army of 40,000 men would be wiped out in its present position near Manassas. On 8 March, Private Sam Hill and the 6th Louisianans were ordered to dismantle the camp that had been their home since July the previous year, and prepare to march 25 miles south of Manassas to the Rappahannock river. Leaving behind nearly everything of value, including precious batteries, food supplies and arms, Johnston's army trudged along single-track roads under incessant rain. Many fell sick with chills and diarrhoea. 'I remained doing what I could,' wrote Sam's sister, Mary Sophia Hill, about her own activities during the dreadful trek through knee-deep mud. She had left the regiment in December in order to visit New Orleans, 'to see my sister, and get money from Ireland'. The blockade prevented her remittance from coming in, but Mary still raised $150 in donations for the regiment and obtained several boxes of clothes and medicines. Her efforts went for nought, however; by the time she eventually reached Virginia all but one of her trunks had been stolen. The old civilities of the South were gradually giving way to a harsher reality. Richmond itself was under martial law.

Sam Hill's brigade finally reached its new camp on the south bank of the Rappahannock on 17 March, acting as the rearguard while the rest of Johnston's army continued on to Orange Court House, an Italianate building in a town of that name, with sweeping steps and a rectangular bell tower not unlike some of the grand residences in New Orleans. Mary managed to find rooms in a little cottage nearby. Here was a pleasant place to rest, even under the leaden skies of a wintry spring. Although the Louisianans were waiting for orders, Mary was kept busy with wounds and injuries, often the result of fighting among Major Chatham Roberdeau Wheat's 1st Louisiana Special Battalion. The Louisiana 'Tigers' were such a lawless lot that the commander of the Louisiana Brigade had two of them executed by firing squad. Major Wheat was a veteran of Garibaldi's Sicily campaign and in March he received a visit from a friend he had not seen since leaving Italy. The visitor was Henry MacIver, the young man who had annoyed William Howard Russell by asking for directions on how to sneak across Federal lines after Bull Run. MacIver had managed to escape from his prison cell in Alexandria, steal the clothes and weapon of a Union soldier and slip into Confederate territory. After briefly being detained as a Yankee spy, MacIver was finally able to achieve his wish and joined the Confederate army. He was made a cavalry instructor with the rank of lieutenant and attached to General Thomas J. 'Stonewall' Jackson's staff.

General McClellan was embarrassed that Joe Johnston, whose timely arrival at Bull Run caused the Federals to flee, had now succeeded in moving to a new, unknown position. The Confederate's actions led McClellan to alter his plans and adopt a far more radical strategy involving the transportation by sea of 100,000 soldiers, plus supplies, horses and equipment, to Fortress Monroe on the tip of the Virginian peninsula. From there the army would march 70 miles west to capture Richmond. The first troops began to be shipped out from Alexandria on 17 March. Edward Dicey was able to join a group of observers that included Nathaniel Hawthorne, who had become a great friend, but Russell was once again forced to stay behind. On 24 March, he wrote in his diary that it was 'One of the saddest days I have had in all my life, and Heaven knows I have had some sad ones, too'.[39] Russell was referring to an article in the *New York Herald* that accused him of having speculated on

the Stock Exchange using information obtained from the British legation during the *Trent* affair. The paper printed a copy of a telegram sent
by Russell to his friend, the lobbyist Sam Ward, which appeared to support the allegation. But it was false. All Russell had done was telegraph
Ward in New York ahead of the official announcement that the Commissioners were being released. This was perhaps unwise, but Russell
claimed that the news was all over Washington by the time he sent the
notice. Ward had a copy of the real, undoctored telegram, which proved
Russell's innocence of any financial dealings, but no newspaper would
print his explanation.

Russell was mortified by the slur on his character, especially after
Lord Lyons let it be known that he regarded the telegram as a gross
breach of trust. Not surprisingly, Francis Lawley sympathized with Russell's predicament and tried to smooth his relations with the legation.
But Russell found Lawley's earnest attempts to help almost as humiliating as the original slander. It was not comfortable to be told to stay
away 'as far as you can, from the British Legation, during the next five
or six weeks', and to refrain 'from any step which, however remotely,
has the appearance of a desire to push yourself into the old relations'.
Although the attachés claimed they believed Russell's protestation of
innocence, he feared they would never fully trust him again. He was
lonely and fed up. His friend William W. Glenn, a Southern journalist,
offered to provide him with safe passage to the Confederacy. Russell
was tempted, but decided 'I could not, I think, with honour or propriety
go South immediately after so long a residence among the Northern
armies'.

Lyons forgave Russell and, at the end of March, invited him back to
the legation for dinner. Russell was doubly grateful, not only for the
rehabilitation of his character, but also because it gave him the opportunity to corner Edwin Stanton and embarrass him into writing out
a pass then and there. Stanton was, however, determined to confine
Russell to Washington, even if it meant revoking the pass of every war
correspondent in the country. On 2 April 1862 the War Department
announced that it would no longer recognize press passes and all reporters currently following the army in Virginia were to return to Washington
or be arrested.[40] After two days of uproar, the Department clarified its
stand so that only foreign journalists were affected. Russell wrote to
Stanton on the 2nd, pleading with him to reconsider: 'I can not conceive

Sir, the object of such conduct.' What, he asked, was the 'cause for the change on your part towards me'.[41] Stanton never replied. By now Russell had written to Lincoln, four generals, Seward, Sumner and 'innumerable Senators', all without success.

'In the South,' Russell wrote ruefully, 'the press threatened me with tar and feathers . . . the Northern papers recommended expulsion, ducking, riding rails, and other cognate modes of insuring a moral conviction of error.' He would not have allowed himself to be cowed by these threats. But he accepted defeat, 'when to the press and populace of the United States, the President and the Government of Washington added their power'. Sam Ward tried hard to dissuade Russell from leaving and complained to Seward that Stanton had 'tomahawked' the North's most valuable foreign asset.[42] The Secretary of State paid scant attention to Russell's departure. Stanton's appalling blunder of driving away the world's most famous war correspondent would only become clear later on when the North had no foreign journalists reporting from its side.

Russell set sail for England on 9 April on board the *China*. 'I saw the shores receding into a dim grey fog,' he wrote; 'our good ship pointing, thank Heaven, towards Europe.'[43] His wife and children had not seen him for over a year, his financial affairs were in a deplorable state, and his career, so it seemed to him, was crumbling. Russell used his final dispatch from New York, on 3 April, to explain to readers why he was abandoning his assignment. They were probably more forgiving than his employers, John Delane and Mowbray Morris, who both sent frantic letters begging him to continue at his post. 'It is lamentable that at such a time we should be practically unrepresented,' grumbled Delane, since J. C. Bancroft Davis had also resigned, on grounds of ill health. *The Times* did agree to honour the £1,340 that Russell had paid out of his own pocket while in America, but took nearly two years to verify every receipt and expense.[44]

Years later, Lord Lyons told William Howard Russell that his presence in Washington during the first year of the war had greatly enlivened the legation and that it was a duller place after he left. Lyons's irritation with Russell over the telegram scandal had been less to do with the offence than with its timing. Lyons was in the middle of secret negotiations with Seward on a joint slave trade treaty when the *New York Herald* published its accusation against Russell. Lyons could not afford to have the legation dragged into a disreputable row when so much depended on discretion and staying out of the public eye.

Lyons had always believed a slave-trade treaty between the two countries was impossible. Only three years before, the mere possibility that the Royal Navy might try to stop an American vessel to search for slaves was sufficient to provoke threats of war. Britain had backed down and the slave trade had flourished. There was scant hope in London that the Lincoln administration would have Congressional support to revisit so contentious an issue. In May 1861 Seward had tried to skirt round Congress by offering to sign a secret memorandum allowing the Royal Navy to stop and search suspected American slavers. But since the offer had coincided with his menacing dispatches to Adams, Lyons and Lord Russell had agreed that Seward's word was 'worth little or nothing' when it came to Anglo-American relations.[45] They had misjudged the sincerity of Seward's intentions, however. The secret memorandum idea was no trick on his part, even if he had not thought through the impact on the public if a Royal Navy vessel sailed into New York harbour with a captured slaver in tow.

The slave trade issue returned when Captain Nathaniel Gordon was sentenced to death on 7 February by a New York court for the crime of participating in the Atlantic slave trade. It was the first successful prosecution of a slave trader for forty-four years, and outcry for Lincoln to pardon Gordon was considerable but not deafening. Lord Lyons wondered whether this was a sign he should speak to Seward about a treaty. Slave-trading was on the increase again, since blockade duty had taken away US navy ships that had been patrolling the west coast of Africa.[46] The only practical way to stop it was to give the Royal Navy the right to challenge slavers flying the American flag.

With relations between the legation and the State Department still in a honeymoon period after the *Trent* affair, Lyons suggested to Lord Russell that they revive the slave trade question while Seward was still 'in the mood'.*[47] As it turned out, Seward had also been toying with the

---

* One of the biggest areas of contention between Lyons and Seward had recently been removed when the War Department assumed responsibility for political arrests. 'I think it is well that the arrests should be withdrawn from Seward,' Lord Lyons had written on 18 February; 'he certainly took delight in making them, and, I may say, playing with the whole matter. He is not at all a cruel or vindictive man, but he likes all things which make him feel that he has power.'

idea of resurrecting negotiations, but neither Lyons nor Seward had given the issue quite the attention that Lord Russell had obviously expended. On 28 February 1862 he surprised Lyons with a printed draft of a slave trade treaty, with all the provisions and exclusions that the Americans might demand already included. Russell also gave Lyons discretionary power on any changes, so that momentum would not be lost. Seward's reaction to the document would show him in his best light, as a gifted politician whose creative manipulation of people and issues could bring about results that were otherwise unobtainable.

Seward liked the proposed treaty and was determined to have it ratified. His abhorrence of the Atlantic slave trade became evident to the journalist Edward Dicey, who went to dinner at his house on 22 March, when the secret negotiations were under way. It was another of Seward's foreign military dinners: Colonel De Courcy, General Blenker and his aide de camp, Prince Felix Salm-Salm of Prussia, were also present. Poor Fanny Seward had taken a violent dislike to De Courcy: 'He appeared very well as long as he kept still and did not say much at the dinner table,' she wrote. 'But after dinner his brilliant capability of making himself disagreeable showed forth with undimmed luster. Added to being ill bred, awkward, and a terrible stare-er, he has the distinction of one of the most ugly and repulsive of faces.' Dicey was also falling in Fanny's estimation until she scrambled her knitting and he sat on the floor to help her untangle the mess.[48] After dinner, Dicey stayed behind after the others had left and discussed the slave trade with Seward. The journalist did not pick up that the Secretary of State was speaking in the past tense: 'The Republican Administration would have merited the condemnation of every honest man if whatever else it had left undone, it had not put a stop to the Slave Trade.'[49]

The 'whatever else' referred to Lincoln's failed attempt to win support from the border States for a gradual emancipation bill.[50] In January, Carl Schurz, the US Minister in Spain, had visited the White House to discuss the reasons for the North's unpopularity in Europe. After being told by Schurz that it was a mistake to hide the anti-slavery aims of the war, Lincoln replied:

'You may be right. Probably you are. I have been thinking so myself. I cannot imagine that any European power would dare to recognize and aid the Southern Confederacy if it becomes clear that the Confederacy stands for slavery and the Union for freedom.' Then he explained to me that, while a distinct anti-slavery policy would remove the foreign danger ... he was in doubt as to whether public opinion at home was yet sufficiently prepared for it. He was anxious to unite, and keep united, all the forces of Northern society and of the Union element in the South, especially the Border States, in the war for the Union. Would not the cry of 'abolition war,' such as might be occasioned by a distinct anti-slavery policy, tend to disunite those forces and thus weaken the Union cause? This was the doubt that troubled him, and it troubled him very much.[51]

The objections of the border States to any form of emancipation within their own State lines forced Lincoln to go far more slowly than he wished. To avoid the same difficulties as Lincoln, Seward asked Lyons to play an elaborate game of subterfuge with him. In a brilliant political manoeuvre, he used the border States' traditional antipathy towards England to trick them into supporting the slave trade proposal. He altered the wording of the draft so that the proposal came from the United States to Great Britain, rather than the reverse. Then he added a ten-year limit to the treaty, and asked Lyons to make objections to it at first, only to allow himself to be publicly beaten down by the force of Seward's arguments. 'Mr Seward's long experience of the Senate, and his well-known tact in dealing with that Body, gives his opinion on such a point so much weight,' explained Lyons to the Foreign Office on 31 March, 'that I naturally thought it prudent to be guided by it.' Lord Russell responded drily that credit for the treaty was 'immaterial' to Her Majesty's Government so long as the slave trade was suppressed.[52] Lyons dutifully performed his role as directed by Seward, and grudgingly 'changed' his mind after a testy exchange of notes.

The Cabinet was unanimous in its congratulation of Seward, with the exception of Gideon Welles, who would not be dissuaded that Britain had an ulterior motive in agreeing to the treaty. 'Yesterday was the anniversary of my arrival three years ago at Washington,' Lyons wrote to Russell on 8 April. 'I celebrated it by signing the Treaty for the Suppression of the Slave Trade.'[53] Nothing, except permission to go home, could have given him greater satisfaction. 'Weary years they have been in many respects,' he wrote, but the treaty made them seem worth the sacrifice. April was a good month for the abolitionists; a week later, on the 16th, President Lincoln signed into law a bill abolishing slavery in

Washington (Sumner had accused him of being the largest slave-owner in America for his delay in freeing the 3,000 slaves in and around the capital). At the beginning of the war 'it was the fashion amongst English critics', wrote Edward Dicey, 'to state that the whole Secession question had no direct bearing on nor immediate connection with the issue of slavery. As to the letter, there was some truth in this assertion; as to the spirit, there was none.' Finally, one year after the Federal evacuation of Fort Sumter, the 'letter' and the 'spirit' of the 'Secession question' were converging.

Five Miles from Richmond

Shiloh – Fall of the Crescent City – The 'Woman Order' –
Vizetelly's change of heart – 'Percy, old boy!' – Lord Edward is
duped – General Lee takes the field – The Seven Days' Battles –
McClellan retreats – 'This is Butler's doing'

Lyons and Seward were quietly congratulating one another over the success of the slave trade bill when the North won its first major victory of
the war on 7 April 1862, at the Battle of Shiloh. The battle, which took
place on Tennessee's southern border, was a first on several counts. It was
the first time Americans witnessed the mass slaughter that comes with
large-scale combat. It was also the first intimation that no single battle, no
matter how terrible, would end the war; and for young Henry Morton
Stanley of the Dixie Grays, it was 'the first time that Glory sickened me
with its repulsive aspect, and made me suspect it was a glittering lie'.[1]

More than 100,000 soldiers fought in the two-day battle. Stanley's
side was led by CS General Albert Sidney Johnston – who was regarded
by his Northern opponents as the ablest general in the Confederacy –
and CS General Beauregard, the hero of Fort Sumter and Bull Run.
They had hoped to launch a surprise attack against US General Grant
while he rested his army of 40,000 men along the wooded ravines of the
Tennessee river at Pittsburg Landing. 'Shiloh', which means 'place of peace'
in Hebrew, was a small Methodist church where Brigadier General William T. Sherman's division had set up camp.

Johnston had chosen to attack Grant at Pittsburg Landing because
he knew that an additional 25,000 reinforcements under US General
Don Carlos Buell were coming from Nashville. Once the two armies
combined, Grant's numerical superiority would be overwhelming and

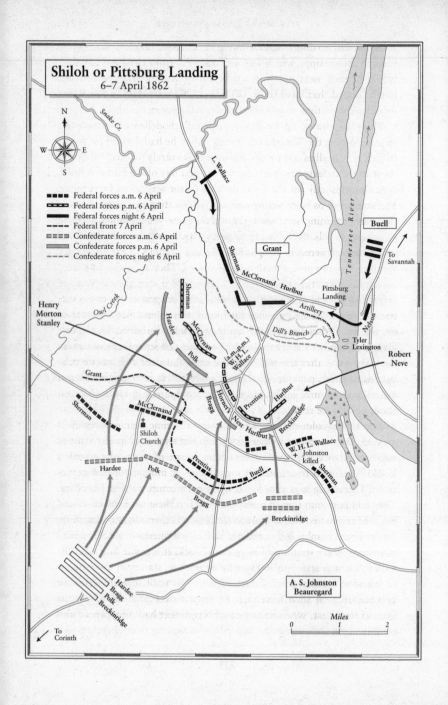

Shiloh or Pittsburg Landing
6–7 April 1862

N

Snake Cr.

■■■■ Federal forces a.m. 6 April
□□□□ Federal forces p.m. 6 April
■■■ Federal forces night 6 April
– – – Federal front 7 April
▨▨▨ Confederate forces a.m. 6 April
▨▨▨ Confederate forces p.m. 6 April
– – – Confederate forces night 6 April

L. Wallace

Tennessee River

Buell

Grant

To Savannah

Sherman

McClernand   Hurlbut

Pittsburg
Landing

Artillery

Nelson

Henry
Morton
Stanley

Owl Creek

Sherman

Hardee

McClernand

Polk

Dill's Branch

Tyler

Lexington

(a.m.,p.m.)
W. H. L.
Wallace

Robert
Neve

Grant

Bragg

Hornet's Nest

Prentiss

Hurlbut

Sherman

McClernand

Shiloh
Church

Hurlbut

Breckinridge

W. H. L. Wallace

Johnston
killed

Hardee

Polk

Prentiss

Buell

Sherman

Bragg

Breckinridge

Hardee
Bragg
Polk
Breckinridge

A. S. Johnston
Beauregard

To
Corinth

Miles
0   1   2

Johnston had no doubt that capturing the strategic railroad junctions at Corinth, Mississippi, which was only 22 miles from Pittsburg Landing, would be their next object. Johnston's own army was 44,000-strong, but he hoped that General Van Dorn and the survivors of Pea Ridge would arrive in time to give him additional support.

The plan, drawn up by Beauregard, was modelled on Napoleon's strategy during the Waterloo campaign, when he had divided his forces to pick off the allies one by one. Historic plans rarely translate well, and those of the defeated even less so; yet the first day of the battle, 6 April, began promisingly for the Confederates. Grant was taken by surprise. Sherman's troops were sitting by their tents, eating their breakfasts in the warm morning sun, when the Rebels came yelling and whooping out of the woods. 'Stand by, Gentlemen,' Stanley's captain had ordered while they gathered in formation. The boy standing next to Stanley stooped down to pick a small posy of violets. 'They are a sign of peace,' he told Stanley. 'Perhaps they won't shoot me if they see me wearing such flowers.' Impulsively, Stanley also stuck a sprig in his cap. Once they charged, 'We had no individuality at this moment ... My nerves tingled, my pulses beat double quick, my heart throbbed loudly, and almost painfully,' Stanley recalled. The Rebel yell jerked him out of his fear. 'The wave after wave of human voices, louder than all other battle-sounds together, penetrated to every sense ...' He remembered he was not alone but surrounded by 400 other companies. 'I rejoiced in the shouting like the rest.'[2]

The Union soldiers had fled Shiloh by the time Stanley's regiment arrived. The Confederates were stopped in their tracks by the sight of such abundance. Here was a neat little village of tents, many with a smoking stove in front, and all surrounded by mounds of new equipment. Everything was superior to their own camp, even the bedding. The sudden resumption of cannonfire recalled them to their senses and the soldiers moved off. A short while later, whether it was five minutes or five hours Stanley did not know, he heard a piteous cry behind him. 'Oh stop, *please* stop a bit.' He glanced back. It was the boy with the violets. He was standing awkwardly on one leg, staring at the remains of his foot.[3] Henry Stanley continued to run until something hit his belt-buckle with such force that he flipped over and landed on the ground head first. When he came to, his regiment had disappeared and all was silent.

As he stumbled through the forest, he almost fell again, tripping over a body lying face up. The eyes of the dead soldier seemed to stare back at him. With a shock, Stanley recognized him as the 'stout English Sergeant of a neighbouring company . . . This plump, ruddy-faced man had been conspicuous for his complexion, jovial features and good humour.' The more he ran the more bodies he encountered. The dead, he recalled, 'lay thick as the sleepers in a London park on a Bank Holiday'. The rest of the day became a series of wordless images. By the time he found his company again only fifty men remained.

Johnston and Beauregard's Waterloo strategy fell apart in an area known as the 'Hornet's Nest', where a sunken road acted like a defensive trench for Federal troops, enabling them to hold steady for six hours against dozens of Confederate assaults. General Johnston was killed leading the final charge; a bullet tore through an artery in his leg, causing him to bleed to death in minutes. The Union soldiers holding the Nest surrendered at 5.30 p.m.; but by then Grant had formed a new defensive line along the river. He had been driven back two miles but his army was still intact. 'We've had the devil's own day, haven't we?' remarked Sherman to Grant after the fighting stopped. '"Yes," he said, with a short, sharp puff of the cigar; "Lick 'em tomorrow, though."'[4]

Grant always used simple language when he spoke; the 40-year-old general was a quiet, plain figure whose forcefulness and intelligence were cloaked behind an unassuming manner. Associates struggled to describe him: 'he is rather under middle height, of a spare, strong build; light-brown hair, and short, light brown beard,' wrote an aide to General Meade. 'His face has three expressions: deep thought, extreme determination; and great simplicity and calmness.' Unlike McClellan, Grant had never aspired to become an American Napoleon; he had not even intended to become a professional soldier. 'A military life had no charms for me,' Grant wrote of his time at West Point, 'and I had not the faintest idea of staying in the army even if I should be graduated, which I did not expect.' But Grant remained in the army for eleven years, fighting in the Mexican–American War of 1846–8, and subsequently spending the next six years on mindless garrison duty, developing and failing to conquer a drink habit. Although happily married to his wife, Julia, and a devoted father to their four children, Grant floundered in civilian life. One year he was reduced to pawning his watch to buy Christmas presents for the family. When the war broke out, Grant was working as clerk in his father's tannery in Galena, Illinois – a humble climbdown for the former captain. Within six months of volunteering, however, Grant had risen from colonel to brigadier general and, in addition to his old nickname in the army of Sam – for his initials U. S. (Uncle Sam) – had acquired the new national nickname of 'Unconditional Surrender Grant', because of the terms he had offered to the defeated Confederates at Fort Donelson.[5]

Sherman's short conversation with Grant on the night of the 6th was actually one of the first between them. Sherman had suffered a nervous breakdown during the autumn of 1861 and had only recently returned to duty. Sherman was the opposite of Grant in mannerisms; his tall, wiry frame was always moving, he gesticulated as he spoke and often worked himself up into an excitement during conversation. But in many ways the pattern of his life was similar to Grant's: Sherman had also struggled in civilian life; he too loved his wife and adored his children; and he had also fought his own private battles of the mind. The latter forged an unbreakable bond between them. Sherman later remarked: 'Grant stood by me when I was crazy and I stood by him when he was drunk. And now we stand by each other always.' In turn, Grant said of him: 'Sherman is impetuous, faulty but he sees his faults as well as any man.' Both were realists, neither was an abolitionist, and each approached the task of warfare in the same relentless and dogged spirit. Sherman had briefly wondered if they should retreat on the 6th, until speaking to Grant reaffirmed his resolve.

During the night, US General Buell and his reinforcements sailed down the river to Pittsburg Landing. By contrast, flooded roads and a damaged rail system meant that Van Dorn's battle-ravaged Confederate army was still sitting 250 miles away in Little Rock, Arkansas. This was good news for William Watson and the 3rd Louisiana Regiment, who were spared the fight, but it was a disaster for Beauregard. The weather turned, and a harsh downpour pelted the living and the dead. Flashes of lightning revealed the presence of wild pigs, which had been attracted by the smell of fresh meat. Neither side had expected such high numbers of casualties and many of the 10,000 wounded were left out on the field all night, their screams so terrible that a Confederate soldier wrote, 'This night of horrors will haunt me to my grave'.[6]

For many of the reinforcements, including an Englishman named Robert Neve of the 5th Kentucky Volunteers, this was their baptism of war. 'Boys,' said his commander in the morning, just before sending the regiment off into the woods, 'we shall beat them today, for their general is killed. He was shot yesterday in leading a charge.' The news had no real meaning for Neve except that his side was apparently doing better than the Rebels. Yesterday, the Confederates had attacked; today it was their job to return the favour. Neve's regiment surged through the woods like hunters flushing out their prey. Occasionally, a stray shell interrupted their momentum. With every foothold gained, Neve's confidence rose; fighting was not so bad after all. The exhausted Confederates made a game effort to repel the invaders. Henry Morton Stanley's company marched forward in skirmishing order. The young soldier stood in a daze until his captain barked, 'Now, Mr Stanley, if you please,' which mortified him. He rushed blindly forward, straight into a pocket of Federal soldiers from Ohio. Two of them wanted to shoot him immediately, but an officer saved his life. As he was marched off to the Union camp, they chatted about 'our respective causes, and, though I could not admit it', he wrote later, 'there was much reason in what they said'. The slavery question 'could have been settled in another and quieter way, but they cared all their lives were worth for their country'.[7]

General Beauregard ordered his army to retreat to Corinth, more than 20 miles away. In the confusion after the battle, hundreds of wounded men were left behind, along with the abandoned wagons and artillery guns that had become stuck in the mud. Beauregard's reputation for tactical genius was also a casualty, although Grant's received a knock, too, for the way he was taken unawares on the first day. The total number of casualties was staggering: more than 23,000 men, or 25 per cent of the forces engaged.

Shiloh was not the only blow to the Confederacy. That same day, the famously abrasive and arrogant commander US General John Pope captured another strategic point – Island No. 10 on the Kentucky–Tennessee border. Edward Dicey had travelled west to Cairo, a commercial depot on the Mississippi river just above the Mason–Dixon line. He watched as great hospital steamboats disgorged their wounded from Shiloh and Island No. 10. 'All day and all night long you heard the ringing of their bells and the whistling of the steam.' Piles of coffins waited on the jetty, 'with the dead men's names inscribed upon them, left standing in front of the railway offices'.[8]

*

In Virginia, General McClellan had already landed two-thirds of his army at Fortress Monroe, which guarded the entrance to Hampton Roads, and was marching up the peninsula towards Richmond when the Confederate Secretary of the Navy, Stephen Mallory, sent a small fleet to attack the remainder of the ship transports. On 11 April, the *Merrimac*, accompanied by six vessels, steamed towards the Federal fleet and its *Monitor*. Francis Dawson had been assigned to the *Beaufort*, which, despite its grand-sounding name, was only a small tugboat with one gun. 'The general idea was that the *Monitor* would be overwhelmed by the combined attack,' wrote Dawson. But the *Monitor* refused to leave the cover of Fortress Monroe, disappointing HMS *Rinaldo* and two French warships that had moved in to observe the fight. One of the Confederate gunboats did manage to capture three transports, which elicited an indiscreet cheer from the *Rinaldo*, but otherwise little was achieved in the expedition. When Dawson returned to the base he was relieved to learn that he was being transferred. Captain Pegram had been given command of an ironclad in New Orleans, and Dawson was to join him.[9]

The French Minister, M. Mercier, visited Richmond a few days later on 16 April, expecting to hear talk of surrender.[10] Instead, that afternoon, the Confederate Congress – which had only 26 Senators and 135 Congressmen – passed a draft law conscripting all able-bodied men between 18 and 35. When Mercier met with his old friend Judah Benjamin, who had been transferred by Davis from the War Department to the State Department in March, he was told that the South would fight to her last breath. Northerners were 'a people for whom we feel unmitigated contempt as well as abhorrence', Benjamin declared with uncharacteristic heat.[11] Sitting in the new Confederate Secretary of State's spacious but austere office in the former US Customs House, Mercier realized that Benjamin was hoping that the French could be enticed into breaking the blockade in return for cotton and the promise of a free-trade agreement. But Mercier knew it was not France that needed persuading.

When Mercier returned home to Washington on 24 April, Lyons went to see him immediately, worried lest his impetuous colleague had made promises to the Confederates that would undo their joint policy of neutrality. Mercier was more excited than usual. He spoke eloquently of the Southern spirit and the reasons why France and Britain should cease dallying and recognize her independence. The South was preparing to recoup its losses, he insisted. Even now, the Confederates were on the verge of completing a second ironclad that would render New Orleans invincible to naval attack. Moreover, they were prepared to lose Richmond, Tennessee, 'New Orleans and all their seaports, and indeed the whole of the coast'.[12] Even as Mercier was talking, a fleet of US gunboats were bearing down on New Orleans, having subdued the supposedly impregnable forts that defended her.

The city officially surrendered on 26 April. The train on which Francis Dawson and his friend Captain Pegram were travelling was within 20 miles of New Orleans when it pulled into a side track. To their astonishment, train after train came rumbling past in the other direction, each one packed with evacuating soldiers. 'There was no choice for us but to go back to Virginia,' Dawson wrote. The much-vaunted ironclad that should have been Pegram's next command was out of their reach. 'The journey back was worse than the journey down, as the delays were multiplied,' Dawson remembered. Despite Mercier's optimism, this last defeat was sending waves of panic through the South. 'New Orleans gone – and with it the Confederacy,' came the anguished cry of the diarist Mary Chesnut.[13] Rumours that General McClellan was almost at Richmond sent people rushing out of the city. Clerks packed up the government archives and prepared them for removal; President Davis put his wife and children on the train for Raleigh, North Carolina.[14]

For six days, until the arrival of US General Benjamin Butler and his 15,000 troops, New Orleans was a city on the verge of anarchy. Fires burned unchecked; looters roamed at will; all commerce, including the delivery of foodstuffs, abruptly stopped. Rioters stormed the Mint and one, William Mumford, succeeded in tearing down the US flag that had been installed on US Admiral David Glasgow Farragut's orders. It was then dragged through the streets of the city. In retaliation, Farragut warned that he was sending his men ashore and would bombard the city unless the US flag was flown from City Hall. The desperate Mayor turned to the foreign Consuls to save New Orleans from immolation. He begged them to send the 4,500-strong European Brigade, which was made up of foreign neutrals who were not liable for the draft but who had volunteered for civil defence duty.[15] The arrival of the French warship the *Milan* allayed the Consuls' trepidation over sending a group of middle-aged 'merchants, bankers, underwriters, judges, real-estate owners and capitalists' into riot duty. The Brigade proved to be a poor substitute; as darkness descended each night, recalled an observer, the city glowed by the light of the arsonist's torch and the faint but urgent ringing of fire bells wafted out across the water.[16]

On 1 May, 2,500 Northern soldiers marched through rubble and rubbish-strewn streets to take up positions in the chief public buildings. The residents of the magnificent St Charles Hotel were turfed out to make way for General Butler and his retinue, while the Customs House became his headquarters. Butler let it be known that, henceforth, every citizen would live and abide by his rules alone. 'The hand that cuts your bread can cut your throat,' he announced.*[17] A successful lawyer by profession, Ben Butler could fight hard and dirty when circumstances demanded. Force of will and astute back-room tactics had won him the military command of the New Orleans operation – a remarkable feat considering that his two previous commands had been marred by breathtaking incompetence.

Among Butler's first acts was the capture and execution of William Mumford, who was strung up from the same flagpole that had flown the desecrated US flag. He also issued a raft of edicts. Any house used by sharpshooters would be destroyed.[18] Shopkeepers who refused to sell to Union officers would have their goods confiscated. Overt displays of partisanship would be judged without mercy – a woman who laughed loudly at a passing Union funeral cortège was sentenced to two years' imprisonment.[19] Almost anyone who wished to do business in the city was first required to take an oath of allegiance.

Nor was Butler the least troubled by diplomatic niceties. When the Consuls protested against their citizens having to take loyalty oaths, he invited them to leave the city. He declared all foreign funds in their safe-keeping to be Confederate contraband and therefore liable to seizure. Union soldiers forced their way into the Dutch consulate, and bullied the hapless Consul into opening his vault. When Butler attempted the same with the French consulate, however, Count Mejan reminded him that a French ship-of-war was moored on the river. Butler also punished

---

* Butler was one of the first politicians to be made a general in the volunteer army. It was his success in raising regiments – and his support for the war as a Democrat – rather than any previous military experience which won him the rank. He had joined the Massachusetts militia as a 21-year-old, and had risen to become a brigadier general without ever hearing a shot in battle.

the members of the British Guard (a company in the European Brigade), who had sent their uniforms and weapons to friends in the Confederate army. Two were imprisoned and another thirty-seven were forced to leave the city.[20]

Lord Lyons thought it was 'very imprudent' for the British Guard to engage in such un-neutral behaviour, but he was sufficiently alarmed by Consul Mure's reports to order the *Rinaldo* to proceed to the city. New Orleans had always been a byword for lawlessness and truculence and the absence of menfolk had little effect on cowing its abandoned wives and daughters. They wore Confederate colours, sang songs, hissed, spat, turned their backs and on one famous occasion dumped the contents of a chamber pot on Union soldiers. In retaliation, on 15 May Butler issued General Order Number 28, which held that 'hereafter, when any female shall by word, gesture, or movement, insult or show contempt for any officer or soldier or the United States, she shall be regarded and held liable to be treated as a woman of the town plying her avocation'. Washington dismissed the document as a crude piece of Southern propaganda until newspapers from New Orleans confirmed it.[21]

Butler's 'Woman Order' galvanized the South more effectively than any speech or partial victory might have achieved.[22] The Confederate armies in the West had become demoralized after the recent spate of defeats. The loss of Island No. 10 had increased Federal control of the Mississippi river to within attacking distance of Memphis, the Confederacy's fifth largest city and the river gateway into Mississippi. Many of the regiments in General Beauregard's army had come to the end of their twelve-month terms and wanted to return home. One of his corps commanders, Braxton Bragg, who was promoted to general after Shiloh, refused to let them go and, to make his point, deserters were shot without trial. William Watson's 3rd Louisianans were among the twelve-month regiments. The men were furious with Bragg until the 'Woman Order' became known. 'The feeling of indignation which was roused by Butler's acts overcame in a great measure the disaffection that had been fast spreading through the army,' wrote Watson. 'Many were roused to a spirit of revenge . . . not that they hated Davis and his Bragg the less, but that they hated Lincoln and his Butler the more.'[23]

By mid-May Beauregard's Army of the Mississippi had swelled to around 70,000 Confederates. But he was facing a massive new entity called the Army of the West, which had 120,000 soldiers. The US general leading this army was Henry Halleck, the second most senior general after McClellan. Known as 'Old Brains' for his treatise on military theory, Halleck had taken charge after Shiloh as the senior general, and had combined the three Federal forces under Buell, Grant and Pope. Although Halleck was moving slowly towards Corinth, Mississippi, Beauregard did not think that the time he had in hand would allow him to prepare any better for the Federals' arrival. He understood the city's importance to the South. 'If defeated here,' he wrote to Jefferson Davis after the army had retreated to Corinth from Shiloh, 'we lose the whole Mississippi Valley and probably our cause.'[24] But given the choice between railroads and men, Beauregard chose the latter. His chief concern now was to save his army.

Halleck arrived at the outskirts of Corinth on 26 May. The pickets in Watson's regiment traded jokes and insults with their Northern counterparts. 'We were glad to hear they had an abundance of coffee,' wrote Watson, 'as we trusted that it would fall into our hands.' In just a few more days Corinth would be completely surrounded and no more supplies would reach Beauregard's wilting army. On the 29th Watson was on a picket duty when his squad was late returning and became lost in the darkness. 'We therefore concluded to seek out a quiet, snug place in the woods and lie down till daylight.' The next morning they awoke to an unnatural silence. Walking back to camp they discovered it was empty. During the night Beauregard had succeeded in evacuating his entire army. It was one of the greatest military manoeuvres of the war. Like most of the rank and file, Watson had been utterly ignorant of Beauregard's elaborate plans to deceive Halleck.

Watson and his men headed off in the direction of Corinth. There they found the railroad and walked along its broken track. Every now and then they came across large groups of Confederate deserters. They were mostly volunteers from Bragg's division – Tennessee men whose main concern now was to protect their farms and families from looting soldiers. Watson did not blame them. He too wished to return home to New Orleans. The Queen's proclamation of neutrality meant that the new conscription law could not apply to him. 'I now considered that I had faithfully fulfilled my engagement to the Confederate States, and trusted they would do the same by me.'[25]

General Halleck's soldiers marched into Corinth on 30 May, only to find a filthy ghost town. The General was furious at being denied his great battle, but 'most of the men and officers were glad of it', wrote Robert Neve of the 5th Kentucky Volunteers. The Englishman wrangled a pass into town and went scavenging around the defensive works, kicking over discarded treasures and occasionally finding something interesting, like a bowie knife. 'I also found a note directed to General Halleck. It said: "If you think there is no HELL or here-after, follow us. Yours, Blythe's Regiment, Mississippi Volunteers."'[26]

The peaceful capture of Corinth did not result in the praise Henry Halleck had expected. Indeed, quite the reverse. The Chicago *Tribune* sneered at his 'barren triumph' and called it 'tantamount to a defeat'.[27] Newspapers across several States followed suit. The acrimony over the Confederates' retreat revealed Halleck's poor relationship with the press. Reporters wishing to follow his army were firmly discouraged from making the attempt, as Frank Vizetelly discovered.[28] It had felt like a deep personal sacrifice to say goodbye to his friends in the Army of the Potomac. 'I was proud of the position I had achieved among them,' he wrote. During the past twelve months, 'I have sought my fortune with the soldiers of the Potomac ... so thoroughly had I become identified with them that numbers of the officers and – I am not ashamed to say it – men, looked upon me as an old friend'.[29]

On 14 May Vizetelly informed readers of the *Illustrated London News* that he had transferred from the US army to the US navy. 'The last you heard of me, [I] was waiting in St Louis for a reply from General Halleck,' he wrote. The response to his request had been disappointing; Halleck had not officially barred him from the Army of the West, but had forbidden him from using government transport. It amounted to the same thing, Vizetelly pointed out, since he could not paddle a canoe, 'charter a steamer specially to carry me, or swim up the Ohio and Tennessee Rivers', just to follow the army. Happily, he discovered that the naval authorities were indifferent to his presence. Vizetelly was granted permission to observe the river operations on the Mississippi.

'Leaving St Louis late in the afternoon,' wrote Vizetelly, 'I found myself steaming down its rapid current in one of those floating palaces.' There seemed to be no 'shore' along the river; 'nothing but submerged forests for miles and miles back, with here and there a clearing showing the locality of a plantation'. His destination was Fort Pillow, the last Confederate obstacle before Memphis. Vizetelly remained on board for six weeks as the Union fleet wound its way down the river. Despite the growing heat, he was often confined to his tiny cabin, as sharpshooters hidden in the tangled thickets along the river proved to be too accurate for safety. Vizetelly was convinced that the South was wasting her men on a losing cause. 'We find that each day the North is developing her gigantic resources,' he wrote. The South had no shortage of brave men, 'but her army is growing weary'. 'I have spoken with numerous desert-ers, prisoners, and others, and they have, with few exceptions, expressed themselves heartily sick of the war.'* [30]

At daybreak on 6 June, the Union and Confederate flotillas steamed towards each other in their final confrontation. As Memphis came into

Confederate sharpshooters firing from the banks of the Mississippi
at the Federal fleet, by Frank Vizetelly

* Northerners had pointed out to Vizetelly the staggering disparities between the two sides. The last economic figures before the war showed that the Southern States had 18,026 'industrial establishments', and the North, 110,274.[31]

view, Vizetelly saw that there was a line of eight Confederate vessels waiting to block them. High above, stretched out along the bluff in front of the city, were thousands of spectators. Their cheers turned to wails as the Confederate fleet was smashed to pieces. 'Never was a success so complete and so cheaply purchased by the victors; never an enemy so humiliated,' Vizetelly wrote in jubilation. 'The stars and bars have been trailed in the dust ... verily the Memphians have eaten dirt.'[32]

Destruction of the Confederate 'cottonclads' off Memphis, by Frank Vizetelly

However, when the readers of the *Illustrated London News* next heard from their war correspondent, Vizetelly was suffering from a crisis of conscience. 'Your readers must understand that I never saw anything of Southern people until I landed at Memphis,' he wrote. 'A "peculiar institution" of theirs had prejudiced me somewhat against them, and I believed from all I heard that the Secession movement was but skin deep after all.' But 'in Memphis and its immediate neighbourhood I made it my business to mix with all classes and test their loyalty or disloyalty ... all were clamouring for separation. If then, such are the sentiments of the entire South, and defeat does not bring them nearer to the Union, what is to be the result of all this bloodshed?'[33] For the first time he questioned whether he had been supporting the right side.

Vizetelly was not the only Briton to undergo a change of heart in June.

Henry Morton Stanley, formerly of the Confederate Dixie Grays, joined the Union army on 7 June. Stanley had been sent to Camp Douglas, outside Chicago, along with hundreds of other Confederate prisoners.[34] About 26,000 men were sent there during the war; at least 6,000 never came out. The inmates called it '80 acres of hell'. 'The appearance of the prisoners startled me,' Stanley recalled. Every man was filthy, emaciated and crawling with vermin.[35] To reach the latrines Stanley was forced to step over half-naked men lying in great puddles of faeces, either too weak or delirious to move themselves. 'Exhumed corpses could not have presented anything more hideous than dozens of these dead-and-alive men,' he wrote. 'Every morning, the wagons came to the hospital and dead-house, to take away the bodies; and I saw the corpses rolled in their blankets, taken to the vehicles, and piled one upon another.'[36]

More than 300 of the 8,000 prisoners in the camp claimed to be British subjects, and a group of them demanded to see the British Consul, John Wilkins. He turned to Lord Lyons for advice. Surely, Wilkins asked, they should try to secure the release of those who had been forcibly conscripted into Confederate service. Lyons encouraged him to 'exert all his influence unofficially in their favour', but he deemed it hopeless to use official channels since it would be impossible to prove whether a man had enlisted willingly or not.[37] The Consul argued and pleaded to see the British prisoners, but the authorities would not allow him inside the camp.[38] Stanley solved his own predicament by switching sides and enlisting for three years in Battery 'L' of the 1st Illinois Light Artillery. The 'increase in sickness, the horrors of the prison, the oily atmosphere, the ignominious cartage of the dead, the useless flight of time, the fear of being incarcerated for years ... so affected my spirits that I felt a few more days of these scenes would drive me mad'. He had never cared about politics anyway; 'there were no blackies in Wales.'[39] In mid-June the battery was shipped to Harpers Ferry in West Virginia, where Stanley was hospitalized for dysentery on the 22nd. Soon afterwards he went for a stroll around the hospital grounds, and did not return. He went home to Wales, eager for now to get as far away from the war as possible.

Stanley was lucky not to have been assigned to Battery 'K', which was sent to Tennessee to help US General George W. Morgan seize the Cumberland Gap from Confederate control. The Gap was a mountain pass through the Appalachians, where Virginia rubbed borders with Kentucky and Tennessee. The harsh Cumberland Mountains suddenly parted there, as though a spade had dug a 1,000-foot-deep slice through the rock, allowing the aptly named Wilderness Road to wind its way down to the rich basin known as the Blue Grass region. General Morgan realized that the Confederate stronghold could not be taken by a direct attack. The only option was to split up his brigades and have them clamber up and over the Cumberland Mountains along mule tracks, so they could launch a surprise assault on the Confederates from the other side.

The ex-British magistrate Colonel John F. De Courcy was ordered to lead his brigade through a steep gorge, flanked by sheer rock on one side and the Cumberland river on the other. It had been eight months since he had been given command of the 16th Ohio Volunteers. His men were pleased to have one of the best drillmasters in the Union as their colonel. But the ways of the British army were not those of a volunteer regiment, and the Ohioans considered him unduly harsh and exacting. He was no more popular with them than he was with Fanny Seward. De Courcy was at his best commanding larger forces where individuals were less likely to be the victim of his harsh comments. But General Morgan had realized that a soldier of De Courcy's experience made him invaluable and had promoted him to brigade commander.

The trek took more than two weeks and cost De Courcy many of his horses and all his supply wagons, which either broke or became lodged in the rocks. The brigades were weary and hungry when they reunited on the other side of the Gap on 18 June. The next day they discovered that the terrible odyssey had been for nothing. The Confederates, believing that General Morgan possessed a force of more than 50,000, had abandoned the Gap.[40] Nevertheless, Morgan became emotional when he reflected on the hardships endured by De Courcy's troops. 'Pardon me for speaking of the heroic bearing and fortitude of the Seventh Division,' he wrote to General Buell and Secretary Stanton. 'A nobler band never marched beneath a conquering flag.' He singled out De Courcy in particular, and asked that he be promoted to brigadier general. 'He is an accomplished officer and is every inch a soldier.' His request was ignored.

McClellan's peninsula campaign to capture Richmond was already under way by 20 June, although not in the manner expected by the US War Department. McClellan was laying elaborate sieges to Yorktown (where the British army had surrendered in 1781) and Williamsburg, towns that the three British military observers with him believed could have been taken with a bit of dash and very little fuss. They held their tongues though, and whenever anyone asked them for their opinion they confined themselves to praising the General's wonderful job in transforming civilians into soldiers. This was exactly what Lord Palmerston wanted. He later reminded Lord Russell that all officers observing 'federal forces in the field ... should be Strictly cautioned not to make any Criticisms which might be useful to the Federals in pointing out to them Faults or Imperfections ... The Federals are luckily too vain to attach much value to the opinions of Englishmen, but our officers might be told to open their Eyes and Ears and to keep their mouths Shut.'*41

A combination of poor intelligence-gathering and McClellan's own paranoia had led him to believe that he was heavily outnumbered by the Confederates defending Richmond. His demands for reinforcements brought about the deployment of the 1st New Jersey Cavalry, known as the Cavaliers, which had been left behind to guard Washington. The morale of the regiment had improved since the arrival of Sir Percy Wyndham, a 29-year-old English soldier of fortune, on 19 February, who had been assigned as its colonel by the War Department in an attempt to resolve the regiment's officer problems. Few men would have willingly accepted such an unhappy outfit, but Sir Percy was not the reflective kind. In the words of one officer, 'he strode along with the nonchalant air of one who had wooed Dame Fortune too long to be cast down by her frowns'.42

The regiment found Sir Percy's eccentricities rather endearing: dark hair crowned his head in a Byronic wave; a moustache and beard extended from his lips like bushy Christmas trees. He seemed to love dressing up and would change his uniform on the flimsiest of excuses. He looked younger than his years, even though he had been a soldier since the age of 15 and had served in the French, Austrian and British armies.43 Wyndham's parentage was dubious and his knighthood Italian (bestowed upon him by King Victor Emmanuel for his services during Garibaldi's campaign), but his skills and bravery were authentic. Although he dressed like a dandy, he possessed a temper that terrified the men. When enraged – which was apparent by the way he twiddled his moustache – Sir Percy was capable of anything, so much so that

---

* The Prince de Joinville excused McClellan's performance, claiming that the General had been constantly hamstrung and interfered with by Washington.

officers from other regiments insisted on wearing side arms when around him. The men learned how to drill because if one person made a mistake, he would force the entire regiment to keep repeating the manoeuvre until they dropped from fatigue. But instead of hating him, the soldiers felt an extraordinary sense of pride. 'Under our new Colonel our affairs have improved so much that we consider ourselves equal to almost any Cavalry Regiment in the field,' wrote its surgeon.[44]

The regiment was en route to the Army of the Potomac when a special messenger arrived with instructions to turn around and head for the Shenandoah Valley as quickly as possible, where it was to join a force under US General McDowell, of Bull Run fame. Jefferson Davis's military chief of staff, Robert E. Lee, had ordered Stonewall Jackson to create a diversion in the Shenandoah Valley so that Lincoln would not dare to send all the soldiers at his disposal to McClellan. The valley was like a gently undulating corridor with high, wooded mountain ranges on either side. The Shenandoah Valley Turnpike stretched for 125 miles, making it an ideal conduit for an invading force.

Jackson, a dour Presbyterian who rarely spoke, even to explain his orders, had originally been sent to defend the valley's abundant orchards and lush pastures. His performance in Virginia during the winter had been lacklustre, but since the beginning of McClellan's peninsula campaign he had beaten every force sent to stop him. He disabled one Federal army, under Fremont, on 8 May. Next he turned on US General Nathaniel P. Banks on the 23rd at Front Royal. This was Sam Hill's, and the 6th Louisianans', first experience of fighting. Their commander, Dick Taylor, recorded in his memoirs that at midday on the 23rd they were marching along a road heading north, when

> there rushed out of the wood to meet us a young, rather well-looking woman, afterward widely known as Belle Boyd. Breathless with speed and agitation, some time elapsed before she found her voice. Then, with much volubility, she said we were near Front Royal, beyond the wood; that the town was filled with Federals, whose camp was on the west side of the river, where they had guns in position to cover the wagon bridge, but none bearing on the railway bridge below the former ... All this she told with the precision of a staff officer making a report.[45]

It has been disputed whether Belle Boyd's courageous dash through active battle lines did indeed provide Jackson with new intelligence, but it was certainly news to Taylor, who ordered his troops to storm the town. The Federals surrendered after five hours of fighting. Colonel Henry Kyd Douglas, a childhood friend of Belle Boyd's, bumped into her 'standing on the pavement in front of a hotel, talking with some few Federal officers (prisoners) and some of her acquaintances in our army . . . as I stooped from my saddle she pinned a rose to my uniform, bidding me remember that it was blood-red and that it was her "colours"'.[46]

Two days after the Confederates' success at Front Royal, Sam Hill's brigade tore through Winchester, liberating it from Federal occupation. Mary Sophia Hill heard that Sam had been killed, 'so off I started for Staunton', she wrote, 'nearly crazy'. She eventually found Sam in a makeshift hospital. He was dirty and in shock, but his wounds were not life-threatening. She became determined to have him transferred out of his regiment.[47]

On 1 June Sir Percy and his rerouted Cavaliers arrived at Strasburg, to the west of Front Royal, just as Stonewall Jackson's troops were evacuating the area. Turner Ashby, a recently promoted Confederate brigadier general, was picking off Union soldiers who had the ill luck to advance too far forward. Sir Percy was fed up with hearing about the 'Black Knight of the Confederacy', as Ashby was called, and had declared to a journalist covering Federal movements that he was going to 'bag' the Rebel. Shortly after breakfast on 6 June, Sir Percy learned that one of Stonewall Jackson's wagon trains was stuck in the mud on the road to Port Republic, guarded by just a handful of Ashby's men. His orders did not include mounting offensives, but he could not resist the prize. Just before 2 p.m., he ordered his cavalry into formation and started off at a gallop in the direction of the stranded wagons. But Ashby and his cavalry were actually grazing their horses not far away. As Sir Percy galloped towards the woods straddling the road, he was stopped by a fierce countercharge from Ashby. The regiment's colours, sixty-four Cavaliers and Sir Percy himself were captured. The Englishman was furious with the behaviour of his troops, who he felt had barely put up a fight.[48] 'He would have stopped right there in the road and engaged in fisticuffs if he could have found a partner,' wrote a Confederate soldier.[49]

Sir Percy was still seething with rage when he arrived as a prisoner at the Confederate base, where his voice was immediately recognized by an old comrade from the Garibaldi campaign, Major Roberdeau Wheat of Virginia. According to Dick Taylor, Wheat shouted, 'Percy, old boy.' 'Why,

Bob,' the other rejoined. Wheat good-naturedly chided him for fighting on the 'wrong' side, and then stepped aside so that the Colonel could be brought before Stonewall Jackson.[50] That evening, while the two men were chatting in Jackson's office, news came that Turner Ashby had been shot through the heart during a later skirmish. A member of Jackson's staff quickly led Sir Percy away so that the General could be alone.[51]

By sunset on 9 June, the bulk of the Union forces in the Shenandoah Valley were in full retreat. A newspaper in Richmond declared: 'Strange as it may appear, news from the armies within five miles of [this city] is of secondary importance. Invariably the crowds which daily flock around the bulletin boards ask first "What news of Jackson?"'[52] With only 17,000 troops at his disposal, Jackson had succeeded against a combined Union force three times his strength, attacking it piecemeal and making full use of the valley's terrain. Yet the events taking place around Richmond were just as significant; on 31 May, CS General Joseph E. Johnston had launched an attack against McClellan's army. Known as the Battle of Fair Oaks, or Seven Pines, the campaign failed in all its objectives, but it did produce one stroke of luck for the Confederacy: the obstinate and increasingly ineffectual General Joe Johnston was struck by a bullet. President Davis replaced him with General Robert E. Lee, who had never before commanded troops in battle. He will 'be timid and irresolute in action', sneered US General McClellan when informed of Lee's appointment.[53]

Spring flooding postponed further movement by either army; and the lull had all Washington on tenterhooks. The five miles between McClellan and the city of Richmond seemed a mere hop and a skip to victory. Seward boasted to Charles Sumner that the war would be over in ninety days or less. Lord Lyons could not help wondering whether he was about to miss its most exciting moment. He had at last received permission to take a holiday, and was leaving on 18 June. Life in Washington was no 'bed of roses', he had often told his sister. But it was not until May that he had finally summoned up the nerve to ask Lord Russell for a leave of absence.[54] Lyons had grown despondent waiting for an answer; 'my chance of getting home seems less and less as I reflect upon it,' he wrote to his sister.[55] By the beginning of June he had persuaded himself that his case was hopeless. Then, on the 6th came Lord Russell's letter granting him three months' leave.[56]

Lord Lyons's final week in Washington started out well, with only the usual routine work.[57] This satisfactory state of affairs was ruined by the arrival of Lord Edward St Maur, a younger son of the Duke of Somerset, First Lord of the Admiralty. It was Lord Edward's older brother, Lord St Maur, who had briefly fought as a Red Shirt under Garibaldi. Lord Lyons thought that Lord Edward was risking his career in the Foreign Service for a cheap thrill and warned him that the presence of a British Cabinet Minister's son could lead to all kinds of unexpected trouble. But even he had not anticipated Lord Edward falling into the hands of Consul Bernal in Baltimore and his secessionist cronies. The Southern journalist W. W. Glenn remembered his first meeting with Lord Edward St Maur very well. 'He was quite young,' he wrote, 'and had a great dread of having his name in the newspapers ... on account of his father's position in the English Cabinet ... He was quite Northern [supporting] too.' Glenn had plans for the youth, however.

> I determined to devote myself to giving intelligent Englishmen every facility for acquainting themselves thoroughly with the true condition of Southern affairs and the spirit of the Southern people ... it might prove useful to make so intelligent a convert. Lord Lyons of course attempted to dissuade him from carrying out his project, and went as far as to tell Lord Edward that if he was caught and thrown into prison, he need expect no aid from him as Minister. Lord Lyons from the beginning did everything he could to prevent the slightest offense being given to the Federal Government ... He made later several remonstrances to me through his attachés.[58]

Dread at what might happen to Lord Edward overshadowed Lyons's otherwise joyful departure on 18 June. In Washington, President Lincoln shook his hand and asked him to convey 'his good intentions towards the people of Great Britain'. When Lyons reached New York, Seward stopped by his hotel to say goodbye. He promised that if anything did arise between the two countries while Lyons was away, he would place the matter on hold until his return.[59] Lyons was touched by these displays, although he had no illusion that the goodwill towards him was anything other than temporary and capricious. If he, rather than Mercier, had visited Richmond to explore the views of the Confederate government, the result would have been expulsion from the country and an apology demanded from Britain. The contrast between the public's attitude towards Britain and France also disturbed him. The French attempt to topple the Mexican government in the spring, Lyons noticed, had been accepted with an angry shrug, even though it mocked American claims to be the sole power in the region.* They 'are more civil to France than to England', he asserted to Lord Russell, 'partly because they never will have, do what she will, the same bitterness against her as they have against England'.[60]

Lord Edward knew that crossing the lines into Southern territory might be risky, but 'there is no imprudence in what I am doing – I have asked good advice', he assured his parents on 19 June. 'I do not intend to get into any chance of difficulties.'[61] Nor did he; Glenn's contacts proved their worth and Lord Edward was safely deposited in Richmond on 26 June. He did not think it odd that, with the Confederacy fighting for its life, President Davis would make the time to see him. Lord Edward was, perhaps, too young and naive to realize what the presence of an English Cabinet Minister's son would mean to Southerners. All Lord Edward had to do was say his name and government officials, staff officers and influential citizens opened their doors to him. 'There is a remarkably friendly feeling towards England . . . the only sign of ill-feeling that exists is on the subject of recognition,' he not surprisingly concluded. 'I saw and talked to everybody, I was very kindly treated indeed.'[62]

He was so well treated that other British subjects – many of whom were desperately trying to find any means of leaving the South – became quite jealous. The Confederates deliberately shielded him from the hardships and persecution often suffered by ordinary Britons. A young Scottish journalist named Gabriel Cueto, for example, had been held without charge since May.[63] Lord Edward never heard about him, and Cueto's case did not receive a mention in England either, although he would spend nine months in a Confederate prison essentially for speaking his mind.[64] An English governess named Catherine Hopley, who was stranded in Richmond, thought it was outrageous that 'Lord Seymour' [sic] should be able to obtain a passport from the Confederate government without any trouble', while the rest of them were left to rot in the

---

* France's invasion of Mexico made the presence of de Joinville and the Orleans exiles politically embarrassing and they departed from America at the end of June. But de Joinville continued to defend McClellan from abroad, publishing a long pamphlet entitled *The Army of the Potomac*, which appeared the following October.

city. 'I went the first thing in the morning, to see Mr Cridland,' she wrote, 'at what the "blockaded British subjects" used to call "anything but the Consolation Office".' She also visited the Confederate Secretary of War, George Randolph, and the Navy Secretary, Stephen Mallory, and offered herself as a courier to Europe. But both men scarcely looked up from their papers. Their curt dismissal was especially wounding since 'I was sympathising so deeply with them all, and wishing I could take messages and letters to England for them, and feeling worthy of being trusted even with the gravest secrets'.[65]

The Confederates did not require Miss Hopley's services when their own native-born women were perfectly willing to carry out danger-ous operations. Mrs Rose Greenhow, the Washington hostess who had exposed herself to Northern wrath by passing military secrets to the South, had arrived in Richmond after months of house arrest and then incarceration in a Federal prison. President Davis made a point of call-ing at her hotel and was shocked to see the ravages wrought by her ordeal. She had the air of someone 'shaken by mental torture', he wrote sadly to his wife.[66] Moreover, she was homeless and penniless. Judah Benjamin promptly sent her $2,500 as a mark of the Confederacy's gratitude.

Lord Edward's arrival had coincided with the beginning of General Lee's counter-offensive against McClellan. Bored of his leaky tugboat, Francis Dawson resigned from the Confederate navy to join an artillery battery commanded by Willie Pegram, a nephew of Captain Pegram. On 26 June, Pegram's battery was ordered to cross the Chickahominy river, north-east of Richmond. According to Lee's plan, the troops under General A. P. Hill (to which the battery belonged) were to form one element of a four-part attack against McClellan's somewhat incoher-ently placed divisions. If all went well for Lee, the Federal invaders would be attacked on every side and would disintegrate.

But one vital piece was missing: Stonewall Jackson and his men had not yet arrived from the Shenandoah Valley. After anxiously waiting until three in the afternoon, General Hill ordered his men to begin their assault without him. 'The guns were instantly loaded, and the firing began,' Dawson recalled. 'A solid shot bowled past me, killed one of our men, tore a leg and arm from another, and threw three horses into a bloody, struggling heap. This was my chance, and I stepped to the gun and worked away as though existence depended on my labours.'[67] He

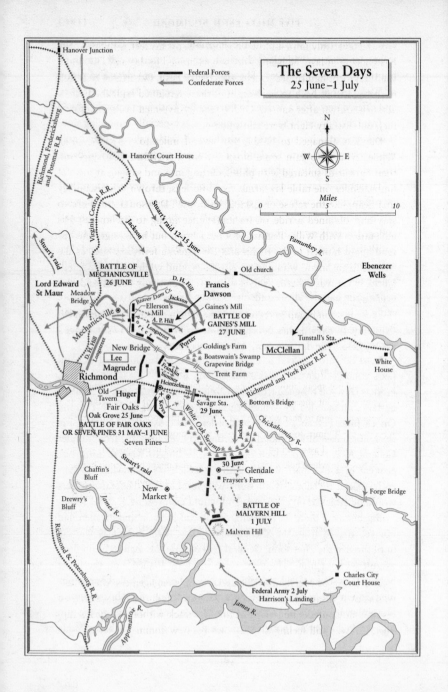

The Seven Days
25 June – 1 July

Federal Forces
Confederate Forces

Hanover Junction

Richmond, Fredericksburg
and Potomac R.R.

Hanover Court House

Virginia Central R.R.

Stuart's raid 12–15 June

Jackson

Stuart's raid

BATTLE OF
MECHANICSVILLE
26 JUNE

Lord Edward
St Maur

Meadow
Bridge

D. H. Hill

Jackson

Francis
Dawson

Beaver Dam Cr.

Ellerson's
Mill

A. P. Hill

Gaines's Mill

Old church

Pamunkey R.

Ebenezer
Wells

Mechanicsville

D. H. Hill

Longstreet

Longstreet

Porter

BATTLE OF
GAINES'S MILL
27 JUNE

Porter

New Bridge

Golding's Farm

Boatswain's Swamp

Grapevine Bridge

Trent Farm

Tunstall's Sta.

McClellan

White
House

Lee

Magruder

Richmond

Franklin

Sumner

Heintzelman

Richmond and York River R.R.

Old
Tavern

Huger

Keyes

Fair Oaks

Savage Sta.
29 June

Bottom's Bridge

Oak Grove 25 June

BATTLE OF FAIR OAKS
OR SEVEN PINES 31 MAY–1 JUNE

Seven Pines

White Oak Swamp

Jackson

Chickahominy R.

Chaffin's
Bluff

Stuart's raid

30 June

Glendale

Drewry's
Bluff

James R.

New
Market

Frayser's Farm

Forge Bridge

Richmond & Petersburg R.R.

BATTLE OF
MALVERN HILL
1 JULY

Malvern Hill

Charles City
Court House

James R.

Federal Army 2 July
Harrison's Landing

Appomattox R.

N
W   E
S

Miles
0   5   10

worked feverishly until a blow knocked him off his feet. 'That Britisher has gone up at last,' he heard. Dawson examined his leg and saw that a shell fragment had ripped away six inches of flesh. But strangely, he felt nothing. 'I went back to my post, and there remained until the battery was withdrawn after sunset.' Of the seventy-five men in Pegram's battery, only twenty-eight were still standing.

Dawson managed to hobble for several miles to a field hospital. While trying to obtain some morphine for a friend he saw surgeons, their bare arms smeared with blood, cutting into and sawing at rows of limbs. Under one table lay 'arms, feet, and legs, thrown promiscuously in a heap, like the refuse of a slaughter house'. Dawson decided not to stay and obtained a ride on an ambulance going to Richmond. His adventures with Willie Pegram had been brief, but he was gratified to read about himself in the Richmond *Despatch*, a few days later, as the 'young Englishman' who had 'received a wound while acting most gallantly'.[68] He was a hero, as tens of pretty young lady-nurses told him every day.

Dawson soon began to regret his fame. When one of his friends in the Confederate navy, James Morgan, came to visit him, Dawson begged for his help. 'The day was hot,' Morgan recalled,

> and I found my friend lying on a cot near the open front door, so weak that he could not speak above a whisper, and after greeting him and speaking some words of cheer I saw that he was anxious to tell me something. I leaned over him to hear what he had to say, and the poor fellow whispered in my ear 'Jimmie, for God's sake, make them move my cot to the back of the building.' I assured him that he had been placed in the choicest spot in the hospital, where he could get any little air that might be stirring; but he still insisted that he wanted to be moved, giving as a reason that every lady who entered the place washed his face and fed him with jelly. The result was that his face felt sore and he was stuffed so full of jelly that he was most uncomfortable . . . Shaking with laughter, I delivered his request to the head surgeon, who pinned a notice on Dawson's sheet to the effect that 'This man must only be washed and fed by the regular nurses.'[69]

The Battle of Mechanicsville, as Dawson's engagement was called, was a costly disappointment for Lee. Jackson's failure to arrive on time resulted in Confederate troops having to attack without adequate support. Lee was still feeling his way into his new command, but the one quality he did not lack was determination. The following day General Hill's troops once again led the assault. But by now Jackson and his men, including the Louisiana Brigade, had arrived and they too rushed into battle. Seeing his men stagger beneath a barrage of fire, Major Wheat galloped in front of the Louisiana Tigers, urging them to follow. Both he and his horse were immediately riddled with bullets. The fighting continued so hotly that Wheat's body lay where it fell for twenty-four hours.

For seven days, beginning on 25 June, Lee and McClellan clashed along the Chickahominy river, around the perimeter of Richmond, in one bloody encounter after another. Although McClellan lost none of these battles, he was unnerved by Lee's attacks and began retreating southwards, away from Richmond. Lee wanted to demolish 'those people', as he referred to the Federals, with another all-out attack on 1 July. By now, the Union army was entrenched around Malvern Hill, 15 miles south-east of Richmond. The terrain favoured the Federal soldiers sitting atop the 150-foot-high plateau. McClellan still had 115,000 men with 100 pieces of artillery and, unlike their general, their nerves were holding steady.

The Confederate attack was so disjointed that isolated brigades ran forward only to be chewed up by artillery fire. This 'was not war – it was murder', a Confederate general later wrote of Lee's failed assault. The Louisianians (minus Sam Hill, who was happily drawing up maps, thanks to some clever wrangling by his sister) were mauled by Irishmen in blue, including the New York 69th. The total Confederate loss on this terrible day was 5,500, nearly twice the number of casualties sustained by the Federals.*

About a quarter of Lee's 80,000-strong army was either dead or wounded. McClellan could have ordered a counterattack, and many of his generals urged him to do so, but he had apparently lost the will to fight. The next morning, 2 July, the mist lifted from the battlefield to reveal so many bodies that the terrain appeared to be masked by a bloody quilt. Some were dead but many still crawled feebly like stricken insects. Despite having inflicted a stunning blow against Lee's army,

---

* Among the Union wounded was 21-year-old Herbert Gladstone, a cousin of William Gladstone, the Chancellor of the Exchequer, who had joined the 36th New York 'British Volunteers' the previous year. He survived an agonizing journey back to Washington with a bullet lodged in his left leg, after which his family in England lost track of him. Efforts to locate him were unsuccessful.

McClellan continued his retreat, and the Seven Days' Battles were a strategic victory for Lee, even with his heavy losses. On 3 June McClellan had been five miles from Richmond; on 3 July he was 30. The casualties for the two sides amounted to more than 35,000 men.

McClellan left behind a treasure trove for the under-supplied Confederates. 'All along the road,' wrote an English observer, 'cartridge boxes, knapsacks, blankets and coats may be picked up. The rebels, as they pass, generally cast away their own worse equipments and refit ... Here were cartridge boxes, unopened and perfectly new.'[70] Five days later, on 8 July, Lincoln sailed down to Harrison's Landing on the James river in order to see the situation for himself. His impatience with McClellan was echoed all over the North. Only the General seemed to think that his withdrawal was nothing other than a 'change of base'. The rest of the country called it a reckless squandering of a brilliant opportunity to capture Richmond and win the war.

Lord Edward St Maur set off for Washington after the Seven Days' Battles and arrived under a flag of truce at McClellan's camp on 15 July. He had planned to stay for some time, but his admission to having observed the campaign from the 'other side' provoked a reaction from the Union officers 'which was really childish', he protested to his father. Unwisely, he fell into arguments with them about the reasons for the war and other sensitive subjects. Lord Edward's opinions had undergone a complete transformation, just as the Southern propagandist W. W. Glenn had hoped. 'I did not start with any feeling one way or the other,' he insisted, 'but I defy any candid man to go south, without being convinced that this war must end in separation.' If the split did not happen soon, he expected it to become a long and 'very cruel war'. He had heard from Southern officers that there had been instances of Louisianian regiments killing their prisoners. 'This', decided Lord Edward, 'is Butler's doing.'

12

The South is Rising

*Beast Butler – Palmerston is offended – Hotze and Spence join
forces – Lindsay goes too far – The* Alabama *escapes – Déjà vu at
Bull Run*

'Beast Butler', as the South dubbed US General Ben Butler, was enjoying
what the Scotsman William Watson called a 'perfect reign of terror' over
New Orleans. Watson had received his discharge from the Confederate
army at Camp Tupelo and set off by train and steamboat to the city.
During his journey south, he witnessed unsettling scenes, including Federal soldiers marching onto a plantation and putting down a slave revolt
at gunpoint, and Confederate 'guerrillas' using women and children as
human shields. When he reached New Orleans, Watson went straight to
the Consul, George Coppell, to ask for a certificate of British nationality. 'He informed me that the certificate would be of no use or protection,
if I violated neutrality. I then looked about for a day or two to see the
state of things under Butler's rule'.[1]

Watson found a city ruled by whim – the whim of a Union soldier, a
Butler-appointed bureaucrat or judge, or an anonymous informer. 'Butler
continued to hunt for treason, and all material that could contribute to
it he confiscated. He found it existed extensively in the vaults of banks,'
wrote Watson, 'in merchants' safes, in rich men's houses, among their
stores of plate and other valuables.'[2] A judicial ransom system was in
effect. Men of means would be arrested on some unknown charge, and
their wives prevailed upon to secure their release by handing over thousands of dollars to a 'fixer' who happened to know the right judge.

Watson had only been in the city for a few days when he experienced
Butler's methods for himself. It began with a thoughtless comment he

made in a café. A short while later Watson was accosted on the street by three men and forcibly marched to the Customs House. He was questioned by detectives who 'seized my pocket-book, as they had seen in it treasonable documents in the shape of bank-notes'. He asked to see a lawyer and to have his arrest made known to the British Consul, which made his interrogators laugh. After a night behind bars, Watson was taken to see General Butler on the charge of having expressed 'treasonable language'. Years later, the memory of his interview still made Watson bitter. Butler's head 'was large and flabby', he wrote scathingly, 'and nearly destitute of hair – except a little at the sides, which was just the colour of his epaulets'. The General jeered at him and asked if he knew why he was there. 'I said I was a British subject, and would have counsel to attend to my case. "Oh, a British subject of course," roared he. "I know that they are all British subjects now in New Orleans."'

Butler's manner throughout the interview led Watson to expect a lengthy prison term. Instead, he was sent before a judge, who examined his certificate of nationality and then offered him some words of advice about incautious jokes in a city under martial law. 'I was quite astonished at having got off so easily.' His pocketbook was also returned, with some of the money still there, 'which was considered a most extraordinary and unaccountable circumstance'.[3] Watson wondered if the presence of the *Rinaldo*, lately arrived on Lyons's orders, had anything to do with his swift release. Butler, he thought, made a great deal of noise about foreigners and the interference of foreign powers, particularly 'John Bull'. But it was all calculated to frighten, rather than eradicate, the foreign population. Nevertheless, Watson was determined to leave New Orleans. All he had to do was find a weakness at one of the checkpoints and sneak past the guards. One sultry summer's day, Watson and two friends set off for a picnic and simply carried on walking.

On 13 May 1862, almost three weeks after Butler's arrival in Louisiana, Henry Adams was surprised by the spectacle of his father performing a victory dance in the hall at the legation. 'We've got New Orleans,' Charles Francis Adams shouted. Henry ran out of the house to look for Thurlow Weed. Finding him 'near his hotel, I leaped out of the cab, and each of us simultaneously drew out a telegram which we exchanged ... I went round to the Diplomatic Club and had the pleasure of enunciating my sentiments'.[4] That evening, Weed's celebrations at the Reform Club were underscored by the shrill cry of newspaper boys who passed beneath the windows, shouting, 'Rumoured Capture of New Orleans'. Even more gratifyingly, the next day *The Times* admitted that it had been 'mistaken' in accepting Southern assurances that the city would never fall. William Howard Russell added spice to the mix by reminding readers of McClellan's 'magnificent army', which 'hated them like the devil and would want to have something to do' once the war was over. Russell's warning appeared to strike a chord. At a reception on 15 May, John Bright wagged his stodgy finger at Henry, saying, 'If you Americans succeed in getting over this affair, you mustn't go and get stuffy to England. Because if you do, I don't know what's to become of us who stood up for you here.' Henry laughed and replied that Bright would be welcome as a member of Congress.[5]

News of the victory had reached London on the anniversary of Charles Francis Adams's arrival in England. The coincidence seemed fitting; life in England had grown quite bearable of late. 'There is just now', Adams wrote to Charles Francis Jr., 'nobody who professes to think well of the South.'[6] It helped that they had moved to a new residence in Upper Portland Place. Situated between Regent's Park and Regent Street, the house at no. 5 enjoyed unobstructed light that streamed through the full-length windows all day long. An invigorated Adams told his mortified secretaries that from now on they were going to behave like gentlemen and cease turning their offices into 'slut holes'. Confident in her improved surroundings, and armed with a new cook, Mrs Adams held her first 'At Home'. To the family's relief, recorded Benjamin Moran, 'it was quite largely attended'.[7]

With the season in full swing and a house now suitable for entertaining, Henry was disappointed by his lack of friends. 'I can't succeed in finding any one to introduce me among people of my own age', he complained to his brother Charles.[8] He sensed he had made a fool of himself when an acquaintance introduced him to William Howard Russell. Rather idiotically, Henry began blathering away about the pity of his returning to England. Russell looked 'embarrassed' at this, and then laughed, remarking 'that personally he was glad [to be home], but he regretted having lost the chance of showing his goodwill to us by describing our successes'.[9] Russell ended the conversation by pointedly saying he would like to call on Henry's father.

William Howard Russell was anxious to clear his name with Adams. It was only once he arrived home that Russell realized the extent to which *The Times* had slanted his reports. The diarist Henry Greville, whose friendship with Fanny Kemble made him take an interest in American affairs, was shocked to learn of Russell's belief 'that the North will in the end carry all before them'. 'If this be his opinion,' wrote Greville on 10 May, 'his correspondence must have been carefully cooked before insertion, for nothing that has appeared in it can bear this construction.'[10] Delane had no use for Russell now that he was in England and stopped taking his articles on the war. The rebuke was not unduly troubling for Russell, however, since he was able to return to his job as editor of the *Army and Navy Gazette*. Nor did he regret his decision to leave America; less than a month after his arrival, he suffered the loss of his 1-year-old son, Colin, and the total collapse of Mary, his wife. The children were now utterly dependent on him. Fortunately, Delane soon forgave Russell; 'here you are and we must make the best of it,' he wrote, and *The Times* awarded Russell a pension of £300 a year for life.[11] Delane resumed commissioning him for special assignments, but the ban on American subjects remained in place.

Charles Francis Adams now almost looked forward to his interviews with the other Russell, the Foreign Secretary. They were more like jousts than conversations; 'about once a week', joked Henry, 'the wary Chieftain sharpens a stick down to a very sharp point, and then digs it into the excellent Russell's ribs'.[12] The Foreign Secretary enjoyed returning the compliment, and it was not uncommon for the meeting to conclude with an invitation to continue the argument over dinner. On 19 May, all five members of the Adams family went to Pembroke Lodge in Richmond Park for an outing with the Russells. 'One year ago, yesterday,' the Minister wrote in his diary, 'I went over this same ground on a very chilly day.' Then he had been nervous about meeting Lord Russell; but now, he decided, 'Lord and Lady Russell are pleasanter as seen in their domestic life than elsewhere. No family is more thoroughly a home circle.'[13] The harmonious relations between the legation and the Foreign Office were sufficiently encouraging for Henry to write to his brother on 6 June that the Confederate Commissioner was no longer a threat to them; 'I hear very little about our friend Mason ... He has little or no attention paid him except as a matter of curiosity.'

A week later, however, General Butler's 'Woman Order' became known. The British were shocked by the implication behind Butler's promise to treat 'any female' who insulted a Northern soldier as a 'woman of the town plying her avocation'. The press was not appeased when Lord Russell explained, during a heated debate in the House of Lords, that Butler was probably extending a law already used to curb prostitution to include Southern women who breached the peace in other ways. Even papers that normally supported the North condemned the Order. For Confederate sympathizers in Parliament, it was a gift that they shamelessly exploited. William Gregory conjured up for his fellow MPs images of women, not unlike their own wives and daughters, being thrown to the mercy of the very dregs of society. Lord Palmerston was unable to restrain himself. 'Sir,' he declared, 'an Englishman must blush to think that such an act has been committed by one belonging to the Anglo-Saxon race.' His sincere outrage struck a chord in the House of Commons; previously neutral MPs began to wonder whether Britain had a moral duty to intervene in the conflict.[14]

This latest innovation in modern warfare was, Palmerston told Russell, 'without example in the history of nations'.[15] The more he thought about it, the more he wished to make an official remonstrance to the North. When Russell would not agree, he went ahead anyway. 'Even when a Town is taken by assault,' he protested in a letter to Charles Francis Adams on 11 June, 'it is the Practice of the Commander of the conquering army to protect to the utmost the Inhabitants and especially the Female Part of Them.' By contrast, Butler was handing over the women of New Orleans 'to the unbridled license of an unrestrained soldiery'.[16]

The US Minister did not know what to make of the protest. The letter was marked 'confidential', and yet it did not seem like a private matter. A professional diplomat might have been more cautious in his response, but Adams had only his instincts and twelve months' experience to guide him. Rather than try to avoid a row, as Lyons would have done, Adams bristled with self-righteous indignation. 'My relations with the Prime Minister can never again be friendly,' he wrote in his diary.[17] Over the next few days he badgered Palmerston with demands for a clarification of his comments. After Adams twice called at his office to complain, Lord Russell realized that the Minister had been pushed to some sort of breaking point. At the second visit, Russell tried to calm him down by agreeing that 'the thing was altogether irregular'. Adams went home elated. 'I now saw that I had all the advantage,' he wrote on 19 June. Meanwhile, Russell suggested to Palmerston that he withdraw his letter. But, once the Prime Minister sensed that Adams was turning the incident into a battle of wills, he refused. The most he could stomach was an ambiguous reply that admitted nothing. Unfortunately, Adams could not resist having the last word. In his final letter, he declared that henceforth he would only accept letters from Palmerston that came through official channels.

Henry was proud that his father had forced Palmerston into a retreat. Benjamin Moran was enthralled by the drama, and thought Adams 'had managed the affair with great skill'.[18] But in truth it was a small victory. The next time the two men encountered one another, Adams noticed that Palmerston deliberately ignored him.[19] Invitations to Lady Palmerston's parties also ceased.

Whatever the provocation, now was not the time for Adams to quarrel with the Prime Minister; the Cabinet was assessing the economic damage caused by the cotton famine. A report by the Poor Law Board read to the Commons in May revealed a bleak picture of inadequate public help and growing private misery. In twelve months the number of charitable cases had risen from 40,000 to 150,000. More than 400,000 workers were either unemployed or working part time, causing great hardship for a further 1.5 million people whose care or livelihoods were dependent on them.[20] Journalists were beginning to write accounts of their tours to the hardest-hit towns, pricking consciences with their descriptions of once-proud industrious families who were forced by 'the iron teeth of poverty' to accept weekly handouts of food and coal.[21]

The US Consuls' descriptions of the suffering in Lancashire convinced Seward that the British would not hesitate to interfere in the war if the alternative meant starvation across wide swathes of England. Thurlow Weed had been urging him since the spring to show that the North was prepared to help Britain overcome the Southern cotton embargo. 'Let the enemy refuse [to send] the cotton,' he advised him.[22] In May, Seward declared the four Southern ports under US control were open for cotton export. But his scheme failed when the Treasury throttled the plan with too many regulations. The initiative therefore lay with the South, and Judah Benjamin was determined to use it. A year ago, the Confederate Cabinet had attempted to wield cotton like a blunt instrument. No one had listened to Benjamin's objections then. But now he was Secretary of State and could introduce a more sophisticated cotton policy without hindrance or argument since Southern coffers certainly needed the revenue.[23]

Benjamin was still hoping that he could bribe France with cotton, but he could not be sure. The Emperor Napoleon's invasion of Mexico also raised the interesting possibility that France might need Southern help in securing its conquest. The problem for Benjamin was his inability to communicate with his Commissioners in a timely fashion. James Mason had yet to receive a single dispatch (although one sent in April eventually arrived in late June), and Slidell was in a similar position.[24] Benjamin was obtaining most of his news from journals and old newspapers. But he was pleased to see that even without his supervision the Commissioners and propaganda agents were making great strides in their efforts to influence public opinion. James Spence and Henry Hotze had become a formidable team. Spence had offered his services to Mason back in April. All he asked for in return was the promise that after independence the South would appoint him as its financial agent. This would help him to recoup some of his losses caused by the 1857 panic. 'I assume', he had written boldly,

> that it will be of value to your Government to have on this side a man of intellect, zealous in their cause, fertile in expedients, vigorous in action, of wide mercantile experience; one accustomed to deal with large and difficult things, able to influence public opinion through the press, and not afraid of any encounter as a speaker. In what measure I may claim to possess some of these, it is not for me to say. I simply state facts, easily verified, from which to draw your conclusions.*[25]

Liverpool was the perfect arena for Spence's genius as a propagandist and social organizer. 'We are southern almost to a man,' a Liverpudlian friend confirmed to the MA Richard Monckton Milnes. 'There is even a secret club here – they call it the "Wig-Wam" ... in this club all the Southern news is discussed, southern newspapers find their way and arrangements are made for sending arms and ammunitions ... No club was ever more practical or more secret: large contributions are constantly

---

* In the same letter, Spence also suggested that the Southerners consider changing their name from Confederate States to 'Southern Union', which sounded better to English ears. When Mason forwarded his request to Benjamin, he asked the Secretary of State not to take offence. Spence's objection to the word 'Confederacy' sounded lunatic, Mason admitted, but he was speaking 'from an English business point of view'. He assured Benjamin that, on all other matters, Spence was a 'man of large research, liberal and expanded views'. Moreover, he had close ties to *The Times*, and his book *The American Union* continued to outsell every other work on the subject.[26]

coming in.'[27] The manufacturing areas around the city were also fertile territory; Spence engaged two veteran strike leaders, William Aitken and Mortimer Grimshaw, to organize mass demonstrations in the worst hit cotton districts. Their motives may have been tinged by a desire to revive their glory days, but they were also passionately against the sacrifice of English cotton workers for the benefit of Northern capitalists.

Hotze naturally gave the protest meetings great prominence in his new weekly, the *Index*. He had started the journal at the end of April with the help of donations from friends in order to have his own vehicle for reporting Anglo-American matters. It was designed to be cosmopolitan and worldly, as though its Southern sympathies were an inconsequential and harmless feature rather than the sole *raison d'être* of the paper. Hotze explained to a potential writer that for the *Index* to be respectable it had 'to be tolerant and yet not indifferent; to be moderate and yet have strong convictions, to be instructive and yet not dull . . .' Above all, the information had to be dressed 'in the most attractive manner' and displayed 'in the most accessible way'.[28]

The *Index* did not require a large circulation so long as it was read in all the clubs and by MPs. Hotze sought out contributors with deliberate calculation. He wanted writers with connections to other newspapers, rather than ardent partisans. The more they wrote for him, he reasoned, the more they would absorb Confederate views, which would in turn carry over into their articles for other newspapers. British journalism was a small enclave within the already small world of educated society.[29] Once inside the charmed circle, Hotze discovered it was easy to influence content without being obvious. Newspaper editors were so eager for American news that they would take his manufactured 'letters from a traveller' and rejig them to appear as editorials or reportage.[30] One of Hotze's favourite methods was to supply an acquaintance with fresh information, in the shape of a pro-South editorial that required little editing. If the article was printed, Hotze would always insist that the submitter should keep the 10 guinea fee. For the moment, Hotze was concentrating on two themes that he thought would resonate with English readers: the needless suffering of cotton workers, and the 'blood' relationship between the Southern gentry and their British cousins.[31]

Henry Adams thought the tone of the *Index* was 'so excruciatingly never conquer' that 'one is forced to the belief that they think themselves very near that last ditch . . .'[32] He discounted the Confederates' methods at his peril, however. Seward's emissary, Thurlow Weed was not a clubbable man in the English sense and Grub Street hacks prided their independence too much to accept his money.[33] He was an expert at pulling the more vulgar levers of corruption, but the subtle game of co-opting English journalists had eluded him. When Weed departed from England at the beginning of June, it was with a sense of regret that he had only partially fulfilled his mission. On a personal level, he was confident that his conversations with various editors and politicians had disabused them of the more pernicious myths about Seward. On the other hand, Weed knew that his efforts to establish a Northern lobby similar to Henry Hotze's stable of propagandists and of opinion-formers had failed.

There was more disappointment for Weed once he arrived home and discovered that his control over the New York press had slipped during his absence. His views on Britain had mellowed during his time abroad, yet he found editors resistant to the idea of adopting a more benign view of Anglo-American relations. Bravely, Weed took on the burden himself and published an open letter to New York City's Common Council, in which he urged his countrymen to reconsider their hostility to England. Regarding the *Trent* affair, 'I am bound,' he asserted, 'in truth and fairness, to say, that that Government and people sincerely believed that *we* desired a rupture with *them*, that we sought occasion to taunt and snub them'. Moreover, America's recent behaviour towards Britain included supporting Russia in the Crimean War, the expulsion of the British Minister on a technicality, and Seward's oft-repeated claim that one day Canada would belong to the United States: 'Some of these grounds of complaint were, as we know, well taken.' He begged his fellow New Yorkers to remember that 'the Union has many ardent, well-wishing friends in England, and can have many more if we act justly ourselves'.[34]

Though wise and admirably sane, Weed's letter failed to address the intense bitterness caused by *The Times* and other newspapers. Edward Dicey was disconcerted when he visited the house of a Northern acquaintance who forced him to gaze at the portrait of a young man. ' "How", he said to me, "would you like, yourself, to read constantly that that lad died in a miserable cause, and, as an American officer, should be called a coward?" ' Dicey admitted that 'I could make no adequate reply'.[35] The fact that many American newspapers were just as rude about Britain was a rather hollow argument in the face of such grief.[36] The US Consul in Paris, John Bigelow, warned Lord Russell that it made Americans deeply

resentful to learn from the British press 'that we are barbarians, that our
system of government is a nuisance, that our statesmen are knaves or
imbeciles . . .'.[37] The British consulate in New York noticed that ordinary
Britons suffered every time there was a controversy in the press, and
Lord Edward St Maur wrote home about a new term being bandied
about the city: 'Anglo-Rebels'.[38]

Despite Butler's offensive 'Woman Order', the MP William Schaw Lindsay was discovering just how difficult it could be to turn goodwill into
action. Nine-tenths of the members, he insisted to James Spence, were
'in favour of immediate recognition'. Spence thought he should wait for
a Confederate victory before forcing a vote but Lindsay disagreed; his
interviews with Emperor Napoleon in April had made it clear that the
only impediment to Southern independence was the British Cabinet.
As proof, he could point to the leading article in Le Constitutionnel on
1 June, which appeared to argue that France should offer to mediate in
the conflict without bothering to wait for Britain.* On 17 June Lindsay
sent an arrogant letter to Russell, warning him that the government
would look weak and foolish if its foreign policy ended up in the hands
of backbenchers like himself. 'Within the next fortnight', he boasted,
support for the Confederacy would be unstoppable. James Mason fervently hoped that his friend was right. He was feeling rather downcast
by their lack of progress. 'We must wait for "King Cotton"', he wrote to
Slidell on 19 June, 'to turn the screw still further.'[40]

Two weeks later, Mason's wish seemed close to being granted. The
supply of cotton bales went down while the number of workers on poor
relief jumped by another 11,000.[41] There were more mass meetings in
Lancashire. Even though the results of these meetings were often ambiguous, they were sufficiently heated to alarm the Union's supporters.† Lord

---

* Le Constitutionnel was generally considered to be the mouthpiece of the French govern-
ment. This 'seems like a preparation of the public mind for a mediation on the part of
France in the American conflict', noted the diarist Henry Greville on 2 June, 'and to-day The
Times has put forth a leader strongly advocating it'.[39]
† Although the strike leaders Aitken and Grimshaw were able to call out large meetings all over
Lancashire, achieving an unambiguous vote in favour of Southern independence was proving
to be a considerable struggle. A meeting in Ashton, which was one of the most deprived towns
in the area, ended with a resolution in favour of recognition for the Confederacy, but someone
from the floor successfully tacked on an amendment that urged Britain and France to 'crush the
abettors of slavery and oppression'.[42]

Lyons had only been home for a few days, but he immediately grasped the seriousness of the situation. He reported to William Stuart, Secretary of the legation, that cotton was, 'the real question of the day'. Obviously, Lyons was powerless to do anything from England, but, he told Stuart, 'If you can manage in any way to get a supply of cotton for England before the winter, you will have done a greater service than has been effected by Diplomacy for a century.'[43] The Duke of Argyll, John Bright and Richard Cobden all wrote to Charles Sumner, begging him to use his influence in facilitating the flow of cotton from the South.[44]

The US legation was in a high state of anxiety. They had hoped to derail Lindsay by exposing the MP as an arms supplier or blockade-runner for the South, but discreet enquiries into his business dealings revealed that the shipping magnate was scrupulously honest.[45] Their best hope lay in a military success. '[We are] waiting the event of the struggle at Richmond,' Henry told his brother on 4 July.[46] London was swirling with rumours that McClellan had been defeated by Lee. 'No one but me is sorry for it,' wrote Lord Lyons; until now he had not understood how sharply public opinion had turned against the United States.[47] Despite the wild ups and downs of the past twelve months he had never ceased to hope that the two countries might form some sort of an alliance, but 'public opinion will not allow the Government to do more for the North than maintain a strict neutrality,' he wrote pessimistically on 5 July, 'and it may not be easy to do that if there comes any strong provocation from the US'.[48] Adams tried dropping heavy hints to Seward that the North could not afford to alienate Europe while her armies looked so vulnerable. The 'insurgent emissaries' here, he warned on the 11th, were eager to seize on 'every act' that might 'cast odium on the Government'.[49]

After the latest news put McClellan in full retreat, Lindsay decided that the time for his motion had come. But over the next few days, the 'nine-tenths' he had boasted of began to doubt the wisdom of forcing the government's hand. After initially encouraging him, the Tory leadership came to its senses and realized that the war brought out too many conflicting passions to unify the Opposition. 'In fact, it seems that there is nothing good to be got out of this American question,' wrote a senior Tory on 14 July.[50] Lord Lyons was also quietly lobbying senior politicians against making any change to the current policy.[51]

Lindsay began to feel uncomfortable. Perhaps, he admitted, Spence was right after all; they needed something exceptional to sweep members off their collective feet. Two days later the longed-for moment arrived when Parliament received the official figures on employment in Lancashire. The report was sufficiently dire to revive Lindsay's courage. He announced that he would be introducing a debate on the Civil War on 18 July. While Lindsay was composing his speech, a report reached London that Lee had defeated the Federal army in the Seven Days' Battles. Henry Adams stared in amazement at the bold headline of his evening paper, '"Capitulation of McClellan's Army. Flight of McClellan on a steamer. Later from America." This astounding news for a moment made me almost give way,' he wrote.

William Forster MP came rushing to the legation to find out if it was true. 'Such odd things have occurred of late, that we can't be sure now that our generals won't run away from their own soldiers,' wrote Moran bitterly.[52] Charles Francis Adams received Forster in his study, looking ashen. 'This has gone so far', he wrote in his diary, 'that I think I should be glad to be relieved of the mission. Nothing but a sense of duty to the public reconciles me to the trial a moment longer.'[53] 'Things look well for Lindsay's motion tonight,' gloated James Mason.[54] *The Times* helped maintain the appearance by suppressing information that contradicted the surrender report.[55] The legation, however, had the latest newspapers from New York. 'A single glance at dates showed us that it was an utter swindle,' wrote Henry; 'we had bulletins from McClellan two days later than the day of the reported surrender.'[56]

Adams was aghast at how quickly the falsehood was spreading, and asked William Forster to take the American newspaper to the House so that MPs could see for themselves that the Federal army had retreated but was still intact. Benjamin Moran went along to watch and was surprised by the enormous crowd that had turned up for the debate. There was much jostling between Northern and Southern supporters over seats in the gallery. James Mason had a shouting match with the doorkeeper and had to be rescued by William Gregory, who led him to the floor. Moran was pleased to see that the Southern Commissioner was wearing the wrong type of coat for the occasion. The only people not present were Adams and Lord Lyons, who both stayed away deliberately.

Adams might have felt calmer if he had known that the McClellan rumour would not affect the government's policy. Three weeks earlier, Lord Palmerston had candidly informed the Confederate agent Edwin De Leon that the Federals could be pushed back and Washington besieged and it would still not be enough to guarantee recognition.[57] The knowledge would have saved Lindsay from making a fool of himself. He was such a poor speaker anyway that several members went off for a drink until he had finished. Moran seethed as he listened to the debate, forgetting that politicians generally consider foreign countries to be fair game. No speaker challenged Lindsay's assertion that slavery was not the cause of the war or that the North was fighting out of greed and a desire for power. At half past one in the morning, Lord Palmerston rose slowly from his seat and the boisterous House fell silent. The 78-year-old politician surveyed his listeners with a grandfatherly air. He reminded the House that a report of the debate would be read in America and would probably offend both sides. But, more important, there had never been 'a contest of such magnitude between two different sections of the same people'. Recognition or mediation was not something to be considered lightly. It was for the government alone to decide 'what can be done, when it can be done, and how it can be done'. The House burst into applause. 'As I came away,' recorded Moran with satisfaction, 'I met Mason alone, looking sullen and dejected.'[58]

With remarkable persistence, James Mason presented the Foreign Office a week later with a formal demand for recognition. The document was accepted without comment. Yet the debate had helped to shape public opinion in a way that was advantageous to the South. First, as Adams complained to Seward, the Confederates had succeeded in positioning themselves as the underdogs and victims in the war.[59] Second, more dangerous still, they had made the idea of British mediation seem like a humanitarian duty to end the bloodshed. Make the war about slavery, Adams urged Seward, otherwise the government could end up caving in to pressure.[60] After the debate, Lord Russell admitted to Lyons that he was astonished by the passions it had stirred. 'The great majority are in favour of the South,' he concluded. Furthermore, 'nearly our whole people are of [the] opinion that separation wd be [of] benefit both to North and South'.[61]

Russell's concern about national sentiment may have blinded him to more practical and immediate issues, such as the Confederates' violations of the Foreign Enlistment Act. Charles Francis Adams had repeatedly asked him to investigate reports of a formidable cruiser that was under construction at Lairds' shipyard. His Consul in Liverpool, Thomas Haines Dudley, had amassed such damning evidence that only

an outright partisan – as the customs collector of Liverpool happened
to be – could claim with a straight face that the mysterious No. 290 at
Lairds was simply a merchant ship of unusual design.[62] The vessel was
ready to depart before Russell finally realized the danger, and he ordered
all the relevant documents to be delivered immediately to the law officers. This was on 23 July. Over the next six days a tragi-comedy unfurled
without anyone realizing its true import until it was too late. The papers
arrived at the house of the Queen's Advocate, Sir John Harding, on the
day he suffered an irreversible nervous breakdown. Meanwhile, an
anonymous Confederate sympathizer in the Foreign Office alerted James
Bulloch that his ship was about to be seized. Harding's illness created a
bureaucratic vacuum. In the ensuing muddle of confused responsibilities
and departmental paper shuffling, the Confederates bribed a local customs official and quietly sneaked the No. 290 out of Liverpool. By the
time the telegram ordering her arrest reached Liverpool on 31 July, the
steamer was on her way to the Azores. There she would receive her
guns, a new captain and a new name: the CSS *Alabama*. Northern shipping was about to face its greatest threat since the war of 1812.

Russell still thought the best hope for ending slavery was for the North
and South to separate.[63] Like many Englishmen he assumed that the
effect of international moral pressure and domestic enlightened opinion
would eventually force Southern leaders to abolish slavery, just as Tsar
Alexander II had abolished serfdom in 1861. Gladstone shared his view;
he was one of the few members of the Cabinet who had actually read
James Spence's *The American Union* and the debate on 18 July sent him
spinning further into the Confederates' arms. Gladstone had fallen in
love with the humanitarian argument. 'It is indeed much to be desired',
he wrote to a friend on 26 July, 'that this bloody and purposeless conflict should cease.' Four days later, a mutual acquaintance succeeded in
placing Henry Hotze next to him at dinner. The evening passed like a
dream for Hotze; Gladstone hung on his every word. By the end of the
night they were discussing where the boundary ought to lie between the
two Americas, and whether it would be better to divide the border States
in half.[64]

  Gladstone would not be the first English politician or the last to fall
under the spell of a foreign agent. But the way Henry Hotze played him
was especially masterful. In his report after their 'chance' meeting, Hotze

described to Judah Benjamin how he carefully drove the conversation to make it seem as though Gladstone was in control. 'I purposely abstained from introducing any topic,' he wrote on 6 August; he allowed Gladstone to waffle on about 'supposed difficulties' over the Confederacy's border. Then, when he thought the moment was right, Hotze casually referred to the South's (non-existent) intention to revalue its currency to make it more favourable for the pound, 'a prospect which I knew would be peculiarly agreeable to him'. Over the next few days he commissioned sympathizers to write articles that discussed the South's economic policies, hoping that they would keep Gladstone's interest alive. This was Hotze's usual tactic. 'Thanks to friends', he continued, he knew which arguments appealed to individual Cabinet members, 'and to these from week to week I devoted myself'. The results appeared to be promising. 'Just as I close this,' finished Hotze, 'a reliable friend steps in to inform me that there have been three successive cabinet meetings ... and that each time the cabinet was evenly divided, Mr Gladstone leading the party in favour of recognition.'[65]

Hotze's 'reliable friend' had given him an accurate report of the state of opinion in the Cabinet. Leading the faction against immediate recognition was the pugnacious Duke of Argyll, who resented Gladstone's attempt to browbeat them with fallacious moral arguments. 'I retain my opinion unchanged,' wrote the Duke after a bruising correspondence with Gladstone; no war 'has been more just or more necessary ... It is not inconsistent to sympathize with revolts which are just, and to fight against other revolts which are unjust.' In his usual blunt way, Argyll informed Gladstone that he was deceiving himself if he believed that separation was good for the 'anti-slavery cause'.[66]

Argyll's reproach stung Gladstone, but the latter was mollified by his success with Palmerston, who 'has come exactly to my mind', he told his wife after the final Cabinet meeting of the session.[67] Palmerston, in fact, did not share Gladstone's moral qualms; and he certainly did not wish to fight a war on behalf of the South. But if the Confederates continued their run of victories, and the North proved obdurate, he could see no reason why the question should not be considered. The French had been advocating October – when the cotton season was normally in full swing – as the time for Europe to decide, which seemed reasonable to Palmerston.[68] Gladstone had also succeeded in pricking Russell's conscience. Though he saw the complications and subtleties of the question that the crusading Chancellor of the Exchequer conveniently ignored, Russell was also becoming bewitched by the siren call of the humanitarian argument. On 6 August Russell suggested to Palmerston that they try to bring the opposing sides to an armistice. But, he asked on reflection, 'On what basis are we to negotiate?' It seemed to him there was little hope that Lincoln 'and his Democracy will listen to reason'.[69]

The deliberations in the Cabinet soon leaked out; the *New York Times* reported that the Great Powers were contemplating mediation. France and Russia were said to be keen; England was apparently undecided.[70] Without Lord Lyons to reassure him, Seward assumed the worst. Senator Orville Browning bumped into him at Lincoln's office and asked him point-blank 'if there was any danger of intervention in our affairs by England and France. He said there was,' recorded Browning, 'unless volunteering went on rapidly, and our army was greatly increased.'[71] Seward sent one of his wrap-the-world-in-flames dispatches to Adams, hoping that it would scare the British into inaction. He also rather cleverly sent out a circular on 8 August to all Consuls in Europe offering inducements to immigrants seeking work opportunities in America.

The circular, No. 19, seemed innocent enough, but it was actually a back-door route for army recruitment. Consulates were encouraged to display information on the cash bounties awarded to volunteers. Seward knew the game he was playing. 'Nobody is authorised to do anything or pay anything, for once entering into this kind of business there would be no end of trouble,' he warned his Consul in Paris, since official recruitment was illegal; but 'to some extent this civil war must be a trial between the two parties to exhaust each other. The immigration of a large mass from Europe would of itself decide it.'[72]

Throughout August, every utterance and report from England was picked over and analysed for clues. It was at this precise moment that the irascible John Roebuck decided to try his hand at Anglo-American relations. The Liberal MP was growing old and change frightened him. Anything that retarded the modernizing, democratizing tendencies of the United States seemed like a cause worth supporting. Forgetting that the South was also a democracy, he championed its independence because separation would hurt the North. On 14 August Roebuck and Palmerston attended the same banquet in Sheffield. Knowing that the Prime Minister's presence would ensure that the speeches were reported in the press, Roebuck theatrically turned to Palmerston and exhorted him to admit that the South's time had come. 'The North will never be our friends,' he bellowed, to a few 'hear, hears'. 'Of the South you can make friends. They are Englishmen; they are not the scum and refuse of Europe.' The Mayor of Manchester leaped to his feet and shouted over the boos and cheers, 'Don't say that; don't say that. Roebuck responded, 'I know what I am saying. [The South] are Englishmen, and we must make them our friends.'[73]

Reports of the Manchester banquet confirmed Northern fears and revived Southern hopes. Palmerston was no longer 'considered [by Southerners] as the personal enemy of the confederacy – a most rabid abolitionist – who is suppressing the sympathies, which England would otherwise show for the south'.[74] All over the South, people waited anxiously for foreign news, many believing that their fate hung on his change of view. General Beauregard received a letter from a Confederate colonel in Tennessee who had read an editorial that appeared to answer their prayers (it was probably one of Henry Hotze's plants): 'The *London Post* (Palmerston's organ) has a most significant article, indicating our early recognition in plain terms as inevitable,' the officer wrote to Beauregard on 7 August. 'All the signs indicate, I think unmistakably, an early action on the part of England and France, but you will remember that I have always said the same – yes, I have always held that it was inevitable and the only way that this war could be ended.'[75]

McClellan's failure to capture Richmond had convinced Lincoln that there was no real substance or drive to the General. McClellan looked and talked the part, he realized, but lacked the will to *act*. Without even bothering to consult him, Lincoln announced McClellan's demotion on 11 July. He lost his position as general-in-chief of the US armies, which was given to 'Old Brains' Henry Halleck, whose commanders out West had produced the victories at Shiloh and Island No. 10; and he was ordered to merge his army with General John Pope's, which was fighting in northern Virginia. This new mammoth army would be commanded by Pope, not McClellan.

Lincoln had to have a military victory; volunteering practically ceased after the Seven Days' Battles and the 600,000 extra soldiers he requested were not stepping forward without the lure of large bounties. Furthermore, he knew that if he played the emancipation card while the North appeared to be losing the war, it would be interpreted at home and abroad as the desperate move of a floundering government; in Seward's words, 'our last shriek on the retreat'.[76] Lincoln had accomplished as much as he could for the moment: Washington was now in line with the rest of the Union and free of the taint of slavery; among the recent bills passed by Congress was a law prohibiting the return of fugitive slaves to their masters, and another allowing 'persons of African descent' to join the army. But Lincoln had not been able to persuade the border States to accept emancipation in return for compensation for their slaves; slavery remained legal in the United States.

Notwithstanding the installation of Henry Halleck as the new general-in-chief, August turned out worse for the North than July. Despite the capture of three important Southern ports, the 'Anaconda' strategy of a total blockade of the South's coastline was far from being achieved.* Nor had the North (with the exception of New Orleans) been able to extend its control of the Mississippi river beyond the border States. Worse, even gains had slipped into losses. Kentucky and Tennessee looked vulnerable once more.

Jefferson Davis had replaced the popular General Beauregard following his retreat from Corinth with the widely disliked Braxton Bragg. At the end of July Bragg had taken his army on a 700-mile manoeuvre into Kentucky, where he intended to install a pro-Southern governor. If the Confederacy could secure this border State, he reasoned, the others might follow. Halleck had sidelined Grant after Shiloh and put his faith in General Buell, whose timely arrival on 6 April had saved the Federal army from defeat. But Buell was fretting uselessly, sending his troops hither and thither without actually trying to intercept Bragg. Robert Neve of the 5th Kentucky Volunteers had vivid memories of the relentless marching: of the thirst, the hunger and the ever-present dust. He recalled with sadness a man they 'found dead on the road who had died through excessive fatigue. As the army passed along there, he laid like a dog as if no one cared who he was. It was', he wrote, 'a bad sight to see a poor soldier die in such a way.'[77] While Neve and thousands like him laboured to keep moving under the broiling sun, Confederate raiders preyed on Buell's weaker outposts.

---

* Although General Winfield Scott's 'Anaconda Plan' to isolate and squeeze the South was never formally adopted, this effectively became the strategy of the war.

On the far eastern side of Kentucky, the small Federal force that had wrested the Cumberland Gap from the Confederates was itself surrounded. Colonel De Courcy's commander sent a desperate telegram to the War Department on 10 August, warning that their supplies would last three weeks at best. That was his last communication with the outside world. A few hours later, Confederate guerrillas organized by John Hunt Morgan and his English staff officer, Colonel George St Leger Grenfell, cut their telegraph line. The beleaguered Federals had no way of knowing whether help would come; still, when the Confederates ordered their surrender, they replied defiantly: 'If you want this fortress, come and take it.'[78] Morgan and his raiders ignored the challenge, confident that starvation would do the work for them.

Lincoln's Cabinet was grim when it learned that a Confederate army was marching unopposed towards Kentucky. As Lincoln's frustration with Buell increased, he turned to General Pope to stop the run of bad news. Pope, at least, claimed to be thirsting for battle. The self-promoting victor of Island No. 10 had recently boasted to the press that his soldiers only ever saw the backs of the enemy. Pope liked to make 'hard war'. Unlike McClellan, he was less concerned about keeping casualty figures to a minimum, nor did he believe in protecting civilians from the ravages of war. He wanted Southerners to suffer because he thought it would make them more willing to surrender. But in one important sense Pope was just the same as McClellan: he misunderstood his opponent.

The Seven Days' Battles had brought out the fighter in Lee. The once cautious officer had undergone a metamorphosis into a general who was resolute and audacious. He had private reasons, too, for wanting to throw the Federals out of Virginia. At the start of the war he had lost the family home of Arlington, across the river from Washington. Shortly after the Seven Days' Battles, his other home, the White House plantation in central Virginia, was burned to the ground by Federal soldiers, forcing his wheelchair-bound wife, Mary, to seek refuge in Richmond.[79]

Lee divided his army of 50,000 into two 'wings' so that he could attack Pope from several directions, a risky tactic given his inferior numbers. Stonewall Jackson was given command of one, and General James 'Old Pete' Longstreet, who had performed well during the Seven Days' Battles, the other. Jackson's division struck first, tearing into Pope on 9 August. He launched another surprise attack against Pope two weeks later, and followed it up on the 27th with a raid on Pope's supply depot at Manassas Junction. 'Huzza,' crowed John Jones, the usually cynical clerk at the Confederate War Department. 'The braggart is near his end.'[80]

Jackson's raid had given away his position; Pope ordered his commanders to prepare the men for battle. The name Manassas conjured up dreadful memories for the North. 'Everything is ripe for a terrible panic,' Charles Francis Adams Jr. wrote to his father from Washington. 'I have not since the war began felt such a tug on my nerves.'[81] Pope's numbers were superior but not overwhelming to Jackson's. McClellan had played into Lee's hands; mortified by his demotion, he had resisted for as long as possible Halleck's orders to reinforce Pope. He knew that a battle was fast approaching and wanted to watch his rival 'get out of his scrape by himself'. Among the reinforcements who did reach Pope, however, was Sir Percy Wyndham, who had been exchanged and was able to rejoin his regiment just in time to participate in the 'scrape'.*

The Second Battle of Bull Run began piecemeal on 28 August and roared into life on the 29th. In the thirteen months since the first battle, the armies had grown in size and the men had become hardened and more experienced. Once again, Henry House Hill was the scene of bitter fighting, although this time it was the Federals who held the hill and the Confederates who were cut down trying to dislodge them. Pope had no idea that Lee and Longstreet had arrived with the other half of the Army of Northern Virginia. After the firing drew to a halt on the evening of the 29th, Pope was so confident he had won that he sent a dispatch to Washington announcing his victory. He was unprepared for the full Confederate assault the following day. At 7 p.m. on the 30th a shocked and disconsolate Pope reluctantly ordered his army to retreat.

The 1st New Jersey Cavalry were massed behind a thickly wooded forest, with orders to stop the retreat from turning into a rout, but as tens of soldiers became hundreds and then thousands the regiment lost its cohesion. Stray gunfire contributed to the Cavaliers' difficulties. Above the din came the order to fall back, which some of the riders interpreted to mean they could gallop off, touching a nerve with Sir

---

* The North and South copied the European system of parole and exchange of prisoners. Prisoners gave their word – their parole – not to take up arms until they were formally exchanged for an enemy prisoner of equal rank. If the wait for exchange was going to take more than a few days, parolees could go home or to a parole camp and wait until they received notice that the paperwork had been completed.

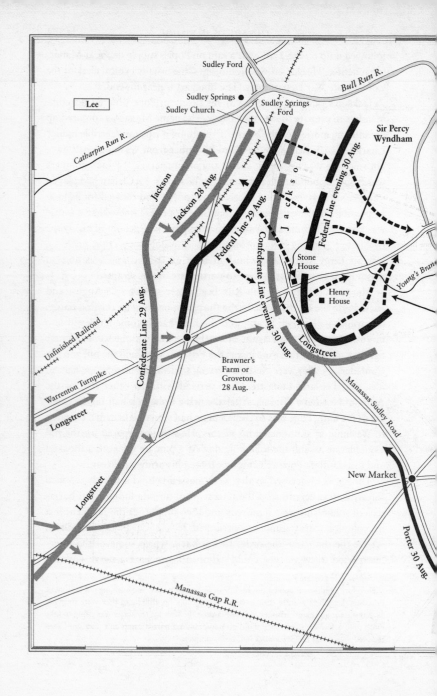

Lee

Sudley Ford

Bull Run R.

Sudley Springs

Sudley Church

Sudley Springs Ford

Catharpin Run R.

Sir Percy Wyndham

Jackson

Jackson 28 Aug.

Federal Line 29 Aug.

Jackson

Federal Line evening 30 Aug.

Confederate Line 29 Aug.

Confederate Line evening 30 Aug.

Stone House

Young's Bran[c]

Henry House

Unfinished Railroad

Longstreet

Brawner's Farm or Groveton, 28 Aug.

Manassas Sudley Road

Warrenton Turnpike

Longstreet

New Market

Longstreet

Porter 30 Aug.

Manassas Gap R.R.

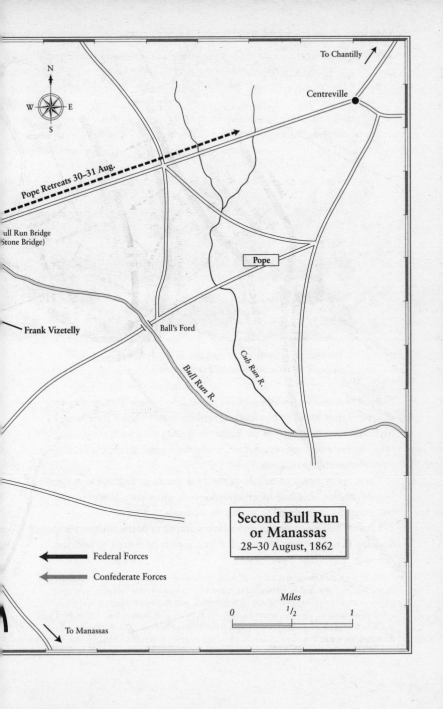

To Chantilly

Centreville

Pope Retreats 30-31 Aug.

N
W E
S

ull Run Bridge
Stone Bridge)

Pope

Frank Vizetelly

Ball's Ford

Bull Run R.

Cub Run R.

**Second Bull Run
or Manassas**
28–30 August, 1862

Federal Forces

Confederate Forces

Miles

0   1/2   1

To Manassas

The Federal army makes its stand on Henry House Hill,
Second Bull Run, by Frank Vizetelly

Percy. The familiar twiddling of his moustache began. Threatening to
shoot any man who disobeyed, he forced the men to bring their horses
back into line and perform the action as though they were on parade.
'The twirl of that long moustache', wrote the regiment's chaplain, 'was
more formidable than a rifle.'[82]

There were 5,000 casualties at the First Battle of Bull Run; at the
Second, 25,000. Lee had lost proportionately more men, however, and
his army was in no shape to pursue the Federals.*

Lincoln had eaten dinner at Secretary Stanton's house on the 30th,
thinking that Pope was his man. But by the time he retired to bed, the

---

* Among the Confederate prisoners was the accident-prone Garibaldi veteran Lieutenant
Henry MacIver, who had received a bullet in the wrist. An Irish Federal surgeon bandaged
his arm with more skill than he could have hoped for, and afterwards MacIver was transferred to Alexandria. He was, wrote his biographer, 'somewhat dismayed to find himself
face to face with his old jailer . . . he saw that the man recognised him as his former prisoner
the instant they met.'[83]

news had come through of the army's defeat. Once again, the residents of Washington woke up to the sight of leaderless soldiers pouring through the streets, filthy, hungry and clearly in search of a drink. Only this time behind them came wagon after wagon of the wounded and dying. 'So,' lamented the treasurer of the US Sanitary Commission, George Templeton Strong, 'after all this waste of life and money and material, we are at best where we were a year ago.'[84]

13

Is Blood Thicker than Water?

*The possibility of intervention – Lee invades the North – Antietam,
the bloodiest day – Dawson experiences Northern hospitality – The
splendours and shortages of Richmond – Meeting the Confederate
generals*

'The suspense was hideous and unendurable,' Henry Adams recalled, as
he waited for news from America.[1] On 9 September 1862 came a telegram from Reuter's agency announcing a victory for US General Pope
at Bull Run. 'This has been a Red Letter Day,' Moran wrote euphori-
cally. 'If this be true it is the beginning of the end.'[2]

Four days later Moran learned they had been misled; Pope had been
defeated and the Confederate army was just 20 miles from Washington.
'My heart sunk within me,' he wrote. 'The rebels here are elated beyond
measure. The Northern people are looked upon as cravens, and the
Union is regarded as hopelessly gone.' He was alone at the legation; the
Adamses were away and Charles Wilson had taken a leave of absence
'for his health'. With no one to act as a moderating influence on his
behaviour, Moran happily insulted a British army officer who called at
the legation to volunteer for the Federal army; 'they think we are unable
to attend to our affairs, and that they can settle them,' he remarked
testily.[3] But what galled him even more was the tone of the papers,
which were 'prating about our being of the same blood' while simultaneously enjoying the 'North's hour of disaster and adversity'.[4] Moran
was not exaggerating the satisfaction in pro-Confederate circles. 'I cannot help hoping that the bold move of the Confederates has been more
successful than is yet acknowledged,' General Grey wrote to his brother
Earl Grey on 11 September. 'I do not know any piece of news that would

give me more satisfaction than to hear that the Confederate Army were in possession of Washington.'[5]

The Adams family said goodbye to their hosts and returned to London as soon as they heard the news. Mrs Adams told Moran that it would have been 'torture' to remain since there were Confederate sympathizers among the house party. Henry suffered pangs of guilt that so many were risking their lives while he was fighting the battle of the drawing rooms. 'After a sleepless night,' Henry subsequently wrote of his younger self, 'walking up and down his room without reflecting that his father was beneath him, he announced at breakfast his intention to go home into the army.'[6]

Lord Russell had been wavering over whether Britain should intercede, until he received the reports about the Second Battle of Bull Run.[7] Charles Francis Adams had come away from their meeting on 4 September thinking it was business as usual since Russell had assured him 'I [could be] quite at ease in regard to any idea of joint action of the European powers in our affairs. I laughed and said I was in hopes that they all had quite too much to occupy their minds ... to think of troubling themselves with matters on the other side of the Atlantic.'[8] But a day later, the Confederate Commissioner in Brussels, Ambrose Dudley Mann, reported that he had just received a letter from his informant in London, 'an influential Englishman', who wrote that there was 'a steady progress of opinion in one direction' regarding Palmerston and Russell. As to the latter, 'I am informed upon the most credible authority, [Russell is] perfectly satisfied that there is not so much a shadow of a chance for the Yankees to overpower the united and resolute South, and that he would not be opposed to intervention if a reasonable hope could be entertained of its acceptance by the administration at Washington.'[9]

Whether or not Russell was 'perfectly satisfied' before Second Bull Run, afterwards he became a thorough convert to the idea that the war must be stopped. 'I agree with you that the time is come for offering mediation to the United States Government, with a view to the recognition of the independence of the Confederates,' he wrote to Palmerston on 17 September. 'I agree further, that in case of failure, we ought ourselves to recognize the Southern States as an independent state.' Russell ordered their Ambassador in Paris, Lord Cowley, to have a quiet word with the Foreign Minister, Édouard Thouvenel, about cooperation from the Emperor.[10]

*

For the Confederates, Lee's victory at Second Bull Run was the signal to begin creating a groundswell of public sympathy in favour of Southern recognition. In France, John Slidell had heard through intermediaries that the Emperor would not state publicly that the powers should intervene until he had received unambiguous reassurances from Britain that it would follow suit. Henry Hotze put his stable of writers to work. 'Since one journalist usually writes for several publications,' he explained to the Confederate Secretary of State, Judah P. Benjamin, 'I have thus the opportunity of multiplying myself, so to speak, to an almost unlimited extent.' He was not worried about 'the sympathies of the intelligent classes [which] are now intensified into a feeling of sincere admiration'. But James Spence's failure to stir up unrest in the manufacturing districts made Hotze fear that the working classes were implacable enemies of the South. 'I am convinced', he admitted, 'that the astonishing fortitude and patience with which they endure [the cotton famine] is mainly due to a consciousness that by any other course they would promote our interests.'[11]

Hotze was overestimating his success with the 'intelligent' classes and underestimating the unpopularity of the North among the workers. But what united all the classes in England, regardless of his efforts, was an ingrained hatred of slavery; the institution was an insurmountable stumbling block. Slidell and Mason could and did mislead potential Southern sympathizers when the occasion demanded. Camouflaging the South's total dependence on slavery was the only way, for example, that Slidell was able to persuade the veteran abolition campaigner Lord Shaftesbury to give them his support. Slidell had targeted Shaftesbury because 'His peculiar position as the leader of an extensive and influential class in England, and the son-in-law of Lady Palmerston gives a value and significance to his opinions beyond that of a simple member of the House of Lords', he explained to Benjamin. But the relationship almost foundered in September when Shaftesbury asked him, in all innocence, 'if the [Confederate] President could not in some way present the prospect of gradual emancipation. Such a declaration coming from him unsolicited would have the happiest effect in Europe ...' Slidell circumvented the question by replying that abolition was an issue for the individual States to decide, and he could not speak for all of them.[12] Slidell was grateful that Lincoln was still publicly maintaining an ambivalent stance on slavery.[13] On 19 August Lincoln declared in a letter published by the *New York Tribune*, 'If I could save the Union without freeing any slave I would do it, and if I could save it by freeing all the slaves I would do it.'* It enabled Slidell to suggest to Lord Shaftesbury that the chances of emancipation 'were much better if we were left to ourselves than if we had remained in the Union'.[14]

Slidell heard from Shaftesbury that a decision regarding Southern recognition was 'close at hand, a very few weeks at the furthest'. Ironically, of all the concerns that might delay or precipitate the decision, Palmerston and Russell never mentioned slavery or public opinion as being among them. They were far more worried that the North would simply reject Britain's offer to mediate. The Duke of Argyll had warned Palmerston at the beginning of September that the Americans would never accept any interference from Europe. 'I think it right to tell you of a letter we have had from Sumner,' wrote the Duke on 2 September. 'He says that there is NO THOUGHT of giving up the Contest. He speaks, indeed, as if doing so were simply impossible.' It would therefore 'be folly, I think, to attempt any intervention'.[15]

But there had been more momentous news from America since Russell and Palmerston had agreed to hold a Cabinet meeting on the subject. CS General Lee had apparently marched with his Confederate army into Maryland. 'The two armies are approaching each other to the North of Washington and another great conflict is about to take place,' Palmerston wrote to Russell on 22 September. 'Any proposal for mediation or armistice would no doubt just now be refused by the Federals. [But] If they are thoroughly beaten ... they may be brought to a more reasonable state of mind.'[16] Two days later, on the 24th, Palmerston informed a delighted Gladstone about the mediation plan. 'The proposal would naturally be made to both North and South,' he wrote. 'If both accepted we should recommend an Armistice and Cessation of Blockades with a View to Negotiation on the Basis of Separation.' If only the South accepted, 'we should then, I conceive, acknowledge the Independence of the South'. Russell had suggested that the Cabinet

---

* Lincoln continued to be hamstrung by the opposition to emancipation from influential leaders such as John Hughes, the Archbishop of New York, who had already issued this warning: 'We Catholics ... have not the slightest idea of carrying on a war that costs so much blood and treasure just to gratify a clique of Abolitionists in the North.' With elections coming up, and the military tide against him, Lincoln felt that he could not afford to alienate anyone.

meeting should be held at the end of October, but Palmerston was now thinking it should be sooner. 'A great battle appeared by the last accounts to be coming on . . . a few Days will bring us important accounts.'[17]

Britain was waiting for news even as thousands of American families were already grieving after the single bloodiest day of the war. Forty-eight hours after his victory at Bull Run, Robert E. Lee had indeed ordered his Army of Northern Virginia to move north. On 4 September his exhausted and underfed troops traversed the Potomac river into the border State of Maryland. Lee's plan was to reach Pennsylvania, cut the rail links there and isolate Washington from the rest of the country. He understood as well as the Confederate government that Europe was waiting for a clear-cut victory, but this was not the reason behind his decision to invade the North. He hoped that the very presence of Confederate soldiers on Northern soil would give President Davis the authority to demand 'of the United States the recognition of our independence'.[18] If that failed, Lee thought it would be a sufficient shock to the North to turn the upcoming elections, which included several State governorships, in favour of the anti-war Democrats.

On 12 September Lincoln overruled his Cabinet and reinstated General McClellan to lead the Army of the Potomac. The soldiers trusted Little Mac, as they called him, and Lincoln felt strongly that this was no time for Washington to play favourites. Among the troops who chased after Lee were Ebenezer Wells of the 79th New York Highlanders and George Herbert of the 9th New York Volunteers. Five major battles and twelve engagements in eighteen months had drained the regiments of their lifeblood. In the words of one chronicler, the Highlanders had withered to a 'body of cripples'.[19]

Ebenezer Wells had been wounded during the Second Battle of Bull Run. 'My Sargent said to me, Wells, leave the field,' he recalled. 'I said what for, he pointed to my leg. I looked and saw blood, I soon felt where it came from: I had been shot in the side . . . [in] the intense excitement of that minute I only remember of having felt a slight stitch.' He was well enough to join the exodus from Washington a week later. The knowledge that McClellan was their leader 'revived the spirits of the men and without any rest we marched into Maryland'. It was probably fortunate that McClellan preferred to move his army at a crawl rather than a jog. Once again, the General's remarkably inefficient intelligence had magnified Lee's forces to twice their actual size, causing McClellan to become hyper-cautious.

Ill-fortune was dogging Lee at every turn. His army should have had at least 15,000 more men, but many had straggled to the point of desertion, or refused on principle to invade the North. Lee himself began the incursion with a nasty fall that left both his hands in splints. Generals Jackson and Longstreet also suffered minor but incapacitating injuries. All three therefore had to be conveyed through Maryland in ambulances, rather than gallantly leading their men on horseback. As the shoeless army tramped its way through the quiet countryside, it became clear that the Marylanders would not rise up or even offer breakfast to the Confederates. The men had to feed themselves with unripe apples and green corn snatched from the fields.[20] Lee naturally worried about his supply line. Aware that there were Federal forces behind him that could cut off his army, he decided that he would have to neutralize the threat they posed before he proceeded further north. He would have to detach his small army into even smaller, autonomous divisions – a risky manoeuvre – but it had worked against Pope, and Lee believed that he had the initiative.

On 13 September, the 27th Indiana Volunteers trailed into an abandoned Confederate camp outside Frederick. Four of them lay down on the grass to talk and rest in the late summer haze. One soldier, a future president of Oregon State University, noticed a yellow envelope lying in the field.[21] Inside, the group found three cigars and Lee's detailed plans for the next four days. The document, entitled Special Orders 191, was speedily relayed up the chain of command to McClellan. Almost as quickly, a Confederate sympathizer galloped off to report the news. At first, McClellan believed the orders were a trick, but a captain from Indiana recognized the handwriting and could vouch that the copyist on Lee's staff had been a friend before the war.[22] 'I have all the plans of the rebels, and will catch them in their own trap,' McClellan telegraphed Lincoln. 'Will send you trophies.'[23]

McClellan delayed his move for two days, even though his 95,000-strong Army of the Potomac was facing a Confederate force of only 18,000. By 16 September Lee had managed to reunite two-thirds of his divided army and take up a position around a quiet Maryland village named Sharpsburg. About a mile away, on the other side of Antietam Creek, McClellan's soldiers gathered in readiness. 'Our Brigade stole into position about half-past 10 o'clock on the night of the 16th,'

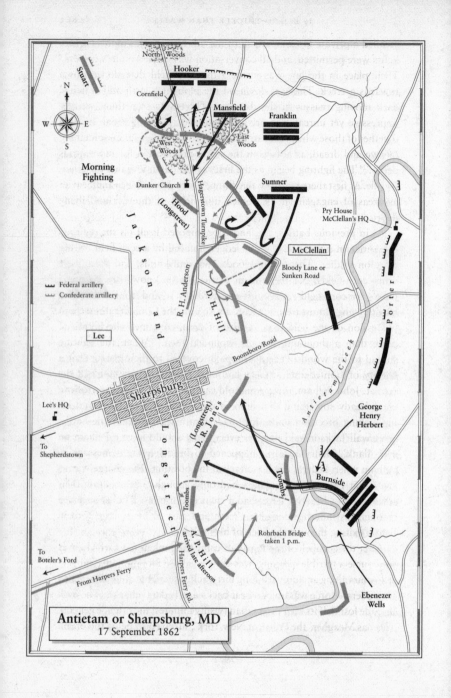

Antietam or Sharpsburg, MD
17 September 1862

Stuart

North Woods

Hooker

Cornfield

Mansfield

Franklin

Morning Fighting

West Woods

East Woods

Sumner

Dunker Church

Hood (Longstreet)

Pry House McClellan's HQ

Jackson and

Hagerstown Turnpike

McClellan

Bloody Lane or Sunken Road

Federal artillery
Confederate artillery

R. H. Anderson

D. H. Hill

Porter

Lee

Boonsboro Road

Antietam Creek

Sharpsburg

George Henry Herbert

Lee's HQ

D. R. Jones (Longstreet)

To Shepherdstown

Longstreet

Toombs

Toombs

Burnside

Rohrbach Bridge taken 1 p.m.

Toombs

A. P. Hill arrived late afternoon

Harpers Ferry Rd.

Ebenezer Wells

To Boteler's Ford

From Harpers Ferry

recalled a private in Company G of the 9th New York Volunteers. 'No lights were permitted, and all conversation was carried on in whispers.' Their place in the line was inside a thin cornfield that sloped down towards a creek. They sat down on the ploughed earth and watched dark moving masses in the distance. 'There was something weirdly impressive yet unreal', the private continued, 'in the gradual drawing together of those whispering armies under cover of the night – something of awe and dread, as always in the secret preparation for momentous deeds.'[24] The fighting began as the first rays of dawn revealed the countryside. At first there was sporadic firing, which grew louder and heavier as areas of engagement blossomed into fields of thunder and flying debris.

As in previous battles, the landscape imposed itself on the fighting. 'At Antietam it was a low, rocky ledge, prefaced by a corn-field,' wrote a Union soldier. 'There were woods, too, and knolls, and there were other corn-fields; but the student of that battle knows one cornfield only – *the* corn-field . . . about it and across it, to and fro, the waves of battle swung almost from the first.' By 10 a.m. the Confederates were in possession of the field that, instead of corn, contained the bodies of more than a thousand dead or wounded men.[25] When the fighting shifted to the woods, Federal troops discovered to their horror that a battery of Confederate artillery had been swiftly moved to block the retreat. John Pelham, the 24-year-old captain in charge of the artillery, was already something of a hero in the South. During Antietam, his unflinching precision under fire made him a legend. After the battle, Stonewall Jackson said of him, 'every army should have a Pelham on each flank'. Henry MacIver happened to be delivering a message to Pelham when Federal cavalry attacked the position. The charge was so swift that Pelham and his men had only enough time to draw their revolvers. But MacIver never had a chance to use his: a bullet smashed through his mouth, taking four teeth and part of his tongue with it, before exiting through the back of his neck.[26]

After the cornfield and the woods came the sunken road which, over the course a terrible morning, was christened the Bloody Lane. For several hours along an 800-yard-long dirt track, a small but well-entrenched Confederate force was able to beat back each Federal charge. (The Irish Brigade lost half its men in less than twenty minutes; the brigade general, Thomas Meagher, 'the Prince of New York', survived by being too drunk to ride.) But eventually they were overwhelmed and surrounded. 'We were shooting them like sheep in a pen,' recalled a private from New York.[27] The break in the Confederate line offered McClellan a clear way through; he could have destroyed Lee's centre and then turned to crush each wing. Yet McClellan never called forward his reserves.

In the afternoon, the hardest part of the fighting was at Rohrbach Bridge, which spanned Antietam Creek and led directly towards the Confederate brigades under General 'Old Pete' Longstreet. Ambrose Burnside, who had led the Union capture of Roanoke in February, now commanded McClellan's 9th Corps, which included both the 9th New York and the 79th Highlanders. The bridge in question was only 12 feet wide but 125 feet long. Burnside divided his corps, sending some, including the 9th, to ford the river further down; the rest, along with the 79th, he ordered to charge across the bridge. The Confederates easily repulsed each assault until the 79th ended up having to trample over the bodies of their comrades in order to reach the other side.

For three hours various regiments made disjointed attempts to fight their way across Burnside's Bridge, as it became known. 'We had a heavy struggle crossing Antietam Creek,' George Herbert told his brother Jack. He had been in charge of the battery that was covering the ford, and had watched as his friends waded through waist-deep water while bullets and shells picked them off one by one. The 9th was the first to reach the far bank. As soon as they were reunited they were ordered to storm the Confederate position on the other side of a ploughed field. It was three in the afternoon. 'When the order to get up was given, I turned over quickly to look at Col. Kimball, who had given the order, thinking he had suddenly become insane,' wrote the regiment's historian. 'I was lying on my back ... watching the shells explode and speculating as to how long I could hold up my finger before it would be shot off, for the very air seemed full of bullets.'[28] The men around him were similarly battle-crazed. One wrote how 'the whole landscape for an instant turned slightly red'.[29]

The regiment managed to stagger on until they were within 50 yards of the Confederates. The two sides stared at each other and then roared into hand-to-hand combat. It was the Confederates who turned and fled towards Sharpsburg. The officers leading the 9th struggled to restrain their troops from chasing after them and finally resorted to taking out their revolvers and threatening to shoot.[30] But at 4.30 p.m. the Union victors were blindsided by a fresh attack from Confederate reinforcements. The last of Lee's divided forces had arrived at the battlefield, and the 9th had no choice but to retreat. Some of the men cried as they stumbled back down the hill. McClellan had failed to send reinforcements. When a courier from Burnside arrived with a plea for men and guns, McClellan replied: 'Tell General Burnside this is the battle of the war . . . Tell him if he cannot hold his ground, then the bridge, to the last man! – always the bridge! If the Bridge is lost, all is lost!' Burnside held the bridge but little else.[31]

'Antietam was a fearful struggle,' wrote Ebenezer Wells. During the night of the 17th he had led his team of wagons to a hill; 'the thickest of the fight had been just there. The road ran parallel with a stone wall which formed a good breastwork for the Southerners, and it was a heavy slaughter for our men . . . It was a moonlit night, and I went to speak to a man sitting across the wall. I wondered what he stayed for.' Wells addressed a few words to him, only to realize that he was dead. 'He must have been killed instantly, as he was in nearly an upright position as though in the act of climbing over. The bodies were piled up in heaps all about us.'[32] Nearly 6,000 men lay dying or dead in ditches and creeks, around fences and knolls, under trees, and across blackened fields. Another 17,000 were either waiting for medical attention or receiving what passed for care under hideous conditions.[33] Remarkably, Henry MacIver was alive. He had been dragged from the field and carried to a nearby house. By the time he was seen to, he had almost drowned in his own blood. To prevent him from choking to death, the doctor put a silver tube down his throat.

McClellan was so dazed by the scale of the battle that he did nothing to impede Lee's retreat across the Potomac river into Virginia. The shocking number of casualties on 17 September would make Antietam the single costliest day of the war. Twenty-five thousand men were killed, wounded or missing. McClellan had lost nearly 15 per cent of his men; Lee, almost a quarter. The Confederate General might have been defeated once and for all, with his army destroyed, if McClellan's attacks had been better coordinated. McClellan had shown that he could take a strong hand and throw it away. Yet Antietam was still a victory of sorts for the North because Lee's invasion had been halted. Although McClellan made the fatal mistake of allowing Lee to escape, he had pricked the aura of invincibility that had grown around the Confederates since the

Seven Days' Battles. He had proven that the Army of Northern Virginia could be stopped.

A few days later, when both armies had deserted the battlefield, the Marquess of Hartington went to inspect the site in order to give a report to his younger brother, Lord Edward Cavendish, who was serving in one of the regiments sent out to defend Canada during the height of the *Trent* affair. Hartington had been in the United States for nearly a month, avoiding his expensive mistress, Catherine Walters (whom he affectionately called Skittles). Now, he walked over the silent terrain in appalled wonder. 'In about seven or eight acres of wood,' he reported to his father, the Duke of Devonshire, 'there is not a tree which is not full of bullets and bits of shell. It is impossible to understand how anyone could live in such a fire as there must have been there.'[34]

Lord Hartington's impression of Washington after the Battle of Antietam was that it resembled a vast camp. 'You see hardly anything but soldiers and baggage-wagons, and stores moving up to the troops ... Washington is now completely surrounded by [forts], I think there are between forty and fifty,' he wrote on 29 September 1862. 'No drink is allowed to be sold, and, though the place is full of soldiers, it is very quiet.' He admired the bearing of the volunteers and thought it 'a great pity that such fine material should be thrown away, as they very likely may be, by having utterly incompetent officers'.[35] Naturally, he was entertained by Seward, Lincoln and a host of Washington dignitaries who had become friends with his other brother, Frederick, during the latter's visit in 1859. By now the Americans were used to titled foreigners in their midst. Seward reminisced at length about his stay in England and the titled personages he had met. Lincoln was civil 'and also told us stories. I said I supposed we had come at a bad time to see the country, and he said, "Well! He guessed we couldn't do them much harm."' Secretary of War Stanton revolted Hartington for being a 'most atrocious snob', worse even than Seward. General McClellan, he thought, was quiet and modest in comparison but Hartington was surprised by the General's hatred of abolitionists.[36]

Lincoln regarded Antietam as the victory he had been waiting for in order to issue his preliminary Emancipation Proclamation. 'I think the time has come now,' he told the Cabinet after the announcement on 22 September. 'I wish it were a better time. I wish that we were in a better condition.' But, he continued, 'I must do the best I can and bear the responsibility of taking the course which I feel I ought to take.' The Proclamation declared that, on 1 January 1863, all slaves in the rebellious parts of the country would be 'forever free'.[37] Lincoln also included the prospect of compensated emancipation for slave-owners – and emigration for freed blacks – in order to soften the objections of both Democratic voters and the border States. Seward had his reservations but supported the President. On 26 September he told his daughter that he hoped the Proclamation had not been issued prematurely.[38]

Francis Dawson learned about the Emancipation Proclamation from his prison guard. His bravery had earned him a commission as a 1st lieutenant of artillery. 'The cup of my happiness was full,' he wrote in his memoir. 'My new uniform was a gray tunic with scarlet cuffs and scarlet collar; an Austrian knot of gold braid on each arm . . . gray trousers with broad red stripes.'[39] The Englishman had acquired legions of admirers. 'I am very highly thought of here; pardon the apparent egotism of the remark,' he wrote candidly to his mother. 'I have a troop of wealthy and influential friends here who will do anything for me. Mr Raines of whom I have spoken to you before has even expressed a wish to adopt me as a son.'[40] His popularity was a blessing, since he had not actually received any pay, and inflation was already turning ordinary articles into priceless objects. He was dismayed to discover that a plain calico shirt cost twenty Confederate dollars (about £2).

Dawson went to Richmond to receive his orders and, while there, had his portrait taken; 'if I am killed it shall be sent to you,' he promised his mother. From anyone else such words might have been mere bravado, but Dawson was serious. He astonished the chief of ordnance, Colonel Gorgas, by informing him that he did not wish to be relegated to the rear. The Colonel complied. 'He gave me a letter to General Longstreet, requesting that, if any particularly hazardous service should fall within the line of my duty, it might be given to me.'[41] Gorgas had assigned him as brigade ordnance officer, under Colonel Manning, in Longstreet's division.[42] But during his first assignment in early September, Dawson was captured along with the wagons he was taking to Longstreet's camp. By morning the prisoners were in Pennsylvania on their way to Harrisburg. Dawson's fresh-looking uniform and general foreignness once again attracted attention. The Union officers escorting the train took such a liking to him that he was able to borrow one of their blankets and a spare toothbrush. But by the journey's end Dawson discovered that it was possible to be too popular. When they reached Harrisburg one of the officers insisted on showing him around the town. The commandant thought this was a doubtful idea but the US captain was adamant. Supper in the town's principal hotel passed without incident. Unfortunately this only emboldened the US officer:

After supper [Dawson recalled], we walked out to the front of the hotel, where my companion slapped me on the shoulder and said in a loud voice: 'Here is a real live Rebel officer! The first man that says a word to him I will knock his damned head off!' This was not a very pacific speech to make to a crowd of fanatical Pennsylvanians, who had just heard that the battle of Sharpsburg [Antietam] had begun.[43]

From the hotel they went to a music hall. They entered as the performers were leading the audience in a rendition of 'The Union and McClellan forever'. Undaunted, the captain escorted Dawson down the aisle to the front row, calmly ignoring the growls and murmurs from the crowd. 'By this time,' he noticed, 'my companion was decidedly exhilarated.' Dawson had no choice but to wait and see what suicidal escapade the captain would think up next. About half an hour later the officer jumped from his seat and shouted at the top of his voice that he would beat any man who laid on a finger on his friend. His action unleashed the crowd. Just before Dawson lost consciousness he heard shots being fired. When he recovered he learned that the commandant had come looking for them. The captain had emerged barely alive. It transpired that he had a notorious drinking problem.

Dawson was almost relieved when he reached the relative safety of Fort Delaware. The grim fort-turned-prison was situated in the middle of the Delaware river, on a swamp-infested island known locally as Pea Patch. The only other inhabitants beside the inmates and guards were malaria-carrying mosquitoes and rats. As an officer, Dawson was housed inside the fort rather than in one of the wooden barracks outside. 'The Time dragged heavily,' he wrote. Ninety unwashed men were crammed into a 30-foot room and never allowed out except for meals, which were short and sparse. After three weeks he was paroled and shipped back to Richmond.

He arrived in the city on 6 October. 'I can hardly realize now', he wrote, 'that the time, counted by days and weeks, was really so short.

And yet, it must have been so.' There was an air of anxiety in Richmond that he had not felt before. All leave had been cancelled and uniformed men were thronging the streets. The hotels were full and there was nowhere for him to stay. The wounded from Antietam filled every spare bed and couch in the city. More than 10,000 soldiers were being treated in Richmond's hospitals. Having heard that there was a shortage of nurses, Mary Sophia Hill temporarily left Sam and went to help at Chimborazo, which had grown so quickly since its establishment in 1861 that in a few more months it would be the largest military hospital in the world.

Dawson could not rejoin Longstreet's army until his exchange was official, which would not be until the end of November, but he was able to wangle a military pass from Colonel Gorgas, who recognized that the foreign volunteer could simply resign if he became fed up. Dawson left the city to visit the Pegrams. Though he did not like to admit it, he was in love – in love with the South, with its people, its culture and, at this particular moment, with Miss Pegram. 'You will think me partial, but it is not so,' Dawson insisted in a letter to his mother. Yet he could not help dwelling on certain attributes of Captain Pegram's niece: 'Loving brown eyes, perfect hands and a rich mass of glorious auburn hair.'[44] The delightful Miss Pegram had nursed him during his convalescence in the summer, and was pleased to so do again.

Dawson's departure from Richmond at the beginning of October coincided with the arrival of Francis Lawley and Lieutenant Colonel Garnet Wolseley. They had met in Baltimore shortly before the Battle of Antietam when they were trying to slip into the Confederacy, the former to report for *The Times*, the latter, who was stationed in Canada, to satisfy his curiosity about volunteer armies. The 29-year-old Wolseley had been among the first wave of soldiers sent out by the British government during the *Trent* affair. After the possibility of war had subsided, Wolseley continued to be fascinated by the events south of the border. 'It is not easy to describe the breathless interest and excitement with which from month to month, almost from day to day, we English soldiers read and studied every report that could be obtained of the war as it proceeded,' he wrote later. Wolseley badgered his superiors until he and a friend secured a two-month leave of absence.[45] They then flipped a coin to decide who would go north and who would have the harder task of going south. Wolseley 'won' the South.[46]

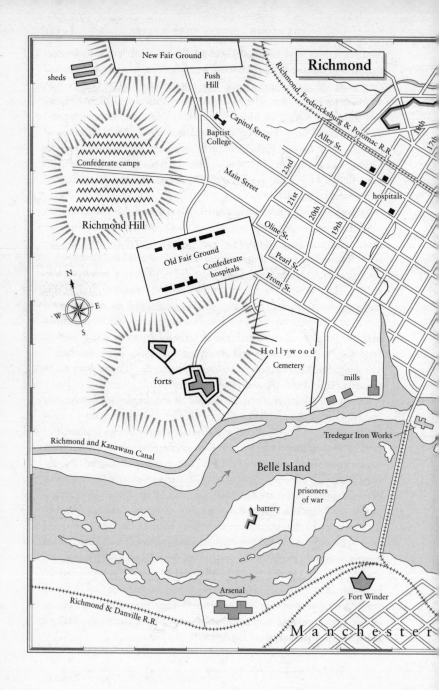

Richmond

New Fair Ground

sheds

Fush Hill

Capitol Street

Baptist College

Confederate camps

Main Street

Richmond Hill

Old Fair Ground

Confederate hospitals

Richmond, Fredericksburg & Potomac R.R.

Alley St.

hospitals

23rd

21st

20th

19th

Oline St.

Pearl St.

Front St.

18th

17th

N
E
W
S

forts

Hollywood Cemetery

mills

Richmond and Kanawam Canal

Tredegar Iron Works

Belle Island

battery

prisoners of war

Arsenal

Richmond & Danville R.R.

Fort Winder

M a n c h e s t e r

Shockoe Creek

fort

fort

earthworks and batteries

16th
15th
14th
13th
12th
11th
10th
9th
8th
7th
swamp

Virginia Central R.R.

Confederate
camps

6th

Jefferson Davis's
house

5th

The Capitol

Capitol Square

Government
House

Alms House

Main Street

Church Hill

Old
St John's
Church

depot

J a m e s

Libby Hill

falls

Railroad Bridge

rapids

Mayo's Bridge

R i v e r

canal

foundry

depot

Haxall Mills

earthworks

During the summer, *The Times* had offered Lawley the now-vacant post of special correspondent. The middling poet and bon vivant Charles Mackay had replaced Bancroft Davis in New York and was supplying the paper with business and political analysis.* But Delane needed the eyewitness reports previously supplied by Russell. Lawley knew nothing about military matters, but in two other important respects he had changed a great deal since February. He was a hardier traveller, and he had decided that the South had a right to independence. No single event was responsible for Lawley's apostasy, but the Anglophobia displayed before and during the *Trent* affair, not to mention the untrammelled hounding of his friend William Howard Russell, had helped to convince him that a strong Confederacy was essential if the North's aggressive tendencies were to be restrained.[47]

Just surviving the tortuous journey past Federal pickets and scouting parties into Confederate territory was an education for Lawley. W. W. Glenn's contacts were finding it harder to slip back and forth. Lawley had never before shared a room, let alone a bed, with several dirty strangers. In his autobiography, Field Marshal Viscount Wolseley, as he was to become, recalled with amusement being woken up in the middle of the night by Lawley, who was standing in the corner of the farmer's shed where they were sleeping, frantically waving his stick at the rats scurrying over his feet. Less comical was their train ride from Fredericksburg to Richmond. The travellers had to squeeze in beside hundreds of amputees who were being conveyed to hospitals in the city. The men lay stretched across the seats and were bumped and jolted continuously. 'That train', wrote Wolseley, 'opened Frank Lawley's eyes to the horrible side of war, made all the more in this instance because no chloroform or medical supplies of any sort were available.'[48]

When Lawley and Wolseley reached Richmond, they were lucky to secure an attic room in the Exchange Hotel. Frank Vizetelly, they learned, had snagged the last remaining bed at the Spotswood, the Willard's of Richmond. He was glad of their company and went with them

---

* Mackay had been a footsoldier in the army of underpaid hacks until 1843, when, at the age of 29, he made his reputation with a book called *Extraordinary Popular Delusions and the Madness of Crowds*. But in his heart he always considered himself a poet rather than a journalist. He did not intend to do any travelling for *The Times*. He had toured the United States in 1858 and felt that he had experienced enough trains and American hotels to last him a lifetime.

to the War Secretary's office to obtain a travel pass. The sight of the captured flags of the enemy lying in heaps on the floor shocked Wolseley but he held his tongue while they received their papers and letters of introduction. The following day, 9 October, the little party set off to find General Lee's headquarters.

Wolseley came away with fragmentary but vivid impressions of the city. Richmond had hardly changed since Charles Dickens had described it in 1842 as 'delightfully situated on eight hills, overhanging the James River'. It was still a city of churches rather than saloons, and despite the arrival of five railway lines over the past thirty years the pace of life remained slow and decorous. The residents prized the city's reputation as the premier cultural centre of the South. Richmond boasted five daily newspapers, a literary journal, several theatres and an academy of fine arts. The city did share one characteristic with Washington: its hotels were similarly uncomfortable and dirty. But otherwise, the capitals were a study in contrasts. Washington was a city built to order, as yet lacking in history or tradition; Richmond was formed shortly after the first settlers arrived in Jamestown and its history was indistinguishable from many of the most famous events of the Revolutionary era. Patrick Henry's famous 'Give me Liberty or Give me Death' speech in 1775 was made in St John's church on Broad Street.

Unlike the domeless Capitol building in Washington, Richmond's neoclassical Capitol was not only finished but also widely admired and imitated. Designed by Thomas Jefferson, it stood proud on the highest hill of the city, within a 12-acre park called Capitol Square, dominating the skyline like the Parthenon on the Acropolis. Here, in a cluster of classical buildings, lay the seat of the Confederate government. The Confederate White House was situated four blocks away, in an Italianate mansion that had been donated to the government by the owner.

Richmond was built on a rising slope and its streets were regular and easy to navigate. The industrial district – the flourmills, tobacco- and wheat-processing plants and the ironworks – was down by the river. Shops and businesses of the better class were below Capitol Square, along Main Street, and the residential neighbourhoods were on the crests of the hills. The city's busiest slave-auction house, owned by Robert Lumpkin, was only three blocks from the Capitol. Wolseley avoided it when he went exploring, though it was almost the only establishment in town with goods to sell. The bookshops were empty of

View of Richmond from the west, by Frank Vizetelly, who sketched
his own image on the left, under the tree

books, and the general stores were denuded of everyday items like shoe
polish and pins.

Before they left, Lawley gave his *Times* dispatch to the French Consul, who was less of a stickler than Consul Moore when it came to
preserving the sanctity of the diplomatic bag. Like Wolseley, Lawley had
noticed the effects of the blockade, but airily dismissed them in his article as merely depriving Southerners of a few unnecessary luxuries. Nor
did it matter, he declared, that Confederate soldiers often had to march
without shoes, hats or coats: 'These men, many of them bearing some of
England's most honoured names, and descended from England's best
families, are in the field, and have been so for 19 months, fighting against
[Northern] mercenaries!' (The article prompted the paper's managing
editor, Mowbray Morris, to remind Lawley that they required his news-
gathering skills, rather than his opinions, since they had plenty of the
latter at home.)[49] Had he read the dispatch, Consul Moore would have
been infuriated by Lawley's insouciance. The beleaguered diplomat was,
at this moment, writing pathetic letters to the Foreign Office saying he

was understaffed, overwhelmed and unable to buy even such commodities as coal for the office: 'I leave it to your Lordship to judge if we are not entitled to extra aid.'[50]

Lawley had never had to suffer a moment's hardship that was not the direct result of his own profligacy. Perhaps this was why he came to idolize the Confederate army. The young plantation aristocrats who so readily sacrificed everything for the sake of an ideal put his own idle existence to shame. Many of them, like the ambulance driver who conveyed Lawley and his friends away from Richmond, were utterly ill suited for soldiering. The driver, the son of a wealthy farmer, had accepted the relatively menial occupation because his battle wounds were too severe to allow him to continue to fight. Yet he had no idea how to look after himself, even to the extent of becoming drenched because he had never had to fetch his own blanket before.[51]

Observing the Southerner's inability to shift for himself, Wolseley decided that the difference between a professional army and a collection of armed volunteers was, for want of a better term, the existence of *esprit de corps*. Without it, as he and other English observers noticed, nothing worked as it should.[52] There appeared to be little internal cooperation or forward thinking. Regiments would march along muddy roads, making them worse, without stopping to lay new tracks so that the next regiment would not become bogged down. Wolseley admitted to feeling 'sorely puzzled' about the South. Slaves were referred to as 'servants', and white servants as 'the help', but the euphemisms were simply window dressing the obvious. Its people combined genteel manners with ancient barbarism; they were brave in the face of appalling deprivation, and personally charming even when proclaiming their bitterness at being betrayed by their British cousins.[53]

As the three Englishmen travelled to General Lee's headquarters near Winchester, they were treated to the full glory of Virginia in the autumn, the gentle golden light reminding Wolseley of a country scene from a Claude painting.[54] When they arrived at Lee's camp in the Shenandoah Valley in mid-October, Wolseley and Lawley were surprised by its spartan appearance. The headquarters was nothing more than eight pole tents placed in a row on hard, rocky ground. Horses roamed loose, wagons were pitched willy-nilly and were clearly serving as makeshift beds for some of the officers.

Lee himself inspired a strong reaction in the travellers; indeed, Wolseley developed an immediate case of hero-worship. Though still recovering the use of his hands, the Confederate General was a 'splendid specimen of an English gentleman, with one of the most rarely handsome faces I ever saw ... You only have to be in his society for a very brief period to be convinced that whatever he says may be implicitly relied upon.' Wolseley recognized in Lee a military genius: 'I never felt my own individual insignificance more keenly than I did in his presence.'[55] Lawley was equally enthusiastic. Lee was 'impressive and imposing', he wrote, 'his dark brown eyes remarkably direct and honest as they meet you fully and firmly ... It is certain that General Lee has no superior in the Confederacy and it may be doubted whether he has any equal.'[56] Vizetelly quickly set about sketching a portrait of him for English readers while Lee conversed with the visitors. Not once, Lawley and Wolseley observed, did the General express any bitterness towards the North, even though his homes had been pillaged without restraint. Nor did Lee discuss the recent battle at Antietam.

Unable to spare even a single tent for the travellers, Lee gave them a two-horse wagon so that they would be able to visit the camps of the other generals. 'Upon leaving him,' wrote Wolseley, 'we drove to Bunker's Hill ... at which place Stonewall Jackson, now of world-wide celebrity, had his headquarters.' The normally taciturn Jackson made a particular effort with his guests, and even reminisced about his time in England, leading them to think that his reputation for moroseness was rather overblown. The General talked so much that the three visitors never had the chance to ask him anything. 'As we rode away,' wrote the Confederate officer escorting the group, 'I said: "Gentlemen, you have disclosed Jackson in a new character to me, and I've been carefully observing him for a year and a half. You have made him exhibit *finesse*, for he did all the talking to keep you from asking too curious or embarrassing questions. I never saw anything like it in him before."'[57]

Jackson's ruse did not prevent the visitors from making their own judgements. Lawley noticed that the General had achieved a kind of mythical stature. Civilians flocked to his camp just for a glimpse of the great man; even his staff regarded him with reverence. The journalist thought it was dangerous that the hopes of so many should rest on just one commander. Yet he could understand why. Jackson lived the part. 'Dressed in his grey uniform,' wrote Wolseley, 'he looks the hero that he is.'[58]

General Longstreet was their final stop on the tour, and could only suffer by comparison to Lee and Jackson. Lawley, however, saw much to praise. 'His frame is stout and heavy, his countenance florid and cheery, and eminently English in appearance.'[59] They watched a review of 10,000 of his soldiers. 'Among this body there were no shoeless or barefooted sufferers,' wrote Lawley, 'a finer or more spirited body of men has never been assembled together on the North American continent.' According to Wolseley, the boots and shoes had only recently arrived in a large shipment from England.

Wolseley's leave was coming to an end and he had to begin his journey home. He was only able to achieve a brief glimpse of Lee's cavalry commander, J. E. B. ('Jeb') Stuart. The travellers arrived at his headquarters, an elegant plantation house called the Bower, to discover that the famed general was off on a raid in Pennsylvania. The Bower's owners were still there, as were numerous pretty female relatives whose chief *raison d'être* appeared to be making the officers comfortable. Stuart returned on 10 October with 1,200 captured horses and not a single man lost. Wolseley observed the riders galloping home and was impressed by their superiority to Northern cavalry, 'who can scarcely sit on their horses, even when trotting'.[60]

CS General Jeb Stuart scouting in the neighbourhood of Culpepper
Court House, Virginia, by Frank Vizetelly

Francis Lawley and Frank Vizetelly were a great hit among Stuart's
staff. Lieutenant Colonel William Blackford recalled the officers' delight
when they returned to camp on 16 October, and found the journalists
waiting to meet them. 'These gentlemen were often after this our guests,
and we all became very fond of them,' he wrote. They already had a
Prussian officer serving as a volunteer aide, Major Heros von Borcke,
and were used to eccentric foreigners.[61] A partially recovered Henry
MacIver was also pottering in and out of Stuart's camp, trying to be useful but more often simply passing the time with friends from his Garibaldi
days. He was delighted to see Vizetelly again. The hard-drinking journalist 'was the most interesting narrator I have ever listened to around
a campfire', wrote Blackford.

> There was not a disreputable or reputable place of prominence in the civil-
> ized world that he did not know all about ... We had a shrewd suspicion
> that he drew a little on his imagination for his facts, but what difference did
> that make to us. Late into the night we all sat around the embers of our fire

out under the grand oaks listening to the fascinating tales he told, his expressive countenance and gestures giving full effect to his words by their play. Mr Lawley was an exceedingly intelligent and refined Englishman and in another style we enjoyed his instructive conversation very much, but Vizetelly was fascinating.[62]

Blackford and von Borcke invited them to pitch their tents on the vacant plot next to their own. 'Regularly after dinner,' von Borcke recalled, 'our whole family of officers, from the commander down to the youngest lieutenant, used to assemble in [Vizetelly's] tent, squeezing ourselves into narrow quarters to hear his entertaining narratives.'[63]

Night amusements in the Confederate camp, by Frank Vizetelly

During the journey home, Wolseley mused on the scenes he had witnessed down south. He had seen many armies, 'but I never saw one composed of finer men, or that looked more like *work*', he wrote. 'Any one who goes amongst those men in their bivouacs, and talks to them as I did, will soon learn why it is that their Generals laugh at the idea of Mr Lincoln's mercenaries subjugating the South.'[64] By the time he reached Montreal he had made up his mind to campaign for Southern recognition. Wolseley was aware that the question remained open in Britain. Like so many Englishmen, he assumed that slavery would quickly die out after independence. The real moral issue, in his eyes, was how long the suffering should be allowed to endure. In a bid to reach the widest possible audience, he decided to write an essay for the literary *Blackwood's Magazine*, entitled, 'A Month's Visit to the Confederate Headquarters'. 'The first question always asked me by both men and women was,' he declared in the article, 'why England had not recognised their independence ... Had we no feelings of sympathy for the descendants of our banished cavaliers? Was not blood thicker than water?'[65]

14

A Fateful Decision

British reaction to Antietam – Gladstone's Newcastle speech –
Battle in the Cabinet – The Emperor proposes joint intervention –
Russell turns tail

Britain did not receive word of Antietam until the very end of September. 'I hope more than I dare express,' wrote Charles Francis Adams in his diary on the 29th. 'For a fortnight my mind has been running so strongly on all this night and day, that it seems to almost threaten my life.' His son Charles Francis Jr., now Lieutenant Adams in the 1st Massachusetts Cavalry, had last written to the family to say that his regiment was joining the Army of the Potomac in Maryland. The following day, the 30th, the legation heard that Lee's advance had been stopped. 'But [McClellan] failed to follow it up and let them escape,' raged Benjamin Moran.[1] Adams was also disappointed. Nor were his fears allayed about his son. It was several more days before they received a letter from Charles. His regiment had sat on their horses in readiness while shells exploded on the surrounding hills, but McClellan never sent them into battle.

Reports of the terrific slaughter at Antietam shocked the nation; the 25,000 casualties on a single day seemed almost inconceivable, especially when compared to the 25,000 Britain suffered during the entire Crimean War.[2] 'The Federals in their turn have had a victory; and so it goes on; when will it end? Fanny Kemble says not until the South is coerced back into the Union,' wrote Henry Greville, reflecting the horror felt by many people at the thought that the war might continue for many months more.[3] Five days later, on 5 October 1862, there was a second uproar in the press, this time over Lincoln's Emancipation Proclamation. As Seward had feared from the outset, the Proclamation was widely denounced as a cynical and desperate ploy. Charles Francis Adams understood its symbolic importance, but even pro-Northern supporters could not understand why Lincoln had allowed the border States to keep their slaves, unless the emancipation order was directed against the South rather than slavery itself. 'Our people are very imperfectly acquainted with the powers of your Federal Government,' explained the anti-slavery crusader George Thompson to his American counterpart, William Lloyd Garrison. 'They know little or nothing of your constitution – its compromises, guarantees, limitations, obligations, etc. They are consequently unable to appreciate the difficulties of your president.'[4]

"NOT UP TO TIME;"
Or, Interference would be very Welcome.

As the French and British governments ponder intervention,
Punch argues the time is now

The *Spectator* declared itself to be disappointed with the Proclamation: 'The principle is not that a human being cannot justly own another,' it insisted, 'but that he cannot own him unless he is loyal to the United States.'[5] For the radical MP Richard Cobden, the moral contradiction proved that 'the leaders in the Federal government are not equal to the occasion'.[6] *The Times* went further and accused Lincoln of inciting the slaves in the South to kill their owners, imagining in graphic terms how the President 'will appeal to the black blood of the African; he will whisper of the pleasures of spoil and of the gratification of yet fiercer instincts; and when blood begins to flow and shrieks come piercing through the darkness, Mr Lincoln will wait till the rising flames tell that all is consummated, and he will rub his hands and think that revenge is sweet'.[7]

ABE LINCOLN'S LAST CARD; OR, ROUGE-ET-NOIR.

Punch portrays Lincoln's Emancipation Proclamation as a last desperate move

Lord Palmerston reacted to the two announcements with a far cooler head than either Russell or Gladstone. All along he had been a proponent of mediation while the outcome of the war seemed obvious. But Lee's check at Antietam, regardless of his escape across the Potomac river, had revealed a serious weakness in the Confederate army. The Prime Minister's confidence in the mediation plan was further shaken by a strong remonstrance from Lord Granville, the Liberal leader in the House of Lords, who argued in a letter to Russell on 27 September that any sort of interference in the war – no matter how good or charitable the intention – would only result in Britain becoming dragged into the conflict. 'I return you Granville's letter which contains much deserving of serious consideration,' Palmerston wrote to Russell on 2 October. 'The whole matter is full of difficulty, and can only be cleared up by some more decided events between the contending armies.'[8]

Russell had come to the opposite conclusion. He wanted the Cabinet meeting to discuss mediation brought forward by a week, from 23 October to the 16th. The news of Antietam and the Emancipation Proclamation had convinced him that only Britain had the power to stop the humanitarian crisis unfolding in America. The answer to Granville's objections, he thought, was to build an international alliance involving France and Russia to force the warring sides to agree to an armistice. 'My only doubt is whether we and France should stir if Russia holds back,' he told Palmerston.[9]

Gladstone was also moved by his belief that a humanitarian crisis was at hand, though he saw two – the one in Lancashire as well as the one in Virginia. Unlike Russell and Palmerston, he did not think that the Confederates had suffered a significant setback at Antietam. 'It has long been clear enough', he wrote, 'that secession is virtually an established fact.' When Gladstone talked about the undecided questions in America he meant whether 'Virginia must be divided, and probably Tennessee likewise'.[10] He impatiently brushed aside the Duchess of Sutherland's objections, telling her that 'Lincoln's lawless proclamation' would be far more destructive to America than a separation between the States. When the Duchess informed her son-in-law, the Duke of Argyll, about this latest twist to Gladstone's view of the war, the Duke sent him a blistering rebuke. 'I would not interfere to stop [the war] on any account,' he wrote. 'It is not our business to do so; and even short-sightedly, it is not our interest. Do you wish, if you could secure this result tomorrow, to see the great cotton system of the Southern States restored? Do you wish to see us almost entirely dependent on that system for the support of our Lancashire population? I do not.'[11] But the combination of his worries about Lancashire and his disgust with the Emancipation Proclamation pushed Gladstone over the edge. On 7 October, the day after the Proclamation appeared in *The Times*, he went to Newcastle to attend a banquet in his honour. He had been thinking all day about 'what I should say about Lancashire and America: for both these subjects are critical'.[12] Gladstone later told his wife that the acoustics were terrible and he had struggled to make himself heard. It would have been better for him, perhaps, if he had not been heard at all. The words that caught everyone's attention were these: 'We may have our own opinions about slavery; we may be for or against the South, but there is no doubt that Jefferson Davis and other leaders of the South have made an army; they are making, it appears, a navy; and they have made what is more difficult than either; they have made a nation.' They were telegraphed all over Europe almost before Gladstone had sat down. Dudley Mann in Brussels wrote to Richmond that same night: 'This clearly foreshadows our early recognition.'[13] Thirty-four years later, Gladstone admitted that his speech was a mistake of 'incredible grossness'. 'I really, though most strangely, believed that it was an act of friendliness to all America to recognise that the struggle was virtually at an end.' He hated to think of the damage he had caused, 'because I have for the last five-and-twenty years received from the . . . people of America tokens of goodwill which could not fail to arouse my undying gratitude'.*[14] But at the time he was unrepentant until Russell pointed out to him that he had created a controversy where none had existed.

Benjamin Moran worked himself up into one of his customary rages after he read the morning news on the 8th. Adams was not sure what to think. He knew enough about British politics now to realize that it would be highly unusual for a change in Cabinet policy to be announced in this way. The press seemed hesitant as well. When Adams saw William Forster four days later, he revealed that Seward had given him secret instructions that he was to withdraw from his post if recognition or intervention became government policy. Forster thought this was something the Foreign Office ought to know before it made any irretrievable decisions. But, Adams wondered, was this the Foreign Office at work, or

---

* Two years after the conclusion of the war, in 1867, Gladstone admitted in a letter to the American author and abolitionist Charles Edwards Lester: 'I had imbibed, conscientiously if erroneously, an opinion that 20 or 24 millions of the North would be happier, and would be stronger . . . without the South than with it, and also that the negroes would be much nearer to emancipation under a Southern Government than under the old system of the Union, which had not at that date (August, 1862) been abandoned . . . As far as regards the special or separate interest of England in the matter, I . . . had always contended that it was best for our interest that the Union should be kept entire.'

just Gladstone? Feeling depressed, he cheered himself up with a trip to the theatre to see *Our American Cousin*. 'The piece has no literary merit whatever,' he wrote. 'I laughed heartily and felt better for it.'[15]

It seemed to Adams that his question about the Cabinet's intentions was answered a week later when Sir George Cornewall Lewis gave a speech in Hereford, contradicting Gladstone's claim that the South was an established nation. His speech received favourable comment in the North and caused uproar in the South. Gladstone's 'made a nation' remark was forgotten. Britain was the clear leader in Europe, complained the influential *Richmond Enquirer*: Lewis had extinguished the light and closed 'the last prospect of European intervention . . .'[16] At home, a relieved Adams decided that Gladstone spoke only for himself in Newcastle and 'had overshot the mark'.

After these two conflicting statements there were no more public comments by any of the Cabinet. But furious arguments were taking place behind the scenes. Gladstone and Lewis had long been rivals. Only one of them could become Palmerston's heir and each was conscious of the other's near presence. Allowing his emotions to cloud his judgement was exactly what the aloof and scholarly Lewis expected of Gladstone. Russell, whenever he thought that the liberal Whig traditions of the house of Bedford were at stake, did the same, and this, Lewis knew, was their weak point.

Russell issued a memorandum to the Cabinet on 13 October that laid out why they should intervene and settle the war. Lewis pounced on it and wrote a scathing counter-memorandum on the 17th, pointing out that it was not a debating club that would be receiving the mediation proposal, but 'heated and violent partisans' who would reject it in an instant. The South would not be grateful for the help, thought Lewis, and the North would swear vengeance on Britain.[17]

Many years later, Henry Adams decided that the real reason why the Cabinet fell into such a muddle over the American question was because the English were, by habit, eccentric:

> The English mind took naturally to rebellion – when foreign – and it felt
> particular confidence in the Southern Confederacy because of its combined
> attributes – foreign rebellion of English blood – which came nearer ideal
> eccentricity than could be reached by Poles, Hungarians, Italians or French-
> men. All the English eccentrics rushed into the ranks of the rebel

sympathizers, leaving few but well-balanced minds to attach themselves to the cause of the Union ... The 'cranks' were all rebels ... The Church was rebel, but the dissenters were mostly with the Union. The universities were rebel, but the university men who enjoyed most public confidence – like Lord Granville, Sir George Cornewall Lewis, Lord Stanley, Sir George Grey – took infinite pains to be neutral for fear of being thought eccentric. To most observers, as well as to *The Times*, the *Morning Post*, and the *Standard*, a vast majority of the English people seemed to follow the professional eccentrics; even the emotional philanthropists took that direction ... and did so for no reason except their eccentricity; but the 'canny' Scots and Yorkshiremen were cautious.[18]

Senior Tories also voiced their concerns after they discovered that Russell was on the verge of approaching the French with his intervention plan; the Opposition still maintained its stance that Britain should avoid becoming entangled with either side. Lord Derby had no doubt, wrote Lord Clarendon, 'we should only meet with an insolent rejection of our offer'.[19] But Russell was no longer listening to his critics. He had already made overtures to the Emperor via the British Ambassador in Paris, Lord Cowley. However, the French Cabinet was undergoing one of its periodic crises, and the Foreign Minister was clearing his desk for his successor. The Confederate Commissioner in Paris, John Slidell, was in a state of nervous excitement. By now, he wrote to the Confederate Secretary of State, Judah P. Benjamin, on 20 October, 'I had hoped to have had it in my power to communicate something definite as to the Emperor's intentions respecting our affairs'. Instead, everything seemed to be in confusion. Slidell's informants were giving him conflicting accounts of the two countries' intentions. All he knew for certain was that the Emperor was their friend and that Lord Lyons most decidedly was not. Slidell ended his letter with the rueful admission: 'I have no dispatches from you later than 15 April.'[20]

It was mortifying to James Mason to hear that John Slidell was having another interview with the Emperor. The Confederates in England envied Slidell for his easy access to senior French politicians. 'I have seen none but Lord Russell,' Mason admitted to his wife, and that was 'now nearly a year ago'.[21] Henry Hotze had to scavenge for news, seizing on scraps and titbits from friends with 'connections to high places' without ever quite knowing whether he was receiving supposition or fact. He was mesmerized by the unprecedented Cabinet brawl over the recognition question. 'This species of ex-parliamentary warfare was opened with the sparring between Mr Roebuck and Lord Palmerston,' he wrote. 'Since then it has grown more serious, and in the case of Mr Gladstone and Sir George C. Lewis into almost open animosity.' In trying to divine the future, Hotze put great weight on the news that Lord Lyons was still in London. He hoped it meant that the Cabinet was teetering on the side of the South. He tried giving a gentle shove by encouraging his 'allies in the London press' to increase their output. Some writers, including one at the Tory-leaning *Herald*, were even willing to let Hotze dictate their articles. There was, however, one person whom Hotze wished he could silence. 'I almost dread the direction his friendship and devotion seem about to take,' he confessed. James Spence had been inspired by the Emancipation Proclamation and was now convinced that the South should issue one of her own. Hotze was furious with Spence for bringing the subject into public view again, but was at a loss how to divert him.[22] Mason was encountering a similar problem from his friends in the Tory Party, who were trying to extract a pledge from him that the South would renounce slavery.

Hotze's fears that the slavery question might prevent recognition were allayed after he learned that the Cabinet meeting and Lyons's departure had again been postponed. This, he thought, was proof that intervention was imminent. In fact, the meeting of 23 October had not been so much delayed as sabotaged. Palmerston had become alarmed by Russell's apparently blind enthusiasm for the mediation plan. 'I am very much come back to our original view of the matter, that we must continue merely to be lookers-on till the war shall have taken a more decided turn,' he told Russell on 22 October. Rather than argue with Russell face to face, Palmerston stayed away from the Cabinet meeting, which meant that nothing official could be decided. The members who did turn up argued heatedly with Russell and Gladstone, both of whom were so shaken by the experience that each afterwards wrote a detailed defence of his position. Russell was especially upset with Lewis, whose memorandum had made him look foolish. The document accused him of propositions 'which I never thought of making', Russell wrote grumpily to Palmerston.[23] He was beginning to feel cornered. A visit from Charles Francis Adams on the same day as the aborted Cabinet meeting only served to increase his discomfort.

Adams had finally given in to his anxiety and had sought an official interview with Russell. He waited restlessly on the day of the 23rd, watching the hours tick by until it was time for him to leave for his three o'clock appointment. He was disappointed when he arrived at the Foreign Office to find several Ambassadors lolling about the antechamber, still waiting for their meetings. Seeing his pained look, one of them tried to cheer him up but soon relinquished the attempt. Adams did not see Russell until half past four. By then he had rehearsed his position so many times that he was able to put his question to Russell as effortlessly as an afterthought. They were speaking about Lord Lyons, who had called on Adams that morning, and Adams casually 'expressed the hope that he might be going out for a long stay. I had indeed, been made of late quite fearful that it would be otherwise. If I had entirely trusted to the construction given by the public to a late speech, I should have begun to think of packing my carpet bag.' Just as casually, Russell replied that Gladstone had been misunderstood and that the Cabinet's position remained unchanged. They talked on but Adams was so relieved he no longer felt the need to press the issue, except to remark that the North would not take kindly to Gladstone's speech.[24] Russell did not detain him, equally relieved that he had been able to lie while sticking to the letter of the truth.

Lord Lyons left for New York on 25 October. 'I have sent off Lyons without instructions,' Russell informed Palmerston, 'at which he is much pleased.'[25] Lyons had never ceased waging his discreet but determined campaign, speaking quietly to senior Tories and Liberals about the folly of interfering in the war. He felt a profound sense of loyalty and gratitude to Russell, but he refused to acquiesce in a policy that he believed to be morally and practically wrong. The cancellation of the Cabinet meeting signalled to him that the proposal had died. 'I am quite satisfied with the course the government means to take at present with regard to American politics – which diminishes the annoyance of going back,' Lyons told his sister on the 24th. During their four months together they had talked frequently about his coming home, and he promised, 'My object now will be to bring my mission to America to an end as soon as I can with credit and propriety.' They probably both knew that this was a vain hope.[26]

Lyons was also mistaken about Russell's proposal. It was napping rather than dead or dying. John Slidell's informant wrote on 28 October: 'I have just returned from Broadlands . . . and have also seen several leading political men in town. My impression is that little or no progress has been made as regards your question.'[27] During the last week of October the memorandum war continued as more Cabinet members felt compelled to state their positions. When Russell received George Grey's letter on the 28th, he thanked him 'for writing me a letter instead of printing a Memorandum', and compared it to Lewis, 'who sprang a mine on me'. But why, he asked, did people think inaction was morally superior to intervention? 'If a friend were to cut his throat,' he wrote, 'you would hardly like to confess, "he told me he was going to do it, but I said nothing as I thought he would not take my advice."'[28] Clarendon observed that 'Johnny always loves to do something when to do nothing is prudent'.[29] When Lord Lyons realized that Russell had not abandoned his plan, he sent him repeated warnings 'that at this moment Foreign Intervention, short of force, could only make matters worse'.[30]

Russell was still feeling put upon when Lord Cowley sent him the news that the Emperor had ordered his new Foreign Minister to approach Britain with a proposal of Anglo-French intervention. Russell was delighted. Once again he could be an Angel of Peace and prevent any further bloodshed in America. 'Was there ever any war so horrible?' he asked Cowley, rhetorically.[31] Now he could call a new Cabinet meeting and his plan would have to be discussed. Palmerston had the opposite reaction. If the North wished to waste the lives of thousands of immigrant Germans and Irishmen, it was not, he decided, England's business to interfere. Moreover, his suspicion of anything French made him sceptical of the proposal. The French have no morals, he told Russell, and would probably agree to all kinds of egregious provisions for slavery. 'The French Government are more free from the shackles of principle and of right and wrong on these matters, as on all others than we are,' he insisted.[32]

By 7 November, rumours about the Emperor's proposal had leaked to the press. Adams's spirits sank in proportion to the rise among Confederates. Russell was like a child anticipating a birthday. After reading that a mass meeting of cotton workers in Oldham had passed a resolution in favour of intervention, Russell could not help asking the Mayor what had changed in the district. Nothing, the Mayor replied; the gathering was small compared to previous American war meetings in Oldham, and had been intentionally packed with Confederate supporters. (James Spence's agents provocateurs, Aitken and Grimshaw, were so disheartened by their inability to form a genuine social movement

ONE HEAD BETTER THAN TWO.

LOUIS NAPOLEON. "I SAY, HADN'T WE BETTER TELL OUR FRIEND THERE TO LEAVE OFF MAKING A FOOL OF HIMSELF?"

LORD PAM. "H'M, WELL, SUPPOSE YOU TALK TO HIM YOURSELF. HE'S A GREAT ADMIRER OF YOURS, YOU KNOW."

Punch's characterization of Louis-Napoleon advocating a joint approach – Palmerston holding back, November 1862

that they ceased their activities shortly afterwards.) But in London, James Mason was growing more optimistic. 'The cotton famine', he was pleased to report, 'is looming up in fearful proportions.' He added that 700,000 workers were currently living off charity, and that typhoid appeared to be on the rise. 'The public mind is very much agitated and disturbed at the fearful prospect for the winter, and I am not without hope that it will produce its effects on the counsels of the Government,' he wrote.[33] The effects were not as great as he believed: every economic indicator showed that the country was absorbing the cotton shock, and civic and Church leaders were confident that mass unemployment in

Lancashire could be alleviated if private individuals throughout the country donated sufficient funds to help the workers. Lord Derby set the example with a donation of £12,000, the largest ever given by one person to a particular cause at that time. He was the chairman of the Central Relief Fund that was overseeing the efforts of 143 committees to collect money and clothing. The workers were unemployed but many were not sitting idle; Harriet Martineau and others were organizing schemes to help them learn new trades and skills. The sewing and cooking schools, she noted, were proving to be especially popular with the women.[34]

Charles Francis Adams had been so satisfied with Lord Russell's explanation that he saw no reason to alter his holiday plans. He was in Tunbridge Wells with his family when the Cabinet met on 11 November to debate the French proposal. Benjamin Moran was equally sanguine. 'Lord Russell gave Mr Adams assurances at their last interview that nothing would be done without notifying him,' Moran wrote in his diary on the 11th. 'I rest undisturbed . . . I infer the French proposal will be rejected.'[35] But while he was pottering about the empty legation, there was open war in the Cabinet. George Cornewall Lewis and the Duke of Argyll were the leaders of the opposition to Russell and Gladstone. The week before, Lewis had sent round a second memorandum – this one over 15,000 words long – which answered every single one of Russell's and Gladstone's arguments. He had also enlisted his son-in-law, the gifted lawyer William Vernon Harcourt, to write a companion piece for The Times, under the pseudonym 'Historicus'.

Russell's ship was sinking, though he steadfastly remained at the helm. He opened the Cabinet meeting by explaining his position once again. When he had finished, he turned expectantly to Palmerston. Russell's desperate glare told him that retreat was impossible. The cornered Prime Minister made a few half-hearted comments about not letting Lancashire down. 'I do not think his support was very sincere,' wrote Lewis, 'it certainly was not hearty. The proposal was now thrown before the Cabinet, who proceeded to pick it to pieces. Everybody present threw a stone at it of great or less size, except Gladstone, who supported it, and the [Lord] Chancellor and Cardwell, who expressed no opinion.'[36] As they debated throughout the morning and into the following day, it became obvious to Lewis that Russell had been rather too forward with the French and feared the consequences of declining their offer. But he remained unmoved by Russell's embarrassment or his dread of annoying France. Lewis scolded Russell for his unrealistic faith in the ability of outsiders to impose peace on America: 'What would an eminent diplomatist from Vienna, or Berlin, or St. Petersburg know of the Chicago platform or the Crittenden compromise?' The idea of the Great Powers dictating the terms of agreement between the North and South was ludicrous.[37] He continued to harry the Foreign Secretary until, in Gladstone's words, 'Lord Russell rather turned tail. He gave way without resolutely fighting out his battle.' Not surprisingly, Gladstone was disgusted with his colleagues. 'But I hope', he wrote to his wife, '[the French] may not take it as a positive refusal, or at any rate that they may themselves act in the matter. It will be clear that we concur with them, that the war should cease.'[38]

Russell hoped that his reply to the Emperor on 13 November was open-ended and flattering enough to soften the awkward fact that his offer was being turned down. Napoleon was indeed annoyed with the Foreign Secretary, especially since the Russians had also been lukewarm about his proposal. But the Emperor's anger paled beside that of the Confederates, who still perceived Russell as their arch-nemesis. Henry Hotze's self-confidence suffered a precipitate blow. He wondered whether his attempts to manipulate opinion had backfired. Worse still was the shock at discovering that the government had a far greater control over the press than he had ever imagined. Once it was announced that the French proposal had been declined, Hotze could not find a newspaper willing to print his attack on Lord Russell, not even *The Times*.[39]

There is no single reason as to why the Cabinet voted against intervening in the war. Economically, it did not make sense to interfere; militarily, it would have meant committing Britain to war with the North and once again risking Canada and possibly the Caribbean for uncertain gains; politically, there was no support from either party or sufficient encouragement from the other Great Powers apart from France; and, practically, the decision to intervene would have required a majority consensus from a Cabinet which had never agreed on the meaning or significance of the war. But there is also an individual whose name is rarely mentioned and yet who deserves his place among the reasons – and that is Seward. From the beginning of the war, eighteen months earlier, Seward had warned Britain to stay out of the conflict or face the consequences. His bluster and posturing had driven away a potential ally but the message was heard. A few months after the Cabinet discussion, William Harcourt joked to Lewis that it was 'a little amusing that the whole wrath of the South and the imputation of being the real obstacle to Intervention should fall on Lord John. It only shows how little is known of the real history of affairs . . . It reminds me of what Sir R. Walpole said: "don't tell me of history; I know that *can't* be true."'[40]

When Charles Francis Adams returned from Tunbridge Wells in mid-November, he straight away paid a visit to Russell's house in Chesham Place. Naturally, they discussed Britain's reply to the Emperor. Adams told him, 'I hoped it would open the eyes of the [American] people to their mistake as to the disposition of the Emperor and make them more liberal to England.' Russell's hearty assent to this was no doubt driven by a combination of guilt and embarrassment. Adams mistakenly thought it was due to the Foreign Secretary having scored a diplomatic coup. 'His Lordship seemed a little elated by his paper and was more cordial than usual,' he wrote in his diary on 15 November. 'He alluded to the alleged audience granted to Mr Slidell . . . and said that if the Queen had granted any such to Mr Mason there would have been no end to the indignation in America. I said, yes.' As November drew to a close, the public's interest in the intervention question waned. In spite of himself, Russell was being credited with having behaved with propriety. Even some British Confederate sympathizers agreed with the government's decision to remain neutral.[41] Only the ever-optimistic James Mason still believed that 'events are maturing which must lead to some change in the attitude of England'.[42]

PART TWO
Fire All around Them

15

Bloodbath at Fredericksburg

Lincoln suffers at the polls – the Battle of Fredericksburg – the Senators attempt a coup – The Marquis of Hartington's conversion – Victory or annihilation

Lord Lyons returned to Washington on 12 November 1862, having spent a few days in New York speaking to Democratic and Republican leaders. He was relieved to find that they were far more willing to share their personal views than the politicians in the capital, who were wary of appearing to be too familiar with him. The 'Peace Democrats' had performed well in the November elections, picking up the governorships of New York and New Jersey as well as taking control of several State legislatures. Their declared aim of peace and compromise over slavery chimed perfectly with the large number of Northern voters who had felt blindsided by Lincoln's Emancipation Proclamation. McClellan's failure to chase after Lee following the Battle of Antietam in September had also contributed to a growing doubt in the North over whether the war was worth the enormous sacrifice in human lives. There had been nine major battles during the past eleven months, resulting in more than 150,000 casualties between the two sides, and yet there was no indication that any end was in sight.

Across the Atlantic, the results of the mid-term elections seemed much worse to Charles Francis Adams than they really were – the Republicans still controlled Congress by a large majority – and his bitterness towards Lincoln threatened to overwhelm his peace of mind. Benjamin Moran was shocked by Adams's indiscreet tirades against the administration (though he secretly enjoyed them, too) and recorded each outburst with relish. 'Mr Adams had a long talk with me about Lincoln,' he wrote in his diary on 19 November:

> He thinks the recent political defeats a natural result of his management. [Lincoln's] whole course from the beginning has been unstatesmanlike, and nothing in his Presidential career was more stupid than the selection of his Cabinet. He appointed Mr Welles without knowing anything about him, and took the others in an equally haphazard way. The conversation satisfied me that Mr Adams regards Lincoln as a vulgar man, unfitted both by education and nature for the post of President, and one whose administration will not be much praised in the future.[1]

Ordinarily, Adams would never have confided in a gossipy malcontent like Moran. But despite having made a large circle of acquaintances during the past eighteen months he felt as friendless as the day he arrived in London. The US Minister in Spain, Carl Schurz, pitied his social isolation. Adams 'performed his social duties with punctilious care', Schurz wrote after a brief visit to England, but parties at the legation were hardly popular events. Adams was not 'a shining figure on festive occasions [and] lacked the gifts of personal magnetism or sympathetic charm that would draw men to him.'[2] The rest of the family also had trouble adapting to English life. His wife Abigail felt upstaged by the social success of the American expatriate Mrs Russell Sturgis, whose soirées were a feature of the season. But it was Henry who was suffering the most from his inability to carve a place for himself in English society. Although he had relinquished the idea of joining the US army like his brother, he was unhappy and restless. 'I have steadily lost faith in myself ever since I left college,' he confessed to Charles Francis Jr. on 21 November, 'and my aim is now so indefinite that all my time may prove to have been wasted.'[3]

The frustration and sense of alienation at the US legation were not all that dissimilar to the loneliness experienced by Lord Lyons and his staff in Washington. Lyons's new first attaché, 25-year-old Edward Malet, had been warned by his friend William Kennedy, who had been seconded to the legation in September, to prepare himself for ghastly weather and few distractions.* 'However,' Kennedy added, 'there is lots

---

* The previous incumbent, William Brodie, had pleaded with the Foreign Office to send him anywhere so long as he could escape Washington.

of work to do and so one has no time to walk about or grumble, especially as we dine every night with [the Minister].'[4] Since Malet had been serving as an unpaid attaché at the British legation in Petropolis, Brazil, where the Emperor Pedro II kept his summer residence, he could hardly wait to experience the so-called discomforts of Washington. A salary of £300, and his promotion to 'the most important mission next to the Embassies', were, Malet wrote happily to his parents, more than enough compensation.

Lord Lyons's dislike of change, particularly with regard to his own staff, made him prickly towards Malet at first, even though the young attaché's background echoed his own. Malet's father, Sir Alexander, was currently serving his tenth year as Minister to the German Federation, placing upon his son the same burdens of expectation and family tradition that had overshadowed Lyons's early career.[5] This unacknowledged connection between them may have been another reason why Lyons was so much harder on Malet than on the others. Malet often had his draft letters returned for rewriting, accompanied by such acerbic comments as 'Brevity is the soul of wit, but I object to absolute nonsense – L.'[6]

Malet found that Kennedy had not been exaggerating about the long hours. 'I have only visited one American house,' he wrote to his mother after a month in the capital. The glorious days of the 'Buccaneers' were already over. Lyons worried about the lack of distractions for his staff: 'nothing whatever in the shape of amusement for them, little or no society of any kind now; no theatre, no club.'[7] But the truth was that the attachés rarely stopped for lunch let alone had time to visit the theatre. Their first break from their desks came at 7 p.m. when they dashed to Willard's to gulp down as many cocktails as they could before returning to the legation at eight for dinner with Lyons. In addition to the daily bundles of diplomatic correspondence which required copying and filing, the attachés were also handling hundreds of cases on behalf of British subjects who were seeking redress or protection from various authorities; and in the past year a very large number of cases had arisen which concerned missing, conscripted, injured or dead British volunteers. Most week-nights Malet was obliged to return to the chancery after dinner and continue working until past midnight. But his situation was different from Henry Adams's in one important respect; the presence of ten bachelors gave the legation in Washington a rather hearty feel, not unlike an undergraduate college or an officers' mess. There was none of the poisonous claustrophobia that infected the legation in London. Nor did Malet have to live with his parents; he was able to rent a spacious house with Kennedy just down the street from the legation, at 227 H Street North. It came with a garden and entertaining rooms large enough to inspire him to try his hand at decorating. He was quite pleased with the results: one room was pink with gold buds, the other white 'with lots of small gold stars'.[8] All that was lacking were the people to fill them. Malet passed his precious spare time wandering up and down Pennsylvania Avenue, watching 'the queerest figures I ever saw in my life – and nearly always troops of prisoners being taken from one place of confinement to another'.[9]

The latest prisoners to arrive in Washington were Confederates captured during a skirmish on 2 November 1862 at Snickers Gap, one of the three main passes in the Blue Ridge Mountains that linked the eastern part of Virginia with the Shenandoah Valley. General McClellan's new plan involved advancing along the base of the Blue Ridge, methodically taking each gap, until he reached the Manassas Gap railroad; once there, he intended to decide whether to attack a portion of Lee's army which was known to be only 25 miles away – or avoid a fight and march east to the town of Fredericksburg, which lay along the bank of the Rappahannock river, 60 miles due north of Richmond. In his telegram to Lincoln that afternoon, McClellan made his usual plea for more men and cavalry, though 'I will do the best I can with what I have got,' he added.[10]

   Lincoln was no longer interested in McClellan's best. He had already made up his mind to dismiss the General after the mid-term elections, and appoint a successor who was less preoccupied with manoeuvring and more interested in attacking. On the night of 7 November McClellan was writing a letter to his wife when two visitors knocked at his door. Snow covered their clothes and their faces were raw from the cold; McClellan realized that this was not a courtesy call. The older of the two, General Catharinus P. Buckingham, had come by special train from Washington to deliver the order from Lincoln, removing McClellan as commander of the Army of the Potomac and instituting General Ambrose Burnside in his place. 'I read the papers with a smile,' wrote McClellan, and 'turned to Burnside [who was standing next to Buckingham] and said, "Well Burnside, I turn the command over to you."'[11] McClellan told his wife, 'they have made a great mistake,' and in his heart Burnside suspected it too. Although his victory at Roanoke the previous spring had raised his reputation with Lincoln, Burnside's limitations as a military leader had been revealed by his muddled thinking during the Battle of Antietam. Many soldiers broke ranks and tried to touch McClellan's boots as he rode out of the camp and into retirement on 9 November. He had failed to lead them to victory but his commitment to their welfare had touched their lives in ways that only the soldiers themselves could appreciate.

Sir Percy Wyndham was disgusted by what he considered to be incompetent army management by the War Department. He had been seconded against his wishes to General Franz Sigel's 11th Army Corps in early September, and given temporary command of the cavalry brigade, which was on guard duty in northern Virginia.[12] Bored by his new command, Sir Percy asked General Samuel P. Heintzelman of the 3rd Army Corps for his help in obtaining a transfer. He was especially annoyed that connections seemed to count far more than merit: 'the names of a great many Colonels in the service have been recommended to the President for Promotion,' he wrote, but 'I, not being acquainted with any political parties or person of influence, naturally have no chance of being recommended in like manner. I would consider it a lasting favour if you would use your influence in obtaining me a position, and if possible in your own command.' Heintzelman was experiencing his own difficulties with High Command and had no influence to spare; so bitter were the rivalries in Sigel's corps that a jealous officer sabotaged Sir Percy Wyndham's request by accusing him of disloyalty. 'I hear it from a field officer of cavalry that Wyndham said to him in the presence of a private of his Regiment that he would soon as leave to fight for the Confederates as for the Union, and that he would if our Government did not give him what he wanted,' claimed the embittered informer.[13]

Even the jovial English lieutenant of the 9th New York Volunteers, George Henry Herbert, was becoming disillusioned, despite his recent promotion to ordnance officer for the division. 'The system is radically wrong,' he complained. 'With the exception of a few regiments, officers and men treat one another as equals, no punishments are inflicted. The private under you today may, if a friend of his gets into office, be a Colonel in another regiment tomorrow.'[14] Herbert's experience was confirmed by an English military observer who was fascinated by the different styles of leadership of the two armies. In the South, though many officers were just as unqualified as their Northern counterparts, the plantation system fostered a strong sense of social hierarchy. 'The Regimental Officers are mostly men of Known families in the districts from whence the regiment is raised,' he wrote, 'and the "mean whites" look up to and obey the sons of the Great Planters'. In the North, it was not uncommon for the soldiers to disregard 'their Captains and their Lieutenants, whom they regard as equals'.[15]

Herbert had just returned from Washington after requisitioning stores for the regiment when he heard the news about General McClellan. Apart from General George Getty, the commander of his division, who was a professional soldier, Herbert had little faith in his superiors, and certainly none in General Burnside after Antietam. 'Everything is rotten to the core,' he repeated to his brother Jack. 'Generals are appointed, I guess, on account of incapacity. Most or at least many are such as no gentleman can serve under and retain self-respect.'[16]

Burnside decided to head straight for Fredericksburg and use pontoon bridges to cross the Rappahannock river. With luck he would be on the other side before Lee even knew where the Federal army had gone. From there it would be a straight movement along the Richmond–Fredericksburg railroad. Each regiment was to have twelve days' rations, which Burnside considered more than sufficient for the enterprise. Lincoln had some misgivings about a plan that placed so much emphasis on timing but he acquiesced, only urging Burnside to move as quickly as possible.

First nature and then Washington, however, began to thwart Burnside at every turn. As soon as the soldiers began their march the clouds gathered and dumped a steady, hard rain on their heads. 'Talk about roads,' Herbert commented to his brother, 'it would do your heart good to see this specimen of a Virginia dirt road. I suppose you have often heard of mud knee deep. You will find it literally deeper than that. It took me 2½ hours to ride seven miles. This is a singular soil. It is a crust of clay over quicksand. As soon as it is thoroughly wet the sand settles, and the first thing you know you break through the crust and down you go four or five feet.'[17] Nevertheless the Army of the Potomac managed to arrive at Fredericksburg in good time on 20 November, only to find that the pontoons were notably absent. Burnside refused to consider an alternative plan and so the entire army waited for the missing pontoons for the next two weeks. Herbert was furious: 'all this time was spent by the rebels in fortifying the hills in rear of the town, mounting heavy guns, etc. And a splendid job they made of it.'[18] Meanwhile, the soldiers used up their rations and discovered that administrative bungling meant no more were coming. Herbert's New York Zouaves celebrated Thanksgiving on 27 November with a feast of water: even the hardtack (a form of dry biscuit) and coffee had run out. The misery of the army's situation led to pilfering and fights between regiments. Ebenezer Wells's Highlanders had a vicious struggle with the 2nd Michigan for the last remaining wood fence in the vicinity, each being desperate to chop it up for firewood.[19] There was so much sickness in the camps that Herbert wondered if more than half the army was actually present for duty.

Behind the Confederate lines, Francis Dawson reported to General James 'Old Pete' Longstreet's headquarters on 6 December, and realized after his brief and unceremonious meeting with the General that his history as an English volunteer held no interest for him. Longstreet maintained a professional relationship with his staff members, which, for a junior officer such as Dawson, meant almost no personal contact at all. Adding insult to his lowly status was the discovery that he was expected to do the work of three men: 'Colonel Manning had no taste for anything but marching and fighting, and Lieutenant Duxberry was too fond of pleasure and show to be of much practical use,' wrote Dawson. 'The whole responsibility in the Ordnance Department of Longstreet's Corps devolved upon me.'[20]

Lee was incredulous that Burnside was still seriously contemplating Fredericksburg as a crossing place. He ordered Longstreet's 1st Corps into position along a 7-mile range of wooded hills that overlooked Fredericksburg and the Rappahannock river. The batteries were clustered thickly, ready to fire on the plain below. When Longstreet asked his artillery commander whether any more guns were needed, the officer replied, 'A chicken could not live on that field when we open on it.'[21] The Confederate army was so well entrenched above the town that a Federal advance seemed completely implausible. Yet 'the Yankees were in plain view on the other side' of the area and 'evidently very active', wrote Heros von Borcke, Jeb Stuart's Prussian volunteer aide, after his reconnaissance. US General Edwin Sumner sent orders to the Mayor to evacuate all civilians. The majority of the inhabitants of the eighteenth-century town were women and children. 'I never saw a more pitiful procession than they made trudging through the deep snow,' wrote a Southern artilleryman:

There were women carrying a baby in one arm, and its bottle, its clothes, and its covering in the other . . . Most of them had to cross a creek swollen with winter rains, and deadly cold with winter ice and snow. We took the battery horses down and ferried them over, taking one child in front and two behind, and sometimes a woman or a girl on either side with her feet in the stirrups, holding on by our shoulders. Where they were going we could not tell, and I doubt if they could.[22]

Sheet ice coated the roads, making the horses fearful and skittish. Reconnaissance 'was anything but pleasant', wrote von Borcke.[23] But the atmosphere at General Stuart's camp remained almost festive. The Maryland journalist William W. Glenn had sent across two more English visitors to the Confederacy. Captains Lewis Phillips and Edward Wynne had succumbed to the temptation that was affecting so many British officers in Canada, to slip through Northern lines for a peek at the Confederate army.[24] Wynne fell ill when they reached Richmond, leaving Phillips to continue by himself. Phillips found the Confederate officers touchingly keen to demonstrate to him the quality of their men. Borcke recalled the Englishman watching a shabbily dressed South Carolina brigade parade before him in a marching style that would have earned swift punishment if performed on British soil, and pronouncing with perfect sincerity that he was impressed.[25]

The picket lines of the two armies had come so close to each other that Rebel and Federal soldiers could jokingly trade insults across the river. Sam Hill's regiment, the 6th Louisianans, enjoyed a brief bartering system with unknown Union pickets, exchanging letters and tobacco for coffee and old editions of *Harper's Magazine*. One letter actually reached its destination in New Orleans.[26] On the night of 10 December word spread through the Confederate camp that ammunition was being doled out among the Yankees, indicating that a battle was imminent.[27] The officers at Stuart's headquarters decided that there was still time to take Captain Phillips to a country ball that was being held nearby. The 10-mile wagon ride to the plantation was a rash and dangerous journey to attempt – several of the Confederates were flung with their musical instruments into a snow bank when the wagon veered off the frozen road, but, laughing and bleeding, they righted the vehicle and continued. After another hour of bumps and near misses they arrived at the house. Borcke recalled that 'the mansion was brilliantly lighted up, many fair ones had already assembled and the whole company awaited, with impatience and anxiety, the arrival of their distinguished guests and promised music'. They danced quadrilles and Virginia reels until the small hours. 'Our English captain', wrote von Borcke, 'entered into the fun quite as heartily as any of us.'[28] By the time they had returned to camp it was almost daybreak; muffled sounds were coming from Federal lines.

General Burnside had ordered his engineers to begin throwing pontoons across the Rappahannock. Fog emanating from the river gave them some cover, but the soldiers remained at the mercy of Confederate sharpshooters. Burnside's response was to shell the town, giving those who had refused to leave their homes a taste of what was to come. Having fiddled and fretted for more than two weeks, he was now impatient to move. His intelligence reports wrongly implied that Lee's army was in poor condition, lacking in artillery and at only half its normal 72,000 strength. The Army of the Potomac was, on paper at least, almost twice the size and equipped with 350 heavy guns. Burnside's natural optimism increased as his army began crossing the river. Lee could hamper the Federals' progress but he lacked the firepower to mount an effective counter-offensive.

Burnside thought he could surprise Lee with a brilliant, sweeping attack.[29] Lee, on the other hand, was confident that the Federal advantages in troops and artillery were more than offset by his own high defensive position above the town; all he had to do was wait for the Army of the Potomac to expose itself on the plain. By 9 o'clock on the evening of 12 December, George Herbert and the 9th New York Volunteers were among the 50,000 Union troops in control of the town. Herbert was shocked to learn that a family friend was among the 500 Confederate prisoners but was unable to speak to him before they were transported to the rear.[30]

The following morning, 13 December, Captain Phillips solemnly shook hands with Jeb Stuart's officers and set off in search of Robert E. Lee. In the meantime the two journalists, Lawley and Vizetelly, were having breakfast with the General and his staff. Lee appeared calm while they waited for the dawn mist to clear from the plains below. His hat and coat were spotless and, as always, the only sign of his rank were three stars on his collar. After breakfast the party rode the length of the Confederate line, looking down at the Federals below as they prepared to march out of Fredericksburg. Longstreet's 1st Corps remained spread

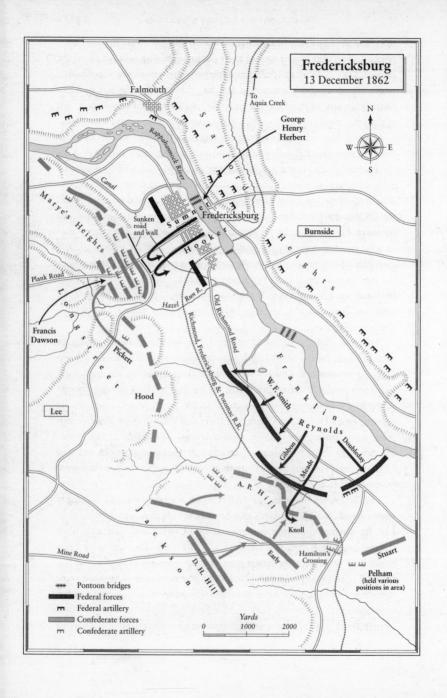

Fredericksburg
13 December 1862

Falmouth

To Aquia Creek

George
Henry
Herbert

N
W · E
S

Rappahannock River

Canal

Marye's Heights

Sunken
road
and wall

Fredericksburg

Burnside

Stafford
Heights

Plank Road

Sumner

Hook

Hazel Run R.

Old Richmond Road

Francis
Dawson

Longstreet

Pickett

Hood

Lee

Richmond, Fredericksburg & Potomac R.R.

Franklin

W. F. Smith

Reynolds

Gibbon

Meade

Doubleday

A. P. Hill

Jackson

Knoll

Mine Road

D. H. Hill

Early

Hamilton's
Crossing

Stuart

Pelham
(held various
positions in area)

Pontoon bridges
Federal forces
Federal artillery
Confederate forces
Confederate artillery

Yards
0   1000   2000

out, but his artillery was massed in tight formation along a low ridge called Marye's Heights, which faced the centre of the town. The gently sloping plain would provide little cover for the Federal advance. Lawley told his readers, 'it is no wonder that every Southerner from the Commander-in-Chief down to the youngest drummer-boy, understood the strength of the ground, and contemplated the coming shock of battle with serene confidence and composure.'[31]

As soon as the shelling began, the skyline of Fredericksburg was transformed from quaint rooftops and spires into a broken, flaming ruin. Herbert tried to describe to his brother what happened next. 'Two miles back of the town, the ground rises gradually and forms a semi-circular range of hills somewhat in this form.' He drew a rough sketch. 'This semi-circle was a mass of guns. The fire of which crossed in every direction and completely swept the plain.' The range was Marye's Heights and at its base lay a sunken road behind a 4-foot-high stone wall. Impregnable to rifle fire, the wall provided almost total cover to the Confederates crouching behind. Regiment after regiment was sent up the plain without adequate protection as generals tried to interpret Burnside's confused battle plan. One body of soldiers crammed into the relative safety of an isolated house. When it became full, those forced outside tried to create a protective barrier with human corpses, or took refuge behind dead horses.[32]

'General George W. Getty, my division commander, and myself', wrote Herbert's brigade commander, Colonel Rush Hawkins, 'were on the roof of the Slaughter house, a high residence at the lower end of the city ... From this prominent position our repeated repulses and the terrible destruction of the Union troops had been witnessed.' At three o'clock the two officers were ordered to send in Getty's division. 'The order was obeyed but not until I had tried to induce General Getty against its obedience and general waste of life.'[33] The instructions became muddled as couriers failed to return and anyone with a horse was commandeered to deliver messages. Ebenezer Wells happened to be at Getty's headquarters and was beckoned over by a general. Someone handed him field glasses, and a distant spot was pointed out on the plain. He was so shocked by what he saw that he almost stumbled. 'I was ordered to go and deliver my verbal despatch ... and if shot it was to be my dying words for it to be carried on,' he recalled.[34] Wells was one of the few who returned unscathed but the fate of his message is unknown. George Herbert's regiment misinterpreted their orders to

mean they were to advance to a nearby battery rather than towards
Marye's Heights. As it turned out, this saved their lives – the only
instance of Burnside's inability to communicate with his officers proving to be fortuitous. The moral, declared a young British army officer
who studied the battle twenty years later, was: 'Let your instructions be
explicit, plainly-worded and capable of no double construction.'[35]

Lawley and Vizetelly watched, awestruck, as six Federal advances
were mown down by a combination of Longstreet's artillery and the
Rebel troops behind the stone wall. 'From the point where I stood, with
General Lee and Longstreet,' wrote Vizetelly, 'I could see the grape, shell,
and canister from the guns of the Washington artillery mow great avenues in the masses of Federal troops rushing to the assault, while the
infantry, posted behind a breastwork just under the battery, decimated
the nearest columns of the enemy.'[36] Looking through his field glasses at
the carnage below, Lee commented, 'It is well that war is so terrible – we
should grow too fond of it.'[37] Francis Dawson was stationed just out of
range to hear Lee's remark. In any case, he was almost spellbound by
the battle: 'Never in my life do I expect to see such a magnificent sight
again,' he wrote to his mother; 'the whole scene of conflict was before
our eyes, and at our feet, the glorious sun shining as tho' bloodshed and
slaughter were unknown on the beautiful earth; the screaming of shells
and the singing of the rifle bullets adding a fearful accompaniment to
the continued booming of the heavy guns.' He saw the Federal army
hurl itself at the Confederate guns. 'It was thrilling to watch the long
line advance, note the gaps in the array, as the wounded fell or else
staggered to the rear, and see the gallant remnant melt away like snow
before our withering fire,' he wrote. The Irish Brigade's distinctive green
and gold flag made its charge one of the easiest to follow from start
to terrible finish. George Hart, an English volunteer in the 69th, wrote
bitterly: 'It was not a fight, it was a massacre.'[38]

The guns began to silence as night drew in. At 9 p.m. Colonel Hawkins
interrupted the generals as they were planning the next day's attack. 'I
listened until I was thoroughly irritated,' he wrote. None of them seemed
to have grasped the day's defeat. Exasperated, the colonel took out his
pencil and drew a diagram of what the Confederates would likely do
to a second attack. This brought them to their senses. But although they
were now unanimous about a withdrawal, no one wanted to go to
Burnside's headquarters with the request. Hawkins took it upon him-

The bombardment of Fredericksburg, Virginia, by
the Federals, December 1862, by Frank Vizetelly.

self, riding in pitch-blackness through mud and debris to Burnside's
camp. He arrived before the General himself and waited. 'As [Burnside]
came through the door he said: "Well, it's all arranged; we attack at
early dawn, the Ninth Corps in the centre, which I shall lead in person";
and then seeing me he said: "Hawkins, your brigade shall lead with the
9th New York on the right of the line, and we'll make up for the bad
work of to-day."' Undaunted, Hawkins launched into a calm but
emphatic explanation as to why there could be no second attack. The
unanimous agreement of the generals forced Burnside to concur.
Strangely, there were still regiments who had yet to fire a shot; Charles
Francis Adams Jr. had spent all day in the woods, reading the poems of
Robert Browning while he waited for orders.

'A ride along the whole length of the lines told a sad tale of slaughter,'
wrote Lawley. 'It is doubtful whether any living pen could do justice to
the horrors.' But 'when the eye had once rested upon the fatal slope of
Marye's Heights the memory became fixed upon the spot'. Fourteen
Federal brigades had been thrown at the wretched stone wall. 'There, in

every attitude of death, lying so close to each other that you might step from body to body, lay acres of the Federal dead.'[39] Vizetelly stopped counting the bodies when he neared 700. Intermingled with the dead were the wounded and dying. With no truce agreed, they could not be rescued from the field. Their screams and moans filled the cold night air. The survivors huddled together in ravines, behind walls and at the bases of trees for warmth, forbidden to light fires lest they provide a target for the enemy. As the dead stiffened in the freezing temperatures they were propped up to look like sentries.[40]

All day on the 14th Lee waited for Burnside to resume the offensive. But, instead of fighting, Union soldiers turned what had been casual looting of Fredericksburg into a full-scale rampage. The historian of Ebenezer Wells's regiment claims that the three terrified women discovered by the 79th in a filthy coal cellar were treated with kind respect. If so, they were among the few who were not taunted or molested. Soldiers went from house to house, stripping the valuables and methodically smashing the rest. The streets became blocked with broken detritus; everything from pianos to petticoats lay in mangled heaps across the roads. The anarchy horrified and disgusted many Federal soldiers but the destruction continued throughout the day. Even Martha Washington's tomb was ransacked and used for target practice. In the night, the madness below seemed to be reflected in the sky – the Northern Lights had never been seen so far south, and bright-red tongues of light flickered and crackled over the soldiers' heads. When dawn came the rising sun revealed a remarkable change on the battle plain. Hardly a shred of blue remained. The dead had been stripped naked by Confederates seeking to exchange their tattered uniforms for good northern cloth.

Lee was still waiting on the 15th when Burnside requested a flag of truce for burial and retrieval. Lee acquiesced, which, according to Wolseley, was a tactical mistake of the gravest kind. In his history of the battle, written in 1889, Wolseley would describe the general's actions as 'inexplicable'. 'Burnside's army was at Lee's mercy', wedged tight between the Confederates and an unfordable river. Lee should have launched an all-out attack and obliterated the mighty Army of the Potomac while it remained vulnerable. Such a decisive victory, Wolseley believed, would have convinced the European powers that neutrality was no longer an option. The Lincoln administration might well have fallen and with it the national will to prosecute the war.[41] But Lee always contended that he had no means of knowing the true extent of Burnside's losses on 13 December. The Confederates had suffered nearly 5,000 casualties – a total that seemed high until they learned that the Federals had experienced another Antietam-style bloodbath with casualties approaching 13,000. While Lee hesitated, Burnside was able to carry out a rapid and silent retreat during the night. The Confederates awoke on the 16th to discover that they were alone.

Mary Sophia Hill went to Fredericksburg to offer her help and found it a ghost town: 'If ever you saw a city of desolation it was this.'[42] Every house was perforated by cannonballs; whole streets lay in rubble. But when Captain Phillips, who had been reunited with his friend Captain Wynne, went down into the town to investigate, they discovered it was far from empty. Major von Borcke accompanied them, recalling in his memoirs, 'A number of the houses which we entered presented a horrid spectacle – dead and wounded intermingled in thick masses.'

As they trod carefully over human debris, Phillips suddenly grabbed von Borcke's arm and pointed to the body of a soldier who was missing a part of his skull: 'Great God, that man is still alive!' His cry caused the soldier to open his eyes and stare 'at us with so pitiable an expression that I could not for long after recall it without shuddering'. Helpless, the men knelt down and stayed with him for a moment.*[43] Francis Lawley was gripped by similar scenes in other parts of the town. 'Death, nothing but death everywhere,' he wrote afterwards; 'great masses of bodies tossed out of the churches as the sufferers expire; layers of corpses stretched in the balconies of houses as though taking a siesta . . . horrified and aghast at what I saw, I could not look.'[44] Sickened by the unrelieved suffering around him, he returned to Richmond without waiting for his friends.

The first of the wounded began to arrive in Washington on 14 December. These were the men who could drag themselves off the battlefield and board steamers without assistance. It was another two days before the seriously injured were brought from the field hospitals. An English military observer at one of these hospitals thought he had never witnessed anything so barbarous:

---

* Jeb Stuart took a grim satisfaction from Wynne and Phillips's reports: The 'Englishmen here', he wrote to General Lee's eldest son, George Washington Custis Lee, 'who surveyed Solferino [the battle which inspired Henry Dunant to found the Red Cross] and all the battlefields of Italy say that the pile of dead on the plains of Fredericksburg exceeds anything of the sort ever seen by them'.

There were about 60 surgeons without coats (chiefly French, German and Irish), covered in blood and dirt, chatting, arguing, and laughing and swearing, and cutting and sawing more like the devils and machines than human beings. Large heaps of legs, and arms were piled here and there, all sizes, and stages of decomposition . . . I thought I could stand a good deal but . . . I felt myself grow pale and dared not speak for a few minutes.[45]

It seemed incredible that any patient could leave such a place alive.

The hospital ships disgorged thousands of stretchers along the crowded waterfront. The wounded lay on the ground for hours until ambulance drivers heaved them onto wagons and ferried them to various hospitals around the city. The new pavilion-style hospitals advocated by Florence Nightingale were being built as quickly as possible. The haste produced careless mistakes: one hospital was left without a mortuary, forcing administrators to stack the dead in an adjacent lot until burial; another was placed next to an open sewer. The newest hospital, Lincoln General, opened the week of Fredericksburg, but even though it had a capacity of 2,575 patients, the number of casualties far exceeded the available beds: hotels, churches, warehouses and even a floor of the Patent Office were converted into makeshift wards. The novelist Louisa May Alcott had been a nurse for all of three days when a line of carts drew up outside the old Union Hotel in Georgetown. The ballroom became Ward Number One with forty beds. The filthy, blood-smeared arrivals were undressed and washed before they were allowed to lie on the sheets. Miss Alcott amazed herself by performing the task without shuddering. Then a British surgeon dressed their wounds. 'He had served in the Crimea,' she wrote, 'and seemed to regard a dilapidated body very much as I should have regarded a damaged garment; and, turning up his cuffs, whipped out a very unpleasant looking house-wife [sewing kit], cutting, sawing, patching and piecing, with the enthusiasm of an accomplished surgical seamstress.'[46]

The vast need for surgeons and medical personal had opened the doors to any foreign doctor with a degree and a proficiency in the English language. Though not in the same numbers as foreign soldiers, they came by their tens and hundreds to Washington. Until two months before, 25-year-old Charles Mayo had been the house surgeon at the Radcliffe Infirmary in Oxford. There were loud protests from the staff and patients when the popular and well-respected doctor announced his intention to go to America to gain more medical experience.[47] After seeing Mayo's qualifications, the new surgeon general, Dr William Hammond, who was valiantly trying to overhaul the entire system, offered him charge of 125 beds at the Armory Square Hospital in Washington. This was not what Mayo had in mind and he politely declined the offer, preferring to sit the assistant-surgeon examination instead. But to his chagrin his marks were so high that the president of the examining board put in a special request for Mayo to be stationed in the capital.

In the aftermath of Fredericksburg, Mayo worked all day and long into the night, hurrying

> from place to place to the assistance of maimed and exhausted men, pursued all the while by messengers with notice of fresh arrivals . . . scarcely a hotel or boarding-house in the city but contained someone that required the doctor's help. It became impossible to keep a detailed visiting list, or to remember the names of one's patients. 'Lieutenant A and five others, Colonel B and six others; Captain C and four others,' are specimens of the kind of record that had to suffice for the contents of a particular house or hotel.[48]

Occasionally, he remembered men by their stories; like the wounded officer in the Irish Brigade who was saved by the butt of his revolver, which took the full force of a Minié ball. But for the most part, he was too busy to become friendly with his patients. He noticed that many of them arrived dying from tetanus – the result of incompetent butchery at the field hospitals, he concluded. There was nothing he could do for these wretched men except try to ease their pain. One particular case stayed in his memory: a healthy young major with a botched amputation who lingered for several days, eventually dying in the arms of a kind and decent hotel-keeper who could not bear the thought of her guest dying alone.

Washington was in an uproar over Fredericksburg, and General Burnside was accused of criminal stupidity. 'What astonishes me is that such a battle should ever have been fought,' the new attaché Edward Malet wrote to his father; 'I do really think that all those men who fell were murdered.'[49] Lincoln's reputation as a war leader suffered a serious blow. The President wrung his hands as he listened to accounts of the battle, repeatedly asking, 'What has God put me in this place for?'[50] For many people, not just in the capital but also throughout the country, the answer was obvious; it was time for Lincoln to make way for a successor. The treasurer of the Sanitary Commission, George Templeton Strong, wrote in his diary on 18 December that 'Old Abe's grotesque genial Western' jokes simply nauseated him now; 'if these things go on we shall have pressure on him to resign.'[51] Three days later Strong recorded with surprise that it was Seward and not Lincoln who had resigned. 'Edward Everett and Charles Sumner are named as candidates for the succession. I do not think Seward a loss to government,' he wrote. 'He is an adroit, shifty, clever politician . . . He believes in majorities, and it would seem, in nothing else.'[52]

A campaign to oust Seward had been gaining momentum for several months. The previous September, Lincoln had fended off an anti-Seward delegation from New York that claimed to represent the wishes of five New England governors, by declaring that the administration would collapse without him. The statement was debatable, since Seward's power had shrunk considerably since the heady days in December 1860 when he boasted to his wife that the future of the government rested on his shoulders.[53] Seward had successfully forged a close relationship with Lincoln as his second-in-command and confidant, but his relations with the rest of the Cabinet had actually worsened during the past two years. The other members resented the way Seward had managed to insinuate himself into Lincoln's inner circle. They disliked arriving at Cabinet meetings and finding him already there, or, when they left, watching him stay behind for a private 'chat'. Gideon Welles's diary was peppered with fulminations against Seward and his wish 'to direct, to be the Premier, the real Executive'.[54] The Treasury Secretary, Salmon Chase, whose views on emancipation were far more radical than Seward's, loathed him so heartily that he seized every opportunity to undermine the Secretary of State. He repeatedly used the phrase 'back-stairs influence' when referring to Seward, until it took on a life of its own and became a universal cry.

Charles Sumner had been hoping for some time that Seward would make a mistake that would finish him permanently. He believed that such a moment had come after the publication in early December of the State Department's diplomatic correspondence for the first half of 1862. By now the State Department was overseeing 480 consulates, commercial agencies and consular agencies abroad, and the literature Seward offered to the public was extensive. The British section contained letters from Charles Francis Adams that the Minister had never imagined would become public. Benjamin Moran arrived at the legation on 22 December to find Adams mortified to the point of tears after the London press gleefully published some of the juicier anti-British dispatches, which included his complaints about *The Times* 'and the sympathies of the higher classes', whom Adams accused of 'longing to see the political power of the United States permanently impaired'.[55]

Seward's decision to publish every letter was 'almost amounting to insanity', Moran declared savagely. 'Mr Adams thinks his usefulness at this post is destroyed ... At one time during the day I thought he seriously contemplated resigning, and I told him he could not be spared – that it was his duty to remain ... This he agreed to ... But that he would be more guarded in his future Dispatches to Mr Seward.' Where, Adams wondered, was Seward's sense of tact or diplomacy? 'I scarcely imagine it wise in diplomatic life to show your hand in the midst of the game.'[56] Now that the whole country knew that he accused the aristocracy of wishing 'to see the Union shattered', Adams doubted if polite society would ever receive him again.*

Sumner was only interested in one letter – a dispatch sent to Adams on 5 July 1862 – in which Seward betrayed his contempt for the hard-line abolitionists and their universal emancipation agenda.† This, Sumner believed, would be sufficient to ruin Seward in the eyes of the radical wing of the Republican Party. All he needed was an event or catalyst to mobilize his fellow Senators – which had been provided by the disaster at Fredericksburg.

On the evening of 16 December the thirty-two Republican Senators gathered for a meeting in the Senate reception room to discuss their response to the defeat. Lincoln did not escape censure, but the general feeling in the chamber was that the President's mistakes were – as Chase repeatedly charged – the direct result of Seward's baleful influence.

---

* Seward's printed correspondence provided some of the most interesting reading the Foreign Office clerks had seen in years. But Lord Lyons adopted a judicious view of the letters. '[Seward's] tone towards the Foreign Powers has, however, become much more civil than it appeared in the correspondence printed last year,' he pointed out to Lord Russell. As for Adams and his indiscreet comments. Lyons thought he showed 'more calmness and good sense than any of the American Ministers abroad. He is not altogether free from a tendency to small suspicions – but this, I think, proceeds from his position, not from his natural character – it is, too, a very common mistake of inexperienced diplomats.'[57]
† The line which really upset Sumner was this: 'the extreme advocates of African slavery and its most vehement opponents were acting in concert together to precipitate a servile war – the former by making the most desperate attempt to overthrow the federal Union, the latter by demanding an edict of universal emancipation.'[58]

Ironically, Seward's deliberate attempt to foster an aura of power and mystique about himself, which William Howard Russell had noticed in 1861, now told against him. By the end of the meeting, all but four of the Senators had agreed that Lincoln should be confronted about Seward. In Sumner's view, the Secretary of State's own words had damned him by revealing his lack of commitment to the war. But there was a deeper intent among some of the Senators: Seward would only be the first casualty. The other moderates in the Cabinet would follow and then Lincoln himself, leaving the way clear for Chase to become President with a Cabinet of fellow radicals.[59]

One of Seward's few remaining friends on Capitol Hill had sneaked out of the Republican meeting to warn him of the impending coup. His immediate reaction was to resign first in order to deny his enemies the satisfaction of seeing him humiliated.[60] By the time Lord Lyons heard about the Senators' attack their delegation had already met with a plainly distressed Lincoln on 18 December and presented their demands for Seward's removal and a reorganization of the Cabinet.[61] Lincoln had been able to parry their claim that the Cabinet was divided, but had no answer to Sumner's accusation that Seward was sending 'offensive dispatches which the President could not have seen, or assented to'.[62] To buy time, he invited them to resume the discussion the following day.

Lyons still regarded Sumner as a reliable ally in Anglo-American controversies, but he thought the Republican Party as a whole combined an unhealthy mix of zealotry and ignorance that made them unpredictable. 'We may have to be ready for squalls,' he wrote to Lord Russell on the 19th. That evening, Lincoln received the Republican delegation for the second time. But he had a surprise for the plotters. He had invited the Cabinet – with the exception of Seward – to hear their allegation that the Secretary of State had usurped its powers. It was an awkward moment for Chase, who, even more than Sumner, had been the prime mover behind the attempted coup. He panicked over whether to portray himself as loyal to Lincoln, which would mean denying the Senators' allegations that the Cabinet was disgruntled, or to throw in his lot with the delegation and support its claims. He lost his nerve and pretended to be surprised that there were rumours against Seward. His cowardice abashed several of the Senators, but not Charles Sumner, who angrily repeated his previous complaints about Seward's record. Still, when confronted with testimonials that the Cabinet was united behind

Lincoln, the majority of the delegation felt too embarrassed to insist on Seward's removal. The meeting adjourned at one in the morning with nothing actually decided.

Lyons thought that the outcome would depend on whom Lincoln could least afford to lose; 'a quarrel with the Republican Members of the Senate is a very serious thing for him.' As two more days slipped by without any definite news Lyons pondered a future without his erstwhile nemesis. 'I shall be sorry if it ends in the removal of Mr Seward,' he wrote a little ruefully on Monday, 22 December. 'We are much more likely to have a man less disposed to keep the peace ... I should hardly have said this two years ago.'[63] But that afternoon he paid a visit to the State Department and to his relief found Seward back at his desk, behaving as if nothing had happened. Over the weekend, just as Seward had started to accept the coup against him, and Lincoln had begun to rationalize to himself why his chief ally in the Cabinet had to be sacrificed to placate the radicals, Chase had become frightened that Seward's friends and supporters would take their revenge on him. To save himself, he offered his resignation in the hope that this would clear him of any imputation of harbouring ambitions for the Presidency. Lincoln realized that Chase had lost his nerve. In a deliberate show of authority, the President rejected his resignation, replied that both Secretaries were indispensable and declared all discussion about a Cabinet reorganization at an end. The Senators' protest had achieved precisely the opposite effect of what they had intended. But it was obvious, Lyons wrote to Lord Russell on 26 December, that 'Mr Seward was plainly not in a position to make any concessions at all to neutrals'.[64] He would not dare risk his remaining political capital on helping Britain to obtain cotton, or indeed on helping Britain at all.

That same day, the 26th, President Jefferson Davis told Southerners to relinquish their hope for British intervention. He was speaking to the legislature in his home state of Mississippi at the end of a morale-boosting tour through the western parts of the Confederacy. Davis did not need to rouse his listeners' indignation – many already had first- or second-hand knowledge of the devastation wrought by Union armies. Nor did he need to warn them against complacency: beyond Virginia, the South was shrinking as more and more territory came under Federal control. What the lean and shabbily dressed listeners required from their President was reassurance that the North might smash their homes but not their moral purpose. Davis damned Northerners as the blighted offspring of Cromwell's fanatical Roundheads. It was in their blood to oppress others, he declared. Their ancestors 'persecuted Catholics in England, and they hung Quakers and witches in America'. The liberty-loving South could never live in harmony with such monsters of intolerance. But, having given his audience its dose of tonic, Davis proceeded to administer a series of bitter pills. The last, and most shocking to the once-mighty kings of cotton, was the fact of the South's utter isolation. 'In the course of this war our eyes have often been turned abroad,' admitted Davis:

> We have expected sometimes recognition, and sometimes intervention, at the
> hands of foreign nations; and we had a right to expect it ... but this I say:
> 'Put not your trust in princes,' and rest not your hopes on foreign nations.
> This war is ours: we must fight it out ourselves. And I feel some pride in
> knowing that, so far, we have done it without the good will of anybody.[65]

The Marquis of Hartington was moved by Davis's speech. He and his travelling companion, Colonel Leslie, had arrived in Richmond on 23 December, five days after leaving Baltimore in the dead of night. Hartington had wanted to ask the US Government's permission to cross into the South but the legation had warned him against the idea. 'They said they thought it was very doubtful,' he explained to his father, the Duke of Devonshire, 'and if we were refused there would be more difficulty in going out on our own hook.' He promised they would not resist if they were captured during the attempt.[66] Fortunately, with the assistance of the ubiquitous Maryland journalist W. W. Glenn, they had been able to travel from one safe house to the next without encountering any Federal patrols.

The difference between the countryside of Maryland and that of Virginia was striking. 'The country looks terribly desolated,' wrote Hartington. 'The fences are all pulled down for firewood, a good many houses burnt, and everything looking very bare.' The contrast between Baltimore and Richmond was even greater. The Southern capital had doubled in size in less than two years, but was worse off in every aspect. Hartington was surprised by the shoddy appearance of all classes. 'They have had no new clothes since the war began,' he wrote, 'and are not likely to get any till it is over.' Yet 'these people say they are ready to go on for any length of time, and I believe many of them think the longer the better, because it will widen the breach between them and the Yankees, against whom their hatred is more intense than you can possibly conceive.'[67]

Hartington had arrived in America in August with no strong feelings about the war. After a couple of weeks in New York he felt 'inclined to be more a Unionist than I was'. The moderation of New Yorkers impressed him since 'I believe, if they could lick them, and the South would come back to-morrow, they would be willing to forget everything that had happened, and go on as usual'. But as he saw more of the North he became less certain about the point of the war. 'I understand nothing about it, and I can't find anybody except Seward who even pretends that he does ... They mix up in the most perplexing manner the slavery question, which they say makes theirs the just cause, with the Union question, which is really what they are fighting for.'[68] He found the Peace Democrats he spoke to in the North a rather unattractive lot, which made him waver: 'I think their arguments are weak and their objects not by any means desirable,' he wrote from Chicago in mid-October.[69]

But once Hartington reached Virginia it took less than a week for him to be won over. Like Frank Vizetelly and Francis Lawley before him, he was smitten. 'I hope Freddy [his younger brother, Lord Frederick Cavendish] won't groan much over my rebel sympathies, but I can't help them,' he wrote to his father on 28 December 1862. 'The people here are so much more earnest about the thing than the North seems to be, that it is impossible not to go a good way with them, though one may think they were wrong at first.'[70] The Southerners were certainly putting on a good show for him. He was introduced to Jefferson Davis and his Cabinet, who seemed like moderate and sensible men to him, fighting the laudable cause of self-determination; had taken to Lee and Jackson, who were modest in victory; and had been shown a couple of carefully selected plantations. 'The negroes hardly look as well off as I expected to see them,' he wrote afterwards, 'but they are not dirtier or more uncomfortable-looking than Irish labourers.' Southern fears of a 'servile insurrection' inspired by Lincoln's Emancipation Proclamation had proved to be unfounded.*[71] On the 29th Lawley accompanied him and Colonel Leslie to Jeb Stuart's headquarters. Forewarned by a

---

* In New Orleans, Acting Consul George Coppell had tried to obtain permission for British subjects to arm themselves in case of a race riot against whites.

telegram from Lawley, the officers ransacked their own belongings to provide the party with comfortable accommodation. Scarce luxuries like blankets and stoves were sacrificed for the visitors. The fattest turkey in the camp was killed and plucked for dinner. Hartington appreciated their efforts, and endeared himself to his hosts by insisting 'we should not make any change for them in our ordinary routine, but let them fare exactly as the rest'. To demonstrate his sincerity he helped to beat the eggs for 'a monster egg-nog'.[72] But as Hartington joined in the revelries, he suddenly realized the scale of suffering it would require to crush the spirit of rebellion. The South 'can never be brought back into the Union except as conquered provinces', he wrote, 'and I think they will take a great deal of conquering before that is done'.[73]

16

The Missing Key to Victory

*New Year's Day – Heartbreak at Vicksburg – General Banks
assumes command at New Orleans – The* Alabama *embarrasses
the US navy – Seward returns to his old ways*

The English volunteer Dr Charles Mayo finally took a rest from work on New Year's Day to attend the public reception at the White House. By the time he reached the front of the queue outside the Blue Room, Lincoln had been shaking hands for more than two hours without a break. 'His presence is by no means majestic,' wrote Mayo, 'and I could not but pity the poor man, he looked so miserable.'[1] A journalist observing the occasion wrote that Lincoln's gait had become 'more stooping, his countenance sallow, and there is a sunken, deathly look about the large, cavernous eyes'.[2] The President had also hosted the official reception for dignitaries, foreign diplomats and politicians earlier in the day. It was the only occasion when the Ministers were expected to wear their dress uniforms to the White House. Notwithstanding the finery on display, the atmosphere had been subdued. Seward hardly left Lincoln's side, Lyons noticed, and made no attempt to engage his colleagues in conversation.

Once the White House had emptied Lincoln could concentrate on the immediate problem at hand: General Burnside had called in the morning to offer his resignation. Though the President had lost confidence in Burnside's capabilities he was not sure that it would be right to give the Army of the Potomac its third leader in three months. Over the past few days, telegrams had been arriving from out west which filled him with anxiety. The Federal armies in Mississippi and Tennessee both appeared to be on the brink of defeat.

*

New Year's Day reception at the White House, by Frank Vizetelly

Only five months earlier, Lincoln had complained that Europe concentrated far too much on the North's failures in the east and entirely ignored the great successes it enjoyed in the west, where Federal armies were 'clearing more than 100,000 square miles of country'.[3] But since then the US navy had been unable to take control of the Mississippi river, and General Grant had failed to capture the river port of Vicksburg, his next objective. For as long as Vicksburg stayed in Confederate hands, the mighty Mississippi remained the South's most precious supply route and means of communication between its eastern and western parts. The significance of the river as the economic backbone of America was no mere story to Lincoln; during his youth he had worked on it, travelling on flatboats from Illinois down to New Orleans. 'Vicksburg is the key,' he had told his generals in 1861. 'The war can never be brought to a close until that key is in our pocket . . . We can take all the northern ports of the Confederacy, and they can defy us from Vicksburg.'*[4] Since that discussion, the Federal army had grown to just under a million men,

---

* Confederate President Jefferson Davis also had emotional ties to Vicksburg. His family home, Brierfield plantation, was only 20 miles south of the town along a part of the river

twice the Confederate total of 464,000. Lincoln wanted this numerical superiority exploited; a week of Fredericksburgs would wipe out Lee's Army of Northern Virginia but cause only a dent in the North's fighting capacity.

Vicksburg was roughly equidistant between Memphis, Tennessee and New Orleans; the next fort was Port Hudson, 150 miles further south, which guarded the approach to Baton Rouge, Louisiana. Nicknamed the 'Hill City' before the war, but now referred to as the Gibraltar of the Mississippi,* Vicksburg owed its defensive strength to the spectacular geography of the Mississippi Delta. Situated along a sprawling chain of hills overlooking a sharp bend in the river, surrounded by alligator-infested swamps and densely wooded bayous whose emerald-coloured waters obscured a netherworld of poisonous snakes and snapping turtles, there were few approaches to Vicksburg which could not be defended from the town. Before the war Vicksburg had been a thriving commercial centre of 4,000 inhabitants, with six newspapers, several churches of different denominations and even its own synagogue. But now its purpose was simply strategic: to be defended or captured at all costs.

The lack of progress in opening up the Mississippi river had political and military implications that Lincoln could not afford to ignore. The Democratic politician-turned-general John McClernand warned that if control of the river were not soon achieved the Midwestern States of Ohio, Illinois and Indiana might lead a second mass exodus from the Union, creating a separate Confederacy of the Northwest, which would make its own peace with the South.

There was also the problem of General Ben Butler down in New Orleans, whose eight-month rule had resulted in a profoundly alienated population as well as a raft of missed opportunities to gain more of the Mississippi. Lincoln decided to replace Butler with another political general, Nathaniel P. Banks. Though his military record was not inspiring – Stonewall Jackson had thrashed his first army in the summer

---

known as Davis Bend. He described Vicksburg as the 'nail-head that held the South's two halves together'.

* The phrase referred to the Great Siege of Gibraltar during the American War of Independence. Though vastly outnumbered and outgunned, the besieged British forces on the Rock had defied a combined Spanish and French invasion fleet for three years and seven months, one of the longest sieges in history.

of 1862 – Banks was a popular and respected Massachusetts politician. From humble beginnings as a bobbin boy in a cotton factory, he had risen through his own talents to become the Speaker of the House of Representatives. His leadership qualities were not in question, nor was his honesty – an important consideration after the accusations of corruption levelled against Butler.

The immaculately dressed and well-spoken Banks (he had carefully erased all traces of his working-class roots) appeared to be the perfect choice. His political connections meant that he had no trouble working with the Governors of New York and New England to recruit an entirely new army of volunteers; he had already displayed his tact and administrative skills after he was sent to quell unrest in Maryland in 1861; and he was ambitious for military glory. Lincoln gave Banks two objectives when he asked him to go to New Orleans in November 1862: militarily, the General was to lead his army up the Mississippi, sweeping away Confederate resistance as he proceeded, until he joined forces with General Grant at Vicksburg, some 225 miles to the north. Politically, he was to ensure the election of a new, pro-Northern legislature in Louisiana that would enable the State to be readmitted to the Union.

Lincoln adopted the same pragmatic approach when General McClernand asked permission to raise an army of volunteers from the Midwest, with the sole aim of attacking Vicksburg. The President believed that the political gains to the administration from McClernand's project outweighed any potential annoyance that might be felt by the army chiefs. However, Lincoln underestimated how much Halleck and Grant – neither of whom had any liking for enthusiastic amateurs, regardless of their political usefulness – would resent the encroachment on their authority. Grant immediately made plans to reach Vicksburg before McClernand. He ordered his trusted general, William T. Sherman, to take 33,000 men and sail down the Mississippi to about 15 miles north of Vicksburg, where he was to leave the river and enter its tributary, the Yazoo. There was a bluff along a bend in the Yazoo that was easy to scale and would allow Sherman to follow an overland route to the town. Grant intended to march towards Vicksburg with the rest the army, luring the Confederates into a battle and thus leaving the way open for Sherman. The operation began on 20 December 1862 as a fleet of troop ships, floating hospitals and gunboats set sail from Memphis. But while Sherman was travelling downriver, Confederate raiders destroyed Grant's supply base, forcing him to turn back towards Tennessee. Sherman continued on his mission, unaware that he would be facing the enemy alone.

The floating attack force came to a halt on Christmas Day, a few miles short of the proposed bluff. The sinking of a gunboat, the USS *Cairo*, revealed the existence of underwater mines around an area of the Yazoo known as Chickasaw Bayou. Still ignorant of Grant's return to base, Sherman decided to alter his plan slightly and disembark at Chickasaw. There was more swamp than dry land here, but above the bluffs were the Walnut Hills and a road that led straight to Vicksburg. Sherman was not fazed by his first solo mission under Grant: he knew that the Walnut Hills were largely devoid of Confederate troops and assumed that the taking of the bluffs would be achieved in a matter of hours. But he waited four days before launching the attack, giving ample time for the Confederates to prepare a defence. Sherman's plan would now require the troops to cross a wide open plain while being shot at from above, echoing Burnside's folly at Fredericksburg. In his memoirs, Sherman described his division commander, Brigadier General George Morgan, cheerfully receiving the order of battle with the words, 'General, in ten minutes after you give the signal I'll be on those hills.'[5] Morgan's memory of the meeting on 28 December was rather different: he had tried to dissuade Sherman from the idea, warning him that a direct frontal attack would turn the gloomy swamps of the bayou into a mass grave. But Sherman was suffering from an excess of bravado, not uncommon among generals when given their first independent command. 'Tell Morgan to give the signal for the assault,' he ordered an aide. 'We will lose 5000 men before we take Vicksburg, and may as well lose them here as anywhere.'[6]

The battle commenced the following day, 29 December. Morgan was furious with Sherman. The men to be lost were *his* men, the survivors of the Cumberland Gap and the harrowing retreat through barren wilderness. Colonel John F. De Courcy was commanding Morgan's 3rd Brigade. His sense of duty forbade him from questioning his orders, but, knowing what was about to happen, he insisted on hearing the orders from Morgan himself: '"General, do I understand that you are about to order an assault?" To which I replied, "Yes; form your brigade,"' Morgan recalled many years later. 'With an air of respectful protest he said: "My poor brigade! Your order will be obeyed, General."' De Courcy had also been changed by his experiences at the Cumberland Gap; gone was the martinet and in its place a commander whose loyalty to his regiment was reciprocated by the men.

General Morgan watched as the brigade charged through the marshes into the freezing water. 'All the formations were broken,' he wrote. 'The assaulting forces were jammed together, and, with a yell of desperate determination, they rushed to the assault and were mowed down by a storm of shells, grape and canister, and minie-balls which swept our front like a hurricane of fire.'[7] De Courcy raced back and forth as he tried to keep cohesion to the regiments. Some managed to cross the small river in front of the bluffs, only to become trapped, others fell back, while a few remained on the near side. After the battle Morgan and De Courcy were accused of failing to put more muscle into the attack, and Sherman was especially critical.[8] Yet a survivor from De Courcy's regiment, the 16th Ohio, wrote afterwards that they were so close to the enemy that they could not retreat without being shot in the back, 'so there was nothing left for us to do except to surrender'.[9] Sherman was pacing up and down at his headquarters when Morgan went to see him about collecting the wounded from the field. Unable to accept the extent of his failure, Sherman at first refused a flag of truce, condemning many of the wounded to death and the rest to capture. His initiation into independent command had cost the lives of 1,800 men, half of them from De Courcy's 3rd Brigade.[10]

Five days later, on 3 January, De Courcy and his shattered regiments slunk into camp at Milliken's Bend, Louisiana. The army was divided into those who believed Morgan and De Courcy, who hotly asserted that they did move forward (and had the casualties to prove it); and those who accepted the account of Brigadier General John Thayer, who claimed that he had passed them with his soldiers while they cowered in the first rifle pits. The dispute would never be resolved; years later, Private Owen Hopkins of the 42nd Ohio Infantry wrote that De Courcy's brigade had followed behind his own, 'but the boys pressed forward so vigorously in the daring onset that it was difficult to tell who was in the advance'.[11] The growing dissension in the camp was halted by the arrival of General McClernand; in his pocket was an order, inveigled out of President Lincoln, assigning all of Sherman's troops to his command. Ever mindful of his future political career, McClernand had a grand vision to implement. He informed a stunned but helpless Sherman – who had known nothing about McClernand's visit to Washington – that the force was going to be renamed the Army of the Mississippi, with Sherman and Morgan as the two corps leaders under him.

McClernand was not as inept as his contemporaries claimed.[12] He did at least recognize a superior soldier when he saw one and was willing to listen to Sherman. At the start of the Chickasaw expedition, a Confederate raid had captured one of the Federal steamers and taken it to Fort Hindman some 40 miles up the Arkansas river, which fed into the Mississippi. Sherman now suggested to McClernand that they capture the fortification. It held no more than 5,000 troops, but its strategic location enabled the Confederates to sneak onto the Mississippi at will, wreaking havoc on Federal ships, before escaping back up the Arkansas. This was the time, urged Sherman, when they had 32,000 men at their disposal, to erase this Confederate menace.

The Federals landed 3 miles below Fort Hindman on 10 January. Morgan ordered De Courcy to hold his brigade at the rear, guarding the boats against an ambush, while the rest of the army began its assault. Admiral David Dixon Porter's gunboats hammered their target – which was not much more than a bastioned dugout – with continuous fire for twenty-four hours. When Sherman gave the order for an all-out attack the following day, there was only half-hearted firing from the fort. The first advance brought the soldiers to within 'hand-shaking distance of the enemy', according to Brigadier General Morgan, but 'the fight continued with sullen stubbornness'. Several times a white flag appeared only to be hastily hauled down. Realizing that a little more effort would tip the scales, Morgan sent orders for De Courcy to march his brigade into action. The troops emerged from the woods along the riverbank and charged, double file, towards the fort. Within minutes another white flag appeared on the parapet and this time it remained.[13]

The attack resulted in a thousand Federal casualties, almost ten times the number inflicted on the Confederates. But McClernand and Sherman had netted nearly 5,000 prisoners, depriving Arkansas of a quarter of its troops. Although Grant initially blasted the operation as a monument to McClernand's vanity, after a few days' reflection he accepted that it had given a much-needed victory, both tactically and psychologically, to the army. On 17 January a snowstorm turned the blackened terrain into a dazzling white as the troop ships steamed back down the Arkansas river to the Mississippi. The commanders took advantage of the quiet hours during the journey to compose their reports. Admiral Porter laid the entire blame for Sherman's failure at Chickasaw on De Courcy: 'All this was owing to Colonel De Courcy (who has since resigned) not following General Blair, who had no difficulty in getting into the works of the enemy,' he asserted in his letter to the Secretary of the Navy, Gideon Welles. 'But for the want of nerve in the leader of a brigade, the army should have succeeded.' Further down the fleet, Brigadier General Morgan sat in his cabin writing precisely the opposite report. De Courcy's 'gallant brigade lost 580 men at Chickasaw Bluffs', he observed, 'and, with Blair's brigade, bore the brunt of that hard-fought but unsuccessful day. Col John F De Courcy deserves promotion.'[14]

Morgan loyally defended his subordinate even after the *New York Herald* published an excoriating account of the disaster, which again named De Courcy as the chief culprit. Everybody and everything associated with De Courcy suffered by association. On 31 January he sent a list of recommended promotions to the Adjutant General. A passionate plea on behalf of the men accompanied the letter. 'I have to add', he wrote, 'that these recommendations are made by me after mature and most deliberate reflection and consideration. I shall never recommend for promotion anyone I do not deem worthy of it.'[15] No reply was forthcoming. Even if the authorities had been predisposed to listen, the army was once again undergoing reorganization. Grant had managed to block McClernand and had taken control of the Army of the Mississippi himself so he could merge it with the other Federal forces in the area.

De Courcy had indeed tried to resign, as Porter mentioned in his letter, but the request had been denied. His longing to escape his present location was exacerbated by the wretchedness of camp conditions. Rain had followed the snow in a grey downpour that continued day after day. The ground beneath the tents flooded, causing the camp's rudimentary latrines to overflow and poison the water wells.[16] The only dry land was occupied by hospitals and graves, which presented the men with a choice of sleeping among the dead or alongside the barely living. Yet Grant could not afford to have his army lie idle while they waited for the weather to cooperate. His best course of military action was politically impossible, since it would mean starting the campaign afresh and leaving the vicinity of Vicksburg. This the Northern public would have interpreted as another defeat. So Grant had the men begin several canal projects in the somewhat forlorn hope of engineering an alternative route to the town. The men were sent out with shovels and ordered to dig. Sherman thought the whole enterprise was 'a pure waste of human effort'.[17]

Every officer in De Courcy's regiment fell ill with swamp fever, and De Courcy himself lasted just two weeks before suffering a total collapse. The army doctor took pity on him and recommended his removal from the camp. The patient had suffered much 'both in body and mind', he wrote on 14 February 1863, making him prey to 'typho-malarial fever'. A few days later De Courcy joined a wagon train heading east. He would not see his old regiment for many months. His destination was Cincinnati, Ohio, 700 miles from Vicksburg, and the long journey was almost as hard as the life he left behind. By the time he was examined by another doctor, on 14 March, his body had become skeletal in appearance. He was immediately placed on sick leave and declared unfit for duty for sixty days.

At the War Department in Washington, reports of Grant's futile engineering works caused alarm, especially since there were rumours that the General was drinking again. Lincoln had already been forced to step in and countermand an order by Grant that threatened to have serious political repercussions. General Order No. 11, which Grant issued in late December, had called for the arrest and expulsion of all Jews in the parts of Mississippi and Tennessee under Union control.* Lincoln revoked the order two weeks later, leaving it to General Halleck to explain to Grant about the wisdom of proscribing 'an entire religious class, some of whom are fighting in our ranks'. But the reversal was too late for local Jewish communities, including thirty families in Paducah, Kentucky, who were driven from their homes and dumped into riverboats bound for Ohio.[18]

Lincoln and his Secretary of War, Edwin Stanton, decided to send Charles A. Dana, a former journalist and troubleshooter for the War Department, to Grant's headquarters. The reason given was the Department's concern about inefficiencies in the paymaster service, but in reality Dana's mission was to be the eyes and ears of the administration. There were too many calls in Washington for Grant's removal for Lincoln simply to do nothing. The Vicksburg campaign had assumed even greater importance since the Battle of Murfreesboro in central Tennessee on New Year's Day. US General William Rosecrans and Confederate

---

* Grant apparently believed that 'Jewish peddlers' were to blame for the army's supply problems.

General Braxton Bragg had fought one another to a stalemate. Each had lost a third of his army, putting both out of action for many months; crucially, neither general would be able to send reinforcements to Vicksburg. When Dana reached the main army camp at Milliken's Bend, just above Vicksburg, Grant and his staff chose the wise course of bringing him into the military family. Dana was allowed full access to everything that was happening in the Army of the Tennessee, and soon came to admire Grant as a resourceful and determined leader.

Francis Lawley also visited the Vicksburg area during the great digging operations. Naturally, he did not go near Grant's headquarters and so had no measure of the man who was staking his reputation and career on Vicksburg's capture. In Lawley's opinion, the town was impregnable. 'The swollen state of the river, the dreary wastes of oozy swamp and fen,' he wrote for *The Times*, were more powerful weapons 'than sword or bullet'. Through his telescope he could see the parlous state of the soldiers in the Federal camps.[19] Lawley departed for Atlanta confident that Grant would never succeed.

General Banks's army in New Orleans – which he called the 19th Corps – consisted of fifty-six regiments, many of them less than four months old and totally ignorant of military life. One of the newest regiments was the 133rd New York Infantry Volunteers, also known as the 2nd Metropolitan Guard because the recruits were mostly New York policemen; tough, working-class men whose fighting skills had been honed against the feral gangs which terrorized lower Manhattan. The 133rd were bemused and dismayed to have a British army officer as their commander. Colonel L. D. H. Currie, as he liked to style himself, was the young officer whom William Howard Russell had referred to in his diary as laughing ruefully at the total lack of military discipline in McClellan's army. The 31-year-old career soldier and veteran of the Crimea* had been sent to Brigadier

---

* During the Crimean War, the 19th Foot was sent to the evocatively named Calamity Bay, where it took part in the bungled fight against the Russians for the Alma heights. Currie was brought down by a bullet that tore a large hole through his left foot. He was rescued from the field, conscious, and therefore able to prevent the regimental surgeon from amputating his foot. For several months Currie lay festering in the notorious Scutari hospital until he was rescued by his brother, who brought him home on a stretcher. Currie made it his mission to walk again. Through sheer force of will he dragged himself on crutches to the medal

General W. F. 'Baldy' Smith's division, where he quickly showed himself to be far too useful to be relegated to administrative work. By the beginning of 1862 Currie was taking part, if not taking the lead, in cavalry expeditions against Confederate pickets in northern Virginia.[20] When McClellan was threatening Richmond in June, Currie's unflappability stood him in good stead after his horse was killed from under him. By July there was a groundswell of support for giving Currie a regiment of his own. Four generals, including McClellan, sent letters on his behalf. 'I believe him capable of filling any military position which may be assigned to him,' wrote Major-General William B. Franklin.[21]

Whether Currie was capable of commanding the unruly 133rd remained to be seen. Already annoyed at having been assigned to a foreigner, the regiment saw nothing positive about being in New Orleans. The women still turned their backs and scowled at the slightest provocation. The male inhabitants seemed to divide into two distinct species: those who wished to fleece them, and those who were waiting for an opportunity to kill them. The city was like a poisonous flower, beautiful to behold but dangerous to the touch. General Butler had cut down the murder rate but every other vice had been allowed to flourish. Banks was appalled to discover that many of the stories that had reached him were true. Federal officers treated private property in the Crescent City as though it was theirs for the taking. A family might receive an eviction notice with orders to move out the same day, taking nothing except clothes and necessities. The new occupier would move in the following day and the plundering would begin.

The Scotsman William Watson observed Banks's attempt to impose civic order on the city and almost felt sorry for him. The Northerner was, wrote Watson, 'altogether too mild a man to grapple with the state of things then existing in New Orleans'.[22] 'Everybody connected with the government has been employed in stealing . . .', a horrified Banks wrote to his wife in mid-January. 'Sugar, silver plate, horses, carriages, everything they could lay their hands on.' He also discovered that nothing happened without a bribe. Among his first directives was an order for all officers to leave civilian accommodation and return to army

---

ceremony at Buckingham Palace on 19 May 1855. His ashen countenance so alarmed Queen Victoria that she asked to be kept informed of his recovery.

quarters.[23] Mary Sophia Hill had recently returned to New Orleans carrying hundreds of messages and letters for the marooned families of Confederate soldiers, and was similarly appalled by the moral degradation that had spread through the city.

The 133rd were sent north to Baton Rouge, where Currie did his best to continue training the men, teaching them the rudiments of drill. By the end of January he was just beginning to make some headway when he learned that the War Department had received serious allegations against him. A former member of the regiment had been trying to persuade his old colleagues to make a joint protest against Currie. When he failed to whip up enough support, he went ahead on his own, concocting an absurd list of crimes allegedly committed by the Colonel. Currie knew he would be exonerated if the authorities questioned his fellow officers. But he recoiled at the thought of an investigation. It would, he was sure, undermine his hard-won authority. Moreover, he found the whole affair deeply offensive. 'I have been engaged in a humble way, but to the best of my ability in suppressing rebellion, and maintaining constitutional government, which is scarcely compatible with such charges,' he wrote to his superiors; 'if, after a life of fourteen years of active employment in a profession of honour, my character requires defence, it is not worthy of it.' They agreed. On 4 February 1863 Currie's commander declared that no notice should be given to the allegations.[24]

Currie's exoneration was followed by an order to lead a scouting expedition through the bayous west of Baton Rouge. After Vicksburg, the Mississippi river meandered for about 150 miles, until it reached another deep bend carved into 80-foot-high bluffs. Here the little town of Port Hudson was perched on top of the eastern bank, the perfect site for heavy artillery to bombard enemy ships as they slowed down to navigate the sharp turn. The bastion not only kept the Federal army bottled up between New Orleans and Baton Rouge, it also protected the Confederates' chief supply route west of the Mississippi. The romantically named Red River, so called for the rust-coloured clay along its northern banks, flowed from the corner of northern Texas all the way down and across Louisiana, finally emptying into the Mississippi just above Port Hudson. It passed through some of the most fertile regions of the Confederacy. If Banks could take Port Hudson he would also have access to the Red River, its grains and cattle and, most important of all, its rich cotton plantations.

Since Banks could not approach Port Hudson from the Mississippi, he wondered if he could bypass the area altogether by exploring a way through the maze-like bayous and lesser tributaries which fed the river. Currie's regiment was sent on a two-week trek through densely wooded swamps and across alligator-infested rivers. They were not only prey to the wildlife but also to local Confederates who lay in wait for them. One private was killed and two others were snatched during an ambush. The men returned at the end of February, nervous and physical wrecks. They were 'used up', in Currie's words: 'In my opinion the country is impracticable for all arms of the service.'[25]

There was no alternative but to face Port Hudson's batteries. Banks invited his naval counterpart, Admiral Farragut, to his headquarters at the St Charles Hotel to discuss a joint assault. The General knew that his troops were no match for a seasoned Confederate army, but they could provide cover for Farragut's warships. Banks would attack Port Hudson from the land, hopefully causing enough confusion to allow the navy to steam up the river. The great question hung on Banks's ability to deliver a solid enough diversion.[26]

Just how green some of his troops were had been demonstrated on 20 February when a small detachment sent to the levee to oversee the departure of Confederate prisoners bound for Baton Rouge was responsible for a disgraceful incident. As word spread through the city that Rebel officers were being escorted onto steamboats, thousands of well-wishers, most of them women and children, ran down to see them off. Mary Sophia Hill was among them. Weeping and cheering, they waved red handkerchiefs in mass defiance against displays of Confederate sympathy. The Union troops soon lost control of the crowd, which heaved and swayed with emotion. Panicking, the Federal officer in charge sent an urgent request for more troops, who arrived with bayonets fixed. They came 'at a canter', recalled Mary. 'The guns were rammed and pointed at this helpless mass of weakness.' The women were literally beaten back from the levee. 'As I never yet ran from an enemy,' she continued, 'but always faced them, I walked backwards, with others, to some warehouses, where we were again chased by Federal officials in uniform.'[27]

No one was killed but there were cuts and broken bones; and with every retelling the officers became more brutal and the danger more desperate. Once again the Northern occupiers had succeeded in presenting

'Scene on the Levee at New Orleans on the Departure of
the Paroled Rebel Prisoners', February 1863

themselves in the worst light. Southern newspapers sarcastically labelled the affair 'La Bataille des mouchoirs'. Banks's reputation plunged: 'Some say Banks never saw a battle, as he was always running; but he did, he won this, which is well remembered,' wrote Mary scornfully.[28]

The navy was also contributing its share of frustration and disappointment to Lincoln. On 11 January 1863 the CSS *Alabama* attacked the US blockade at Galveston, Texas. Once a forsaken collection of wooden buildings along a dreary sandbar that stretched for 27 miles, Galveston had become a boomtown in recent years, sporting large modern warehouses and New Orleans-style mansions. Profits from shipping cotton – three-quarters of Texas's produce passed through the seaport – had paid for colonnades of palm trees and lush oleanders to line streets that had formerly been tracks in the grass. The US navy had begun blockading Galveston in July 1861, and a Federal force had briefly held the port until CS General John Magruder (nicknamed Prince John by his enemies on account of his flashy behaviour in front of ladies) recaptured the town on New Year's Day in 1863. Reinforcements to the naval blockade had just arrived when Captain Raphael Semmes and the *Alabama* cautiously approached the Union fleet.

In only six months the *Alabama* had become the most famous ship afloat. The entire English-speaking world knew her history, beginning with her audacious escape from under the noses of the British authorities. In addition to her aura of daring she was beautiful to behold. The 54-year-old Semmes loved the *Alabama* from the moment he first saw her. During his thirty-seven years in the navy, he had never sailed on such a well-crafted vessel. 'Her model was of the most perfect symmetry,' he wrote, 'and she sat upon the water with the lightness and grace of a swan.'[29] The Confederate navy agent, James Bulloch, had asked Lairds to build him a ship that could survive the harshest of conditions for months on end. He knew that the *Alabama* would never have a homeport or a regular source of supplies.[30] The result was a 230-foot vessel with three masts, built for roving and raiding, capable of sail and steam power, equipped with two engines, a liftable screw propeller and eight powerful guns. Her cabins could comfortably accommodate twenty-four officers and a crew of 120.

Semmes had been in command of the CSS *Sumter* until the vessel required such extensive repairs that in the summer of 1862 he was forced to sell her in Gibraltar. When he and his second-in-command,

1st Lieutenant John Kell, arrived in England, Bulloch realized that they were the obvious choice to take command of the *Alabama*. The new crew soon nicknamed their captain 'Old Beeswax' on account of his highly waxed moustache. The sharpened tips – which looked both debonair and frighteningly precise – were symbolic of the divergent nature of his character: Semmes was always perfectly correct and mild-mannered in his demeanour but behind the mask was a stern and relentless fighter. He had strong literary and intellectual tastes and, in contrast to many of his peers in the navy, had no trouble adapting to home life when on furlough. During the long gaps between his deployments at sea, Semmes had established his own law practice. He was also a successful writer, having published two well-received memoirs of his experiences during the Mexican–American War.

Despite frequent buffetings from rough weather and unruly sailors, Semmes soon imposed his will on the ship. The seamen were almost all British, 'picked up, promiscuously,' wrote Semmes, 'about the streets of Liverpool . . . they looked as little like the crew of a man-of-war, as one can well conceive. Still, there was some *physique* among these fellows, and soap, and water, and clean shirts would make a wonderful difference in appearance.'[31] The officers, on the other hand, were mostly Southerners, the notable exceptions being the master's mate, 21-year-old George Townley Fullam from Hull, and the assistant surgeon, David Herbert Llewelyn, a vicar's son who had recently completed his residency at Charing Cross hospital.[32] Semmes considered the *Alabama* to be a ship of war rather than a privateer, and demanded navy-style obedience from the men. 'My code was like that of the Medes and Persians – it was never relaxed,' he wrote. 'I had around me a staff of excellent officers, who always wore their side arms, and pistols, when on duty, and from this time onward we never had any trouble about keeping the most desperate and turbulent characters in subjection.'[33] The highest wages of any fleet and the promise of fantastic amounts of prize money also helped to maintain discipline.

On 5 September the *Alabama* scored its first capture, an unarmed whaler, which was raided for supplies and then set alight. The merchant crew was allowed to go ashore in its whaleboats. Those men were lucky; other crews were held prisoner below deck until Semmes could unload them at a neutral port. By Christmas the *Alabama* had successfully pounced on ten US ships.[34] One capture often led to another since

Semmes would use the information gleaned from logbooks and time tables to chase after sister ships. But at Galveston Semmes was offered a different opportunity: to prove to the world that the *Alabama* was capable of much more than merely preying on civilian ships. For the first time, she was meeting adversaries of her own class.[35]

As soon as Semmes caught sight of the five blockading ships in front of Galveston, he ordered the *Alabama* to retreat slowly, hoping to entice one of the vessels into a chase. The Federal captain of the *Hatteras* took the bait, believing that he had caught a blockade-runner in the act, and hardly noticed that Galveston was becoming smaller and smaller in the distance. 'At length,' described Semmes, 'when I judged that I had drawn the stranger out about 20 miles from his fleet, I furled my sails, beat to quarters, prepared my ship for action, and wheeled to meet him.'[36] The ships faced each other nose to nose, a mere hundred yards apart and yet only partially visible in the clear, moonless night. Using a bullhorn, the warship challenged first, ordering the unknown vessel to identify herself. Semmes cheekily shouted back, 'This is her Britannic Majesty's steamer *Petrel*.' There followed an awkward pause while the captain of the *Hatteras* pondered his next move. He had no wish to provoke the Royal Navy but there was something suspicious about the ship floating before him. After some rapid calculation of consequences, he announced he was sending over a boarding party. Semmes called back that he was delighted, thus buying the *Alabama* a few precious minutes to load her guns. They heard orders being shouted and the creaking sound of a boat being lowered into the water. This was the signal for 1st Lieutenant Kell to cry out, 'This is the Confederate States Steamer *Alabama*!' followed by a broadside from the cannon. The captain of the *Hatteras* quickly returned fire. Each time the *Alabama* landed a shell on her adversary, one of the sailors was heard to shout, 'That's from the "scum of England".'[37] In less than fifteen minutes the *Hatteras* was completely disabled and started to sink. The survivors from the ship were picked up and held in the brig until the *Alabama* docked at Port Royal in Jamaica on 20 January.

If that not were not enough to shake the US navy's morale, a week later the blockading fleet at Mobile Bay in Alabama failed to stop the midnight escape of the infamous CSS *Florida*, the ship originally known as the *Oreto*. After her hurried exit from Liverpool in March 1862, the vessel had suffered one setback after another. The British authorities in

Nassau detained her for nearly four months, although the courts there finally determined that she was not in defiance of the Foreign Enlistment Act. But once free, Captain Maffitt lost half his crew to yellow fever, including his own stepson. Even when the *Florida* eventually sailed into Mobile in September, she continued to be dogged by misfortune. It took three months before the repairs to her damaged hull were completed. Finally, on 17 January 1863, nine months after leaving Liverpool, the *Florida* began its long-delayed career as a Confederate commerce raider. Two days later, Captain Maffitt captured his first prize, a cargo ship bound for New York.

The Confederate gains at sea were taking place at a sensitive time for Anglo-US relations. For the past two months a group of twelve New York businessmen, calling themselves the New York International Relief Committee, had been soliciting donations for Lancashire's suffering cotton workers.[38] On 9 January the *George Griswold* set sail carrying a large cargo of provisions which included 13,000 barrels of flour and 500 bushels of corn, all paid for by the Committee. The ship was bedecked with symbols of Anglo-American friendship, including the flags and pennants of the two nations. As the *Griswold* was towed out of New York harbour she received salutes from the British vessels that had gathered to see her off. Four more ships soon followed the *Griswold*; the irony that they could be captured and destroyed by the *Alabama* was not lost on the Northern press, nor on Seward.*[39]

The Secretary of State used the public's resentment regarding the *Alabama* and the *Florida* to his advantage. Over the New Year, he had met with Senator James Grimes, chairman of the Naval Affairs Committee, and persuaded him to propose an armed response against Britain. There was nothing anti-British in Seward's motives. His only concern was how to shore up his weak position among Republicans; with any luck, Sumner would oppose Grimes's measures and look like an apologist for England, costing him popularity in the press. After the Galveston attack by the CSS *Alabama*, Grimes announced that he was reviving the bill to allow President Lincoln to issue letters of marque. It was necessary to arm civilian privateers, he argued, because the Confederates were

---

* Lord Lyons naturally took heart from the *Griswold*, perhaps far too much. The ship was proof, he told Russell, that Americans liked to complain about Britain, but behind the posturing 'there lies a deeper and more enduring feeling of good will and kindly affection, which will be a lasting bond of feeling between the two kindred nations.'

building their own fleet in England. Lincoln should have the power 'to let slip the dogs of war' against them.[40]

As Seward had hoped, Charles Sumner could not resist attacking such a poorly conceived idea. 'This revival of Letters of Marque is [Seward's] work. I have protested to the President against their issue, but I fear that I shall not entirely succeed,' he complained to John Bright. 'There is not a Senator – not one – who is [Seward's] friend politically, the larger part are positively, and some even bitterly against him ... In the House of Reps., he has no friends; nor among his colleagues of the cabinet.' Lord Lyons was crestfallen once he realized that Seward had resorted to the same anti-British line that had made the first year of the war so acrimonious and difficult. 'It looks like a return to the old bluster,' he wrote sadly. 'Whether he does it to recover his position with the Radical party and with the people at large ... or ... he really thinks he can frighten England and France with his privateers, I can not say. He is more cordial than ever with me personally, and I do my best to prevent his getting into hot water either with France or with me.'[41]

Sumner was speaking the truth, however, when he warned Bright that the Confederate navy programme had to be stopped: 'The feeling towards England runs high and I hear it constantly said that war is inevitable unless those ships now building are kept from preying on our commerce.'[42] Northern newspapers were blaming the *Alabama* and the *Florida* for the precipitous decline of US shipping (rather than the lack of Northern investment in the merchant marine).[43] 'England will be hated for it, till the last American now on the stage goes to his grave,' threatened the *New York Times*.[44]

17

'The Tinsel has Worn Off'

Democrats versus Republicans – Burnside in the Virginian mud –
Arrival of General Hooker – Mosby's raid – A crisis of conscience –
Volunteering for the South – An encounter with Stonewall Jackson

Lincoln's troubles made the Democrats bolder in their denunciation of Republican 'fanaticism' for persisting with the war. 'You have not conquered the South,' thundered Clement Vallandigham in the House on 14 January 1863. 'You never will.'[1] The Ohio Congressman and leader of the Peace Democrats had been unseated by the Republicans in the Congressional elections, and this was his farewell speech. Though far from being an Anglophile, Vallandigham was deliberately echoing the Earl of Chatham's warning to the House of Lords during the American War of Independence: 'My Lords, you cannot conquer America!' Although Vallandigham had been defeated in the violent and expensive contest, he was confident that his opposition to the war – and Lincoln's Emancipation Proclamation – would win him the governorship of Ohio in ten months' time. 'Sir,' he concluded, 'there is fifty-fold less of anti-slavery sentiment to-day in the West than there was two years ago; and if this war be continued, there will be still less a year hence.'*

Vallandigham's 'make peace now' speech was received by a public still trying to comprehend the staggering death toll from Fredericksburg, Chickasaw Bluffs and Murfreesboro. Discontent with the war, wrote Lyons on 10 February, 'is undoubtedly increasing, and if we have

---

* Vallandigham revelled in being called a 'Copperhead', a term used by the Republicans to imply that the Peace Democrats were like copperhead snakes, ready to strike on behalf of the South without warning – and by the Democrats themselves to symbolize their commitment to freedom and State rights, since copper pennies bore the word 'liberty' on them.

no success before the Spring ... it will be impossible to keep up the numbers of the Army.'* One hundred and thirty regiments were about to reach the end of their term of enlistment, George Herbert's among them. 'I am waiting as impatiently as you can for 4th of May,' the Englishman wrote to his mother. Like most of his comrades, he had no intention of re-enlisting: 'The tinsel has worn off the thing,' he admitted.[2] Congress was aware that it had a potentially crippling manpower shortage and was preparing a bill for a national draft.

The recent spate of defeats was not the only reason for the lack of enthusiasm for volunteering. The War Department's mishandling of wounded soldiers had become a national scandal. Dr Mayo never saw the gross abuses of the system, since he was caring for officers well enough to recuperate in private establishments, but another English doctor, 25-year-old Charles Culverwell, was a reluctant witness to the neglect suffered by soldiers who were sent to the convalescent hospitals.[3] Ironically, Culverwell had never wanted to be a doctor. He was addicted to the theatre, but his father had pleaded and 'reasoned with me, until at last he suggested a compromise. "Get your diplomas; get a means of livelihood at your fingers' ends, and then you may do whatever you like."'[4] Culverwell dutifully qualified, married in 1860, became a father himself and supported his family as a doctor by day, while acting at night under the stage name 'Charles Wyndham'. The public was unconvinced by either role. 'No patient darkened my door,' he wrote, and the theatre company went bankrupt in August 1862. There are conflicting accounts as to why he enlisted as a surgeon in the Federal army.[5] But regardless of whether he went freely or was pushed by his family, Culverwell later claimed that he relished the prospect of adventure: 'I was bound for America, the land of freedom where equality was adored, favouritism abhorred ... I was convinced that on my arrival there I had only to hold up my little finger and every State in the Union would rush at me with a commission.' He arrived in America in October 1862 with

---

* Dr Mayo was shocked when he visited Congress. 'In both houses,' he wrote, 'the occupation of members seemed to consist of calling each other traitors.' He was a witness to some of the least edifying scenes in Senate history. On 27 January 1863 Senator Willard Saulsbury made his infamous harangue from the Senate floor. He was, recorded the doctor, 'in a state of hopeless drunkenness, and insisted on making a speech, and when rebuked by the chairman and threatened with removal by the sergeant-at-arms, drew and cocked his revolver, and threatened to shoot any body who interfered with him'. The stand-off continued for some time until Saulsbury was persuaded to leave.

just $45. The rest of the family's savings was left with his wife Emma, who remained in London, pregnant with their second child. They had agreed she would come out as soon as he was financially secure.

The plan went awry from the beginning. Culverwell had come without letters of introduction: they were offered to him, including one to General Nathaniel Banks, but he had turned them down. Not knowing what else to do, Culverwell parked himself in the public sitting room at Willard's hotel and placed his illustrated book on surgery on his knees. He sat there reading for two days, hoping that someone would ask him if he was a doctor. At the end of the second day he noticed an elderly gentleman being approached by autograph seekers. He recognized the face but could not recall the name; this was enough to give him courage. His heart beating with excitement, Culverwell went up to him and asked for help. The stranger politely declined. Not knowing what else to do, Culverwell returned to the public room the following day. This time, the elderly gentleman sought his eye and asked him:

> 'How was it you were so foolish to come to America without letters? They are absolutely indispensable here.' I explained to him that I was stupid enough to believe America different from other countries, and the mere fact of introductions being used in Europe stamped them as superfluous here. I told him that a letter to General Banks which had been offered to me, I had even refused to wait for, as it had come from Paris. 'I know General Banks,' he replied; 'I'll give you a letter to him if you like, but I shall be bound to say I know nothing about you.' 'So long as I am able to get to him,' I said, 'I should ask for nothing more.'[6]

Culverwell discovered that the kind stranger was none other than the impresario P. T. Barnum. His letter opened the way to an appointment as acting assistant surgeon, a position that allowed the holder to resign and rejoin at will. But Barnum's influence evidently had its limits: Dr Culverwell was sent to one of the contraband camps near Alexandria, the most unpopular posting in the medical corps. He lasted two weeks in the pestilential and stinking shanty town that contained the South's runaway slaves.* His

---

* It was General Butler who allegedly invented the term 'contraband'. He was the commandant of Fortress Monroe in 1861 when three runaway slaves arrived asking for sanctuary. When their former Southern masters requested their return, Butler refused, arguing that slaves were 'contraband of war', since the South was using them as 'tools' to sustain the war effort. The term stuck.

request for a transfer resulted in the army's second most unpopular assignment: duty at Camp Convalescent, Fort Ellsworth, known locally as 'Camp
Misery', where wounded soldiers too sick to be discharged instead died of
neglect. 'We don't get any vegetables at all,' wrote an inmate of Camp Convalescent. 'We are in tents, five in each tent, no beds ... we don't get our
cooking done ... it is one of the meanest places I have come across ...
They need not talk of the misery of the rebels, let them come down here
and it will open their eyes.'[7] Culverwell lasted for two months before he
could stand it no longer and asked to be transferred. This time the authorities were merciful and on 20 January 1863 he was sent to Jefferson
Barracks in St Louis, Missouri, one of the largest military hospitals outside
Washington.

It was not only the sick who suffered deprivations. Theft and bureaucratic incompetence were so widespread throughout the army that the
soldiers were often short of basic supplies such as fuel, blankets and fresh
food. Lorenzo D. Sargent, the new colonel of Charles Francis Adams Jr.'s
regiment, the 1st Massachusetts Cavalry, exemplified one of the criticisms made by British military observers of the Northern system of
command: he fraternized with the lower ranks as a way of showing solidarity with the men, but failed to concern himself with their physical or
moral welfare. 'He considers himself a tactician and yet he could not drill
a corporal's guard without making ludicrous blunders,' Charles Francis
Jr. wrote to his family. 'His mistakes on the drill ground, his theories of
war and his absurdities in camp are ... the laughing stock of the regiment ... He has already cost us the best officers in our regiment, and we
all fear that he will ultimately ruin it.'[8]

Charles Francis Jr.'s frustration with the lack of accountability in the
army was a common complaint among the soldiers; recruits were deserting in Virginia at the rate of a hundred a day. There were frequent fights
and disturbances in the camps. Percy Wyndham's cavalry brigade was in
a state of uproar after he gave the colonel of one of his regiments a ferocious beating and threatened to shoot him if he continued to disobey
orders. The officers in the brigade retaliated by petitioning the War
Department for the right to wear side arms in his presence. Disgusted
with his men and with the failure of leadership from above, Sir Percy
resigned his command on 18 January 1863.[9] But General Heintzelman
considered his skills and experience too precious to lose. 'Colonel

Wyndham is such an excellent Cavalry officer when under the orders of a suitable commander and has behaved so gallantly on frequent occasions,' he wrote, 'that I would most reluctantly see his resignation accepted. His service with the main army in the front would I am satisfied be eminently valuable.'[10] The army accepted his suggestion of returning Wyndham to the 1st New Jersey Cavalry, where he was still liked and admired.

General Burnside knew that his generals were conspiring against him and that he had to act swiftly before his army disintegrated. To save his command and the army's morale, he decided to challenge the Confederates again but from a different vantage point several miles north of Fredericksburg. George Herbert predicted disaster, yet the weather seemed to favour the General, remaining cold and dry while the troops packed their belongings and tore down the camps. In the pre-dawn hours of 20 January, the men stood in smart rows with three days' rations in their packs, ready to march across the Rappahannock. However, by mid-afternoon they felt the first spots of rain on their heads; by late evening they were struggling against a steady downpour. 'In two hours the roads were impassable,' wrote Herbert.[11]

George Herbert watched as mules sank up to their necks in mud. Every few yards, the New York Zouaves had to dig themselves out and then attempt to free the artillery, which was mired in three or more feet of icy sludge. Ebenezer Wells of the 79th Highlanders watched helplessly as a loaded wagon slid off the side of a cliff, pulling six horses to their death. 'We let it go for it was bitter cold,' he recalled. The men concentrated on survival. 'I was nearly frozen to death, if I had have given way to sleep which seemed to almost overpower me I never should have felt any more pain. I cut my thumb thinking it would cause circulation,' he wrote. 'I felt as though I could cry aloud in despair.' To survive, Wells lay down next to his horse, Bill, who had been trained to perform circus tricks, 'putting my feet between his hind legs, my body against his and my face in his breast.'[12]

Burnside admitted defeat after forty-eight hours and ordered his men to return to their original campsites. Dubbed the 'Mud March' by the army and the press, this was his final debacle as commander of the Army of the Potomac. By 27 January the General and a few loyal staff members were on a train bound for New York. General 'Fighting Joe' Hooker (a nickname that would return to haunt him) took Burnside's

place. Hooker's intrigues against Burnside had been notorious throughout the army. When George Herbert learned the news, he put the
promotion down to 'right smart bobbery' and thought his 'appointment
will create a great disturbance'.[13] Charles Francis Adams Jr. told his
brother Henry that Lincoln had created more problems for himself by
selecting a man 'who has not the confidence of the army'.[14]

Hooker was a heavy drinker, and although his name did not inspire
the slang term for prostitute, as is popularly believed, his headquarters
often resembled a saloon bar in the worst part of town. The qualities
that had caught Lincoln's attention were his energy and ambition, which
were on display as soon as he took control of the Army of the Potomac.
On 5 February the soldiers learned that they were being divided into
eight numbered corps, with their own badges and insignia. Hooker also
created a separate cavalry corps under General George Stoneman, just
as Lee had done with Jeb Stuart. In one stroke Hooker eliminated the
muddles and regimental rivalries that had driven Percy Wyndham into
an armed stand-off against his fellow officers. Charles Francis Adams Jr.
revised his earlier opinion, writing happily, 'At last we are coming up
and winning that place in public estimation which we have always felt
belonged to us of right.'[15]

Dr Mayo visited the Army of the Potomac during Hooker's reorganization. He had been promoted from assistant to staff surgeon and now
served on the three-member board that certified volunteer surgeons.
Mayo was interested to see how Hooker was managing the health of the
soldiers. 'I was here able to see how the wheels of the medical department of an army of more than a hundred thousand men are kept in
motion by their chief director, Dr Letterman – an able manager, if ever
an army had one.' With Hooker's support, Dr Jonathan Letterman insti-
gated a new, healthier regime. The railway line was repaired and supplies
were being brought quickly and efficiently to the front. 'The army was
now therefore pretty comfortable,' wrote Mayo.

> All had tents, or shelter of some kind, and plenty of rations ... Almost all
> had built themselves fireplaces and chimneys ... and had plenty of fuel to
> keep themselves warm. In fact, as camp life goes, there was little to complain
> of but the mud, which was certainly some of the dirtiest (always excepting
> that of Washington), brownest, deepest, stickiest, and most ubiquitous that
> can be conceived.[16]

He could not say the same for the inhabitants of Fredericksburg, who were surviving on twice-weekly handouts of food. Mayo watched as huddled figures, including children, sat for hours in the snow by the banks of the river, a fishing rod in one hand and a bucket in the other. Before Mayo returned to Washington he paid a visit to the Irish Brigade. So many of its officers had passed through his care after Fredericksburg that he felt a special affection for the men. It was melancholy for him to walk through the half-empty camp. Fewer than 600 of the 1,100 remained; yet they were, he wrote in astonishment, 'as jovial and hospitable as ever'. The marked lack of bitterness among the brigade even extended to its wounded.*

Aside from the downpours and sticky sludge, the chief impediments to Hooker's massive reorganization were the Confederate raids on outlying camps. They occurred without warning, and though little was taken except for a few wagons or an unlucky soldier on picket duty, the effect on Federal morale was severe. Hooker had been in command for less than a week when, on 29 January 1863, a small force led by one of the most effective Confederate outfits – John Singleton Mosby and his Partisan Rangers – pounced on the Federal pickets guarding Percy Wyndham's base around Fairfax Court House. Nine horses and their riders were captured. Wyndham ran to his horse and marshalled 200 cavalrymen to chase after Mosby, but the raiders had vanished into the darkness. The raids against the Federals had made Mosby a hero among Virginians, which surprised everyone who had known him before the war. A lawyer by profession, he was small and thin, slightly hunched, and very plain with straw-like hair and a narrow, hatchet face. He looked more like 19 than his real age of 30, but his unprepossessing exterior belied a superior ability to infiltrate enemy lines and cause mayhem. His surprise attacks were forcing Federal authorities to divert large numbers of troops into wasteful defensive operations.

On the evening of 8 March, Mosby and twenty-nine volunteers set

---

* These included former employees from the Irish estate of William Gregory, the leading Confederate sympathizer in Parliament. Gregory's gamekeeper, Michael Conolly, had followed his family to America and volunteered for the North. His action cost him his arm at Fredericksburg. Several of Conolly's cousins were also wounded, but his two brothers had come out of the battle unscathed. 'As for my part,' Conolly wrote to Gregory from his hospital bed, 'I will not be able to join the company again.'

off towards Fairfax Court House for a second time. He had devised a plan to sneak into Wyndham's headquarters and kidnap him from his bed. Mosby had not told the men what he aimed to do, since he reasoned that they would have undoubtedly refused so suicidal a mission. It was a frosty, pitch-black night, which helped the marauders slip past Federal pickets. Mosby knew exactly where to find the gaps in the line. 'We passed along close by the camp-fires, but the sentinels took us for a scouting party of their cavalry,' he wrote. 'I had felt very cold in the early part of the night, but my blood grew warmer as I got farther in the lines, and the chill passed away. I had no reputation to lose by failure but much to gain by success.' It was midnight when they reached the village of Fairfax. Mosby's men were shocked when they realized where they were, but not more so than the Federal guards, who at first refused to believe what was happening.[17]

Mosby quickly organized his men into raiding parties; one to gather the prisoners, the other to collect the horses. The telegraph lines were cut, and the operator subdued. The Confederates moved stealthily from house to house, rousing officers from their beds with the warning they would be shot if they made a noise. Mosby waited impatiently for Wyndham to appear. 'But for once fortune had been propitious to him,' recalled Mosby. Wyndham had taken the train for Washington that afternoon. The raid on his house only produced two sleepy staff officers and Wyndham's uniform, which Mosby decided to keep as a trophy. As he prepared to leave with his dumbfounded prisoners, who outnumbered the Confederates four to one, Mosby was told that Brigadier General Edwin Stoughton was billeted in the town.[18]

The 25-year-old Stoughton was as famous for his unlikely promotion as he was for his high living. He should not have been in Fairfax at all since his brigade was 5 miles away, but the General liked his independence. The two-storey brick house that served as his headquarters was never empty or silent. Unable to resist the challenge, Mosby tricked his way inside by claiming to have a dispatch from the 5th New York Cavalry. He then grabbed the surprised officer, 'whispered my name in his ear, and told him to take me to General Stoughton's room. Resistance was useless and he obeyed.' Stoughton was sleeping off a rowdy night. Mosby woke him by spanking his bottom. 'He asked in an indignant tone what all this meant. I told him that he was a prisoner, and that he must get up quickly and dress. I then asked him if he had ever heard of "Mosby", and he said he had. "I am Mosby," I said.' Stoughton intrigued his captor by taking such inordinate care in getting dressed that one of the Confederates standing guard politely handed him his watch after he left it on the bureau.[19]

Sir Percy Wyndham was humiliated. It hardly mattered that he was in Washington at the time. He felt unable to face his men again. For three weeks he hid himself away, ignoring orders to return to his regiment, the 1st New Jersey Cavalry. A final order, underlined 'commandatory', roused him from his funk. Still preoccupied with thoughts of revenge, Wyndham sought permission to form his own regiment of ranger scouts. When his request was denied he asked for and obtained a leave of absence.

Abraham Lincoln apparently laughed when he heard about Stoughton's capture, joking, 'I can make a better general in five minutes, but the horses cost one hundred and twenty-five dollars apiece.'[20] Yet behind the ludicrous picture of a general being taken from his own bed was the worrying possibility that anyone could be Mosby's next victim. The military authorities ordered a thorough review of Washington's defences. New men were put in command; the outposts were strengthened and pulled closer together; a new system of passwords was introduced. Just in case Mosby had designs on the capital, troops guarding the chain bridge, one of the chief bridges linking Washington with Virginia, were ordered to remove the planks every night.

The authorities suspected that Mosby was receiving local assistance. Fearing it could be anyone and everyone in Virginia, they issued a blanket warning to commanders to have their men on high alert at all times. Sentries had strict injunctions to reject 'it's me' or 'we're with the 4th' and other such casual identifications. Any information that might be helpful to the enemy, such as duration of stays and destinations, was deliberately withheld from the troops. The tightening net closed on the two British captains, Lewis Phillips and Edward Wynne, during their return journey to the North. Phillips's luck had always been better than his companion's and he made it through to Maryland; but Wynne was caught while crossing the Potomac river. The legation learned of his arrest a few days later. 'He seems to have behaved very foolishly,' wrote the new attaché Edward Malet. 'He gave himself up to the federal

The chain bridge across the Potomac above Georgetown,
looking towards Virginia, by Frank Vizetelly

pickets . . . [and] being brought before the commanding officer seems to
have chaffed him and tried to carry matters with a high hand.'[21] Wynne
maintained that he had said nothing objectionable beyond admitting he
had been 'very well treated whilst in the South' and was therefore grateful to its people. It is unlikely he stopped there, however, since he was
soon brought under guard to Old Capitol prison in Washington.

Lord Lyons forbade the attachés from writing to Wynne or making it
seem as though the legation had any interest in his release. He had 'had
some trouble', explained Malet to his family, 'as the government are
very much put out at our soldiers going South and then returning rampant secessionists and now that they have caught one they wish to make
an example of him'. The Old Capitol prison was a decaying, makeshift
jail in the middle of Washington. Once a school, it had become an
unsavoury haven for snakes and vermin when the authorities began
using it to house political prisoners. Nothing was done to delouse or
repair the inside; the windows were simply boarded up and a fence

erected at the back. Smugglers, blockade-runners, suspected Rebel sympathizers, spies and the odd Federal military offender soon joined the political prisoners. They smoked and played cards all day long, waiting to be charged, or released, or sometimes executed. Captain Wynne was 'prisoner no. 6'. Malet visited him several times, bringing him cigars and newspapers. He tried to cheer him up, pointing out that the officials had allocated Wynne a private room. His efforts had little effect; Wynne shunned the other prisoners, preferring to sit in his cell, plotting his escape.

The Marquis of Hartington and his friend Colonel Leslie were exploring Charleston when they learned about Wynne's imprisonment. The Charlestonians 'are much better off here than at Richmond for most things', Hartington observed to his father. 'Though most people have removed their property and slaves . . . in case of an attack by the enemy.' But being 'better off' was not the same as being comfortable. Hartington was more candid about the situation to his mistress, Skittles: 'I have lost all my luggage, & I can't get any things here; at least very few things; & I have had to get along on one suit of clothes for a fortnight & shall for some time longer . . . We have had some hunting as they call it, but it is not much like Leicestershire.'[22] Apart from the ruined areas from the fire in 1861, the city was clean and orderly. The hotels were not crammed with shabby refugees like those in Richmond. But there was no escaping the fact that Charleston was under siege. The cost of living had risen eightfold since April 1861. Consul Bunch had reported to the Foreign Office that salt was seventy times more expensive, there was no coal at any price and the only cloth available for purchase was sailors' blue serge.

Hartington had been inclined to sail out of Charleston in a blockade-runner, since 'there is scarcely any risk at all of being taken in one of them, especially in running out, and it would not do us much harm if we should be caught as they could only take us to some other port and then let us go'.[23] Now he feared the ignominy of his position if he were to be thrown into the Old Capitol like Wynne. With the help of their new friends, Hartington and Leslie devised an overland route that relied on safe houses all the way to Washington. On 9 February Edward Malet was woken by sinister noises coming from his garden. He went outside to investigate and found Hartington and Leslie prowling in the back.

They were terrified of being caught by the police; Captain Wynne had escaped from the Old Capitol prison earlier that day, causing a hue and cry in the capital.*

Malet took Hartington and Leslie in for the night. 'The best advice we could give them', he wrote, 'was to be off as fast as possible and stop nowhere till they were in New York.' The travellers regaled Malet with stories of their adventures, prompting him to comment: 'They are enthusiastically secesh† and describe as magnificent the behaviour of everyone in the south.' Malet joked with them, but his laughter was not as whole-hearted as it would have been a few months before. Many years later he could still recall the moment he switched his sympathies from the South to the North. 'I, together with one or two other Secretaries, received an invitation to go to a ball at the front,' he wrote. First they saw a review of the army, then,

> at about nine o'clock we sallied forth to the ball, which took place in a huge tent. All the belles of Washington were present, and on entering we found ourselves in the presence of a brilliant throng. A quadrille was going on, couples were advancing and receding in the graceful maze of the dance, when, to our great surprise, the music suddenly stopped, the dancers drew back to either side, making a way down the centre, and the strains of our beloved, 'God Save the Queen', struck up as, escorted by our hosts, we walked down the avenue formed by the dancers.

Malet was almost moved to tears. 'Think of the stupendous struggle in which the North was engaged, the high tide of national feeling, the distrust with which Great Britain was regarded at the time, – yet here, in the centre of the vast host which represented the fighting power of the North, a small knot of Englishmen, whose only title to regard was that they belonged to the legation.'[24]

Hartington and Leslie arrived in New York a week after their rescue by Malet. They had traversed almost 300 miles without incident, but Hartington made up for it now by creating a supremely embarrassing one: he attended a ball given by the Rothschilds' banker August Belmont, and either accidentally or purposefully sported a Confederate badge on

---

* Wynne had escaped by 'breaking out a panel in his door'. He was one of only four escapees in the prison's history. Wynne always insisted that he acted on his own and the legation's records are silent on the matter.
† Slang for secessionist.

his lapel. However, when a Union lieutenant on sick leave angrily confronted him, Hartington apologized and removed it (not wishing to be thought of as anti-Northern, even though his sympathies now lay with the South).* Just before he set sail from New York on 25 February, Hartington described his feelings in a letter to his father:

> I suppose there will be an early debate on America, but perhaps it is just as well for me not to be there as I might be tempted to speak, and my opinions are all so mixed up and confused that I should probably make a mess. Besides, notwithstanding my confusion I am very decidedly Southern in the main, & from what I see that would not at all suit my constituents. How they can be so idiotic as to admire Lincoln and his emancipation proclamation, & how they can talk such nonsense as they do about emancipation I cannot understand, & I shall have to tell them so.[25]

The more the blockading squadron tried to tighten its grip, the more Charlestonians enjoyed watching the blockade-runners evade them and triumphantly steam into the harbour. The ships not only brought precious supplies but also news and, from time to time, British volunteers for the army. One of the first to arrive in January was Captain Stephen Winthrop, from Warwickshire and formerly of the 22nd Regiment of Foot, who braved the winter mud to seek out Robert E. Lee in Camp Fredericksburg. The General welcomed Winthrop with great courtesy, though he neither needed nor wanted another volunteer on his staff. After a short deliberation over what to do with the Englishman, Lee sent him to General Longstreet with his regards.

Winthrop was shortly followed by two more volunteers: Henry Wemyss Feilden of the Black Watch, and Bradford Smith Hoskins, formerly of the 44th Regiment of Foot and the Garibaldi Guard. The latter ended up with Jeb Stuart, who sent him to replenish John Mosby's staff; Feilden was assigned to the defence of Charleston. His background was similar to Colonel Currie's. Both men were public-school educated career officers with a strong sense of personal honour and public duty.

---

* Hartington's faux pas took on a life of its own. The lapel badge story was repeated ad nauseam as incontrovertible proof of the English aristocracy's hatred of the United States. The American poet and literary critic James Russell Lowell included the incident in his diatribe against European arrogance in his essay 'On a Certain Condescension in Foreigners' (1869), changing the story slightly in order to have Lincoln meet Hartington after the ball and deliberately insult him for having shown disrespect towards the North.

After leaving Cheltenham College in 1857, Feilden had joined the Black Watch, properly known as the 42nd Royal Highlanders. He spent his nineteenth birthday in India, preparing to recapture Cawnpore, the scene of one of the worst massacres of British civilians. His twenty-first was celebrated in China, while floundering in the deep swamp that surrounded the Taku Forts – it was here that US Commodore Josiah Tatnall disobeyed the order to be a mere observer and sent aid to the British forces.

Feilden's grandfather, Sir William, was a mill owner from Blackburn, Lancashire, who had made a fortune in the cotton business. But as Henry was the second of seven children and one of four sons, there was never any doubt he would have to earn his living. He sold his commission in 1860 and returned to England in the hope of going into business. Four years of hard fighting had matured Feilden in unexpected ways; in addition to possessing considerable courage and self-confidence, he felt a strong sense of compassion for the weak and vulnerable. Many years later, Rudyard Kipling, one of Feilden's closest friends, said of him, 'I don't believe the Colonel ever gave a man a shove downwards in all his life.'[26]

The family connection with Southern cotton made Feilden all the more susceptible to Confederate propaganda. He believed the canard that the South would abolish slavery once independence had been achieved. Shorn of its moral perils, the South looked immensely attractive, especially through the sympathetic reports of Vizetelly and Lawley.[27] Feilden resolved to run the blockade with a cargo of supplies, sell them at a profit and then join the Confederate army. But once he arrived at Bermuda, Feilden discovered that Francis Lawley's claims about Charleston being an open port were a gross exaggeration. It took three attempts and two different captains before he reached the Confederacy at the end of January.

Feilden eventually arrived at Richmond on 15 February 1863. 'The city is one great camp,' he wrote to his aunt:

> Indeed the whole country is, everyone is a soldier, and everyone is trying for military distinction. The demand for appointment as officers is enormous, so many thousand have extraordinary claims on the Executive that it is impossible to do one half of them justice. I saw at once that my chance of getting a military appointment was very small, and indeed I could not

24. Confederate President Jefferson Davis (1808–89). Davis seemed an ideal choice for the Confederate Presidency, having served as a Senator for Mississippi and as Secretary of War under President Franklin Pierce, but he was notoriously thin-skinned and incapable of delegating. Davis was shocked and disappointed when Britain failed to recognize Southern independence.

25. The inauguration of Confederate President Jefferson Davis in Montgomery, Alabama, on 18 February 1861. Davis used his speech to prepare Southerners for war: 'We have entered upon the career of independence, and it must be inflexibly pursued.'

26. The Confederate White House, Richmond, Virginia. The Davis family lived here from 1861 to 1865. Tragedy struck in 1864 when five-year-old Joe Davis was killed by a fall from the first-floor balcony.

27. Richmond, Virginia, during the war. Known as the 'City of Seven Hills', it was named after Richmond in London because the view of the James river from its highest hill reminded the city's founder, William Byrd, of the Thames from Richmond Hill.

28. General Robert E. Lee (1807–70), Confederate commander of the Army of Northern Virginia. The South's most famous general was admired by both sides during the war, and British travellers were invariably star-struck when introduced to him. Lieutenant-Colonel Garnet Wolseley of the British army wrote that Lee was 'a splendid specimen of an English gentleman, with one of the most rarely handsome faces I ever saw ... You only have to be in his society for a very brief period to be convinced that whatever he says may be implicitly relied upon.'

29. General Thomas J. 'Stonewall' Jackson (1824–63), Confederate commander of the famous Stonewall Brigade, Lee's cavalry corps, who earned his nickname during the First Battle of Bull Run. He went on to form a successful partnership with Lee until his death from friendly fire at Chancellorsville in 1863. On hearing that Jackson's arm had been amputated, Lee replied: 'He has lost his left arm; but I have lost my right arm.'

30. Arlington, Virginia, plantation home of General Robert E. Lee before the war, seized by the Union in 1861.

31. General Josiah Gorgas (1818–83), Confederate chief of ordnance. He kept the Southern armies supplied with arms throughout the war despite the blockade and an immense shortage of raw materials.

32. Judah P. Benjamin (1811–84), Confederate Secretary of State. Known as 'Jefferson's Pet Jew', Benjamin served Davis unquestioningly and even took the blame for mistakes which were not his own. The blockade prevented him from directing an effective or timely foreign policy.

33. Stephen Mallory (1817–73), Confederate Secretary of the Navy, one of the longest-serving members of President Davis's Cabinet. Mallory's strategy of building the Confederate navy in Great Britain almost brought the Northern and British governments to war.

34. James Dunwoody Bulloch (1823–1901), (*left*) with his half-brother Irvine. Bulloch was the Confederacy's chief secret agent in England and architect of the programme to build Confederate commerce raiders in Britain and France. 'He is the most dangerous man the South have here and fully up to his business,' claimed the head of the US secret service in Europe.

35. Henry Hotze (1833–97). Hotze was sent to England to be the chief Confederate propagandist in Europe and founded the pro-Southern journal *Index*. He was an expert at influencing public opinion: an editor 'should see with the eyes of the public, and hear with the ears of the public, and yet have eyes and ears of his own'.

36. James Murray Mason (1798–1871), Confederate Commissioner in England. Mason and his fellow commissioner John Slidell were sailing to Europe to take up their posts when their ship, the British mail packet *Trent*, was stopped by Captain Wilkes of the US navy. Britain demanded an apology for the 'attack' on her mail ship and the release of the two men. The *Trent* affair very nearly took the US and Britain to war.

37. John Slidell (1793–1871), Confederate Commissioner in France. 'He is an excellent judge of mankind, adroit, persevering, and subtle, full of device, and fond of intrigue,' wrote William Howard Russell. If Slidell were shut up in a dungeon he 'would conspire with the mice against the cat rather than not conspire at all'.

MR. LAIRD'S SHIP-BUILDING YARD, LIVERPOOL.—(SEE PRECEDING PAGE.)

38. The shipyard of the Laird Brothers, Liverpool, builders of the CSS *Alabama*. The cotton trade had helped to make Liverpool rich and given it deep ties with the South. The majority of blockade-runners sailed from Liverpool, and Fraser, Trenholm, the Confederacy's bankers, had their offices at 10 Rumford Place. Lord Russell complained that the city was 'addicted to Southern proclivities, foreign slave trade, and domestic bribery'.

39. Federal troops marching through New Orleans. Before the war New Orleans was the fourth largest city in the country and the South's premier port. It also had the largest immigrant population of the South.

40. Charles Francis Adams Jr. (1835–1915), (*second from right*) the only son of Charles Francis Adams to volunteer during the war, who rose from 1st Lieutenant of the 1st Massachusetts Cavalry in 1861 to Colonel of the 5th Massachusetts (Colored) Cavalry in 1865 and led one of the first coloured regiments through Richmond after its fall on 3 April 1865.

41. Henry Adams (1838–1918). Henry accompanied his father, Charles Francis Adams, to London as his private secretary and later recorded his isolation and loneliness in *The Education of Henry Adams*. 'Every young diplomat,' he wrote, 'and most of the old ones, felt awkward in an English house from a certainty that they were not precisely wanted there, and a possibility that they might be told so.'

42. Charles Francis Adams (1807–86), US Minister to Great Britain. Adams was the son and grandson of US ministers and presidents. Though he was dutiful, honest and hardworking, his family legacy cast a shadow over his entire life. 'Charles Francis Adams naturally looked on all British [statesmen] as enemies,' wrote Henry Adams.

43. Henry Feilden (1838–1921), British volunteer in the Confederate army. He was surprised to discover that he was not the only Englishman to offer his services to the South: 'A good number have, prior to this, come out to this country,' he wrote in 1863, 'and I believe have been obliged to serve as volunteers in the Army or on some General's staff until they have proved themselves fit for something.'

44. Francis Dawson (1840–89), British volunteer in the Confederate navy and subsequently the Confederate army. 'My idea simply was to go to the South, do my duty there as well as I might, and return home to England.' In fact, Dawson stayed in the South after the war and became editor of the Charleston *News and Courier*.

expect it otherwise. I paid a visit to the Secretary of War, presented my letter to him and other influential men, was told that if possible something would be given to me, and I received from all of them that kindness and courtesy so distinctive in the Southern gentlemen. A good number of Englishmen have, prior to this, come out to this country, and I believe with very rare exceptions they have been obliged to serve as volunteers in the Army or on some General's staff until they have proved themselves fit for something.

A Confederate sympathizer in Nassau had asked Feilden to deliver a box of goods to Stonewall Jackson in camp at Hamilton's Crossing near Fredericksburg. Eager to meet the General, Feilden set off on the 50-mile journey as soon as there was a lull from the rain and snow. But 'the day I went to camp the rain came down with redoubled fury, as if it was proud of showing the earth's dirty face, and dissipating the white mantle of snow', he wrote.

> I stumbled through mud, I waded through creeks, I passed through pine-woods. Wet through I got into camp about 2 o'clock and made my way to a small house – the General's Head Quarters. I wrote my name, gave it to an orderly and was immediately told to walk in. The General rose and greeted me warmly – he is so simple and unaffected in his ways and habits. I cannot illustrate this better than by telling exactly what he did – he took off my wet overcoat with his own hands, made up the fire, brought wood for me to put my feet on to keep them warm whilst my boots were drying, and then began asking me a great many questions on many subjects. We had a very pleasant conversation till dinnertime when we went out and joined the members of his staff. At dinner the General said Grace in a fervent, quiet manner that struck me much; there is a something about his face that you cannot help reveren-cing. He is a tall man, well and powerfully built but thin, with a brown beard and hair; his mouth is very determined-looking, the lips thin and compressed firmly together; his eyes are blue dark, with a keen and searching expression in them; his age is 38 and he looks about 40. I expected to see an old, untidy-looking man, and was surprised and pleased with his looks.

Henry returned to his room after dinner. The General sought him out again and offered his bed to share:

> I thanked him very much for the courtesy, but said goodnight, and slept in a tent, sharing the blankets of one of his aides-de-camp. In the morning at

breakfast I noticed the General said Grace before the meal with the same fervour as I had remarked before. An hour or two afterwards it was time for me to return to the Station. This time I had a horse, and I turned up the General's Head Quarters to bid adieu to him. His little room was vacant so I stepped in and stood before the fire: I noticed my great coat stretched before the fire on a chair. Shortly after the General entered the room. I was saying goodbye, and as I finished he said, 'Captain, I have been trying to dry your great coat, but am afraid I have not succeeded very well.' That little act shows the man, does it not! To think that in the midst of his duties, with the cares and responsibilities of a vast army on his shoulders, with the pickets of a hostile army almost within sight of his quarters, he found time to think of and to carry out these little acts of thoughtfulness!

Feilden had never encountered such personal courtesy from a British general. He returned to Richmond desperately hoping that the Confederate War Department had accepted his application. He would have accepted anything and was thrilled with the offer of a captaincy and the position of assistant adjutant general in Charleston. In only a few weeks he had become as ardent a Confederate as any native-born Southerner. For the first time in years Feilden felt at home: 'I am tired of going to sea myself, I am sick of seeing new places,' he wrote, 'never did I feel happier than at the present moment.' He was an efficient adjutant and quickly made friends among his fellow officers; General Beauregard pronounced himself satisfied with the latest addition to his staff.

Charleston society was delighted with the handsome and personable English captain. 'The people are the kindest I ever met,' Feilden wrote in wonder, unaware that he was making up for the loss of Consul Bunch, whose recent departure from the city had left a void that he filled perfectly. (Though the 'cotton is king' attitude of the South had never ceased to irritate the Consul, he was heartbroken to receive the Foreign Office's order to return to England.[28]) Feilden's lodgings were in one of the boarding houses used by English blockade-runners. This gave him unfettered access to breakfast, lunch and dinner. Until then, he told his aunt, he had been eating the diet of ordinary Southerners: 'coffee made out of rye, or else water, crackers and old bacon or tough meat. The people of the South are suffering very much for want of good food.'[29]

Neither the threat of attack nor the scarcity of luxuries had diminished Charleston's social calendar. Francis Lawley attended a ball, before setting off on his travels through the western part of the Confederacy, and was impressed by the Southerners' determination to keep up appearances; the shimmering silks and starched collars defied the truth of the two-year blockade. It was as though the closer the city came to danger, the more its inhabitants clung to their old habits. 'I am finishing off this scrawl as the gentleman who is taking this to England leaves tomorrow,' Feilden wrote on 4 March 1863. 'We are living here very comfortably and enjoying ourselves, although every day we expect to be attacked by the Yankee Armada.'[30]

18

Faltering Steps
of a Counter-Revolution

Attack on Charleston – British public opinion begins to change –
The illustrious Maury, Pathfinder of the Seas – Espionage – Lord
Russell is thwarted by John Bright – Wilkes again

The 'Yankee Armada' set sail for Charleston at the beginning of April 1863. Frank Vizetelly was still in the city and could hardly wait for the clash to take place. His reports for the *Illustrated London News* became increasingly one-sided as he watched the city prepare for the attack. 'I have every faith in the result of the coming encounter,' he wrote, 'for never at any time have the Confederates been more determined to do or die than they express themselves now.'[1] More important than the Confederates' determination, however, was the lack of preparedness of the US invasion force. Dr Mayo inspected the fleet of seven monitors* and two ironclads before it left the Washington Navy Yard 'and sincerely pitied those who had to go to sea in it'. The decks of the monitors were barely a foot above water. He thought the slightest turbulence would probably swamp the vessels and send them to the bottom of the sea.[2] Admiral Samuel F. Du Pont was similarly pessimistic about his fleet, but the public clamour to capture and punish Charleston for starting the war was gathering force. Lincoln interpreted Du Pont's reluctance as McClellan-like timidity. 'Doom hangs over wicked Charleston,' boomed the *New York Herald Tribune* on the eve of the fleet's departure. 'If there is any city deserving of holocaustic infamy, it is Charleston.'[3]

---

* Monitor ships were different from ordinary ironclads on account of their heavy guns, revolving turrets and flat bottoms, which enabled them to lie low in the water.

Confederates sinking torpedoes by moonlight in the harbour channel,
Charleston, May 1863, by Frank Vizetelly

Du Pont's fleet sailed into the harbour on 7 April. At 3 p.m. urgent
peels rang across the city, alerting the inhabitants to take cover. Confident in Beauregard's defences, many chose to watch from rooftops and
balconies rather than hide in their houses. Frank Vizetelly ran from the
Charles Hotel down to the Battery Promenade, where he jostled with
the spectators for an unobstructed view of Fort Sumter. 'I sketched
the scene,' he wrote for the *Illustrated London News*, 'and finished the
drawing in the evening, while the garrison of Fort Sumter were repairing the damages.' Admiral Du Pont's prediction that his fleet would be
overwhelmed was soon fulfilled. The fight lasted a mere two and a half
hours. But in that time his fleet was crippled and his best ironclad frigate, the *Keokuk*, was sunk.

'I don't think the Yankees can capture Charleston, do what they will,'
Henry Feilden wrote after the battle. 'In six weeks more the unhealthy
season will come on, and the scoundrels will die on this coast like rotten
sheep.' It was his firm belief that the South would win its independence
by Christmas. In the meantime, he planned to convert his entire savings
into Confederate currency while it was still cheap to buy. Vizetelly was
similarly ebullient about the South's prospects for victory. 'The fight
may be renewed at any moment if the Federals have the stomach for the

attempt,' he informed his readers back home, 'but I think they have suffered too much . . .'[4]

The US Secretary of the Navy, Gideon Welles, was furious with Du Pont for failing to put on a better show. Embarrassed by yet another naval defeat, he wondered whether it was even worth making a further attempt: 'Nothing has been done, and it is the recommendation of all, from the Admiral down, that no effort be made to do anything,' Welles wrote gloomily in his diary. 'I am by no means confident that we are acting wisely in expending so much strength and effort on Charleston, a place of no strategic importance. But it is lamentable to witness the . . . want of zeal among so many of the best officers of the service.'[5]

Vizetelly's triumphant reporting of the Union's repulse contributed to the sour mood in Washington. The Secretary of War, Edwin Stanton, was an avid reader of the English press, particularly those journals that were sympathetic to the South. Stanton would shut his office door, settle down on the sofa, and spend the afternoon discovering from Britain's finest journalists why the North deserved no pity, and why he, especially, was the worst sort of bungler. According to one of his clerks, it was almost a form of relaxation for him.[6]

Contrary to Stanton's belief that all England sympathized with the South, support for the North was growing. The London Consul Freeman H. Morse, whose duties had expanded to include propaganda and public agitation, told Seward that there had been a 'revolution' since Lincoln's Emancipation Proclamation.[7] Despite the initial scepticism towards the Proclamation, and the best efforts of *The Times* to portray it as a cynical ploy to encourage race riots, or at the very least force Southern soldiers to return to their homes to protect their families, the message that the war had a moral purpose seemed to be reaching the British public.

Among the initial signs was a rise in pamphlets and books putting forward the case for the North. James Spence's seemingly unassailable arguments in *The American Union* for recognition of the South were picked apart to devastating effect by the economist John Elliot Cairnes in his book *The Slave Power*, which appeared in the autumn of 1862 and went through several editions after the Emancipation Proclamation. Cairnes was followed by the actress Fanny Kemble, who published her diary, *Journal of a Residence on a Georgian Plantation in 1838–1839*, written during her exile on her former husband's slave plantation in Georgia; and William Howard Russell, whose account of his stay in America, entitled *My Diary North and South*, verified many of her observations.[8] The *Spectator* journalist Edward Dicey also wrote a travelogue – *Six Months in the Federal States* – which tried to correct many of the distortions and caricatures about Northern culture that pro-Southern journalists had propagated. An increase in the number of volunteers calling at the legation reflected the changing perception of the war. 'Applications for service in our army strangely fluctuate,' wrote Benjamin Moran in his diary on 14 January 1863. 'For some time past they have been but few. Since the announcement of the President's determination to adhere to his emancipation policy they have again become numerous and today we have had a French and British officer seeking employment.'[9] Moran was surprised by the wide range of motives and financial circumstances of these would-be volunteers; as far as he could tell, some were genuine idealists, but others were simply looking for an escape from their daily existence. Another surprise was waiting for him when he went to church. The vicar had never mentioned the war before, but on this Sunday he announced during prayers, 'our hearts in this great contest are with the North', which was answered with a deep 'Amen' from the congregation.[10]

'Emancipation Meetings continue to be held in London every week, sometimes four or five a week at some of which two and three thousand people have been present and in a majority of cases unanimously with the North. Other portions of the country are following the example of this city and holding meetings with about the same result,' Consul Morse reported to Seward.[11] James Spence spoke passionately at an anti-slavery meeting in Liverpool but to his surprise, he failed to convince a mixed audience of merchants and tradespeople that the South would also abolish slavery as soon as it won independence.[12] The public was far more interested in hearing from President Lincoln than from Spence. Encouraged by Charles Sumner, Lincoln had written an eloquent letter to the 'Workingmen of Manchester' thanking the cotton workers for their patience and sacrifice. 'Whatever misfortune may befall your country or my own,' declared the President, 'the peace and friendship which now exist between the two nations will be ... perpetual.'[13]

Morse was being helped by Peter Sinclair, a formidable and energetic Scotsman who had spent the past six years building a Canadian-American temperance organization called 'Bands of Hope'. Sinclair had lately returned to England with the specific intention of giving his aid to the North. 'Mr Sinclair has been laying facts, figures and arguments before a committee of the old Emancipation Society, one of the most influential organizations in England,' Morse informed Seward in January. Even though some veteran campaigners like Bishop Samuel Wilberforce and Lord Shaftesbury remained unconvinced (much to Henry Hotze's glee), Sinclair had been remarkably successful in convincing a wide range of individuals – including 'merchants, bankers, lawyers, literary men, etc.' – that abolition was only possible in a united America. The hitherto pacifist British and Foreign Anti-Slavery Society changed its stance and became actively involved in the counter-propaganda war, secretly supplying Moran with information about Confederate activities in the financial markets.[14] Sinclair was also the leading organizer of the Emancipation Society's massive demonstration at Exeter Hall on 29 January. Henry Adams managed to secure a seat at the meeting and was thoroughly uplifted by the experience. The politicians, Henry told his brother afterwards, were going to have to listen to their constituents or risk being 'thrown over'.*

Henry Adams had cheered up considerably since September, when the powerfully connected Lichard Monckton Milnes made the improvement of the 25-year-old's social life his pet project.[15] But his father continued to be tormented by doubts and anxieties; Charles Francis Adams felt especially angry towards Seward. It was not only the dispatches publication fiasco. On 28 January the legation received a telegram from the Secretary of the legation, Charles Wilson, announcing his imminent arrival in London. Benjamin Moran was in despair. Adams was horrified. Both had assumed that Wilson would never return from his government-funded vacation in Chicago. Neither could stand working with the uncouth and obnoxious Secretary, whose only reason for being at the legation originated from a serpentine bargain between Seward and Lincoln over patronage. Without consulting or explaining his thoughts to Moran, Adams decided that the best way to keep Wilson

---

* Henry Adams was like his father in his tendency to exaggerate the division of opinion between the social classes. Friends, neighbours and even families disagreed with one another, such as the Devonshires at the top of the scale – where Hartington leaned towards the South, and his brother Lord Frederick Cavendish towards the North – and the Collings family at the lower end, where Jesse Collings, a hardware merchant, assailed the local press with letters in support of the North, and his brother Henry, a commercial sailor, joined the Confederate navy and fought on board the CSS *Merrimac*.

at a distance – without its looking like a direct snub – was to exclude both legation Secretaries from all social functions. Moran was crushed when he discovered that the Adamses were entertaining behind his back. 'This is a deliberate slight,' he raged in his diary. 'All other Ministers invite their secretaries to their state dinners; but it seems to be a pleasure to ours to degrade his by acts of omission.'[16] Charles Francis Adams was far too preoccupied to notice Moran's wounded dignity. A thick, yellow fog had descended on London, quite different from the usual kind at this time of year. It made the day seem like endless night, and the world outside even more claustrophobic than the world within. The sense of being trapped exacerbated Adams's fears; he was dreading the opening of Parliament on 5 February and could think of little else.

As it happened, although several speakers referred at length to the American war, there were no clarion calls for immediate recognition of the South, or hints from the government about a change in policy. The issue was certainly alive: in the Lords, the Earl of Carnarvon asked Lord Russell to explain Britain's position on the fate of Her Majesty's subjects currently held without trial in Northern prisons.[17] But America did not seem to resonate in Parliament as it had done before Christmas. Adams mentally thanked the Poles for their revolution on 22 January 1863, which was keeping the House distracted.

Adams was also nervous about his meeting with Lord Russell on 7 February, the first since the publication of his uncomplimentary dispatches, and he expected some sort of rebuke or coldness. 'I was a little prepared to find him rather more reserved than heretofore,' Adams wrote in his diary. 'In his place I think I should have been so. But so far as I could see there was no difference.' (Adams might have felt differently towards Russell had he known of the Foreign Secretary's strenuous efforts to unite the Cabinet behind his mediation plan.) The fog dissipated, 'yet I felt rather sad', Adams confessed in his diary. 'The unsettled condition of our public affairs and the doubt that overhangs the future both financially and morally cast a shadow upon everything.'[18] When he did venture out, Adams was not particularly sociable. Even dinner at the Argylls' was a chore for him, though he liked them as a rule. 'The Duchess is an interesting woman, but she is not very easy in conversation. She labors at starting subjects without knowing how to keep them going. He is much in the same way,' he complained on 11 February, forgetting that a conversation requires two willing partners.[19]

Great emancipation meeting held at Exeter Hall, March 1863

Nearly three weeks later, Adams came face to face with Lord Palmerston at a royal levee. The two had not spoken to one another since the 'Butler letters' the previous June. 'Of course I was called to decide something, so I made a formal bow and put out my hand.' To Adams's relief, 'He bowed in return and took my hand so that no perceptible difficulty took place. Most of the other Cabinet members treated me with great cordiality.'[20] Adams was still trying to make sense of the encounter when he received an invitation from Lady Palmerston, the first in over a year. 'This was certainly a change,' he wrote in puzzlement, unaware that Benjamin Moran had left his card at Cambridge House. The dictates of diplomatic protocol obliged Lady Palmerston to respond to the gesture by inviting the Assistant Secretary to her next party, which she could not do without also including the senior members of the legation. But it cannot be said that Adams made the most of the opportunity. Afterwards he wrote, 'The same old crowd and the same people whom I did not know.'[21] Although Adams often spoke as though he cared nothing for social advancement, Benjamin Moran was not fooled: 'One of the leading characteristics, if not the leading one of English society,' he wrote in his diary, 'is its perfect exclusiveness. To get through this barrier is almost impossible. Americans who try it once and fail, generally stop; but not the Adamses. Their desire to get thro' the charmed wall and into the circle is a disease ... altho' they are constantly pretending they are indifferent to it.'[22]

The Confederate Commissioner James Mason had never seen the inside of Cambridge House, and was thus denied the luxury of being bored by the Palmerstons' parties. During the past twelve months Mason's most intimate encounter with the higher echelons of government had been the thirty minutes he had spent in Lord Russell's office shortly after his arrival. On the other hand, Mason could boast that he had seen the Egyptian Hall of the Mansion House in the City of London many more times than Adams, since the South enjoyed strong support from financial institutions with historic ties to the cotton industry.

The Lord Mayor's banquet on 11 February 1863 came just at the right time for Mason; Russell had become more elusive than ever. Mason did not know what to make of this 'strange contumacy from such a quarter'. To make sure his correspondence was not falling victim to Federal skulduggery, he had had his secretary personally deliver the last

Confederate letter to the Foreign Office. That had been more than a month earlier. The banquet at the Mansion House appeared to confirm Mason's belief that the Foreign Secretary was out of step with the rest of the country. 'When my name was announced by the Mayor, it was received with a storm of applause,' Mason wrote in his diary. He was invited to address the hall, and elicited loud cheers each time he referred to the commercial ties between the City and the South, confirming his belief that he had acquitted himself rather well. One of James Spence's friends had been among the guests and was convinced that he had witnessed a momentous event. 'My dear Spence,' he wrote the next day,

> I was at the Mansion House last night and heard the Lord Mayor virtually recognize the South in the quietest and most inoffensive way that could be imagined ... As I came out I rubbed shoulders with Captain Tinker, Grinnell's partner and I said, jocularly, 'Well, you see the Lord Mayor has been and gone and done it.' He laughingly replied, 'Oh yes, it's all over now.' Depend on it, this expression of opinion from the heart of England's middle classes must tell. It will reverberate thro' the land and find an echo.[23]

The only Southerner in England who did not rejoice after the Lord Mayor's banquet was Commodore Matthew Fontaine Maury, who thought that Mason was wasting his time. 'Many of our friends here have mistaken British admiration of Southern "pluck", and newspaper spite at Yankee insolence as Southern sympathy. No such thing,' Maury had written to a friend in late January. He was adamant: 'There is no love for the South here. In its American policy the British Government fairly represents the people ... there is no hope for recognition here, therefore I say withdraw Mason.' After the banquet Maury wrote: 'We are gaining ground here, it is true, but before we can expect any aid or comfort we must show our ability to get along without it – then it will be offered right and left.'[24]

Matthew Maury would have been a much better Southern Commissioner than William Yancey or James Mason. He was one of the Confederacy's few international heroes, having received six honorary knighthoods, a clutch of medals, seals and membership of several Royal Societies for his contribution to the study of oceanography. Maury's research of sea charts and weather patterns had enabled him to uncover the hidden pathways of the sea, taking the guesswork out of trade routes and opening the oceans to further exploration. It was Maury's discovery of the North Atlantic shelf that had emboldened Cyrus Field to lay his ill-fated telegraph cable in 1858.

But in America, Maury's blunt and often captious behaviour had made him as many enemies as admirers. The navy pushed him into retirement, although it relented and made him a commander after he fought to be readmitted. When the war began, Maury was 55 years old, happily married and the father of nine children, having run the Naval Observatory in Washington for nearly seventeen years. But on 20 April 1861, though he neither owned slaves nor approved of slavery, Maury chose his native State of Virginia over his loyalty to the Federal government. He walked out of the Observatory for the last time, with tears streaming down his face, leaving on the desk his sword, naval uniform and a letter of resignation to Abraham Lincoln.

Maury soon discovered that old quarrels had not died with the new Confederacy. It was unfortunate that his future had ended up in the hands of three of his greatest rivals: Jefferson Davis, Judah P. Benjamin and Stephen Mallory. Maury's pioneering work on torpedoes and mines received scant official support. When he received his orders in August 1862 to go on a purchasing mission to London, Maury had assumed it was an attempt to consign him to oblivion.[25] He knew there was already a crowd of agents in England competing with each other for scarce resources. After long, anguished discussions, Maury and his wife Ann agreed that their youngest child, 13-year-old Matthew junior, known as Brave, would accompany him to England. The rest of the family would try to live quietly in northern Virginia.

Maury and young Brave travelled to Charleston to wait for room to become available on a steamer running the blockade. As the weeks passed, Maury became a frequent guest at Ashley Hall, home of George A. Trenholm. Built in the Regency style according to Southern taste, the house was a skilful combination of intimidation and opulence. Few families could maintain such an establishment in the present times, but the blockade had transformed Trenholm from the chairman of a middle-sized shipping firm into the wealthiest man in the South. Life at Ashley Hall was not only untouched by the war, it was better than ever. Dinner guests were treated to delicacies that had not been seen in Charleston since 1861. Maury hardly noticed 17-year-old James Morgan at the other end of Trenholm's dinner table, looking uncomfortably hot in his woollen naval uniform. A random series of events had brought Morgan to Trenholm's door. Since helping his English friend, Francis Dawson, escape the over-enthusiastic nursing of some female volunteers, Morgan had been transferred from one ship to another. His current posting was on a little ironclad still in dry dock. With nothing to do and nowhere to go, Morgan had taken to roaming aimlessly around Charleston until Trenholm took him under his wing. On the sultry night that brought Maury and Morgan together for the first time, Trenholm turned to the youth and 'asked me if I would like to go abroad and join a cruiser', recalled Morgan. 'On being assured that I would give anything to have the chance, he returned to Commodore Maury and resumed his conversation about the peculiarities of the "Gulf Stream."' The next morning Morgan received orders from the Secretary of the Navy to accompany Maury to London. There, he was to report to James Bulloch for further instructions.[26]

Maury's worst fears about his mission had been confirmed when he arrived in England in late November 1862. The Confederates were low on funds and had been surviving on credit since the previous summer. Caleb Huse had warehouses full of precious guns, medicines, blankets and shoes for Lee's army that he could not afford to ship. James Bulloch himself had two half-completed ironclad rams at the Lairds shipyard in Liverpool, costing £94,000 each, which would never leave dry dock if he did not pay up in time. In Scotland, two agents for the Confederate navy, one of them the hapless James North, were in an equally perilous relationship with the shipwrights on the Clyde. If these ships could be let loose upon the Federal navy, they would, in Bulloch's words, 'sweep away the entire blockading fleet of the enemy'.[27] The modifications he had suggested would enable his cruisers to fight in any waters. Mobile, heavily gunned and armed with menacing iron rams, they were a new breed of fighting machine. But in the meantime Bulloch had until March to find the final instalment.

Bulloch was polite to Maury, but clearly regarded him as an added burden. Apart from the financial headache of yet another agent seeking pay and expenses, he feared that every new Confederate operation threatened the security of his own. Shortly before Maury's arrival, Bulloch had informed Richmond via a secure channel that sneaking the ships past the British authorities would be difficult, 'and will require to be conducted with such caution and secrecy that I fear to mention the plan even in this way'. The chief British ports had received orders to prevent the departure of any other *Alabama*s. Hampered by one of the worst winters in many years, the builders had put up temporary sheds and were using expensive gaslight in order to work round the clock. Even so, construction was coming on slowly.[28] 'Have tried very hard to hasten the completion, but insurmountable difficulties have occurred,' Bulloch wrote in code, trusting that the cipher had not been broken by Federal agents. 'No armoured ships for Admiralty have ever been completed in time specified: whole character of work new, and builders cannot make close calculations: great labour and unexpected time required to bend armour-plates: and the most important part of the work, the riveting, is far more tedious than anticipated.'[29]

The first attempt to solve the Confederates' debt crisis was made by James Spence and William Schaw Lindsay MP. Spence had at last achieved his wish to be appointed the South's financial agent for Europe. Eager to untangle the Confederates' wayward affairs, he and Lindsay had come up with the ingenious idea of floating cotton bonds on the London market, neatly sidestepping the fact that two-thirds of the Confederacy's wealth was tied up in slaves and land. As long as the Southern government could guarantee the flow of cotton to England, it would be a cheap way of raising money. Mason enthusiastically endorsed the idea. But Spence was outmanoeuvred by John Slidell and Caleb Huse, who championed an alternative loan proposal by the French banker Frédéric Emile, Baron d'Erlanger. There were several reasons why Slidell preferred to work with the Frenchman. Erlanger et Cie was one of the great European banking houses, similar to the Rothschilds' and Barings, and had lent money to the French government. Moreover, the Baron was desperately in love with Slidell's daughter, the beautiful Mathilda. He had been introduced to her during a business trip in New Orleans and had never recovered from the meeting (the two were married in October 1864).[30]

Spence and Slidell fought over the Erlanger proposal throughout January 1863. The Baron was amazed to have his dealings questioned by a provincial businessman and flicked Spence's questions aside. Such disrespect only angered Spence all the more: he refused 'to be treated with something like polite contempt', he told Mason. 'I am not the man to take it easily.' He had no choice. The Confederate Secretary of State, Judah P. Benjamin, did not like the terms of the Erlanger loan, particularly the 5 per cent commission, but he was anxious to drag the Emperor into closer ties with the Confederacy. On 29 January the Confederate Congress voted to approve the Erlanger loan.[31]

The real threat to Bulloch's ironclad rams, however, was not the lack of funds but Federal infiltration of his inner circle. The US Consuls Thomas Haines Dudley and Freeman Morse had finally succeeding in placing an agent close to the confederates' centre of operations.[32] Soon Morse and Dudley were able to relay precise descriptions of the blockade-runners leaving England, making it easier for the ships to be intercepted.*[33] One capture resulted in the loss of sorely needed provisions Maury had bought for his family.[34] Another netted the North a large cache of documents, which on inspection turned out to be two months' worth of official correspondence between Richmond and the Confederates in England. Among the revelations was James Spence's employment by the South, which ruined his cover as a disinterested advocate.

The Consuls also exposed the Cunard shipping line as the secret carrier of Confederate dispatches between Nassau and England, and even uncovered how the *Alabama* was able to send and receive messages. 'It has all the time been a mystery to me how Capt. Semmes? could get his letters and papers,' wrote the agent known only as WFGA. The system turned out to be quite simple. The lighthouse keeper on the Hole in the Wall, at the south end of the Abacos Islands in the Bahamas, was being paid to act as a go-between: every two weeks the *Alabama* would sail by and exchanges would be made.[35] The Confederate operations might have been completely compromised were it not for the parsimonious attitude of the US State Department. Espionage was an expensive game and the two Consuls were always running out of money. Seward had not increased their budget for some time, his estimation of their work having been coloured by one or two blunders that had undermined their credibility.

'Think British Government will prevent iron ships leaving,' Bulloch

---

* The Consuls reported on 9 January 1863, for example, 'an armed steamer is to leave Liverpool to-morrow with important dispatches from Commodore Maury (who is still in England), Mason, and Slidell. A man by the name of Hope is the bearer of these dispatches and will go out on the steamer.'

informed Richmond on 3 February, 'and am much perplexed; object of armoured ships too evident for disguise.'[36] The only Confederate project that had not been compromised was Matthew Maury's. Using privately financed cotton bonds, he had bought a Scottish steamer, called the *Japan*, which could be easily converted into a fighting ship. A colleague in the Royal Danish Navy was generously helping to oversee the conversion on the Clyde. But Northern agents heard rumours about the ship once Maury began to assemble a crew and arrange for the delivery of guns and supplies. He needed fifty seamen and twenty-one officers. There were nine Confederate naval officers scattered around London, living in boarding houses under assumed names. Maury used his rank to commandeer them for the *Japan*. That still left eleven vacancies that had to be filled with British officers. It was hardly ideal for the Confederates to be in the minority on their own cruiser, but the imminent threat of exposure left him with no other choice.

Maury was finalizing the last details for the *Japan*'s departure when permission to sell cotton bonds through the Erlanger banking house finally arrived from Richmond. Erlanger issued the prospectus on 18 March. The public's response was little short of frenzied, which made Spence's objections look self-serving. By the third day more than $16 million worth of bonds had been sold.[37] In his report, James Mason admitted that there had been 'a strong opinion in moneyed circles of the City that the enterprise was a hazardous one, and likely to fail in the market'. But the Confederates had managed to overcome the City's scepticism by touting the loan as a risk-free investment. Mason assured subscribers that no matter which side won the war, the bonds would always have to be honoured.[38]

'Cotton is King at last,' crowed Mason.[39] 'It is financial recognition of our independence,' John Slidell declared to Richmond.[40] His sentiments were echoed in London. Confederate sympathizers raised the issue of recognition in the Lords on 23 March, but Russell made a forceful speech that put an end to the debate before it had even properly started. Charles Francis Adams was surprised and thought it the best Russell had given on the war.[41] He did not know, of course, that Sumner was sending hysterical letters to the Duchess of Argyll and other English friends, warning them to be prepared for Northern privateers preying on English ships; or that Lord Lyons had advised Russell to treat the Confederate activities in England as a real threat to peace.[42] 'The outcry in America about the *Oreto* and the *Alabama* is much exaggerated,' Russell replied to Lyons, 'but I must feel that her roaming the ocean with English guns and English sailors to burn, sink and destroy the ships of a friendly nation, is a scandal and a reproach. I don't know very well what we can do.'[43] After Richard Cobden bluntly spelled out the danger of being a passive observer, Russell decided that the House of Commons should debate whether the current Foreign Enlistment Act needed to be strengthened.

Russell asked Charles Francis Adams what he wanted the government to say in the debate, to which Adams replied they 'should declare their disapproval of the fitting out of such ships of war to prey on American commerce'. Russell thought this was eminently sensible and relayed the message to Palmerston just before the Commons discussion on 27 March 1863. The House knew that Lairds had built the *Alabama* and was in the process of building more like her. 'I think you can have no difficulty in declaring this evening', Russell wrote to Lord Palmerston, 'that the Government disapprove of all such attempts to elude our law . . .'[44]

'The government itself is getting alarmed,' Freeman Morse wrote excitedly to Seward on the morning of the debate. 'This country is now thoroughly agitated on what they call the American question . . .'[45] The debate began with William Forster asking the government whether new laws were required to prevent the Confederates from building their warships in Britain. There should have been no difficulty except that no one had counted on John Bright appearing in the Commons. Adams had tried to dissuade him from speaking, knowing how Bright's 'help' often had the opposite effect. The night before, Bright had enjoyed a standing ovation at a trade union meeting when he roundly denounced the 'privileged class' for being foes of freedom. Still intoxicated by the cheers of his audience, he gave a similar-sounding speech to the House, forgetting that his listeners were members of this afflicted class. They should have 'looked in the faces of three thousand of the most intelligent of the artisan classes in London, as I did', he told an indignant House, 'and heard their cheers, and seen their sympathy for [America]'.[46] Bright was answered by John Laird, who had spent the evening hearing himself denounced as a cheat and warmonger. After pointing out that his firm had been approached by both the North and the South at the beginning of the war, 'I have only to say that I would rather be handed down to posterity as the builder of a dozen *Alabamas*, than as the man who applies himself deliberately to set class against class,' he bellowed, to the accompaniment of cheers from both sides of the House.[47]

In addition to dragging the shipbuilding question into his own class war, Bright also challenged Palmerston to apologize to the Americans. That promptly killed any hope of the House voting to strengthen the Foreign Enlistment Act. Rather than voicing his disapproval of Confederate evasions of the law, Palmerston declared he would never amend Britain's laws simply to satisfy international pressure.[48] Seizing this as their cue, Confederate sympathizers introduced a new subject in the debate: the US navy's harassment of British merchant ships. Adams believed that Bright had provided Palmerston with an excuse to avoid strengthening the Act. 'Had he been really well disposed he never could have written me the private note which caused our differences last year,' he wrote bitterly.[49]

Furious that John Bright's blundering speech had thwarted the government's attempt to strengthen the Foreign Enlistment Act, Russell ordered his staff to treat seriously all allegations against suspect ships. It was not long before the government had details of several Confederate vessels. Matthew Maury's *Japan* on the Clyde was one of the first to be unmasked. Maury learned that the project was out in the open from a report in the newspapers. He immediately sent orders for the cruiser to leave England whatever her condition. The crew and stores were to sail on a separate ship and rendezvous in neutral waters. A messenger delivered a cryptic note to the lodgings where James Morgan had been hiding since his arrival in England. He was ordered to proceed with the utmost care to a house in Little St James's Street, where a 'Mr Grigson' would give him further instructions. Morgan hurried through the streets, hoping that he was not being followed. At the house he found a half a dozen nervous Confederate officers. They jumped every time there was a knock at the door, fearing it was Consul Morse with the police. Nobody dared leave the house until well after sunset.

At half-past nine that evening [wrote Morgan] we all proceeded to a railway station where we took a train for White Haven, a little seaport about an hour's ride from London. There we went to a small inn, where we met Commander Maury, Dr. Wheeden, and Paymaster Curtis, and were soon joined by others – all strangers to me. We waited at the inn for about a couple of hours; there was little, if any, conversation, as we were all too anxious and were all thinking about the same thing. In those two hours it was to be decided whether our expedition was to be a success or a failure. If Mr. Adams, the American Minister, was going to get in his fine work and balk us, now was his last opportunity.[50]

The Foreign Office had already issued instructions to detain Morgan's vessel. But by some mysterious chance, the telegram remained in an outbox until after the port's telegraph station closed for the day. The delay enabled the *Japan* to escape in the early hours of 1 April 1863.[51] Eight days after leaving England, off the coast of Brittany, Matthew Maury's cousin Commander William Lewis Maury hoisted aloft the Confederate flag and the *Japan* began its service as the CSS *Georgia*.

The appearance on the high seas of a third Confederate commerce raider ratcheted up the already high tension between the United States and Royal navies. The US blockading squadron at Mobile, for example – still smarting from the embarrassment of having allowed the CSS *Florida* to escape – started firing live rounds at passing Royal Navy vessels, each time claiming to have mistaken the unambiguous appearance of a British warship for a civilian blockade-runner.* Conversely, British frigates patrolling the Caribbean were as unhelpful as possible towards the US vessels trying to chase down blockade-runners.

Admiral Milne, commander-in-chief of the Royal Navy's operations in North America and the West Indies, was annoyed by his officers' failure to maintain a strictly neutral stance. He despised the blockade-runners and had ordered the fleet to refrain from giving them any assistance. Sometimes the so-called offence against the US was simply tactless behaviour, such as the fraternization between British crews and the CSS *Alabama* when she sailed through Jamaican waters in January. But at other times Milne detected more than a hint of partisanship. In February he removed the HMS *Petrel* from Charleston after Captain George W. Watson and his officers became far too friendly with the blockaded townspeople.[53] The last straw was a clearly biased report by

---

* In New Orleans, a young sub-lieutenant on shore leave from HMS *Galatea* was beaten up and thrown into the stocks. An investigation revealed that he had been strolling down Canal Street singing Rebel songs. The dim-witted officer defended his conduct, saying, 'I did call them stinking cowards but that was nearly all.'[52]

Watson about the weakness of the blockading fleet. Milne upbraided him for 'mixing himself so conspicuously and unnecessarily with the Confederate authorities', and ordered Watson to a remote part of the Caribbean. 'I cannot trust him either at Nassau or on the American coast,' Milne complained on 20 March to Sir Frederick Grey of the Admiralty.[54] Milne also punished the captain of HMS *Vesuvius*, who had agreed to transport $155,000 in specie past the blockade at Mobile because, allegedly, it was interest owed to bond-holders in Britain. (Fearful of the reaction in Washington, Lyons promptly dismissed the British Consul who had arranged it.)

Milne made it his general rule to adopt a lenient approach regarding complaints about American harassment of 'innocent' cargo ships. He also held firm even when the US navy widened its net to include merchant ships sailing between the West Indies and the Gulf of Mexico. The chief destination of these ships was Matamoros, a miserable, drought-ridden town on the Mexican border, about 30 miles from the mouth of the Rio Grande. White, powdery dust covered every surface in Matamoros, including the hair and clothes of the inhabitants, making them look like the walking dead. The town would have dissolved back into the scrubland were it not directly across the river from Brownsville, Texas, another little miserable town whose existence was saved by the Civil War.

These two places, more than 1,500 miles from Richmond, were the only open gates into the Confederacy. The narrow, winding Rio Grande was a neutral river and so, according to international law, could not be blockaded. At first the North paid little attention to Matamoros. It was situated in a barren waste that spread for hundreds of miles; there were no port facilities or roads, and its only connection to Brownsville was a rickety ferryboat. But even with these obstacles, cotton sellers were prepared to risk their lives hauling long wagon trains across the Texas plains and over the river. By early 1863 nearly 200 ships a month were calling at Matamoros, bringing supplies to the Confederacy and in return leaving with cotton.

Although he could not admit to it publicly, Russell was anxious for the sake of the British cotton industry that this tiny chink in the blockade should stay open. He ordered Lyons to protest against the US navy's habit of seizing any British ship heading towards Mexico. There was no way of proving whether the guns and *matériel* were destined for the South or for the beleaguered Mexican government, whose twelve-month resistance against the French invasion force was showing signs of fatigue. But Milne was loath to interfere with the practices of the US navy; HMS *Phaeton* was already cruising in the Gulf as a friendly reminder of British neutrality. The only help that Milne was prepared to give to British merchantmen was the advice to anchor on the Mexican side of the Gulf, where the US navy was powerless to molest them.

The fate of several British merchant ships was already worrying the Foreign Office – and the readers of *The Times* – when Admiral Charles Wilkes once again exercised his uncanny ability to create an international crisis. Learning that a British-owned merchant ship called the *Peterhoff* was leaving the Danish island of St Thomas to sail to Matamoros, Wilkes ordered the USS *Vanderbilt* to stop her as soon as she left the harbour. As the *Vanderbilt* approached, one of the *Peterhoff*'s passengers was observed throwing a large packet into the water. Her captain was nowhere to be seen since he was busy burning papers in his cabin. The captured ship was brought to Key West in Florida on 10 March 1863, where the British Vice-Consul said that the vessel could not possibly have been involved in anything so low as blockade-running since Captain Stephen Jarman was a lieutenant in the Royal Naval Reserve. Moreover, she had been transporting the Lloyds insurance agent for Matamoros and a bag of mail from the Post Office. The return of the mail became an instant cause célèbre in England. The poisonous combination of Charles Wilkes and British property provoked *Trent*-like hysteria, with the press insisting that national honour was at stake.[55]

Lyons warned Russell that the mood of the Northerners was just as violent.[56] Whatever their disagreements over the war and the merits of abolition, they were united by their resentment against Britain. 'Everybody is furious with England and with everybody and everything English,' Lyons wrote sadly.[57] The Northern press was claiming that the British were building a navy for the Confederates, supplying their armies, lending them money and providing moral if not actual support to the *Alabama*, *Florida* and *Georgia*. Lyons telegraphed Admiral Milne to make his fleet battle-ready – once again the signal for war would be: 'Could you forward a letter for me to Antigua?'[58] Milne complied, though he was fearful that putting his ships on alert would provoke the very collision he was labouring so hard to prevent.

"BEWARE!"

Keeper. "HE AIN'T ASLEEP, YOUNG JONATHAN; SO YOU'D BEST NOT IRRITATE HIM."

Punch warns the United States not to iritate the British Lion, May 1863

19

Prophecies of Blood and Suffering

Blockade-running becomes a serious business – Two cautionary tales – Seward is courageous – General Longstreet feeds an army – A murder – Hooker's 'perfect plan'

In London, Benjamin Moran laughed sourly when he read the naive response of the British Vice-Consul in Florida to the allegations against the *Peterhoff*. There was no doubt Captain Jarman had been blockade-running; Moran had in his possession a copy of the subscription letter offered by the *Peterhoff*'s owners, which stated that the purpose of the voyage to the West Indies was to supply arms to the Confederacy in exchange for cotton. Nor could the uproar over Admiral Wilkes's action disguise the fact that Bermuda and the Bahamas had become the chief supply depots for the South.

The Bahamas was the preferred route for commercial blockade-runners because of its proximity to the Southern coast. It took only three days to sail from Nassau to the main Southern ports. The same trip from Bermuda – which was almost 900 miles due east of Charleston – took at least five days and sometimes more in poor weather. But by late 1862 Josiah Gorgas, the Confederate chief of ordnance, had realized that Bermuda's relative inaccessibility was an advantage for his government since the competition for docking facilities and warehouses was less fierce. The Ordnance Department's small fleet of blockade-runners used the tiny island of St George, which lay at the top end of the archipelago. Its port was closer to the open sea than the main island's, and the approach from the South was an easy passage through crystalline waters. On the return journey, the ordnance fleet unloaded its cargoes at Wilmington in North Carolina, rather than sailing to Charleston, which was expensive and crowded. Though not as convenient as Charleston – Wilmington was 25 miles from the sea, on the east bank of the Cape Fear river – the port could be reached via two different approaches and enjoyed the advantage of being guarded by Fort Fisher, whose large guns could hit any blockader attempting to enter the river.

Unloading cotton from blockade-runners at the port of
Nassau, by Frank Vizetelly

The supply system between Bermuda and Wilmington was growing so rapidly that in early 1863 the Ordnance Department appointed Major Norman Walker to oversee its operations on the island. From his headquarters at the Globe Hotel on St George, the industrious Walker arranged for 80,000 Enfield rifles, 27,000 Austrian rifles and 21,000 muskets to be shipped in February alone. He also filled orders for steel, copper and saltpetre, and sent hundreds of cases packed with screwdrivers, cartridges, buckles, stirrups, percussion caps, buttons and all the other daily necessities required by the Confederate armies. Soon the US Consul in Bermuda reported that Confederate steamers were coming and going with the regularity of a mail ship.[1] Resented by the locals for his attempts to interfere with this lucrative trade, the Consul's life became a daily round of harassment both petty and great. One morning in March a group of 'colored blockade running seamen' took their revenge by loudly singing Confederate songs beneath his window.[2]

The Globe Hotel was a three-storey stone building, painted a pretty shade of pink and adorned with black shutters. Built in 1699 as a residence for the Governor, it was one of the oldest houses on the island. With each change of ownership the place had become a little more run-down and frayed about the edges, and was currently a boarding house run by a widow and her three spinster sisters. But 'it was a Palace to me', wrote Walker's pregnant wife, Georgiana, who arrived on 24 March 1863 with three young children in tow and what remained of their belongings. (One bag contained the Confederate flag and a pouch filled with Virginian soil. Georgiana intended to give birth with the flag draped symbolically above the bed and the soil placed underneath to ensure that the baby was a true Virginian.) Desperate to join her husband in Bermuda, Georgiana had approached every blockade-runner in Wilmington, pleading to be taken on as a passenger, until finally the captain of the *Cornubia*, the leading steamer in the Ordnance Department's squadron, had taken pity on her. Georgiana became the first woman to run the blockade.

At times Georgiana could count as many as a dozen Confederate flags in the harbour. Some of the vessels' captains were Southern but many were British, usually Royal Naval Reserve officers. One, the Hon. Augustus Charles Hobart-Hampden, a younger son of the 6th Earl of Buckinghamshire, even resigned his commission to dedicate himself to blockade-running, and there seemed to be no shortage of thrill-seekers from either branch of Her Majesty's forces. On the steamship from Halifax to Liverpool in November, Matthew Maury and James Morgan had been surprised to learn that among the passengers was a group of English army officers who had used their leave to try blockade-running. The Earl of Dunmore, who became friendly with Maury and Morgan, boasted of his capture and confinement in a Northern prison. The Earl had 'passed through the Federal lines and gone to Richmond and thence to Charleston', wrote a clearly impressed Morgan.

He had travelled incognito, under his family name of Murray. The boat he took passage on successfully eluded the Federal fleet off Charleston, but an outside cruiser captured her the very next day. The prisoners were of course searched, and around the body of 'Mr. Murray,' under his shirt, was found

wrapped a Confederate flag – the flag of the C.S.S. *Nashville*, which had
been presented to him by Captain Pegram. Despite his protestations that he
was a Britisher traveling for pleasure, he was confined, as 'Mr. Murray,' in
Fort Lafayette. The British Minister, Lord Lyons, soon heard of his predicament and requested the authorities in Washington to order his release,
representing him as being the Earl of Dunmore, a lieutenant in Her Majesty's
Life Guards. But the commandant of Fort Lafayette denied that he had any
such prisoner and it required quite a correspondence to persuade him that a
man by the name of Murray could at the same time be Lord Dunmore.[3]

Lord Lyons implored his staff to discourage their friends and acquaintances from visiting the Confederacy. Two months after Edward Malet's
midnight encounter with Hartington, the legation attaché was again called
to the aid of an English civilian. The Federal security measures implemented after Mosby's raid had snared another victim: George Alfred
Lawrence was famous throughout England as the author of *Guy Livingstone*. Published in 1857, the novel eulogized a handsome, daredevil
Guards officer who defies social convention to the point of blackguard-
ism, but ultimately knows right from wrong. Five years later, Lawrence's
dashing alter ego still haunted its sedentary creator. In December 1862
Lawrence shocked his wife and friends by announcing his intention
to serve as a volunteer staff officer to General Lee. In contrast to the devil-
may-care Guy, Lawrence had carefully planned his adventure. He obtained
highly laudatory letters of introduction, including one from James Mason,
made financial provisions for his family, and had secured an appointment
from the *Morning Post* as its Southern correspondent.

Lawrence was greeted with adulation by the young attachés at the
legation. Lord Lyons invited him to dinner, although he was not as taken
with the author as his impressionable staff, one of whom supplied Lawrence with the address of the ever-obliging journalist W. W. Glenn. This
time, however, Glenn regretted his involvement: Lawrence was captured
on 10 April a few miles from the last Federal outpost in West Virginia.
He was highhanded with his Federal interrogator and melodramatically
refused to answer questions except to say, 'I am the author of *Guy Livingstone* and other works of fiction. I took no letters from Baltimore to
carry and none were found on me.'

According to the army report, hidden among Lawrence's personal
belongings was a letter from Mr Glenn, giving directions on where to

find his guide, 'and the route to take, the persons to trust and to avoid . . . it reflects a disloyal and traitorous light'. There was also a scurrilous verse in his handwriting: 'Jeff Davis rides a white horse, Abe rides a mule, Davis is a gentleman, Abe a fool.' William Seward was robustly unsympathetic when Lord Lyons wrote to him about releasing Lawrence from Old Capitol prison.

The publicity attending Lawrence's arrest was deeply embarrassing for Lord Lyons. He also feared what the English papers would say once it became known that the 'author of *Guy Livingstone*' was being held in prison without charge. Despite persistent prodding by Lyons to bring Lawrence to trial or else release him, Seward did nothing for two months. The Secretary of War, Edwin Stanton, insisted that Seward make an example of Lawrence, and showed his anger by refusing to grant any more passes to British military observers, including Lieutenant Colonel James Eli Crowther, who had been sent by the British army as an official observer.*

George Lawrence whiled away his time in prison writing irritable letters to Lyons, swearing that there was not 'a shadow of foundation' to the charge he had sought to join the Confederacy. The attachés visited him weekly, bearing little care packages, which the guards kept for themselves. Lawrence loathed his loquacious cellmate, whose 'narrative riches about matched those of the knife-grinder'.[5] His sole consolation, he wrote, was the occasional sight of a beautiful female prisoner who once threw him a white rose from her window. Apart from this innocent little romance, Lawrence kept to himself. When Seward finally ordered his release in June, Lawrence returned to New York a chastened man. Henceforth he would continue his campaign against the North from the safety of his study.

Lord Lyons might have been more persuasive with Seward if Lawrence's arrest had not coincided with that of another adventure-hungry Briton. The 20-year-old Alfred Rubery was one of life's nincompoops. The death of his father, John Rubery, the largest umbrella manufacturer

---

* Stanton was like Seward in his inability to resist an aristocratic title. He granted a visitor's permit to Lord Abinger, who was stationed in Canada with the Scots Guards. Abinger went down to the Army of the Potomac, was treated to a grand review, and had his photograph taken with Hooker's staff. His discreet and affable nature meant no one among his hosts had the faintest idea of his true feelings. In contrast to the neutral Crowther, Abinger was thoroughly sympathetic to the South. The previous April he had invited Commissioner James Mason to dine at the regimental mess in Eastbourne. Mason was most gratified to have the notice of a Scottish peer and recorded every detail of the outing in his diary.[4]

in Birmingham, had given him a modest independence. Leaving his older brother to manage the family business, Alfred went to San Francisco in the summer of 1862 with dreams of making his fortune in mining. He had not been in the city for long when he fell into a barroom argument with a Federal officer. Young Rubery had visited the South before the war. Naturally, as one who owed his wealth and social position to factory smoke, he idealized Southern society and thought it the most perfect on earth. He said all this and more to the incensed Lieutenant Tompkins, who happened to be the descendant of a New York State Governor. 'High words followed,' according to witnesses, 'and Tompkins made a remark that touched Rubery's honor. The latter simply said, "You will hear from me, sir," and left the room.'⁶

The virtually friendless Rubery needed a second for his duel with Tompkins. An acquaintance put him in touch with Asbury Harpending, a Confederate veteran who had fought at Shiloh. Only a year older than Rubery, Harpending seemed to be living proof that fantasies can come true. Brought up in Kentucky, he had run away from home as a teenager and made his way to Mexico, where he discovered a gold mine, becoming rich overnight. But the chronic anarchy and violence that bedevilled Mexico soon separated Harpending from his new source of wealth. Undaunted, when the war began he went to San Francisco with fresh schemes in mind. His first idea was to organize a chapter of the Knights of the Golden Circle, a secret pro-Southern society, and have each member recruit 100 volunteers. This, he reckoned, would give him a big enough force to seize California's government buildings and declare the State's allegiance to the South. When that failed, he somehow got himself to Richmond, where he wrangled an officer's commission in the Confederate navy.

Harpending returned to San Francisco with a new plan. He and a friend named Ridgley Greathouse were going to charter a ship, sail it into Mexican waters and lie in wait for the Pacific Mail steamer and its cargo of California gold. After offloading the passengers, they would equip the steamer as a privateer and send the gold to Richmond. Thus armed, they would prey on Californian cargo ships and, with luck, disrupt the supply of gold to the North. The only hitch to the plan was the $25,000 required to see it through to execution. Harpending was therefore delighted to meet the pro-Southern and apparently well-heeled Rubery.

First Harpending had to rescue his friend from the duel with Tomp-kins. Alfred Rubery's physical prowess lagged far behind his enthusiasm. 'I tried him at pistol practice,' recalled Harpending, 'and found that, with extra good luck, at ten paces he could hit a barn.' The American could fast-talk his way out of anything; he used his gift now to make the duel disappear. With Tompkins safely dispatched, the three conspirators began looking for a suitable ship. They soon happened upon the *J. M. Chapman*, a 90-ton schooner that had just made a record-breaking voyage from New York. As soon as ownership was transferred to them, they proceeded to hire a crew and purchase enough firepower to make a formidable warship. 'It only remained to secure a navigator who could be implicitly trusted,' wrote Harpending. When none materialized they were forced to engage William Law, a sea captain and ex-slave trader who had been dismissed by the Pacific Mail Company. Law had only eight fingers and 'was the most repulsive reptile in appearance that I ever set eyes on', wrote Harpending. His antipathy proved to be well founded.

The day of departure was set for 15 March 1863. The night before, Harpending and Rubery hid in a dark alley behind the American Exchange Hotel, waiting for the crew to arrive. They then divided into three squads to avoid suspicion, 'slipped through the dimly lighted streets, past roaring saloons and sailor boarding houses' and reached an unfrequented part of the waterfront unnoticed, where the privateer was moored. Rubery and Harpending 'were exultant'. But

> when we scrambled aboard the *Chapman*, Greathouse was pacing the deck in agitation. Law was not there. I experienced a shock such as a man receives when a bucket of ice water is emptied on him in his sleep. The sug-gestion of treachery could not be avoided. We cast loose from the wharf and anchored in the stream. But we were helpless. We could not sail with-out our navigator. We had nothing to do but wait.[7]

Shortly after dawn the three conspirators awoke to find the *Chap-man* surrounded by US gunboats. The authorities had been keeping careful surveillance for several days. Rubery and Harpending had neg-lected to supply the local revenue officers with a cargo manifest, thereby piquing official interest in the mysterious boxes that were being loaded in such a hurry. The luckless three were taken to Alcatraz, where Rubery was soon visited by Consul William Lane Booker, who thought him to be a rather unsympathetic, cocky youth who fully deserved his punishment. 'He has nothing to complain as to his treatment, Booker reported to Lord Russell, 'beyond being deprived of his liberty.'[8] The evidence against Rubery was so overwhelming that Lyons made no attempt to intervene on his behalf. While searching through Rubery's baggage the Federals had found a plan for capturing San Francisco's forts, a proclamation to the people of California, urging them to join the Confederacy, and a declaration of allegiance for those who did.

Rubery's family could not accept that their little Alfred had played a central role in the conspiracy. For the past three months he had been spinning a tale to them about a mining venture in Mexico. Determined to prove his innocence, they showed the letters to Birmingham's two MPs, John Bright and William Scholefield. Neither shared the Ruberys' delusion: 'They seem to be wholly unaware that he can have committed himself so as to justify his arrest,' wrote Scholefield pityingly.[9] '[Alfred] must be wonderfully stupid to have engaged in any conspiracy,' decided John Bright, 'and yet I hear that he is sharp and clever, and was educated at the London University.' The Rubery name and fortune carried sufficient weight in Birmingham to make it impossible for the MPs to ignore the family's request for help. John Bright reluctantly wrote to Charles Sumner, 'Is it too much for me to ask you to procure his liberation on condition that he shall at once return to England?'[10] It was. Rubery remained at Alcatraz.

Lord Lyons refused to let either George Lawrence or Alfred Rubery disrupt his enjoyment of the first days of spring. It was not only possible but also delightful to walk down streets abloom with flowering trees. The great drying-out attracted crowds of tourists and distinguished visitors to the city. Seward's house became lively again and 19-year-old Fanny Seward briefly relinquished her reserve to enjoy a brief flirtation with an English naval surgeon on leave from the USS *Commodore Morris*.

Washington society turned out en masse, including President Lincoln, to watch the self-styled 'youngest star in the world', John Wilkes Booth, play Hamlet at Grover's Theatre. Dr Charles Culverwell observed Booth's debut in the capital. Having heard that the lesser parts were open to audition, Culverwell took a leave of absence and auditioned under the name 'Charles Wyndham'. To his great surprise, he won the part of Osric. On the handbills for the play Culverwell was described as: 'Charles Wyndham: first appearance of a gifted young actor'. After the opening night on 14 April 1863, no one noticed Osric, but Booth received praise from every quarter. Many years later, Culverwell still retained vivid memories of his brief encounter with Booth:

> During my introductory rehearsal I wandered about the stage and finally chose an advantageous position at a little table where I could command a good view of all the proceedings. John Wilkes noticed me there and smiled . . . The courtesy and kindness shown to me by John Wilkes made way for friendship between us, and we frequently were together after the play. He was a most charming fellow, off the stage as well as on, a man of flashing wit and magnetic manner. He was one of the best raconteurs to whom I have ever listened. As he talked he threw himself into his words, brilliant, ready, enthusiastic. He could hold a group spellbound by the hour at the force and fire and beauty of him . . . as an actor, the natural endowment of John Wilkes Booth was of the highest. His original gift was greater than that of his wonderful brother, Edwin . . . He was the idol of women. They would rave of him, his voice, his hair, and his eyes. Small wonder, for he was fascinating . . . Poor, sad, mad, bad, John Wilkes Booth . . . [11]

Lord Lyons was never given the opportunity to watch Booth play Hamlet; a careless clerk in the Foreign Office had forwarded the legation's correspondence to the printers of the parliamentary 'blue book' without first removing the censored passages. Its arrival in mid-April caused such controversy that Lyons suffered the same hideous embarrassment that had ruined Charles Francis Adams's Christmas. 'The goodwill to me personally, which miraculously survived so long, seems at last to have sunk altogether,' wrote Lyons. The political damage was also considerable. The 'blue book' had offended or alienated both supporters and enemies alike: 'Unluckily the book contains just the passages in my dispatches which are most irritating to each of the parties, and which it is most inconvenient to them to have published.'[12]

Lyons was especially worried about how the 'blue book' would affect his relationship with Seward. He had heard that the Secretary was annoyed and feared that it made him appear weak in his dealings with the diplomatic corps. Lyons also braced himself for a difficult time over the *Peterhoff* affair, with Seward making public threats and statements about what the United States would and would not stand for, similar to his recent grandstanding about letters of marque. But Seward surprised him; rather than allowing the controversy to take on a life of its own, he courageously defied the objections of the Cabinet and returned the *Peterhoff*'s captured mailbag to Lyons. He even prevailed upon his rival Gideon Welles to transfer Admiral Wilkes to the Pacific Ocean, where there were fewer opportunities to cause trouble. The US Navy Secretary grudgingly gave the order but in secret Welles fantasized about the dire retribution awaiting Britain – 'Years of desolation, of dissolution, of suffering and blood'.[13] Welles's supporters started a whispering campaign against Lyons. 'Among other devices', wrote Lyons, 'is that of representing me as having made the most violent and arrogant demands about the *Peterhoff*.' This led to an unpleasant encounter with Charles Sumner at a dinner party. The Senator dragged Lyons into a corner and proceeded to rail at him for overstepping his prerogative. Lyons was dumbfounded at first, and then swore he had never made anything resembling a demand. He finally offered to show Sumner copies of his correspondence with Seward.[14]

Lyons wondered whether he was wasting his efforts to bolster good relations between the two countries. 'One hardly knows whether to wish the North success or failure in the field,' he had written to Russell during the *Peterhoff* affair.[15] Yet the Confederacy was equally bitter against England, Lyons learned from the diplomatic bags which occasionally made it out of the South.* 'It ought to have been known here from the first, but was not, that England could be no friend to the Confederacy or its cause,' declared the *Richmond Enquirer*, for example. 'We have been long in finding out the truth and, before we would admit it, have endured some humiliations and insolent airs on the part of that Power, which surprised us very much, but ought not to have done so. At last the thing has become too clear.'[17]

Southern rage against Britain placed Francis Lawley in a difficult position. He had completed his tour of the Confederacy and returned to

---

* It was no longer the exception but the rule for British subjects to be conscripted into the army or jailed if they refused. By some miracle Lord Lyons received a letter from a Yorkshire lad in a Southern jail in Mississippi. The writer was desperate for help: 'I was, like a very dog, ordered to "fall in",' he wrote, 'and were sent to this place and placed in artillary [*sic*] companies. I again told my captain of my immunity from the service but it availed nothing ... I was sick from exposure and sent to hospital where I have been ever since, except the last two weeks when I was arrested and sent to Jail, where I now write this, charged with cursing the Confederacy and trying to escape the place, which they term desertion.'[16]

Richmond at the end of March, but his report for *The Times* was taking longer than usual to compose. Anything less than unqualified praise, Lawley had discovered, was not tolerated by his hosts. He confided his exasperation to William Gregory: 'I cannot impress upon you the difficulty which I find in the discharge of my present office, in avoiding topics which will be calculated to ruffle the amour propre ... of the most susceptible people and government on earth.'[18]

Lawley still believed in the purity of the Southern planter class as the epitome of all that was noble and intelligent in the human race. But in his opinion the rest of the Southern population was going to the dogs: 'Richmond and in a less degree, Charleston and Mobile, strike me as immense gambling booths.' He would know – many of his friends and acquaintances, including Judah Benjamin, made up the chief clientele of Richmond's illicit 'hells'. Profiteering, corruption and hoarding were rampant. Lawley felt a visceral disappointment whenever he observed Southerners behaving like ordinary human beings in time of war, and he tried as much as possible to shut his eyes to the messy aspects of the South. He required moral clarity from the Confederates, especially now that the North was growing stronger and more aggressive. Part of him was confident that 'Fighting Joe' Hooker stood no chance against Lee. But he had seen enough of the Federal army to have doubts, even if he preferred not to express them out loud. 'My sole and only hope is in the demoralization of the Yankees but I have little faith in it,' he wrote to Gregory. 'The truth is that the Yankee fights much better than he has been represented as fighting.'[19]

On 2 April 1863, a few days after Lawley had unburdened himself to Gregory, there were bread riots in Richmond. The Confederate capital was a microcosm of the many hardships being endured across the South; hunger and disease were spreading. Smallpox had invaded the poorer neighbourhoods as more refugees arrived, begging for space, even if it meant sleeping outside on a porch or in a garden shed. Everything was scarce. Women who before the war bought only the finest scented soaps from France were using soap made from kitchen grease mixed with lye. Ordinary articles such as pins and buttons were so hard to come by that John Jones, the diarist in the Confederate War Department, walked to work every day with his eyes fixed on the ground hoping to find some carelessly dropped treasure in the gutter.

Lee's Army of Northern Virginia was also suffering; the men had been on half-rations for so long that many were showing the first signs of scurvy. There were still plenty of foodstuffs in southern Virginia and North Carolina, particularly in the fertile tidewater regions near the coast, but for the past year transportation had become almost impossible. The Federal occupation of Norfolk, Suffolk, Plymouth, Washington and New Bern – all of them strategically important towns along the south-eastern seaboard – was choking the Confederate supply line. On the morning of the bread riots in Richmond, General Longstreet – Francis Dawson's new commander – received permission to attack Suffolk. The Union garrison there was weakly held and Longstreet believed he could take it with 20,000 men. The Confederate General had hoped to launch a surprise attack, but an intercepted message alerted the Federals to his plan.

Washington promptly dispatched thousands of troops to strengthen the garrison, forcing Longstreet to alter his battle plan from an attack to a siege. The no-longer-plump Englishman, George Herbert of the 9th New York Volunteers – Hawkins' Zouaves – was among the reinforcements. The regiment was thunderstruck by its mobilization. The men had only six weeks left before the terms of their enlistment expired. They had expected to remain in camp at Newport News, Virginia, where the most strenuous activity of the day was a game of baseball against the 51st New York. The men 'are all anxiously looking forward to our final march up Broadway', Herbert told his mother. Few of them intended to re-enlist: Herbert was already planning his future in England. 'I guess I shall have somewhere about $400 when I am mustered out and the more gold falls the richer I shall be,' he mused on 31 March.[20]

Eleven days later, on 11 April, Herbert and his comrades disembarked at Portsmouth Naval Yard. The regiment stood listlessly under pelting rain as enquiries revealed that Suffolk was already under siege by Longstreet's forces. The trains had been cancelled and there were no available wagons. The soldiers were forced to march 27 miles over railroad sleepers, loaded down with all their equipment. It was dark by the time they reached the Suffolk camp. No one had bothered to prepare for the regiment's arrival so the men went from tent to tent, seeking a place to sleep. Lieutenant Colonel Edgar Kimball found an old friend from the Mexican War and spent a few hours warming himself with his tent companion's whisky.

A little after 2 a.m. Kimball remembered his orders to report to General

George Getty's headquarters. On the way, however, he came across General Michael Corcoran, the boisterous commander of the Irish Brigade. In one version of what happened next, Kimball went to the aid of a sentry who was shouting at several men on horseback. Corcoran, on the other hand, claimed that Kimball suddenly emerged from the darkness and grabbed his bridle, demanding that the countersign be given. But according to all versions of the incident, Corcoran refused to give it, saying, 'I am General Corcoran and staff.' This was not enough for Kimball, who began brandishing his sword, whereupon Corcoran shot him at point-blank range. Journalists at the camp rushed to telegraph the news of his death.

Kimball's insistence on the proper countersign was initially commended as a wise precaution when the guerrilla John Mosby was about: 'Under the circumstances, with a Rebel force in close proximity, an enemy might have said the same thing,' wrote a New York correspondent. But when the Zouaves learned of their colonel's death, many of them picked up their weapons and started for Corcoran's camp. Fearing a riot, General Getty had the bugle sounded for assembly, which the men instinctively obeyed. He sat on his horse in front of the regiment and made a conciliatory speech, promising that there would be an investigation into Kimball's shooting. The soldiers calmed down as they listened. At first they were rather pleased to hear that the General was sending them away from the camp at once. A few hours later, when they had reached Fort Nansemond, the men realized that the General had ordered them to the 'extreme front'. The Zouaves spent the next twenty-two days under continuous fire from Confederate rifle pits, 'so fully occupied with the enemy in front', wrote the regiment's historian, 'that if his satanic majesty had wished to brew mischief he could have found no heart or hands in the regiment to do it for him'. None of the regiment was allowed to attend Kimball's funeral in New York on 20 April.[21]

As more Union troops were sent to reinforce Suffolk, Longstreet realized that his small army would soon be radically outnumbered. He saw no reason to continue the siege, since enough bacon and grain to feed Lee's army for two months had been collected during his so-called 'Tidewater Campaign'. Longstreet was preparing to withdraw his men when a telegram arrived on 3 May 1863 ordering his immediate return to the Army of Northern Virginia: 'Fighting Joe' Hooker was on the move. Longstreet tried to move as quickly as he could without jeopardizing the safety of the long wagon trains filled with supplies. George Henry Herbert's term of enlistment ended on the same day as Longstreet's retreat. The Zouaves threatened to mutiny if they were kept at Suffolk a minute longer, sufficiently alarming the authorities into providing troop transports to take the regiment straight to New York.

Longstreet doubted that he would reach Lee in time to help him stop General Hooker's advance. Suffolk was more than 150 miles from Fredericksburg and 'Fighting Joe' had been counting on this when he devised his battle plan. The two armies had passed the winter facing one another across the banks of the Rappahannock river. Hooker tried to give the impression that he was contemplating another frontal assault of Fredericksburg to hide the fact he was looking for places to ford the river upstream. Richmond was still his objective, and the Confederate army was still blocking the way; but Hooker's strategy – one of the boldest on the Union side for the entire war – involved a sophisticated deception. He intended to force the Confederates out of their entrenched position at Fredericksburg by attacking them simultaneously from several different directions. To achieve this, he needed to disguise the whereabouts of his army until it was too late for Lee to do anything other than react defensively.

Hooker knew that the Army of the Potomac had a two-to-one advantage over Lee, whose Army of Northern Virginia numbered fewer than 65,000 men. The Union General thought he could increase the odds even more by sending his 12,000-strong Cavalry Corps on raiding parties around Richmond, with instructions to 'Let your watchword be fight, fight, fight'. He wanted the cavalry to isolate Richmond from the rest of the State, causing panic in the capital and, with luck, forcing Lee to detach a part of his army for its defence. Sir Percy Wyndham's regiment had a merry time ripping up railroads and cutting communications north of Richmond, rarely encountering opposition. Predictably, Wyndham went too far and began thinking up his own assignments, which led to his arrest for insubordination; after vigorous protests by his supporters he was released with a censure for disobeying orders.

Hooker was in a jubilant mood once the Army of the Potomac started moving on 29 April. Leaving 40,000 troops at Fredericksburg under the capable command of General 'Uncle John' Sedgwick, he ordered the rest, numbering almost 80,000 men and officers, to cross the Rappahannock river at two different places and rendezvous at Chancellorsville, nine miles west of Fredericksburg. The name applied not to a village but to a clearing in a wood that stretched out for 70 square miles in such dense thickets that locals simply labelled it 'the Wilderness'. A cross-roads cut through the middle of the clearing, passing close to an old brick mansion named Chancellor House. Here Hooker and his staff set up their temporary headquarters, flushing the indignant female inhabit-ants out of the parlour to their bedrooms on the floor above. He was ready to launch his surprise attack. 'My plans are perfect,' he declared on the eve of the battle, 'may God have mercy on General Lee, for I will have none.'[22]

20

The Key is in the Lock

A great gamble – Death of Stonewall Jackson – Grant reaches
Vicksburg – Arthur Fremantle meets the famous Colonel Grenfell –
Feilden in love

The discovery that Hooker had divided his army and was intending to crush him like a nut between two hammers came as a tremendous shock to Lee, who was unused to being tricked by his Federal opponents. Having weighed the various risks and options for his army, he decided that the greatest danger came from Hooker's advancing forces rather than the 47,000 Federals still remaining at Fredericksburg. Lee also avoided the trap of dispatching part of his army to defend Richmond, having correctly guessed that the Federal cavalry raids around the capital were nothing more than a feint. Even so, he could only afford to leave 10,000 men to hold Fredericksburg. The remaining 52,000 he ordered to turn around and take up defensive positions just beyond Chancellorsville. Lee planned to attack Hooker's troops as they emerged from the Wilderness, using the advantage of surprise.

The fighting began on 1 May 1863. At Fredericksburg, General Sedgwick fired some artillery at the Confederates and engaged in a few skirmishes. It was hardly the aggressive movement envisaged by 'Fighting Joe' Hooker, but to the raw and untested 2nd Lieutenant Henry George Hore it seemed as though he had participated in a marvellous triumph. Hore had joined Sedgwick's staff only a few weeks earlier, having sailed from England to do his part in freeing the slaves. 'We are victorious and captured [the Confederates'] batteries, men and all,' Hore wrote in the afternoon to his cousin, Olivia: it had been 'the Battle of Fredericksburg the Second'.[1]

Francis Lawley had rushed from Richmond as soon as he heard that Hooker was on the march but was disappointed that the Wilderness's impenetrable scrub made it impossible for him to see what was happening. What blinded him also hindered Hooker's generals as they tried to lead their men through the woods. At 2 p.m., after meeting relatively light pockets of resistance from the Confederates, Hooker suddenly called off the advance and ordered his army to retreat back to Chancellorsville. His commanders begged him to continue fighting. Hooker was obstinate: 'I have got Lee just where I want him,' he told General Darius Couch, who walked away from the meeting convinced that 'Fighting Joe' 'was a whipped man'. Hooker was never able to explain his decision afterwards except to say that all of a sudden he lost faith in himself.[2]

That night, Lee and Stonewall Jackson discussed how to take advantage of their adversary's hesitation. They agreed to divide the already outnumbered army into even smaller segments. Jackson would take 30,000 men and march around Hooker's army, relying on local guides to find a way through the Wilderness and surprise him from the rear, while Lee would remain in front with just 15,000 troops. In any other battle the opposing cavalry would have spotted such a manoeuvre, but Hooker's was miles away, destroying barns and canals.

When Hooker was informed that large troop movements were taking place he decided that it meant the Confederates were retreating back to Fredericksburg. It never occurred to him that Lee would attempt an attack from two different directions, using the same divide-and-surprise tactic that he himself had intended to employ. The next day, 2 May, at 5 p.m., just as the Federals were sitting down to cook their dinners, Stonewall Jackson ordered his men to charge. 'Swift and sudden as the falcon sweeping her prey, Jackson had burst on his enemy's rear and crushed him before resistance could be attempted,' wrote Francis Lawley in a sudden fit of poetry.[3] The rout was so complete that an entire wing of the Union army collapsed and ran back towards headquarters, some two miles away. The first Hooker learned of the battle was when one of his staff officers happened to walk out on to the veranda. '"My God, here they come!" he shouted.'[4] The lines between the two armies became blurred as the twilight turned to darkness.

Hooker was not beaten yet, however. Though strangely passive with regard to his immediate danger, he had no trouble directing the operations at Fredericksburg. Furious that Sedgwick had been poking rather

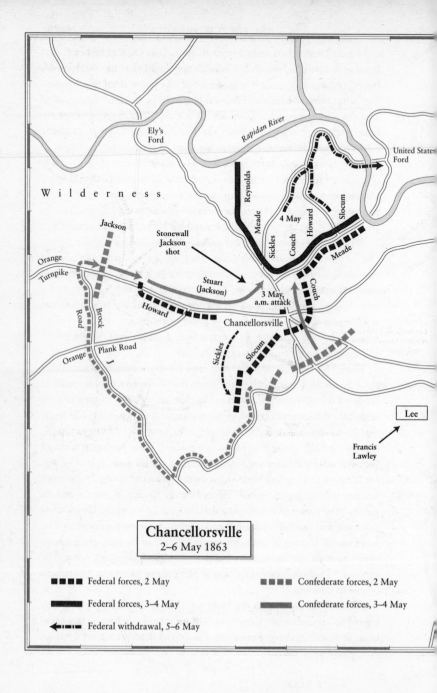

W i l d e r n e s s

Ely's Ford

Rapidan River

United States Ford

Jackson

Orange Turnpike

Road

Brock

Orange Plank Road

Stonewall Jackson shot

Stuart (Jackson)

Howard

3 May, a.m. attack

Chancellorsville

Sickles

Slocum

Reynolds

Meade

Sickles

4 May

Couch

Howard

Slocum

Meade

Couch

Lee

Francis Lawley

Chancellorsville
2–6 May 1863

■■■■ Federal forces, 2 May

■■■■ Federal forces, 3–4 May

◄■■■ Federal withdrawal, 5–6 May

■■■■ Confederate forces, 2 May

■■■■ Confederate forces, 3–4 May

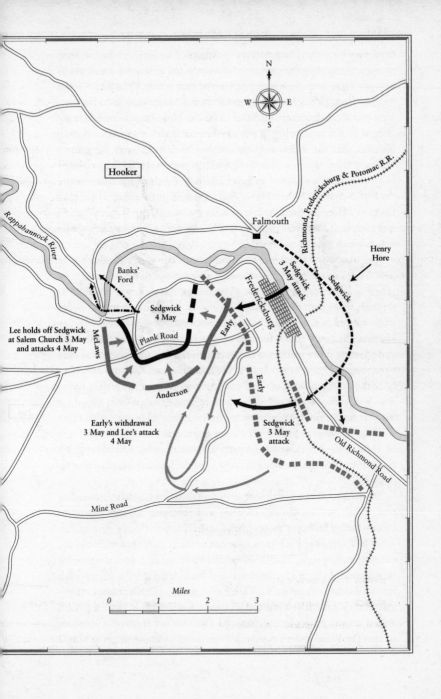

Hooker

Rappahannock River

N
W   E
S

Richmond, Fredericksburg & Potomac R.R.

Falmouth

Henry Hore

Banks' Ford

Sedgwick 3 May attack

Sedgwick

Sedgwick 4 May

Fredericksburg

McLaws

Plank Road

Early

Lee holds off Sedgwick at Salem Church 3 May and attacks 4 May

Anderson

Early

Early's withdrawal 3 May and Lee's attack 4 May

Sedgwick 3 May attack

Old Richmond Road

Mine Road

Miles

0   1   2   3

than smashing the Confederates' positions, Hooker sent him a terse message demanding the capture of the town and instructed the message-bearer to stay until Sedgwick had moved into action.[5] The direct order had its effect. Henry Hore was up early on 3 May, riding hard between Sedgwick's headquarters and the batteries. Now he saw real fighting instead of the tepid firing of the day before. It was a shock for him to discover that the Rebel soldiers handled their rifles with far greater accuracy than his own side. Sedgwick's troops were flailing until the Federal artillery unleashed its guns. There was such a long delay before the first explosions, wrote Hore, 'that I thought [the Rebels] would take the guns before we fired. At last came the word: "Depress pieces" and I quite felt sick, they were just about fifty yards or so from my horse who was as much excited as myself.'

The next hour was Hore's initiation into the sordid truth of war. 'Good God, my dear girl, it was awful,' he admitted to his cousin Olivia. 'Their dead seemed piled heaps upon heaps, the shot went right clear through them, completely smashing the front of the columns.' Sedg-wick ordered ten regiments to charge across the plain towards Marye's Heights, the same attack formation that had decimated the Irish 69th and so many other regiments in December. But this time there was only a thin line of Confederates behind the famous stone wall, and in half an hour the attackers were up and over, lunging forward with their bayo-nets. Sedgwick was so excited that he tore a page from a letter meant for his wife and scribbled an order for more artillery. He gave it to Hore with the command to ride as fast as he could and return with every gun he could find. A fellow officer named Hansard, who had abjured his home State of South Carolina in support of the Union, offered to accom-pany him.

The two officers were almost at the rear when a Confederate raiding party came crashing through the trees with terrifying whoops and yells.[6] Hore wheeled his horse around, hoping that Hansard was with him. But when he looked behind him he saw one of the raiders spur his horse on, reaching out to grab Hansard's bridle. Hore made a split decision to turn around. As he did so, the two riders struggled and fell to the ground. Hansard landed on his back. While he lay prone, a Confederate cavalry-man whipped out his sword and plunged it into his chest. Hore watched, aghast, as the raider leaned forward and tore off Hansard's shoulder straps. The Rebel locked eyes with Hore and shook the straps at him. 'I now felt as if he or I must be killed,' wrote Hore. Time slowed and each movement became exaggeratedly clear in his memory. He pulled out his revolver and galloped towards the cavalryman. 'I had made up my mind I would kill him if I could.' The Rebel either had no gun or forgot he had one. When Hore was sure he would not miss, he fired straight at him: 'This did not take 30 seconds,' he wrote, 'not near so long as it takes me to write. I sighted him along the barrel of my revolver and if I had not killed him the first time would have shot again, for H[ansard] was a good friend to me.'[7]

Hore remembered little else of that day. Once the Federal army had breached Marye's Heights the Confederates pulled back towards Chancellorsville, making a new stand in the woods around Salem church. Though still outnumbered, the Confederates managed to hold down Sedgwick's troops. Hore was confused and thought that the Confederate retreat meant another victory. 'They have not gained (the Rebels I mean) a single yard,' he wrote, 'and we don't mean they shall', not realizing that, in Hooker's plan, Sedgwick should have been at Chancellorsville by now, helping to smash Lee's little army. By this time, Hooker was sorely in need of Sedgwick. Shortly after 9 a.m. on the morning of the 3rd, a Confederate cannonball had smashed into the veranda of Chancellor House, knocking Hooker unconscious. Though still groggy after coming to, he insisted on resuming command, much to the dismay of his staff. Contrary to his generals' wishes, Hooker ordered a general retreat.

Shortly after Hooker's departure, Chancellor House went up in flames.* Lee trotted up to the burning house as Confederates came running towards him, cheering and shouting wildly. Behind them the Wilderness had been transformed into a roaring furnace, trapping the lost and wounded. Men closest to the conflagration could see figures waving in the inferno. Union and Confederate soldiers braved the searing heat to pull out anyone they could. Two enemies fought together to rescue a trapped youth: 'The fire was all around him,' recalled the Federal soldier. They could see his face: 'His eyes were big and blue, and his hair like raw silk surrounded by a wreath of fire.' In vain, they burned their hands trying to reach him. 'I heard him scream, "Oh Mother,

---

* Mrs Chancellor and her six daughters were rescued by one of Hooker's aids, Lieutenant Colonel Joseph Dickinson. He disobeyed orders and remained with the women until they were safely across the Rappahannock, earning their eternal friendship and gratitude.

O God." It left me trembling all over, like a leaf.' The defeated rescuers fled the forest. Although it was agony to open their fingers, 'me and them rebs tried to shake hands'.[8]

There was no cathartic pain for Henry Hore. On the night of the 4th, taking advantage of the full moon, he led a burial party to look for Hansard's body. They found him lying next to the dead Rebel. Hore dug a grave and buried Hansard but deliberately left the Mosby raider to rot out in the open. 'My dear Cousin you must think me quite savage,' he wrote afterwards in the bleak surroundings of an old barn, 'but the carnage of this frightful war and the horrid sights I see every day made me indifferent to human life. At one time I should have never thought of killing anyone, but now can shoot a man without a shake of my hand. I think I am writing to you more as if you were a hard hearted man than a very pretty girl.' Every now and then, Hore interrupted his letter to give a sip of water to his friend, Lieutenant Bowen, who lay bleeding in the corner. 'He wants to know who I am writing to, so I said it was to my cousin in England. He has just said: "Don't tell them we are beaten, Harry, the papers will let them know that."'

On 5 May the balmy weather was replaced by lashing wind and rain. The Confederate commanders informed Lee that another attack was beyond their men's strength. The storm provided the Union army with perfect cover as it slowly crawled back over the Rappahannock river. Charles Francis Adams Jr.'s cavalry regiment was on the other side, part of the skeleton force of mounted troops Hooker had kept behind. He initially discounted the tales from the abject stragglers who stopped to ask for food or shelter, but 'in the afternoon came the crusher', he told his father. They received the order to saddle up and return to their old camp. They found it 'deserted, burned up, filthy, and surrounded with dead horses. We tied up our horses and stood dismally round in the pouring rain.'[9]

Henry Hore arrived at Fortress Monroe on Hampton Roads a few days later, on 9 May, a young man no longer.[10] The magnitude of Hooker's defeat was numbing: 17,000 casualties to Lee's 13,000, without gaining the slightest moral or tactical advantage. Lincoln was horror-struck when he read the telegram, exclaiming, 'My God, my God, what will the country say?' The press was predictably harsh: 'Everybody feels', wrote Joseph Medill, the editor of the *Chicago Tribune* and a close friend of the President's, 'that the war is drawing to a disastrous and disgraceful termination.'[11] The *New York World* railed that the 'gallant Army of the Potomac' had been 'marched to fruitless slaughter' by 'an imbecile department and led by an incompetent general'.[12]

The country's frustration with its leaders only made the gratitude felt towards the volunteers all the deeper and more profound. A flotilla of boats swarmed the troop ship carrying the 9th New York Volunteers as it approached the Battery at the southern tip of Manhattan. Thousands of well-wishers lined the pier, throwing flowers and waving flags, and a military band escorted the soldiers along Broadway to Union Square. The men were still wearing their filthy uniforms from the siege at Suffolk, but their dishevelled appearance seemed to delight the crowds. This was the enthusiastic reception that the 700 survivors of the regiment had been imagining for weeks. On 20 May 1863, George Henry Herbert handed over his weapon at the Armoury, shook hands with his comrades one last time and walked away. After a disastrous beginning that had made him the butt of the regiment's jokes, Herbert had grown to love his life in the army. He sailed for England richer by $400, ready to start life afresh.

Lee had maintained a sanguine demeanour throughout the battle – until the moment he learned that Stonewall Jackson had been shot. Jackson had been reconnoitring positions when he accidentally galloped into his own picket line. The nervous Confederate guards shot blindly at the group, killing several riders and striking Jackson. Two bullets had torn through his left arm; another had hit his right wrist. He was also dragged along by his horse and dropped by his stretcher-bearers. The damage to his left arm was irreparable; the limb had to be amputated the next morning. Lee sent Jackson a message via the chaplain, begging him to recover quickly, adding, 'He has lost his left arm, but I have lost my right arm.' As soon as doctors deemed he could be moved, Jackson was loaded onto an ambulance and taken on a 27-mile journey to a plantation at Guinea Station.

Francis Lawley followed behind, arriving at the plantation on 7 May. Jackson had been moved to the estate office where he could recuperate in private. 'With a beating heart I rode up to ask after him,' wrote Lawley. The doctor stepped outside so that he could speak plainly: the General's wife and infant daughter were inside. Jackson had appeared to be recovering but late the previous night the classic signs of pneumonia had set in. Lawley knew what this meant: 'I gave up all hope of his recovery.' The news was so powerful that he felt winded. He sat heavily on the ground with 'a mist in my eyes and a sense of suffocation rising in my throat'.[13]

Lawley could not bear to wait for the end, and boarded one of the trains taking the wounded back to Richmond. On 8 May he sent a letter to the Confederate Secretary of War, James Seddon, warning him of Jackson's desperate condition. Two days later, on the 10th, Jackson died. Lee cried when he learned the news; there was not a man or woman, North or South, who failed to understand the meaning of Jackson's death or his vital importance to the Confederacy.*

The loss of Jackson posed a dilemma for Lawley. If he made too much of it in his reports, readers might think that the South had suffered a mortal blow. Yet here was an opportunity to create a mythic figure whose heroic end would elevate the entire Southern cause. Lawley did his best, eulogizing Jackson as both an earthly saint and military genius whose death would only inspire the South to 'deeds of more than mortal valor'. (Unfortunately, the blockade was playing havoc with Lawley's dispatches; his obituary of Jackson reached London before the news of his shooting.[15])

Lawley was so concerned about presenting Jackson's death in the best possible light that he deliberately obscured the gravity of the situation out west. On 19 May 1863 he finally revealed to the English public that Vicksburg might not be impregnable after all. The news was 'contrary to my own and the general anticipation', Lawley admitted at the end of yet another article on Stonewall Jackson. US General Grant had won a series of tactical victories, beginning with a successful night raid by the Union navy on 16 April, which enabled the fleet to steam up the Mississippi river, past Vicksburg's thirty-one guns. Grant stopped all the useless digging and canal building and set his army loose against the Confederates. On 1 May his troops crushed the small force holding the town of Port Gibson, 30 miles south of Vicksburg. Suddenly it was as though the wind was at their backs. The Federal army raced towards Vicksburg, fighting four battles in seventeen days, swatting aside the Confederates' resistance. US General Sherman razed most of Jackson, the capital of Mississippi, on 14 May, in a fiery portent of what was to come in 1864.

---

* In his history of the Civil War, Winston Churchill wrote: 'Chancellorsville was the finest battle which Lee and Jackson fought together. Their combination had become perfect.'[14]

Grant's success frightened Richmond, but there was no agreement on how he should be stopped. Longstreet thought they should provoke a battle against the Union Army of the Cumberland, which was stationed in Tennessee. This, he argued, would force Grant to divide his forces between the two theatres. Jefferson Davis wanted to send reinforcements to the two Confederate generals defending Mississippi, John Pemberton and Joseph E. Johnston (now fully recovered from his bullet wound). But Lee had his own plan, one so bold and risky that its very audaciousness made any other suggestion appear timid and lacklustre. He proposed to lead his army north again – for an invasion of Pennsylvania. The State was unprotected; Hooker would have to withdraw from Virginia to defend Washington. At the very worst the North would look vulnerable to its own citizens and, possibly, in the eyes of the international community, incapable of winning the war. The Confederate Cabinet debated Lee's proposal for two days and at last agreed, with only the Postmaster General, John Reagan, dissenting. Davis decided that Vicksburg would have to be reinforced with regiments from all parts of the South except Virginia.

In May 1863 Frank Vizetelly was on board one of the relief trains carrying troops to Vicksburg. He was going out west, Vizetelly informed his readers, because 'The campaign in the valley of the Mississippi will, I believe, decide the duration of the war.'[16] He offered no explanation as to why he had missed the Battle of Chancellorsville. Given the state of his debts and his propensity to fall off the wagon, Vizetelly's absence and his sudden decision to go to Vicksburg were probably connected. The train juddered slowly across Georgia and Mississippi, the track so worn and buckled in places that it was derailed three times. On the last, Vizetelly was thrown hard against the carriage and suffered a concussion. For an hour or two he thought his arm was broken and was relieved to find it only badly bruised. The engineers managed to keep the train going until they reached Jackson, Mississippi, 45 miles east of Vicksburg. Sherman's departure was so recent that the city was still burning. Nothing of any value was intact, certainly nothing that might repair the damaged train. 'The Yankees were guilty of every kind of vandalism,' Vizetelly wrote with indignation. 'They sacked houses, stole clothing from the negroes, burst open their trunks, and took what little money they had.' Now he was not sure where to go. The news from

Train with reinforcements for CS General Johnston running off the tracks in
the forests of Mississippi, by Frank Vizetelly

Vicksburg was ominous. The Federal army had surrounded the hilltop
town: CS General John Pemberton's army of 30,000 men was holed up
inside, along with 3,000 luckless civilians. The Confederate army had
enough rations to last sixty days. The fatherless families who cowered
in its midst, on the other hand, had only their gardens, their fast-
emptying cupboards and, in the final resort, their pets. Vizetelly decided
he had no choice but to stay in and around Jackson. His exploration
of the surrounding countryside revealed dozens of dismal encampments,
where women and children had clustered together for protection. It was
an unexpected sight, he wrote; 'Ladies who have been reared in luxury'
were living rough like country peasants, 'with nothing but a few yards of
canvas to protect them from the frequent thunderstorms which burst in
terrific magnificence at this season of the year over Mississippi.'[17]

Only two months before, Northern newspapers had branded Grant
a failure and a drunk. But since then he had marched 130 miles and

won every battle. Charles A. Dana, the observer sent by Lincoln and Stanton to Grant's headquarters, had seen much that troubled him: the callous, even brutal, attitude towards the sick appalled him, but he never saw Grant incapacitated. In fact, closer acquaintance made Dana appreciate the General's particular genius for waging war without ever faltering or second-guessing himself. This determined quality was indispensable once Grant reached Vicksburg: his first assault on 19 May was a dismal failure. A thousand Federal soldiers fell in the attack but not a foot was gained. On the second attempt, three days later, he lost another 3,000 men. Grant insisted that the army remain where it was. But he also refused to request a flag of truce to allow the wounded to be collected. The injured lay strewn among the dead for two days. The only witness to their suffering was the harsh sun, which putrefied the dead and flayed the living. Finally driven mad by the screams and stench from the ditches, the Confederates sent a message to Grant, begging him 'in the name of humanity' to rescue his men.[18]

It then dawned on Grant that all he had to do was be patient and starve out the inhabitants. Inside the town, no one believed such a calamity would come to pass. General Pemberton and his men were waiting for General Johnston to lead his army to their rescue. But the cantankerous Johnston had warned Pemberton not to retreat to Vicksburg, and now that it had happened, he wrote off the town and the army as lost. Nothing, not even urgent telegrams from President Davis and Secretary of War Seddon, could make Johnston change his mind and risk his small force of 24,000 men against a Federal army three times the size. His one concession was to send out a request for volunteers to sneak supplies through the Federal lines into Vicksburg. Vizetelly accompanied some of the missions. These forays were exceedingly dangerous. The scouts had to crawl on their hands and knees in the dark for miles, 'avoiding every gleam of moonlight, and prepared at any moment to use the revolver or the knife'. Many previous attempts, Vizetelly informed his readers, had ended with the volunteers being either captured or shot. During one particular mission, the intrepid band scrambled along gorges and through pathless woods until they were 12 miles from Vicksburg. There they left Vizetelly and disappeared into a ravine. 'As I lay on the ground in the calm, quiet night I could distinctly hear sounds of musketry between the loud booming of mortars,' he wrote. Whether that meant success or failure he could not tell and would not know until the next day.[19]

Shells continually rained down on Vicksburg, shaking nerves and buildings alike. Parishioners of St Paul's Catholic church attended Mass even though the church was dangerously situated on one of the highest points of the town. On one occasion a shell crashed through a window and exploded above the altar. Stunned but unhurt, Father John Bannon managed to calm his screaming congregation and continue with the service.[20] The townspeople retreated to their cellars and to caves dug deep into the hillside, but there was no respite from the thunderous noise. Afterwards witnesses wrote in wonder at the little touches of comfort people added to their caves. As the siege went on rugs, chairs and even beds were dragged underground. But bravado, enterprise and fortitude ultimately gave way to hunger, fear and despair.

The barrage was not all one way. As long as they had shells, the gunners in Vicksburg had their choice of sitting targets outside. Each time he led his wagon trains out to forage, Ebenezer Wells, the English wagon master of the New York 79th, bade a final farewell to his friends. On several occasions he returned to camp with bullets lodged in his saddle and blanket. 'Our over-tasked mule-teams', wrote an officer, 'were obliged to drag all the supplies under a broiling sun from the reeking banks of the Yazoo, or over the long road that wound through the hilly and desolate region.'[21] Sometimes Wells's teams made it back to the camp but not the sorely needed supplies, which had been left behind, along with a team of wounded or dying mules.

Among the Federal soldiers who held their breath as cannonballs whizzed over their heads was the Oxford doctor Charles Mayo. He was furious to be at Vicksburg. One of his former patients, Major-General George Hartsuff, had invited him to join his headquarters at Louisville, Kentucky. Mayo received permission for the transfer and was set to leave when he discovered that a clerk had written down the wrong department on his orders, sending him to General Grant instead of General Burnside. Hartsuff advised Mayo to go to Vicksburg anyway and wait for him to sort out the clerical error with the surgeon general.

Mayo caught typhus as soon as he arrived on 1 June. He put on a brave face for his family's sake, telling them that he had a nice tent 'pitched with that of the Medical Director of the Corps, under a pair of fine beech-trees on a hill', neglecting to mention that there were nine

Confederate scouts with percussion-caps for the garrison of Vicksburg,
running the Federal pickets, by Frank Vizetelly

others in the tent. He had been placed as staff surgeon-major and medical inspector of the 13th Army Corps, with 25,000 men under his care. Mayo found the survivors of the 22 May assault in a wretched state, many having been left to the mercy of unwilling and unsympathetic civilians. Ever practical, he immediately set about imposing some order on the shambolic situation. He had all the wounded collected and placed together under an open shed made of rough poles and boards. For beds, he copied an innovation found in a deserted Confederate camp and used cane poles and strips of bark plaited together to make a mat. The contraption was strong enough to support a man's weight and flexible enough to conform to his body.

The army medical department was more of a hindrance than a help to him. But 'we had one excellent and trustworthy friend', he wrote, 'namely, the Sanitary Commission'. The volunteer organization had depots and agents for every army in the field. 'The principal agent with Grant's army was a thoroughly good fellow, and consequently was of very great use to us, indeed without the aid of his supplies the sick must

have suffered far more than they did,' Mayo wrote. The medical department always had an excuse, and whatever it did send was never enough.
By contrast, the Sanitary Commission agent was so determined to secure
the very best for the injured that he even managed to haul ice from
Cincinnati to the camp, an unimaginable luxury in the searing heat. 'But
no man alive could have counteracted the effects of that climate,' wrote
Mayo. 'Malaria, salt pork, no vegetables, a blazing sun, and almost poisonous water, are agencies against which medicine is helpless. They soon
began to tell on myself, as they did on others much more nearly accustomed to the climate. The hope of being recalled also vanished.'[22]

Mayo's sense of duty kept him at his post but, by the middle of June,
he realized that if he did not do something about his situation he would
be dead by the autumn. He had become used to the constant shelling, but
the malarial conditions were sapping his strength. 'Vicksburg still holds
out,' he wrote miserably to his sister on 19 June. A week later Mayo had
become so desperate that he sent a plea for help to Lord Lyons. It embarrassed him to write to the Minister, particularly as Lyons had urged him
not to accept an officer's commission since it would put him beyond the
help of the legation: 'I was led to believe that I should have no difficulty
in getting an order of transfer to a climate in which I could be of some
use; if I had thought that they had intended to leave me here I would
have left the service rather than come. Now, however, I cannot pass the
lines of the army.' Mayo begged Lyons to pass on his letter of immediate
resignation to the Secretary of War. 'The reason why I apply to your
Lordship is that I know no other means of getting any attention paid
to my communication; nor would any communication addressed to
government officials be allowed to leave this dept except through the
military authorities, who are bound by the strict orders mentioned above
to obstruct it.'[23]

While Mayo looked to Washington for deliverance, the wilting Federal army turned its eyes to the South. Grant had been expecting General
Banks to steam up the Mississippi river; he was meant to have taken
Port Hudson by now and opened the way for joint river operations
against Vicksburg. Where was he? Washington had been asking the
same question. General Henry Halleck sent two angry letters to Banks,
expressing his disappointment 'that you and General Grant are not acting in conjunction'.[24] Banks had captured Alexandria, the State capital
of Louisiana, but Halleck dismissed this as a selfish quest for glory. The

judgement was unduly harsh; Banks was trying to devise a way of capturing Port Hudson that did not require a river attack. His first attempt on 27 May had resulted in almost 2,000 casualties compared to a Confederate loss of only 235. The total repulse mirrored Grant's disaster at Vicksburg a few days earlier, but Banks, at least, was prompt in retrieving the wounded.

Staff at Banks's headquarters noticed a precipitous drop in morale after the failed attack. The men had lost not only confidence in their General but also in themselves. Banks, on the other hand, saw no reason why he should not be more successful the second time around. He brought in additional artillery so that by 11 June he had more than 130 guns. Ever punctilious, he sent a letter to Confederate General Franklin Gardner inside the fort at Port Hudson, suggesting that he surrender to 'avoid unnecessary sacrifice of life'. Gardner declined, even though his men were already exhausted and starving.

On the 14th, Banks attacked Port Hudson for the second time. Colonel Currie's luck ran out at a place called 'Priest Cap'. His division commander, General William Emory, was hit first; the Englishman took his place, shouting 'Get on, Lads' as he ran forward towards the fort. Within minutes Currie was struck by bullets to both arms. Almost a hundred members of the 133rd went down behind him. Some 4,000 Federals were either killed or wounded that day.

Currie was rescued by his own men and dragged back to safety. His wounding came as a terrible blow to the regiment. He was no longer considered alien but eccentric; his English manner of speaking was regarded as quaint rather than foreign. General Emory wrote to him from his own hospital bed, saying,

> I shall now have the pleasure of making an earnest personal appeal to the president for your promotion for your splendid heroism on the 14th at Port Hudson – Although I had myself fallen long before your assaults, yet from the commencement until you fell, the agony of my own position was relieved by your heroic words of command, all of which were distinctly audible until you fell.

Another officer asserted that everyone was convinced 'the works of the enemy in your front would have been carried by your regiment, had you not so soon been wounded'.[25]

A hospital ship transported Currie down to New Orleans, where he

remained for a few weeks until he was well enough to be sent to Philadelphia to recuperate. It would be several months before he rejoined his
regiment. The survivors of the 133rd went about their duties without
enthusiasm. 'I think the hope of taking the port without force is a forlorn one,' wrote the regiment's assistant surgeon. 'General Banks has
offered a promotion and medals to one thousand who will volunteer to
storm their works . . . We can see their camps and their soldiers and also
the Secesh flag very plainly. We have the Fort completely surrounded
but I suppose they have enough provisions inside to last them probably
a year.' When the regiment left Baton Rouge there were 800 men and
officers; 'now we scarcely number 400'.[26] But Banks had no intention of
withdrawing until Port Hudson surrendered.

The Union and Confederate forces remained in their respective fortifications, slowly shrinking through disease and malnutrition. The only
general with the ability to move was Joseph Johnston, and he was in a
state of passive dejection. He had repeatedly urged Pemberton to evacuate Vicksburg, arguing that the town could always be retaken but his
army was irreplaceable. Grant's siege made escape impossible now; an
English army officer travelling through Mississippi asked Johnston
about his plans. The General replied, 'he was too weak to do any good,
and he was unable to give me any definite idea as to when he might be
strong enough to attack Grant'.[27] The officer, Lieutenant Colonel Arthur
James Lyon Fremantle, had arrived in the South on 8 April. This was the
first time he had encountered anything less than total optimism and
determination from a Confederate general. Fremantle's initial response
to the war had been one of casual interest. 'In common with many of my
countrymen, I felt very indifferent as to which side might win,' he wrote,
'but if I had any bias my sympathies were rather in favour of the North,
on account of the dislike which an Englishman naturally feels at the
idea of slavery.' His support for the North did not, however, survive
Seward's early misfires in international diplomacy: 'Soon a sentiment of
great admiration for the gallantry and determination of the Southerners, together with the unhappy contrast afforded by the foolish bullying
conduct of the Northerners, caused a complete revulsion in my feelings,
and I was unable to repress a strong wish to go to America and see
something of this wonderful struggle.'[28]

The 26-year-old officer applied for a leave of absence from his regiment, the Coldstream Guards, which had been stationed in Canada

since the *Trent* affair. In contrast to many of his fellow officers, Fremantle was only prepared to enter the South in a manner that did not violate the rules of neutrality. This ruled out running the blockade or slipping through Federal lines from the North. Such circumspect behaviour was typical of the young man. A keen sense of military honour was ingrained in the Fremantle family. His grandfather and father had both served in the army, and all his brothers were officers too.

Fremantle had been posted to Gibraltar as the assistant military secretary to the Governor when the US navy chased Commander Raphael Semmes in his first commerce raider, the CSS *Sumter* into port in January 1862. Semmes vividly remembered their meeting. The Governor sent Fremantle to present a memorandum to Semmes which outlined the strict rules of neutrality the authorities intended to observe towards both navies while the Federals and Confederates remained at Gibraltar. Having warned Semmes that no breech would be tolerated, Fremantle then confessed to him 'that he was an ardent Confederate, expressing himself without any reserve, and lauding in the highest terms our people and cause. He had many questions to ask me, which I took great pleasure in answering.'[29] Semmes probably gave Fremantle the idea of reaching the Confederacy via Mexico, where there was no blockade and therefore no laws against crossing into Southern territory.

The route from Matamoros through the Texas desert to San Antonio was exceptionally arduous. Fremantle may have chosen the most honourable way but it was also the most dangerous. The law, where it existed at all, was rough and imprecise, and Fremantle was careful to travel in company. His first act on reaching San Antonio was to sell his heavy trunk, along with most of his belongings. It made him less likely to be robbed, and it was obvious he was not going to need any formal attire.

Fermantle was 90 miles from Alexandria on 10 May when he encountered a pathetic trail of refugees fleeing the city after Banks's capture. He grew anxious that he might become trapped on the west side of the Mississippi and made a dash across the river. A Confederate steamboat took him part of the way, but for the final 30 miles he had to paddle upstream in a skiff with six other men. Fremantle finally reached Jackson, Mississippi on 18 May. By now he had only a small bag and the clothes on his back. As he walked past the still-smouldering Catholic church and the ruins of what had once been Jackson's principal hotel,

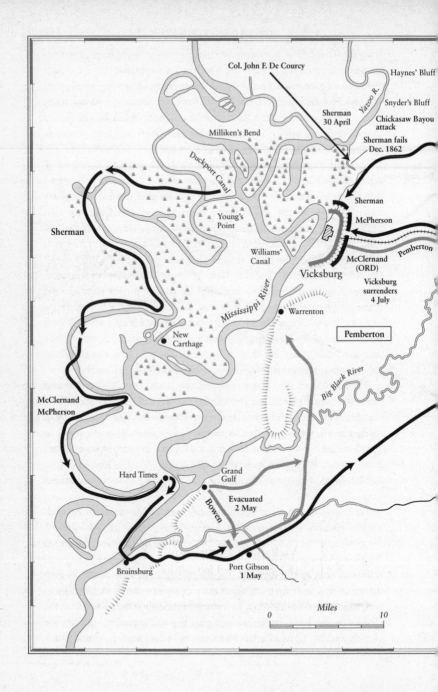

Col. John F. De Courcy

Haynes' Bluff

Snyder's Bluff

Sherman
30 April

Chickasaw Bayou
attack

Sherman fails
Dec. 1862

Yazoo R.

Milliken's Bend

Duckport Canal

Young's
Point

Sherman

Sherman

McPherson

Williams'
Canal

McClerland
(ORD)

Pemberton

Vicksburg

Vicksburg
surrenders
4 July

Mississippi River

Warrenton

Pemberton

New
Carthage

McClernand
McPherson

Big Black River

Hard Times

Grand
Gulf

Evacuated
2 May

Bowen

Bruinsburg

Port Gibson
1 May

Miles

0   10

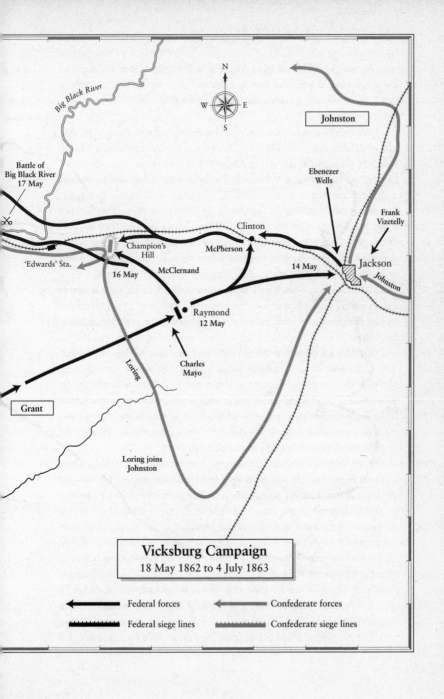

Big Black River

Battle of
Big Black River
17 May

Clinton

McPherson

Champion's
Hill

'Edwards' Sta.

16 May

McClernand

14 May

Ebenezer
Wells

Frank
Vizetelly

Jackson

Johnston

Johnston

Raymond
12 May

Loring

Charles
Mayo

Grant

Loring joins
Johnston

Vicksburg Campaign
18 May 1862 to 4 July 1863

Federal forces Confederate forces

Federal siege lines Confederate siege lines

he fell into the hands of local vigilantes who were eager to hang some-one. He was saved by an Irish doctor who pushed his way through the crowd, saying. 'I hate the British Government and the English nation, but if you are really an officer in the Coldstream Guards there is nothing I won't do for you.'[30]

Once the mob was satisfied that Fremantle was not a spy he was allowed to continue on his way. He reached General Johnston's head-quarters a couple of days after Grant's first assault on Vicksburg. The General seemed a little detached: 'He talks in a calm, deliberate and confident manner,' wrote Fremantle; 'to me he was extremely affable, but he certainly possesses the power of keeping people at a distance when he chooses, and his officers evidently stand in great awe of him.' When Johnston told Fremantle that they had nothing compared to the Federals, the British officer realized that he was speaking the literal truth. 'At present his only cooking-utensils consisted of an old coffee-pot and frying pan – both very inferior articles.' When they sat down to eat, Fremantle discovered 'there was only one fork (one prong deficient) between himself and Staff, and this was handed to me ceremoniously as the "guest"'.[31]

Fremantle encountered the same polite behaviour wherever he went. The Confederates were curious about him, and he was constantly pep-pered with questions, such as whether the Coldstream Guard really wore scarlet into battle. Inevitably someone always asked him whether he thought that British soldiers could fight as well or better. During one train journey there was a lively debate in the carriage as to whether the British could have defeated Lee at Fredericksburg.

On 28 May Fremantle arrived in Chattanooga, Tennessee, where General Bragg and his long-suffering army were encamped. He was not the only visitor at Bragg's headquarters. The staff introduced Fremantle to an unexpected guest: three days earlier, Clement Vallandigham, the dissident Democrat and leader of the so-called Copperheads, had been unceremoniously dumped in front of Confederate pickets and ordered by his Federal guards not to turn back. The exiled politician was out-raged at his treatment by the US government. On 1 May he had attended a rally in Ohio where he gave one of his usual anti-war speeches. It was a deliberate provocation, and General Burnside – who had been transferred to run the Department of Ohio, which oversaw all mili-tary matters across seven States from Wisconsin to West Virginia – fell into the trap. On 4 May Burnside sent soldiers to Vallandigham's house in Dayton. They smashed down his back door and dragged the politician off to a waiting train. Vallandigham's arrest had the effect that he was hoping for: newspapers throughout the Midwest declared him a martyr to free speech and freedom of conscience. Burnside hastily assembled a military tribunal of eight army officers to 'try' the case. It was a farce, Vallandigham indignantly told Fremantle; one of the officers was not even American. (The unknown officer was Colonel John Fitzroy De Courcy, who had returned to duty and was anxious to be of use to Burnside in the hope it would lead to his reinstatement with the 16th Ohio.)

The tribunal listened to the evidence for two days and came to a unanimous agreement on the defendant's guilt. They had more difficulty deciding what to do with him. One judge thought he ought to be shot, another suggested exile; eventually they agreed he should be imprisoned in a fort somewhere.[32] But the ensuing national uproar over Vallandigham's trial severely embarrassed the administration and Lincoln swiftly commuted the sentence to banishment. Yet Vallandigham had no wish to be in the South. He had been made, in Fremantle's words, 'a destitute stranger' in his own country. General Bragg was puzzled how to treat his reluctant visitor; Vallandigham's platform of compromise and reunion was no more popular in the South than Lincoln's policy of forced reunion. He was relieved to learn that Vallandigham wished to travel to Bermuda, where it would be possible for him to take ship to Canada. Vallandigham preferred not mix with his hosts while they waited for permission from Richmond to allow him to travel to Wilmington. He did not consider himself a Confederate sympathizer and was not interested in meeting foreign supporters of the South; he politely declined an introduction to the sole English volunteer on Bragg's staff.

Colonel Fremantle, on the other hand, was delighted to meet his compatriot. 'Ever since I landed in America, I had heard of the exploits of an Englishman called Colonel St. Leger Grenfell,' he wrote on 30 May, two days after his arrival at Bragg's headquarters. 'This afternoon I made his acquaintance, and I consider him one of the most extraordinary characters I ever met. Although he is a member of a well-known English family, he seems to have devoted his whole life to the exciting career of a soldier of fortune.' Grenfell was Bragg's inspector-general of cavalry, having left the raiding outfit led by the Confederate guerrilla John Hunt Morgan the previous Christmas. Fremantle was surprised to learn that Grenfell was 55 years old and that he had a wife (who had thrown up her hands some years before and was running a successful girls' school in Paris) and two grown-up daughters.[33] Grenfell told Fremantle that he had fought the Barbary pirates in Morocco, followed Garibaldi in South America and joined the Turks against the Russians in the Crimea. The last was undoubtedly true, as he had been Colonel De Courcy's brigade-major in the Turkish Contingent.[34] Neither Grenfell nor De Courcy ever knew that their paths had again crossed during the Federal occupation of the Cumberland Gap.

'Even in this army,' wrote Fremantle,

> which abounds with foolhardy and desperate characters, he has acquired the admiration of all ranks by his reckless daring and gallantry in the field. Both Generals Polk and Bragg spoke to me of him as a most excellent and useful officer, besides being a man who never lost an opportunity of trying to throw his life away. He is just the sort of a man to succeed in this army, and among the soldiers his fame for bravery has outweighed his unpopularity as a rigid disciplinarian. He is the terror of all absentees, stragglers and deserters, and of all commanding officers who are unable to produce for his inspection the number of horses they have been drawing forage for.

Grenfell always wore a red cap, which made him conspicuous in battle and therefore more esteemed among the officers. Forty years later, Bragg's cavalry chief, Major-General Joseph Wheeler, still retained his admiration for the Englishman. He wrote to Grenfell's daughter in 1901, telling her, 'your father was one of the bravest and best officers in the Confederate Army. A man of chivalry and generosity. If he had a fault it was his great fondness for adventure.'[35]

Grenfell took Fremantle on a tour of the outposts. During the ride he was frank about the army's deficiencies, as well as his own troubles: 'He told me he was in desperate hot water with the civil authorities of the State, who had accused him of illegally impressing and appropriating horses, and also of conniving at the escape of a Negro from his lawful owner, and he said that the military authorities were afraid or unable to give him proper protection.' Three days later, on 3 June, 'Grenfell came to see me in a towering rage,' wrote Fremantle. He had been arrested. 'General Bragg himself had stood bail for him, but Grenfell was naturally furious at the indignity. But, even according to his own account, he seems to have acted indiscreetly in the affair of the Negro, and he will have to appear before the civil court next October. General Polk and his officers were all much vexed at the occurrence.'[36] Bragg's surety was misspent. A week later, Grenfell packed his bags and disappeared. No one heard anything of him for three months.

By then, Fremantle had already left for the East. After another tortuous train ride, which had the single distinguishing feature of a female soldier in their midst, he arrived at Charleston.* One of the first people to greet him was Captain Henry Feilden. Fremantle was amazed to come across another English volunteer. 'A Captain Feilden came to call upon me at 9 a.m,' he wrote in his diary. 'I remember his brother quite well at Sandhurst.'[37] The younger Feilden seemed entranced with the South. Naturally, Freemantle could not know of the momentous event that had taken place in Feilden's life that week: Miss Julia McCord of Greenville, South Carolina, had visited the office, seeking a military pass to visit her brother.

* While Fremantle was in Charleston, the local newspapers reported: 'The Western army correspondent of the "Mobile Register" writes as follows:–The famous Colonel St. Leger Grenfell, who served with Morgan last summer, and since that time has been Assistant Inspector-general of General Bragg, was arrested a few days since by the civil authorities . . . If the charges against him are proven true, then there is no doubt that the course of General Bragg will be to dismiss him from his Staff; but if, on the contrary, malicious slanders are defaming this ally, he is Hercules enough and brave enough to punish them. His bravery and gallantry were conspicuous throughout the Kentucky campaign, and it is hoped that this late tarnish on his fame will be removed; or if it be not, that he will."'

The Eve of Battle

A message to the shipbuilders – British reaction to Jackson's death – Henry Hotze resurgent – All eyes on Lee – Sir Percy Wyndham finds glory at Brandy Station – A lost boy

'My father heard about your going out to America to see me,' the Marquis of Hartington wrote to Skittles after his return to London in early spring. 'He has been told all about the whole thing, which he had no notion of before ... [and] is in a terrible state about it,' he added disingenuously. 'I told him you had given me up and he knows that I am very unhappy.' The truth, as they both knew, was that he was gently putting his mistress aside, or at least was trying to, with so far limited success.[1] Yet Hartington would not have the luxury of dithering for much longer; he had received an invitation from Lord Palmerston to join the government, which would mean assuming greater responsibilities while enjoying fewer of life's pleasures. 'I think it would be a most horrible nuisance,' he wrote.[2] On 13 April 1863, however, the decision was made for Hartington by the unexpected death of George Cornewall Lewis, the Secretary for War.* Earl de Grey was promoted from Under-Secretary to Secretary, and Hartington was offered de Grey's former position, an honour not even he could refuse.[3]

---

* It was the second tragedy to strike the Lewis family. Lewis's daughter had died in childbirth some weeks before, leaving the infant son to be brought up by her grieving husband, William Vernon Harcourt. The double loss (Lewis had been like a father to Harcourt) led to Harcourt's temporary withdrawal from public life. He stopped writing his pro-Northern essays, which had appeared in *The Times* under the pen name 'Historicus'. He remained a widower until 1876, when he married Elizabeth Motley, the daughter of the American historian John Lothrop Motley.

A certificate for the Seven Per Cent Cotton Loan, signed by Emile Erlanger and J. Henry Schroeder, and by Colin McRace and John Slidell for the Confederacy

The Confederates in England had reviled Lewis ever since his speech against recognition the previous November. They were not sure what de Grey or Hartington might achieve for their cause, but the simple fact of there being two more known supporters in positions of power was enough to rescue the Confederates from their gloom. Nothing had gone right for them since the launch of the Erlanger-sponsored cotton bonds in March, and these had ultimately proven to be a disappointment. Rumours spread by Federal agents that Jefferson Davis intended to default on the bonds had caused the price to plummet. Only secret buying on a massive scale by the Confederates was keeping them at a reasonable level. Charles Prioleau, the director of Fraser, Trenholm, was beside himself. 'All the "warm Southern men" sold right and left,' he complained.[4]

The secret ship-construction programme had also suffered a spate of reversals. A week after the *Georgia*'s escape on 1 April, Matthew Fontaine Maury learned that John, his eldest son, was missing at Vicksburg and presumed dead. 'Oh my dear, dear wife,' he wrote, 'my heart is gone from me.'* Maury's only mementoes of his lost son John were a short letter and his old winter coat, which had been shortened to fit 12-year-old Brave; this at least 'has its memories', he wrote.[5] Heartbroken, Maury abandoned London and went with Brave to live in Bowdon, on the outskirts of Manchester, refusing to see anyone except his closest friends. Almost simultaneously, the government impounded the *Alexandra* in Liverpool, which Fraser, Trenholm had intended to donate to the Confederate navy; and James Bulloch heard that the former paymaster of the *Alabama*, a man called Clarence Yonge, had decided to exact revenge for his dismissal by telling both the Federals and the British government everything he knew about the Confederates' operations.

Bulloch tried to guess what his enemies would learn from Yonge. The Lairds rams currently under construction would be safe, he thought, since Yonge had left England the previous July: 'I do not think he was ever in the Birkenhead works, or that he has any personal knowledge of what is going on there. He surely can have no knowledge of the *Alexandra*.'[6] But the government's evident willingness to use Yonge to build its case against the *Alexandra* made Bulloch fearful that the era of

---

* John had disappeared while leading a reconnaissance mission at Vicksburg. A friend on the Federal side made enquiries but could find no record of his capture. An investigation after the war found evidence that he had run into a Federal scouting party, which shot him and dumped his body.

legal loopholes and fly-by-night escapes had passed. He became convinced of this towards the end of April, after Charles Francis Adams was allowed to commit a serious diplomatic blunder without incurring any official sanction.

Shortly after the seizure of the *Alexandra*, Adams had written in his diary, 'The course of the government has raised the whole hive of sympathizers, as it was never stirred before. What with the case of the *Alexandra*, and that of the *Peterhoff* . . . the effect is to stimulate ill temper [and] the greater the necessity of keeping as quiet and calm as possible.'[7] But instead of heeding his own advice, Adams became entangled in a blockade-running scandal involving two American gun-runners who were shipping arms to Mexico. Admiral Wilkes's capture of the *Peterhoff* had made insurance for sailing in Mexican waters prohibitive for small firms. The gun-runners, General Juan Napoleon Zerman and Colonel Bertram B. Howell, asked Adams to provide them with an affidavit stating they were aiding the Mexicons and not the South. This, they hoped, would lower their insurance premium since their ship would no longer be at risk of capture by the US navy. In spite of Moran's warnings, Adams not only provided Howell and Zerman with a letter of indemnity, but also embellished it with pointed jabs at Lloyds for underwriting 'dishonest enterprises' such as blockade-running.[8] As is so often the case with compromising letters, one copy became several. The letter went from Lloyds to the owners of the *Peterhoff*, thence to the Foreign Office, and finally to *The Times*.

The press called Adams a hypocrite for protesting against British arms sales to the South while secretly helping Americans to supply Mexico. One newspaper wondered if he was selling protection; another accused him of plotting to drive British shipping from the Americas. *The Times* returned to its favourite theme of Northern hypocrisy. The paper often reminded its readers of the example set during the Crimean War, when President Franklin Pierce had rebuffed Britain's protests over the shipments of American-made weapons to the Russians with the retort: 'Americans sold munitions of war to all buyers without troubling themselves about the ports to which the goods would be consigned, or the purposes to which they would be put.'

This, and no more, is what we have done ourselves [argued *The Times*]. We have served the Federals and we have served the Confederates, each customer according to his wants. The Federals wanted weapons to equip an army. The Confederates wanted a ship to begin a navy ... the Washington Government will find it hard to impeach as a crime what is simply a repetition of its own deliberate proceedings.*[9]

The French also issued a strong protest over Adams's letter to the US Minister in Paris. The Foreign Office was incensed with Adams and thought 'his explanation of it ... very lame'. The embarrassed Ministry desperately tried to stave off a debate on the subject but finally yielded on 23 April. Aided by the Tories, pro-Southern MPs excoriated the government for allowing the North's envoy to become 'the Minister for Commerce in England'. One sarcastically remarked that Adams's notion 'of honesty and neutrality is remarkable. Every thing is honest to suit his own purposes.' Some of the speeches that followed were so insulting towards the North that the Speaker of the House later apologized to Adams. Calm was restored only after Palmerston and Russell assured their respective listeners in the Commons and the Lords that Seward would disavow Adams's 'extraordinary' and 'unwarrantable' act.

The government had to work hard to stifle the controversy, muzzling its party members and planting stories in the press that the Foreign Office was satisfied with Adams's protestations of innocence. Palmerston twisted Delane's arm into having *The Times* imply that Howell and Zerman had tricked Adams. But none of these efforts to protect Adams diminished his sense of grievance. He remained convinced that his behaviour had been above reproof and for weeks afterwards badgered Lord Russell to retract his speech in the Lords. Henry Adams loyally supported his father, telling his brother Charles Francis Jr., 'When the whole *Peterhoff* story is told, we shall reverse everything and overwhelm these liars.'[10] Nevertheless, he could see that his father was floundering, and was relieved when the prominent New York lawyer William M. Evarts arrived on 1 May. Evarts was one of Seward's closest political confidants and had been sent by him to liaise with the Crown prosecution lawyers in the *Alexandra* trial. But instead of bolstering Charles Francis Adam's confidence, Evarts's arrival had sent him into further decline: he was the fourth US agent to arrive that spring. Henry could joke

* The pro-Russian President Pierce further irritated Britain and France by offering to mediate an armistice between them and Russia.

about having a 'complete Cabinet of Ministerial advisers and assistants', but he was not the one whose competence appeared to be in doubt.

Hartington's maiden speech as the new Under–Secretary for War took place on 14 May 1863. He managed to arrive late for the debate – regarding a bill to regulate the country's volunteer militias – and without his papers, but the House appeared to accept his apology once he demonstrated a sound grasp of the subject. The Confederate sympathizers in the Commons held their breaths, waiting to see whether he might use the opportunity to praise the South; finally, after keeping them in suspense until the end of his speech, Hartington fulfilled their hopes by making a long and favourable comparison between English volunteer soldiers and the brave fighting material he had recently seen in the Confederacy. By itself, Hartington's speech was a minor event, but its timing turned out to be extremely fortunate for the South, coming as it did four days before the news of Lee's victory at Chancellorsville. James Mason's supporters in Parliament were so elated that they immediately laid plans to rattle the government again about Admiral Wilkes and Northern interference with British ships in the West Indies. In France, a friendly meeting with the Spanish Ambassador lifted Commissioner Slidell's spirits.

It was the news of Stonewall Jackson's death, however, which made the Confederates spring into action. They were amazed and delighted by the spontaneous outpouring of public grief in England. Newspapers carried long eulogies to the fallen hero; *The Times* even compared Jackson's death to Admiral Nelson's at Trafalgar. Flags flew at half mast at many cotton mills. Public expressions of sympathy were hastily drawn up for Jackson's widow. The unexpected intensity of the reaction delivered the Confederates from their despair even as it threw the US legation and its supporters into deeper vexation. The querulous Liberal MP John Roebuck, whose youthful affection for America had changed in his old age to a blazing dislike, held a mass meeting in Sheffield that voted to recognize the Confederacy. A few days later, on 1 June, the pro-Confederate owner of the *Saturday Review*, Alexander Beresford Hope, formed a committee calling itself the 'British Jackson Monumental Fund'. Beresford Hope, whose support for the Confederacy stemmed from a misguided belief that its political system was more aristocratic than the Union's, announced that the fund was going to commission the Irish sculptor

John Foley, designer of the Albert Memorial in Hyde Park, to make a statue of Stonewall Jackson which would be presented to the people of Virginia upon completion.* Not to be outdone, publishing houses hastily called for biographies of the General. The race was won by the English governess stranded in Richmond during Lord Edward St Maur's visit, Catherine Hopley, who pipped the competition with her *Stonewall Jackson,* published in August.[12]

The Confederates also regarded it as a good sign that the newest of their three cruisers, the *Georgia,* had made contact with the *Alabama* in Brazil. The vessels had met in the harbour of Bahia quite by chance. 'Day broke and we found ourselves very near two men-of-war,' wrote James Morgan.

> What was their nationality? It seemed an age before the hour for colors arrived, but when it did, to our great delight, the most rakish-looking of the two warships broke out the Stars and Bars! 'It is the Alabama!' we gasped, and commenced to dance with delight. The officers hugged one another, each embracing a man of his own rank, except the captain and myself. Like the commander, I was the only one of my rank aboard, so I hugged myself.[13]

The ship-owner William Schaw Lindsay had succeeded William Gregory as the Confederacy's chief political lobbyist in the Commons. He was a safer choice than Roebuck, less volatile and more popular among his fellow MPs. Lindsay was elated by the commotion over Jackson's death, believing it meant the country was ready to recognize Southern independence. He invited Mason and Roebuck down to his estate in Surrey for a concentrated weekend of plotting. The three of

---

* The wealthy Beresford Hope and his brother-in-law Lord Robert Cecil, the future Marquis of Salisbury and Prime Minister, were both haunted by the fear that American-style democracy might one day infect British politics. But whenever Beresford Hope adopted a cause, he embraced it with fanatical intensity. He romanticized the South to an absurd degree, publishing three pamphlets in support of its independence. 'I honestly and entirely believe,' he wrote, 'that the cause which will tend to the confirmation of all the evils of slavery, is that of the North, and that the cause which is most likely to prove a benefit to the slave, and in the end relieve him of his shackles, is that of the South.' The statue of Stonewall Jackson was not finished until 1874. But Beresford Hope had remained committed to the project and paid the shipping costs. The unveiling ceremony took place in Richmond, Virginia the following year in front of 50,000 people, including many survivors of Jackson's command.[11]

them mulled over their various options. Should they approach the Tories first? Or try to persuade the Emperor to rekindle the idea of an Anglo-French initiative? The Poles were still agitating for independence from Russia; what did this mean for British foreign policy? After many hours of intense discussion, the three men agreed upon an ambitious plan. The English MPs would be in charge of whipping up public support, to which James Spence and Henry Hotze would contribute their own unique skills. Roebuck also agreed to approach the Tories to find out whether they would be willing to make recognition a party issue. Mason, meanwhile, was to go to France and meet with Slidell, who, with luck, might be able to elicit a message of support from the Emperor.

Roebuck wasted little time. In the first week of June he met with Benjamin Disraeli, who said all the things that an Opposition leader would when offered the chance of attacking the government, without actually committing himself or his party to a change in their policy of non-interference in the American war. But this was encouragement enough for Roebuck, who gave notice in the House of his intention to revisit the question of recognition. The debate was slated for the end of June. The Confederates took the news with a degree of caution. Roebuck was an asset to the extent that the MP represented himself as a Man of the People, but (in the words of one observer) vanity was 'written all over his face when you came near it'. They trembled at the idea of letting Roebuck loose in the Commons without an explicit move by the French beforehand. John Slidell drew up a memorandum for Louis-Napoleon's attention, which outlined all the reasons why an independent South suited French interests, and requested an interview.

When Mason returned to England he found Waterloo Station plac-arded with posters depicting the British Union Jack crossed with the Confederate flag. Hackney cab drivers were displaying the emblems in miniature. Hotze was working at a feverish pace, distributing posters, placards and circulars up and down the country. The *Morning Herald* and the *Standard* agreed to print editorials demanding recognition every other day until the debate. Spence was also in his element. During the past two years he had changed from being a businessman of no great talent or success into a canny political operator, respected by the South-erners in England and feared by the Northern lobby. For the new push in Parliament, Spence formed two separate organizations. One was a respectable club, called the Manchester Southern Club, whose purpose was to distribute Confederate material in the north of England. The other was his own private army of agitators. The group successfully broke up an abolitionist meeting at the Manchester Free Trade Hall. 'These parties are not the rich spinners but young men of energy with a taste for agitation but little money,' Spence wrote to Mason.

> It appears to my judgment that it would be wise not to stint money in aiding this effort to expose cant and diffuse the truth. Manchester is naturally the centre of such a move and you will see there are here the germs of important work – but they need to be tended and fostered. I have supplied a good deal of money individually but I see room for the use of 30 or 40 pounds a month or more.[14]

Almost no one outside the legation had the least suspicion that public opinion was being cleverly manipulated. 'The intelligence of the country is now unanimous in our favor,' Henry Hotze wrote proudly. He was exaggerating his success, but there had been an undeniable shift back towards the South since the initial excitement aroused by Lincoln's Emancipation Proclamation at the beginning of the year. Hotze's genius lay in his understanding of who and what constituted fashionable opinion. He knew how to portray the South in ways that appealed to particular constituencies, such as the clergy, university students, journalists, actors and artists, whom he considered to be natural proselytizers as well as role models. The Ladies' London Emancipation Society tried to beat Hotze at his own game by distributing more than 100,000 copies of excerpts from Fanny Kemble's plantation diary, but neither they nor the indefatigable Harriet Martineau could match Hotze's tentacle-like connection with the press. By early May, Martineau had given up trying to change the North's poor image in England and was concentrating on the message 'that it is not necessary to admire the Yankees very much to be on their side in the quarrel'.[15]

Hotze was being helped, of course, by the absence of pro-Northern English journalists covering the war in America. Since Charles Mackay's arrival in America to replace the *Times*'s ailing New York correspondent, J. C. Bancroft Davis, he had been obediently sending back articles that showed the North in a poor light. The managing editor, Mowbray Morris, was pleased with the reports, telling Mackay, 'Your views are entirely in accordance with those of the paper and I believe of the

Southern refugees camping in the woods near Vicksburg, by Frank Vizetelly

majority in this country.'[16] (The Mowbray fortune had disappeared almost overnight after emancipation released the slaves on the family's sugar plantation in the West Indies.) Francis Lawley was treading a far more precarious line. He was writing his reports to make it seem as though a Confederate victory was inevitable; but he was also trying to force the government's hand by provoking public outrage over Southern suffering. (Henry Adams was one of the few people who saw through him. 'His dread of the shedding of blood makes him wonderfully anxious for intervention,' he commented sarcastically to Charles Francis Jr. 'Mr. Lawley's humanity doesn't quite explain his earnestness.'[17])

The combination of Lawley's eyewitness reports and Frank Vizetelly's emotive drawings acted powerfully on the public conscience. 'I assure you the sympathy of all England is with the South and I think justly so,' a housekeeper from Manchester informed her relatives in Michigan. '[The Northerners] are jealous of us as a mightier nation and hate us because we do not take their part, but it is a family quarrel and they must make it up themselves.'[18] At the other end of the social spectrum, the Hon. Lucy Lyttelton, at the time an impressionable 22-year-old debutante, was shocked to discover that not everyone supported the South. 'During dinner America was the topic,' she wrote in her diary on 13 June 1863 while staying with the Duchess of Sutherland at Cliveden. 'The Duke and Duchess [of Argyll] are Northern! in their sympathies.' Lucy did not feel confident enough to argue with them or with the widowed William Harcourt, the other guest present. 'It does make one's heart ache to think of such grief,' she wrote; 'he joins in conversation, and puts on no affectations of sorrow; but his face tells it all. The little baby lives.'[19] Henry Hotze could not have hoped for a more positive reception to his propaganda. On 19 June the *Bradford Observer* asked how was it that the South won the moral argument: 'We have men really wishing for the universal abolition of slavery expressing earnest wishes for the success of the section of a nation who are the most deeply tainted with the crime of slavery.'

Yet the Confederate lobby was still not satisfied. There was a rumour going around the Tory Party that the Emperor would not openly support the South. Roebuck and Lindsay agreed they had to receive a personal assurance from Louis-Napoleon himself before they exposed themselves to the massed ranks of the House. John Slidell prepared the ground for their meeting during his own interview with the Emperor on 18 June. Once again Louis-Napoleon said he hoped the South would win, not least because he considered the Confederates more supportive of his own venture in Mexico. He also agreed to allay the fears of the two English MPs. Slidell could almost hear the trumpets of independence in his ears. Two days later, on 20 June, Roebuck and Lindsay went to the Tuileries. James Spence had run through all the possible arguments with Roebuck in advance. The Emperor reassured them that he had not changed his mind. However, he added, his Cabinet was opposed to any sort of formal communication with London. It feared that Lord Russell might use the offer as leverage to gain favour with Seward. The French Ambassador had been instructed to make only an informal approach about a joint move between the two countries.

In London, James Spence attended a campaign dinner for nearly sixty guests given by Beresford Hope. He sat between the publisher John Murray and the Whig politician Lord Elcho, both of whom made flattering remarks about his *Times* articles. But Spence could not enjoy himself while the Tories' participation remained an open question. 'The news by the mail may have a good effect if important,' he wrote to Charles Prioleau.[20] The Confederate lobby discussed whether they should go ahead without the Conservative Party and simply rely on the Emperor's promised support. Mason, Hotze and Spence were also worried about the *Alexandra* trial, which they feared might throw out something embarrassing or prejudicial at precisely the wrong moment.

The trial began on 22 June, with the Crown prosecution laying out the facts against the ship. Lord Russell had moved the trial to London, certain that Liverpool would never allow a conviction against one of its own. The city, he wrote in exasperation, was 'addicted to Southern proclivities, foreign slave trade, and domestic bribery'.[21] The *Alexandra* was, said the Solicitor-General, Sir Roundell Palmer, obviously a vessel built for war. To bolster his argument, he produced Clarence Yonge, the ex-paymaster of the *Alabama*, who admitted that James Bulloch and Fraser, Trenholm were in cahoots and confirmed that Confederate naval and military officers had the run of the company's headquarters. But Sir Hugh Cairns, Bulloch's defence lawyer, mercilessly tore Palmer apart. Despite the best efforts of Consul Dudley, the American lawyer William Evarts, the Home Office's Secret Service, the chief law officers and a Confederate turncoat, all the evidence produced was circumstantial. After three days of testimony, the case went to the jury on 25 June. Guided by the presiding judge, Justice Pollock (who happened to be a great friend of Lindsay's as well as a stickler for legal precedent), the jury found against the Crown; the seizure of the *Alexandra* was ruled to have been illegal. The Confederates and their supporters were jubilant. Pollock had interpreted the Foreign Enlistment Act to mean that only fully armed ships were covered under the law; 'war-like' ships could be built without interference. But James Bulloch knew in his heart that the case was only a temporary victory. Lord Russell demonstrated his determination to win by ordering Palmer to appeal the ruling.

The day after the acquittal London heard stunning news from America. General Lee was marching towards Maryland, or possibly Washington. 'The English hope it will be our destruction,' wrote Benjamin Moran in his diary.[22] Lee's invasion thrilled the Confederate lobby. The timing could not have been more auspicious for them. They had already decided to prepare the way for Roebuck's motion by having one of Gregory's friends in the Lords, the Marquis of Clanricarde, ask Russell whether the French had made any sort of important proposal that ought to be made known to the country. This, they thought, would force Russell's hand.[23]

On 26 June 1863 Clanricarde fired the first salvo and asked Russell whether he had received a communication from the French. Russell replied he had not. This rather flustered Clanricarde, who tried to retrieve the situation by asking whether the noble lord thought it was time to recognize the South. Russell replied that he did not, and so ended the exchange. This was not how the Confederates had expected the day to end. Either Russell or the Emperor was lying to them. In Paris, Slidell paid a hasty visit to the Foreign Minister, who assured him that a note had indeed been sent to Baron Gros, the French Ambassador. In London, Roebuck went to see the Ambassador, who could only say that he had not made a formal approach to Russell, which the Englishman already knew.

Louis-Napoleon had actually instructed his Ambassador to speak to Palmerston about jointly recognizing the South but the Prime Minister was ill with gout. Baron Gros, unsure whether he was required to convey the same message to the Foreign Secretary, merely met with Lord Russell instead but dropped a hint about the Emperor's intentions and left it at that. All this nudging and nodding was creating a scenario for a perfect tragicomedy of errors, unless decisive reports arrived from America.[24]

Henry Adams suddenly realized the danger confronting the Northern lobby. He did not rate John Roebuck as a politician but he knew that the combination of the Confederates winning the *Alexandra* case and the stirring news about Lee might just tip the House into taking action. The latest reports from America spoke of a significant cavalry engagement in Virginia – the largest yet in the war – but it appeared to have been inconclusive. 'Mr Roebuck has come back, big with the fate of nations,' Adams told his brother Charles Francis Jr. 'Evidently there is a crisis coming at home, and events here will follow, not lead, those at home.'[25]

With some trepidation, given John Bright's previous performance in the Commons, the pro-Northern lobby asked him to lead the counterattack against Roebuck and Lindsay. Bright agreed, though he was worried

that another military victory by Lee would make any further debate about
recognition a pointless exercise. He was having dreams about the war
where he was surrounded by telegrams that he could see but not read.[26]
The reports from America caused 'great anxiety' to Bright, who wrote to
Charles Sumner on 27 June:

> Roebuck brings on a motion on Tuesday, the 30th for the 'recognition' of
> the South. I had hoped that before that news might have reached us of the
> fall of Vicksburg, in which case, I believe, the proposition would not have
> been made: Now, it will be made and discussed, and there are some men in
> the House whose voice will be very unfriendly to your country . . . the bad
> news, or the appearance of it this morning, will tend to stimulate the friends
> of the South here.[27]

Charles Francis Adams asked Bright to attend a working dinner on
the night of the 27th. Several of Seward's recent emissaries were present,
including William Evarts, John Murray Forbes and William H. Aspinwall.* A sense of grievance against the Lincoln administration weighed
down the conversation. 'The impression here is that your Government
is incapable, that it lacks two essential qualities, foresight and force,'
Bright explained to Sumner. 'Among the Americans here, friends of the
North, there is great want of confidence in your Cabinet at Washington,
and I cannot but feel that great losses of men, and means, and long
delays, and apparent mismanagement, must have the effect of creating
a disgust with the war.'[28]

Having witnessed the British government's difficulties, Evarts thought
that Washington was not giving Lord Russell the credit he deserved for
his attempts to secure a conviction against the *Alexandra*'s owners.
Forbes and Aspinwall concurred; they were returning to America in a
few days and intended to speak to Seward about his role in the British
public's negative perception of the North. The profound suspicion
Seward inspired in England was brought home to them during their

---

* John Murray Forbes and William Aspinwall were two wealthy businessmen and philanthropists who had arrived in the spring bearing $10 million in government bonds. Seward
had sent them to England on a secret mission to purchase any ships that could be used by
the Confederates for their navy. Only a handful of people were meant to know the details,
but Forbes and Aspinwall had been in England for less than a week when *The Times*
received a tip-off. Thwarted by their exposure, they gave a considerable tranche of their
money to Consuls Dudley and Morse for their espionage operations – with more immediate
and probably far more effective results.

negotiations with Barings Bank over a large loan to the Federal government: Barings agreed to the deal only after the financial agents gave their word that Seward would not be allowed to issue letters of marque against British merchant ships.[29]

Forbes and Aspinwall left for New York on 30 June, the day of Roebuck's motion in the Commons, but a few hours too early to know the results of the debate. In America, the last newspaper reports placed the Confederate army near the border of Pennsylvania. Harrisburg, the State's capital, was standing by to evacuate the legislature. The Confederates in London were feeling confident; Roebuck did not know that Bright was to be his opponent in the House. When asked by a Southerner whether he would fear such an encounter: '"No, sir!" said Roebuck sententiously. "Bright and I have met before. It was the old story – the story of the sword-fish and the whale! No sir! Bright will not cross swords with me again!"'[30]

The death of Stonewall Jackson had not dented the Confederate army's confidence, even though Lee had been forced into a drastic reorganization to make up for the loss of his best general. He created three infantry corps, one under 'Old Pete' Longstreet, and the others under Richard Ewell and A. P. Hill. Jackson's cavalry was assigned to Jeb Stuart. Longstreet had already demonstrated his abilities; the rest would have to prove themselves on the field. But at least Lee had sufficient stores and enough men, 80,000 in all, to justify leading the army into enemy territory.

Thirty days of hot, cloudless skies had left Virginia parched and dry. As the Army of Northern Virginia marched away from Fredericksburg during the first week of June, rising columns of dust betrayed its movements to General Hooker's scouts. Hooker realized that Lee was heading north, and assumed that the Confederates were going to attack Washington. He was prevented from discovering his mistake for several days by the newly appointed A. P. Hill, who had been ordered to block the Federals at Fredericksburg for as long as possible. The strategy worked in so far as it occupied the attentions of US General 'Uncle John' Sedgwick, but Lee had underestimated the strength and size of Hooker's Cavalry Corps, who were also on the hunt.

The debonair Jeb Stuart had passed the time since Chancellorsville organizing grand reviews of his troops. His headquarters was in Culpep-per County, 30 miles east of Fredericksburg on the other side of the Rappahannock river, where the Orange-and-Alexandria railroad passed through a small village at Brandy Station.[31] The grandest of the reviews was on 5 June, involving all 10,000 soldiers and the horse artillery, fol-lowed by a ball in the evening. Thousands of spectators watched as Stuart put on a performance of knightly dash worthy of *Ivanhoe*. There were even buglers and flower girls who scattered petals before Stuart's arrival.

When Lee and his army reached Culpepper Court House on 9 June Stuart put on another review, this time without the flower girls. But the feeling among the observers was that the cavalry general had become far too interested in showmanship for his own good. Lee commented acidly to Stuart about a Northern commander who had also bedecked himself with flowers – just before a defeat. Francis Lawley wrote damn-ingly that Stuart was 'much too fond of frolics and dancing and being flattered'.[32] As soon as the performance ended, the men dispersed in readiness for the long march in the morning. Lee planned to take the army across the Blue Ridge Mountains into the Shenandoah Valley and head due north; Stuart was meant to be diverting attention rather than attracting it, so that Lee would have time to put sufficient distance between himself and his pursuers.

At 4.30 in the morning on 9 June, the first divisions of US General Alfred Pleasonton's 11,000-strong cavalry corps splashed across the Rappahannock on a mission 'to disperse and destroy the rebel force' at Culpepper. Stuart's antics had led the Federal cavalry straight to him; but Hooker's information was several days old and he was unaware that the entire Army of Northern Virginia was nearby, or that it was about to begin the journey northward. Woken by the sound of firing, Stuart scrambled out of his tent on Fleetwood Hill, which over-looked Brandy Station, and shouted to his officers to block the river fords. He was too late; half the Federal cavalry was already across the river.

Sir Percy Wyndham, restored to brigade command and in high spir-its, led the second half of the corps, which forded the Rappahannock mid-morning. He was trotting towards Brandy Station when an artil-lery gun on top of Fleetwood Hill began firing shells at their feet. There was only the one gun at Stuart's headquarters, but Wyndham could not know that. He shouted for the brigade to halt and take up a defensive position. A Federal artillery gun was pointed in the offending direction and fired back. Half an hour later the 1st New Jersey Cavaliers made the first of six charges against Stuart's position on Fleetwood Hill. Wyndham had trained his men to use their sabres, which at the time they had scoffed at as fancy Old Worldism, but now that they were fighting up close with the horses wheeling and rearing, the sabre proved by far the most effective weapon. Their Confederate opponents were outraged and bewildered; one of them shouted, 'Draw your pistols and fight like gentlemen!'[33]

The thunderous galloping of thousands of horses caused a swirling brown cloud to envelop the hill as cavalry units charged and counter-charged one another for almost seven hours. At various times during the day each side briefly gained control of the crest. The Confederates captured Wyndham's artillery and two of his best officers were killed, yet the 1st New Jersey Cavaliers fought on until they were surrounded and their only path of retreat was through the enemy. Wyndham remained in command, despite a bullet having sliced through his calf, until all his men were off the hill and safely back across the Rappahannock.

Wyndham exhorted the regiment to take pride in its performance. Though they had not taken possession of the hill, his troops had behaved nobly, he wrote the following day, 'standing unmoved under the enemy's artillery fire, and when ordered to charge, dashing forward with a spirit and determination'.[34] The Battle of Brandy Station fulfilled Wyndham's dream of leading his own cavalry charge. The disappointments and frustrations of the past year were eclipsed by the brilliant performance of his troops under fire. The exhausted soldiers relished his delight. Wyndham 'paid the regiment the highest compliments for its steady and dashing charges', wrote one of his officers to the Governor of New Jersey on 10 June. 'He goes to Washington today [to hospital]. We hope he will soon return, as he cannot be spared from his command.'[35]

The Battle of Brandy Station was a turning point for the Federal cavalry. Though its 866 casualties were nearly twice as many as the Confederates', the Union cavalry had come of age. Even Charles Francis Adams Jr., whose squadron played only a small part in the fighting, gained confidence from the fight. But for Pleasonton's mistiming of the two river crossings, he told Henry, they would have 'whipped Stuart out of his boots'.[36] Charles Francis Jr. was right. If Pleasonton had co-ordinated the corps better so that the two divisions had attacked simultaneously rather than six hours apart, Stuart would have been smashed to pieces. Reflecting on the battle many years later, one of Stuart's officers commented that Brandy Station 'made the Federal cavalry'.[37] Similarly, the battle ruined Jeb Stuart's aura of invincibility; the fact that he had ultimately held his ground did not excuse his carelessness in allowing the surprise attack, or lessen the shame of his having to call on infantry reinforcements for help.

Lee could not afford to let the near-debacle at Brandy Station slow the momentum of his army. The departure for Maryland proceeded as planned. The 2nd Corps under Ewell headed towards the lower Shenandoah Valley, with Longstreet following close behind. On 13 June the 3rd Corps slipped away from Fredericksburg, leaving their Federal opponents to discover that the week-long sparring had simply been a feint rather than the preparation for a large battle. General Hooker realized he had been tricked but his latest intelligence only told him the Confederate army was somewhere in the Shenandoah Valley. The best he could do was to keep the Army of the Potomac moving north while protecting Washington against surprise attacks.

The skirmishing at Fredericksburg had been a gentle introduction to warfare for Company F of the 7th Maine Infantry, a company of new recruits that arrived in Virginia on 23 May 1863. Walking fresh into a battle-hardened regiment was not usually a pleasant experience for recruits. But the newest and youngest member of Company F had no difficulty in endearing himself to his comrades. Nineteen-year-old Frederick Farr was a runaway from England who had enlisted under the alias Frederick Clark. His father was the celebrated epidemiologist William Farr, who pinpointed the cause of the great cholera epidemic of 1848. The last Farr senior had heard from his son was in January, when Frederick wrote to say he was studying hard for his civil service exams. Three weeks later, on 26 February, Frederick had secretly boarded the *Anglo-Saxon* for Portland, Maine.

Back at home, Dr Farr called at the US legation to swear an affidavit that Frederick was under age and had enlisted without his parents' permission. He also fired off letters to his Northern friends in the US Sanitary Commission and the Statistics Office begging for their help. Joseph Kennedy of the Census Bureau petitioned Seward, Lyons and even General Hooker on Farr's behalf. Kennedy tried to have Frederick transferred to General Pleasonton's staff, where his own son was an aide, and engaged a local lawyer in Maine to visit the boy. The lawyer returned with unexpected news: the youth had only ever wanted to be a soldier and had refused his help. 'He is very popular with his superior officers and is as disinclined to leave the service at present as they are indisposed to part with him.' All the lawyer could do for now was ask the regiment's colonel and the Governor of Maine (both of whom were personal friends) to take an interest in Frederick's welfare.[38]

On 8 June Joseph Kennedy cornered Lord Lyons at a ball given by the Brazilian Minister. Kennedy pressed Farr's case until Lyons explained that even in the best circumstances – where the law had been clearly transgressed – his appeals to Seward often failed to win a release.[39] That day Lyons had been shown one of the saddest letters yet received by the legation. A Miss Hodges in Baltimore had written about her fiancé, Bradford Smith Hoskins, who had been killed on 30 May during a skirmish between Federal cavalry and Mosby's rangers. Hoskins had been in America for less than six months, and with Mosby for only six weeks. Federal troopers had carried the mortally wounded officer into a nearby farmhouse belonging to the Green family, who took pity on the Englishman, dying so far from home, and buried him in their family plot in the cemetery across the way. Unfortunately, the Federals' magnanimous gesture was undermined by the theft of his personal effects. Miss Hodges begged Lord Lyons to track down the missing articles and have them returned to Hoskins' father in England. The Minister dutifully began the laborious task of finding the thief.*[41]

Lyons was longing for a respite from the daily grind of appeals and rejections. He half hoped that the rumours of an imminent attack by the Confederates were true. 'There is some chance of communication

---

* Several months went by as the case moved slowly down the chain of command until it reached the colonel of the 5th New York Cavalry. He discovered that it was one of his troopers who had taken the bag. The article was proffered up, with Hoskins' belongings still inside, and passed back up the chain to Washington. It was a melancholy triumph for Lyons, but he was glad to inform the Revd Hoskins in Kent that his son's belongings were on their way home.[40]

between Washington and the North being interrupted, as it was at the beginning of the war,' Lyons wrote to his sister on 16 June. 'The interruption of my correspondence for a few days would be a most enjoyable relief to me.'[42] But he suspected there was no real danger, except to Lee. Lyons thought the General had made 'a perilous move' by launching another invasion, even though the mere suggestion of his coming had created panic in Washington. Sir Percy Wyndham was ordered out of his bed and told to round up all available horsemen for the city's defence.

Crossroads at Gettysburg

The anguish of Charles Francis Adams Jr. – Colonel Fremantle
meets Robert E. Lee – The view from the oak tree – The Federals
hold – Lawley's painful duty

Fremantle's train pulled into Richmond on the morning of 17 June 1863, while over a hundred miles away the Army of Northern Virginia was crossing the Blue Ridge Mountains into the Shenandoah Valley. Francis Lawley had already left Richmond, hoping to reach Lee before the army disappeared entirely. He was weighed down by a sense of foreboding, even though his reports maintained their jaunty tone. His boast that 'Vicksburg will never fall' was simply propaganda, he had admitted to the Marquis of Hartington in a confidential letter of 14 June. It looked increasingly doubtful that the besieged town could withstand Grant for much longer. 'If it falls the Confederacy may hold out and will strive to hold out for years,' he wrote. 'But bisected & perforated everywhere by its enemies its fortunes will be at zero. No successes which Lee can gain in Virginia will be set off against the fall of Vicksburg.' Mindful of Hartington's new position as Under-Secretary for War, Lawley appealed to his military instincts, urging him to lobby for Southern recognition so that Britain would have an ally if the North turned its million-strong army towards Canada.[1]

'I hear everyone complaining dreadfully of General Johnston's inactivity in Mississippi, and all now despair of saving Vicksburg,' Fremantle wrote in his diary. He had spent his first day in Richmond visiting with as many government officials as would receive him.*[2] He eventually

---

* Despite not having met a single Southerner who was prepared to free his slaves under any conditions, Fremantle wrote after his visit to Charleston: 'I think that if the Confederate States were *left alone*, the system would be much modified and amended.'

managed to gain access to the Confederate Secretary of State, Judah P. Benjamin – 'a stout dapper little man' in Fremantle's opinion – whose ante-room was crowded with supplicants waiting for an audience. Benjamin gravely pressed upon him England's moral responsibility in allowing the bloodshed to continue – one word about recognition and the war would end, he claimed. When Fremantle brought up the spectre of Britain losing Canada if she grappled with the North, Benjamin laughed at the possibility: 'They know perfectly well you could deprive them of California ... with much greater ease.' This was a novel idea that Fremantle was too polite to pursue.[3]

After their interview, Benjamin escorted Fremantle to Davis's house. The President served him tea, the first Fremantle had seen during his travels, while they discussed the risks to England if she supported the Confederacy. Although Davis avoided talking about the current fighting, he alluded bitterly to the suffering wrought by Union armies. His own family had been made homeless after Federal soldiers torched his brother's plantation in Mississippi, having forced the tearful occupants onto the lawn to watch the destruction. He defended the behaviour of Confederate soldiers and denied that they shot men who surrendered. (The fate of Negro regiments at Charleston and also Port Hudson in 1864 would put the lie to this.) This gave Fremantle the opportunity to question him about Colonel Grenfell's legal trouble with the State authorities. 'He was very sorry when I told him,' wrote Fremantle, as 'he had heard much of his gallantry and good services'.[4] But Davis was not unduly troubled by Grenfell's departure; there seemed to be no shortage of foreign volunteers.*

'When I took my leave about 9 o'clock, the President asked me to call upon him again,' wrote Fremantle. He felt sorry for him; Davis looked much older than his fifty-five years. He face was lined and emaciated, his eyes were evidently hurting him, yet 'nothing can exceed the charm of his manner, which is simple, easy, and most fascinating.'[6] This was an uncharacteristic description of a man who was generally considered to be haughty and cold, and too enamoured of his military record during

---

* Only the week before, on 9 June, a letter from Lieutenant Sydney Herbert Davies had appeared on his desk. Davies had resigned from his regiment in Canada in order to carry secret dispatches to the South. 'I have now the honour to apply for a major's commission in the CSA,' he wrote. 'I am in possession of a first class certificate as an instructor of musketry and am not ignorant of warfare.' He was rewarded with a commission of 1st lieutenant.[5]

CS General Longstreet's corps crossing the Blue Ridge from the Shenandoah
to the Rappahannock, by Frank Vizetelly

the Mexican–American War to listen to the advice of his generals. On
the night of 19 June there was an explosion of thunder and lighnting over
Richmond. The clattering of rain followed by a rush of cool air made a
pleasant end to Fremantle's last hours in the city. He was packing in
preparation for a dawn departure by train to Culpeper, where he hoped
to obtain a horse and ride to Lee's headquarters at Berryville.

The drought also broke at Middleburg, near the northern Virginia
border, finally ridding the countryside of its pervasive smell of rotting

horses.[7] Water flowed through the camp of the 1st Massachusetts Cavalry, flooding the tents, many of which stood empty. Charles Francis Adams Jr. was alone in his, struggling to make sense of the past forty-eight hours. Only four days ago he had been studying William Howard Russell's published diary for accuracy and bias, wondering if the authorities had forgotten the regiment's existence. After the Battle of Brandy Station, General Pleasonton had ordered the cavalry to pursue the Confederate army into the Blue Ridge Mountains and bring him definitive intelligence of its direction. Jeb Stuart had placed his troopers in front of the three mountain gaps to hold them off. Both he and his men were trying to blot out their recent near-humiliation; Pleasonton's cavalry were no less determined to prove that they were the Confederates' equals or better. The 1st Massachusetts Cavalry had always previously ended up on the sidelines or been held in reserve, but this time they were assigned to Kilpatrick's brigade, and sent to break the Confederate hold at Aldie, the northernmost gap in the Blue Ridge. They roared into the village on the morning of the 17th, easily driving off the Rebel pickets, but when they turned back for another sweep they were hit by a countercharge of Confederate reinforcements. Charles Francis's squadron became trapped at the foot of a hill. 'My poor men were just slaughtered and all we could do was to stand still and be shot down,' he wrote in anguish to his brother Henry. 'In twenty minutes and without fault on our part I lost thirty-two as good men and horses as can be found in the cavalry corps. They seemed to pick out my best and truest men, my pets and favourites. How and why I escaped I can't say, for my men fell all around me.'[8] He was wracked by guilt and grief over his losses. The army's leaders were butchers, he wrote bitterly to Henry; the 'drunk-murdering-arson dynasty' of Hooker and the rest had to be expelled before they did Lee's work for him.

Jeb Stuart succeeded in driving the Federals away from the passes, but he could not prevent General Pleasonton from obtaining the information sought by Hooker. By 22 June the Federals knew for certain that Pennsylvania and not Washington was Lee's objective. Stuart was unsure what Lee wished him to do in the face of so many threats – should he guard the gaps, follow the Confederate army up the Shenandoah Valley, or create a diversion and try to maintain the deception that the Capital was in danger? Lee sent him two notes on 22 and 23 June which the cavalry commander interpreted to mean that he could use his own judgement, provided he rejoined the main body of the army in good time. Stuart decided to go riding and raiding in between the Federal army and Washington.[9]

Fremantle at last arrived at Lee's headquarters at 9 a.m. on 22 June. He recognized the General immediately but refrained from going up to him. The expression on Lee's face discouraged frivolous interruption. Instead, Fremantle asked a member of his staff where he might find Francis Lawley. After introducing him to Lee's aides, Lawley invited Fremantle to join them for breakfast. There was another guest at the table, a Prussian captain named Justus Scheibert, who was an official observer from the

Royal Prussian Engineers. The conversation centred mostly on Jeb Stuart and his successful repulse of Pleasonton's cavalry at the mountain passes. For the moment, at least, Stuart's reputation was on a reprieve. But he had lost one of his most popular volunteers – the Prussian soldier Heros von Borcke, who had been severely wounded at Aldie.

Lawley understood Fremantle's desire to meet Lee but persuaded him to wait until the atmosphere was less frenetic. He suggested they leave the camp and deposit themselves 10 miles further north, at Winchester, where there would be decent lodgings and a blacksmith for Fremantle's suffering horse. They spent the next couple of days together, exploring the battle-scarred countryside and staying out of the Confederates' way. The houses looked bleak and dilapidated, with those still inhabited being used as hospitals for the wounded. The travellers visited the mud hole that had once been Commissioner Mason's elegant plantation. 'Literally not one stone remains standing upon another,' wrote Fremantle, surprised at the vitriol behind the Federal attack.

On 24 June, leaving Lawley to write his *Times* dispatch, Fremantle went foraging for their horses, without success. He eventually found virgin grass four miles out of town but all the hay and corn had been seized long ago. He was experiencing on a small scale one of Lee's greatest anxieties: how to feed his army. As usual, Lawley hid the situation from his readers. He conceded that the Southern army was 'still ragged and unkempt' but declared that all had good shoes, and the animals were 'for the most part sleek and fat'. Lawley was unable to finish his report that day or the next. He became so ill, probably with dysentery, that they had to stay behind in Winchester even though the Confederate army had resumed its northward progress. On 25 June Lawley forced himself to mount his horse and they rode all day in the rain, trying to catch up with Lee. They managed to pass some divisions of Longstreet's corps, but the generals had already crossed the Potomac.

'It was a dreary day! The rain was falling in torrents,' recalled Francis Dawson. 'General Lee, General Longstreet and General Pickett were riding together, followed by their staffs. When we reached the Maryland shore we found several patriotic ladies with small feet and big umbrellas waiting to receive the Confederates who were coming a second time to deliver downtrodden Maryland.' One of the four women held an enormous wreath which had been intended to adorn the neck of Lee's horse, Traveler, but its size frightened the animal and it was handed to one of the General's aides to carry. More ladies greeted them at Hagerstown, just south of the Pennsylvania State line. This time one of them asked for a lock of Lee's hair, which he refused and offered one of General George Pickett's instead. 'General Pickett did not enjoy the joke,' wrote Dawson, 'for he was known everywhere by his corkscrew ringlets, which were not particularly becoming when the rain made them lank in such weather as we then had.'[10]

Lawley and Fremantle rode into Hagerstown late Friday night on 26 June. They had almost caught up with the army, but Lawley was so weak that he slumped alarmingly on his horse. Fremantle's had gone lame; 'by the assistance of his tail, I managed to struggle through the deep mud and wet,' he wrote, until, after 17 very long miles, they bribed a Dutchman with gold to let them stay the night. 'I dared not take off my solitary pair of boots, because I knew I should never get them on again,' recorded Fremantle. Twenty-four hours earlier, in England, *The Times*'s managing editor, Mowbray Morris, was writing optimistically to Lawley to keep going for just a little bit longer. The only real hardship was the blockade, he asserted; once that was raised 'your position will be comparatively easy and your work pleasant'.[11]

The following day Lawley was too ill to be moved. Deciding that his friend required medical attention, Fremantle took Lawley's horse, which seemed marginally less likely to collapse, and set off in search of Longstreet. He found him after only an hour. Longstreet immediately sent an ambulance to fetch Lawley, and invited Fremantle to join his mess during the campaign. He informed the surprised Englishman that they had already crossed into Pennsylvania, Maryland being only 10 miles wide at this point. They were heading towards Chambersburg, a small town 20 miles from Hagerstown.

After a couple of days' observation, Fremantle believed he was witnessing a rare event in military history: an invasion unadorned by mass rape and murder. In fact, Northern blacks were robbed, assaulted and in some cases forced at gunpoint into slavery. But since these crimes happened along the fringes of the army, Fremantle only saw minor infractions such as fence-breaking or Northern whites being forced to accept worthless Confederate dollars for their goods. Fremantle thought they were remarkably ungrateful for the restrained behaviour 'and really appear to be unaware that their own troops have been for two years treating Southern towns with ten times more harshness'.[12] Francis Dawson felt proud to

be riding in Longstreet's corps. 'The army behaved superbly in Pennsylvania,' he declared. 'The orders against straggling and looting were strict.'
He saw Lee dismount in front of a field of broken rails and tidy them up
himself: 'It was the best rebuke that he could have given to the offenders.'
When the army entered Chambersburg, Dawson was surprised to see
young men lolling on street corners. Suddenly Lee's invading army of
60,000 seemed small and vulnerable; there were no 'spare' men in Virginia. Dawson visited the prison where he had been held after the Battle
of Antietam. There were Yankee prisoners in the yard and for a brief
moment he wanted to pelt them with stones, as had been done to him.

To maintain order, Lee had decreed that only generals and their staff
were allowed into Chambersburg without a special pass. But this official reassurance was not enough to calm the townspeople: all the shops
and hotels were closed and shuttered. The commissary officers could
not find anyone willing to sell provisions, though they threatened to
seize them by force if necessary. Lawley was recuperating at the Franklin Hotel, which was kept locked to casual passers-by. Fremantle had to
hammer on the doors, shouting that he was an English traveller, until
they were cautiously opened.

Fremantle went to Lawley's room to give him the latest news and
discovered that the journalist was not alone. An Englishman dressed in
the full uniform of the Hungarian hussars was sitting in the chair,
recounting his journey through the lines. He had crossed into the South
in late May, aided as usual by the Maryland journalist W. W. Glenn, in
the hope of meeting the famous Robert E. Lee. Fremantle could not stop
himself from smiling; the 38-year-old Captain Fitzgerald Ross had spent
the past thirteen years in Austria and had succumbed to the country's
fondness for military pomp. He was dressed as though he were on parade, and brushed aside Fremantle's warning that the Confederates would
tease him mercilessly.

All day during the 28th and 29th, Fremantle walked quietly among
the Confederates, observing the unhurried preparations to move further
north. The army corps was dispersed for miles around, employed in the
unending search for food and water. The Confederate army had marched
more than 90 miles from its base at Fredericksburg. Every bullet and
shell had been brought with them in long wagon lines. Despite these
difficulties, Longstreet's headquarters had a relaxed air about it. The
normally taciturn General passed the early part of the evening with

Fremantle, reminiscing about his time in Texas. But shortly after the Englishman departed, Longstreet received another visitor, a scout, who brought devastating news. The Union army had crossed into Maryland and was only days if not hours behind them.

Jeb Stuart was meant to be Lee's eyes and ears, but at this precise moment the cavalryman was 55 miles away, his progress slowed by 125 captured wagons. He was rather pleased with his expedition; on 28 June he had come within six miles of Washington, sending tremors down Pennsylvania Avenue. Lord Lyons ordered his staff to pack their bags in case they needed to make a hasty departure. No one in the legation believed that the Federal cavalry in the capital would be a match for Jeb Stuart's. Since being hustled back onto duty, Sir Percy Wyndham had succeeded in rounding up 3,000 riders. But he had only found horses for two-thirds of them. (In his search for more, some of his actions had bordered on outright theft, earning him powerful enemies in the capital.)

Lee had no means of sending a message to Stuart, but he dispatched hurried instructions to his generals, who were spread out in a 45-mile radius, to collect their scattered corps and meet outside the village of Cashtown, eight miles west of Gettysburg. On 30 June, Lee heard that 'Fighting Joe' Hooker had resigned after a petty quarrel with General-in-Chief Henry Halleck, and been replaced by George Gordon Meade. Lee was not happy with the change; Hooker would have been a far weaker opponent. Meade was a veteran of the Mexican–American War, a no-nonsense professional soldier whose hair-trigger temper had earned him the nickname 'The Old Snapping Turtle'. Fremantle accompanied Longstreet to Lee's headquarters while he was in the midst of moving his headquarters closer to Gettysburg. Ten different roads went through the town, making it a useful launch site for a confrontation with the Federal army. Lee betrayed no sign of anxiety to Fremantle, who, like many observers, thought him 'the handsomest man of his age I ever saw'. He was wearing his customary long grey jacket and wellington boots, both of which were surprisingly clean.

One of the Confederate brigades had spotted Union cavalrymen lurking around Gettysburg. When Lee received the news, all knew that a battle was imminent. Still elated by the recent victory at Chancellorsville, Lee's officers had no doubt about the outcome. Lawley was equally optimistic. Though weak, he had managed to eat breakfast in the hotel dining room in Chambersburg with Captain Ross on 1 July. The complaints and anti-Southern comments of the other diners, all locals, so irritated Lawley that, to Ross's acute embarrassment, he held a twenty-dollar Confederate bill aloft and declared 'in a month it would be worth more than all their greenbacks in the North put together'.[13]

As Lawley and Ross were eating their breakfast, four Confederate infantry brigades set off in search of a warehouse reputed to be full of shoes. Three miles from Gettysburg they stumbled into the 1st Cavalry Division of the Union army. Thus began the Battle of Gettysburg, without the orders or knowledge of the two commanders. It was eleven o'clock when the faint echoes of artillery fire alerted Lee to the battle taking place. He was furious at this unexpected development, which added to the difficulties forced upon him by not knowing where his enemy lay or how many he faced. At this moment there were in fact more Confederates than Federals at Gettysburg – a massed attack could have captured the town.

An hour later, at noon, Longstreet was marching at the head of his corps towards Gettysburg. Fremantle followed on horseback while Lawley and Captain Ross travelled at the back of the wagon line. 'At 2 p.m. firing became distinctly audible in our front,' wrote Fremantle. Soon they passed a ghastly parade of stretchers and the walking wounded coming the other way. The soldiers were so accustomed to such scenes that they barely glanced at them. Finally, at 4.30 p.m., the travellers found General Lee on the top of Seminary Ridge, observing the battle below.

Fremantle climbed to the top of an oak tree in order to obtain a better view of the Federal defences. The town lay within an undulating basin, surrounded by ridges and boulder-strewn hills. Lee had realized that control of these ridges was paramount; as at Fredericksburg, whoever held the high ground outside the town had the advantage. General Ewell's orders were to drive the Federals from Cemetery Ridge, 'if possible'. Fatally for Lee's plans, Ewell decided it was not possible, and remained where he was.[14] Nevertheless, when the firing withered away at dusk the Confederates appeared to have won the day. They had lost 6,000 men compared to the almost 9,000 casualties suffered by the Federals, and the town was theirs.

The Union army, however, had seized the best defensive positions around the perimeter of hills and ridges south of Gettysburg, near the local cemetery. That evening Fremantle and Lawley witnessed a tense debate between the Confederate generals. 'The enemy's new position', reported Lawley later, made Longstreet fear that a direct assault would

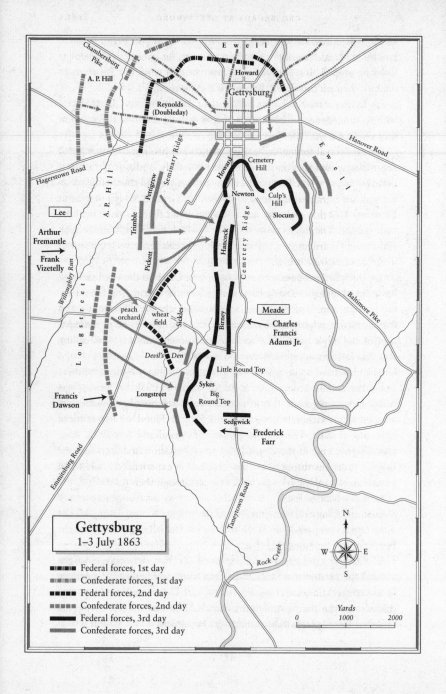

Gettysburg
1–3 July 1863

- ▪▪▪▪ Federal forces, 1st day
- ▪▪▪▪ Confederate forces, 1st day
- ▪▪▪▪ Federal forces, 2nd day
- ▪▪▪▪ Confederate forces, 2nd day
- ▪▪▪▪ Federal forces, 3rd day
- ▪▪▪▪ Confederate forces, 3rd day

Chambersburg Pike

A. P. Hill

Reynolds (Doubleday)

Ewell

Howard

Gettysburg

Hanover Road

Hagerstown Road

Seminary Ridge

Pettigrew

Howard

Cemetery Hill

Ewell

A. P. Hill

Lee

Trimble

Newton

Culp's Hill

Slocum

Arthur Fremantle

Frank Vizetelly

Pickett

Cemetery Ridge

Hancock

Willoughby Run

Baltimore Pike

peach orchard

wheat field

Sickles

Birney

Meade

Charles Francis Adams Jr.

Devil's Den

Longstreet

Little Round Top

Francis Dawson

Longstreet

Sykes

Big Round Top

Sedgwick

Frederick Farr

Emmitsburg Road

Taneytown Road

Rock Creek

N
W   E
S

Yards

0   1000   2000

be too dangerous. He wanted Lee to move the army to a better location and force Meade to come after them. But Lee disagreed. 'The enemy is here,' he argued; 'if we do not whip him, he will whip us.' They would renew the attack tomorrow. Lawley thought Longstreet was right, ignorant as he was of the risk such a move would entail when the Confederates had no intelligence of Meade's numbers or position other than what they could see with their own eyes.

'The universal feeling in the army was one of profound contempt for an enemy whom they have beaten so constantly, and under so many disadvantages,' wrote Fremantle. But never before had the disadvantage been one of terrain or information. When US General Meade arrived at Cemetery Hill that night, he was relieved to find that his army held the high ground. The ridge occupied by the Federals was several miles long, and in some parts more than 140 feet high. Lee's army was spread out in a thin semicircle below.

Yet the four European observers nevertheless shared the Confederates' optimism. Lawley's malady had returned, but he insisted on breakfasting at 3.30 a.m. with the Prussian observer Scheibert, Fremantle and Captain Ross, who had shaved and waxed his moustache in anticipation of the day's battle. He made silly comments about Mars calling which the others accepted in good humour.

They returned to Fremantle's oak tree on Seminary Ridge and there found Lee and his generals discussing the plan of attack. Longstreet was still trying to persuade Lee to retire from Gettysburg. Fremantle was amused to see Generals Longstreet and John B. Hood whittle at sticks while they talked. The habit struck him as peculiarly American. Ross soon lost interest in the Confederates' conversation and stared at the Federal positions through his field glasses. He experienced a jolt when he saw them looking straight back at him through their own.[15]

In the morning, despite being ordered to move his troops into attack formation, Longstreet procrastinated for several hours, giving Meade more time to prepare. Federal reinforcements had been arriving throughout the night, including the 7th Maine Infantry (and the English runaway Frederick Farr), which was sent to shore up the extreme end of the Union line. 'Order from General Gibbon read to us,' recorded a private in one of the Minnesota regiments occupying Cemetery Ridge. 'He says this is to be the great battle of the war and that any soldier leaving the ranks without leave will be instantly put to death.'[16]

The concentration of troops now numbered 60,000 Confederates and 85,000 Federals, yet all was quiet on 2 July until late afternoon. Bored with waiting, Ross and Fremantle left the other two by the tree and went exploring. They bumped into two members of Longstreet's staff. One of them, Colonel James B. Walton, was in charge of the reserve artillery. The Confederates shared their cherries with them and afterwards they all went for a dip in the stream. When the Englishmen returned to the oak tree, Jeb Stuart had at last reappeared with the missing cavalry. Lee was so angry he could barely acknowledge him.

'No one would have imagined that such masses of men and such a powerful artillery were about to commence the work of destruction,' wrote Fremantle. 'We began to doubt whether a fight was off to-day at all.' The sudden explosion of Confederate artillery at 4.45 p.m. gave the answer. An hour later Longstreet ordered his corps to storm the Federal defences. Fremantle was amazed by Lee's behaviour once the fighting began. The general sat by himself on a tree stump. No one spoke to him. He received only one report and sent just one message. He had become an observer in his own battle. 'I know not whether I am mistaken,' Lawley wrote later. 'Lee struck me as more anxious and ruffled than I had ever seen him before, though it required close observation to detect it.'[17] In previous battles, Lee had encouraged his subordinates to use their initiative, but at Gettysburg the practice allowed for increased confusion. Without a leader to coordinate its movements the Confederate assault was like a random firecracker display. To add to the strangeness of the scene, a Confederate marching band 'began to play polkas and waltzes, which sounded very curious, accompanied by the hissing and bursting of shells'.[18]

The cannonade sounded 'one deep prolonged bellowing roar', wrote Lawley. 'A thick canopy of smoke, constantly rent by bright darting flashes of flame, cast its dense pall over the struggling, bleeding thousands who toiled and died in its centre.'[19] Lee's plan called for a specific type of attack known as 'en echelon', meaning that the divisions were to attack in sequence, parallel to one another – first hitting the south side of Meade's line which held Little Round Top hill, and then the north side which overlooked the cemetery near the town. En echelons were complicated, requiring precision timing and execution; it would have been a risky manoeuvre for Lee under the best of circumstances and to attempt one now, when two of his three corps commanders were new and untried, was asking a great deal. The Federals had orders to hold Little Round Top 'at all hazards'; Father William Corby, one of the chaplains of the Irish Brigade, climbed to the top of a boulder and called out that any soldier killed on the battlefield would be given a full Christian burial, but God help those who ran away.[*][20] Almost half the brigade was killed or wounded that day in the infamous Wheat Field, which lay near the bottom of Little Round Top hill. Meanwhile, General Ewell's attacks against Meade's northern lines along Cemetery Hill teetered on the brink of victory but fierce Federal counterattacks drove the Confederates back to the town. When the sun went down each army had suffered almost 10,000 casualties.

Lee was haemorrhaging men yet he still believed that one more assault would dislodge the Federals and allow him to pick off the fleeing divisions one by one. He wanted all 65 batteries of 282 guns ready and primed for action for the next day, 3 July. Longstreet had argued against fighting the Federals at Gettysburg, and now vehemently protested against Lee's proposal to attack the Union centre, which, as far as he could tell, would simply be a repeat of Fredericksburg, only this time with the Confederates on the plain and the Federals firing at them from above. Lee was confident that if he sent Jeb Stuart to attack Meade from behind at the same time as the assault in the front, the Federals would be too confused to repel both.

General Meade sensed that Lee was going to throw at him everything within his grasp. Conscious that he was the sixth general to lead the Army of the Potomac, he invited all the generals to a war council at the little white farmhouse that served as his headquarters. The dozen or so commanders discussed whether to retire or continue the battle and then took a vote: they would remain at Gettysburg for one more day and, since they held the higher ground, allow Lee to launch another attack.[21]

The Confederate reserve artillery was ordered into position, facing the centre of Meade's line. One of the English volunteers who had run the blockade in the spring, Captain Stephen Winthrop, was assigned a battery and told to bring it to Captain Charles W. Squires of the Washington Artillery. Although he had been appointed to Longstreet's staff in late April, Winthrop had only arrived at his headquarters a day or so

---

[*] Gettysburg, like Antietam, Fredericksburg and Chancellorsville, had its own lexicon of horrors where thousands died contesting a patch of ground: the Wheat Field, Devil's Den and the Peach Orchard.

before the battle and the order flummoxed him. He tried to memorize the directions, but it proved impossible to navigate the country roads without a map. He became lost and did not arrive until midnight. Squires was so angry that he had Winthrop placed under arrest. The unlucky Englishman was held under arms until the morning, when Colonel Walton came to his rescue.[22]

Early in the morning the four observers joined Lee's and Longstreet's staff as they reconnoitred the battleground, the first time the Confederates had done so since the battle erupted. It was unnerving for Fremantle to walk past the bodies of fallen soldiers, some of whom turned out to be still alive, opening their eyes as they heard him approach. The conspicuous party attracted the attention of a sharpshooter, which led to an encounter with a hidden battery. A few shells whizzed over their heads. One landed on a Federal field hospital, trapping the wounded inside when the building went up in flames.

Although Lee had wanted simultaneous artillery and infantry attacks, Longstreet was inordinately slow in placing his men. As a result, all the fighting that morning took place in one location, around Cemetery Hill. By noon, there were 3,500 casualties. Hundreds of horses were dead or dying, including sixteen killed by a shell in the yard next to Meade's farmhouse. Then the battlefield went silent for a while, which allowed the midday sun to clear the enveloping smoke, and the next stage of Lee's mangled plan went into motion. Francis Dawson was recovering from dysentery, but even in his weakened state he worked feverishly to transport ordnance to the 164 artillery crews facing the Federal centre line: 'Every arrangement was made to shell the enemy's position, on Cemetery Hill, and follow this up by an attack in force,' he wrote. 'Three or four hundred pieces of artillery were being fired as rapidly as the cannoneers could load them. Being in the centre of the front line, I had an excellent view of the fight.'[23]

Leaving Lawley and Scheibert at their post by the oak tree, Fremantle and Ross went down into the town, thinking that the view from the cupola above Ewell's headquarters would offer a spectacular panorama. The idea became less attractive as shells began bursting from all directions. They had managed to reach the tollgate when flying shrapnel sliced into their guide. A little boy who had latched on to them began screaming and laughing hysterically each time another shell burst. Fremantle realized they had to get away as quickly as possible. But at the next explosion the child darted off before they could stop him. 'I never saw this boy again, or found out who he was,' wrote Fremantle sadly.[24]

The two observers were still dodging shells when Longstreet finally ordered his corps to prepare for the attack. The Federal guns had stopped firing, leading him to assume that his own barrage had successfully destroyed their defence. He did not know that his artillerists' aim had been slightly off, or that the Federals were simply conserving their ammunition for the expected assault. The Confederates, on the other hand, had used up all their long-range shells. Longstreet's artillery chief, Edward P. Alexander, begged him to call the charge before the Federal guns started up again.

Dawson watched as 14,000 Confederate soldiers assembled in the woods. One division, led by the ringletted George Pickett, was almost exclusively Virginian. Prayers were read to the brigades, as though the men were receiving the last rites. 'This is a desperate thing to attempt,' Dawson heard one of the brigadier generals remark. 'Just then,' Dawson continued, 'a hare which had been lying in the bushes, sprang up and leaped rapidly to the rear. A gaunt Virginian, with an earnestness that struck a sympathetic chord in many a breast, yelled out: "Run old heah; if I were an old heah I would run too." '[25]

The Federals could not see the Confederates massing in the woods across from them. 'From our position the eye ranged over a wide expanse of uneven country, fields broken by woods, showing nowhere any signs of an army movement, much less of conflict,' Charles Francis Adams Jr. wrote in his memoirs. Even at the height of the battle, Gettysburg seemed pleasingly pastoral: 'a quiet, midsummer, and champagne country. Neither our lines nor those of the enemy were visible to us; and the sounds of battle were hushed.' When the Confederate artillery fire began, Charles Francis Jr. and the survivors of the 1st Massachusetts Cavalry had been lying on the grass, near their horses, while they waited for orders. The thick heat and soft buzzing of insects acted as a kind of soporific. 'Lulled by the incessant roar of the cannon,' he recorded, 'while the fate of the army and the nation trembled in the balance, at the very crisis of the great conflict, I dropped quietly asleep. It was not heroic; but it was . . . war.'[26]

Forty-seven Confederate regiments spaced a mile apart began advancing across the 1,400-yard field which lay in front of Cemetery Ridge.

Francis Lawley – too ill to climb the tree himself – shouted up to Justus Scheibert to describe the charge to him. The Prussian started a running commentary, full of technical descriptions, prompting Lawley to bellow at him in frustration to use layman's terms, but Scheibert was at a loss for further words, having never witnessed such butchery. The closer the Confederates stumbled towards the concave Federal line the easier targets they presented. Fremantle entered the wood where Pickett's division had gathered only a few minutes before. Federal shells were bringing down huge tree limbs, and yet the wood was full of grey-clad soldiers, 'in numbers as great as the crowd in Oxford Street in the middle of the day'. Then he saw that every single one was wounded.[27]

The woodland scene confused Fremantle. When he found Longstreet, who was sitting on a rail at the edge of the wood, he made an exceptionally thoughtless comment. 'Thinking I was just in time to see the attack,' he wrote contritely, 'I remarked to the General that "I wouldn't have missed this for any thing."' Longstreet gave a hollow laugh, '"The Devil you wouldn't! I would like to have missed it very much; we've attacked and been repulsed; look there!"'[28] Longstreet asked wearily for a drink and Fremantle offered him a sip of rum from his flask. Scattered in heaps and fragments below were nearly 7,000 Confederate soldiers. George Pickett had lost two-thirds of his division, including all thirteen colonels. 'I suppose that I was the first man to whom Pickett spoke when he reached the line,' wrote Francis Dawson. 'With tears in his eyes, he said to me: "Why did you not halt my men here? Great God, where, oh! where is my division?" I told him that he saw around him what there was left of it.'[29]

Fremantle was surprised by Longstreet's calm demeanour. A Federal charge at this moment would have smashed the Confederate army to pieces. When one general protested that he could not gather his men, Longstreet sarcastically told him not to worry; the enemy would do it for him. Lee came riding up the hill to help rally the soldiers. 'His face, which is always placid and cheerful, did not show signs of the slightest disappointment,' wrote Fremantle. His only concern was to ready a line of defence. Lee asked Colonel Alexander whether they had enough ammunition to repel a Federal attack. The artillerist gave a bleak answer. Lee bravely acknowledged his part in the failed charge. 'It was all my fault this time,' Lee told the dazed fugitives from Pickett's charge; 'form your ranks again when you get back to cover.'[30] At 7.30 p.m., when he was certain that there would be no more fighting that day, Fremantle returned to camp to describe the recent events to Lawley.

On the following day, 4 July, the battlefield was soaked by a long, steady downpour. 'Many dear friends had yielded up their young lives during the hours which had elapsed,' wrote Charles Francis Jr., 'but, though twenty thousand fellow creatures were wounded or dead around us, though the flood-gates of heaven seemed open and the torrents fell upon the quick and the dead, yet the elements seemed electrified with a certain magnetic influence of victory, and, as the great army sank down over-wearied in its tracks, it felt that the crisis and danger was passed – that Gettysburg was immortal.'[31]

Lee now had just one aim – to retreat with the remnants of his army before Meade attacked. Seventy thousand Confederates in all had fought at Gettysburg; only 48,000 were leaving. The Federal army had one field hospital for every 12,000 soldiers; the Confederates simply gathered as many of the injured as they could and loaded them onto wagons. Thousands were left behind, and countless men died from their wounds or starved to death waiting for someone to rescue them. Two weeks after the battle, a civilian accidently found one of the abandoned camps. A party was sent to collect the survivors. A shocked witness wrote:

> One boy without beard was stretched out dead, quite naked, a piece of blanket thrown over his emaciated form, a rag over his face, and his small, thin hands laid over his breast. Of the dead none knew their names, and it breaks my heart to think of the mothers waiting and watching for the sons laid in the lonely grave on that fearful battlefield. All of those men in the woods were nearly naked, and when ladies approached they tried to cover themselves with the filthy rags they had cast aside. The wounds themselves, unwashed and untouched, were full of worms. God only knows what they suffered.[32]

Lincoln would never forgive Meade for not driving after Lee. But the Union commander had lost a quarter of his army: 23,000 men were dead, wounded or captured. His generals supported his decision to wait until they were sure of Lee's movements. A temporary halt while the injured were removed and the supply trains arrived did not seem like an intolerable delay. The Federal cavalry caught up with the Confederates two days later. 'As we approached Hagerstown, we heard some fighting ahead, between our cavalry and a cavalry force of the enemy. I rode ahead to see if any artillery was needed,' wrote Colonel Alexander.

> During the day I had an accession to my staff. Capt. Stephen Winthrop ... on the march from Gettysburg [had] negotiated with Gen. Sorrel, Longstreet's adjutant, to be transferred to me. Sorrel asked me if I would consent – which I did very willingly, and he joined me about noon on the 6th. He was well built, stout & very muscular, good grey-blue eyes, a full, oval face, with a British mouth and nose, good natured, jolly, & brave. He was an excellent and admirable representation of his country ... That very afternoon he got a chance to show the stuff he was made of.[33]

Winthrop was returning with a fresh horse from Alexander's reserve when he rode into one of Jeb Stuart's regiments as it prepared to attack a Federal battery. He introduced himself and asked to carry their colours. The Confederates were too surprised to decline his request. He positioned himself at the front of the charge and leaped forward. 'Winthrop's horse was killed by canister quite close to the guns, but the charge was repulsed. He got another horse, and went in a second charge,' recalled Alexander. Though armed with only his sabre, he rode into the body of the Federal cavalry and plunged his sword into one of them – 'coming out with his sabre bent & bloody all over'. Winthrop went off to look for Alexander, satisfied that his honour had been redeemed after his humiliating arrest at Gettysburg.

'The March back to the Potomac was dreary and miserable indeed,' wrote Dawson. 'The rain fell in torrents. The clothing of the men was worn and tattered, and too many of them were without shoes. It was a heart-breaking business, and gloom settled down upon the army.' A trail 18 miles long slowly ground through the mud to Hagerstown in Maryland. During the journey Longstreet talked to Fremantle and Lawley about the reasons for the Confederate defeat, placing the failure on numbers rather than tactics.[34] 'He said the mistake they had made was in not concentrating the army more, and making the attack yesterday with 30,000 men instead of 15,000,' reported Fremantle. 'The advance had been in three lines, and the troops of Hill's corps who gave way were young soldiers, who had never been under fire before.' Longstreet would retract this opinion after the war, however, writing in his own memoirs that 40,000 men 'could not have carried the position at Gettysburg'.[35]

Lawley, Fremantle, Ross and Scheibert arrived at Hagerstown on the 7th. They took rooms together at the Washington Hotel.[36] Lawley had a hard task ahead of him and was left alone by the others so he could write in peace. He could not disguise the grief in his heart: 'For the first time during my residence in Secessia,' he began, 'it is my province to record, as having happened under my own eyes, a failure of the Confederate arms.'[37]

23

Pressure Rising

Fiasco at the House of Commons – Vicksburg surrenders – An economy without cotton – Rioting in New York – A summer jaunt – Rose Greenhow's diplomatic mission

The House of Commons was full on Tuesday evening, 30 June 1863, when Henry Adams entered the Strangers' Gallery, pretending to ignore the Southerners seated around him. According to the latest news from America, Lee's army had marched without hindrance all the way to Pennsylvania. But the news appeared to be having a dampening effect on support for Roebuck's motion – several MPs had questioned the need for a debate on recognition when the Confederacy was on the verge of winning independence without English help. It was yet one more dilemma weighing on Roebuck's mind when he entered the Commons. Earlier that day in the House of Lords, Russell had denied for a second time that the Emperor had written to him about recognizing the South.

James Spence had always felt uncomfortable with Roebuck as the South's main spokesman in the Commons, but even he never imagined the extent to which the MP would self-immolate that evening. Roebuck's speech began unpromisingly with an overflow of bile before descending into such balderdash that he alienated his listeners. There were cries of 'No!' when Roebuck insisted that Negroes were worse off in the North than in the South where 'black children and white children are brought up together. I say it without fear of contradiction from any one whose contradiction is worthy of notice . . . There is a kindly feeling in the minds of the Southern planters towards those whom England fixed there in a condition of servitude.' But the real damage came towards

the end when he referred to his interview with Louis-Napoleon. Roebuck explained afterwards that Russell's denial had given him no choice
because his own honour was at stake. But rather than simply saying in
a few words that France was eager to cooperate on a policy of recognition, Roebuck gave a blow-by-blow description of their interview,
including Louis-Napoleon's complaints about double-dealing by the
Foreign Office.

At that moment he was doomed, and the Confederate lobby discred-
ited. Roebuck had broken a cardinal rule: he, a backbencher, had wedged
himself into the middle of Anglo-French relations. Although Lord Robert Cecil defended Roebuck's good intentions and Henry Morgan-Clifford
spoke of the 'barbarity' of the Federal army that disgusted 'even the
Negroes', the Tories abandoned Roebuck to his fate – MPs known to
sympathize with the South expressed their disapproval of the motion,
and the under-secretaries from the Home and Foreign Offices were
robust in their criticism of his interference. Gladstone's telling-off was
merciful by comparison, though the Cabinet was furious with Roebuck
for dredging up the question of recognition. But there was more to
come. John Bright had watched his prey stagger and bleed from a thousand little cuts before he moved in for the kill. He recalled with biting
sarcasm that 'only about two years ago' Roebuck had stated categorically, 'I have no faith in the Emperor of the French', and yet here he was
appearing before the House as the emissary of 'the great French ruler'.
As to the confusion between Roebuck and the Foreign Office over what
the Emperor had actually communicated:

> I will say this in justice to the French Emperor, that there has never come
> from him, nor from any one of his ministers, nor is there anything to be
> found in what they have written, that is tinctured in the smallest degree with
> that bitter hostility which the hon. and learned Gentleman [Mr Roebuck]
> has constantly exhibited to the United States of America and their people.[1]

Observing Roebuck's humiliation, Henry Adams wrote that Bright
'caught and shook and tossed Roebuck, as a big mastiff shakes a wiry,
ill-conditioned, toothless, bad-tempered Yorkshire terrier'. His crushing of
the MP was so complete that Henry 'felt an artistic sympathy with Roebuck, for, from time to time, by way of practice, Bright in a friendly way
was apt to shake him too, and he knew how it was done'. A Southerner

described it as 'the most deliberate and tremendous pounding I have ever witnessed'.[2] The House adjourned for the night, leaving Roebuck's motion prostrate on the floor.

There was consternation in Whitehall and the Quai d'Orsay as to how Anglo-French policy could have degenerated so swiftly into public farce. The French Foreign Minister, Édouard Drouyn de Lhuys, dispatched a telegram to Ambassador Gros in London asking for an explanation of the British government's denial.[3] At the Foreign Office, Lord Russell asked Lord Cowley, Britain's Ambassador to France, whether he had knowledge of a proposal from the Emperor. Russell vaguely recalled Baron Gros's aside about the Emperor's support for Southern recognition, but it had never occurred to him to treat it as an official communiqué to the government. Just as troubling to the Cabinet was the claim in Roebuck's speech that Louis-Napoleon had complained of his peace overtures being ridiculed by the British. The Foreign Office clerks were ordered to comb through every diplomatic dispatch of the past twelve months to see if there was any truth to the allegation.

When Mason reported the debacle to Slidell, his chief concern was whether they would be able to procure written evidence to prove Roebuck's claim. James Spence and William Gregory, on the other hand, wanted only to be rid of the controversy; they pleaded with Roebuck to withdraw his motion. 'The members are 10 to 1 in favour of the South,' wrote Spence to Commissioner Mason, but the minute the Emperor of France was dragged into the debate, the issue became a matter of national pride and 'on this point the vote might be 5 to 1 against Southern interests'.[4] Roebuck, as Spence had feared, would not be swayed, nor would he listen to Palmerston, who wrote to him on 9 July saying he was welcome to make his motions in support of the South, but he was treading on dangerous ground when he interfered in matters of state. Roebuck was defiant. That same day *The Times* predicted the capture of Washington by Lee.[5]

On Friday, 10 July Roebuck tried to resume his motion only to find himself blocked by his friends. William Schaw Lindsay urged him to wait until after the arrival of the *Scotia* in three days' time – bringing definitive news of Lee's victory – which would cast the debate in an entirely different light. The Confederates added their own entreaties, terrified that Roebuck was on course to destroy the South's political chances in the Commons permanently. In Henry Hotze's opinion, the question of recognition would 'never again receive serious attention, even if a man could be found bold enough to broach it after the experience of the last two weeks'. All he desired now was a 'decent retreat' before the House had the opportunity to vote down Roebuck's motion.[6]

The Times helped the Confederates by printing an editorial on Monday, 13 July, urging Roebuck to withdraw his motion. Finally, Roebuck listened to the pleas from the chorus around him. That same evening he announced to the House his decision to withdraw his motion. Benjamin Moran was in the gallery, watching as the Southern lobby squirmed during Roebuck's speech. William Lindsay spoke immediately after, telling Members that whatever else they thought of his friend, he was not a liar; the Emperor truly had told them of his desire to recognize the South. The speech was 'a long rambling half mad jumble', wrote Moran, 'which the House alternately laughed and jeered at. Then Palmerston rose, and while patting the two dupes on the head, expressed the hope that the unusual proceedings ... would never be repeated.'[7] The Confederates were never happier to see a motion die.

Charles Francis Adams attended a reception at Lord Derby's later that night, his recent depression almost lifted by the Confederate fiasco in the Commons. The Tories pressed him for news, forcing him to admit that, like them, he was waiting for the Atlantic steamer to arrive. But when the *Scotia* did come, on Thursday, 17 July, the reports about the battle at Gettysburg were unclear. Adams could not tell whether Lee had suffered a defeat or merely been checked for a day or so. *The Times* hedged but leaned towards a momentary delay. Two days later, however, Henry Adams came down to breakfast and found his father reading the victory telegram from the State Department. 'I wanted to hug the army of the Potomac,' Henry wrote of his joy at that moment. 'I wanted to get the whole of the army of Vicksburg drunk at my own expense. I wanted to fight some small man and lick him.' The telegram announced not only Lee's retreat from Gettysburg but also the fall of Vicksburg.

An uneven line of soiled white flags had signalled the surrender of Vicksburg on 4 July. As the medical inspector of the 13th Army Corps, Dr Charles Mayo was among the first wave of Federal officers sent to inspect the situation inside the town. Seven thousand mortar shells had been lobbed into Vicksburg during the forty-three-day siege. In some

Rebels marching out of Vicksburg and stacking arms

streets every single house had been hit; shattered glass and wooden shards lay strewn everywhere. 'The blackened ruins that had once been houses' made Mayo wonder how Londoners would fare in similar circumstances. 'We knew quite well that the besieged would be unable to take charge of their own. As it was we found their sick in a most miserable plight,' he wrote. 'The state of their hospitals was such that a regard for our own safety compelled us to place them in the hands of our own medical officers for instant purification and speedy abolition. They had come to the end of their resources. About 15,000 men fit for duty was all that remained of Pemberton's army: his sick numbered 6000 or 7000.'*[8]

The fighting was not over, although Pemberton had finally given up Vicksburg, General Johnston had no intention of surrendering

---

* While Mayo was exploring Vicksburg, he was the subject of cheerful conversation at home. On 11 July 1863 the *Medical Times and Gazette* reported on the dinner held by the Southampton Medical Society: 'Mr Dayman spoke at length: "A son of one of their old associates, Mr. Mayo, of Winchester (hear, hear), was at that moment with the army in America." – [A deeply-toned Voice: Yes, but on the wrong side – laughter.] "There were no wrongs on the side of Surgery." (Hear.) [A Voice: I should prefer his being in the south. Another Voice: The north is more bracing, and laughter.] "Their young friend, Dr. Chas. Mayo, was with the army in North America." – [A Voice: The right man in the right place,

the regiments under his control. He decided to make a stand at Jackson, whose citizens were still struggling to resurrect the city after its occupation in May. Frank Vizetelly reluctantly decided that it was time for him to leave before the Federals seized control of the last railroads going east. He made it out just in time: on 7 July 46,000 US troops, led by General Sherman himself, crossed the Big Black River and were only 20 miles from Jackson. But the journey quickly became a nightmare once the parched and dusty soldiers discovered that the retreating Confederates had fouled all the wells. Sherman was forced to send his mule teams back to the Big Black to collect drinking water for his thirsty army. At Jackson, he encountered another problem: the Confederates were too well entrenched to be dislodged by anything except a sustained artillery barrage – the kind that required much more ammunition than the Federals had brought. It took less than an hour for the Union batteries to fire all their available shells. Sherman hastily sent his ordnance officers to round up all the army's reserves. In the meantime the guns remained silent.

---

and laughter.] "He was gone out as a volunteer Surgeon, taking with him no prejudiced views of the supremacy of Military Surgery, but content to carry into the field the principles which had made his father ... Might their young friend do justice, not only to Hampshire, but also to England." (Applause).'

The surrender of Vicksburg – view of the city from the riverbank showing part
of the river batteries

Helpless until the ammunition arrived, the soldiers fortified their
positions with heavy bales of cotton, brought in from the surrounding
countryside by heavily guarded wagon trains. Undaunted by the capture of the previous wagon train, Ebenezer Wells set off with his despite
having an escort that was only half-strength. 'I was about six miles out,
riding along in front of my teams,' he wrote, when 'I was startled by a
shot passing close to me.' It seemed to be coming from a nearby cornfield. One of the guards became frightened and jumped into a wagon. As
he landed his gun went off, firing a bullet into Wells's best friend. Torn
between saving the wounded officer and protecting the supply train,
Wells shouted for the wagons to keep moving without him and carried
his friend to the edge of the road. 'I knelt beside him while he told me
his last message home,' he recorded. The officer begged him to send his
watch and bible home to his family. 'Then, asking me to take his hand
but not to move it for the pain, he told me to go as I was in danger.'
Wells reluctantly galloped off after his wagons. Travelling down the

same road on the return journey, he was horrified to see a large red stain where his friend had been lying. 'By great favour the General allowed me to have a funeral,' wrote Wells. The ammunition had arrived and the guns were firing when the burial took place, the priest's words drowned out by the roar of the artillery.[9]

The next day, 17 July 1863, a lone black civilian was spotted walking away from the city, carrying a white flag.[10] Johnston had led his army out during the night, leaving Jackson silent and empty but for a few hundred frightened citizens. The Federals marched in, capturing some Confederate stragglers, among them an Englishman named Captain Frederick Hampson of the 13th Louisiana Regiment. Two years later, after he had escaped to England, Captain Hampson still shuddered at his treatment:

> When captured by the enemy I was stripped of my clothes, even my shoes then robbed of my money, watch and rings. [I] was then marched a distance of 45 miles to Vicksburg BAREFOOT, and on the route was grossly insulted by the privates and some officers of the Federal Army: I experienced fearful suffering from hunger, exposure and thirst, not being allowed to leave the

ranks, and when we bivouacked [we had] no tents or covering to protect us from the weather: it raining almost all the time ... I remained in their hands until about the middle of August, when I succeeded with two more brother officers in effecting my escape from Vicksburg, thence to New Orleans, and from there made the best of my way (via New York by water) to England.[11]

Ebenezer Wells had fallen victim to 'Mississippi fever' and was too ill to celebrate the Federal capture of Jackson, becoming another of the delirious, groaning soldiers whom Dr Mayo tried to keep alive long enough to be transported to the North. Mayo had more than five hundred patients in his field hospital, with ninety of them under his personal care. He was no longer living in a tent, but on a steamboat next to the hospital ships. Lord Lyons's reply to his letter reached him there. Though disappointed by the Minister's refusal to pass on his resignation, Mayo was gracious in his response, apologizing for placing him in an uncomfortable position: 'Of course I had no right to expect any other reply than that which I have just received,' he replied to Lyons in late July. 'Two months of sickness in a climate like this, incurred through a blunder made by a Washington office-assistant do not tend to improve a man's temper, nor to reconcile him to his position. I intend to leave this district with or without orders, at the first opportunity.'[12]

'The fall of Vicksburg has made me ill all the week,' James Spence wrote to Mason.[13] The Times downplayed the news at first; but on 23 July Charles Francis Adams noted that the paper 'condescends to admit this morning that Vicksburg is taken'. Three days later, The Times was also forced to concede the Federal capture of the Mississippi river – Port Hudson had surrendered to General Nathaniel Banks on 9 July after a forty-eight-day siege.

As soon as Henry Hotze recovered from the shock of the news – no one had expected Vicksburg to surrender, let alone General Lee to falter – he began rallying his supporters in the press. It was imperative that they halt the now precipitous slide of Confederate bonds. 'You will not be surprised that I am giving to my operations an extension which only the urgencies of the crisis could warrant,' he informed the Confederate Secretary of State, Judah P. Benjamin. Hotze had pulled off the extraordinary feat of persuading a religious publishing house to include in every publication, religious and non-religious, for the next two months a Southern pamphlet entitled, 'Address to the Christians throughout the World'. Signed by the ninety-six clergymen of Richmond, Virginia, the 'Address' urged fellow Christians to protest against Lincoln's Emancipation Proclamation.[14] Hotze estimated that it would be read by two million people.[15] This and the obvious shock felt by the public were his only comfort.

There was outrage in the legation at the lack of enthusiasm in England over the Northern successes. *The Economist* described Lee's defeat as a tragedy because it meant a prolonging of the war.[16] 'The salons of this great metropolis are in tears,' Adams wrote cynically in his diary. 'Tears of anger mixed with grief.' He was still smarting over the ignominious end to Mrs Adams's weekly parties; not even Benjamin Moran bothered to attend the final one.* The Assistant Secretary had ceased to attend out of protest, having been cast into a jealous agony ever since George Sheffield, one of Lord Lyons's unpaid attachés, visited the legation and innocently revealed that Lyons invited the junior diplomats to every dinner. Moran blamed Henry Adams for stealing his rightful place. Ironically, Henry had recently written to Seward's son, Frederick, pleading for an increase in salary in recognition of Moran's services: 'he is an invaluable man,' he wrote, 'a tremendous worker, and worth any ten ordinary officers to Government, but here he has borne nine tenths of the labour of the Legation for seven years, and gets for it a miserable pittance of $1500 a year; about enough to support a respectable cab-driver in this city.'[17]

Unaware of Henry's intercession on his behalf, Moran behaved towards him with appalling rudeness and spite. It pained him to watch Henry slowly navigate his way into English society and start to enjoy a real life outside the legation. The younger Adams had become a member of the Cosmopolitan Club, which did not have permanent premises like Brooks's or Boodles, but whose members were all notable figures on the literary or political stage. Henry was mystified why Lord Frederick

---

* Adams had also cancelled the legation's Fourth of July celebration. The previous year's dinner had been a desultory affair. He expected this year's to be no better, and he feared a visit from the popular orator Henry Ward Beecher, brother of the author Harriet Beecher Stowe, who was visiting England on a lecture tour. Beecher was rousing the British public but for all the wrong reasons, telling a gathering of temperance campaigners, for example, that the North was losing because its army officers could not stay sober.

Cavendish had championed his admission: 'whether he feels his conscience touched by the vagaries of his brother Hartington; or whether he desires to show a general and delicate sympathy with our position,' he wrote to Charles Francis Jr., 'I don't know and can't guess.' But more important even than joining a club or being proposed by a peer, Henry had finally made a genuine friend, Charles Milnes Gaskell, known as Carlo, the son of James Gaskell, a Yorkshire MP and supporter of the North. The friendship, wrote Henry Adams, 'affected his whole life'.[18]

The season was drawing to a close. 'The streets are full of Pickford's vans carting furniture from the houses, and Belgravia and May Fair are the scene of dirt and littered straw,' Henry wrote to his brother. He knew he would miss the excitement. Despite everything, he liked going about in London society, 'and some day in America,' he wrote, 'I may astonish myself by defending these people for whom I entertain at present only a profound and lively contempt.'[19]

Their father was looking forward to the summer recess: though the year had begun disastrously, none of it now seemed to matter. 'The great causes of our apprehension have died away,' he wrote. 'The cotton famine and Lancashire distress have not proved such serious troubles as we had feared.'[20] Newspapers no longer carried alarming reports of protest meetings and 'disturbances' in the mill towns. The Earl of Derby's Central Committee was efficiently distributing almost £500,000-worth of charity and the Poor Law Board was overseeing a £2 million public works programme in Lancashire, paying the unemployed cotton workers to build sewers, pave roads and create public parks and recreation grounds.[21] Some mills were using cotton from India – even though it was of inferior quality to Southern cotton – which had almost doubled imports from 536,000 bales in 1861 to over a million in 1863. Moreover, there were plenty of opportunities for workers who were willing to move away from the cotton districts. The British linen and woollen industries were enjoying a renaissance, for example, the profits from blockade-running were swilling around Liverpool, and the armaments industry was having its best year ever.[22] The latest figures showed that even with the dragging effects of the Morrill Tariff, the value of British trade was rising and would top £444 million for 1863. All of these developments were an encouraging counterbalance to the troubles of the cotton industry.

*

The legation was settling into its usual summer routine when Benjamin Moran noticed something strange. He wrote on 27 July: 'the steamer this week brought no Despatches whatever. This never occurred before in my time.'[23]

The abrupt silence had been caused by the complete breakdown of civic order in New York. For five days, between 13 and 17 July, the city lay at the mercy of 50,000 rioters who exacted a gruesome revenge on the two classes of persons they considered most responsible for the war: Negroes and those who defended them. There had been signs of working-class resentment ever since the Draft Act became law on 3 March 1863. In theory it provided Washington with more than three million potential new soldiers; in practice it netted about 100,000 reluctant conscripts and 70,000 substitutes. The draft applied to all able-bodied white males between the ages of 20 and 45, but the exemptions for particular family circumstances, such as only sons with widowed mothers to support – as well as the provision which allowed a man to purchase a substitute for $300 – mostly benefited the middle classes and native-born Americans.[24] (For immigrant labourers earning an average of 85 cents a day, the sum of $300 was a cruel joke.) Nowhere was the resentment greater than among the 200,000 Irish immigrants of New York, many of whom felt that they had been enticed into emigrating so that they could provide 'food for [gun]powder'. The editor of the *Freeman's Journal*, a popular Irish newspaper in New York, demanded to know why the Irish were expected 'to go and carry on a war for the nigger'.[25]

Although aliens were specifically excluded from the draft, the State Department had recently tightened the rules and increased the burden of proof required from resident foreigners.* Consul Archibald was struggling to keep pace with the demand for his help. There had been a sharp increase since the spring in the number of 'crimpings', kidnappings and illegal conscriptions of British subjects. The latest complaint to reach the consulate involved three Caribbean sailors who had disappeared

---

* British residents were required to go in person to the New York consulate to receive a Certificate of Nationality, which could be presented to the Enrollment Board. Each person had to sign an affidavit and bring a witness who could corroborate his statement. The fee for the certificate was $3, which Archibald generally waived. He tried to make the process faster but the enrolment offices frustrated his efforts. There was one in every district of the city, and all demanded slightly different criteria for proof of exemption. Archibald was overwhelmed.

from the *Mary Harris* only to reappear as unwilling seamen on board USS *Tulip*. Archibald wondered whether the recent strike by Irish dock workers had something to do with the *Tulip* case; the shipyard owners had brought in contrabands – freed slaves – to replace the workers. The combination of the looming draft and black strike-breakers was an especially inflammable mix. The working-class Irish community was outraged that the draft only applied to whites and feared that cheaper – and better educated – black workers were out to steal their jobs.

On Saturday, 11 July 1863 the authorities chose a half-developed block of Manhattan – 47th Street and Third Avenue–to hold the first of two lotteries for the draft. Colonel Robert Nugent of the Irish 69th New York Volunteers had been asked to oversee the lottery in the hope that this would calm Irish objections. But no other preparations had been made in case there was violence; there were only 800 policemen on duty for the entire city, and almost every New York regiment was at Gettysburg with General Meade.[26] The drawing of names passed without incident, however. There were a few more fires than usual over the weekend, and the crowds watching them seemed to be on the large side, but the authorities had no hint of what was about to happen on Monday.

When the famous *Great Eastern* – the largest passenger ship in the world – docked at New York on Sunday night, the disembarking passengers felt an air of menace from the onlookers. The financial agents John Murray Forbes and William H. Aspinwall were among them; in Forbes's trunk were $6 million-worth of bonds. He was standing on the quayside, fearful that he was about to be mugged, when an Irish cab driver recognized him from a goodwill visit Forbes had once paid to his regiment and offered to take him anywhere he wanted. 'We rattled safely over the rough, dark streets, and I was soon glad to deposit my charge among the heaps in the old Brevoort House [Hotel],' wrote Forbes.[27] A few hours later, Lieutenant Colonel Fremantle's train pulled into New York from Pennsylvania. He had said farewell to his friends on 9 July when the Confederate army was still resting at Hagerstown in Maryland and turned back towards the North. Fremantle's steamship, the *China*, was scheduled to depart for England on Wednesday, 15 July, and until then he had arranged to stay at the Fifth Avenue Hotel on Madison Square. Even though the city was searingly hot, Fremantle walked the length of Broadway on Monday. 'On returning to the Fifth Avenue,' he wrote, 'I found all the shopkeepers beginning to close their stores, and I perceived by degrees that there was great alarm about the resistance to the draft which was going on this morning.' Inside the hotel he found a scene of pandemonium, with terrified guests begging the equally frightened concierges for protection. A mob had torched several blocks nearby and was holding back the fire brigade. Fremantle decided it would be better to wander around anonymously rather than be trapped or cornered in the hotel: 'I walked about in the neighbourhood, and saw a company of soldiers [from the invalid corps] on the march, who were being jeered at and hooted by small boys, and I saw a negro pursued by the crowd take refuge with the military; he was followed by loud cries of "Down with the bloody nigger! Kill all niggers!" etc.'[28]

The British Consul was able to rescue Ann Anderson, a Barbadian ship's cook, who was being chased down West Street by a mob. Fortunately, she had time to hammer on the doors of the consulate at No. 10 and be pulled to safety. Twenty blocks north from Fremantle's hotel, at 43rd and Fifth, stood the Colored Orphan Asylum, home to 237 Negro children aged 12 and under. Three thousand rioters gathered at the front, forcing the asylum superintendent hurriedly to evacuate the small occupants out through the back. One little girl was left behind. She was found cowering under her bed by the rioters and beaten to death.[29]

Further downtown, another mob, heavily armed and 10,000-strong, appeared in front of the police headquarters on Mulberry Street and was confronted by 200 club-wielding policemen. After twenty minutes of hand-to-hand fighting, the mob turned tail.[30] The violence was sporadic but clearly the result of direction. Small working parties cut down the telegraph poles along Third Avenue, isolating each of the twenty-six police precincts from central command. Others stopped the railroad cars and pulled up the rail tracks. Rioters broke into the Armoury on 21st Street and Second Avenue, helping themselves to the rifles and carbines within. A separate mob headed over to Newspaper Row, across from City Hall Park, where the *Tribune* and the *New York Times* had their offices. The *Times* editor, Henry Raymond, kept the crowd at bay with three borrowed Gatling guns, but the *Tribune* building had only a small band of policemen guarding its entrance.[31] Rioters burst through the doors to find that the staff had used bales of newspaper to barricade the stairs. Unable to push their way through, the mob set fire to the counters and went off in search of other prey.

By sunset, the orange sky was streaked with columns of black smoke.

Hiding inside the St Nicholas Hotel, the Mayor of New York, George Opdyke, and the US army general in command of the Department of the East, John Ellis Wool, passed their responsibilities back and forth as a group of prominent citizens implored them to declare martial law. At 9.30 p.m. the New York head of the telegraph service, Edwin Sanford, sent a wire to Washington from Jersey City, whose station was still operating: 'In brief the city of New York is tonight at the mercy of a mob whether organized or improvised, I am unable to say ... The situation is not improved since dark. The program is diversified by small mobs chasing isolated Negroes as hounds would chase a fox.'

There were fires burning uncontrollably all over the city. Establishments that employed blacks as well as whites, such as bars and brothels, were particularly targeted. Dr Elizabeth Blackwell feared for the Infirmary and ordered the servants to close the shutters and lock the doors. Every light was extinguished, leaving the occupants sitting in darkness as the muffled but unmistakable shouts of a lynch mob torturing its victim could be heard through the walls. Some of the white patients became hysterical, begging Dr Blackwell to save the hospital by expelling the black occupants. She had almost succeeded in calming them down when one of the contraband patients went into labour. Terrified that the woman's cries might be heard from outside, Dr Blackwell and two nurses carried her to the back of the Infirmary. There, in a semi-lit room, they worked all night to deliver the baby.

Meanwhile, mobs were prowling the waterfront, attacking British vessels known to have black crew-members. One black sailor was lynched and another suffered life-threatening injuries. Archibald turned the consulate into a safe house, but with limited space at his disposal he had to ask the legation in Washington for help. Although there were no carriages or omnibuses running, an intrepid secretary at the consulate managed to reach Jersey City to send a ciphered telegram from Archibald to Lord Lyons: 'I consider a man-of-war essential here immediately to receive and protect British Black crews.' Lyons replied that the HMS *Challenger* was on its way, but the warship would not reach New York for at least another twenty-four hours. Archibald could not wait that long. In desperation, he contacted the French consulate, which arranged for Admiral Reynaud to offer the *Guerriere* to British blacks. The French frigate steamed into the harbour, opened the gun ports and let down rope ladders. The captain shouted through his megaphone that all coloured Britons were to board the vessel by order of Consul Archibald. Seventy-one black British sailors clambered aboard, and a further seven British vessels moored alongside her.

The violence on Tuesday included mass looting and more raids on the armouries. Rioters sacked Brooks Brothers, burned the 26th Precinct house, destroyed the Harlem river bridge, demolished the Washington Hotel and attacked the Mayor's house. Fifty to sixty thousand people were said to be out on the streets; barricades were being erected at various points in the city to hinder the movement of police. 'Immediate action is necessary, or the Government and country will be disgraced,' Edwin Sanford telegraphed the War Department. The Governor of New York, Horatio Seymour, declared a state of insurrection and also asked Washington for troops. A politician to his fingertips, he assured the angry crowd outside City Hall that he was their friend and supporter against the draft but his appeal failed to stop the violence. Finally, late on Tuesday night, Washington ordered five regiments to the city.

'Wednesday begins with heavy showers, and now, (ten a.m.) cloudy, hot, and steaming,' wrote the treasurer of the US Sanitary Commission, George Templeton Strong, in his diary; 'there will be much trouble today.'[32] When Fremantle went down for breakfast he found soldiers guarding the hotel (Robert Lincoln, the President's eldest son, was coming home from Harvard and happened to be one of the guests). But outside, the immediate streets were deserted; the entire city appeared to be in the middle of a mass exodus. There were no carriages and he had to walk down to the waterfront. 'I was not at all sorry to find myself on board the *China*,' wrote Fremantle, his final memory of the city was of 'a stone barricade in the distance, and [the sound of] firing going on'.[33] The mob and the military had evidently found one another.[34]

At mid-morning a small funeral cortège started out from West 53rd Street. Dr Charles Culverwell's wife, Emma, could no longer wait for the rioting to subside. Their 3-year-old daughter had died on Sunday of infant cholera. Emma did not know where Charles was, although he had promised to come to them. Terrified for herself and her surviving daughter, she attempted to slink unnoticed past the rioters. They barred her way, forcing Emma to plead for permission to bury her child.[35] All this time Culverwell had been begging his hospital superiors in St Louis to grant him compassionate leave. In desperation he annulled his contract on 16 July, donned civilian dress and headed for New York.

By Wednesday night HMS *Challenger* had still not appeared; however, a US warship had joined the *Guerriere* and was training its guns on Wall Street to deter an attack on the financial district. On Thursday, rioters discovered they were fighting not just a few brave souls but 10,000 veterans of Gettysburg. During the night there was a final, bloody convulsion at Gramercy Square on 20th Street, which left one soldier and fifteen rioters dead. But at noon on Friday the roars and explosions ceased as suddenly as they had begun; Elizabeth Blackwell unlocked the doors of the Infirmary for the first time in forty-eight hours. Edwin Sanford telegraphed Washington at 3.45 p.m. that the 'city continues very quiet'. George Templeton Strong blessed the change in weather: 'rain will keep the rabble quiet tonight.'[36] Early estimates put the death toll at anywhere from 100 to 1,000 people, but the physical devastation was obvious. Whole blocks had been burned and more than 300 buildings destroyed.[37] Among the homes that had been ransacked was Colonel Nugent's – a punishment for his role in enforcing the draft.

'It is a fact that the rioters have been almost entirely Irish,' Archibald wrote to Lord Russell, and their fury towards 'the poor Negro people' had not abated simply because of the presence of troops.[38] HMS *Challenger* arrived on Saturday and accepted transfer of the refugees from the *Guerriere*. The seventy-one coloured seamen remained sequestered below for several days. 'There are, however, many lawless characters still about the wharves,' Archibald wrote on 20 July, 'and the masters assure me that it is not safe for the Negro sailors to return to their own vessels.'[39] Although the Consul was due to take his annual leave, he remained in the smouldering city until he was confident that the danger had passed.

Lyons had not heard from Seward during the crisis; violence had flared in other parts of New York and the Secretary's own house in Auburn was attacked. The incident was relatively small – a rock hurled through a downstairs window – but for several nights Frances Seward had stayed awake, waiting for the sound of breaking glass. Be prepared for the loss of our home, Seward wrote stoically to his wife; if the war brings an end to slavery, 'the sacrifice will be a small one'.[40]

Despite Archibald's brave conduct during the riots, British subjects 'are far from being pleased either with HM Government or with HM Minister here', Lord Lyons told Lord Russell on 24 July. No one thought that the legation was doing enough to protect Britons from the rampant

"ROWDY" NOTIONS OF EMANCIPATION.

" THE mob on the corner, below my house, had hung up a negro to the lamp-post. In mockery, a cigar was placed in his mouth. * * * For hours these scared negroes poured up Twenty-seventh Street, passing my house. * * * One old negro, 70 years old, blind as a bat, and such a cripple that he could hardly move, was led along by this equally aged wife with a few rags they had saved, trembling with fright, and not knowing where to go."—MANHATTAN's *Letter in the Standard, July 30th.*

Punch accuses President Lincoln of doing nothing to save free
blacks from the rioting Irish

cheating and illegal conscriptions that accompanied the latest draft effort. 'If I have not succeeded as well as I ought, I have done more than most people, who knew everything about the difficulties, expected,' insisted Lyons. 'I have taken more pains myself about it, and given Mr Seward more trouble about it, than about any matter which I have had to treat with him.'[41] The legation staff was working late into the night, trying to keep abreast of the rapidly increasing number of case files. Few cases, if any, were straightforward.[42] Young Frederick Farr refused to be helped. He ignored the attachés' enquiries and would not respond to letters from his father's friends. 'That is a queer boy of yours,' one of them wrote to Dr Farr in exasperation; 'I have not been able to draw a line from him.' Farr's commanding officer reported that the boy was 'in excellent health and spirits' after Gettysburg and only wanted to be left alone.[43]

Lyons knew there was nothing to be gained from telling British subjects that they should count themselves fortunate to be in the North and not in the South, where the situation was far worse. In addition to being tricked or beaten into joining regular regiments, Britons were being rounded up to man 'home defence militias' and there was nothing the Consuls could do about it; Judah P. Benjamin expelled Consul George Moore from Richmond in June for allegedly exceeding the limits of his purview. One of the very few British conscripts to escape to the North, a Mr R. R. Belshaw, thanked Lyons 'for the interest which you have taken in my case', but, he complained, 'Thousands of British subjects are daily suffering in the Confederate army as I have done and yet there is no relief; though England speaks she says nothing.'[44]

Lyons did not have a satisfactory answer for Belshaw; the diplomatic situation in the South was beyond his control and yet somehow still perceived by Washington and London as his responsibility.* Lord Russell pondered whether they ought to send a military agent or commissioner to Richmond, going the same route as Fremantle in order to avoid running the blockade, but Lyons persuaded him against the idea. The North would object, and the Confederate government would no doubt ignore the agent as it did the Consuls. Seward was adamant that any attempt to contact the Southern authorities would be regarded by the United States as an act of deliberate provocation, if not war.

Lyons did not understand what drove the Secretary of State. Sometimes they seemed to be in the most perfect harmony. Tucked away in the Seward archives are private letters showing that Lyons often coached Seward on how to frame his official responses to British complaints.[46] But Seward was always playing more than one game at a time. In early August he asked Lyons if Britain would be prepared to join the US in fighting the French takeover of Mexico. 'It would no doubt be a relief to Mr Seward,' Lyons reported after the interview, if Britain assumed the burden of defending the Mexicans – and the Monroe Doctrine – against the Emperor's imperialist designs. But 'England would run the greatest risk of being ultimately sacrificed without scruple by the United States'.[47]

Four days later, on 7 August, Lyons was distressed to see his suspicions

* The Secretary of the Navy, Gideon Welles, had a strangely inflated idea of Lyons's power. It was mortifying, he complained, 'the extent Lord Lyons shapes and directs, through the Secretary of State, an erroneous policy to this government.' The CSS *Florida* had recently sailed within 60 miles of New York, leaving a trail of burning ships and bruised egos in her wake. Welles sent six cruisers to chase after the elusive Captain Maffitt and his crew, but a false lead had led them up the East Coast towards Nantucket. This, too, was somehow Lord Lyons's fault.[45]

confirmed. 'An impending quarrel with England is allowed to be put forward as a lure to Volunteers for the Army,' he informed Russell. Seward's latest dispatch to Charles Francis Adams predicted war if the British government failed to halt the Confederates' shipbuilding programme. Seward knew that Adams would never show such a threatening letter to Lord Russell; and Lyons knew it too, telling Russell, 'It will not, I suppose, be communicated to you, but will first see the light when Congress assembles in December.'[48]

Lyons was about to leave for a short visit to Canada when Seward waylaid him with a proposition to spend the last two weeks of August exploring northern New York State: all the foreign Ministers had been invited. Lyons could think of few things worse than being dragged through the wilds with the very people he wished to escape. But, he confessed in a private letter to Lord Russell, Seward 'has made such a point of my going with him, that it has been impossible to get off without telling him plainly that I'd not choose to travel with him. This of course I could not do; and he deserves some consideration from us.'[49]

Lyons would not have felt so guilty if he had known the reasons behind Seward's invitation. The Secretary of State had been entertaining for some time the idea of a summer jaunt with the diplomatic corps, which would allow him to demonstrate his charming side and the North's booming economy all at the same time; but he only went forward with his plan when he needed a cover for visiting Judge Samuel Nelson of the Supreme Court. Opponents of the draft were mounting legal challenges and the administration wanted to be sure that the court would make the right decision. Judge Nelson happened to live in Cooperstown, upstate New York.

On 15 August the large party of diplomats and officials boarded a special train for New York; Lyons had brought along two attachés so he would not have to do all the talking. Contrary to his fears, Seward behaved with impeccable manners throughout the journey; ice cream was provided when it was hot, and carriages for those who preferred to explore sitting down. This rarely seen side of Seward touched Lyons. The Secretary of State was incurably vain, he told Russell, but the more one knew of him, the more there was 'to esteem and even to like'. The trouble lay in Seward's tendency to overplay his hand, which required Lyons to exercise his 'patience and good temper to be always cordial with him'.[50]

The two-week excursion finished with a visit to Niagara Falls on 25 August. Seward had a long conversation with Lyons before the Minister departed for Canada. He began by referring to the problem of British antipathy towards the North. Lyons assured him that the pro-Southern feeling would dissipate as soon the war ended, since there would be 'nothing to keep it alive. I told him that the important point was public opinion in the United States.' But Seward insisted that something had to be done to change British opinion: 'The President could not travel, and the United States had no Princes.' Lyons listened, wondering where this was leading. Then it dawned on him that Seward was floating the idea of a goodwill visit to England. The prospect seemed baffling and Lyons suspected Seward was thinking more of his domestic audience, perhaps for a future presidential run. Guessing how the Cabinet would react to such a tour, Lyons gently discouraged the plan. When he heard of it, Palmerston was indeed horrified: 'I hope Seward will not come here,' he wrote to Lord Russell. The visit would not change British policy – except for the worse if Seward said something silly. 'He is . . . vulgar and ungentlemanlike and the more he is seen here the less he will be liked.' He would drink brandy with 'some editors of second rate newspapers', and be fêted by the manufacturing towns, but 'I doubt whether Seward would be very well received in Society'.[51] Seward soon dropped the idea – to a silent chorus of relief in England.

After the tour's conclusion, Lyons travelled to Canada in the hope of finally obtaining some rest from his labours. But there he found that the conflict was being enacted in miniature north of the border. Crimpers and recruiters were doing a brisk business along the border towns, turning Canadian public opinion dangerously pro-Southern. The authorities suspected the Confederates were planning to use Canada as a base for operations, although so far there was little proof to support these fears.

The idea of launching raids from Canada had indeed been suggested to Jefferson Davis, but he remained undecided, worrying that the international community would regard such a move as a last, desperate measure. For the moment, Davis had decided to pursue an alternative course. The North was constantly sending emissaries to meet with influential members of British society, and he was sure that the South had suffered as a result. To redress the balance, Davis had asked Rose Greenhow – whom he remembered as one of the most powerful hostesses in Washington before the war – to travel to England and to France with the express purpose of explaining the case for Southern independence. Slidell would help her gain an audience with the Emperor, but the rest would be up to her own efforts.

Rose had been living quietly since her arrival in Richmond in June the previous year. Between looking after 10-year-old Rose, and writing a memoir of her imprisonment in Washington, she had managed to make a semblance of a life for herself. But she had not been happy. The Southern ladies had not welcomed her into their circle – Mary Chesnut waspishly described Rose as 'spoiled by education – or the want of it'.[52] President Davis's request was a welcome rescue not only from her grinding day-to-day existence, but also from the petty disapproval of Richmond society.

There were no other travellers at the Mill's House Hotel when Rose arrived in Charleston during the second half of July; the other guests were all black-marketeers of some description. Within hours of unpacking, she received a visit from General Beauregard. Knowing that she had a direct link to President Davis, he gave her a frank report of the situation and explained why he needed more artillery. The Federal bombardment was about to resume, and this time the Confederates expected it to continue until the city surrendered.

Rose's next guest was Frank Vizetelly. 'He gives me all that he gathers, altho' under the seal of confidence as I told him I should tell you,' she informed President Davis. Vizetelly believed that the shortage of drinking wells around Jackson, Mississippi, would soon exact a crushing toll on Grant's army, having witnessed 'eight men within a space of thirty feet fall down from want of water'. This fact alone, he told her, guaranteed that CS General Johnston would not be driven out of the city. But in fact, even as Vizetelly spoke, the Confederates were retreating from Jackson and in a few hours the city would be in flames.

> Best of all [concluded Rose], this man's account inspired me . . . with great hope – and he thinks that the tighter we are pressed the better our chance of recognition – He says that the European world will never allow the reconstruction of the American Union – that their sympathies are naturally with the Anglo-Saxon race who are represented in the South . . . He says he is very glad that I am going to England as he knows I will be useful, and gives me some very good letters.

Before he left, Vizetelly handed Rose an article he had written for the *Charleston Courier*. It was one of several he was preparing to send to the Southern press, under a pseudonym, giving his view of the situation in the West. 'He thinks our people unduly depressed now by the events at Vicksburg,' Rose explained to Davis.[53] Vizetelly's passionate advocacy of the Southern cause had temporarily robbed him of his critical faculties. Every judgement, every prediction he made to Rose would turn out to be wrong.

Rose soon came to the conclusion that Charleston harbour was useless as a means of escape, and she boarded a train with little Rose for Wilmington. Her rooms at the Mill's House Hotel did not remain empty for long. On 7 August Fitzgerald Ross and Captain Scheibert checked into the hotel, having left Francis Lawley behind in Richmond. The journalist had pushed himself to the brink of collapse at Gettysburg and was too weak to travel. The pressure of maintaining an optimistic tone in his *Times* reports was also taking its toll on him. Lawley avoided discussing specifics in favour of general articles about Southern pluck and Lee's 'genius', which, he declared, would prevent the North from ever having a decisive military victory.* These were familiar sentiments to his readers, perhaps too familiar. Anthony Trollope was disappointed: 'We must be poles asunder,' he wrote of Lawley, 'till some future day when, after the end of all the bloodshed, we shall be able to talk over it all in cool philosophy.'[54]

Fitzgerald Ross recognized Vizetelly from Lawley's description when the journalist showed up at Mill's House Hotel for dinner. According to Scheibert, 'this hotel had the best service of any tavern' in the South. It charged the highest prices, too: $100 per person for a three-course meal.[55] General Beauregard welcomed Vizetelly's new friends when they called at his headquarters, and introduced them to the English officer on his staff. Henry Feilden was growing used to his role as Beauregard's talking piece and cheerfully gave a tour of the preparations against the next phase of the Federal siege. The Consuls observed with alarm that more warships were sailing into the harbour. The city itself was obvi-

---

* Charles Francis Adams Jr. was inclined to agree with Lawley. Writing from his sodden camp in Virginia on 23 July, he told his father 'that Lee's army at Gettysburg was in every respect superior to the Army of the Potomac . . . The spirit of his army was much better than that of ours . . . You will ask why we were not defeated then at Gettysburg? We just escaped it by the skin of our teeth and the strength of our position.'

ously the next objective. The British Consul, Henry Pinckney Walker, sent a message to the legation in Washington which somehow slipped through, beseeching Lord Lyons to send a British warship to rescue the 'several thousand' British women and children who were in the direct line of fire.*[56]

At 10.45 p.m. on 21 August, a note from US General Quincy Adams Gillmore was delivered to Beauregard's headquarters, announcing the imminent bombardment of the city. He had forgotten to sign it, so no one took the threat seriously. Three hours later the shelling began. 'At first I thought a meteor had fallen; but another awful rush and whirr right over the hotel and another explosion beyond, settled any doubts I might have had,' wrote Vizetelly. He threw on his clothes and ran down the stairs, fighting his way past hysterical businessmen. 'One perspiring individual of portly dimensions was trotting to and fro with one boot on and the other in his hand, and this was nearly all the dress he could boast of ... Another, in a semi-state of nudity with a portion of his garments on his arm, barked the shins of everyone in his way in his efforts to drag an enormous trunk to the staircase.'[57] Out in the street women were running in all directions, their heads ducked, some carrying children in their arms. Many people were stampeding towards the station, in a wild hope that a train would be waiting to convey them away. Vizetelly found Ross and Scheibert coolly standing around in the Mill's House bar. He persuaded them to go down to the promenade, where they would have a better view of the bombardment. To their surprise, a large crowd had already gathered there. For an hour they stood out under the open canopy of stars, with Vizetelly and Ross taking bets as to whether the shells would fall short and land on their heads.[58]

The next morning General Beauregard sent a furious note to Gillmore demanding a halt to the firing until all the civilians could be evacuated. The British Consul called on General Gillmore under a flag of truce with a similar request. The Federal commander granted a cease-fire of twenty-four hours before resuming the bombardment. After three weeks of continuous shelling the excitement wore thin, and the three friends began to discuss their departure from Charleston. On 14

---

* The British Consul was exaggerating; the number was less than a thousand. Lyons's chargé d'affaires, William Stuart, telegraphed Admiral Milne for his advice. Milne replied in the negative. It would be unthinkable, he wrote, to send in a ship now and interfere with Federal naval plans.

Downtown Charleston under fire from Union forces, by Frank Vizetelly

September Ross and Vizetelly bade farewell to Scheibert, who was returning to Prussia. 'I fear our troubles have only begun,' Thomas Prioleau wrote to his cousin Charles Prioleau, the head of Fraser, Trenholm in Liverpool. 'The fire brought against us is immense and incessant, yet we do not despair.'[59]

---

* Francis Lawley's optimistic reporting about the shelling of Charleston did not deceive William Howard Russell: 'such rubbish!' he wrote in his diary on 28 September. 'I really believe on the U.S. question the great John Bull has lost his head and is distracted by jealousy to such an extent that it has not only ceased to be just and generous but to be moderately reasonable.'

24

Devouring the Young

*Rose Greenhow sails to England – The British government vs. the
rams – Commissioner Mason leaves his post – A new breed of
volunteer – General Bragg's justice*

The blockade-runner *Phantom* was the only ship to escape from Wilmington on the night of the 5 August 1863. Rose Greenhow and her daughter were on board. 'We passed the *Elizabeth* and the *Hebe*, who had each got aground, but our anxiety was too great on our own account to bestow much thought upon our friends,' she wrote in her diary; 'the Yankees threw up rockets, which revealed to us the fact that we were in the midst of five of the "blockaders".' After rounding Cape Fear with the pursuers mercifully far behind, 'Capt. Porter had a mattress spread upon deck, upon which I lay,' Rose continued in her diary, 'watching the moon which had risen and was shining gloriously high in the Heavens, and pitying myself as the victim of that most unfortunate infirmity of seasickness.' Little Rose also felt wretched and 'crouched by my side, amidst the cotton bales which crowded the deck'.[1]

The *Phantom* sailed unmolested into St George's harbour, Bermuda, on 10 August 1863. Rose's steamship to England was not leaving for three weeks, which gave her ample opportunity to study Major Walker's shipping operation. 'The entire trade of the island is Confederate,' she remarked. The willingness of the British authorities to ignore his activities was a reflection of Bermuda's desperate plight before the war. A devout believer in 'the wise and beneficial system of servile labor', she hoped that the British now regretted their folly in abolishing slavery in 1833. Had it not been for the Confederate community on the island, all of whom shared her prejudices, Rose would have been unhappy during her stay; living cheek by jowl with a free black population seemed unnatural and offensive to her. But in contrast to her treatment at Richmond, Rose was the centre of attention in St George. 'She is one of the most beautiful women I ever saw,' gushed Georgiana Walker. 'She knows this and like a sensible woman, does not pretend to think the contrary.'[2] The fact that Rose was travelling on a diplomatic mission made her seem even more glamorous.

Rose had expected to be in Liverpool by 11 or 12 September at the latest, and was taken by surprise when the captain announced that he was changing their destination. The *Harriet Pinckney* was a new Confederate steamer, he explained, and too precious to risk becoming 'Yankee prey' on the return journey. They were heading south instead, to Falmouth on the coast of Cornwall. 'This was unexpected to us all,' she wrote in her diary, 'and everyone set to work to know where Falmouth was and what sort of a place.'[3] The captain was being overly cautious; the closest threat to the *Pinckney* was the USS *Kearsarge*, which was sailing around the Azores in the hope of finding one of the Confederate raiders.

Captain Maffitt would not have sailed the CSS *Florida* into Brest, France, had he known that his arrival would attract the attention of Federal agents, putting in jeopardy the six Confederate raiders under construction at Nantes and Bordeaux.* James Bulloch had moved his operations across the Channel after the detention of the *Alexandra* in the spring. The Emperor had given his permission for the switch to France with the proviso that if the United States uncovered the existence of the Confederate ships, the authorities would deny all knowledge of the programme.[4] Lucien Arman, owner of the largest shipbuilding firm in the country, was building four *Alabama*-style raiders for Bulloch in Bordeaux, and had also helped to arrange the contract for the two smaller ships at Nantes.

The obliging Arman – whose wealth and position had grown in step with the Emperor's desire to modernize his navy – also introduced Bulloch to the brokerage firm of Bravay and Company. Monsieur Bravay agreed to buy the Confederate rams nearing completion at the Laird

---

* Maffitt could not resist lingering in the Channel in the hope of snatching a last-minute prize, and was rewarded for his daring with the *Anglo-Saxon*, a US ship carrying coal to New York. He removed the passengers, appropriated the coal and burned the ship. The Royal Navy was affronted by Maffitt's cheek at carrying out a raid so close to British waters and sent a frigate to patrol the area. But by then Maffitt had docked at Brest.

shipyard in Liverpool for a nominal sum (plus a large commission), and maintain that they were destined for his client, the Pasha of Egypt. The intricate web of deception had been working well until the *Florida* sailed imprudently into Brest with its Confederate flag flying from the mast. The Foreign Minister, Drouyn de Lhuys, was furious and proceeded to sit on Captain Maffitt's request to use the port's repair facilities for four days before reluctantly assenting on the condition that it was kept secret from the American legation.

In London, the *Florida*'s arrival went almost unremarked amid the furore over the imminent departure of the Lairds rams. Charles Francis Adams had warned Lord Russell that their very existence presented the greatest threat to Anglo-American relations since the *Trent* affair. Two ram-raiders could not, of course, win the war for the Confederacy, but they could threaten the Federal stranglehold on Charleston or Wilmington. Moreover, argued Adams, if the rams were allowed to leave, there would be nothing to prevent the Confederacy from building twenty more in Britain. War between America and England would be unavoidable if the government failed to clamp down on all Confederate violations of British neutrality; and this, he was convinced, would never happen under Lord Palmerston.

Adams's view was a common one among Americans in Europe. William Howard Russell was appalled by the cynicism of his friend John Bigelow, the former editor of the *New York Evening Post* and current US Consul in Paris. There was nothing machiavellian about the British government's slowness in taking action, Russell contended: 'Our Foreign Enlistment Act requires revision and was meant for slow coach times. Steam, cupidity and commercial genius . . . are too much for it nowadays.'[5] Richard Cobden had also spoken to Bigelow, thinking that he might be more open to argument than Adams. But Bigelow would not be persuaded. 'I told him the impression was becoming quite general among Americans on both sides of the Atlantic that Palmerston and *The Times* were plotting for a war with the United States,' he reported to Seward on 17 April.[6]

US Consul Dudley in Liverpool had uncovered every aspect of the Confederates' operations: how they recruited sailors, who paid them and when, how they procured supplies and on which vessels the cargoes sailed. But he had failed to unearth a single piece of written evidence against the rams that could be presented in a court of law. The Lord

Mayor of London warned the Home Office that it would be a waste of time sending government agents to investigate Lairds, since nothing would be found. But Lord Russell ignored the advice, which he believed to be tainted by the Mayor's pro-Southern bias, and sent the agents anyway. 'I think sometimes', Dudley wrote to Seward, 'that the whole community are banded together to assist [the Confederates] and to baffle us.'[7] The hostility experienced by pro-Northerners in Liverpool could be overwhelming at times: 'I have ... done myself a great deal of damage,' complained one of Dudley's informants.[8]

The Duke of Argyll noticed Charles Francis Adams's agitation when the US Minister and his family went to stay in Scotland in the middle of August. One morning after breakfast Adams had a frank conversation with the Duke about the probability of the North declaring war if the government allowed the rams to depart. He was surprised to discover that he was not the first to say so. 'He said that he had received a letter from Sumner,' wrote Adams on 28 August 1863, 'dwelling very strongly on the danger of war.' Adams was too circumspect to discuss Seward's latest dispatch (the threatening and bombastic letter Lord Lyons had seen earlier in August), but he hinted that there were instructions he was deliberately holding back for the moment. Adams, however, had no way of knowing that Seward was actually quite sanguine about the rams. 'The English Ministry are our friends,' Seward had recently admitted to the Navy Secretary, Gideon Welles. The very day Adams poured out his fears to the Duke, Seward told Welles to cease worrying, because 'the armored vessels building in England will not be allowed to leave'.[9] Adams's continual fretting about the rams ruined the enjoyment of his visit to Inveraray Castle and he left for London on 31 August, thinking he would never see Scotland again. This, he decided, would not be a great loss: 'Half of it is fit only for the habitation of the beasts and the birds. The other half has nothing especial to recommend it either.'[10]

Benjamin Moran was hysterical when Adams arrived back at the legation on 3 September. One of the Laird rams had actually been taken for a test run, yet Lord Russell had replied to Adams's latest protest with what seemed to Moran the usual empty assurances. The legation was reliving the escape of the *Alabama*. The effect on Adams was dramatic. He sent a warning to Russell that day, and a stronger one the next. On the 5th, having received nothing but a bland note in reply, he lost his temper. 'This is war,' he wrote to Russell, war by stealth and deceit. If the government allowed the two rams to depart, to destroy New York and Boston at will, the United States would retaliate. If the circumstances were reversed, Adams declared, Britain would do the same. He would communicate his government's response forthwith.[11]

Adams assumed that Lord Palmerston was interfering – or worse, restraining Lord Russell from responding properly. It would have been far better for his peace of mind and the future of Anglo-American relations had he been kept informed of the strenuous efforts of the Home and Foreign Office clerks to find a legal way of stopping the rams. Since June, the government had been secretly conducting an international investigation into their true ownership. The British Consul in Egypt had been ordered to prise the truth out of the Pasha as to how he had become mixed up with the Confederates. The information trickling in only heightened Russell's suspicions about Bravay and Co. Palmerston agreed that he, too, was worried about 'this ship building business'. Yet there was no obvious remedy: Seward's threats and Adams's letters made it politically impossible for them to amend the Foreign Enlistment Act without appearing to bow to US pressure; Lord Chief Justice Pollock had not shown the slightest sympathy towards the government's delicate position; and the law officers, including the Attorney General and the Solicitor General, were anxious that no further cases should come to court.

The Cabinet's concern had increased in August after Richard Cobden shared with them his most recent correspondence from Charles Sumner. The Senator, reported Cobden, had made a volte-face about England and instead of being her chief ally in the capital was now her loudest critic. Sumner appeared to be so bent on revenge for Britain's accumulated wrongdoings that Cobden had felt constrained to remind him, 'We have been the only obstacle to what would have been almost a European recognition of the South.'*[12] The more Russell heard about the state of

---

* The Duke of Argyll told Sumner that he would not show his letters to Lord Russell because the Foreign Minister would dismiss them as gibberish. The Duchess also tried to reason with him. 'I like you to be quite frank with me, but wish you did not hope for what is impossible,' she wrote earnestly. 'I sent some of the newspaper extracts you sent me to Lord Russell.' He replied: 'We must be neutral ... We do not "fit out ships by the dozen," and Mr. S. must know the allegation to be untrue. One – two – three ships may have evaded our laws, just as the Americans evaded the American laws during the Canadian Contest ... You will have seen that the Government did their best in the *Alexandra* case. As to the iron-plated ships, there seems to be great difficulty in getting at the truth.'

opinion in the North, the less he agreed with the advice of the law officers to wait until there was positive proof against the rams. Finally, on
31 August, the Foreign Office received a telegram from the British Consul in Egypt, confirming that the Pasha story was a ruse. Still the legal
advisers to the Customs and Treasury departments rejected his entreaties for action.

Although he was still on holiday in Scotland, Russell telegraphed
his Under-Secretary for Foreign Affairs, Austen Henry Layard, on 3 September to say that he would return to London for a confrontation with
the law officers if necessary. Palmerston concurred with Russell: the
Confederates were dragging the government into 'neutral hostility'. He
considered the possibility of having to pay damages to Lairds worth the
risk – it would certainly be cheaper than footing the bill for a war with
the United States.[13] Layard obediently sent the detention order that day.
Fearful that his telegram might lose itself – in the way that unpopular
messages were wont to do in the Treasury Department – he wrote again
two days later.[14] His persistence paid off and a customs official informed
Lairds of the order.

Lord Lyons's Secretary of the legation, William Stuart, received
instructions to explain to Seward that the vessels were being detained
even though the government did not expect a favourable decision from
the courts. Unfortunately, no one remembered to share this concern
with Charles Francis Adams, or indeed apprise him of the recent developments regarding the rams. Russell's sudden reticence may have been
prompted by a fear of leaks, or a desire to wait until he had definite
news, but most likely he had become annoyed with the aggressive tone
of Adams's letters and had decided that the Minister could afford to
wait a little while.

Over the next two weeks, there was frenetic correspondence between
the Cabinet as it debated whether the detention order had been the right
step. As if to remind the Ministry how fraught the issue remained in
Parliament, the *Liverpool Courier* declared on 12 September that a government that truckled to US pressure was worthy of impeachment. The
next day Palmerston suggested to the First Lord of the Admiralty,
the Duke of Somerset, that the navy should purchase the rams from
M. Bravay, which would avoid the embarrassment of another legal
battle. At the very least, he wrote in all seriousness, 'we are short of
iron clads and it takes time to build them'. The rams would be a useful

addition to British naval capacity just in case '[the Federals] should be disposed and able next year to execute their threatened vengeance, for all the forbearance we have shown them'.[15]

In October, Captain Hoare, the Royal Navy attaché to the British embassy in Paris, visited M. Bravay with a line of credit and a list of questions. Their conversation left Hoare with no doubt of the rams' true ownership. The Frenchman's grimaces were irritating but illuminating – had James Bulloch witnessed this display of self-important puffery, he would have been furious at Bravay's indiscretion. Nevertheless, the Frenchman refused to sell the rams at any price and Hoare returned home with nothing except a poor opinion of the Confederates' dealings. By coincidence, British crewmen from the *Florida* arrived in Liverpool during the same week of Hoare's meeting with Bravay. Captain Maffitt had let them go to save money, but everyone, including Consul Dudley, assumed they were coming to take the rams out of the Lairds shipyard while there was still time. This mistaken belief sent officials into a frenzy. Russell saw another *Alabama* incident in the making and wanted the Marines to become involved; the Home Office ordered the Liverpool constabulary to keep a close watch on the sailors.[16] (When the truth eventually became known, the authorities decided there were far too many to prosecute for violating the Foreign Enlistment Act, much to the legation's annoyance.)

If Lord Russell had expected gratitude from Charles Francis Adams he was soon disabused. The US Minister was only just beginning to express his pent-up frustration with the British government. Ignorant of Russell's marathon negotiation with the law officers, Adams assumed that it was his 'war letter' that had frightened the English into action, and he fired another cannonade of unfortunate remarks on 16 September: 'If Her Majesty's Government have not the power to prevent the harbours and towns of a friendly nation from being destroyed by vessels built by British subjects, and equipped, manned, and dispatched from her harbours,' he raged, 'then . . . all international obligations, whether implied or expressed, [are] not worth the paper on which they are written.'[17] His letter was passed around the Cabinet, accompanied by various noises of disgust and outrage. 'It seems to me that we cannot allow to remain unnoticed his repeated and I must say somewhat insolent threats of war. We ought, I think, to say to him in civil Terms "you be damned",' declared Palmerston. Russell thought the same. In his reply on 25 September he dispensed with the usual expressions of 'regret and concern' and went straight to the point. 'There are, however, passages in your letter,' he wrote, which 'plainly and repeatedly imply an intimation of hostile proceeding towards Great Britain on the part of the Government of the United States unless steps are taken'. These threats would not be tolerated: Her Majesty's Government will never 'overstep the limits of the law' for the sake of appeasing another government, and 'they will not shrink from any consequences of such a decision'.[18]

Adams came to his senses after he received Russell's indignant reply and hastily apologized for his letter. But Henry Adams was unrepentant. 'They meant to play us, like a salmon,' he told Charles Francis Jr., until their father's threat of war ended 'the little game ... Undoubtedly to us this is a second Vicksburg. It is our diplomatic triumph, if we manage to carry it through.'[19] It was Russell's fault that the legation wrongly assumed Adams had scored a victory over him. His pride had brought him the worst of all outcomes: his efforts unacknowledged, his reputation tarnished, and the government made to look weak. Adams's apparent diplomatic coup was naturally the talk of Washington. William Stuart was so alarmed that he spoke to Seward's son, Frederick, on 18 September, to explain the real sequence of events. But the myth of the British lion cowering under the onslaught of the American eagle had already taken hold.

Seward could not resist making capital out of England's embarrassment. He had asked Thurlow Weed to plant newspaper stories about the dangerous rams in England, so that he could fight a 'battle' and emerge the victor. Gideon Welles was infuriated by the ease with which his rival manipulated the news. 'I am under restrictions which prevent me from making known facts which would dissipate this alarm,' he wrote in his diary. 'It does not surprise me that the *New York Times* ... and all the papers influenced by Seward should be alarmed. [He] knows those vessels are to be detained, yet will not come out and state the fact, but is not unwilling to have apprehension excited. It will glorify him if it is said they are detained through protest from our minister.'[20]

Charles Sumner unwittingly played into Seward's hands. The rage and paranoia that had recently alarmed his friends burst into public view on 10 September. Several thousand people crowded into Cooper

Union in New York to listen to him deliver a four-hour tirade against Britain. 'I am disappointed and disgusted with Sumner's own conduct,' wrote Lord Lyons after he had read the speech in full.[21] Its real purpose, he believed, was to strengthen Sumner's position against Seward. If the rams were stopped, people would remember the Cooper Union speech as being instrumental in the diplomatic victory. But if the warships were allowed to set sail, Sumner would be able to point to his speech as proof that he, at least, had been willing to confront the British. The vehement denunciations of Britain were baffling to Sumner's friends. Some attributed his excess of feeling to his old head injury, others, to grief over the recent death of his brother; all agreed on the calamitous damage to his reputation. Having positioned himself as the voice of moderation, his new bellicosity made him look like the worst kind of political opportunist. Lord Lyons would never trust him again. 'I had hoped better things of him,' he wrote.[22] The distinguished and respected Edward Everett accused Sumner of 'muckraking' for the sake of his ambition. One of the few letters of approval came from Seward, who, with exquisite irony, sent Sumner his hearty congratulations.[23]

The Economist announced that there was no hope for Anglo-American relations if a 'friend' like Sumner could make such a hostile speech. He was condemned in every English newspaper.[24] The Argylls tried to make excuses for him, but to Northern supporters in England Sumner was now a liability. 'Sumner seems to have been trying to demolish himself for some time past,' wrote Harriet Martineau. 'He has done it now.'[25] His accusation that the British government was conniving with the Confederates had to be answered, which Russell duly did in a widely praised speech. Sumner became agitated by the criticism coming from the other side of the Atlantic and obstinately stuck to his position, even after he learned that Russell had detained the rams *before* his Cooper Union speech. Protests from English acquaintances simply made his declarations more extreme. 'If Russell wants cotton, let him withdraw all support . . . for the Rebellion,' he ranted to John Bright, who, for all his faults, pandered to no man and refused to play along with Sumner's characterization of Russell.[26]

Adams was disappointed that few people in England other than his own son gave him credit for stopping the rams. But a bruised ego was the least of his worries. On 28 September, Moran recorded that the legation

messenger had grievously swindled the family. Letters had been intercepted, Adams's wine cellar ransacked, money taken and even cheques
forged. Feeling that their sanctuary had been violated, Mrs Adams was
already pining to leave London when an anonymous letter arrived at
the legation:

> Dam the Federals
> Dam the Confederates
> Dam you both
> Kill you damned selves for the next *10* years if you like; so much the better
>   for the world and for England. Thus thinks every Englishman with any
>   brains. NB.PS. We'll cut your throats fast enough afterwards for you if
>   you aint tired of blood, you devils.[27]

This decided the matter. Adams found a large seaside retreat for rent in
St Leonards-on-Sea, near Hastings. There, he led Henry and Brooks into
the slate-blue water for bracing plunges before breakfast.[28] It was a
relief to leave behind the chaos and discord of the legation. 'My state
of depression of spirits is becoming chronic,' he wrote in his diary in a
rare moment of self-reflection. 'This way of living does not suit me, and
the condition of public as well as of my private affairs at home is not
satisfactory.'[29]

Adams's chief solace was that his difficulties paled besides those of
the Confederates. Mason had announced on 21 September that he was
closing the commission. Benjamin Moran was almost sorry to see him
go: 'Mr Mason was the unfittest man they could have sent here, and has
proved an ignominious failure.'[30] Mason's English friends had feared
just such a reaction to his departure and had entreated him to stay; the
press, including *The Times*, considered his resignation ill-judged. But
Mason was acting on Judah Benjamin's instructions. The Confederate
Secretary of State had ordered him to relocate to France under the new
designation of 'special commissioner to the Continent', and to give as his
reason for the move Southern dissatisfaction with Britain.[31] Yet the state
of affairs in France was no better for the Confederates. A disgruntled
clerk at the offices of Bravay and Co. had passed incriminating documents to the US legation. The French authorities naturally professed to be
shocked to learn that the Confederates were using their dockyards, and
the Foreign Minister, Drouyn de Lhuys, glibly assured William L. Dayton,
the US Minister in Paris, that there would be a thorough investigation

into the matter. The deception granted Bulloch a reprieve but it was no guarantee that his construction programme would be allowed to continue.

There was a funereal atmosphere at James Mason's house in Sackville Street when Rose Greenhow arrived for dinner on 17 September. She had seen him the day before. 'He was very kind – and we had a long talk,' she wrote in her diary.[32] Mason apologized for leaving her in such an awkward position. She had been expecting to make a life for herself in London as the Confederate commission's political and social hostess, re-creating her role in Washington before the war, and his departure would be depriving her of an essential platform for her mission. Mason had also performed a vital function for the Confederates and their sympathizers in England by keeping the personal differences between them to a sustainable level. It had not mattered quite so much that James Spence dismissed Henry Hotze's propaganda journal, the *Index*, as a waste of time and money, or that Hotze considered Spence to be a deluded abolitionist, when there was a third party to keep them apart. How they would work together once he was in France had not been resolved. Spence and Hotze vied with one another to help Rose. Spence took her to Richard Bentley and Sons, the publishers of Charles Dickens, who eagerly bought the memoir she had been writing in Richmond, *My Imprisonment and the First Year of Abolition Rule at Washington*. Hotze trumpeted Rose to the readers of the *Index* as one of the great martyrs of the Southern cause, a heroine whose 'spirit and talent [were] not common even among women of the South'.[33]

For all of Hotze's genius at shaping public opinion, he failed to understand the gravity of the situation in Liverpool. 'The Rams in the Mersey are more than ever the centers of attention. The efforts of the Government to insure their detention are really ludicrous,' he sneered to Benjamin. Bulloch, on the other hand, saw nothing amusing about the government's actions. On 8 October Russell decided that Lairds could not be trusted and he changed his detention order to outright seizure. The Duke of Argyll congratulated Russell and urged him not to regret defying the law officers: 'They would never have advised you to do what you have so rightly done,' he wrote. 'I say, three cheers for the House of Russell.'[34] Palmerston agreed with Argyll that there 'was no moral Doubt that [the rams] are intended for Confederate service'. Even the Queen became involved, telling Gladstone that the rams business should not be allowed 'to endanger the Government'. Despite her concern, Gladstone thought 'she did not appear to lean towards over-conciliation of the Federal Government'.[35] James Bulloch insisted in his memoirs that he never intended the rams to sneak out of England. If this was so, Lairds had done him a disservice with their suspicious activity.

The task of guarding the rams was one of the least rewarding experiences of Captain Edward Inglefield's career in the Royal Navy. He and his men were threatened wherever they went in Liverpool. An intelligent and empathetic officer, he realized that the anger directed towards them stemmed chiefly from a fear that the 500 craftsmen working on the rams would lose their jobs, and he advised the Home Office to allow the work to continue until the ships were completed. Inglefield deliberately refrained from putting on a show of force: he moored his sloop at some distance from the rams, carried nothing more threatening than an umbrella, and ordered his men to remember that on this mission they were peace-preservers not war-makers. It was a sensible but hazardous move. One ram looked primed to leave: 'her turrets are very nearly completed, and excepting stores she can be ready for sea almost any day,' he reported. 'I have taken upon myself not to permit the boilers to be run up, or the fires laid even for presumed experimental purposes.'[36]

Bulloch was surprised that the government had seized the rams without first obtaining legal sanction; nor had charges been filed against Lairds. After a month went by without any sign of legal action he began to wonder if the process was being deliberately drawn out in order to give the law officers more time to prepare their case. On 28 October 'Historicus' attacked the rams in The Times (this was Vernon Harcourt's return to print after the death of his wife in April), condemning the Confederates' illegal use of British shipyards and arguing for a determined response from the government. Bulloch realized that 'Historicus' was preparing public opinion for the government's clampdown on Confederate operations in England; whether or not the rams case went to court, they would never be allowed to leave. The following day brought more disappointing news. The CSS Georgia had dropped anchor at Cherbourg, in so dilapidated a state as to be on the verge of sinking. The raider had destroyed nine ships during her six-month adventure. But according to Lieutenant James Morgan the final weeks had resembled a gothic horror story, full of madness and savagery. Captain Maury had

The Royal Navy keeping watch over the Laird rams in the Mersey

suffered a nervous breakdown near the Cape of Good Hope and the enforcement of discipline had fallen to the charming but weak Lieutenant Evans. There were constant fights and several attempted mutinies: 'Things had gone from bad to worse than bad until one day some of the stokers discovered that a coal bunker was all that separated them from the spirit-room,' wrote Morgan;

and inserting a piece of lead pipe into the hole they got all the liquor they (temporarily) wanted. This they distributed among the crew and soon there was a battle royal going on the berth deck which the master-at-arms was unable to stop ... Here was a pretty kettle of fish! ... I suddenly leaped upon the man and bore him to the deck, where, in a jiffy, the master-at-arms placed the bracelets on his wrists. The other mutineers, quietly extending their arms in sign of submission, were placed in irons, and confined below. The discipline of the ship needed as much repairing as the vessel did herself. It was time the *Georgia* sought a civilized port for more reasons than one.[37]

Clerks at Fraser, Trenholm had carefully stored the crew's letters, to be distributed on their eventual return to port, and receiving news from home helped calm the febrile atmosphere on the ship. 'There was great rejoicing for all save me,' recorded Morgan after the letters were delivered to Cherbourg. He had received two: the first told of the death of his brother George, a captain serving in the 1st Louisiana Infantry in Virginia; the second, that Gibbes, his other brother and a captain in the 7th Louisiana, had died a prisoner of war on Johnson's Island in Lake Erie. Morgan's adventures at sea suddenly seemed trivial to him after the terrible news from home. From this moment, his one ambition was to return to the South and fight the Federals.

In the south-west, the capture of Vicksburg and Port Hudson had brought a temporary quiet to the Mississippi region. General Banks's 19th Corps returned to camp, and the 133rd New York Volunteers, Colonel Currie's regiment, resumed its garrison duty in Baton Rouge. Currie had recovered from his wounds and, much as he retained a fondness for his men, he loathed inaction more and had applied for a transfer. 'I have at least one strong arm left,' he wrote to Thurlow Weed, 'and I am only desirous that any merit I may possess . . . may meet with equal favor with my compeers.'[38] Currie's eagerness to be in the thick of danger was rare: most of the injured and sick wanted to be as far away from the fighting as possible.

Ebenezer Wells and Dr Charles Mayo were both sent north, Wells to a hospital in Kentucky and Mayo to Saratoga Springs in New York to recover from typhus. His last weeks in Vicksburg had been a blur to him, but the illness saved his life in an unexpected way. On 18 August Mayo had become so unwell that a friend insisted he spend the night in town with him, rather than on his ship, the *City of Madison*. During the night there was an explosion on the *Madison* which claimed the lives of all those on board. After this near-brush with death, the authorities finally took pity on Mayo and shipped him out of Vicksburg. The War Department accepted Mayo's resignation from the army on 8 September, although it was another two weeks before he was well enough to sail for England on the 22nd, never to return to America.*

Mayo's quiet departure contrasted with the noisy and sometimes violent integration of the thousands of new army recruits produced by the draft, many of whom were determined to desert at the first opportunity. Even the volunteers were often cynical about their situation. 'As I fully

---

* Nine years later, in 1872, while taking a break between wars, an old friend from the Vicksburg campaign went down to Oxford to pay Dr Mayo a visit. The friend was General Sherman.

intend to desert if I don't get good treatment, I enlisted under the name of Andrew Ross,' James Horrocks wrote to his parents on 5 September 1863. The 19-year-old had run away from Lancashire to escape the financial burden and shame of having fathered an illegitimate child.[39] Volunteering in the Federal army seemed like an excellent prospect to the prodigal son: 'I shall get when mustered in $200 from the state of New Jersey, 50 dollars from Hudson City (where I enlisted) and 25 dollars from the Government. This, together with a month's pay in advance, will make $288 cash down,' he told his parents. 'I shall be able to save more money as a soldier than as a clerk with 400 dollars a year (that is a pretty good salary in New York).'[40]

Horrocks was surprised by the large number of foreigners who had enlisted with him. 'The Company I am in is a motley assembly – Irish, Germans, French, English, Yankees – Tall, Slim, Short, and Stout. Some are decently behaved and others uncouth as the very devil,' he wrote home. One-fifth of the regiment was English, including all the sergeants. Nevertheless, he was pretending to be a Scot in order to avoid the anti-English prejudice among the Americans.[41] The desertions began as soon as the men received their bounty money; but, far from deserting himself, Horrocks was sent out with several others to find the absconders and returned with more than a dozen. The ecstatic spirit of patriotism and duty that had animated the first wave of volunteering in 1861 had died out; Horrocks's desire 'to keep myself pretty secure and safe' reflected the feelings of a large minority of the new soldiers, especially among the conscripts.

In the South, where there were neither untapped reserves of young men nor legions of foreigners arriving each week, part-time raiders and guerrilla outfits were playing an increasingly important role in the war effort. Northern Virginia, where Charles Francis Adams Jr. was stationed, was Mosby country. The eastern shore of the Chesapeake Bay, 200 miles to the south, had become John Yates Beall country. As with Mosby, the war had enabled the 28-year-old Beall to redefine himself. His father's death when Beall was 20 had forced him to sacrifice a promising legal career in order to care for his widowed mother and five younger siblings. Service in the Confederate army had provided an honourable escape route from domestic responsibilities until a bullet to his right lung seemed to cut short his military career.

Beall moved to Canada in 1862, where he tried to establish a business selling game, until a friend told him about the Confederate navy operations in England. It sounded so exciting that he wanted to 'join them and take of their fortune for good and evil'.[42] In the time it took Beall to reach Richmond in February 1863 he had changed his mind about going to England, and instead saw himself as a water-born version of John Mosby. The Confederate Navy Secretary, Stephen Mallory, was sceptical of the idea. He appointed Beall acting master on 5 March – the usual commission for gentleman volunteers – but gave him no other help or encouragement: Beall would have to supply his own boat, uniform, weapons and volunteers, none of whom could be eligible for conscription. Furthermore, although they would be able to keep whatever booty they captured, they would not be paid.

Beall set about recruiting from the groups still open to him – the middle-aged, stranded foreigners and wounded veterans like himself. By September 1863 his Confederate Volunteer Coast Guard, or 'Beall's Party' as it was known, had grown to eighteen and included two newspaper editors and their apprentices, a couple of sailors, and two Scotsmen: Bennet Graham Burley and John Maxwell. Burley had recently been imprisoned in Castle Thunder, the converted warehouse in Richmond that housed spies and political prisoners. The 23-year-old Glaswegian had arrived in the South the previous year, bearing designs for a powerful underwater limpet mine, which in theory could penetrate armour plating. (The explosive device had been invented by his father, Robert Burley Jr., the owner of a tool-making factory, who, unable to secure commercial interest in his invention at home, had given the plans to his son to take to America.)

Bennet Burley had chosen the South on the assumption he would have a better chance of being noticed. His hunch was correct, though for all the wrong reasons. Fortunately, the new chief of the Confederate navy's Bureau of Ordnance and Hydrography, John M. Brooke, was also an inventor. As soon as Brooke saw Burley's plans, he knew that the youth was no spy and arranged for his release. Having regained his freedom, Burley displayed the daring and initiative that later made him one of the most famous war correspondents of his generation and persuaded Brooke to let him test the mine on a Federal ship. John Maxwell was assigned to help Burley carry out his mission, but Burley's father had missed something in the design and at the final moment they were unable to ignite the fuse.

The mine's failure to explode merely whetted Burley's and Maxwell's appetite for danger, and they officially joined Beall's Party on 13 August 1863, the day their navy commissions as acting master came through. Having acquired two small boats, the black-painted *Raven* and the white *Swan*, the raiders went on to harass Federal shipping around Cape Charles and Fortress Monroe so successfully that a joint US military and naval expedition was ordered to find them.[43] Beall's dream of emulating Mosby had come true.

John Mosby himself had received a bullet wound in August and had only recently returned to active duty. He decided to prove his recovery by reprising his spectacular raid against Sir Percy Wyndham in March. This time the target was Francis Pierpont, the Governor of pro-Union West Virginia, who was staying in temporary quarters in Alexandria. The raid was unsuccessful but it reminded Wyndham, whose recovery from his leg wound had been reported with great excitement by local newspapers, that the contest between them was still alive.[44]

Wyndham's New Jersey Cavaliers were camped at Bristoe Station, right in the centre of Mosby country, but Wyndham was unable to indulge his fantasies of revenge, having again been moved up to brigade command. US General Meade had ordered his Cavalry Corps to find out where Lee was moving with the Army of Northern Virginia. Despite almost constant skirmishing with Jeb Stuart's troops, the cavalrymen were able to report that Lee had dispatched General Longstreet and the 1st Corps to an unknown destination. 'I should be glad to have your views as to what had better be done, if anything,' Meade asked General Halleck on 14 September. Lincoln wondered what Meade was waiting for: 'he should move upon Lee at once,' the President wrote impatiently to Halleck.[45]

Meade did indeed move, but slowly and deliberately, to the relief of the Confederates. President Davis and General Lee had decided there was no alternative to sending Longstreet to Tennessee, which was in danger of being captured by US General Rosecrans and his Army of the Cumberland. If Rosecrans succeeded, yet more vital railroads would be lost, railroads that were Virginia's only lifeline to the much-reduced Confederacy. Tennessee lay across the top of the South like an elongated anvil, touching the borders of Arkansas, Mississippi, Alabama, Georgia, North Carolina and Virginia: the Confederates feared that its conquest would allow the North to carve up the South like a joint of beef. The implications of such a disaster added to the Richmond Cabinet's anguish after the summer of defeats. The chief of ordnance, Josiah Gorgas, mourned in his diary: 'Yesterday we rode on the pinnacle of success – today absolute ruin seems to be our portion. The Confederacy totters to its destruction.'[46]

During July, Rosecrans had pushed his Confederate adversary, Braxton Bragg, into the eastern corner of Tennessee. Bragg still held Chattanooga, with its all-important rail depots, but the irascible General was leading a demoralized army that had already been defeated twice in battle. Bragg's bullying manner made him despised by his officers and loathed by the men. 'I had seen men shot, and whipped, and shaved, and branded,' wrote Sam Watkins, a private in the 1st Tennessee Infantry Regiment. He thought he was used to Bragg's ways but at Chattanooga worse was to come. He watched the hanging of two 'Yankee spies'. 'I saw a guard approach,' he wrote, 'and saw two little boys in their midst ... I saw that they were handcuffed. "Are they spies?" I was appalled; I was horrified; nay, more, I was sick at heart ... the youngest one began to beg and cry and plead most piteously ... The props were knocked out and the two boys were dangling in the air. I turned off sick at heart.'[47]

25

River of Death

Colonel De Courcy wins and loses – Longstreet arrives at Chick-
amauga – The Confederate generals' revolt – Two English travel-
lers – Contrasting goodwill tours – 'They are all down on us'

The timing of Longstreet's arrival in Chattanooga depended on eastern
Tennessee remaining under Southern control. If the railroads or the
road through the Cumberland Gap stayed open, Longstreet would be
able to reach General Bragg in a matter of days. If these were closed, the
only other possible train route went south through the Carolinas, west
through Georgia, and finally north to Chattanooga, taking at least a
week, if not two. However, Federal forces led by General Burnside captured Knoxville, Tennessee on 2 September 1863, cutting the Virginia–
Tennessee rail link. This left the Cumberland Gap, which had been
guarded by a garrison fort of 2,500 Confederates since starvation drove
out Colonel De Courcy in 1862. The new Confederate commander at
the Gap, Brigadier General John Frazer, was struggling: only two regiments were in a fit state for duty; the other two had been so depleted by
illness and desertions that they were in a state of near mutiny. Frazer
had been receiving conflicting orders about whether to evacuate or
defend the fort. In the end he decided to fight.[1]

Burnside did not want to be caught up in an arduous struggle for a
single pass when he had an ideal candidate for the task in Colonel De
Courcy, whose familiarity with the area was unmatched. Burnside assigned
to him an independent brigade of 1,700 men, with orders to attack the
Confederates from the northern side of the Gap. For De Courcy, the command signalled that his rehabilitation was complete, and his reputation
no longer tainted by the accusations of cowardice at Chickasaw Bluffs.

De Courcy's happiness was short-lived. He discovered after the expedition had begun that his brigade consisted of the flotsam and rejects of Burnside's army; one regiment was just three months old, another, a mere two weeks. Worse still, the ordnance supplies had failed to arrive on time. His artillery regiment had lost most of its guns; his two cavalry regiments had no revolvers, and the infantry regiments were down to thirty bullets per man. Their bread ration was enough to last them for four days, perhaps seven if cut in half. De Courcy ordered a slow march, hoping that the rations and munitions would catch them up along the way. None came. By 7 September, De Courcy had grown so outraged by the lackadaisical incompetence of Federal headquarters in Kentucky that he was bombarding them with hourly messages, demanding to know, in the strongest language possible, when he could expect the arrival of his supplies. His brigade had now crossed the Cumberland Ford, and the Gap was less than half a day's march away.[2]

When he learned that no wagons had been dispatched because the commissary officer in Kentucky had been on a drunken spree for several days, the best and worst aspects of De Courcy's character came to the fore. 'What is to be done?' he wrote to a member of Burnside's staff on 7 September. 'My men will begin to get sick before many hours for want of bread. Little corn here, and I have only ammunition enough to bluster with and persuade the enemy to evacuate or capitulate if he be so inclined but I cannot make a serious attack.'[3]

De Courcy's first instinct was to telegraph his resignation. But as he thought about his predicament he realized that the Confederates had no means of knowing the state of his forces. This gave him the idea of deceiving the Confederates into thinking his brigade was four times the size – by having his men march in a continuous loop within earshot of the fort. Thus heartened, he made the fatal mistake of falling in love with his cleverness and when help arrived, in the form of a cavalry brigade under General James M. Shackelford, De Courcy became worried that he would interfere. He should have dispatched a messenger to explain his intentions. Instead, he sent a letter asking Shackelford to stay out of the Gap because, 'I fear you have not been made acquainted . . . that I am fully acquainted with all the roads and locations on both sides of the gap, and further that I have been in the military profession almost continuously since my sixteenth year.' Shackelford ignored De

Courcy and sent a message to General Frazer ordering him to surrender, which he refused to do.

Between his furious telegrams to Kentucky and his tactless behaviour to Shackelford, De Courcy was leaving a trail of ill will.[4] On 8 September De Courcy sent a final communication to General Frazer. The situation was hopeless, he said. The fort was surrounded and any attempt to fight their way out would only result in 'a cruel loss of life'. All this time the same Federal regiments had been marching round and round, making it seem as though the Confederates were facing several thousand men. He naturally hedged when Frazer replied, asking to know the number of Federal troops opposing him. For twenty-four hours the Confederate General held firm, but after a day of absolute stillness – De Courcy would not even allow the men to load their rifles in case one of the new recruits accidentally pulled the trigger and started a firefight – Frazer's nerve started to buckle. De Courcy thoughtfully sent back the Confederate go-between with a gift of two gallons of good whisky. He followed up with a note: 'It is now 12.30 p.m., and I shall not open fire until 2 p.m., unless before that time you shall have struck all your flags and hoisted in their stead white flags in token of surrender.'[5]

During these tense negotiations General Burnside had marched up from Knoxville, Tennessee with an additional infantry brigade. He, too, sent a demand for surrender to General Frazer. By now the Confederate had received three orders in three days from three separate forces. As far as he knew, tens of thousands of Federal troops were poised to blow his position to pieces. Frazer drank De Courcy's whisky and considered his options. In the meantime, an irritated Burnside tried to assert his authority over the situation. He was incensed to learn that De Courcy had ignored Shackelford's command. Ignorant of the Colonel's plan and the reasons behind it, Burnside regarded his action as veering close to insubordination.

At three o'clock on 9 September, Frazer ordered his staff to run up the white flag. De Courcy's troops fell into line and marched into the fortified camp, singing 'The Girl I Left Behind Me'. The Confederates were unaware that their Federal captors were carrying unloaded rifles. The soldiers looked at the small force with astonishment; one shouted, 'Where are the rest of the men?'[6] De Courcy went to find Frazer, who was sitting in his tent, the last of the whisky in one hand, his snuffbox in the other. In the meantime, a quarter of the Confederates quietly slipped away from the Gap, taking their guns and knapsacks with them. De Courcy was not interested in the loss of four hundred or so prisoners. He had captured the pass without firing a single bullet. He savoured the moment. 'The whiskey worked,' he remarked, according to one of his aides.[7] When Richmond learned of the surrender, Josiah Gorgas recorded in his diary that the Cumberland Gap had been given away by 'a drunken Brigadier, named Frazer'.[8]

Burnside trotted up the road an hour later, expecting to see the Confederates in formation and Frazer standing at the front, ready to hand over his flag. The sight of De Courcy walking around as though he owned the place made Burnside snap. Enraged, he ordered two officers to escort the Colonel back to his camp. The following day De Courcy was taken to Kentucky under armed guard. The charge was insubordination, but the rumour swirling through the ranks was that he had colluded with General Frazer to let the prisoners escape. No charges were actually brought against him, but once again he was in limbo and his character under suspicion. On 18 September 1863 De Courcy wrote to the assistant adjutant general on Burnside's staff, pleading for a court of inquiry so he could clear his name. An investigation 'has now become absolutely necessary to save my character – as an officer and a gentleman'.[9]

Down in Louisiana, the 16th Ohio Volunteers received a vague report that De Courcy was no longer on detached duty with Burnside. They still missed him. 'Hear that Col DeCourcy is ordered back to his regiment,' wrote the regiment's drummer in his diary on 21 September 1863. 'Hope it is true.'[10] In Kentucky, Burnside's harsh treatment of De Courcy won the Colonel a large degree of sympathy. 'It is stating the case very mildly to say that the officers of De Courcy's brigade were highly indignant at this summary way of dealing with the leader – a leader whose sterling qualities they had seen occasion to admire,' wrote Lieutenant Colonel Robert McFarland of the 86th Ohio Infantry. The officers wrote a protest on De Courcy's behalf and sent it to President Lincoln. Even Burnside's own staff felt that the summary arrest without charge was an overreaction to the incident. One of the assistant adjutant generals, Lieutenant Colonel Charles Loring, added his voice to the clamour: 'I feel for him that he would suffer under very grave imputations if the circumstances of the case be not made publicly known.'[11]

But the protests only annoyed Burnside all the more. He refused to grant De Courcy's request for a court of inquiry. Instead, on 29 September, Burnside distributed a public letter which lambasted De Courcy for his arrogant behaviour.[12]

The detour forced on Longstreet by the capture of the Cumberland Gap meant changing trains at least ten times to reach Chattanooga. 'Never before were such crazy cars – passenger, mail, coal, box, platform, all and every sort, wobbling on the jumping scrap-iron – used for hauling soldiers,' recalled one of his aides.[13] The men were not bothered by their unorthodox conveyances, and even enjoyed themselves. 'When we reached South Carolina we received attentions which had long ceased to be common in Virginia,' wrote Francis Dawson. 'A number of ladies were waiting for us on the platform, armed with bouquets of flowers and with well filled baskets of cake, fruit, and more substantial fare. There was an abundance, too, of lemonade for the dusty soldiers.'[14] But to Mary Chesnut, who caught a glimpse of the rumbling cavalcade, the sight was macabre. Miles of flatcars passed by, with 'soldiers rolled in their blankets lying in rows with their heads all covered, fast asleep. In their grey blankets packed in regular order, they looked like swathed mummies.' The sight made her sad: 'All these fine fellows were going to kill or be killed. Why?'[15]

The imminent arrival of more Confederate troops renewed Bragg's confidence. A battle was imminent, but he would no longer be fighting a numerically superior enemy. Rosecrans had divided his army into three isolated forces. If Bragg could lure each of them in turn into one of the deep valleys that marked the terrain around Chattanooga, he might be able to destroy the entire Federal army. His plan depended on General Burnside remaining in Knoxville, and on his own Confederate generals following his exact orders. Burnside obligingly fiddled and fussed, but Bragg's second requirement proved to be impossible. The Confederate commander had made himself so despised that his generals ignored him, allowing opportunities to attack to slip through their grasp. Bragg desperately needed Longstreet, if only to restore order and spirit to his army.

When news of Longstreet's departure for Tennessee reached Charleston, Vizetelly and Fitzgerald Ross took the first available train to Georgia, accompanied by a British army officer named Charles H. Byrne, who had run the blockade in order to join the staff of the renowned Irish Confederate general Patrick Cleburne. The travellers arrived in Augusta on 15 September. The town owed its prosperity to the Savannah river; 'most of the goods which run the blockade into Charleston and Wilmington are sold by auction here, whence they are dispersed all over the interior,' reported Ross, whose appetite for running after the action remained strong despite the misery of Gettysburg. 'We found several English friends in Augusta engaged in the blockade-running business.' An invitation to stay proved too tempting to resist and the three companions had such a merry time that they were caught by surprise when Longstreet's train passed through on 19 September. Realizing that they were in danger of missing the battle, they begged a ride on the next train. On the 20th they lurched to a halt outside Ringgold, several miles south of Bragg's army, unable to travel any further because of broken track. It was obvious from the crowded pens of Federal prisoners in the middle of the town that the battle for east Tennessee had already begun.

Longstreet arrived at Bragg's headquarters near the Chickamauga river ('River of Death' in Cherokee), just before midnight on 19 September; the bulk of his troops were with him, although the artillery train carrying Francis Dawson was still en route. Bragg had mismanaged the first day of fighting, making uncoordinated attacks which were readily crushed by the Federals. For the morrow, he told Longstreet, the army was to be divided into two, with Longstreet commanding one wing and General Leonidas Polk the other, in order to hit Rosecrans in synchronized blows, left and right.[16] The blows did take place, but, because of a combination of undelivered orders, misunderstood directions and the difficulty of operating in a thickly wooded terrain that screened parts of the fighting, the synchronization did not. Even so, Longstreet was magnificent. While Bragg was panicking and calling the battle lost, 'Old Pete' realized that the Federal line had split and sent in his wing to exploit the opportunity. The Confederates almost succeeded in breaking Rosecrans's entire army. But one US general, George H. Thomas – who was henceforth known as 'the Rock of Chickamauga' – held his position and prevented a total Federal disaster.

It was late afternoon when Vizetelly and Ross heard about Longstreet's assault. Vizetelly decided to rush to the front, appalled that he was missing the battle. They did not arrive at Longstreet's camp until evening: 'We had walked a dozen miles,' wrote Ross, 'and, not knowing

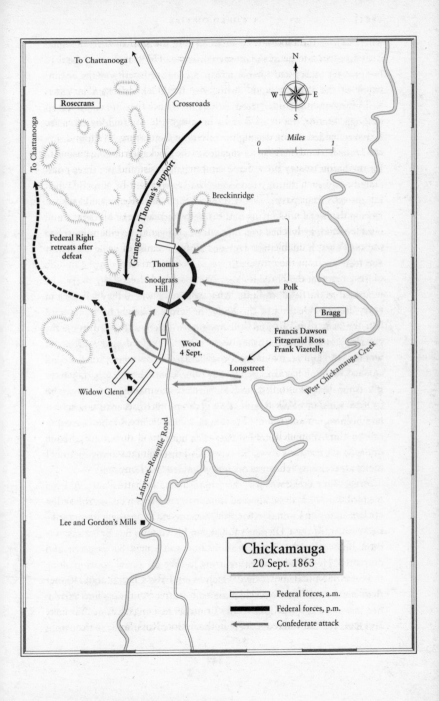

To Chattanooga

Rosecrans

Crossroads

N
W   E
S

Miles

0   1

To Chattanooga

Granger to Thomas's support

Breckinridge

Federal Right
retreats after
defeat

Thomas

Snodgrass
Hill

Polk

Bragg

Francis Dawson
Fitzgerald Ross
Frank Vizetelly

Wood
4 Sept.

Longstreet

West Chickamauga Creek

Widow Glenn

Lafayette–Rossville Road

Lee and Gordon's Mills

Chickamauga
20 Sept. 1863

☐ Federal forces, a.m.

■ Federal forces, p.m.

→ Confederate attack

where to find our friends, we concluded to stay where we were all night.' They had missed one of the most dramatic and bloody days of the war. Longstreet's attack had spread mass panic among his opponents, reminiscent of the Federal flight during the Battle of Bull Run in 1861. Rosecrans's army, and indeed Rosecrans himself, had fled to Chattanooga, leaving the Confederates in possession of his deserted headquarters. As soon as it was light, the companions resumed their search for Longstreet. 'We had been very much disappointed at being too late for the battle,' wrote Ross, 'but I think what we saw today rather moderated our regret.' In all, 36,000 men had been killed or wounded during the two-day fight, nearly a third of the total who had taken part. During the night, while Ross and Vizetelly had slept, the battlefield had been a hive of activity as small details of soldiers and civilians searched for survivors, holding their lanterns aloft to avoid treading on hands and feet.

The Confederate private Sam Watkins had helped to carry the wounded to the field hospitals. 'Men were lying where they fell, shot in every conceivable part of the body,' he wrote afterwards. 'Some with their entrails torn out and still hanging to them and piled upon the ground beside them, and they were still alive.' He passed a group of women who had been looking for relatives. One of them cradled a dead soldier's head on her lap, crying, 'My poor, poor darling! Oh, they have killed him, they have killed him!' He turned away, but there was nowhere to look without being assaulted by gore and terror. A man whose jaw had been torn away, leaving his tongue lolling from his mouth, tried to talk to him. Another stumbled past with both his eyes shot out, though one was still hanging down his cheek. 'All through that long September night we continued to carry off our wounded,' he recorded.[17]

Bragg was transfixed by the bloodshed. Longstreet argued, even pleaded with him, to be allowed to launch another attack on the Federals before they had time to fortify Chattanooga, and briefly thought he had persuaded the General to follow up his victory. But Bragg saw the thousands of corpses, the dead horses and shattered wagons, and despaired. He ordered the entire army to take up a new position along the crest of Missionary Ridge, which overlooked Chattanooga. Rather than endure another battle, he planned to starve Rosecrans into surrender, just as Grant had done to the Confederates at Vicksburg. Vizetelly and Ross realized that they were in the midst of an uproar in the camps and that the troops were furious with their leader. 'I do not know what our Generals thought,' wrote Sam Watkins. 'But I can tell you what the privates thought ... We stopped on Missionary Ridge, and gnashed our teeth at Chattanooga.'[18] Watkins would have been gratified to know that Bragg's commanders shared his outrage. Several of them were discussing with Longstreet whether they should risk their careers by sending an official complaint to Richmond.

Vizetelly was circumspect in his report of the Battle of Chickamauga for the *Illustrated London News*. He made no mention of the generals' revolt against Bragg, or that Longstreet was leading the cabal.[19] His shame at having arrived late may have pushed him to go beyond his usual exuberance in camp. Every night he sang songs and entertained the senior officers as though his life depended on their enjoyment. The Confederates were mystified by the riotous visitor who could drink them all under the table, but deeply appreciative of his efforts. 'It was no uncommon thing to see a half dozen officers, late at night, dancing the "Perfect Cure" which was one of the favourite songs ... in the London music halls, and was introduced to our notice by Vizetelly,' wrote Francis Dawson, who was thrilled to share his tent with him.[20] Years later, Longstreet's artillery chief, Edward P. Alexander, could still remember Vizetelly teaching them the words to 'Tiddle-i-wink'.* 'He was really a man of rare fascination and accomplishments,' reminisced Alexander. 'He made great friends everywhere, but especially in Longstreet's corps.'[21]

The evening frolics could not mask the fact that the Confederate Army of Tennessee was in crisis. Bragg had suspended two popular generals, Polk and Thomas Hindman, for their failure to carry out his orders during the battle. Longstreet had secretly sent an official complaint to Richmond against Bragg and was waiting for a reply. The fourteen other senior generals were on edge, as Francis Dawson discovered. He had been made acting chief of ordnance while his superior, Colonel Peyton T. Manning, recovered from a head wound, and his temporary promotion gave him a seat at the staff dinners. One night Major Walton,

---

* The Confederates loved this song, which Vizetelly had composed himself: ' 'Twas in the Atlantic Ocean in the equinoctial gales; / A sailor he fell overboard, amid the sharks and whales. / And in the midnight watch his ghost appeared unto me; / Saying I'm married to a mermaid in the bottom of the sea. CHORUS: Singing Rule Britannia! Britannia rule the waves. / Britons never, never, never will be slaves.'

who I had always disliked heartily [wrote Dawson], said that when the Confederate States enjoyed their own government, they did not intend to have any damned foreigners in the country. I asked him what he expected to become of men like myself, who had given up their own country in order to render aid to the Confederacy. He made a flippant reply, which I answered rather warmly, and he struck at me. I warded off the blow, and slapped his face.

The next morning, Dawson asked Ross to deliver his challenge to Major Walton. Ross had relished the prospect of a duel but was deprived of the spectacle by Walton's offer of a written apology. Dawson waited for two days. When none came, he sent Ross to see Walton again. The Major informed him that he had changed his mind. Delighted, Ross responded that the Major must chose his weapons since the challenge still held. 'This brought Walton to terms,' wrote Dawson, 'and he made the apology I required.'[22] Dawson felt vindicated but he still had to dine with Walton every day. On 29 September 1863 he wrote to his mother: 'Last night I was dreaming of you and it makes me feel very sad to be here entirely alone.' Were it not for the English visitors in the camp his life would have been intolerable. 'This is the one great source of pleasure to me,' he admitted.[23]

The tensions in Bragg's army increased until on 5 October twelve generals signed a petition asking for him to be removed from his command. Francis Lawley hoped that Longstreet would take over from General Bragg. 'I have done my very utmost to get him to the helm,' he wrote to a friend. 'The disappointment and indignation of his own corps, if he is put under Bragg, will be great and dangerous.'[24] Lawley was still feeling weak as well as unappreciated by his employers; he had recently received a reprimand from Mowbray Morris at The Times, who, in a momentary pang of editorial responsibility, had asked him to tone down his 'extravagant partiality to the Southern Cause'.[25]

Lawley arrived from Richmond just as Bragg learned of the attempted coup against him. He was unsurprised by the 'heartburning recrimination' which had infected all ranks of Bragg's army.[26] When Jefferson Davis arrived at the camp on 9 October, Lawley assumed that the President had made the difficult journey expressly to remove the unpopular general. 'The conclusion is irresistible', he told Times readers in his new spirit of semi-impartiality, 'that General Bragg failed to convert the most headlong and disordered rout which the Federals have ever seen . . . into a crowning victory like Waterloo.' Cold, driving rain accompanied

Davis's visit. Francis Dawson had to dig a trench around their tent to keep the water from flooding in during the night. The rain did not deter wild hogs from feeding on the dead, but most other activity ceased. The guns could not be moved, the wagons became stuck. 'Few constitutions can stand being wet through for a week together,' wrote Ross. They were fortified, however, by the box of provisions Lawley had brought with him from Virginia. He had also arrived with a spare horse which enabled the observers to follow President Davis as he visited the different headquarters. Davis stayed for five days, and every day the generals, the travellers, indeed the entire army, expected an announcement.

On 22 September 1863 the telegraph office in Washington had erupted into frenzied activity as the first reports came through from Chickamauga. The message from General Rosecrans was blunt: 'We have met with a serious disaster.'[27] The news was bewildering to the Cabinet. Their most recent message from Rosecrans had announced his effortless capture of Chattanooga. Although Lincoln and General Halleck had been concerned that General Burnside was taking too long to march from Knoxville to join forces with Rosecrans, it had never occurred to them that the Army of the Cumberland was in any real danger from Bragg. Tennessee had appeared to be falling like a neat row of dominoes, especially now that the Gap was in Federal hands. Indeed, Lincoln was so confident that he had started to make plans to strengthen Tennessee's pro-Northern State government.[28]

The rest of the Cabinet had shared Lincoln's optimism. William Seward had been feeling sufficiently cheerful to allow his work to be interrupted by a visit from Leslie Stephen. The Englishman had arrived in Washington with a letter of recommendation from John Bright. The future editor of the *Dictionary of National Biography* (and father of Virginia Woolf) was, at the age of 31, entering the final months of his phase as an Anglican clergyman. Recently, he had suffered a crisis of faith and was on the verge of leaving the Church and his academic post at Trinity Hall, Cambridge. His wild red hair and unkempt beard made him an alarming figure, but the combination of being a friend of John Bright and the cousin of the pro-Northern journalist Edward Dicey overcame Seward's resistance. He invited Stephen to accompany him to the White House. A Cabinet meeting was slated to begin in half an hour, but in the intervening time Seward introduced Stephen to Lincoln as a friend of the 'great John Bright'. 'Bright's name is a tower of strength in these parts,' Stephen wrote in surprise to his mother:

> They all talked of him with extraordinary admiration, and I was obliged to conceal the very distant nature of my relations to him by ingenious prevarication. I said that I had not seen him since the end of the Parliamentary session, as I had been absent from England since that time, and I did not let on that I had only seen him once, two years before that epoch, and then from the gallery of the House of Commons when he was on the floor.[29]

British descriptions of Lincoln had led Stephen to expect a clumsy elephantine figure of bizarre proportions, not the 'benevolent and hearty old gentleman' who laughed and smiled so readily. 'I felt quite kindly to him,' Stephen recorded. He thought Lincoln was far more impressive than Seward, whose initial good impression was undermined by his fatal propensity to swagger. 'He is a little, rather insignificant-looking man, with a tendency to tell rather long-winded and rather pointless stories,' wrote Stephen dismissively. 'He rather amused me by the coolness with which he talked about government affairs to me as a total stranger. Within five minutes after he saw me he said that if England permitted the rebel rams to start, they would declare war.'[30]

Taking advantage of the military pass Seward had written out for him, Stephen had visited General Meade's headquarters in Virginia, where no one, either during the journey or in Meade's camp, believed him when he said that England remained unconvinced that slavery was the real cause of the war. 'They perfectly laugh at me,' Stephen wrote to his mother after he had arrived in New York at the end of September. 'I might as well tell them that in England we did not think the sun is the cause of daylight.' Nor did Americans believe him when he tried to explain the confusion which had led many Englishmen to support the South. 'Assuming that Englishmen had really understood the nature of the quarrel, I should feel ashamed of my country myself. Of course, I know they didn't,' he added, 'but it is no use trying to drive that into Americans, it only produces shrugs of their shoulders and civil grins.'[31]

Leslie Stephen left New York at the end of September, feeling more depressed than ever. He had not seen anything to make him more reassured about American or English public opinion. 'I am in rather a bad temper this morning,' he wrote on 28 September after seeing an except from the conservative-leaning *Morning Herald* in one of the New York papers.

'They write to say that we ought to send out ironclads for the South because we are certain to go to war with the North anyhow, and because the South are our natural friends.' He was determined to combat such misapprehensions but he doubted it would make a difference. 'I almost dread coming back to England to be in my usual position of a minority of one,' he admitted.[32]

Exasperation with English attitudes to the war had also led an acquaintance of Stephen's, Henry Yates Thompson, to visit America in order to gain first-hand knowledge about the situation. His own family had fallen victim to the fashionable moralizing which dismissed the North as an empire-seeking nation of hypocrites and elevated the South as the last bastion of a pre-industrial paradise. 'I am quite staggered by your letter,' he had written crossly to his mother from Philadelphia on 19 September in response to her comment that Northern racism was as bad if not worse than Southern slavery. 'If you really think slavery pleas-anter, all I say is you don't know what slavery is,' he raged. 'I am so certain myself of the good to humanity of this War that, if the North were not winning, I should be inclined to volunteer myself, and have a shot at some of those accursed people you are all praising so loudly.'[33]

The 24-year-old had recently passed an excruciating week in Boston as the guest of the eminent Edward Everett, whose son William had been in the year below him at Cambridge. Two of William Everett's brothers had been picked by the draft, causing considerable grief in the household, when Thompson arrived. Everett could not have been a more gracious host, but William Everett became very bitter and talked incessantly about how much he had hated his time in Cambridge and what torture it had been to listen to English opinion about the war, causing Thompson to worry whether he had misunderstood his invitation to stay.

Thompson arrived in Washington at the beginning of October, shortly after Stanton had ordered 20,000 reinforcements to General Rosecrans at Chattanooga. He visited Seward on the 2nd: 'I was quite shocked by his appearance: he was so bowed,' he wrote to his brother Sam. 'I was told afterwards that he has a son very ill just now with one of the armies. If I had known that before, I should not have gone ... The photo-graphs of Seward look quite different from how he really appears now.'[34] Thompson did not feel comfortable bothering Seward for a pass to Meade's headquarters, nor did he try to impose himself on the Presi-dent. His only sight of Lincoln was a glimpse of a cadaverous face through the window of a carriage, its wheels churning such a cloud of pale dust that the cavalry trotting behind looked like the four horsemen of the Apocalypse. Thompson was right to avoid the White House; the Lincolns were in silent mourning for the unmentionable side of Mary's family. Her brother-in-law, Confederate General Todd Helm, had been killed at the Battle of Chickamauga. Three of Mary's brothers had already died for the South.[35] Thompson stayed only a few days in the city and then headed out west.

Henry Yates Thompson's departure from Washington coincided with the return of Lord Lyons from his holiday in Canada. The Minister had spent the past week in New York, taking the temperature of the city. 'It is a pity I cannot come here oftener,' he told Lord Russell. 'This is so much the best place for obtaining a knowledge of what is going on in the political world.'[36] It was a strange time for Lyons to make a visit. Tiffany and Co. was flying the Russian flag on the front of its building and American and Russian flags lined the whole of Broadway.

Two weeks earlier, four Russian warships had sailed into New York harbour. Their appearance took the country by surprise. The press speculated that the Tsar had sent the fleet as a goodwill gesture to the North. Some people even wondered whether he was making a covert offer of military aid – 'Thank God for the Russians,' wrote Gideon Welles in his diary. But when Seward questioned the Russian Minister Baron Stoeckl about the fleet's visit, the Baron was vague. The real reason was that the Tsar had sent his fleet to North America in order to keep it ready in case hostilities resumed against England and France. The Russian admiral of the fleet had orders to give every impression of military support short of actually lying.[37]

The city organized a parade and an elaborate banquet in honour of the Russian visitors. In the midst of the excitement the arrival of Admiral Milne on the flagship HMS *Nile* was hardly reported in the press. It was the first visit by a British admiral since the War of 1812, and a genuine gesture of goodwill which Milne and Lyons had been planning for several weeks. But the Russian presence crushed their hopes of making a strong impression on the American public. In contrast to the throngs who visited the Russian ships, not a single vessel approached the *Nile*. The closest Milne came to a public honour was a dinner party given for him and Lady Milne at Cyrus Field's house in Gramercy Park. The Admiral did not mind the indifference shown to his visit, though Lyons was disappointed, given the multiple occasions on which Milne had restrained his officers and pun-ished those who displayed less than strict neutrality in the conflict. Milne instinctively warmed to the energy and spirit of the North.[38]

Before the end of Milne's visit the commander of the Brooklyn Navy Yard came to his senses and invited the Admiral for a tour. Milne was introduced to Major-General Irvin McDowell of Bull Run fame and other official dignitaries. 'Although on our arrival there was evidently much coolness,' Milne reported to the Duke of Somerset, 'yet before we left the tide in our favour had evidently turned.' As Lyons had discovered for himself during their first meeting in Canada, it was impossible not to like and respect the Admiral.

Washington was more welcoming towards Admiral Milne. Seward once again set aside his work for the mixed pleasure of escort duty, and Gideon Welles suspended his loathing of Britain for the hour he sat next to Milne at a dinner at Willard's.* The Navy Secretary had a good mem-ory for courtesies as well as slights: the previous July, HMS *Phaeton* happened to sail past the US Virgin Islands on Independence Day. Mind-ful of Milne's order to show respect when in American waters, the captain had surprised the Federal warship moored in the harbour by hoisting the US flag and firing a twenty-one-gun salute.

Admiral and Lady Milne sailed back to Canada on 12 October. 'I believe my visit has done much good in many ways, and I would strongly recommend that such visits should be repeated,' he wrote to the Duke of Somerset.[39] The British weekly newspaper in New York, the *Albion*, thought Milne deserved official praise for his courage in forcing the issue. 'And now that the ice is broken, we trust that hereafter and in happier times, the British Admiral commanding . . . may make frequent visits to this port.'[40] He could see that Americans cared about British opinion to an astonishing degree. Yet this vital part of diplomatic rela-tions was left solely to the whim of the press. The Admiral did not know of Henry Hotze's existence but he was coming to the realization that Britain could no longer talk Ambassador to Cabinet and assume that public relations did not matter. If nothing else came from Milne's visit, his sober assessment of Britain's unpopularity gave credibility to Lyons's repeated warnings to the Foreign Office. As if to underline the point, the

* George Templeton Strong had sat next to Seward at the same dinner and been reluctantly impressed by the Secretary of State, writing afterwards, '[I] am satisfied there is more of him than I supposed. He is either deep or very clever in simulating depth.'

Treasury Secretary, Salmon Chase, made a bizarre speech in Ohio shortly after Milne's visit about wanting to seize 'Old Mother England by the hair' and give her a good shaking.

Lyons and, lately, the Foreign Office had come to believe that Seward was Britain's best hope for keeping relations level between the two countries and both were rooting for him in his ongoing battles with Gideon Welles and Charles Sumner.[41] (No one outside the British government knew that Seward was giving Lyons off-the-record advice on how to forestall some of the Congressional attacks on British interests.[42]) Contemplating the immediate future, Lyons saw only dangerous corners and looming obstacles now he knew for certain 'that Mr Sumner and the ultras will make another onslaught on Mr Seward when Congress opens'.[43] Worse still was Baron Mercier's revelation that he had requested a leave of absence. His wife had put up with Washington for his sake, Mercier explained to Lyons, but she could stand it no longer. Lyons could not help himself but he hoped that the French Foreign Ministry would share his anxiety and consider Mercier too important to be replaced.

When trouble for Lord Lyons did come, it was from the South rather than the North. On 23 October, he read in the *National Intelligencer* that the four remaining British Consuls had been ordered to leave the Confederacy in retaliation for Britain's alleged support for the North.[44] The Consuls' unceasing efforts on behalf of conscripted Britons had been an irritant to the Confederate State Department for more than a year, and they made convenient scapegoats that Judah Benjamin had no scruple about using. Acting Consul Allan Fullarton in Savannah had provided the excuse when on 3 October he sent to Richmond a belligerent protest on behalf of six drafted British subjects. Four days later, on 7 October, Benjamin convened a special Cabinet session to discuss the Consuls. Jefferson Davis was conveniently in Tennessee with General Bragg, and therefore protected from any international outcry which might follow. The decision to expel them was apparently unanimous.[45] If Benjamin did not gain any popularity by the move, at least he did not lose any, and he doubted that the Confederacy would suffer either.

The troubles endured by the Scotsman William Watson showed the importance of the Consuls to the British community. Tired of struggling to find work in the South after leaving the Confederate army, Watson had decided to try his hand at blockade-running. During the summer he sailed from New Orleans to Belize. There, fear of the Confederate commerce raiders had led to a glut in cheap US-owned ships for sale. He bought a flat-bottomed vessel, christened her the *Rob Roy* and headed for the Gulf of Mexico. When Watson eventually reached Galveston he discovered that the city was barely functioning. 'It was now virtually in ruins, and the grass was growing in the streets,' he wrote. Anarchy and martial law ruled simultaneously.

Watson was powerless to prevent a local Confederate commander from impounding the *Rob Roy* for defence duty. But he had faith in Consul Arthur Lynn. 'When I saw that gentleman and reported the matter he was a little surprised, but said he would scarcely be much astonished at anything these people – the Confederates – would do. They were now desperate, and would not let any regard for international law or individual rights interfere with any project they meant to carry out.'[46] In the face of Consul Lynn's protests, CS General Magruder promised that he would release the *Rob Roy* if an alternative vessel could be found.[47] Naturally disappointed by this response, Watson went to Magruder's headquarters himself. The officers were sarcastic towards him until he was recognized by a former member of the 2nd Texas Regiment. 'I was quite astonished at the great effect which this little incident had upon the demeanour of the officials towards me,' wrote Watson. The *Rob Roy* was returned and Watson was again free to face the ordinary hazards of blockade-running.[48]

Several weeks passed before Consul Lynn learned of Benjamin's order for the British Consuls to leave, and, when he read the order itself, he noticed that his name had been left off the list. He decided to remain at his post until circumstances changed. Consul Frederick Cridland in Mobile had also escaped Richmond's notice and was determined to stay. Every white male between the age of 16 and 60 was being conscripted. 'Letters are received and applications are made to me daily by British subjects to interfere and prevent their being forced into military service, but I cannot assist them,' he wrote on 14 November. Yet he hoped that his presence still retained some moderating effect. Cridland's letter caused much indignation in the Foreign Office over the plight of Britons in the South; it sickened Lord Lyons each time a letter appeared from the Confederacy pleading for help that he was unable to give.*[49]

---

* When HMS *Virago* eventually made it through to Mobile in January 1864, Consul Cridland told the captain that he had not heard from the Foreign Office for six months. Later, in April, a pathetic message from Consul Lynn miraculously arrived in Washington, begging

Most Southerners did not believe that British residents were suffering at all. Southern newspapers rarely if ever reported when Britons were chained to wagons and dragged through the town to encourage 'volunteering', or hung upside down and repeatedly dunked in water, or threatened with being shot through the knees.[50] The War Department clerk John Jones almost envied them. 'The expulsion of British consuls will immediately be followed by another exodus,' he wrote contemptuously in his diary. 'Already passports are daily applied for, and invariably granted by Mr. Assistant Secretary Campbell. The enemy, of course, will reap great benefit from the information conveyed by these people, and the innumerable brood of blockade-runners.'[51]

In one of the rare letters to reach the outside, Cridland told Lord Russell that the South was turning into one vast prison, with the British at the mercy of the wardens and inmates.

> My power of description is inadequate to convey to Your Lordship a proper idea of the present state of morals here [he wrote]. In the camps a man has to carry on his person all his property for nothing is safe when a soldier's back is turned – Education is at a stand still and the principal thought is how to make what will prevent starvation. Finally, the hatred publicly expressed against England by the press, and the people who are informed by Editors and others that Great Britain is the principal cause of the war, makes it far from pleasant to be known here as a British subject and in some instances no language or threats seem sufficient to express the growing enmity.[52]

The British community in Galveston sent a petition to Lord Russell, begging for a man-of-war to take them to any British colony. The Foreign Office received another from a desperate group in Virginia whose applications for passports had been refused. 'They are all down on us here,' cried one of the petitioners whose brother had been murdered for 'being British'. 'There is no justice for us.'[53]

---

for guidance: 'If I am however, to remain at my post it would afford me sincere gratification if Your Lordship would direct me what course to pursue'. The Consuls in the South could not know of the extraordinary efforts made by the Foreign Office in trying to reach them. Lyons pleaded unsuccessfully with Seward to allow a special envoy through the blockade so that Britain could make a direct protest to the Confederate government.

26

Can the Nation Endure?

Jefferson Davis's choice – Saved by the 'Cracker Line' – Lincoln addresses the country – Fighting in the clouds – The centre breaks – The South holds

Francis Lawley had been so sure that Jefferson Davis would dismiss General Bragg that in his *Times* dispatch on 8 October 1863 he wrote as though an announcement was imminent. Yet Bragg's removal was not preordained. The Battle of Chickamauga had been a stunning victory for the South – the only one since Chancellorsville in May. Longstreet had complained to the Secretary of War, James Seddon, 'that nothing but the hand of God can help as long as we have our present commander', without reflecting how his doom-laden letter would appear to the world beyond Tennessee and Georgia. To Davis, the charge seemed self-serving and melodramatic; he agreed with Bragg that it would have been impossible for his shattered army to chase after US General Rosecrans – even for the 10 miles to Chattanooga. Furthermore, aside from the obvious dangers presented by the Confederates' internal disputes, the Army of Tennessee looked not only secure but on the verge of another success.

Chattanooga was not quite a one-horse town, but with little more than 2,000 residents it certainly did not have the resources to feed and shelter an army of more than 50,000. The Tennessee river looped the town in a U-bend on three sides, with the fourth, which faced south, overlooked by an undulating chain of mountains. At the south-western end rose Lookout Mountain, which towered 2,000 feet above the town; towards the north-eastern end the six-mile-long Missionary Ridge gently curved around like a natural amphitheatre. Since Bragg held both these high points and the railroads in the valley, the Federals' only safe supply

Chattanooga and the Federal lines from the lower ridge of
Lookout Mountain, by Frank Vizetelly

route was a single road through back-country which eventually reached
Chattanooga via the far side of the Tennessee river. During the rainy
season, which was just beginning, the road was expected to become an
impassable mud track, leading to inevitable starvation for the Federals.

President Davis had already demonstrated his willingness to be firm
with generals who opposed him. Despite public criticism he had shunted
aside both Joe Johnston and P. G. T. Beauregard. But with Bragg, a man
he liked and trusted, Davis was strangely protective. Not even the shocking number of Confederate casualties of Chickamauga – higher than
those suffered by Lee at Gettysburg and far higher than those suffered
by Rosecrans – shook Davis's faith in him. After allowing the unhappy
generals to air their objections for a couple of days, Davis climbed atop
the appropriately named 'Pulpit Rock' on Lookout Mountain and made a
brief but spirited defence of Bragg to the Confederate troops assembled

below, warning his listeners that 'he who sows the seeds of discontent and distrust prepares for the harvest of slaughter and defeat'. Davis may have felt that there was no other credible alternative to General Bragg, but the Army of Tennessee disagreed. When Davis boarded his return train on 14 October 1863, much of the army's will to fight went with him. Instead of giving him three cheers, soldiers shouted 'send us something to eat, Massa Jeff. I'm hungry! I'm hungry!' (Bragg's ability to manage the supply operations for the army was no better than his skills as a leader of men.) The news of Davis's decision spread so quickly that two days later Consul Cridland wrote to Lord Russell from Mobile, Alabama that everyone was in despair because President Davis was 'retaining General Bragg in command against all opposition'.[1] Bragg's retribution was swift. The leading rebels found themselves sidelined or dismissed; Longstreet's command was reduced to the 15,000 soldiers who had accompanied him from Virginia and he was sent to guard Lookout Mountain, as far away from Bragg as possible.

Lawley, Vizetelly and Ross stayed with Longstreet for another week, loyally enduring the short rations and incessant rain until they could stand it no longer. Vizetelly completed a couple more sketches and Lawley one more dispatch, this time not even trying to sugar over his contempt for Bragg. There was no compelling reason for them to remain but leaving proved more difficult than they expected, as the few trains running from Chickamauga station were reserved for the sick and wounded. Ross solved the problem by making friends with the stationmaster, who retained a proud memory of being inspected by Lord John Russell at the beginning of the war. At first 'I tried to explain that he might be mistaken', wrote Ross, who realized that the man had confused Lord Russell with William Howard Russell. Since the stationmaster found them room in a covered wagon (which only let in the rain at the corners), he decided to drop the point.[2]

They arrived back in Augusta, Georgia two days later, on 24 October. To their relief, the Planters' Hotel had rooms for all of them. 'A clean bed with actual sheets,' exclaimed Lawley, 'plenty of water to wash in, decent food, a table to write on, candles' – these were luxuries for a man 'who has long floundered in the mud of General Bragg's camp'.[3] The weather was less harsh, too, and a gentle autumn wind replaced the cruel downpours in Tennessee. The men passed the afternoons on their hotel balcony in shirtsleeves, smoking and chatting. They tried out the local theatre and discovered it to be quite passable. Vizetelly's only complaint was the tea served at the Planters', which was so weak he wondered how it managed to reach the spout.[4]

Little news filtered down to Augusta from Bragg's camp, and certainly none from the besieged Federals in Chattanooga. The three friends were unaware that Washington had sent 23,000 troops from the Army of the Potomac to reinforce Rosecrans. Lincoln had acted decisively; there was only one general he truly believed in, and he called upon him now. Ulysses S. Grant was summoned from his headquarters in Cairo, Illinois and ordered to Chattanooga. Lincoln had written to Grant after Vicksburg, 'When you turned northward, east of the Big Black, I feared it was a mistake. I now wish to make the personal acknowledgement that you were right and I was wrong.'[5] The President showed his newfound faith in Grant by placing him in overall command of the three main Federal armies in the west.

Lincoln was taking a risk by interfering with the Army of the Cumberland. 'Old Rosy' as the soldiers called Rosecrans remained beloved by the men; he had meticulously looked after their welfare and many of them were sorry to see him dismissed. 'Worst of all,' wrote the English volunteer Robert Neve of 5th Kentucky Volunteers, worse than the short rations, lack of blankets and leaking tents, 'was the order for General Rosecrans to be relieved. It was read to us on parade.'[6] Rosecrans's popularity with the soldiers was the chief reason why Lincoln waited until after the election for State Governor in Ohio on 13 October to dismiss him, fearing that to do otherwise could push the soldier vote towards Vallandigham (who lost by a wide margin). But once the election was out of the way, he agreed that General Rosecrans could be replaced by the 'Rock of Chickamauga', General George Thomas, who had prevented a complete Federal rout at Chickamauga.

The Confederate siege of Chattanooga was so tight that after a mere three weeks sutlers in the town were charging six cents for a mouthful of bread – the usual price for two loaves. In the animal pens, the horses and mules were staggering around in the last throes of starvation. Every building in the town had been transformed into a makeshift hospital, except for the Catholic church where Rosecrans worshipped. Grant arrived at Chattanooga on 23 October, still using crutches after a fall from his horse in August. But the painful injury had not affected his vigour or determination. The 23,000 reinforcements from Virginia had arrived, led by a chastened 'Fighting Joe' Hooker. General Sherman's corps was coming from Mississippi. Grant was confident he could best his opponent; the real enemy he feared was Tennessee's geography. Somehow he had to ferry food and grain to Chattanooga before the entire Army of the Cumberland collapsed or surrendered.

If Rosecrans had at least been able to hold on to Lookout Mountain, the situation facing the Federals would not have been so dire. With the Confederates now in possession of it, all the southern routes into the town, including the river, roads and railway, were exposed to sniper fire. But the engineers of the Army of the Cumberland had come up with a plan. It required a furtive night expedition along the Tennessee river, beneath the Confederate guns on Lookout Mountain. If successful, they would be able to build a pontoon bridge two miles up river, where a bend in the river would put the Federal forces beyond the reach of artillery fire.

At 3 a.m. on 27 October fifty pontoon boats, each carrying twenty-four soldiers and two rowers, silently paddled past the Confederates. Robert Neve was in the fourth boat. 'It was a fine moonlit night and very still,' he wrote. 'We passed down very quiet and could even see the Rebel pickets standing before their fires. It did not create any alarm.'[7] They seized the landing with relative ease, driving back a small Confederate counterattack with few losses. 'The next job was to cut down all trees ... all day long we had to work felling trees and making small breastworks. Here we were all but starving. Rations were very short.' A Confederate attack was expected and it came at midnight on the 28th. This should have been Longstreet's second triumph at Chattanooga – his opportunity to defeat Grant without having to engage in a major battle. But Longstreet had not been paying attention to the Federal inroads along the southern end of the valley, and he made a serious mistake now by sending only four brigades against the attack force. The Confederates were easily over-whelmed and had to retreat back up Lookout Mountain.

The next day the first supply wagons carrying hardtack (called 'crackers' by the army) and dried beef came rolling through along the 'Cracker Line'. The route stretched back for hundreds of miles. In northern Kentucky, a partially restored Ebenezer Wells led a wagon train of more than 2,000 pack animals, fighting fever and exhaustion to keep the supplies moving. Robert Neve soon noticed the difference in his rations. Over the next two weeks more supplies arrived, including fresh vegetables and new uniforms. 'Our rations were getting better, and we felt better as well.' His regiment was so close to the Confederate pickets that they agreed to take turns on picket duty. 'We would wave each other's caps and then exchange newspapers.' The reversal of their fortunes was complete; it was now the Confederates who were outnumbered, starving and miserable, and the Federals who were growing in confidence and strength.

General Bragg grasped the magnitude of Longstreet's mistake in fail-ing to prevent the Federal bridgehead into Chattanooga, but his reaction to the disaster was perverse. Instead of trying to plug the gap, or reinforce his position, Bragg chose to send Longstreet away, along with 20,000 men, on an expedition to take Knoxville, Tennessee from General Burn-side. There was some rationale to the decision: if Burnside could be forced back to central Tennessee, the Confederates would have repos-session of the three railways which passed through Knoxville and the all-important Cumberland Gap, which would restore the quick route to Virginia. But at best the mission was a dangerous sideshow when Federal supplies and troops were pouring into Chattanooga.

Bragg relished the thought of Longstreet having to operate on his own, hoping that this would expose some of his rival's weaknesses. 'One of General Longstreet's most serious faults as a military commander was shown at this time,' admitted Francis Dawson. Longstreet made few preparations for the campaign, and never bothered to speak to Dawson about ordnance. 'Not one word was said to me by him on the subject. I had an inkling, however, of what was going on, and obtained ample supplies. Had I not done so, we should have been in an awkward predicament by the time that we reached Knoxville. Had anything been lacking, it is certain that the blame would have been placed on me.'[8] The army reached its destination with less than half the number of wagons and animals required for a campaign. But Dawson's prescience protected him from Longstreet's growing fury as the General watched his army wilt under the twin assaults of hunger and cold.[9] The capture of a Federal wagon train on 15 November eased some of the pain.

Longstreet desperately wanted to avoid a siege and hoped to make Burnside fight him outside the town. On 16 November, he thought he had succeeded. Burnside's army was strung across a narrow valley outside of Knoxville; a 'beautiful position' for taking, recalled a Confederate officer. But the situation began to go wrong almost at once. When the cannons opened fire Dawson was horrified to discover that the ammunition he had worked so hard to acquire was defective. Instead of raining fire and shot upon the enemy, the shells exploded prematurely or not at all. Two days of fighting ended with severe losses to the Confederate corps. The English captain serving on Colonel Edward Alexander's staff, Stephen Winthrop, was severely injured while attempting to rescue a fallen comrade.

Longstreet vacillated while his enemy built stronger defences. 'There was a good deal of delay, for one reason and another,' wrote Dawson, 'and we were so near the town that we could hear the tunes played by the band at Fort Sanders. The favourite air then was: "When this Cruel War is Over."'[10] Longstreet had assured Bragg that Knoxville would be captured long before Grant's reinforcements arrived at Chattanooga. This was impossible now that Burnside occupied the town. But since he had not heard from Bragg for several days, Longstreet wrongly assumed there was no imminent danger to the besiegers.

Francis Lawley, Frank Vizetelly and Fitzgerald Ross left Georgia in early November once they knew for certain that General Longstreet would not be returning to Chattanooga. Vizetelly and Ross set off for Charleston, while Lawley, who was mystified by his friends' enthusiasm for danger, headed for Richmond. Charleston was again being bombarded; if the Federals succeeded in taking the city it would be one more disaster that Lawley would have to fudge for his readers. The strain of always putting the best face on Confederate fortunes was beginning to show in his most recent dispatches. When he arrived in Richmond on 14 November, Lawley wrote a report for *The Times* which admitted far more than he perhaps realized. The enemy, he wrote, 'hems in the edges of the "rebellion" on every side'. The North had surrounded the South 'with a cordon of vessels so numerous as for the first time in 30 months to make access to the Confederate coast really dangerous and difficult'.[11]

Lawley thought the city looked beautiful. A light dusting of snow covered most reminders of the war and imparted charm to even the most dilapidated buildings. President Davis had returned to Richmond a few days earlier, having toured Charleston's defences and delivered an encouraging speech to its embattled citizens. During his absence the Confederate Cabinet had learned that the precious Lairds rams were almost certainly lost to them. The Secretary of the Navy, Stephen Mallory, still hoped that James Bulloch would find a way to rescue the vessels; with the exception of the *Alexandra*, the agent had always come through. But the rest of the Cabinet thought the news vindicated its decision to expel the British Consuls. They were convinced that the Royal Navy could have broken the blockade at any time during the past three years if the British had been truly in favour of Southern independence.

The existence of the British blockade-runners made no difference to Southern resentment towards Britain – though without them Lee's army would have been suffering even greater privations. Lee had not fought a battle since Gettysburg and yearned to launch an attack against General Meade and the Army of the Potomac. It went against the grain with him to remain on the defensive, but, as he had explained to his wife in late October, 'thousands were barefooted, thousands with fragments of shoes, and all without overcoats, blankets or warm clothing. I could not bear to expose them to certain suffering on an uncertain issue.'[12]

General Meade was troubled by many worries, but the condition of his army was not among them. At the beginning of October a scandal had threatened to tarnish the reputation of the cavalry corps but was quickly hushed up by the War Department. All the cavalry knew about it was that Sir Percy Wyndham had been escorted to Washington under armed guard. It was not clear why he had been removed. The War Department refused to say anything more than that he was relieved 'for the time being'. Sixteen years later, in 1879, the *Decatur Daily News* of Illinois ran an article which claimed to clear up 'an old mystery'. Apparently, two unnamed informants had accused Wyndham of plotting to surrender his regiment to the Confederates for $300,000. 'Mr Stanton could not, getting his information as he did, place Col. Wyndham under arrest ... so the only road open was to remove him from command.'[13] The informants had first approached Secretary Chase with the accusation, who took the matter to Stanton. They claimed to have a letter from the Confederate Secretary of State, Judah P. Benjamin, which laid out a strategy to entice Wyndham into surrendering his cavalry.[14] The War Department does not seem to have investigated whether Wyndham actually considered the bribe, nor was he interrogated about the letter.

Speculation about Wyndham's removal from active duty was rife: Lord Lyons received protests from the public after stories appeared in the New York press which accused him of being the instigator. 'I have to say that there is no foundation whatever for the assertion made respecting me,' Lord Lyons wrote to a Mr John Livingston in New York. He had not, as Livingston claimed, solicited or made 'representations of a disparaging character against that brave officer'.[15] On 5 November, the *New York Times* intervened unexpectedly – probably at Seward's behest – with an article on the controversy which explicitly denied Lord Lyons's involvement and repeated the War Department's stance that the Colonel was on temporary relief from duties. It would turn out to be a very long relief.

The Union cavalry wondered about the unexplained removal of its most colourful brigade leader; Wyndham's habit of twiddling his moustache whenever he became angry was remembered with humour rather than the fear it once provoked. The corps would have been happy to have him back, especially after it suffered a humiliating defeat by Jeb Stuart's troopers at Buckland Mills on 19 October, which was dubbed 'Buckland Races' by the Confederates after the Federals were chased up country for several miles. Meade was summoned by Lincoln for an interview in Washington and given to understand that he was expected to destroy Lee, not play cat-and-mouse with him. The result of the meeting was a small engagement near Fredericksburg on 7 November, which netted Meade more than 1,600 prisoners, eight battle flags and four cannons.

The Secretary of War, Edwin Stanton, remained unimpressed and wanted Meade to push harder. Nothing about the situation in Virginia pleased him. But on 14 November Stanton received one piece of news which did give him satisfaction: the combined land and sea force sent to capture the Confederate raider John Yates Beall had at last succeeded in cornering its prey. Bored of lying low in Richmond, Beall had resumed his raids on 10 November. He managed to seize just one vessel before his whereabouts were exposed and the full might of the North pounced on the little band. Bennet G. Burley was one of only two who managed to escape. Beall and his crew were taken to Fort McHenry in Baltimore were they were kept in manacles for six weeks, until the Confederate Secretary of the Navy, Stephen Mallory, ordered eighteen Federal prisoners of war – picked at random – to be similarly shackled in retribution, which led to a relaxation of their treatment.*

'I have seen your dispatches,' Lincoln telegraphed Meade after the fight at Fredericksburg, 'and I wish to say, "Well done!"' He then wrote to Burnside at Knoxville, giving him the news about Meade's success and asking pointedly: 'let me hear from you.'[16] Lincoln was also waiting anxiously for news from General Grant: the 'Cracker Line' had saved the Army of the Cumberland from starvation but far more was at stake than a battle over logistics. 'If we can hold Chattanooga and eastern Tennessee,' Lincoln had written to Rosecrans before the General's removal, 'I think the rebellion must dwindle and die.'[17]

On 19 November the President was going to Gettysburg – whose 23,000 Federal casualties in July remained the highest of any battle of the war – to speak at the dedication of the town's new war cemetery. The solemn and painful task was made worse by the uncertainty in the West; Lincoln would have to address the mourners with Rosecrans's disaster at Chickamauga still fresh in their minds. However, Lincoln did not wish to dwell on the dangers facing the country, or why duty had to be its

---

* Unwilling to volunteer for the regular Confederate army, Burley briefly tried his hand at journalism before turning to the stage. He joined the New Richmond Theatre, run by the British theatre manager Richard d'Orsay Ogden. Burley's first role was a small part in the aptly named *The Guerillas*, a Confederate melodrama set during Stonewall Jackson's military campaign in 1862.

own reward at such a time. He already had a theme for the speech, one advocated three months earlier by Seward's financial emissary to London, John Murray Forbes, whose perspective on the meaning of the war had sharpened during his travels abroad. 'John Bright and his glorious band of English republicans can see that we are fighting for democracy,' Forbes had written to Lincoln on 8 September. 'After we get military successes, the mass of the Southern people must be made to see this truth, and then reconstruction becomes easy and permanent.'[18]

A large retinue accompanied Lincoln to Gettysburg, including Seward, several Governors and Senators, and the French Minister, Henri Mercier; but not Lord Lyons, who did not receive an invitation. Although the reasons for the visit were sombre, the crowds greeted Lincoln with enthusiasm and queued in large numbers to shake his hand. The principle speaker at the ceremony was not the President but the great orator Edward Everett, whose age and infirmities were sadly evident in parts of his speech. Everett spoke for more than two hours during the unusually hot afternoon, tripping up occasionally and at one point confusing Meade with Lee.[19]

The audience steeled itself for another long speech, not knowing that Lincoln had been asked by the organizers to be short and concise. The two-minute address was over so quickly that the photographer did not have time to focus his lens, and many among the 15,000 listeners had not yet settled down. Lincoln himself believed that his words had fallen flat. Several newspapers criticized him for failing to live up to the occasion.[20] Antonio Gallenga, a temporary correspondent for *The Times*, thought that Lincoln's speech had been a total failure. English readers were told that the 'imposing ceremony' was 'rendered ludicrous by some of the luckless sallies of that poor President Lincoln'.[21] But Lincoln's private secretary, John Hay, recorded in his diary that the President spoke 'in a firm free way, with more grace than is his wont'.[22] Edward Everett had no doubts about the momentous nature of Lincoln's speech. He congratulated Lincoln, confessing that he wished he had come 'as near to the central idea of the occasion, in two hours, as you did in two minutes'.[23] Everett realized that Lincoln had captured the essential nature of the war. In a mere 272 words, the President had defined the moral purpose of the country's existence – democracy, freedom, equality – not only for the mourners at Gettysburg but for every subsequent generation of the American people. The Revolution of 1776 had brought forth:

a new nation, conceived in liberty, and dedicated to the proposition that all men are created equal. Now we are engaged in a great civil war, testing whether that nation, or any nation so conceived and so dedicated, can long endure.

We are met here on a great battlefield of that war. We have come to dedicate a portion of it as a final resting place for those who here gave their lives that that nation might live. It is altogether fitting and proper that we should do this.

But in a larger sense, we can not dedicate – we can not consecrate – we can not hallow this ground. The brave men, living and dead, who struggled here, have consecrated it far above our poor power to add or detract. The world will little note, nor long remember, what we say here, but can never forget what they did here. It is for us, the living, rather, to be dedicated here to the unfinished work which they who fought here have so nobly advanced. It is rather for us to be here dedicated to the great task remaining before us – that from these honored dead we take increased devotion to that cause for which they here gave the last full measure of devotion; that we here highly resolve that these dead shall not have died in vain; that this nation, under God, shall have a new birth of freedom; and that this government of the people, by the people, for the people, shall not perish from the earth.

*

Henry Yates Thompson arrived at Bridgeport, Alabama, 47 miles downstream from Chattanooga on Friday, 20 November, carrying a letter of introduction from Edward Everett to Dr John Newberry, the head of the Western Department of the Sanitary Commission. It was late, so instead of continuing his journey to the Commission's headquarters, Thompson bedded down in one of their tents at Bridgeport. 'Before I went to sleep,' he wrote, 'I heard a solemn thudding sound outside. I asked my companion what was it and he said: "Oh, the last of Sherman's men crossing the pontoons." '[24]

Grant had been waiting for Sherman's troops to arrive before he made his attack against General Bragg. By 21 November he had accumulated more than 60,000 men. Staring down at them from Lookout Mountain and Missionary Ridge was a diminishing army of 33,000 Confederates. The 'Cracker Line' had answered the Federal hunger pains, but no such relief had come to Bragg's army. 'Never in all my

45. A coloured regiment poses for the camera. By the end of the war there were more than 180,000 coloured troops serving in the Union army. Their entry in the US army was slow and difficult and did not begin until Congress passed an Act in July 1862 that allowed them to enlist.

46. Group of 'contrabands', Cumberland Landing, Virginia. Escaped slaves were not sent back to the South because they were classed as 'contraband of war', meaning that they were part of the Southern war effort and were therefore liable for 'confiscation'. Thousands of slaves from Virginia fled to shanty towns around the outskirts of Washington.

47. A slave auction house in Atlanta, Georgia.

48. The Rohrbach Bridge. During the Battle of Antietam on 17 September 1862 the bridge became known as Burnside's Bridge, after US General Burnside ordered his men to cross it while being fired upon by the Confederates from the bluffs above the river.

49. The dead after the slaughter at Antietam. The battle ended in a draw and was the single bloodiest day of the war. The two sides combined suffered more than 25,000 casualties.

50. President Lincoln and US General McClellan meeting after the Battle of Antietam. Lincoln was furious with McClellan for not pursuing General Lee and crushing the Confederate army while it was in retreat.

51. General Ambrose Burnside (1824–81), commander of the US Army of the Potomac for less than three months. His exuberant facial hair allegedly gave rise to the term 'sideburns'.

52. Fredericksburg. CS General Robert E. Lee won a stunning victory over Burnside at the Battle of Fredericksburg on 13 December 1862. Burnside ordered the Federal soldiers to charge across a plain overlooked by a seven-mile range of wooded hills filled with Confederate artillery. When asked if any more guns were needed, the artillery officer in charge replied, 'A chicken could not live on that field when we open on it.'

53. Marye's Heights. The famous stone wall along the heights at Fredericksburg gave the Confederates perfect protection while they fired upon the Federals below. Burnside sustained 12,600 casualties to Lee's 5,000.

54. Admiral Raphael Semmes (1809–77), who commanded two commerce raiders of the Confederate navy. His exploits on the CSS *Alabama* inspired the Junior United Service Club of Great Britain to present him with a 'magnificent sword, which had been manufactured to their order in the city of London, with suitable naval and Southern devices'.

55. Commander Matthew Fontaine Maury (1806–73), Confederate navy, nicknamed 'pathfinder of the seas' for his study of ocean currents which made travel easier and faster. Maury was sent to England during the war to purchase commerce raiders for the Confederate navy.

56. Lieutenant James Morgan (1845–1928), Confederate navy, friend and future brother-in-law of the English Confederate volunteer Francis Dawson. Morgan served on Commander Maury's commerce raider the CSS *Georgia*, whose cruise ended in madness and savagery after only six months at sea.

57. Colonel John Fitzroy De Courcy (1821–90), 31st Baron Kingsale, (*left*) British volunteer in the Union army and colonel of the 16th Ohio Infantry. In 1863 De Courcy captured the Cumberland Gap from the Confederates with a force less than half the size of his opponents by tricking them into believing they were surrounded by a huge army.

58. Colonel Sir Percy Wyndham (1833–79), British volunteer in the Union army, knighted by King Victor Emmanuel for his services during the Garibaldi campaign to liberate southern Italy, and colonel of the 1st New Jersey Cavaliers. Sir Percy only ever twiddled his moustache when angry.

59. Dr Charles Culverwell (1837–1919), British volunteer surgeon in the Union army, who yearned to become an actor and between campaigns appeared several times on the stage, including with John Wilkes Booth in *Hamlet* at Grover's Theatre. 'They would rave of him, his voice, his hair, and his eyes. Small wonder, for he was fascinating . . . Poor, sad, mad, bad, John Wilkes Booth.' After the war Culverwell became Sir Charles Wyndham, one of the most successful actors of his generation.

60. Battle of Gettysburg, 1–3 July 1863. The bloodiest battle of the Civil War resulted in more than 43,000 casualties. CS General Robert E. Lee withdrew first, giving the psychological edge to US General George Meade.

61. Little Round Top, Gettysburg. US Colonel Joshua Chamberlain and his 20th Maine held Little Round Top for Meade, depriving Lee of the high ground that the Confederate General needed in order to seize control of the battle. Chamberlain later received the surrender of Lee's army in 1865.

62. Secretary of State William Seward taking a party of diplomats to see Trenton Falls in New York on 18 August 1863. (*left to right*) William Seward, Secretary of State, Russian Minister Baron Stoeckl, Nicaraguan Minister Luis Molina, British Minister Lord Lyons, French Minister M. Mercier, German Minister Rudolph Schleiden, Bertinatti (Italian legation), Swedish Minister Count Piper, M. Bodisco (Russian legation), George Sheffield (British legation) and Mr Donaldson (US State Department).

63. Rose Greenhow (1817–64), Confederate spy and envoy, with her daughter Little Rose, in a photograph taken in Federal prison. Jefferson Davis sent her to England in 1863 in the hope that she would persuade either Lord Palmerston or Emperor Napoleon III (who was then the Emperor of the French), to recognize Confederate independence.

64. Belle Boyd (1844–1900), Confederate heroine, spy, prisoner, and dispatch carrier for the Confederate government. Belle's attempt to run the blockade out of Wilmington in 1864 was foiled by the Federal blockade. She fell in love with her captor and they were married in St James's Church, Piccadilly.

65. General Braxton Bragg (1817–76), Confederate commander of the Army of the Tennessee and the most unpopular general in the South. His subordinates wrote to Richmond in October 1863, after the Battle of Chickamauga, asking for a different leader, but Davis insisted that Bragg stay.

66. Civilians hunting for souvenirs the day after the Battle of Chattanooga on 25 November 1864. General Bragg had to retreat, throwing away the victory of Chickamauga in September, and opening the way for a Federal invasion of the Deep South.

whole life do I remember of ever experiencing so much oppression and humiliation,' wrote the Confederate private Sam Watkins. 'The soldiers were starved and almost naked, and covered all over with lice and camp itch and filth and dirt. The men looked sick, hollow-eyed, and heart-broken, living principally upon parched corn, which had been picked out of the mud and dirt under the feet of officers' horses.'[25]

Thompson and Dr Newberry boarded a steamboat for the last leg of the journey. It was another two days of arduous travel before they reached Chattanooga on 22 November. That day Bragg stacked the cards against himself still higher by sending two more divisions to Knoxville. 'I had a fine view of the whole Rebel position on Missionary Ridge about three miles distant across a wooded valley,' wrote Thompson on the 23rd:

> The pickets and the skirmishers of both sides were behind their respective rifle pits in the valley below us and the Rebel pickets were plainly visible from Fort Wood, about half a mile from where I stood. All those round me were expecting immediate fighting. Soon I saw a sight I shall never forget. The whole Union army in the town – about 25,000 men under General Thomas – left their tents and huts and marched out past Fort Wood in long winding columns creeping into the valley and into line of battle round the town. From Fort Wood it all looked like a great review. But it was in deadly earnest.

Thompson was observing Grant's test of Bragg's resolve, to see whether the Confederate General was prepared to fight over Chattanooga or was planning to withdraw. The Union line charged towards Orchard Knob, a fortified hillock at the base of Missionary Ridge. The Confederates in the rifle pits were as mesmerized as Thompson by the bright spectacle rushing towards them, and fled. Federal Private Robert Neve was surprised to take the hill so easily: 'We kept rushing on until we got in sight of their works, which we took with little opposition, and captured a number of prisoners. I took two myself,' he added. Thompson watched as the prisoners were brought in and noticed that they were 'rough and ragged men with no vestige of a uniform'. During the night, while Neve lay shivering on the ground listening to every rustle and snap, Thompson rolled bandages for the Sisters of Mercy. He had not expected so much noise nor, perhaps, so much blood. 'This is war with a vengeance,' he wrote.[26] The men had seemed universally brave and determined. Robert Neve could have enlightened him that nothing was ever uniform in battle: 'I noticed in this fight that several officers and men got sheltered behind the trees, and kept waving their hats and cheering men up to a great degree, not even caring about firing a shot at the enemy.'[27]

After breakfast on 24 November, Thompson returned to Fort Wood to watch the second day of the Battle of Chattanooga. Bragg had managed to recall one of the two divisions sent to Knoxville – General Patrick Cleburne's – and had placed it at the far end of Missionary Ridge to shore up his right. Grant's overall plan for the day was simple: to capture the extreme ends of Bragg's position and then take the middle. 'Fighting Joe' Hooker's day had come.

> I began to think nothing was doing [wrote Thompson] when at about midday, when I was dividing my lunch with one of the gunners on the fort, heavy reports of cannon and musketry from Lookout Valley made all of us hurry to that side of Fort Wood. I joined two officers looking through telescopes towards Lookout Mountain and we soon saw Hooker attacking, his men plainly visible to us sweeping round the steep face of Lookout.
>
> Close by me was General Grant in a black surtout with black braid on and quite loose, black trousers and a black wideawake hat and thin Wellington boots. He looked clean and gentlemanly but not military having a Stoop and a full reddish beard, the moustache much lighter than the ends which were trained to a peak.
>
> We saw Hooker's men fall back once – then they advanced again. After some little suspense we saw the Rebels run round the face of Lookout near the top and Hooker's line advance after them, rifles popping all along the face of the mountain and guns shelling the retreating Rebels from Moccasin Point and Fort Negley. An officer beside me with a telescope cried out: 'There they are and the Rebels are running.' His glass was pointed to the steep face of Lookout more than half way up – and there sure enough, just three miles from us along the sparsely wooded face of the mountain, we saw a running fight with the Rebels retreating before Hooker's men.
>
> When Hooker's men planted that large U.S. flag near the top of the mountain, the whole of the troops, and the people in and around Chattanooga, who must number some 60,000 at least, seemed to hurrah together.
>
> The only man who seemed unmoved was General Grant himself, the prime author of all this hurly burly. There he stood in his plain citizen's clothes looking through his double field-glasses apparently totally unmoved.

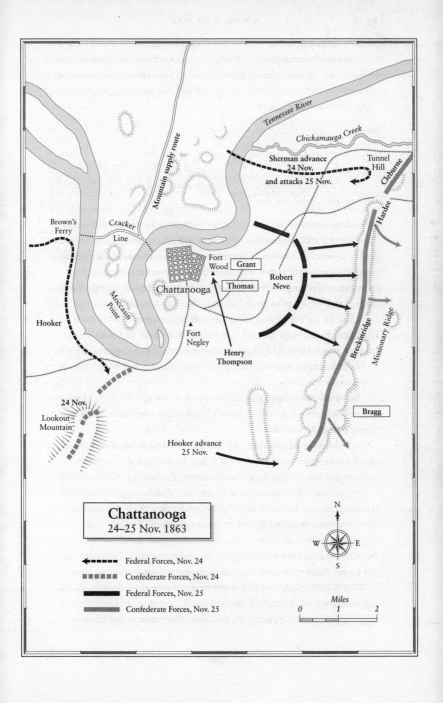

Tennessee River

Chickamauga Creek

Sherman advance
24 Nov.
and attacks 25 Nov.

Tunnel
Hill

Cleburne

Mountain supply route

Brown's
Ferry

Cracker
Line

Hardee

Fort
Wood

Grant

Robert Neve

Chattanooga

Thomas

Moccasin
Point

Breckinridge

Missionary Ridge

Hooker

Fort
Negley

Henry
Thompson

24 Nov.

Bragg

Lookout
Mountain

Hooker advance
25 Nov.

Chattanooga
24–25 Nov. 1863

N
W · E
S

- ◀ ▬ ▬ ▬ Federal Forces, Nov. 24
- ▪ ▪ ▪ ▪ ▪ Confederate Forces, Nov. 24
- ▬▬▬ Federal Forces, Nov. 25
- ▬▬▬ Confederate Forces, Nov. 25

Miles

0   1   2

I stood within a few feet of him and I could hardly believe that here was this famous commander, the model, as it seemed to me, of a modest and homely but efficient Yankee general. I stood next to General Grant for quite some time. If the battle had been a pageant got up for my benefit I could not have had it better.

Thompson had witnessed the 'Battle Above the Clouds', so called because a light fog had formed on parts of the mountain during the fight, obscuring the valley below. Hooker's victory had been achieved with surprisingly little cost; the casualties, including the missing and captured, were fewer than 2,000. The following day, the 25th, was supposed to be Sherman's turn for glory. Grant expected his man, who had served him so well at Vicksburg, to complete the rout and drive the Confederates off Missionary Ridge. But Sherman's adversary was General Patrick Cleburne, a former corporal in the 41st (Welsh) Regiment of Foot, who was the best commander in the Army of the Tennessee. Cleburne's new British volunteer aide-de-camp, Captain Charles H. Byrne, who had accompanied Ross and Vizetelly on their journey from Charleston in September, described the fight for his friends. 'Three times did they charge our position, and three times were they repulsed,' he wrote. 'The third charge was the most determined of the lot. They managed to reach the crest of the hill, and there they fought us for about two hours at a distance varying from twenty to thirty paces; – so close were they that our officers threw stones.'[28] Byrne's horse was shot in the neck. But rather than abandon his comrades, he chose to remain and fight on foot.

The bravery and sacrifice of Cleburne's soldiers became immaterial after Grant exploited the fact that Bragg had allowed the centre of the Confederate line to thin dangerously during the fight to only 15,000 men. At Gettysburg, the Confederate charge at Meade's centre had proved fatal because Lee failed to dent the Federal strength; but here there was a genuine weakness and Grant prevailed. General Thomas's division of 25,000 rose from the base of Orchard Knob and smashed through the Confederate defences at the top of the ridge. No one had ordered the men to go that far; a rage and madness simply took hold of them. 'We had all got mixed up,' wrote Robert Neve. 'Every man done as he liked, firing to the best advantage until we got twenty yards from the top. Someone cried out, "Fix bayonets!" and "Forward to the charge." The

Confederates ran, 'leaving cannon, wagons, horses, tools and everything. It was a perfect rout.'*[29] Four thousand Confederates were captured on the ridge, twice the number of casualties for the battle.

Bragg was powerless to halt the men as they came hurtling down the other side of the mountain towards Ringgold. Sam Watkins saw him ride. 'Bragg looked scared. He had put spurs to his horse, and was running like a scared dog . . . Poor fellow, he looked so hacked and whipped and mortified and chagrined at defeat, and all along the line, when Bragg would pass, the soldiers would raise the yell . . . "Bully for Bragg, he's hell on retreat."'[30] The only division that did not panic was Cleburne's, which held off the Federals long enough to enable the bulk of Bragg's army to escape off the mountain. The Confederates managed to stay ahead of their pursuers, crossing through Ringgold Gap into Georgia towards the station town of Dalton. Grant did not have the wagons and supplies for an incursion into enemy country and forbade his generals from pursuing the Confederates past Ringgold.

Henry Yates Thompson explored Bragg's deserted headquarters two days after the battle, on 27 November. Since the 25th he had been helping Dr Newberry by identifying the dead and pinning their names to their jackets. The first slain Federal he found turned out to be called 'John Bull'. As Thompson wandered among the bullet-scarred trees, picking up souvenirs, he stumbled across a pile of bodies. He had not noticed them at first because their faded uniforms were the same colour as the leaves. They had no hats or shoes.

> I went on to a knoll commanding the ridge in both directions [he wrote]. I found two Rebels – one dead and one just alive unattended since the battle. I gave the wounded man what brandy I had left in my flask and he spoke a little. His brains were protruding – the wound was in the back of his head. He seemed thankful for the brandy. I minced and mixed some meat, onions and biscuit and put water with them. He tried to eat but could not chew. A Federal came to help and washed his face.

---

* This was also Robert Neve's final day of the war. Already sick with dysentery, he was sent to hospital after the battle and was never again well enough to fight. He mustered out of the army in September 1864 and returned to England. His health permanently damaged by the war, he died in his mid-thirties in 1879, and his wife, Charlotte, successfully applied to Washington for her widow's pension.

While combing through the field, Thompson had a second shock. He saw two children, a little girl and boy, scavenging among the dead. They were collecting bullets. 'The little girl said she lived "over there", pointing to Bragg's headquarters. She had been in the house all through the battle,' he wrote. No one seemed to be responsible for them. The children seemed unaware of the danger which had passed over their heads, or of the perilous future which awaited them once the soldiers were no longer around to share their rations.[31] The pageantry Thompson had seen from afar had darkened to a scene of horror. 'The impression left on me by my walks the next day through those blood-stained woods', he wrote later, 'fixed a conviction in my mind, a conviction of the absolute and essential wickedness of those who talk lightly of war and still more of those who lightly begin a war.'[32] Thompson was ready to return home. 'Now I am tired to death,' he wrote. His ship was not leaving until 23 December, but Thompson felt he had witnessed enough suffering and intended to spend the final weeks of his stay in America visiting friends and enjoying himself as a tourist. His opinion of the United States had grown even higher now that he understood the great suffering endured by its people.

'God be praised for this victory, which looks like the heaviest blow the country has yet dealt at rebellion,' George Templeton Strong wrote in New York after hearing the news from Chattanooga. 'Meade's army again reported in motion and across the Rapidan,' he added to his diary entry. 'The nation needs one or two splendid victories by its Eastern armies to offset those gained in the West.'[33]

Two days later, on 29 November, General Longstreet received a wire from Jefferson Davis, confirming the Confederate defeat at Chattanooga and ordering him to abandon his siege at Knoxville so that he could provide support to Bragg. The telegram had come an hour too late for 800 Confederate and 13 Federal soldiers. One of the worst-planned assaults of the war had just taken place in front of Burnside's defences. Francis Dawson was so sickened by the fiasco that he could not bear to write about it in his memoir. All he could say about the twenty minutes of slaughter was that Longstreet's attack 'failed utterly'.

The Confederates began to march away from Knoxville on 4 December. Fearing that General Sherman was on his way to help Burnside, Longstreet decided it would be safer to retreat further east rather than head south towards Georgia. 'The men suffered frightfully,' wrote Dawson. 'It is no exaggeration to say that on such marches as they were obliged to make in that bitter weather they left the bloody tracks of their feet on the sharp stones of the roads.' Longstreet was stricken with remorse and self-doubt, and wished to be relieved of command. His request was denied, but President Davis did accept General Bragg's resignation. The General blamed the defeat on the cowardice of his troops and the personal animosity of his commanders, without ever examining his own part in either cause. President Davis had no other alternative than to recall his stubborn opponent General Joe Johnston and order him to take command of Bragg's Army of Tennessee.

In the Federal army, General Burnside, too, asked to be relieved. He was satisfied that his reputation as a commander had been redeemed by the capture of the Cumberland Gap and the defence of Knoxville. No longer would he be known solely for the disaster at Fredericksburg and the humiliating 'Mud March' of January 1863. The real victor of the Cumberland Gap, Colonel De Courcy, was also determined to leave the army. The War Department was not interested in deciding the contest between a departing general and his disgruntled colonel and had never responded to De Courcy's complaints. He was saved from becoming bitter by the loyal support and admiration of the soldiers who had been with him on the campaign. 'It was the unanimous opinion of the officers in De Courcy's brigade that this trouble actually grew out of jealousy caused by the brilliant result of De Courcy's tactics,' Lieutenant Colonel McFarland of the 86th Ohio Infantry later claimed. 'It will be borne in mind that 2,500 men, well protected by rifle-pits, forts, and cannon, had surrendered to 800, who were without effective support of any kind.'[34] The injustice meted out to De Courcy so grieved his old regiment that on 19 December the officers and men of the 16th Ohio Volunteer Infantry presented him with a commemorative sword, sash and belt. Captain Hamilton Richeson declared:

> Officers there are who command the confidence of those under them, but who cannot win their respect. Others have the respect of the men but not their confidence. You, sir, not only possess the confidence, but also the respect of the soldiers of your regiment . . . Indeed, through all the vicissitudes, dangers, privations and vexations of a soldier's life, while you were with the regiment you made so perfect, your conduct was admirable.[35]

De Courcy had always hoped that he would win their respect, though devotion had seemed out of the question because of his famously disciplinarian style. The 16th's parting gift demonstrated that he had achieved far more than he had believed possible. 'If I did well it was because they did better,' he replied. 'Under fire they were ever firm, cool and self-reliant.' De Courcy's Civil War experiences had been harsh and frequently heartbreaking, but by no means in vain. The soldiers he had tried so hard to mould into idealized versions of British troops remained proudly and defiantly true to their American roots; rather, it was De Courcy himself who was transformed into an officer and leader worthy of his men.*

General Meade had suffered the misfortune of embarking on his new campaign against Lee the day after eastern newspapers reported Grant's boast that his army was 'driving a big nail in the coffin of the rebellion'. Meade had learned that the Confederate Army of Northern Virginia, which was barely more than half the size of the 80,000-strong Army of the Potomac, was encamped in two separate locations some 30 miles apart. His plan was to creep across the Rapidan river, strike at one Confederate corps with all his might, and then quickly go after the other. But gross incompetence by one of his generals, who became lost, and bad weather which slowed down the others, wrecked Meade's beautiful design. By the time all the Federals were across the river and in place, Lee had his full army ready and properly entrenched. The area, known as Mine Run, was only eight miles from Chancellorsville. It was a thickly wooded area divided by a stream which ran into the Rapidan river. When Meade surveyed his army's position on 30 November he knew in his heart that he had failed. Though Lee had fewer than 50,000 men at his disposal, they were expertly placed behind impregnable defences. A soldier from Massachusetts looked across at the Confederate works and 'felt death in my very bones'.[37]

---

* In early 1864 De Courcy submitted his resignation. He received an ordinary discharge on 19 February, which, after protests, was amended to an honourable discharge on 3 March. He was 44 years old. More than half his life had been spent in the service of one army or another, and he could not imagine beginning a new life in business or farming. De Courcy chose to go home, to England. His future prospects were slim. But there was still one career open to him: he could marry well. On 10 May 1864 De Courcy married Elia, Comtesse du Bosque de Beaumont, a French widow of independent means.[36]

Meade made the courageous decision to call off the attack, though he knew he would be dubbed a coward by the Northern public. He quietly pulled his army back over the Rapidan. During the retreat a sudden freeze almost paralysed the Army of the Potomac. The 7th Maine Infantry, young Frederick Farr's regiment, suffered its worst night of the war as it crossed the Rapidan on 1 December. 'We halted after marching for a short time, and the night being intensely cold we made fires,' wrote a friend of Frederick's. 'This was the last that has been seen or heard of him. It is supposed that wearied out by the exceptional hardships he had undergone, he fell asleep by one of the fires and did not awake till the rebel cavalry came up to him and took him prisoner, as the Rebs followed close at our heels.'[38] No one had received word from Frederick, but it was assumed that he was in one of the prisons near Richmond.

The Army of the Potomac retired to its winter camps, which were spread out between the two 'Raps', the Rappahannock and Rapidan rivers. The Army of Northern Virginia followed suit on the other side of the Rapidan, and out west the opposing armies under Grant and Johnston did the same. There would be no more fighting until the spring. Although the Federal offensive in Virginia had not materialized, it was Lee rather than Meade who was on the defensive, and the same pattern was being repeated all over the South. Charleston held, despite the continued bombardment of its forts, but the question was for how much longer. Wilmington was still open but Mobile and Galveston, though nominally under Confederate control, were receiving only a trickle of blockade-runners. John Jones, the War Department clerk in Richmond, had heard that the capture rate was one in four blockade-runners; 'we can afford that,' he wrote.[39] But Jones had also heard in the War Department that soldiers were threatening to desert in order to feed their families and protect their farms. Grant's victory at Chattanooga had given the Union a base from which to attack not only the heart of the South, but also its munitions and gunpowder factories in Georgia.

Fredericksburg, Chancellorsville and Chickamauga – the three Confederate victories in 1863 – had not taken the South one step closer to independence, whereas Gettysburg had restored the morale of the Northern public, and Vicksburg had showed that victory was possible. 'The signs look better,' Lincoln wrote after the Mississippi river was reopened to travel and commerce. 'The Father of Waters again goes unvexed to the sea.' Much of Mississippi, Tennessee, West Virginia and Virginia north of Fredericksburg were under Union control; the Gulf and the Atlantic coasts were also closed off from the Confederacy; and Texas, Arkansas and most of Louisiana were inaccessible to Richmond. But these advantages seemed less certain when the core of the Confederacy – Virginia, the Carolinas, Georgia and Alabama – remained intact; two formidable Confederate armies and the great Robert E. Lee were still at Davis's disposal; and the fighting spirit of the South remained unbroken.

PART THREE
If Only We Are Spared

27

Buckling under Pressure

Time for a vacation – The Alabama *– The Irish – Confederate woes in Europe – The Liberal government clings to power*

'They are wearing out, down there,' Henry Adams wrote to his brother Charles Francis Jr., after *The Times* published Francis Lawley's reports from Tennessee. 'He says it took him forty hours to go by rail the hundred and thirty miles from Atlanta to Chattanooga, in the filthiest, meanest cars he ever saw.'[1] The effects of the Federal blockade were far worse than Henry knew. The Confederate government cupboards were practically bare: in recent months the purchasing orders for its agent James Bulloch in Liverpool had broadened from military supplies to include such ordinary items as 'one dozen erasers', 'two dozen memorandum books of different sizes, and 12 dozen best lead pencils'.[2]

Francis Lawley was feeling worn out himself, after three years of reporting from the field, and had decided to take a leave of absence in the New Year. He stayed in the Confederate capital over Christmas while his friends Frank Vizetelly and Fitzgerald Ross went to the headquarters of the Confederate general Jeb Stuart near the Orange Court House in Virginia. The celebrations were not as jolly as the previous Christmas, though Stuart chivalrously lent them his own tent, and Ross was delighted to meet Stuart's new assistant inspector general of the Cavalry Corps, Colonel George St Leger Grenfell. After their visit Ross wrote that the English cavalry officer had 'told us some capital stories of his various adventures ... The Colonel ... has only lately been transferred to this army, and looks back with regret to the stirring and fighting time when he was with [General John Hunt] Morgan in the West ... [they] adored their "fighting old Colonel", and would have followed him anywhere'.[3]

Grenfell had failed to achieve the same popularity among Stuart's men. When the Englishman had resurfaced in Richmond after his mysterious disappearance from Bragg's army, his value as an expert cavalryman had persuaded the Confederate authorities not to prosecute him for his original crime of helping a slave to escape, or for having jumped bail ahead of his trial. But Grenfell's placement on Stuart's staff in September had caused fierce resentment among the tight-knit group. By the time Ross met Grenfell, the Colonel had become so fed up with his treatment that he was on the verge of joining forces again with General Morgan. The Kentucky raider's recent escape from a Federal prison in Ohio had raised his reputation in the South still higher, and hundreds of volunteers were answering his invitation to form a new guerrilla outfit.[4]

After Christmas, Ross and Vizetelly returned to Richmond to say goodbye to Lawley. Though his spirits were waning, those of Richmond society were not; amateur theatricals were the craze that winter. Vizetelly had been the mainstay of every production – painting the scenery, rehearsing the songs, adapting the parts and sometimes even acting. On 12 January 1864 he performed in a comedy before a select audience that included President Davis and General Stuart. Vizetelly's part 'was to dandle and stifle the cries of a screaming baby', wrote the diarist Mary Chesnut, while three soldiers behind a curtain simulated the child's cries. 'When Mr Vizetelly had exhausted all known methods of quieting an infant (in vain), his despair was comic. He threw the baby on a chair and sat on it,' prompting great roars of laughter.[5]

Two weeks after Lawley left for England, Vizetelly realized that he, too, was exhausted and should return home to rest before the fighting resumed in the spring. In his last dispatch from the South, Vizetelly admitted that his two years in the Confederacy had affected him more than any other assignment; 'every soldier of the army of Northern Virginia was a comrade. We had marched many weary miles together, and I had shared in some of their dangers,' he wrote. 'This brought me nearer to them than years of ordinary contact could have done.' As he rode away from Jeb Stuart's camp in late January, Vizetelly stopped to look back at the little gathering of tents, suddenly afraid for 'the many friends who were lying there, some of whom would breathe their last in the first glad sunshine of [the] coming spring'.[6]

*

Winter quarters of Jeb Stuart's cavalry, by Frank Vizetelly,
who sketches himself on the left

As Lawley and Vizetelly made their separate journeys across the Atlantic,
each having run the blockade at Wilmington, news of the CSS *Alabama*'s
latest raids on Northern ships was spreading. Captain Raphael Semmes
daily expected to see a Federal fleet bearing down on the *Alabama*, but
none came. 'My ship had been constantly reported, and any one of his
clerks could have plotted my track . . . so as to show [Gideon Welles] . . .
where I was bound.' Instead, laughed Semmes, the US Navy Secretary
played an endless and unwinnable game of chase. All Semmes had to do
was estimate how long it would take for intelligence of his whereabouts to
reach Washington, and make sure he left ahead of his pursuers.[7]

Since the Confederate commerce raider's launch in 1862, Semmes had
burned or released on bond forty-two vessels, sunk the gunboat USS *Hatteras* at Galveston, and converted one captured vessel into a satellite raider
(the *Tuscaloosa* would have a short career of six months and take only
one prize). But by the summer of 1863 the *Alabama* and its crew had
begun to show signs of battle fatigue. Still searching for prey, Semmes
sailed down to Cape Town, South Africa, where to his surprise and relief
he and his crew were fêted as heroes. Nothing so exciting or glamorous

had visited Cape Town for a very long time and the residents of this lonely outpost of the British Empire could hardly believe their good fortune. They were so welcoming – inviting the Southerners on big-game and ostrich hunts – that twenty-one sailors deserted, leaving Semmes with a serious shortage of men. After much scraping around, his executive officer, 1st Lieutenant John McIntosh Kell, was only able to find eleven replacements. Fortunately, two Prussian naval officers who had been shipwrecked near Cape Town also joined as master's mates.[8] The appearance of the gunboat USS *Vanderbilt* off the Cape put an end to the *Alabama* crew's two-month respite from their harsh life at sea. At midnight on 24 September the ship set sail during a heavy gale for the fertile hunting grounds of the Far East, where Semmes knew he was not expected.*

An article entitled 'Our Cruise' in the *Southern African Mail* by George Townley Fullam, one of the English officers on board the *Alabama*, eventually reached England in the autumn. Fullam described the ship's adventures from her narrow escape out of Liverpool in July 1862 to her glorious entry into Cape Town twelve months later. Embarrassingly for the British government, Fullam claimed that someone in Her Majesty's Customs had alerted the Confederates to the *Alabama*'s pending seizure, allowing her to get away in time. Not surprisingly, the US legation was incensed by this revelation. Charles Francis Adams ordered the article to be printed as a pamphlet and arranged for a copy to be sent to Lord Russell with a strongly worded complaint attached.

Although Russell insisted to Adams that the British government could not be held responsible for the depredations of the *Alabama*, privately he was worried that the United States might carry out its threat – first made by Seward and Adams in 1862 – to sue Britain for damages after the war.[10] Russell discussed with the law officers whether they should bar the raider from all British ports around the world, but in their opinion such a move could be interpreted as an admission of guilt. The Duke of Argyll thought Russell was being too timid and argued that the government

---

* That same night, in the Kell household, far away in McIntosh County, Georgia, 6-year-old Jonny Kell cried as his mother buried his little sister, Dot, near the house. His younger brother, 3-year-old Munroe, was too shocked to speak. Jonny frightened his mother by saying he wished to join 'little Sissy' in heaven. Four days after her daughter's death, Mrs Kell was relieved to hear that Munroe had regained his words. 'Jonny, you may have my marbles,' he said, 'I don't want them any more.' That evening he showed the classic signs of diphtheria. He was dead by the morning. 'Oh God have mercy on my desolate broken heart,' wrote Lieutenant Kell's despairing wife. 'He has been gone so long, so long! Three long sad years.'[9]

NEUTRALITY.

Mrs. NORTH. "HOW ABOUT THE *ALABAMA*, YOU WICKED OLD MAN?"
Mrs. SOUTH. "WHERE'S MY RAMS? TAKE BACK YOUR PRECIOUS CONSULS—THERE!!!"

The Union and the Confederacy both rail at a determinedly
calm John Bull, *Punch*, November 1863

should not only keep the *Alabama* from British ports, but also ban all
blockade-runners from the West Indies. As a less drastic alternative, the
Duke suggested that blockade-runners should be banned from using the
Royal Naval Dockyard in Bermuda for repairs and coaling, but even this
seemingly sensible suggestion was deemed too risky by the law officers.
Russell was relieved when an alleged violation of British neutrality at
Queenstown, Ireland – involving the USS *Kearsarge* and sixteen Irish
stowaways – for once reversed the direction of complaints, giving him
the opportunity to play the injured party with the US legation.*

* Captain John Ancrum Winslow had been searching for James Morgan's ship, the *Georgia*,
when storm damage forced the USS *Kearsarge* to put into Queenstown, Ireland, on 3 November for emergency repairs. While it was there, a local newspaper printed a story that it had
come expressly to enlist volunteers. The following day the *Kearsarge* was surrounded by rowing boats filled with men clamouring to be chosen. The *Kearsarge* set sail on 5 November with
sixteen extra men. Winslow's explanation of the incident failed to say how the sixteen climbed
aboard unnoticed and managed to find such perfect hiding places on an unfamiliar ship.

The British government was fully aware that large numbers of Irishmen were enlisting in the Federal army; Consul Archibald had observed the crowds at Castle Garden, the immigration depot on the southernmost tip of Manhattan, and estimated that every week 150 Irish labourers were stepping off the boat and into the arms of recruiters.[11] A Home Office clerk compiling passenger statistics first spotted the phenomenon in April 1863, when he noticed a sharp increase – it had almost tripled since 1862 – in the number of single, male travellers. The shipping lines were asked to resubmit their passenger lists in case there had been an error. In Ireland, local squires and magistrates were directed to make discreet enquiries in their districts as to who was leaving and why. The results showed that between January and November 1863, when the USS *Kearsarge* docked at Queenstown, more than 80,000 jobless males had emigrated from Ireland. After carefully reviewing all the statistics from the past three years, the Home Office discovered that the actual increase in the emigration of unmarried Irishmen was roughly 10,000 a year (a figure the government decided it could accept without too much heartache).[12]

The Confederate government was also concerned about the vast influx of Irish immigrants to the North, and in August 1863 sent its propagandist in France, Edwin De Leon, to Ireland, where he diligently spent several weeks publishing articles about the horrors of the war. James Mason followed in September, but his findings confirmed their worst fears. The Irish were so poor after two failed harvests, Mason wrote to the Confederate Secretary of State, Judah P. Benjamin, on 4 September 1863, 'that the temptation of a little ready money and promise of good wages would lead them to go anywhere'.[13] But the Draft Riots in New York in mid-July had given Benjamin hope that it was not too late to stem the tide. The accusation that the US government was throwing its Irish immigrants into the slaughtering pen was gaining credibility following the near-obliteration of the Irish Brigade at Fredericksburg and Gettysburg. He dispatched to Ireland two more agents, Lieutenant James Capston, a former Dubliner, and Father John Bannon of Vicksburg, with orders to discourage Irish immigration using all the means at their disposal.

The exposure of the stowaways on the *Kearsarge* had been Lieutenant Capston's first success. But he could not uncover any proof for the Home Office that Captain Winslow had acted deliberately, nor did he find evidence of official Federal recruiting in Ireland. (The US government had no need to send over agents when there were plenty of unscrupulous entrepreneurs ready to assume the risk themselves in return for a large cut of the bounty paid for volunteers.*) Capston and Bannon soon gave up that particular line of attack and concentrated instead on spreading anti-Northern propaganda. The two Confederate agents tried to tap into nationalist sentiment by comparing the South's fight for independence with Ireland's; and distributed thousands of hand-bills, warning potential emigrants that they would end up as cannon fodder if they went to the North. Father Bannon also used his Church connections to ensure that the injustices endured by the Irish community in the North were broadcast from the pulpit. Although emigration continued apace, the agents successfully rubbed off any glamour in volunteering for the North.

The danger of having their arms shipments seized by the US navy, and their commerce raiders impounded by the government, had driven the Confederates' activities in Britain underground. 'The cheapest and most favorable market, that of England, was well nigh closed to the Confederacy, while the United States were permitted to buy and ship what they liked, without hindrance, and at the ordinary current prices,' complained James Bulloch in his memoirs.[14] Matthew Fontaine Maury had hoped to launch a second Confederate cruiser, the CSS *Rappahannock*, but he had been forced to send the vessel from Sheerness, Kent, on 24 November 1863 with its hull and boilers still needing work simply to prevent its seizure by the authorities. The cruiser just managed to reach Calais, where it had remained since December, awaiting repairs.

The blockade was also drastically inhibiting the South's communications. Rose Greenhow had been in Paris since December, trying to arrange an interview with Emperor Napoleon III: 'I would write you many interesting particulars,' she wrote to a friend in Virginia, 'but the

---

* On 11 March 1864, for example, 120 Irish labourers stepped off the *Nova Scotia* in Portland, Maine, expecting to begin work on the railroads. They were unaware that Mr Finney, their agent, had been arrested in Ireland for illegal recruiting. They were taken by train to Boston, where they were locked in a warehouse and given nothing but whisky. Two days later an official recruiter arrived, backed by the police, who blocked all the doors so that the men could not escape. So outrageous was the scheme that local Irishmen battled with the police and broke open the warehouse. But their intervention was too late for Thomas Tulley and six other hostages. Despite the British Consul's vigorous protests, and a prompt complaint by Lord Lyons, the men were shipped off to the 20th Maine regiment in the Army of the Potomac.

publication of the late intercepted letters is a good warning to me to be careful. If you will get from Mr. Benjamin a cipher and use my name as the key, I can then tell you many things.'[15] The 'intercepted letters' were those from the CSS *Robert E. Lee*, which had been caught on 9 November 1863 on its twenty-first trip between Wilmington and Nassau. The US navy also captured the Confederate Ordnance Department's two remaining supply ships the same night, but the real prize was the *Lee*. On board were two lieutenants from the Royal Artillery, the Belgian Consul and a mailbag containing dispatches from Mason for the Richmond Cabinet.[16] The mailbag had also included the private correspondence of Edwin De Leon, which revealed every aspect of his propaganda campaign, from his attempts to bribe French journalists to his methods of spreading disinformation. But by the time De Leon's letters had appeared in the New York and London press the disgraced agent was already on his way back to the South, having been dismissed by Jefferson Davis, not for the exposure but for criticizing Judah P. Benjamin, who had taken the side of John Slidell in the acrimonious relations between the two agents.

Slidell had refused to work with De Leon after he learned that the propaganda agent had opened and read Confederate dispatches intended for him alone. Convinced that De Leon was after his position, Slidell tried to undermine him at every opportunity. He was equally hostile towards Rose Greenhow and discouraged his wife from helping her find a school for her daughter. (Eventually Rose accomplished the task on her own, placing little Rose in the Convent du Sacré Cœur, a Catholic boarding school with many foreigners among its 200 girls.[17]) Slidell's suspicions about De Leon were groundless, but he was right to be fearful of interference from Rose: 'I have come to the conclusion that we have nothing to hope from this side of the Channel,' she wrote to Davis on 2 January 1864.[18] The French mission was a waste of time and resources, she concluded: Slidell cared more about his social life than Confederate diplomacy, and Mason's grasp of French was too poor for him to be effective in Europe. She advised Davis to recall Slidell and send Mason back to London before the work of two years withered on the vine.

Rose thought Louis-Napoleon's sympathy was entirely mercenary: 'they want tobacco now quite as much as the English want cotton ... and I believe that if we were to stop the going out of either cotton or tobacco, it would have more effect than anything else.'[19] Having failed to reach the Emperor through friends or contacts, she audaciously wrote to him on 11 January, requesting a meeting, and much to Slidell's annoyance was granted an interview at the Tuileries on the 22nd. The little drama was observed by the Maryland journalist W. W. Glenn, who, having spirited Lawley, Vizetelly and a host of other British visitors across Southern lines, was now in Paris visiting a friend. Glenn's own feelings about Rose were ambivalent – he had seen her once before in Mason's company and thought her 'a handsome woman, rouged and elaborately gotten up' – but he was still amused by Slidell's consternation over her success with the Emperor:

> Slidell, the moment he heard she was to have an audience, was so afraid of the apparent influence of the woman . . . that she might injure him at Richmond by her letters, or on her return home, and thus perhaps effect his recall which he by no means desired, that he immediately went and left his card; and although he had declared she should not set . . . foot in his house or know his family, he sent Mrs S to call upon her too. When she went to have her interview, Mr S sent Eustis, his secretary of legation, with her to present her. She had them in fact all at her feet.[20]

Louis-Napoleon was not only charming and sympathetic – taking the Confederate heroine's hand and gently seating her on a cushion next to him – but he also surprised her with the depth of his knowledge about the war. 'Tell the President,' she recorded him saying, 'that I have thoughts on his military plans – he has not concentrated enough. The Yankees have also made true blunders. If instead of throwing all your strength upon Vicksburg you could have left that to its fate and strengthened Lee so as to have taken Washington, the war would have ended.' He continued to be charming even when she asked him directly whether he would recognize the Confederate States. 'I wish to God I could,' Louis-Napoleon apparently answered. 'But I cannot do it without England.'[21] At the end of their conversation the Emperor escorted her to the door and shook her hand. He seemed to be offering hope and for a short while Rose was elated by the interview. She wrote in such glowing terms to Georgiana Walker in Bermuda that her friend recorded in her diary:

> Mrs. G. is much delighted with her visit to Paris, & considers her mission to have been a successful one. She had an audience of the Emperor, & was

treated with marked attention. She says she advocated our cause warmly &
earnestly, & left not one point uncovered; that the Emperor received her as
one directly from the President; & bade her tell the President that his sympathy was all with him, & that he should do all in his power to aid him.
The Empress says, 'His Majesty is not averse to interviews with beautiful
escaped prisoners'. I have since heard that Mrs. Greenhow had attended a
Ball at the Tuileries, & had supped in the room & perhaps at the table with
their Majesties.[22]

But in reality the Emperor had only uttered the same platitudes that
Slidell had heard a dozen times before, and once Rose was able to reflect
on the interview she realized that she too had been fobbed off: 'My
belief is the stronger now that our only chance of recognition must now
come from England and that, that is the place to which our efforts must
be directed.' She returned to London on 6 February 1864. 'I left my little
one behind and my heart was heavy,' she wrote in her diary.[23] James
Bulloch, who had arrived in France on 27 January, escorted her to the
station, helped her onto the train and deposited her in the carriage
reserved for women travelling alone. Aware of the heavy burdens upon
him, Rose was touched by his courtesy.

Bulloch was too discreet to unburden himself, but he was that day
suffering 'a greater pain and regret than I ever thought it possible to
feel'.[24] He had crossed the Channel in a last-ditch effort to save the rams,
which were still being held at Lairds in Liverpool. Since they belonged
to a French subject, M. Bravay, the Emperor could, in theory, request
their return to France. But Louis-Napoleon refused to intervene. Slidell
assumed that the Emperor was simply paying lip-service to Northern
demands, but Bulloch knew better. 'There was a good deal said about
the personal sympathy of the Emperor for the South; and his earnest
desire that by some means or other we might get our ships out,' he
wrote angrily after the war, but 'the sympathy and hope were sheer
mockery'.[25] The day after Rose's departure, on 7 February, Bulloch sent
a letter to Bravay authorizing him to sell the Lairds rams as quickly as
possible. (It took several months, but after considerable haggling the
Admiralty bought the ships for £180,000.) Bulloch's distress was not
only for the loss of the rams; Slidell had decided that the ship-construction
operation was jeopardizing his relationship with the Emperor and
ordered Bulloch to sell the unfinished ironclads in Bordeaux. Determined

not to be thwarted, Bulloch pretended to acquiesce while he sought a broker who would agree to buy the vessels on paper only.

Even legitimate Confederate enterprises were buckling under pressure. The price of the Confederate cotton bond had dropped precipitously from £70 to £34 after Grant's victory at the Battle of Chattanooga, and now fluctuated around the £50 mark. The cost of shipping supplies to the Confederacy and the increasing likelihood of capture were wiping out the profits of blockade-running.[26] For the first time since the war began, the survival of Fraser, Trenholm and Co. – the Southern shipping firm and financial clearing house for the Confederacy in Europe – appeared to be in doubt. 'Every consignment to us is closely scrutinized and anything at all suspicious would be seized at once,' Charles Prioleau in Liverpool explained to a would-be arms supplier. Nor could he extend further credit to the Confederate government, not even to purchase replacement blockade-runners for the Ordnance Department. Prioleau calculated that if every available cotton bale arrived at Liverpool, the company would still be owed £70,000.

> If there is anything that could make me despair of the Republic it is this [Prioleau wrote to George Trenholm in Charleston]. Look at all the intercepted correspondence and what does it show? That every individual who comes to this country has but one aim and object namely to get as large an amount of plunder as possible out of every operation, the government in all cases bearing the cost . . . I do candidly believe, though perhaps I ought not say so, that the Government has not been served with perfect and unswerving integrity . . . by any agents except yourself, Bulloch and FT and Co and what is the result? We are all reduced to a condition of equal inefficiency and disgust . . . I will still do all in my power so to arrange matters as to enable myself to buy you at least one boat, but you will see yourself from what I have written that it cannot be depended on.[27]

The Confederate propaganda agent Henry Hotze had made a similar complaint to Benjamin about dishonest agents in his end-of-year letter in 1863. Six months earlier he had suggested that Richmond should assume control of all the Confederacy's international dealings, from arms supplying to blockade-running. Now he begged Benjamin to do it before the market damned the Confederacy for good. 'Prohibit the exportation of cotton, except for Government account,' he wrote.

'Prohibit the importation of luxuries on any pretence, and import shoes and clothes as well for the citizens as the Army.' Most important of all, he urged him to void all contracts that had not been negotiated by Colin McRae, the South's official purchasing agent.[28] With cotton selling for more than 23s. a pound (five years before it had been worth only 7d.), there were vast profits awaiting the Confederate government if it could put an effective system in place.

Hotze also wanted to be rid of James Spence, whose support for the abolition of slavery had become a burden and an embarrassment for the Confederates in England. The ardent supporter of Southern independence was roaring up and down the country in preparation for the opening of Parliament in February. Spence had studied the methods of the anti-slavery societies and was imitating them to good effect: publishing pamphlets before each meeting, preparing fact sheets for the local press, circulating petitions during the meeting and creating local affiliates of his Southern Independence Association.[29] The aim, he told Lord Wharncliffe, the head of the Manchester affiliate, was to make it seem as though pro-Southern feeling was increasing, since nothing should be allowed to dampen the already fragile spirits 'of our people who of late have had much to dismay them'. But all the good work had been ruined, in Hotze's opinion, by the Association's anti-slavery manifesto, which stated explicitly: 'The Association will also devote itself ... to a revision of the system of servile Labour, unhappily bequeathed to them by England, in accordance with the spirit of the age, so as to combine the gradual extinction of slavery with ... the true civilisation of the negro race.'[30] This, Hotze believed, was unacceptable and far outweighed Spence's success in attracting four peers and nine MPs to the committee.

James Mason hastily wrote to Benjamin from France that he had been unable to prevent the anti-slavery manifesto: the Southern Independence Association represented the 'views of Englishmen addressed to English people ... it was in vain to combat their "sentiment". The so-called "antislavery" feeling seems to have become with them a "sentiment" akin to patriotism.'[31] Mason's defence was not enough to save Spence's position as the South's official financial agent, and his operations were transferred to Colin McRae. But Benjamin was so flattering and apologetic in his letter of dismissal on 11 January that the Confederacy was able to retain Spence's goodwill. 'As a man of the world,' Benjamin wrote, 'I would meet you on the most cordial terms without the slightest reference to your views on this subject; but that, "as a member of a government," it would be impossible for me to engage you in its service after the publication of your opinions.'[32] It helped that Benjamin agreed to reimburse him for the money he had expended on propping up the South's declining bonds.

Hotze would have been disappointed but not distraught if Spence had dropped all connection with the South, since there was a new organization afoot which had nothing to do with Liverpool businessmen. The Society for Promoting the Cessation of Hostilities in America had been started by Matthew Maury and the Revd Francis W. Tremlett, the vicar of St Peter's, Belsize Park, London, whose church had become the favoured place of worship for Confederate naval officers abroad. The Society was overtly Christian, directed at ordinary people rather than politicians, and pacifist in its aims. Its purported aim was to halt the bloodshed in the South – by harnessing the power of public outrage through mass petitions to Parliament.

'It is a singular feature of this struggle in America, that its merits should be debated at popular meetings held all over this kingdom,' Adams wrote to Seward a few weeks before the opening of Parliament. 'The associations of sympathizers with the insurgents have of late been assiduously engaged in sending paid agents to deliver lectures in behalf of their cause at various places. This has given occasion to counter efforts. Frequently discussions are held by representatives of both sides. I very much doubt whether anything precisely similar ever took place before.'[33]

Adams knew that the Confederacy's supporters were waiting for the new parliamentary session with great anticipation. The Liberal government appeared to be tottering towards collapse: the Tories had won every by-election since 1859, cutting Palmerston's majority in the Commons to 44. Several junior government ministers were close to resigning, and Palmerston had become mixed up in a bizarre divorce case.* Worse, Russell had exposed the government to withering criticism in the press for his inept intervention between the Danes and the Germans in their

---

* The 80-year-old premier had been cited as the guilty party in the divorce proceedings of Timothy O'Kane against his wife Margaret, prompting the society joke: 'She was Kane, but was he Able?' Benjamin Disraeli grumpily predicted that the case – though spurious – would do wonders for Palmerston's popularity, and no doubt give him a sweeping victory at the next election.

war over the duchy of Schleswig-Holstein.* Seward had also contributed to the British government's weakness. 'That Solomon has ... exercised his usual indiscretion,' raged Moran on 11 February 1864 after Seward included in the official publication of the State Department's correspondence for 1863 dispatches that were never sent to the Foreign Office, such as his provocative July letter on the Lairds rams.[34]

By playing fast and loose with the State Department record of official dispatches, Seward had made any British concession seem like weakness in the face of Northern threats. Russell insisted in the House of Lords that he knew nothing about the bellicose July dispatch, and that his decision to detain the rams was based on sound legal advice rather than fear of Northern retribution, but he was not believed and the government was damaged. The Tories repeatedly asked for an exact accounting of the time line between Adams's threat of war and the detention of the rams; cried shame about the mistreatment of British prisoners; and demanded an immediate investigation into US recruiting schemes in Ireland. The more Russell protested the less he seemed to be in control of the situation. Lord Derby accused him of having made Britain a laughing stock in the eyes of the world through his meddling in foreign affairs. Russell, declared Derby to gales of laughter in the Lords, was no better at directing events than Bottom in A Midsummer Night's Dream.[35]

Fortunately for the government, the Tories did not mind castigating Russell for his handling of the Northerners, but they had no desire to be seen as the defenders of slavery, or of rebellion.[36] Nor were they sure that it was in their interest to take power at this precise moment: 'Johnny seems to have got into such a muddle in every part of the world,' Lord Derby wrote to Disraeli. 'But how far are we prepared to take the responsibility of the consequences of success?' He was by no means confident that his party had enough support in the House for a change of ministry.[37]

Henry Hotze grasped the subtlety of Lord Derby's position after watching him lead the assault on Russell from the Lords. 'Their object is rather to embarrass the Government than to attack it seriously,' he

---

* Palmerston began the government's troubles by declaring in the House of Commons in July 1863 that if Denmark were attacked by Germany, Great Britain would come to her defence. But once the Germans began to make good on their threats – invading Holstein in December 1863 and Schleswig in February 1864 – thanks to Russell's maladroit dealings with Louis-Napoleon it was Britain who stood alone, and dared not risk sending troops in support of Denmark.

informed Benjamin.[38] The American question was tossed like a ball in between weightier debates about the oppressed Poles and the German invasion of Denmark. Hotze watched anxiously as the Tories' appropriation of the Lairds rams controversy undermined the purpose of the Southern Independence Association, turning its meetings into a reflection of the power struggle in Westminster. Nothing could be agreed upon between the Association's Tory and Liberal members, so nothing was achieved; and several prominent Liberal supporters left after a scathing attack on their anti-slavery credentials by Goldwin Smith, the Regius Professor of History at Oxford, in a pamphlet entitled, 'A Letter to a Whig Member of the Southern Independence Association'.

On 23 February the US legation held its breath after the Tory Opposition forced a vote in the Commons to have all the papers regarding Adams and the Lairds rams made public. The government defeated the motion by a narrow margin of 34 votes. Confronted by the possibility of a change in government, Charles Francis Adams decided that he preferred Palmerston to survive. Adams still attended Lady Palmerston's weekly parties with gritted teeth, but the sight of the 80-year-old Prime Minister standing jauntily at the top of the grand staircase no longer oppressed him. 'At one time, I thought it would be better for our interest in America that he should go out,' Adams wrote in his diary. 'Of late, I have changed my mind. The Ministry have now gone as far as any Ministry would be likely to do.'[39]

Adams's usual cynicism about British politics was in partial abeyance due to a happy family event. Charles Francis Adams Jr. had at last taken his furlough and come to England. The term of the 1st Massachusetts Cavalry had expired at the end of 1863, but Charles had encouraged his company to follow his example and re-enlist. 'They seem to think that I am a devil of a fellow,' he wrote. 'These men don't care for me personally. They think me cold, reserved and formal. They feel no affection for me, but they do believe in me, they have faith in my power of accomplishing results and in my integrity.'[40]

Benjamin Moran envied Charles Francis Jr.'s assured deportment. 'He is a sturdy weather tanned man of about 30 years – stout and strong with a bald head; and is a good deal taller than either his father or his brother Henry . . . [and] is coming to Europe to dip into English society,' he wrote in his diary. Moran's hope that it would only be a little dip was soon dashed. 'Mr Adams can't introduce his secretaries to their rights,' he thundered, 'but he and his wife go out of their way to *stuff* their son into every possible house in London, when he really has no business there.'[41] At a party given by Lady de Grey, Moran sidled up to a crowd that included the poet Robert Browning and the artist John Everett Millais. 'When, Lo! Mrs Adams appeared forcing her way through followed by the Captain at her apron string. I was disgusted,' he wrote. 'She was in her element and talked as loud and vulgarly as ever. Holding her finger up and shaking it towards him, she said, "here Charley, here, here," and on his joining her presented him to Browning and Tom Hughes [the author of *Tom Brown's Schooldays*] . . . I got out of the way and went down stairs.'[42]

Moran was outraged when 'the Captain' failed to pay a visit to the legation offices. 'He is pure Adams,' Moran wrote spitefully. But his opportunity for revenge on the family came sooner than he expected: Charles Francis Adams wished to take both his sons to the Queen's levee on 2 March. 'This morning,' wrote Moran on 1 March, 'Mr H. B. Adams came into the Legation and rather insolently insisted that he was entitled to outrank us at Court.' Henry ought to have known that Moran would not allow a threat to his rank as Assistant Secretary to pass unchallenged. As a mere private secretary, Henry had no official rank.

'I even questioned the propriety of his going to Court at all – to say nothing about his right,' recorded Moran. With extraordinary timing, Sir Edward Cust, the Queen's Master of Ceremonies, called at the legation at the height of the argument and confirmed that the right of attendance was extended only to daughters of Ministers, not to sons or private secretaries. Naturally exceptions were allowed, but unofficial private secretaries such as Henry Adams would certainly be ranked behind the last attaché or Assistant Secretary. Moran had been waiting to hear this ever since Henry's arrival. The look of triumph on the Secretary's face was too much for Henry and he swore never to go to Court again. 'I don't think anyone will regret that decision,' wrote Moran smugly.[43]

Shortly after the altercation with Moran, Henry and Charles Francis Jr. left for Paris, 'a city for pleasure', wrote Charles Francis.[44] The brothers took every advantage of their freedom. Charles recorded that they spent their last night in the company of beautiful Burgundy 'and started for London smiling and happy with wine'. He was sober, though a little jaded, for his presentation at Court on 12 March. During the carriage ride he annoyed Moran by grumbling about the occasion. 'This cant is abominable,' wrote Moran afterwards. 'If he didn't know what he was going for, why in the name of decency did he go?'[45] Henry was still smarting from the argument and stayed at home.

Henry Hotze was pleased when he heard that the Revd John Sella Martin and Andrew Jackson, both former slaves, had ended their lecture tours and were going home to America. Their presence had threatened to overshadow his successful infiltration of the downmarket press. With sufficient funds, the South could be parlayed into a national cause, Hotze often told Benjamin:

> The North has two papers, one 3-penny and one penny paper, which it subsidizes lavishly. We also have two, a 3-penny one and a penny one, and in respectability, standing, and influence no one would venture to institute even a comparison between the respective champions. We have moreover the advantage over the subsidized writers of the North that our cause is pleaded with the force of personal conviction and with the zeal of personal friendship and political sympathy ... In the neutral press, both daily and weekly, we have also important connections, equally honorable, while the North, beyond its own organs, has nothing. All this, I unhesitatingly declare, is due to the *Index*.[46]

Hotze was also looking for ways to dilute the impact of Henry Yates Thompson's articles in the press. Since his return from the battlefields of eastern Tennessee, Thompson had been writing for the *Daily News* and touring the country, giving talks about his experiences in the North, somewhat to his family's embarrassment. Leslie Stephen was another irritant, since he was unafraid to take on the South's supporters at Cambridge and force them to defend their views on slavery ('I can actually bear testimony [to them] that you are human beings (more or less), that you smoke like Christians,' he joked to James Russell Lowell in Massachusetts).[47] Neither man was an eccentric or a fanatic, and their opinions on the war could not easily be dismissed. Hotze hoped that Colonel Fremantle's *Three Months in the Southern States*, which had been published just before Christmas, would become so popular that dissenting voices would be ignored.[48] Still, even Fremantle's book contained passages that upset Hotze. At James Mason's request, Fremantle had removed passages that made the South seem foreign to English eyes, but he refused to take out his impressions of Southern slavery.[49]

Lawley's arrival in England in February briefly revived Hotze's hope of a propaganda coup. The journalist had been travelling for nearly three weeks and the enforced rest had restored him to health. William Howard Russell saw him twice in the same week and noted that he was 'in splendid fettle, grey but as clear and handsome as paint'. His eloquent reports of the Confederacy's sufferings had won him a following of swooning females, but Russell was not deceived. Lawley, he wrote, was as 'hard as nails'.[50] However, Lawley could not afford to bring public attention to himself lest he alerted his creditors. The best he could do for Hotze and the Confederates during the short time he dared spend in England was to speak privately to his former colleagues in Westminster. None of these meetings produced anything of substance, although his interview with Disraeli on 19 February had seemed promising at the time.[51]

At the beginning of March Lawley passed through Paris on his way to Italy. Slidell reported to Benjamin that Lawley 'had a long and very interesting interview with the Emperor. The conversation turned entirely upon American affairs and was most satisfactory ... the Emperor is prepared to take any action in our favor in concert with England, but adheres to his determination not to move without her cooperation.'[52] *The Times* barely touched on American affairs while its special correspondent was away, and when it did, Hotze found the articles quite unsatisfactory. His impatience was shared by the managers of *The Times*. Mowbray Morris reluctantly granted Lawley an extra month's holiday in return for his promise to be in Virginia before the start of the spring campaigns.[53]

On 25 March Charles Francis Adams Jr. set sail back to the United States. The brothers had been surprised by how much they enjoyed each other's company. Henry even accompanied him to Liverpool, and waited on the tugboat as Charles Francis's steamer pulled out of sight. 'Henry nodded to me good-bye from the tug,' wrote Charles Francis, 'and I, with a bitter taste ... in my mouth, was off for home.'[54] His departure from Britain was followed a few days later by that of Rose Greenhow, for France. Little Rose sobbed when her mother appeared at the convent. Her distress made Rose dread the inevitable parting. 'I know I ought not to be miserable,' Rose wrote in her diary as she reflected on the decisions that had brought them to Europe, 'and yet I am, and tears which I try to keep back flow down my cheek and blind me.'[55] On 2 April she celebrated little Rose's eleventh birthday with the one gift that her daughter craved above all: her undivided attention.

Most of the time, Rose's apartment at the Amarante Hotel was crowded with visitors. James Bulloch was among her callers, having paid a secret visit to the unfinished corvettes in Bordeaux and Nantes. James Spence was also in Paris, visiting Mason. Spence's latest scheme was a grand charity bazaar to raise money for Confederate prisoners. He had heard that the US Sanitary Commission was organizing some sort of fair in New York and John Bright was signing autographs for sale. Spence planned to hold a bigger and splashier event in Liverpool, and had already enlisted the Marchionesses of Bath and Lothian to serve as patrons.[56]

'Public opinion has quite come round to the belief that the North is staggering under its last efforts,' Spence wrote optimistically to Mason on his return to England. 'The Ministry here, too, is in a shaky state . . . I have a strong opinion that this will be the last year of Lord Russell's reign.' The government could not shake off the Lairds rams issue, though Palmerston tried to dispel the perception that the Ministry was in cahoots with the North by frequently condemning US recruitment of Irish labourers who 'enlist in some Ohio regiment or other, and become soldiers with the chance of plunder, and God knows what besides'.[57] Henry Hotze likened the nightly debates in Parliament to a public 'ducking' of the Ministry.[58]

Slidell heard rumours that Palmerston was saying it was time the American war was brought to an end, but he was now counting the days to a Tory government and no longer cared about what the Prime Minister might or might not be feeling. Henry Hotze was also hoping that the Tories would deliver a final blow to the Liberals, if only to see them humiliated for 'their callous subordination of all other interests to those of party'.[59] The Confederates' desire for change was shared by many of the unemployed workers in Lancashire. John Ward, the loom weaver from Clitheroe, had reached the end of his endurance.

> It has been a very poor time for me all the time owing to the American war, which seems as far of being settled as ever [he wrote in his diary on 10 April]. The principle reason why I did not take any notes these last two years is because I was sad and weary. One half of the time I was out of work and the other I had to work as hard as ever I wrought in my life and can hardly keep myself living. If things do not mend this summer I will try somewhere else or something else, for I can't go much further with what I am at.[60]

28

A Great Slaughter

Grant takes command – A disastrous campaign – Lord Lyons labours on – The new volunteers – Return to the Wilderness – An unstoppable force

General Ulysses S. Grant arrived in Washington on 8 March 1864 to accept his promotion to lieutenant general. In giving him command of all the Union armies in the field, Lincoln promised that he would not interfere as long as the strategy remained one of relentless attack. They both knew that the South could not possibly compete with the North for manpower or resources.[1] The Capitol's gleaming new dome – finished on 2 December 1863 – was a powerful advertisement of the healthy state of the US Treasury, especially compared to the hyperinflation and financial chaos that was crippling the South.*

Yet the year had not begun well for the North: the Confederate cavalry under General Nathan Bedford Forrest had hampered Sherman's attempts to wreck Mississippi's rail system; a Union incursion into Florida was beaten back in late February; and in Charleston the Federal navy encountered a new and potentially devastating weapon of war: the submarine. The experimental CSS *H. L. Hunley* – named after its inventor – sank the gunboat USS *Housatonic* during an evening attack on 17 February. (All but five of the Federal crew survived but the *Hunley* mysteriously sank during its return journey to Fort Moultrie, drowning

---

* At the start of the war in 1861, one dollar in gold had equalled $1.10 in Confederate dollars; three years later in 1864, it equalled $20. At the same time, in the North, one gold dollar equalled $1.55 in US greenbacks in 1864.

the six sailors inside. The tragedy dissuaded the Confederates from building any more.)

Grant had prepared a strategic plan for the next phase of the war: to subdue the western half of the Confederacy first before moving east to crush Lee's Army of Northern Virginia. But he discovered on his arrival in Washington that Lincoln's promise not to meddle in military actions contained qualifications. Lincoln, along with General Henry Halleck (who had been relegated to the newly created administrative post of chief of staff), wanted a major push up the Red River into Texas.

The fertile cotton plantations along the Red River were too enticing for the administration to ignore. Lincoln also liked the idea of keeping troops in Texas just in case the Confederates attempted to join forces with the French in Mexico. The fall of Mexico City in June 1863 had effectively ended the Franco-Mexican War, although the victorious French army was still fighting the defeated Juarist regime in parts of the country. Archduke Ferdinand Maximilian, the younger brother of the Austrian Emperor Franz Joseph I, had been cajoled by Louis-Napoleon into accepting the imperial crown of Mexico and was due to arrive in the country sometime in April.* Even though Grant did not think either reason was sufficiently compelling to deprive him of the forces he needed for an attack against Mobile, Alabama – which he considered a vital stepping-off point for capturing the rest of the State – Lincoln and Halleck went ahead with their plan anyway.

On 12 March US General Nathaniel Banks's troops began slogging from Franklin, Louisiana, towards Shreveport, the Confederate capital of Louisiana since the capture of Alexandria in 1863. The campaign was a joint army–navy expedition, with Admiral David Dixon Porter leading a flotilla up the Red River to converge with Banks at Shreveport. Some of the infantry regiments were only two months old. The 17th Infantry Corps d'Afrique, for example, was made up of freed slaves

---

* The Emperor of the French breezily assured Maximilian that the United States was 'well aware that since the new regime in Mexico is the work of France they cannot attack it without immediately making enemies of us'. But Seward had nonetheless let it be known through the US Minister in Paris that the United States would never recognize a French puppet regime in Mexico – which put Louis-Napoleon in a bind and complicated his relations with the Confederates. He could only support the South if its victory was assured, otherwise the new Emperor of Mexico would have a powerful and vengeful United States as his neighbour.[2]

from Nashville, Tennessee. Its officers were white volunteers from across the North, among them Dr Charles Culverwell from New York.* The generous signing bonus of $227 had persuaded him to apply for the post, part of which paid for his photograph in a new uniform purchased specially for the expedition. Many years later, he made light of his participation in the Red River campaign, joking that he had expected to show off his crisp, new jacket to the inhabitants of captured Confederate towns, only to find that the opportunity never came.

Few excursions in the war encountered so many mishaps or ended so ignominiously as Banks's Louisiana campaign. Yet the start had been exceptionally smooth; he reached Alexandria on 26 March and immediately began to organize elections for the new pro-Union State legislature. But from then on, nothing went right. This plan to revive economic ties between Southern plantation owners and the North was undone by Admiral Porter's officers, who seized all the cotton for themselves before the official cotton brokers, who accompanied Banks, had the chance to transact any legitimate business. Even the Red River turned against him; instead of rising to its usual winter levels it began to shrink at a rapid rate. Porter just managed to haul his vessels over the rapids above Alexandria before the fast emerging rocks made the journey impossible. The US fleet ground to a halt near Grand Ecore, a small trading town perched atop a 90-foot bluff, more than 70 miles from Shreveport. Banks was able to push his army a little further up the river, but the single-track route he had chosen turned the journey into a slow-moving haul through foul slurry.

The Confederate General Richard (Dick) Taylor ended Banks's advance at the Battle of Mansfield on 7 April, some 40 miles south of Shreveport. Taylor had only 8,000 men against 12,000 Federals, but he was one of

---

* After the death of his child during the Draft Riots in July, Culverwell had accepted a post at MacDougal hospital in the Bronx, New York, so he could be close to his family. Still determined to try his luck as an actor, he had resigned in the autumn to join Mrs John Wood's company at the Olympic Theatre in Manhattan. He promised his long-suffering wife that it would be his final attempt to conquer the stage. Mrs Wood had given him the role of the ardent young poet in the burlesque *Brothers and Sisters*. Culverwell had never performed such lengthy speeches before and his nervousness grew in anticipation of the first night. His opening speech began with the line: 'Drunk with enthusiasm I . . .' On 8 October, Culverwell leaped on stage and declared, 'Drunk.' With that he died a thousand deaths, unable to utter another word. The next morning 'Ma Woods' dismissed him and Culverwell returned to the Federal army.[3]

the ablest generals in the South and had already demonstrated his aggressive fighting skills while serving under Stonewall Jackson in 1862. In this campaign, Taylor also benefited from having several excellent subordinates, including the French aristocrat Prince Camille de Polignac (affectionately dubbed 'Prince Polecat' by his Texan troops), who had volunteered for the South in 1861. The Confederates cost the Federals 2,000 men at Mansfield; the loss shattered Banks's confidence in the mission and he ordered a general retreat, much to the chagrin of his own troops. His men never forgave him for making them look like cowards, and whenever he passed by marching columns he was greeted with rude songs and catcalls. Prevented from fighting the real enemy, Federal soldiers punished the surrounding communities instead, leaving a swathe of burning homesteads all the way back to Alexandria. Porter's fleet was now stranded above the rapids, forcing Banks to stay put with his glowering army until the Red River rose or someone found a way to carry the ships over the rocks.

Towards the end of April, with Porter's ships still floating in three feet of water rather than the usual nine, Colonel Joseph Bailey, the acting military engineer of the 19th Corps, devised a complex plan for damming the river to create a surge over the falls. 'This proposition looked like madness, and the best engineers ridiculed it,' wrote Admiral Porter in his report. But Bailey convinced his superiors that the plan would work. On 30 April 3,000 Federal troops began hacking and sawing. 'Trees were falling ... quarries were opened; flat-boats were built to bring stone down from above, and every man seemed to be working with a vigor I have seldom seen equalled,' wrote Porter. He singled out a few officers and regiments for praise, in particular the 133rd New York and its English colonel, L. D. H. Currie, adding: 'the noble men who succeeded so admirably in this arduous task, should not lose one atom of credit so justly due them.'[4] With his wounds healed, Currie had decided against transferring to another command and was back once more with his men, guiding them through the perils of Banks's final campaign.

On 1 March Confederate troops near Richmond stopped a bold attempt by a small Union cavalry outfit to liberate the Federal prisoners in Belle Isle camp on the James river. One of the leaders of the expedition, Colonel Ulric Dahlgren, was killed during the retreat. Southerners were appalled that Dahlgren, who had strong family ties to the Confederacy, would turn against his own kind. Even more shocking was the discovery of papers on his body that outlined a plan to massacre the entire Confederate Cabinet.[5]

The days of 'Rosewater chivalry' were at an end, declared the *Richmond Enquirer* on 5 March; henceforth the Confederacy must fight 'barbarity with barbarity'.[6] A week after Dahlgren's raid, Davis summoned Captain Thomas Hines, who had masterminded the prison escape of the Kentucky raider General John Hunt Morgan, to a secret meeting in Richmond. He ordered Hines to travel to Canada via Chicago and other cities in the north-west to recruit propagandists and fighters for the South. Once in Canada, his mission was to collect the scattered survivors of Morgan's command, plus any displaced Southerners or former prisoners of war, and encourage them to rejoin the Confederate army. Hines could, in the carefully chosen words of the Confederate Secretary of War, James Seddon, by 'any fair and appropriate enterprises of war' engage in 'any hostile operation' against the North.[7]

Hines presented Colonel Grenfell with a dilemma after he invited his former comrade to join his operations in Canada. At first, Grenfell felt honour-bound to keep his promise to serve Morgan as his adjutant general.[8] But the offer of adventure proved too enticing, and two weeks after Captain Hines received his departure orders Grenfell resigned his commission and announced he was leaving the Confederacy. The resignation was obviously a contrivance, both to extricate him from his commitment to Morgan and as part of a scheme to make it appear as though he was disenchanted with the South. His official disengagement from the Confederacy would theoretically enable Grenfell to travel without hindrance through the North, picking up information for Hines all the while.[9]

The Confederate government's willingness to violate British neutrality in Canada had increased after the unexpected arrival on 1 April of a special messenger sent by Lord Lyons, carrying a letter from Lord Russell to Jefferson Davis. Seward had permitted this first and only direct communication between London and Richmond, no doubt amused by its humiliating contents for the South. Russell had written a remonstrance to Davis for using British ports to build Confederate warships, and, in his inestimable way, had managed to prick every sensitive part of Southern pride. The worst insult for Davis was Russell's continual reference to 'the so-called Confederate States'. It was a week before Davis could bring himself to answer Russell's letter, and even then he was so offended that he had his private secretary write on his behalf. In future, Davis dictated to the secretary, any communication containing the phrase, 'so-called Confederate States', would be returned without a reply. British neutrality, he raged, was nothing more than 'a cover for treacherous, malignant hostility'.[10]

On 7 April Davis sent a wire to Colonel Jacob Thompson, a former Cabinet Secretary under President Buchanan, and veteran of Vicksburg, who had returned to his plantation in Oxford, Mississippi after its surrender. It read: 'If your engagements will permit you to accept service abroad for six months, please come here immediately.'[11] Thompson arrived a few days later and accepted the appointment of 'Commissioner for Special Service in Canada'. The post was quite unlike Mason and Slidell's in Europe. Davis was not interested in playing diplomatic games. Instead, Thompson's mission was to foment anti-Northern feeling in Canada until it created a crisis in Anglo-American relations. Davis also wanted him to supervise Thomas Hines's propaganda operations in the north-west. The existence of the Knights of the Golden Circle and its recent offshoot, the Sons of Liberty, had convinced Benjamin and Davis that there were tens of thousands, if not hundreds of thousands, of disaffected Midwesterners who, with the right encouragement and sufficient funds, would take up armed resistance against the Republican administration.[12]

Jacob Thompson was an intelligent man, but a poor judge of character and given to impulsive behaviour. With proper oversight and a sufficiently large organization behind him, he might have been a good choice for the post. But the deputy selected by Davis was Clement C. Clay, a popular Alabama Senator before the war, whose poor health and obsession with appeasing his spoilt wife made him an unsuitable candidate for any sort of clandestine operation. Thompson needed a stronger and steadier hand than Clay's, someone with more caution and a more cynical attitude towards the self-described Confederate agents currently making a nuisance of themselves in Canada. Davis had also entrusted Thompson with $1 million in gold, far too large a sum to be under the control of one person.

Thompson and Clay ran the blockade at Wilmington on 5 May without encountering any particular difficulty, despite Judah P. Benjamin's indiscreet letter to Slidell in Paris. 'We have sent Jacob Thompson of Mississippi and Clement C. Clay of Alabama to Canada on secret service,' he had written on 30 April, 'in the hope of aiding the disruption between the Eastern and Western States in the approaching election at the North. It is supposed that much good can be done by the purchase of some of the principal presses, especially in the North-West.'[13]

A second important decision Jefferson Davis made in April was to recall General Beauregard from Charleston. Although Davis still loathed the Creole general, he had bowed to his friends' urgings to make use of Beauregard's popularity as the victor of First Manassas (Bull Run). Davis's own popularity had suffered since Bragg's defeat at Chattanooga, emboldening his enemies in the Confederate Congress. Davis could not afford to allow politically connected generals like Beauregard to remain disaffected.[14]

The news that he was being transferred to the command of the military operations in North Carolina and southern Virginia below Richmond caught Beauregard by surprise. Although he had felt sidelined in Charleston, he was anxious about leaving when the Federals were building up their fleet for another assault. He had so little confidence in his replacement, General Sam Jones, that he decided not to take all his staff with him, in the hope that some continuity would be maintained. The English volunteer Captain Henry Feilden, whose admiration for the departing commander bordered on hero-worship, was crestfallen to learn that he was one of those staying behind. The General called him to his office on 19 April to explain the situation, promising to send for Feilden if his new appointment became permanent. 'I don't think I have any chance of getting to Virginia with him for some time, though I flatter myself that he has too much regard for me to debar me from sharing the privations and dangers of the field with him,' Feilden wrote after the meeting.[15]

This was not what the recipient of the letters wished to hear. Feilden had recently become engaged to 26-year-old Julia McCord, the daughter of the late Congressman David James McCord – known in his day as Handsome Davy – who had been a powerful figure in South Carolina politics during the 1830s. Julia should have been brought up amid great comfort and security, but the early death of her parents had robbed her of both. Before meeting Feilden she had lived quietly and obscurely with a spinster cousin in Greenville, South Carolina.

Julia had fallen in love with Feilden when she visited his office in June 1863 to obtain a military pass to visit her half-brother. (She preserved the little piece of paper for the rest of her life.) Her effect on Feilden was equally dramatic: 'I have only one thing to say and that is you must have no doubts of my love for you, darling,' he promised in one of his earliest letters to her. 'Don't be afraid, dearest, of my love to you fading,' he repeated in another. 'You are so good and kind. I am only afraid I don't show my love to you sufficiently, but wait till I go up to Greenville with you and I shall be as attentive to you as you can desire.'[16] His protectiveness towards her extended to playing down the dangers that faced Charleston. 'Don't be alarmed about my overworking myself, the business of the office is already decreasing,' he lied on 30 April. As soon as various troop movements had been completed, 'we shall have a very quiet summer'.[17] But with Beauregard gone, a Federal fleet of almost fifty ships gathering outside the harbour and General Jones so short of manpower that the city's fire brigade was being used in place of real soldiers, there was no chance of a quiet or peaceful summer.[18]

'I doubt whether people in Europe are aware of the extent of the progress of this country in military strength,' Lord Lyons had written to Russell during Grant's Chattanooga campaign. In answering Russell's question as to whether Britain could still defeat the United States in a war, Lyons had replied that any British invading force would be outnumbered 'by five to one' and would have no chance of winning. But he did not 'think the government here at all desires to pick a quarrel with us or with any European power'.*[19] Lyons's conviction that an Anglo-American war was now unlikely did not mean that he was any less disappointed by his failure to change US attitudes to Britain. 'It is not my purpose here to explain the bitter feelings of the great majority of the American people against England,' he wrote to Russell on 25 April. 'The feeling is the less to be combated, because it is utterly unreasonable and utterly regardless of facts or arguments.'[20] Recently, the *New York Times*

* Lord Lyons accepted the extra burdens placed upon the legation because of the war, but he refused to spy for the Foreign Office. When Lord Russell asked him to obtain drawings of the American-made Parrot gun, a new invention which showed destructive promise, he answered: 'I consider it to be of the utmost importance that not only this Legation should not be employed in such practices, but that both myself and every other member of it should be absolutely and bona fide without any knowledge of their existence.'

had speculated with undisguised glee on the hope of a war between Britain and Germany if Palmerston were to stand firm on his promise to side with Denmark against Germany in the territorial dispute over Schleswig-Holstein. A new German navy would arise, the newspaper predicted, 'manned, equipped, and armed' in American ports.[21]

Lyons was not sure that he could stand living in Washington for much longer. He particularly missed the company of Henri Mercier, who had returned to France on New Year's Eve. ('His wife was so miserable here that she could bear it no longer,' Lyons told his sister.[22]) Without the Merciers, Lyons's intimate social circle had contracted to the Russian Minister Baron Stoeckl and his American wife Elisa. More seriously, Lyons had grown to dislike his work at the legation: 'The business becomes more troublesome and tiresome everyday – requiring constant and minute care, but not being interesting, except from the fear that despite all my attention, something may go wrong, and bring about serious evils.'[23] In early spring Lyons wrote a frank letter to Lord Russell expressing concern that he was no longer fit for the post. 'I am worn out, and utterly weary of the whole thing,' he confessed. 'The people here too are beginning to get very tired of me; and I feel that if I can by any means get through this summer without breaking down in health, and without getting in to any very serious scrape, it will be as much as I shall be able to do.' Lyons did not wish to resign from the Foreign Office. 'The Profession is too important to me, and too interesting to me, but in truth I feel that during the past five years I have gone through as much or more than my mind or body is equal to.'[24] Russell replied sympathetically and emphatically that Lyons belonged in Washington.

The legation staff were also tired, and demoralized by their inability to help or make contact with British subjects in the South. The anguish of ignorance was a common lament among families in Britain with relatives in Confederate prisons. Dr William Farr had tried every possible approach to obtain news of his son, Frederick, who had been captured the previous December. After being informed by the legation that there was no communication between Washington and Richmond, he had befriended the Confederate community in England in the hope that someone would be able to pass along information. In late February, an agent working with the purchasing agent Caleb Huse wrote to the assistant commissioner of exchange in Richmond, Captain William Hatch, saying that 'a good friend of our cause' was seeking to know if his son was still alive.[25] There were more than twenty prisons in and around Richmond. It would take some time for Captain Hatch to discover the whereabouts of Private Frederick Farr and, even if he was found, to convey the news to England. While the Farrs waited for news, not even knowing if the search was indeed under way, Frederick became ill with typhus – a disease endemic in the filthy and overcrowded Southern prisons – and died on 23 March 1864.

'Suppose I were ill for a week,' Lyons's attaché Edward Malet wrote despairingly to his mother. 'I think it is rather hard upon me, for a Legation ought not to be left in such a condition that it cannot get on without one man.'[26] The Foreign Office had refused to increase the number of attachés and yet had denied them holiday leave on the grounds that the legation was dangerously overstretched.[27] Most of the new work was coming from a steep rise in forced-enlistment cases and arrests of British subjects for desertion. 'Every effort has been made by us to obtain redress for those which have appeared to be well founded,' Lyons assured Lord Russell. 'In few cases, however, have our efforts produced any satisfactory results.' The form was always the same:

> The remonstrances addressed by me to the Sec of State are duly acknowledged and transmitted to the War or the Navy Department. The Department orders an investigation ... I do my best to elicit the truth, and to obtain evidence – a controversial correspondence between the US government and me ensues. The Department always claims that the men were willing volunteers; the Government accepts the statement, and the men are retained.[28]

Lyons cited as an example the case of 16-year-old Henry Usher, the grandson of Admiral Usher, who was kidnapped by crimpers while on his way to a job interview at the British consulate in New York. With the legation's help, Consul Archibald had eventually tracked Usher down in Beaufort, South Carolina, where the boy had been enlisted in the 5th New York Heavy Artillary as 'John Russell'.[29] This had been in January, and four months later the War Department was still dragging its feet.

If it required strenuous efforts to rescue a British subject from the armed services, the circumstances had to be extraordinary for a Briton to be released from prison – such as the Presidential pardon given to Alfred Rubery the previous December. Rubery's guilt in the attempted seizure of the *J. M. Chapman* in California was undeniable but the request for his release had come from John Bright, whose photograph was currently hanging above the mantelpiece in Lincoln's office. The official decree announcing the pardon declared that the President's decision should be regarded 'as a public mark of the esteem held by the United States of America for the high character and steady friendship of the said John Bright'. The unabashedly pro-Southern Rubery also had his $10,000 fine commuted so long as he left the country within thirty days and made no attempt to help or enter the Confederacy.*

Lyons would never have championed Rubery's release if it had been up to him; as a rule, he refused to bother Seward with cases involving self-described British Confederate volunteers. 'To do so', Lyons told Lord Russell, after the Foreign Office forwarded a protest from Private Joseph Taylor, a Yorkshireman who had been incarcerated in Fort Delaware since Vicksburg, 'could in fact hardly fail to cause annoyance. There are, I am sorry to say, a very large number of British Subjects who are Prisoners of War as Mr Taylor is, and who, like him, entered the Confederate Service in disobedience to the Queen's commands, and in defiance of Her Majesty's warning that they would do so at their peril.'[31] However, Seward was not entirely deaf to or blasé about the myriad injustices created by the war. British prisoners of war in Federal hands were given the option of swearing an oath of allegiance to the United States in exchange for their release.†[32] Hundreds of British prisoners took advantage of the oath – including Private Taylor, who by late spring was back home in Yorkshire, where he joined the local constabulary.

---

* Bright also used his influence to rescue 17-year-old Alfred Massey Richardson. Alfred had been working for the chairman of the Union and Emancipation Society of Manchester. The previous August, his head filled with ideas about freeing the slaves, Alfred and a friend, Stephen Smelt, had run off to New York. They both joined the 47th New York Volunteers, but not before being beaten up and robbed of their bounty money. 'Can you undertake to obtain [Richardson's] discharge?' Bright wrote to Sumner on the same day that Lincoln signed Rubery's pardon. 'I think Mr Stanton will be able to spare so young a boy, if you apply to him.' Sumner took Bright's request literally and secured the release of Richardson but neglected to mention young Smelt, to the grief of his parents.[30]

† The North had ceased conducting prisoner exchanges with the South, ostensibly in protest against Confederate mistreatment of coloured soldiers. But with 611,000 men under arms, the North could afford to have several thousand penned up, whereas the South, whose total armed force did not exceed 277,000, could not. Many British prisoners were relieved by the halt to the exchanges. Presented with the choice between a Federal prison and return to the South, they often preferred to stay in prison.

Lyons suspected that forced enlistments in the Federal army would continue until the War Department ceased to regard the practice as a necessary evil to make up for the shortfalls in the draft. But there were signs that the sheer volume of crimping was beginning to have an adverse impact on the army. After watching the execution of two such victims for attempting to desert, General Isaac Wistar sent a protest to General John Dix in New York about the dishonest recruiting practices in the city:

> Nearly all are foreigners, mostly sailors both ignorant of and indifferent to the objects of the war in which they thus suddenly find themselves involved [he wrote]. Two men were shot here this morning for desertion; and over thirty more are now awaiting trial or execution. These examples are essential as we all understand but, it occurred to me, General, that you would pardon me for thus calling your attention to the great crime committed in New York of kidnapping these men into positions where, to their ignorance, desertion must seem like a vindication of their rights and liberty.*[33]

The lax discipline and poor attitude of the new recruits and draftees was also a problem for the Federal army. 'If I was in England or in the English service I should consider that it was a shame and a sin to desert,' wrote the English volunteer James Horrocks. But here, 'in the land of Yankee doodle', desertion is 'regarded universally as a *smart thing* and the person who does it a *dem'd smart fellow*'.[34] Yet Horrocks was a soldier of uncommon ability and rectitude compared to James Pendlebury, who enlisted as a private in the 69th New York Infantry on 27 January. Pendlebury was an unemployed mill worker from Lancashire with a family, a drink problem and a gammy leg. At home he used to spend every night in the pub, boring the regulars until 'one day I was talking energetically about the Slaves and full of fire when my comrades said I ought to go to America', recalled Pendlebury. 'One said he would give me twopence if I would go and others also offered pennies.'[35]

Pendlebury collapsed upon arriving in New York, and spent several weeks in hospital. After his discharge he was arrested for drunkenness

---

* The passenger line Cunard, for example, was losing sailors faster than it could replace them. The company's chairman, Sir Edward Cunard, ordered his lawyers to help rescue the drafted men, although he despaired at finding many of them. 'The truth is that the English are in a much worse position here than any other nation,' he wrote to an MP. Cunard acknowledged that Consul Archibald was working hard but Lord Lyons, he complained, was 'entirely too easy going and diplomatic'.

in Jersey City. The judge agreed to waive the fine if Pendlebury enlisted: 'A policeman came with me to see that I really did enlist. However, when I went under the standard, I was too short. They ... ran me down to Williamsburg and there I was big enough to join the 69th New York Irish Brigade ... On joining I got 400 dollars down, so I thought I would send it home.' Instead, he spent it on whisky. When the money ran out, Pendlebury's ailments returned. The members of the Irish 69th were familiar with the problem.

> Now if there is a drinker here [wrote Pendlebury], he will know how dreadful he feels after a spree, when he is nearly dying and can't get any more drink – that was how I felt. When [the guard] answered I looked up into his face and said, 'Can you save a life because I fear I shall be dead before morning.' He asked me what I meant, so I told him. He then poured me a tea cup of whisky and I drank it and fell asleep.[36]

Pendlebury had found a home for himself and, despite his English nationality, his Irish comrades accepted him among their ranks, preferring an alcoholic volunteer to a reluctant conscript. [37]

Edward Lyulph Stanley, the headstrong younger son of the British Postmaster General Lord Stanley, arrived in Washington on 14 April 1864, having spent three weeks in New York listening to strangers make pointed comments about England's treachery.* He had not been the slightest bit fazed, being able to hold his own in any arena. According to family lore, when young Lyulph was 5 years old, 'he was one day naughty and scolded by his mother; when she had finished, he said, "Proceed, you interest me."'[39] 'Stanley is a clever young man,' wrote Lord Wodehouse after being introduced to him in 1862, '& will be very pleasant when he has rubbed off a little juvenile conceit, which however is pardonable, as he has just taken a first class at Oxford. He is a staunch Northerner which is singular and a finer Radical. I like to see a young man begin with rather extreme opinions. They "tone" down fast enough.'[40]

---

* When Fitzgerald Ross arrived in New York at the end of April, he was warned by the *Times* correspondent Charles Mackay not to discuss the war or politics in New York because of the vicious differences in opinion. 'It is considered very mauvais genre' to bring up either topic, he wrote. The safest way to begin a conversation was 'to abuse England, which everyone is glad to do, and as everybody agrees on this point, there is no difference of opinion'.[38]

But Stanley was showing no signs of toning down. He visited the Adamses before his departure and exhausted them all with his rapid, earnest talk about American politics.[41]

Seward was treated to a similar verbal onslaught when he invited Stanley to dinner on 17 April. In contrast to Lord Edward St Maur, Stanley saw no need to be circumspect simply because of his father's position in Palmerston's Cabinet, and grilled Seward on every subject that arose. 'Mr. Seward struck me as sharp and on the whole a kindly amiable man,' wrote Stanley after the encounter, 'but rather shrewd than really able or wide in his views, and prone to be captious and technical instead of statesmanlike in his way of handling great questions.' He was far more impressed by Lincoln, who, he wrote, 'spoke very reasonably and without any vulgarity tho' with some quaintness and homeliness of expression'.[42] The President obviously warmed to the Englishman since he allowed his private secretary, John Hay, to take the next morning off to show Stanley around Washington. (They went to General Lee's former home, Arlington, which by Stanley's standards was 'dirty and small'.) Hay's opinion of England had been coloured by Lawley's reports, Stanley noticed with regret. He discovered, like every visitor before him, that 'Americans see hardly any English newspaper but *The Times*', 'which is considered here as the true exponent of English opinion'.

Stanley had come to America to learn how British supporters might help the soon-to-be-emancipated slave population, but he was not averse to visiting the front lines, too. On 22 April he took the train to Brandy Station in Culpeper County, Virginia, to visit the Army of the Potomac. Waiting for him at the station was Charles Francis Adams Jr. Captain Adams's contempt for his commanding officers had finally made him accept a transfer to General Meade's cavalry escort, which meant that he was in a position to introduce Stanley to both Meade and General Grant. The former, wrote Stanley, was 'a thorough gentleman and very captivating', the latter, 'very modest and unassuming in manner' but clearly a man of 'character and a will of his own'. In conversations about the future of Negroes in the army, Grant was honest about his initial doubts and why he had changed his mind in their favour after observing how well they fought as soldiers at Vicksburg.

Stanley spent two days with Charles Francis Jr. The monotony of camp life surprised him: the soldiers' daily routine seemed cheerfully domestic, and wintertime relations between the Federal and Confederate armies were strangely cordial. 'I am told there is a most friendly feeling between the [opposing] armies,' wrote Stanley; 'it is almost impossible to prevent their mixing, and exchanging coffee and tobacco and playing cards together, though there are very strict orders against it.'*[43] Unlike every other visitor to the Army of the Potomac before him, he had no interest in staying to watch it fight. He was anxious instead to visit New Orleans, to see how the city's emancipated blacks were faring under Northern rule. He left Meade's headquarters as hundreds of covered supply wagons were being assembled in long lines.

Charles Francis Jr. was not sure whether they were preparing to attack Lee or taking precautionary measures in case of a sudden move by the Confederates. 'The feeling about Grant is peculiar,' he noticed; 'a little jealousy, a little dislike, a little envy, a little want of confidence.' A 'brilliant success will dissipate the elements', he thought, but until then Grant would be regarded as an interloper.[44] Grant was also taking over at a time when the term of enlistment for thousands of soldiers was about to expire. The 79th Highlanders had only two weeks more to serve, and their dress uniforms had already been bought for the parade up Broadway. They were furious at being sent to Virginia; during a parade review, the regiment marched past Grant in silence, refusing to answer the call for three cheers.

Banks was still struggling against the Red River when Grant decided that the spring campaign should be directed against the South's two largest armies, Lee's and Johnston's. There were to be no more uncoordinated battles in various parts of the South. On 3 April 1864 he ordered Sherman to leave Chattanooga and head with his 98,000 men for Atlanta, Georgia. 'You, I propose to move against Johnston's army,' Grant told Sherman, 'to break it up and get into the interior of the enemy's country as far as you can, inflicting all the damage you can against their war resources.'[45] Once Atlanta had been taken, Sherman was to march across

---

* Some authorities were content to turn a blind eye to even flagrant fraternization. 'Our regiment had plenty of coffee but not tobacco,' wrote James Pendlebury. 'We made boats of paper and floated the boats containing the article we wished to exchange down to the other side. One day we ran short of paper and one of the Confederates offered to swim across the river if he would not be taken prisoner. This was cordially agreed upon, but the officer in charge on our side did not carry out his promise and the man was taken prisoner. He was taken to General Hancock's quarters and the general very kindly let him go back.'

the State to Savannah and then up the coastline, through the Carolinas to Virginia, where he was to join Grant at Richmond.

Theoretically, Grant had 185,000 soldiers with which to attack Lee, but political considerations had whittled down that number to a little over 100,000. The Secretary of War, Edwin Stanton, insisted on keeping back 20,000 for the defence of Washington; and a further 65,000 were divided between the Army of the James, led by General Butler (of the New Orleans 'Woman Order' fame), and the Army of West Virginia, under the command of the German General Franz Sigel. To his frustration, Grant discovered that these 'political' generals not only owed their ranks to Lincoln but were also protected by him and could not be shunted aside, despite their proven inabilities in the field.

Grant tried to limit their potential for disaster by giving Butler and Sigel mere supporting roles in his spring campaign. Their objective would be to deprive the Confederate Army of Northern Virginia of its supplies, while Grant went after Lee himself. 'Beast' Butler started out first on 3 May with 30,000 soldiers, along with their horses and heavy guns, crammed into an assortment of steamboats and ferries for the two-day journey up the James river towards Richmond. As there was only a light smattering of Confederate forces south of Richmond, there was no reason why Butler could not disembark his army at one of the many landings along the river and march unmolested all the way to the capital. Grant wanted Butler to plant his forces just below Richmond, blocking every route from the south and west. If Butler had been acting solely at his own discretion, Grant might have been worried. But two veteran commanders had been appointed as Butler's subordinates to prevent him from wrecking the venture.

The 5th Battery New Jersey Light Artillery, containing the English Private James Horrocks, was among the regiments placed under Butler's command. When Horrocks saw Butler in person he was startled by his notorious ugliness. 'Imagine a bloated-looking bladder of lard,' he wrote to his parents. 'Call before your mental vision a sack full of muck ... And then imagine four enormous German sausages fixed to the extremities of the sack in lieu of arms and legs.'[46] Butler had been ordered to drive hard towards Richmond, smashing the rail link between Petersburg and Richmond as he went. But Horrocks did not notice any particular sense of urgency after his regiment arrived on 5 May at a deserted City Point, less than 25 miles from the Confederate capital.

The day was warm and sunny, far too pleasant to waste idling on the banks. 'I took a walk with another fellow,' wrote Horrocks. 'We passed several little shanties, and at every one the soldiers . . . were ransacking and taking everything worth taking.' Horrocks and his friend hurried on. 'We walked on about a mile and a half and then came to a fine residence of a planter, in which about a dozen soldiers were making free with everything.' As they approached the gate, a couple of soldiers came out, laden with struggling livestock. A headless lamb was slung over the shoulder of one, its neck still dripping with blood. The grey-haired owner of the house sat hunched on the doorstep, moaning as Horrocks stepped around him. Once inside, he heard screams and the crashing of wood as soldiers forced open every door and cupboard. The black house servants were cowering in the corner of the parlour while the elderly wife of the owner shouted hoarsely at the men to leave. Horrocks walked down the hall to escape the noise. 'In the next room, which was extremely well furnished, was a piano. I sat down and played Home, Sweet Home! with variations.' The playing soothed him and, without another thought, he joined in the looting. 'I took a flute and a package of beautiful wax candles and a piece of scented soap.' He also found a wad of Confederate notes, which he was about to pocket when the old lady entered the room and shamed him into putting them back. Suddenly, Horrocks wished to slip away as quickly as possible.

The troops were starting to move out when Horrocks returned to the landing place. No one had missed him. They marched for several hours through thick, piney woods. 'Every now and then we passed some poor fellow who had given out and lay on the side of the road with his knapsack and musket alongside of him and then we passed portions of their kit . . . scores of blankets and overcoats, and boots and shoes.' Like Frederick Farr, these men had been left behind, 'thrown away', in Horrocks's words, 'in order to lighten the load'.[47] Horrocks promised his parents that he would take the greatest care with his life; he expected to be fired at soon and was curious how it would feel. 'When I have felt it, I will tell you how it is.'[48]

Horrocks's eagerness to encounter Confederate bullets was delayed by General Butler, who, instead of blocking the approaches to Richmond from the south and west, had become diverted by the non-existent need to build fortifications and trenches, giving the Confederates enough time to insert General Beauregard's small force of 18,000 men between the US Army of the James and the capital. Butler's failure to reach Richmond meant that Grant would be setting his spring campaign into motion with his plan damaged from the outset.

The Army of the Potomac began moving on 4 May. If Grant's ultimate objective was to reach Richmond, Lee's was just as straightforward: to hold down the enemy long enough to convince the Northern public to vote for a pro-peace President in the November election. He was relieved when his scouts confirmed that the Federals had crossed the Rapidan river and were marching along the Germanna Plank Road. The route Grant had chosen passed through the Wilderness, whose dense wasteland had helped to give the Confederates their victory at the Battle of Chancellorsville in 1863.

Instead of marching quickly through the Wilderness, the Federal commanders took a leisurely pace so that by midnight the advance of the army was still less than halfway through. In the darkness, there was many a startled yell as an accidental kick or stumble over a mound of leaves revealed the human remains beneath. Many soldiers were too frightened to sleep that night, but not the new volunteer James Pendlebury, who lay down on the ground, curled up like a dog. Pendlebury had made the beginner's mistake of throwing away his knapsack during the hot and tiring march. 'In throwing away the knapsack I also threw away my cartridge box,' he wrote. During the night, Captain O'Neill 'came and wakened me with his foot, and, handing me a cartridge box, said, "Here take that, and don't ask any questions." He had stolen it from one of the other men because he was so fond of me.'⁴⁹

Pendlebury's regiment was part of General Hancock's 2nd Corps, one of the first to enter the Wilderness on 4 May. There was no possibility he would be able to hide from the fighting once it began. 'This was my first battle and I can't say that I was a brave man, for I wished I was at home,' he wrote in his memoir. 'But after I had fired a few times I began to get accustomed to the work and soon I had no fear about me.' His baptism started at 4 p.m. on 5 May. Lee had succeeded in placing two of his three corps inside the Wilderness though General Longstreet was still a day's march away. Forty thousand Confederates pitched into 70,000 Federals. Just as Lee had hoped, the Union regiments lost their sense of direction, firing wildly into the trees and charging hither and thither. At sunset many soldiers had no idea where they were, and resorted to lying behind improvised breastworks. There was nothing to

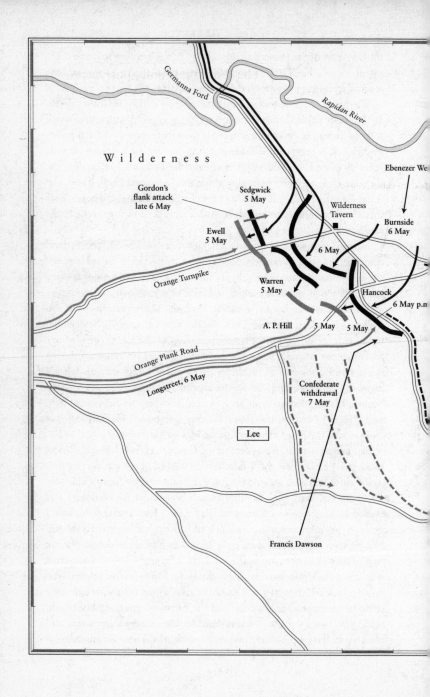

Germanna Ford

Rapidan River

Wilderness

Gordon's
flank attack
late 6 May

Sedgwick
5 May

Wilderness
Tavern

Ebenezer We

Burnside
6 May

Ewell
5 May

6 May

Orange Turnpike

Warren
5 May

Hancock

6 May p.m

A. P. Hill

5 May   5 May

Orange Plank Road

Longstreet, 6 May

Confederate
withdrawal
7 May

Lee

Francis Dawson

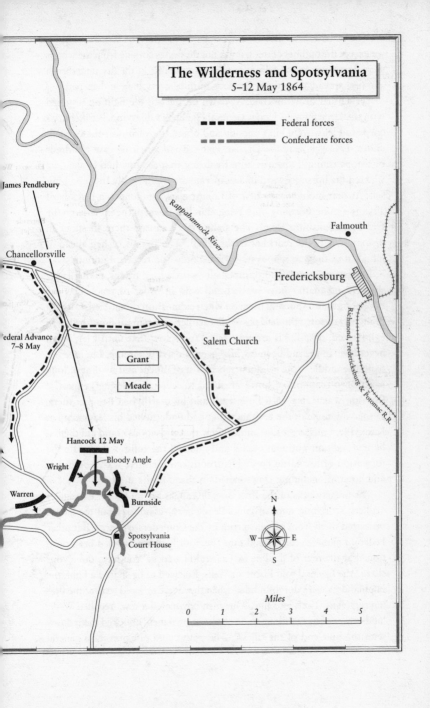

The Wilderness and Spotsylvania
5–12 May 1864

- - - Federal forces

- - - Confederate forces

James Pendlebury

Rappahannock River

Falmouth

Chancellorsville

Fredericksburg

Federal Advance 7–8 May

Salem Church

Grant

Meade

Richmond, Fredericksburg & Potomac R.R.

Hancock 12 May

Bloody Angle

Wright

Warren

Burnside

Spotsylvania Court House

N
W E
S

Miles

0   1   2   3   4   5

see except the outlines of tree trunks. But the noises coming from the woods were terrifying. As at Chancellorsville, stray sparks lit the dry underbrush and fires spread along the forest floor, burning everything in their path.

Yet neither army flinched. At dawn on the 6th the fighting resumed with the same ferocity. Under General Hancock's direction, Pendlebury's corps suddenly found its cohesion and began to overpower the Confederates. Lee was near the Orange Plank Road when he saw hundreds of troops running towards him. Realizing that the line had broken, he spurred his horse forward in a desperate attempt to rally the men himself. At that moment, the first of Longstreet's regiments – a brigade of Texans – came storming up, having marched through the night from the Old Fredericksburg Road. The sight of Lee caused them to shout in dismay, 'Lee to the rear! Lee to the rear!'[50] The Texans rushed ahead of him; but of the 800 who went forward only 300 returned unhurt.

Longstreet's corps had tramped along little-used tracks, taking every shortcut no matter how snarled and wild in order to reach Lee, the boom of gunfire spurring them on when exhaustion threatened. Captain Francis Dawson, who had passed his artillery examination in April, was exhilarated, despite his arduous ride. 'You know that until I left I had never been in the saddle in my life,' he wrote to his parents, 'but in sober truth the saddle is the headquarters of a staff officer and by dint of long practice you cannot fail, however stupid, to become moderately expert.'[51] Dawson was riding with Longstreet and his staff when Lee met them. Displaying none of the hesitancy that had undermined his leadership at Knoxville, Longstreet saw immediately that the woods could aid them if he ignored conventional tactics and allowed the terrain to dictate the formation of his battle line.[52] His troops ran forward, with Longstreet and his staff, including Dawson, riding ahead of the surge.

The breastworks of the Irish Brigade caught fire under the barrage of artillery, scorching some of James Pendlebury's comrades, but the flames protected them from being overrun by the Confederate charge. But other Federal regiments turned and ran. The 79th Highlanders had been positioned at the rear of the line by General Hancock. 'You have done your share,' the General told Ebenezer Wells. Relieved to be spared a fight, the Highlanders were dumbfounded when they were ordered to beat the fleeing regiments back into line. 'Our men bayoneted a few,' recalled Wells, 'and others of us not liking to do so to our own men, knocked them down with the butt end of the rifles.'[53] The 79th could not prevent a general rout, however, and by late morning the Orange Plank Road belonged to the Confederates. Longstreet had smashed the Federal line with a pan-ache that recalled Stonewall Jackson's stunning victory the previous May at Chancellorsville. Dawson trotted up behind Longstreet as the General led a small group of staff and commanders along the road. The Confeder-ates were congratulating one another on their signal success.

Though it was a date few liked to remember, it was exactly a year and a day since General Jackson had been accidently shot while scout-ing three miles further west, near the Orange Turnpike Road. The Orange Plank Road was similarly hemmed in by trees, which made it difficult for the isolated pockets of Confederate troops on either side to see one another. 'There were but about eight of us together, all mounted,' described Dawson. '*Without a moment's warning* one of our brigades about 2000 strong, only 50 or 60 yards distants [*sic*] poured a deliber-ate fire into us.' 'Friends', shouted one of Longstreet's officers, too late. Seconds later, four of the eight were on the ground. Three were dead or dying; Longstreet was slumped over his saddle, choking and coughing up blood. Dawson and two others lifted him from his horse and carried him over to a large tree. 'My next thought was to obtain a surgeon,' continued Dawson, 'and, hurriedly mentioning my purpose, I mounted my horse and rode in desperate haste to the nearest field hospital. Giv-ing the sad news to the first surgeon I could find, I made him jump on my horse, and bade him, for Heaven's sake, ride as rapidly as he could to the front where Longstreet was. I followed afoot.'[54]

Dawson arrived as Longstreet was being carefully laid in an ambulance. The General had been hit by a single bullet, which passed through his neck and out of his right shoulder. He was bleeding heavily but conscious. Dawson joined the silent group riding in the ambulance. They met Lee on the way to the hospital. 'I shall not soon forget the sadness in his face,' wrote Dawson, 'and the almost despairing movement of his hands, when he was told that Longstreet had fallen.' Longstreet's appearance convinced Lee that the Wil-derness had claimed his other most reliable commander. Visibly shaken, he rode away to assume control of Longstreet's attack. But Lee could only guess what Longstreet had planned to do, and not all of it made sense to him. It was four o'clock when he gave the order to attack, several hours after Longstreet had intended his final assault to begin. During the delay, the Fed-erals had regrouped and were prepared for the onslaught. The firing ceased at nightfall with neither side conceding their ground.

The following day, 7 May, saw skirmishes but no real fighting. The two armies needed time to replenish their ammunition, fill places left by the dead and wounded, and to eat and sleep after two days of continuous fighting. In the past forty-eight hours 11,000 Confederate and 17,500 Federal soldiers had been killed or wounded in the Wilderness. Troops in the Army of the Potomac watched with a baleful eye as the supply wagons were hitched to horses and led towards the rear. They took it as a sign that Grant had ordered a retreat, just like Hooker after Chancellorsville and Burnside after Fredericksburg. The casualties from the battle were certainly enough to make most commanders unwilling to risk another clash with Lee, but Grant was different from his predecessors. The wagons were moving because Grant was continuing the advance to Richmond. He informed General Meade that the entire army must be on the march by midnight. Once the long lines began moving, Grant took his place at the front so that the men would know he was leading them towards, rather than away from, battle.

Lee was prepared for the news. He knew he was facing a far tougher opponent than his previous adversaries. He assumed Grant was heading for the crossroads at Spotsylvania Court House – the road south from there was the swiftest route to Richmond – and raced to get there ahead of him. Over the next couple of days, the two armies converged on Spotsylvania, skirmishing all the way.[55] Lee managed to stay in front, but barely: using bayonets and tin cups, his army hastily dug itself in along the intersection at the Court House in a thin line that extended for about three miles. The Confederates braced for Grant's attack on the 10th. During the afternoon, Union regiments clambered through the woods out into the open, in an attempt to punch a hole in Lee's defences. The Confederate line bulged in the middle where the ground was higher than the rest of the undulating landscape. Here, at a point dubbed the 'Mule Shoe' because of its U-shape, a Federal attack succeeded in capturing 1,200 prisoners, temporarily threatening the integrity of Lee's line. A simultaneous attack on the Confederate position around the Spotsylvania Court House was led in part by the 79th New York Volunteers. Though Ebenezer Wells was furious at being in the front lines when his release was less than three days away, he feared being called a coward even more than dying.[56] But here the Confederates held their position and the attack ended at darkness with nothing achieved. The Highlanders were kept at the front lines until the final minute of their enlistment, when the regiment was ordered to march to Fredericksburg with 200 prisoners in tow.

Grant tried to shake Lee from Spotsylvania by sending Major-General Phil Sheridan and 10,000 cavalrymen to attack the Confederate defences in front of Richmond. The raid forced Lee to dispatch Jeb Stuart and 4,500 troopers to pursue the Federals, and the two cavalry forces clashed on 11 May at Yellow Tavern, only six miles from Richmond. Stuart received a fatal shot in his stomach as he attempted to rally his outnumbered corps. Sheridan could have destroyed Stuart's cavalry, but Lee's nephew, Fitzhugh Lee, known as Fitz, immediately took charge and was able to effect a skilful retreat.

When first checked by Lee, Grant had sent a telegram to General Halleck in Washington, which read in part: 'I propose to fight it out on this line [of attack] if it takes all summer.' He showed his determination by launching a second attack against the 'Mule Shoe' on 12 May. The nature of the ground invited the attackers in, but getting out – especially once the earth had been churned to mud – was almost impossible. The Highlanders had escaped by a hair's breadth – a day that cost the two armies more than 10,000 men. The brutal hand-to-hand fighting between the Federals and Confederates led to the area being christened the 'Bloody Angle'. 'Rank after rank was riddled by shot and shell and bayonet-thrusts, and finally sank, a mass of torn and mutilated corpses,' recalled a horror-struck member of Grant's staff who witnessed the assault. 'Then fresh troops rushed madly forward to replace the dead, and so the murderous work went on.'[57]

The Army of the Potomac had suffered twice as many casualties as the Army of Northern Virginia since 5 May. A rough estimate showed that on 13 May, 83,000 Federals remained of the 119,000 who had crossed the Rapidan river on the 4th. But Lee had not only lost a quarter of his army: a third of his commanders were also gone, and more responsibilities were devolving onto his shoulders. Grant, on the other hand, though he did not want for commanders, had far too many who were a positive help to the enemy. Nothing useful had come out of General Sigel's Shenandoah Valley campaign, and General Butler had become trapped behind his trenches, eight miles south of Richmond. He had fought so feebly that even James Horrocks could see that the Army of the James was poorly led. 'There is no confidence felt in the *beast* at all,' he informed his father.[58]

Grant's reaction to the failure of Sigel and Butler was to push his own soldiers to march faster and fight harder. Only four days after the fighting at the Mule Shoe the Army of the Potomac began another move southwards. The effect on the army, wrote Charles Francis Adams Jr. to his father, was almost the same as real victory, 'when in fact it has done only barren fighting. For it has done the one thing needful before the enemy – it has advanced. The result is wonderful ... It is in better spirits and better fighting trim today than it was in the first day's fight in the Wilderness.'[59]

'Defiance to her Enemies'

Garibaldi's visit – James Mason falls for the trick – Battle in the
English Channel – A tale of corruption in New Orleans – The
Beautiful Belle – A fatal arrogance

The English were shocked by the descriptions of the fighting in the Wilderness and at Spotsylvania. 'There has been a great deal of news from America this week,' wrote the Lancashire cotton worker John Ward on 29 May 1864, 'giving an account of some of the most terrific battles with the most terrible carnage and slaughter for eight days that has ever been known in the world, and with little result.'[1] The parents of Frederick Farr believed that their son's incarceration in a Confederate prison was a blessing compared to what he might encounter at the Wilderness, until they learned of his death.* Dr Farr tried to take solace from the knowledge that his son died peacefully, rather than in agony on the battlefield. Most newspapers described the duel between Grant and Lee as a festival of slaughter. In *The Times*, Charles Mackay compared Grant to Javert from Hugo's *Les Misérables*: 'But still he holds his way undaunted, seeing nothing, caring nothing, but Richmond.'[3] The *Standard* claimed with pardonable exaggeration that there had been more casualties in the past two weeks than during the Napoleonic

---

* 'Although the news is not official – it comes through an authentic channel,' Frederick's distraught father wrote on 30 May 1864. 'Now he is beyond all our anxiety and rests – we humbly hope – in heaven.' Three weeks later, the family received a condolence letter from the wife of one of the officers in Frederick's regiment. In the short time she had known the boy, wrote Ellen Bacon, his love of army life had been striking. He had turned down two offers of an honourable discharge. The officers had tried to protect him from harm: 'They often occupied him in writing, and sought other ways to lighten his duties. He seemed content and really appeared to like the Service.'[2]

and Crimean wars combined.[4] The 'unprecedented death toll' in May was a popular subject with newspaper editors and cartoonists. 'It is mortifying that we get no telegrams direct from officials at Washington,' complained Benjamin Moran. 'If we had reports of our own to give early to the press, we could greatly modify opinion here.'

Moran had been in an especially foul mood since Giuseppe Garibaldi's visit to England in April. The 'Great Liberator' of southern Italy had come at the private invitation of the Duchess of Sutherland, although the half-million spectators who lined the streets to greet his arrival made it seem as though the entire nation had turned out to honour him. Thousands also attended the Duchess's reception for Garibaldi at Stafford House on 13 April. Moran had longed to go, and the entire Adams family was invited, but not the legation Secretaries: 'Mr Adams could have obtained us an invitation just as easy as not,' fumed Moran. He finally managed to catch a glimpse of Garibaldi when the General was out riding: 'It struck me . . . that Henry B. Adams was paraded at Stafford House to visit Garibaldi . . . [I] could only see him in the street from the top of a brick pile.'[5]

The Civil War was barely mentioned during Garibaldi's visit, though the Confederates lived in fear that he might stir up public opinion by saying something in favour of the North. Henry Hotze's propaganda skills were needed more than ever, but he was in France trying to revive the newspaper contacts abandoned by Edwin De Leon. Francis Lawley was also abroad, unable to return to London after his interview with the Emperor for fear of alerting his creditors. Vizetelly was in England, but since his arrival in mid-April he had divided his formidable energy between his favourite literary haunts, the Cheshire Cheese public house in Fleet Street and the Savage Club in Drury Lane. He had not thought about the Confederacy except to let Francis Dawson's family know that 'he is very much liked, and is a very good officer, and, I have no doubt, will make his way'.[6]

The Confederate agent James Bulloch felt stymied at every turn; even though the decision against the *Alexandra* had been overturned on appeal it was too late to resurrect his dream of a British-built Confederate navy.*

---

* The Confederates had used every possible trick, including jury tampering, to influence the outcome of the court cases. On 17 May 1864, for example, Charles Prioleau directed one of their agents to make sure there was a favourable decision in an upcoming court case: 'The

The Confederate cruiser *Georgia*

In France, the Marine Department had ordered the two unfinished vessels in Nantes to be detained. 'Every pledge has been violated, and we have encountered nothing but deception and duplicity and are now their victims,' Bulloch wrote indignantly of the French.[8] He understood better than Slidell that the Confederacy was simply a pawn in the Emperor's grand designs for Mexico. Only three raiders remained afloat: the *Georgia*, currently under refurbishment in Cherbourg, the *Alabama*, whose last known whereabouts put her near Cape Town, and the *Florida*, which was thought to be near Bermuda. Bulloch hoped to keep them all at sea, if only to deter investors from using US shipping firms. He would rather have sold Matthew Maury's unseaworthy *Rappahannock*, still at Calais, and use the money to repair the *Georgia* but was overruled by the senior Confederate naval commander in Europe, Commodore Samuel Barron, who decided to do the opposite and strip the *Georgia* of her fittings and use them on the *Rappahannock*.

enclosed list contains the names of the Juries to try the case on the 6 June. It is important to know the sympathies of as many of them as possible ... find out whether any of them or how many are, by opinion or interest, enemies to the cause of the defendants or the contrary ... Any expenses incurred we will of course discharge – you have carte blanche in this respect.'[7]

The empty *Georgia* crept out of Cherbourg on a moonless night and arrived in Liverpool on 2 May. 'She was a poor miserable little tin kettle of a craft, but I loved her,' wrote Lieutenant James Morgan. 'My life, as the youngest of her officers, and the only one of my grade, had been very lonely, still she had been the only home I had known for thirteen months.'[9] On his first night ashore he went to the theatre: 'as soon as my gray uniform was noticed a whisper went through the audience that the *Alabama* had arrived in the port. Someone proposed three cheers for the *Alabama*, and they were given with a will.'[10] An evening of applause – and then only because of mistaken identity – was Morgan's chief reward for the nine vessels captured by the *Georgia*. The ship was decommissioned on 10 May. The crew assembled on the quarter-deck as the Confederate flag was lowered for the last time. 'We bade good-bye to our shipmates,' wrote Morgan, who was more determined than ever to return home, 'many of us never to meet again.'[11] James Bulloch sold the *Georgia* for £15,000. It was not a bad sum, considering his options. He planned to purchase several more blockade-runners with the money, hoping that the vessels would pay for themselves after a couple of runs, or else be converted by Southern engineers into gunships.[12]

The faithful William Schaw Lindsay MP wrote to James Mason after the *Georgia*'s sale, begging him to return to England. The movement was adrift without him, he confided. Lindsay tried to instil a sense of urgency in his friend: 'Matters seem to be coming to a crisis on the other side of the Atlantic ... the question is quite ripe for fresh agitation, and from experience I find that that agitation must be started by a debate in Parliament.'[13] The British government's majorities in both Houses were so slim that Palmerston was desperately casting about for allies. He was furious with Gladstone, who gave a speech in the Commons on 11 May that deeply antagonized the conservative wing of the Liberal Party. Like the speech in Newcastle in 1862 when he jumped ahead of government policy by declaring the South 'a nation', Gladstone again appeared to go to the furthest reaches of political reform, arguing that the upper-working-classes deserved the vote because of their patience during the economic hardship caused by the American Civil War. Palmerston dashed off a sharp reprimand on 12 May: 'Your speech may win Lancashire for you, though that is doubtful, but I fear it will tend to lose England for you' – and the government, he could have added.[14]

Two weeks later, Lindsay sent Mason stunning news. The Prime Minister had invited him to a private meeting on 26 May, to discuss the wording of a resolution to offer mediation between the warring States. Lindsay never considered whether Palmerston might be trying to buy off the pro-Southern MPs in Parliament. 'You should come here as soon after receipt of this letter as possible,' Lindsay begged Mason. Palmerston had even indicated he was open to a meeting with the Confederate Commissioner, but Mason refused to come to London unless summoned by the Prime Minister himself.

The Confederate Commissioner's obduracy was shaken by a letter from the Revd Francis Tremlett, the vicar of St Peter's, Belsize Park. Tremlett reminded Mason that he had started the Society for Promoting the Cessation of Hostilities in America a few months before, and 'as you were good enough to get us a good lift some little time since ... I feel that you would naturally like to know what we have been doing with the money'. Mason hardly remembered the Revd Tremlett, although the vicar kept open house for any Confederate in need; and he was astonished to learn that the Society was organizing a deputation to meet Lord Palmerston.[15] He also discovered that Tremlett had been working with Commodore Matthew Maury for several months until illness had curtailed Maury's activities.

Tremlett's organization was not lobbying MPs and peers for Southern independence per se; the vicar knew that such activity would imply an acceptance of slavery. Instead, the Society presented itself as a religious body whose sole aims were peace and the revival of Lancashire's cotton trade. But Tremlett candidly admitted to Maury on 1 June 1864,

> I want your help much; for (between ourselves), I am the Society so far as work is concerned ... I can't get any help that is not purely mechanical. The result is that I am obliged to spend hours and hours in the House of Commons, not only looking up members, but coaching them up also. I find they are as stupid in American affairs, except Lord R. Cecil, Lindsay, Gregory, and a few others, as any outsiders can be.[16]

Tremlett intended to lead deputations to Russell as well as Palmerston; 'of course I shall have enough to do to look up influential people to form the Deputation, but if I can't find these, I will go even if I have to go alone,' he told Maury. 'I want someone who thoroughly understands the American questions and will not be put down by Lord

R[ussell]. You see then, my dear Maury, how essential it is that you or Mason should be here just at present. You may know of persons whom I do not know, because persons talk to you on American affairs as a thing of course, which they do *not* to me.'[17]

Mason left Paris within a day of receiving Tremlett's letter and arrived in London on 5 June. As soon as Palmerston learned of Mason's presence, he knew that the Confederacy's supporters in Parliament would not dare risk their chances of a pro-Southern resolution by voting with the Tories to bring down the government. He now strung them along, continually requesting delays to Lindsay's resolution for British mediation in the war. The Confederate lobby nervously discussed the import of this and decided that the Prime Minister was waiting for news from Virginia. They were also reassured by Henry Hotze, who had heard from a source that the Opposition was again considering its own motion for Southern recognition. 'Indeed, I am satisfied that so general, almost universal, is popular sentiment in England with the South,' Mason wrote to Judah P. Benjamin on 9 June, 'the ministry, even if disposed to resist, would have to yield to the popular sentiment.'[18]

During the second week of June the reports from America seemed to confirm Mason's optimism. He regularly called at Rose Greenhow's lodgings in Mayfair to discuss the latest telegrams. 'He agrees perfectly with me in considering the news excellent,' she recorded in her diary after they read in the press that Grant and Lee had clashed again on 3 June, just south of Spotsylvania at a crossroads called Cold Harbor.[19] According to the reports, 7,000 Federals had fallen in less than an hour while trying to drive the Confederates from their fortified trenches.* Mason did not bother with Tremlett's Society after he learned about Grant's setback, even though Lord Russell had agreed to meet the vicar's 'deputation'.

The Confederates noted every utterance and passing remark which indicated a politician's preference for one side or the other, while remain-

---

* For several days after the battle, Grant refused to call a temporary truce to allow the wounded to be retrieved. By the time he changed his mind it was too late for many of the trapped and helpless soldiers. After the war, Grant expressed his remorse for the unnecessary suffering he had caused at Cold Harbor. Among those affected by his actions was Seward, who – for the second time in the war – spent several sleepless nights waiting to learn the fate of his son, Captain William Seward Jr. He had read in the newspapers that two captains from his son's corps had been wounded at Cold Harbor, but neither had been named.[20]

ing blind to the obvious pressures squeezing the government. 'A few feeble barks have been raised against us, but without much effect as far as I can see,' Henry Adams wrote airily to Charles Francis Jr. on 10 June.[21] For the past six weeks a conference of nine European powers had been meeting in London to try to settle the dispute between the Germens and the Danes, but Lord Russell's efforts to impose a resolution were going spectacularly badly: the German powers – Austria and Prussia – had announced their intention to disregard all previous treaties regarding the sovereignty of Schleswig-Holstein and Denmark was refusing to accept Russell's offer of mediation. Britain was suddenly looking less like a Great Power that could dictate the destiny of Europe than a weak and blustering island nation.

The *Alabama* was spotted outside Cherbourg harbour on 10 June 1864, having spent six months in the Far East followed by a return visit to Cape Town. The ship looked battered and dirty. 'Our bottom is in such a state that everything passes us,' Captain Semmes had written in his journal on 21 May. 'We are like a crippled hunter limping home from a long chase.'[22] The last four months of her two-year voyage had pushed the vessel and her crew past endurance. The *Alabama*'s seams were opening; damp and mould had invaded every corner, including the magazine that housed Semmes's dwindling supply of gunpowder. The repairs would take at least a month, providing he had the cooperation of the French. He was worried that they were going to turn him away. 'The last batch of newspapers captured were full of disasters,' Semmes wrote in his memoirs. 'Might it not be, that, after all our trials and sacrifices, the cause for which we were struggling would be lost? . . . The thought was hard to bear.'[23]

The French port admiral informed Semmes that he had made a mistake in choosing Cherbourg over Le Havre. Cherbourg was a naval station and subject to government oversight; Le Havre was a commercial port with many private docks where the *Alabama* could have settled without interference. The admiral could not allow Semmes to dry-dock his ship without permission from the Emperor, who was enjoying a brief sojourn in the country. While they waited for the Emperor's return to Paris, USS *Kearsarge* sailed into view (the American legation in Paris having alerted Captain Winslow to the arrival of the *Alabama*). Although Captain Winslow led his crew in a rousing cheer when he announced they were going to fight the *Alabama* at last, he was feeling as exhausted as Semmes. 'I find I have not the health that I had,' he wrote on 13 June. 'I am fast running down hill.'[24]

'Here we are,' wrote Semmes's English assistant surgeon, David Herbert Llewellyn, to one of his old colleagues at Charing Cross Hospital. 'An enemy is outside. If she only stops long enough we go out and fight her. If I live, expect to see me in London shortly. If I die, give my best love to all who know me.'[25] Semmes could have waited for the Emperor's permission to dry-dock, but he deliberately chose to fight the *Kearsarge*. 'The two ships are so equally matched that I do not feel at liberty to decline it,' Semmes wrote in his journal, ignoring the difference between the *Kearsarge*'s spruce condition and the *Alabama*'s dilapidated state.

> Accordingly, on Sunday morning, June 19th, between 9 and 10 o'clock [recalled Lieutenant John Kell], we weighed anchor and stood out of the western entrance of the harbor, the French iron-clad frigate *Couronne* following us. The day was bright and beautiful, with a light breeze blowing. Our men were neatly dressed, and our officers in full uniform. The report of our going out to fight the *Kearsarge* had been circulated and many persons from Paris and the surrounding countryside had come down to witness the engagement.[26]

Seven miles beyond French waters, the *Kearsarge* floated quietly while Captain Winslow carried out the Sunday inspection of the ship and crew. The routine seemed no different than the week before, except that today the guns were loaded and, perched high above the deck, special lookouts were scanning the horizon.[27] The *Alabama* sailed into view with a growing flotilla of spectator ships behind her. A band aboard one vessel played 'Dixie'; on another the crew gave 'three cheers for the *Alabama*'. In the few moments left before battle stations, Semmes made his final speech to the crew, telling them:

> Remember that you are in the English Channel, the theatre of so much of the naval glory of our race, and that the eyes of all Europe are at this moment upon you. The flag that floats over you is that of a young Republic, who bids defiance to her enemies, whenever, and wherever found. Show the world you know how to uphold it![28]

When the two ships were a mile apart, they turned broadside to broadside and began firing at each other in classic duelling fashion. Dr Llewellyn was operating on a wounded sailor when a shell burst open the wardroom, sweeping the table and patient from under him.[29]

Two more struck the *Alabama*'s pivot gun, killing its crew. Just one of the *Alabama*'s shells scored a direct hit on the *Kearsarge* – landing on the sternpost – but it failed to explode. The *Kearsarge* demolished the *Alabama* in less than an hour. Only when the vessel was clearly listing did Semmes give the order to abandon ship. Nine of the crew were dead; at least two dozen more lay wounded about the deck. Dr Llewellyn came up to help load the worst injured onto a dingy. The master's mate, George Fullam, was ordered to row to the *Kearsarge* and request assistance. According to eyewitnesses, an uninjured sailor tried to leap into the dingy but was held back by Llewellyn: '"See," he said, "I want to save my life as much as you do, but let the wounded men be saved first."' He refused the occupants' request to row over with them to the *Kearsarge*. 'We can make room for you,' argued Fullam. 'I will not peril the wounded men, was his reply.'[30]

Once Captain Winslow accepted that the white flag was not a trick he dispatched two boats to rescue survivors before they were dragged under by the vortex swirling around the stricken ship. Two French boats also arrived to help, as did the *Deerhound*, an English pleasure yacht. They were unable to save seventeen of the crew, including two of the black sailors serving on board, nor Dr Llewellyn, who was last seen holding on to two cartridge boxes.*[31] Captain Semmes was among the forty-two survivors who were rescued by the *Deerhound*. The *Kearsarge* picked up another seventy, three of whom died soon after being brought on deck. One of the French boats delivered its human cargo to the *Kearsarge*; the other headed to shore. But the owner of the *Deerhound* asked Semmes for directions, to which he managed to splutter 'any part of Great Britain'. Captain Winslow was outraged when he realized that she was sailing towards England, but there was nothing he could do to prevent the Confederates' escape.

The *Alabama*'s crew received a heroes' welcome on their arrival at Southampton. 'One thing is very noticeable that the destruction of the *Alabama* is much lamented by a majority of this people,' Consul Zebina

---

* Llewellyn's self-sacrifice revived the complaints of Charles Mayo and others about the shabby treatment meted out to doctors by the British army and Royal Navy. 'There has been a stupid jealousy set on foot between "combatant" and "non-combatant" officers,' declared the *Daily Telegraph*. 'We are carefully taking measures to keep men like Llewellyn out of our ranks, and drive them to Confederate cruisers, foreign service – anything and everything sooner than the regiments and ships where they are officially snubbed.'

Eastman remarked crossly to Seward. 'The London *Standard* says, "Every TRUE Englishman will regret to learn that the gallant *Alabama* has gone to her last resting place."'[32] The Cabinet's view regarding the *Alabama*'s demise was more practical. Lord Russell hoped that Adams would cease making claims for compensation, though he doubted the Northerners would be bought off that easily. Palmerston, as usual, asked what lessons could be learned for the navy: 'The Fate of the *Alabama* certainly shews that the days of unprotected wooden ships are fast fading away, and it makes one rather uneasy about the fore and aft unprotected parts of the [iron-hulled, armour-plated warship HMS] *Warrior*,' he warned the Duke of Somerset.[33]

Henry Adams was disgusted with the way the papers were 'trying to make a sea-lion of this arrant humbug'.[34] On 24 June an advertisement appeared in the *Telegraph* asking for contributions from army and navy officers to a fund to replace the sword lost by Semmes when the *Alabama* went down. The press interest was so great on both sides of the Channel, and the reports so detailed and numerous, that Édouard Manet was able to paint a depiction of the battle which persuaded people he had witnessed it himself.[*][35] Captain Semmes and Lieutenant Kell recuperated at the Revd Tremlett's vicarage while the papers debated the significance of the *Alabama*'s role in the war. In two years the cruiser had captured or destroyed a total of sixty-five US ships, causing more than $5 million-worth of losses to the Northern merchant marine trade. Had Britain behaved with propriety, was she blameless over the *Alabama*, asked several newspapers. The Duke of Argyll pressed the Cabinet for an answer. 'It will be found important to be able to say that we did our best to protest against the legitimacy of such proceedings,' he had warned shortly before the duel. Otherwise 'in the first war in which we are engaged, "Alabamas", will certainly be fitted out against us from neutral ports'.[36]

When news of the *Kearsarge*'s victory reached Washington, Gideon Welles ordered the Navy Department to fly its largest Union flag. In

---

* Yet many of the details in the press were wrong. Henry Adams read that Semmes hid under a tarpaulin during the battle. Across the Atlantic, the Confederate arms agent Edward C. Anderson mistakenly believed that his son had been killed. 'My worst fears are realized and my noble boy is no more,' he wrote. 'According to the newspaper account which is all I have of the battle, my darling son was blown overboard by a shell, leaving his leg on deck. The news came like an earthquake upon me . . . My darling boy is the only officer killed in [the] battle.'

Baltimore harbour, US troop ships sailing past HMS *Phaeton* hooted and chanted the *Alabama*'s name.[37] Glad to have something other than casualty lists and homecoming parades to report, the *New York Times* discussed the sinking of the *Alabama* for several weeks.*

The best that could be said for Grant in June was that he remained undaunted despite having lost 55,000 men since May. But the sheer fact he was still marching forward was vitally important for Northern morale in the light of the humiliating end to General Banks's Red River campaign. Lincoln's ability to shield his friend did not extend to outright disaster, and Banks's replacement to lead the 19th Corps, Major-General Edward Canby, was appointed even before the defeated Federals arrived back in New Orleans.

Banks retained his title of Commander of the Department of the Gulf, but his role was purely administrative. General Canby began a complete reorganization of his army. Among the changes was the formation of a 'marine brigade' under Colonel L. D. H. Currie, whose task was to guard the Mississippi river from guerrilla attacks.[39] Dr Charles Culverwell, however, chose to return to his family. May was the start of the sickly season, when swarms of mosquitoes rose like shimmering clouds out of the swamps. But the only assignment that would take him back to New York was escort duty for eleven soldiers who had become insane during the Red River campaign. Only seven survived the journey. Culverwell could cope no longer, and he resigned from the army for good shortly afterwards. Culverwell returned to England, never again to repeat the experiment of military life or indeed of being a doctor.†[40]

---

* The 79th New York Highlanders had their homecoming parade up Broadway and soon dispersed. 'We were mustered out of the service June 9th, 1864,' recalled Ebenezer Wells. 'I stayed a few weeks in N.Y. then returned to England, being away 4 years and 5 months.' The adjustment to civilian life proved to be hard. But eventually Wells found peace through prayer and a sense of pride that he had fought on the side of justice. '[I] have marched in triumph amid the plaudits of noble hearts, have felt the throb of nobility and patriotism as I fought for country dear,' he wrote, 'and have come back to my own home to receive the kiss of love.'[38]

† Using his stage name of Wyndham, Culverwell toiled steadily in the world of provincial theatre while he built up his skill and reputation. When he visited America again in 1870, it was as Charles Wyndham – one of the leading comic actors of his generation. Shortly before he was knighted in 1902, Wyndham gave a fundraising speech on behalf of the British soldiers fighting in the Boer War: 'I served with the Federal forces during the longest and most bitter conflict of modern days. Then I learned for the first time, and at first hand, what war really means, war – which if it does not make life worth the living, at least makes death worth the dying.'

The return of General Banks to New Orleans coincided with Edward Lyulph Stanley's arrival in the city. The Englishman was told that Banks had been labouring hard to improve the condition of freed slaves, having established nine military schools to teach literacy to the black recruits and ninety-five regular schools for black children.[41] But Stanley quickly realized that the white population were putting up a fierce resistance to Banks's reforms. 'The whites here have been accustomed to maltreat the negroes without any notice being taken of it,' he observed to his family on 17 May.[42] He went to a supposedly well-run plantation – the same one visited by William Howard Russell in 1861 and the Marquis of Hartington in 1862 – and thought it exposed the myth of 'the contented slave'. He was appalled by the dirty state of their hovels, by their despair, and fear of him as a white man. 'I am quite satisfied that [the plantation] is being very badly managed in the interest of the negro,' he declared.[43]

Stanley doubted how much more Banks could achieve without the wholehearted support of his staff. One New Orleans resident admitted to Stanley that she preferred the certainty of Butler's misrule to the arbitrary and capricious administration that now governed the lives of ordinary citizens. Banks had little control over his subordinates, she complained; rather than step in to curb abuses, 'he was so undecided and would keep putting you off, and giving you no satisfactory answer'.[44]

Mary Sophia Hill, the former British schoolteacher who had become a Confederate nurse after her twin brother, Sam, enlisted in the army, was one of the victims of General Banks's poor administration. She had left the South after the Battle of Gettysburg to visit relatives in Britain. But on her return to New Orleans in the spring of 1864 she had found herself under increasing scrutiny from Federal officials. 'Imagine how my English blood boiled with indignation at being treated like a criminal,' she complained to her brother on 20 May. 'I will never forget it to [sic] the Yankees – never; not that it would be possible for me to hold them in greater contempt than I do at present.'[45]

Mary had attracted attention because she always seemed to have a letter or parcel to deliver to someone in the city. She received two visits from a stranger, named Ellen Williams, who offered to convey any letters to the South since she was departing for Galveston. Ellen also tried to give her a note from CS General Taylor addressed to a Mrs Hill, which

Mary refused to take: 'I told her I was not Mrs Hill and the letter was not for me.' But Mary injudiciously gave her three letters, including one for Sam. A few days later, on 26 May, Mary came home to find a Captain Frost from the provost office waiting in the parlour. He bundled her into a cab and drove her to the women's prison on Julia Street.

The jailer, Mr Laurence, took a hearty dislike to the new prisoner and her repeated declarations of British nationality. He boarded up Mary's window, removed the sheets from her bed and prevented her from having contact with her sister or brother. 'I often wonder since [how] I kept my senses,' she wrote later, 'for many have lost their reason for less cruelty.' The main charge against her, she eventually learned, was that of passing information to the enemy. 'I wrote to Mr Coppell, acting Consul, who wrote me word he would attend to my case: it was not necessary to see me. I differed with him. It was his duty to see me and hear what I had to say, he knowing me to be a British subject.'*[46] After three weeks of solitary confinement, Mary was allowed a visit from her sister and brother-in-law, who were so appalled by her condition that they forced the authorities to allow her to be seen by a doctor. 'Had it not been for him, I would have died,' she wrote.[47] She was held in prison without being officially charged or given a date for her trial, while she grew weaker and more desperate by the day.

Mary Sophia Hill was not the only nuisance to the Federal authorities. Belle Boyd, the Confederate spy and heroine of the Battle of Front Royal in 1862, was also in custody. Her ability to prise information out of impressionable Federal soldiers was legendary. It was only with the greatest reluctance that Stanton had sanctioned Belle's release from prison the previous December after she contracted typhoid.

Belle had recuperated in Mobile, Alabama under the care of Mary Semmes, the wife of Captain Semmes, who 'treated me with as much

---

* Coppell had received Mary's distress call when he was himself at a particularly low ebb. He had been working without pay since September 1861. 'I should not have troubled your Lordship on this occasion but that my individual resources . . . are inadequate to the present large demands upon them,' he had written to Russell on 20 May. Knowing it would be some time before he received a reply, he laboured at his duties with waning enthusiasm. (When his letter eventually arrived in London the Foreign Office was amazed that he had never said anything before. No one had bothered to check whether the legation or London was meant to be paying his salary. Russell immediately granted him £350 per annum, and £200 war allowance.)

attention as though I had been her own daughter'. Mary's tales of the *Alabama* inspired her to try a new kind of adventure and she wrote to Judah Benjamin, offering to carry Confederate dispatches to England. Benjamin was delighted and provided Belle with $500 in gold, a letter of introduction to Henry Hotze and passage on a blockade-runner out of Wilmington. As dawn broke on her twentieth birthday, 9 May 1864, the *Greyhound* carried Belle and two other passengers past the blockade out into the open sea. She did not get very far; the USS *Connecticut* captured the *Greyhound* at 1.40 p.m. on the following day.

The US naval officer in charge of taking the *Greyhound* to Boston, Lieutenant Samuel Hardinge, was a handsome young fellow without a girl back home. He did not know, at first, that the widowed 'Mrs Lewis' was the infamous Belle Boyd – and by the time he discovered her true identity he was so besotted that she was able to persuade him that the captain of the *Greyhound* ought to be released. Hardinge took Belle shopping for clothes when the *Greyhound* stopped briefly in New York, and finished by proposing marriage to her when the vessel docked at Boston. 'So generous and noble was he in every thing,' Belle wrote later, 'that I could not but acknowledge that my heart was his. I firmly believe that God intended us to meet and love.'[48]

This had not, however, been the intention of the War Department. Gideon Welles ordered Lieutenant Hardinge's arrest. 'My dear Miss Belle, It is all up with me,' he wrote dejectedly on 8 June. 'The Admiralty says that it looks bad for us; so I have adopted a very good motto, viz: "Face the music!"'[49] Welles and the War Secretary, Edwin Stanton, were incensed that Belle had managed to make both their departments look foolish, and were determined it should never happen again. The provost marshal in Boston received a telegram ordering her immediate removal to Canada, and 'if I was again caught in the United States, or by the United States authorities, I should be shot', she wrote. Two days later she was on the train to Montreal, missing Hardinge, but excited at the 'delightful prospect of breathing free Canadian air'.[50]

Stanton had been in the midst of deciding what to do with Miss Boyd when one of his clerks informed him that an Englishman, a former volunteer in the Confederate army, was asking for an audience. The military governor of New York, General Dix, had hesitated to accept Colonel Grenfell's tale about his disenchantment with the South, and had sent him to Washington to apply directly to the War Department for permission to travel through the North as a tourist. Annoyed at the presumption on his time, Stanton nevertheless agreed to see Grenfell, out of curiosity. Two days later, on 13 June, Grenfell was shown into Stanton's office.[51]

Stanton received Grenfell with a stenographer present, which ought to have been a warning that this was not the time to play games. Heedless of the danger, Grenfell behaved like a second-string actor at his grand moment. He not only offered the incredulous Secretary 'inside' information about Lee's army, but also professed himself ready to join the US army. Stanton declined the offer. But he did extract a promise from Grenfell to make no further contact with nor provide any help to the Confederacy. The Colonel left Stanton's office believing that his performance had been masterful. He had received permission to travel anywhere in the North without having to register his presence with the local provost marshals. It had not occurred to Grenfell that the authorities could keep watch on him by other means. His mission accomplished, Grenfell returned to New York, where his new friend, Fitzgerald Ross, was waiting to begin their tour of northern New York and Canada, unaware of the sinister reason for the journey.

30

'Can We Hold Out?'

*A Welsh visitor to Washington – Tit-for-tat – Return of Lawley
and Vizetelly – An intolerable stench – Battle of the crater – The
Negro regiments – Devastation in the Valley*

On 22 June 1864, Griffith Evans, a Welsh army veterinary surgeon
stationed in Canada, called at the British legation in Washington seeking
advice on how to reach the front. Lyons explained that it was doubtful
Seward would give him an official pass. 'Lord Lyons entertained me
very hospitably,' wrote Evans. 'He took my hand in both his when I left,
and gave it a good shaking.' Evans felt sorry for him: 'He looks a kind,
good natured middle-aged man who was staggering under the burden
of safeguarding the rights and liberties of nearly 3 million British subjects.' Evans was shocked to learn that crimping was never punished,
nor legal redress available for the victims:

> The usual mode is to drug the food or drink, whether it be alcohol or tea.
> The person loses consciousness and recovering some time after in a distant
> place finds himself dressed in the US uniform, he remonstrates but is assured
> he enlisted himself, finds some money in his pocket which he is told is part
> of his bounty, and that he has spent or lost the rest. Such are the complaints
> received daily. All the Embassy can do is to request the War Department to
> investigate the case, to give it a fair trial and report. Some are then retrieved
> and some not, but none of those relieved get Army compensation.[1]

Lyons did not discuss his civil cases with Evans. That week, British
subjects in Memphis had protested to him about a rule that banned
their employment unless they joined the Federal militia; a black Canadian had been arrested for breaking the State of Delaware's ban on

coloured people; and Mary Sophia Hill had written to him from prison, begging for his intercession. 'Imagine, my Lord, a woman and a British subject so threatened,' she cried. 'My object in writing this letter is to ask Your Lordship to see justice done me and to protect me until I am proved as not belonging to the Glorious Flag of Old England.'[2]

Consul Coppell admitted to Lyons that he had failed to visit the prisoner, but 'From personal knowledge I do not think the case one for Your Lordship's interference'.[3] Lyons had no reason to doubt him. Experience had taught the Minister that cases such as Mary's usually came with a long and tangled history of mutual antipathy between the prisoner and the authorities. He would not help her while there were others who were truly innocent and helpless. William Seward was amazed by Lord Lyons's tenacious advocacy for such pathetic cases. The old rules of warfare had been swept away, he told him during a contentious interview. Seward pointed to the latest news from Charleston, where the Confederates had moved fifty Northern officers to a converted prison, in direct range of the US gunboats.

General Sam Jones in Charleston had decided it was time for the Federals to feel what the city's civilian population had been enduring for the past eight months, and fifty Federal prisoners of war (all officers) had been moved to a converted prison in one of the most heavily shelled neighbourhoods. He knew that an attempt to capture the city was still being prepared – his scouts had reported that thirteen warships and forty-six troop transports were anchored less than 100 miles away in Port Royal Sound, which had been captured by the Federals early on in the war.[4] But the timing of the attack remained a mystery. Captain Henry Feilden was not taking any chances: he had drawn up a will in Julia's favour, even though their wedding had not yet taken place. If he were to be killed now, he told her,

> I should feel as if I was leaving a wife behind in you, and it is my duty to attend to your wants. I thought of you, darling, last night whilst I was sitting out on the ground, I thought of you and felt happy to be able to render my small mite in defence of your country. You will trust me dearest, wont you, to love you ever as I do now, whatever happens if I am alive you will be protected ... someone who will think of nothing else for the rest of his life but making you happy.[5]

General Beauregard had recommended Feilden for promotion:

> Though I do not think there is much chance of their refusing it, personally
> I do not care whether they do or do not [Feilden admitted]. I really look
> forward to the war ending this year, and if . . . [only] we are spared to one
> another, we shall be able to settle so comfortably in Charleston. I will go
> into some business and work very hard, and then I shall have you to com-
> fort me and inspire me. Then you will be able to amuse yourself with all
> your old friends and acquaintances. Dearest Julie, if I can only make you as
> perfectly happy as we mortals can expect to be, I shall have no other wish
> on this earth.[6]

Feilden's respect for General Jones plummeted after the Federal officers were used as human shields. He had urged Jones to reconsider the
order, pointing out that retaliation would probably follow. 'My argument then and now was the homely adage that "two wrongs can never
make a right",' he related to Julia.[7] Feilden was so troubled that on
30 June he went down to check on the Federal prisoners. He wore his
best uniform for the visit, 'to show that we are not quite ragged yet in
the Confederacy'. There were five generals among the fifty officers.
Feilden struck up a conversation with General Truman Seymour, who
was so interesting and pleasant that he regretted the folly of General
Jones all the more: 'I hardly ever met a Yankee before, never a Yankee
General and thought the contact would make one's flesh crawl, but
strange to say, I could not blow Seymour from a gun or hang him without a good deal of repugnance. Indeed, I felt more inclined to ask him
to dinner and show him around Charleston.'[8]

Feilden's prophesy of retaliation was soon fulfilled. The commandant
of Fort Delaware, on Pea Patch Island in the Delaware river, received an
order to select fifty officers from among the 12,500 Confederate prisoners and dispatch them to one of the captured forts in Charleston harbour
so that they would be in the line of Confederate fire. The inmates
assumed that there would be more random selections in the future, and
the thought spurred many to look for a way of escape. There was only
one route out, however, through sewage drains that led to the Delaware
river. Among the six prisoners willing to try was Bennet G. Burley, who
had been captured on 12 May 1864 while planting torpedoes on the
Rappahannock river. When Burley was searched they found an unusual
pass that granted him the freedom to cross Southern lines at will. Regular

soldiers did not carry such passes. Burley was labelled a spy and treated accordingly.

Burley weighed the risks and decided that his prison conditions could not significantly worsen if he tried to escape and was recaptured. One night, when the drains were full and water was seeping up through the floor, Burley and his five comrades prised open the grille in their barracks and, taking a big breath, lowered themselves into the pitch-dark pipe. Burley's powerful physique enabled him to thrust his body along for 25 yards until he reached the end and could heave himself into the rushing river. Only one other Confederate managed the same feat. Burley was rescued by a passing sailing boat, telling the crew that he had capsized while night-fishing, which the captain either believed or chose not to question. He was taken to Philadelphia and from there headed north, aiming for Canada where he would be safe.

In Virginia, the Army of the Potomac was edging towards Richmond. 'We must destroy this army of Grant's before he gets to the James River,' Lee had urged General Jubal Early on 29 May. 'If he gets there, it will become a siege, and then it will be a mere question of time.'[9] Two weeks later, on 12 June, the Federals had not only reached the James but also crossed it, using pontoon bridges. Now only the small town of Petersburg, population 18,266, lay between Grant and the Confederate capital.[10] The town straddled the five remaining railways and two main roads that connected Richmond to the rest of the State. From 15 to 18 June, Grant ordered a continuous wave of attacks, losing more than 10,000 men over four days, without breaking the Confederate defences. 'We have assaulted the enemy's works repeatedly and lost many lives, but I cannot understand it,' Charles Francis Adams Jr. wrote in anguish to his father on 19 June. 'Why have these lives been sacrificed? Why is the Army kept continually fighting until its heart has sickened within it? I cannot tell . . . Grant has pushed his Army to the extreme limit of human endurance.'[11]

The US generals complained that their troops had lost their courage for frontal assaults. The men would make a show of going forward before hunkering down under cover. Grant tried one last time before he accepted the necessity for a long siege. He dispatched Sheridan on another cavalry raid, with orders to attack Lee at his vulnerable points – the bridges, water tanks and supply lines. On 22 June Grant ordered an assault against one of the five railroads. The 69th New York Volunteers were among the attackers.

> Our Captain asked permission to lead us [wrote James Pendlebury]. He had been under arrest for some time and told me that he had a foreboding that in the next encounter he would be killed ... As we were entering into the charge he received a shot and fell at my side. I turned and said, 'Captain, are you mortally wounded?' He said, 'I am Jimmy, don't leave.' There was one thing I had learnt always to have beside me, which I knew was most refreshing; I carried a supply of water because the first thing men who are wounded cry for is water. The captain thanked me for it and I stood beside him. I, myself, was so very thirsty that I lay down and literally slaked up every drop of water that I found in the imprint of a horse's shoe in the clay. I forgot it was muddy I was so thirsty. I gave to my Captain many a drink during the throes of death. I turned him over many times and did all I could for him. After a while I got him on my shoulder and carried him into the shelter of the trees out of the sound of the whizzing bullets. I really thought I would never get out alive. By and by the Captain died and I got him on my back and carried him back to our works. We buried him in the breast works in front of Petersburg, Virginia.

Grant ordered a second charge, but many of the troops were done with fighting. The 69th were drunk before the attack – Pendlebury wandered forward in a daze, thinking he would dodge Confederate bullets if they came – and the men were captured en masse.[12]

The Confederates were no less shaken by the six weeks of relentless fighting. Francis Dawson had suffered so many near-misses that he was certain the next bullet would find him.[13] But his spirits had recovered since the return of Lawley and Vizetelly, who ran the blockade at Wilmington together on 5 June. Vizetelly had brought with him a letter from Dawson's mother. 'Little did I think, when years ago, I saw drawings and sketches in the [London] Illustrated by our "special artist F. Vizetelli", or even when we had many a frolic together in the mountains of Tennessee,' Dawson wrote home on 26 June, 'that he, the same joyous, corpulent artist would have proved a source of such happiness to my dear parents and myself.' Dawson's happiness was complete after Vizetelly drew a picture of his corps on a midnight march through burning woods.[14]

'I am satisfied General Grant will make no more onslaughts upon the

A corps of the Confederate army marching by night
through burning woods, by Frank Vizetelly

Confederate breastworks,' Lawley wrote from Lee's headquarters on
27 June. 'Weeks and weeks will probably pass without amending Grant's
prospects before Petersburg.' The Confederates' defences stretched for
over 30 miles in a protective semicircle of trenches and bomb-proof
shelters, connected by walkways that in some places were 6 feet deep
and up to 12 feet wide. Lawley recognized that the real danger to the
Confederacy came from Sherman in Georgia. Only CS General Joseph E.
Johnston and the Army of Tennessee stood between Sherman and
Atlanta, the last strategic target of the South. The great question on
Lawley's, indeed, everyone's mind, was whether the Northern electorate
would decide to end the war before Sherman reached Virginia.

Three days later, on 1 July, Lee's artillery commander, General
Edward P. Alexander, arrived at the Confederate headquarters with disturbing news. He had seen activity that convinced him the Federals were
digging a tunnel under their trenches. Lawley asked him how long it
would have to be to clear their works: 'I answered about 500 feet,' Alexander recalled. '[Lawley] stated that the longest military tunnel or gallery

View of Petersburg from CS General Lee's headquarters – watching
the Federals through binoculars, by Frank Vizetelly

which had ever been run was at the siege of Delhi, and that it did not
exceed 400 feet. That it was found impossible to ventilate far greater
distance.' Alexander reminded him that the average coal mine went
much further and it would not be too taxing for the Federals to ask any
volunteer from the Pennsylvania mines about ventilation. Lee had no
option but to wait and see who would turn out to be right.[15]

Lawley and Vizetelly suffered as the summer heat cast a pall over the
trenches. To pass the time, Vizetelly drew portraits of Lee and his staff
watching the Federals through field glasses. The biggest excitement was
the arrival of a captain from the British army, G. T. Peacocke, who
reported for duty as a volunteer aide to General Pickett.[16] Lawley filled
his reports with stories of 'African savagery' and Federal brutality
towards women and children, but neglected to describe the hunger that
now afflicted Lee's army. One of the more colourful English blockade-
runners, the Hon. Augustus Charles Hobart-Hampden, the third son of
the Earl of Buckinghamshire, whose later exploits with the Turkish navy
won him the title 'Hobart Pasha', visited the front lines in July. He came

armed with boxes of sausages and sardines, which were naturally gobbled up by the grateful Confederates. 'For months past [they] had tasted nothing but coarse rye-bread and pork washed down with water,' wrote Hobart-Hampden. 'There were several Englishmen among the officers composing the staff,' he added with surprise. 'I often wonder what has become of them.'[17]

Hobart-Hampden saw Petersburg and Richmond, where nearly every other female was dressed in deep mourning, and even snatched a half-hour conversation with Lee himself, yet still he believed Lawley's optimistic prediction of Southern victory. 'Though a line of earthworks hurriedly thrown up in a few hours at Petersburg was nearly all that kept Grant's well-organised army from entering the capital; though the necessaries of war, and even of life, were growing alarmingly short,' he wrote after the war, 'still everyone seemed satisfied that the South would somehow or other gain the day.' Lawley he could excuse, since the journalist was 'so carried away by his admiration of the wonderful pluck shown by the Southerners ... whereas all of us ... should have seen the end coming months before we were obliged to open our eyes to the fact it was come'.[18]

The Welsh army veterinarian, Griffith Evans, had obtained an observer's pass from the Medical Department, and was visiting the Federal lines at the same time that Hobart-Hampden was with the Confederates. He too had little sense that the South was struggling when he arrived at Petersburg. His first visit was to General Butler's camp on 3 July, where the flies were already a pestilence (they were the biting kind and 'are very troublesome indeed', James Horrocks complained to his brother[19]). All day long, wrote Evans, the men sat in their fetid dugouts, sweltering in the heat, until the night shift relieved them. It was a dreadful existence and he pitied them. Soldiers talked to him about the 'fearful slaughtering' they had witnessed in vague tones, 'as if they wished to forget it'.

Driving around the countryside, Evans thought he had never beheld anything so hideous, so redolent of biblical destruction: 'Fences pulled down for fuel, the crops in the fields trodden down, houses deserted or occupied by troops, or burnt down, thousands of recent graves of men killed or died lately, and those so shallow that the stench from them was in places intolerable. Dead cattle and horses, men's accoutrements, etc., strewn about, etc. etc. It was indescribable and the effect was sad and sickening.'[20] He could not imagine how the soldiers would tolerate their conditions for much longer.

A rumour was spreading through the camps during Evans's visit. The army discouraged discussion of it, but the news eventually leaked out. Sir Percy Wyndham had ridden into the camp of the 1st New Jersey Cavaliers, insisting that he was once more their colonel. Although the men knew that the New Jersey State legislature had petitioned Washington for Wyndham's reinstatement for the second time on 4 June, there had been no indication that Stanton had changed his mind. After a tense stand-off, the lieutenant colonel of the regiment ordered the arrest of Wyndham, who refused to leave quietly. Wyndham created such uproar that General Meade had him escorted to Washington under guard on 1 July. His discharge papers were waiting for him when he arrived. On 5 July 1864 Sir Percy Wyndham was officially mustered out of the army, and strongly encouraged to leave town.*

Griffith Evans's own return to Washington was impeded by a Confederate

---

* Sir Percy briefly attempted to run a riding academy for cavalry officers in New York. Its failure led him to return to Italy to serve on Garibaldi's staff for the next couple of years. Ever the roving adventurer, he moved to south-east Asia, starting a humorous journal in India, the *Indian Charivari*, and a logging business in Mandalay, Burma. He was killed in Mandalay at the age of 49 in 1879, while demonstrating a hot-air balloon of his own design, which exploded in mid-air.

raid on the perimeter. The audacious attack, led by Jubal Early, was an attempt by Lee to force Grant into detaching part of his army to defend Washington. 'There is a large Confederate force within three or four miles of Washington, and some perhaps think they will make an attempt to take the town today,' Lord Lyons informed his sister on 13 July. But though there was panic in the city, the legation was not even bothering to pack up the archives. 'Even if the town was taken my physical comfort would not be likely to be disturbed,' Lyons decided. 'I don't really expect to have to move, and I daresay you will hear next week that things have lapsed into their odious condition.'

Lyons was far more worried about the state of his staff. He repeatedly told the Foreign Office that it could no longer assign the same number of attachés to Washington as it did to Ulan Bator. The Secretary, William Stuart, and one of the junior staff had left before the arrival of their replacements. 'The heat is overpowering,' Lyons wrote to Lord Russell. 'I am anxiously looking out for [their] arrival ... and I hope they will be immediately followed, if they are not accompanied, by one or more Third Secretaries or Attachés – otherwise the whole Legation will be knocked up.'[21] A letter from Joseph Burnley, the new Secretary, brought terrible news: he was coming out with his wife and children. 'A dreadful prospect for me – and still worse for him, poor man,' wrote Lyons. No woman had disturbed the monastic peace of the legation for the past five years.[22] Lyons set about trying to dissuade Burnley from bringing his family. He could, with complete honesty, describe the lonely existence of a British diplomat in Washington. With Henri Mercier gone, and the Russian Minister, Baron Stoeckl, on leave for the summer, Lyons had not received a single invitation to dinner for weeks.[23]

Griffith Evans was concerned for Lyons when he visited the legation on 20 July, though the Minister sheepishly declined his sympathy. Evans should reserve his pity for the country's leaders, Lyons told him: 'Mr Lincoln is not the man to look at that he was four years ago.' The Welshman realized the truth of this statement when he visited the White House a few days later. He walked through the 'Grand Reception Room', which he thought was 'very seedy looking', into Lincoln's office without anyone challenging his presence. Lincoln was so exhausted and put-upon that he did not think to ask why a stranger was in his office. 'He shows marks of mental overwork,' decided Evans after a few minutes' conversation.[24]

The pressures on Lincoln were increasing. Grant's failure to capture Richmond and Jubal Early's raid near Washington had shaken the Cabinet's confidence. The tense divisions between the members resurfaced in violent quarrels and a resumption of the old plots and counter-plots against one another. Seward, whose son Will had been wounded while defending Washington against Early, turned some of his frustration on Lord Lyons. He rudely dismissed as exaggeration the Minister's complaints that the Central Guard House in Washington was using water punishments against alleged deserters. Lyons had evidence from six separate cases, and was outraged by the State Department's explanation that a cold shower was pleasant in the summer. Turning water cannon on prisoners was not 'in conformity with any law or regulations', he bluntly wrote to Seward on 25 July. It was used for one reason only: 'for the purpose of extorting, by the infliction of bodily pain, confessions from persons suspected of being deserters'.[25] Nor was this his only complaint against the army. That same week, Lyons received evidence from the New York consulate of British subjects being hung by their thumbs until they agreed to sign confessions of desertion.

The legation's only success in July was the rescue of Admiral Usher's grandson, Henry, who had walked into the New York consulate on the 13th, painfully thin and a little unsteady on his feet. 'Usher has been for about a week in hospital in this place, too ill to report to me until today,' recounted the deputy Consul. Now they had him, they were not allowing him out of their sight. One of the clerks went to the ticket office to purchase a berth for the boy. Another stayed by him until he boarded the steamer. The attachés celebrated the news that young Usher had departed from New York with a drink at Willard's.

The President has 'called for 500,000 more recruits', Lyons reported to London on 22 July. 'It will depend very much on the events of the present campaign whether he gets them.'[26] Thurlow Weed believed this new draft to be an act of political suicide.[27] The army knew little of Grant's intentions and its spirits sank as the soldiers broiled and sweated in their camps, waiting for orders. 'Here we are just where we have been so long and no one knows anything,' Charles Francis Adams Jr. complained to his brother. 'I am tired of the Carnival of Death.'[28]

Charles Francis was unaware that the 500-foot tunnel at Petersburg was almost complete. In a couple more days, Grant intended to blow up the centre of the Confederate lines. In preparation for the daring assault Grant ordered a diversionary attack north of the James river, close to Richmond. The troops selected for the mission included Colonel L. D. H. Currie and the 133rd New York Volunteers, lately arrived from Louisiana. Grant wanted Lee to be caught between defending Richmond and defending Petersburg, and, with luck, ruffled into making mistakes. But it was the Federals who ended up committing the errors by their failure to plan adequately for the assault. Colonel Currie, who had been appointed acting commander of the 3rd Brigade, 1st Division, discovered that many of his troops were new recruits. He became increasingly worried the more he witnessed their lethargic response to his orders. The men had been assigned to hold one of the creeks that fed the James, but at the first sign of trouble they broke cover and ran for their lives. 'Colonel Currie is as much annoyed at the conduct of his troops as myself,' reported his commanding officer: 'They had the most explicit instructions from Colonel Currie, who even went so far as to tell them if they broke, the troops in the rear had orders to fire on them.'[29]

Currie's threats could not match the actual feel of gunfire for many of these men.* General Weitzel, the acting chief of staff for the 19th Corps, vigorously defended Currie's conduct to his irate superiors. He 'bears three honorable wounds,' Weitzel wrote indignantly, 'and is promoted for gallantry. He was Major-General Smith's adjutant-general all through the campaigns of the Army of the Potomac.' But Currie was denied the opportunity to correct the poor impression made by his raw troops. The next day, on 27 July, he was ordered to take his brigade to Washington in anticipation of another attack by Jubal Early. Two days later, on 29 July, the diversionary expedition was abandoned and the Federals recrossed the James river; the mine tunnel was scheduled to explode in a few hours' time.

A hitch had been discovered, however. The troops specially trained for the mission happened to be from coloured regiments, and all of a sudden it seemed politically hazardous to use them; white regiments

---

* Some of them were victims of crimpers, like 21-year-old Edward Sewell from Ipswich, who had arrived in 1862 to work as a mechanic for a New York firm. He had been kidnapped in May while riding on the train to work: 'I sat by myself in the corner and believe I began to doze [wrote Sewell]. About three or four in the afternoon I woke up and found myself on board a steam-packet on its way to Hart's Island . . . I found that I was then in uniform as a soldier, and had been robbed of my money, jewels, and clothes, except a ring on my finger.'[30]

were substituted in their place. Notwithstanding Grant's declaration that 'they will make good soldiers', there was still widespread resistance to the idea of blacks in uniform, as well as doubts about their abilities. 'Can a Negro do our skirmishing and picket duty?' asked Sherman rhetorically. 'Can they improvise bridges, sorties, flank movements, etc., like the white man? I say no.'[31] The second-class status of the coloured regiments was reflected in their pay for the first two years – which stayed at $7 a month, only just over half the $13 paid to whites – until Congress rectified the inequality. Yet the number of black volunteers was increasing, from none before 1862, to 15,000 in 1863, to more than 100,000 by the summer of 1864. Moreover, they were not only serving their country, they were dying for it too, and at a higher rate than white soldiers. The Confederates rarely took black prisoners alive.*

At 4.45 a.m. on 30 July the fuse was lit and four tons of gunpowder exploded underneath two unsuspecting South Carolina regiments. Two hundred and fifty men were buried instantly; several hundred others were blown to fragments. The hole formed by the explosion was more than 150 feet long, 97 feet wide and 30 feet deep. 'Into this crater', wrote General Alexander, 'the leading [Federal] division literally swarmed, until it was packed about as full as it could hold.'[32] The Federal soldiers were trapped as the Confederate regiments on either side of the crater formed a new defensive line and trained their guns into the crater. Alexander's English staff officer, Stephen Winthrop, and three others ran to one of the artillery pieces that was still working and started firing. The Federal soldiers were slaughtered like animals in a pen. Almost 4,000 were lost in the debacle, including most of the black troops who were sent in after the white regiments. 'The effort was a stupendous failure,' wrote Grant.[33]

Francis Lawley was two miles away at Lee's headquarters when he heard the muffled boom and saw the 'dark curls of smoke' billowing from the crater. He embellished the fiasco in his report to give a false picture to British readers of white bravery and black cowardice. 'The panic-struck negroes', he lied, 'crowded into the empty crater of the mine, and cowered down in abject terror.' While he was crafting his

* A notorious example of Confederate rage against black soldiers had taken place only three months before, on 12 April, at Fort Pillow in Tennessee. The Federal force of approximately 262 black and 295 whites surrendered to General Nathan Bedford Forest. But fewer than 75 black soldiers walked out alive.

Times dispatch, a messenger arrived with the news that Jubal Early had torched the Pennsylvanian town of Chambersburg. Lawley added this to the end of his report, to show that Lee still retained the ability to attack Northern targets: 'Richmond never laughed more scornfully at the puny onslaught of her foe.'[34]

'We have met with a sad disappointment at Petersburg,' Seward wrote to his wife on 5 August. 'And now we have to deal with a disappointed, despondent, and I fear discontented people, who expect the Administration to guarantee success.'[35] Lincoln travelled down to Fort Monroe for a private conference with Grant. The General blamed the War Secretary, Edwin Stanton, for insisting 'that defending Washington was more important than chasing the enemy, even if it allowed Early to feint and pounce wherever he chose'.[36] A few days after the meeting, Grant had his way and General Phil Sheridan was allowed to lead a force of 40,000 men into northern Virginia. Sheridan's instructions were clear: to make the fertile Shenandoah Valley unfit for human habitation and destroy Jubal Early's army. Grant's precise words were for Sheridan 'to follow him to the death'.[37] The key was mobility, which could only be achieved if Sheridan's supply lines kept up with him. The 'thankless and arduous' task of guarding the continuously moving wagon trains was given to Colonel Currie.[38]

Lee had hoped that Early's raids would force Grant to send reinforcements to northern Virginia; he was even prepared to sacrifice a whole division of his army if it diverted the Federals away from Petersburg and Richmond. Francis Dawson was among the cavalry force under General Fitz Lee that arrived in the Shenandoah Valley on 8 August. 'I then realized, as never before', wrote Dawson, 'the devastation of war ... The brutal Sheridan was carrying out his fell purpose ... columns of smoke were rising in every direction from burning houses and burning barns.'[39] Yet he prevaricated to his parents, telling them the Confederacy was 'tattered but like our soldiers it stands well'.[40]

The detachment of 40,000 Federal troops made little difference to Grant's strength in southern Virginia, whereas Lee needed every man in the trenches. Grant was relentless, probing and attacking any perceived weakness in the Confederate defences. '[He] is a man of such infinite resource and ceaseless activity,' wrote Charles Francis Adams Jr. admiringly on 13 August. 'Scarcely does one scheme fail before he has another on foot; baffled in one direction he immediately gropes round for a vulnerable point elsewhere – that I cannot but hope for great results the whole time. He has deserved success so often that he will surely have it at last.'[41]

General Butler's Army of the James finally had worse things to worry about than the biting flies. 'We have had no fighting here since I last wrote,' James Horrocks admitted to his parents just before the army was deployed on 14 August. 'We have been remarkably quiet. I believe we have not fired a shot nor had a shot fired at us for over a month.' But Horrocks came down with typhus and did not take part in the march to Deep Bottom (so named after a deep bend in the James river about 11 miles south-east of Richmond) where Grant planned to mount a second attack – the first had ended badly on 27 July – against Lee's defences at Chaffin's Bluff.[42] Horrocks's illness saved him from participating in what turned out to be the second of three assaults at Chaffin's Bluff. On this occasion, a lack of proper planning meant that the ships carrying the troops along the river were too big to dock at the designated landing areas. The schedule for the operations was thrown into disarray and the Confederates succeeded in driving the Federals back to the river.

Among the 3,000 Federal casualties on 14 August was Robert Moffat Livingstone, the 18-year-old son of Dr David Livingstone, the celebrated missionary and explorer. The boy had been missing for over a year. Livingstone had ordered Robert to sail from England and join him in Kilmane, Portuguese East Africa, in early 1863, but the wayward youth had changed his mind and only journeyed as far as Natal, South Africa, where he absconded with the ship's money box.*[43] Robert worked his passage to America and joined the 3rd New Hampshire Infantry in January 1864, enlisting under the name of Rupert Vincent. His regiment had suffered several losses at Deep Bottom, including their colonel, Josiah Plimpton; but it was actually heatstroke which felled Robert, a common problem that week. He was taken to a field hospital, where he became lost in the system for more than a month, leading his commanding officers to assume he had deserted. At least his family now knew where he was; Robert had

* Since the death of Livingstone's wife Mary in 1862, relations between father and son had become strained to breaking point. Dr Livingstone had not seen his son – or any of his children – for several years, though he continued to send them long, disapproving letters from East Africa. Robert was a restless, lonely boy – 'dour, determined, impulsive', was how one contemporary described him. Far from acceding to his father's wish for him to train as a doctor, Robert wanted to join the army or navy. At one point, he absconded from school and became lost for a short time in the underworld of Limehouse in London, where sailors' hostels operated side by side with opium dens and brothels.

finally written to his favourite sister, confessing that army life was not at all what he had envisioned.[44] 'Robert has gone all to the bad,' lamented Dr Livingstone when he heard the news. Despite his grief, Livingstone did not give up on him entirely and resolved that if Robert behaved himself, he would try to help him obtain an officer's commission.[45]

The heat that had put Robert in hospital was reaching some of the highest temperatures in recent memory. Lawley wrote in The Times that the past twenty days had been the worst he had ever known. 'Night and day the mercury of the Fahrenheit has touched 90, and has sometimes gone considerably above that figure.' Visiting Richmond, he saw that people cleaved at all times to the shady side of the streets, flitting like 'pale shadows' under the harsh sun.[46] 'The drought still continues to the total destruction, I fear, of all crops, especially of our vegetables,' the Confederate chief of ordnance, Josiah Gorgas, wrote despairingly.[47] Naturally, this was not something that Lawley cared to admit, and in his next dispatch he managed to turn every adversity into a seeming virtue. 'Lee has, as usual, the odds against him,' he allowed, 'and yet at no moment has the confidence of Secessia in the security of Richmond and Petersburg been more serene.'[48] The true feelings of 'Secessia' were more accurately expressed by Gorgas, who wrote in his diary on 29 August: 'Can we hold out much longer?'[49]

31

The Crisis Comes

Not enough men – Lincoln upholds the message of Gettysburg –
Lord Lyons insists – Colonel Grenfell's new mission – Failure of
the Copperheads

The South was nearly bankrupt. In mid-July President Davis persuaded George A. Trenholm to take over from Christopher Memminger as Secretary of the Treasury – even though the businessman told him frankly that it was too late to improve the Confederacy's finances. Its rampant inflation and crippling shortages were evidence of an economy that was no longer functioning. The South's military position also looked critical, especially in the West, and on 17 July 1864 Davis removed General Joe Johnston from command of the Army of Tennessee. The Cabinet unanimously backed the decision. General William T. Sherman had invaded Georgia on 7 May with a force of 100,000 men, and for the past three months Richmond had been expecting to hear of a great battle between the two armies. But Johnston had insisted on pursuing a strategy of attrition – arguing that he could wear Sherman down through defensive manoeuvring, and then attack once the numerically superior Federals were too weak to resist.

The problem for Johnston was that whenever he settled his men into a seemingly impregnable position, Sherman simply marched around him and continued towards Atlanta. Johnston succeeded in having one battle of his choosing, at Kennesaw Mountain on 27 June, less than 30 miles from Atlanta, but Sherman easily absorbed the 3,000 casualties and moved forward. Johnston abandoned the mountain, but before he could establish a new defensive line the Federals had crossed the last natural barrier before Atlanta – the Chattahoochee river – on 8 July.

Now there were no more mountains or rivers to stand in the way of Sherman's advance. Losing Atlanta would not only be politically disastrous: Davis knew that its capture would 'open the way for the Federal Army to the Gulf on the one hand, and to Charleston on the other'. The South would be split in two: 'It would give them control of our network of railways and thus paralyze our efforts.'[1] Davis replaced Johnston with one of his subordinate commanders, 33-year-old General John Bell Hood, who had been lobbying for weeks to be allowed to wage a more aggressive campaign.

Atlanta was not the only city under threat. Mobile's defences were crumbling, and the survival of Charleston – where the Federal bombardment was under way – rested on Fort Sumter continuing to keep the enemy out of the harbour. Captain Henry Feilden was fighting his own battles with the Ordnance Department for more guns (there was still no word of his promotion, despite General Jones having added his own letter of recommendation to General Beauregard's). He did not wish to sound defeatist, but if Mobile were to fall, Feilden told General Gorgas, 'Farragut's fleet would be set at liberty for operations to the eastern coast, and there can be little doubt that Charleston would be the first place assailed . . . in our present position, I feel deeply apprehensive as to the result of a grand naval attack.'[2]

Feilden was unable to press his point further; in August he was sent on a special mission to Florida. 'Throughout this State but especially on the Coast there are large numbers of deserters and desperadoes who have fled from our armies and hid themselves in these almost inaccessible wilds,' he explained to Julia. 'The General now wishes to apply the policy of reconciliation, and I shall go down amongst them as an ambassador. I think with good care we may have some success, but they will be a hard crowd to deal with.'[3] Feilden kept Julia amused with wry descriptions of his journey along the country roads of the Deep South. He made a brief stop in Savannah, Georgia, where he stayed at a plantation remarkably untouched by the war. His bedroom, he told Julia, was decorated with French china: 'You will think me very foolish perhaps noticing all these things, but I am so fond of pretty house arrangements.' While he was there, he dined with an ageing officer who remembered selling cotton to his grandfather, old Sir William Feilden.[4]

The South could not afford Feilden to return empty-handed. It had run through its reserves of able-bodied men and there were now so few officers left that one of the Confederate brigadier generals killed at Deep Bottom was only 24 years old. The War Department clerk John Jones had heard that General Bragg was recommending 'publication be made here, in the United States, and in Europe, encouraging enlistments of foreigners in our army'.[5] Bragg had probably been inspired by the unexpected arrival in Richmond of four Polish army officers in early August who claimed that thousands of Polish exiles would fight for the South in return for grants of land after the war. The manpower shortage was so acute that Davis was willing to believe them; he authorized the South's financial agent in Britain, Colin McRae, to spend £50,000 to charter transport ships for the Poles allegedly waiting to enlist.[6] Judah P. Benjamin also agreed to Henry MacIver's request for passage on a blockade-runner so he could return to Scotland and raise volunteers for the Confederacy. (The arrangement brought to a close the Scottish officer's disappointing career in the Confederate army, which had ended with him sidelined to provost marshal duties, and beset with health problems brought on by syphilis.[7])

The Confederate Navy Department was not lacking men but ships. At the beginning of August the Confederate Navy Secretary, Stephen Mallory, detached the *Tallahassee* from the fleet defending Wilmington and sent it on a commerce raid up and down the East Coast. The vessel was a former blockade-runner purchased by Mallory from an English blockade-running firm and converted into a raider. The *Tallahassee* destroyed twenty-six vessels during its nineteen-day voyage – Northern papers reacted as though the entire eastern seaboard were under attack – but the brief sensation was won at a terrible cost to Southern supplies. Lee had argued strongly against the plan and his fears were proved right. The *Tallahassee* consumed the last of Wilmington's supply of smokeless coal, forcing blockade-runners to burn the more conspicuous black variety, which led to the capture of seven ships. The Federal navy took advantage of the *Tallahassee*'s absence to double the size of the blockading fleet around Wilmington. Fresh sailors were sent to the US navy ships, including Henry Morton Stanley, whose previous history as a Confederate *and* Federal deserter was unknown to the authorities.*

---

* Stanley had returned to the North from Wales in January 1863, having failed to be reconciled with his family or to find satisfactory employment. But he had fared no better in

The *Tallahassee* was an embarrassment to Lord Lyons as well as the Navy Department. The Northern press, Lyons informed Russell, constantly referred to the vessel as the 'Anglo-Rebel pirate'. He suspected that the stalemate in Virginia and Georgia had created more than the usual need to find scapegoats, and advised the Foreign Secretary to refrain from making any sort of public statement about American affairs. 'I should say the quieter England and France were just at this moment the better.' The subject was too volatile, especially since the 'Peace Party' was becoming bolder in its demands for an armistice. Lincoln's popularity had fallen precipitously since the slaughter in Virginia and the fiasco of the crater explosion at Petersburg. The latest news from Atlanta was also disappointing: Sherman had defeated Hood in three separate engagements and yet the city remained in Confederate hands. Newspapers throughout the North harped on the administration's failures: 'Who shall revive the withered hopes that bloomed at the beginning of General Grant's campaign?' asked the Democratic *New York World*. 'Who is responsible for the terrible and unavailing loss of life . . . after the opening of a campaign that promised to be triumphant?'[9] Lyons feared that 'Mr Lincoln's chance of the Presidency for a second term seems vanishing.'[10]

Jefferson Davis had been praying for this moment: the Northern public and press were growing weary of the war. His original belief that Southern independence would be achieved through British recognition had been proved wrong and his hopes in Lee delivering independence through his victories had been dashed, but he still had faith that the South would prevail if it could break the Northern will to fight. He now realized that Britain's neutral stance was not a curse but a boon to the Confederacy, since Canada was the perfect staging post for waging psychological warfare against the North. The Special Commissioners in Canada, Jacob Thompson and Clement C. Clay, could move about with relative ease, and even if they failed to inflict serious damage on Northern targets, their activities might provoke Washington into declaring

---

America, and after working at various jobs he joined the US navy on 19 July 1864. He was assigned to the USS *Minnesota* as a ship's clerk, a light position that would only expose him to danger if the vessel received a direct hit. Otherwise, he anticipated a summer of little excitement other than the occasional chase of an unarmed blockade-runner.[8]

VERY PROBABLE.

Lord Punch. "THAT WAS JEFF DAVIS, PAM! DON'T YOU RECOGNISE HIM?"
Lord Pam. "HM! WELL, NOT EXACTLY—MAY HAVE TO DO SO SOME OF THESE DAYS."

Punch's view that Britain (Palmerston) will soon have to recognize the
Confederacy (Jefferson Davis)

war against Britain. Davis was sure that recognition of the South would
be among the first – if not the first – step that Britain would take against
the North.

Thompson and Clay had quickly realized that they would never work
well together, but they had created enough separation between their
projects to minimize potential friction. Clay preferred to work with
James Holcombe, a former law professor at the University of Virginia,
who had been in Canada for the past five months on a separate mission
for the Confederate State Department.*[11] Clay was hoping to romance

---

* On 7 December 1863 seventeen Confederate sympathizers – many of them British – had
boarded the steamer *Chesapeake* in New York and hijacked it once they were in international

disaffected Northern politicians into believing that an armistice was in the interests of both sides. It seemed to him that the peace advocates were willing to believe almost anything. 'We have not dispelled the fond delusion of most of those with whom we have conversed, that some kind of common government might – at some time hereafter – be established,' he wrote archly to Benjamin.[12] One of these intermediaries convinced the editor of the New York *Tribune*, Horace Greeley, that Clay and Holcombe had been given the authority to negotiate peace terms with the North.[13] Greeley used the power of his newspaper to confront Lincoln over his reluctance to consider the Confederates' terms: 'I entreat you to submit overtures for pacification to the Southern insurgents,' he urged melodramatically. 'Our bleeding, bankrupt, almost dying country also longs for peace.'[14] The public, Greeley insisted, would vote for a Democratic President in November if Lincoln seemed to care more about war than peace.

Lincoln knew enough about the Confederate Commissioners in Canada to be certain that political embarrassment rather than peace was their goal, but he also knew that he could not afford to be portrayed as deaf to potential overtures from the South. Yet there were no terms that the South could offer – other than the abolition of slavery and restoration of the Union – that he would accept. In contrast to many Northerners, and even some conservative Republicans, Lincoln's belief in the principles articulated at Gettysburg – liberty and democracy – was unshakeable and he would not trade them for peace, or for his re-election in November.

Lincoln skilfully wrong-footed Greeley by inviting him to be the North's representative in these apparently genuine discussions for peace. Greeley had no choice but to accept and on 18 July, with Lincoln's private

---

waters. The intention was turn the vessel into a privateer, but the adventure quickly degenerated into farce. The *Chesapeake* ran out of coal and most of the crew deserted. The vessel was captured by a US warship and towed into Halifax harbour on 15 December. Once it became known that a Canadian was among the prisoners, a furious crowd took over Queen's Wharf, determined to free him. Five more US navy ships appeared in the harbour and a tense stand-off ensued. Finally, on 19 December, the US naval officers bowed to pressure and all the prisoners were rowed to shore, whereupon the crowd 'rescued' the Canadian. Holcombe had been ordered to find any legal argument, no matter how weak, to claim the *Chesapeake* as a Southern prize. But to his embarrassment he discovered that none of the *Chesapeake* privateers were actually from the South, and the Confederates had no claim to their services or the vessel.

secretary, John Hay, accompanying him as a witness, he met with Clay and Holcombe on the Canadian side of Niagra Falls. Hay was carrying a letter from Lincoln to the Commissioners, addressed 'To Whom It May Concern'. It offered them safe conduct to Washington to discuss the war under the following terms: 'the integrity of the whole Union, and the abandonment of slavery'; no other condition would be acceptable. The discussion unfolded much as Lincoln had expected, with Clay admitting that he had no authority to negotiate a peace and Greeley and Hay returning empty-handed. But the Confederates had prised out of Lincoln a statement about slavery, and its fundamental place in the war, that could only make him more unpopular with the great mass of voters in the West who still thought they were fighting for the Union rather than abolition.

The 'To Whom It May Concern' letter was indeed the last straw for some Lincoln supporters. The treasurer of the US Sanitary Commission, George Templeton Strong, thought 'his letter ... may cost him his election. By declaring that abandonment of slavery is a fundamental article in any negotiation for peace and settlement, he has given the disaffected and discontented a weapon.'[15] Charles Francis Adams Jr. was shocked by the palpable sense of defeat among the Cabinet when he visited Washington at the end of August. (He was on furlough, recovering from an attack of jaundice caused by malaria.) He had transferred from Meade's staff to an all-black regiment, the 5th Massachusetts (Colored) Cavalry, and was waiting to take up his commission as lieutenant colonel in September. His own convictions about the aim of the war and the necessity of seeing it through remained strong despite his recent experiences in Virginia; but a meeting with Seward left him deeply concerned. 'His tone was very different from that of last spring,' Charles Francis Jr. wrote to his father on 20 August, 'when he seemed to me so buoyant and confident of the future ... I was pained to feel how discouraged he was. He too gave me the impression which all here do, of "going it wild" and not seeing where this thing is going to come out.'[16]

Contrary to Charles Francis Jr.'s fears, Seward was one of the few politicians not scheming to replace Lincoln or flirting with ideas for a negotiated peace. But 'the Tide is setting strongly against us', warned the editor of the New York Times, Henry Raymond, on 22 August. As chairman of the Republican National Committee, Raymond's views carried substantial weight. He saw no hope for Lincoln, barring a sudden military success, unless the administration declared its willingness to consider reunion with slavery intact.[17] Even Edwin Stanton, whose longevity at the War Department owed much to his loyalty to Lincoln, decided that it might be worth finding out from the Confederate Commissioners what sort of terms the South would be willing to discuss. On 19 August 1864, Judge Jeremiah Black, a moderate Democrat and old friend of Stanton's, visited Commissioner Thompson in Toronto. Three days after the meeting, Thompson wrote to Mason and Slidell in France that Stanton had sent Black to him because he had lost all confidence in the Republicans' re-election. 'Judge Black has come to me to learn the state of feeling in the Confederate States, and to know whether I was able to say if negotiations for peace could be opened without the ultimatum of final separation.'[18] Stanton never did learn the answer, because on 22 August the *New York Herald* exposed the meeting, which frightened him into repudiating any connection with the visit. Facing treachery in his Cabinet, abandoned by the Republican National Committee and excoriated in the press, Lincoln believed that his chances of re-election were slim. Yet 'I honestly believe that I can better serve the nation in its need and peril than any new man could possibly do', he told Thaddeus Kane, the chairman of the House Ways and Means Committee.[19] The following day, the 23rd, Lincoln put his Cabinet to the test: he asked them to demonstrate their loyalty by signing their names at the bottom of a covered document. They did not know it, but each man was committing himself to the war until the last day of the Lincoln Presidency, assuming the Democrats won the White House in November:

> This morning, as for some days past, it seems exceedingly probable that this Administration will not be re-elected [read the memorandum], then it will be my duty to so cooperate with the President elect, as to save the Union between the election and the inauguration; as he will have secured his election on such ground that he can not possibly save it afterwards.[20]

While these sombre proceedings were taking place in Lincoln's office, across the parched park of Lafayette Square Lord Lyons was writing his assessment of the President's future. The situation was indeed bleak. 'Now, Mr Lincoln's star is very pale. The new loan lags – the pay of the Armies is in arrear – and the Conscription ... will be made under the most unfavourable circumstances.' But 'there is still a *possibility*', Lyons insisted to Lord Russell, 'of some military successes before the winter, which might make a great change in public feeling'.[21] Lyons had hoped for some sign of progress before he left for Canada to discuss with the Governor General, Viscount Monck, how to restrain Confederate operations in North America. The trip had been planned since July, but Lyons was loath to leave the legation before at least some of his cases were settled. 'I heartily wish I could get away from Washington, and go at once to Canada,' he had written to Russell on 9 August, 'but with two Members of the Legation away on account of their health, and two more ailing, I am afraid the work cannot be done at all without me ... I am a little nervous, too,' he admitted, 'as to my own position with reference to quite a new man.' Lyons was still not yet sure whether the married Joseph Burnley was the right fit for the legation.[22]

The unresolved cases included that of Mary Sophia Hill, who had written again to the legation. She had been tried in a military court and a verdict had apparently been reached. 'But no official statement has been made, or any public verdict given, nor can I get any satisfaction,' she wrote in a shaky hand on 20 August:

> I have been tried according to their own laws, and after four weeks, common justice, I should think, would demand a verdict ... the shocks my nervous system has received from the confinement and from the rough treatment I received from my jailer and assistant, as well as the excitement of my trial, and now four weeks suspense as to result, will make me an invalid for life and has very nearly upset my reason. I am not, never ever have been, guilty of the charges brought against me ... But there seems a spirit of bitterness against HM's subjects here, and very little law or justice for them.[23]

Lyons agreed that the law and justice were becoming two quite separate entities for British subjects. Whether Mary was as innocent as she claimed would make no difference, he was quite certain, to her treatment by the military authorities. It was only a gross injustice – resulting in the death of a conscripted Briton – that had recently forced a change in the War Department's approach to disputed enlistments so that alleged British subjects were removed from the battlefield while their cases were under review.* But Lyons was feeling overwhelmed and

---

* The victim was Andrew Cunningham, a British subject who had been kidnapped and forced into the 39th New York Volunteers on 8 January 1864. Lyons was alerted to his

disheartened. 'Since my return to Washington last October,' he wrote frankly to Lord Russell, 'it has been as much or more than I have been able to do, to keep the daily business from getting into arrears and confusion. I have had to work so incessantly at the pumps to prevent the water rising above my head, that I have not been able to think of any measure for stopping the leak.'[25]

At the end of August Lyons decided he could not take another day in the capital: 'The thermometer in the House literally stands as high at midnight as at noon.' He ordered his two favourite attachés, Edward Malet and George Sheffield, to be ready to leave for Canada with him on the 30th. The new Secretary, Joseph Burnley, would just have to do his best.

The Canadian authorities had warned London that the Confederates in British North America were not only 'hostile in spirit' to the North but also 'prepared to give expression to that hostility in overt acts'.[26] Fitzgerald Ross was astonished by the brash behaviour of the Confederate community on the Canadian side of Niagara Falls. He and Colonel Grenfell had arrived at Clifton House hotel in mid-July to find the hotel awash with conspiracies. 'The "season" had hardly yet commenced,' wrote Ross, but the place was so busy that it seemed to be in mid-flow. Scores of survivors from John Morgan's failed raid into Kentucky were hanging around the colonnaded hotel and were 'delighted to meet their old Colonel again'. In his travel account, Ross tried to make the meeting sound coincidental and harmless. The Morgan raiders passed the time 'talking Secesh politics and plotting mischief against the Yankees', he wrote, as though the conspirators were nothing more than nostalgic veterans who liked to reminisce about the glory days and plan the occasional nuisance.[27]

Ross's breezy memoir left out the real details of their stay at Niagara. It was the week of Commissioners Clement C. Clay and James Holcombe's peace conference with Horace Greeley; it was also the week that Grenfell

---

plight on 11 February and immediately petitioned for his release. The facts regarding Cunningham's kidnap were never in dispute, but even so the usual delays followed. Finally, on 7 June 1864, after considerable nudging from Lyons, Seward gleaned from the War Department that Cunningham's release had been ordered. Six weeks went by without further communication on the subject. Seward had completely forgotten about Cunningham when, on 23 July 1864, he received a sheepish note from Charles Dana, Assistant Secretary of War. They had been unable to find Private Cunningham because he had been killed in battle on 10 May 1864, four weeks before his discharge.[24]

was reunited with the Confederate agent Thomas Hines.*[28] Grenfell sent a mysterious letter from Niagara to his daughter, Mary. 'There is still work to be done and I am awaiting events,' he wrote, before warning her that he was planning to disappear 'for a month or so I hope, before I again get into the saddle . . . It is impossible to give a safe opinion upon what may take place in the South within the next three months, but they cannot subjugate it, never, never!'[29] Ross parted from Grenfell at the end of July and returned to England in the autumn, intending to write a book about his adventures in the South. He never imagined that the 'mischief' had actually grown into a conspiracy involving the exiled Copperhead, Clement Vallandigham, and the underground group the Sons of Liberty.

Vallandigham had been living a lonely and frustrating existence in Windsor, Ontario, since his expulsion to the South in 1863 and subsequent escape on a blockade-runner to Bermuda. Windsor's chief recommendation was its location along Canada's southern boundary, facing Detroit. Vallandigham's suite on the second floor of the Hirons House hotel afforded him a fine view of the forbidden fruit across the river. The hotel was also situated next to the ferry landing, which made it convenient for pilgrimages by Copperheads and loyal allies in the Democratic Party.[30] Desperation had driven Vallandigham to accept an offer from the Sons of Liberty to become its 'Supreme Grand Commander'. The original Sons of Liberty was a revolutionary organization formed before the War of Independence to demoralize and intimidate the loyalist supporters. In its new incarnation, the Sons of Liberty combined paramilitary aims with Masonic-like rituals, complete with secret signs, elaborate initiations and large stockpiles of weapons in several States.

Far more popular in the Northwest than anywhere else in the country, the Sons of Liberty nevertheless attracted an eccentric constituency and its numbers fluctuated wildly from a few thousand across the country to 18,000 in Indiana alone.[31] The grand commander of the organization, an Indiana printer named Harrison H. Dodd, needed Vallandigham

---

* The Confederate government believed there were 400 escaped prisoners of war hiding out in Canada and Nova Scotia. James Holcombe had been ordered to advertise in local newspapers that he had the means to pay for their passage home. But his efforts to locate the missing 400 yielded only six Confederates. Hines, on the other hand, had no trouble locating the survivors of Morgan's brigade, whom he trained for his operations against the North.

since the Sons of Liberty was in danger of collapsing unless it could find a national figure sufficiently credible to attract more members. Vallandigham needed the Sons of Liberty almost as much; his resounding defeat in the 1863 election for State Governor of Ohio had been a major setback. General McClellan looked certain to win the Democratic Party's nomination for President unless Vallandigham used the organizing capabilities of the Sons of Liberty to force his way into the selection process.

Thompson's and Captain Hines's first meeting with Vallandigham took place at Windsor on 11 June 1864. 'On my arrival here I heard that there was such an organization as the Order of the Sons of Liberty in the Northern States, and my first effort was to learn its strength, its principles, and its objects, and if possible to put myself in communication with its leading spirits,' Thompson reported back to Judah P. Benjamin. 'This was effected without much difficulty or delay. I was received among them with cordiality, and the greatest confidence at once extended to me.' His investigations into the Society revealed that the membership was not as large as Vallandigham had boasted to him, but

> its organization was essentially military. It had its commanders of divisions, of brigades, of regiments, of companies. The belief was entertained, and freely expressed that by a bold, vigorous, and concerted movement the three great Northwestern States of Illinois, Indiana, and Ohio could be seized and held. This being done, the States of Kentucky and Missouri could easily be lifted from their prostrate condition and placed on their feet, and this in sixty days would end the war.[32]

Vallandigham was hedging his bets. He was hoping to lead the Democrats to victory in the Presidential election, but was prepared to reap the fruits of an armed uprising of the Northwest if his political ambitions failed. He was counting on Thompson to provide the arms and explosives for his members.

Thompson did not care whether Vallandigham wanted reunion or Southern independence so long as he was committed to fomenting a revolution in the North. He agreed to fund a joint venture between his Confederate raiders and Vallandigham's Sons of Liberty to make a coordinated attack on the three prisoner-of-war camps in Illinois and Indiana. The prisoners would provide a ready army to help the conspirators stage a *coup d'état* in the Northwest, and, as soon as this was accomplished, they would return to the South to help finish the war. Thompson hoped that the prison break would bring an additional 50,000 fighters to the Confederacy.

Captain Hines, Colonel Grenfell and some sixty former members of Morgan's brigade were to attack the prisons; the Sons of Liberty would have the responsibility for rounding up the chiefs of the local legislatures and disposing of them. 'All they need now is an "occasion", as they style it, to rise and assert their rights,' Thompson had reported to Benjamin on 7 July.[33] There was no attempt at any strategic planning, no discussion as to which camps would be liberated first or how the army of liberated prisoners would be fed, transported and clothed; but this did not stop Thompson from writing hundreds of thousands of dollars' worth of cheques. Confederate sympathizers and corrupt middlemen shipped cartloads of revolvers hidden in boxes marked 'Sunday school books' to Ohio and Indiana. New York proved to be especially fertile ground for obtaining illicit guns and ammunition.

All the Confederates had assigned themselves aliases, which fooled no one and only served to give the conspirators a false sense of security. 'Dear Hunter [the alias used by Thomas Hines],' wrote Grenfell on 31 July from Collingwood on the Canadian side of Lake Huron, 'there is fair fishing round the place but better further North ... if any news write immediately.'[34] Grenfell was waiting for Hines to give him the signal to go south to Toronto, which was the agreed rendezvous point for the plotters. However, the date for the uprising was proving to be difficult to pin down with the Sons of Liberty, and the 'occasion' had been pushed back several times. Vallandigham had returned to Ohio, hoping to be arrested by the authorities, in the belief this would provoke a public backlash violent enough to spark a revolt. But to his dismay, Lincoln gave orders for the troublemaker to be ignored, which deprived Vallandigham of the intoxicating power of indignation. Ironically, Grant's military failures in Virginia had also weakened the Sons of Liberty's resolve since public weariness with the war made it seem likely that democracy rather than conspiracy would soon bring peace. Representatives for the Sons of Liberty tried to cancel the mission, telling Hines and Thompson on 8 August: 'the more we think of it the more thoroughly are we convinced that it will be unsuccessful.'[35]

The organization had been successfully infiltrated and arrests were already beginning to take place, including those of fifty leading men from the Sons of Liberty in Kentucky on 30 July. Two days later the

State's grand commander, Judge Joshua Bullitt, was seized as he stepped off the ferryboat on his return from a conference with Thompson and Hines in Canada. A search of his belongings revealed a satchel full of gold, a cheque for $10,000 signed by Jacob Thompson and many incriminating papers.[36] The leaders of the Indiana chapter, including Harrison Dodd, were arrested three weeks later. The Confederates were equally guilty of jeopardizing the mission. They knew US detectives were tailing them but failed to alter their behaviour. The same basic ciphers were used, the same routines followed and there was much careless talk in public places. By now the Federal authorities had a clear idea that some sort of attack on Camp Douglas was being planned in a joint Copperhead–Confederate operation.

Thompson and Hines would not be put off, however, and managed to prise out of the Sons of Liberty a new date for the uprising. It would now take place on 29 August in Chicago during the Democratic national convention. The obvious wavering of the Sons of Liberty made the Confederates anxious, but they reckoned that even if only half the promised 5,000 members actually came there would still be a reasonable chance of success. Hines sent out the long-awaited signal for his followers to convene in Toronto. On 24 August Thompson handed Hines his written orders and $24,000 to cover the expenses of the mission. Over the next few days Grenfell and sixty others slipped into Toronto. Each man was provided with $100 in cash, a pistol, ammunition and a return train ticket to Chicago. Hines outlined the plan: they were to travel inconspicuously, in groups not larger than three or four. Once in Chicago they would meet at Richmond House hotel for the rendezvous with the Sons of Liberty. One force would make for Camp Douglas to liberate its 5,500 inmates. The other would travel 200 miles west to Rock Island Barracks to release its 9,000 Confederate prisoners.

Grenfell left with Hines and a couple of others on 26 August. He chose as his costume for the occasion a grey hunting suit, in the same hue as the Confederate uniform, two sporting guns and a yellow-spotted hunting dog – a loud disguise entirely characteristic of him. When one of Grenfell's travelling companions pointed out that the suit would probably cause him to be arrested the minute he stepped off the train, he replied: 'I have my English papers, and my gun and my dog, and if they ask me what I am doing, I will say I am going hunting.'[37] The party reached Chicago on 28 August and proceeded straight to Richmond

House. Grenfell signed the register under his own name. Hines, on the other hand, kept to his alias of Hunter. The Confederates had a suite of rooms – all labelled 'Missouri Delegation' – which was deemed a sufficient disguise to allow them to blend in with the thousands of real delegates who were crowded four to a room in the city's overburdened hotels. (The plumbing, which had so irritated Anthony Trollope during his stay in the city, remained unimproved.)

That night, the Confederates and Sons of Liberty met for the first time since the secret conferences in Canada. They revealed 'that something had gone wrong'; no orders had been sent to the 40,000 members in Ohio or the 50,000 in Indiana. By way of exculpation they pointed out that the mission had already been exposed in several newspapers and that Camp Douglas had received additional Federal troops.[38] The Confederates were incensed. It seemed impossible that the hundreds of thousands of dollars funnelled to the Sons of Liberty would fail to produce a single fighter. Outside the hotel windows the city was heaving with anti-war protesters, many of them obviously wearing side arms. At least some of them, Hines insisted, would be eager to see a little action.

The embarrassed conspirators agreed to supply the Confederates with 500 men by the following evening. The Camp Douglas plan would be abandoned, and the less guarded prison at Rock Island would become the sole target. Under the new plan, one of Hines's deputies, John Castleman, and twenty Confederates would accompany the Sons of Liberty, while Hines and the remaining fifty would provide support by cutting the telegraph wires and stopping all trains in and out of Chicago. With the help of the prisoners from Rock Island Barracks, they would commandeer the trains and head 200 miles south to Springfield, the State capital. In a few hours Illinois would be theirs.

The Confederates waited uneasily for the sun to set. Outside, excited crowds tramped to and from the convention hall. Vallandigham avoided Richmond House: he was far too busy squeezing and working the delegate system. Prison breaks and political assassinations could not have been further from his mind. Only Charles Walsh, the leader of the Chicago chapter of the Sons of Liberty, and a couple of sidekicks bothered to return to Hines's rooms. He did not have 500 men, or 100 men or even 50 men, although Walsh thought he might be able to find 25 if given enough time. When the Confederates insisted this was not enough, Walsh suggested 8 November – the day of the election – as the new date for the prison liberation. Hines agreed through gritted teeth, swearing he would hold them to the day no matter what the cost. Once the Sons of Liberty left, the Confederates passed the rest of the night pondering their options. The snippets of news that filtered along the corridors of the hotel indicated that Vallandigham had failed to derail McClellan's bid for the nomination. Just about every expectation held by Hines, Grenfell and the rest had turned out to be wrong. There were no seething undercurrents of revolution, no paramilitary organization of well-armed fighters, no willingness in any quarter to take risks.

It was too dangerous for the Confederates to remain in Chicago. Hines outlined their choices during a noisy meeting of the disappointed volunteers: they could use their tickets to return to Canada; attempt to sneak home; or stay with him and hide out in southern Illinois until 8 November. Twenty chose Canada; another twenty-five said they would go south. The rest agreed to help Hines build a force from scratch among the Illinois members of the Sons of Liberty. Grenfell, as usual, made a fourth choice. He would maintain the hunting charade and shoot prairie chickens around Carlyle, Illinois, until called to duty.[39] 'Tell the girls I am alive and well, although engaged in rather dangerous speculations, which you will know more of, probably, bye and bye,' he wrote on 31 August to the Grenfell family business manager in London.

> The North West states are ripe for revolt. If interfered with in their election they will rise. All this is in favour of the South . . . We are on the eve of great events. Abe Lincoln will either have made peace, or made himself a military dictator, within the next two months. In the latter case the N.W. Provinces secede, and there comes a row. Either course aids the South.[40]

Jacob Thompson shared Grenfell's delusion that the Northwest was smouldering with revolutionary aims. The Copperhead leaders were cowards, he claimed to the Confederate Secretary of State, but 'the feeling with the masses is as strong as ever. They are true, brave, and, I believe, willing and ready.'[41] Indeed, Thompson was angry with Hines for giving up so quickly on the Chicago expedition. He refused to work with the Confederates who returned to Toronto, calling them 'deserters'. Thompson blamed everyone for the mission's failure, including Clay and Holcombe, whom he accused of weakening the Copperheads' resolve by having dangled the prospect of a negotiated peace at the Niagara Falls conference in July.

Thompson had become a bitter and vengeful man since his arrival in Canada; during his absence from home, Federal soldiers had burned his Mississippi plantation and assaulted his wife. Isolated from friends and family and surrounded by like-minded fugitives, Thompson turned his personal grievances into an excuse to inflict the greatest possible suffering on the North, and in particular on Northern civilians. Nothing, he complained to Clay, should distract the Confederates from delivering the message of violence.

32

The Tyranny of Hope

Clinging to power – How to orchestrate a public protest – Rose
Greenhow makes her decision – Petitioning for peace – Atlanta

Lord Palmerston was facing the prospect of defeat in the twilight of his parliamentary career. 'They [the Opposition] have had their Meeting and have agreed upon a vote of Censure,' Palmerston wrote to Gladstone on 28 June 1864 after Lord Russell's peace conference in London ended, embarrassingly for the British government, without an armistice agreement between the Germans and the Danes. 'We shall want a great Gun to reply to Disraeli. Would you be ready to follow him?'[1] As much as it pained Palmerston to write these words to his most troublesome member of the Cabinet, he could not escape the truth that it was his own pugnacious declaration last July – that Denmark could always rely on Britain's support – which had started the government's woes. The Danes had believed him; the French resented him, but the Germans knew he was bluffing – even if it was some months before Palmerston realized it himself. Queen Victoria was still devoted to the land of her late husband and was prepared to do almost anything to prevent 'Lord Pilgerstein and Johnny', as she derisively termed Palmerston and Russell, from standing in the way of German interests – even though the Prince of Wales's wife, Alexandra, was a Danish princess.

There was a national uproar after Palmerston and Russell announced that Britain would not fight alongside the Danes after all. Whether the government's course was right or wrong mattered less than the obvious fact that it was a complete reversal from the one originally proposed. On 4 July Disraeli introduced in the House of Commons a resolution against the government. 'In England every other topic of interest has been adjourned to await the issue of the parliamentary battle which commences this evening,' the Southern propagandist Henry Hotze reported to Judah P. Benjamin, 'and yet I am more than doubtful about the result.' The Tories were destitute of policies; 'the chief end of its tactics is to get into office without committing itself on either of the two great questions ... the American and the Danish.' This, feared Hotze, could be their undoing.[2]

Henry Adams was tickled to be so close to and yet untouched by the Liberals' political crisis. 'Everyone who has an office, or whose family has an office, is in a state of funk at the idea of losing it,' he chuckled to Charles Francis Jr. Recently he had been feeling flat and 'more and more doubtful every day as to what life is made for', he had confided to his brother. 'I am getting old, and must be at work. The *chef* can do without me, if he only tries.'[3]

The parliamentary debates on the censure continued for four days. Gladstone did indeed fire his big guns in the Commons, though in his diary he complained, 'I threw overboard all my heavy armament and fought light.'[4] The speech sealed his position as the undisputed leader-in-waiting of the Liberal Party, although it was not strong enough to silence the government's critics. 'I wish either that one could put one's nerves into one's pocket ... or that one could run away from the future,' Henry wrote to his brother on 8 July. 'The division takes place tonight, and the excitement in society is tremendous.' Their father had heard that the government was down to a majority of two or four votes in the Commons. He was surprised to find himself hoping that the Liberals would pull through.

The Confederate Commissioner James Mason was still waiting for the interview with Palmerston that William Schaw Lindsay had promised in June. The Prime Minister had played his part with finesse, making no commitments to the pro-Southern faction in Parliament, while ensuring that the Tories could not offer them anything that was not already under discussion. Rose Greenhow had become close to the Opposition through a fortuitous friendship with the Tory hostess Lady Chesterfield, and was convinced that the Confederates were wasting their time with the Liberals.[5] Despite telling Mason everything she heard in Lady Chesterfield's drawing room, she could not shake his faith in Palmerston. 'Saw Mr Mason who was very busy,' Rose wrote on 8 July. 'He does not think we have anything to gain by a change in ministry. [For] Queens sake!'

Adams finished his work early that night so he could watch the government fight for its life. In the Lords, Russell gave a speech that even his supporters thought 'rather feeble'. 'It was amusing', wrote a listener, 'to hear Lord Russell refuting in his speech all his own arguments in the Cabinet for war.' Argyll was a little too forceful to be effective, but the government was helped by the absence of Lord Derby, who was laid up with gout.[6] In the Commons, Adams squeezed into the Strangers' Gallery at 5 p.m. and sat through seven speakers while waiting for Palmerston to make his stand. It was past midnight when the Prime Minister finally rose to address the House. He was obliged to defend the outcome of the London peace conference as if no promises had ever been made to Denmark, and the German rebuff had never happened. More humiliating still, when he listed the government's achievements during the past four years, he could think of few examples that had not originated from Gladstone's tax-cutting measures rather than from himself or Lord Russell.

'He is not a good speaker, his manner is hesitating,' Adams wrote in his diary, which was true of Palmerston at the best of times. 'And yet I cannot doubt', he added reluctantly, 'that he makes the only real leader now to be found in English politics.'[7] The division took place at half past two in the morning, with the Tories confident that they had the votes. Mrs Greenhow waited impatiently at her lodgings: 'I am anxious for news from Parliament,' she wrote in her diary. 'I am afraid the Government will have a majority.' Both Houses divided at the same moment. The Peers went against the government by a majority of 9 votes; but in the Commons, the Tories discovered that a handful of MPs had switched sides during the debate, uneasy that the price of government would mean effectively declaring that Britain was no longer a Great Power but a feeble, blustering bully. The Liberals survived by a majority of 18 votes.

'Had the scale turned the other way, the scene would have been worth staying to see,' wrote Adams, who left before the result was called. His early departure meant that he missed a first in the history of the Commons. As soon as the numbers were called, Palmerston clambered up the stairs on his gouty foot to the Ladies' Gallery to embrace his wife in plain view of the House. She cared as much as Palmerston himself, that when he did go out of politics, it would be on his own terms.[8]

With the parliamentary crisis safely passed, the Confederate lobby at Westminster stepped forward to claim its reward from Palmerston.

Lindsay's resolution for mediation was to be the climax of a week of carefully orchestrated events. The Confederate lobby had reasoned – justifiably – that the previous failures in the Commons had been exacerbated by the problem of individuals acting on their own. In order to succeed, they had to appear united, representative of the entire country and popular among MPs of all persuasions.

For several weeks, Spence's Southern Independence Association had been distributing petitions and resolutions throughout England calling for British intervention in the war. These were intended to represent the voice of the ordinary public – some of them, like the Manchester petition, contained more than 5,000 signatures.[9] Next, Mason was to have his interview with Palmerston, followed by the deputation from the Revd Tremlett's peace society. Separately, representatives from the cotton factories were to deliver a 90,000-strong petition to Russell. Only then, after the government had heard from the rich and the poor, from manufacturers and merchants, all demonstrating that the country desired action on behalf of the South, would Lindsay put forward his resolution.

The plan began well. At Henry Hotze's instigation, *The Times* reported that the Northern armies had been checked on every front. Lindsay took Mason to see Palmerston at Cambridge House on 14 July: 'I was received with great civility, and after the ordinary topics of salutation Lord P. commenced the conversation,' Mason wrote afterwards to Judah P. Benjamin. Palmerston seemed interested in the South's military options but became evasive when Mason asked him for a definite answer as to whether Britain would join with Napoleon in offering to broker an armistice. (If Mason had paid any attention to recent debates in Parliament, he would have realized that the idea of an Anglo-French alliance on practically any issue was preposterous.) He tried not to be disappointed by the interview but it seemed hardly worth the seven-week wait. Afterwards, James Spence made a valiant attempt to find something positive, telling Mason that Palmerston 'could not but be influenced in his own mind by the remarks you would make to him' and was sure to pay greater attention than 'that piece of small human pipe clay, Lord Russell'.[10]

Palmerston was no less opaque when the Revd Tremlett and James Spence arrived the following day with the delegation from the Society for Promoting the Cessation of Hostilities in America. Tremlett had collected an impressive group that included six MPs and the president of the Royal College of Surgeons. Palmerston listened politely but quipped, 'Those who in quarrels interpose, Will often wipe a bloody nose,' and sent them on their way. The 'human pipe clay', Lord Russell, presented a more sympathetic demeanour to the factory workers who visited the Foreign Office on 18 July. Their petition described the poverty and hunger endured by those in the once-profitable cotton trade, and begged Russell to 'enter into concert with other European powers, with a view to restore peace on the American continent'. But he was just as vague as Palmerston over when international mediation might be appropriate. The signals were clear to those who knew how to read them. The managing editor of *The Times*, Mowbray Morris, wrote to Lawley that afternoon: 'This Government will not be moved from its policy of non-intervention in America, and it is not likely that its Danish experiences will give Earl Russell a taste for further meddling.'[11]

It would have been sensible for Lindsay to retreat at this moment. The orchestrated displays of public feeling had failed to create the momentum needed to push the government behind his resolution. There were only a few days left of the parliamentary session and the House was already half deserted. But the dogged MP would not give up, knowing that if he withdrew his resolution now, there would not be another opportunity to debate intervention for several months. While Lindsay pondered how best to use the limited means at his disposal, Rose Greenhow continued to plead with every member of the government who happened to come her way. She cornered Gladstone at a dinner given by Lord Granville on 21 July and reminded him that less than two years before he had declared the Confederacy a nation. 'Your sympathies have been with us of the South, but your Government have aided the Yankees,' she scolded. 'Your neutrality is a farce.' Gladstone parried her accusations with a mixture of humour and obfuscation. Recognition, he told her, would not help the South and would only make the North angry.

Rose tried again on 24 July when Lady Chesterfield brought her to Lady Palmerston's final party of the season and introduced her to the Prime Minister. Rose was annoyed that he used the same arguments as Gladstone. 'Talked a good deal with him,' she wrote in her diary. 'He asked me how I got over. I said, "Run the blockade."' The next afternoon, Lindsay finally raised the subject in the House of Commons, though he was now certain of the answer. He did not bother trying for a resolution, but simply asked Palmerston the same question put by Mason during his private interview eleven days earlier: whether the government had any intention of 'acting in concert with the other powers of Europe ... to bring about a suspension of hostilities'. The curt response he received was the same: there was 'no advantage to be gained' by doing so, even though 'Her Majesty's Government deeply lament the great sacrifice of life and property in America and the distress which that war has produced in this country'.[12]

'Thus has terminated an operation which has cost much labor and money to somebody or other,' was Charles Francis Adams's sarcastic epitaph.[13] He had paid little attention to the Confederates after Palmerston's successful repulse of the Tory attack, being more concerned with the worsening asthma of his daughter Mary. He blamed the London fogs for undermining her health, and added the crime of bad weather to the long list of malicious and treacherous acts that Britain would one day be called upon to answer for.[14] Adams also seemed to draw comfort from his belief that the British upper classes were united in favour of slavery and injustice. He wasted much time and effort in July arguing with Lord Russell, despite all evidence to the contrary, that the rescue of the *Alabama*'s officers had been pre-arranged with the owner of the *Deerhound*. Adams was so intent on proving a conspiracy that he neglected to make capital out of the genuine scandal surrounding the *Alabama*: that Southern officers had saved each other and left the English seamen to drown. Adams also squandered an opportunity to undermine accusations of Northern arrogance and hypocrisy when, on 28 July, the Commons debated the problem of British workers being kidnapped or tricked into the Federal army. Instead of supplying Northern supporters with information on the latest efforts to stop the abuse, Adams took umbrage against the tone of the complaints and insisted it proved the intent of 'the higher classes' to destroy the Union.[15]

Rose Greenhow suffered from the same wilful blindness as Adams, though she confused sympathy for Southern suffering (her own in particular) with acceptance of Southern slavery. Few people had the nerve or desire to challenge her fantasy, though the Duchess of Sutherland snubbed Rose in the most pointed manner possible when Lady Chesterfield introduced them at the Kensington horticultural show. Rose was able to comfort herself with the observation that the Duchess's girth and 'gaudy apparel' compared badly with her own remarkably youthful appearance. She had greater trouble putting aside her embarrassment at an incident during a dinner given by Lord Granville's sister, Lady Georgiana Fullarton. An unnamed earl had pressed her relentlessly on the subject of slave families, until she lost her temper and shrilly revealed the ugly prejudices of her native country. Rose sensed the alienation of her audience and was furious. It was at moments like this that she hated the English almost as much as the North.

'My heart yearns to stay and also to go,' she wrote in her diary after the prorogation of Parliament. Her diplomatic mission appeared to have fizzled out into something resembling a goodwill tour. She had not extracted any new promise from the Emperor nor had she helped Mason and Lindsay achieve any material change in government policy. 'I thirst for news from home. The desperate struggle in which my people are engaged is ever present,' she wrote unhappily. Rose's book sales had brought her more than £2,000, money she preferred to distribute in the South rather than waste on yet another jolly but meaningless outing with her Tory friends. But Mason and Spence were disappointed when Rose announced her decision to return to the South. She countered Spence's protests by assuring him that she would not be gone for long. After all, her elder daughter, Florence, had recently joined her in England, and she could not leave little Rose (who was still uncertain about boarding-school life) for too long.*

Rose would be joining an exodus of Southerners. Captain Semmes was also making arrangements to go home, though he knew that prison and possibly execution were likely if he was caught by the Federals. He was more than a little in love with Louisa Tremlett, the Revd Tremlett's sister, and, unwilling to leave just at the moment, had accepted the Tremletts' invitation to accompany them on a walking tour of Europe. Other survivors of the *Alabama* had already left, as had Lieutenant James Morgan of the ill-fated *Georgia*. Rose braved the Channel crossing one more time in order to say farewell to her daughter. They went shopping and Rose bought her a watch, 'which made her very happy'. It was one of the few times the child smiled. 'My little darling very miserable

---

* Rose was not alone in feeling guilty about her comfortable life in Britain. When Matthew Fontaine Maury read that the birthday present of his youngest child was to be allowed to eat until full, he confessed to the Revd Tremlett how he 'felt as if I must choke with the sumptuous viands set before me on the Duke [of Buckingham]'s table'.[16]

that I am going away,' wrote Rose on 28 July. Two days later, she took little Rose back to the convent 'and left her sobbing bitterly. It was a heavy trial . . . my heart is very sad.'

Rose was, as usual, desperately seasick during the Channel crossing: 'I got a bench on deck, and seated my maid and lay with my head on her lap.' She arrived back at 34 Sackville Street on 1 August to find London almost empty. 'The season [is] over . . . Houses shut up. Streets blocked with baggage,' she wrote with a tinge of regret. Georgiana Walker, the Confederate exile in Bermuda, had recently arrived with her children and was staying in lodgings on the floor below (she had come to England to consult an ophthalmologist about her younger daughter's failing eyesight). The glamour surrounding Rose as she made her final farewells put Georgiana in awe of her: 'The Lords and Ladies and Duchesses are her constant visitors,' she wrote in her diary, 'and her invitations to dinner parties and balls innumerable.'[17] James Mason was also leaving town: 'I propose for the next two or three months to visit different points in England and in Ireland, not to return to London unless specially called,' he informed Benjamin on 4 August.[18]

Charles Francis Adams was about to go on holiday as well, albeit with reluctance. He liked London when it was empty: 'to me it is usually a period of the most pleasant relief and satisfaction,' he wrote in his diary. 'Were my family contented I would cheerfully remain, at least during the warm weather.'[19] But the family were most definitely not: 'Mary and I are plotting to make sure that this be our last season,' Henry wrote to Charles Francis Jr. 'All this however is as yet unknown to the family, and much depends on Loo.' Loo was Henry's married sister, Louise Kuhn, who came with her husband Charles in July for an extended visit.[20] Ironically, Henry did not need his sister's help to persuade their father. Adams was longing for a 'release from a continuance at this post before another season'.[21]

Now that the era of perpetual crisis had passed, both Charles Francis Adams and Henry were restless. They were becoming bored, too, with many of their friends, but lacked the confidence to make further inroads among 'the fashionable'. Neither felt that English society had learned to treat the Adams family with the proper respect. Rose Greenhow, at least, knew how to treat the Adams *amour-propre*. Fearlessly, she visited the legation on 11 July, shortly before her departure for the South, to procure a parole for Lieutenant Wilson, one of the *Alabama*'s officers, who needed medical attention. Adams was unable to resist her flattery and handed to her one of the few victories during her time in England.

Rose spent her final evening in London with her elder daughter Florence. 'Until the last minute she had hoped that I would not go,' she wrote in her diary. 'But alas, inexorable destiny seems to impel me on.' Mason accompanied Rose to Glasgow, where the blockade-runner the *Condor* – the newest addition to the blockade-running fleet of Alexander Collie, an English shipbuilder – was preparing to leave on 10 August. The commander was Captain William N. W. Hewett, the same captain who had taken Mason and Slidell to England after the conclusion of the *Trent* affair. He was using the alias Samuel S. Ridge. 'I like his looks and am quite sure he will not lose his vessel if courage and coolness will save it,' decided Rose. Only when she was completely alone on board the vessel did the enormity of her decision begin to weigh upon her. 'A sad, sick feeling crept over me of parting, perhaps forever, from many very dear to me,' she wrote. 'A few months before I had landed as a stranger; I will not say in a foreign land, for it was the land of my ancestors ... But I was literally a stranger in the land of my fathers and a feeling of cold isolation was upon me.'

Henry Hotze had also decided to leave England for a short while, in order to expand his operations into Europe. He had pulled off a great triumph in France by cultivating Auguste Havas, the proprietor of the Havas Agency, the sole telegraphic and foreign news service in the country. 'All translations from papers in other languages ... are made for the whole French press [by] ... Havas,' Hotze explained to Benjamin. Its monopoly on foreign news was complete and unassailable: 'whatever is not contained in the "Blue Sheet" of Havas can only by the merest accident reach the columns of a French paper, and, on the other hand, whatever is there contained can scarcely escape the notice of every editor in the Empire. Here, then, is the true focus of centralization.'[22]

Hotze's journal the *Index* was paying for itself. Circulation was increasing, as were revenues, and Hotze no longer had to write the majority of articles himself. The Southern poet John R. Thompson had agreed to come over from Richmond to help him, and Hotze had prevailed on John Witt, a nephew of the scientific racialist George Witt, to become the magazine's new editor. A more ardent believer in the Confederate cause could not have been found; better still in Hotze's opinion, Witt – who was the same age as Henry Adams – was placing his considerable talents at the *Index*'s disposal for the meagre sum of £300 per annum.

'My work being thus, both in England and France, reduced within manageable dimensions,' Hotze told Benjamin. 'I feel able ... to devote some efforts to a field hitherto entirely neglected.' Hotze's aim was to spread uncertainty in the European financial markets regarding the North's ability to pay its bonds. He had also heard that Poles were being recruited in Germany to fight for the Federal army. This, he thought, he could deal with quite easily by sending across John Witt to entrap a recruiter. Hotze had already dispatched the amenable Witt to Ireland on a mission to expose the activities of Federal recruiters there. 'One conviction for violation of the Foreign Enlistment Act would make considerable noise,' he explained to Witt. 'Engage the services of a first rate detective ... find some intelligent, non-commissioned officer ... who could play the part of a decoy duck at the proper time.'[23]

Although British subjects were more likely to be forced into the Confederate than the Federal army, the South's isolation from Europe meant that such reports rarely reached the outside world. As far as the British public was aware, the kidnaps, beatings and torture of immigrants were all a Northern phenomenon. The Manchester Southern Independence Association had made the advertising of such stories its chief project for the summer. For once, *Punch* showed common sense by remarking, 'We imagine that the number is really rather small, but it is well that emigrants should be warned.'[24]

The perception that crimping was rampant in the North lent veracity to Robert Livingstone's explanation to his father of how he became a Federal soldier. 'I went to Cape Town where your agent Mr Rutherford advised me to find employment on board a brig which brought me to Boston,' Robert wrote from his hospital bed. 'Here I was kidnapped and one morning ... I found myself enlisted in the US army.' He passed over his alias of 'Rupert Vincent' by claiming, 'I have changed my name, for I am convinced that to bear your name here would lead to further dishonour to it.' Robert swore to his father that he was an unwilling combatant and a penitent son.[25] Dr Livingstone tried to suppress his doubts and accept the letter at face value. 'Our Robert is in the Federal Army ... he was kidnapped he says,' he told a friend.[26]

Livingstone joined the queue of anxious relatives making enquiries at the legation. 'We get daily applications as to the fate of persons in our

SOMETHING FOR PADDY.

O'CONNELL'S STATUE (log). "IT'S A *REPALER* YE CALL YOURSELF, YE SPALPEEN, AND YOU 'RE GOIN' TO
DIE FOR THE *UNION*."

Punch's caricature Irishman is lured to fight for the Union (*left*), while the
Church (*right*) urges him to stay

army, and I have a great deal to do to answer them,' Benjamin Moran
recorded in his diary. 'It is curious how variable is the nature of the
enquiries addressed here. At one time the letters all run on employment
in the army – at another on free emigration – and now on the fate of
relatives in our service.'[27] The other change Moran noticed was much
more disturbing to him: for no apparent reason that he could discern,
the public had gone wild over a petition addressed to the US government asking for the bloodshed to end. London had been placarded with
advertisements for the so-called 'Peace Address': 'not only are the walls
covered with big posters inviting people to sign,' he wrote, 'but men are
sent around from house to house in lanes and allies [*sic*] for signatures.

The address is a most insulting one to the loyal American people, and is being extensively subscribed by children and fools. Shop girls and servants are inveigled into placing their names to it.'[28] The US Consuls reported similar scenes in their districts, commenting in wonder on 12 August, 'The country between the Rappa hannock and the Potomac has become as familiar to the English public as the space between St Paul's and South Kensington.' In Ireland, priests were reading the petition during the Sunday sermon and urging parishioners to sign. The 'Peace Address' was in the form of a letter claiming brotherhood with the American people. The alleged author was Thomas Bentley Kershaw, a Manchester cotton factory foreman. Thomas Dudley ordered his agents to uncover the identity of his financial backers. Consul Eastman in Bristol thought Kershaw was the front man for an international conspiracy directed at wavering voters in the North. He commented to Seward on 24 August, 'You will observe that under all these rumours of peace, there lies coiled the insidious project of Southern independence.'[29]

Charles Francis Adams told Seward that the real instigators of the Peace Address had to be 'the rebel emissaries themselves', never imagining that the Confederate lobby was furious with Kershaw for diverting the public's energy into a scheme that had no chance of achieving its goal. Spence had tried everything short of sabotage to discourage him.[30] 'Mr K. is a man of much energy and some ability but little judgment – very little,' he wrote angrily, his antipathy towards Kershaw all the greater because of the latter's lower-middle-class origins.[31] William Schaw Lindsay would never have allowed the peace petition to continue but a stroke in August had disabled him and his recovery was uncertain. The loss of Lindsay as a friend and guide made Mason even more reluctant to concern himself with British affairs. Rather than interrupt his pleasant idyll in the country, he left the matter to Henry Hotze's discretion.

Hotze had initially refused to give Kershaw any assistance in collecting signatures. The master propagandist knew that a peace petition from England would incite Northern Anglophobia without adding a single vote to the Democrats.[32] He was cross with Matthew Fontaine Maury, who was the sole Confederate to encourage Kershaw, and thought it typical of him to take the opposite line from his fellow exiles. It was Maury's nature to believe that no one in power was listening to him or taking his work seriously. Maury was so proud of the peace petition that he sent several copies to his cousin Rutson Maury in New

York, declaring: 'Counting all who are represented by the societies, firms, etc. that have already signed; the signatures obtained in England represent several millions of her Majesty's subjects.'[33] Hotze would have been very angry had he known about the copies. He was running his own peace campaign, writing letters and articles under various aliases for newspapers throughout the North. Kershaw's only usefulness to the Southern cause was in his keeping the issue alive among the 'shop girls and servants'. But even then, there were cheaper ways of attracting public sympathy than the £150 it cost to distribute the petition.*[34]

Hotze was one of the first people to see Belle Boyd when she arrived from Quebec in early August. Though she had destroyed her dispatches when the *Greyhound* was captured by the Federals, Belle still possessed Benjamin's letter commending her to Hotze's protection. It was only natural that she would seek him out now that she was friendless and penniless. In a surprising twist, Hotze was himself holding a letter for Belle. 'Upon opening it, I found that it was from Mr Hardinge, informing me that he had come to England,' wrote Belle in her memoir, 'but not being able to learn my whereabouts, had proceeded to Paris, in the faint hope of finding me there. I was deeply touched at this new proof of his honest attachment, and immediately telegraphed a message to him, stating where he would find me in London.'[35]

Belle and Acting Ensign Samuel Hardinge had spent a total of three weeks in each other's company. They might have married without Hotze's encouragement, but the propagandist worked so swiftly that neither was allowed the opportunity to have second thoughts. Hotze arranged the entire wedding. He booked the church, invited the guests and, most important of all, tweaked the interest of the press by portraying the young lovers as a modern day Romeo and Juliet. The nuptials took place at St James's, Piccadilly, on 24 August 1864. The main newspapers, including several in France, carried gushing accounts of the day, complete with a lengthy history of the brave and beautiful bride and her stalwart groom. Belle was inundated with wedding presents, which was fortunate, since the couple were beginning married life with nothing except the public's goodwill.

Benjamin Moran noted the Confederate wedding in his diary: 'It

---

* When Kershaw eventually arrived in Washington with his petition in October, he was told that the US government did not accept foreign petitions from non-accredited individuals. After waiting for a few days, he gave up and returned home.

seems the rebel strumpet Belle Boyd was married at St James' Church, Piccadilly, to-day to some poor idiot. He is said to be a deserter from our Navy by the name of Hardinge.'³⁶ Moran was alone at the legation; the Secretary, Charles Wilson, had left for Chicago on 17 August, having decided that an honest day's work could not be half as trying as another hour spent in Moran's company. Naturally, Moran was frightened that Henry Adams was angling for the vacant post, unaware that Henry had not only refused it but insisted to Seward that Moran was the only suitable candidate.

The Adams family returned to London on 3 September, still anxious about Mary's health.* London would not begin to revive until the autumn and, until then, offered few distractions for the family. The most exciting part of the day was the arrival of the post, though the news from America made them despair. 'Of course, if things were going well at home, we could resign ourselves even to London in September,' admitted Henry to a friend. 'But all our correspondents except [his brother Charles Francis] are in the depths of despondency, and announce discomfiture at the elections.'³⁷ The North was suffering from war malaise, Charles Francis Adams wrote in his diary. 'All accounts agree in saying that the President is deserted and his re-election in great danger.'³⁸

On 11 September rumours reached London that Sherman had captured Atlanta. The effect on the legation was electric, even though they had to wait a full week before receiving confirmation of the news. The reports were 'doubted by The Times and disbelieved in the City', Henry told his brother Charles. For the past month the press had been castigating Lincoln for his refusal to concede defeat. Even William Howard Russell had written in the Army and Navy Gazette: 'The Northerners have, indeed, lost the day solely owing to the want of average ability in their leaders in the field.'³⁹ The Confederates and their supporters tried to play down the strategic importance of Atlanta. Slidell assured the Emperor, during a chance conversation at the races, that Sherman's latest advance would be a pyrrhic victory for his overstretched and under-supplied forces. The Emperor 'expressed his admiration and

---

* The holiday had been a trial: Henry did not mind his brother-in-law, Charles Kuhn, but his sister Loo had turned into a peevish invalid. Rather like Alice James, the intelligent, thwarted sister of Henry and William James, Loo was too wealthy to have an occupation and too clever to be happy without a purpose other than herself. 'She is evidently much bored by our life,' Henry commented drily to Charles Francis Adams Jr.

astonishment at what we had achieved', the Commissioner reported to Benjamin. But, he added: 'A year ago I should have attached some important political signification to this incident.'[40]

The price of Confederate bonds dipped, but did not collapse, however, and James Spence was relieved to see that donations to the Confederate charity bazaar he was planning to hold in Liverpool were not affected. The 'Peace Address' continued to attract thousands of signatures, despite a strong counter-appeal by the Union and Emancipation Society. But Hotze knew that Atlanta's fall would boost the chances of Lincoln winning a second term, and hastened his departure to Germany: 'It is from Germany that the enemy must next spring recruit another army,' he wrote. 'It is upon Germany that he relies for the gold to carry on the war.'[41]

Georgiana Walker and her family also left England. Her husband, Norman, had arrived at the end of August, driven from Bermuda by an outbreak of yellow fever. The Confederates agreed that he should make Halifax, Nova Scotia, his new base for supplying the South until it was safe to return to the Caribbean. On 30 September the family set sail for Canada on the *Europa*. The chief drawback to the vessel, wrote Georgiana, was the number of 'Yankee' passengers. 'But I must admit that they behaved themselves as well as Yankees can behave and exhibited that respect for us, which all Yankees feel for Southerners.'[42] She was expecting to be miserable in Halifax, until she remembered that Rose Greenhow might still be there, waiting for a blockade-runner to take her to Wilmington. The thought of being with her friend gave Georgiana hope that everything would turn out well.

33

'Come Retribution'

Burley and Beall are reunited – Lord Lyons meets Feo – Shipwreck – Charleston under siege – Northern ambivalence – The enemy in ashes

Lord Lyons arrived in Montreal on 15 September 1864 with his two favourite attachés, George Sheffield and Edward Malet. Simply being away from the unhealthy climate of Washington was enough to restore Malet's health: 'A change of air is all I wanted,' he informed his mother, 'and I now feel as if I had never been ill.'[1] But Lyons, he noticed, remained weighed down by his fear that many tedious discussions awaited him in Quebec about Federal crimping and Confederate plots.

The Governor General of Canada, Viscount Monck, was in many ways as isolated as Lord Lyons. Though he was blessed with a genial manner and patrician ease at social gatherings, his determination to avoid showing favouritism towards any party forced him to maintain a degree of aloofness from the Canadians, who could sense that he looked askance at their internal quarrels. Monck thought his Ministers were among the most small-minded men he had ever encountered. None of them, he wrote in a confidential letter to London, 'is capable of rising above the level of a parish politician'.[2] It had been clear to him since his arrival three years earlier that the endemic suspicion and jealousy between Canada's provinces had been disastrous for the country's development. To survive and flourish, Monck believed, these separate provinces had to be persuaded that their future prosperity depended upon confederation; and he had thrown himself into the project with energetic zeal.* He hoped that at the very least political unity would strengthen Canada's relations with the United States, and possibly even make the colonists more willing to pay for their own defence – an object dear to London.

Lord Monck had been concerned about Southern violations of British neutrality ever since the Confederate agents had appeared in the spring, petitioning – without success – to have five additional ships sent to patrol the Great Lakes. Personally, he was pro-Northern rather than neutral (or even pro-Southern like many Canadians), and was doing his best to discourage the Confederacy from sending its agents to Canada. In November 1863 he had foiled a Southern plot to attack the Federal prison camp on Johnson's Island in Lake Erie off Sandusky, Ohio, successfully dampening the Confederates' interest in launching raids from Canada against the North until now.[3]

During the summer Commissioner Jacob Thompson had revived the plan to liberate the prisoners on Johnson's Island. The days when almost any force could have taken the island were long past, but the prison was still an enticing prospect for the Confederates because its position in Sandusky Bay was close to the Canadian border. Sandusky itself was a minor little town; Charles Dickens had paid a fleeting visit in 1842 and thought the place bleak and the population 'morose, sullen, clownish and repulsive'.[4] But to the fugitive slaves who escaped captivity via the 'underground railroad' to Canada, Sandusky represented their last stop before freedom. The US authorities had chosen Johnson's Island for the opposite reason; without a boat, it was the last stop to nowhere.

The island's prison was badly built and poorly maintained: the latrines lacked drainage and the barracks had no running water. But the suffering of the 2,500 Confederate prisoners had only really begun in the spring, when the War Department decreed that conditions should mirror those of Southern prisons; food parcels were confiscated and prisoners were forbidden to supplement their rations except by capturing rats (which

---

* The 4th Viscount Monck exceeded all expectations when he took up the governorship. He had only accepted the post because his Irish estates were so encumbered with debt that it was either Canada or bankruptcy. He had never displayed the least talent for politics or administration before; yet Palmerston had seen something in Monck that he liked and his perspicacity was rewarded. Monck was a diligent, discreet and scrupulously honest public servant who led the way to the British North American provinces becoming the Canadian Confederation in 1867.

were, however, plentiful). The inmates were weak and diseased. Yet these were the men Jacob Thompson intended to use to bring terror to the United States' northern border.

The iron-hulled gunboat USS *Michigan* had been patrolling Sandusky Bay since Monck's exposure of the first Confederate plot against Johnson's Island. Before then, it had been employed to make draft protesters in Detroit think twice before they rioted.[5] The warship had never fired its guns and was too unseaworthy for deployment in a battle, but since she was the only naval vessel on Lake Erie, whoever sailed her controlled the lake. In mid-July Thompson believed he had found the right man to capture the vessel.

Twenty-seven-year-old Charles H. Cole was a mystery to everyone who knew him. He lied about his war record, hiding the fact that he had been cashiered from the Confederate army in 1863 for dishonesty.[6] He had never held a leadership role, and yet in July he managed to dupe Thompson into giving him $4,000 to investigate the various possibilities for seizing the *Michigan*.[7] Cole used the money to entertain his girlfriend to a luxurious holiday tour around the Great Lakes before finally settling down to business on 11 August and booking a room for 'Mr and Mrs Cole' in one of Sandusky's better hotels. The West House overlooked Sandusky Bay, offering its clientele an unobstructed view of Johnson's Island and the USS *Michigan*, which was usually anchored near by. Cole's reports to Thompson were sufficiently optimistic to elicit the order that he should spend whatever it took to bribe the officers or purchase the *Michigan* outright. 'He thinks everything looks favourable and is sanguine of success,' Thompson told Clement Clay on 13 August 1864. Cole opened an account in one of the local banks, letting it be known that he represented an oil company from Pennsylvania, and began distributing his largesse among the *Michigan*'s officers. None responded to his cautious overtures. Even the captain, John C. Carter, who resented sailing around an empty lake while his peers were off chasing Confederate raiders, was beyond reach.

Cole wrote to Thompson in August, telling him that he was ready to lead a team of Confederates to capture the vessel. The claim may have been nothing more than a manoeuvre to gain more time and funds. If so, he was caught out when Thompson not only ordered him to proceed but also sent him one of his best volunteers, John Yates Beall, late of Chesapeake Bay.[8] Cole realized once he met Beall that his comfortable little set-up was at an

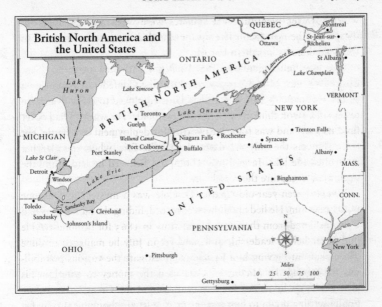

end. Beall had crossed into Canada hoping to start his own privateering operations on the Great Lakes, but dropped the idea after hearing about the Johnson's Island plan from Thompson. 'I immediately volunteered,' wrote Beall, 'and went to Sandusky, Ohio, to meet Captain Cole, the leader. We arranged our plans, and separated. Cole stayed at Sandusky. I came to Windsor to collect men, and carry them to the given point.'[9]

Beall remained in Windsor until the beginning of September, carefully working out the details of the plan with Thompson. He was overjoyed when Bennet G. Burley arrived after a difficult journey through the North. Burley's British nationality meant he could purchase the equipment and weapons required without inviting suspicion, and Cole's role was gradually reduced until his sole contribution was to arrange an evening of diversions for the *Michigan*'s crew.[10] Some were to be entertained on shore, the rest plied with drink on the vessel. While Cole was intoxicating the crew, Beall and his team were to capture the local Sandusky ferryboat called the *Philo Parsons* and, on Cole's signal, to sail alongside the *Michigan* and climb aboard. Then, with the element of surprise on their side, they would fire on the garrison guarding Johnson's Island, blow open the walls and release the prisoners.

On 17 September, two days before the date appointed for the raid, one of Beall's volunteers betrayed the group to the Provost Marshal of Detroit. Captain Carter of the *Michigan* was initially sceptical of the report, until he remembered that Cole had arranged a party for the *Michigan*'s crew at an inn on the outskirts of Sandusky. On the morning of the 19th, Carter sent to the West House hotel a trusted officer, who lured Cole onto the *Michigan* on the pretext of asking permission for the entire crew to attend the party. As soon as he was on the vessel, Cole was arrested and searched for papers. The documents Cole was carrying were not particularly revealing, but that did not stop him from confessing everything to Captain Carter. He also admitted that he had intended to abscond with Thompson's money before carrying out the final part of the plan to rescue the prisoners.[11]

In the meantime Beall and Burley had boarded the *Philo Parsons*, fully confident Johnson's Island would be theirs by midnight. Burley persuaded the ferry captain to make an unscheduled stop at Sandwich, on the Canadian side of the river, to pick up three friends, one of whom he said was disabled; the ship's clerk noticed that the disabled man was miraculously cured as soon as the vessel started moving again. At the next stop, another sixteen men climbed aboard, bringing a large wooden trunk with them. The *Philo Parsons* continued chugging quietly along its scheduled route until 4 p.m., when the trunk was opened and Burley handed out two dozen revolvers and hatchets. Within half an hour all the passengers and crew were locked in the cabin. No one had been hurt, although a few shots had been fired.

Beall and Burley congratulated themselves on a superbly run operation. All that they had to do was drop off the prisoners on one of the deserted islands in the lake and wait for Cole's signal to attack the *Michigan*. By 6 p.m., however, the plan was falling apart. Beall discovered from the engineer that there was no more wood, since it was company policy to take on only enough fuel for the scheduled trip. The raiders had no choice but to sail to the nearest fuelling station, on Middle Bass Island. While they were loading the wood another ferry, the *Island Queen*, docked beside the *Philo Parsons*. Seeing the puzzled look on its captain's face, Beall ordered his men to seize the steamer. The fight proved much more difficult than they expected; among the passengers were twenty-six Federal soldiers on an illicit jaunt. Vicious hand-to-hand fighting ensued between the soldiers and Confederates and the *Island Queen*'s engineer was shot in the face. It was thirty minutes before the last man surrendered.

Beall, with his strong sense of chivalry, refused to allow the passengers to be molested. One turned out to be carrying $80,000 in his baggage, which he offered to share with Beall in exchange for his life. The Confederate haughtily explained that he was conducting a rescue mission, not a robbery, and all property was safe except for the ships themselves and their day's takings, which were legitimate prizes. As soon as there was sufficient wood on board to restart the engines, Beall ordered the passengers off the boat, first exacting a promise from each one to keep silent for the next twenty-four hours.

It was 9 p.m. when the Confederates finally sailed within sight of the *Michigan*. She had changed position since the morning and was facing the prison; ominously, her gun ports were open and steam was rising from her funnel. The raiders waited for Cole's signal. Burley's anecdotes of previous raids failed to impress the worried men, and after an hour they began to argue that they should turn back. None of them knew Beall or Burley well enough to risk their lives in what increasingly appeared to be a compromised mission. Beall pleaded and threatened without success. The ringleader of the mutineers explained they had nothing against him – they even admired him – but they were not prepared to die for him. When Beall asked if they were willing to put their opposition down in writing, they not only agreed but all seventeen signed their names. The statement declared the mission to be hopeless: 'We ... take pleasure in expressing our admiration of the gentlemanly bearing, and courage of Captain Y. Bell [*sic*] ... but ... we cannot by any possibility make it a success, and having already captured two boats, we respectfully decline to prosecute it any further.'[12]

Beall and Burley had little choice but to abort the mission. When the sun rose on Tuesday, 20 September 1864, the *Philo Parsons* lay partially submerged a few miles from Windsor. The Confederates had stripped her of everything valuable, including three mirrors and the piano from the saloon. Beall was already on his way to the northern wilds of Ontario; Burley went east to hide out with friends in Guelph, near Toronto.

The legation in Washington informed Lord Monck of Beall's raid by coded telegram. Anxious to forestall Northern accusations of connivance or indifference, he ordered the Canadian Rifles stationed at Windsor to provide all possible assistance to the US authorities. Lord Lyons had only been at Spencer Wood, the Governor's official residence in Quebec, for two days and the news from Lake Erie so depressed him that he retired to bed with a crushing headache. The unwelcome discovery that there was a large number of house guests also staying had already put him in a delicate state. He did not reappear for twenty-four hours.

Lyons roused himself for an excursion to Chaudière Falls but he remained apart from the group and left them wondering when he failed to appear at the picnic lunch. Their suspicion that he was avoiding them was close to the mark. He would have stayed away from dinner, too, if he could have done so without offence. Just before the gong, there was a savage encounter between a house cat and a lapdog belonging to one of the guests. 'With difficulty the animals were quieted, and we went in to dinner,' recorded Lord Monck's sister-in-law, Frances Monck, whose husband, Colonel the Hon. Richard Monck, was the Governor General's brother and military secretary. 'Lord L.'s amusement was great; he went on all the evening alluding to the battle.'[13]

Feo Monck, as she was always known, was a force of nature, though a gentle one, who was perpetually missing trains, losing hats and spilling anything hot and full to the brim. She was intelligent, too, though it could be difficult to tell behind the endless little dramas that punctuated her day. Feo and Lyons soon discovered that they shared the same dislike of hot weather, cold weather, exercise and boats, and thereafter, as his attachés observed, he was a changed man. Sheffield and Malet had always assumed that Lord Lyons disliked women; but around Feo he revealed a hitherto unknown repertoire of after-dinner songs and became a tireless raconteur of hilarious anecdotes from the annals of diplomatic history. The more Feo laughed at his puckish comments the wittier he became. 'If you could hear Lord L.'s odd, grave, inquiring way of saying these things you would laugh as much as I am now laughing,' she wrote in her letter-journal after they had spent a week exploring the majestic rivers of Quebec.

By the time the house party visited Shawinigan Falls, the second highest waterfall in Canada after Niagara, Lyons had thrown off the last traces of reserve, removing his boots and stockings and splashing about the shallow rocks like a child. 'Lord L. has travelled much, but he says he never saw a more exquisite view than that day,' recorded Feo. 'When we had feasted our eyes on the Falls, and picked leaves, we went to our grand lunch laid on a table made with boards by the servants and boat-men. The sun was burning hot and the day perfection.' During the long journey home 'we talked and sang, and Lord L. repeated poetry'.[14]

Lyons could not be so free when they visited Montreal and Niagara Falls. 'We are to go to the Cataract House at Niagara on the American side,' wrote Feo, 'as the Confederate people are met at the Clifton House [on the Canadian side], and Lord L. does not wish to seem to watch them.'[15] For once, Lyons's caution made things worse; it would have been better if he had made a great show of watching them, and sent a clear message to Jacob Thompson and his cohorts that their illegal operations in Canada would not be tolerated. But he was struggling both physically and mentally; only Feo Monck and the attachés knew how much he dreaded his return to Washington. During one of their final excursions, he persuaded her to hide with him instead of meeting a deputation of local worthies who had gathered to greet their boat. 'He gave me his arm,' wrote Feo, 'and we ran off out of the ship, and got into a cab with-out waiting for any of them,' leaving the Mayor standing disconsolately on the wharf. As the date of his departure on 12 October drew near, he became increasingly reckless and led Feo into all sorts of scrapes. On an outing to Lake Ontario they climbed up a steep ledge overlooking the lake, ignoring the prominent danger sign, and 'we stood there', recalled Feo, 'clinging to the railing till we saw a policeman coming, and were so afraid of being scolded that we jumped down and ran away!'[16]

Rose Greenhow had arrived at Halifax on 6 September 1864, and had been forced to wait for nearly three weeks, while the *Condor* re-coaled and took on supplies before she could begin the final part of her journey to Wilmington, North Carolina. Two more passengers were joining her: the Lieutenant Wilson whose parole she had obtained from Charles Francis Adams, and the Confederate Commissioner James Holcombe, who had decided that he did not wish to participate in Thompson's or Clay's operations. The long delay until the *Condor*'s departure on 24 September was enough time for the US Consul in Halifax to learn the names of the passengers and the ship's destination. As soon as the vessel steamed out of the harbour, he sent a telegram to Washington warning the Navy Department to ready the fleet at Wilmington. When the *Condor* reached Cape Fear in the small hours of 1 October, every available blockader was waiting.

A storm was brewing as the vessel approached the Carolina coast. The roiling sea favoured the *Condor*, and Captain Hewett was able to slip past the first line of blockaders. But as they approached New Inlet – the closer of the two entrances to Cape Fear river – Hewett saw that the sheer number of blockaders crowding around the entrance would make it impossible for him to escape detection. The USS *Niphon* was the first to spot the *Condor* and at 3.30 a.m. the chase began. The *Niphon* ploughed through the waves, firing her guns in a steady roll. The *Condor*'s passengers cowered beneath the deck, listening to the explosions above their heads. Suddenly, the ship lurched hard to starboard and crashed to a stop. The pilot had mistaken the wreck of the *Night Hawk*, which had been chased down the previous night, for a Federal ship and turned hard to avoid it, hitting a sandbank in the process.

The *Condor* was close enough to Fort Fisher for its guns to afford her some protection against the *Niphon*. Captain Hewett thought he might still be able to make the final dash in a few hours, once the tide had lifted his ship off the bar, but he could not guarantee that it would hold against the pounding of the waves, or that the rest of the fleet would not join the *Niphon*. Rose Greenhow and James Holcombe both became hysterical. She was carrying dispatches from Mason and Hotze for Richmond, as well as £2,000 in gold, the entire profits from her book, and was rapidly becoming panic-stricken at the thought of being a Federal prisoner again.[17] Since the shore was only a few hundred yards away, she begged Captain Hewett to let down a rowing boat. Holcombe added his pleas. At first Hewett refused but when two sailors volunteered to row he relented.

Rose, Holcombe, Wilson and the *Condor*'s pilot clambered with great difficulty into the rolling boat with the oarsmen. Rose had left everything on the ship except a copy of her book, the dispatches and the money, which was in a pouch secured by a chain. As they neared the surf a wave flipped over the boat, spilling the passengers into the water. The men were able to swim to the surface and cling to the side of the boat, but Rose never reappeared. An hour later, the tide brought the rowing boat in, allowing the battered and exhausted survivors to hobble onto the beach. Captain Hewett and his crew were rescued at dawn, although the *Condor* was left stuck in the sand.

Rose's body was found in the morning by Thomas Taylor, an English blockade-runner who had gone down to the beach to supervise the salvage operation of his own vessel.* He had her body carried to Fort Fisher, where the commandant's wife, Mrs Lamb, prepared it for transportation to Wilmington. The following day, 2 October, the city gave Rose a state funeral: church bells tolled as her flag-draped coffin led an immense cortège, headed by representatives from the Confederate War Department, the army and the navy. Mindful that she was being buried without her family present, the president of the Soldiers' Aid Society preserved Rose's hair for her daughters, 'in case we ever hear from them'.[19]

Rose Greenhow's death was a brutal reminder to Wilmington's inhabitants that the Federals were tightening their grip. Francis Lawley had become worried for its safety after his visit in mid-September. 'There is abundant cause for thinking that Wilmington is the great thorn in the flesh of the Federals at this moment,' he wrote on 24 September. 'We shall witness a desperate attack upon this place within the next seven weeks.'[20] This was also the view of General Beauregard, who was growing exasperated by the lack of defensive preparations in both Wilmington and Charleston, and had written to Captain Henry Feilden, urging him to try his utmost to shake 'the authorities of Charleston' out of their complacency.[21]

Beauregard's letter had been waiting for Feilden when he returned to Charleston from his secondment to General John K. Jackson. Though his mission to bring back Confederate deserters from Florida was arduous and uncomfortable, the worst that had happened to him was the loss of a ring given to him by Julia.† She had been talking about a grand wedding after the war, but Sherman's capture of Atlanta had convinced Feilden that it would be foolish to delay any longer. Charleston's defences were holding for the moment, but seventy days of continuous shelling had left parts of the city in utter ruin – Feilden was not sure where they

---

* The vessel was the *Night Hawk,* which had confused the pilot on board the *Condor.* Thomas Taylor was the 'supercargo', the officer in charge of a ship's cargo. Though only 24, Taylor had the highest success rate of any English blockade-runner. But his luck had run out the night before the *Condor*'s arrival. The *Night Hawk* was chased onto a sandbar and boarded by Federal sailors, who 'acted more like maniacs than sane men, firing their revolvers and cutting right and left with their cutlasses', recalled Taylor. After beating up the crew, they set fire to the ship and left, not caring whether the blockade-runners burned or drowned. Taylor had wanted to fight the flames but his men dragged him onto the rowing boat, 'though the boiling surf seemed more dangerous to my mind than remaining on the burning ship'.[18]

† Feilden promised the family he had stayed with in Florida that he would send them a reward if they ever found the ring. Two years after the end of the war, he received a small package with the ring inside. He kept his promise and sent all the money he could afford.

would live after the wedding. (Lieutenant James Morgan of the defunct *Georgia* was dismayed when he visited Charleston during Feilden's absence and found many of the streets covered over with grasses and vines. 'I felt ashamed of my new uniform,' he wrote, after seeing the ragged state of the troops guarding Wilmington and Charleston.[22] Morgan had never imagined that conditions aboard his ship would compare favourably with those in the local barracks.)

Feilden was so accustomed to keeping up a positive front for Julia that a general vagueness was creeping into all his letters. He gave his family every pertinent detail about his fiancée except her surname, and Lady Feilden was obliged to send an engagement present of gloves and a parasol addressed simply to Miss Julia. Feilden laughingly reassured Julia that the omission had not been for want of love. His feelings for her would never alter, he promised, nor would he ever give her a moment's distress by flirting or looking at another woman. 'My wife will never be afraid of my misbehaving in that manner,' he wrote firmly.[23]

Feilden's steadfast nature was one of the qualities that endeared him to his superiors. He had never complained about the state of headquarters, even though his commanding officer, General Roswell S. Ripley, was a drunk and his staff not much better. It was nevertheless a great relief to him when Ripley was replaced at the beginning of October. 'General Beauregard has recommended that Colonel Harris be promoted to the rank of Major General, and that the defence of Charleston be handed over to him,' Feilden wrote excitedly to Julia. The change in command almost certainly guaranteed his promotion:

> Col. [D. B.] Harris told me that he had told General Beauregard that he would only accept the command under certain conditions, and one of them was that he should select his own staff, and not have Ripley's crowd palmed off on him. In that case he will apply for me as his [Assistant Adjutant] General. It will be a capital thing for me if all this happens; it will give me my promotion to a Majority and put me in a position where I shall not be ranked by every ignoramus who has got influence enough to be placed on the staff of the Department of SC., Ga., & Fla. Colonel Harris is a splendid officer and just the man I should like to serve under. Charleston, with him in command, would make a splendid fight.[24]

Feilden's belief in the South was unshaken by the recent downturn in her fortunes. 'I was intended to live in the midst of all these troubles,' he wrote, 'for I can keep up my spirits under all circumstances.' True to form, his subsequent letters were all about their wedding.[25] But the flow of letters between Charleston and Greenville ceased in early October. Yellow fever had spread to the staff headquarters and Colonel Harris was among the first to be struck with the disease. Feilden nursed him day and night for a week, but Harris was beyond help and died on 10 October. Feilden stayed up for two nights, guarding the body from the depredations of rats and dogs until Harris's family could claim it. He had lost not only a friend but also his best chance of promotion.

General Beauregard's choice to replace Harris was Lieutenant General William J. Hardee, a veteran of the Mexican–American War and the author of a drill manual read by both armies. Hardee had been looking for a new post since falling out with General Hood in Georgia and came with his own staff of trusted and experienced officers. Feilden's friends were determined to ensure that Hardee realized he was gaining an officer of exceptional quality. 'I wish particularly to commend him to your consideration as highly capable for the duties of the Adjutant General,' wrote Colonel Thomas Jordan, Beauregard's chief of staff, to General Hardee on 12 October. 'He is of English birth and education and has seen service in the British Army. At first he was on inspection duty, but I had him transferred to my office, where he became my right-hand man – and I can recommend him as a judicious, well-informed, well trained staff officer.'[26] The letter languished in Hardee's 'to consider' pile. The General was appalled by the bedraggled state of his new troops and immediately launched a campaign for supplies. The soldiers lacked blankets and coats; 'very many of my men are absolutely barefooted,' he complained to Richmond on 19 October.

Francis Lawley had seen for himself the weakened state of the Southern armies. It went against the grain with him to dwell on the Confederacy's deprivations but he could no longer ignore the truth. 'I cannot be blind to the fact, as I meet officers and privates from General Lee's army,' he wrote to Lord Wharncliffe from Richmond on 12 October, 'that they are half worn out, and that, though the spirit is the same as ever, they urgently need rest.' Their diet for the past 160 days had consisted of bread and salted meat, while the enemy had at its command 'all that lavish profusion of expenditure and the scientific experience that the whole civilized world can contribute'.[27] However, when Lawley praised 'the patience and self-denying endurance of the

Rendezvous of CS General Mosby's men above the Shenandoah Valley,
by Frank Vizetelly

troops' he was stretching an ideal already abandoned by his friends.
Earlier in the week, the chief of ordnance, General Josiah Gorgas, had
privately conceded that the soldiers' spirits were almost beyond saving:
'Our poor harrowed and overworked soldiers are getting worn out with
the campaign. They see nothing before them but certain death, and have,
I fear, fallen into a sort of hopelessness, and are dispirited. Certain it is
that they do not fight as they fought at the Wilderness and Spotsylvania.'[28]

Frank Vizetelly witnessed the battles between Jubal Early's similarly
exhausted Confederates and Sheridan's hard-driving cavalry in the
Shenandoah Valley. Early was relying on the help of John Singleton
Mosby and his Partisan Rangers to harass the Federals, and at first
Vizetelly was dazzled by Mosby, whose guerrilla raids reminded him of
the daredevil spirit of Jeb Stuart. 'His achievements are perfectly marvellous,' wrote Vizetelly after hearing how the Rangers swooped down
on a 600-car Federal wagon train in mid-August and captured the entire
contents, suffering only two casualties in the raid.[29] Mosby had been

able to outlast his former rival, Sir Percy Wyndham, but his new opponent, the English Colonel L. D. H. Currie, could not be tricked into making the sort of mistakes that had been Wyndham's undoing. Although Currie could not prevent Mosby's raids, he kept the wagon trains moving and intact. Nor were the raiders much help to Jubal Early in a real cavalry battle. Early had lost an entire brigade in a combined US cavalry and artillery attack on 24 September.* Since then, he had only been able to mount insignificant skirmishes against Sheridan, who was carrying out Grant's order to lay waste to the region. Vizetelly had covered many campaigns but none that so explicitly targeted the enemy's will to fight. The sight of emaciated women pleading with soldiers for bread to feed their children led him to accuse US troops of deliberately causing mass starvation among the civilians. Sheridan's declaration that 'the people must be left nothing but their eyes to weep with over the war' was repeated many times in the British press. This sort of 'wanton destructiveness', asserted the editor of the *Illustrated London News*, is 'unknown to modern warfare'.†30

There was nowhere safe for refugees any more: families who thought they would find sanctuary in Richmond risked losing their adolescent sons to the Confederate army. Despite President Davis's dictum against 'grinding the seed corn of the Republic', boys as young as 15 were now being rounded up and marched to the trenches. 'No wonder there are many deserters – no wonder men become indifferent as to which side shall prevail,' wrote the War Department clerk John Jones bitterly.31 Nevertheless, those who risked the journey to Richmond sometimes met with surprising generosity. 'Virginians of the real old stock', in Mary Sophia Hill's words, gave her a corner to sleep in when she arrived ill and penniless in early October. The military tribunal in New Orleans had returned a guilty verdict with the recommendation of imprisonment for the duration of the war. But her defence lawyer, a 'Union man' named

---

* During a battle on 24 September 1864 at Front Royal, an English volunteer substitute, Private Philip Baybutt (1844–1907), seized the regimental flag of the 6th Virginia Cavalry. The prize enabled him to receive the only medal of honour awarded to a British subject during the Civil War.
† Sheridan ordered his troops to hang prisoners of Mosby's Rangers rather than treat them as prisoners of war, and six were executed on 22 September 1864. Mosby retaliated and executed five Union prisoners, chosen at random, on 6 November. A week later he wrote to Sheridan, suggesting that they call a truce on the executions.

Punch's terrifying depiction of the human cost of the Civil War, September 1864

Mr Christian Roselius, had protested against the sentence and won a commutation to banishment from New Orleans. Consul Coppell also interceded on her behalf, offering to buy passage for Mary on the *Sir William Peel*, which was about to depart for England, but General Banks

refused, saying, 'she will have to run the blockade. She will have plenty of trouble; perhaps it will teach her to behave herself the rest of her days.'[32]

'He had his desire,' recalled Mary. 'I did have plenty of trouble.' Despite the insistence of the new legation Secretary, Joseph Burnley, that 'everything that could be done in this matter has been done', Mary was carried across the picket lines into Confederate territory and left by the road to fend for herself.[33] Mary never revealed how she made the 1,000-mile journey from New Orleans to Richmond without a horse or money, but the memory continued to haunt her and she was driven to seek justice after the war.

Mary had arrived in Richmond shortly after the Federals captured another of the forts guarding the approach to the capital on 29 September. The enemy, wrote John Jones on 4 October, 'is now within five miles of the city, and if his progress is not checked, he will soon be throwing shells at us ... Flour rose yesterday to $425 a barrel, meal to $72 a bushel.'[34] Mary risked her life to look for her twin brother Sam, who had been sent to the trenches with the other engineers in his office. While crossing a pontoon bridge she stood aside to allow General Lee to ride past. 'I consider it an honor,' she wrote, 'and a great one too, to have seen the General of the age, Robert E. Lee, the soldier's friend, the Christian warrior.'[35]

Lee had grown used to such hero-worship; his determination to endure the same hardships as his men was widely known, though it had not deterred Southerners, particularly women, from delivering food and gifts to his tent. But another side to Lee had become apparent of late. No man, not even the great 'Christian warrior', could withstand the relentless attrition of troops, supplies and options without showing the strain. Francis Dawson was taken to Lee's mess and subjected to a tirade of sarcastic remarks:

> It was the most uncomfortable meal that I ever had in my life [he wrote]. My frame of mind can be imagined when General Lee spoke to me in this way: 'Mr Dawson will you take some of this bacon? I fear that it is not very good, but I trust that you will excuse that. John! Give Mr Dawson some water; I pray pardon me for giving you this cup. Our table service is not as complete as it should be. May I give you some bread? I fear it is not well baked, but I hope you will not mind that.' Etc., etc., etc.; while my cheeks were red and my ears were tingling, and I wished myself anywhere else than at General Lee's headquarters.[36]

Only a month of fighting weather remained. On 7 October 1864 Lee ordered his final large-scale assault of the year, sending two divisions along Darbytown Road with orders to flush the Federals out of their new position. They started off well and overran the first line of trenches, capturing more than 300 soldiers in the process, among them the English fugitive Robert Livingstone, who had been released from hospital on 30 September and had only rejoined the 3rd New Hampshire Volunteer Infantry the day before. As Livingstone was marched away he could hear his side responding with a massive barrage of fire. The Confederates were faltering; Lee galloped towards the retreaters, waving his hat and shouting for them to make another stand. On previous occasions the very sight of him had been enough to stem a flight, but this time the men continued to run.

Grant was sufficiently encouraged by his troops' handling of the Confederate attack to order a follow-up assault on 13 October, but this time the Federals were driven back by the defenders. 'We have had a pretty brisk little fight today,' Dawson wrote to his mother that evening. 'Grant has been feeling our lines on this [north] side of the River; he made but two attacks on our ranks and each time was easily repulsed.' The setback to the Federals had an immediate effect on the Confederates' spirits. Dawson was almost giddy: 'There are croakers [pessimists] everywhere ... but you must not allow any of them to persuade you that we are, as the Yankees say, "in our last ditch."' Moreover, his commander had returned: 'I am happy to say that General Longstreet reported for duty today, his right arm and hand is still paralyzed from his wound but he could not be kept back any longer ... he is a tower of strength to our cause, and he returns at a good time.'[37]

Dawson's optimism was a testament to his ignorance of the true state of the Confederate defences. He had laughed at the sight of black regiments during the recent fighting in and around Darbytown Road, and considered their deployment proof of the North's weakness. But more experienced Confederate officers acknowledged their heroism and were asking why the South did not employ their slaves to solve the manpower shortage.* General Lee was considering the idea, although he did not say so in public.

Edward Stanley was fascinated by the North's ambivalence to Negro regiments. Even some members of the Adams family were shocked by Charles Francis Jr.'s transfer to a black regiment. 'His uncle, Mr Sidney Brooks, was I hear very disgusted that his favourite nephew would do this,'

---

* The coloured troops in the Darbytown Road engagements received fourteen of the sixteen medals of honour awarded to black soldiers during the Civil War.

wrote Stanley. 'I am glad he has done this as the more people of position take these commands, the more it tends to raise the Negro.' Stanley thought the experience would be good for Adams himself, who 'was not quite free from the American prejudice against and repugnance to Negroes'. Charles Francis Adams Jr. had not regretted his decision in the previous September to transfer to the 5th Massachusetts (Colored) Cavalry, but he shared General Sherman's doubts that black troops would ever be the equal of white. The 'nigs' were 'angelic', he told Henry Adams after the regiment had sustained nineteen casualties and three dead in fighting at Petersburg on 15 June. But 'the rugged discipline which improves whites is too much for them. It is easy to crush them into slaves, but very difficult by kindness and patience to approach them to our own standard.'[38]

Stanley had finished his tour of the North more pessimistic about the future of the freedman than when he started. Day-to-day relations between blacks and whites had the feel of an awkward jig to him. He had visited a school in Boston where a 'quadroon' pupil was made to sit by herself, as though separated from the other girls by a cordon sanitaire.* The sight convinced him that the racial integration of the US army was vital to reforming American society. He knew this would not happen overnight, but he had been encouraged by the number of white soldiers willing to join coloured regiments, especially among the foreign volunteers who wanted to become officers.

Private James Horrocks was among the whites applying to transfer to a coloured regiment. 'What do you think about it?' he asked his parents, as he weighed the army's unequal treatment of coloured regiments against the possible improvement of his prospects:

> Chances of being shot greater; accommodations and comforts generally smaller, but pay much larger than what I have now. No horse to ride but a uniform to wear. And above all – an *Officer*'s real shoulder straps and the right of being addressed and treated as a gentleman, with the advantage of better society, and if I like it, this is a position I can hold for life, being

---

* Ernest Duvergier de Hauranne, a French journalist and liberal politician, was in New York on a similar cultural voyage as Stanley. He observed: 'Between Broadway and the Hudson River there exists a filthy, rundown neighborhood inhabited by Irish immigrants and colored people exclusively. It is impossible to imagine anything more depressingly poor ... From time to time one sees with amazement a trolley car ride by which carries a sign: "Colored People Admitted." What in the world can be the meaning of this? Are there separate laws here for Negroes? No, but public prejudice persecutes them more powerfully, more tyrannically even than law.'[39]

United States troops, while Volunteers will undoubtedly be disbanded when the war is over.*[40]

Horrocks's confidence that peace could not be far away received a boost on 19 October at the Battle of Cedar Creek in the Shenandoah Valley. The Confederates under Jubal Early surprised the Federals in a dawn attack, routing two of Sheridan's corps and destroying their camps. But in the afternoon, Sheridan led a crushing counterattack, capturing hundreds of prisoners and most of Early's artillery. It was the Confederate General's third and final battle against Sheridan in the Shenandoah Valley. Every battle had been a Federal victory, and Early could not afford to risk another encounter. 'We have only pistols, sabers and old fashioned rifles,' wrote a Confederate cavalryman. 'Above all, we have not enough food to keep the horses up.'[41] Sheridan had achieved his purpose; the verdant Shenandoah Valley was now a wasteland of burned fields and ruined homesteads.

Sheridan's success in Virginia made some newspapers uneasy. 'The laying waste of the Shenandoah Valley will undoubtedly call out acts in retaliation equally terrible', predicted the *Detroit Free Press* as reports began to filter through to the North of a Southern movement to exact revenge.[42] On 15 October the *Richmond Whig* urged Davis

to burn one of the chief cities of the enemy, say Boston, Philadelphia, or Cincinnati. If we are asked how such a thing can be done, we answer, nothing would be easier. A million of dollars would lay the proudest city of the enemy in ashes. The men to execute the work are already there. There would be no difficulty in finding there, here, or in Canada, suitable persons to take charge of the enterprise and arrange its details ... New York is worth twenty Richmonds. They have a dozen towns to our one; and in their towns is centered nearly all their wealth. It would not be immoral and barbarous. It is not immoral nor barbarous to defend yourself by any means or with any weapon the enemy may employ for your destruction.

The Confederacy's mood of despair and outrage would soon be reflected in its new cipher key, which would be altered from 'Complete Victory' to the more ominous-sounding 'Come Retribution'.

---

* For example, the English volunteer Thomas Beach, who had adopted a new identity as a Frenchman named Henri Le Caron, was able to leap from being a private in the 15th Pennsylvania Cavalry to a lieutenant in the 15th US Colored Infantry.

34

'War is Cruelty'

The Confederates invade Vermont – Colonel Grenfell's mistake –
War at sea resumes – The impact of Lincoln's re-election – March
to the sea – Death in a prison camp

Instead of feeling restored by his holiday in Canada, Lord Lyons felt incapacitated by intense bleakness. Nothing inappropriate had taken place between him and Feo Monck; nor did he ever expect to see her again. But she had awakened something in him, a half-realized sense of liberty that would not be stifled and yet could not be indulged, and the prospect of Washington seemed intolerable. Lyons could no longer avoid the truth: he did not belong in America, where his quiet eccentricities were out of step with the harsher rhythms of the young Republic. The legation had been a haven for the past four years, but even this was about to be taken away from him as it was time for his staff, including Edward Malet, to be transferred to new posts. In a couple of months Lyons would have to start all over again, with a new set of faces.

Lyons's visit to New York in mid-October was uneventful until the night of the 20th, when he attended a dinner party where the guests included General John Dix, the military governor of New York State. Suddenly a messenger burst into the room and handed a telegram to the General, who read it and rushed out. He returned half an hour later to berate the astonished Lyons: twenty or so Confederate raiders had crossed the border from Canada and had attacked the Vermont town of St Albans, looting more than $200,000 from its three main banks, setting fire to the square and killing one citizen. He told Lyons that he had sent a force back across the border with orders to capture the raiders dead or alive. The news immediately conjured up in Lyons's mind the spectre of another international crisis: if the North invaded British soil and seized the Confederates, the British government would have to protest and demand an apology along with restitution of the prisoners. The United States would refuse, forcing the government into an ultimatum – probably followed by a declaration of war.

Lord Monck had foreseen the same catastrophic chain of events and ordered the Montreal police to find the Confederates before they fell into the Northerners' hands. Thirteen raiders were caught within forty-eight hours, but the US posse found their leader, Bennett Young, hiding in a farmhouse. Young – who had participated in the Chicago convention plot – might have swung from a tree were it not for the intervention of a British army officer who happened upon the scene and persuaded the furious Northerners to escort the prisoner to the local garrison. Monck telegraphed the news to Seward, assuring him that the Confederates would remain in custody while the courts examined the case for their extradition. He hoped this swift action would forestall any thoughts of Northern retaliation.

The St Albans raid had been organized by the Confederate Commissioner Clement C. Clay without the knowledge of Jacob Thompson, who was furious it had been kept from him. Thompson's own plots were nearing fruition and promised to be far more destructive and violent than mere banditry against a US border town. He feared that this further violation of British neutrality would lead to increased cooperation between the Canadian and Northern authorities, and create more obstacles for his operatives. As far as Thompson could tell, Canadians remained broadly supportive of the South and he wanted nothing to jeopardize their goodwill. Halifax was still 'intensely Southern', according to Georgiana Walker, who had arrived with her family on 11 October. (For her, Rose Greenhow's death overshadowed the actions of a few hotheads. 'My thought flew at once to the poor little orphan at the Sacré Coeur, now bereft of Father, Mother, Friends,' she wrote, 'truly [reliant] on the cold charities of the world.'[1])

General Sheridan was expanding the definition of 'total war' to include deliberate starvation and the destruction of civilian property. Jacob Thompson was taking it in another direction: that of terror and mass murder. He was far more systematic than any of the other Confederate agents working in Canada, and had the men and resources to mount large-scale campaigns.*[2] Thompson had several schemes under way in late October, including a second attempt against the USS *Michigan* by John Yates Beall and Bennet G. Burley, which involved the purchase and arming of a civilian steamer; but Thompson's chief plot was an undertaking in conjunction with the Northern Sons of Liberty to start a revolution on 8 November, Election Day.

Two more members from General John Hunt Morgan's defunct brigade had been sent by Jefferson Davis to help Thompson: Lieutenant Colonel Robert Maxwell Martin and Captain John William Headley. They had originally hoped to lead the supposed uprising talked up so persuasively in June by Vallandigham, but Copperhead enthusiasm for conspiracies had subsided once Sherman's and Sheridan's victories exposed the weakness of the Confederacy. By the beginning of November the number of cities involved in the Confederate Sons of Liberty plot had shrunk to just two: Chicago and New York. 'We were told that about 20,000 men were enlisted in New York under a complete organization,' recalled Captain John Headley. 'It was proposed by the New York managers to take possession of the city on the afternoon of Election Day and, in order to deter opposition, a number of fires were to be started in the city.' As in the Chicago plot, the prisoners at Fort Lafayette would be freed, and the city's authorities, both military and civilian, either murdered or thrown in prison.[3] The Confederates expected the rest of New York State to follow or be taken as easily as the city.

Lord Monck was throwing the meagre resources at his disposal into surveillance operations against the Confederates, but his system was grossly inferior to the Federals'. Alerted by the US Consul in Halifax, Seward was able to telegraph General Dix on 2 November: 'This department has received information from the British Provinces to the effect that there is a conspiracy on foot to set fire to the principal cities in the

---

* A completely separate operation, led by a Kentucky doctor, Luke P. Blackburn, had been inspired by the yellow fever epidemics in Bermuda. Dr Blackburn was an expert on the disease and twice in 1864 offered his services to the Bermudan authorities, once in the spring and once in the autumn. Believing, mistakenly, that yellow fever could be transmitted via the clothes of deceased victims, Blackburn nursed the dying patients and then stored their belongings in large trunks. He had them transported to Halifax, where another agent shipped them to Washington to be auctioned off to unsuspecting civilians. Blackburn's ignorance that yellow fever is spread via mosquito bites rather than human contact saved the lives of hundreds if not thousands. Blackburn's plot was exposed after the war but he escaped punishment and became Governor of Kentucky in 1879.

Northern States on the day of the Presidential election.' The warning was followed by the dispatch of General Butler and 5,000 troops, who marched into New York on 7 November. The New York Copperheads met Thompson's guerrillas that day and told them to go back to Canada, as no subversive would dare show his face while Butler was in town. But Martin and Headley would not be put off that easily and extracted from the Copperheads a new date for the uprising: Evacuation Day on 25 November, so called because it was the day the British army evacuated Manhattan during the Revolutionary War.

Although the New York plotters had postponed their plan, the Chicago conspiracy was still in play, despite the arrest of John Castleman, Captain Thomas Hines's deputy, on 2 October. Castleman's place was taken by the English volunteer Colonel Grenfell. 'We have all got to live a certain time,' Grenfell wrote to his daughter on 11 October, 'and when the end comes what difference will it make whether I lived in London or Illinois?'[4] The new plan was relying on the help of 1,200 Copperheads – a much smaller number than before – to launch a four-pronged attack on Camp Douglas. Once armed and liberated, the Confederate prisoners were supposed to break open the other prison camps in the State while the Copperheads, led by Grenfell, created a diversion throughout Chicago with fires and incendiary bombs. Hines expected to raise an army of 25,000 Confederate prisoners of war to capture Illinois.

The Commandant of Camp Douglas, Colonel Benjamin Sweet, had informants inside the prison who were keeping him abreast of the conspiracy, but he did not know the full details of the plot until a Confederate turncoat named Maurice Langhorne called at his office on 5 November and offered to go undercover for him. Langhorne had briefly served under CS General Morgan and had no difficulty reconnecting with his former comrades. Grenfell was particularly incautious and freely discussed the plot not only with Langhorne but also with a second informant, who was sent by Colonel Sweet to verify the information.

Shortly after midnight on 7 November, US troops arrested the leader of the Copperheads; another detachment went after Thomas Hines, although he managed to hide. A third went to the Richmond House hotel in search of Grenfell. A fellow conspirator had managed to get a note to him first, which read: 'Colonel – you must leave tonight. Go to Briggs House,' but Grenfell ignored the warning. The arresting officers found the note when they entered his room. He was sitting by the fire, fully dressed, though he could have run from the hotel at any time during the previous three hours.[5] Whether he was feeling ill (he was still recovering from influenza) or was simply overconfident, his inaction led him to becoming an inmate of Camp Douglas rather than its liberator. He was put in a special cell reserved for spies and irregular combatants – next to the latrines.

The legation read about the arrests on the morning of the election, but Lord Lyons himself was unaware of the failed plot. He had collapsed on 6 November. 'Two days after you left,' George Sheffield wrote to Edward Malet, 'Lord Lyons gave up the work of the legation to Burnley, and I am sorry to say, has been seriously ill.'[6]

Lord Lyons's last act of business before his collapse was to speak to Seward about the problem of Confederate operations out of Canada. Seward believed his assurances that Lord Monck was trying his best to discourage them, and as a show of good faith gave him a copy of the government's vehement protest before it was sent to Charles Francis Adams in London. Lyons was grateful, since it would allow Lord Russell sufficient time to compose his response before it was officially delivered. 'He said that it would be impossible to resist the pressure which would be put upon the government ... if these incursions from Canada continued,' Lyons reported confidentially to Lord Russell on 28 October.[7] A way had to be found to stop Thompson and his agents.

Seward's protest to Lord Russell arrived at the legation while Adams was out of London. The family had moved to Hanger Hill House, a handsome Georgian mansion in the village of Ealing.* The apparent certainty of a Democratic victory, before the good news of Atlanta, had made Charles Francis Adams lackadaisical about coming into London. Benjamin Moran was exasperated: 'This conduct is cruel, for it keeps me in suspense, and prevents me from doing my work,' he complained in his diary.[8] He did not deny that the State Department dispatches

---

* Formerly the home of Lady Byron, its current owners advertised Hanger Hill as a healthy retreat from London with the convenience of being only six miles from the city's centre. Henry Adams liked Hanger Hill's aristocratic pretentions, but the unrelieved proximity to his family was a trial. Mary was weak and querulous, and 'Loo will bore herself to death,' he told his brother, Charles Francis Jr.

often contained a 'vast deal of lofty nonsense', but Moran had always fulfilled *his* duty and expected Adams to do the same.*

'Mr Adams got a letter this morning from Mr Dudley reporting a suspicious vessel,' Moran recorded on 8 October. 'I thought we should send the Niagara after her, but he said no.' Moran revelled in injured silence when it was discovered that the vessel had been carrying the crew for the *Shenandoah*, James Bulloch's replacement for the *Alabama*. The forced sale of the French ships had provided Bulloch with a large reserve of cash that he used to purchase a ready-built steamer.[9] The greatest challenge for Bulloch was how to assemble the Confederate officers in one place without someone talking or being discovered. In order to forestall potential leaks, Bulloch had furnished each crew member with explicit instructions. 'You will proceed to London by the 5 o'clock train this afternoon,' Bulloch informed 1st Lieutenant William Whittle on 6 October 1864,

> and go to Wood's Hotel, Furnival's Inn, High Holborn. Take a room there and give your name as Mr. W. C. Brown if asked. It has been arranged for you to be in the coffee room of the hotel at 11 o'clock a.m. precisely to-morrow, and that you will sit in a prominent position, with a white pocket handkerchief rove through a buttonhole of your coat, and a newspaper in your hand. In this attitude you will be recognized by Mr. Richard Wright, who will call at the appointed hour and ask you if your name is Brown. You may say yes, and ask his name; he will give it, and you will then retire with him to your room, hand him the enclosed letter of introduction, and then, throwing off all further disguise, discuss freely the business in hand.[10]

Whittle and his fellow Confederates obeyed their orders and the *Shenandoah* sailed secretly from London on 8 October. But after the transfer of arms and crew had been made in neutral waters on the 19th, the new commander of the cruiser, James Waddell, discovered that the stabilizers

---

* Benjamin Moran was especially irritated when Adams missed a visit to London in order to stay with the Duke of Devonshire at Chatsworth. Adams had steeled himself for a miserable time, not knowing whether the other members of the family would include the pro-Southern Marquis of Hartington, or the pro-Northern Lord Frederick Cavendish. Hartington was not there, and Adams found the Duke to be quite likeable: 'During my stay I have been favorably impressed with the character to this family,' he wrote in his diary. Without realizing it, he recognized in the Duke the same characteristics that marked his own relations with strangers: 'There is an absence of assumption which approaches almost shyness in performing the duties of the position.'

for the gun carriages were missing. Without them, the guns would go crashing backwards every time they were fired. But this was the least of Commander Waddell's problems. He had only 43 officers and men for a ship designed to carry a crew of 150.[11] The equipment had been salvaged from other Confederate ships, and in the rush to acquire guns and ammunition ordinary necessities such as tables and chairs had been forgotten. Waddell was so concerned by the shortages that he contemplated abandoning the cruise, but his small crew persuaded him that they would be able to manage. Most were used to far worse deprivations, especially the transfers from the *Alabama*. 'Every officer and man "pulled off his jacket and rolled up his sleeves,"' recalled Lieutenant Whittle, 'and with the motto, "do or die", went to work at anything and everything.' They captured their first prize, the *Alina* from Maine, on 30 October. With a little encouragement, seven sailors from the *Alina* agreed to serve on the *Shenandoah*, giving hope to the overworked crew that more would follow.

James Bulloch argued that his little navy's record was spotless and that his raiders had attacked the Northern shipping trade without ever harming passengers or crew.[12] But there was nothing heroic about commercial warfare, and in real engagements the Confederate cruisers fared badly. On 7 October the USS *Wachusetts* had captured the CSS *Florida* – the last of the original three commerce raiders – in the Bay of San Salvador, Brazil, without firing a shot.[13] Bulloch's real contribution to the South was his supply operation, which, under the steady direction of the Confederate agent Colin McRae, was working twenty-four hours a day. Since the beginning of autumn, McRae and Bulloch had sent more than five miles of wire, eight pairs of engines, six torpedo boats, four steamers for the navy, three British engineers and a large quantity of miscellaneous goods, including three unmarked boxes sent by Matthew Maury that contained the parts for a new kind of electromagnetic mine.[14]

Maury had 'locked myself down' in an 'experimental establishment of my own', as he told Louisa, the sister of the Revd Tremlett.* But he

---

* Maury was working on improvements to his mines and what he termed torpedoes, which were immobile electrical mines intended to detonate upon contact. Unfortunately, he failed to take into account the impracticality of using new technology that could not be easily replicated or repaired. Stephen Mallory could not afford to waste his dwindling resources on such rarified warfare. But the British army had plenty of resources, and General Sir John Burgoyne of the Royal Engineers supplied Maury with acid, batteries, insulated wire and all other necessary ingredients for mine manufacturing without asking too many questions about how much was actually required for experimental use.

did take one day off to visit the Confederate bazaar in aid of the Southern Prisoners' Relief Fund.[15] Despite James Spence's fear that the bazaar would have too many contributors and not enough buyers, more than 2,000 visitors crammed into Liverpool's St George's Hall on 18 October. Inside the neoclassical building were twelve stalls, representing the twelve Confederate States (though the twelfth, Kentucky, had actually remained in the Union). Confederate flags and portraits of Southern generals lined the walls. 'This is purely an enterprise gotten up by English gentlemen and ladies, sympathizers with the South and of their own prompting,' James Mason told his wife with great pride.[16] Spence had accumulated an extraordinary array of donations, from Robert E. Lee's pipe to wooden crosses made from the wreckage of Fort Sumter. In addition to persuading local businesses to donate all the food and drink, he arranged for a number of concerts to take place throughout the four days.[17] (Raphael Semmes had departed for the South on 3 October; or else Spence would have tried to make use of him as another attraction.) Encouraged by the large crowds, the organizers extended the fair from four to five days. Even after deducting expenses their final profits were more than £17,000.

Although many newspapers accepted the organizers' claim that the bazaar was an exercise in charity rather than political propaganda, Northern supporters were not deceived. Benjamin Moran prayed to heaven that retribution would fall upon the English. 'When the day of reckoning comes,' he wrote to Dudley on 1 November, 'I hope I shall be oblivious of mercy towards this government. As usual they will whine and sniffle for kind treatment and bring up the old Boston twaddle about the same Shakespeare, the same Milton, the same race and the same language.'[18] Moran's desire to be merciless was granted a week later when Samuel Hardinge, Belle Boyd's new husband, paid an unexpected visit to the legation. He came 'begging for a loan today', Moran recorded in his diary on 7 November 1864. 'He looks like a traitor – is tall and about 21 years of age. He professes to be loyal.' Moran triumphantly turned him away, but Hardinge returned the next morning, offering to spy for the Federals. Moran was supercilious: 'I gave him no encouragement. He is evidently in very straightened [sic] circumstances, and wants money. After associating with rebels and marrying a spy, it is rather cool impudence in him to come here to beg. His coming here is proof to me that the rebels are in very great pecuniary troubles in

London.'[19] Hardinge returned to America shortly afterwards – without Belle. He was arrested on his arrival in the North and taken to Old Capitol prison, where he was told he would remain at the discretion of Edwin Stanton, the Secretary of War.

The irony for the Confederates was that the bazaar had been too successful. The outpouring of support for the South by the British public would make it impossible for the US government – had Seward been so inclined – to allow the distribution of the fund to Confederate prisoners without suffering a loss of face. 'It would be a great relief to us if we could get permission to act openly,' Spence wrote to Lord Wharncliffe on 2 November after he realized that the fund was in danger of turning into a thankless burden.*[20] He suggested that they write a letter to Charles Francis Adams, asking leave to send 'an accredited agent' on a tour of Northern prisons. At the very least it would demonstrate the organizers' good faith to the British public. The bazaar committee had already purchased 2,000 blankets, 10,000 socks and 5,000 shirts, which were boxed and ready to be shipped. Wharncliffe duly wrote to Charles Francis Adams on 9 November begging him to show pity on 'the suffering of American citizens, whatever their State or opinions'.[21] Adams tersely replied that the matter was for the State Department to decide, not the legation, and refused to answer any further correspondence on the subject. (Adams did not feel the least guilty about turning away the pro-Southern supporters: he had his hands full with cases he considered to be far more deserving.)

Henry Hotze was too absorbed by his own troubles to help Spence. His plan to step back from the day-to-day running of the *Index* had backfired in a spectacular fashion.† The staff had revolted against John Witt, the new editor, imperilling Hotze's plan to expand his operations.[23]

---

* Spence had already assumed the task of unravelling Rose Greenhow's estate on behalf of her daughters, and baulked at taking on any more work. 'She had faults, but who has not,' Spence had written to Wharncliffe after learning of her death. His reference to her 'faults' was a delicate allusion to the distrust she inspired in Francis Lawley and others as a shameless manipulator of men. President Davis's wife, Varina Davis, could only feel so much pity for Rose: 'her poor wasted beautiful face all divested of its meretricious ornaments and her scheming head hanging helplessly upon those who but an hour before she felt so able and willing to deceive.'
† Percy Gregg, whom Hotze had always suspected of being slightly unhinged, had started the trouble by refusing to allow Witt to edit his copy. Witt had retaliated by dropping his leaders altogether – with good reason: they were the ravings of a violent racist. 'Of the passages altered or omitted there is scarcely one that I would have let stand,' Hotze admonished Gregg

Nor had anything come of his attempt to create a recruiting scandal in Ireland. Hotze had in fact discovered a genuine fraud in England involving three con artists from New York who enticed several hundred workers over to America on a false glass-manufacturing contract. But the press had shown only perfunctory interest in the case. The Tories were content to let it alone as well; Lord Derby had come to the conclusion that Palmerston had no intention of calling an early election. He ordered the party 'to sit still' and allow the government to tear itself apart.[24]

Palmerston was not in the least interested in petty recruiting scandals, except as a counter-argument to Northern complaints about the *Alabama*; he was only concerned with the Civil War in so far as it revealed a new military threat to Britain. 'If the Americans go to war with us,' Palmerston wrote to the First Lord of the Admiralty, the Duke of Somerset, 'they will send out a swarm of fast steamers ... sturdy enough to escape from our cruisers, and strong enough to capture any merchantman.'[25] The obvious answer was to build more ironclads. 'We must keep Pace with France, America and Russia,' he urged Gladstone shortly before the Presidential election. 'Whatever may be the Number of men in our Army and Navy, it is absolutely necessary that they should be armed with the best weapons which the Ingenuity of the Day has been able to invent.'[26] When Russell received Seward's protest about the Confederates' use of Canada on 10 November, Palmerston reacted as though it was only a matter of time before the US navy's new monitor-class gunboats seized control of the Great Lakes. Worried that the Americans could close off access to the St Lawrence river that connected the Great Lakes to the Atlantic, he suggested to the War Secretary Lord de Grey that the river be protected by 'floating batteries and heavy guns' powerful enough to 'smash and sink monitors'.[27] 'Any Reduction of our real Naval Force,' Palmerston warned Somerset, 'in the face of all the warnings we have of contingent hostility on the part of the Federal States of North America would be taking upon ourselves a very dangerous responsibility.'[28]

Adams too was worried by the aggressive language in Seward's protest

---

on his return from Germany. 'There are some I could mention to you which I should consider almost fatal to the paper.' Hotze had never intended the *Index* to be a pulpit for slavery. He was trying to massage not bludgeon public opinion. 'It is a matter of real disappointment to me that one of my chief calculations, resting upon you, threatens to fail.'[22]

to Lord Russell. He knew the Foreign Secretary well enough now to be certain that the dispatch would be counterproductive. 'Latterly the tone of the Government has been growing a little less friendly,' mused Adams. 'The mischief is, that to declare hostilities, would only be playing into the rebel hands.'[29] Unaware that Russell had already received an unofficial copy of the protest via Lord Lyons, Adams decided to rephrase Seward's letter before delivering it to the Foreign Office.

Adams was still struggling to find the right tone for the 'improved' dispatch when the *Canada* arrived on 21 November, bringing the results of the Presidential election. Lincoln had carried all but two States, though a few went Republican by the slimmest of margins, including New York State, by less than 1 per cent of the popular vote. 'Thus has the country passed safely through the most grave of its trials since the first outbreak of the war,' wrote Adams with relief in his diary.[30] The British press concentrated on Lincoln's victory and ignored the Confederate government's latest message to Europe, which came in the form of a manifesto demanding immediate recognition. The South's request for 'justice' from Great Britain, while it was deploying guerrillas and agents provocateurs in Canada, received a cold response from Lord Russell.[31] In the circumstances, James Mason was fortunate to have any response at all. France, Sweden and the Papal States were the only other countries to acknowledge receipt of the manifesto.[32]

All of a sudden Adams felt free. For the past three years his life had been blighted by fear and anxiety. Lincoln's re-election – which would not have happened if the war were still going badly – seemed to herald the end of perpetual crisis. 'The responsibility attending this post declines steadily with the progress of the war,' Adams wrote in his diary. He felt the change justified his asking Seward 'about the possibility of my being relieved in the spring'. When Henry Adams heard the news of the election he feared his father would be too reticent in his request, and asked Charles Francis Jr., 'should you go to Washington, try and have a talk with Seward about our affairs'.[33]

Adams delivered his amended version of Seward's protest on Confederate–Canadian operations to Lord Russell on 25 November. His lingering misgivings about deserting the legation fell away once he learned that Russell had not only received Seward's protest via Lord Lyons but also had already replied. 'Mr Adams is very angry with Mr Seward about his conduct,' reported Benjamin Moran. 'His labor was all thrown away and he is made to look like a fool. It was a trick that no man but Seward could have played with Mr Adams.'[34]

'This election has relieved us of the fire in the rear,' Charles Francis Jr. wrote to Henry Adams on 14 November, 'and now we can devote an undivided attention to the remnants of the Confederacy.'[35] The Democrats' hopes of winning the White House had been upended by the twin victories of Sherman in Atlanta and Sheridan in the Shenandoah Valley. Grant's tenacity had made the Copperheads appear defeatist if not unpatriotic, and the same message of 'peace now' that had been so popular during the summer had alienated all but the Democrat's core supporters in the autumn. Ordinary Federal soldiers shared Charles Francis Jr.'s determination to finish the war; 78 per cent had voted for Lincoln. The Democratic candidate General McClellan had counted on the army without considering the psychological cost to men who were fighting for victory rather than peace. Even many Federal prisoners of war 'voted' for Lincoln. James Pendlebury had been a prisoner at Andersonville, considered to be the worst of the Confederacy's prisons, since his capture in June. Unable to cope with the sheer number of prisoners, the commandant of Andersonville, Henry Wirz, had allowed a small delegation to travel to Washington with a petition to resume the exchange system.[36] The failure to gain a response led to a second prison being built near by to take some of the overflow. 'We moved to Millen and while there I voted for Abraham Lincoln,' Pendlebury wrote in his memoirs. 'Our Captains allowed us to as they were anxious to carry McLennon [sic] because Abe Lincoln was a Republican and McLennon a Democrat. Now 19 out of every 20 voted for Lincoln so we were all "docked" rations.'* The defiance shown by Pendlebury was all the more remarkable given that the Federal soldiers knew Lincoln had refused to

---

* Hundreds of Federal prisoners took part in the sham vote. According to an early chronicler of Kansas State history, 'When Sherman started on his march to Savannah the rebel authorities believed that a detachment of the Federal army would be sent to release the prisoners at Andersonville. Accordingly, in October 1864, [several Kansan prisoners] were taken to Milledgeville, Georgia, and from there to Savannah. While at Milledgeville, the Union prisoners went through the form of casting their votes at the general election. The soldiers in the field were given the privilege of voting for President . . . The rebels were very much interested in the outcome, and advised those who wanted the war to come to a speedy close to vote for McClellan. However, the result of this balloting was about two to one in favor of Lincoln.'[37]

THE FEDERAL PHŒNIX.

The Federal Phoenix rises again, according to *Punch*, from the flames
of States rights, free press and the Constitution

resume prisoner exchanges until the Confederates treated white and
black prisoners on an equal basis. On some days, there were more than 150
burials at the prison: 'We would fight like wild beasts that we might carry
out the body of a fellow prisoner, because on those occasions we would get
into the woods and come back with a supply of firewood with which to do
our cooking.'[38] After the prisoners were forbidden to go into the woods,
they fought for the 'privilege' of taking the bodies to the carts since it was
their only opportunity to scavenge for clothing.

The needless suffering of prisoners was a frequent accusation hurled
at both administrations. But Lincoln and Grant were also blamed for
deliberately sacrificing thousands of Northern soldiers in order to

prevent the South from replenishing its empty ranks. The Regius Professor of History at Oxford University, Goldwin Smith, was on a lecture tour of the US and took the opportunity to visit a prison camp in Chicago and a prison hospital in Baltimore. He thought neither unduly harsh, whereas the sight of returning Federal prisoners from Andersonville made him shudder: 'I put my finger and thumb round the upper part of a large man's arm,' he wrote. 'It must be said that Grant was partly responsible, if, as was understood, he refused to exchange prisoners. No laws of war surely can warrant the retention of prisoners whom a captor cannot feed.'* 39

Goldwin Smith's popularity in the US was second only to John Bright's on account of his vigorous pamphleteering in support of the North, and he was entertained during his tour by a plethora of Senators and generals.40 Before the election he stayed with Charles Sumner, who ranted so obsessively about Seward's blunders as Secretary of State that Smith was glad to escape. Afterwards, when Smith was in Washington, he stayed with Seward and realized that not all of Sumner's criticisms were unfair. Seward had fallen into the old habit of drinking and talking too much: he is 'the least cautious of diplomatists', recorded Smith. With regard to Lincoln, Smith noted that the English perception of the President as an 'ungainly and grotesque' figure was largely correct, 'but on the face instead of levity, sat melancholy and care'.41

The escalating tension along the Canadian border was a significant factor in Seward's return to bad habits. He needed to talk to Lord Lyons and was frustrated by his mysterious illness. In the beginning he had heard that it was typhoid; then the diagnosis changed to neuralgia or dyspepsia or a combination of both. Whatever it was, the Minister was unable to leave his room or receive visitors. Seward had taken Lyons for granted for so long that he was shocked to discover how quickly matters could deteriorate when the British Minister was absent. Seward broke protocol by writing directly to Lord Monck, rather than via the legation, urging him to act swiftly and publicly before John Yates Beall's latest Lake Erie venture – known to be centred around an armed and reinforced steamship – created a mini-war on the Great Lakes.42 Monck did not appreciate being accused of dilatoriness when he was devoting

---

* By the middle of 1864 the South had become so desperate for men that Davis agreed to a simple exchange – soldier for soldier – without regard to race. Prison exchanges resumed in November, albeit slowly.

the greater part of his day to thwarting the Confederates (he even sent a chronology to Lyons showing how and when he had responded to each event) but he was not as attuned to Northern public opinion as Seward. The Secretary of State knew there was trouble brewing long before the *New York Times* came out in favour of a retaliatory war: 'Let it come,' declared the newspaper. 'We were never in better condition for a war with England.'[43] Seward could only hope that his letters were being put into Lord Lyons's hands.[44]

Seward could at least take satisfaction from the growing dissension within the Confederate Congress over the war; calls for peace were appearing in the Southern press with increasing frequency. He was heartened, he wrote to his wife, 'in the discovery that division is at last breaking out among the rebels'.[45] Davis had been travelling through the remnants of the Confederacy, giving speeches to the public and meeting with State Governors in private, several of whom were on the verge of withdrawing their cooperation. Desertion was endemic, yet 85 per cent of Mississippi's white adult male population was in the army, which made a mockery of Davis's exhortation to Confederate women in his speech to Congress on 7 November to 'use your influence to send all to the front'.[46] Varina Davis discerned a greater willingness in Richmond to cabal against her husband. 'The temper of Congress is less vicious,' she wrote, 'but more concerted in its hostile action.'[47] The Confederate Congress had reacted angrily as a body to Davis's proposal to appropriate 40,000 slaves as a supplement to the army. They would be diggers, cooks and porters, rather than soldiers, but their contribution would be significant enough to earn them their freedom after the war. The War Department clerk John Jones took Davis's proposal as a sign that normal life in the Confederacy was disintegrating.[48] Wood was $100 a cord and coal cost $90 a load, both beyond the means of a civil servant. When Confederate soldiers received their pay, which was not often, they encountered the same frustrating experiences as Jones. Captain Francis Dawson's monthly salary of $150 allowed him to purchase new trousers for $100, but not a new pair of boots, which cost $350. Dawson prayed that his current boots would see him through the final weeks of the autumn campaign. 'After the 15th November, Richmond is safe,' he informed his mother. For then the weather would be the Confederacy's best defence.

The Army of Northern Virginia was stretched like an elastic band along mile after mile of trenches and fortifications. Lee had already moved his headquarters to be closer to Petersburg, where Grant had made the greatest gains in territory. Dawson's prophecy was accurate almost to the day. The Federals settled into their winter dugouts during the second week of November. Private James Horrocks and the 5th New Jersey Light Artillery actually built little wooden cabins, complete with windows and brick chimneys.

> Thank goodness I have a nice, warm log shanty to live in [he wrote to his parents]. Already the winter of Virginia begins to commence. This season is characterized chiefly by perpetual rain, and penetrating cold that pierces through one's clothing and makes one shiver. Mud of a sticky character takes one up to the knees and it is no rare occurrence to get up to the middle in it ... The state of the ground renders the movement of Artillery almost impossible.[49]

General Longstreet occasionally ordered a round of artillery fire to keep the Federals on their toes, but his batteries were no less mud-bound than those of his opponents. The relative quiet enabled him to reorganize his staff. There were several promotions and requests for transfers, including one by Francis Dawson. Longstreet had never shown the least interest in the Englishman but suddenly became indignant when Dawson was appointed chief ordnance officer on General Fitz-hugh Lee's staff. 'General Fitz Lee heard of me through some of our mutual English friends and made application for me,' Dawson explained to his mother. Dawson was delighted to be able to say goodbye to his uncongenial messmates. He had been casting about for a new position since June without much success. 'Although I have suffered but little,' he wrote to his mother on 25 November, 'it is useless to deny that there is considerable jealousy displayed towards an Englishman.'[50]

Dawson felt welcomed by his new mess officers from the beginning. 'A better set of fellows on Fitz Lee's staff it would have been difficult to find,' he wrote. 'There was no bickering, no jealousy, no antagonism.' The camaraderie he had craved – 'we lived together as though we were near relatives' – made up for the hardship of his new post. Dawson had to work twice as hard with a smaller staff and no logistical support: 'I found that it was no joke to organize the Ordnance Department of a couple of Divisions of Confederate Cavalry, but I adapted myself to circumstances.'[51]

Lee had sent his nephew to reinforce Jubal Early's shattered army in the Shenandoah Valley, where there was clearly going to be no winter lull. General Sheridan's reputation so terrified civilians that the women of Harrisonburg had petitioned the government for the right to organize themselves into a regiment for local defence.[52] Their bravery inspired Dawson to chide his mother for complaining about his father's debts: 'Tell him for me to keep a stout breast,' he wrote. 'Only think of the misery and desolation of this fair land and all will seem light by comparison.'[53]

In Georgia, General Sherman had initiated his own version of scorched-earth tactics. The Federal Army of the Tennessee had occupied Atlanta since 2 September; finally, on 15 November, Sherman gave the order to evacuate. His next destination was the city of Savannah, 285 miles to the east. He did not expect much resistance from Lee, who could not afford to detach a single regiment from the siege around Petersburg; nor was he frightened of General Hood and his little Army of the Tennessee, which was lurking somewhere in the countryside. Before he left Atlanta he set the city on fire, and expelled its remaining residents, telling the Mayor: 'War is cruelty, and you cannot refine it.'[54] Five thousand houses were burned to the ground in a single night. 'Behind us lay Atlanta,' as the army began to march, Sherman recalled in his memoirs, 'smouldering and in ruins, the black smoke rising high in air, and hanging like a pall over the ruined city.'

Sherman's plan for Georgia was effective and simple. He divided his army into two wings and cut a devastating trough more than 50 miles wide through the State. Foragers, known as 'bummers', had broad orders to do as they pleased short of mass rape and murder. Fearful that the Federals might first head south towards Andersonville, which was only 120 miles from Atlanta, Commandant Wirz sent hundreds of prisoners on forced marches to various locations around the State. He could not feed them all anyway; James Pendlebury received a pint of corn for a four days' march. 'A poor fellow asked if he could lie beside me and in the morning he was dead,' he wrote. 'During that march I don't think beasts could have been more savage.'

The economic catastrophe caused by Sherman's march sent immediate ripples across the South. At Salisbury prison, North Carolina, where Robert Livingstone had been sent in October, 10,000 prisoners were living outdoors in a large pen. 'Some dug holes in the ground to shelter themselves from the cold winds at night,' wrote Archibald McCowan, a Scotsman who arrived at the same time as Livingstone. As the rations grew smaller and smaller, the prisoners feared that the Confederates would starve them to death before the war ended. Walking past the prison well on 24 November, McCowan noticed a small group of prisoners lounging round, each carrying a club made from a tree branch. 'One of these men was very conspicuous on account of his uniform; the red breeches and Turkish cap of a Zouave regiment.' Suddenly, the group attacked the prison sentries. 'Each of the other conspirators knocked down his man and with the arms thus obtained they rushed to the large gate which generally stood open to allow teams to pass in and out,' wrote McCowan.[55] The other prisoners joined in. Two of the guards were killed before the sentries on the other side of the pen realized what was happening. In a few minutes every prisoner was running towards the gates. McCowan had intended to join the mêlée but a friend grabbed him by the arm and pulled him down, '"Stay where you are you damn fool", he said.' The Commandant climbed to the roof and turned the prison's howitzer onto the crowd below. McCowan waited until all was silent before raising his head. He could see a number of bodies sprawled on the ground. 'I learned later that 15 prisoners were killed and about 60 wounded, not one of whom knew anything about the matter.' Robert Livingstone had tried to run away with the others and had been shot down. He lived for ten days before dying of his wounds on 4 December, when his body was dumped in a trough alongside the other casualties of the failed rebellion.

35

'The British Mark on Every Battle-field'

The plot against New York – A parting of friends – Congress retaliates – A Christmas gift – Wilmington falls – One last attempt

The Confederate leader of clandestine operations in Canada, Jacob Thompson, was still confident in his designs for a campaign of terror, despite the failure of his agents on Lake Erie and in Chicago. He had particular faith in John Yates Beall and Bennet Burley and believed that their new scheme – to purchase and convert a steamer into a warship – had a far greater chance of succeeding than the ill-fated attempt to seize the *Philo Parsons*. Burley had been working at a foundry in Guelph, Ontario, overseeing the construction of the cannon and torpedoes that were to be fitted to the converted steamship. 'Everything is going on finely and I anticipate having the things finished early, perhaps this week,' he had reported in October.[1] Beall was waiting to captain the vessel as soon as it was delivered to Port Colborne, at the southern end of the Welland Canal on Lake Erie, some 30 miles west of Buffalo.

Beall's plan called for the steamer, renamed the CSS *Georgian*, to receive its battering ram and cannon at Colborne. The ram was designed to sink the USS *Michigan*, and the cannon was to be used against the undefended cities along Lake Erie from Buffalo to Detroit. But when the *Georgian* sailed onto Lake Erie on 1 November, it seemed as though every household within a 200-mile radius of Colborne knew of her arrival. 'The whole lake shore was a scene of wild excitement,' Thompson wrote to Judah P. Benjamin. 'At Buffalo two tugs had cannon placed on board . . . Bells were rung at Detroit . . . The bane and curse of carrying out anything in this country is the surveillance under which we act.'[2]

To make matters worse, the *Georgian*'s propeller broke and a replacement had to be brought from Toronto. But the conspirators believed they were safe after the authorities searched the vessel and, since the weaponry had not yet been delivered, found nothing suspicious.

By 16 November, the *Georgian* had been repaired and was sailing west towards Sarnia on Lake Huron to pick up the rest of her weaponry when Monck's agents finally achieved their first success against the Confederates. They intercepted the shipment before it reached Sarnia and found a large quantity of arms in three boxes marked 'potatoes'. The trail led straight back to Burley, who was arrested in Guelph the following day and taken to Toronto to face an extradition trial to the United States. At first, the detectives thought they had captured Beall, and their confusion enabled him to go into hiding before they realized their mistake. The rest of the *Georgian*'s crew also scattered, leaving only Burley to take the blame for the plot. Thompson was prepared to kill civilians for the cause of Southern independence, but he was less insouciant about risking the lives of his own men. He hastily wrote to the Confederate Navy Secretary, Stephen Mallory, asking him to forward documents proving Burley's naval commission so that the charge of piracy – which carried a death sentence – could not be made against the Scotsman.[*3]

Disappointed by the sudden unravelling of the Lake Erie plan, Thompson waited anxiously for the outcome of the plot to set New York alight on 25 November. There had been no word from Lieutenant Colonel Robert Martin or Captain John Headley since their aborted attempt on the 7th. But the departure of General Butler and his Federal troops on 15 November gave Thompson hope that they would still carry out the mission. The small Confederate cell was more determined than ever 'to let the Government at Washington understand that the burning homes in the South might find a counterpart in the North', as Headley recalled.[4] They were planning to use a new kind of incendiary

---

* With great difficulty and expense, Jacob Thompson managed to send a message to Richmond using the latest techniques in photography. The message – a request for written evidence of Burley's naval commission – was written in extra large letters, photographed, and the negatives reduced to the size of five thumbnails, which were then placed under the cloth covering of the messenger's jacket buttons. 'I (afterwards) met J Davis at a dinner,' recalled the photographer. 'I asked him if he remembered the button message, and he seemed much pleased to meet the author of it.' Stephen Mallory and Jefferson Davis both supplied the affidavits requested by Thompson. Davis claimed to have ordered the *Philo Parsons* expedition, and Mallory provided proof of Burley's naval commission.

bomb based on Greek fire – a mixture of phosphorus and carbon bisulphate – which could be transported easily in small bottles and used to produce a powerful explosion when exposed to air. The targets were the city's hotels. The conspirators were to travel around with large satchels, and one by one leave the bottles in pre-booked bedrooms.

On 24 November, the day before the attack, Headley picked up the chemical concoction from a Southern sympathizer, and carried it in his suitcase on a streetcar up the Bowery:

> I soon began to smell a peculiar odour – a little like rotten eggs – and I noticed the passengers were conscious of the same presence. But I sat unconcerned until my getting off place was reached, when I took up the valise and went out. I heard a passenger say as I alighted, 'there must be something dead in that valise.'[5]

Only six of the original eight took part on the 25th, two having lost their nerve. Each man put ten bottles of the Greek fire in a satchel and spread out through the city. They visited nineteen hotels in all, as well as two theatres and Barnum's Museum. But the Confederates had ignored the basic rule of arson – that fire requires oxygen to burn – and had planted the Greek fire in locked bedrooms and closed cupboards, causing the flames to peter out of their own accord.

One of the hotels set on fire, the Lafarge, was adjacent to the Winter Garden Theatre at Broadway and 31st, where the three Booth brothers, Edwin, Junius Brutus and John Wilkes, were playing together for the first and last time in their careers, giving a charity performance of *Julius Caesar* to raise money for the Shakespeare Statue fund for Central Park; John Wilkes Booth was playing Mark Antony and his more famous brother Edwin was Brutus. John Wilkes, a member of the Sons of Liberty, was already deep into his own plot, although at this time the scheme was limited to kidnapping Lincoln and forcing the release of all Confederate prisoners in exchange for his freedom. Booth had been meeting Confederate agents in Canada, but the fragmented structure of their operations meant that he knew nothing about the New York conspiracy, and the arsonists were unaware whose life they were risking when they set fire to the Lafarge. As news rippled across the auditorium that the hotel next door was burning, there were screams from the audience and people began to rise from their seats. 'The panic was such for a few moments that it seemed as if all the audience believed the entire building in flames,' reported the *New York Times*. But in that split second between calm and a stampede, Edwin Booth stepped forward and reassured the audience that the theatre was not itself on fire: 'In addition ... Judge McCunn rose in the dress circle, and in a few timely remarks admonished them all to remain quietly in their places, and at the same time tried to show them the danger which would attend a pell-mell rush for the doors, and especially the uselessness of it.'[6]

The fires had caused mass panic throughout the city, but no recorded deaths. By the following evening, newspapers were carrying full descriptions of the six suspects, who all decided to leave for Toronto on the 11 o'clock train. They slipped into their berths and waited, fully dressed and armed, in case detectives boarded in pursuit. Much to their surprise, they reached Canada without being recognized. US detectives came looking for them but returned to New York empty-handed.* General Dix announced that 'such persons engaged in secret acts of hostility' would be caught, tried and executed 'without the delay of a single day'.[8] The treasurer of the US Sanitary Commission, George Templeton Strong, thought the arson attempt proved 'that the South is thoroughly rotten, and the Confederacy a mere shell'.[9] Such was the fear in the city that several newspapers called for Southern citizens to be rounded up and expelled, and Dix ordered all Southern refugees to register their names with the police department.

In the midst of the public outpouring of anger against the South (and at the British for harbouring the conspirators in Canada) Mary Sophia Hill turned up without warning at the New York consulate to request Archibald's assistance. She had come to complain about her trial and banishment from New Orleans, but Consul Archibald was less interested in the dangers she had overcome to reach New York than in the threat to her safety now that she had arrived. He purchased a ticket for her on the next steamship to England and made sure that she was on it.

Lord Lyons had not left his bedroom for more than a month; all the while Seward had continually assumed that in one more week or so the

---

* Only one of the arsonists was caught and tried for the crime: Robert Cobb Kennedy, an Irishman, who was picked up by detectives in Detroit on 29 December 1864. He was tried in New York and sentenced to hang on 25 March 1865. Kennedy went to the gallows insisting that the plot was a legitimate act of war in retaliation for Northern atrocities, and that he had intended to destroy buildings rather than kill civilians.[7]

Minister would reappear looking tired, perhaps, but otherwise well. He was shocked when Lyons informed him on 4 December that he was leaving for England in two days' time. 'I agree with you that it is best that you go away for a time,' Seward answered Lyons's note by return messenger. 'And yet I feel that my cares and difficulties will be seriously increased by your withdrawal.'[10]

Lord Russell had hoped to keep Lyons in Washington for the duration of the war, and was still counting on him making a full recovery after a month or two in England. He made it clear to Lyons that this was a respite rather than a transfer from his post. But the Minister cared only that he was going home; he wrote to his sister, telling her to prepare an extra place for Christmas dinner.[11] The doctors had diagnosed his headaches as neuralgia, and he had been warned that the pain could become worse before it went away. Fortunately, his worries about the transatlantic crossing were soothed by George Sheffield, the last of the old guard at the legation, who offered to escort the invalid home. The suddenness of the decision – there were no farewell banquets and no time to engrave a watch or some such memento – imparted a sense of crisis to the news. On 5 December, the morning after he received Lyons's note, Seward wrote to Charles Francis Adams, urging him to impress on Lord Russell 'how deeply this incident is regretted by this government, and how desirous we are for Lord Lyons's recovery and return to our country'.[12]

A week later, on 12 December, Lyons was helped up the gangplank of the *China* in New York by Sheffield. Within only a few hours of the Minister's departure, Seward's fears about his burdens increasing came true. The extradition trial in Montreal of the St Albans raiders ended suddenly after the magistrate in charge of the case, Judge Charles Coursol, ordered their discharge on grounds so technical that the explanation introduced a new and arcane area of debate for the Canadian judiciary. The pro-Southern audience in the courtroom swarmed the prisoners, cheering and shouting as they were led down the steps. By the time the news reached Lord Monck in Quebec City, the raiders had fled the area. General Dix had no qualms about sending his troops into Canada to find them. 'All military commanders on the frontier' were ordered to chase and, if necessary, shoot the Confederate guerrillas 'wherever they may take refuge'. But even before Dix issued his proclamation, Monck had ordered new arrest warrants. 'The police are making every effort to prevent their escape,' he informed the legation.[13]

Monck's attempt to demonstrate his seriousness to Seward was undermined by an incident three days later which once again involved John Yates Beall. On 16 December a small team led by Beall tried to intercept a train taking seven Confederate generals from Johnson's Island prison to Fort Lafayette in New York. They failed to stop the train or find the generals, and two US detectives captured Beall and another guerrilla on the American side of Niagara. 'All the efforts of Confederates . . . had failed,' lamented Captain Headley. 'Now many of our best men were in prison. Burley at Toronto. Cole at Sandusky. Young and his comrades at Montreal. Beall and Anderson in New York City. Grenfell, Shenks, Marmaduke, Cantrill and Travers at Chicago.'[14]

John Yates Beall suffered the same fate as Robert Cobb Kennedy, one of the New York arsonists. He was taken to New York, where he was found guilty by a military court of spying and piracy, and executed on 24 February 1865. Right up until the last moment he refused to accept the charges against him – claiming he was a Confederate naval officer and neither a spy nor a pirate. 'It is murder,' he is alleged to have said before mounting the gallows. 'I die in the service and defence of my country.'

Beall's conviction not only appeared to validate the desperate measures called for by General Dix, but also lent strength to those who argued that Britain deserved to be punished for allowing these plots to be nurtured in her territories.* Yet Seward, who might have been expected to inflate his rhetoric for maximum effect, surprised observers by moving swiftly to maintain calm along the Canadian border. He countermanded General Dix's order, though he begged the legation Secretary, Joseph Burnley, to keep quiet about it until the fuss had died down. Seward also laboured hard to manage the increasingly belligerent stance against Britain adopted by Congress. Charles Sumner's transformation into Britain's harshest critic was now complete and he was leading the Senate movement for retaliatory steps to be taken against the mother country. His first target was the ten-year-old Reciprocity Treaty – a free-trade agreement with Canada – that was scheduled to

---

* Anti-British feeling reached new heights. In Washington, for example, two policemen ambushed Arthur Seymour, one of the junior Assistant Secretaries at the legation, beating him almost senseless. The two policemen – and the magistrate who acquitted them – were caught in a lie when they claimed that Seymour admitted in court he was drunk on the evening. Seymour had actually just finished work and was on his way to dinner.

end in June 1865. Using his position as chairman of the Foreign Relations Committee, Sumner pushed through a resolution for the treaty's suspension after June; he also attacked the Rush–Bagot Treaty of 1817, which limited the militarization of the Great Lakes, and prepared a list of grievances, beginning with the Queen's proclamation of neutrality in 1861, which he intended to be the basis of a campaign for massive financial restitution from Britain.

Charles Francis Adams Jr. had breakfast with Sumner in Washington in December and thought him half-sane at best, 'and now out-Sumners himself'.[15] The Senator's brave and often lonely fight to achieve equal rights for Negroes had become lonelier of late because of his tendency to alienate potential allies.[16] Rather than being an asset in the White House's campaign to pass the 13th Amendment, which expanded the Emancipation Proclamation to all US States and not just those in rebellion, he was regarded as an obstacle to the deal-making which had to be done to achieve its passage. The Senate had passed the Amendment in April 1864, but it had stalled in the House until now.

Sumner's power in the Senate was waning; Lincoln no longer listened or trusted him (Sumner's frequent appearances at the White House were due to Mary Lincoln, whom he assiduously courted). Seward no longer feared him, but, according to Charles Francis Jr., would exile Sumner as a Minister to Anywhere, if he could. Lyons had come to Washington believing that Sumner was the greatest man in American politics. Five years later, he considered him to be a self-aggrandizing, sneaky Savonarola who tainted the very causes he affected to espouse. 'If that man ever gets into power he will, under some highly moral pretence, sacrifice the highest public interests to his position,' Lyons complained to Professor Goldwin Smith, who happened to be a fellow passenger on the *China*. Of all public men in Washington, 'he is the one for whom I have brought away the least respect'.[17] Lyons's regard for Seward, on the other hand, had matured from barely concealed contempt to admiration. After an acrimonious beginning each had learned and benefited from their forced collaboration. The politician had become a true statesman, the diplomat a true ambassador.

The chief defect of Jacob Thompson's plots, in the opinion of the Confederate government, was that they were not working. Thompson defended his record to the Confederate Secretary of State, Judah P.

Benjamin: 'I have relaxed no effort to carry out the objects the Government had in view in sending me here. I had hoped at different times to have accomplished more, but still I do not think my mission has been altogether fruitless.'[18] Benjamin disagreed and appointed his replacement, telling Thompson in December:

> From reports which reach us from trustworthy sources, we are satisfied that so close espionage is kept upon you that your services have been deprived of the value which is attached to your further residence in Canada. The President thinks, therefore that as soon as the gentleman arrives who bears this letter ... that you transfer to him as *quietly* as possible all of the information that you have obtained and the release of funds in your hands and then return to the Confederacy.[19]

The 'gentleman' was Brigadier General Edwin Gray Lee, a cousin of Robert E. Lee. Edwin Lee suffered from chronic lung disease and was no longer fit for active service, but he had experience in clandestine operations. He found on his arrival in Canada, however, that Thompson was not prepared to leave quietly or hand over control.

Jefferson Davis and Judah P. Benjamin knew that the Canadian operations were their only means of striking directly into the North. The South's last remaining army in the west, the Army of Tennessee under Joe Johnston's successor, John Hood, was smashed to pieces over the course of seven battles between September and November – in the last, the Battle of Franklin on 30 November, the attack of the Southern army was so ill-planned and uncoordinated that General John M. Schofield was able to inflict one of the bloodiest defeats of the war. Six Confederate generals were killed, including Patrick Cleburne, the highest-ranking Irish general in the South.* From then on, Sherman was determined to reach the

---

* Cleburne was the first Southern general to argue that the slaves should be promised their freedom if they fought in the army. On 2 January 1864 he wrote to General Joe Johnston: 'Our country has already some friends in England and France, and there are strong motives to induce these nations to recognize and assist us, but they cannot assist us without helping slavery, and to do this would be in conflict with their policy for the last quarter of a century. England has paid hundreds of millions to emancipate her West India slaves and break up the slave trade. Could she now consistently spend her treasure to reinstate slavery in this country? But this barrier once removed, the sympathy and the interests of these and other nations will accord with our own, and we may expect from them both moral support and material aid. One thing is certain, as soon as the great sacrifice to independence is made and known in foreign countries there will be a complete change of front in our favor of the sympathies of the world.'[20]

Atlantic coast as quickly as possible. 'I can make this march, and make Georgia howl!' he assured Grant. 'I propose to ... make its inhabitants feel that war and individual ruin are synonymous terms.'[21] Leaving General Thomas behind to destroy the remnants of Hood's army, Sherman was able to move forward between 10 and 15 miles a day, and cause at least $1 million-worth of damage to Georgia. He entered Savannah on 21 December 1864, having completed his 300-mile 'march to the sea' in thirty-six days. He telegraphed Lincoln: 'I beg to present you as a Christmas gift the City of Savannah, with one hundred and fifty guns and plenty of ammunition, also about twenty-five thousand bales of cotton.'

Richmond did not learn of Savannah's capture for several days. But the Confederate government was transfixed by the threat towards its last open port. '[Federal] Troops are moving toward Wilmington from here,' wrote the chief of ordnance, Josiah Gorgas, 'and a heavy armament has departed from Hampton Roads, supposed to be destined to the attack of that place. The great trouble to be met now is to feed the army here while the railroads southward are being repaired.'[22] The situation was now desperate: the supply of food for the army would not even last the month without additional deliveries from Bermuda. The commissary-general, Lucius Northrop, turned to Thomas Taylor, the English blockade-runner, for help. 'I said I would do my best,' wrote Taylor, 'and after some negotiations he undertook to pay me a profit of 350 per cent upon any provisions and meat I could bring in within the next three weeks!'[23] Taylor set out on the *Wild Rover* and returned from Bermuda on 24 December just as the long-expected assault on Fort Fisher at Wilmington by General Butler and Admiral Porter was about to begin.

Francis Lawley and Frank Vizetelly had both rushed to Wilmington from Petersburg, fearing they would be too late to witness the attack. The largest fleet ever assembled in the war – sixty-four Federal ships in total – was arranged in a three-mile-wide crescent, blocking the entrance to Cape Fear. Opposing them were fewer than 1,000 Confederates manning the fort, some of them boys who had never fired a gun before. (The Confederate navy consisted of only fifty vessels now, and Mallory had not even bothered to send a defence.) 'For five weary hours upon the 24th,' wrote Lawley, 'the iron hailstorm, without one instant's cessation, descended upon or around the fort, tore great rents ... set fire to the wooden quarters of the garrison, swept away every vestige of flag or flagstaff . . . without injuring a hair of the head of its defenders.'[24] The Federals' plan to explode a ship next to the ramparts merely resulted in a loud noise and a great deal of sea spray, but the Confederates' secret weapon – Matthew Fontaine Maury's electro-magnetic mines – also failed, being too complicated and delicate to work properly under fire.

The first wave of US troops fought all Christmas Day, coming within 75 yards of the walls. Rather than being buoyed by their proximity to success, however, General Butler was blinded by the possibility of defeat, and when darkness fell he called off the attack. Admiral Porter was furious. Five hundred properly led men could have taken the fort, he claimed to the Navy Secretary, Gideon Welles. To compound Porter's anger, the *Banshee* 2 and its vital supplies for Lee's army managed to slip past the Federal fleet in the early hours of 26 December. Taylor was fired upon by several gunboats as he dashed towards the fort: 'It was an exciting moment as we crossed the bar in safety, cheered by the garrison,' he wrote, 'who knew we had provisions on board for the relief of their comrades in Virginia.'[25]

The South knew that the Federal attackers would return. 'If Wilmington falls, "Richmond next", is the prevalent supposition,' wrote the War Department clerk John Jones. 'It is unquestionably the darkest period we have yet experienced. Intervention on the part of European powers is the only hope of many. Failing that, no doubt a negro army will be organized – and it might be too late!'[26] President Davis decided to make one last appeal to Britain. With nothing left to offer, and with no threat of blackmail or an Anglo-American war to dangle, Davis resorted to the previously unthinkable: he proposed to abolish slavery in return for recognition of Southern independence. On 27 December 1864 he asked Duncan F. Kenner, one of his few remaining allies in the Confederate Congress, to go to London to speak to Lord Palmerston.* Benjamin promised Kenner that he would prevent Mason and Slidell from interfering, and wrote to the Commissioners on 27 December 1864.[27] He dared not

---

* Kenner was the largest slave-owner in Congress, but this had not prevented him from trying to persuade Davis in early 1863 to ask Britain for recognition in return for gradual emancipation. Like General Patrick Cleburne, Kenner had realized that no British government would sully its anti-slavery record by recognizing the South while she remained a slave-owning nation. In 1863, when her fortunes were at the high-water mark, he believed the South could have made the offer from a position of strength and probably dictated her own terms.

describe the mission in explicit terms in case the letter fell into the wrong hands, but he stated that Kenner's mandate came directly from the President and could not be questioned.[28] Meanwhile, Davis arranged a secret meeting between Kenner and the Confederate Congressional leaders, who reluctantly accepted there was no alternative. Partly to explain his departure, and partly because his position as chairman of the House Ways and Means Committee made him the obvious candidate, Kenner was given additional powers to negotiate a government loan from European banks. Kenner would have authority to sell every last cotton bale in the South, if necessary, so long as he procured new funds for the bankrupt Treasury.

But before Kenner could do any of these things, he first had to find a way of breaking through the Federal stranglehold on the South.

Francis Lawley paid a brief visit to Charleston after the Battle of Wilmington and was sorry that he did: the empty streets reminded him of Boccaccio's description of Florence after the Black Death. Some blocks were nothing more than charred ruins, while others remained eerily pristine with 'vacant verandahs and deserted sun balconies'. There was grace and grandeur amid the ruins – the tall spire of St Michael's Church remained intact, though no one would now dare, as Rose Greenhow once had, to climb the steps for a view over the harbour. 'Nor can any one who visits Charleston to day be blind to the possibility,' he wrote in his *Times* report, 'that before the 13th of April 1865, arrives – the fourth anniversary . . . – a Federal watchman may from this same spire gaze down upon the sun-lit harbour and city beneath him.'[29]

The city was not entirely devoid of troops or civilians: there were still 12,000 soldiers garrisoned in the surrounding area and Henry Feilden was as busy as ever. His wedding to Julia had taken place in Greenville, South Carolina, on 27 October 1864, but he could not allow her to live with him in Charleston. 'How I miss you, dearest, and all your kindnesses and attentions,' he wrote to his wife, who remained in Greenville. 'But it was the right thing to do under the circumstances, for we shall soon have to undertake active operations.' No one was sure whether Sherman would head to Charleston after Savannah, or march to Richmond via Columbia, South Carolina's State capital. Either way, the State and its port were doomed. 'One thing you may be sure of,' promised Henry, 'you will have to be looked after, and I will resign my commission sooner than not be able to do so.' He had persuaded one of the last blockade-runners in Charleston to take out £100-worth of cotton for them. This was all the non-Confederate money they possessed, 'and will give us some little exchange in the hour of need'.[30] Feilden had again been recommended for promotion, this time by General Beauregard and General Hardee. As it was, not only was there no response to the generals' requests, but also Feilden fell victim to the growing confusion in the War Department. He received contradictory orders, sending him hither and thither, much to the annoyance of Hardee and Beauregard, who both wanted him on their staff. He managed to have the orders rescinded but his promotion remained in abeyance.[31]

On 4 January 1865 General Lee detached the veteran South Carolina regiments from his shrinking army and sent them home to defend their State. Feilden was already thinking about evacuation plans. 'If we can't hold Charleston,' he wrote to Julia on the 5th, 'I am very sure we shall not burn it up, because there are now in the city and would be left behind, some 15,000 poor men, women and children and negroes, who cannot possibly leave the city in any case, for they would have no place to go, and would die of starvation.' Julia had fantasies about burning their house rather than letting it fall into Federal hands. 'It would be a good deal like cutting off one's nose to spite the face,' he chided. 'If Charleston is to be burnt, let the Yankees have the disgrace of doing it. Sherman's army will commence active operations in South Carolina in a few days.'[32] Feilden tried to reassure Julia that a Federal occupation would not be as terrible as she feared. He could not comprehend the pent-up rage many Northerners felt towards South Carolina, and Charleston in particular, for being the cradle of rebellion.[33] Nor did he understand the Southern horror of 'Negro troops'. 'I know it would make no difference to me for I lived in places where there was nothing but Negro troops, Nassau for instance,' he wrote to her, 'and I noticed that people; Southerners, English and others seemed to enjoy life just as much as if all the troops in the island were white.'[34]

The South was undergoing a late but hard lesson in the fighting ability of black soldiers as five Negro regiments joined the Federal assault force for the next attack on Wilmington. At four in the morning on 13 January, Admiral Porter's fleet once again appeared on the horizon and by 8 a.m. the first landing transports were disgorging troops onto the beach. Frank Vizetelly had remained at Fort Fisher, hoping to draw a picture of the fighting. His patience was rewarded with a perfect view of the attack. He was able to capture the entire scene for the *Illustrated London News*, from the Federal soldiers landing in the distance, to the Confederates desperately trying to shore up the fort's walls in the foreground.

The fall of Fort Fisher, by Frank Vizetelly

The fort fell two days later on 15 January, although Wilmington itself remained in Confederate hands for the moment. Feilden urged Julia to remain in Greenville. 'The people are now dreadfully scared here,' he wrote on 19 January. 'Many I am sure are sorry that they did not clear out before this. It cannot be long before this city is attacked. I suppose we shall have to yield in the end unless strong reinforcements reach us, of which I see very little hope at present.' Sherman had already set out from Savannah and stories of Federal atrocities were preceding his advance.[35]

Julia may have been safe in Greenville but she was living in the most primitive conditions, without winter shoes or proper undergarments. It was, nevertheless, easier for her to obtain flour and wood than it was for the inhabitants of Richmond. 'We have famine, owing to the incapacity of the government, and the rapacity of speculators,' complained John Jones on 19 January. The city was swirling with rumours. He had heard that Secretary of War James A. Seddon had resigned – which was true – and that Jefferson Davis was going to be replaced by General Lee – which was not, although the Confederate Congress voted to make Lee 'Commander-in-Chief' of all Southern forces. Four days later, on the 23rd, Jones wrote, 'It is rumored that a commissioner (a Louisianan) sailed to-day for England, to make overtures to that government.'[36]

Kenner was not sailing for Europe; he had decided to make the 300-mile journey to New York, and from there attempt to sneak onto one of the fast steamships. He set off on 18 January with two guides, who had been told that 'Mr Kinglake' was going to Canada to assist with the defences of the Confederate prisoners. Their orders were to make haste but also to take extra care to avoid capture. Neither knew that their charge's identity was as fake as his brown wig, nor were they aware that the last messenger to attempt to reach Canada from the South had been captured in Ohio, tried by court martial and sentenced to death.[37]

In Canada, Lord Monck was fighting a rearguard action against pro-Southern prejudice and bureaucratic incompetence in order to preserve British neutrality in the region. Five of the St Albans raiders, including Bennett Young, had been rearrested;* the Montreal chief of police had been forced to resign, the original judge in the St Albans case, Charles Coursol, suspended, the St Albans banks indemnified for the money stolen, the law changed to allow for the expulsion of aliens, and hundreds of troops deployed along the border. On 11 January the judge in Montreal had granted the St Albans raiders a thirty-day recess on the grounds they needed more time to prepare their defence. But Monck hoped this setback would be viewed against the success of the Bennet Burley trial in Upper Canada where Burley's extradition had been ordered on 20 January. Lord Monck signed the extradition papers and on 2 February Burley was taken by special night train to Suspension Bridge station at Niagara Falls. Twenty armed guards rode the train, maintaining vigil until the US agents came on board to collect the prisoner.[38]

The Secretary of the legation, Joseph Burnley, dismissed Burley as an

---

* Jacob Thompson tried to obtain copies of their commissions, just as he had done Burley's, but none of his messengers had succeeded in reaching Richmond.

undeserving case, just as he had done with Colonel Grenfell. 'If my cousin Charles would use his influence with Lord Lyons it might be of use to me,' Grenfell had written in December to the chief clerk of the family firm, Pascoe Grenfell and Co., in London, unaware that Lyons was about to return to England. 'I cannot say more at present. I know not a soul here nor have I a friend.' He ended the note, pathetically: 'I leave it to you to inform my girls of my situation or not, just as you like.'[39] Grenfell's cousin, Charles Grenfell MP, did ask for help from the Foreign Office, which in turn ordered Burnley to raise the case with Seward. The legation Secretary doubted they could do anything for Grenfell, whose guilt was so obvious that 'everything seems to militate against him', but he asked the British Consul in St Louis, Mr Wilkins, to make discreet enquiries.[40] 'You seem to be on such good terms with the Authorities', he explained, 'that I dare say you may be able to effect something privately when I should most likely fail officially.'[41]

Grenfell's former commanding officer, General Joseph Wheeler, later claimed that the Englishman was innocent of the charges. Of the more than 100 conspirators who had been arrested in November, only eight were put on trial in January, and Grenfell was one of them. 'The trial of your grandfather, you must recall,' Wheeler wrote to Grenfell's family, 'was a time when there was most extreme and bitter partisan feeling, and the officials had around them a number of spies who were dishonorable men in the extreme, and who would commit any perjury to secure convictions.'[42] Grenfell was in the most trouble because of the way he had tried to deceive the War Secretary, Edwin Stanton, and his treatment in prison was undoubtedly the harshest, but he made his predicament far worse by his arrogant behaviour. One of Grenfell's greatest weaknesses – the reason his life had been a catalogue of disappointments and bitter feelings – was his delusion that he was a prince among pygmies. He believed he was more intelligent than everyone else, braver, more principled, and certainly more deserving of special treatment. Occasionally, he impressed people with his bravado, but more often he turned them into inveterate foes. If the judge advocate had any animus against Grenfell before the trial, it was increased tenfold after Grenfell mocked him with a silly salute when stating his 'Not Guilty' plea.

Grenfell's British nationality would have worked against him even if he had been a model prisoner. Edwin Stanton wanted Britons in the Confederacy to suffer the same retribution as Southerners. Gideon

Welles agreed and was disgusted with Seward's reluctance to sanction the seizure of British property in Savannah. Stanton told Welles not to worry: Sherman was taking a robust approach towards British cotton merchants who were trying to protect their cotton by 'asserting it had the British mark upon it'. Sherman told them in reply that he had 'found the British mark on every battle-field. The muskets, cartridges, caps, projectiles were all British and had the British mark upon them.'*[43]

There were only eight objections to the resolution when the Senate voted to rescind the US trade treaty with Canada on 12 January 1865. Charles Sumner's anti-British rhetoric was incomprehensible to his friends in England, particularly his slurs against Lord Russell, which were so outrageous that John Bright was forced into the unfamiliar posture of defending the Foreign Secretary's integrity.[44] But Sumner's position did not seem unreasonable, nor unjust, to a Northern public still terrified that there were arsonists and insurgents ready to strike without warning.

When Davis's envoy, Duncan Kenner, reached New York on 6 February, after a hazardous trek through the back roads of Virginia and Maryland, he discovered that the slavery issue had been taken out of his hands. On 21 January the House of Representatives had finally voted – by 119 to 56 – to ratify the 13th Amendment, thus abolishing slavery on American soil. The Confederate Congress, on the other hand, had voted against Davis's proposal to arm the slaves. Kenner also learned that the two governments had engaged in half-hearted peace negotiations on 3 February – known as the Hampton Roads Conference – which collapsed on the first day. These were all good reasons for him to give up, but he was determined to see the mission through to completion. He boarded the Southampton-bound *America* on 11 February, posing as a Frenchman in order to confuse the detectives standing guard at the pier. Kenner believed the fate of the Confederacy lay in his hands: Wilmington was gone, Charleston was tottering. But if Lord Palmerston could be persuaded that there was no longer any moral impediment to Southern recognition, Kenner still had faith that the combination of Britain's navy and Confederate courage would win independence for the South.[45]

---

* General Grant made a similar complaint to Seward, forwarding to him 'specimens of fuses captured at Fort Fisher ... and the statement of Co. Tal P. Shaffner that the same were manufactured at the Woolwich Arsenal, England, an arsenal owned and run by the British Government'.

36

'Richmond Tomorrow'

The truth cannot be hidden – A late success for Bulloch – Hysteria over Canada – Arrival of Davis's envoy – A hard line – Lord Lyons retires (temporarily)

Lord Lyons had been miserable for much of the journey home. Almost worse than the headaches was the persistent feeling that he had failed. He feared that he had ruined his prospects by leaving Washington and doubted that the relationship of mutual respect he had built laboriously between the legation and the State Department would survive his absence. Lyons's former attachés were also anxious about their chief's legacy being undone. 'There appeared the other day in the paper, a list of acts of the United States Government which showed their ill will to England,' Edward Malet wrote to him from Frankfurt. 'There were about eight and I was delighted to see that they had all taken place after your departure from Washington.' The 'Buccaneers', as the attachés once styled themselves, had complained constantly of overwork while they were there, but their new assignments made them miss the cama-raderie of the legation. 'When we were very jolly in the evening we always used to sing, "yonder lies the whiskey bottle empty on the shelf"' sighed Malet.[1]

Lyons looked so ravaged when he arrived at the Foreign Office on Christmas Eve 1864 that Lord Russell was startled. He promised Lyons that his post in Washington would remain open until either his health was restored or he chose to give it up of his own volition. This reassur-ance lifted a great weight off Lyons; for the first time in many weeks he did not feel as though he had thrown away his career in a moment of weakness. A few days after the interview, Lyons composed his final report on American affairs, and wrote letters of recommendation for his long-suffering staff. There was much he regretted about the war, but it had served a purpose, he told Russell. Amid all the horrors and iniquities 'there appears to be one gleam of consolation', he thought, for 'slavery seems to be doomed'. Jefferson Davis's proposal to employ 40,000 slaves as auxiliary soldiers showed that 'the South appears to be seriously disposed to arm and free, and grant land to a large number of slaves; and if this be done, the emancipation of the whole body of slaves must follow'.[2]

The Southern Independence Association was delighted that the South was finally coming round to Britain's way of thinking, and composed a congratulatory address to President Davis on his boldness. To many people, however, the idea seemed far-fetched: nothing but sheer desperation would make them relinquish 'the services' of their slaves, Lord Palmerston told John Delane, the editor of The Times, 'but one can hardly believe that the South [sic] men have been so pressed and exhausted'. Delane was inclined to agree until he learned that General Sherman had reached the outskirts of Savannah. 'The American news is a heavy blow to us as well as to the South. It has changed at once the whole face of things,' Delane wrote to his deputy editor on 25 December. 'I have told Chenery to write upon it.' The next day, he sent another note: 'I am still sore vexed about Sherman, but Chenery did his best to attenuate the mischief.'[3] James Spence also tried to play down the news, telling Lord Wharncliffe on 5 January 1865 to look out for his article in The Times: 'You will find I do not attempt to deny the Federal success in Tennessee or the danger of Savannah, which I assume to be likely to fall [the news of Christmas Eve had not yet reached Britain], but I hope to show that public opinion overestimates the importance of the events and that upon the whole the year's campaign is a failure on the part of the Federals.' Spence disliked writing such obvious propaganda for the South, 'but then,' he reasoned, 'it is at such a time – the hour of need – that a friend is of value. When the South is victorious they can do without one's aid.'[4]

The fall of Savannah was not the only disaster that James Spence was trying to present in a more favourable light. His Confederate prisoners' bazaar had inspired the London office of the US Sanitary Commission to publish a pamphlet on Southern prison conditions.[5] Neither Spence nor Wharncliffe had stopped to consider whether highlighting the plight of Confederate prisoners might backfire if anyone queried the South's own record, though their campaign had worked so well at first that Mrs Adams asked Charles Francis Jr. whether it was official policy to mistreat Confederate prisoners.[6] Lord Wharncliffe tried to calm the public outcry by forwarding letters to the press from English volunteers who had suffered in Federal prisons, but it was too late to reverse the damage.*[7] Families with relatives in Southern prisons, including Dr Livingstone, began to insist that as British subjects they should be released at once under the prisoner exchange system. Livingstone was relieved. 'The adjutant of Robert's Regiment says he is sure that Robert was not left dead or wounded, the day he was captured in a skirmish before Richmond,' he wrote to a friend on 4 January. 'They are negotiating for exchange and will give him the "consideration his family merits."'[8] Another father with a missing son, Thomas Smelt, wrote directly to Abraham Lincoln, begging him 'as a parent from a parent, that my son may be sent back to me, he has surely fought well and suffered much for your cause and deserves so much'.[9]

James Spence did not realize how badly the Southern cause had suffered until *The Times* began to turn down his propaganda articles without explanation. After being met with silence for more than a week Spence conceded that his influence with the paper was at an end. 'I doubt if they will insert anything more on the subject,' he wrote to Lord Wharncliffe on 16 January. 'I see but one thing now that can save the South and that is arming the negroes. Tho' I have always expected they would do it, I am growing fearful lest they invited those fatal words – "too late".'[10]

James Bulloch did not accept that time had run out on the Confederacy, especially since – after the disappointments of the previous year – he

---

* One letter came from police constable Joseph Taylor, late of Company F, 5th Louisiana, who wrote to Lord Wharncliffe on 5 January: 'As one who has opposed the Northern Armies from Cedar Mountain fight which took place in August 1862 up to the Battle of Gettysburg, Pennsylvania, July 1863, and taken prisoner the day after that great Battle had terminated, I think it my duty to make this humble protest against the assertion of Mr. Seward that the prisoners taken by the Federals are so well treated that they are suffering no privations.' Another English recipient of Lord Lyons's aid, Captain Hampson of the 13th Louisiana Regiment, wrote: 'Looking in today's *Standard*, I wish so far as lies in my power to corroborate [Taylor's] statement in regard to the treatment of Confederate prisoners by the Federals. I have had personal experience of their kindness (!) to their fellow being whilst in their hands and prisoner.'

was experiencing a late surge of success.[11] The *Ajax*, one of two river steamers he had commissioned to defend the entrance to Wilmington, sailed from Glasgow undetected in the second week of January. 'It is quite impossible to predict what may have transpired when you reach Nassau,' Bulloch told the captain of the vessel, Lieutenant John Low. 'Should [Wilmington] have been taken by the enemy ... you will then proceed with the ship to Charleston, SC ... You may find Charleston itself closed to you, in which case there will remain no port on the Atlantic coast of the Confederate States into which you can take the *Ajax*.' But even then Bulloch wanted Low to find a way to use the ship against the North: at the very least she could bring cotton out from Texas or Florida.[12]

He was already thinking of weapons other than cruisers to send across the Atlantic: his two remaining blockade-runners, for example, were useless for fighting but could easily be deployed as rocket launchers against fishing towns in New England.[13] Bulloch had also managed to buy back one of the French ironclads that had been sold after the Emperor ordered the secret construction programme to end.* The cruiser, which he had decided to christen the *Stonewall*, was coming from Copenhagen, and Bulloch had arranged for a ship with a crew and arms to meet her in neutral waters. After waiting two weeks for news that the transfer had taken place, Henry Hotze suggested to Bulloch on 25 January that they should go ahead and announce the existence of the CSS *Stonewall*. It would, he argued, cause panic on the East Coast and force the US navy to send ironclads to New York, opening the way for the *Stonewall* when she reached Wilmington.[14] Hotze's *Index* had been heavily advertising the *Shenandoah*'s last known captures for that very reason, unaware that the raider was now anchored at Port Phillip Bay,

---

* In late December Bulloch triumphantly informed Mallory that he was on the verge of a significant breakthrough. He had always assumed that the French-made cruisers were lost to them. After the Emperor had ordered their sale one had been bought by the Prussians, the other by the Danes, to be deployed at sea against each other, but the contest never took place because the Danes were defeated before they received the ship and it became clear to M. Arman, the ship's builder, that the Danes had no use for his expensive vessel when it finally arrived in Copenhagen. Rather than insisting on the sale, Arman devised an outrageous plan to sabotage the ship during her trials, thereby providing the unsuspecting Danes with a legal excuse to break the contract. He already knew, of course, of a buyer who would pay twice the amount he had agreed with the Danes for such a powerful ship. Bulloch agreed to pay an exorbitant 455,000 francs for the return of the vessel.

four miles from Melbourne, bereft of coal and in serious need of refurbishment. The Australians were delighted to be front-row spectators for a change, and thousands were visiting the bay in the hope that the notorious Captain Semmes of the *Alabama* was the new commander of the *Shenandoah*.[15]

The diehards had no trouble accepting Hotze's propaganda. His own staff believed him. John Thompson wrote in his diary: 'Am told we shall soon hear something of importance. I think it refers to an ironclad from Europe to attack Boston and New York.'[16] The shipping owner Alexander Collie ridiculed James Spence for being 'blue'. 'We might be prepared to hear of Wilmington and Charleston being captured, and of Richmond being evacuated,' Collie wrote to Wharncliffe on 23 January; 'but, in spite of it all, the South will wear the North out and gain its independence.' In the meantime, he was expecting his steamers to begin taking 'three or four cargoes monthly for the next four months'.[17]

The *Stonewall* was in greater danger than either Bulloch or Hotze knew. Her arrival at Quiberon Bay, on the south coast of Brittany on 24 January, was telegraphed to the US Minister in Paris. Mr Dayton was no longer in charge of the US legation, having died under mysterious circumstances in December; John Bigelow, the Consul in Paris, had been promoted in his place. A man of far greater intelligence and vigour than Dayton, Bigelow almost succeeded in scuppering the mission by his protests to the French authorities. But one of the worst storms in recent memory ultimately achieved his work for him; on 29 January, only a day after the *Stonewall* sailed from Quiberon, the ship's bridge was smashed to pieces by giant waves. Unable to sail on to Wilmington, Captain Page took the damaged vessel to Ferrol, on the Spanish coast, and waited for repairs. Twenty-four hours later Europe learned that the Federals had captured Wilmington's only defence, Fort Fisher.

'Glorious news reached us today,' Benjamin Moran wrote in his diary on 30 January 1865. 'The rebels are tired and will come back soon [into the Union].' Bulloch pressed on, however, and sent an engineer to Ferrol to oversee the *Stonewall*'s repairs. 'The fall of Fort Fisher seriously deranges our plans for sending supplies, but all of us who are charged with such duties will speedily consult and make new and suitable arrangements,' he promised Mallory.[18] Mason was also defiant, telling Benjamin that the Southerners in England approved of the Congress's declaration on 13 December 1864 to fight on 'at whatever cost or hazard'.[19]

The Economist criticized the public's overreaction to the news of Fort Fisher, since the South 'still have large armies in the field, they have still the ablest generals of the Republic in their ranks', but most other papers now declared the Confederacy to be without hope.[20] It was common knowledge that the South would not be able to survive without its imports. During the past four years, 60 per cent of the Confederacy's rifles had come through the blockade, 75 per cent of her saltpetre and 30 per cent of her lead, and, particularly after 1862, the blockade-runners had become the South's lifeline.[21] Consul Thomas Dudley in Liverpool had recently completed his statistics for 1864 and amassed evidence against 113 steamships and 304 sailing vessels. Despite the US navy's efforts, the South had managed to export 124,700 bales of cotton in return for meat, shoes, arms, medicines and all other necessities of war. A total of 303 steamships had successfully run into Wilmington during the war, more than twice the number that reached Charleston.[22] The port had become indispensible to the Confederacy. On 15 February Consul Dudley reported that the blockade-running business had died almost overnight.

It had taken four years and 700 US ships at a cost of $567 million to close every Southern port. During that time there had been 6,316 attempts and 5,389 runs past the blockade. The average capture rate for the whole war was only 30 per cent, but this figure hides the increasing success of the Federal navy over time. In 1861 roughly nine out of ten blockade-runners reached their destinations, but by 1865 the number was only one in two. Although criticized as inept at the time, it is now clear that the blockade played a clear and vital role in the Northern war effort. Guns, meat and shoes could be shipped in on the blockade-runners, but not the heavy cargoes such as iron rails, telegraph poles and train carriages that the South needed in order to move its armies, feed its people, communicate long distances and transport supplies. These hammer blows to the South cost only 10 per cent of the total expenditure of the war; except for Rose Greenhow and a few others, almost no one was killed; and a mere 132,000 sailors were employed by the navy compared to 2.8 million soldiers in the army.[23]

Mrs Adams, Henry, Mary and Brooks left London on 1 February to begin a tour of the Continent. The family had given up the house in Ealing in the expectation that Charles Francis Adams would follow them soon, assuming that Seward would grant his request and appoint a successor.

They also were hoping for a visit from Charles Francis Jr., who had surprised them by becoming the colonel of his regiment and proposing marriage to Mary Hone Ogden all in the same month.

'Neither *Henry* nor Brooks Adams had the decency to bid me goodbye,' Moran raged in his diary. 'I didn't expect so much civility from the boy, but I did from Henry.' He was equally incensed with his new Assistant Secretary, Dennis Alward, for ingratiating himself so easily into Adams's favour. 'Mr Adams is very civil, but it is the smile of the ogre,' he wrote. The Minister had wounded Moran to the quick by inviting Alward to ride in his carriage and, at a reception given by the Countess of Waldegrave, had taken 'special pains to introduce Mr Alward to everybody and equal pains not to introduce me at all'.[24]

Parliament resumed for business a week later on 7 February. 'I have no reason to anticipate any modification in the policy of the ministry toward us,' wrote Mason to Judah P. Benjamin. 'Still, as we have a large body of earnest friends and sympathizers in both houses, it may be that something will arise during the session of which advantage can be taken.'[25] The 'something' was the universal consternation over Congress's repeal of the two treaties with Canada, particularly the Rush–Bagot Treaty, which limited the naval power on the Great Lakes. On the evening of the 7th, Lord Derby attacked the government in the House of Lords for its failure to reinforce Canada's defences on the Lakes: 'If you allow the neighbouring Power to have a preponderating force there, you place Canada at the disposal of the United States.'* MPs in the Commons painted an equally apocalyptic vision; one Welsh MP insisted that 'the act of the President of the United States in tearing up these treaties without ... any expostulation, any argument, any correspondence, on the subject is an act of such unmistakable hostility that it really amounts almost to a declaration of war'.[27] The hysteria in Parliament alarmed Adams, who warned Seward on 9 February: 'The insurgent emissaries and their friends are busy fanning the notion that this is a

---

* Defending British North America against the United States was the best reason for creating the Dominion of Canada, in Derby's opinion. 'Under these circumstances, I see with additional satisfaction that which is probably the most important part of the Royal Speech – I mean the announcement that Her Majesty has given her sanction to the proposed federation of the British North American Provinces. I hope I may regard that federation as a measure tending to constitute a Power strong enough, with the aid of this country, which I trust may never be withdrawn from those provinces, to defend themselves against any aggression.'[26]

THE THREATENING NOTICE.

ATTORNEY LINCOLN. "NOW, UNCLE SAM, YOU'RE IN A DARNED HURRY TO SERVE THIS HERE NOTICE ON JOHN BULL. NOW, IT'S MY DUTY, AS YOUR ATTORNEY, TO TELL YOU THAT YOU *MAY* DRIVE HIM TO GO-OVER TO THAT CUSS, DAVIS——" *(Uncle Sam Considers.)*

Punch depicts Lincoln advising restraint on the move to punish Canada by ending the free trade treaty, February 1865

prelude to war the moment our domestic difficulties are over.' With uncharacteristic force, he charged the Secretary of State to remember that the future of Anglo-American relations lay in his hands. 'Nothing but an extraordinary error in policy', he declared, could turn the sincere desire in Britain for peace into a determination for war.[28]

All of Adams's meetings with Lord Russell since December had been very satisfying. The Foreign Secretary had taken care to explain the government's position regarding the Confederate operations in Canada, and what steps had been taken to prevent them. They had both agreed that the two countries had survived far worse aggravations. 'We had heretofore passed through so many troubles during this war,' Russell told Adams, 'so we might safely get over this one.'[29] But in late January Russell's tone had become anxious; he requested clarification on twelve US steam launches under construction in British dockyards, and whether they were for military or civilian use. Adams realized that the government's concern was whether they would be used, not against the South, but on the Great Lakes against the British. Palmerston was genuinely alarmed. 'There is something mysterious about these launches,' he wrote to Russell. 'Could they have not got them sooner, more cheaply and as good in their own dockyards? What they are really meant for one cannot say. Their size is quite enough for carrying guns, and it is probable they are destined to cover the landing of troops on our shores in the Lakes.'[30]

The Cabinet agreed that Quebec should be fortified as quickly as possible: the navy's budget was increased, and the Queen warned on 12 February that the country was preparing for war. Her private secretary, Lieutenant General Charles Grey, argued unsuccessfully for a pre-emptive strike.*[31] Although the Queen deprecated the idea, she shared Grey's anxiety, acknowledging in her diary 'the impossibility of our being able to hold Canada, but we must struggle for it'.[32] Lord Lyons was summoned to the palace to give his assessment of the United States' intentions. Still in the grip of mental exhaustion and in great pain from his neuralgia, he could not help sounding bleak. Lyons 'seemed bitterly disgusted with his post at Washington and with the dreadful people he has had to deal with – so insincere and ungentlemanlike', the Queen recorded after the interview. 'He thinks the position a dangerous one, but does not believe in a war [between the Americans and] us, at least he hopes it may not come to it.'[33]

Lord Russell had been sincere when he told Adams in December that responsibility for preventing an Anglo-American war rested on the two of them finding 'a safe issue from this, as we had from so many other troubles that had sprung up during this war'.[34] In mid-February, he decided to send a protest to the Confederate government over its blatant abuse of British neutrality. Unlike the previous remonstrance sent in 1864, this one would be dispatched to Washington with a request that

---

* A short time later, the Duke of Somerset received a parcel containing the plans of the US navy's latest ships and their torpedoes. They had been secretly obtained by the master ship-builder Donald McKay, who resided in New York but whose heart and family remained in Nova Scotia.

the US government pass the letter on to Richmond. Russell first showed the document to Charles Francis Adams. It was addressed to Mason, Slidell and Dudley Mann, and laid out three specific charges against the Confederate government: the 'unjustifiable and manifestly offensive' abuse of the Foreign Enlistment Act to build warships in British ship-yards; the instructions given to Confederate cruisers that 'set aside some of the most settled principles of international law'; and the raids by Ben-net G. Burley and others that had been planned and executed in Canada. These showed 'a gross disregard of her Majesty's character as a neutral power, and a desire to involve her Majesty in hostilities.'[35]

Adams was astonished by the passion in Russell's voice; 'he read it over slowly and deliberately,' the Minister recorded in his diary and during the subsequent conversation agreed with him 'that it looked ill' when juries repeatedly acquitted Confederate offenders. 'People here now took sides, almost as vehemently on our questions as we did our-selves. It was to be regretted, but there was no help for it,' Russell had argued, which received the blunt riposte from Adams that if Britain had become embroiled in the Prussian–Danish war, 'in two months, Prussia would have been fitting out fast steamers in the port of New York, and we should not have been able to stop them. His Lordship candidly enough admitted that the idea had occurred to him.'[36] 'This conference was one of a most friendly character,' Adams wrote to Seward, 'and con-vinced me that whatever might be the desires of the French emperor, nothing but the grossest mismanagement on our part would effect any change in the established policy of this ministry towards us.' Over the next few days, Adams repeated his warnings with greater vehemence:

> I need not explain to you that the impression is sedulously kept up that your own feelings are strongly hostile to this country. I find this to prevail even among a large class of persons wholly friendly to us. I have combated it with them in vain. I do not think it is so much entertained by ministers as it was. In this respect, the presence of Lord Lyons has done some good.[37]

Adams wondered whether Seward was even bothering to read his reports, since the Secretary of State rarely responded to specific points and had ignored Adams's request to leave London.[38]

The news that the US Congress had ratified the 13th Amendment, abol-ishing slavery, had an even greater effect on British public opinion than the North's recent military victories. No amount of sneering by Henry Hotze in the *Index* could diminish the moral grandeur of emancipation. He had been counting on the memoirs of Fitzgerald Ross and of Belle Boyd to create a sensation – and a diversion – but neither book was ready for publication. 'I can do no better though I have tried very hard,' Ross explained to his publishers. 'Is it the general experience of authors that the preface is the most difficult part of the book to write?'[39] Belle Boyd was being helped with her book by the writer George Augustus Sala, who may also have become her lover; if he did, the affair was suddenly complicated by the return of Belle's husband, Sam Hardinge, who had been released without explanation from Fort Delaware on 8 February, and had arrived in London with his health completely broken down.* Belle included Hardinge's prison diary in her memoirs, but there is no record of what happened to him once he reached England; he simply disappeared and was never mentioned again. She was similarly tight-lipped about the birth date of her daughter, Grace.[41]

James Mason was in Paris with Dudley Mann and Slidell, composing a joint response to Lord Russell's protest, when Duncan Kenner arrived on 24 February.[42] The Commissioners could not believe that the South they remembered would genuinely consider emancipation; to them, it was the core of Southern identity.[43] Yet Mason had recently received a letter from his eldest son, Lieutenant James M. Mason Jr., who fully embraced the idea of offering freedom to the slaves in return for their fighting for the Confederacy: 'with proper discipline they will fight as well as any mercenaries,' he insisted. His regiment, the 42nd Virginia Infantry, had almost starved while fighting General Sheridan in the Shenandoah Valley, and was hardly better off in Petersburg. He doubted any of them could survive another winter of such suffering: 'if the North continues her present energy, the long night of ruin, misery and agony will surely come unless indeed, you in Europe, do something for our aid.'[44]

Kenner had risked his life to deliver Davis's proposal of emancipation in return for recognition, and it did not matter to him whether the

---

* Sala had reported on the war for the *Daily Telegraph*. In the introduction he provided for Belle's memoir, *Belle Boyd in Camp and Prison*, he claimed that she possessed scandalous information about members of Lincoln's administration. Whether or not this was really the case, he helped her to draft a threatening letter to Lincoln on 24 January, in which she offered to suppress her memoir if Hardinge was released by the beginning of March. 'I think it well for you and me to come to some definite understanding,' Belle had written boldly.[40]

Commissioners were relieved or outraged.[45] Slidell realized that they had no choice, and on 4 March he had an interview with the Emperor, who repeated his condolences and sent the Commissioner on his way. But Mason still could not bring himself to accept the truth; he accompanied Kenner to London and tried to keep him distracted with business arrangements for the Confederate cotton loan. Kenner could not be deflected from his real purpose for long, however, and he insisted that Mason arrange the meeting with Lord Palmerston.

The Confederate Commissioner reluctantly complied, but he had one more trick up his sleeve. At the last minute he succeeded in persuading Kenner to step aside and allow him to make the representation, on the grounds that the mission required the skills of an experienced diplomat. Mason met with Lord Palmerston on 14 March 1865. By his own account, he prevaricated for almost twenty minutes before finally asking whether 'there was some latent, undisclosed obstacle on the part of Great Britain to recognition'. Palmerston had already divined the real purpose of the conversation and replied without hesitating that slavery had never been the obstacle. Mason was elated until he recounted the conversation to a friend, Lord Donoughmore, who told him that Palmerston had said this precisely to forestall a last-minute appeal from the South: slavery had *always* been the chief impediment to recognition. The South had squandered her only chance of achieving it by not emancipating the slaves in 1863, when Lee was the undisputed victor on the battlefield. For a brief moment, Mason feared that he had been responsible for ruining the South's last hope of survival, and wanted to see Palmerston again so he could be much clearer this time, but Donoughmore assured him that 'the [opportunity] had gone by now, especially that our fortunes seemed more adverse than ever'.[*46]

Hotze informed his editorial staff that 'the Confederate funds in Europe were in a state of bankruptcy ... and the Index would probably be discontinued in two or three months'. 'This greatly disconcerted me,'

* The former Confederate Secretary of State Robert M. T. Hunter stated the conundrum in stark terms on 7 March 1865, during the Confederate Senate debate on whether to use slave soldiers. 'To arm the negroes is to give them freedom,' he told the Chamber. 'If we are right in passing this measure, then we were wrong in denying to the old Government the right to interfere with the institution of slavery.' He, for one, was not prepared to be a hypocrite. But the majority of the Senate chose survival over principle. They all knew that General Lee was desperate to have the Negro recruits for his army. A week later, on 13 March, the Confederate House of Representatives followed suit after a raucous and bitter debate.

wrote his deputy John Thompson, 'as I am at a loss to know how to live when my salary is cut off.'[47] The Confederates in London were further demoralized by the debate in the Commons on the night of the 14th about the proposed cost of Canada's defences. Benjamin Moran observed the proceedings from the Strangers' Gallery, expecting to hear the North denounced or the South eulogized. To his surprise, Southern recognition was not even mentioned and 'the marked feature was the tone of respect towards the US, Mr Lincoln and Mr Seward. This was in wonderful contrast to the jeers, the sneers and the disrespect common in that House on all occasions when these names were mentioned two and three years ago ... Forster made a speech that amounted to eloquence. I didn't think he had it in him.'[48]

The revolution in British attitudes towards the North and South was also apparent in the Foreign Office's approach to persons who had run afoul of the US authorities, as Mary Sophia Hill found to her disappointment. 'I should like my trial denounced,' she had written to Lord Wharncliffe in February. 'I feel assured British Statesmen will see simple justice done.'[49] Mary had written in a similar vein to Lord Russell: 'I have come to this country for the purpose of carrying my case personally to your Lordship, and to ask for justice to be done me, and though but a humble individual, I feel assured not all is in vain. England's flag protects her subjects, wherever they may be scattered.'[50] But he did not feel inclined 'to ask for justice', and after reviewing all the documents in Mary's case, nor did Russell's legal advisers. 'Her whole story is, moreover, extremely improbable,' insisted the Attorney General on 18 March:

> It is not true, as she says, that she was acquitted; she was found guilty, and banished. It is certainly not improbable that she may have been rudely treated by the United States authorities; but the British Consul and Lord Lyons appear to have done all that was in their power to save her from the consequences of her own (to say the least) very imprudent acts. We are clearly of opinion, that there is no ground for your Lordship's interference in this matter.[51]

Robert Burley, Bennet's father, encountered a similar response to his requests. Frightened by the execution of John Yates Beall, Bennet's friend and co-conspirator, Burley senior had enlisted the help of his local MP, Robert Dalglish, as well as William Forster, to take up the case with the Foreign Office and the American legation.[52] (Fitzgerald

Ross became concerned for Colonel Grenfell and asked his publisher to remove all references to his friend from his memoir.) He also made a heartfelt appeal to Lord Russell to save his son. The Foreign Secretary scribbled on the back of Burley's letter: 'inform him a copy of his letter will be sent to Washington with instructions to do the best for his son.'[53] Translated, it meant the government would not contest the charges.

Russell was so anxious about the apparent rise in Northern hostility towards England that he asked Lord Lyons to cut short his recuperation and return immediately to Washington. But to his surprise, instead of dutifully agreeing, Lyons resigned from the diplomatic service. 'Lord Russell has been extremely kind to me, and so indeed has every one,' Lyons wrote to his former Secretary of the legation, William Stuart. Seward's subsequent letter especially moved him: 'I accept your farewell with sincere sorrow,' the Secretary of State wrote on 20 March. 'But I reconcile myself to it because it is a condition of restoration of your health.' Seward promised that Anglo-American relations would prosper after the war, although it saddened him that Lyons would not be around to enjoy the moment when the two countries 'are reconciled and become better friends than ever ... But God disposes.' It was bittersweet for Lyons to read these words. 'I confess that I do not feel so much relief or even pleasure as might have been expected,' he told Stuart. 'I seriously thought of offering to go back immediately when I heard the decision of the Cabinet.' That decision was the appointment of Sir Frederick Bruce, the former Minister to China, as the new head of the Washington legation. It was not Bruce that troubled Lyons but the reality of being replaced. He even missed 'my Washington Mission'. In Lyons's reply to Seward he reflected on 'the friendly and unconstrained terms on which we were', and how much good they had produced. 'I am most anxious that my successor's intercourse with you should be placed at once on the same footing.'[54]

'You are about to proceed to Washington at a very critical period,' Russell informed Sir Frederick on 24 March 1865.[55] There were not only 'a vast number of difficult and complicated questions' to be resolved, but also the problem of American anger towards Britain. Seward's most recent salvo clearly reflected the state of public opinion, regardless of whether it accurately portrayed his own feelings. '[The dispatch] is hostile in the extreme to England,' complained Benjamin Moran, 'and gives color to the idea so prevalent here that he really wants to quarrel with

Great Britain. The fact is, Seward is always doing some absurd thing, and often behaves like a child.'[56] Lord Russell had come to a similar conclusion about Seward some time ago, which was why he warned Bruce on no account to mention the *Alabama* or allow Seward to speak to him about reparations for the Confederate cruisers built in Britain. If Seward brought up the Confederate cruisers, Bruce was to declare the subject beyond his remit.[57] That night, Benjamin Moran encountered Lord Lyons and Sir Frederick Bruce together at the French embassy ball. Lyons smiled when Moran asked how he had enjoyed Washington, and replied with monumental understatement, 'he had had a very satisfactory time in the US, although rather hard worked'.[58]

Charles Francis Adams was amused by the government's 'singular panic in regard to what will be done by us, after restoration [of the Union]. A week or two since you could not drive the notion out of their heads that we were not about to pounce at once upon Canada.'[59] But Adams took the greater satisfaction from seeing the humiliation of his former adversaries:

> one thing seems for the present to be settled. That is, that no hope is left for any aid to the rebel cause. England will initiate nothing to help them in their critical moment ... The voluminous intrigues of the rebel emissaries have been completely baffled, their sanguine anticipations utterly disappointed. They have spent floods of money in directing the press, in securing aid from adventurers of all sorts, and in enlisting the services of ship and cannon builders with all their immense and powerful following, and it has been all in vain. So far as any efforts of theirs are concerned, we might enter Richmond tomorrow. This act of the drama is over.[60]

37

Fire, Fire

Tom Conolly MP crosses the bar – Welly! – The last train out –
Richmond burns – Grant breaks Lee's line

Henry Feilden reluctantly accompanied General Hardee as the Confederate army abandoned Charleston on 17 February 1865. 'I cannot bear to think of leaving this dear old city which has been defended so long and gloriously,' he wrote sadly to Julia. 'I have given our house to an English family who will endeavour to save it for me.' But he warned her that 'we are going to see hard times'.[1] His last view of the city before its fall was of golden flames flickering against the night sky as great fires consumed the wharves: the retreating Confederates had deliberately torched the remaining cotton and set fire to ships in the harbour. He was unaware that this 'magnificent sight' had led to a horrific tragedy: a large crowd of civilians, mostly women and children, had been foraging in a warehouse that contained a lethal combination of food and gunpowder when it exploded, killing 150 and leaving many more to die in agony.[2]

Federal troops entered Charleston on 18 February and almost immediately went on the rampage. The contents of the houses, including pianos and four-poster beds, were either plundered or destroyed depending on the humour and taste of the invaders. Consul Henry Pinckney Walker reappeared and invited any British subjects in the city to register at the consulate, although he did not offer the building as a refuge.[3] Some women were not only afraid to leave their houses, but were unable to do so, since looters had stolen their dresses.

It was ten days before Feilden had another opportunity to write. During that time he had not changed his clothes nor slept in a real bed. 'I do not know how much more we have to endure,' he wrote on the 28th, 'but as far as I am concerned I am a stronger Southern Man at this moment than ever I was before, and I shall not give up till the very last moment.'[4] His devotion was not a universal feeling among the retreating Confederates. General Hardee had come down with typhus shortly before the order to evacuate, and was barely able to walk let alone inspire courage or fortitude among his demoralized troops. Months of defensive duties had made the soldiers unfit for forced marches, and the struggle through frozen swamps in unceasing downpours caused many to faint with exhaustion. Whole companies disappeared in the darkness.[5] The officers' ability to prevent desertion during daylight was hardly more successful and the small army was losing almost 200 men a day. Hardee's destination was a small town north of Wilmington called Fayetteville, North Carolina, an important supply base for the Confederates. General Johnston – whom Lee had recently reinstated – had ordered all available troops to meet there to make a last stand against Sherman's advancing forces.

Confederate regiments were already gathering at Fayetteville when Thomas Conolly, an Anglo-Irish MP from County Kildare, Ireland, arrived on 2 March. Conolly had invested in the blockade-runner *Emily II* and sailed to Bermuda with her, intending to run the blockade at Wilmington. A less eccentric character might have chosen to return home after the fall of Fort Fisher, but Conolly saw no reason to let a Northern victory get in the way of his visiting 'Dixie'. Leaving the *Emily II* at Nassau, he persuaded Captain Maffitt, who was taking his ship the *Owl* to Havana, to make a slight detour by way of the North Carolina coast and drop him off somewhere near Cape Fear. On 26 February Conolly and two friends climbed into a skiff and rowed through the pouring rain, over the sandbar and into the neck of the Shallotte river, some 37 miles north of Wilmington. Soaked to the skin and hungry, they called at several houses until they found someone willing to give them shelter for the night.[6]

It was only after he landed that Conolly learned of General Sherman's arrival in South Carolina. The news made him drop his plans to tour Charleston in favour of reaching Richmond as quickly as possible. He arrived at Fayetteville on 2 March to find it mobbed with wagons and soldiers. 'The bar-room of the large Hotel is crowded with men in uniform, and a fine young fellow, very handsome, is hobbling about on a new wooden leg,' Conolly jotted in his diary. The three travellers passed two days in the town, while Conolly tried to negotiate the purchase of a horse. 'So we make the best of it,' he wrote, 'and order a banjo band and whiskey to our room and ask all the wounded officers about and have a capital evening's amusement up to 1 o'clock dancing and singing . . .'[7] Two days later, they ran into Frank Vizetelly, who obligingly offered to take them to Richmond.

The small party arrived at the capital on 8 March. Conolly's penchant for bright red breeches looked incongruous amid the browns, greys and deep mourning. 'The aspect of Richmond at this time is wretched,' he wrote. 'Shops with nothing in them except enough to show how miserably they are run out. Stores with open doors and empty bales and broken up packing cases and dirty straw.' Government clerks were quietly packing their archives in anticipation of having to leave the city. Vizetelly deposited Conolly at the Ballard Hotel and went in search of Francis Lawley. The Ballard was 'now miserably furnished, scarcely anything in the bedrooms except the beds and a few broken chairs,' Conolly recorded. The carpets had been torn up and sent to the army for coats. 'Almost all the crockery in the Hotel is cracked and broken, and we had to buy 3 tumblers for our room at 25 dollars each.' He was annoyed to discover that a bottle of brandy set him back $60.[8]

The first resident to receive a visit from Conolly was the wife of James Mason, the Confederate Commissioner in London. 'Plucky dear old Lady,' he wrote. She was nursing her son, James M. Mason Jr., who was one of the few survivors of a recent skirmish against General Sheridan.[9] The day had been proclaimed by Davis as one of fasting and prayer, and Conolly confined himself to muffins for tea, followed by oysters and cocktails. During the next few days he attached himself to various generals, his open and liberal purse helping to soften any objections to his presence. His persistence paid off and, on 13 March, he received an invitation to supper at the Confederate White House at 9 p.m.

Conolly was impressed by President Davis's calm demeanour: 'I never saw quiet determination more strikingly manifest in any person than in Jeff Davis,' he wrote. 'His conversation is easy, copious in illustration from foreign countries, and rich and animated!' Varina Davis, on the other hand, was less adept at hiding her true thoughts; though obtuse at times, Conolly knew when he was being put down: 'Mrs Davis is a very different character,' he decided; 'a great talker and very bitter. She is calculated to damage any cause however good.'[10]

Had Conolly appeared a day later, it is unlikely that the Davises would have invited him to dinner. Lord Russell's protest to the Confederate Commissioners was delivered to Richmond on 14 March, the morning after. 'Britain gives us a kick while the Federal generals are pounding us,' the War Department clerk John Jones wrote bitterly.[11] But by then, Conolly had already left the capital and was being entertained by General Lee at Petersburg. Conolly's reaction to meeting Lee was similar to Colonel Wolseley's in 1863. Even in the hour of his greatest trial, Lee still retained an aura of magnificence. 'The Hope of His Country is also the handsomest man in all that constitutes the real dignity of man that I ever saw,' wrote Conolly. Lee looked immaculate. His uniform fitted perfectly, his beard was neatly trimmed.

> We visited him at his quarters, a neat farm house with a willow tree in its first spring leaves before the door, and apple trees round the gable used for tying up numerous courier horses [Conolly recorded]. General Lee rises gracefully from his pine table and welcomes me cordially – half an hour easy conversation and as I excuse myself on account of his pressing business he asks us to dinner at 3.30.[12]

The General drew the line at allowing Conolly to stay the night and General Pryor's wife was prevailed upon to take him in. 'You may imagine my sensation at receiving the following note,' she recorded:

> 'General Lee has been honored by a visit from the Hon. Thomas Connolly, Irish MP from Donegal. He ventures to request you will have the kindness to give Mr Connolly a room in your cottage, if this can be done without inconvenience to yourself.' Certainly I could give Mr Connolly a room; but just as certainly I could not feed him! The messenger who brought me the note hastily reassured me. He had been instructed to say that Mr Connolly would mess with General Lee.[13]

But she was quickly won over by Conolly's charm: 'The MP proved a most agreeable guest,' she wrote, 'a fine-looking Irish gentleman with an irresistibly humorous, cheery round of talk.'[14] During Conolly's final dinner at Petersburg, Lee opened a bottle of 'very old Madeira'. 'Excellent! Just 2 glasses,' wrote Conolly mournfully, not realizing that he had consumed all the vegetables and the only turkey in the mess. After saying goodbye to Lee, who gave him his photograph and a Confederate flag, Conolly braved a storm to attend a party at Petersburg with 'some nice young fellows' and a bevy of pretty ladies.

67. Jacob Thompson (1810–85), Confederate Commissioner in Canada. Jefferson Davis gave him $1 million in gold to fund secret operations against Northern targets, both civilian and military. Thompson's plots became increasingly destructive and terror-driven as the war progressed.

68. Clement C. Clay (1816–82), Confederate Commissioner in Canada. Clay was sent out at the same time as Jacob Thompson, but they were temperamentally unsuited to working together and operated out of different cities.

69. Confederate plotters meeting on the Canadian side of Niagara Falls, July 1864. (*left to right*) George N. Sanders, Captain John B. Castleman, Colonel George St Leger Grenfell, British volunteer in the Confederate army, and Captain Thomas H. Hines. Together they hatched a plot to take Chicago and liberate the Confederate prisoners in the surrounding camps. Castleman and Grenfell were captured, but only Grenfell was sentenced to death. He drowned while trying to escape from the harshest Federal prison in the US, Fort Jefferson, on the Dry Tortugas in the Gulf of Mexico.

Among the innovations of the American Civil War was the use of observation balloons, heavier and more accurate artillery and the reliance on railways to mass-transport troops and arms.

70. Mounted cannon – the 'Dictator', most powerful mortar in the war, so heavy it had to be fitted to a specially reinforced railway car.

71. Massed field artillery.

72. A Federal observation balloon.

73. US Lieutenant General Ulysses S. Grant (1822–85), centre, whose victories in the Western theatre of the Civil War led to President Lincoln appointing him general-in-chief in March 1864. Grant was relentless in war and magnanimous in victory.

74. Battle of Cold Harbor, 31 May–3 June 1864. The fourth phase of US General Grant's campaign against CS General Lee ended in defeat for the Union. Grant was labelled 'Butcher Grant' because of the high number of Federal casualties. The fighting took place over the same area as the Battle of Chancellorsville in 1863, and soldiers could not help treading on human remains.

75. CSS *Alabama*. In twenty-two months the Confederate commerce raider covered more than 75,000 miles, captured or sank sixty-five Northern merchant ships, destroyed $5 million-worth of Northern goods, and caused a massive sell-off of US merchant marine.

76. CSS *Stonewall*. A Confederate ironclad ram, she was commissioned by James Bulloch in England and built in France, though delays prevented her from reaching the South before the end of the war.

77. The crew of the USS *Kearsarge*. The USS sloop-of-war, commanded by Captain John Winslow, defeated the CSS *Alabama* in an extraordinary duel in the English Channel on 19 June 1864.

78. Fort Sedgwick, the bomb-proof Union quarters at Petersburg, called 'Fort Hell' by its occupants. Opposite was Fort Mahone, known as 'Fort Damnation'. The siege of Petersburg cost the lives of 70,000 soldiers in nineteen separate battles.

79. The trenches at Petersburg. Between June 1864 and April 1865 the two armies were spread out in a maze of trenches stretching for more than thirty miles. 'All day long,' wrote a British observer, 'the men sat in their fetid dugouts, sweltering in the heat, until the night shift relieved them . . . Soldiers talked about fearful slaughtering they had witnessed in vague tones, as if they wished to forget it.'

80. Charleston at the end of the war. Charleston was regarded with special hatred by Union forces because it was here that the war began on 12 April 1861, when CS General Beauregard fired on the Federal-held Fort Sumter, forcing its surrender. 'If there is any city deserving of holocaustic infamy, it is Charleston,' declared the *New York Herald Tribune*.

81. Richmond after its fall on 3 April 1865. Fire threatened to engulf the entire city and the Federal invaders became firefighters, saving what they could. Fifty-five blocks, the entire business district, went up in flames.

82. and 83. Victory parade of the US army down Pennsylvania Avenue and the front of the Capitol on 24 May 1865. More than 620,000 soldiers and 50,000 civilians died in the war. At least a further 470,000 soldiers were wounded or maimed, including 50,000 amputees. The North lost 10 per cent of its white males aged 20–45; the South lost 30 per cent.

84. Lincoln Memorial, old Calton Cemetery, Edinburgh. On the west side, the inscription reads: 'Unveiled 21st August 1893. This plot of ground given by the Lord Provost, Town Council of Edinburgh to Wallace Bruce, US. Consul as a burial place for Scottish soldiers of the American Civil War 1861–5.' On the east: 'To preserve the jewel of liberty in the framework of peace. Abraham Lincoln.' Around the base: 'Suffrage – Union – Education – Emancipation.'

85. The British Stonewall Jackson Memorial, Richmond, Virginia. The inscription on the plaque reads: 'Presented by English gentlemen, as a tribute of admiration for the soldier and patriot, Thomas J. Jackson, and gratefully accepted by Virginia in the name of the Southern people. Done A. D. 1875, in the hundredth year of the commonwealth. "Look! There is Jackson, Standing like a Stone-Wall."'

The Confederate Congress was holding what would turn out to be its last session when Conolly returned to Richmond on 18 March. Four days earlier, the politicians had agreed to allow owners to volunteer their slaves as soldiers, having voted unanimously 'to prosecute the war with the United States until ... the independence of the Confederate States shall have been established'. But today the members adjourned with no thought of when they would meet again.[15] The city was tense and quiet as the residents waited to learn whether General Joe Johnston would stop Sherman's advance now that Fayetteville had fallen to the Federals. 'If Sherman cuts the communication with North Carolina,' wrote John Jones, 'no one doubts that this city must be abandoned by Lee's army.'[16]

'We are falling back slowly before Sherman,' Feilden had scribbled in a pencilled note to Julia on 13 March. 'I hope that we may have a victory over this man Sherman. I should like to pursue him from here to South Carolina.'[17] None of the Confederate generals, including Hardee, had expected Sherman to make it through the Carolina swamps so quickly, if at all. The right wing of Sherman's army was within marching distance of Raleigh, North Carolina's capital. In desperation, Hardee deployed his outnumbered and weakened forces in a surprise attack against Sherman's left flank on 16 March.

The ambush slowed Sherman just enough for Johnston to organize his army into battle formation at Bentonville, North Carolina. There, for three days, beginning at dawn on 19 March 1865, a force of 20,000 Confederates struggled against an army three times its size. The disparity between the two armies was exacerbated by the Confederates' muddled organization, but Johnston suddenly showed his critics that he could fight – and fight hard – when pressed. By 21 March Johnston's army had suffered more than 2,500 casualties, to the Federals' 1,500. Feilden was talking to General Hardee when a stray shot struck the tree beside them. The next bullet passed through Feilden's sleeve 'near enough to jar my funny bone' and hit his horse, Billy, in the leg. The wound was just bad enough to prevent him from riding the horse in the next cavalry charge. Hardee's 16-year-old son, Willie, begged to take part, and, in the heat of the moment, Hardee nodded his assent and kissed the boy farewell. A short while later, a Texas Ranger brought Willie back, shot through the chest. 'He was a mere schoolboy,' wrote Feilden in anguish. 'He was as gallant a little fellow as ever fired a musket.'

The tragedy made him long to be with Julia: 'Oh! My precious one, if we are only spared to meet again, and live together, what happiness it will be,' he wrote. 'I don't care how poor we may be. It will be the greatest blessing this earth can afford us.'[18]

After the Battle of Bentonville, Sherman continued his march towards Richmond while the Confederates retreated to Raleigh, North Carolina – Johnston was apparently too stunned to consider pursuit. He telegraphed Lee: 'Sherman's course cannot be hindered by the small force I have. I can do no more than annoy him.' Lee realized that in a few days he would be facing the combined forces of Grant, Sheridan and Sherman, and he began planning the Army of Northern Virginia's evacuation from Petersburg. He knew that Richmond would then fall to the Federals, but if his army remained intact the South would still have its fighting capability. On 25 March, he launched a surprise attack against the Union Fort Steadman, on the east side of Petersburg, hoping to distract Grant long enough to enable the rest of the Confederate army to retreat southwards, towards North Carolina. The assault was an outright disaster, costing Lee 4,000 casualties against the Federals' 1,500, without any weakening of Grant's line.

Tom Conolly was in Richmond during the attack, but the news of its failure made no difference to his confidence in the ultimate outcome of the war: 'Richmond thy sun is not setting, rather the Day is just about to break over your hero-crested virgin hills!' he wrote in his diary, adding for good measure: 'Always darkest before the dawn! What a dawn, Independence!' Late on the 25th he received a note, inviting him to visit Mrs Mason's house. '"Welly" is to be there!' wrote Conolly in surprise, learning for the first time that his friend Lieutenant Llewellyn Traherne Bassett Saunderson of the British army's 11th Hussars had arrived in the South at the same time as him, hoping to volunteer on General Lee's staff.[19]

The following day, 26 March, Conolly went to church, where the vicar's sermon sent him to sleep; 'I hate argument, I like faith much better!' Conolly was oblivious to the fact that the city was emptying around him. Jefferson Davis had overridden his wife's protests and instructed her to take the family to Charlotte, North Carolina, 300 miles to the south-west, and to go further, if necessary. Their furniture was sent to auction, and Varina distributed various mementoes to friends and servants. Davis also asked his private secretary to accompany the family to

safety. He gave Varina all his gold save for one five-dollar piece and a
small Colt pistol, which she was to use in the 'last extremity'.

The CSS *Georgia*'s former lieutenant, James Morgan, met the Davis
family at the station. In his wildest dreams he had never imagined
himself as personal guard to a mother and her small children. When
summoned by the Confederate Navy Secretary, Stephen Mallory, to the
Navy Department, he thought it was for some infraction: 'I at once
began to think of all my sins of commission and omission. To my surprise, he told me that I was to accompany Mrs. Jefferson Davis south,
and added, with a merry twinkle in his eyes, that the daughters of the
Secretary of the Treasury [George Trenholm] were to be of the party.'
(Morgan had become engaged to Trenholm's younger daughter, Helen,
whom he had met in Charleston on the night of his introduction to
Matthew Fontaine Maury.)

As Morgan observed the parting between Jefferson and Varina, he
realized that the Davises were behaving as though it was their final
moment together as a family. The two eldest children clung to their
father, crying to stay with him. Davis kissed them all again, stroked the
baby that lay asleep on a bench, embraced his wife, wished Morgan and
the Trenholm girls a safe journey, and walked heavily down the carriage
steps. What should have been a six-hour train journey took more than
four days. When the creaking train pulled into Charlotte a furious mob
surrounded the carriage.

> I closed the open windows of the car so that the ladies could not hear what
> was being said [recalled Morgan]. We two men were helpless to protect
> them from the epithets of a crowd of some seventy-five or a hundred black-
> guards, but we stationed ourselves at the only door which was not locked,
> determined that they should not enter the car. Colonel Harrison was
> unarmed, and I had only my sword, and a regulation revolver in the holster
> hanging from my belt. Several of the most daring of the brutes climbed up
> the steps, but when Colonel Harrison firmly told them that he would not
> permit them to enter that car the cowards slunk away. When the disturbance
> had quieted down Mrs. Davis, her sister, and her children left the train.

The city's residents were frightened of showing courtesy to Varina and
furious with her husband for mismanaging the war. 'Mrs. Davis would
have been in a sad plight if it had not been for the courage and chiv-
alric courtesy of a Jewish gentleman, a Mr. Weil,' wrote Morgan, 'who

hospitably invited her to stay at his home until she could make other arrangements. May the God of Abraham, Isaac, and Jacob bless him wherever he is!'[20]

Jefferson Davis waited anxiously in the Confederate capital while Lee sought to delay Grant's encirclement of Petersburg. The Army of Northern Virginia had dwindled to no more than 35,000 men, while Grant's Army of the Potomac had grown to over 125,000. President Lincoln was less than 20 miles from Richmond, having travelled from Washington on the *River Queen* to visit Grant's headquarters at City Point on the James river. (Mary and Tad accompanied him for the first days, but Mary behaved so strangely – raving at the slightest provocation – that she was encouraged to stay in her cabin.) Lincoln's greatest concern was that peace, which seemed so close now, should not be a pyrrhic victory for the North. 'I want no one punished,' he told Sherman and Grant. Their armies were to be restrained from violence or vengeance. When asked about President Davis, Lincoln expressed a wish that the Confederate leader would emigrate, unnoticed and unmolested.

Lee and Grant had fought each other over 700 square miles of territory since 9 June 1864; more than 70,000 soldiers had died in nineteen separate battles. Now, the struggle had narrowed to the possession of the Five Forks crossroads, 15 miles from Petersburg. Lee needed to hold it just long enough for his forces to escape from Petersburg using the Southside Railroad. Tom Conolly was again at Lee's headquarters, where he watched the General outline the battle plan to his staff, using a stick and a 'mud map'. Conolly remained with Lee, rather than following Generals Fitz Lee and Pickett to Five Forks, and was rewarded with the spectacle of a skirmish between two picket lines.

> This pleased him so much [wrote General Wilcox], that he offered his service to me for the coming campaign, and said if I would permit him he would remain with me until its close. I accepted his tender of service, and told him I would make him one of my volunteer aides. He thanked me, and asked if I would let him go under fire. I replied that it would hardly be possible for him to escape being under fire. He said he would return to Richmond, get his baggage and report to me early Monday morning [3 April].[21]

At Five Forks, Fitz Lee and Pickett had orders to hold the crossroads 'at all hazard'. Welly had been placed on Fitz Lee's staff, where he was delighted to discover another British volunteer, Francis Dawson. They rose at 3.30 a.m. on 31 March and 'after a rough breakfast we all went down to General Pickett's headquarters where a Council of War took place. We remained here for 3 hours or so, smoking and telling stories in a downfall of rain the whole time.'[22] Years afterwards, Dawson also remembered the terrible rain that had chilled him to the bone. He had tried to keep warm by gulping coffee out of an old tin cup before the fighting commenced, and scalded his lips in the process. Later in the morning another moment seared itself into his memory: 'It was very difficult to rally the men,' he wrote.

> One fellow whom I halted as he was running to the rear, and whom I threatened to shoot if he did not stop, looked up in my face in the most astonished manner, and, raising his carbine at an angle of forty-five degrees, fired it in the air, or at the tops of the pines, and resumed his flight. It made me laugh, angry as I was.[23]

Towards sundown, General Fitz Lee's men made a final, desperate charge against Sheridan's line. One bullet struck an overhanging branch just as Dawson lowered his head to ride under the tree; the next tore into his shoulder.

'Bad news from Pickett,' recorded Welly on 1 April. 'He has lost 5,000 men out of 8,000, and the remainder are cut off from us.' The two generals, Fitz Lee and Pickett, had ridden off to a picnic, having assumed that Sheridan would spend the day entrenching his men. Far from it: Sheridan launched a surprise attack. 'We had no idea that the enemy were so close to us,' wrote Welly; 'when all of a sudden about 250 Yankees let drive at us, it was so sudden that nobody could help being startled. I looked round and the whole regiment had disappeared.' Sheridan captured more than 4,000 prisoners at Five Forks. As the scattered Confederates found one another, Welly was relieved to learn that 'Dawson, one of my brother ADCs', had not been killed, but sent to Richmond at Fitz Lee's insistence.[24]

Dawson arrived in the city so befuddled with morphine that he was oblivious to the turmoil in the streets. At dawn on Sunday, 2 April, Grant ordered an all-out attack on Lee's defences, smashing through at almost every point. Lee realized he had to retreat immediately or risk being surrounded and captured. He ordered the troops to evacuate and sent a telegram to Davis, advising him to leave Richmond. The message was

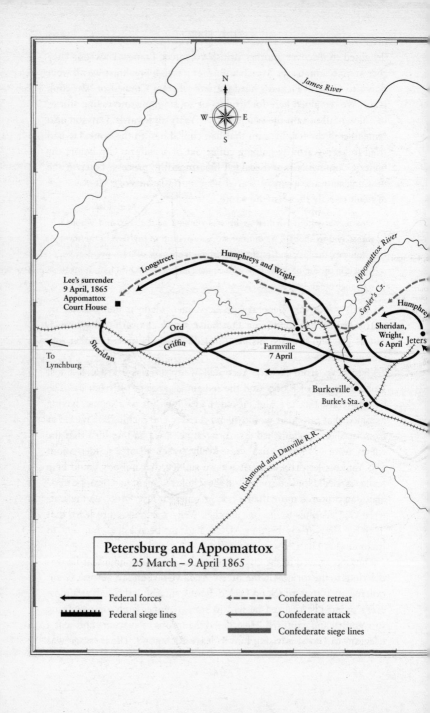

James River

N
W E
S

Longstreet   Humphreys and Wright

Appomattox River

Seyler's Cr.

Lee's surrender
9 April, 1865
Appomattox
Court House

Humphrey

Ord

Sheridan,
Wright, 6 April

Griffin   Farmville
Sheridan   7 April   Jeters

To
Lynchburg

Burkeville
Burke's Sta.

Richmond and Danville R.R.

Petersburg and Appomattox
25 March – 9 April 1865

⟵━━━ Federal forces   ⇠- - - Confederate retreat

▮▮▮▮▮ Federal siege lines   ⟵━━ Confederate attack

▬▬▬▬ Confederate siege lines

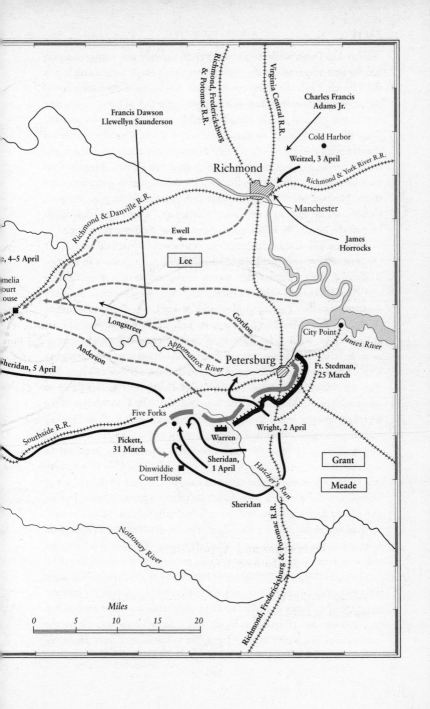

Richmond, Fredericksburg & Potomac R.R.

Virginia Central R.R.

Charles Francis Adams Jr.

Cold Harbor

Francis Dawson
Llewellyn Saunderson

Weitzel, 3 April

Richmond

Richmond & York River R.R.

Manchester

James Horrocks

Richmond & Danville R.R.

Ewell

Lee

, 4–5 April

melia
ourt
ouse

Longstreet

Anderson

Gordon

Appomattox River

City Point

James River

Petersburg

Ft. Stedman, 25 March

heridan, 5 April

Southside R.R.

Five Forks

Pickett, 31 March

Warren

Wright, 2 April

Sheridan, 1 April

Grant

Meade

Dinwiddie Court House

Sheridan

Hatcher's Run

Nottoway River

Richmond, Fredericksburg & Potomac R.R.

Miles

0   5   10   15   20

delivered to Davis while he was at church. Conolly was sitting in a pew nearby and observed the sexton whisper in his ear. 'He rises and leaves the Church. Then the same operation to one and a second member of the government, both follow suit; people begin to whisper . . . they rose in tens and 20s and left the Church, outside the secret was soon abroad.' Only the most faithful remained for communion. Conolly fought his way through the streets – 'a regular stampede has begun' – to the home of his friends, Mrs Enders and 'her nice pretty daughters'. He promised the distraught women he would spend the night, guarding the house for them. Having satisfied himself that they were safe for the moment, Conolly set off in search of Francis Lawley and found him packing his bags at the hotel: 'We take a parting cup to our next merry meeting.'

Jefferson Davis was also packing. Trains were being laid on to take the government and the Treasury to Danville, 40 miles south-west of Richmond. There was pandemonium in the city. People were fighting and clawing at each other to escape the city; 'on horseback, in every description of cart, carriage and vehicle,' wrote Lawley, 'on canal barges, skiffs, and boats'. Stephen Mallory and Judah P. Benjamin were already at the station, waiting for the rest of the Cabinet. Mallory had sent an order to Raphael Semmes, who had been placed in charge of Richmond's water defences after his return to the South in November 1864, to destroy the fleet of nine ships on the James river and take his force to wherever Lee established his new headquarters. The Confederate Navy Secretary had not heard from James Bulloch in weeks. Each day he had waited for a telegram announcing the arrival of the CSS *Stonewall*, but despite Bulloch's efforts the cruiser had only set sail from Spain on 28 March. Mallory had no idea of the whereabouts of the CSS *Shenandoah* (the raider was in the Pacific, near the Eastern Caroline islands, south of Guam), nor did it matter now. Judah Benjamin was inscrutable, but he, too, had to accept that his final gamble had failed. Even if Duncan Kenner had succeeded in obtaining Southern recognition from Palmerston in exchange for emancipation – which Benjamin seriously doubted after receiving Lord Russell's protest – it was too late for the Confederacy.

The trains began rumbling out of Richmond at 11 o'clock. First went the government train, followed by the Treasury's, and finally the government archives. Every car was crowded with refugees; more were riding on the roofs and clinging on to the sides. Some of the guards on the trains were boys, barely in their teens. 'Up to the hour of their departure from Richmond,' insisted Francis Lawley, 'I can testify that Mr Davis and the three most prominent members of his Cabinet went undauntedly forth to meet the future, not without hope that General Lee would be able to hold together a substantial remnant of his army.'[25]

Tom Conolly stood by the front window of the home of the Enders family, keeping watch while the women lay on the sofas behind him, 'and weep and sob till their hearts seem breaking'. Francis Lawley also remained awake. 'During that memorable night there was no sleep in Richmond,' he wrote. 'In front of every Government bureau, of every auditor's office, around the Capitol, and upon each side of Capitol-Square, the glare of vast piles of burning papers turned night into day.' The last regiments to leave Richmond had orders to destroy the ordnance depots to keep them from enemy hands, and to dispose of the city's liquor supply. In a well-intentioned but disastrous move, the Confederates emptied hundreds of whisky kegs onto the streets. 'Women and boys, black and white, were seen filling pitchers and buckets from the gutters,' wrote John Jones in his diary.[26]

Both Conolly and Lawley heard the explosions, which seemed to shake every building in Richmond to its foundations.

> As I walked up between 5 and 6 in the morning of Monday, the 3rd, to catch the early train [wrote Francis Lawley], a vast column of dense black smoke shot into the air ... as the eye ranged backwards along the James River, several bright jets of flame in the region of Pearl and Cary streets augured the breaking forth of that terrible conflagration which subsequently swept across the heart of the city. As the train moved off from the Fredericksburg depot about 6 o'clock, I parted with Mr Conolly, the Member for Donegal, who had passed a month in Richmond, and was upon this eventful morning still undecided whether to follow General Lee's army or to strike northwards like myself.[27]

In the commercial district, hardly a single pane of glass remained unbroken, and from Main Street to the canal nearly a thousand buildings were on fire. The bridges were also destroyed. This, together with the 'roaring and crackling of the burning houses ... made up a scene that beggars description and which I hope never to see again', wrote a departing Confederate officer; 'a city undergoing pillage at the hands of its own mob, while the tramp of a victorious enemy could be heard at its gates!'[28] Lawley was overwhelmed at the sight. For the past four years he had venerated the South; he had perjured himself on its behalf, and had perpetuated a dream only to watch helplessly now as it transmogrified into a nightmare. 'Hell is empty, and all the devils are here,' he quoted from *The Tempest*.

Conolly returned to his hotel at sunrise, shoving at anyone who attempted to get in his way. Hundreds of fires were still burning. He had almost reached the building when he heard a cry, 'the Yankees, the Yankees'. The city's bleary-eyed residents were astonished to see a combination of white and Negro regiments from the US Army of the James – Butler's old army – riding through the streets. Many were singing 'John Brown's Body' as they marched. The scene helped to make up Conolly's mind to quit the Misses Enders and by mid-morning he was riding for Fredericksburg. Already a Federal flag was hanging from the rooftop of the Capitol. 'The ensign of our subjugation,' lamented a female resident, but its appearance represented salvation just as much as disaster.[29] The US general leading the Federal entrance, Godfrey Weitzel, hurriedly ordered his officers to organize teams of firefighters. The hotels, the banks, the better class of shops, the warehouses, depots and hundreds of private houses were either charred heaps of brick or empty edifices. Fifty-five blocks in the centre of Richmond had disappeared, but Weitzel's men saved many more.

Hundreds of families collected in Capitol Square, sitting in huddled groups, with the detritus of destruction around them, waiting miserably for the Federals to take charge of their future. Hour by hour, order was gradually restored to the streets. By 10 p.m., when Charles Francis Adams Jr. led the 5th Massachusetts (Colored) Cavalry into the city, an unofficial curfew made the place seemed deserted. 'To have led my regiment into Richmond at the moment of its capture is the one event which I should most have desired as the culmination of my life in the Army,' he admitted to his father. 'For the first time I see the spirit of the Virginians, the whole people are cowed – whipped out.'[30]

Abraham Lincoln arrived at the city a few hours after Charles Francis Jr., on the morning of the 4th.[31] The black population was anything but 'whipped out'. They clustered about him, shouting ecstatically, touching his clothes and shaking his hand; he protested when some knelt down as he passed. Lincoln entered the Confederate White House and looked around Davis's office, even sitting in his chair. He seemed tired and worn to those around him. Victory was at hand, but not yet in his hands – not until the surrender of Lee's army, he reminded a Confederate delegation who called on him to discuss Virginia's political future. During the afternoon Lincoln toured hospitals and prisons, showing a gentle courtesy to Federals and Rebels alike. He displayed a magnanimity towards the defeated Confederates that was conspicuously absent among his colleagues in the Cabinet.

Lee would be able to keep fighting if he could reach North Carolina and consolidate his army with the survivors of General Joe Johnston's. He ordered his commanders to head 40 miles west, towards the court house at Amelia Springs, where the scattered fragments of the Army of Northern Virginia could regroup and distribute supplies for the long journey ahead. But Grant was in pursuit; his forces moving so swiftly that Quartermaster Sergeant James Horrocks (since his promotion in March) returned from his furlough in New York to find his camp deserted. Not knowing where the 5th New Jersey Light Artillery had gone, he walked into Richmond and spent the night on the floor in one of the bedrooms in the Confederate White House. 'So I had the honor of sleeping in the house of Jeff Davis,' he wrote to his brother, 'if there is any honor in that.'[32]

38

'A True-born King of Men'

Lincoln in Richmond – Appomattox Court House – A final salute – From actor to assassin – Punch apologizes – The American example – Flight to the interior – Vizetelly's fifty-pound note

On 5 April 1865 Abraham Lincoln spent his second day in Richmond, riding about in an open carriage. His bravery terrified the Presidential retinue, but it no doubt contributed as much to the city's return to order as any overt display of arms. The aftermath of Richmond's burning was also observed by Thomas Kennard, an English railway engineer, who was so eager to be a part of the momentous events in Virginia that he had chartered a private yacht to take him and a small group of British and American tourists along the James river to the Confederate capital. They wandered through the streets, shocked to find 'that nearly half the city has been reduced to ashes', though they thought the Federal soldiers' behaviour was exemplary.

> No pillage or destruction of property had taken place [wrote Kennard], and, to the great honour of the Federal arms be it fairly said, never before did cities like Petersburg and Richmond, entered by excited troops after years of siege, suffer to so trifling an extent. Tobacco was the only temptation that could not be resisted. There was not a whisper amongst the inhabitants conversed with, other than that they had been treated in the most humane and proper manner. We can all certify to the fact that out of the thousands upon thousands of troops we have seen only one man has been detected the worse for drink. This is accounted for by the fact that spirits are forbidden both in the army and navy on service. One could not fail to remark the deep mourning worn by the ladies moving about the streets, or

the careworn expression of their countenances. The 'darkie' element, on the contrary, was decidedly jubilant.[1]

Lincoln stopped at Capitol Square, on his way to General Weitzel's headquarters in the former Confederate White House, and addressed a crowd of newly freed slaves: 'My poor friends, you are free,' he said, 'free as the air. You can cast off the name of slave and trample upon it . . . Liberty is your birthright.' But later, at the close of his meeting with Weitzel, Lincoln urged the General to treat the defeated white population with tact: 'If I were in your place,' the President told him, 'I'd let 'em up easy, let 'em up easy.'[2]

Lincoln was impatient for peace and he urged General Grant, in a telegram on 6 April, to finish off Lee's army before it escaped to Georgia: 'nothing . . . is to delay, hinder, or interfere with your work.'[3] Grant had heard from Sheridan that the Confederates had massed at Amelia Court House, 40 miles west-north-west of Petersburg, and were desperately foraging for food in the surrounding countryside as their supplies had failed to arrive. Grant realized immediately that his adversary had only one course of action: 'It now became a life and death struggle with Lee to get south to his provisions.'[4] More than a million and a half rations of bread and meat were waiting for the famished Confederates at Danville, 100 miles away on the Virginia–North Carolina border. 'The soldiers are in a dreadful state from hunger,' Welly wrote in his diary on the 6th. Lee had heard that the road to Danville was blocked, but there were 80,000 rations at Farmville, only 18 miles from his present position; this had to be the next destination or else his men would either collapse from starvation or desert.

Francis Lawley had changed his mind about fleeing immediately to New York, and had returned to observe the final scene of the drama that had absorbed his life since becoming the *Times*'s special correspondent. 'All day long upon the 6th, hundreds of men dropped from exhaustion,' he wrote, 'and thousands let fall their muskets from inability to carry them any further.'[5] Lee pleaded with his son, Rooney, who was commanding a division of the cavalry corps, to keep up its spirits: 'don't let it think of surrender. I will get you out of this.'[6] But Sheridan pounced on the Confederate army as it retreated across Sayler's Creek. Two divisions, amounting to almost a quarter of Lee's forces, were cut off from their comrades; here, beside a naked line of trees, occurred the

Richmond, Virginia, after capture by the Federals, by Thomas Kennard

final battle between the Army of the Potomac and the Army of Northern Virginia.

> Shells screaming, passed us, some bursting a few feet off us, volley of bullets coming in every direction [wrote Welly]. Every now and then, I heard bullets go with a *thud* into some unfortunate soldier, who would give a scream and all was over. I had a very narrow escape by a Parrot shell passing within 2 inches of my head and bursting within a foot of me, by coming in contact with a tree, a piece of it killing a man about a hundred yards off. It certainly was very exciting. People may talk about hunting, but a good battle is a 100 times more exciting.[7]

The surrounded Confederates tried to fight their way through, many resorting to fists and teeth if they had no weapons.* But after five hours

---

* A former British army officer in the Confederate army, Henry O'Brien, lay among the wounded, left for dead by his comrades. He had not expected the war to come to this: 'I came to this country last winter,' he explained a few weeks later from prison, his life having been saved by a Federal surgeon. '[I ran] the blockade at Wilmington, NC through a love of adventure and a desire of seeing something of active service on this continent.'[8]

the two divisions surrendered, making prisoners out of nine Confederate generals (including Custis, Lee's eldest son) and almost 8,000
soldiers. The grey countryside turned black from the smoke rising from
burning wagons. Lawley looked about him and saw 'exhausted men,
worn-out mules and horses, lying down side by side – gaunt famine
glaring hopelessly from sunken lack-lustre eyes – dead mules, dead
horses, dead men everywhere – death, many times welcomed as God's
blessing in disguise'.[9]

Lee dragged the remains of his army across the Appomattox river
and reached Farmville on 7 April. The precious rations were waiting for
him, but also the news that the way ahead to Appomattox Station,
25 miles west from Farmville – where the rest of his supplies had been
sent – was blocked by Sheridan. Straggling had diminished Lee's army
to fewer than 13,000 men, yet when he received a note from Grant on
the evening of the 7th, asking for surrender to avoid 'any further effu-
sion of blood', he tried to use the correspondence to buy time while his
officers looked for an escape route to Danville. That night General Fitz
Lee sent Welly to deliver a note to his uncle, Robert E. Lee, who was,
wrote the British officer, 'quite calm, although the Army is in such a
state'.[10] The next day was even worse for the Confederates. 'No food,

and marching all day. It is a fearful sight to see the state of our Army, hundreds upon hundreds lying in the road, not able to move from hunger and fatigue,' wrote Welly. 'The enemy surround us on all sides.' Lee's army was so depleted that one brigade had only eight men.[11]

During the night of 8 April, Lee's senior commanders, Longstreet, Gordon and Fitz Lee, gathered in a copse near Appomattox Court House to discuss the possible courses left open to them. Fitz Lee did not wish to be a part of any surrender and informed his uncle that he would take the remainder of his corps and flee southwards. But the others were prepared to surrender with Lee if their final attempt to escape failed. Though there were only 10,000 soldiers present for duty against a pursuing force of 116,000, the generals agreed there should be one last attempt to break through Grant's encirclement. 'At 6 a.m., our line of battle is formed,' wrote Welly. 'The whole line move forward under heavy shelling from the enemy, our men seem mad with rage, they charge the enemy who are ten times their number, and drive them before them, killing all that come in their way, taking no prisoners, but for all that it is no good, the enemy's reserve come up and our men have to retreat, but they do it only inch by inch.'[12]

At 8.30 a.m. Lee was informed that Gordon's attack had failed and the troops were falling back towards Longstreet's position, which was itself under fire from Federal forces. 'Then,' said Lee, 'there is nothing left for me to do but to go to General Grant, and I would rather die a thousand deaths.'[13] He had prepared for this moment, and had dressed before the battle in his best uniform, with red sash, ceremonial sword and gold scabbard (the last given to him by a group of English female admirers).[14] Welly was still exchanging fire with Federal soldiers when Fitz Lee received Lee's dispatch that he was surrendering the army that day.

When the Union and Confederate generals gathered at 1 p.m. in the parlour of Wilmer McLean's brick house, a short distance from Appomattox Court House, Grant was struck by the extreme contrast between Lee's immaculate clothes and his own 'rough travelling suit' (which was only a private's uniform adorned with the stars and epaulettes of a lieutenant general). Lee had just two officers with him; Grant was accompanied by Generals Sheridan, Ord and Porter and most of his staff, but the witnesses stood back respectfully as the two men chatted for a while, as though the occasion was no more than two veterans meeting for the first time since the Mexican–American War. 'What General Lee's feelings were I do not know. As he was a man of so much dignity, with an impassible face, it was impossible to say,' wrote Grant in his memoirs, 'but my own feelings, which had been quite jubilant on the receipt of his letter, were sad and depressed.'[15] Finally, Lee could take the suspense no longer, and brought the subject round to the surrender.

At four in the afternoon, Lee and his aides stepped out onto the sun-lit porch of the McLean House, the document of surrender signed. Grant had offered generous terms: the Confederates were to lay down their weapons in perpetuity, but in return the officers could keep their horses and side arms, and all could return to their homes unmolested. Grant had also offered to send rations to the famished Confederates. Lee mounted his horse, Traveller, and rode towards his own lines. 'As the great Confederate captain rode back from his interview with General Grant,' wrote Francis Lawley,

> the news of the surrender acquired shape and consistency, and could no longer be denied. The effect on the worn and battered troops – some of whom had fought since April 1861 ... passes mortal description. Whole lines of battle rushed up to their beloved old chief, and, choking with emotion, broke ranks and struggled with each other to wring him once more by the hand. Men who had fought throughout the war, and knew what the agony and humiliation of the moment must be to him, strove with a refinement of unselfishness and tenderness which he alone could fully appreciate, to lighten his burden and mitigate his pain. With tears pouring down both cheeks, General Lee at length commanded voice enough to say: 'Men, we have fought through the war together. I have done the best that I could for you.'[16]

Lawley did not stay to watch the defeated Confederates stack arms and surrender their regimental flags on 12 April. He was in New York, finishing his report on Richmond's evacuation, when the ceremony took place. His refusal to witness the final moments of the Army of Northern Virginia meant that he deprived himself of an experience that would have helped to heal rather than increase his sorrows. There was none of the crowing or ritual humiliation that he had feared; indeed, as the first line of Confederates stepped forward to deliver their weapons – members of Stonewall Jackson's old brigade – the Federal guard stood to attention and presented arms, inspiring the Confederates to do the same – 'honor answering honor', in the words of the attending Federal general, Joseph Chamberlain.[17]

Word of Lee's surrender spread quickly throughout the South. 'We were brought into the 4 mile camp at Vicksburg and I was lying there when news came of General Grant's great victory,' wrote James Pendlebury of the New York 69th Irish Regiment. He had survived three months of relentless marching from one makeshift prison to another until his rescue by Federal troops. Sick and weak as he was, Pendlebury dragged his emaciated frame to the Vicksburg Court House and rang the bell, which was answered by a volley of cannonfire off the surrounding hills. But in Richmond, the 100-gun salute was ignored by the long shuffling lines of residents queuing at US Sanitary Commission depots for their rations. Francis Dawson had regained consciousness, although he was incapacitated by the bullet wound to his shoulder. 'What would you think of me were I to return to England, poorer than when I left her shores?' he wrote to his mother. He felt not just the defeat of the Confederacy but a sense of personal failure: 'My life has been a useless one, productive only of grief to others whom I love the best and remorse to myself.' He had always promised his mother that his absence from London would not leave her in want; however, his 'worldly possessions' now consisted of 'a postage stamp and what was left of a five dollar greenback that a friend in Baltimore had sent me'.[18]

Further south, at Danville, Jefferson Davis, his Cabinet, and an escort of sixty midshipmen from the Confederate naval academy, boarded their trains again, this time for Greensboro in North Carolina, where the armies of Beauregard and Johnston were said to remain intact. 'People in the army wonder at my good spirits,' Feilden wrote to Julia from his makeshift camp at Hillsborough, North Carolina, 'for all that I cannot shut my eyes to our condition, though perhaps after all it is more philosophic to try and not think, but to float down with the current.'[19] But, like Dawson, Feilden was prepared for a prolonged resistance to Federal rule. 'To tell the truth,' he wrote, 'I would sooner be killed in this war than leave the country in its present distress of my own accord.' Davis shared his sentiments, and when he reached Greensboro the Confederate President became indignant with Beauregard and Johnston for telling him there was no alternative to asking Sherman for his terms of surrender. Davis insisted that the war was by no means over, not when there remained two undefeated Confederate armies – Johnston's in North Carolina and General Edmund Kirby-Smith's west of the Mississippi.[20] Driven by Davis's determination to fight on – and a fear that they would all be hanged for treason if caught by the Federals – the remaining members of the Confederate Cabinet began making preparations to leave Greensboro on 14 April. They were being hunted by Federal forces, but one determined seeker had already found them, though he was a friend: Frank Vizetelly had been trying to catch up with Davis since the fall of Richmond and was the only journalist to reach him.

Abraham Lincoln had been in Washington for five days on 14 April when he convened the Cabinet to discuss the terms for readmitting the Southern States to the Union. The only member not at the meeting was William Seward, who was bedridden after suffering a carriage accident on 5 April that had left him with a dislocated shoulder and a broken jaw. His wife and daughter, Frances and Fanny, were nursing him. 'His face is so marred and swollen and discolored that one can hardly persuade themselves of his identity,' his wife Frances wrote to her sister, nor was he able to communicate except by grunting.[21] Bereft of his closest ally, Lincoln found it much more difficult to persuade the Cabinet of the wisdom of showing clemency towards the South. He even advised the War Secretary, Edwin Stanton, to allow the Confederate plotters in Canada to escape to Europe. Stanton wanted Jacob Thompson arrested and tried in the US. 'Best to let him run,' countered Lincoln.[22]

The President felt there was something particularly momentous about this day – Good Friday. He was not sure what to expect, he told the Cabinet, perhaps news of Johnston's surrender or the capture of Jefferson Davis, but the night before he had dreamed his recurring dream – the one which always seemed to precede good news – where he was sailing 'with great rapidity towards an indefinite shore'.[23] When he joined Mary Lincoln for a carriage ride a couple of hours later, Lincoln was even more emphatic about his feelings: 'I consider *this day*, the war has come to a close,' he told her. 'We must *both* be more cheerful in the future – between the war and the loss of our darling Willie – we have both, been very miserable.'[24]

That evening the Lincolns went to Ford's Theatre to watch Laura

Keane in her one-thousandth performance of Tom Taylor's *Our American Cousin*.* All of Washington knew that Lincoln was going to be there, and many people had bought tickets just so they could catch a glimpse of him. The information helped John Wilkes Booth to make up his mind; his previous attempts to kidnap the President had all been thwarted by faulty intelligence or human failure. Months of frustration had exacerbated his already volatile nature, and tonight he was determined 'to live in history'.[25] He expected three deaths to occur simultaneously: Lincoln's by his hand, Vice-President Johnson's by the hand of George Atxerodt, and Seward's by the hand of Lewis Powell; and he had prepared a statement in advance for the *National Intelligencer*, justifying the murders. The three men started out together, but George Atxerodt could not bring himself to perform the task and retreated to a hotel bar. At 10 p.m. Powell called at Seward's house, claiming to have brought medicine from the doctor. A servant took him to the third floor, where Fanny and a male nurse were tending to Seward. But Frederick, Seward's younger son, became suspicious and refused to let Powell enter the patient's room. Throwing off his pretence, Powell attempted to shoot Frederick and, when the gun failed to go off, used it to beat him into a state of unconsciousness. Easily dispensing with the nurse who opened the door to investigate the noise, Powell ignored Fanny and went straight for Seward, who struggled to defend himself as Powell hacked at his head and neck with his bowie knife. Fanny's screams alerted Seward's older son, Augustus, who rushed into the room and tried to grab the knife. Powell slashed at him wildly; breaking free of Augustus's grip, he hurled himself down the stairs and out of the house, stabbing a State Department messenger who happened to call at the wrong time.

A few minutes later, just after the curtain had risen for the third act of *Our American Cousin*, Booth talked his way into the Presidential box and fired a single shot into the back of Lincoln's head. Before anyone could stop him, Booth leaped over the balustrade and onto the stage, the petrified actors watching helplessly as he hobbled out the back. Lincoln was carried to a house across the street, where he lingered, unconscious, for nine hours, his decline observed by the Cabinet and

---

* Her first performance, on 15 October 1858, had coincided with Lincoln's final US Senate election debate against Stephen A. Douglas. Although Douglas went on to represent Illinois in the Senate, Lincoln's extraordinary eloquence and clarity regarding the future of slavery had catapulted him to national prominence.

several doctors. Mary Lincoln became so hysterical that she was removed from the room several times, and was absent when Lincoln took his final breath at twenty-two minutes past seven in the morning.

Seward lived; his throat had been slashed several times and his right cheek nearly sliced off as he tried to fight his attacker. Frederick was in a coma, his skull broken in two places, and Augustus had suffered two stab wounds to the head and one to his hand. The Secretary of State drifted in and out of consciousness for several days, unaware that Lincoln was dead or that Andrew Johnson had been sworn in as the 19th President of the United States. Although propped up on pillows so he could watch Lincoln's funeral procession on 19 April, Seward admitted later that the black funeral plumes passing beneath his window had caught his eye but failed to register with him as anything significant or untoward.[26]

On 21 April Lincoln's funeral train pulled away from Washington station at 7 a.m. and began its 1,700-mile journey to Springfield, Illinois.* That day, in Virginia, the raider John Singleton Mosby disbanded his Partisan Rangers, although Mosby himself refused to give his parole. His two British volunteers confounded the Federals by asking for safe passage to Canada. The following day, General Fitz Lee wrote his final dispatch to Robert E. Lee, commending each of his staff officers 'and Captain Llewellyn Saunderson, who, having just arrived from his native country, Ireland, joined me previously to the fall of Petersburg, and remained with me to the last'.†[27] Lincoln's train had reached Albany, the State capital of New York, when Joe Johnston surrendered his army to Sherman on 26 April. The one important difference to the terms that Grant had offered Lee was Sherman's agreement to provide transport for the Southern troops from distant States. Henry Feilden had only 100 miles to travel in order to reach Julia in Greenville, South Carolina, so he set off on his own horse.

---

* Consul Archibald broke Foreign Office protocol for the first time in his life to attend a memorial service organized by the British community in New York. He defended his action to Sir Frederick Bruce, arguing that to have stayed away would have offended not only his own sensibilities but the entire city's.
† A paroled Confederate general, Cadmus Wilcox, who bumped into Tom Conolly in New York on 22 April, wrote: '[I] met Conley the first night. He gave an amusing account of his leaving Richmond in the night and his difficulties in reaching the Baltimore-Ohio railroad. He urged me to go to Ireland with him and, supposing I wanted money, offered me his purse freely.'

I have not heard anything about you for so long [he wrote] that I have been quite miserable. You are aware I suppose that the war has ended in this part of the country, and that we have given in on this side of the Mississippi. Considering the position we were in, General Johnston made excellent terms with Sherman for the army – that is to say – that we are not to be molested by the Yankee Government, and our personal property is respected. No one else in the country has any guarantee for either life or property, except from the magnanimity of our enemies, which does not amount to much. The feeling of indignation in the North against our late leaders is described by the Yankee officers as intense. General Schofield (a very old friend of General Hardee's) who now commands North Carolina advised him to leave the country at once. My own opinion is that our prominent men will be treated with great severity, if not executed ... The death of Lincoln was looked upon by our army as a great misfortune for the South. If he were alive we should have had no difficulty in getting terms.[28]

The flight of John Wilkes Booth, the man behind the South's 'great misfortune', also came to an end on 26 April. (Lewis Powell, the attempted murderer of Seward, had been caught ten days earlier.) Booth and another accomplice were found in a barn a few miles south of Port Royal, Virginia, by a detachment of twenty-six Federal soldiers. When Booth refused to surrender they set fire to the barn in the hope of flushing him out; but one of the soldiers, Boston Corbett, shot him in the neck while he remained inside. Corbett's desire for glory deprived the mourning nation of the chance to obtain justice for its slain President.

Lincoln's funeral train finally reached its destination at Springfield, Illinois on 3 May 1865. After a twelve-day journey through more than 440 cities and towns, the bodies of Lincoln and his son Willie, who had died in 1862, would now be laid to rest in Oak Ridge Cemetery.

England was already 'staggering', according to Benjamin Moran, over the news of Lee's surrender, when the telegram announcing the assassination of President Lincoln arrived on 26 April. John Bright felt 'stunned and ill' when he heard the news. He was in mourning for his best friend, Richard Cobden, who had died on 2 April, three weeks too soon to celebrate 'this great triumph of the Republic', and his brother-in-law Samuel Lucas, the owner and editor of the *Morning Star*, who had died on the 16th. 'I feel at times as if I could suffer no more and grieve no more,' wrote Bright in his diary. 'The slave interest has not been able to destroy the nation, but it succeeded in killing the President.'[29] 'I was horror struck,' recorded Moran, 'and at once went up with Mr Alward [the new Assistant Secretary] to announce the intelligence to Mr Adams. He turned as pale as death.' Within a few hours the legation was overrun with visitors. Adams had expected to see Bright and Forster, and possibly Lord Houghton (formerly Richard Monckton Milnes), but certainly not the Duke of Argyll or Lord Russell, who showed 'as much sympathy as he was capable of'.[30] Lord Lyons also made a special trip to London to pay his respects and obtain news about Seward.

The British press was united over the tragedy of Lincoln's violent death. Newspapers that had routinely criticized the President during his lifetime rushed to praise him. On 28 April and again on 1 May, *The Times* printed long eulogies to the late President. 'The feeling which the death of Mr Lincoln has excited in England is in no degree confined to the advocates of the Northern cause, it has shown itself just as strongly among the friends of the South,' the paper declared. 'We feel confident that a sorrow in which both nations may without exaggeration be said to share cannot pass without leaving them better acquainted with each other, and more inclined to friendship ... than they were before.'* This was a wild hope and the editors knew it; William Howard Russell could not help writing smugly in his diary: 'Had *The Times* followed my advice how different our position would be – not only that of the leading journal but of England!'[31]

Despite being the primary instigator and cause of the *Times*'s wildly biased reporting of the war, Francis Lawley escaped vilification because he was not a journalist by profession. The paper's New York correspondent, Charles Mackay, on the other hand, was castigated for betraying his trade. The *Spectator* accused him of doing 'probably more than any other single man to diffuse error concerning the great issue involved, and to imperil the cause of human freedom'.[32] The *Times*'s managing editor, Mowbray Morris, belatedly realized the damage caused to the paper's reputation by its pro-Southern reporting and dismissed Mackay from his post in a scathing letter which laid the entire blame for the *Times*'s position on his shoulders alone:

* Leslie Stephen prepared a devastating critique of the *Times*'s reporting on the American Civil War, which he published later that year under the title 'The Times and the American Civil War'. The 33-page pamphlet carefully dissected each report and essay for its bias and misrepresentation of facts.

It is my painful duty to inform you that a successor will shortly be dispatched from England to take your place. This result which I greatly deplore has been brought about by your blind and unreasonable condemnation of all public men and measures on the Federal side. It seems to us that you have persistently and wilfully shut your eyes to all facts and signs which did not tend to the support of your foregone conclusions ... You have presented the English public with a distorted picture of the Federal cause, and have, as I believe, contributed very largely to produce the exasperation which you allege to exist in the American mind against the English. Moreover your letters have been deficient in the qualities of a sound foreign correspondent. They have contained but a few facts and a great deal of wild declamation.[33]

The Economist also felt obliged to explain away its previous condemnations of Lincoln, claiming that over the past four years 'Power and responsibility visibly widened [Lincoln's] mind and elevated his character'.[34] But it was *Punch* that performed the greatest volte-face. Three weeks earlier, on 8 April, the magazine had placed Lincoln in a gallery of April Fools that included Napoleon III and the MPs Roebuck, Bright and Disraeli. The combination of embarrassment, shame and shock that Lincoln was killed while watching his play moved Tom Taylor, the magazine's senior contributor, to browbeat his colleagues into giving him a free hand to compose an abject apology and homage to the late President. The editor, Mark Lemon, supported him, telling the staff, 'The avowal that we have been a bit mistaken [over Lincoln and the war] is manly and just.' Taylor did not hold back. 'Between the mourners at his head and feet, / Say, scurril-jester, is there room for *you*?' he asked contritely. Lincoln 'had lived to shame me from my sneer, / To lame my pencil, and confute my pen, / To make me own this kind of prince's peer, / This rail-splitter a true-born king of men. / My shallow judgment I had learned to rue.'[35]

Moran's usual cynicism was temporarily overcome when he attended a mass meeting at St James's Hall, Piccadilly on 30 April:

The room was draped in black and three United States flags were gracefully entwined in crape at the east end of the room. The floor, the balcony, the galleries, and the platform of the great hall were literally packed with ladies and gentlemen ... the warmth of the applause, the earnest detestation of the murder, and the condemnation of slavery made me inwardly vow that hereafter I would think better of the feelings entertained towards us by

BRITANNIA SYMPATHISES WITH COLUMBIA.

Britannia sympathizes with Columbia, *Punch*, May 1865

Englishmen than ever before. And that if ever any chance of quarrel should occur between the two Countries, and I should hear an uninformed countryman of mine denouncing honestly and mistakenly, the spirit of England towards us, the recollection of what I saw then would nerve me to declare that we had friends in England in our day of sorrow, whose noble sympathy should make us pause.[36]

He wrote even more fulsomely the following day, after observing the speeches in the House of Commons and the House of Lords. Russell's speech exceeded Moran's expectations, not on account of the expected praise of Lincoln, but because the Foreign Secretary answered the charge of hypocrisy that had dogged the North and Lincoln from the outset of the war.[37] 'Many persons were eager for the immediate abolition of slavery,' admitted Russell, but:

I remember that Lord Macaulay once declared that it would have been a great blessing if the penal laws against the Roman Catholics had been abolished from the time of Sir Robert Walpole, though Sir Robert Walpole would have been mad to propose a measure for that purpose. So it was with regard to President Lincoln. Whatever may be the horror of slavery, I believe he was perfectly justified in delaying the time.

Moran felt liberated by Russell's speech:

As an American I felt proud of the self-made Illinois Lawyer, who by his honesty, his singlemindedness, and his love of freedom, had extorted words of admiration from the two greatest deliberative assemblies in the world. Yes, that crowded House of English Lords – the proudest nobles in the world – pressed forward to hear the respective chiefs of their parties speak words of praise of Abraham Lincoln.[38]

The US Consuls described extraordinary scenes at public meetings. A resident of Liverpool, arguably the most pro-Southern city in Britain, recorded with surprise that the news 'has turned all sympathy towards the North. Immense meetings on the subject have been held almost everywhere in England and the Queen herself has addressed a letter of condolence to Mrs Lincoln.'[39] Adams began to think that Lincoln had done more for Anglo-American relations by his death than by any other act during his life. Yet he also noticed that British admiration of Lincoln had not altered the political class's ambivalent attitude towards the American political system. On 3 May, three days after Russell's speech on Lincoln, the House of Commons debated a long-delayed reform bill to extend the right to vote to leaseholders in properties worth £6 per annum. A second debate followed on 8 May; the Civil War and American democracy were referred to a total of thirty-seven times both in support of and against the bill.[40] The House ultimately voted against it by 288 to 214, but Adams was relieved that no one during the debates had mentioned Canada or the threat of a US invasion, strengthening his hope that 'the popular current is now setting strongly towards America, and if it continues will work a most decided change in the political future here. Nothing will contribute more to it than the singular career of Mr Lincoln as the impersonation of democracy.'[41]

The great change in attitudes towards the North did not mean that the Confederates in England were being cast aside by their friends, however. James Spence disbanded the pro-Southern associations, because, he explained to a former member, it would be wrong to continue public action on behalf of the South: 'I feel, too, that Englishmen cannot now take further part in this direction with propriety.' But his personal loyalty to Mason was undiminished, and he was among those who offered to establish a subscription fund on the Confederate agent's behalf. (The Southern Commissioner was too proud to accept such charity.) 'The British believe that resistance is hopeless,' Mason wrote to Judah P. Benjamin on 1 May; 'and that the war is at an end – to be followed, on our part, by passive submission to our fate. I need not say that I entertain no such impression, and endeavor as far as I can to disabuse the public mind.'[42] The South's other chief agents in England – James Bulloch, Henry Hotze, Colin McRae and Matthew Maury – were far more realistic. Hotze trimmed his staff on the *Index* and began looking for financial backers, announcing that the journal's new cause would be the protection of 'white man's government', against the 'Africanization' of America.[43] Maury sent a formal letter of surrender to the US navy, promising to desist from all acts of aggression against the United States. Bulloch and McRae girded themselves for prolonged litigation from creditors both real and predatory on account of the Confederacy's unpaid bills. (Some firms, such as the London Armoury Company, which had turned away business in order to fulfil its lucrative orders from the Confederacy, would quickly go bankrupt.) The certainty that an investigation into their books would absolve them from wrongdoing counted for little against the knowledge that their personal sacrifices for the South had been to no avail.

John Slidell wrote to Mason from Paris, urging him to open his eyes to the South's defeat: 'We have seen the beginning of the end. We are crushed and must submit to the yoke. Our children must bide their time for vengeance, but you and I will never revisit our homes under our glorious flag.'[44]

Jefferson Davis finally accepted defeat on 3 May. He had been constantly on the move since leaving Greensboro on 14 April, and had reached Washington, in north-east Georgia. Right up until the day before, Davis had insisted to the cluster of Cabinet members and generals surrounding him that resistance was not just possible but also a duty. He had carried on the normal functions of government, issuing orders and signing papers – albeit by the roadside instead of at his desk – as if it would only be a matter of time before the Confederacy was made whole again. Frank Vizetelly was present to sketch him doing so. 'This was probably the last official business transacted by the Confederate Cabinet and may well be termed "Government by the roadside",' the war artist wrote next to his drawing.

'Three thousand brave men are enough for a nucleus around which the whole people will rally when the panic which now afflicts them has passed away,' Davis had told a member of his cavalry escort. The officer was speechless for a brief moment before replying that the 3,000 troops guarding the Confederate President would risk their lives to save his, 'but would not fire another shot in an effort to continue hostilities ... Then Mr Davis rose and ejaculated bitterly that all was indeed lost. He had become very pallid, and he walked so feebly as he proceeded to leave the room that General Breckinridge [the new Confederate Secretary of War] stepped hastily up and offered his arm.'[45] Even then, Davis did not relinquish all hope. A few hours later he was approached by Lieutenant James Morgan of the CSS *Georgia*, who had come in search of him after Varina Davis had relieved him of his escort duty.

Jefferson Davis signing acts of government by the roadside, by Frank Vizetelly

I begged him to allow me to accompany him, but he told me that it would be impossible, as I had no horse [recalled Morgan]. He spoke to me in the most fatherly way, saying that as soon as things quieted down somewhat I must make my way to the trans-Mississippi, where we still had an army and two or three small gun-boats on the Red River, and in the mean time he would give me a letter to General Fry, commanding at Augusta, asking him to attach me temporarily to his staff.[46]

The Confederate Cabinet began to break up as soon as the fugitives crossed into Georgia on the 3rd. They were worn down by fatigue and fear. 'I am as one walking in a dream, and expecting to wake,' wrote General Josiah Gorgas.[47] Vizetelly drew one last picture of the complete party as it rode through the woods, and then Gorgas, Judah Benjamin and Stephen Mallory all set out on their own. A novice rider, Benjamin was physically incapable of keeping up with Davis and had struggled for the past few days. He assumed the disguise of a French businessman, bought a horse and buggy, and went off in the direction of Florida, where he hoped to take passage on a boat to the Caribbean.

Flight of Jefferson Davis and his Cabinet over the Georgia Ridge, five days before his capture, by Frank Vizetelly

'I saw an organized government . . . fall to pieces little by little,' wrote Captain Micajah Clark, Davis's former private clerk, who had been placed in charge of the Confederacy's travelling Treasury three days earlier. Vizetelly's final sketch showed Davis in Washington, Georgia on 4 May, shaking hands with the officers of his guard. 'It was here that President Davis determined to continue his flight almost alone,' wrote Vizetelly. 'With tears in his eyes he begged them to seek their own safety and leave him to meet his fate.' The journalist thought that Davis had been 'ill-advised' to travel with so large a retinue when there was a $100,000-bounty on his head.

With the Postmaster General, John H. Reagan, his three aides and a small cavalry detachment Davis headed southward, expecting to catch up with Varina and the children in a day or two. He hoped that the wagons carrying the last of his government's funds – $288,022.90 in gold and silver coins – would reach a port and from there be transported to England, where it could be used to fund Southern resistance against Washington.* Davis now realized the extreme folly of attracting attention, and made up a new identity as a Texas politician on his way home. Vizetelly's presence only endangered the party and the journalist accepted that it was time for him to leave. Just before he rode away, sometime on or shortly after 5 May, Vizetelly pressed a fifty-pound note in Davis's hand, which would be enough to pay for the entire family to sail to England, third class.[48]

The next time Vizetelly had a report of his progress it was from the news wires, announcing Davis's capture on 10 May. The Federal commander at Hilton Head, South Carolina, signalled:

> Jeff Davis, wife, and three children; C C Clay and wife, Reagan, General Wheeler, several colonels and captains, Stephens (late Vice-President) are now at Hilton Head, having been brought here from Savannah this afternoon. They were captured by 130 men, 5th Michigan Cavalry, 120 miles south of Macon, Ga., near Irwinville. They had no escort, and made no resistance. Jeff. looks much worn and troubled; so does Stephens.[49]

The new British Minister, Sir Frederick Bruce, informed London of the development. 'There is no doubt that the Confederacy as a political body is at an end,' he wrote to Lord Russell. He strongly advised that

---

* The bulk of the money disappeared and has never been found.

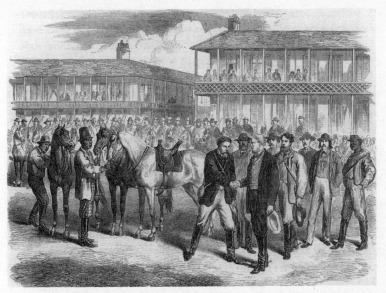

Jefferson Davis bidding farewell to his escort two days before his capture,
by Frank Vizetelly

Britain refuse port entry to the two Confederate cruisers still at large, unless she desired to irritate the US government. 'The moment is a critical one,' Bruce warned on 16 May.[50] The CSS *Stonewall* had tried to obtain coal at Nassau and been sent on her way. The ship managed to make it to Havana, where its presence embarrassed the authorities for a few days until definitive news arrived of the Confederacy's collapse.*

Bruce had been in Washington since 8 April, although he had not yet been presented to Lincoln when the President was assassinated on 14 April. Since then, Bruce had waited anxiously to learn what the new administration's attitude would be towards Britain. A large banner had been draped across the State Department, proclaiming: 'Peace and good

---

* The Scotsman William Watson was in Havana trying to salvage some of his profits from his blockade-runner the *Rob Roy* when the *Stonewall* sputtered into the harbour. 'As for the large fleet of blockade-running steamers thrown idle at Havana, it would be difficult to say what became of them all,' wrote Watson. He was disappointed to discover that exorbitant taxes and charges had reduced his share to a sum comparable to the average yearly wage of a ship's master.[51]

will to all nations, but no entangling alliances and no foreign interven-
tions,' which did not inspire him with confidence.[52] He was relieved
when Johnson went out of his way to reassure him of his cordial feelings towards Britain.[53] 'I have not been accustomed to etiquette,' Johnson
admitted when Bruce was presented to him, 'but I shall be at all times
happy to see you and prepared to approach questions in a just and
friendly spirit.'* Charles Sumner had offered to be an intermediary
between the British legation and President Johnson, but Bruce was loath
to call upon him despite his admiration for the Senator's historic battle
against slavery. There was something about Sumner's insistence that no
one else in Washington was capable of discussing foreign affairs that
made Bruce doubt his motives. 'It struck me', wrote Bruce, 'that the drift
of his conversation was to lead me to the conclusion that I should enter
into confidential communication with himself. This I am reluctant to
do, as long as there is hope of Mr Seward being able shortly to resume
his duties.' He disliked 'the want of frankness in him', and suspected
that Sumner was trying to discover his weaknesses in order to exploit
them later.[55]

Bruce could see that the overwhelming desire in the country was for
peace, and no longer feared for the safety of Canada, although there
were still serious frictions between Britain and America which remained
unresolved. 'The feeling against blockade runners, and foreigners who
have served in a civil or military character in the South, is so strong as
to make a fair trial almost hopeless,' he wrote to Russell. 'These cases
require great delicacy in handling – for to insinuate unfairness on the
part of the officers composing their Military Commissions, would render the execution of a sentence only more certain.' Reflecting on Colonel
Grenfell, who had been the only defendant in the Chicago conspiracy
trial to receive the death sentence, Bruce thought that people were
'against leniency where a foreigner is concerned and the Government
will not openly thwart the popular sentiment in that respect'.[56] Bennet

---

* In contrast to 'plain and quiet Lord Lyons', Bruce was 'white-haired, white-whiskered,
round-cheeked, with rich dark eyes, hearty, [and] convivial', wrote Oliver Wendell Holmes,
the future Supreme Court Justice. Bruce was a clever choice as Minister; his successful partnership with Anson Burlingame, the US Minister in China, had already made him popular
with the administration. Moreover, Bruce liked Americans, having served on a previous diplomatic mission to Washington in 1842; he felt comfortable among them, and preferred the
raw energy of the New World to the stuffy hauteur of the Old. Holmes was amazed to discover that Bruce was 'pretty freely outspoken for our side as if he were one of us'.[54]

Burley's trial would take place soon, and Bruce expected a similar outcome.

Bruce felt pity for the defeated South but his overriding fears were for the coloured population of the United States, whose future seemed so uncertain. 'The antagonism [against] the Negro breaks out constantly,' he wrote to Lord Russell. In Manhattan, a delegation of black New Yorkers was denied the right to walk behind Lincoln's funeral cortège. When the White House intervened, a police escort had to protect the black marchers from the violence of the mob. 'At Philadelphia,' continued Bruce, 'though the Abolition element is strong, the pretension of the coloured people to ride in the railway cars are strenuously resisted, and threaten to end in serious riots.' He had also heard that Tennessee had barred the testimony of black witnesses except in trials involving black defendants.[57]

Many Southerners assumed that Northern fury would result in the execution of all the leading Confederates. Henry Feilden had heard that President Johnson was 'burning with hatred against the South' (which was untrue, though Johnson did exclude plantation owners of estates worth more than $20,000 before the war from pardon), yet his own experiences showed him there was hope of eventual reconciliation between the two sides. He encountered mostly kindness from Federal troops as he slowly made his way to Charleston. Two Northern officers 'acted as well as they could and were as kind and accommodating as possible', he told Julia. 'For instance they insisted on paying all the expenses. We helped them to drink three bottles of whiskey en route. At Branchville they got the US officer to put our horses on the car and saved us 65 miles ride. By the way,' he added, 'the 102nd US Colored troops gave us lunch there.'[58]

President Andrew Johnson proclaimed a general amnesty on 29 May 1865, three days after the surrender of the last Southern army in the field, General Edmund Kirby-Smith's Army of the Trans-Mississippi. The war was officially at an end, but for many people it was not over. During the past four years Dr Elizabeth Blackwell had rarely been absent from her work, training nurses at the New York Infirmary for Women; she tried to explain her state of mind to Barbara Bodichon, her friend in England:

> You cannot hardly understand and I cannot explain how our private lives
> have all become interwoven with the life of the nation's. No one who has

not lived through it can understand the bond between those who have . . . Neither is it possible without this intense and prolonged experience to estimate the keen personal suffering that has entered into every household and saddened every life . . . The great secret of our dead leader's popularity was the wonderful instinct with which he felt and acted . . . he did not lead, he expressed the American heartbreak . . . it has been to me a revelation to feel such influence and to see SUCH leadership. I never was thoroughly republican before . . . but I am so, thoroughly, now.[59]

Epilogue

Going home, staying on – A transatlantic cable – The Alabama
*claims – Sumner's demands – Impasse – Last chance at Geneva –
Conclusion*

On 23 May 1865 more than 150,000 soldiers began marching down
Pennsylvania Avenue to the White House in a grand review of the Union
armies. The parade lasted for two days, and even then the spectators
lining the route saw but a fraction of the victorious Northern forces.
General Ulysses S. Grant – who would succeed Andrew Johnson as
President in 1868 – was now the commander-in-chief of the largest
army in the world with 1,034,064 soldiers at his disposal.[1]

Yet a mere eighteen months later, Grant's forces would consist of just
54,302 men in the regular Federal army, and 11,000 (most of whom
were US coloured troops) in the volunteer army.[2] The navy was also
shrinking, selling its warships as quickly as the market allowed until
by 1870 only fifty-two of the original 641 vessels remained.[3] The rapid
pace of demobilization reflected the country's desperate yearning for
peace. In the aftermath of the war a different kind of volunteer stepped
forward, one motivated by a sense of debt to the nation's fallen, whose
mission was not to kill but to collect statistics, identify remains and
re-inter, in military cemeteries, thousands of rotting and neglected corpses.[4]
The renowned Civil War nurse Clara Barton founded the Office of Correspondence to help families in their search for soldiers who were missing
and presumed dead.[5] A total of 360,222 Federal soldiers were known to
have died during the past four years, and another 271,175 had been
injured or maimed. To Colonel L. D. H. Currie, the British commander
of the 133rd New York Metropolitan Guard, this terrible human toll

meant the loss of all but one of the regiment's founding officers. To the former British prisoner Private James Pendlebury of the 69th New York Irish Regiment, it meant returning to his regiment after ten months in captivity to find that he recognized less than half the faces.

The demobilized forces benefited from a steady economy and abundant land. The continuous influx of immigrants during the war – more than 800,000 by most accounts – had not crowded out the labour pool, and many of the British volunteers, including Colonel Currie, saw America as offering greater opportunities than the old country.[6]

The errant father Private James Horrocks would not have returned to England even if he could. He stayed in the US army until November 1865, by which time he had earned both the officer's commission he coveted and a considerable sum of money. 'I have paid all my debts,' he wrote to his family on the 27th, 'bought ... an excellent suit of citizen's clothes and everything I stood in need of and have still above $400 left.' Horrocks joined the million-plus veterans who sought to make a new life for themselves after their wartime experiences. But his hopes of making a fortune were never quite realized: he married a woman from California, settled in St Louis, Missouri, and passed into middle age as an accountant in a credit agency. Despite having no legitimate children of his own, Horrocks refused to acknowledge the illegitimate son in England whose birth had driven him from his home and into the ranks of the Federal army.[7]

Other British volunteers became true Anglo-Americans in the manner of Dr Elizabeth Blackwell, who moved easily between the two countries until she fell out with her sister Emily over the management of the New York Infirmary, and went to live permanently in England in 1869. The most colourful example of this new breed was the serial deserter Henry Morton Stanley. He jumped ship from the USS *Minnesota* in February 1865 and spent the next two years pursuing various ventures in America, including gold prospecting in Colorado, while simultaneously trying to launch a career in journalism. His ability to spin a tale eventually brought him to the notice of James Gordon Bennett, the editor of the *New York Herald*, who hired him as a foreign correspondent. In 1871 Stanley set off on his famous expedition through present-day Tanzania to find the missing missionary Dr David Livingstone – father of Robert who had died in a Confederate prison camp shortly before the war's end. After spending almost two decades in Africa, Stanley returned to

England in 1890, where he subsequently became an MP and was knighted in 1897.

The Britons who chose to go home took back with them not just memories (and in some cases wounds) but also new attitudes based on American ideals. James Pendlebury received $875 from the army, which he spent in two weeks, and had to work his passage across the Atlantic. But his experiences had changed him for the better. 'What did I learn from all this?' he asked in his memoirs. 'I have learned that I never need want for bread as long as I have health and strength ... Nothing that is honest demeans a man and if he does not like his work; well, let him mend himself as soon as he can. This is what I learned in America ... today, through going to America I am an independent gentleman.' Pendlebury became a successful businessman and tried hard to stay off drink. In 1877 he took his family to the Isle of Man, where, according to his obituary, he purchased a mansion and became 'a prominent figure at many public meetings ... (unafraid) to express his opinions in the most vigorous language'.[8]

The America that Pendlebury was describing did not extend to the South. Eighty-eight per cent of America's wealth now resided in the North; in the cotton States there was neither the industrial base nor the manpower to fuel economic growth. One in four white Southern males between the ages of 17 and 45 – some 258,000 – had been killed in the war and at least 260,000 had suffered debilitating injuries.[9] Nine thousand miles of railtrack had been destroyed, three-quarters of the South's merchant shipping was gone, and almost all the banks had been emptied of specie. Without slavery, the entire commercial infrastructure of the South collapsed. For the first year after the war bartering was commonplace in many villages and communities. The labour-intensive cotton plantations were worth only a third of their pre-war value, and even the parts of the South which had been untouched by actual fighting were soon brought to poverty and ruin. Frances Butler, Fanny Kemble's youngest daughter, had never shared her mother's pro-Northern sympathies, and in 1865 returned with her father to the family rice plantation in Georgia. For the first couple of years she lived in utter squalor.

> So I cook, and my maid does the housework, and as it has rained hard for three days and the kitchen roof is half off, I cook in the dining-room or parlour. Fortunately, my provisions are so limited that I have not much to

cook; for five days my food has consisted of hard pilot biscuits, grits cooked in different ways, oysters, and twice, as a great treat, ham and eggs. I brought a box of preserves from the North with me, but half of them upset, and the rest were spoilt. One window is entirely without a sash, so I have to keep the shutters closed all the time, and over the other I have pasted three pieces of paper where panes should be ... I think if it rains much more there will not be a dry spot left in the house.[10]

The exploitative aspects of Reconstruction – the punitive taxes, questionable expropriations and legal chicanery that often ran unchecked – also hindered the South's recovery. Captain Henry Feilden, the English volunteer on General Beauregard's staff in Charleston, lost the title to his house, forcing him to live apart from his new wife Julia. He went to Orangeburg, some 70 miles from Charleston, where he tried to set up a wagon-hauling business, while Julia remained in Greenville with her aunt.[11] They endured the arrangement for a year before accepting defeat and moving to England. Feilden was reinstated in the British army and served as paymaster in the 18th Royal Hussars. In later life, he combined his military service with a second career as a naturalist and eminent polar explorer. The marriage was a happy one, though childless, and a timely bequest in 1901 brought them a beautiful seventeenth-century house in the village of Burwash, Sussex. There, Rudyard Kipling and Feilden became neighbours and close friends. After Feilden's death in 1921, Kipling wrote, 'He was the gentlest, gallantest English gentleman who ever walked.'*[12]

Francis Dawson, General Fitz Lee's English ordnance officer, was also reduced to manual labour. As soon as his shoulder wound had recovered he worked as a field hand on a plantation near Richmond. The job sustained him until businesses began to reopen and his education made him a desirable employee. In 1866 he joined the staff of the Richmond *Examiner* for a short time before becoming the assistant editor of the Charleston *Mercury*. Unlike Feilden, however, Dawson not only made the South his home, but played a significant part in its revival as the editor of the Charleston *News and Courier*. He married as his second

* The poet Algernon Swinburne also became friends with Feilden. 'I defy you not to like him if you knew him,' Swinburne wrote to a friend in 1867; '[he is] one of the nicest fellows alive, and open as such men should be, to admiration of all fallen causes and exiled leaders. I am not saying they are equal in worth – heaven forbid – only I must say that failure is irresistibly attractive, admitting as I do the heroism of the North.'

wife (the first having died young) the writer Sarah Morgan, older sister
of his long-time friend, Lieutenant James Morgan – who rounded out
his own picaresque career by becoming the US Consul-General to Australia. Dawson was playing an increasingly prominent role in Democratic
politics when he was killed on 12 March 1889 during an argument with
a neighbour. Southern culture had always been more aggressive than
Northern, but the weakening of social and official authority after the
Civil War had led to even greater levels of violence. Dawson's contribution to the pacification of the South had been a long campaign against
duelling, an effort which the jury repaid by acquitting his murderer.

Neither of the two British participants in Jacob Thompson's guerrilla
war against the North – Colonel George St Leger Grenfell and Bennet
G. Burley – ever returned to the South. Grenfell's death sentence was
commuted to life imprisonment at Fort Jefferson in the Dry Tortugas
islands, 70 miles west of the Florida Keys in the Gulf of Mexico. His
cellmates were the four conspirators in Abraham Lincoln's assassination
who did not receive capital sentences. One, Dr Samuel Mudd, who
treated the injured John Wilkes Booth during the actor's flight from
justice, became good friends with Grenfell; and in 1867 he sent a
description of Grenfell's treatment to his brother-in law:

> Colonel St. Ledger Grenfel [*sic*] is kept in close confinement under guard. A
> few days ago, being sick, he applied to the doctor of the Post for medical
> attention, which he was refused, and he was ordered to work. Feeling him-
> self unable to move about, he refused. He was then ordered to carry a ball
> until further orders, which he likewise refused. He was then tied up for half
> a day, and still refusing, he was taken to one of the wharves, thrown over-
> board with a rope attached, and ducked; being able to keep himself above
> water, a fifty pound weight was attached to his feet. Grenfel is an old man,
> about sixty. He has never refused to do work which he was able to perform,
> but they demanded more than he felt able, and he wisely refused. They
> could not conquer him, and he is doing now that which he never objected
> doing.[13]

On 6 March 1868 Grenfell tried to escape from Dry Tortugas along with
three other prisoners. They were caught in a storm and the little boat
disappeared. Afterwards there was the occasional 'sighting' of Grenfell
but there is little doubt that he drowned somewhere in the Gulf.

Burley had better luck than Grenfell. He had been incarcerated in

Port Clinton, the capital of Ottawa County, Ohio, and was awaiting his second trial (the first having resulted in a hung jury), when, in September 1865, a well-wisher brought him an apple pie to celebrate the start of apple-picking season. Hidden beneath the crust was a sharpened iron file. Burley escaped to Detroit where he was able to cross the river to Canada and to freedom. He became a journalist and in 1881 settled down to a long career as the foreign correspondent for the London *Daily Telegraph*. Burleigh (he changed the spelling) was joined at the *Telegraph* by George Augustus Sala (Belle Boyd's sometime protector) and Francis Lawley, who had returned to England shortly after Appomattox. Dropped by Sala, Belle took advantage of the general amnesty declared by President Johnson in 1866 to go back to the United States, where she earned a living as an actress until her marriage in 1869 to Lieutenant John Swainston Hammond, a former British volunteer in the Federal army.[14] Lawley's return to England had a less happy outcome: his creditors continued to pursue him, and the salary he earned from writing about the turf (a subject he knew well) was not enough to stave off bankruptcy. There were still outstanding debts against his estate when he died in 1901. His fellow pro-Southern journalist, Frank Vizetelly, continued as a war artist and was killed in 1883 while covering the fighting in the Sudan between the Anglo-Egyptian army under William Hicks (Hicks Pasha) and the Mahdi rebels.

Canada was a popular hiding place for many Southern fugitives: Jefferson Davis resided there for a time after his release from prison in 1867. At first it had seemed likely that the former Confederate President would be tried and executed for masterminding Lincoln's assassination. But when no evidence could be produced against him, the grounds for trying him became more complicated. The question was still unresolved when Davis was given bail on 13 May 1867. It was a further two years before the threat of legal action against him and thirty-seven other Confederate leaders, including Robert E. Lee, was dropped by the government. Davis lived on for another twenty years, beset by financial misfortune and family tragedies, but a defiant symbol of the Confederate States to the last. Lee, in contrast, was a firm advocate of reconciliation. He became president of Washington College, in Lexington, Virginia, a post he held until his death in 1870.

The last Confederate War Secretary, John Breckinridge, and the Commissioners James Mason, Clement C. Clay and Jacob Thompson also returned to the US from Canada once they were confident of receiving an amnesty. Despite his leading role in the Confederates' terror operations in Canada, Thompson was never prosecuted for his crimes. He chose Memphis, Tennessee as his new home, his wealth mysteriously untouched despite the war – there was always speculation that some of his fortune came from the $1 million entrusted to him by the Confederacy in 1864.

Thompson was extremely fortunate, especially so in light of the terror and destruction he had tried to inflict upon the North. His colleagues in Europe never dared return to the United States since they were not included in any of the official pardons. Ambrose Dudley Mann, the Commissioner in Brussels, and John Slidell, the Commissioner in Paris, stayed in France; the Confederate financial agent Colin McRae emigrated to Belize, and the chief of Confederate operations abroad, James Bulloch, remained in Liverpool. His brother, Irvine, was one of the last Confederates to surrender when his ship the CSS *Shenandoah* sailed into Liverpool on 6 November 1865.* Both Bullochs are buried at Toxteth Park Cemetery, Liverpool.

The former Confederate Secretary of State, Judah P. Benjamin, also died abroad. He arrived in England in July 1865, after a harrowing escape from Florida, and retrained as a barrister. In 1868 he published a treatise on commercial law, popularly known as 'Benjamin on Sales'; the book's immediate success assured him financial stability for the rest of his life. Striving to put the past behind him (and burdened by many secrets), Benjamin generally avoided the other Confederate exiles. He made no effort to see Henry Hotze despite their close relationship during the war. Hotze, in any case, had no interest in refashioning himself to suit the times; he remained an unapologetic supporter of slavery and the creed of white supremacy. But his hope of publishing a magazine dedicated to crushing the aspirations of freed blacks was soon quashed, and he became a propagandist for hire, working for any government or ruler who required his arts. He died in Zug, Switzerland, in 1887.[15]

---

* The *Shenandoah* had been at sea for a year when Captain Waddell finally brought her back to England, six months after the war's end. During that time the cruiser had captured thirty-eight ships, the majority of them Northern whalers, and taken more than a thousand prisoners. Waddell had believed that the South would continue to fight after Lee's surrender. It was the capture of President Davis – which he learned from the British bark, *Barracouta*, on 2 August 1865 – that persuaded him to surrender too.

Lord Lyons died a few months after Hotze, having served in the Foreign Office for forty-eight years – the last twenty of them as the British Ambassador to France, the highest-ranking post in the diplomatic service. Once Lyons had recovered from the neuralgia that had forced him to leave Washington, he found that retirement was far worse than being overworked and eagerly accepted Lord Russell's offer in October 1865 of the embassy in Constantinople. Lyons himself was too modest to recognize his altered standing in the Foreign Office, but instead of the lonely mid-level diplomat who had incited derision at Washington he was now a highly respected representative of Her Majesty's Government, whose dignified though conciliatory approach in delicate situations made him invaluable. He was rewarded with the Paris embassy after only a year in Constantinople, and there he spent the remainder of his life, in great comfort and satisfaction, served faithfully by several of his former attachés at the Washington legation.

In his own way, Benjamin Moran also reached the summit of his capabilities – if not his ambitions – when in 1876, after twenty-three years at the US legation in London, he was sent to run the US legation in Lisbon, where he showed that he was not without talent as a diplomat. The *New York Times* described him as 'one of the most capable and experienced diplomats in the service of the United States'.[16] He ruled over his little kingdom for six years, gleefully bullying his staff, until his retirement in 1882, when he returned to England and passed the last four years of his life in Braintree, Essex. At his death, the humble printer's son from Chester, Pennsylvania was praised by the London *Times* as the 'ablest and most honest' representative the United States had ever sent to Great Britain.[17]

On 27 July 1866 Cyrus Field stood on the deck of the *Great Eastern*, watching through his binoculars as engineers hauled the transatlantic cable ashore at Heart's Content, Newfoundland. Finally, after five attempts in nine years, a cable sturdy enough to withstand the rigours of the Atlantic was laid along the 1,800-mile under-sea shelf between Ireland and Canada. The cable's first message, sent through on the 28th, announced the signing of the peace armistice between Prussia and Austria. The Americans had been as surprised as the rest of Europe by the speed and efficiency with which Prussia had defeated Austria in the

Seven Weeks' War. The Battle of Sadowa on 3 July had involved nearly 500,000 soldiers, the largest concentration of troops to date in either Europe or America. The Prussian military observers in the US during the Civil War had been impressed by how rapidly armies and artillery could be transported by rail, and during the past year the Prussian War Minister had created a Field Railway Section, modelled on the Union Construction Corps. The Prussians had also benefited from the close attention they had paid to Civil War developments in artillery and communications.[18]

The second message to reach Newfoundland was from Queen Victoria to President Andrew Johnson, congratulating him 'on the successful completion of an undertaking which she hopes may serve as an additional bond of Union between the United States and England'. At the moment it was just a hope: Austria's recent defeat had added another layer of complexity to a relationship that was already tense due to the unresolved issues left by the American Civil War. Prussia's emergence as the dominant military nation among her neighbours was redrawing the balance of power in Europe. France was now menaced by a credible threat, and the German confederation no longer answered to Vienna but to Berlin. It was too soon to tell how these changes would affect Britain and America, but British politicians were worried that it would be the same old story of England facing two threats at once. 'It is the unfriendly state of our relations with America that to a great extent paralyses our action in Europe,' Russell's replacement as Foreign Secretary, Lord Clarendon, would shortly admit. 'There is not the smallest doubt that if we were engaged in a Continental quarrel we should immediately find ourselves at war with the United States.'[19]

During a Commons debate on 13 March 1865, Lord Palmerston had tried to brush away the many crises of the past four years by putting them down to a family quarrel: 'the North wished us to declare on their side and the South on theirs, and we wished to maintain a perfect neutrality.' But this simplification of the arguments between the two countries carried no weight outside the Commons, and little even there. According to The Times, and a majority of the British public, both sides had behaved badly. The United States had never supported Britain in any war, including the Crimean, and yet neither the North nor the South had seen the contradiction in demanding British aid once the situation was reversed. Both had unscrupulously stooped to threats and black-mail in their attempts to gain support, the South using cotton, the North using Canada. Both were guilty in their mistreatment of Negroes, both had shipped arms from England and both had benefited from British volunteers. In America, the perception that Lord Russell had behaved like a villain and that the British ruling classes had schemed with the Confederacy to overthrow the Union in the hope of destroying democracy was so pervasive that the historian George Bancroft digressed upon it during his eulogy on Lincoln before Congress on 12 February 1866.[20] Bancroft, like his compatriots, believed that the declaration of neutrality had been nothing more than an underhand attempt at recognizing the independence of the South; that the British government had connived with the Confederates to send out the commerce raiders; and the blockade-runners had been allowed to operate with impunity because they enabled the South to keep fighting long after its own supplies were exhausted.

Senator Charles Sumner played a discreditable part in promulgating the myth that Britain had acted maliciously and illegally in awarding belligerent status to the South. His friends in England, especially the Duke and Duchess of Argyll, felt betrayed by his attacks. 'You know how heartily my Duke has been with you all through,' the Duchess protested on 4 July 1865. 'You know how ... fair a man Sir George Lewis was, you know that there were others true to you ... I protest again against your supposing it a proof of Lord Russell's ill-will, when [belligerent status] was a Cabinet measure. As to the haste, I suppose there would have been less of it, if the consequence attached to it by you had been foreseen.'[21] Lord Russell was so incensed by the repeated slurs on his motives and intentions towards the North that he rejected Charles Francis Adams's proposal in the summer of 1865 for an international arbitrator to consider American claims against Britain. Russell has since been criticized for being stiff-necked and arrogant, and is often blamed for being the main reason why the *Alabama* claims controversy dragged on for seven more years.[22] Yet, at the time, Russell was devastated to have his honour called into question. Arbitration by a foreign government, he told the Chancellor of the Exchequer, William Gladstone, in September 1865, would be humiliating to England and to himself; it would mean asking whether 'he was diligent or negligent in the execution of the duties of his office'. In his replies to Adams, Russell complained that his successes against the Confederates counted for nothing, whereas his failures – none of which he believed were his fault – counted for everything. Palmerston's death on 18 October, which elevated Russell to the Prime Ministership once again, removed the only person who would have had weight and influence to show Russell that there could be another approach to the claims.

William Henry Seward never accused Britain of having collaborated with the South. But he steadfastly maintained that relations could not be cordial until reparations had been paid for the *Alabama*'s depredations and an apology given for Britain having bestowed belligerent status on the South. For most of 1865 the injured Secretary of State was content to allow Charles Francis Adams a free rein in his dealings with Lord Russell – as long as these points were not conceded. Seward did not have strength to resort to the kind of bluster which had marked his first year in office. Physically, he would never return to his old self. His right arm was useless and speaking was difficult; 'few of his old friends could meet him without a shock,' wrote his son. However, it was the family tragedy which followed Powell's attack that inflicted the greatest damage on Seward. His sons Fred and Augustus slowly recovered from their wounds, but Frances, Seward's wife, went into a rapid decline and died on 21 June, less than three months after the assassination attempt. Their relationship had been complicated though not unloving, and her loss severed Seward from what he had always considered to be the better part of himself. Almost immediately after Frances' death, it became clear that his daughter Fanny's health had also been affected and she began to succumb to the tuberculosis which would kill her the following year.

Seward's troubles increased in 1866 as he struggled to find his footing in President Johnson's administration.[23] Having been partly responsible for the pro-war Tennessee Democrat's appointment as Lincoln's Vice-President, Seward had wrongly assumed that Johnson would follow his lead or at least listen to his advice. Instead, Johnson had stubbornly pursued his own line – which leaned decidedly towards maintaining the egregious status of the black population in the South. Johnson's attempts to obstruct Reconstruction lost him the support of the Republicans. The relationship between the White House and Congress deteriorated so quickly that in March 1866 Johnson vetoed the new Civil Rights Bill which, among other guarantees, awarded full US citizenship to American blacks. Congress responded by overturning his veto. Seward tried to serve Johnson as faithfully as he had served Lincoln, but even the British Minister, Sir Frederick Bruce, noticed the lack of rapport between them and wondered whether the President regarded Seward more as an obstruction than a help.

Bruce had no doubt that Seward was determined to keep the peace between England and America, but what other plans the Secretary of State was harbouring remained a mystery to him. Charles Francis Adams, however, soon divined exactly what game Seward was playing: the protests over belligerency and the *Alabama* claims were leverage to force Britain to make territorial concessions to the US. Seward had heard that there was support in British Columbia for annexation by America and this had given him the idea that perhaps all of Canada and possibly even parts of the Caribbean might be obtained for the Union. There was 'no prospect coming to an agreement', he told Adams on 2 May 1866, even though the American Minister had been saying for some time that 'the line of difference between the two countries was becoming thinner and thinner'.[24]

A month later, between 31 May and 7 June, Seward's machinations were upset by a series of raids across the US–Canadian border. This time the guerrillas were not a handful of Confederates but several thousand Fenians, Irish-Americans committed to Irish independence, who intended to conquer or hold Canada hostage until Britain proclaimed Ireland a free state. The existence and aims of the 50,000-strong Fenian Brotherhood (many of whom were US army veterans) had never been a secret. The previous autumn its leaders had approached Seward and Johnson asking to know how the US would react to the establishment of an Irish republic on Canadian soil, and had received the ambiguous answer that the government would 'acknowledge accomplished facts'. The Fenians had read into this the notion that the US would send troops north in support, once the initial invasion had taken place.

The US did end up sending troops, but it was to arrest rather than to help the Fenians. In the first week of June the USS *Michigan* once more sailed forth to keep the peace on Lake Erie, on this occasion intercepting several hundred Fenians as they attempted to cross the Niagara river.* Seward was furious at having to side with Canadian and British troops against Irish-Americans, a community whose votes he deemed vital to the Johnson administration. He knew this would create a fierce reaction but the US could not allow the raids to take place while pursuing claims against Britain for 'past injuries and damages' caused by her failure to behave with strict neutrality. 'Thus we have seen ruinous British warlike expeditions against the United States practically allowed and tolerated by her Majesty's government,' Seward fulminated in a dispatch to Adams, 'and we have seen similar attempts in this country against Great Britain disallowed and defeated.'[25] Seward's acute feeling for public sentiment, especially the fluctuations in American Anglophobia, was demonstrated by Congress's reconsideration of the country's neutrality law. On 26 July 1866, two days before the completion of the transatlantic cable, the House of Representatives voted unanimously to remove restrictions on Americans building or selling warships to foreign belligerents. In effect, they were warning Britain that in her next conflict she could expect hundreds of *Alabama*s sent from US shores to destroy her merchant marine.

Seward was prepared to wait, confident, as he told Adams, that ultimately the *Alabama* claims would be settled 'by such acquisition from England as would enable us to round off our North-Western territory'. Early in 1867 his desire for peaceful expansion into Canada appeared to be on the verge of fulfilment after the Russians offered to sell 'Russian America' (Alaska) to the United States. With remarkably little haggling, Seward brought down the asking price to $7.2 million and signed the treaty of sale with the Russian Minister on 30 March. 'I know that Nature designs that this whole continent, not merely the thirty-six States, shall be, sooner or later, within the magic circle of the American Union,' Seward declared to an audience in Massachusetts. But to his surprise, the public disagreed and he was harshly criticized in the press for wasting millions on a distant 'icebox'. The prospect of having a US border to the north and south of them did not encourage the Canadians to seek their absorption within 'the magic circle'. On 1 July 1867 British North America became the Dominion of Canada,

---

* The Fenian movement was also crippled by the successful infiltration of spies and informants. The most famous British spy was Henri Le Caron (the former Thomas Miller Beach), whose experiences as a volunteer in the Federal army brought him into early contact with many Fenians, thus earning their complete trust – and ensuring their failure.

initially a confederation of four provinces – Ontario, Quebec, New Brunswick and Nova Scotia – under a single Canadian parliament.[26] It looked probable that the other provinces, including British Columbia, would soon seek to join Canada rather than the Union.

The existence of a united, largely self-governing Canada allowed the new British government, led by the Tory Prime Minister Lord Derby (Lord Russell having lost the general election in 1866), to breathe a little easier. Derby's Foreign Secretary Lord Stanley hoped that Seward would realize that his plan to extract territory in exchange for dropping the *Alabama* claims had been compromised, and would finally agree to begin negotiations. Stanley, Charles Francis Adams had noted in his diary in the spring of 1867, had little reason to be defensive about Britain's actions during the war and was more willing than Russell to discuss the two countries' differences. But no British politician was prepared to 'confess a wrong and sell Canada as the release from punishment', nor was the Derby government any more prepared than its predecessor to revisit the question of belligerent rights.[27] Seward's response was uncompromising: 'I feel quite certain that the balance of faults has been on the side of Great Britain,' he told Adams on 2 May 1867 in a dispatch for communication to Lord Stanley. 'Thus the whole controversy between the two states must remain open indefinitely.'[28]

The British hoped that Seward was bluffing, but his recent dealings with France suggested that he was not. Louis-Napoleon had secretly asked Seward at the end of 1865 whether the US would recognize the validity of Emperor Maximilian's rule in Mexico in exchange for a complete withdrawal of the French army. Seward had not only turned down the offer, but allowed General Grant to send 30,000 US troops under Phil Sheridan to the Rio Grande, where they provided arms and training to the Juarist rebels. Prussia's victory over Austria in 1866 convinced Napoleon that Mexico was a distraction compared to the threat on his doorstep posed by German militarization. He informed Maximilian that the French army would remain in Mexico only until March 1867, when he would have to chose between maintaining his throne unaided or abdication. Napoleon urged him not to be proud and to abdicate, but Maximilian would not hear of leaving and paid for his misplaced idealism with his life. His rule collapsed within weeks of the French leaving Mexico, and despite a heroic rescue attempt by Prince Felix Salm-Salm,

a former Prussian volunteer in the Federal army and Colonel of the 68th
New York Infantry, Maximilian was captured and executed by the victorious Benito Juárez on 19 June 1867.*

However, Canada was not Mexico, and the Fenians in the US were
never thought to be as dangerous as the Juarists. The British desire to
resolve the *Alabama* claims controversy came more from a growing
sense that bygones should be bygones. 'Surely it is time to forget ancient
differences,' asked the Duke of Argyll at a public breakfast in London in
honour of the American abolitionist William Lloyd Garrison on 29 June
1867, just ten days after Maximilian's death.

> This country desires to maintain with the American people not merely rela-
> tions of amity and peace; it desires to have their friendship and affection.
> (Cheers.) It is not merely that that country has sprung from us in former
> times. It is that it is still to a great extent springing from England. (Hear,
> hear.) It is hardly possible to go into any house of the farming class ...
> without being told that a brother or a sister, a daughter or a son, has gone
> to the United States of America ... (Cheers.) I think we ought to feel, every
> one of us, that in going to America we are going only to a second home.
> (Cheers.)[29]

The breakfast was a final gathering of the old guard of pro-Northern
supporters and included – in addition to some of the more obvious
names such as John Bright, William Forster and Lord Houghton –
Edward Lyulph Stanley, John Stuart Mill and William Vernon Harcourt
('Historicus' in *The Times*) as well as the veteran black abolition campaigners Sarah Parker Remond and the Revd J. Sella Martin. Lord
Russell was initially not invited, an omission which hurt him deeply.
Too embarrassed to explain that Garrison subscribed to the American
view, that Russell had supported the South during the war, the organizers quickly 'found' his invitation. Russell then took advantage of the

* As a veteran of the Federal army, Prince Salm-Salm was almost unique among the 2,500
Americans who went to Mexico after the Civil War. The exodus there of ex-Confederates
was orchestrated by Matthew Fontaine Maury, who offered his services to Emperor Maximilian in June 1865, and was appointed Imperial Commissioner of Immigration. Most
settled near Cordoba in a specially designated area known as the Carlotta Colony, where
they eked out a miserable existence for a couple of years before returning to the South.
Another 9,000 Southerners moved to Brazil, where slavery remained legal, and about 1,000
went to British Honduras, now Belize. The community at Forest Home in Punta Gorda died
out and its cemetery is now a tourist attraction.

occasion to offer a public apology for his failure to understand why Lincoln did not simply abolish slavery in 1861:

> Distance and want of knowledge of the circumstances of America made me fall into error in that respect ... I did not do justice to the efforts made by the United States, but I am now persuaded that President Lincoln did all that it was possible to do, and that we are bound to give our tribute of admiration to the excellent policy which the President and his Government pursued.

Russell's attempt to make amends impressed Charles Francis Adams and John Bright but not Seward, whose continued intransigence puzzled British friends of the North.[30] Shortly before Christmas, Seward fatally undermined Adams's confidence in his judgement by proposing that Britain could relinquish the Bahamas in exchange for settling the *Alabama* claims. Instead of asking for permission to return home, Adams informed Seward that he was resigning, effective 1 April 1868.

Once it became known that the American Minister was retiring after seven years in London, Adams's stiffness and unsociability were no longer deplored but admired as proof of his integrity and demonstrable fairness towards England.[31] By April 1868 there had been four Prime Ministers in three years: Palmerston, Russell, Derby and Benjamin Disraeli; Adams's longevity at the legation during a period of such rapid political transition changed his public persona from that of a Yankee crank to a pillar of the diplomatic community. Ever nervous of making speeches, he turned down the numerous offers to hold a banquet in his honour, but that did not mean he was insensible to the plaudits which came his way. Lord Russell's speech in the House of Lords on 27 March 1868 gave Adams the most satisfaction of all. 'Here I may say I cannot mention that gentleman's name without expressing my high esteem and respect for him,' declared Russell. 'He did everything which honour and good faith and moderation could prescribe.[32]

Adams had tried hard to resolve the contentious relations between the United States and Britain during his last three years in London, and he was annoyed when Seward informed him shortly before his retirement that there was room for negotiation after all: it 'is plain that Mr Seward has opened his eyes to the proximity of his term', Adams commented cynically in his diary.[33] Seward was indeed becoming conscious of his legacy; he had served as Secretary of State for almost a decade, but the past three years under Johnson had been a crushing disappointment. Seward's political reputation had been tarnished by his ill-judged attempts to play the conciliator between Johnson and his critics. In May 1868 Johnson survived an attempt by the Senate to remove him by impeachment for 'high crimes and misdemeanors', but only by one vote. 'I have always felt that Providence dealt hardly with me in not letting me die with Mr. Lincoln,' Seward remarked bitterly. 'My work was done, and I think I deserved some of the reward of dying there.'[34] Seward was frequently accused of being drunk in public during the latter half of Johnson's Presidency. 'He no longer seemed to care,' wrote Henry Adams, who visited Washington in 1868; 'he asked for nothing, gave nothing, and invited no support; he talked little of himself or of others, and waited only for his discharge.'[35] This was an exaggeration – Seward cared a great deal – but he had lost the facility of keeping his friends loyal and his enemies afraid. 'His trouble', sneered a critic, 'is not that the party to which he once belonged is without a leader, but that he wanders about, like a ghost – a leader without a party.'[36]

General Grant's election to the Presidency in November 1868 opened a fresh path of negotiations for both countries, but for Seward it meant that he had only four months left in office to engineer one final diplomatic triumph. It was not only the *Alabama* claims and the question of belligerent rights which was aggravating British–American relations: the boundary dispute over San Juan Island had remained unresolved since the destruction of Farmer Cutlar's potatoes by Charles Griffin's pig in June 1859; Britain's insistence that British nationality could not be exchanged for another was also a growing source of friction because of the number of Irish emigrants to the US who claimed American citizenship; and the Canadians were making life difficult for American fisherman who strayed into their waters. The new Minister to the Court of St James's, Reverdy Johnson, who had arrived in London in late August, took to heart Seward's instruction to be flexible. He achieved agreements over San Juan and the naturalization question with the Tory government before its defeat in December, and signed a convention of understanding over the *Alabama* claims with the new Liberal government under Gladstone on 14 January 1869. The Johnson–Clarendon Treaty, as it was called, agreed that all British and American claims for compensation would be considered by an arbitration committee appointed by both countries; but it did not address the *Alabama* claims per se nor the issue of belligerency.

Seward was nervous about what the Senate might do to the treaty, and kept the details secret for as long as possible. Bruce's successor in Washington, Sir Edward Thornton, feared that Seward had miscalculated by withholding information. The increasingly anti-British tone in the capital arising from the prolongation of the *Alabama* dispute required the kind of political skills that the outgoing Secretary of State had long lost. The difference between the Seward of 1862, who had successfully thwarted the Senate's opposition to the Anglo-US Slave Trade Treaty, and the Seward of 1868, who was unable to find more than a single ally for the Johnson–Clarendon Treaty, was stark. The treaty was rejected in the Senate by 44 votes to 1; the triumphant architect of Seward's humiliation in the Senate was his old rival, Charles Sumner.

On 13 April 1869 Sumner gave an address to the Senate in which he laid the entire cost of the war after Gettysburg in 1863 at Britain's feet. He estimated the financial damages caused by the Confederate commerce raiders to be $15 million, and added a further $2 billion for the indirect damages caused by Britain's 'un-neutral neutrality'. As a proportion of Britain's GDP, the same figures today would be £300 million for the commerce raiders and £411 billion for the indirect costs.[37] Sumner also demanded an unreserved admission of guilt and an apology from Britain, followed by a new treaty to arrange for the reparations. The speech rescued Sumner's flagging political career. It was one of the only instances in his life where he correctly judged the prevailing public opinion and successfully capitalized on it to increase his power in Washington. A few weeks later, Sumner gave another speech in which he spoke of Britain's complete withdrawal from the Americas. It was the kind of political opportunism that Seward had employed during his heyday – pursuing a largely pragmatic course in foreign relations in private while making extreme and bellicose statements in public. Until that moment, Sumner's influence with the new Grant administration had looked tenuous but now he had national popularity as well as his chairmanship of the Foreign Relations Committee to reinforce his bargaining power with the President.

To best his rival, Charles Sumner had used Seward's favourite political tool of combining public demagoguery against England with private messages of goodwill. He was aided by the fact that Grant's attitude towards England was cool, even bordering on hostile, and that both the new President and his Secretary of State, Hamilton Fish, were fascinated by the possibility of absorbing Canada into the United States.* But the price of US bonds dropped by 10 per cent on the London Stock Exchange after the publication of Sumner's speech, suddenly calling into question the £300 million worth of British investment in the United States.[39] It also soon became apparent to Fish, as it had to Seward, that the demand for an apology from Britain for declaring neutrality was a self-imposed limitation on American foreign policy. When Cuban rebels attempted to wrest independence from Spain in late spring of 1869 Fish had to persuade Grant that it was impossible for the US to award them belligerent status without destroying its own claims against Britain.

Sumner's resurgence in Washington did not last long. He overplayed his hand as chairman of the Foreign Relations Committee by making it abundantly clear that the administration could not make the smallest decision on foreign policy without his assent. The first sign of trouble flared in the summer of 1869 when Sumner's handpicked successor to the US legation in London, the historian John L. Motley, ignored the State Department's instruction to leave the belligerency claim alone and instead parroted Sumner's *Alabama* claims speech at the Foreign Secretary, Lord Clarendon. Under any other circumstances Motley's insubordination would have cost him his position, but Fish dared not risk alienating Sumner. The Senator's vice-like grip on the administration was reflected in the parts of President Grant's annual message to Congress in December 1869 that touched on America's foreign relations, especially the harsh condemnation of Seward's failed Johnson–Clarendon Treaty.[40] Fortunately, Seward was not in Washington to hear his efforts so condemned, having already left the country on a fourteen-month world tour.

It was Sumner's active opposition to Grant's plan to purchase Santo Domingo during the first half of 1870 that sealed his downfall. In a

---

* In late March 1865 President Lincoln had discussed the *Trent* affair with General Grant, making it clear that Britain deserved to be punished: 'We gave due consideration to the case, but at that critical period of the war it was soon decided to deliver up the prisoners. It was a pretty bitter pill to swallow, but I contented myself with believing that England's triumph in the matter would be short-lived, and that after ending our war successfully we would be so powerful that we could call her to account for all the embarrassments she had inflicted upon us.'[38]

clear challenge to the Massachusetts Senator, Grant ordered Minister Motley's recall from London, although it was six months before the administration found a candidate who was willing to accept the post. Fish's determination to break free of Sumner's control removed the impasse between Britain and America over the *Alabama* claims. The timing could not have been better: Gladstone's Foreign Secretary in 1870, Lord Granville, was as anxious to find common ground with the US Secretary of State as Fish was with him. Gladstone was naturally inclined to pursue a conciliatory policy with the United States, but Prussia's resounding victory over France at the Battle of Sedan on 2 September 1870 and the astonishing capture of Louis-Napoleon were equally compelling reasons for Britain to revisit the *Alabama* claims. The balance of power in Europe was dramatically altered by the collapse of the Second Empire and its unstable replacement, known as the Third Republic. For London, the fear that American raiders would set sail to attack its commercial ships at the first sign of European hostilities was a powerful encouragement to negotiate with the Americans.

Even without the irritations caused by Sumner, Washington also had strong reasons to reopen negotiations with Britain. The Canadian government's denial of fishing rights or entry into its ports for American fisherman had to be addressed before the economic consequences became a political liability to Grant's re-election chances in 1872. The administration had also discovered that no European bank would renegotiate a lower interest rate on America's foreign debts until the country's uncertain relationship with Britain had been resolved.[41] The sudden political will in Britain and America to end the differences between them produced one of the most remarkable and successful international conventions of the nineteenth century. 'We are taking several bites out of that big cherry,' Granville wrote triumphantly to John Bright in October 1870; 'reconciliation with the States.'[42] Two teams, each consisting of five commissioners, met in Washington on 24 February 1871. By all accounts, the commissioners got on remarkably well; the British were surprised to discover that their American counterparts were 'a very gentlemanly good set of fellows socially'; and that Hamilton Fish was 'quite English in manner and appearance'.[43] In only nine weeks the two teams negotiated agreements on over forty separate points from San Juan Island's boundary to the protection of international copyrights. Just as important, each side obtained a much-wanted victory: the US received an expression 'in a friendly spirit' of regret for the escape of the *Alabama* 'under whatever circumstances'; and Britain wrangled a strict agreement on the rules of neutrality which would ensure that there would never be any US-built *Alabama*s deployed against British shipping. The sheer comprehensiveness of the Treaty of Washington settled most disputes, potential and historical, for the next twenty years. Fish also used Sumner's inevitable objections to the negotiations, since America's right to Canada was not part of the discussion, to engineer the latter's removal as chairman of the Foreign Relations Committee.

The Treaty of Washington established two tribunals, one to arbitrate the claims of private individuals against the United States for actions committed during the Civil War, and the other, to rule on the *Alabama* claims. At the first, Mary Sophia Hill finally had her say in court. In fact, she said far too much and her claim was dismissed on 15 November 1871 for indecorous language. Undaunted, she appealed the decision: 'I leave my case in your honorable hands, feeling that justice, even at this late hour, will be done me, and the insult to our flag, through me, be canceled, as England always has and always will protect the most humble of her subjects. As I said before, my health is ruined, so I do not consider the damage of two thousand pounds excessive.'[44] This time, the Court decided that £2,000 *was* excessive but otherwise found in her favour, and on 5 January 1872 awarded her $1,560 in damages.

The *Alabama* claims tribunal met in Geneva in December 1871. Charles Francis Adams was called out of retirement to represent the United States on the panel of five international judges who were to decide on the case. Adams had not wanted the appointment and when he met his fellow judges he thought his worst fears confirmed. The British representative, Lord Chief Justice Sir Alexander Cockburn, had so short a temper that he seemed unbalanced, while the three other judges – a Swiss, a Brazilian and an Italian – had varying degrees of familiarity with English. America and Britain each sent two legal teams to argue their respective sides. The proceedings started calmly enough until the British team discovered in early January 1872 that Sumner's claims for $2 billion – at 7 per cent interest – had been included by the Americans for arbitration. They demanded that the claims be excluded, and the

Americans responded with equal vehemence that they stay and be decided upon by the judges. There was outrage in Britain when the news became known. Gladstone declared in the House of Commons on 7 February 1872 that the government would be 'insane to accede to demands which no nation with a spark of honour or spirit left could submit to even at the point of death'. France, after all, had paid less than half that sum to the victorious Prussians.

Grant could not have dropped the claims for $2 billion, even if he wanted to, without jeopardizing his re-election hopes in November. Yet the idea that the *Alabama* and her sister ships, the *Florida*, *Georgia* and *Shenandoah*, were responsible for prolonging the war by two years was patently ludicrous. The proceedings had been stalled for almost six months when Lord Russell surprised the Liberal government by spearheading a movement in the House of Lords for the British team to return home until the Americans had withdrawn the demand. The Foreign Secretary, Lord Granville, understood that Russell was upset, but he could not allow the former Foreign Secretary's hurt feelings to become a fatal obstruction, and possibly leave the government vulnerable to a vote of no confidence.

It was Charles Francis Adams who rescued the tribunal from its imminent collapse (and the Liberals from Russell's umbrage). Realizing that neither government could be seen to back down, he took it upon himself to persuade the other judges that the 'indirect claims' argument had no validity in international law and therefore had to be excluded from consideration. 'My Dear Bright,' wrote Lord Granville happily on 12 June 1872, 'we are on the eve of a probable and satisfactory settlement of the Alabama question . . . this course has been secretly prompted by Adams.' But three days later there was still no word from Geneva on whether the judges had agreed to Adams's proposition. 'Arbitration meeting at Geneva today, and we waited for news,' recorded William Forster in his diary. After five hours 'we had exhausted subjects of talk, and were listlessly looking at one another . . . we took three chairs on to the terrace outside the cabinet room, one for each of us and one for the chess-board. We had three games, and, alas! [Granville] won two of them. Still no telegram.' It was another twenty-four hours before Forster heard that Adams had been successful.[45]

Three months later, on 14 September 1872, the tribunal ruled that Britain owed $15.5 million, including interest, for the damage caused by the three Confederate cruisers. Ironically, the sum was $500,000 more than the amount first proposed by Charles Sumner in 1869.* The American press complained that it was too little, and the British press that it was too much, but there was a shared sense of pride in both countries that a high moral precedent had been set in allowing disputes to be resolved in an international court rather than on the battlefield.[46] Without Adams's bravery and initiative the proceedings would have collapsed – with calamitous results for Anglo-American relations. Adams is usually praised on the unfounded assertion that he prevented Britain from supporting the South, whereas his real triumph – when he transcended his own limitations and acted with visionary patriotism – was the fruit of his actions during June 1872. Before Adams returned home he briefly visited England in order to say a last farewell to Lord Russell, and to reassure him that his reputation had not been sullied by Britain's expression of regret for the escape of the *Alabama* or by the payment of the claims. This act of generosity towards Russell caused Adams to arrive back in the United States too late to say goodbye to Seward, who died on 10 October 1872. The former Secretary of State's death received respectful attention but not the national mourning that he deserved, considering his service to the country. Seward was too complex and contradictory a person to be easily categorized. He was not, as is now sometimes claimed, one of the greatest Secretaries of State in US history; his chronic and sometimes dangerous manipulation of foreign relations to boost his domestic agenda precludes him from that title. But after a disastrous beginning at the State Department he became essential to the preservation of peace between America and Britain. His restraint of the forces that could have destroyed the fragile neutrality of the British government remains one of his outstanding achievements.

Two months after the ruling in Geneva, Sergeant Gilbert H. Bates, formerly of the 1st Wisconsin Heavy Artillery Regiment, travelled to Britain on a personal goodwill mission. Starting in Scotland on 6 November 1872, Bates walked the length of the country, bearing aloft the Stars and Stripes, to prove to Americans that the British bore no ill will towards the United States. He had performed a similar feat in 1868, marching through the South from Vicksburg to Washington. At Bolton, Bates was accosted by a man who declared that he too was a Federal

* Britain actually paid out $8,070,181, since the US agreed to give Canada $5.5 million for the right to fish in its waters and also paid $1,929,812 in compensation as a result of rulings at the Mixed Commission on British and American claims.

veteran and wished to carry the flag through the town; it was James Pendlebury. Surprised, Bates handed him the flag and Pendlebury was allowed to have his moment of glory. Bates received a hero's welcome when he reached London on 30 November. Addressing an appreciative crowd in front of the Guildhall in the City, he declared:

> It has been asserted by the press that this is a Yankee test of English feeling towards the States, but as far as I am concerned, it is no test. It is only a proof that I was right . . . when I said the English people respected America . . . I have met with nothing but the kindest treatment. I have not had even a cross look from any one. My own countrymen on the other side of the Atlantic have been watching the progress of the tour of my flag with the greatest interest, and therefore I am gratified that the English people have proved that I was right.[47]

The resolution of the *Alabama* claims brought the Civil War chapter of British-American history to a close. The pre-war resentment between the two countries had finally played itself out and a new, less hysterical and suspicious relationship was forming. Thirteen years later, in 1885, Ulysses S. Grant could write about the two countries in his memoirs with hope instead of rancour.

> England's course towards the United States during the rebellion exasperated the people of this country very much against the mother country [he wrote]. I regretted it. England and the United States are natural allies, and should be the best of friends. They speak one language, and are related by blood and other ties. We together, or even either separately, are better qualified than any other people to establish commerce between all the nationalities of the world.[48]

*

Almost immediately after the war, the British writer William Michael Rossetti (brother of the artist Dante Gabriel) tried to explain its impact on English public opinion in an essay for the American *Atlantic Monthly*. Rossetti claimed never to have seen his compatriots so animated 'in connection with any other non-English occurrences': the entire country had divided over the merits of the Civil War, and whether abolition, democracy, the Union or the right to self-determination had been the real principle at stake. Expressions such as '"I am a Northerner", and "I am a Southerner"' were 'as common on Englishmen's lips as "I am a Liberal or "a Conservative"'.[49] It has been the purpose of this book to restore to view the Anglo-American world that Rossetti described.

After the Civil War and the resolution of the *Alabama* claims, the simmering tensions which had regularly flared into full-blown crises between Washington and London became a thing of the past – although the relationship remained complicated and not always cordial. 'I fear that a good deal of feeling against England – mind you, none whatever against an Englishman – still foolishly exists in certain quarters of our purely American communities,' wrote Theodore Roosevelt to the British historian James Bryce in 1889, though he added: 'But they are perfectly ready to elect Englishmen to office.'[50]

In 1925, the US consulate in London collected information on British Civil War veterans for the Federal Pensions Bureau for the last time. By then the largest survivors' organization in the country, the American Civil War Veterans (London Branch), had dwindled from 140 members to a mere 24 ex-soldiers and 21 widows. But already in histories of the war it was as though the British volunteers in the Union and Confederate armies had never existed.[51] This is not to say that Britain was rubbed out of the Civil War, far from it: 1925 was also the year that the first major study of Anglo-American relations during the war was published – E. D. Adams's *Great Britain and the American Civil War*. After Adams came a trickle and then a flood of books on the subject as the role of international diplomacy gained ever greater prominence in the historiography of the Civil War. 'No battle,' observed Allan Nevins, author of the eight-volume series *Ordeal of the Union*, in 1959, 'not Gettysburg, not the Wilderness, was more important than the contest waged in the diplomatic arena and the forum of public opinion.' The seemingly inexhaustible scholarly interest in these two areas continues to endorse the truth of Nevins's insight. But studies of movements, forces, factors and political calculations ultimately have to be anchored by individual experience. *A World On Fire* has been an attempt to balance the vast body of work on Anglo-American history in the 1860s with the equally vast material left behind by witnesses and participants in the war – to depict the world as it was seen by Britons in America, and Americans in Britain, during a defining moment not just in US history but in the relations between the two countries.[52]

The histories of the British participants, in what is and always will be an American story, brings the sharper focus that often comes with distance. Though united by language and a shared heritage, the Britons in America were nevertheless strangers who happened to find themselves, for a variety of reasons, in the midst of great events. Their simultaneous involvement and detachment (even when their observations turned out to be misleading or mistaken) provide a special perspective on the war, one that by definition was not possible for native-born Americans.[53] There were also many instances when the intimate access granted to British observers meant that they were the only independent witnesses to record a particular event – such as William Howard Russell on President Lincoln's first White House dinner, or Frank Vizetelly on the flight of Jefferson Davis after the fall of Richmond. For this reason, their accounts remain not only fascinating but invaluable relics of the Civil War.

Rossetti concluded his essay about Britain and the American Civil War with an apology which speaks for all those authors who venture into this complex history: 'for anything I have said which may possibly sound egotistic or intrusive, I – still more for anything erroneous or unfair in my statements or point of view, – I must commit myself to the candid construction of my reader, be he [or she] American or English.'[54]

Notes

ABBREVIATIONS

B L   British Library

B D O F A   *British Documents on Foreign Affairs: Reports and Papers from the Foreign Office Confidential Print*, ed. Kenneth Bourne and D. Cameron Watt (Frederick, Md., 1986–)

M H S   Massachusetts Historical Society

M P U S   *Message of the President of the United States*, 37th Congress (Washington, 1862)

N A R A   National Archives and Records Administration, Washington

O R   Official Records

O R N   Official Records Navy

P R F A   *Papers Relating to Foreign Affairs Accompanying the Annual Message of the President of the United States*

P R O   Public Record Office

PROLOGUE

1. Virginia Clay-Copton and Ada Sterling, *A Belle of the Fifties: The Memoirs of Mrs Clay of Alabama* (New York, 1904), pp. 116, 118.

2. *New York Times*, 19 February 1859.

3. Mrs Roger A. Pryor, *Reminiscences of Peace and War* (New York, 1905), p. 57.

4. C. Vann Woodward (ed.), *Mary Chesnut's Civil War* (New Haven, 1981), p. 367.

5. Lyons nevertheless understood the importance of providing excellent food and wine at the legation dinners. Hence the chef was from Paris and the wine from his own family cellars. Source: Brian Jenkins.

6. James J. Barnes and Patience P. Barnes (eds.), *Private and Confidential: Letters from British Ministers in Washington to the Foreign Secretaries* (Selinsgrove, Pa., 1993), p. 213, Lyons to Lord Malmesbury, 12 April 1859.

7. Raymond A. Jones, *The British Diplomatic Service* (London, 1983), p. 99.

8. Calvin D. Davis, 'A British Diplomat and the American Civil War: Edward Malet in the United States', *South Atlantic Quarterly*, 77/2 (1978), p. 166.

9. 863,409 British and 1,611,304 Irish, PRO FO115/394, f. 216. Two-thirds of these 'British' expatriates were actually Irish immigrants, who harboured a visceral hatred towards the mother country. Nevertheless, they enjoyed the same protection by HM Minister as the 98 Scots in Dakota and the 23,848 Englishmen in Massachusetts. Recently, the Foreign Office had recognized that the legation's staff of five was too small and a sixth attaché was on his way. Although the British government promulgated the official line of 'once a Briton, always a Briton', in practice Lyons was not expected to take up the cases of naturalized British subjects.

10. H. C. Allen, *Great Britain and the United States* (New York, 1955), p. 361. In 1819, the Foreign Secretary, Lord Castlereagh, warned his new British Minister: 'the jealousies as yet imperfectly allayed inclines the Government of the United States to maintain . . . [to us] a tone of greater harshness than towards any other Government whatever. The American people are more easily excited against us and more disposed to strengthen the hands of their Ministers against us than against any other State.'

11. George Washburn Smalley, *Anglo-American Memories* (New York, 1912), p. 174.

12. Lord Newton (ed.), *Lord Lyons: A Record of British Diplomacy*, 2 vols. (London, 1914), vol. 2, p. 214.

13. John Evan (pseudonym of Evan John Simpson), *Atlantic Impact* (London, 1952), p. 210. This oft-repeated description of Lyons may possibly be apocryphal but the spirit of the story remains true.

14. The Admiral became his son's champion: 'Had it not been for your visit to England at the critical moment,' he wrote to his father from his new post in Florence, 'I should now have been no more than simple Secretary of Legation.' Newton (ed.), *Lord Lyons*, vol. 1, p. 7.

15. Scott Thomas Cairns, 'Lord Lyons and Anglo-American Diplomacy during the American Civil War', Ph.D. thesis, London School of Economics, 2004, p. 58.

16. As quoted in Brian Jenkins, *Britain and the War for the Union*, 2 vols. (Montreal, 1974, 1980), vol. 1, p. 44.

17. Sarah Agnes Wallace and Frances Elma Gillespie (eds.), *The Journal of Benjamin Moran, 1857–1865*, 2 vols. (Chicago, 1948, 1949), vol. 1, pp. 504–5, 8 February 1859.

18. Newton (ed.), *Lord Lyons*, vol. 1, p. 14, Lord Lyons to Lord Malmesbury, 29 May 1859.

19. Charles Dickens, *American Notes for General Circulation* (London, 1842; Penguin Classics, 2000), p. 129.

20. Edward Dicey, *Spectator of America*, ed. Herbert Mitgang (Athens, Ga., 1971), p. 62.

21. Ibid., p. 65.

22. Michael Burlingame (ed.), *Lincoln's Journalist: John Hay's Anonymous Writings for the Press, 1860–1864* (Carbondale, Ill., 1998), p. 50.

23. William Howard Russell, *My Diary North and South*, ed. Eugene H. Berwanger (New York, 1988), p. 41, 26 March 1861.

24. Clay-Copton and Sterling, *A Belle of the Fifties*, p. 139.

25. Mrs Clay recalled that Lyons said, 'Ah, Madam! do you remember what Uncle Toby said to his nephew when he informed him of his intended marriage?' She, presumably not having read *Tristram Shandy*, had no idea what was coming next. 'Then, without waiting for my assent, he added, "Alas! alas! quoth my Uncle Toby, you will never sleep slantindicularly in your bed [any] more!"' Ibid.

26. Hudson Strode (ed.), *Private Letters of Jefferson Davis* (New York, 1966), p. 105, Varina Davis to Jefferson Davis, 10 April 1859.

27. Wilbur Devereux Jones, *The American Problem in British Diplomacy, 1841–1861* (London, 1974), p. 172. Napier was blamed for having given too much away to the Americans, including recognition of the Monroe Doctrine when the issue was not even under discussion.

28. Barnes and Barnes (eds.), *Private and Confidential*, p. 214, Lyons to Lord Malmesbury, 21 June 1859.

29. Newton (ed.), *Lord Lyons*, vol. 1, p. 14, Lord Lyons to Lord Malmesbury, 30 May 1859.

30. James O'Donald Mays, *Mr Hawthorne Goes to England* (Ringwood, 1983), pp. 156–8.

CHAPTER 1. THE UNEASY COUSINS

1. Wilbur Devereux Jones, *The American Problem in British Diplomacy, 1841–1861* (London, 1974), p. 169, Lord Derby to Lord Malmesbury, 11 October 1858.

2. Kenneth Bourne, *The Foreign Policy of Victorian England, 1830–1902* (Oxford, 1970), p. 334, Lord Palmerston to Lord Clarendon, 31 December 1857.

3. In 1807, HMS *Leopard* was prowling off the coast of Virginia when it came across the USS *Chesapeake*. The *Leopard* fired on the *Chesapeake* after the vessel refused to heave to, killing three American sailors and wounding a further eighteen. Only one deserter was found.

4. Paul Leicester Ford (ed.), *The Writings of Thomas Jefferson, 1807–1815*, vol. 9 (London, 1898), p. 366, Jefferson to William Duane, 4 August 1812.

5. Thomas Low Nichols, *Forty Years of American Life*, 2 vols. (London, 1864), vol. 1, p. 409.

6. Jasper Ridley, *Palmerston* (New York, 1971), pp. 270–74, Palmerston to Russell, 19 January 1841.

7. Evelyn Ashley, *The Life and Correspondence of Henry John Temple, Viscount Palmerston*, 2 vols. (London, 1879), vol. 1, p. 408, Palmerston to H. S. Fox, 9 February 1841.

8. The raid had taken place in 1837. The USS *Caroline* was carrying supplies to pro-American Canadian insurgents. Tired of troublemakers fostering rebellion south of the border, a group of armed men seized the *Caroline*, killing an American sailor in the process, and sent it over Niagara Falls. While hogging his bar-stool, McLeod boasted that he was the killer. In truth, he was a pathetic fantasist.

9. James Chambers, *Palmerston: The People's Darling* (London, 2004), p. 199.

10. Ridley, *Palmerston*, p. 273.

11. The border dispute over New Brunswick and Maine was settled by the British Minister Lord Ashburton, and the Secretary of State, Daniel Webster.

12. H. C. Allen, *Great Britain and the United States* (New York, 1955), p. 136.

13. Ibid., p. 123

14. Betty Fladeland, *Men and Brothers* (Champaign, Ill., 1972), p. 351.

15. Annie Heloise Abel and Frank J. Klingberg (eds.), *A Sidelight on Anglo-American Relations, 1839–1858* (Lancaster, Pa., 1927), p. 40.

16. Elizabeth Cady Stanton, *Eighty Years and More: Reminiscences, 1815–1897* (New York, 1898), pp. 71–92.

17. Jean Fagan Yellin, 'Harriet Jacobs and the Transatlantic Movement', in *Sisterhood and Slavery: Transatlantic Antislavery and Women's Rights. Proceedings of the Third Annual Gilder Lehrman Center International Conference at Yale University* (New Haven, 2001), p. 7.

18. Allen, *Great Britain and the United States*, p. 198.

19. William Brock, 'The Image of England and American Nationalism', *Journal of American Studies*, 5 (Dec. 1971), Edward Everett, speech at Bristol, 1842, p. 227.

20. Nichols, *Forty Years of American Life*, vol. 1, p. 398.

21. Allen, *Great Britain and the United States*, p. 147, quoting the *Edinburgh Review*, 1820.

22. It was often pointed out that Louisiana would still belong to the French if Barings Bank in London had not financed the purchase, selling more than $9 million worth of the $11 million bonds.

23. Charles Dickens to Macready, 22 March 1842, quoted in Walter Allen, *Transatlantic Crossing: American Visitors to Britain and British Visitors to America in the Nineteenth Century* (New York, 1971), p. 236.

24. What Seward actually believed in has been the subject of intense historical debate. In a speech in 1853 he declared it was his aim that the Republic 'shall greet the sun when he touches the tropics, and when he sends his gleaming rays towards the polar circle, and shall include even distant islands in either ocean'. But Ernest Paolino argues that by 1857 Seward had abandoned the idea of annexing Canada by force. For one thing, a trip to Labrador convinced him that the Canadians would never accept it. Nevertheless, he liked to talk as though he believed it was just a matter of time, if only to annoy the British. In 1860 he made a speech which congratulated the Canadians for 'building states to be hereafter admitted into the American union'. Ernest N. Paolino, *The Foundations of the American Empire* (New York, 1973), p. 8.

25. G. H. Warren, *Fountain of Discontent: The Trent Affair and Freedom of the Seas* (Boston, 1981), p. 56.

26. Henry Adams, *The Education of Henry Adams*, ed. Ernest Samuels (repr., Boston, 1973), p. 102.

27. David Herbert Donald, *Charles Sumner and the Coming of the Civil War* (New York, 1961), pp. 295–6.

28. *Letters of Sir George Cornewall Lewis*, ed. Sir G. F. Lewis (London, 1870), pp. 390–92, Lewis to the Hon. Edward Twisleton, 21 January 1861.

29. *Illustrated London News*, August 1856, pp. 121–2. The Duchess of Sutherland made it a point of duty to support black performers who came to England. In 1853, for example, she invited Elizabeth Taylor Greenfield, known as the 'Black Swan', to perform a concert at Stafford House in the presence of Queen Victoria. The event was so celebrated that it was turned into a song, 'The Other Side of Jordan' (1853).

30. *George Douglas, Eighth Duke of Argyll (1823–1900): Autobiography and Memoirs*, ed. the Dowager Duchess of Argyll, 2 vols. (London, 1906), vol. 1, p. 412.

CHAPTER 2. ON THE BEST OF TERMS

1. Kathleen Burk, *Morgan Grenfell, 1838–1988* (Oxford, 2002), p. 20.

2. John M. Taylor, *William Henry Seward: Lincoln's Right Hand* (New York, 1991), p. 107.

3. Jay Sexton, *Debtor Diplomacy* (Oxford, 2005), p. 138.

4. Playing to the gallery, Seward had urged President Buchanan to give Britain one year to withdraw entirely from Central America. If she refused, he argued, the United States would have the right to annex Canada. Cuba had become the largest importer of slaves after Brazil, prompting Lord Palmerston to order the Royal Navy to surround the island, if necessary, and board any suspicious-looking ship, whatever the colour of its flag. By May 1858, the Royal Navy had boarded 116 suspected slave ships, of which 61 were American-owned. The New York press, in particular, raised an outcry, and the Secretary of State, Lewis Cass, demanded that Britain stop such activities immediately. Senator James Murray Mason had steered a bill through the Senate to send a US naval squadron to the Caribbean. The British government backed away from a confrontation and ordered the Royal Navy to desist from the practice. Palmerston was outraged by Derby's pusillanimity. But he placed the greater blame on the United States. Hugh Thomas, *The Slave Trade* (New York, 1997), p. 764.

5. Edwin G. Burrows and Mike Wallace, *Gotham* (New York, 1999), p. 676.

6. H. C. Allen, *Great Britain and the United States* (New York, 1955), p. 158.

7. Frederick W. Seward (ed.), *Seward at Washington* (New York, 1891), p. 372.

8. Taylor, *William Henry Seward*, p. 113.

9. H. F. Bell, *Lord Palmerston*, 2 vols. (London, 1936), vol. 2, p. 253. Her mother

had been the great Lady Melbourne, a political hostess whose influence in the 1780s was second only to the Duchess of Devonshire's.

10. John Prest, *Lord John Russell* (London, 1972), p. 134. 'You give great offence to your followers,' his exasperated brother, the Duke of Bedford, once complained, 'by not being courteous to them, by treating them superciliously or de haut en bas, by not listening . . . to their solicitations, remonstrances, or whatever it may be . . .'

11. Ibid., p. 349.

12. Beverly Wilson Palmer (ed.), *The Selected Letters of Charles Sumner*, 2 vols. (Boston, 1990), vol. 1, p. 24, Sumner to Duchess of Argyll, 22 May 1860.

13. Seward (ed.), *Seward at Washington*, p. 390.

14. Sarah Agnes Wallace and Frances Elma Gillespie (eds.), *The Journal of Benjamin Moran, 1857–1865*, 2 vols. (Chicago, 1948, 1949), vol. 1, p. 545, 21 May 1859.

15. Ibid., p. 558, 23 June 1859.

16. Ibid., p. 504, 8 February 1859.

17. K. Theodore Hoppen, *The Mid-Victorian Generation* (Oxford, 1998), p. 202.

18. James Matlack Scovel, 'The Great Free Trader by his own Fire Side', *Overland Monthly and Out West Magazine* (1893), p. 129.

19. Seward (ed.), *Seward at Washington*, p. 380. Deborah Logan (ed.), *The Collected Letters of Harriet Martineau*, 5 vols. (London, 2007), vol. 4, p. 180, Martineau to Henry Reeve, 6 July 1859. Seward also told Harriet Martineau that he believed Sumner's ailments were mostly psychological.

20. Wilbur Devereux Jones, *The American Problem in British Diplomacy, 1841–1861* (London, 1974), p. 200.

21. Massachusetts Foundation for the Humanties: http://www.mfh.org/specialprojects/shwlp/site/honorees/remond.html, Sarah Parker Remond to Abby Kelly Foster, September 1858. Sibyl Ventress Brownlee, 'Out of the Abundance of the Heart: Sarah Ann Parker Remond's Quest for Freedom', Ph.D. thesis, University of Massachusetts, 1997, p. 119.

22. Wallace and Gillespie (eds.), *The Journal of Benjamin Moran*, vol. 1, p. 608, 22 November 1859.

23. Ibid., p. 614, 10 December 1859.

24. Ibid., p. 616, 16 December 1859.

25. Brownlee, 'Out of the Abundance of the Heart', p. 136.

26. David Herbert Donald, *Charles Sumner and the Coming of the Civil War* (New York, 1961), p. 348.

27. Taylor, *William Henry Seward*, p. 114.

28. James J. Barnes and Patience P. Barnes (eds.), *Private and Confidential: Letters from British Ministers in Washington to the Foreign Secretaries* (Selinsgrove, Pa., 1993), p. 223, Lord Lyons to Lord Russell, 6 December 1859.

29. Mason's report was published in June 1860.

30. Mrs Roger A. Pryor, *Reminiscences of Peace and War* (New York, 1905), p. 98.

31. Rose Greenhow, *My Imprisonment and the First Year of Abolition Rule at Washington* (London, 1863), p. 192.

32. Martin Duberman, *Charles Francis Adams* (New York, 1961), p. 213.

33. Greenhow, *My Imprisonment*, p. 192.

34. Ernest Samuels (ed.), *Henry Adams: Selected Letters* (Cambridge, Mass., 1988), p. 21, Henry Adams to Abigail Adams, 13 February 1860.

35. Duberman, *Charles Francis Adams*, p. 21.

36. Charles Francis Adams would have argued back that he had not been a slouch during his adulthood: he served in the Massachusetts State legislature for five years, and was twice an unsuccessful candidate for Vice-President, in 1848 and 1872.

37. San Juan Island remained under joint military occupation for the next twelve years. Then, after Britain and the United States signed the Treaty of Washington, the San Juan Island question was referred to Kaiser Wilhelm I. He established a three-man arbitration commission, which studied the issue for almost a year. On 21 October 1872 the commission ruled in favour of the United States. A month later, the Royal Marines packed their bags, said goodbye to their American friends, and marched out of the English camp for the last time. Two years later, the American camp was abandoned.

38. PRO 30/22/34, ff. 130–33, Lyons to Russell, 10 April 1860.

39. PRO 30/22/34, ff. 149–50, Lyons to Russell, 22 May 1860.

40. As recently as 2 March Sumner had told her: 'I incline now more than ever to think that Seward will be [our candidate].' Palmer (ed.), *The Selected Letters of Charles Sumner*, vol. 1, p. 19.

41. No one had actually counted the Prince's entourage, so it came as a terrible shock when there were too many bodies for too few beds. Buchanan gallantly offered up his room and slept on a sofa in the corridor.

42. Stanley Weintraub, *Edward the Caresser* (New York, 2003), p. 68.

43. Ibid., p. 71. The issue of slavery would force itself upon the Prince one more time, in the North. On 18 October 1860 a delegation of African-Americans presented him with 'An Address of Colored Citizens of Boston to the Prince of Wales', which offered 'their profound and grateful attachment and respect for the Throne which you represent here, under whose shelter so many thousands of their race, fugitives from American slavery, find safety and rest . . . and where the road to wealth, education, and social position, and civil office and honors is as free to the black man as to the white.' *Anti-Slavery Advocate*, 2/403/50, 1 February 1861.

44. Weintraub, *Edward the Caresser*, p. 73.

45. Edward Dicey, *Spectator of America*, ed. Herbert Mitgang (Athens, Ga., 1971), p. 11.

46. Lloyd Morris, *Incredible New York* (New York, 1951; repr. Syracuse, NY, 1996), p. 24.

47. Weintraub, *Edward the Caresser*, p. 76.

48. The 69th Regiment New York State Militia was the nucleus for the 69th New York State Volunteers, which was itself one of the three founding Irish regiments of the famous New York Irish Brigade.

49. Seward (ed.), *Seward at Washington*, p. 455.

50. Palmer (ed.), *Selected Letters of Charles Sumner*, vol. 1, p. 23, Sumner to Seward, 20 May 1860.

51. Glyndon Van Deusen, *William Henry Seward* (Oxford, 1967), p. 231.

52. Hallward Library, University of Nottingham, Newcastle, NEC/10885/134, Duke of Newcastle to Sir Edmund Head, 5 June 1861.

53. Sir Theodore Martin, *The Life of His Royal Highness the Prince Consort*, vol. 5 (New York, 1880), p. 204.

54. Ibid.

55. Martin Crawford, *The Anglo-American Crisis of the Mid-Nineteenth Century: The Times and America, 1850–1862* (Athens, Ga., 1987), p. 76, Morris to Bancroft Davis, 30 October 1860.

56. Lord Newton (ed.), *Lord Lyons: A Record of British Diplomacy*, 2 vols. (London, 1914), vol. 1, pp. 27–8, Lyons to Duke of Newcastle, 29 October 1860.

57. Crawford, *The Anglo-American Crisis of the Mid-Nineteenth Century*, p. 10, 12 October 1860.

58. Newton (ed.), *Lord Lyons*, vol. 1, p. 29, Lord Lyons to Duke of Newcastle, 10 December 1860.

CHAPTER 3. 'THE CARDS ARE IN OUR HANDS!'

1. Wilbur Devereux Jones, *The American Problem in British Diplomacy, 1841–1861* (London, 1974), p. 198.

2. Ibid.

3. *BDOFA*, Part 1, ser. C, vol. 5, p. 162, law officers of the Crown to Lord John Russell, 7 December 1860.

4. Sarah Agnes Wallace and Frances Elma Gillespie (eds.), *The Journal of Benjamin Moran, 1857–1865*, 2 vols. (Chicago, 1948, 1949), vol. 1, pp. 751, 753, 7 December, 11 December 1860.

5. Ibid., p. 765, 9 January 1861.

6. *The Times*, 9 January 1861.

7. *Illustrated London News*, 19 January 1861.

8. William S. Walsh, *Abraham Lincoln and the London Punch* (New York, 1909), p. 20.

9. Brian Jenkins, *Britain and the War for the Union*, 2 vols. (Montreal, 1974, 1980), vol. 1, p. 86. And *BDOFA*, Part 1, ser. C, vol. 5, pp. 169–70, Lord Lyons to Lord John Russell, 18 December 1860.

10. Glyndon Van Deusen, *William Henry Seward* (Oxford, 1967), p. 240.

11. Frederick W. Seward (ed.), *Seward at Washington* (New York, 1891), p. 487.

12. Ernest Samuels (ed.), *Henry Adams: Selected Letters* (Cambridge, Mass., 1988), p. 32, Henry Adams to Charles Francis Adams Jr., 9 December 1860.

13. Charles Francis Adams Jr., *Charles Francis Adams, 1835–1915: An Autobiography with a Memorial Address* (Boston, 1916), p. 82.

14. Charles Francis Adams Jr., 'The British Proclamation of May, 1861', *Massachusetts Historical Society Proceedings*, 48 (1915), pp. 190–241, at p. 216, Lord Lyons to Lord John Russell, 4 February 1861.

15. PRO Kew, 30/22/35, ff. 16–19, Lyons to Lord John Russell, 12 February 1861. Lord Newton (ed.), *Lord Lyons: A Record of British Diplomacy*, 2 vols. (London, 1914), vol. 1, p. 30, Lord Lyons to Lord John Russell, 7 January 1861.

16. *BDOFA*, Part 1, ser. C, vol. 5, p. 181, Russell to Lyons, 20 February 1861.

17. Charles M. Hubbard, *The Burden of Confederate Diplomacy* (Knoxville, Tenn., 1998), p. 27.

18. Doris Kearns Goodwin, *Team of Rivals* (New York, 2005), p. 316.

19. Michael Burlingame, *Abraham Lincoln*, 2 vols. (Baltimore, 2008), vol. 2, p. 98.

20. 'He is obtrusive,' complained Welles, 'assuming and presuming, meddlesome, and uncertain, ready to exercise authority always, never doubting his right until challenged; then he becomes timid, uncertain, distrustful, and inventive of schemes to extricate himself . . . I think he has no very profound or sincere convictions.' *Diary of Gideon Welles*, 3 vols. (Boston, 1911), vol. 1, pp. 134–40.

21. *BDOFA*, Part 1, ser. C, vol. 5, Lyons to Russell, 18 March 1861.

22. Lynn M. Case and Warren F. Spencer, *The United States and France: Civil War Diplomacy* (Philadelphia, Pa., 1970), p. 130. Norman Ferris maintained that the various accounts of the dinner by the foreign Ministers were too dissimilar to be trustworthy. I believe that the sense in all of them is the same: Seward did not like their answers and became aggressive. Norman B. Ferris, 'Lincoln and Seward in Civil War Diplomacy: Their Relationship at the Outset Reexamined', *Journal of the Abraham Lincoln Association*, 12 (1991), p. 21.

23. Newton (ed.), *Lord Lyons*, vol. 1, pp. 31–4, Lyons to Russell, 26 March 1861. Norman Ferris disputes Lyons's account but his argument is not persuasive.

24. David Donald, *Charles Sumner and the Coming of the Civil War* (New York, 1961), p. 383.

25. Adams, *Charles Francis Adams, 1835–1915*, p. 108.

26. MHS, Adams MSS, Diary of Charles Francis Adams, 28 March 1861.

27. David H. Donald, *Lincoln* (New York, 1995), p. 285.

28. Interestingly, Jack Shepherd, *The Adams Chronicles* (New York, 1975), p. 358, Martin Duberman, *Charles Francis Adams* (New York, 1961), p. 257, Philip Van Doren Stern, *When the Guns Roared: World Aspects of the American Civil War* (New York, 1965), p. 35, and Donald, *Lincoln*, p. 321, take the account from Charles Francis Adams Jr.'s biography of his father, but it differs in minor but significant aspects from Adams's diary.

29. Alan Hankinson, *Man of Wars: William Howard Russell of 'The Times', 1820–1907* (London, 1982), p. 152.

30. C. Vann Woodward (ed.), *Mary Chesnut's Civil War* (New Haven, 1981), p. 67, 4–10 June 1861.

31. Hankinson, *Man of Wars*, p. 157, Mowbray Morris to Russell, 4 April 1861.

32. Wiltshire and Swindon RO, 2536/10, Edward Best to Aunt Sophia, 10 May 1861.

33. William Howard Russell, *My Diary North and South*, ed. Eugene H. Berwanger (New York, 1988), p. 42, 26 March 1861; dashes added for clarity.

34. Ibid., p. 47, 28 March 1861.

35. Ibid.

36. MHS, Adams MSS, Diary of Charles Francis Adams, 31 March 1861.

37. Charles Francis Adams, Jr., *Charles Francis Adams, 1835–1915: An Autobiography* (Boston, 1916), pp. 112–3.

38. Van Deusen, *William Henry Seward*, p. 270.

39. Edward L. Pierce (ed.), *Memoir and Letters of Charles Sumner*, 4 vols. (Boston, 1894), vol. 4: *1860–1870*, p. 29.

40. The crux of his proposal was America's engagement with Europe. Seward stated that he 'would demand explanation from Spain and France, categorically, at once. I would seek explanations from Great Britain and Russia, and send agents into Canada, Mexico and Central America, to rouse a vigorous continental spirit of independence on this continent against European intervention. And if satisfactory explanations are not received from Spain and France, would convene Congress and declare war against them.' This was a scattergun approach, indicative of Seward's state of mind. At least regarding Spain, he did have a valid issue. With extraordinary timing, Spain had just annexed Santo Domingo – a direct snub to the Monroe Doctrine. But the others were mere wishful thinking.

41. Patrick Sowle, 'A Reappraisal of Seward's Memorandum of April 1, 1861, to Lincoln', *Journal of Southern History*, 33/2 (May 1967), pp. 234–9.

42. Russell, *My Diary North and South*, p. 66, 9 April 1861.

43. Ibid., p. 77, 15 April 1861.

44. Martin Crawford (ed.), *William Howard Russell's Civil War: Private Diary and Letters, 1861–1862* (Athens, Ga., 1992), p. 43, William Howard Russell to Lord Lyons, 19 April 1861.

45. Russell, *My Diary North and South*, p. 92, 18 April 1861.

46. Ibid., p. 95, 20 April 1861.

47. There is a still a lively debate as to whether the US was right or wrong to have chosen a blockade over port closures. As Howard Jones has noted, the US Constitution deemed that all ports must be treated on an equal basis. Lincoln did not have the legal power to close only the Southern ports and leave those in the North open. He would either have to shut every port in the country, or declare that Northern ports were exempt from closure since they were not part of the United States, which would have been absurd. Jones, *Blue and Gray Diplomacy* (Chapel Hill, NC, 2009), p. 56.

48. A letter of marque (marque meaning 'frontier') was a cheap way for countries without a navy to wage war against an enemy's shipping. By international law,

any captain with a vessel could become a privateer if issued with one. Thus shielded by the law, he could roam the sea, seizing enemy ships and taking them before an Admiralty court. There it would be decided whether or not the ship was a legal prize and not, for example, the property of a neutral state. If judged a legal prize, the ship would be condemned and captain and crew entitled to its profits. Roland R. Foulke, *A Treatise on International Law*, 2 vols. (Philadelphia, 1920), vol. 2, p. 244. The last country to offer letters of marque was Mexico in 1847.

49. The Declaration had four salient points: 1. Privateering is, and remains, abolished; 2. The neutral flag covers enemy's goods, with the exception of contraband of war; 3. Neutral goods, with the exception of contraband of war, are not liable to capture under enemy's flag; 4. Blockades, in order to be binding, must be effective. Also, the Declaration was only binding upon countries which had signed the treaty.

50. Adams, 'The British Proclamation of May, 1861', p. 218.

51. Ibid., p. 220, Lord Lyons to Lord John Russell, 6 May 1861.

52. In Lyons's words, 'it may be impossible to deter this Government from offering provocations to Great Britain, which neither our honour nor our interest will allow us to brook.' Ibid., p. 83, Lord Lyons to Lord John Russell, 20 May 1861.

53. Ibid., p. 229, Lord Lyons to Lord John Russell, 6 May 1861.

54. Adams, *Charles Francis Adams, 1835–1915*, p. 89.

55. Russell, *My Diary North and South*, p. 126, 7 May 1861.

56. Ibid., p. 104, 27 April 1861.

57. *The Times*, 30 April 1861.

58. Russell, *My Diary North and South*, p. 119, 5 May 1861.

59. *The Times*, 7 May 1861.

60. Russell, *My Diary North and South*, p. 124, 7 May 1861.

61. Adams, 'The British Proclamation of May, 1861', p. 207, Consul Bunch to Lord John Russell, 28 February 1861.

62. Russell, *My Diary North and South*, p. 128, 7 May 1861.

63. Crawford (ed.), *William Howard Russell's Civil War*, p. 52, 7 May 1861.

64. Robert Douthat Meade, *Judah P. Benjamin: Confederate Statesman* (Baton Rouge, La., 2001), pp. 172, 175.

65. Russell, *My Diary North and South*, p. 128, 7 May 1861.

66. Meade, *Judah P. Benjamin*, p. 172.

67. Ibid., p. 166. During his long imprisonment after the war, Jefferson Davis allegedly told his doctor that he had wanted to send three million bales of cotton to Europe before the blockade took effect. It never happened because he 'had not time to study and take the responsibility of directing until too late.' *Prison Life of Jefferson Davis* by Dr Cravens, quoted in *Confederate Veteran*, 24 (1916), p. 207. Douglas B. Ball also exonerates Davis and instead blames the Secretary of the Treasury, Christopher Memminger, for being short-sighted and vacillating on the subject until it was too late: *Financial Failure and Confederate Defeat* (Champaign, Ill., 1991), pp. 88–96. Where the ships would have come from to load 3 million bales, however, is not clear.

68. Russell, *My Diary North and South*, p. 130, 7 May 1861.

69. F. L. Owsley, *King Cotton Diplomacy* (2nd edn., Chicago, 1959), p. 24, 4 June 1861.

CHAPTER 4. EXPECTATIONS ARE DASHED

1. William S. Walsh, *Abraham Lincoln and the London Punch* (New York, 1909), p. 24.

2. *MPUS*, no. 330, Dallas to Seward, 9 April 1861.

3. Donald Bellows, 'A Study of British Conservative Reaction to the American Civil War', *Journal of Southern History*, 51/4 (Nov. 1985), pp. 505–26, at p. 511.

4. *MPUS*, no. 330, Dallas to Seward, 9 April 1861.

5. Brian Jenkins, 'Sir William Gregory: Champion of the Confederacy', *History Today* 28 (1978), p. 323.

6. Charles Francis Adams Jr., 'The British Proclamation of May, 1861', *Massachusetts Historical Society Proceedings*, 48 (1915), pp. 190–241, at p. 209, Bunch to Russell, 21 March 1861.

7. Sarah Agnes Wallace and Frances Elma Gillespie (eds.), *Journal of Benjamin Moran, 1857–1865*, 2 vols. (Chicago, 1948, 1949), vol. 1, p. 809, 13 May 1861.

8. PRO 30/22/21, ff. 469–71, Palmerston to Russell, 27 April 1861. They were flummoxed by having no American to speak to on the issue. On 5 May (f. 472), Palmerston wrote to Russell that he had received a visit from an agent of the Rothschilds, who read a letter from August Belmont urging mediation: 'I stated to him also the obvious objections to any step on our part at the present moment but I admitted the great importance of the matter and it desires to be fully weighed and considered.' Palmerston suggested they could try communicating 'confidentially with the South by the men who have come over here from there; and with the North by Dallas who is about to return in a few days. Dallas, it is true, is not a political friend of Lincoln and on the contrary rather leans to the South, but still he might be an organ, if it should be deemed prudent to take any step.'

9. PRO NI T/1585A, Private John Thompson to father, 28 April 1861.

10. *Illustrated London News*, 4 May 1861.

11. *The Economist*, 4 May 1861.

12. *Saturday Review*, 30 March 1861.

13. Wallace and Gillespie (eds.), *The Journal of Benjamin Moran*, vol. 1, p. 796, 5 April, 1861, p. 799, 18 April, 1861, p. 802, 27 April 1861.

14. A. L. Kennedy (ed.), *My Dear Duchess: Social and Political Letters to the Duchess of Manchester, 1858–1869* (London, 1956), p. 154, Lord Clarendon to Duchess of Manchester, 8 May 1861.

15. British Sessional Papers, 1861, vol. LXIII, Command Paper No. 2910, pp. 210–11, 3 May 1861.

16. *Letters of Sir George Cornewall Lewis*, ed. G. F. Lewis (London, 1870), pp. 395–6, Lewis to Sir Edmund Head, 13 May 1861.

17. K. D. Reynolds, *Aristocratic Women and Political Society in Victorian Britain* (Oxford, 1998), p. 124, Duchess of Sutherland to Gladstone, 25 May 1861, BL Add. MS 44325, ff. 137–9, and Duchess of Sutherland to Gladstone, 28 May 1861, f. 144.

18. BL Add. MS 44531, Gladstone to Duchess of Sutherland, 29 May 1861.

19. *BDOFA*, Part 1, ser. C, vol. 5, p. 199, Lord John Russell to Lord Lyons, 11 May 1861.

20. Even before the Proclamation, the Secretary of War, Simon Cameron, had gently but firmly to reject offers from Canadians who were eager to raise regiments for the North. OR, ser. 3, vol. 1, ser. 122, no. 6.

21. After the war, the United States claimed that Britain had acted without provocation and with malign intent. However, as D. P. Crook, C. F. Adams Jr. and others argue, the Cabinet had more than enough information and reason to take this route. Lord Russell knew by 11 May, thanks to the Consul in New York, that Lincoln had proclaimed the blockade and called for 75,000 soldiers – and that the Confederacy had a President, functioning legislature, a constitution, judges, customs officers, armies and a flag. See, for example, D. P. Crook, *The North, the South, and the Powers 1861–1865* (New York, 1974), *passim*.

22. ORN, ser. 2, vol. 3, p. 215, Yancey and Dudley Mann to Toombs, 21 May 1861.

23. Henry Adams, *The Education of Henry Adams*, ed. Ernest Samuels (New York, 1973), p. 116.

24. MHS, Adams MSS, Diary of Charles Francis Adams, 11 July 1861.

25. The legation shuttled first to 7 Duke Street on 20 May, and then to 17 St George's Place on 1 June. The building was adequate but on the small side. The house he found for his family, 52 Grosvenor Square, had also been his grandfather's residence during his posting in London.

26. W. C. Ford (ed.), *Letters of Henry Adams, 1858–1891*, 2 vols. (Boston, 1930–38), vol. 1, p. 90, Henry Adams to Charles Francis Adams Jr., 16 May 1861.

27. Quoted in Asa Briggs, *Victorian People* (London, 1954), p. 206.

28. T. Wemyss Reid, *Life of the Right Honourable William Edward Forster* (London, 1888), p. 333, Forster to Ellis Yarnall, 10 May 1861.

29. Adams, *The Education of Henry Adams*, p. 124.

30. Trinity College Library, Cambridge, Houghton MS CA9/66, Monckton Milnes to Sir Charles J. MacCarthy, 25 June 1861.

31. *George Douglas, Eighth Duke of Argyll (1823–1900): Autobiography and Memoirs*, ed. the Dowager Duchess of Argyll, 2 vols. (London, 1906), vol. 2, p. 170, Argyll to John Motley, 14 May 1861.

32. MHS, Adams MSS, Diary of Charles Francis Adams, 15 May 1861.

33. Ibid., 16 May 1861.

34. Ibid.

35. Charles Vandersee, 'Henry Adams behind the Scenes: Civil War Letters to Frederick W. Seward', *Bulletin of the New York Public Library*, 71/4 (1967), p. 248. Otherwise, Henry had written to Frederick Seward, every staff member would be new, and 'you will see at once what a position the Embassy would be in'.

36. G. P. Gooch (ed.), *The Later Correspondence of Lord John Russell, 1840–1878*, 2 vols. (London, 1925), vol. 2, p. 320, Russell to Lord Cowley, 13 June 1861.

37. MHS, Adams MSS, Diary of Charles Francis Adams, 18 May 1861.

38. Edward L. Pierce (ed.), *Memoir and Letters of Charles Sumner*, 4 vols. (Boston, 1894), vol. 4: *1860–1870*, p. 31, Argyll to Sumner, 4 June 1861.

39. Gooch (ed.), *The Later Correspondence of Lord John Russell*, vol. 2, p. 320, Russell to Lord Cowley, 13 June 1861.

40. Hansard, 3rd ser., vol. 163, col. 277, 30 May 1861.

41. C. Vann Woodward (ed.), *Mary Chesnut's Civil War* (repr. New Haven, 1981), p. 67.

42. Seward's new accommodation was called the 'Old Club House'. Two years before he moved in, it was the scene of Daniel Sickles's notorious murder of Phillip Barton Key, his wife's alleged lover. Sickles shot Key in cold blood on the street in front of the house, and his victim was carried inside where he bled to death in the room which became Seward's parlour.

43. David Herbert Donald, *Charles Sumner and the Rights of Man* (New York, 1970), p. 21.

44. Ibid., p. 25.

45. *Tropic Wind, Hiawatha, Octavia* and *Haxall*.

46. *BDOFA*, Part 1, ser. C, vol. 5, p. 209, doc. 172, Lyons to Russell, 2 May 1861.

47. Adam Gurowski, *Diary from March 4, 1861 to November 12, 1862* (Boston, 1862), pp. 37–50.

48. PRO 30/22/35, ff. 96–8, Lyons to Russell, 4 June 1861; PRO 30/23/35, ff. 99–100, Lyons to Russell, 10 June 1861.

49. George Templeton Strong, *Diary of the Civil War 1860–1865*, ed. Allan Nevins. (New York, 1962), p. 145, 22 May 186.

50. G. H. Warren, *Fountain of Discontent: The Trent Affair and Freedom of the Seas* (Boston, 1981), p. 84.

51. MHS, Adams MSS, Diary of Charles Francis Adams, 1 June 1861.

52. Ford (ed.), *Letters of Henry Adams*, vol. 1, p. 93, Henry Adams to Charles Francis Adams Jr., 10–11 June 1861.

53. Designed by Isambard Kingdom Brunel, the ship was five times the size of its nearest rival. In addition to the 2,000 troops on board, there were more than 470 women and children, 122 horses and 400 crew, making a total of more than 3,000. During the voyage, two women gave birth, and five stowaways were discovered.

54. MHS, Adams MSS, Diary of Charles Francis Adams, 12 June 1861.

55. Allan Nevins, *The War for the Union*, 4 vols.; vol. 2: *War Becomes Revolution 1862–1863* (New York, 1960), p. 245.

56. MHS, Adams MSS, Diary of Charles Francis Adams, 5 June 1861.

57. W. C. Ford (ed.), *A Cycle of Adams Letters, 1861–1865*, 2 vols. (Boston, 1920), vol. 1, pp. 13–15, Charles Francis Adams to Charles Francis Adams Jr., 21 June 1861.

58. Ibid., pp. 19–22, Charles Francis Adams to Charles Francis Adams Jr., 18 July 1861.

59. MHS, Adams MSS, Diary of Charles Francis Adams, 17 June 1861.

60. Carl Schurz, 'Reminiscences of a Long Life', *McClure's*, 26/1 (Nov. 1905), p. 642. Schurz went on to say: 'I left Mr. Adams with the highest impression of his patriotism, of the clearness and exactness of his mind, of the breadth of his knowledge, and his efficiency as a diplomat . . . He was, in the best sense of the term, a serious and sober man. Indeed, he lacked some of the social qualities which it may be desirable that a diplomat should possess. While he kept up in London an establishment fitting the dignity of his position as the representative of a great republic and performed his social duties with punctilious care, he was not a pleasing after-dinner speaker, nor a shining figure on festive occasions. He lacked the gifts of personal magnetism or sympathetic charm that would draw men to him.'

61. MHS, Adams MSS, Diary of Charles Francis Adams, 18 August 1861.

62. Ibid., 5 June 1861.

63. Ford (ed.), *A Cycle of Adams Letters*, vol. 1, p. 7, Charles Francis Adams to Charles Francis Adams Jr., 7 June 1861.

64. Adams, *The Education of Henry Adams*, pp. 197, 196, 134.

65. Wallace and Gillespie (eds.), *The Journal of Benjamin Moran*, vol. 2, 25 June 1861, p. 834.

66. MHS, Adams MSS, Diary of Charles Francis Adams, 18 June 1861.

67. Wendy Hinde, *Richard Cobden* (New Haven, 1987), p. 305. 'As for the separation of the States,' he wrote, 'if I were a citizen of a free state, I should vote with both hands for a dissolution of partnership with the slave states.'

68. Hansard, 3rd ser., vol. 163, col. 192, 28 May 1861.

69. Ford (ed.), *A Cycle of Adams Letters*, vol. 1, pp. 13–15, Charles Francis Adams to Charles Francis Adams Jr., 21 June 1861.

70. J. A. V. Chapple and Arthur Pollard (eds.), *The Letters of Mrs Gaskell* (New York, 1997), pp. 654–8, Gaskell to Charles Eliot Norton, 10 June 1861.

71. Belle Becker Sideman and Lillian Friedman (eds.), *Europe Looks at the Civil War* (New York, 1960), p. 62, Darwin to Asa Gray, 5 June 1861.

72. Clare Taylor, *Britain and American Abolitionists: An Episode in Transatlantic Understanding* (Edinburgh, 1974), p. 407, R. D. Webb, 16 July 1861.

73. 2 February 1861. But far more inflammatory had been Seward's recent note, sent to all foreign governments, asking them to refuse asylum to escaped slaves.

74. *Englishwoman's Journal*, June 1861.

75. ORN, ser. 2, vol. 3, p. 202, Yancey, Rost and Dudley Mann to Toombs, 15 July 1861.

76. William L. Yancey Papers, Alabama Department of Archives and History, Yancey to R. Chapman, 3 July 1861.

CHAPTER 5. THE REBEL YELL

1. Martin Crawford (ed.), *William Howard Russell's Civil War: Private Diary and Letters, 1861–1862* (Athens, Ga., 1992), p. 58, 21 May 1861.

2. William Howard Russell, *My Diary North and South*, ed. Eugene H. Berwanger, (New York, 1988), p. 172, 1 June 1861.

3. Crawford (ed.), *William Howard Russell's Civil War*, p. 59, 24 May 1861.

4. Ibid., p. 58, 25 May 1861.

5. Out of a total population of 168,675, 66,268 were immigrants.

6. Crawford (ed.), *William Howard Russell's Civil War*, p. 62, 29 May 1861.

7. *The Times*, 22 May 1861. For a fascinating discussion on the ethnic components of Louisiana's regiments, see Ella Lonn, *Foreigners in the Confederacy* (Chapel Hill, NC, repr. 2001), pp. 100–113.

8. PRO FO 5/788, f. 171, Mure to Lord John Russell, 9 July 1861.

9. Russell, *My Diary North and South*, p. 166, 27 May 1861.

10. William Watson, *Life in the Confederate Army: Being the Observations and Experiences of an Alien in the South during the Civil War* (London, 1887; repr. Baton Rouge, La., 1995), pp. 122, 397.

11. Pembrokeshire RO, HDX/559/52, William Benyon to brother Thomas in Wales, 15 May 1861.

12. Nathaniel Cheairs Hughes Jr. (ed.), *Sir Henry Morton Stanley, Confederate* (Baton Rouge, La., 2000), p. 95.

13. The other problem for Mure was the harassment of black British subjects. He arranged for a black Crimean War veteran to be spirited out of the city, and paid $17.40 from consulate funds to secure the release of Alexander White, another black British subject languishing in jail. PRO FO 5/788, f. 171, Mure to Lord John Russell, 9 July 1861. Russell, *My Diary North and South*, p. 171, 1 June 1861.

14. Mary Sophia Hill, *A British Subject's Recollections of the Confederacy* (Baltimore, 1875), p. 7, 8 June 1861.

15. Ibid.

16. Ibid., p. 60.

17. Ibid., p. 8, 20 June 1861.

18. Columbia University, Blackwell MSS, Elizabeth Blackwell to Barbara Bodichon, 23 April 1861.

19. William Quentin Maxwell, *Lincoln's Fifth Wheel* (New York, 1956), p. 6.

20. Ibid., p. 8.

21. Columbia University, Blackwell MSS, Elizabeth Blackwell to Barbara Bodichon, 6 June 1861.

22. Ibid.

23. Dorothy Clarke Wilson, *Lone Woman* (Boston, 1970), p. 388.

24. Columbia University, Blackwell MSS, Elizabeth Blackwell to Barbara Bodichon, 6 June 1861.

25. Wellcome Institute, Verney MS 8999/24, Florence Nightingale to Sir Henry Verney, 11 June 1861.

26. Columbia University, Blackwell MSS, Elizabeth Blackwell to Barbara Bodichon, 6 June 1861.

27. Henri Le Caron, *Twenty-Five Years in the Secret Service: The Recollections of a Spy* (16th edn., London, 1893), p. 10.

28. PRO 33/22/39, f. 71, Archibald to Lord John Russell, 24 April 1861.

29. PRO FO282/6, ff. 335–46, Archibald to Lord John Russell, 24 April 1861.

30. PRO FO282/6, ff. 350–51, d. 20, Archibald to Lord Lyons, 29 April 1861.

31. Some, like Mr Murphy from Petersfield, England, were running away from debts, wives and other burdens. His wife tried everything to locate him, even writing to President Lincoln to ask 'Your Majesty' for help since 'myself and dear baby are starving . . . Should he be with any of your magistys [*sic*] regiments will you send the word.' NARA, RG94, entry 416, box 47, 1861 E–K, S. 396, Mrs E. Murphy to President Lincoln, 29 August 1861.

32. Corcoran's insubordination led to his arrest and appearance before a court martial. He was in limbo, still under arrest but with no trial in sight, until the battle of Fort Sumter. Corcoran immediately offered the services of the 69th. This posed an uncomfortable dilemma for the authorities until Governor Morgan issued a pardon and the charges against Corcoran could be dismissed.

33. Richard Demeter, *The Fighting 69th: A History* (Pasadena, Calif., 2002), p. 59. The 69th's flag boldly proclaimed the allegiance of its members. Made of green cloth, at the top was the Fenian symbol of the sunburst, in the middle a golden harp, and along the bottom a wreath of shamrocks.

34. BL Add. MS 415670, f. 214, Herbert to mother, 18 July 1861.

35. Wiltshire and Swindon RO, 2536/10, Edward Best to Aunt Sophie, 10 May 1861.

36. PRO FO282/8, ff. 22–4, Edward Archibald to Lord John Russell, 26 April 1861.

37. The best history of the British origins of the 36th New York Volunteers can be found at: http://www.conversantcomm.pl/36thNY/History2.htm.

38. *Boston Herald*, 20 April 1861, p. 4, col. 1.

39. *Albion*, 25 May 1861.

40. New York Historical Society, *Narrative of Ebenezer Wells* (c. 1881), n.pp., c. 2 June 1861.

41. Ibid.

42. Russell, *My Diary North and South*, p. 225.

43. *Roxbury City Gazette*, 27 June 1861, p. 2.

44. *Illustrated London News*, 6 July 1861, p. 22.

45. James M. Perry, *A Bohemian Brigade: The Civil War Correspondents* (Hoboken, NJ, 2000), p. 190.

46. *Illustrated London News*, 3 August 1861, p. 121.

47. Ibid., p. 22, 6 July 1861.

48. Crawford (ed.), *William Howard Russell's Civil War*, p. 74, Russell to J. C. Bancroft Davis, 22 June 1861.

49. W. H. Russell, *My Diary North and South* (London, 1863), p. 377. Berwanger's 1988 abridged edn. does not include this observation.

50. Crawford (ed.), *William Howard Russell's Civil War*, p. 80, 4 July 1861.

51. Russell, *My Diary North and South*, ed. Berwanger, p. 255.

52. Crawford (ed.), *William Howard Russell's Civil War*, p. 79, 3 July 1861.

53. Russell, *My Diary North and South*, ed. Berwanger, p. 227.

54. W. C. Ford (ed.), *A Cycle of Adams Letters, 1861–1865*, 2 vols. (Boston, 1920), vol. 1, p. 15, Charles Francis Adams Jr. to Charles Francis Adams, 2 July 1861.

55. Doris Kearns Goodwin, *Team of Rivals* (New York, 2005), p. 364.

56. PRO 30/22/35, Lord Lyons to Lord John Russell, 20 July 1861.

57. Allan Nevins, *The War for the Union*, 4 vols.; vol. 1: *The Improvised War 1861–1862* (New York, 1959), p. 214.

58. William Mark McKnight, *Blue Bonnets o'er the Border: The 79th New York Cameron Highlanders* (Shippensburg, Pa., 1998), p. 23.

59. Russell, *My Diary North and South*, ed. Berwanger, p. 240, 13 July 1861. Russell also doubted that any army could reconquer so vast a territory as the South. 'It is one thing', he opined in *The Times*, 'to drive the rebels from the south bank of the Potomac, or even to occupy Richmond, but another to reduce and hold in permanent subjection a tract of country nearly as large as Russia.' *The Times*, 18 July 1861.

60. John Bakeless, *Spies of the Confederacy* (New York, 1970), p. 10.

61. The value of her work has since been questioned, but there is no doubt that she was able to send advance warning to General Beauregard to prepare for the imminent arrival of the Federal army in Virginia. Edwin Fishel, *The Secret War for the Union* (New York, 1996), p. 59.

62. Hill, *A British Subject's Recollections of the Confederacy*, p. 8, 4 July 1861.

63. Russell, *My Diary North and South* (1863), p. 438. Berwanger's 1988 abridged edn. does not include this exchange.

64. Russell, *My Diary North and South*, ed. Berwanger, p. 266.

65. Ibid., p. 266.

66. *The Times*, 6 August 1861.

67. *Illustrated London News*, 10 August 1861, pp. 143–5.

68. James M. McPherson, *Battle Cry of Freedom* (London, 1988), p. 342.

69. McKnight, *Blue Bonnets o'er the Border*, p. 27.

70. Ibid., p. 28.

71. Russell, *My Diary North and South*, ed. Berwanger, p. 268.

72. New York Historical Society, *Narrative of Ebenezer Wells*.

73. *The Times*, 6 August 1861.

74. Russell, *My Diary North and South*, ed. Berwanger, p. 277.

75. Hill, *A British Subject's Recollections of the Confederacy*, p. 10.

CHAPTER 6. WAR BY OTHER MEANS

1. *The Times*, 6 August 1861.

2. William Howard Russell, *My Diary North and South*, ed. Eugene H. Berwanger (New York, 1988), p. 278.

3. Allan Nevins, *The War for the Union*, 4 vols.; vol. 1: *The Improvised War 1861–1862* (New York, 1959), p. 221.

4. The Confederates suffered 400 killed, 1,600 wounded, and the Federals, 625 killed, 950 wounded and 1,200 captured. James M. McPherson, *Battle Cry of Freedom* (London, 1988), p. 347.

5. James McPherson, *Tried by War* (New York, 2008), p. 41.

6. New York Historical Society, *Narrative of Ebenezer Wells* (c. 1881), n.pp., 15 August 1861.

7. Martin Crawford (ed.), *William Howard Russell's Civil War: Private Diary and Letters, 1861–1862* (Athens, Ga., 1992), p. 110, 26 August 1861.

8. Camille Ferri Pisani, *Prince Napoleon in America*, trans. Georges Joyaux (Bloomington, Ind., 1959), p. 100.

9. Crawford (ed.), *William Howard Russell's Civil War*, p. 100, 7 August 1861.

10. West Sussex RO, Lyons MSS, Box 299, 5 August 1861.

11. Pisani, *Prince Napoleon in America*, p. 113.

12. Ibid., p. 130.

13. Jeff Kinard, *Lafayette of the South* (College Station, Tex., 2001), p. 19.

14. PRO 30/22/35, Lord Lyons to Lord Russell, 6 September 1861. Bunch had been entrusted with secret negotiations between the South and Britain and France to end privateering. This too was exposed in the diplomatic bag.

15. Another piece of bad luck was Robert Mure's surname – the same as the Consul's in New Orleans. US newspapers erroneously claimed that the two men were related, which made it look as though the British Consuls in the South were in cahoots with each other against the North.

16. West Sussex RO, Lyons MSS, Box 299, Lord Lyons to sister, 23 August 1861.

17. Alan Hankinson, *Man of Wars: William Howard Russell of 'The Times', 1820–1907* (London, 1982), p. 170.

18. Russell, *My Diary North and South*, pp. 301, 305.

19. The letter was purportedly from an English soldier, R. Young Atkins, 'late of the Garibaldi Brigade', who fought at Bull Run. The real Atkins was from Cork, his name was Richard Goring, and whether he wrote any of the rubbish in the letter remains doubtful.

20. C. Vann Woodward (ed.), *Mary Chesnut's Civil War* (New Haven, 1981), p. 159, 23 August 1861.

21. Brian Jenkins, *Britain and the War for the Union*, 2 vols. (Montreal, 1974, 1980), vol. 1, p. 154. It was a coincidence that John Bright broke his public silence about

the Civil War just three days before the news of Bull Run. Neither the timing nor his views found favour with the voters of Rochdale and the Radical candidate lost the election.

22. Stanley Morison, *The Times: The History of The Times. The Tradition Established, 1841–84* (London, 1939), p. 367.

23. Durham University, General Charles Grey MSS, GRE/D/VI/6, General Grey to 3rd Earl Grey, 31 August 1861.

24. Susan St John Mildmay and Herbert St John Mildmay (eds.), *John Lothrop Motley and his Family: Further Letters and Records* (London, 1910), p. 112.

25. BL Add. MS 415670, f. 216, George Henry Herbert to Jack, 12 October 1861.

26. He had allowed his mind to wander during drill practice. Unfortunately, wrote the regimental historian, when the order to march was given he 'failed to move, and as a consequence the regiment "stood fast" while all the other regiments moved off. For an instant the General seemed paralyzed with astonishment.' He then bellowed at the top of his voice, '"Move! Move! For God's sake, you little bandy-legged man, move!" Herbert moved.' When the practice was over, 500 men turned in Herbert's direction and shouted in unison, 'Move. Move, you little bandy-legged man.' Matthew J. Graham, *The Ninth Regiment New York Volunteers* (Lancaster, Ohio, repr. 1997), p. 66.

27. BL Add. MS 415670, f. 216, Herbert to Jack, 18 July 1861.

28. Sarah Forbes Hughes (ed.), *Letters and Recollections of John Murray Forbes*, 2 vols. (New York, 1900), vol. 1, pp. 234–5, Charles Francis Adams to J. M. Forbes, 30 August 1861.

29. MHS, Adams MSS, Diary of Charles Francis Adams, vol. 76, 6 August 1861.

30. Deborah Logan (ed.), *The Collected Letters of Harriet Martineau*, 5 vols. (London, 2007), vol. 4, p. 283, Martineau to Henry Reeve, 28 July 1861.

31. *Morning Star*, 15 July 1861.

32. *Letters, Speeches, and Addresses of August Belmont* (n.p., 1890), p. 77, Belmont to Seward, 30 July 1861.

33. *Illustrated London News*, 10 August 1861.

34. ORN, ser. 2, vol. 3, p. 247, Lord Russell to Yancey, Rost and Dudley Mann, 24 August 1861.

35. James D. Richardson (ed.), *A Compilation of Messages and Papers of the Confederacy Including the Diplomatic Correspondence, 1861–1865*, 2 vols. (Nashville, Tenn., 1905), vol. 2, p. 53, Yancey and Dudley Mann to Robert Toombs, 1 August 1861.

36. Charles McCaskill, 'An Estimate of Edwin DeLeon's Report of his Service to the Confederacy', MA thesis, University of South Carolina, 1950, p. 24.

37. ORN, ser. 2, vol. 3, p. 233, Dudley Mann to Toombs, 3 August 1861. Dudley Mann continued: 'The modus operandi would be this: That you should employ a strictly trustworthy individual to prepare a short statement of the most important occurrences, and transmit it per Cunard steamer to us, under cover to "M'Iver,

agent Cunard Packets, Queenstown, Ireland." Reuter will give him directions to telegraph the contents to us the moment the steamer touches at that place. If it were deemed important to communicate twice a week, then a dispatch might be sent to "Joseph Sharpe", Southampton, England.'

38. Sarah Agnes Wallace and Frances Elma Gillespie (eds.), *The Journal of Benjamin Moran, 1857–1865*, 2 vols. (Chicago, 1948, 1949), vol. 2, pp. 868–9, 26 August 1861.

39. NARA, M.T-396, roll 4, US Consul in Leith to Seward, 29 August 1861.

40. For example, Edward Anderson complained, 'I called last night on Mr Yancey to protest against his recommendation of English adventurers for appointment in the Confederate Army. The case in point was that of a young man who for some days had been hanging around my quarters seeking to get a recommendation to the authorities in Richmond, and who from all I could gather was an unprincipled trifling fellow. I had refused to endorse him and he went from me to Yancey who, without any knowledge whatever of the man, gave him letters to the Secy of War which procured him employment as an officer. I subsequently learned that this fellow turned out a Yankee spy.' W. S. Hoole, *Confederate Foreign Agent: The European Diary of Major Edward C. Anderson* (Tuscaloosa, Ala., 1976), pp. 43–4, 7 August 1861.

41. Joseph A. Fry, *Henry S. Sanford: Diplomacy and Business in Nineteenth-Century America* (Reno, Nev., 1982), p. 50.

42. McPherson, *Battle Cry of Freedom*, p. 318.

43. Frank J. Merli, *Great Britain and the Confederate Navy* (Bloomington, Ind., 1965), p. 17.

44. R. I. Lester, *Confederate Financing and Purchasing in Great Britain* (Charlottesville, Va., 1975), p. 148.

45. James D. Bulloch, *The Secret Service of the Confederate States in Europe*, 2 vols. (New York, 1884), vol. 1, p. 32.

46. McCaskill, 'An Estimate of Edwin DeLeon's Report of his Service to the Confederacy', p. 22.

47. At 10 Rumford Place.

48. David Hepburn Milton, *Lincoln's Spymaster: Thomas Haines Dudley and the Liverpool Network* (Mechanicsburg, Pa., 2003), p. 29.

49. ORN, ser. 2, vol. 2, pp. 83–7, James Bulloch to Mallory, 18 August 1861.

50. Fry, *Henry S. Sanford*, p. 37.

51. Harriet Chappell Owsley, 'Henry Shelton Sanford and Federal Surveillance Abroad, 1861–1865', *Mississippi Valley Historical Review*, 48 (Sept. 1961), p. 212.

52. Ibid., pp. 212–13.

53. Anderson never told Huse that his original mission had been to report on the latter's operations and, if necessary, send him home. Huse's determination to beat out Federal competition looked like reckless spending to the Confederate authorities, who had no idea of the obstacles impeding their agent. Some even suspected him of harbouring Union sympathies because he did not hate all Northerners. But

after three weeks' acquaintance Anderson was able to report that Huse's only defect was that he sometimes lacked discretion.

54. Neill F. Sanders, 'Consul, Commander and Minister: A New Perspective on the Queenstown Incident', *Lincoln Herald*, 81/2 (1979), pp. 102–15, at p. 103, Sanford to Seward, 4 July 1861.

55. Owsley, 'Henry Shelton Sanford and Federal Surveillance Abroad', p. 214.

56. Hoole, *Confederate Foreign Agent*, p. 64, 26 September 1861.

57. Ibid., p. 36, 25 July 1861.

58. Samuel Bernard Thompson, *Confederate Purchasing Operations Abroad* (Gloucester, Mass., 1973), p. 16.

59. Owsley, 'Henry Shelton Sanford and Federal Surveillance Abroad', p. 214.

60. Warren F. Spencer, *The Confederate Navy in Europe* (Tuscaloosa, Ala., 1983), p. 18.

61. David Hollett, *The Alabama Affair: The British Shipyards Conspiracy in the American Civil War* (Wilmslow, 1993), p. 16.

62. OR, ser. 1, vol. 4, no. 127, p. 577, L. P. Walker to Caleb Huse and Edward Anderson, 17 August 1861.

63. ORN, ser. 2, vol. 2, pp. 83–7, James Bulloch to Stephen Mallory, 18 August 1861.

64. Neill F. Sanders, 'Lincoln's Consuls in the British Isles, 1861–1865', Ph.D. thesis, University of Missouri, 1971, p. 34.

65. Peter Barton, 'The First Blockade Runner and the "Another Alabama": Some Tees and Hartlepool Ships That Worried the Union', *Mariner's Mirror*, 81 (1995), pp. 45–64.

66. F. L. Owsley, *King Cotton Diplomacy* (2nd edn., Chicago, 1959), p. 233.

67. Stephen R. Wise, *Lifeline of the Confederacy: Blockade Running during the Civil War* (Columbia, SC, 1988), p. 24.

68. Anthony Trollope, *North America* (repr. London, 1968), p. 20.

69. New York Historical Society, *Narrative of Ebenezer Wells*, 13 October 1861. Despite the relative disappointment of Lewinsville, McClellan decided that the 79th merited the return of its colours. They were handed over during a solemn ceremony.

70. Vizetelly provided the *Illustrated London News* with a sketch of the wounded being greeted by General McClellan. The accompanying description was completely over the top: 'He raised his hat as each poor fellow was borne from the ambulance to the hospital; and many whose eyes were fast glazing in death raised themselves . . . and smiled a last smile at their young and beloved General.'

71. Russell, *My Diary North and South*, p. 318, 10 October 1861.

72. Ibid., p. 313, 11 September 1861.

73. Crawford (ed.), *William Howard Russell's Civil War*, p. 125, Russell to Delane, 13 September 1861.

74. John Black Atkins, *The Life of Sir William Howard Russell*, 2 vols. (London, 1911), vol. 2, p. 72.

75. Nevins, *The War for the Union*, vol. 1, p. 300. McClellan actually had 152,000, but one-third were absent, under arrest or otherwise unfit for duty.

76. PRO FO 5/779, desp. 131, Consul Archibald to Lord Russell, 25 September 1861. By late summer, Archibald was making the five-hour journey to Lafayette on a weekly basis. He discovered extreme malnutrition among the men. Their food allotment should have been worth 43 cents a day, but theft by the guards reduced this to 10. Eugene H. Berwanger, *The British Foreign Service and the American Civil War* (Lexington, Ky., 1994), pp. 53–4.

77. Ibid., p. 55.

78. On 25 September, Benjamin Moran wrote: 'We have some very fine young fellows to see us for service in our army.' Two days later, he wrote again: 'There were several fine gentlemanly Englishmen here today.' Wallace and Gillespie (eds.), *The Journal of Benjamin Moran*, vol. 2, pp. 883, 884, 25 September, 27 September 1861.

79. Adams wrote that he was plagued with visitors because of 'the notice current in the papers that I have authority to engage officers for the American service. The wish for adventure and pay is great in all the countries of Europe. I see something of it from almost every nation.' MHS, Adams MSS, Diary of Charles Francis Adams, vol. 76, 30 September 1861. Adams had to be extremely careful lest he attract the same charge of recruiting which led to the English Minister, John Crampton, being expelled from Washington during the Crimean War. As far as he was concerned, the would-be Federals could do whatever they wished so long as the legation was not made a party to their plans.

80. Russell, *My Diary North and South*, p. 291.

81. One issue of *Frank Leslie's Illustrated Newspaper* listed the Count de Sayre, the Baron de Schonen, and Major-General Charles F. Havelock of the Imperial Ottoman Army, all arriving simultaneously in Washington. Ella Lonn has identified dozens of British officers and soldiers of fortune who held positions of responsibility in the Union army. Two of the most distinguished were Robert Johnstone and John Lambert. Ella Lonn, *Foreigners in the Union Army and Navy* (New York, repr. 1969), p. 283. Robert Johnstone was Lieutenant Colonel of the 5th New York Cavalry until August 1863. When questioned about his reasons for joining, he explained that all his life he had delighted in anything big, and that he could not remain idle while so big a nation was being split asunder. And John Lambert was a captain in the 33rd New Jersey Volunteers who became acting inspector general on General David Hunter's staff.

82. New York State Library, Edwin Morgan MSS, box 19, f. 11, L. D. H. Currie to Governor Morgan, 2 March 1863.

83. PRO 30/22/35, Lord Lyons to Lord Russell, 9 September 1861. (The origin of the anecdote remains a mystery. Lord Lyons merely wrote: 'Seward exercises upon the reports of spies and informers, the power of depriving British subjects of their liberty, or retaining them in prison, or liberating them, by his sole will and pleasure.')

84. Berwanger, *The British Foreign Service and the American Civil War*, p. 53.

85. *BDOFA*, Part 1, ser. C, vol. 5, p. 307, Lord Lyons to Lord Russell, 6 September 1861.

86. Crawford (ed.), *William Howard Russell's Civil War*, p. 150, Russell to Delane, 14 October 1861.

87. Ibid., p. 125, Russell to Delane, 13 September 1861.

CHAPTER 7. 'IT TAKES TWO TO MAKE A QUARREL'

1. Hudson Strode, *Jefferson Davis: Confederate President*, 3 vols. (New York, 1959), vol. 1, p. 141.

2. W. S. Hoole, *Confederate Foreign Agent: The European Diary of Major Edward C. Anderson* (Tuscaloosa, Ala., 1976), p. 66, 26 September 1861.

3. Harriot Chappell Owsley, 'Henry Shelton Sanford and Federal Surveillance Abroad, 1861–1865', *Mississippi Valley Historical Review*, 48 (Sept. 1961) p. 215.

4. Joseph A. Fry, *Henry S. Sanford: Diplomacy and Business in Nineteenth-Century America* (Reno, Nev., 1982), p. 45.

5. Sarah Agnes Wallace and Frances Elma Gillespie (eds.), *The Journal of Benjamin Moran, 1857–1865*, 2 vols. (Chicago, 1948, 1949), vol. 2, p. 899, 31 October 1861.

6. MHS, Adams MSS, Diary of Charles Francis Adams, 21 September 1861.

7. MHS, Charles Francis Adams, Notebook Reminiscences, 18 September 1867. Russell was able to reassure Adams that Britain had no intention of going to war with Mexico.

8. MHS, Adams MSS, Diary of Charles Francis Adams, 1 October 1861.

9. James D. Bulloch, *The Secret Service of the Confederate States in Europe*, 2 vols. (New York, 1884), vol. 1, p. 115.

10. Hoole, *Confederate Foreign Agent*, p. 82, 15 October 1861.

11. Wallace and Gillespie (eds.), *The Journal of Benjamin Moran*, vol. 2, p. 892, 17 October 1861.

12. PRO 30/22/35, ff. 295–300, Lyons to Russell, 22 October 1861.

13. Martin Crawford (ed.), *William Howard Russell's Civil War: Private Diary and Letters, 1861–1862* (Athens, Ga., 1992), p. 159, Russell to J. C. Bancroft Davis, 19 October 1861.

14. PRO 30/22/35, ff. 229–40, Lyons to Russell, 6 September 1861.

15. James M. McPherson, *Battle Cry of Freedom* (London, 1988), p. 357.

16. These included a letter sent to all the Governors of States that possessed a port or coastal city, telling them to be prepared for a foreign invasion.

17. Sumner certainly knew the truth about France. Harriet Martineau wrote to him, 'I know that our Cabinet has had, and still has, the utmost difficulty in preventing the French and Spanish governments from breaking the blockade.' Deborah Logan (ed.), *The Collected Letters of Harriet Martineau*, 5 vols. (London, 2007), vol. 4, p. 307, Martineau to Sumner, *c.* November 1861.

18. *BDOFA*, Part 1, ser. C, vol. 5, doc. 336, pp. 331–2, Lyons to Russell, 28 October 1861.

19. PRO 30/22/35, ff. 263–78, private, Lyons to Russell, 4 October 1861.

20. E. D. Adams, *Great Britain and the American Civil War*, 2 vols. in 1 (New York, 1958), vol. 1, p. 194.

21. PRO 30/22/35, ff. 340–44, Lyons to Russell, 6 December 1861.

22. Adams, *Great Britain and the American Civil War*, vol. 1, p. 194.

23. University of Southampton, Palmerston MSS, PP/GC/LE/144, Lewis to Palmerston, 3 September 1861.

24. *Reynolds's Newspaper*, 29 September 1861.

25. W. C. Ford (ed.), *A Cycle of Adams Letters, 1861–1865*, 2 vols. (Boston, 1920), vol. 1, pp. 48–50, Henry Adams to Charles Francis Adams Jr., 28 September 1861.

26. Wallace and Gillespie (eds.), *The Journal of Benjamin Moran*, vol. 2, p. 911, 25 November 1861.

27. He gave one of his typical barnstorming speeches, eliciting cheers from the audience. However, Yancey overplayed his hand and referred to the South as 'the land of the free and the home of the oppressed', which prompted *Punch* to remind him that the whites were the free and the blacks were the oppressed. Winthrop Donaldson Jordan and Edwin J. Pratt, *Europe and the American Civil War* (New York, 1931), p. 23.

28. ORN, ser. 2, vol. 3, pp. 222–3, Yancey and Mann to Robert Toombs, 15 July 1861.

29. R. J. M. Blackett, *Divided Hearts: Britain and the American Civil War* (Baton Rouge, La., 2001), p. 138.

30. 'I often think of you, and wonder what your feelings are with regard to the fearful events now happening,' Wilding told Hawthorne. In a long letter, he analysed the current situation thus: 'The anti-slavery people profess to believe that slavery has nothing to do with the struggle; that the Federal Government are no more contending for the abolition of slavery than are the Confederates. They won't see that the contest is for the abolition of slavery in the only way that reasonable men in America have ever supposed it possible, by confining it to its present limits; and that the South, rather than submit to that, will, if they can, destroy the Union. There are many reasons for this feeling in England. In the first place, I believe Englishmen instinctively sympathize with rebels – if the rebellion be not against England. A great many also desire to see the American Union divided, supposing that it will be less powerful, and less threatening to England. All the enemies of popular government – and there are plenty even in England – rejoice to see what they suppose to be the failure of Republican institutions.' Julian Hawthorne (ed.), *Nathaniel Hawthorne and his Wife*, vol. 2 (Boston, 1884), pp. 165–6, Wilding to Hawthorne, 14 November 1861.

31. Ford (ed.), *A Cycle of Adams Letters*, vol. 1, pp. 52–3, Charles Francis Adams Jr. to Henry Adams, 6 October 1861.

32. Ibid., pp. 61–3, Henry Adams to Charles Francis Adams Jr., 25 October 1861.

33. Russell told an audience in Newcastle on 14 October, 'I cannot help asking myself as affairs progress in the conflict, to what good can it lead?' According to *The Times*, Russell then warned his listeners that a moment might come when intervention in the American war would be inevitable. After all, the paper reported him as saying, the war was not about slavery but about one side fighting for 'empire, and the other for independence'. (In fact, Russell had said 'power' rather than 'independence', which was less inflammatory. But someone at the paper had decided the phrase was too anodyne.) Norman Ferris, *Desperate Diplomacy: William H. Seward's Foreign Policy, 1861* (Knoxville, Tenn., 1976), p. 238, fn.

34. *Illustrated London News*, 2 November 1861.

35. Michael Burlingame and John R. Turner Ettlinger (eds.), *Inside Lincoln's White House: The Complete Civil War Diary of John Hay* (Carbondale, Ill., 1997), p. 26, 12 October 1861. Seward claimed absurdly to his wife on 29 October that the wicked machinations of Britain 'made it doubtful whether we can escape the yet deeper and darker abyss of foreign war'.

36. The Consuls for Belfast, Glasgow and Dublin all wrote strong letters on the subject.

37. John M. Taylor, *William Henry Seward: Lincoln's Right Hand* (New York, 1991), p. 192.

38. MHS, 'Bright–Sumner Letters, 1861–1872', October 1912, pp. 93–165, Bright to Sumner, 20 November 1861. But if the *Leicester Guardian* was anything to go by, there was still an opportunity to influence public opinion towards the North: 'By the domestic fireside, on the exchange, and in the counting house ... every tide of events has been anxiously watched,' it commented. The emotional response to the war was not 'on account of the great commercial interests involved but the feeling that those taking part in the contest are bone of our bone, and flesh of our flesh'. Blackett, *Divided Hearts*, p. 6.

39. Crawford (ed.), *William Howard Russell's Civil War*, p. 165, Russell to J. C. Bancroft Davis, 6 November 1861.

40. Ibid.

41. PRO FO5/779, desp. 164, Archibald to Lyons, 2 November 1861. PRO FO282/9, f. 79 d. 163, Archibald to Lyons, 1 November 1861.

42. Seward has 'the power', Lyons added angrily, 'of depriving British Subjects of their liberty, or retaining them in prison or liberating them by his own will and pleasure'. PRO FO282/9, f. 79, d. 163, Archibald to Lyons, 1 November 1861.

43. Anthony Trollope, *North America* (repr. London, 1968), p. 139.

44. Edward Chalfant, 'A War So Near', *Journal of Confederate History*, 6 (1990), p. 146.

45. Hoole, *Confederate Foreign Agent*, p. 88.

46. Stephen R. Wise, *Lifeline of the Confederacy: Blockade Running during the Civil War* (Columbia, SC, 1988), p. 54.

47. New York Historical Society, *Narrative of Ebenezer Wells* (c. 1881), n.pp., c. 9 November 1861.

48. Hoole, *Confederate Foreign Agent*, p. 101.

49. James P. Gannon, *Irish Rebels, Confederate Tigers* (Mason City, Iowa, 1998), p. 10.

50. Mary Sophia Hill, *A British Subject's Recollections of the Confederacy* (Baltimore, 1875), p. 60.

51. Quoted in Robert Douthat Meade, *Judah P. Benjamin: Confederate Statesman* (Baton Rouge, La., 2001), p. 182.

52. Hoole, *Confederate Foreign Agent*, p. 102.

53. MHS, Adams MSS, Diary of Charles Francis Adams, vol. 76, 2 November 1861.

54. Wallace and Gillepie (eds.), *The Journal of Benjamin Moran*, vol. 2, p. 908, 19 November 1861.

55. Edward Chalfant, *Both Sides of the Ocean* (New York, 1982), p. 316.

56. PRO FO198/21, p. 10, Lord Russell to Adams, 28 November 1861.

57. Henry Adams, *The Education of Henry Adams*, ed. Ernest Samuels (repr. Boston, 1973), p. 119.

58. Wallace and Gillespie (eds.), *The Journal of Benjamin Moran*, vol. 2, p. 913, 27 November 1861.

59. John Evan, *Atlantic Impact* (London, 1952), pp. 83–4. Karl Marx was scathing about Seward. His article for *Die Presse* on 28 November claimed, 'We regard this latest operation of Mr. Seward as a characteristic act of tactlessness by self-conscious weakness simulating strength. If the naval incident hastens Seward's removal from the Washington Cabinet, the United States will have no reason to record it as an "untoward event" in the annals of its Civil War.'

60. MHS, Adams MSS, Diary of Charles Francis Adams, vol. 76, 27 November 1861.

61. Ibid., 29 November 1861.

62. *The Times*, 29 November 1861.

63. James Chambers, *Palmerston: The People's Darling* (London, 2004), p. 487, Palmerston to the Queen, 5 December 1861.

CHAPTER 8. THE LION ROARS BACK

1. William Howard Russell, *My Diary North and South*, ed. Eugene H. Berwanger (New York, 1988), p. 325, 16 November 1861. Russell made a mistake and called Macfarland, McClernand.

2. *BDOFA*, Part 1, ser. C, vol. 5, pp. 361–2, Lord Lyons to Lord Russell, 19 November 1861.

3. *New York Times*, 18 November 1861; *Sunday Transcript*, 17 November 1861.

4. For example, Seward's son, Frederick, who was Assistant Secretary of State, wrote to the US Consul in Havana on 22 November: 'It gives the Department

pleasure to acknowledge the great importance of the service which has been rendered by Captain Wilkes to his country'. D. P. Crook, *The North, the South, and the Powers, 1861–1865* (New York, 1974), p. 115.

5. Charles Wilkes was the great-nephew of 'Wilkes and Liberty' John Wilkes, the cheery eighteenth-century rogue who, in spite of himself, became a martyr and hero for political radicals opposing George III.

6. Allan Nevins, *The War for the Union*, 4 vols.; vol. 1: *The Improvised War 1861–1862* (New York, 1959), p. 388.

7. Russell, *My Diary North and South*, p. 327, 19 November 1861.

8. *The Times*, 3 December 1861.

9. B. J. Lossing, *A Centennial Edition of the History of the United States* (Chicago, 1876), p. 587.

10. Howard K. Beale (ed.), *The Diary of Edward Bates* (Washington, DC, 1933), p. 202, 19 November 1861.

11. Stephen W. Sears, *The Civil War Papers of George B. McClellan: Selected Correspondence, 1860–1865* (New York, 1989), p. 136, McClellan to Mary Ellen, 17 November 1861.

12. PRO 30/22/35, ff. 317–23, Lyons to Russell, 22 November 1861.

13. Although the South was collectively holding its breath, in South Carolina a lonely General Robert E. Lee sent a little bouquet of violets to his daughter, and the following advice to his wife: 'You must not build your hopes on peace on account of the United States going into a war with England ... Her rulers are not entirely mad, and if they find England is in earnest ... they will adopt [peace]. We must make up our minds to fight our battles and win our independence alone. No one will help us.' Robert E. Lee, *Recollections and Letters* (New York, repr. 2004), pp. 51–2.

14. Anthony Trollope, *North America* (repr. London, 1968), p. 138.

15. PRO FO519/178, Lord Clarendon to Lord Cowley, 29 November 1861, quoted in Crook, *The North, the South, and the Powers*, p. 131.

16. As the Duke of Argyll wrote from France: 'If such an act as that committed by the *San Jacinto* be allowed, I see nothing which would prevent any European Government seizing on board of our ships any refugees from their revolted provinces, who might be coming to England (as many do) to excite popular sympathy with their cause.' *George Douglas, Eighth Duke of Argyll (1823–1900): Autobiography and Memoirs*, ed. the Dowager Duchess of Argyll, 2 vols. (London, 1906), p. 180, Duke of Argyll to Gladstone, 7 December 1861.

17. John Morley, *The Life of William Ewart Gladstone: 1809–1872*, 2 vols. (London, 1908), vol. 2, pp. 73–4, Gladstone to Argyll, 3 December 1861.

18. Sir Theodore Martin, *The Life of his Royal Highness the Prince Consort*, vol. 5 (New York, 1880), p. 349. Prince Albert continued: 'we are therefore glad to believe that upon a full consideration of the circumstances, and of the undoubted breach of international law committed, they would spontaneously offer such redress as alone could satisfy this country, viz. the restoration of the unfortunate passengers and a suitable apology.'

19. 'I think now the American Government', he wrote, 'under the inspiration of Seward will refuse us redress. The prospect is melancholy, but it is an obligation of honour which we cannot escape.' PRO Cowley MSS, FO519/199, Russell to Lord Cowley, 7 December 1861.

20. Brian Jenkins, *Britain and the War for the Union*, 2 vols. (Montreal, 1974, 1980), vol. 1, p. 212.

21. Nancy Mitford (ed.), *The Stanleys of Alderley* (London, 1968), p. 270, Lord Stanley to Lady Stanley, 2 December 1861.

22. For some reason, he has generally been misidentified as Seymour Conway, although W. H. Russell refers to him properly as Conway Seymour.

23. G. P. Gooch (ed.), *The Later Correspondence of Lord John Russell, 1840–1878*, 2 vols. (London, 1925), vol. 2, p. 321, Lord Russell to Lord Clarendon, 6 December 1861. In fact, Lord Clarendon thought that Russell was generally far too namby-pamby with Seward. 'I don't like the low tone taken by Johnny,' he told the Duchess of Manchester; 'he is right not to be quarrelsome but humility is not the way to keep vulgarity & swagger in order & there is not a despatch from that beast Seward that does not contain some menace to us.' A. L. Kennedy (ed.), *My Dear Duchess: Social and Political Letters to the Duchess of Manchester, 1858–1869* (London, 1956), p. 208, Clarendon to Duchess of Manchester, 25 December 1862.

24. Desmond McCarthy, *Lady John Russell*, p. 260, Lady John to Lady Dumferline, 13 December 1861.

25. *Letters of Sir George Cornewall Lewis*, ed. Sir G. F. Lewis (London, 1870), pp. 405–6, Lewis to Twistleton, 5 December 1861.

26. The purchases were actually a coincidence. At the start of the war, the United States had 3 million pounds of saltpetre in reserve, which was all that had been left over from the Mexican–American War. The US navy commissioned Lammot Du Pont to replenish the country's supply before the *Trent* incident took place. It just so happened that he began loading his prodigious cargo on 28 November, the day after Britain received news of the seizure. Once the ban was in effect, Charles Francis Adams advised Du Pont to offload the saltpetre surreptitiously in limited amounts in order to avoid flooding the market.

27. Regis Courtemanche, *No Need of Glory: The British Navy in American Waters* (Annapolis, Md., 1977), p. 59.

28. Mitford (ed.), *The Stanleys of Alderley*, p. 271, Lord Stanley to Lady Stanley, 4 December 1861.

29. Ibid., p. 271, Lord Stanley to Lady Stanley, 6 December 1861.

30. Somerset RO, Somerset MSS, d/RA/A/2a/34/7/1, Admiral Milne to Duke of Somerset, 24 January 1861. Milne also feared the loss of the West Indies as a possible result of the war: 'The defence of our West India Islands, also Brunswick, Nova Scotia, Newfoundland, and the St Lawrence in spring, causes me much anxiety, but in so far as the force at my disposal will admit I will do all I can to defend them from aggression, but your Grace and the members of the Board must

be aware the large naval force which these defensives will require, and that the efficiency of our ships will in a great measure depend on the supply of coal at the various stations.' 22 December 1861.

31. Kenneth Bourne, 'British Preparations for War with the North, 1861–1862', *English Historical Review*, 76/301 (Oct. 1961), pp. 600–632, at p. 609.

32. Some pessimists within the War Office feared that victory would be impossible without a deus ex machina-like intervention, such as General McClellan refusing to part with any troops until spring, Confederate activity tying down the majority of Federal troops, a cold winter inhibiting deployment, or New England States such as Maine turning against the Union.

33. *Army Historical Research*, vol. 19, pp.112–14, Lieutenant Colonel G. J. Wolseley to Major Biddulph, 12 December 1861.

34. G. H. Warren, *Fountain of Discontent: The Trent Affair and Freedom of the Seas* (Boston, 1981), p. 130.

35. Mitford (ed.), *The Stanleys of Alderley*, p. 274, Lord Stanley to Lady Stanley, 20 December 1861.

36. Bourne, 'British Preparations for War with the North, 1861–1862', p. 616.

37. Owen Ashmore (ed.), 'The Diary of James Garnett of Low Moor, Clitheroe, 1858–65', vol. 2: 'The American Civil War and the Cotton Famine, 1861–65', *Transactions of the Historic Society of Lancashire and Cheshire for the Year 1971*, 123 (1972), pp. 105–43, at p. 114, 3 December 1861.

38. MHS, Adams MSS, The Diary of Charles Francis Adams, 9, 11 December 1861.

39. W. C. Ford (ed.), *A Cycle of Adams Letters, 1861–1865*, 2 vols. (Boston, 1920), vol. 1, pp. 75–7, Henry Adams to Charles Francis Adams Jr., 30 November 1861. Although Bright claimed to have a poor opinion of Lord Lyons, whom he had met once, when he had the opportunity to speak with him properly, he decided that Lyons was 'a sensible man, calm of temper and serious'. R. A. J. Walling (ed.), *The Diaries of John Bright* (New York, 1931), p. 407.

40. T. Wemyss Reid, *Life of the Right Honourable William Edward Forster* (London, 1888), p. 344, Forster to his wife, 4 December 1861.

41. *Spectator*, 7 December 1861. Bright was fortunate that no one knew or remembered how he had warmly greeted Senator Slidell when the latter visited England a few years before. Then, he wrote in his diary: 'Thro' the Park with Cobden. With him afterwards to dine at Fenton's Hotel with Mr. Brown, M.P. Among those present was Mr. Slidell, American Senator, who appeared to be a sensible man with more of the Englishman than American in his manners.' Walling (ed.), *The Diaries of John Bright*, p. 151.

42. Deborah Logan (ed.), *The Collected Letters of Harriet Martineau*, 5 vols. (London, 2007), vol. 4, p. 312, Martineau to Henry Reeve, 4 December 1861.

43. Sarah Agnes Wallace and Frances Elma Gillespie (eds.), *The Journal of Benjamin Moran, 1857–1865* 2 vols. (Chicago, 1948, 1949), vol. 2, p. 922, 12 December 1861.

44. Warren, *Fountain of Discontent*, p. 142.

45. Wallace and Gillespie (eds.), *The Journal of Benjamin Moran*, vol. 2, p. 923, 14 December 1861.

46. 'I am here quietly waiting the developments of events over which I have no control,' Adams complained to Motley, the Minister to Austria, 'and in which I had no participation.' Edward Chalfant, *Both Sides of the Ocean* (New York, 1982), p. 346.

47. Weed had assumed that Seward's trip to London in 1859 had been a success. Instead, he discovered that 'every idle word he spoke here, in society, is treasured up and a bad meaning given to it. For example, he made enemies of a Noble Household for laughing at the enormous sums of money paid for Paintings. At another Dinner Table he gave offense by insisting that English Books were absurdly expensive, and that American re-productions were just as good, etc etc etc.' Such boorish behaviour would not have won Seward friends anywhere. In the first instance, he betrayed himself to be a philistine, and in the second, unscrupulous, since the American reproductions were cheap only because they were printed in defiance of copyright, thus depriving English authors of their royalties.

48. University of Rochester, Rochester, NY, Rush Rhees Library, Seward MSS, Mission Abroad, 1861–1862 [microform]; a selection of letters from Archbishop Hughes, Bishop McIlvaine, W. H. Seward and Thurlow Weed, Weed to Seward, 18 December 1861.

49. *The Times*, 6 December 1861.

50. University of Rochester, Rochester, NY, Rush Rhees Library, Seward MSS, Weed to Seward, 10 December 1861.

51. 'I am placed in a predicament almost as awkward as if I had not been commissioned here at all.' OR, ser. 2, vol. 2, p. 1123, Adams to Seward, 11 December 1861. Warren, *Fountain of Discontent*, p. 164.

52. Ibid., p. 152.

53. T. C. Pease and J. Randall (eds.), *The Diary of Orville H. Browning, 1850–1881* (Springfield, Ill., 1925–31), 10 December 1861, p. 50.

54. Beverly Wilson Palmer (ed.), *The Selected Letters of Charles Sumner*, 2 vols. (Boston, 1990), vol. 1, p. 82, Sumner to Duchess of Argyll, 18 November 1861.

55. Ibid., pp. 88–9, Charles Sumner to Francis Lieber, 24 December 1861.

56. Jay Sexton, *Debtor Diplomacy* (Oxford, 2005), p. 96.

57. Columbia University, Blackwell MSS, Blackwell to Bodichon, 30 December 1861.

58. Frederick W. Seward (ed.), *Seward at Washington* (New York, 1891), p. 32.

59. Pease and Randall (eds.), *The Diary of Orville H. Browning*, p. 51, 15 December 1861.

60. Russell, *My Diary North and South*, p. 331, 16 December 1861.

61. Martin Crawford (ed.), *William Howard Russell's Civil War: Private Diary and Letters, 1861–1862* (Athens, Ga., 1992), p. 207, Russell to John T. Delane, 20 December 1861.

62. The mood in the Senate was no different. Senator Orville Browning, for example, was adamantly against any kind of settlement. 'We were clearly right in what we did,' he insisted. England could send as many the troops she liked. 'We are determined, at all hazards, to hold on to the prisoners . . .' Pease and Randall (eds.), *The Diary of Orville H. Browning*, p. 50, fn.

63. The United States did not have a naval plan against Britain. Admiral Milne, on the other hand, had already put his fleet on alert. His instructions from London were to end the blockade of the Southern ports (without directly cooperating with the Confederacy). How he achieved this was to be his own affair. Courtemanche, *No Need of Glory: The British Navy in American Waters* (Annapolis, Md., 1977), p. 59, Admiral Milne to Sir Frederick Grey, December 1861. Milne's strategy depended on a three-pronged attack. One force, under Commodore Dunlop, would sail from Vera Cruz and clear the Federal navy from the Gulf. The larger, Milne's, would attack the US blockading fleet and then proceed up the coast to the north-east, where it would establish a blockade of the major northern ports. Milne would be able to count on reinforcements, a sufficient number of coaling vessels and a working dockyard in Bermuda. He thought that his plan had, in the short term, a good chance of success. A mere three months later, however, after the launch of the USS *Monitor*, he felt that the advantage had started to turn in favour of the North and he looked back to the *Trent* affair as Britain's most favourable moment.

64. Crawford (ed.), *William Howard Russell's Civil War*, p. 207, Russell to John T. Delane, 20 December 1861.

65. Michael Burlingame, *Abraham Lincoln*, 2 vols. (Baltimore, 2008), vol. 2, p. 224.

66. Palmer (ed.), *Selected Letters of Charles Sumner*, vol. 2, p. 87, Sumner to Bright, 23 December 1861. 'Are Mr. Mason and Mr. Slidell so irresistibly eloquent that we must not run the danger of hearing them speak?' asked the Duchess of Argyll in one of her letters to Sumner. MHS, Argyll Letters, p. 93, Duchess of Argyll to Charles Sumner, 8 December 1861.

67. James J. Barnes and Patience P. Barnes (eds.), *Private and Confidential: Letters from British Ministers in Washington to the Foreign Secretaries* (Selinsgrove, Pa., 1993), p. 273, Lyons to Russell, 23 December 1861.

68. Palmer (ed.), *Selected Letters of Charles Sumner*, vol. 1, pp. 88–9, Charles Sumner to Francis Lieber, 24 December 1861.

69. Ibid. Opinion remains divided on the issue. At one extreme are those who believe that the North would have crushed the Royal Navy, destroyed 'the façade of British military preeminence' and rocked 'the foundations of British economic primacy'; at the other: humiliation for the North and swift independence for the South. The strength of these wildly divergent arguments depends, in part, on how long the war might have continued. Nevertheless, the evidence does suggest its own story, one in which all sides come out the worse for wear – except for the

South. See e.g. Russell F. Weigley, *A Great Civil War* (Bloomington, Ind., 2000), p. 81; Andrew Wellard, 'After the *Trent*, or Third Time Lucky?', *Crossfire*, 62 (April 2000).

70. Beale (ed.), *The Diary of Edward Bates*, p. 216. Meanwhile, in England, people were beginning to worry that her naval superiority was not nearly superior enough. On the same day as the American Cabinet discussions, *The Times* warned that the North had extraordinary maritime resources. Furthermore, 'Our adversaries will lose not a moment after the declaration of war in pressing forward the construction and equipment of cruisers and it must be expected that many of these vessels will, as in the last war, elude the blockade and prowl about the ocean in quest of prey ... It is quite possible that while England is ruling undisputed mistress of the waves a Yankee frigate may appear some fine morning off one of our ports and inflict no slight damage upon us.'

71. James M. McPherson, *Battle Cry of Freedom* (London, 1988), p. 444. The result of the crisis was the Legal Tender Act of February 1862, which – *inter alia* – created a national paper currency, unleashed the power of government bonds, and provided the Treasury with the money to pay its bills.

72. The way Seward framed the discussion, the *Trent* was really a continuation of the old impressment argument – the one that had led to war in 1812. Then it was over Britain stopping American ships and removing British deserters. Now, alleged Seward, the United States had inadvertently performed a similar violation that he was delighted to rectify, and in so doing, establish once and for all a fifty-year-old American principle. It was complete legal nonsense. The *Trent* had nothing to do with impressment. But the argument sounded stirring and patriotic, and was guaranteed to go down well with the public. Seward threw in a couple of other arguments for good measure, about ambassadors and dispatches being fair game on the high seas and other such dubious nonsense.

73. David H. Donald, *Lincoln* (New York, 1995), p. 323.

74. Russell, *My Diary North and South*, p. 333, 26 December 1861.

75. Many years later Trollope wrote in his autobiography: 'I was at Washington at the time, and it was known there that the contest among the leading Northerners was very sharp on the matter. Mr Sumner and Mr Seward were, under Mr Lincoln, the two chiefs of the party. It was understood that Mr Sumner was opposed to the rendition of the men, and Mr Seward in favour of it ... I dined with Mr Seward on the day of the decision, meeting Mr Sumner at his house, and was told as I left the dining room what the decision had been.' Anthony Trollope, *An Autobiography*, ed. Michael Sadleir (New York, 1923), p. 166.

76. Doris Kearns Goodwin, *Team of Rivals* (New York, 2005), p. 400. See Logan (ed.), *Collected Letters of Harriet Martineau*, vol. 4, *passim*, for Martineau's references to the plans and the advice.

77. Pease and Randall (eds.), *The Diary of Orville H. Browning*, 27 December 1861, p. 519.

78. Barnes and Barnes (eds.), *Private and Confidential*, p. 274, Lyons to Russell, 31 December 1861.

79. Edward L. Pierce (ed.), *Memoir and Letters of Charles Sumner*, 4 vols. (Boston, 1894), vol. 4: *1860-1870*, p. 59.

80. Warren, *Fountain of Discontent*, p. 20.

81. David Herbert Donald, *Charles Sumner and the Rights of Man* (New York, 1970), pp. 43-4.

82. Adam Gurowski, *Diary from March 4, 1861 to November 12, 1862* (Boston, 1862), p. 165.

CHAPTER 9. THE WAR MOVES TO ENGLAND

1. *Transactions of the Historic Society of Lancashire and Cheshire*, John Ward Diary, 171 Cont A, 1 January 1862.

2. Seward countered that he had been on tenterhooks himself, until they convened on Christmas Day: 'Remember, that in a Council like ours, there are some strong wills to be reconciled.' But Weed was not satisfied. The legation had been the last to know of the Commissioners' release; even the clerks in the City were better informed. 'I do not see how I could have prevented the difficulties which attended the delay and suspense in the *Trent* affair. The telegraph outstrips the mails – and I cannot send despatches or receive them by telegraph,' rejoined Seward. Weed would not back down, insisting that Seward should have at least written privately to Adams, rather than leaving him in complete suspense. Margaret K. Toth (ed.), *Mission Abroad, 1861-1862* (Rochester, NY, 1954), Seward to Weed, 22 January, 30 January and 7 March 1862.

3. Sarah Agnes Wallace and Frances Elma Gillespie (eds.), *The Journal of Benjamin Moran, 1857-1865*, 2 vols. (Chicago, 1948, 1949), vol. 2, p. 940, 8 and 9 January 1862.

4. *Letters of Lord St Maur and Lord Edward St Maur* (London, 1888), p. 245, Duke of Somerset to Lord Edward St Maur, 12 January 1862.

5. Nancy Mitford (ed.), *The Stanleys of Alderley* (London, 1968), p. 281, 19 February 1862, Jonny Stanley to Maude Stanley.

6. Wellcome Library, RAMC.75, f. 2107, Sir Anthony Jackson, January 1862.

7. *Illustrated London News*, 11 January 1862. Later, when the extent of American anger became clear, it defended Britain's response: 'And if the British people misinterpreted the sentiments of the Americans with regard either to slavery or secession, the Americans very palpably misinterpreted those of the British people and Government in the affair of the *Trent*.' Ibid., 19 April 1862.

8. Charles Francis Adams Jr., 'The Trent Affair: An Historical Retrospect', *Massachusetts Historical Society Proceedings*, 45 (1912), p. 529.

9. Toth (ed.), *Mission Abroad*, p. 236, Hughes to Seward, 11 January 1862.

10. MHS, Adams MSS, Diary of Charles Francis Adams, 15 January 1862.

11. Edward Chalfant, *Better in Darkness* (New York, 1994), p. 21.

12. Ibid., p. 25.

13. Wallace and Gillespie (eds.), *The Journal of Benjamin Moran*, vol. 2, p. 940, 10 January 1862.

14. Desmond McCarthy, *Lady John Russell*, p. 260, Lady John Russell to Lady Dumferline, 13 December 1861.

15. *Letters of Lord St Maur and Lord Edward St Maur*, p. 245, Duke of Somerset to Lord Edward St Maur, 12 January 1862.

16. MHS, Adams MSS, Diary of Charles Francis Adams, 19 April 1862. His diary for just one week in April, for example, shows that he may have felt lonely, but he was not alone. He went to dinner at Lord Lansdowne's on 1 April, 'the dinner was pleasant without being animated'. From there he went to a glittering reception at Stafford House. The next day he went to a dinner at the Duchess of Somerset's. On the 3rd he went to a reception of the President of the Royal Society at Burlington House. On the 5th, Mrs Adams had her first reception for Americans in London – with about thirty guests. On the 7th he had dinner with the Duke and Duchess of Northumberland, with 'Lord and Lady Macclesfield, Lord Ellenborough, Lord and Lady Colville, Lord and Lady Colchester and Mr and Mrs Spencer Walpole, and one or two others'.

17. David H. Donald, *Lincoln* (New York, 1995), p. 329.

18. Anthony Trollope, *North America* (repr. London, 1968), pp. 139–40.

19. T. C. Pease and J. Randall (eds.), *The Diary of Orville H. Browning, 1850–1881* (Springfield, Ill., 1925–31), p. 520, 28 December 1861. Aware that people were whispering behind his back, in January Seward tried to rouse public support by publishing all of the previous year's correspondence between the State Department and the various legations. He made sure to include the originals of letters that had been toned down. His opponents replied by publishing a pamphlet entitled 'A Review of Mr Seward's Diplomacy' which exposed his considerable blunders. Jay Monaghan, *Diplomat in Carpet Slippers* (New York, 1945), p. 212.

20. Pease and Randall (eds.), *The Diary of Orville M. Browning*, 25 January 1861, p. 527.

21. BL Add. MS 415670, f. 219, Herbert to mother, 14 January 1862.

22. James M. McPherson, *Battle Cry of Freedom* (London, 1988), p. 372.

23. Martin Crawford (ed.), *William Howard Russell's Civil War: Private Diary and Letters, 1861–1862* (Athens, Ga., 1992), pp. 218–19, Russell to Delane, 16 January 1862.

24. *Illustrated London News*, 22 February 1862.

25. Ibid., 22 March 1862.

26. BL Add. MS 41567, f. 221, Herbert to mother, 4 February 1862.

27. Charles F. Johnson, *The Long Roll* (repr. Shepherdstown, W.Va., 1986), p. 93.

28. *Illustrated London News*, 22 March 1862.

29. There were some minor incidents in January and February but Lyons brushed them off. Not serious, but annoying, was Seward's cheeky offer to let British troops travel through Maine to Canada. It was actually a case of lost luggage, but Seward used the incident to make it appear as though he were graciously allowing the British army to disembark in the United States on their way to invade her from Canada.

30. West Sussex RO, Lyons MSS, Box 300, Lord Lyons to Augusta Mary Minna Lyons, 31 January and 7 February 1862.

31. PRO 30/22/36, ff. 27–8, Lyons to Russell, 1 February 1862.

32. Edward Dicey, *Spectator of America*, ed. Herbert Mitgang (Athens, Ga., 1971), p. 90–92.

33. John B. Jones, *A Rebel War Clerk's Diary at the Confederate States Capital*, ed. Earl Schenck Miers (Urbana, Ill., 1958), p. 63, 1 January 1862.

34. C. Vann Woodward (ed.), *Mary Chesnut's Civil War* (New Haven, 1981), 11 February 1862, p. 286.

35. Eli N. Evans, *Judah P. Benjamin* (New York, 1988), p. 146.

36. Crawford (ed.), *William Howard Russell's Civil War*, p. 219, Russell to Delane, 16 January 1862.

37. *Living Age*, 69/3 (Oct.–Dec. 1863), p. 189.

38. Burton J. Hendrick, *Statesmen of the Lost Cause* (New York, 1939), p. 235.

39. When Slidell was a boy, living in the First Ward, his best friend was Charles Wilkes. The friendship was broken when they were teenagers, over the affections of a local girl. They had not seen each other for many years when Slidell became Wilkes's unwilling guest on board the *San Jacinto*.

40. Vann Woodward (ed.), *Mary Chesnut's Civil War*, p. 170, 28 September 1861.

41. Wallace and Gillespie (eds.), *The Journal of Benjamin Moran*, vol. 2, p. 1212, 22 September 1863.

42. Crawford (ed.), *William Howard Russell's Civil War*, p. 61, 25 May 1861.

43. William Howard Russell, *My Diary North and South*, ed. Eugene H. Berwanger (New York, 1988), p. 164, 25 May 1861. Slidell's experience of foreign diplomacy was limited to his eighteen-month stint in Mexico, where he served as the American Minister, 1845–6.

44. *The Times*, 10 December 1861.

45. Francis W. Dawson, *Reminiscences of Confederate Service , 1861–1865*, ed. Bell I. Wiley (Baton Rouge, La., 1980), p. 182, Dawson to mother, 20 February 1862.

46. ORN, ser. 2, vol. 3, encl. no. 3, p. 332, Mason to Hunter, 7 February 1862.

47. Stephen Z. Starr, *Colonel Grenfell's Wars* (Baton Rouge, La., 1971), p. 40.

48. Ibid.

49. E. D. Adams, *Great Britain and the American Civil War*, 2 vols. in 1 (New York, 1958), vol. 1, p. 243.

50. Ibid., p. 263.

51. ORN, ser. 2, vol. 3, p. 343, Mason to Hunter, 22 February 1862.

52. Adams, *Great Britain and the American Civil War*, vol. 1, p. 243.

53. Ibid., p. 261, and Brian Jenkins, *Britain and the War for the Union*, 2 vols. (Montreal, 1974, 1980), vol. 1, p. 253. The blockade issue was further muddied by Northern plans to block up Charleston harbour with a 'stone fleet' – that is, sinking wrecks to make passage impossible – which was considered in England to be short-sighted and inhumane.

54. Toth (ed.), *Mission Abroad*, p. 386, Weed to Seward, 18 February 1862.

55. Seward's continued silence was a gift to the South. *The Economist*, for example, pronounced: 'It is in the independence of the South, and not in her defeat, that we can alone look with confidence for the early amelioration and the ultimate extinction of the slavery we abhor.'

56. Citizenship was not conferred on free blacks until 1866. However, the legation began quietly giving out passports in 1862.

57. MHS, Adams MSS, Diary of Charles Francis Adams, 25 January 1862. Ironically, on 6 March the New York State Chamber of Commerce passed a resolution thanking John Bright for his advocacy of the 'principles of constitutional liberty and international justice for which the American people were contending'.

58. Devon RO, 2065m/cl/29, J. W. Buller MP to Georgiana, 14 March 1862.

59. Toth (ed.), *Mission Abroad*, p. 400, Weed to Seward, 20 February 1862.

60. Charles Vandersee, 'Henry Adams behind the Scenes: Civil War Letters to Frederick W. Seward', *Bulletin of the New York Public Library* 71/4 (1967), p. 249.

61. *MPUS*, pp. 22–3, n. 112, Adams to Seward, 7 February 1862.

62. Stephen B. Oates, 'Henry Hotze: Confederate Agent Abroad', *Historian*, 27 (1965), p. 134.

63. Ibid., p. 135.

64. ORN, ser. 2, vol. 3, p. 347, Hotze to Hunter, 23 February 1862.

65. Wallace and Gillespie (eds.), *The Journal of Benjamin Moran*, vol. 2, p. 961, 6 March 1862.

66. Roundell Palmer, *Memorials*, 2 vols. (London, 1894, repr. 2003), vol. 1, p. 404.

67. Toth (ed.), *Mission Abroad*, p. 463, Weed to Seward, 8 March 1862.

68. MHS, Adams MSS, Diary of Charles Francis Adams, 8 March 1862.

69. ORN, ser. 2, vol. 3, p. 359, Mason to Hunter, 11 March 1862.

CHAPTER 10. THE FIRST BLOW AGAINST SLAVERY

1. John Stuart Mill, *The Contest in America*, repr. from *Fraser's Magazine*, February 1862 (Boston, 1863). The Adams family met John Stuart Mill at a dinner given by the Argylls. Years later, Henry Adams sheepishly admitted that he drank too much wine that night, and 'after dinner engaged in instructing John Stuart

Mill on the peculiar merits of an American protective system . . . Mr Mill took no apparent pleasure in the dispute.' Henry Adams, *The Education of Henry Adams*, ed. Ernest Samuels (repr. Boston, 1973), p. 126.

2. Philip Van Doren Stern, *When the Guns Roared: World Aspects of the American Civil War* (New York, 1965), p. 112.

3. W. D. Jones, 'Blyden, Gladstone and the War', *Journal of Negro History*, 49 (1964), p. 58, fn.

4. *George Douglas, Eighth Duke of Argyll (1823–1900): Autobiography and Memoirs*, ed. the Dowager Duchess of Argyll, 2 vols. (London, 1906), vol. 2, p. 190, 13 May 1862.

5. Jones, 'Blyden, Gladstone and the War', p. 58. Blyden had recently returned from a diplomatic mission to the United States, where he was subjected to the usual treatment meted out to free blacks, such as being denied the right to ride on public buses or eat in white-owned restaurants. He was particularly upset at being denied entry to the House of Representatives. There was no such bar to the Houses of Parliament, which surprised some Northerners. Benjamin Moran laughed at Charles Wilson's annoyance at having to sit beside 'the negro representative from Hayti'. On 6 February he wrote in his diary: 'From what I have been told the black exhibited a good deal better manners than did my fellow secretary. For all his "black republicanism," he clearly indicated by his uneasiness a decided antipathy to "the nigger".'

6. MHS, Adams MSS, Diary of Charles Francis Adams, 16 April 1862. Adams was convinced that Lord Shaftesbury was against the North, and was using his influence with the anti-slavery societies. However, Thurlow Weed became acquainted with Shaftesbury and realized that the Earl, like so many others, had been alienated by the North's willingness to continue slavery.

7. Sarah Agnes Wallace and Frances Elma Gillespie (eds.), *The Journal of Benjamin Moran, 1857–1865*, 2 vols. (Chicago, 1948, 1949), vol. 2, p. 979, 16 April 1862.

8. David Hepburn Milton, *Lincoln's Spymaster: Thomas Haines Dudley and the Liverpool Network* (Mechanicsburg, Pa., 2003), pp. 5–7.

9. Wallace and Gillespie (eds.), *The Journal of Benjamin Moran*, vol. 2, pp. 832–3, 24 June 1861.

10. 'You may rest assured that no proper effort will be wanting on my part to report to you all that can be learned of the doings of rebel agents here,' Consul Morse promised. NARA, T. 168, roll 30, vol. 30, desp. 1, Morse to Seward, 30 January 1862.

11. Milton, *Lincoln's Spymaster*, p. 33.

12. F. L. Owsley, *The CSS Florida* (Philadelphia, 1965; repr. Tuscaloosa, Ala., 1987), p. 22.

13. He definitely could not afford marine insurance. In spite of Weed's conviction that Lloyds was making a handsome profit out of secretly providing insurance to blockade-runners, Huse's experience was that the terms were so outrageous as to be prohibitive. ORN, ser. 4, vol. 1, p. 127, Caleb Huse to Major Gorgas, 15 March 1862.

14. BL Add. MS 38951, ff. 53–5, Lord Hammond to Austen Henry Layard, 20 April 1862.

15. See, for example, MHS, Adams MSS, Diary of Charles Francis Adams, 9 May 1862.

16. PRO FO5/818, Russell to Lyons, 17 April 1862.

17. Napoleon then said the complete opposite to William Dayton, the American Minister: 'Mr Adams tells me', reported Benjamin Moran on 17 April, 'that Louis Napoleon in a personal interview with Mr Dayton expressed his regret at the precipitate recognition of the rebels as belligerents by France and Gt. B., and stated that it was England's work. He is now willing to withdraw it if Gt. B. will also.'

18. Louis Martin Sears, 'A Confederate Diplomat at the Court of Napoleon III', *American Historical Review*, 26/2 (Jan. 1921), pp. 255–81, Slidell to Mason, 12 April 1862.

19. NARA, T. 168, roll 30, d. 1, Morse to Seward, 12 April 1862.

20. Wallace and Gillespie (eds.), *The Journal of Benjamin Moran*, vol. 2, p. 969, 22 March 1862.

21. W. C. Ford (ed.), *A Cycle of Adams Letters, 1861–1865*, 2 vols. (Boston, 1920), vol. 1, p. 133, Henry Adams to Charles Francis Adams Jr., 11 April 1862.

22. Adams, *The Education of Henry Adams*, p. 134.

23. ORN, ser. 2, vol. 2, p. 183, Bulloch to Mallory, 11 April 1862.

24. Wallace and Gillespie (eds.), *The Journal of Benjamin Moran*, vol. 2, p. 978, 14 April 1862.

25. ORN, ser. 1, vol. 1, pp. 745–9, Captain Pegram to Mallory, 10 March 1862.

26. Francis W. Dawson *Reminiscences of Confederate Service, 1861–1865*, ed. Bell I. Wiley (Baton Rouge, La., 1980), p. 32.

27. Duke University, Francis Dawson MSS, Dawson to mother, 16 May 1862.

28. James J. Barnes and Patience P. Barnes (eds.), *The American Civil War through British Eyes*, vol. 1 (Kent, Ohio, 2003), pp. 313–14, Lyons to Russell, 16 March 1862.

29. It is true that wooden ships were defenceless against those made of iron. However, D. P. Crook quotes the *Manchester Guardian* (3 April 1862), one of the few English newspapers to maintain a sense of perspective about the news: 'There may be a certain truth in saying that our whole navy consists of but two men of war [*Warrior* and *Black Prince*]; but it is to be observed that, in the same sense, the French have but one, the Americans have only a gunboat, and no other nation has any navy at all.' Crook, *The North, the South, and the Powers, 1861–1865* (New York, 1974), p. 188. In reality the *Monitor* and the *Warrior* would never have engaged with each other, because the former could only sail in calm water and the latter could only manoeuvre in the open sea.

30. John Black Atkins, *The Life of Sir William Howard Russell*, 2 vols. (London, 1911), vol. 2, p. 93.

31. Martin Crawford (ed.), *William Howard Russell's Civil War: Private Diary*

and Letters (Athens, Ga., 1992), p. 231, Russell to Mowbray Morris, 15 March 1862.

32. Edward Dicey, *Spectator of America*, ed. Herbert Mitgang (Athens, Ga., 1971), p. 149.

33. Lawley's early life is described in Brian Jenkins, 'Frank Lawley and the Confederacy', *Civil War History*, 23 (March 1977), and William Stanley Hoole, *Lawley Covers the Confederacy* (Tuscaloosa, Ala., 1964).

34. Jenkins, 'Frank Lawley and the Confederacy', p. 148.

35. Julia Miele Rodas, 'More than a Civil (War) Friendship: Anthony Trollope and Frank Lawley', *Princeton University Library Chronicle*, 60/1 (1998), p. 42, Lawley to mother, 2 February 1862.

36. Crawford (ed.), *William Howard Russell's Civil War*, p. 230.

37. Alan Hankinson, *Man of Wars: William Howard Russell of 'The Times', 1820–1907* (London, 1982), p. 180.

38. William Watson, *Life in the Confederate Army: Being the Observations and Experiences of an Alien in the South during the Civil War* (London, 1887; repr. Baton Rouge, La., 1995), p. 285.

39. Atkins, *The Life of Sir William Howard Russell*, vol. 2, p. 105, 24 March 1862.

40. Ilana Miller, *Reports from America* (Stroud, 2001), p. 212.

41. Crawford (ed.), *William Howard Russell's Civil War*, p. 235, Russell to Stanton, 2 April 1862.

42. Allan Nevins, *The War for the Union*, 4 vols.; vol. 2: *War Becomes Revolution 1862–1863* (New York, 1960), p. 3.

43. William Howard Russell, *My Diary North and South*, ed. Eugene H. Berwanger (New York, 1988), p. 340.

44. Hankinson, *Man of Wars*, p. 181.

45. A. Taylor-Milne, 'The Lyons–Seward Treaty of 1862', *American Historical Review*, 38/3 (1933), pp. 511–25.

46. The small US fleet known as the Africa Squadron had been patrolling the West Coast since 1860; the largest fleet was the British Preventive Squadron, which had six ships.

47. James J. Barnes and Patience P. Barnes (eds.), *Private and Confidential: Letters from British Ministers in Washington to the Foreign Secretaries* (Selinsgrove, Pa., 1993), p. 280. The source for the footnote on this page is the same.

48. University of Rochester, Fanny Seward Diary, ff. 21–9, 22 March 1862.

49. Dicey, *Spectator of America*, p. 58.

50. Lincoln had calculated that paying owners compensation for all the slaves in the Northern States would cost the equivalent of eighty-seven days of warfare.

51. *The Reminiscences of Carl Schurz*, ed. Carl Schurz, Frederic Bancroft and William Archibald Dunning, 3 vols. (Garden City, NY, 1917), vol. 2, p. 304.

52. Taylor-Milne, 'The Lyons–Seward Treaty of 1862'.

53. PRO 30/22/36, ff. 63–6, Lyons to Russell, 8 April 1862.

CHAPTER 11. FIVE MILES FROM RICHMOND

1. Nathaniel Cheairs Hughes Jr. (ed.), *Sir Henry Morton Stanley, Confederate* (Baton Rouge, La., 2000), p. 129.

2. Ibid., pp. 123, 124.

3. Ibid., p. 126. The boy, Henry D. Parker, aged 18, survived but was discharged from the army on 10 April.

4. Stanley P. Hirshon, *The White Tecumseh* (New York, 1997), p. 120.

5. General Grant was in fact named Hiram Ulysses Grant, but a mistake in his application to West Point resulted in his being known as Ulysses S. Grant.

6. Peter Batty and Peter Parish, *The Divided Union* (London, 1987), p. 80.

7. Hughes (ed.), *Sir Henry Morton Stanley*, p. 136.

8. Edward Dicey, *Spectator of America*, ed. Herbert Mitgang (Athens, Ga., 1971), p. 208.

9. Dawson's propensity for romantic flights of fancy helped him to survive his transition to life as a junior officer in the navy. There was nothing knightly about the first time he tried to climb into bed: 'like one of the heroes of my favorite Marryatt [*sic*], I signalized my entrance into the hammock on one side by pitching out on my head on the other side.' Francis W. Dawson, *Reminiscences of Confederate Service, 1861–1865*, ed. Bell I. Wiley (Baton Rouge, La., 1980), pp. 40–42.

10. Lord Lyons was annoyed by Mercier's visit. It was his firm belief that they should respect the Northern embargo and refrain from any direct communication with the South. He also feared that it would give the impression of a crack in the Anglo-French accord. For that reason alone, Seward was not averse to Mercier's solo mission.

11. Robert Douthat Meade, *Judah P. Benjamin: Confederate Statesman* (Baton Rouge, La., 2001), p. 254.

12. James J. Barnes and Patience P. Barnes (eds.), *The American Civil War through British Eyes*, vol. 2 (Kent, Ohio, 2005), p. 26, Lord Lyons to Lord Russell, 28 April 1862.

13. C. Vann Woodward (ed.), *Mary Chesnut's Civil War* (New Haven, 1981), p. 330, 27 April 1862.

14. Hudson Strode, *Jefferson Davis: Confederate President*, 3 vols. (New York, 1959), vol. 2, p. 246.

15. See Ella Lonn, *Foreigners in the Confederacy* (Chapel Hill, NC, repr. 2001), pp. 113–15, for a discussion on the European Brigade. There were 2,500 Frenchmen, 800 Spaniards, 500 Italians, 400 Germans, Dutch and Scandinavians, and 500 Swiss, Belgian, English, Slavonians and others.

16. Virgil Carrington Jones makes clear that by 30 April New Orleans was relatively calm. 'Truly the backbone of the rebellion is broken,' reported Admiral Porter. Jones, *The Civil War at Sea*, 3 vols. (New York, 1961), vol. 2, p. 138.

17. Robert S. Holzman, 'Ben Butler in the Civil War', *New England Quarterly*, 30/3 (Sept. 1957), pp. 330–45, at p. 335.

18. PRO FO5/848, ff. 403–10, Consul Coppel to Lord Russell, 9 May 1862.

19. Holzman, 'Ben Butler in the Civil War', p. 334.

20. The British Consul tried to protect the 105 British members of Company B. When Butler learned that thirty-nine of them had sent their uniforms and weapons to friends in the Confederate army, he ordered the entire company to appear before him in full kit, or face either expulsion or imprisonment. Two men, according to a petition from the British residents, Samuel Nelson and J. Turner Roe, were arbitrarily arrested and sent 'to work as common laborers on the forts which is tantamount to a death sentence given the weather, conditions etc.' They requested a British warship for protection. PRO FO5/848, ff. 433–9, Petition on behalf of British Residents of New Orleans, 11 June 1861.

21. PRO FO5/830, ff. 346–8, Lord Lyons to Lord Russell, 30 May 1862.

22. Seward dispatched a trusted representative to New Orleans to examine each claim of judicial abuse. It came as no surprise to Butler's critics when every one of his cases was overturned.

23. William Watson, *Life in the Confederate Army: Being the Observations and Experiences of an Alien in the South during the Civil War* (London, 1887; repr. Baton Rouge, La., 1995), p. 371.

24. James M. McPherson, *Battle Cry of Freedom* (London, 1988), p. 416.

25. Watson, *Life in the Confederate Army*, p. 361.

26. 'The Journal of Robert Neve', private collection, p. 40.

27. Shelby Foote, *The Civil War*, 3 vols. (New York, 1986), vol. 1, p. 385.

28. Halleck proclaimed a blanket ban on all journalists and non-combatants on 13 May, on the grounds that Confederate spies were among them.

29. *Illustrated London News*, 26 April 1862.

30. Ibid., 14 June 1862.

31. E. B. Long, with Barbara Long, *The Civil War Day by Day: An Almanac 1861–1865* (New York, 1971; repr. New York, 1985), p. 726.

32. *Illustrated London News*, 19 July 1862.

33. Ibid., 26 July 1862.

34. Camp Douglas was originally a training camp for volunteers; after the capture of Fort Donelson in February, the temporary barracks had been converted to hold enlisted prisoners of war; officers were sent to a separate prison. There Stanley shared a straw pallet with W. H. Wilkes, a Southern nephew of the notorious Charles Wilkes.

35. Hughes, *Sir Henry Morton Stanley*, p. 141.

36. Ibid., p. 146.

37. PRO FO115/300, ff. 151–2, Lord Lyons to Lord Russell, 5 May 1862.

38. See e.g. OR, ser. 2, vol. 4, S. 117, William Hoffman to Edwin Stanton, 28 June 1862.

39. Hughes, *Sir Henry Morton Stanley*, p. 148. Hughes notes that George Levy, the author of the most comprehensive study of Camp Douglas, has serious doubts about Stanley's account. However, there is sufficient evidence to accept that he was there, and did join the 1st Illinois Light Artillery.

40. OR, ser. 1, vol. 10/1, p. 73, Report of Col. John F. De Courcy, 20 June 1862.

41. Hugh Dubrulle, 'A Military Legacy of the Civil War: The British Inheritance', *Civil War History* (June 2003), pp. 153–80. The military observers were genuinely impressed, however. Sir George Seymour wrote to Lord Russell on 9 May 1862: 'I have just seen a letter from an English officer (a man who has seen a great deal of service) who has been taking a look at the Federal army. A finer one – or one better provided with all things necessary he never – he says – saw – and he adds ... "that it would require a force of 100,000 men to keep them out of Canada." Meanwhile he says that he does not trace much hostile feeling towards us, and that he has met with a great deal of civility from the Federal Officers.' PRO 33/22/39, f. 163.

42. Richard Taylor, *Destruction and Reconstruction* (1879, repr. New York, 1992), p. 21.

43. He claimed to be the son of Brigadier Sir Charles Wyndham of the 5th Light Cavalry, and a Frenchwoman named Zoë Vauthrin. His mother allegedly gave birth to him in the middle of the English Channel, on board the *Arab*. But there was no HMS *Arab* in commission in 1833, nor did the Royal Navy have a Captain Charles Wyndham. Nor was he the son, illegitimate or otherwise, of Lord Leconsfield, although there was a Captain Charles Wyndham, killed in action at Jagdalak on 29 October 1841.

44. Edward G. Longacre, *Jersey Cavaliers* (Hightstown, NJ, 1992), p. 47.

45. Taylor, *Destruction and Reconstruction*, p. 53.

46. Ruth Scarborough, *Siren of the South* (Macon, 1997), p. 53. This same Henry Kyd Douglas has been accused of being the man responsible for Robert E. Lee's Antietam battle plans falling into Federal hands. Wilbur D. Jones, 'Who Lost the Lost Order?', *Civil War Regiments: A Journal of the American Civil War*, 5/3 (1997).

47. Mary Sophia Hill, *A British Subject's Recollections of the Confederacy* (Baltimore, 1875), pp. 19, 20.

48. Wyndham's lieutenant colonel reported: 'All the officers, as far as I could see, behaved bravely in trying to rally their men, but to no avail. They retreated without order and in the greatest confusion – for the most part panic-stricken.' OR, ser. 1, vol. 15/1, p. 680.

49. Longacre, *Jersey Cavaliers*, p. 92.

50. Douglas Southall Freeman, *Lee's Lieutenants*, 3 vols. (repr. New York, 1970), vol. 1, p. 432.

51. James I. Robertson Jr., *Stonewall Jackson* (New York, 1997), p. 429.

52. Ibid., p. 449.

53. Wilmer Jones, *Generals in Blue and Gray* (New York, 2006) p. 80.

54. PRO 30/22/36, ff. 87–90, Lyons to Russell, 6 May 1862. 'So strongly have I been impressed with the necessity of being at the seat of Government, that with the exception of the two months ... attendance upon the Prince of Wales, I have been only four nights absent from Washington,' he wrote apologetically.

55. West Sussex RO, Lyons MSS, Box 300, Lord Lyons to Augusta Lyons, 6 May 1862.

56. When Lyons called on Seward to say goodbye, Lyons reassured him it would be far better for him to spend his holiday in England than at an American resort, cut off from both capitals. Seward agreed, reported Lyons. 'There was, [Seward] was happy to say, no difficult question pending between the two governments.' PRO FO5/831, ff. 171–4, Lyons to Russell, 9 June 1862.

57. The legation often acted as a missing persons bureau. Instructions like this one to the consulate in New York were not uncommon: 'to insert in the New York Herald and New York Tribune the following advertisement: "Ashley Norton Jones, otherwise called George Temple, who is believed to be serving in the United States Army, is earnestly entreated, for the sake of his afflicted parents to communicate at once with the Reverend Rush Buel, 44 William Street, Providence, RI. His parents will consult his wishes on all matters. Officers or comrades are requested to call his attention to this notice." Notice should appear every alternative day for a month.'

58. Bayly Ellen Marks and Mark Norton Schatz, *Between North and South: A Maryland Journalist Views the Civil War. The Narrative of William Wilkins Glenn 1861–1869* (Cranbury, NJ, 1976), pp. 64–5, 15 June 1862.

59. Just before he left, on 13 June, Lyons informed the Foreign Office that Congress had voted to recognize the Republics of Haiti and Liberia. Previous administrations had declined because 'those Republics are governed by men of Negro descent'.

60. Lord Newton (ed.), *Lord Lyons: A Record of British Diplomacy*, 2 vols. (London, 1914), vol. 1, pp. 85–6, Lord Lyons to Lord Russell, 16 May 1862.

61. *Letters of Lord St Maur and Lord Edward St Maur* (London, 1888), p. 251, Lord Edward St Maur to Duke of Somerset, 9 June 1862; p. 254, to Duchess of Somerset, 19 June 1862.

62. Ibid., p. 260, Lord Edward St Maur to Duke of Somerset, 25 July 1862. It became a Southern myth that Lord Edward 'fought' alongside General Longstreet in the Seven Days' Battles. By the same token, Lord Edward returned home believing that Southern Anglophobia was a Northern myth.

63. Cueto had arrived in America at around the same time that W. H. Russell gave up trying to follow the Army of the Potomac. Put off by Russell's tangle with officialdom, Cueto decided he would work as a free agent, travelling without passes or letters to wherever the action seemed most exciting. He did not get very far. A Yankee civilian remembered meeting him while they were both imprisoned in Castle Godwin. 'Soon after I learned . . . that Cueto had died of typhoid fever in New York City.' George Washington Frosst, *A South Berwick Yankee behind Confederate Lines (Part II)*. Cueto was in a Confederate prison in North Carolina for eight months before he was able to smuggle out a letter to Consul Bunch in late November 1862. The Consul immediately sent a letter of protest to Judah P. Benjamin, who ordered an investigation into Cueto's arrest.

64. But when Major George Longley started a fight with a Federal officer while travelling on a Northern train, and was arrested for breaching the peace, *The Times* awarded him ample space to complain about his treatment. William Stuart, Secretary of the legation, was much less sympathetic. He refused to protest on Longley's behalf, saying that the Major had failed to mention, 'as stated in Mr Bernal's despatch', 'that you had remarked to Colonel Massey, that you believed the South to be in the right . . . which must have given just grounds to a Federal Officer with whom you were unaquainted'. PRO FO115/340, f. 36, Stuart to Major Longley, 28 September 1862.

65. Catherine Cooper Hopley, *Life in the South from the Commencement of the War by a Blockaded British Subject* (London, 1863, repr. New York, 1971), p. 348.

66. Strode, *Jefferson Davis*, vol. 2, p. 260.

67. Dawson, *Reminiscences*, p. 49.

68. Ibid., p. 51.

69. James M. Morgan, *Recollections of a Rebel Reefer* (Boston, 1917), pp. 226–7.

70. Devon RO, 867B/Z36, entr. 14, 5 July 1862, unknown writer.

CHAPTER 12. THE SOUTH IS RISING

1. William Watson, *Life in the Confederate Army: Being the Observations and Experiences of an Alien in the South during the Civil War* (London, 1887; repr. Baton Rouge, La., 1995), p. 398.

2. Ibid., p. 407.

3. Ibid., p. 413.

4. W. C. Ford (ed.), *A Cycle of Adams Letters, 1861–1865*, 2 vols. (Boston, 1920), vol. 1, p. 146, Henry Adams to Charles Francis Adams Jr., 16 May 1862.

5. Ibid., p. 145.

6. Ibid., p. 137, Charles Francis Adams to Charles Francis Adams Jr., 17 April 1862.

7. Sarah Agnes Wallace and Frances Elma Gillespie (eds.), *The Journal of Benjamin Moran, 1857–1865*, 2 vols. (Chicago, 1948, 1949), vol. 2, p. 996, 6 May 1862.

8. Ford (ed.), *A Cycle of Adams Letters*, vol. 1, p. 145, Henry Adams to Charles Francis Adams Jr., 16 May 1862.

9. Ibid., p. 141, Henry Adams to Charles Francis Adams Jr., 8 May 1862.

10. Countess of Stafford (ed.), *Leaves from the Diary of Henry Greville*, vol. 4 (London, 1905), p. 46, 10 May 1862.

11. John Black Atkins, *The Life of Sir William Howard Russell*, 2 vols. (London, 1911), vol. 2, p. 173.

12. Ford (ed.), *A Cycle of Adams Letters*, vol. 1, p. 142, Henry Adams to Charles Francis Adams Jr., 8 May 1862.

13. MHS, Adams MSS, Diary of Charles Francis Adams, 19 May 1862.

14. *Illustrated London News*, 14 June 1862.

15. H. F. Bell, *Palmerston*, 2 vols. (London, 1936), vol. 2, p. 317.

16. Edward Chalfant, *Better in Darkness* (New York, 1994), p. 39.

17. MHS, Adams MSS, Diary of Charles Francis Adams, 12 June 1862.

18. Wallace and Gillespie (eds.), *The Journal of Benjamin Moran*, vol. 2, p. 1029, 25 June 1862.

19. MHS, Adams MSS, Diary of Charles Francis Adams, 12 July 1862.

20. F. L. Owsley, *King Cotton Diplomacy* (2nd edn., Chicago, 1959), p. 145.

21. Norman Longmate, *Hungry Mills: The Story of the Lancashire Cotton Famine, 1861–5* (London, 1978), p. 95.

22. D. P. Crook, *The North, the South, and the Powers, 1861–1865* (New York, 1974), p. 198.

23. The problem for the North and the South was that the cotton famine had been brought on by a complicated set of circumstances. The distress suffered by the workers was real, but the 'famine' was a combination of overproduction during the previous three years, a surplus of some grades of cotton and a dearth of other grades. As Howard Jones writes, 'The initial surplus led to reduced work time, and its eventual depletion extended the layoffs.' Jones, *Blue and Gray Diplomacy* (Chapel Hill, NC, 2009), p. 227. Also, in the first year of the war, the cotton glut in England was so great that Northern textile mills were actually able to buy surplus British stock and ship it over.

24. Robert Douthat Meade, *Judah P. Benjamin: Confederate Statesman* (Baton Rouge, La., 2001), p. 248.

25. ORN, ser. 2, vol. 3, pp. 402–4, James Spence to James Mason, 28 April 1862.

26. Virginia Mason, *The Public Life and Diplomatic Correspondence of James M. Mason* (New York, 1906), pp. 271–2, Dispatch 9, Mason to Benjamin, 2 May 1862.

27. Trinity College Library, Cambridge, Houghton MS CB36/2[3], Henry Bright to Lord Houghton, 22 July 1862.

28. Library of Congress, Hotze Papers, Private Letter Book, Hotze to John George Witt, 11 August 1864.

29. For example, as Dudley Mann wrote excitedly to Judah P. Benjamin on 15 September 1862, after *Blackwood's* published a long article about Jefferson Davis, written by the Hon. Robert Bourke: '*Blackwood* stands in the same relation to the British periodical press as the *Times* does to the British newspaper press. They are wonderfully influential in molding European opinion; for their power is not confined to Great Britain' ORN, ser. 2, vol. 3, pp. 528–9.

30. OR, ser. 4, vol. 2, pp. 23–5, Edwin De Leon to Judah P. Benjamin, 30 July 1862.

31. Hotze's competitor was a shabby little rag called the *London American*, edited by the eccentric George Francis Train. By coincidence, its offices were one door

down, separated from the *Index* by a tobacconist's. The *Liverpool Mail* once described Train as 'our extremely fast Yankee cousin, famous for making galloping speeches, for writing galloping books, and galloping himself around the world' (4 Feb. 1860).

32. Ford (ed.), *A Cycle of Adams Letters*, vol. 1, p. 153, Henry Adams to Charles Francis Adams Jr., 6 June 1862.

33. ORN, ser. 2, vol. 3, p. 326, Henry Hotze to Robert Mercer Hunter, 1 February 1862.

34. Thurlow Weed, Harriet A. Weed and Thurlow Weed Barnes, *Life of Thurlow Weed*, 2 vols (Boston, 1884), vol. 2, p. 416, Weed to New York Common Council, 1 July 1862.

35. Edward Dicey, *Spectator of America*, ed. Herbert Mitgang (Athens, Ga., 1971), p. 144.

36. For example, the *Illustrated London News* asked on 19 April 1862 why it was that Americans were so sensitive about British criticism – and why the English had such a knack for provoking them with 'ill-timed and unfair comment'. 'The explanation', it decided, 'is to be found in their mutual ignorance of each other's feelings and modes of thought. America does not understand England, and England does not understand America.'

37. 'I am disturbed by the state of feeling which is growing up between our two countries,' he continued. 'It matters not how averse your government or ours may be to war, your people have become so inflamed against us by the daily ministrations of the press that no government will be strong enough to control their resentment. National Library of Scotland, Tweeddale Mun./Yester MSS, (0439)MS14467, ff. 40–43, John Bigelow to Lord Russell, 2 August 1862.

38. For example, on 8 August, Secretary of War Stanton announced that citizens eligible for the draft (which called for 300,000 new soldiers) were forbidden to travel abroad. That day, the British legation sent a report that hundreds of British travellers were being hauled off trains and arrested at quaysides on the pretext of being 'draft evaders'. Among the Britons forcibly removed from a Baltimore train was a Mr Drury, the legation's diplomatic messenger. PRO 30/36/1, desp. 150, William Stuart to Lord Russell, 14 August 1862. *Letters of Lord St Maur and Lord Edward St Maur* (London, 1888), p. 250, n.d, *c.* 1862.

39. Countess of Stafford (ed.), *Leaves from the Diary of Henry Greville*, vol. 4, p. 55.

40. E. D. Adams, *Great Britain and the American Civil War*, 2 vols. in 1 (New York, 1958), vol. 1, pp. 305–7.

41. Brian Jenkins, *Britain and the War for the Union*, 2 vols. (Montreal, 1974, 1980), vol. 2, p. 88.

42. R. J. M. Blackett, *Divided Hearts: Britain and the American Civil War* (Baton Rouge, La., 2001), p. 173.

43. Adams, *Great Britain and the American Civil War*, vol. 2, p. 20, Lyons to Stuart, 5 July 1862.

44. 'I know it will be said that this is giving them the means and money for a pro-longation of the contest,' admitted the Duke. 'But its effect in this way would be comparatively small, whilst it would greatly tend to dissipate the danger which is really a growing one.' MHS, Argyll Letters, p. 99, Argyll to Sumner, 12 July 1862.

45. However, Zebina Eastman obtained circumstantial evidence in November that Lindsay's firm purchased the *Calypso* for blockade-running. NARA, M. T-185, roll 7, vol. 7, Eastman to Seward, 20 November 1862.

46. Ford (ed.), *A Cycle of Adams Letters*, vol. 1, p. 163, Henry Adams to Charles Francis Adams Jr., 4 July 1862.

47. Howard Jones, *Union in Peril: The Crisis over British Intervention in the Civil War* (Chapel Hill, NC, 1992), p. 127.

48. Adams, *Great Britain and the American Civil War*, vol. 2, p. 20, Lyons to Stuart, 5 July 1862.

49. *MPUS*, p. 133, Adams to Seward, 11 July 1862.

50. Crook, *The North, the South, and the Powers*, p. 214.

51. West Sussex RO, Lyons MSS, Box 300, Lyons to sister, 19 July 1862. 'I had a long talk with Lord Palmerston. I had also a sufficiently long conversation with Lord Derby at his own home.'

52. Wallace and Gillespie (eds.), *The Journal of Benjamin Moran*, vol. 2, p. 1037, 17 July 1862.

53. MHS, Adams MSS, Diary of Charles Francis Adams, 17 July 1862.

54. Jones, *Union in Peril*, p. 133.

55. Jenkins, *Britain and the War for the Union*, vol. 2, p. 100.

56. Ford (ed.) *A Cycle of Adams Letters*, vol. 1, p. 167, Henry Adams to Charles Francis Adams Jr., 19 July 1862.

57. OR, ser. 4, vol. 2, pp. 23–5, Edwin De Leon to Judah Benjamin, 30 July 1862.

58. Wallace and Gillespie (eds.), *The Journal of Benjamin Moran*, vol. 2, p. 1044, 19 July 1862.

59. Confederate propaganda had been so successful that the great humanitarian and social reformer Lord Shaftesbury was firmly pro-South on *moral grounds*. He told John Slidell that he 'viewed it as a struggle, on the one hand, for inde-pendence and self-government, on the other, for empire, political power, and material interests'. ORN, ser. 2, vol. 3, pp. 546–8, Slidell to Judah Benjamin, 29 September 1862. Edwin De Leon claimed, 'With the tide of public opinion running so strong in England that even Lord Shaftesbury and Exeter Hall now abandon their Yankee sympathies as untrue . . .' OR, ser. 4, vol. 2, p. 128, De Leon to Benjamin, 30 September 1862.

60. *MPUS*, p. 160, Adams to Seward, 17 July 1862.

61. Quoted in Crook, *The North, the South and the Powers*, p. 219.

62. The reality of the situation, however, was much more complicated than Moran or Dudley allowed. The American Consul in Dundee was probably closer to the mark when he wrote that it was more of a matter of who got to whom first. 'I have reason to believe', he told Seward on 17 June, 'that there are officials in HM

govt that could be very easily induced to take service in the ranks of the U States or the so-called Confederate States quite indifferently.' NARA, M.T-200, roll 3, vol. 3, US Consuls in Dundee, Consul J. B. Holderby to Seward, 17 June 1862.

63. On 1 May 1862 Lord Russell told Lord Lyons that 'separation would be best for the North as well as for the South ... for the future welfare of the free, and for the future emancipation of the slave'. PRO FO/5/189.

64. Philip Guedalla (ed.), *Gladstone and Palmerston, being the Correspondence of Lord Palmerston and Mr Gladstone 1851–1865* (London, 1928), pp. 230–31.

65. ORN, ser. 2, vol. 3, pp. 505–8, Hotze to Benjamin, 6 August 1862.

66. *George Douglas, Eighth Duke of Argyll (1823–1900): Autobiography and Memoirs*, ed. the Dowager Duchess of Argyll, 2 vols. (London, 1906), vol. 2, p. 193, Argyll to Gladstone, 2 September 1862.

67. David F. Krein, *The Last Palmerston Government* (Ames, Iowa, 1978), p. 65.

68. Jenkins, *Britain and the War for the Union*, vol. 2, p. 112.

69. Krein, *The Last Palmerston Government*, p. 66.

70. *New York Times*, 13 August 1862.

71. T. C. Pease and J. Randall (eds.), *The Diary of Orville H. Browning, 1850–1881* (Springfield, Ill., 1925–31), p. 562, 24 July 1862.

72. Charles P. Cullop, 'An Unequal Duel: Union Recruiting in Ireland, 1863–1864', *Civil War History*, 13 (1967), p. 104.

73. Adams, *Great Britain and the American Civil War*, vol. 2, p. 34, fn.

74. *Letters of Lord St Maur and Lord Edward St Maur*, p. 250, n.d.

75. OR, ser. 1, vol. 17/2, p. 671, Thomas Jordan to General Beauregard, 7 August 1862.

76. David H. Donald, *Lincoln* (New York, 1995), p. 366.

77. 'The Journal of Robert Neve', private collection, p. 53.

78. Robert L. Kincaid, *The Wilderness Road* (Middlesboro, Ky., 1966), p. 246.

79. Brian Holden Reid, *Robert E. Lee* (London, 2005), p. 106.

80. John B. Jones, *A Rebel War Clerk's Diary at the Confederate States Capital*, ed. Earl Schenck Miers (Urbana, Ill., 1958), pp. 95–6, 27, 28 August 1862.

81. Ford (ed.), *A Cycle of Adams Letters*, vol. 1, p. 177, Charles Francis Adams Jr., to Charles Francis Adams, 27 August 1862.

82. Edward G. Longacre, *Jersey Cavaliers* (Hightstown, NJ, 1992), p. 100.

83. Captain W. D. L'Estrange, *Under Fourteen Flags: The Remarkable True Story of a Victorian Soldier of Fortune* (Newton Stewart, 1999), p. 80.

84. George Templeton Strong, *Diary of the Civil War 1860–1865*, ed. Allan Nevins (New York, 1962), p. 252, 4 September 1862.

CHAPTER 13. IS BLOOD THICKER THAN WATER?

1. Henry Adams, *The Education of Henry Adams*, ed. Ernest Samuels (repr. Boston, 1973), p. 128.

2. Sarah Agnes Wallace and Frances Elma Gillespie (eds.), *The Journal of Benjamin Moran, 1857–1865*, 2 vols. (Chicago, 1948, 1949), vol. 2, p. 1068, 9 September 1862.

3. Ibid., p. 1058, 22 August 1862.

4. Ibid., p. 1071, 13 and 14 September 1862.

5. Durham University, Gen. Charles Grey MSS, GRE/D/VI/7, General Grey to Henry, 3rd Earl Grey, 11 September 1862.

6. Adams, *Education of Henry Adams*, p. 129.

7. On 2 September the British Ambassador in Paris, Lord Cowley, had heard that opinion in the Cabinet was tilting 'in favour of mediation in America', and that if the Emperor were to announce publicly what he was saying in private to the Confederates, England would probably go along with him. David F. Krein, *The Last Palmerston Government* (Ames, Iowa, 1978), p. 66.

8. *MPUS*, p. 184, Charles Francis Adams to William Henry Seward, 4 September 1862.

9. ORN, ser. 2, vol. 3, p. 524, Dudley Mann to Judah Benjamin, 5 September 1862.

10. Sir Spencer Walpole, *Life of Lord John Russell*, 2 vols. (New York, 1968), vol. 2, p. 349, Russell to Palmerston, 17 September 1862.

11. ORN, ser. 2, vol. 3, pp. 535–536, Hotze to Benjamin, 26 September 1862.

12. Ibid., pp. 546–8, Slidell to Benjamin, 29 September 1862.

13. The Confederates in Europe were helped by recent reports in the European press that showed Lincoln in a poor light as far as abolition was concerned. One referred to Lincoln's meeting on 14 August with a delegation of freedmen. The President had been frank about his fears for them, saying it would be best for everyone if the black population emigrated somewhere else, perhaps Central America. David Donald points out that, despite the message, the fact of the meeting was momentous – African-Americans had always been barred from the White House. David H. Donald, *Lincoln* (New York, 1995), p. 368.

14. In London, William Gregory naively asked the Southern Commissioners whether the Confederacy could not devise an education programme for the slaves so that they might eventually earn enough money to buy their own freedom. He was offered many reasons why this was absolutely impossible. Brian Jenkins, *Sir William Gregory of Coole: A Biography* (Gerrards Cross, 1986), p. 154. The American Consul in Bristol reported that Yancey had been flagrant in his promises, telling one author of a pro-Confederate article that Richmond had given him 'full powers to pledge gradual emancipation to the governments of Europe on condition of their guaranteeing the independence of the Confederate States.' NARA, M. T-185, roll 7, vol. 7, Zebina Eastman to William Henry Seward, 20 October 1862.

15. University of Southampton, Hartley Library, Palmerston MSS, GC/AR/25/1, Argyll to Palmerston, 2 September 1862.

16. PRO 30/22/14D, Palmerston to Russell, 22 September 1862.

17. Philip Guedalla (ed.), *Gladstone and Palmerston, being the Correspondence of Lord Palmerston and Mr Gladstone 1851–1865* (London, 1928), p. 232, Palmerston to Gladstone, 24 September 1862.

18. Thomas Nelson Page, *Lee, Man and Soldier* (New York, 1911), p. 219, Lee to Davis, 8 September 1862.

19. William Mark McKnight, *Blue Bonnets o'er the Border: The 79th New York Cameron Highlanders* (Shippensburg, Pa., 1998), p. 72.

20. Shelby Foote, *The Civil War*, 3 vols. (New York, 1986), vol. 1, pp. 664–5.

21. Wilbur D. Jones, *Giants in the Cornfield* (Shippensburg, Pa., 1997), p. 292.

22. Russell Weigley, *A Great Civil War* (Bloomington, Ind., 2000), p. 148.

23. OR, ser. 1, vol. 19/2, p. 218, McClellan to President, 13 September 1861.

24. Robert Underwood Johnson and Clarence Clough Buel (eds.), *Battles and Leaders of the Civil War*, 4 vols. (Secaucus, NJ, 1985), vol. 2, p. 660.

25. Ibid., pp. 660–61.

26. Captain W. D. L'Estrange, *Under Fourteen Flags, being the Life and Adventures of Brigadier-General MacIver* (Newton Stewart, Wigtonshire, 1999), p. 83.

27. Charles Augustus Fuller, *Personal Recollections of the War* (Fairford, repr. 2010), p. 40.

28. James M. McPherson, *Crossroads of Freedom: Antietam* (Oxford, 2004), p. 127.

29. David L. Thompson, 'With Burnside at Antietam', in Johnson and Buel (eds.), *Battles and Leaders of the Civil War*, vol. 2, p. 556.

30. Matthew J. Graham, *The Ninth Regiment New York Volunteers* (Lancaster, Ohio, 1997), p. 303.

31. James M. McPherson (ed.), *Battle Chronicles of the Civil War*, 6 vols. (Lakeville, Conn., 1989), vol. 2, p. 252.

32. New York Historical Society, *Narrative of Ebenezer Wells* (c. 1881).

33. James M. McPherson, *Battle Cry of Freedom* (London, 1988), p. 544.

34. Devonshire MSS, Chatsworth, 2nd series (340.180), Lord Hartington to Duke of Devonshire, 29 September 1862.

35. Ibid.

36. Ibid.

37. Donald, *Lincoln*, p. 375.

38. Frederick Bancroft, *The Life of William H. Seward*, 2 vols. (Gloucester, Mass., 1967), vol. 2, p. 338.

39. Francis W. Dawson, *Reminiscences of Confederate Service, 1861–1865*, ed. Bell I. Wiley (Baton Rouge, La., 1980), p. 66.

40. Ibid., p. 193, Dawson to mother, 23 April 1863.

41. Ibid., p. 56.

42. S. Frank Logan, 'Frances W. Dawson, 1840–1889: South Carolina Editor', MA thesis, Duke University, 1947, p. 27.

43. Dawson, *Reminiscences*, p. 69.

44. Ibid., p. 190, Dawson to mother, 22 November 1862.

45. Wolseley was not the only British soldier to request a leave of absence in order to observe the war. Captain Edward Osborne Hewett, RE, also travelled around the North during October and November 1862. He wrote a report for the army which is now lost. See R. A. Preston, 'A Letter from a British Military Observer of the American Civil War', *Military Affairs*, 16 (1952), pp. 49–60.

46. James A. Rawley (ed.), *The American Civil War: An English View* (Mechanicsburg, Pa., 2002), p. xiii.

47. Brian Jenkins, 'Frank Lawley and the Confederacy', *Civil War History* (March 1977), p. 149.

48. William Stanley Hoole, *Lawley Covers the Confederacy* (Tuscaloosa, Ala., 1964), p. 15.

49. Ibid., pp. 20–21, *The Times*, 4 November 1862.

50. PRO FO 5.909, ff. 36–7, n. 5, Moore to Russell, 11 January 1863.

51. Anon. (Wolseley), 'A Month's Visit to the Confederate Headquarters', *Blackwood's Magazine*, 93 (Jan. 1863), p. 17.

52. Captain Hewett wrote of Northern officers: 'At the end of a day's march the officers look out for themselves; never see that their men are properly and completely encamped, or fed, much less that the poor horses are fed or looked after; that the men's arms, accoutrements, or artillery or cavalry harness is cleaned or repaired, or in fact anything at all till the general order to fall in for the next day's march.' Preston, 'A Letter from a British Military Observer', p. 53. William Howard Russell had previously noticed that the social hierarchy of the South was replicated in the Confederate army, which shored up the chain of command between officers and men.

53. Wolseley was surprised and amused by the ever-present immediacy of the Revolutionary War. Wherever an Englishman wanders, he wrote, 'his fellow-passengers in railway carriages or stages will invariably begin talking to him about Smiths, Browns, and Tomkinses in the same strain that we are accustomed to hear allusions made to the Pitts and to Marlborough or Wellington ... If this war has no other result, therefore, it will at least afford American historians something to write about, and save them from the puerility of detailing skirmishes in the backwoods or on the highlands of Mexico, as if they were so many battles of Waterloo or Solferino.' Anon. (Wolseley), 'A Month's Visit to the Confederate Headquarters', p. 16.

54. Ibid., p. 14.

55. Ibid., p. 18.

56. Hoole, *Lawley*, pp. 31–2, *The Times*, 30 December 1862.

57. G. F. R. Henderson, *Stonewall Jackson and the American Civil War* (1898; repr. Cambridge, Mass., 1988), p. 554, fn.

58. Anon. (Wolseley), 'A Month's Visit to the Confederate Headquarters', p. 21.

59. *The Times*, 30 December 1862.

60. If Wolseley had seen them in action, he might have revised his opinion. Another English observer thought that neither side was particularly adept at

traditional cavalry engagements. 'They approach one another with considerable boldness, until they get to within about forty yards, and then, at the very moment when a dash is necessary, and the sword alone should be used, they hesitate, halt, and commence a desultory fire with carbines and revolvers ... Stuart's cavalry can hardly be called cavalry in the European sense of the word.' Quoted in Jay Luvaas, *The Military Legacy of the Civil War* (Lawrence, Kan., 1988), p. 21. On the other hand, both sides learned how to use their cavalry as effective scouts.

61. Heros von Borcke had arrived in the Confederacy in early May, via a block-ade-runner called the *Hero*. He was a tall, strapping German with a shock of blond hair and an unintelligible accent. He had decided to volunteer out of bore-dom with garrison duty, or, according to another version, to annoy his father. He was close in age to Stuart, and they became friends immediately. Borcke wrote his own highly coloured reminiscences of his Confederate career. Nevertheless, his wounds were real and a bullet remained permanently lodged in his lung. After his return to the ancestral castle, von Borcke occasionally flew the Confederate flag from the turrets.

62. William Stanley Hoole, *Vizetelly Covers the Confederacy* (Tuscaloosa, Ala., 1957), pp. 58–9.

63. Ibid., pp. 555–6, quoted from Heros von Borcke, 'Memoirs of the Confeder-ate War for Independence', *Blackwood's Magazine*, 99 (Jan.–June 1866), p. 90.

64. Anon. (Wolseley), 'A Month's Visit to the Confederate Headquarters', p. 24.

65. Ibid., pp. 24–5, 29.

CHAPTER 14. A FATEFUL DECISION

1. Sarah Agnes Wallace and Frances Elma Gillespie (eds.), *The Journal of Ben-jamin Moran, 1857–1865*, 2 vols. (Chicago, 1948, 1949), vol. 2, p. 1076, 30 September 1862.

2. Duncan Andrew Campbell, *English Public Opinion and the American Civil War* (Woodbridge, 2003), p. 103.

3. Countess of Stafford (ed.), *Leaves from the Diary of Henry Greville*, vol. 4 (London, 1905), p. 73, 29 September 1862.

4. Clare Taylor, *British and American Abolitionists: An Episode in Transatlantic Understanding* (Edinburgh, 1974), p. 491, George Thompson to William Lloyd Garrison, 25 December 1862.

5. Howard Jones, *Blue and Gray Diplomacy* (Chapel Hill, NC, 2009), p. 232.

6. He added: 'Lincoln has a certain moral dignity, but is intellectually inferior, & as men do not generally measure others correctly who are above their own cal-iber, he has chosen for his instruments mediocre men ... I know the men at the head of affairs on both sides, & I should say that in energy of will, in comprehen-siveness of view, in habits & power of command, & in knowledge of economical & fiscal questions, Jefferson Davis is more than equal to Lincoln & all his

Cabinet.' Elizabeth Hoon Cawley (ed.), *The American Diaries of Richard Cobden* (Princeton, 1952), p. 75, Cobden to Bright, 7 October 1862.

7. *The Times*, 7 October 1862. Even Liberal newspapers were shocked. The *Morning Advertiser* remarked on 6 October: 'We can give no credit to President Lincoln . . . the motive was not any abhorrence of Slavery in itself, but a sordid, selfish motive, nor can we approve the means to which he is prepared to resort.' For Britain, the atrocities committed in the Indian Mutiny were still fresh memories. The suggestion that Lincoln was trying to engineer similar mayhem and bloodshed in the South was enough to stir the public against him.

8. E. D. Adams, *Great Britain and the American Civil War*, 2 vols. (New York, 1958), vol. 2, p. 44. For an in-depth discussion of the 'intervention crisis' the following sources are indispensible: Robert Huhn Jones, 'Anglo-American Relations, 1861–1865, Reconsidered', *Mid-America: An Historical Review*, 45 (Jan. 1963), pp. 36–49; Martin P. Claussen, 'Peace Factors in Anglo-American Relations, 1861–5', *Mississippi Valley Historical Review*, 26/4 (March 1940), pp. 511–22; Henry Adams, 'Why Did Not England Recognize the Confederacy?', *Massachusetts Historical Society Proceedings*, 66 (1972), pp. 204–22; Davis D. Joyce, 'Pro-Confederate Sympathy in the British Parliament', *Social Science* (April 1969), pp. 95–100; Kinley J. Brauer, 'British Mediation and the American Civil War: A Reconsideration', *Journal of Southern History*, 38/1 (Feb. 1972), pp. 49–64; Frank J. Merli and Theodore A. Wilson, 'The British Cabinet and the Confederacy: Autumn, 1862', *Maryland Historical Society* (Fall 1967), pp. 239–62; Robert L. Reid (ed.), 'William E. Gladstone's "Insincere Neutrality" during the Civil War', *Civil War History*, 15/4 (1969), pp. 293–307; Howard Jones, *Union in Peril: The Crisis over British Intervention in the Civil War* (Chapel Hill, NC, 1992); Brian Jenkins, *Britain and the War for the Union*, 2 vols. (Montreal, 1974, 1980); Charles M. Hubbard, *The Burden of Confederate Diplomacy* (Knoxville, Tenn., 1998).

9. Adams, *Great Britain and the American Civil War*, vol. 2, p. 45, Russell to Palmerston, 2 October 1862.

10. Roy Jenkins, *Gladstone* (London, 1995), p. 472.

11. *George Douglas, Eighth Duke of Argyll (1823–1900): Autobiography and Memoirs*, ed. the Dowager Duchess of Argyll, 2 vols. (London, 1906), vol. 2, p. 195, Argyll to Gladstone, 2 September 1862.

12. Jenkins, *Gladstone*, pp. 472, 466.

13. ORN, ser. 2, vol. 3, pp. 549–51, Dudley Mann to Judah Benjamin, 7 October 1862.

14. John Morley, *The Life of William Ewart Gladstone: 1809–1872*, 2 vols. (London, 1908), vol. 2, p. 536, and Henry Steele Commager (ed.), *The Civil War Archive* (New York, 2000), pp. 362–3. The quotation in the footnote below is from *Harper's Magazine*, 54 (1877), p. 111.

15. MHS, Adams MSS, Diary of Charles Francis Adams, 5 October 1862.

16. D. P. Crook, *The North, the South and the Powers, 1861–1865* (New York, 1974), p. 266, 8 November 1862.

17. The literature on the Cabinet discussions during October and November is voluminous. See Adams, *Great Britain and the American Civil War*, vol. 2, p. 52, for a discussion on the memoranda wars.

18. Henry Adams, *The Education of Henry Adams*, ed. Ernest Samuels (repr. Boston, 1973), pp. 183–4.

19. Adams, *Great Britain and the American Civil War*, vol. 2, p. 54, Clarendon to Russell, 19 October 1862.

20. ORN, ser. 2, vol. 3, pp. 560–61, Slidell to Benjamin, 20 October 1862.

21. Virginia Mason, *The Public Life and Diplomatic Correspondence of James M. Mason* (New York, 1906), pp. 371–2, Mason to wife, 18 January 1863.

22. ORN, ser. 2, vol. 3, pp. 565–67, Hotze to Benjamin, 24 October 1862.

23. Adams, *Great Britain and the American Civil War*, vol. 2, p. 56. In his memorandum, written on 25 October 1862, Gladstone insisted, somewhat improbably, that the Americans would not be able to resist 'a general opinion on the part of civilized Europe that this horrible war ought to cease'.

24. MHS, Adams MSS, Diary of Charles Francis Adams, 23 October 1862.

25. Adams, *Great Britain and the American Civil War*, vol. 2, p. 56, Russell to Palmerston, 24 October 1862.

26. West Sussex RO, Lyons MSS, Box 300, Lyons to sister, 24 October 1862.

27. ORN, ser. 2, vol. 3, pp. 542–78, Slidell to Benjamin, 28 October 1862.

28. G. P. Gooch (ed.), *The Later Correspondence of Lord John Russell, 1840–1878*, 2 vols. (London, 1925), vol. 2, p. 331, Russell to Grey, 28 October 1862.

29. Sir Herbert Maxwell, *Clarendon*, 2 vols. (London, 1913), vol. 2, p. 265, Clarendon to Lewis, 25 October 1862.

30. PRO 30/22/36, ff. 281–9, Lyons to Russell, 11 November 1862.

31. Jones, *Union in Peril*, p. 203.

32. Gooch (ed.), *The Later Correspondence of Lord John Russell*, vol. 2, p. 333, Palmerston to Russell, 2 November 1862.

33. ORN, ser. 2, vol. 3, p. 603, Hotze to Benjamin, 7 November 1862.

34. Deborah Logan (ed.), *The Collected Letters of Harriet Martineau*, 5 vols. (London, 2007), vol. 4, p. 365, 17 September 1862.

35. Wallace and Gillespie (eds.), *The Journal of Benjamin Moran*, vol. 2, p. 1088, 11 November 1862.

36. Maxwell, *Clarendon*, vol. 2, p. 268, Lewis to Clarendon, 11 November 1862.

37. Jones, *Union in Peril*, p. 217.

38. Morley, *The Life of William Ewart Gladstone*, vol. 2, p. 538, Gladstone to wife, 13 November 1862.

39. ORN, ser. 2, vol. 3, pp. 610–12, Hotze to Benjamin, 22 November 1862.

40. Quoted in Jones, *Union in Peril*, p. 223.

41. e.g. Keele University, Sneyd MS, S[rs/hwv]/274, Henry William Vincent to Ralph Sneyd, 17 November 1862.

42. ORN, ser. 2, vol. 3, p. 618, Mason to Benjamin, 11 December 1862.

CHAPTER 15. BLOODBATH AT FREDERICKSBURG

1. Sarah Agnes Wallace and Frances Elma Gillespie (eds.), *The Journal of Benjamin Moran, 1857–1865*, 2 vols. (Chicago, 1948, 1949), vol. 2, p. 1092, 19 November 1862.

2. *The Reminiscences of Carl Schurz*, ed. Carl Schurz, Frederick Bancroft and William Archibald Dunning, 3 vols. (Garden City, NY, 1917), vol. 2, p. 246.

3. W. C. Ford (ed.), *A Cycle of Adams Letters, 1861–1865*, 2 vols. (Boston, 1920), vol. 1, p. 195, Henry Adams to Charles Francis Adams Jr., 21 November 1862.

4. Duke University, Malet family MSS, Kennedy to Malet, 15 September 1862.

5. Calvin D. Davis, 'A British Diplomat and the American Civil War: Edward Malet in the United States', *South Atlantic Quarterly*, 77/2 (1978), pp. 160–61. In his memoir, Malet wrote that he always regretted obtaining his first post through his father's influence. 'For many years it did me harm,' he wrote. 'The grade above mine was that of paid attaché, and ten of my juniors were passed to that rank over my head on the ground that I had been appointed when I ought to have been still in the schoolroom.' E. Malet, *Shifting Scenes* (London, 1901), p. 18.

6. Davis, 'A British Diplomat and the American Civil War', p. 171.

7. Ibid., p. 163.

8. Duke University, Malet family MSS, Malet to Lady Malet, 10 February 1863.

9. Ibid., Malet to Lady Malet, 2 December 1862.

10. *The Civil War Papers of George B. McClellan: Selected Correspondence, 1860–1865*, ed. Stephen W. Sears (Cambridge, Mass., 1992), p. 517, McClellan to Lincoln, 2 November 1862.

11. Richard Wheeler, *Voices of the Civil War* (New York, 1990), p. 203.

12. The 12,000-strong corps was principally made up of German immigrants, and most of its commanders were foreign-born. A hero to many German-Americans on account of his military leadership of the Baden revolutionaries in the 1848 Revolution against Prussia, Sigel seemed to attract bad luck in the Civil War. At the Second Battle of Bull Run in August, his soldiers were mangled by the Confederates, resulting in the loss of 2,000 men. Since then, the 11th had been designated the Reserve Grand Division. Some of the German volunteers' English did not run much further than the corps's slogan: 'I fights mit Sigel'.

13. NARA, CB MID64, roll 66, Sir Percy Wyndham to General Heintzelman, 3 December 1862.

14. BL Add. MS 41567, f. 240, Herbert to mother, 3 January 1863.

15. Hugh Dubrulle, 'Fear of Americanization and the Emergence of an Anglo-Saxon Confederacy', *Albion: A Quarterly Journal Concerned with British Studies*, 33/4 (Winter 2001), pp. 583–613, at p. 604, Lt Colonel Henry Malet to Layard, 27 December 1862, BL Add. MS 39104, Layard Papers.

16. BL Add. MS 41567, ff. 236–7, Herbert to brother Jack, 26 November 1862.

17. Ibid.

18. BL Add. MS 41567, ff. 238–9, Herbert to brother Jack, 16 December 1862.

19. William Mark McNight, *Blue Bonnets o'er the Border: The 79th New York Cameron Highlanders* (Shippensburg, Pa., 1998), p. 83.

20. Francis W. Dawson, *Reminiscences of Confederate Service, 1861–1865*, ed. Bell I. Wiley (Baton Rouge, La., 1980), p. 83.

21. Shelby Foote, *The Civil War*, 3 vols. (New York, 1986), vol. 2, p. 22.

22. Wheeler, *Voices of the Civil War*, p. 206.

23. Heros von Borcke, 'Memoirs of the Confederate War for Independence', *Blackwood's Magazine*, 99 (Jan.–June 1866), p. 193.

24. After Wynne and Phillips came Colonel Bramston, followed by Captain Bushby, who 'had just run the blockade into Charleston, after an exciting chase by the Federal cruisers, and could only spare a few days to look at our army ...'. Bushby presented General Lee with a saddle and Stonewall Jackson with a breech-loading carbine. Borcke, 'Memoirs', p. 463.

25. Ibid., p. 194.

26. Mary Sophia Hill, *A British Subject's Recollections of the Confederacy* (Baltimore, 1875), p. 31.

27. Foote, *The Civil War*, vol. 2, p. 26.

28. Borcke, 'Memoirs' p. 196.

29. Nearly three decades later, a young British military historian and disciple of Viscount Wolseley summarized Burnside's mistakes: 'firstly, he underrated his antagonist; secondly, he neglected to reconnoitre as far as was within his power; thirdly, in preference to a line of operations which was feasible and safe, he selected one which ... might possibly lead to terrible disaster.' Lieutenant Colonel G. F. R. Henderson, *The Campaign of Fredericksburg* (London, 1886; privately repr., 1984), p. 36.

30. Mr Goolrick, the British Vice-Consul (who was actually an American citizen) was also among the captives. He had long been an embarrassment to Lord Lyons, providing ample fodder to Northern newspapers who claimed that every British official was rabidly pro-South. Lyons took advantage of his arrest to close the vice-consulate permanently.

31. William Stanley Hoole, *Lawley Covers the Confederacy* (Tuscaloosa, Ala., 1964), p. 39.

32. Robert Underwood Johnson and Clarence Clough Buel (eds.), *Battles and Leaders of the Civil War*, 4 vols. (Secaucus, NJ, 1985), vol. 3, p. 116.

33. Ibid., p. 127.

34. New York Historical Society, *Narrative of Ebenezer Wells* (c. 1881), 11 December 1862.

35. Henderson, *The Campaign of Fredericksburg*, p. 73.

36. *Illustrated London News*, 31 January 1863.

37. Brian Holden Reid, *Robert E. Lee* (London, 2005), p. 144.

38. Chicago Historical Society, George W. Hart MSS, George Hart to mother, 12 January 1863.

39. Hoole, *Lawley*, p. 40.

40. Johnson and Buel (eds.), *Battles and Leaders of the Civil War*, vol. 3, p. 116.

41. James A. Rawley (ed.), *The American Civil War: An English View* (Mechanicsburg, Pa., 2002), p. 158.

42. Hill, *A British Subject's Recollections of the Confederacy*, p. 30.

43. Borcke, 'Memoirs', p. 451. The quotation in the footnote on this page is from Stuart to G. W. C. Lee, 18 December 1862, quoted in *The Letters of General J. E. B. Stuart*, ed. Adele H. Mitchell (n.p.: Stuart-Mosby Historical Society, 1990), pp. 284–5.

44. *The Times*, 23 January 1863.

45. R. A. Preston, 'A Letter from a British Military Observer of the American Civil War', *Military Affairs*, 16 (1952), p. 55.

46. Quoted in Margaret Leach, *Reveille in Washington* (Alexandria, Va., 1962; repr. 1980), p. 276.

47. In contrast to the British army, assistant surgeons in the Northern army were ranked as lieutenants and generally afforded much greater respect. 'The social position of the medical, as compared with the combatant officers, is decidedly good, much better than in our own army,' Mayo explained to British readers in an essay about his experiences. It did not provoke comment that 'any person with decent prospects of success in civil practice should ever think of entering it'. Francis Galton (ed.), *Vacation Tourists, 1862–1863* (London, 1864), p. 376.

48. Ibid., p. 384.

49. Duke University, Malet family MSS, Malet to father, 16 December 1862.

50. Michael Burlingame, *Abraham Lincoln*, 2 vols. (Baltimore, 2008), vol. 2, p. 446.

51. George Templeton Strong, *Diary of the Civil War 1860–1865*, ed. Allan Nevins (New York, 1962), p. 282, 18 December 1862.

52. Ibid., p. 282, 21 December 1862.

53. Frederick W. Seward (ed.), *Seward at Washington* (New York, 1891), p. 487, Seward to wife, 28 December 1860.

54. *Diary of Gideon Welles*, 3 vols. (Boston, 1911), vol. 1, p. 133, 16 September 1862.

55. *MPUS*, p. 160, Adams to Seward, 31 July 1862.

56. MHS, Adams MSS, Diary of Charles Francis Adams, 22 December 1862.

57. PRO 30/22/36, ff. 320–23, Lyons to Russell, 12 December 1862.

58. *PRFA* (1862), p. 124, Seward to Adams, 5 July 1862.

59. Frederick J. Blue, *Salmon P. Chase: A Life in Politics* (Kent, Ohio, 1987), p. 191.

60. John M. Taylor, *William Henry Seward: Lincoln's Right Hand* (New York, 1991), p. 208.

61. David Herbert Donald, *Charles Sumner and the Rights of Man* (New York, 1970), p. 90.

62. Burlingame, *Abraham Lincoln*, vol. 2, p. 453.

63. PRO 30/22/36, ff. 327–30, Lyons to Russell, 22 December 1862.

64. James J. Barnes and Patience P. Barnes (eds.), *The American Civil War through British Eyes*, vol. 2 (Kent, Ohio, 2005), p. 282, Lyons to Russell, 26 December 1862.

65. *Rebellion Record: A Diary of American Events*, ed. Frank Moore, 12 vols. (New York, 1863), vol. 6, p. 299.

66. Devonshire MSS, Chatsworth, 2nd series (340.1831), Lord Hartington to Duke of Devonshire, 18 December 1862.

67. Ibid., Lord Hartington to Duke of Devonshire, 25 December 1862.

68. Ibid., Lord Hartington to Duke of Devonshire, 29 September 1862.

69. Ibid., Lord Hartington to Duke of Devonshire, 17 October 1862.

70. Ibid., Lord Hartington to Duke of Devonshire, 28 December 1862.

71. William Watson was in Baton Rouge, where slaves vastly outnumbered the white population. He watched his friends confront the possibility by speaking directly to their slaves. There seemed to be little desire to leave. 'If we run away, and go to New Orleans, like dem crazy niggers, where is we?' asked one slave wisely. 'If so be we are to get free, we get it anyhow.' William Watson, *Life in the Confederacy: Being the Observations and Experiences of an Alien in the South during the Civil War* (London, 1887; repr. Baton Rouge, La., 1995), p. 430.

72. Borcke, 'Memoirs', p. 458.

73. Devonshire MSS, Chatsworth, 2nd series (340.1831), Lord Hartington to Duke of Devonshire, 28 December 1862.

CHAPTER 16. THE MISSING KEY TO VICTORY

1. Charles Herbert Mayo, *Genealogical History of the Mayo and Elton Family* (privately printed, 1882), p. 230.

2. Doris Kearns Goodwin, *Team of Rivals* (New York, 2005), p. 498.

3. James McPherson, *Tried by War* (New York, 2009), p. 149.

4. Winston Groom, *Vicksburg, 1863* (New York, 2009), p. 132. It is important to note, however, that James McPherson does not believe that Lincoln ever said those words; he concludes that the conversation was fabricated by Admiral David Dixon Porter. Even so, Lincoln himself would have agreed with them. James McPherson, *This Mighty Scourge: Perspectives on the Civil War* (Oxford, 2007), p. 131.

5. *Memoirs of General William T. Sherman* (New York, 1876), p. 291.

6. Robert Underwood Johnson and Clarence Clough Buel (eds.), *Battles and Leaders of the Civil War*, 4 vols. (Secaucus, NJ, 1985), vol. 3, p. 467.

7. Ibid., p. 468.

8. Sherman wrote in his memoirs: 'one brigade (De Courcy's) of Morgan's troops crossed the bayou safely, but took to cover behind the bank, and could not be moved forward. Frank Blair's brigade, of Steele's division, in support, also crossed the bayou, passed over the space of level ground to the foot of the hills: but, being

unsupported by Morgan, meeting a very severe cross-fire of artillery, was staggered and gradually fell back . . . I have always felt that it was due to the failure of General G. W. Morgan to obey his orders, or to fulfill his promise made in person. Had he used with skill and boldness one of his brigades, in addition to that of Blair's, he could have made a lodgment on the bluff, which would have opened the door for our whole force to follow.' *Memoirs*, pp. 291–2.

9. He continued: 'After capture, which was near night, we were marched through a drenching rain to Vicksburg, a distance of eleven miles, hungry and without blankets and were corralled in an old foundry where we laid on the cold wet ground for rest.' Personal papers of Major Milton Mills – 16th OVI, letter from Benjamin Heckert, description of Battle of Chickasaw Bayou, 21 December 1904, doc. B028–01:http://www.mkwe.com/ohio/pages/B028-01.htm.

10. OR, ser. 1, vol. 17/1, p. 650, 29 December 1862.

11. Owen Johnston Hopkins, *Under the Flag of the Nation: Diaries and Letters of a Yankee Volunteer* (Columbus, Ohio, 1961), p. 46. See also the diary of Sergeant Asa E. Sample of the 54th Indiana Infantry, who recorded his part in the Chickasaw assault: 'About this time the rebel batteries opened with canister shot and shell, replied to by our cannon in the rear. The ground before us was completely obstructed by fallen timber for near forty rods (660 feet). Over this we had to pass. Just now General DeCourcey gave the command "advance the 54th and 22nd Kentucky about 50 yards!!" The fallen trees completely mingled the companies of both regiments but onward we went, whiz, boom, boom, went the shells above us, now lying down to evade that bursting burst, now advancing and many falling.' http://www.hoosiersoldiers.com/54THINDIANA/1YEAR/DIARIES/SAMPLE/DIARY-DECEMBER-1862.htm.

12. Allan Nevins, *The War for the Union*, 4 vols.; vol. 2: *War Becomes Revolution 1862–1863* (New York, 1960), p. 386.

13. OR, ser. 1, vol. 17/1, S. 24, pp. 721–4, no. 4, Report by Brigadier General George Morgan, 13th Army Corps.

14. Ibid.

15. Ohio Historical Society, Series 147-74-188, De Courcy to Adjutant General, 31 January 1863.

16. William L. Shea and Terrence J. Winschel, *Vicksburg is the Key* (Lincoln, Nebr., 2003), p. 60.

17. Stanley Hirshson, *The White Tecumseh* (New York, 1997), p. 145.

18. John Y. Simon (ed.), *The Papers of Ulysses S. Grant*, 24 vols. (Carbondale, Ill., 2000), vol. 7, pp. 50–55. After the war, Grant denied that he was anti-Semitic and, to make amends, attended the dedication of the Adas Israel Congregation in Washington DC.

19. William Stanley Hoole, *Lawley Covers the Confederacy* (Tuscaloosa, Ala., 1964), p. 44.

20. OR, ser. 1, vol. 5, S. 5, p. 504. On 8 February, General Smith ended his report on a skirmish around Fairfax Court House by saying, 'Captain Currie, as usual, was everywhere to direct and make successful the expedition.'

21. New York State Library, Edwin Morgan MSS, box 19, f. 11, Currie to Governor Morgan, 2 March 1863.

22. William Watson, *Life in the Confederacy: Being the Observations and Experiences of an Alien in the South during the Civil War* (London, 1887; repr. Baton Rouge, La., 1995), p. 440.

23. Bruce Catton, *Never Call Retreat* (London, 2001), p. 74.

24. New York State Library, Edwin Morgan MSS, box 19, f. 11, Currie to Governor Morgan, 2 March 1863.

25. OR, ser. 1, vol. 15, S. 21, p. 250, telegram from L. D. H. Currie, 26 February 1863.

26. Once Banks had filled all the outposts and boosted the garrisons, his effective fighting force was less than half his 32,000 army. At first he thought that a run up the Mississippi river was still possible with just 12,000 men. Catton, *Never Call Retreat*, p. 76.

27. Mary Sophia Hill, *A British Subject's Recollections of the Confederacy* (Baltimore, 1875), p. 28.

28. Ibid.

29. Raphael Semmes, *Service Afloat: A Personal Memoir of my Cruises and Services* (1868; repr. Baltimore, 1987), p. 402.

30. Charles Grayson Summersell, *CSS Alabama* (Tuscaloosa, Ala., 1985), p. 13.

31. Semmes, *Service Afloat*, p. 405.

32. The officers either knew or were related to one another to a remarkable degree. Fifth Lieutenant Irvine Bulloch, for example, was James Bulloch's younger half-brother; Midshipman Edward Maffitt Anderson was the son of Edward Charles Anderson, who had directed the Confederate navy's purchasing operations so ably in 1861; and Midshipman Eugene Anderson Maffitt was his cousin.

33. Semmes, *Service Afloat*, p. 427.

34. Raimondo Luraghi, *A History of the Confederate Navy* (Annapolis, Md., 1996), p. 227.

35. In truth, the USS *Hatteras* was not such a formidable opponent after all, being little more than a refitted passenger ship with about half the *Alabama*'s firepower. Charles Grayson Summersell (ed.), *The Journal of George Townley Fullam* (Tuscaloosa, Ala., 1973), p. 72.

36. Semmes, *Service Afloat*, p. 543.

37. Norman C. Delaney, *John McIntosh Kell of the Raider Alabama* (Tuscaloosa, Ala., 1973), p. 143.

38. Douglas Maynard, 'Civil War "Care": The Mission of the *George Griswold*', *New England Quarterly*, 34/3 (1961), p. 300.

39. Ibid., p. 303.

40. David Herbert Donald, *Charles Sumner and the Rights of Man* (New York, 1970), p. 109.

41. PRO 30/22/37, ff. 29–30, Lyons to Russell, 24 February 1863.

42. Beverly Wilson Palmer (ed.), *The Selected Letters of Charles Sumner*, 2 vols. (Boston, 1990), vol. 1, p. 148, Sumner to John Bright, 16 March 1863.

43. Brian Jenkins, *Britain and the War for the Union*, 2 vols. (Montreal, 1974, 1980), vol. 2, p. 185. Modern, low-cost, British-built and -owned steamships were monopolizing the Atlantic trade because their American competitors were old-fashioned sailing boats.

44. *New York Times*, 21 November 1862.

CHAPTER 17. 'THE TINSEL HAS WORN OFF'

1. *Speeches, Arguments, Addresses, and Letters of Clement L. Vallandigham* (New York, 1864), p. 430.

2. BL Add. MS 415670, f. 245, Herbert to mother, 10 March 1863. The source for the footnote on this page is Francis Galton (ed.), *Vacation Tourists, 1862–1863* (London, 1864), p. 398.

3. Charles Herbert Mayo, *Genealogical History of the Mayo and Elton Family* (privately printed, 1882), p. 230.

4. Wendy Trewin, *All on Stage: Charles Wyndham and the Alberys* (London, 1980), p. 8.

5. Ibid., p. 11. This says his father encouraged him. But Wyndham himself says the family opposed the move and refused to support him financially. Thomas E. Pemberton, *Sir Charles Wyndham: A Biography* (London, 1904), pp. 8, 33.

6. Trewin, *All on Stage*, p. 18.

7. http://oha.alexandriava.gov/fortward/special-sections/voices/, testimony of William Wallace, 3rd Wisconsin Volunteer Infantry.

8. W. C. Ford (ed.), *A Cycle of Adams Letters, 1861–1865*, 2 vols. (Boston, 1920), vol. 1, p. 206, Charles Francis Adams Jr. to mother, 21 December 1862.

9. Wyndham was always a favourite with the press, and his side was taken by *Dawson's Daily Times and Union*, a popular Indiana newspaper, which declared that the resignation had been a matter of principle since he held Colonel Butler in such low esteem.

10. NARA, CB MID64, roll 66, Report by General Heintzelman, 20 January 1863.

11. BL Add. MS 415670, ff. 242–3, Herbert to Jack, 28 January 1863.

12. New York Historical Society, *Narrative of Ebenezer Wells* (c. 1881), January 1863.

13. BL Add. MS 415670, ff. 242–3, Herbert to Jack, 28 January 1863.

14. Ford (ed.), *A Cycle of Adams Letters*, vol. 1, p. 250, Charles Francis Adams Jr. to Henry Adams, 30 January 1863.

15. Ibid., p. 264, Charles Francis Adams Jr. to Charles Francis Adams, 8 March 1863.

16. Galton (ed.), *Vacation Tourists*, p. 401.

17. Robert Underwood Johnson and Clarence Clough Buel (eds.), *Battles and Leaders of the Civil War*, 3 vols. (Secaucus, NJ, 1985), vol. 3, p. 150.

18. Ibid.

19. *The Memoirs of Colonel John S. Mosby*, ed. Charles W. Russell (Boston, 1917), p. 175.

20. Jeffry D. Wert, *Mosby's Rangers* (New York, 1990), p. 48.

21. Duke University, Malet family MSS, Malet to father, 19 January 1863.

22. Henry Vane, *Affair of State* (London, 2004), p. 62.

23. Devonshire MSS, Chatsworth, 2nd series (340.184), Hartington to 7th Duke, 21 January 1863.

24. Edward Malet, *Shifting Scenes* (London, 1901), p. 25.

25. Devonshire MSS, Chatsworth, 2nd series (340.186), Hartington to 7th Duke, 17 February 1863.

26. University of Georgia Libraries, Athens, Ga., MSS 340, A. Trevor-Battye, 'A Noble Englishman, being Chapters in the Life of Henry Wemyss Feilden', p. 6.

27. Their romanticized portrayal of the Confederacy inspired fiction writers to develop the theme. In 1862 the pulp writer William Stephens Hayward began his series about Captain George, a dashing English adventurer who travels to the South to fight its cause. The popularity of the series prompted a host of imitations, all based in the South.

28. The Charleston Chamber of Commerce and the Society of St George both held farewell dinners for Bunch.

29. South Carolina Historical Society, Feilden–Smythe MSS, Feilden to aunt, 4 March 1863.

30. Ibid.

CHAPTER 18. FALTERING STEPS
OF A COUNTER-REVOLUTION

1. *Illustrated London News*, 16 May 1863. Vizetelly sometimes shocked his Confederate friends by his casual attitude towards strict accuracy. See G. Moxley Sorrel, *Recollections of a Confederate Staff Officer* (Lincoln, Nebr., 1999), p. 205.

2. Francis Galton (ed.), *Vacation Tourists, 1862–1863* (London, 1864), p. 399.

3. Robert N. Rosen, *Confederate Charleston* (Columbia, SC, 1994), p. 99.

4. South Carolina Historical Society, Feilden–Smythe MSS, Feilden to Phil, 16 April 1863. *Illustrated London News*, 16 May 1863.

5. *Diary of Gideon Welles*, 3 vols. (Boston, 1911), vol. 1, p. 276, 20 April 1863.

6. Doris Kearns Goodwin, *Team of Rivals* (New York, 2005), p. 511. Albert E. H. Johnson, 'Reminiscences of the Hon. Edwin M. Stanton', *Records of the Columbia Historical Society* (1910), p. 80.

7. NARA, T. 168, roll 31, vol. 31, doc. 3, Morse to Seward, 3 January 1863.

8. Russell was pleased by his success but annoyed with his publishers. They had

cut out 186 pages, he told the US Consul in Paris, John Bigelow. The book accurately reflected his feelings, except 'I must own I felt more hurt than I can or cared well to say at being refused leave to go with McClellan, as I was most anxious to show it was not my fault that Bull Run No. 1 ended with a panic ... I believe in my heart, however, that I do not entertain the smallest unkindly feeling towards a single citizen of the United States ...' John Bigelow, *Retrospections of an Active Life, Part One, 1817–1863,* 5 vols. (New York, 1909), vol. 1, pp. 605–6. Russell to Bigelow, 25 February 1863.

9. Sarah Agnes Wallace and Frances Elma Gillespie (eds.), *The Journal of Benjamin Moran, 1857–1865,* 2 vols. (Chicago, 1948, 1949), vol. 2, p. 1106, 14 January 1863.

10. Ibid., p. 1110, 21 January 1863.

11. NARA, T. 168, roll 31, vol. 31, doc. 3, Morse to Seward, 3 January 1863.

12. *Illustrated London News,* 7 February 1863.

13. Philip Van Doren Stern, *When the Guns Roared: World Aspects of the American Civil War* (New York, 1965), p. 177.

14. Wallace and Gillespie (eds.), *The Journal of Benjamin Moran,* vol. 2. p. 1108, 16 January 1863.

15. Henry Adams, *The Education of Henry Adams,* ed. Ernest Samuels (repr. Boston, 1973), pp. 142–3.

16. Wallace and Gillespie (eds.), *The Journal of Benjamin Moran,* vol. 2, p. 1121, 14 February 1863.

17. Outraged by the plight of two British subjects imprisoned for alleged desertion, the British Consul in Philadelphia sent an unofficial protest to the State Department. William Seward thought that the letter had to be an exaggeration, at least, he hoped so, but he was sufficiently disturbed to write to the Secretary of War, Edwin Stanton: 'The granite walls of the dungeons are represented to be wet with moisture, the stone floor damp and cold, the air impure and deathly, no bed or couches to lie upon and offensive vermin crawling in every direction. It is also represented that the prisoners are allowed no water with which to wash themselves or change of clothing and are on every side surrounded by filth and vermin.' OR, ser. 2, vol. 5, p. 118, Seward to Stanton, 27 January 1863.

18. MHS, Adams MSS, Diary of Charles Francis Adams, 9 February 1863.

19. Ibid., 11 February 1863.

20. Ibid., 25 February 1863.

21. Ibid., 28 February 1863.

22. Wallace and Gillespie (eds.), *The Journal of Benjamin Moran,* vol. 2, p. 1136, 18 March 1863.

23. Virginia Mason, *The Public Life and Diplomatic Correspondence of James M. Mason* (New York, 1906), pp. 387–92.

24. Warren F. Spencer, *The Confederate Navy in Europe* (Tuscaloosa, Ala., 1983), pp. 135–6, 21 January 1863, 20 January 1863.

25. Ibid., p. 131.

26. James M. Morgan, *Recollections of a Rebel Reefer* (Boston, 1917), pp. 96–7.

27. James D. Bulloch, *The Secret Service of the Confederate States in Europe*, 2 vols. (New York, 1884), vol. 1, p. 272.

28. Ibid., p. 270.

29. Ibid., p. 395, 3 February 1863.

30. There appears to be a great deal of confusion over which Emile Erlanger – the father or son – Mathilda actually married. Charles M. Hubbard, *The Burden of Confederate Diplomacy* (Knoxville, Tenn., 1998), p. 207, says the father, which the family website confirms: http://www.hyde-thomson.com.familytree/default.htm.

31. Judith Fenner Gentry, 'A Confederate Success in Europe: The Erlanger Loan', *Journal of Southern History* (1970), pp. 158–88. Spence always claimed that Erlanger took advantage of the Confederacy, but subsequent studies have shown that the terms of the loan were comparable to, if not more favourable than, those offered to other governments with more grounds for legitimacy.

32. H. B. Wilson was a Canadian who had worked in the shipping industry. He did not arouse the Confederates' suspicion and, within a few weeks of introducing himself, had become a regular at their meetings and dinners. His success opened the doors to other US agents.

33. ORN, ser. 1, vol. 13, p. 640, 9 January 1863. Excerpts of these reports were distributed to the navy, for example: 'Liverpool. January 10 1863: The steamer *Pet* has just cleared and will go to sea this day ... The steamer *Banshee* has gone to-day on a trial trip ... It will not be very many days before she leaves for the South ... The *Peterhoff* went to sea yesterday. I herewith forward an invoice of her cargo, also an invoice and description of the *Sterlingshire*, a sailing bark in the Confederate service. From all I can learn the two steamers may attempt to get into Charleston. They are new, or nearly so, and would make good transport ships.'

34. Frances Leigh Williams, *Matthew Fontaine Maury* (Piscataway, NJ, 1963), p. 403.

35. NARA, T. 168, roll 31, vol. 31, doc. 29, Morse to Seward, 20 February 1863.

36. Bulloch, *The Secret Service of the Confederate States in Europe*, vol. 1, p. 395, 3 February 1863.

37. ORN, ser. 2, vol. 3, pp. 712–16, Mason to Benjamin, 19 March 1863.

38. Stephen R. Wise, *Lifeline of the Confederacy: Blockade Running during the Civil War* (Columbia, SC, 1988), p. 94.

39. Van Doren Stern, *When the Guns Roared*, p. 194.

40. Hubbard, *The Burden of Confederate Diplomacy*, pp. 132–3.

41. E. D. Adams, *Great Britain and the American Civil War*, 2 vols. in 1 (New York, 1958), vol. 2, p. 130.

42. Beverly Wilson Palmer (ed.), *The Selected Letters of Charles Sumner*, 2 vols. (Boston, 1990), vol. 1, p. 154, Sumner to John Bright, 7 April 1863.

43. Lord Newton (ed.), *Lord Lyons: A Record of British Diplomacy*, 2 vols. (London, 1914), vol. 1, pp. 99–100, Russell to Lyons, 28 March 1863.

44. Adams, *Great Britain and the American Civil War*, vol. 2, p. 131.

45. NARA, T. 168, roll 31, vol. 31, doc. 41, Morse to Seward, 27 March 1863.

46. Adams, *Great Britain and the American Civil War*, vol. 2, p. 134.

47. Brooks Adams, 'The Seizure of the Laird Rams', *Proceedings of the Massachusetts Historical Society*, 45 (1911–12), p. 248.

48. 'We have had – I have had – some experience of what any attempt of that sort may be expected to lead to . . .', Palmerston told the House. He was referring to the collapse of his previous premiership in 1859, when MPs punished him for truckling to French demands to curb the freedoms of political refugees living in Britain. Spencer, *The Confederate Navy in Europe*, p. 99.

49. MHS, Adams MSS, Diary of Charles Francis Adams, 28 March 1863.

50. Morgan, *Recollections of a Rebel Reefer*, p. 114.

51. Frank J. Merli, *Great Britain and the Confederate Navy* (Bloomington, Ind., 1965), p. 129.

52. The officer from the *Galatea* was singing the 'Bonnie Blue Flag', which went: 'Hurrah! Hurrah! For Southern rights hurrah! Hurrah for the Bonnie Blue Flag . . .' *BDOFA*, Part 1, ser. C, vol. 6, doc. 193, pp. 146–7, Commodore Dunlop to Admiral Milne, 7 February 1863. In the Caribbean there was also an incident involving HMS *Greyhound*, when the band played 'Dixie's Land' within earshot of a US naval vessel. Commander Hickley immediately raced over to the players and made them follow up with 'My Country, 'Tis of Thee', but the damage was already done.

53. 'Here we are amongst the rebels enjoying ourselves very much,' wrote Henry Gawne to his mother, a week after arriving at the port. 'Everyone here is very hospitable. As much hunting as ever you please and of all descriptions, deer, foxes etc. Several of our officers are away now for four days in the Country hunting. I went out riding last Friday with a Col Browne of the Artillery.' Buckinghamshire RO, Gawne MSS, D115/20 (1), Henry Gawne to Edward Moore Gawne and mother, 6 January 1863.

54. Regis Courtemanche, *No Need of Glory: The British Navy in American Waters* (Annapolis, Md., 1977), p. 117.

55. Newton (ed.), *Lord Lyons*, vol. 1, p. 100, Lord Russell to Lord Lyons, 28 March 1863.

56. PRO 30/22/37, f. 43, Lyons to Russell, 13 April 1863.

57. PRO 30/22/37, ff. 57–60, Lyons to Russell, 5 May 1863.

58. Adams, *Britain and the American Civil War*, vol. 2, p. 140.

CHAPTER 19. PROPHECIES OF BLOOD AND SUFFERING

1. *The Private Journal of Georgiana Gholson Walker*, ed. Dwight Franklin Henderson, Confederate Centennial Studies, 25 (Tuscaloosa, Ala., 1963), p. 13.

2. Kenneth Blume, 'The Mid-Atlantic Arena: The United States, the Confederacy, and the British West Indies, 1861–1865', Ph.D. thesis, SUNY Binghamton, 1984, p. 257.

3. James M. Morgan, *Recollections of a Rebel Reefer* (Boston, 1917), pp. 103–5.

4. PRO FO115/361, f. 3, Stanton to Seward, 15 May 1863. Montreal, where Abinger was stationed, was teeming with Confederate refugees, which further solidified his pro-Southern stand. On his return to Montreal, he married Helen Magruder, the daughter and niece of renowned Confederates.

5. George Alfred Lawrence, *Border and Bastille* (New York, 1864), p. 190.

6. James H. Wilkins (ed.), *The Great Diamond Hoax and Other Stirring Episodes in the Life of Asbury Harpending* (San Francisco, 1915), pp. 66, 74–6.

7. Ibid.

8. PRO FO5/1280, Consul Booker to Russell, 29 June 1863.

9. PRO FO5/1280, Scholefield to Austin M. Layard, 1 May 1863.

10. 'Bright–Sumner Letters, 1861–1872', *Proceedings of the Massachusetts Historical Society*, 46 (1912), pp. 120–22, John Bright to Sumner, 27 June 1863.

11. 'John Wilkes Booth: An Interview with the Press with Sir Charles Wyndham', *New York Herald*, quoted in Gordon Samples, *Lust for Fame* (New York, 1998), p. 113.

12. James J. Barnes and Patience P. Barnes (eds.), *Private and Confidential: Letters from British Ministers in Washington to the Foreign Secretaries* (Selinsgrove, Pa., 1993), p. 320, Lyons to Russell, 13 April 1863, and p. 322, 5 May 1863. The most controversial revelation in the 'blue book' was Lord Lyons's private meeting with New York Democrats in November 1862. The Republican administration put the worst possible interpretation on it, even though Lyons was not doing anything wrong or unusual for a diplomat by talking to the opposition party. 'The Despatches of Lord Lyons prove how difficult it is to become familiar with the public spirit in this country, even for a cautious, discreet diplomat and an Englishman,' wrote Adam Gurowski. 'I am at a loss to understand why Earl Russell divulged the above mentioned correspondence, thus putting Lord Lyons into a false and unpleasant position with the party in power.' *Diary from November 18, 1862– October 18, 1863* (New York, 1864), p. 182.

13. *Diary of Gideon Welles*, 3 vols. (Boston, 1911), vol. 2, p. 250, 1 April 1863. It was no help to Lyons that Welles vehemently opposed Seward on the letters of marque question. His chief objection stemmed from the fact it would remain the purview of the State Department rather than his own.

14. Sumner calmed down a little, but remained adamant that the *Peterhoff*'s mails should have been dealt with by the prize court. Ironically, when the British Cabinet had a chance to consider the *Peterhoff* affair rationally, it too reached the same conclusion. The Lord Chancellor asked: 'What will be most [helpful] for our interest as a future belligerent?' The answer, obviously, was the right to seize the enemy's letters from neutral ships.

15. PRO 30/22/37, ff. 42–3, Lyons to Russell, 7 April 1863.

16. PRO FO115/394, f. 35, B. Lowry to Lyons, 28 May 1863.

17. *Richmond Enquirer*, 3 October 1863.

18. Emory University, Gregory MSS, Lawley to Gregory, 26 March 1863.

19. Ibid.

20. BL Add. MS 41567, ff. 246–7, George Henry Herbert to mother, 31 March 1863.

21. Matthew J. Graham, *The Ninth Regiment New York Volunteers* (Lancaster, Ohio, 1997), p. 420.

22. Bruce Catton, *The Civil War* (New York, 2004), p. 130.

CHAPTER 20. THE KEY IS IN THE LOCK

1. Bernard Price, *Sussex: People, Places, Things* (London, 1975), p. 149.

2. Robert Underwood Johnson and Clarence Clough Buel (eds.), *Battles and Leaders of the Civil War*, 4 vols. (Secaucus, NJ, 1985), vol. 3, p. 161.

3. *The Times*, 11 June 1863.

4. William C. Davis (ed.), *The Civil War: A Historical Account of America's War of Secession* (New York, 1996), p. 114.

5. Jeffry D. Wert, *The Sword of Lincoln* (New York, 2006), p. 246.

6. Henry Hore identified the raiders as belonging to Mosby's Cavalry, and, while there is no reason to doubt his word, it is worth noting that Mosby was at Warrenton Junction, Virginia, on 3 May. See Jeffry D. Wert, *Mosby's Rangers* (New York, 1990), pp. 57–8.

7. Price, *Sussex*, p. 150.

8. Geoffrey C. Ward, Ric Burns and Ken Burns, *The Civil War* (New York, 1990), p. 210.

9. W. C. Ford (ed.), *A Cycle of Adams Letters, 1861–1865*, 2 vols. (Boston, 1920), vol. 1, p. 294, Charles Francis Adams Jr. to Charles Francis Adams, 8 May 1863.

10. Hore returned to England after the war. He joined the Capital and Counties Bank in Chichester, eventually rising to bank manager. He died in 1887. Price, *Sussex*, p. 145.

11. David Saville Muzzey, *The United States of America: Through the Civil War* (New York, 1931), p. 575.

12. Allan Nevins, *The War for the Union*, 4 vols.; vol. 2: *War Becomes Revolution 1862–1863* (New York, 1960), p. 453.

13. *The Times*, 16 June 1863.

14. Winston S. Churchill, *The American Civil War* (New York, 1985), p. 100.

15. Ian F. W. Beckett, *The War Correspondents: The American Civil War* (London, 1997), p. 102.

16. *Illustrated London News*, 8 August 1863.

17. *Illustrated London News*, 29 August 1863.

18. William L. Shea and Terrence J. Winschel, *Vicksburg is the Key* (Lincoln, Nebr., 2003), p. 151.

19. *Illustrated London News*, 29 August 1863.

20. Philip Tucker, 'Confederate Secret Agent in Ireland: Father John B. Bannon and his Irish Mission, 1863–1864', *Journal of Confederate History*, 5 (1990), p. 55.

21. Francis Galton (ed.), *Vacation Tourists, 1862–1863* (London, 1864), p. 412.

22. Ibid., p. 410.

23. PRO FO115/394, ff. 305–7, Mayo to Lyons, 26 June 1863.

24. James G. Hollandsworth Jr., *Pretense of Glory* (Baton Rouge, La., 1998), p. 120.

25. University of Rochester, Rochester, NY, Rush Rhees Library, A.W39 Thurlow Weed MSS, Currie to Weed, 6 August 1863.

26. Huguenot Historical Society, LeFevre/DuBois/Eltin Family Papers/NYUL58T-320-0057, Assistant Surgeon S. E. Hasbrouck to Sol, 133rd New York Volunteers, 16 June 1863.

27. Arthur J. L. Fremantle, *Three Months in the Southern States* (Lincoln, Nebr., 1991), p. 120.

28. Ibid., p. 7.

29. Raphael Semmes, *Service Afloat: A Personal Memoir of my Cruises and Services* (1868; repr. Baltimore, 1987), p. 314.

30. Fremantle, *Three Months in the Southern States*, p. 108.

31. Ibid., p. 117.

32. Frank L. Klement, *The Limits of Dissent* (New York, 1998), p. 168.

33. The details of Colonel Grenfell's life are taken from Stephen Z. Starr, *Colonel Grenfell's Wars* (Baton Rouge, La., 1971), a brilliant piece of detective work on an extremely elusive figure.

34. Fremantle, *Three Months in the Southern States*, p. 149.

35. Starr, *Colonel Grenfell's Wars*, p. 100.

36. Fremantle, *Three Months in the Southern States*, p. 164.

37. Ibid., p. 180.

CHAPTER 21. THE EVE OF BATTLE

1. Henry Vane, *Affair of State* (London, 2004), p. 65.

2. Patrick Jackson, *The Last of the Whigs: A Political Biography of Lord Hartington, Later 8th Duke of Devonshire* (London, 1994), p. 33.

3. 'Bow down ye ignoble hard working members!' the Earl of Kimberley wrote sarcastically in his diary, who thought the position should have gone to him. *Journal of John Wodehouse, First Earl of Kimberley* (Cambridge, 1997), p. 92, 20 April 1863. When Lawley heard the news of Hartington's promotion he sent him the official report on the US attack on Charleston on 7 April. 'A printed copy

of it was handed to me as a favour, and I was told that I might make any use of it in Europe which I tried, short of its publication.'

4. Merseyside Maritime Museum, Fraser, Trenholm MSS, B/FT box 81, p. 111, C. K. Prioleau to J. T. Welsman, 9 May 1863.

5. Frances Leigh Williams, *Matthew Fontaine Maury* (Piscataway, NJ, 1963), p. 409. Maury learned of his son's disappearance on 8 April 1863.

6. Mersey Maritime Museum, Fraser, Trenholm MSS, B/FT box 1/7, Bulloch to Prioleau, 20 April 1863.

7. MHS, Adams MSS, Diary of Charles Francis Adams, 7 April 1863.

8. Martin Duberman, *Charles Francis Adams* (New York, 1961), p. 305.

9. Excerpted in the *New York Times*, 6 December 1862.

10. W. C. Ford (ed.), *A Cycle of Adams Letters, 1861–1865*, 2 vols. (Boston, 1920), vol. 1, p. 275, Henry Adams to Charles Francis Adams Jr., 23 April 1863.

11. The inscription on the plaque reads: Presented by English gentlemen, as a tribute of admiration for the soldier and patriot, Thomas J. Jackson, and gratefully accepted by Virginia in the name of the Southern people. Done A. D. 1875, in the hundredth year of the commonwealth. "Look! There is Jackson, Standing like a Stone-Wall."'

12. Charles P. Cullop, 'English Reaction to Stonewall Jackson's Death', *West Virginia History*, 29/1 (Oct. 1967), pp. 1–5. The Beresford Hope quotation in the footnote on this page is from his *The Results of the American Disruption* (London, 1862), p. 44.

13. James M. Morgan, *Recollections of a Rebel Reefer* (Boston, 1917), p. 126.

14. Library of Congress, Mason Papers, James Spence to Mason, 16 June 1863.

15. *Harriet Martineau: Selected Letters*, ed. Valerie Sanders (Oxford, 1990), p. 201, Martineau to Henry Bright, 3 May 1863.

16. Brian Jenkins, *Britain and the War for the Union*, 2 vols. (Montreal, 1974, 1980), vol. 2, p. 50.

17. Ford (ed.), *A Cycle of Adams Letters*, vol. 2, p. 9, Henry Adams to Charles Francis Adams Jr., 14 May 1863.

18. Joyce Miank Lierley (ed.), *Affectionately Yours: Three English Immigrants, the American Civil War and a Michigan Family Saga* (Omaha, Nebr., 1998), p. 166, Mary Ann Rutter to brother, 24 September 1863.

19. John Bailey (ed.), *Diary of Lady Frederick Cavendish*, 2 vols. (New York, 1927), vol. 1, p. 161. The future Lady Frederick was also Gladstone's niece, which no doubt played a role in her early political education.

20. Merseyside Maritime Museum, Fraser, Trenholm MSS, B/FT box 1/114(a), Spence to Prioleau, 20 June 1863.

21. Wilbur Devereux Jones, *The Confederate Rams at Birkenhead*, Confederate Centennial Studies, 19 (Wilmington, NC, 2000), p. 47.

22. Sarah Agnes Wallace and Frances Elma Gillespie (eds.), *The Journal of Benjamin Moran, 1857–1865*, 2 vols. (Chicago, 1948, 1949), vol. 2, p. 1178, 27 June 1863.

23. F. L. Owsley, *King Cotton Diplomacy* (2nd edn., Chicago, 1959), p. 450.

24. Ibid., p. 461.

25. Ford (ed.), *A Cycle of Adams Letters*, vol. 2, p. 41, Henry Adams to Charles Francis Adams Jr., 26 June 1863.

26. Herman Ausubel, *John Bright: Victorian Reformer* (New York, 1966), p. 136.

27. 'Bright–Sumner Letters, 1861-1872', *Proceedings of the Massachusetts Historical Society*, 46 (1912), pp. 120-22, John Bright to Charles Sumner, 27 June 1863.

28. Ibid.

29. Philip Van Doren Stern, *When the Guns Roared: World Aspects of the American Civil War* (New York, 1965), p. 202.

30. Henry Adams, *The Education of Henry Adams*, ed. Ernest Samuels (repr. Boston, 1973), p. 187.

31. Emory M. Thomas, *Bold Dragoon: The Life of J. E. B. Stuart* (Norman, Okla., 1999), p. 226.

32. Devonshire MSS, Chatsworth, 2nd series (340.195), Lawley to Hartington, 14 June 1863.

33. Edward G. Longacre, *Jersey Cavaliers* (Hightstown, NJ, 1992), p. 144.

34. OR, ser. 1, vol. 27/1, doc. 39, p. 966, 10 June 1863.

35. OR, ser. 1, vol. 27/1, doc. 43, p. 1054, 10 June 1863.

36. Ford (ed.), *A Cycle of Adams Letters*, vol. 2, p. 32, Charles Francis Adams Jr. to Henry Adams, 14 June 1863.

37. Thomas, *Bold Dragoon*, p. 226.

38. British Library of Political and Economic Science, LSE, Farr MSS, GB 0097 Farr/vol. X, Add. 2, ff. 5-25.

39. PRO FO282/10/d.211, ff. 104-11, Archibald to Lyons, 8 July 1863.

40. PRO FO114/402, f. 1038, Lyons to Revd W. E. Hoskins, 3 December 1863. Lyons also passed on two letters from his brother officers, testimonials to how bravely Hoskins fought and died.

41. PRO FO115/394, f. 100, Miss Hodges to Lord Lyons, 8 June 1863. Many years later, Hoskins' family erected a gravestone on his burial plot.

42. West Sussex RO, Lyons MSS, box 301, 16 June 1863, Lyons to sister.

CHAPTER 22. CROSSROADS AT GETTYSBURG

1. Devonshire MSS, Chatsworth, 2nd series (340.195), Lawley to Hartington, 14 June 1863.

2. Arthur J. L. Fremantle, *Three Months in the Southern States* (Lincoln, Nebr., 1991), p. 220. The quotation in the footnote on this page is from p. 191.

3. Ibid., p. 208.

4. Ibid., p. 211.

5. According to William Torens, Davies was sent to the 7th Tennessee Infantry

first, from August 1863 to November 1864, and then became a lieutenant and AAIG to Heth on 30 November 1864.

6. Fremantle, *Three Months in the Southern States*, p. 211.

7. Justus Scheibert wrote eloquently about such damaged terrain: 'Only grunting swine wandered around on level ground, often rooting at the shallow graves and gnawing on bodies which stared with distorted horrible expressions at persons who rode by.' Justus Scheibert, *Seven Months in the Rebel States during the North American War, 1863*, trans. Joseph C. Hayes, ed. William Stanley Hoole (Tuscaloosa, Ala., 2009), p. 33.

8. W. C. Ford (ed.), *A Cycle of Adams Letters, 1861–1865*, 2 vols. (Boston, 1920), vol. 2, pp. 36–7, Charles Francis Adams Jr. to Henry Adams, 19 June 1863.

9. Emory M. Thomas, *Bold Dragoon: The Life of J. E. B. Stuart* (Norman, Okla., 1999), p. 241.

10. Francis W. Dawson, *Reminiscences of Confederate Service, 1861–1865*, ed. Bell I. Wiley (Baton Rouge, La., 1980), p. 91.

11. Morris to Lawley, 25 June 1863, quoted in Brian Jenkins, 'Frank Lawley and the Confederacy', *Civil War History*, 23 (March 1997).

12. Fremantle, *Three Months in the Southern States*, p. 177.

13. Fitzgerald Ross, *Cities and Camps of the Confederate States*, ed. Richard Barksdale Harwell (Champaign, Ill., 1997), p. 42.

14. Historians have since exonerated Ewell. He had less than an hour to get his troops into line and charge the ridge before Federal defenders received thousands of reinforcements. James M. McPherson (ed.), *Battle Chronicles of the Civil War*, 6 vols. (Lakeville, Conn., 1989), vol. 3, p. 69. But when Francis Lawley wrote his report of the day's fighting he repeated without examination the accusation that Ewell had lost the battle through his bungling.

15. Ross, *Cities and Camps*, p. 48.

16. Joseph E. Persico, *My Enemy, My Brother: Men and Days of Gettysburg* (New York, 1988), p. 135.

17. *The Times*, 18 August 1863.

18. Fremantle, *Three Months in the Southern States*, p. 260.

19. *The Times*, 18 August 1863.

20. Susannah Ural Bruce, *The Harp and the Eagle* (New York, 2006), p. 163.

21. Jeffry D. Wert, *The Sword of Lincoln* (New York, 2006), p. 294.

22. 'Rebel Without a Cause – from Shakespeare Country', *Crossfire: The Magazine of the American Civil War Round Table*, 48 (April 1993).

23. Dawson, *Reminiscences*, p. 95.

24. Fremantle, *Three Months in the Southern States* p. 190.

25. Dawson, *Reminiscences*, p. 96.

26. Charles Francis Adams Jr., *Charles Francis Adams, 1835–1915: An Autobiography with a Memorial Address* (New York, 1916), p. 151.

27. Somewhere in the stream was Lieutenant Colonel George T. Gordon of the 34th North Carolina Infantry. He had arrived in the South six months before, a fugitive

from British and Canadian justice. An accomplished fraud, he tricked the authorities into awarding him the rank of major. To his surprise, the war exposed a hitherto completely hidden layer of decency. Promotions followed and by the time of Gettysburg he was a brigade commander. After the war, however, he returned to his old ways.

28. Fremantle, *Three Months in the Southern States*, p. 267.

29. Dawson, *Reminiscences*, p. 96.

30. Edward Porter Alexander, *Fighting for the Confederacy: The Personal Recollections of General Edward Alexander Porter*, ed. Gary Gallagher (Chapel Hill, NC, 1989), p. 266.

31. Adams, *Charles Francis Adams, 1835–1915: An Autobiography*, p. 151.

32. John B. Jones, *A Rebel War Clerk's Diary at the Confederate States Capital*, ed. Earl Schenck Miers (Urbana, Ill., 1958), p. 286.

33. Alexander, *Fighting for the Confederacy*, p. 268.

34. Fremantle, *Three Months in the Southern States*, p. 274.

35. James Longstreet, *From Manassas to Appomattox* (New York, 2004), p. 361. Longstreet added: 'It is simply out of the question for a lesser force to march over broad, open fields and carry a fortified front occupied by a great force of seasoned troops.' Longstreet was stung by the criticisms of his own actions at Gettysburg and energetically defended himself against charges which ranged from treason to arrogance.

36. William Stanley Hoole, *Lawley Covers the Confederacy* (Tuscaloosa, Ala., 1964), p. 63

37. *The Times*, 18 August 1863.

CHAPTER 23. PRESSURE RISING

1. Hansard, 3rd ser., vol. 171, cols. 1827–8, 3 June 1863, John Bright.

2. Henry Adams, *The Education of Henry Adams*, ed. Ernest Samuels (repr. Boston, 1973), p. 461.

3. F. L. Owsley, *King Cotton Diplomacy* (2nd edn., Chicago, 1959), p. 461.

4. E. D. Adams, *Great Britain and the American Civil War*, 2 vols in 1 (New York, 1958), vol. 2, p. 172.

5. Ibid., p. 173.

6. ORN, ser. 2, vol. 3, no. 25, pp. 839–40, Hotze to Benjamin, 11 July 1863.

7. Sarah Agnes Wallace and Frances Elma Gillespie (eds.), *The Journal of Benjamin Moran, 1857–1865*, 2 vols. (Chicago, 1948, 1949), vol. 2, p. 1183, 14 July 1863.

8. Francis Galton (ed.), *Vacation Tourists, 1862–1863* (London, 1864), p. 412.

9. New York Historical Society, *Narrative of Ebenezer Wells* (c. 1881).

10. William L. Shea and Terrence J. Winschel, *Vicksburg is the Key* (Lincoln, Nebr., 2003), p. 185.

11. Sheffield Archives, WHM 461 (24), Hampson to Lord Wharncliffe, 17 January 1865.

12. PRO FO115/395, f. 60, Mayo to Lyons, 24 July 1863.

13. Adams, *Great Britain and the American Civil War*, vol. 2, p. 179.

14. *Historical Collection, Michigan Pioneer and Historical Society*, vol. 29 (Lansing, Mich., 1900), p. 604.

15. ORN, ser. 2, vol. 3, no. 26, pp. 849–51, Hotze to Benjamin, 23 July 1863.

16. W. C. Ford (ed.), *A Cycle of Adams Letters, 1861–1865*, 2 vols. (Boston, 1920), vol. 2, p. 59, Henry Adams to Charles Francis Adams Jr., 23 July 1863; *The Economist*, 1 August 1863, quoted in Hugh Brogan, 'America and Walter Bagehot', *Journal of American Studies*, 11/3 (Dec. 1977), p. 340.

17. Charles Vandersee, 'Henry Adams behind the Scenes: Civil War Letters to Frederick W. Seward', *Bulletin of the New York Public Library*, 71/4 (1967), p. 259.

18. Adams, *The Education of Henry Adams*, pp. 204–5.

19. Ford (ed.), *A Cycle of Adams Letters*, vol. 2, p. 59, Henry Adams to Charles Francis Adams Jr., 23 July 1863.

20. Ibid., p. 54, Charles Francis Adams to Charles Francis Adams Jr., 24 July 1863.

21. Norman Longmate, *Hungry Mills: The Story of the Lancashire Cotton Famine, 1861–5* (London, 1978), p. 205.

22. Lance Davis and Stanley L. Engerman, *Naval Blockades in Peace and War* (Cambridge, 2006), pp. 128–9.

23. Wallace and Gillespie (eds), *The Journal of Benjamin Moran*, vol. 2, p. 1188, 27 July 1863.

24. Allan Nevins, *The War for the Union*, 4 vols.; vol. 2: *War Becomes Revolution 1862–1863* (New York, 1960), p. 120.

25. Susannah Ural Bruce, *The Harp and the Eagle* (New York, 2006), p. 177.

26. Edward Robb Ellis, *The Epic of New York City* (New York, 2005), p. 298.

27. Sarah Forbes Hughes (ed.), *Letters and Recollections of John Murray Forbes*, 2 vols. (New York, 1900), vol. 2, p. 49.

28. Arthur J. L. Fremantle, *Three Months in the Southern States* (Lincoln, Nebr., 1991), p. 300.

29. Ellis, *The Epic of New York City*, p. 305.

30. The description of the Draft Riots is largely taken from the following sources: Ellis, *The Epic of New York City*; Joel Tyler Hedley, *The Great Riots of New York, 1712–1873* (New York, 1873); David Barnes, *The Draft Riots of New York, July, 1863: The Metropolitan Police. Their Service during Riot Week* (New York, 1863); Edwin G Burrows and Mike Wallace, *Gotham* (New York, 1999), pp. 888–99.

31. James M. McPherson, *Battle Cry of Freedom* (London, 1988), p. 610. The Gatling gun had been patented in 1862.

32. George Templeton Strong, *Diary of the Civil War 1860–1865*, ed. Allan Nevins (New York, 1962), p. 339, 15 July 1863.

33. Fremantle, *Three Months in the Southern States*, p. 303.

34. Iver Bernstein, *The New York City Draft Riots* (Oxford, 1990), p. 17.

35. George Rowell, 'Acting Assistant Surgeon', *Nineteenth Century Theatre Research*, 12 (1984), p. 33.

36. Strong, *Diary of the Civil War*, p. 341, 17 July 1863.

37. Ellis, *The Epic of New York City*, p. 315.

38. PRO FO282/8, ff. 325–8, Archibald to Russell, 18 July 1863.

39. PRO FO282/10, ff. 126–7, d. 238, Archibald to Lord Lyons, 20 July 1863.

40. Doris Kearns Goodwin, *Team of Rivals* (New York, 2005), p. 536.

41. Lord Newton (ed.), *Lord Lyons: A Record of British Diplomacy*, 2 vols. (London, 1914), vol. 1, p. 115, Lyons to Russell, 24 July 1863.

42. Northumberland RO, 2179/1, C. A. Race to father, 24 July 1863. Another lost soul in the Federal army was 34-year-old Theodore Lee. Unhappy at home and beset by financial problems, he had fled England because 'I wanted a radical change . . . I needed a change to prevent both mind and body being comfortably boxed up at the expense of my friends.' Joining the Federal army as a substitute had seemed his only option. So far his life was tolerable, he wrote to his brother and sister in England, except that 'the mosquitoes and bugs are terrible at night'. Leicestershire RO, D3796/6, Theodore Lee to his brother and sister, 16 August 1863.

43. British Library of Political and Economic Science, LSE, Farr MSS, Add. 2, J. G. Kennedy to William Farr, 9 August 1863. Sometimes, the case was reversed and the legation was pitted between a penitent son and his furious family. Charles Race, an English sergeant stationed at Fort Monroe, needed all his convage to inform his father that he was still alive: 'With feelings of sorrow which it is utterly impossible for me to describe, I take my pen in a trembling hand to write and let you know where I am,' he wrote on 24 July 1863. 'I went as you are aware to London and, after passing a few miserable days there, a burning sense of shame at the idea of looking anybody in the face again combined, I now think with a kind of insanity, I formed the idea of coming to America . . . I left England whether ever to see you again or not, God only knows.'

44. PRO FO115/395, f. 73, Belshaw to Lyons, 14 August 1863.

45. *Diary of Gideon Welles*, 3 vols. (Boston, 1911), vol. 1, pp. 409–10, 21 August 1863.

46. University of Rochester, Rochester, NY, Rush Rhees Library, Seward MSS, Lyons to Seward, 20 July 1863.

47. PRO FO5/892, ff.17–24, Lyons to Russell, 3 August 1863.

48. PRO 30/22/37, ff. 133–6, Lyons to Russell, 7 August 1863.

49. PRO 30/22/37, ff. 143–6, Lyons to Russell, 14 August 1863.

50. PRO 30/22/37, ff. 147–59, Lyons to Russell, 2 September 1863.

51. PRO 30/22/22, ff. 255–7, Palmerston to Russell, 14 September 1863.

52. C. Vann Woodward (ed.), *Mary Chesnut's Civil War* (New Haven, 1981), p. 664.

53. Duke University, Special Collections Library, Rose O'Neal Greenhow Papers, Greenhow to Jefferson Davis, 16 July 1863.

54. N. John Hall (ed.), *The Letters of Anthony Trollope*, 2 vols. (Stanford, 1983), vol. 1, p. 228, Trollope to Altisidora Annesley, 26 July 1863.

55. Justus Scheibert, *Seven Months in the Rebel States during the North American War, 1863*, trans. Joseph C. Hayes, ed. William Stanley Hoole (Tuscaloosa, Ala., 2009), pp. 132, 140.

56. PRO FO5/907, ff. 179-88, Stuart to Russell, 15 August 1863.

57. *Cornhill Magazine*, 10 (1864), pp. 99-110.

58. Fitzgerald Ross, *Cities and Camps of the Confederate States*, ed. Richard Barksdale Harwell (Champaign, Ill., 1997), p. 107.

59. Merseyside Maritime Museum, Fraser, Trenholm MSS, B/FT box 1/107, Thomas Prioleau to Charles K. Prioleau, 9 September 1863. The comment by Lawley in the footnote is taken from Alan Hankinson, *Man of Wars: William Howard Russell of 'The Times', 1820-1907* (London, 1982), p. 182

CHAPTER 24. DEVOURING THE YOUNG

1. North Carolina State Archives, Private Collections, PC 1226, Rose O'Neal Greenhow MSS, London Diary, p. 3.

2. *The Private Journal of Georgiana Gholson Walker*, ed. Dwight Franklin Henderson, Confederate Centennial Studies, 25 (Tuscaloosa, Ala., 1963), p. 53.

3. Ann Blackman, *Wild Rose: Rose O'Neale Greenhow, Civil War Spy* (New York, 2005), p. 267.

4. Warren F. Spencer, *The Confederate Navy in Europe* (Tuscaloosa, Ala., 1983), pp. 144-76. In addition to Spencer, the other invaluable works on this subject are *King Cotton Diplomacy* by Frank Owsley (2nd edn., Chicago, 1959) and *Great Britain and the Confederate Navy* by Frank J. Merli (Bloomington, Ind., 1965).

5. John Bigelow, *Retrospections of an Active Life, Part One, 1817-1863*, 5 vols. (New York, 1909), vol. 1, p. 632, Russell to Bigelow, 15 April 1863.

6. Ibid., p. 639, Bigelow to Seward, 17 April 1863. Cobden had apparently insisted that 'no English statesman has ever taken more humiliating buffetings' trying to avoid war, 'that there was never a greater mistake. Palmerston does not want war, he wants to maintain power and he knows that a war would shatter his ministry to atoms in an instant.'

7. NARA, M. 141, roll t-25, vol. 25, Dudley to Seward, 15 August 1863.

8. David Hepburn Milton, *Lincoln's Spymaster: Thomas Haines Dudley and the Liverpool Network* (Mechanicsburg, Pa., 2003), p. 107.

9. *Diary of Gideon Welles*, 3 vols. (Boston, 1911), vol. 1, pp. 428, 437.

10. MHS, Adams MSS, Diary of Charles Francis Adams, 28 August 1863.

11. *PRFA*, 1 (1864), p. 367, Adams to Russell, 5 September 1863.

12. 'Letters of Richard Cobden to Charles Sumner', *American Historical Review*, 2 (1897), p. 312, Cobden to Sumner, 7 August 1863. Cobden continued: 'Had England joined France they would have been followed by probably every other

State of Europe, with the exception of Russia. This is what the Confederate agents have been seeking to accomplish. They have pressed recognition on England and France with persistent energy from the first.'

13. PRO 30/22/22, f. 243, Palmerston to Russell, 4 September 1863. In fact, he expected them to lose the case: 'I think you are right in detaining the iron clads now building in the Mersey and the Clyde, though the result may be that we shall be obliged to set them free – There can be no doubt that ships coated with iron must be intended for warlike purposes, but to justify seizure we must, I conceive, be able to prove that they are intended for the use of the Confederates and to be employed against the Federal government, and this may not be easy as it will be to lay hold of them.'

14. Brian Jenkins, *Britain and the War for the Union*, 2 vols. (Montreal, 1974, 1980), vol. 2, p. 290.

15. Somerset RO, Somerset MSS, d/RA/A/2a/39/11, Palmerston to Somerset, 13 September 1863. Palmerston continued: 'if we get these ships they will tend to give us moral as well as maritime strength.' On 2 October, Palmerston was ruminating on the theme of war with the US: 'we shall be pretty well off, I see, by next summer, with an addition for 1865; and there seems no good reason to expect a rupture with France within that period though it would be hazardous to say as much of our relations with the United States.'

16. Detective Officer William Cozens filed the following report: 'On Sunday the 13th instant, 95 men of the crew of the Florida arrived here by Railway from Cardiff the greater portion of them are natives of Ireland and some from various parts of Great Britain, the rest are composed of Germans, Dutchmen and a few Americans.' PRO HO45/7261/122.

17. *BDOFA*, Part 1, ser. C, vol. 6, p. 184, Adams to Russell, 16 September 1863.

18. D. P. Crook, *The North, the South and the Powers, 1861–1865* (New York, 1974), p. 326, *PRFA*, 1 (1864), p. 384, Russell to Adams, 25 September 1863.

19. W. C. Ford (ed.), *A Cycle of Adams Letters, 1861–1865*, 2 vols. (Boston, 1920), vol. 2, p. 82, Henry Adams to Charles Francis Adams Jr., 16 September 1863.

20. *Diary of Gideon Welles*, vol. 1, p. 435, 17 September 1863.

21. PRO 30/22/37, ff. 227–30, Lyons to Russell, 6 November 1863.

22. PRO 30/22/37, ff. 213–16, Lyons to Russell, 23 October 1863.

23. For a fuller discussion of Sumner's motives and the reaction to his speech, see David Herbert Donald, *Charles Sumner and the Rights of Man* (New York, 1970), pp. 126–37.

24. *The Economist*, 3 October 1863.

25. Deborah Logan (ed.), *The Collected Letters of Harriet Martineau*, 5 vols. (London, 2007), vol. 5, p. 31, Harriet Martineau to Henry Reeve, 29 September 1863.

26. Beverly Wilson Palmer (ed.), *The Selected Letters of Charles Sumner*, 2 vols. (Boston, 1990), vol. 2, pp. 197–8, Sumner to Bright, 6 October 1863.

27. Quoted in Sarah Agnes Wallace and Frances Elma Gillespie (eds.), *The Journal of Benjamin Moran, 1857–1865*, 2 vols. (Chicago, 1948, 1949), vol. 2, p. 1220, 8 October 1863.

28. Edward Chalfant, *Better in Darkness* (New York, 1994), p. 69.

29. MHS, Adams MSS, Diary of Charles Francis Adams, 24 October 1863.

30. Wallace and Gillespie (eds.), *The Journal of Benjamin Moran*, vol. 2, p. 1212, 22 September 1863.

31. Benjamin did not have a clear idea, when he sent the dispatch on 4 August, of what Mason's departure would achieve, beyond pinning his hopes on the French to break clear of their alliance with Britain. Charles M. Hubbard, *The Burden of Confederate Diplomacy* (Knoxville, Tenn., 1998), p. 149.

32. North Carolina State Archives, Private Collections, PC 1226, Rose O'Neal Greenhow Papers, London Diary, p. 35.

33. Blackman, *Wild Rose*, p. 271.

34. PRO 30/22/26, Argyll to Russell, 17 October 1863.

35. Philip Guedalla (ed.), *Gladstone and Palmerston, being the Correspondence of Lord Palmerston with Mr Gladstone 1851–1865* (London, 1928), pp. 264–6, Palmerston to Gladstone, 9 October 1863; Gladstone to Palmerston, 8 October 1863.

36. *BDOFA*, Part 1, ser. C, vol. 6, doc. 348, Captain Inglefield to Lord Paget, 1 November 1863; Inglefield to Vice-Admiral Grey, 25 October 1863.

37. James M. Morgan, *Recollections of a Rebel Reefer* (Boston, 1917), p. 164.

38. University of Rochester, Rochester , NY, Rush Rhees Library, A.W39 Thurlow Weed MSS, Currie to Weed, 15 September 1863.

39. Some of James Horrocks's letters were deposited in the Lancashire Record Office, in Preston; the rest are in the Blackburn Museum. In 1982 the curator of the Blackburn Museum, A. S. Lewis, collated the two collections and published them under the title, *My Dear Parents*. The combination of Lewis's scholarship and Horrocks's engaging style makes the book one of the most important eyewitness accounts of Civil War life by an English volunteer. His father owned a cotton mill and had suffered hard during the cotton famine. Horrocks was forced to abandon his studies at the Wesleyan teachers' training college in London and return home to Bolton. The pregnancy of Martha Jane Hammer had added another financial burden. She successfully sued him for financial support. He ran away to America rather than submit to the court, leaving his family with the embarrassment of the unpaid support.

40. A. S. Lewis (ed.), *My Dear Parents* (New York, 1982), p. 23, Horrocks to parents, 5 September 1863.

41. Ibid.

42. Daniel B. Lucas, *Memoir of John Yates Beall* (Montreal, 1865), p. 265.

43. W. W. Baker, 'Memoirs of Service' (property of Mr Jack Beall), p. 21.

44. Jeffry D. Wert, *Mosby's Rangers* (New York, 1990), p. 98.

45. Jeffry D. Wert, *The Sword of Lincoln* (New York, 2006), p. 313.

46. Frank E. Vandiver (ed.), *The Civil War Diary of Josiah Gorgas* (Tuscaloosa, Ala., 1947), p. 55.

47. Sam Watkins, *Company Aytch* (New York, 1999), p. 74.

CHAPTER 25. RIVER OF DEATH

1. Robert L. Kincaid, *The Wilderness Road* (Middlesboro, Ky., 1966), pp. 268–9.

2. Ibid., pp. 263–5.

3. OR, ser. 1, vol. 30, doc. 52, p. 435, De Courcy to Brigadier General Potter, 7 September 1863.

4. William Marvel, *Burnside* (Chapel Hill, NC, 1991), p. 278. For example, De Courcy wrote to Brigadier General Robert Potter on 7 September 1863: 'My sick are filling the houses in my rear, and I have no surgeons or medicines to leave with them. Dr. Wilson can inform you that I foretold this and some of the other disasters which must take place on this line of operations unless commissary, quartermaster's, and medical departments work in a different fashion from what they are now doing.' OR, ser. 1, vol. 30, doc. 52, p. 435.

5. Kincaid, *The Wilderness Road*, p. 271.

6. Ibid.

7. Ibid.

8. Frank E. Vandiver (ed.), *The Civil War Diary of Josiah Gorgas* (Tuscaloosa, Ala., 1947), p. 62, 17 September 1863.

9. NARA, M552, roll 26, Compiled Military Service Record, De Courcy to Colonel Richmond, 18 September 1863.

10. http://www.mkwe.com/ohio/pages/linn-03.htm, 16th Ohio Volunteers, Diary and Letters of Thomas Buchannan Linn, 21 September 1863.

11. NARA, RG9, Loring to Burnside, 18 September 1863.

12. OR, ser. 1, vol. 30/3, doc. 52, p. 943, General Field Orders No. 15.

13. Hudson Strode, *Jefferson Davis: Confederate President*, 3 vols. (New York, 1959), vol. 2, p. 475.

14. Francis W. Dawson, *Reminiscences of Confederate Service, 1861–1865*, ed. Bell I. Wiley (Baton Rouge, La., 1980), p. 100.

15. Mary Boykin Chesnut, *A Diary from Dixie*, ed. Isabella D. Martin and Myrta Lockett Avary (New York, 1905), p. 241.

16. Brian Holden Reid, *The American Civil War and the Wars of the Industrial Revolution* (London, 1999), p. 132.

17. Sam Watkins, *Company Aytch* (New York, 1999), p. 88.

18. Ibid., p. 89.

19. *Illustrated London News*, 26 December 1863.

20. Dawson, *Reminiscences*, p. 102.

21. Edward Porter Alexander, *Fighting for the Confederacy: The Personal Recollections of General Edward Porter Alexander*, ed. Gary Gallagher (Chapel Hill,

NC, 1989), p. 301. Vizetelly's brother claimed that he offered to deliver a message for Longstreet during the battle, since all the other couriers had been picked off by Federal sharpshooters. 'Upon his return to the General's headquarters, Longstreet commissioned him an "honorary captain" in the Confederate States Army.' William Stanley Hoole, *Vizetelly covers the Confederacy* (Tuscaloosa, Ala., 1957), p. 104. It is possible that Vizetelly delivered messages, but not during a battle that he missed.

22. Dawson, *Reminiscences*, p. 102.

23. Ibid., p. 195, appendix: Dawson to mother, 29 September 1863.

24. Emory University, Gregory MSS, Lawley to Gregory, 16 September 1863.

25. Julia Miele Rodas, 'More than a Civil (War) Friendship: Anthony Trollope and Frank Lawley', *Princeton University Library Chronicle*, 60/1 (1998), pp. 39–60, at p. 48, Morris to Lawley, 24 September 1863.

26. Emory University, Gregory MSS, Lawley to Gregory, 16 September 1863.

27. Doris Kearns Goodwin, *Team of Rivals* (New York, 2005), p. 556.

28. Michael Burlingame and John R. Turner Ettlinger (eds.), *Inside Lincoln's White House: The Complete War Diary of John Hay* (Carbondale, Ill., 1997), p. 84, 11 September 1863.

29. Frederic William Maitland, *Life and Letters of Leslie Stephen* (New York, 1906), p. 119.

30. It should be noted that Seward already suspected that the ships had been detained. Leslie Stephen dismissed Seward as a lightweight after he confused John Stuart Mill with Richard Monckton Milnes. Yet Seward was not so different from the MP who remarked to an American visitor that Lee would presumably follow up his Gettysburg victory by taking Washington and New Orleans, since 'New Orleans is about 100 miles from Washington, I think?' J. G. Randall, *Lincoln the President*, 4 vols., vol. 3: *Midstream* (New York, 1953), p. 317.

31. Maitland, *Life and Letters of Leslie Stephen*, p. 122.

32. Ibid., p. 123.

33. *An Englishman in the American Civil War: The Diaries of Henry Yates Thompson, 1863*, ed. Sir Christopher Chancellor (New York, 1971), p. 86.

34. Ibid., p. 98.

35. Randall, *Lincoln the President*, p. 370.

36. James J. Barnes and Patience P. Barnes (eds.), *Private and Confidential: Letters from British Ministers in Washington to the Foreign Secretaries* (Selinsgrove, Pa., 1993), p. 335.

37. Philip Van Doren Stern, *When the Guns Roared: World Aspects of the American Civil War* (New York, 1965), p. 234.

38. 'I never was in such a town or place in all my life,' Milne wrote admiringly. He believed that below the surface of hostility was a deep bond between the two countries that it was his duty to nurture. Somerset RO, Somerset MSS, d/RA/A/2a/34/32, Milne to Somerset, 18 October 1863.

39. Ibid.

40. *New York Albion*, 17 October 1863.

41. PRO 30/22/37, ff. 203-7, Lyons to Russell, 16 October 1863.

42. PRO 30/22/37, ff. 219-26, Lyons to Russell, 26 October 1863.

43. PRO 30/22/37, ff. 203-7, Lyons to Russell, 16 October 1863.

44. PRO FO 5/895, ff. 69-71, d. 758, Lyons to Russell, 23 October 1863.

45. Eugene H. Berwanger, *The British Foreign Service and the American Civil War* (Lexington, Ky., 1994), p. 119.

46. William Watson, *The Civil War Adventures of a Blockade Runner* (College Station, Tex., 2001), pp. 50, 56.

47. PRO FO 5/909, ff. 361-2, Lynn to Magruder, 3 October 1863.

48. Watson, *The Adventures of a Blockade Runner*, p. 58.

49. PRO FO 5/896, f. 40, Lyons to Russell, 6 November 1863. 'My Lord, I have much to say regarding the barbarous manner in which British subjects are treated in the Southern Confederacy,' wrote Mr McIntyre from Alabama on 3 October 1863. His friend, James Maloney, applied for a British passport in 1861 and started for home. The provost marshal arrested him anyway and sent him to General Bragg's army, sneering at 'his damned English protection'. 'I do not know whether your Lordship is acquainted with these facts or not. But if you are . . . it is very strange that something cannot be done to secure for British Subjects that protection which they seek.' In January 1864 the legation had to return the Southern Consuls' pay receipts to London, explaining that Lord Lyons 'has no means of sending these letters to their destination, nor does he know whether the Consular officers to whom they are addressed are still at their posts'. The source for the quotation in the footnote on this page is PRO FO 5/948, f. 57, Lyons to Russell, 19 April 1864.

50. Berwanger, *The British Foreign Service and the American Civil War*, p. 104.

51. John B. Jones, *A Rebel War Clerk's Diary at the Confederate States Capital*, ed. Earl Schenck Miers (Urbana, Ill., 1958), p. 292, 15 October 1863.

52. PRO FO 5/908, ff. 115-17, Cridland to Lord Russell, 14 November 1863.

53. Berwanger, *The British Foreign Service and the American Civil War*, p. 107.

CHAPTER 26. CAN THE NATION ENDURE?

1. PRO FO 5/908, ff. 115-17, no. 30, Cridland to Russell, 14 November 1863.

2. Fitzgerald Ross, *Cities and Camps of the Confederate States*, ed. Richard Barksdale Harwell (Champaign, Ill., 1997), p. 140.

3. *The Times*, 1 December 1863.

4. Ross, *Cities and Camps*, p. 143.

5. John G. Nicolay and John Hay (eds.), *Complete Works of Lincoln*, vol. 9 (New York, 1907), p. 26, Lincoln to Grant, 13 July 1863.

6. 'The Journal of Robert Neve', private collection, p. 140.

7. Ibid., p. 143.

8. Francis W. Dawson, *Reminiscences of Confederate Service, 1861–1865*, ed. Bell I. Wiley (Baton Rouge, La., 1980), p. 105.

9. Jeffry D. Wert, *General James Longstreet: The Confederacy's Most Controversial Soldier* (New York, 1993), p. 341.

10. Dawson, *Reminiscences*, p. 109.

11. *The Times*, 15 December 1863.

12. Bruce Catton, *Never Call Retreat* (London, 2001), p. 273.

13. *Decatur Daily News*, 20 March 1879.

14. David Donald provides the following footnote in his edition of Salmon P. Chase's diary: 'Henry Charles De Ahna wrote the President his version of these events on January 31, 1864: "As Your Excellency probably recollects, it was brought to the knowledge of the Government several months ago, that through a singular mistake in a name, I found myself approached by an agent of the Rebel government and an offer of $50,000 was made to me, if I would undertake to enter into a negotiation with Col. Percy Wyndham and by offering him in the name of the Rebel Government the sum of 100,000 Dollars, would succeed in persuading the said Percy Wyndham to allow himself to be taken prisoner with his whole Cavalry Brigade." De Ahna told his story to V. Hogan, "who was then well known as Secretary Chase's Detective," and he also had an interview with Chase himself, but he claimed that Chase failed properly to investigate the matter.' *Inside Lincoln's Cabinet: The Civil War Diaries of Salmon P. Chase*, ed. David Donald (New York, 1954), p. 316.

15. PRO FO115/400, f. 247, Lyons to John Livingston, 3 November 1863.

16. Nicolay and Hay (eds.), *Complete Works of Abraham Lincoln*, vol. 9, p. 204, Lincoln to Meade, 9 November 1863; Lincoln to Burnside, 8 November 1863.

17. Ibid., p. 154, Lincoln to Rosecrans, 4 October 1863.

18. Sarah Forbes Hughes (ed.), *Letters and Recollections of John Murray Forbes*, 2 vols. (New York, 1900), vol. 2, p. 74, Forbes to Lincoln, 8 September 1863.

19. Michael Burlingame, *Abraham Lincoln*, 2 vols. (Baltimore, 2008), vol. 2, p. 573; Ronald White Jr., *Lincoln* (New York, 2009), p. 604.

20. David H. Donald, *Lincoln* (New York, 1995), p. 465.

21. *The Times*, 4 December 1863.

22. Michael Burlingame and R. Turner Ettlinger (eds.), *Inside Lincoln's White House: The Complete War Diary of John Hay* (Carbondale, Ill., 1997), pp. 112–13, 18–19 November 1863.

23. Burlingame, *Abraham Lincoln*, vol. 2, p. 576.

24. *An Englishman in the American Civil War: The Diaries of Henry Yates Thompson, 1863*, ed. Sir Christopher Chancellor (New York, 1971), pp. 141–2.

25. Sam Watkins, *Company Aytch* (New York, 1999), p. 91.

26. *An Englishman in the American Civil War*, p. 152.

27. 'The Journal of Robert Neve', p. 158.

28. Cleburne realized that he had a volunteer of exceptional quality the moment Byrne presented himself at his headquarters. The General requested a commission

for him on 8 November, writing: 'This young gentleman is eminently deserving. He left England to volunteer his services in our cause. He has been on my staff. I have found him a brave and gallant officer, highly intelligent, and devoted to our cause. I am the more anxious he should be appointed, because he sacrificed the opportunity of being commissioned in the British Service. He passed the examination required to entitle him to be placed on the list of possible appointees, before he left England, which he did upon a limited leave of absence. His leave has now expired, and, as he understands, he had forfeited his chance of being subjected in that service.' Irving A. Buck, *Cleburne and his Command* (Wilmington, NY, 1995), p. 27.

29. 'The Journal of Robert Neve', p. 161.

30. Watkins, *Company Aytch*, p. 95.

31. *An Englishman in the American Civil War*, pp. 166-7.

32. Ibid., p. 18.

33. George Templeton Strong, *Diary of the Civil War 1860-1865*, ed. Allan Nevins (New York, 1962), p. 375, 27 November 1863.

34. R. W. McFarland, *The Surrender of Cumberland Gap* (Columbus, Ohio, 1898), p. 29.

35. For a complete description of the 16th Ohio Volunteer Infantry, De Courcy's career as its colonel, along with scanned documents, muster rolls, and much more, see http://www.mkwe.com/home.htm.

36. Ten years later, De Courcy's cousin died. Thus, *Kind Hearts and Coronets* style, though De Courcy was the fourth child of a second son, he became the 31st Baron Kingsale, Ireland's premiere barony.

37. Jeffry D. Wert, *The Sword of Lincoln* (New York, 2006), p. 321.

38. British Library of Political and Economic Science, LSE, GB 0097, Farr MSS, vol. X, Henry Ezechiel to Mr Murray, 6 January 1864.

39. Jones, *A Rebel War Clerk's Diary*, p. 306, 12 November 1863.

CHAPTER 27. BUCKLING UNDER PRESSURE

1. W. C. Ford (ed.), *A Cycle of Adams Letters, 1861-1865*, 2 vols. (Boston, 1920), vol. 2, p. 106, Henry Adams to Charles Francis Adams Jr., 27 November 1863.

2. ORN, ser. 2, vol. 2, p. 514, Stephen Mallory to Bulloch, 22 October 1863.

3. Fitzgerald Ross, *Cities and Camps of the Confederate States*, ed. Richard Barksdale Harwell (Champaign, Ill., 1997), p. 172.

4. Stephen Z. Starr, *Colonel Grenfell's Wars* (Baton Rouge, La., 1971), pp. 106-7. Ross, *Cities and Camps*, pp. 172-3.

5. C. Vann Woodward (ed.), *Mary Chesnut's Civil War* (New Haven, 1981), p. 337, 12 January 1864.

6. *Illustrated London News*, 2 April 1864, p. 313.

7. Raphael Semmes, *Service Afloat: A Personal Memoir of my Cruises and Services* (1868; repr. Baltimore, 1987), p. 629.

8. They were Baron Maximilian von Meulnier of Bremen and Julius Schroeder of Hanover.

9. Norman C. Delaney, *John McIntosh Kell of the Raider Alabama* (Tuscaloosa, Ala., 1973), p. 153.

10. Charles Francis Adams made the first claim for redress against the *Alabama*, 'for the national and private injuries sustained by the proceedings of this vessel', on 20 November 1862. Russell replied on 19 December, categorically stating that 'Britain cannot be held responsible ... for these irregular proceedings of British subjects', and to claim otherwise would be as reasonable as the British government suing the American 'for the injuries done to the property of British subjects by the *Alabama* ... on the ground that the United States claim authority ... over the Confederate States, by whom that vessel was commissioned'. *PRFA*, 1 (1864), p. 35, Russell to Charles Francis Adams, 22 December 1862.

11. PRO FO282/7 (2), Consul Archibald to Lord Lyons, 9 April 1863.

12. PRO HO45/7261/216, Colonial Office to Home Office, 10 February 1864. Final estimates for Irish-American recruitment throughout the war hover around 140,000 in the Federal army, and between 20,000 and 40,000 in the Confederate. Of the sixteen stowaways on the *Kearsarge*, five were tried in April 1864 for violating the Foreign Enlistment Act. They pleaded guilty to the charge and were released on their own cognizance. By then, Adams thought the government was pursuing the case in order to appear even-handed in its battle to shut down Confederate operations.

13. Charles P. Cullop, 'An Unequal Duel: Union Recruiting in Ireland, 1863–1864', *Civil War History*, 13 (1967), p. 108.

14. James D. Bulloch, *The Secret Service of the Confederate States in Europe*, 2 vols. (New York, 1884), vol. 1, p. 444.

15. Duke University, Special Collections Library, Rose O'Neal Greenhow Papers, Greenhow to Alexander Boteler, 10 December 1863.

16. The captured blockade-runner is incorrectly identified as the *Ceres* in William C. Davis (ed.), *Secret History of Confederate Diplomacy Abroad* (Lawrence, Kan., 2005), p. xxii.

17. Ann Blackman, *Wild Rose: Rose O'Neale Greenhow, Civil War Spy* (New York, 2005), p. 275.

18. Ibid.

19. Lynda L. Crist, Kenneth H. Williams and Peggy L. Dillard (eds.), *The Papers of Jefferson Davis*, vol. 10 (Baton Rouge, La., 1999), p. 143.

20. Bayly Ellen Marks and Mark Norton Schatz (eds.), *Between North and South: A Maryland Journalist Views the Civil War. The Narrative of William Wilkins Glenn 1861–1869* (Cranbury, NJ, 1976), p. 123, February 1864.

21. Quoted in Blackman, *Wild Rose*, p. 279. Samuel W. Richey Confederate Collection, Walter Havinghurst Special Collections, Miami University (Oxford, Ohio), Rose Greenhow to Jefferson Davis, 2 January 1864.

22. *The Private Journal of Georgiana Gholson Walker*, ed. Dwight Franklin

Henderson, Confederate Centennial Studies, 25 (Tuscaloosa, Ala., 1963), p. 74, 8 March 1864.

23. Quoted in Blackman, *Wild Rose*, p. 281.

24. Bulloch, *The Secret Service of the Confederate States of America*, p. 296.

25. Ibid.

26. Stanley Lebergott, 'Through the Blockade: The Profitability and Extent of Cotton Smuggling, 1861–1865', *Journal of Economic History*, 41 (Dec. 1981), p. 876.

27. Merseyside Maritime Museum, Fraser, Trenholm MSS, B/FT box 81, Prioleau to Trenholm, 12 January 1864.

28. ORN, ser. 2, vol. 3, pp. 981–5, Hotze to Benjamin, 26 December 1863.

29. R. J. M. Blackett, *Divided Hearts: Britain and the American Civil War* (Baton Rouge, La., 2001), p. 190.

30. *Index*, 14 January 1863.

31. ORN, ser. 2, vol. 3, pp. 1007–9, Mason to Benjamin, 25 January 1864. For example, Lady Wharncliffe wrote on 30 January 1864: 'To think that having started [the war in 1861 with our friends] here drawn with indignation at the conduct of the Confederates, and that now one should be wishing for their success, slave owners as they are! ... however I am convinced that somehow the knell of slavery is rung.' Durham University, Grey MSS, GRE/G17/21/18–19, Georgiana Elizabeth, Lady Wharncliffe, to Miss Elizabeth Copley.

32. Benjamin to Spence, 11 January 1864, quoted in John Bigelow, 'The Confederate Diplomatists and their Shirt of Nessus', *Century Magazine*, 20 (1891), p. 122.

33. *PRFA*, 1 (1864), p. 44.

34. Sarah Agnes Wallace and Frances Elma Gillespie (eds.), *The Journal of Benjamin Moran, 1857–1865*, 2 vols. (Chicago, 1948, 1949), vol. 2, p. 1263, 11 February 1863.

35. Hansard, 3rd ser., vol. 173, cols. 28–30, 4 February 1864.

36. Wilbur Devereux Jones, *The Confederate Rams at Birkenhead*, Confederate Centennial Studies, 19 (Wilmington, NC, 2000), p. 107.

37. W. G. Wiebe, Mary S. Millar and Anne P. Robson, *Benjamin Disraeli Letters: 1860–1864* (Toronto, 2009), p. 314.

38. ORN, ser. 2, vol. 3, pp. 1060–63, Hotze to Benjamin, 12 March 1864.

39. MHS, Adams MSS, Diary of Charles Francis Adams, 20 February 1864.

40. Ford (ed.), *A Cycle of Adams Letters*, vol. 2, pp. 118–19, Charles Francis Adams Jr. to Charles Francis Adams, 16 January 1864.

41. Wallace and Gillespie (eds.), *The Journal of Benjamin Moran*, vol. 2, p. 1264, 16 February 1864 and 17 February 1864.

42. Ibid., p. 1266, 20 February 1864.

43. Ibid., p. 1269, 1 March 1864.

44. Edward Chase Kirkland, *Charles Francis Adams Jr.* (Cambridge, Mass., 1965), p. 28.

45. Wallace and Gillespie (eds.), *The Journal of Benjamin Moran*, vol. 2, p. 1274, 12 March 1864.

46. ORN, ser. 2, vol. 3, pp. 874–81, Hotze to Benjamin, 27 August 1863.

47. Frederic William Maitland (ed.), *Life and Letters of Leslie Stephen* (New York, 1906), pp. 155–7, Stephen to Lowell, 1 January 1864.

48. The book was far superior to the novelist George Alfred Lawrence's self-pitying account of his capture and imprisonment, called *Border and Bastille*. It was also much more effective as a piece of pro-Confederate propaganda than a work such as *The South As It Is*, by the Revd T. D. Ozanne, who had spent twenty-one years in the South and could not understand why it should be made to suffer all because of 'one social evil'.

49. Hugh Dubrulle, 'Fear of Americanization and the Emergence of an Anglo-Saxon Confederacy', *Albion: A Quarterly Journal Concerned with British Studies*, 33/4 (Winter 2001), pp. 583–613, at p. 594.

50. Brian Jenkins, 'Frank Lawley and the Confederacy', *Civil War History*, 23 (March 1977), p. 158.

51. Ibid.

52. ORN, ser. 2, vol. 3, pp. 1046–7, Slidell to Benjamin, 5 March 1864.

53. Jenkins, 'Frank Lawley and the Confederacy', p. 158.

54. Quoted in Edward Chalfant, *Better in Darkness* (New York, 1994), p. 75.

55. Blackman, *Wild Rose*, p. 284.

56. Library of Congress, Mason Papers, Spence to Mason, April 1864.

57. Hansard, 3rd ser., vol. 173, cols. 1922–3, 14 March 1864, Lord Palmerston.

58. ORN, ser. 2, vol. 3, pp. 1067–9, Hotze to Benjamin, 19 March 1864.

59. ORN, ser. 2, vol. 3, pp. 1077–9, Hotze to Benjamin, 24 March 1864.

60. *Transactions of the Historic Society of Lancashire and Cheshire*, John Ward Diary, p. 176.

CHAPTER 28. A GREAT SLAUGHTER

1. A headcount in the South at the end of 1863 revealed that only 277,000 soldiers remained after three years. President Davis did not dare allow such alarming information to reach the public. The North, on the other hand, had 611,000 men in arms.

2. John Bierman, *Napoleon III and his Carnival Empire* (New York, 1988), p. 234.

3. Thomas E. Pemberton, *Sir Charles Wyndham: A Biography* (London, 1904), p. 27; 'Britons in the Civil War: Sir Charles Wyndham', *Crossfire*, 37 (Nov. 1990).

4. OR, ser. 1, vol. 34/1, p. 219, Report of Admiral Porter, 13 June 1864. 'I trust some future historian will treat this matter as it deserves to be treated,' he declared, 'because it is a subject in which the whole country should feel an interest.'

5. Although Dahlgren's massacre plan could have been a forgery, the South believed that the papers were authentic.

6. Duane Schultz, *The Dahlgren Affair* (New York, 1998), p. 157. Two weeks before Colonel Dahlgren made his doomed ride towards Richmond, the Confederate Congress had secretly approved a bill on 15 February to transfer $5 million

to a Secret Service fund. The bill also authorized the use of covert warfare against the North. The government had finally accepted that Lee could not win the war by himself.

7. Ibid., p. 181.

8. Mabel Clare Weaks, 'Colonel George St Leger Grenfell', *Filson Club History Quarterly*, 34 (1960), p. 11.

9. Stephen Z. Starr, *Colonel Grenfell's Wars* (Baton Rouge, La., 1971), p. 125.

10. Frank Moore (ed.), *Rebellion Record*, ser. 1, 53 vols., vol. 8 (New York, 1883), p. 515, Burton N. Harrison to Lord Lyons, 6 April 1864.

11. Oscar A. Kinchen, *Confederate Operations in Canada* (Hanover, Mass., 1970), p. 36.

12. John Jones passed a pleasant two days in February 1863, working out possible permutations of a three-way partition between the States; John B. Jones, *A Rebel War Clerk's Diary at the Confederate States Capital*, ed. Earl Schenck Miers (Urbana, Ill., 1958), p. 165.

13. James Morton Callahan, *The Diplomatic History of the Confederacy* (Baltimore, 1901), p. 225.

14. Hudson Strode, *Jefferson Davis: Confederate President*, 3 vols. (New York, 1959), vol. 3, p. 35.

15. 'There is no doubt he has got the best military head of any man in this Confederacy, and if he only gets a chance he will make his mark on the enemy this Spring and Summer,' Feilden had written enthusiastically. South Carolina Historical Society, Feilden–Smythe MSS (3), Feilden to Julia McCord, 20 April 1864.

16. Ibid. (10), Feilden to Julia McCord, 29 April 1864.

17. Ibid. (6), Feilden to Julia McCord, 30 April 1864.

18. E. Milby Burton, *The Siege of Charleston* (Columbia, SC, 1982), p. 283.

19. PRO FO 5/896, f. 23, Lyons to Russell, 3 November 1863; the reference for the quotation in the footnote is PRO FO 5/896, f. 33, Lyons to Russell, 3 November 1863.

20. PRO FO 5/948/274, f. 63, Lyons to Russell, 25 April 1864; James J. Barnes and Patience P. Barnes (eds.), *The American Civil War through British Eyes*, vol. 3 (Kent, Ohio, 2005), p. 157.

21. *New York Times*, 2 February 1864.

22. West Sussex RO, Lyons MSS, Box 301, Lyons to sister, 26 December 1863; PRO 30/22/37, f. 63, Lyons to Russell, 24 December 1863.

23. West Sussex RO, Lyons MSS, Box 302, Lyons to sister, 11 March 1864.

24. PRO 30/22/38, ff. 46–9, Lyons to Russell, 17 May 1864.

25. British Library of Political and Economic Science, LSE, Farr MSS, Add. 2, unknown writer to Captain Hatch, 19 February 1864.

26. Duke University, Malet family MSS, Malet to mother, 4 January 1864.

27. Edmund Hammond, the Permanent Under-Secretary of State for Foreign Affairs, had a low opinion of young men who wanted to have a personal life outside the Foreign Office: 'The labour required of the Foreign Office Clerks is great,

the attendance long, and the hours late and uncertain.' *Reports from Commissioners*, 20 vols., vol. 5 (London, 1856), p. 67, Hammond to Horace Mann, 25 June 1855.

28. PRO FO5/949, f. 5, d. 289, Lyons to Russell, 3 May 1864.

29. PRO FO282/10, f. 294, Archibald to Lyons, 30 January 1863.

30. 'Bright–Sumner Letters, 1861–1872', *Proceedings of the Massachusetts Historical Society*, 46 (1912), pp. 93–165, at p. 127, Bright to Sumner, 15 December 1863. Thomas Smelt, the father of young Stephen, wrote to Lincoln on 6 March 1864, imploring him to release his son, who had been drugged and drafted into the army. The humble clerk struggled to express himself: 'I also appeal to you as a Father and man of honour that you take all these circumstances into your consideration, and for the sake of his family, you be graciously pleased to grant this my prayer,' he begged. By the time Mr Smelt's letter had passed from Lincoln's desk to the adjutant general's office, and from there into the hands of the War Department clerks, Stephen had been wounded and captured by the Confederates. Stephen Smelt was a prisoner of war in Andersonville, the prison with the highest death toll in the South. He was beyond the reach of his father or the indifferent Northern authorities. NARA RG 94/SKM 06, Thomas Smelt to Lincoln, 6 March 1864.

31. PRO FO5/898, f. 66, Lyons to Russell, 7 December 1863.

32. The Foreign Office could not, officially, applaud a solution that forced British subjects to pledge their allegiance to a foreign country, but there was relief in London that a hideous injustice against conscripted Britons in the Southern armies had been resolved.

33. Warwickshire RO, CR114A/533/23 (1), Seymour MSS, General Wistar to General Dix, 15 April 1864.

34. A. S. Lewis (ed.), *My Dear Parents* (New York, 1982), p. 67.

35. James Pendlebury MSS, private collection, p. 1.

36. James Pendlebury MSS, p. 2.

37. PRO FO5/1287, d.189, Francis Lousada to Lord Lyons, 11 March 1864 and *passim*.

38. Fitzgerald Ross, *Cities and Camps of the Confederate States*, ed. Richard Barksdale Harwell (Champaign, Ill., 1997), p. 219.

39. Frances Elizabeth Owen Monck, *My Canadian Leaves: Diary of a Visit to Canada, 1865–6* (London, 1891), p. 127.

40. *Journal of John Wodehouse, First Earl of Kimberley* (Cambridge, 1997), p. 75.

41. R. A. J. Walling (ed.), *The Diaries of John Bright* (New York, 1931), p. 271.

42. Edward Lyulph Stanley, 4th Baron Stanley of Alderley, letters from America, Royal Commonwealth Society Library, Cambridge, Stanley to Lady Stanley, 17 April 1864.

43. Ibid. Cambridge, Stanley to Lady Stanley, 27 April 1864.

44. W. C. Ford (ed.), *A Cycle of Adams Letters, 1861–1865*, 2 vols. (Boston, 1920), vol. 2, p. 128, Charles Francis Adams Jr. to Charles Francis Adams, 1 May 1864.

45. OR, ser. 1, vol. 32/3, p. 246, Grant to Sherman, 3 April 1864.

46. Lewis (ed.), *My Dear Parents*, p. 77, Horrocks to parents, 8 May 1864.

47. Ibid.

48. Ibid., p. 78.

49. James Pendlebury MSS, pp. 4–5

50. Shelby Foote, *The Civil War*, 3 vols. (New York, 1986), vol. 3, p. 170.

51. Francis W. Dawson, *Reminiscences of Confederate Service, 1861–1865*, ed. Bell I. Wiley (Baton Rouge, La., 1980), p. 197, Dawson to mother, 1 June 1864.

52. Jeffrey D. Wert, *General James Longstreet: The Confederacy's Most Controversial Soldier* (New York, 1993), p. 385.

53. New York Historical Society, *Narrative of Ebenezer Wells* (*c.* 1881), 5 May 1864.

54. Dawson, *Reminiscences*, p. 197, Dawson to mother, 1 June 1864, and p. 115.

55. Grant was annoyed by the half-hearted performance from his tired army, but, wrote a British military historian in the 1930s, 'It is sometimes difficult to decide where driving force deteriorates into mere pigheadedness and refusal to face unpalatable facts.' Alfred H. Burne, *Lee, Grant, and Sherman* (repr. Lawrence, Kan., 2000), p. 24.

56. New York Historical Society, *Narrative of Ebenezer Wells*, 10 May 1864.

57. Horace Porter, *Campaigning with Grant* (New York, 1906), p. 110.

58. Lewis (ed.), *My Dear Parents*, p. 85, Horrocks to father, 31 May 1864.

59. Ford (ed.), *A Cycle of Adams Letters*, vol. 2, p. 131, Charles Francis Adams Jr. to Charles Francis Adams, 29 May 1864.

CHAPTER 29. 'DEFIANCE TO HER ENEMIES'

1. *Transactions of the Historic Society of Lancashire and Cheshire*, John Ward Diary, pp. 178–9.

2. British Library of Political and Economic Science, LSE, Farr MSS, Add. 2, Ellen Bacon to Farr, 22 June 1864.

3. *The Times*, 27 May 1864. *Les Misérables* had been published in New York to great acclaim in 1862.

4. *Standard*, 24 May 1864. (There were 55,000 estimated casualties at the Battle of Waterloo, 25,416 from the Wilderness campaign.)

5. Sarah Agnes Wallace and Frances Elma Gillespie (eds.), *The Journal of Benjamin Moran, 1857–1865*, 2 vols. (Chicago, 1948, 1949), vol. 2, p. 1283, 14 April 1864; p. 1285, 21 April 1864. This was not Moran's only humiliation that spring. On 18 May, he went to a party in Kensington Palace Gardens. He entered the smoking room to discover that it had been commandeered by Charles Dickens, Wilkie Collins 'and other famous literary men'. Moran would have loved to have stayed but he was shown the door by one of the guests.

6. Francis W. Dawson, *Reminiscences of Confederate Service, 1861–1865*, ed. Bell I. Wiley (Baton Rouge, La., 1980), p. 130.

7. Merseyside Maritime Museum, Fraser, Trenholm MSS, B/FT, box 81, p. 298, Prioleau to Henry Wise, 17 May 1864.

8. Samuel Bernard Thompson, *Confederate Purchasing Operations Abroad* (Gloucester, Mass., 1973), p. 40.

9. James M. Morgan, *Recollections of a Rebel Reefer* (Boston, 1917), p. 180.

10. Ibid., p. 182.

11. Ibid.

12. Warren F. Spencer, *The Confederate Navy in Europe* (Tuscaloosa, Ala., 1983), p. 194. The blockade-running business had remained an exclusive club of a small number of shipping firms. The most accurate calculation to date lists only 111 British-owned ships between 1861 and 1865.

13. Library of Congress, Mason Papers, Lindsay to Mason, 10 May 1864.

14. John Morley, *Life of William Ewart Gladstone: 1809–1872*, 2 vols. (London, 1908), vol. 1, p. 572. Gladstone said he feared the praise as much as the criticism, worrying that it had been taken too literally as a declaration of the rights of man. But the speech is regarded as a watershed. Gladstone later said he was not trying to import 'American principles'; only that the events on the 'other side of the Atlantic' had demonstrated how democracy could strengthen a government and bolster the 'energy given to the action of a nation'. He regarded England as pursuing a middle way between Europe and America.

15. Library of Congress, Mason Papers, Tremlett to Mason, 2 June 1864.

16. Library of Congress, Maury Papers, Tremlett to Maury, 1 June 1864.

17. Ibid.

18. ORN, ser. 2, vol. 3, p. 1144, Mason to Benjamin, 9 June 1864.

19. The name Cold Harbor came from the local tavern, which offered beds for the night, but not hot meals.

20. Frederick W. Seward (ed.), *Seward at Washington* (New York, 1891), p. 223.

21. Ernest Samuels (ed.), *Henry Adams: Selected Letters* (Cambridge, Mass., 1988), p. 68, Henry Adams to Charles Francis Adams Jr., 10 June 1864.

22. Norman C. Delaney, *John McIntosh Kell of the Raider Alabama* (Tuscaloosa, Ala., 1973), p. 157.

23. Raphael Semmes, *Service Afloat: A Personal Memoir of my Cruises and Services* (1868; repr. Baltimore, 1987), p. 750.

24. John Morris Ellicott, *The Life of John Ancrum Winslow* (New York, 1905), p. 179.

25. Frederick Milnes Edge, *The Career of the Alabama ('no. 290') from July 29, 1862, to June 19, 1864* (London, 1908), p. 27, D. H. Llewellyn to Travers, 14 June 1864.

26. Robert Underwood Johnson and Clarence Clough Buel (eds.), *Battles and Leaders of the Civil War*, 4 vols. (Secaucus, NJ, 1985), vol. 4, p. 607.

27. Ellicott, *The Life of John Ancrum Winslow*, p. 193.

28. Charles Grayson Summersell, *CSS Alabama* (Tuscaloosa, Ala., 1985), p. 77.

29. Ibid., p. 78.

30. Edge, *The Career of the Alabama*, p. 28.

31. A week after Llewellyn's death, the doctors and students at his alma mater, Charing Cross Medical School, voted to open a subscription fund in memory of his sacrifice. The public subscription was especially popular with doctors in the Indian army. Enough money was raised to found the Llewellyn Scholarship Prize, and two memorials, one at Charing Cross Hospital and the other at his parish church, Easton, in Wiltshire. The marble plaque at Charing Cross paid tribute to Llewellyn's bravery and sacrifice under fire: IN MEMORY OF DAVID HERBERT LLEWELLYN, FORMERLY A STUDENT OF THIS HOSPITAL AND AFTERWARDS SURGEON TO THE CONFEDERATE STATES WAR STEAMER 'ALABAMA'. AFTER HER ACTION WITH THE FEDERAL STEAMER 'KEARSAGE' OFF CHERBOURG, THOUGH ENTREATED BY THE WOUNDED TO JOIN THEM IN THEIR BOAT, HE REFUSED TO PERIL THEIR SAFETY BY SO DOING, AND WENT DOWN WITH THE SINKING VESSEL, ON 19TH JUNE 1864 IN THE 26TH YEAR OF HIS AGE. THIS TABLET HAS BEEN ERECTED AND A SCHOLARSHIP FOUNDED IN HIS NAME BY HIS FELLOW STUDENTS, AND OTHERS IN ENGLAND AND INDIA TO COMMEMORATE HIS SELF-SACRIFICING COURAGE AND DEVOTION.

32. NARA, M.T-185, roll 8, vol. 8, US Consuls in Bristol, Consul Eastman to Seward, 23 June 1864.

33. Somerset RO, Somerset MSS, d/RA/A/2a/40/10, Palmerston to Somerset, 21 June 1864.

34. W. C. Ford (ed.), *A Cycle of Adams Letters, 1861–1865*, 2 vols. (Boston, 1920), vol. 2, p. 158, Henry Adams to Charles Francis Adams Jr., 24 June 1864.

35. See Beth Archer Brombert, *Édouard Manet* (Chicago, 1997), pp. 159–60, for the reasons why, contrary to popular belief, Manet did not witness the battle. The quotation in the footnote on this page is from W. S. Hoole, *Confederate Foreign Agent: The European Diary of Major Edward C. Anderson* (Tuscaloosa, Ala., 1976), 17 July 1864.

36. Brian Jenkins, *Britain and the `War for the Union*, 2 vols. (Montreal, 1974, 1980), vol. 2, p. 333.

37. A week later, one of the *Phaeton*'s lieutenants was kidnapped and crimped while on shore leave. Consul Bernal eventually rescued him from trench duty outside Baltimore.

38. New York Historical Society, *Narrative of Ebenezer Wells* (*c.* 1881), 9 June 1864.

39. OR, ser. 1, vol. 34/4, doc. 64, p. 138, Canby to Major-General A. J. Smith.

40. Thomas E. Pemberton, *Sir Charles Wyndham: A Biography* (London, 1904), p. 21.

41. James G. Hollandsworth Jr., *Pretense of Glory* (Baton Rouge, La., 1998), p. 211.

42. Edward Lyulph Stanley, 4th Baron Stanley of Alderley, letters from America, Royal Commonwealth Society Library, Cambridge, Stanley to Blanche, 21 May 1864.

43. Ibid., Stanley to Kate, 9 June 1864. When Stanley visited General Banks at his

office on 3 June, the General showed no embarrassment over his recent demotion, though he admitted his frustration with the slow pace of change for former slaves. His main source of pride was the number of Negroes entering the army. The Louisiana Native Guards who fought at Port Hudson had been the first black regiment officially mustered into the army. Since then another thirty black regiments had been formed, with at least 18,000 black recruits, and more were coming.

44. Ibid., Stanley to Blanche, 12 May 1864.

45. Mary Sophia Hill, *A British Subject's Recollections of the Confederacy* (Baltimore, 1875), p. 90.

46. Ibid., p. 62. The source for the footnote is PRO FO5/906, ff. 104–7, d. 2, Coppell to Lord Russell, 20 May 1864.

47. Hill, *A British Subject's Recollections of the Confederacy*, p. 63.

48. Belle Boyd, *Belle Boyd in Camp and Prison* (New York, 1865; repr. Baton Rouge, La., 1998), p. 197.

49. Ruth Scarborough, *Siren of the South* (Macon, Ga., 1997), p. 157.

50. Boyd, *Belle Boyd in Camp and Prison*, pp. 200–203.

51. Stephen Z. Starr, *Colonel Grenfell's Wars* (Baton Rouge, La., 1971), p. 126.

CHAPTER 30. 'CAN WE HOLD OUT?'

1. University College of North Wales, Bangor, Evans MSS 2854, ff. 63–9, *c.* June 1864.

2. PRO FO5/1258, n. 73, enc. 2, Mary Sophia Hill to Lyons, 17 June 1864.

3. PRO FO5/1258, n. 73, enc. 1, Coppell to Lyons, 1 July 1864.

4. E. Milby Burton, *The Siege of Charleston* (Columbia, SC, 1982), p. 285.

5. Just fifteen blockade-runners had been able to get out in May, but Feilden was able to put a few cotton bales on one of them for his own account. 'All my English friends in the Blockade runners came to me for assistance and it was no great return if a bale of cotton was now and again taken out for me', Feilden wrote later. South Carolina Historical Society, Feilden–Smythe MSS (11), Feilden to Julia McCord, 23 May 1864.

6. Ibid., (12), Feilden to Julia McCord, 28 May 1864.

7. Ibid., (14), Feilden to Julia McCord, 18 June 1864.

8. Ibid., (16), Feilden to Julia McCord, 30 June 1864.

9. Jubal A. Early, *The Campaigns of Gen. Robert E. Lee: An Address by Lieut. General Jubal A. Early, before Washington and Lee University, January 19th, 1872* (Baltimore, 1872), p. 42.

10. Holden Brian Reid, *Robert E. Lee* (London, 2005), p. 219.

11. W. C. Ford (ed.), *A Cycle of Adams Letters, 1861–1865*, 2 vols. (Boston, 1920), vol. 2, p. 154, Charles Francis Adams Jr. to Charles Francis Adams, 19 June 1864.

12. James Pendlebury MSS, private collection, p. 7.

13. Francis W. Dawson, *Reminiscences of Confederate Service, 1861–1865*, ed.

Bell I. Wiley (Baton Rouge, La., 1980), pp. 195-6, Dawson to mother, 1 June 1864. His letters occasionally assumed a finality in their tone: 'I feel how much I have sinned against your tender care and loving kindness!' he wrote. 'Forgive me, my dear Parents, every unkind word and harsh thought.'

14. *Illustrated London News*, 6 August 1864.

15. Edward Porter Alexander, *Military Memoirs of a Confederate* (New York, 1907), p. 564.

16. OR, ser. 1, vol. 40/2, doc. 81, order from Secretary of War, 25 June 1864.

17. Augustus Charles Hobart-Hampden, *Hobart Pasha* (New York, 1915), p. 176.

18. Ibid., pp. 180-81.

19. A. S. Lewis (ed.), *My Dear Parents* (New York, 1982), p. 92.

20. University College of North Wales, Bangor, Evans MSS 2854, ff. 74-5, 4 July 1864.

21. PRO 30/22/38, f. 71, Lyons to Russell, 15 July 1864.

22. West Sussex RO, Lyons MSS, box 302, Lord Lyons to Augusta, 13 July and 15 July 1864.

23. Ibid., Lyons to Augusta, 2 June 1864.

24. University College of North Wales, Bangor, Evans MSS 2854, f. 82, 21 July 1864.

25. Mark E. Neely, *The Fate of Liberty: Abraham Lincoln and Civil Liberties* (New York, 1991), pp. 110-11.

26. PRO 30/22/38, f. 74, Lyons to Lord Russell, 22 July 1864.

27. Doris Kearns Goodwin, *Team of Rivals* (New York, 2005), p. 646.

28. Ford (ed.), *A Cycle of Adams Letters*, vol. 2, pp. 168-9, Charles Francis Adams Jr. to Henry Adams, 27 July 1864; Charles Francis Adams Jr. to Henry Adams, 22 July 1864.

29. OR, ser. 1, vol. 40/3, doc. 82, p. 489, General Birney to Foster, 26 July 1864.

30. PRO FO/1281, Memorial of Edward Sewell; Private Sewell of the 93rd New York Volunteers was recovering from dysentery in a military hospital, when he had heard from other patients 'that we were likely to have liberty to go to New York to vote for the President . . . I at once conceived the notion of escaping and gave my name and represented my state to be New York. On the fifth passes were given to us, and on the sixth I and many others went to New York by Railway. I arrived at New York on the seventh. I immediately went to the house of a friend named Eiglaugh. I told him my story and arranged with him, to obtain me a Berth on board a steamer for England.'

31. Howard Westwood, *Black Troops, White Commanders, and Freedmen during the Civil War* (Carbondale, Ill., 1992), p. 32; Gabor S. Boritt, *Lincoln's Generals* (New York, 1995), p. 147.

32. Alexander, *Military Memoirs*, p. 569.

33. Ulysses S. Grant, *Personal Memoirs of Ulysses S. Grant* (New York, 2003), p. 505.

34. *The Times*, 23 August 1864.

35. Frederick W. Seward (ed.), *Seward at Washington* (New York, 1891), p. 238, Seward to Frances, 5 August 1864.

36. Grant, *Memoirs*, p. 506.

37. Adam Badeau, *Military History of Ulysses S. Grant*, 3 vols. (New York, 1885), vol. 2, p. 502.

38. Richard Bache Irwin, *History of the Nineteenth Army Corps* (New York, 1892), p. 442.

39. Dawson, *Reminiscences*, p. 123.

40. Ibid., p. 201, Dawson to mother, 7 August 1864.

41. Ford (ed.), *A Cycle of Adams Letters*, vol. 2, p. 181, Charles Francis Adams Jr. to Henry Adams, 13 August 1864.

42. Lewis (ed.), *My Dear Parents*, p. 92.

43. Timothy Holmes (ed.), *David Livingstone: Letters and Documents, 1861–1872* (London, 1990), pp. 85, 73, Livingstone to James Young, 19 February 1862; Livingstone to James Young, *c.* July/August 1863. The source for the footnote is George Seaver, *David Livingstone: His Life and Letters* (London, 1957), p. 453.

44. William Garden Blaikie, *Personal Life of David Livingstone*, p. 339.

45. Holmes (ed.), *David Livingstone: Letters and Documents*, p. 96, David Livingstone to Charles Livingstone, 2 September 1864.

46. *The Times*, 20 September 1864.

47. Frank E. Vandiver (ed.), *The Civil War Diary of Josiah Gorgas* (Tuscaloosa, Ala., 1947), p. 132, 8 August 1864.

48. *The Times*, 24 September 1864.

49. Vandiver (ed.), *The Civil War Diary of Josiah Gorgas*, p. 137, 29 August 1864.

CHAPTER 31. THE CRISIS COMES

1. James M. McPherson, *Battle Cry of Freedom* (London, 1988), p. 751.

2. OR, ser. 1, vol. 35/2, doc. 66, p. 615, Feilden to Gorgas, 20 August 1864.

3. South Carolina Historical Society, Feilden–Smythe MSS (22), Feilden to Julia McCord, 1 September 1864.

4. Ibid. (20), Feilden to Julia McCord, 26 August 1864.

5. John B. Jones, *A Rebel War Clerk's Diary at the Confederate States Capital*, ed. Earl Schenck Miers (Urbana, Ill., 1958), p. 414, 25 August 1864.

6. Philip Van Doren Stern, *When the Guns Roared: World Aspects of the American Civil War* (New York, 1965), pp. 314–15.

7. ORN, ser. 2, vol. 3, p. 1202, Benjamin to Colin McRae, 6 September 1864.

8. John Bierman, *Dark Safari: The Life behind the Legend of Henry Morton Stanley* (New York, 1990), p. 38. See also Nathaniel Cheairs Hughes Jr. (ed.), *Sir Henry Morton Stanley, Confederate* (Baton Rouge, La., 2000), pp. 150–54.

9. 12 July 1864 and 6 August 1864; quoted in James McPherson, *Tried by War* (New York, 2009), pp. 231–2.

10. PRO 30/22/38, ff. 91–4, Lyons to Russell, 15 August 1864, and f. 95, 23 August 1864.

11. ORN, ser. 2, vol. 3, p. 1032, Benjamin to Slidell, 19 February 1864. The Knights of the Golden Circle also boasted Harpending and Rubery – the California raiders – as members. Other members included Jesse James, John Wilkes Booth and the rampaging Quantrill Raiders in Missouri. The secretive order answered only to itself, but its aims included an independent South, the protection of slavery, and the acquisition of territory from Mexico.

12. OR, ser. 4, vol. 3, pp. 585–6, Clay to Benjamin, 11 August 1864.

13. The Confederates had initiated the contact; it was the idea of Confederate gadfly and sometime agent George N. Sanders, whose dreams and schemes were forever ending in disaster. However, his powers of persuasion were legendary and – to the other Confederates' dismay – Sanders had no sooner arrived in Canada than he latched onto Clay and Holcombe and brought them completely under his sway. He played them like puppets, thoroughly enjoying his power to script the occasion. 'In my long life I have known no counterpart to this man,' recorded an observer. 'He was a constant menace to the interests for which the commissioners were responsible.' Adam Mayers, *Dixie and the Dominion: Canada, the Confederacy, and the War for the Union* (Toronto, 2003), p. 65.

14. Michael Burlingame, *Abraham Lincoln*, 2 vols. (Baltimore, 2008), vol. 2, pp. 669–70.

15. George Templeton Strong, *Diary of the Civil War 1860–1865*, ed. Allan Nevins (New York, 1962), p. 474, 19 August 1864.

16. W. C. Ford (ed.), *A Cycle of Adams Letters, 1861–1865*, 2 vols. (Boston, 1920), vol. 2, p. 182, Charles Francis Adams Jr. to Charles Francis Adams, 20 August 1864.

17. David H. Donald, *Lincoln* (New York, 1995), p. 529.

18. George Congdon Gorham, *Life and Public Services of Edwin M. Stanton*, 2 vols. (New York, 1899), vol. 2, p. 149.

19. Doris Kearns Goodwin, *Team of Rivals* (New York, 2005), p. 648.

20. Library of Congress, Papers of Abraham Lincoln, 'Blind Memorandum', 23 August 1864.

21. PRO 30/22/38, ff. 95–7, Lyons to Russell, 23 August 1864.

22. PRO 30/22/38, ff. 85–90, Lyons to Russell, 9 August 1864.

23. PRO FO5/1258, n. 73, Mary S. Hill to Lord Lyons, 20 August 1864.

24. *Widow of Andrew Cunningham, late a British subject: Correspondence between the State department and the British legation, relative to the claim of the widow of the late Andrew Cunningham, a British subject, improperly enlisted into the military service of the United States. March 5, 1866* (39th Congress, Hse Rep., 1866). Seward promised Lyons that Cunningham's widow would receive his bounty and army pay without delay. But the War Department ignored his repeated requests.

25. PRO 30/22/38, ff. 99–101, Lyons to Russell, 30 August 1864.

26. *BDOFA*, Part 1, ser. C, vol. 6, p. 313, Monck to Cardwell, 26 September 1864.

27. Fitzgerald Ross, *Cities and Camps of the Confederate States*, ed. Richard Barksdale Harwell (Champaign, Ill., 1997), p. 228.

28. Duane Schultz, *The Dahlgren Affair* (New York, 1998), p. 209.

29. Mabel Clare Weaks, 'Colonel George St Leger Grenfell', *Filson Club History Quarterly*, 34 (1960), p. 11, Grenfell to Mary, 18 July 1864.

30. K.W. Wheeler, *For the Union: Ohio Leaders in the Civil War* (Columbus, Ohio, 1968), p. 50.

31. The 'Northwest' encompassed Illinois, Wisconsin, Indiana, Michigan and Iowa, States which not only felt little cultural or political affinity with New England, but also felt unfairly targeted by the tax system. The Knights of the Golden Circle had changed its name first to the Order of the American Knights, and then in 1864 to the Sons of Liberty. Its membership remains impossible to determine, but at its height may have been as many as 300,000. The Sons claimed to have a membership closer to a million.

32. ORN, ser. 1, vol. 3, p. 714, Thompson to Benjamin, 3 December 1864.

33. William Tidwell, *April '65: Confederate Covert Action in the American Civil War* (Kent, Ohio, 1995), p. 130.

34. Weaks, 'Colonel George St Leger Grenfell', p. 10, Grenfell to 'Hunter', 31 July 1864.

35. John W. Headley, *Confederate Operations in Canada and New York* (New York, 1906), p. 225.

36. Oscar A. Kinchen, *Confederate Operations in Canada* (Hanover, Mass., 1970), p. 58.

37. Stephen Z. Starr, *Colonel Grenfell's Wars* (Baton Rouge, La., 1971), p. 172.

38. James Horan, *Confederate Agent: A Discovery in History* (New York, 1954), p. 129.

39. D. Alexander Brown, 'The Northwest Conspiracy', *Civil War Times Illustrated*, 10 (May 1971), p. 16.

40. Weaks, 'Colonel George St Leger Grenfell', p. 11, Grenfell to William Maynard, 31 August 1864.

41. ORN, ser. 1, vol. 3, p. 714, Thompson to Benjamin, 3 December 1864.

CHAPTER 32. THE TYRANNY OF HOPE

1. Philip Guedalla (ed.), *Gladstone and Palmerston, being the Correspondence of Lord Palmerston with Mr Gladstone 1851–1865* (London, 1928), p. 289, Palmerston to Gladstone, 28 June 1864.

2. ORN, ser. 2, vol. 3, pp. 1162–3, Hotze to Benjamin, 4 July 1864.

3. W. C. Ford (ed.), *A Cycle of Adams Letters, 1861–1865*, 2 vols. (Boston, 1920), vol. 2, p. 165, Henry Adams to Charles Francis Adams Jr., 8 July 1864. Edward Chalfant, *Better in Darkness* (New York, 1994), p. 79.

4. John Morley, *The Life of William Ewart Gladstone: 1809–1872*, 2 vols. (London, 1908), vol. 1, p. 563.

5. On 28 June 1864 Rose recorded the following conversation in her diary: 'Called upon Lady Chesterfield. Lady Derby was there, Marchioness of Ailesbury also came in. Much talk upon politics ... I asked, "Will ministers go out?" Answer, "No." The radicals have promised to support the Gov. in their peace policy and there will be a division of 25 or 30 in support. Lady C: "I don't believe they can have such a majority, not more than five or 6." In that case it will be a defeat. Then they will dissolve Parliament and go to the country. They love office too well to go out. Lady C: "They will be hard pressed." Lady A: "Yes but you will see, they will manage it." The discussion is put off for Monday. Lord Derby will man it in the House of Lords. Mr. Disraeli in the Commons.'

6. *Journal of John Wodehouse, First Earl of Kimberley* (Cambridge, 1997), p. 140, 8 July 1864.

7. MHS, Adams MSS, Diary of Charles Francis Adams, 8 July 1864.

8. William Flavelle Monypenny, *Life of Benjamin Disraeli, Earl of Beaconsfield*, vol. 3 (London, 1916), p. 405.

9. Mary Ellison, *Support for Secession* (Chicago, 1972), p. 153.

10. Library of Congress, Mason Papers, Spence to Mason, 18 July 1864.

11. Brian Jenkins, *Britain and the War for the Union*, 2 vols. (Montreal, 1974, 1980), vol. 2, p. 336.

12. *The Times*, 26 July 1864.

13. *PRFA*, 1/2 (1864), p. 229, Adams to Seward, 28 July 1864.

14. Ibid., p. 223, Adams to Seward, 21 July 1864.

15. Ibid., p. 250, Adams to Seward, 29 July 1864.

16. Diana Fontaine Corbin, *A Life of Matthew Fontaine Maury* (London, 1888), p. 223.

17. *The Private Journal of Georgiana Gholson Walker*, ed. Dwight Franklin Henderson, Confederate Centennial Studies, 25 (Tuscaloosa, Ala., 1963), p. 94, 16 May 1864. Rose procured the best ophthalmologist in London for Georgiana's child, who pronounced the condition to be incurable.

18. ORN, ser. 2, vol. 3, p. 1184, Mason to Benjamin, 4 August 1864.

19. MHS, Adams MSS, Diary of Charles Francis Adams, 1 August 1864.

20. W. C. Ford (ed.), *Letters of Henry Adams 1858–1891*, 2 vols. (Boston, 1930–38), vol. 1, p. 441, Henry Adams to Charles Francis Adams Jr., 1 July 1864.

21. MHS, Adams MSS, Diary of Charles Francis Adams, 30 July 1864.

22. ORN, ser. 2, vol. 3, p. 1143, Hotze to Benjamin, 3 June 1864.

23. Library of Congress, Hotze Papers, private letterbook, Hotze to Witt, 18 June 1864.

24. *Punch*, 6 August 1864.

25. Andrew Ross, *David Livingstone: Mission and Empire* (London, 2002), p. 190.

26. Timothy Holmes (ed.), *David Livinstone: Letters and Documents, 1861–1872* (London, 1990), p. 100, Livingstone to W. C. Oswell, 21 October 1864.

27. Sarah Agnes Wallace and Frances Elma Gillespie (eds.), *The Journal of Benjamin Moran, 1857–1865*, 2 vols. (Chicago, 1948, 1949), vol. 2, p. 1327, 16 September 1864.

28. Ibid., p. 1329, 22 September 1864.

29. NARA, M. T. 185, roll 8, vol. 8, Consul Eastman to Seward, 24 August 1864.

30. *PRFA*, 1/2 (1864), p. 313, Charles Francis Adams to Seward, 29 September 1864.

31. Sheffield Archives, WHM 460a/60, Spence to Lord Wharncliffe, 12 December 1864.

32. The Duchess of Sutherland's anti-slavery petition of 1852, 'The Affectionate and Christian Address of Many Thousands of Women of Great Britain and Ireland to their Sisters, the Women of the United States of America', was signed by more than 500,000 British women. It caused considerable offence in both the North and the South. But at least that petition was addressed to the citizens of the United States. Kershaw's intention to present the petition to the Northern government was both preposterous and presumptuous.

33. Corbin, *A Life of Matthew Fontaine Maury*, p. 218, Maury to Rutson Maury, 30 August 1864.

34. Library of Congress, Hotze Papers, Private letterbook, Hotze to Benjamin, 2 September 1864. The reference for the footnote is George M. Brooke Jr. (ed.), *Ironclads and Big Guns of the Confederacy: The Journal and Letters of John M. Brooke* (Columbia, SC, 2002), p. 190, Maury to Jansen, 28 September 1864. 'It is so strange to me that sensible men will require to see ship after ship blown up before they will have faith in submarine mining,' Maury complained to his wife. The enthusiastic attitude of his British friends made the Confederate government appear obtuse by comparison. General Sir John Burgoyne of the Royal Engineers was impressed by Maury's work on the electrical currents of underwater torpedoes, and invited him to cooperate on several experiments of his own. A nearby field in Bowdon became Maury's testing ground for automatic detonators. 'The British Government has appointed a Board to investigate, experiment and report upon Gun Cotton in all its war-like aspects,' Maury informed his friend Jansen. 'They are also moving upon the question of submarine mining and torpedoes.'

35. Belle Boyd, *Belle Boyd in Camp and Prison* (New York, 1865; repr. Baton Rouge, La., 1998), p. 206.

36. Ibid., p. 208; Wallace and Gillespie (eds.), *The Journal of Benjamin Moran*, vol. 2, p. 1317, 25 August 1864.

37. Ford (ed.), *Letters of Henry Adams*, vol. 1, p. 446, Henry Adams to John Gorham Palfrey, 16 September 1864.

38. MHS, Adams MSS, Diary of Charles Francis Adams, 5 September 1864.

39. *Army and Navy Gazette*, 3 September 1864. Not everyone doubted the news.

Northern supporters in Perth, Scotland, celebrated Sherman's victory by flying the American flag and firing the town cannon.

40. ORN, ser. 2, vol. 3, p. 1219, Slidell to Benjamin, 29 September 1864.

41. Ibid., p. 1209, Hotze to Benjamin, 17 September 1864.

42. *The Private Journal of Georgiana Gholson Walker*, p. 112.

CHAPTER 33. 'COME RETRIBUTION'

1. Duke University, Malet family MSS, Malet to mother, 30 August 1864 and 29 September 1864.

2. Brian Jenkins, *Britain and the War for the Union*, 2 vols. (Montreal, 1974, 1980), vol. 2, p. 369.

3. Robin Winks, *Canada and the United States: The Civil War Years* (Lanham, Md., 1988), pp. 143–7. Monck had telegraphed Lord Lyons, who immediately sent a message to Seward, alerting him to the plot. Meanwhile Monck ordered the Welland Canal between Lake Erie and Lake Ontario to be watched for suspicious steamboats. General Cox in Ohio informed Edwin Stanton on 15 November that 'the Rebels who left Windsor to join the raid are returning, saying that the plans are frustrated for the present, and will have to be postponed for a time'. OR, ser. 3, vol. 3, p. 1043, Cox to Stanton, 15 November 1863.

4. Madeline House, Graham Storey and Kathleen Tillotson (eds.), *The Letters of Charles Dickens*, vol. 3 (New York, 1974), p. 207, Dickens to John Forster, 24 April 1842.

5. Bradley A. Rodgers, *Guardian of the Great Lakes* (Ann Arbor, Mich., 1996), p. 84.

6. Charles Frohman, *Rebels on Lake Erie* (Columbus, Ohio, 1975), p. 98.

7. Oscar A. Kinchen, *Confederate Operations in Canada* (Hanover, Mass., 1970), p. 105.

8. Frohman, *Rebels on Lake Erie*, p. 73.

9. John W. Headley, *Confederate Operations in Canada and New York* (Kent, Ohio, 1906), p. 252.

10. Daniel B. Lucas, *Memoir of John Yates Beall* (Montreal, 1865), p. 32.

11. Frohman, *Rebels on Lake Erie*, p. 93.

12. Ibid., p. 80.

13. Frances Elizabeth Owen Monck, *My Canadian Leaves: Diary of a Visit to Canada, 1865–6* (London, 1891), p. 122.

14. Ibid., p. 137.

15. Ibid., p. 148, 4 October 1864.

16. Ibid., p. 170.

17. Ann Blackman, *Wild Rose: Rose O'Neale Greenhow, Civil War Spy* (New York, 2005), pp. 298–9.

18. Thomas E. Taylor, *Running the Blockade* (Annapolis, Md., repr. 1995), p. 123.

19. Blackman, *Wild Rose*, p. 300.

20. *The Times*, 15 November 1864.

21. South Carolina Historical Society, Feilden–Smythe MSS, Beauregard to Feilden, 5 September 1864.

22. James M. Morgan, *Recollections of a Rebel Reefer* (Boston, 1917), pp. 197–8.

23. South Carolina Historical Society, Feilden–Smythe MSS, Feilden to Julia McCord, 27 September 1864.

24. Ibid., Feilden to Julia McCord, 25 September 1864.

25. The wine, for example, was coming from Bermuda, and the ring was being made from the last of his gold sovereigns. Ibid., Feilden to Julia McCord, 27 September 1864.

26. Ibid., Jordan to Hardee, 12 October 1864.

27. *The Times*, 5 November 1864.

28. Frank E. Vandiver (ed.), *The Civil War Diary of Josiah Gorgas* (Tuscaloosa, Ala., 1947), p. 145, 6 October 1864.

29. *Illustrated London News*, 21 January 1865.

30. Ibid., 22 October 1864.

31. John B. Jones, *A Rebel War Clerk's Diary at the Confederate States Capital*, ed. Earl Schenck Miers (Urbana, Ill., 1958), p. 433, 10 October 1864.

32. Mary Sophia Hill, *A British Subject's Recollections of the Confederacy* (Baltimore, 1875), p. 66.

33. PRO FO5/1285, n. 78, Burnley to Russell, 26 September 1864.

34. Jones, *A Rebel War Clerk's Diary*, p. 431, 4 October 1864.

35. Hill, *A British Subject's Recollections*, p. 40.

36. Francis W. Dawson, *Reminiscences of Confederate Service, 1861–1865*, ed. Bell I. Wiley (Baton Rouge, La., 1980), p. 125.

37. Ibid., pp. 201–2, Dawson to mother, 13 October 1864.

38. W. C. Ford (ed.), *A Cycle of Adams Letters, 1861–1865*, 2 vols. (Boston, 1920), vol. 2, pp. 194–6, 18 September 1864. Charles Francis Adams Jr. was vastly overstating the condition of the 5th Massachusetts (Colored) Cavalry, an elite black regiment that included Charles Douglass, the son of the abolition campaigner Frederick Douglass, and Joshua Laurence, father of the poet Paul Dunbar Laurence, whose work was set to music by Samuel Coleridge-Taylor.

39. Ernest Duvergier de Hauranne, *Eight Months in America: Letters and Travel Notes*, 2 vols. (Chicago, 1974), vol. 1, p. 32, 20 June 1864.

40. A. S. Lewis (ed.), *My Dear Parents* (New York, 1982), p. 107, Horrocks to parents, 19 November 1864.

41. James McPherson (ed.), *Atlas of the Civil War* (Philadelphia, 2005), p. 190.

42. Gary W. Gallagher (ed.), *The Shenandoah Valley Campaign of 1864* (Chapel Hill, NC, 2006), p. 212.

CHAPTER 34. 'WAR IS CRUELTY'

1. *The Private Journal of Georgiana Gholson Walker*, ed. Dwight Franklin Henderson, Confederate Centennial Studies, 25 (Tuscaloosa, Ala., 1963), p. 113, 11 October 1864.

2. William Tidwell lists five separate Confederate 'cells' operating in Canada: in Toronto, under Jacob Thompson; in Hamilton, under Cassius F. Lee; in St Catherine's, under Clement Clay; in Windsor, under one Steele; and in Montreal, under Patrick Charles Martin and George N. Sanders. *April '65: Confederate Covert Action in the American Civil War* (Kent, Ohio, 1995), p. 135.

3. John W. Headley, *Confederate Operations in Canada and New York* (New York, 1906), p. 265.

4. Mabel Clare Weaks, 'Colonel George St Leger Grenfell', *Filson Club History Quarterly*, 34 (1960), p. 12, Grenfell to Mary, 11 October 1864. Stephen Z. Starr says it is only speculation that Grenfell was Hines's deputy, although well-founded speculation. *Colonel Grenfell's Wars* (Baton Rouge, La., 1971), p. 183.

5. Stephen Starr writes, 'There is unfortunately no way of discovering what thoughts passed through his mind as he sat quietly in his hotel room in the dreary hours of a November night.' Ibid., p. 203.

6. Duke University, Malet family MSS, Sheffield to Malet, 11 November 1864.

7. PRO 30/22/38, f. 120, Lyons to Russell, 28 October 1864.

8. Sarah Agnes Wallace and Frances Elma Gillespie (eds.), *The Journal of Benjamin Moran, 1857–1865*, 2 vols. (Chicago, 1948, 1949), vol. 2, p. 1341, 19 October 1864.

9. Bulloch's successful manipulation of the legal system made it appear as though there was a vast conspiracy by the British to help the Confederacy. Dudley reported to Seward on 15 November that the owners of the *Laurel* and the *Sea King* were British. They both sailed under the British flag. The sailors were British. 'The armament, shot, shell, guns, powder, and everything down to the coal in the hold are English, all the produce and manufacture of Great Britain. Even the bounty money paid for enlisting the men was English sovereigns and the wages English coin, pounds, shillings and pence. It seems to me that nothing is wanting to stamp this as an English transaction from beginning to end . . .' NARA M. 141, roll t-29, d. 386.

10. ORN, ser. 2, vol. 2, p. 731, Bulloch to Whittle, 6 October 1864.

11. Tom Chaffin, *Sea of Gray* (New York, 2006), pp. 58–64.

12. Chester G. Hearn, *Gray Raiders of the Sea: How Eight Confederate Warships Destroyed the Union's High Seas Commerce* (Camden, Me., 1992), p. 152. The American merchant marine had shipped over 5 million tons before the war. The latest statistics pointed to a decline of 4 million tons.

13. The ship and her crew had been continuously at sea since sneaking out of Brest on 10 February 1864. Yet the flight from the American flag meant that in

eight months the *Florida* had only managed to capture thirteen prizes. Short of coal, and worried that his bored crew might mutiny unless given their shore leave, Captain Charles Morris (Maffitt's replacement) had sailed into Bahia, Brazil, where he was pounced upon by the waiting *Wachusetts*.

14. ORN, ser. 2, vol. 2, p. 736, Bulloch to Stephen Mallory, 20 October 1864. R. I. Lester, *Confederate Finance and Purchasing in Great Britain* (Charlottesville, Va., 1975), pp. 190–91.

15. Virginia Historical Society, Raphael Semmes MSS, MSS1Se535a/53–65, Maury to Tremlett, 23 October 1864.

16. Virginia Mason, *The Public Life and Diplomatic Correspondence of James M. Mason* (New York, 1906), p. 514.

17. John Bennett, 'The Confederate Bazaar at Liverpool', *Crossfire: The Magazine of the American Civil War Round Table*, 61 (Dec. 1999).

18. David Hepburn Milton, *Lincoln's Spymaster: Thomas Haines Dudley and the Liverpool Network* (Mechanicsburg, Pa., 2003), p. 121.

19. Wallace and Gillespie (eds.), *The Journal of Benjamin Moran*, vol. 2, pp. 1346–7, 7–8 November 1864.

20. Sheffield Archives, WHM 460a/47, Spence to Wharncliffe, 2 November 1864. The sources for the quotations in the first footnote are Sheffield Archives, WHM 460a/46, Spence to Wharncliffe, 31 October 1864, and C. Vann Woodward (ed.), *Mary Chesnut's Civil War* (New Haven, 1981), p. 664, Varina Davis to Mary Chesnut, 8 October 1864.

21. Sheffield Archives, WHM 460a/51, Wharncliffe to Adams, 9 November 1864.

22. Library of Congress, Hotze Papers, private letterbook, Hotze to Gregg, 8 October 1864. The journal was moving from its two rooms in Bouverie Street to more spacious premises at 291 Strand, and Hotze could not afford any decrease in the circulation. Yet he must have seen the increasing references in the press to the South as a slave State. On the same day as his reproof to Gregg, a writer in the *Dumfries Standard* declared that he hoped 'the day is not far distant when a deep sense of shame shall be felt in this country for even the partial and temporary sympathy manifested for the pro-slavery States of America'. Loraine Peters, 'The Impact of the American Civil War on the Local Communities of Scotland', *Civil War History*, 49 (2003).

23. The *Index* was printing 2,250 copies a week – an impressive circulation considering that John Bright's *Morning Star* was only 5,000.

24. Angus Hawkins, *The Forgotten Prime Minister*, vol. 2 (Oxford, 2008), p. 291.

25. Somerset RO, Somerset MSS, d/RA/A/2a/40/13, Palmerston to Duke of Somerset, 6 September 1864.

26. Philip Guedalla (ed.), *Gladstone and Palmerston, being the Correspondence of Lord Palmerston with Mr Gladstone 1851–1865* (London, 1928), p. 302, Palmerston to Gladstone, 19 October 1864.

27. Scott Thomas Cairns, 'Lord Lyons and Anglo-American Diplomacy during

the American Civil War', Ph.D. thesis, London School of Economics, 2004, p. 348, Palmerston to de Grey, 11 September 1864.

28. Somerset RO, Somerset MSS, d/RA/A/2a/40/16, Palmerston to Duke of Somerset, 30 November 1864.

29. MHS, Adams MSS, Diary of Charles Francis Adams, 23 November 1864.

30. Ibid., 21 November 1864. While writing about his fears of a Democratic victory, he revealed an ugly prejudice against the Democratic financier Augustus Belmont, whom he slated as 'the German Jew agent of the foreign stockbrokers, the Rothschilds'.

31. Russell thought he was giving more than they deserved when he wrote: 'of the causes of the rupture Her Majesty's Government have never presumed to judge ... Such a Neutrality Her Majesty has faithfully maintained and will continue to maintain.' *A Compilation of the Messages and Papers of the Confederacy, Including the Diplomatic Correspondence, 1861–1865*, 2 vols. (Nashville, 1905), vol. 2, p. 687, Russell to Commissioners, 25 November 1864.

32. E. D. Adams, *Great Britain and the American Civil War*, 2 vols. in 1 (New York, 1958), vol. 2, p. 243. Slidell visited the French Foreign Ministry, thinking that the Foreign Minister wished to discuss the manifesto. Instead, he received an official complaint regarding the forced enlistment of French subjects into the Confederate army. The Minister refused to show any interest in the capture of the CSS *Florida* in neutral waters, or in any other American infringements dangled before him by Slidell.

33. Ernest Samuels (ed.), *Henry Adams: Selected Letters* (Cambridge, Mass., 1988), p. 71, Henry Adams to Charles Francis Adams Jr., 25 November 1864.

34. Wallace and Gillespie (eds.), *The Journal of Benjamin Moran*, vol. 2, p. 1354, 1 December 1864 and 30 November 1864.

35. W. C. Ford (ed.), *A Cycle of Adams Letters, 1861–1865*, 2 vols. (Boston, 1920), vol. 2, p. 223, Charles Francis Adams Jr to Henry Adams, 14 November 1864.

36. The system for exchanging prisoners had worked according to a strict hierarchy: 1 general = 46 privates; 1 major-general = 40 privates; 1 brigadier general = 20 privates; 1 colonel = 15 privates; 1 lieutenant colonel = 10 privates; 1 major = 8 privates; 1 captain = 6 privates; 1 lieutenant = 4 privates; 1 noncommissioned officer = 2 privates.

37. William Elsey Connelley, *A Standard History of Kansas and Kansans*, 5 vols. (New York, 1918), vol. 5, p. 2473.

38. James Pendlebury MSS, private collection.

39. Arnold Haultain (ed.), *Reminiscences by Goldwin Smith* (New York, 1910), p. 336.

40. Goldwin Smith wrote, for example: 'Does the Bible Sanction American Slavery?' (1863), as well as his 'Letter to a Whig Member of the Southern Independence Association' (1864).

41. Haultain (ed.), *Reminiscences by Goldwin Smith*, p. 353.

42. Robin Winks, *Canada and the United States: The Civil War Years* (Lanham, Md., 1988), p. 305.

43. Michael Burlingame, *Abraham Lincoln*, 2 vols. (New York, 2008), vol. 2, p. 740.

44. *PRFA*, 2/2 (1864), p. 760, Seward to Lyons, 3 November 1864.

45. Frederick W. Seward (ed.), *Seward at Washington* (New York, 1891), p. 250.

46. William Cooper, *Jefferson Davis, American* (New York, 2000), p. 539.

47. Bell Wiley, *Confederate Women* (New York, 1975), p. 109.

48. John B. Jones, *A Rebel War Clerk's Diary at the Confederate States Capital*, ed. Earl Schenck Miers (Urbana, Ill., 1958), p. 447, 9 November 1864.

49. A. S. Lewis (ed.), *My Dear Parents* (New York, 1982), p. 108.

50. Francis W. Dawson, *Reminiscences of Confederate Service, 1861–1865*, ed. Bell I. Wiley (Baton Rouge, La., 1980), p. 204, Dawson to mother, 25 November 1864.

51. Ibid., pp. 132–3.

52. Jones, *A Rebel War Clerk's Diary*, p. 456, 5 December 1864.

53. Dawson, *Reminiscences*, p. 205, Dawson to mother, 25 November 1864.

54. Mark Grimsley, *The Hard Hand of War* (Cambridge, 1995), p. 188. In popular myth, thousands of families were driven out into the desolate countryside at the point of the bayonet. In reality, 1,644 people, including 860 children, were put on trains to nearby towns.

55. Archibald McCowan, 'Five Months in a Rebel Prison, 1 October 1864 to 1 March 1865', *Victorian Periodical Review* (1993).

CHAPTER 35. 'THE BRITISH MARK ON EVERY BATTLE-FIELD'

1. Oscar A. Kinchen, *Confederate Operations in Canada* (Hanover, Mass., 1970), p. 117.

2. ORN, ser. 1, vol. 3, p. 718, Thompson to Benjamin, 3 December 1864.

3. Frederick Job Shepard, *The Johnson's Island Plot: An Historical Narrative of the Conspiracy of the Confederates . . .*, ed. Frank H. Severance (Buffalo, 1906; repr. Ithaca, NY, 2007), p. 45.

4. John W. Headley, *Confederate Operations in Canada and New York* (New York, 1906), p. 271.

5. Ibid., p. 272.

6. *New York Times*, 26 November 1864.

7. Edward O. Cunningham, 'In Violation of the Laws of War', *Journal of the Louisiana Historical Association*, 18/2 (Spring 1977), pp. 189–201.

8. *New York Times*, 27 November 1864.

9. George Templeton Strong, *Diary of the Civil War 1860–1865*, ed. Allan Nevins (New York, 1962), p. 522, 29 November 1864.

10. *PRFA*, 2 (1864), p. 370, Seward to Lyons, 4 December 1864.

11. Joseph Burnley, the new legation Secretary, complained that once Lyons fell ill

it became next to impossible to get him to write his letters. An unofficial count by Lord Lyons's biographer revealed a grand total of 8,236 letters written by Lyons since 1861. It was no wonder that he could not face another dispatch.

12. *PRFA*, 1 (1864), p. 370, Seward to Adams, 5 December 1864.

13. PRO FO881/1334, p. 72, Monck to Burnley, 14 December 1864.

14. Headley, *Confederate Operations*, p. 309.

15. W. C. Ford (ed.), *A Cycle of Adams Letters, 1861–1865*, 2 vols. (Boston, 1920), vol. 2, p. 238, Charles Francis Adams Jr. to Henry Adams, 25 December 1864.

16. Sumner's bill to forbid segregation on Washington's streetcars died in the Senate through lack of support.

17. 'Letters of Goldwin Smith to Eliot Norton', *Proceedings of the Massachusetts Historical Society*, 49 (1916), p. 115, Goldwin Smith to Norton, 29 December 1864.

18. Kinchen, *Confederate Operations in Canada*, p. 177; ORN, ser. 1, vol. 3, p. 930, Thompson to Benjamin, 3 December 1864.

19. William Tidwell, James Hall and David Winfred Gaddy, *Come Retribution: The Confederate Secret Service and the Assassination of Lincoln* (Ann Arbor, 1988), p. 203.

20. Cleburne concluded: 'It is said slavery is all we are fighting for, and if we give it up we give up all. Even if this were true, which we deny, slavery is not all our enemies are fighting for. It is merely the pretense to establish sectional superiority and a more centralized form of government, and to deprive us of our rights and liberties. We have now briefly proposed a plan which we believe will save our country. It may be imperfect, but in all human probability it would give us our independence ... Negroes will require much training; training will require time, and there is danger that this concession to common sense may come too late.' OR, ser. 1, vol. 52/2, p. 592, Cleburne to Johnston, 2 January 1864.

21. OR, ser. 1, vol. 39/3, p. 162, Sherman to Grant, 9 October 1864; p. 377, Sherman to Thomas, 20 October 1864.

22. Frank E. Vandiver (ed.), *The Civil War Diary of General Josiah Gorgas* (Tuscaloosa, Ala., 1947), p. 157, 20 December 1864.

23. Thomas Taylor, *Running the Blockade* (Annapolis, Md., repr. 1995), p. 140.

24. *The Times*, 7 February 1865.

25. Taylor, *Running the Blockade*, p. 141.

26. John B. Jones, *A Rebel War Clerk's Diary at the Confederate States Capital*, ed. Earl Schenck Miers (Urbana, Ill., 1958), p. 467, 27 December 1864.

27. ORN, ser. 2, vol. 3, pp. 1253–56, Benjamin to Mason and Slidell, 27 December 1864.

28. Craig A. Bauer, 'The Last Effort: The Secret Mission of the Confederate Diplomat, Duncan F. Kenner', *Louisiana History*, 22 (1981).

29. *The Times*, 8 March 1865.

30. South Carolina Historical Society, Feilden–Smythe MSS, Feilden to Julia Feilden, 21 December 1864.

31. 'It does seem strange,' he wrote on 4 January 1865, in a letter to William

Porcher Miles, the chairman of the House Military Affairs Committee. He had served three different generals and been recommended for promotion on three separate occasions, without success. 'I expect I know more of the localities and the organization of the troops than any other AA general in the office.' NARA, Feilden military records, Feilden to Porcher Miles, 4 January 1865.

32. South Carolina Historical Society, Feilden–Smythe MSS, Feilden to Julia Feilden, 5 January 1865.

33. James Ford Rhodes, 'Who Burned Columbia?', *Proceedings of the Massachusetts Historical Society*, 35 (1901), p. 268.

34. South Carolina Historical Society, Feilden–Smythe MSS, Feilden to Julia Feilden, 5 January 1865.

35. The Hon. Maurice Berkeley Portman, third son of Viscount Portman, and an old friend of Lord Wharncliffe's, had recently arrived from Canada to serve under General Wade Hampton. He told Wharncliffe that the wife of one acquaintance had allegedly been bayoneted to the wall and her house set on fire, another had been 'violated', and a third, stripped and forced to dance for the soldiers. Sheffield Archives, WHM 461 (18), identified by author as Maurice B. Portman, 10 January 1865. Portman's judgement of the situation was utterly absurd. Despite having witnessed the First Battle of Fort Fisher, and visited Lee's headquarters in Petersburg, he still wrote as though the South was going to win.

36. Jones, *A Rebel War Clerk's Diary*, p. 485, 23 January 1865.

37. Bauer, 'The Last Effort', p. 80.

38. National Archives of Canada, Burley, Extradition MSS, sec. C-1, RG 13, vol. 987, Robert Harrison to John Macdonald, 4 February 1865.

39. Stephen Z. Starr, *Colonel Grenfell's Wars* (Baton Rouge, La., 1971), p. 210.

40. See ibid., p. 212, and PRO FO5/1155, on the Grenfell correspondence.

41. Starr, *Colonel Grenfell's Wars*, p. 212.

42. Buckinghamshire RO, D11/1/3.c, memorandum by Joseph Wheeler.

43. *Diary of Gideon Welles*, 3 vols. (Boston, 1911), vol. 2, p. 229, 21 January 1865. The source for the footnote is OR, ser. 1, vol. 46/3, p. 38, Grant to Seward, 19 March 1864.

44. 'Bright–Sumner Letters', *Proceedings of the Massachusetts Historical Society*, 46 (1913), p. 132, Bright to Sumner, 26 January 1865.

45. Bauer, 'The Last Effort', p. 86.

CHAPTER 36. 'RICHMOND TOMORROW'

1. West Sussex RO, Lyons MSS, box 299, Malet to Lyons, 24 February 1865.

2. PRO 30/22/38, Lyons to Russell, 27 December 1864.

3. Arthur Irwin Dasent, *John Thadeus Delane, Editor of 'The Times'*, 2 vols. (London, 1908), vol. 2, p. 135, Delane to Dasent, 25 December 1864; p. 136, Delane to Dasent, 26 December 1864.

4. Sheffield Archives, WHM461/6, Spence to Wharncliffe, 5 January 1865.

5. The controversy rescued the year-old London branch from its torpid existence. New York Public Library, US Sanitary Commission MSS, box 339/120, C. S. P. Bowles to E. C. Fisher, 2 January 1865.

6. W. C. Ford (ed.), *A Cycle of Adams Letters, 1861–1865*, 2 vols. (Boston, 1920), vol. 2, p. 244, Charles Francis Adams Jr. to Abigail Adams, 8 January 1865.

7. A recent traveller to America suggested to Wharncliffe that they donate the money to the US Sanitary Commission. 'I witnessed there on many and various occasions the untiring efforts of this Commission who took care of the sick, wounded and PRISONERS on each side,' the correspondent asserted. Sheffield Archives, WHM461/15, Bower Wood to Wharncliffe, 3 January 1865. The source for the footnote is Sheffield Archives, WHM461/16, PC Joseph Taylor to Wharncliffe, 5 January 1865, and WHM461/24, Captain Hampson, late 13th Louisiana Regiment, to Wharncliffe, 17 January 1865.

8. Timothy Holmes (ed.), *David Livingstone: Letters and Documents, 1861–1872* (London, 1990), p. 102, Livingstone to James Young, 4 January 1865.

9. NARA RG94/skm/414, Smelt to Lincoln, 17 March 1865. Smelt wrote that he had written twelve months previously to get his son discharged on grounds of youth and inability: 'I have today a letter from him, he having been exchanged [from a Confederate prison] and is now at Annapolis – He was wounded in 3 places . . . and lay for two days uncared for on the field of battle, yet singular to relate – lives!' (See also Chapter 28, n. 30.)

10. Sheffield Archives, WHM461/23, Spence to Wharncliffe, 16 January 1865.

11. Not even the knowledge that every dispatch since July 1863 had been lost or captured diminished Bulloch's belief that sea power could save the South. ORN, ser. 2, vol. 2, p. 787, Bulloch to Mallory, 24 December 1864.

12. ORN, ser. 2, vol. 2, p. 787, Bulloch to Low, 8 January 1865.

13. 'If you approve this suggestion, you will please give me the earliest possible intimation of your views,' he wrote to Mallory. ORN, ser. 1, vol. 3, p. 722, Bulloch to Mallory, 10 January 1865.

14. Library of Congress, Hotze Papers, private letterbook, Hotze to Bulloch, 25 January 1865.

15. Two British officers were allowed on board. They were amazed that such a large ship could be managed by so small a crew. The Governor of Australia was perplexed by the *Shenandoah*'s arrival and unsure whether to apply the usual Belligerent Rules or act on his own initiative. He decided to be safe and ordered her departure after re-coaling and carrying out emergency repairs.

16. 'Diary of John R. Thompson,' *Confederate Veteran*, 37 (1929), p. 99, 27 January 1865.

17. Sheffield Archives, WHM461/25, Collie to Wharncliffe, 23 January 1864.

18. ORN, ser. 1, vol. 3, p. 736, Bulloch to Mallory, 11 February 1865.

19. ORN, ser. 2, vol. 3, p. 1260, Mason to Benjamin, *c*. February 1865.

20. *The Economist*, 5 February 1865.

21. Stephen R. Wise, *Lifeline of the Confederacy: Blockade Running during the Civil War* (Columbia, SC, 1988), p. 266, and David Surdam, *Northern Naval Superiority and the Economics of the American Civil War* (Columbia, SC, 2001), p. 87.

22. Lance Davis and Stanley L. Engerman, *Naval Blockades in Peace and War* (Cambridge, 2006), p. 154.

23. See e.g. Surdam, *Northern Naval Superiority*, pp. 207-9.

24. Sarah Agnes Wallace and Frances Elma Gillespie (eds.), *The Journal of Benjamin Moran 1857-1865*, 2 vols. (Chicago, 1948, 1949), vol. 2, pp. 1382, 1373, 1371, 2 February 1865, 6 February 1865 and 23 February 1865.

25. ORN, ser. 2, vol. 3, p. 1260, Mason to Benjamin, *c.* February 1865.

26. Hansard, 3rd ser., vol. 177, col. 27, 7 February 1865, Lord Derby.

27. Ibid., cols. 141-50, 10 February 1865, Sir John Walsh, MP for Radnorshire.

28. *PRFA*, 1 (1866), p. 131, Adams to Seward, 9 February 1865.

29. MHS, Adams MSS, Diary of Charles Francis Adams, 28 December 1864.

30. G. P. Gooch (ed.), *The Later Correspondence of Lord John Russell, 1840-1878*, 2 vols. (London, 1925), vol. 2, p. 336, 7 February 1865. As late as 15 January, Palmerston was still arguing with the Duke of Somerset that Quebec, Montreal, Halifax and Bermuda must all be fortified. 'The warnings of eventual hostility on the part of the United States are not to be disregarded, and the Irish Fenians in North America would give us trouble in Ireland if we had war with America.'

31. Kenneth Bourne, *Britain and the Balance of Power* (Berkeley, 1967), p. 271. The source for the footnote is Somerset RO, Somerset MSS, d/RA/A/2a/270/13, Donald McKay to Rear Admiral Robinson, 14 February 1865.

32. Dean Mahin, *One War at a Time* (Dulles, Va., 1999), p. 226.

33. Scott Thomas Cairns, 'Lord Lyons and Anglo-American Diplomacy during the American Civil War', Ph.D. thesis, London School of Economics, 2004, p. 362, Journal of Queen Victoria, 10 March 1865.

34. *PRFA*, 1 (1866), pp. 69-71, Adams to Seward, 30 December 1864.

35. Ibid., p. 176, Russell to Mason, Slidell and Mann, 13 February 1865. Brian Jenkins, *Britain and the War for the Union*, 2 vols. (Montreal, 1974, 1980), vol. 2, p. 366. The Queen thought it was somewhat undignified to ask for Seward's help in delivering the letter. But Russell replied that if the only reason against sending the letter was 'because we do not like to be thought afraid', he was prepared to suffer that consequence, 'for the humanity of the country'.

36. MHS, Adams MSS, Diary of Charles Francis Adams, 14 February 1865, and *PRFA*, 1 (1866), p. 165, Adams to Seward, 16 February 1865.

37. Ibid., p. 183, Adams to Seward, 23 February 1865.

38. The situation in France also worried Adams after he heard in confidence from General McClellan's former military adviser, the Prince de Joinville, that the Emperor was building a large fleet at Cherbourg which he would be prepared to employ on behalf of the Confederates if Seward showed the slightest inclination to meddle in Mexico.

39. Fitzgerald Ross, *Cities and Camps of the Confederate States*, ed. Richard Barksdale Harwell (Champaign, Ill., 1997), p. xix, Ross to Blackwood, 24 March 1865.

40. Library of Congress, digital MSS online, Papers of Abraham Lincoln, Belle Boyd to Lincoln, 24 January 1864. Sala had a robust view of sex and extramarital relations and Belle was not in a position to dictate their relationship. Sala's contribution to the development of Victorian pornography is well documented, not least his co-authorship of the underground magazine the *Pearl*. After helping Belle, Sala became the ghost-writer for Lieutenant Colonel Heros von Borcke, Jeb Stuart's staff officer, who published his memoir in 1866.

41. See Louis A. Sigaud, *Belle Boyd – Confederate Spy* (Richmond, Va., 1944), pp. 185-7. Sigaud ponders the various rumours and half-truths concerning Hardinge and Grace.

42. 'We all agree, however,' wrote Slidell, 'that the letter of the Secretary for Foreign Affairs is extremely insolent and offensive.' ORN, ser. 2, vol. 3, p. 1263, Slidell to Benjamin, 24 February 1865. Shortly after Kenner's arrival in France, another emissary arrived, the French volunteer in the Confederate army Prince Camille de Polignac, who reached Paris on 21 March 1865, hoping to persuade the Emperor that giving aid to the Confederacy would be beneficial to his long-term plans for Mexico. 'When I left the country on what I expected to be a six month's absence, I was unaware of the hopeless conditions of the affairs in the east,' he wrote subsequently. Jeff Kinard, *Lafayette of the South* (College Station, Tex., 2001), p. 184.

43. 'The rumors lately prevalent coming from the South . . . [have] attracted much attention in England,' Mason wrote to Benjamin. 'Many enquiries have been made of me by our well-wishers whether I thought it would be done. It is considered by them with much favor as a measure . . . whilst in their opinion it would be a first step toward emancipation.' Mason reassured Benjamin that he had disabused them of the idea. ORN, ser. 2, vol. 3, p. 1258, Mason to Benjamin, 21 January 1865.

44. Robert W. Young, *Senator James Murray Mason* (Knoxville, Tenn., 1998), p. 180.

45. Craig A. Bauer, 'The Last Effort: The Secret Mission of the Confederate Diplomat, Duncan F. Kenner', *Louisiana History*, 22 (1981), pp. 67-95.

46. *A Compilation of the Messages and Papers of the Confederacy*, 2 vols. (Nashville, 1905), vol. 2, p. 717, Mason to Benjamin, 26 March 1865.

47. 'Diary of John R. Thompson', p. 99.

48. Wallace and Gillespie (eds.), *The Journal of Benjamin Moran*, vol. 2, p. 1393, 14 March 1865.

49. Sheffield Archives, WHM 461 (31), Hill to Wharncliffe, 17 February 1865.

50. PRO FO5/128, Hill to Russell, 18 February 1865.

51. PRO FO83/2223, Roundell Palmer to Russell, 18 March 1865.

52. PRO FO5/1101, ff. 23-5, Robert Dalglish to Mr Layard, 24 February 1865.

53. PRO FO5/1101, ff. 53–6, Robert Burley to Russell, 25 March 1865.

54. Lord Newton (ed.), *Lord Lyons: A Record of British Diplomacy*, 2 vols. (London, 1914), vol. 1, pp. 139–41.

55. PRO FO5/1009, d. 112, Lord Russell to Sir Frederick Bruce, 24 March 1865.

56. Wallace and Gillespie (eds.), *The Journal of Benjamin Moran*, vol. 2, p. 1395, 17 March 1865.

57. PRO FO5/1009, d. 112, Russell to Bruce, 24 March 1865.

58. Wallace and Gillespie (eds.), *The Journal of Benjamin Moran*, vol. 2, p. 1398, 24 March 1865.

59. Ford (ed.), *A Cycle of Adams Letters*, vol. 2, p. 258, Charles Francis Adams to Charles Francis Adams Jr., 24 March 1865.

60. Ibid., p. 259, Charles Francis Adams to Charles Francis Adams Jr., 24 March 1865.

CHAPTER 37. FIRE, FIRE

1. South Carolina Historical Society, Feilden–Smythe MSS (41), Feilden to Julia, 14 February 1865.

2. E. Milby Burton, *The Siege of Charleston* (Columbia, SC, 1982), p. 321.

3. Walker defended himself to the Foreign Office: 'I have endeavoured, as I had done previously, to perform my consular duties with the utmost strictness and impartiality.' PRO FO5/1015, f. 287, Pinckney Walker to Mr Burnley, 20 February 1865.

4. South Carolina Historical Society, Feilden–Smythe MSS (40), Feilden to Julia, 28 February 1865.

5. Nathaniel Cheairs Hughes Jr., *Bentonville: The Final Battle of Sherman and Johnston* (Chapel Hill, NC, 2006), p. 32.

6. Nelson D. Lankford, *An Irishman in Dixie* (Columbia, SC, 1988), p. 25.

7. Ibid., p. 32, 4 March 1865.

8. Ibid., p. 39, 9 March 1865.

9. Ibid., p. 42, 10 March 1865. A Mrs Brown, according to Lankford, was the one of the couriers who carried messages between Richmond and the Confederates in Canada.

10. Ibid., p. 48, 13 March 1865.

11. John B. Jones, *A Rebel War Clerk's Diary at the Confederate States Capital*, ed. Earl Schenck Miers (Urbana, Ill., 1958), p. 517, 14 March 1865.

12. Lankford, *An Irishman in Dixie*, p. 52, 16 March 1865.

13. Mrs Roger A. Pryor, *My Day: Reminiscences of a Long Life* (New York, 1909), p. 236.

14. Conolly wiled away the time before dinner visiting other camps. At General Heath's, he was surprised to meet Captain Sydney Herbert Davis, the British volunteer who had come to the Confederacy in 1863.

15. At his hotel, Conolly bumped into the Hon. Maurice Berkeley Portman, whose own optimism about the war had been shaken by an encounter with Sheridan's bummers.

16. Jones, *A Rebel War Clerk's Diary*, p. 520, 19 March 1865.

17. South Carolina Historical Society, Feilden–Smythe MSS (45), Feilden to Julia, 13 March 1865.

18. Ibid. (46), Feilden to Julia, 25 March 1865.

19. The Saundersons of Saunderson Castle, County Cavan, were an old Anglo-Irish family with a large fortune to spend. The 24-year-old Welly was the youngest of five brothers, three of whom belonged to the same regiment. 'The trio were not without notoriety and were generally known as Rats No. 1, No. 2 and No. 3,' wrote a historian of the family. 'They were always doing something dangerous.' Conolly was deeply impressed when Welly told him that he had even sold his commission in order to fight with Lee, unaware that the British army officer had something to prove. Welly was desperately in love with Lady Rachel Clonmell, but her father thought he was a wastrel and had refused him permission to set foot in the house, let alone propose marriage. R. Lucas, *Colonel Saunderson: A Memoir* (London, 1908), p. 14. I am indebted to Derek Mayhew for this information.

20. James M. Morgan, *Recollections of a Rebel Reefer* (Boston, 1917), p. 232.

21. *Southern Historical Society Papers*, vol. 4 (Richmond, Va., 1877), ed. Revd J. W. Jones, p. 22, fn.

22. Virginia Historical Society, Diary of Llewellyn Saunderson, MSS5:1Sa877:1, 31 March 1865.

23. Francis W. Dawson, *Reminiscences of Confederate Service, 1861–1865*, ed. Bell I. Wiley (Baton Rouge, La., 1980), pp. 142–3.

24. Virginia Historical Society, Diary of Llewellyn Saunderson, 1 April 1865.

25. *The Times*, 25 April 1865.

26. Jones, *A Rebel War Clerk's Diary*, p. 528, 2 April 1865.

27. *The Times*, 25 April 1865.

28. Edward M. Boykin, *The Falling Flag: Evacuation of Richmond* (New York, 1874), pp. 12–13.

29. Sallie A. Brock, *Richmond during the War: Four Years of Personal Recollections* (repr. Lincoln, Nebr., 1996), p. 367.

30. W. C. Ford (ed.), *A Cycle of Adams Letters, 1861–1865*, 2 vols. (Boston, 1920), vol. 2, p. 263, Charles Francis Adams Jr. to Charles Francis Adams, 10 April 1865.

31. Lincoln and Grant had some memorable conversations during the President's stay on the *River Queen*. Grant asked Lincoln about the *Trent* affair: 'Yes, Seward studied up all the works ever written on international law, and came to cabinet meetings loaded to the muzzle with the subject. We gave due consideration to the case, but at that critical period of the war it was soon decided to deliver up the prisoners. It was a pretty bitter pill to swallow, but I contented myself with believing that England's triumph in the matter would be short-lived, and that after ending our war successfully we would be so powerful that we could call her to

account for all the embarrassment she had inflicted upon us.' Doris Kearns Goodwin, *Team of Rivals* (New York, 2005), p. 711.

32. A. S. Lewis (ed.), *My Dear Parents* (New York, 1982), p. 131, Horrocks to brother Joseph, 8 April 1865.

CHAPTER 38. 'A TRUE-BORN KING OF MEN'

1. *Illustrated London News*, 20 May 1865.

2. Michael Burlingame, *Abraham Lincoln*, 2 vols. (Baltimore, 2008), vol. 2, p. 793.

3. John Hay and John G. Nicolay (eds.), *Abraham Lincoln: Complete Works*, 2 vols. (New York, 1922), vol. 2, p. 669, Lincoln to Grant, 6 April 1865.

4. Ulysses S. Grant, *Personal Memoirs of Ulysses S. Grant* (New York, 2003), p. 593.

5. *The Times*, 25 April 1865.

6. Brian Holden Reid, *Robert E. Lee* (London, 2005), p. 237.

7. Virginia Historical Society, Diary of Llewellyn Saunderson, MSS5:1Sa877:1, 6 April 1865.

8. PRO FO115/448, f. 402, Henry O'Brien to Sir Frederick Bruce, 14 June 1865.

9. Francis Lawley, 'The Last Six Days of Secessia', *Fortnightly Review*, 2 (June 1865), pp. 1–10, at p. 7.

10. General Fitz Lee had taken a liking to Welly – because he behaved 'admirably under fire' and 'was bold, bright, and witty of course'. Fitzhugh Lee, *General Lee* (New York, 1925), p. 387.

11. Burke Davis, *To Appomattox: Nine April Days, 1865* (New York, 1959), p. 282.

12. Virginia Historical Society, Diary of Llewellyn Saunderson, 8 April 1865.

13. James Ford Rhodes, *History of the Civil War 1861–1865* (New York, 1917), p. 434.

14. Frederick Maurice (ed.), *An Aide de Camp of Robert E. Lee* (New York, 1927), p. 273.

15. Grant, *Memoirs*, p. 629.

16. Lawley, 'The Last Six Days of Secessia', p. 9.

17. Jay Winik, *April 1865* (New York, 2001), p. 197.

18. Duke University, Francis Dawson MSS, no. 27, Dawson to mother, 7 April 1865; Francis W. Dawson, *Reminiscences of Confederate Service, 1861–1865*, ed. Bell I. Wiley (Baton Rouge, La., 1980), p. 146.

19. South Carolina Historical Society, Feilden–Smythe MSS (47), Feilden to Julia, 6 April 1865.

20. With the exception of Judah Benjamin, no one thought that this was even a remote possibility.

21. Frederick W. Seward (ed.), *Seward in Washington* (New York, 1891), p. 270.

22. Charles A. Dana, *Recollections of the Civil War* (New York, 1913), p. 274.

23. *Diary of Gideon Welles*, 3 vols. (Boston, 1911), vol. 2, p. 284, 14 April 1865.

24. Burlingame, *Abraham Lincoln*, vol. 2, p. 806.

25. Ibid., p. 814.

26. Seward (ed.), *Seward in Washington*, p. 278.

27. I am indebted to Derek Mayhew for supplying me with this information about his ancestor. The source for the footnote is *Southern Historical Society Papers*, vol. 4 (Richmond, Va., 1877), ed. Revd J. W. Jones, p. 22. Conolly's return to Ireland was reported in the *Donegal Advertiser*, which noted acidly: 'here again, we have him impressing upon the Donegal electors how much better it was for him to go to America than to stay like ordinary members and attend to the dull routine of his parliamentary duties.' NARA, Dispatches, US Consuls in Sheffield, Consul Abbot to Seward, 15 May 1865.

28. South Carolina Historical Society, Feilden–Smythe MSS (48), Feilden to Julia, 4 May 1865.

29. Keith Robbins, *John Bright* (London, 1978), p. 175.

30. MHS, Adams MSS, Diary of Charles Francis Adams, 26 April 1865.

31. Alan Hankinson, *Man of Wars: William Howard Russell of 'The Times'*, *1820–1907* (London, 1982), p. 182.

32. George S. Wykoff, 'Charles Mackay: England's Forgotten Civil War Correspondent', *South Atlantic Quarterly*, 26 (1927), pp. 59–60.

33. *The History of the Times*, vol. 2 (London, 1939), p. 387–8, Morris to Mackay, 21 April 1865.

34. *The Economist*, 29 April 1865.

35. Oscar Maurer, 'Punch on Slavery and the Civil War', *Victorian Studies*, 1/1 (Sept. 1957), pp. 4–28.

36. Sarah Agnes Wallace and Frances Elma Gillespie (eds.), *The Journal of Benjamin Moran, 1857–1865*, 2 vols. (Chicago, 1948, 1949), vol. 2, p. 1419, 30 April 1865.

37. After Russell's speech, Charles Sumner's vituperative attacks on Lord Russell seemed not only childish but unhinged. The Duke of Argyll was mystified why Sumner should take such offence. 'I have always thought you unjust to Lord Russell, because of little irritating speeches and phrases,' Argyll responded after one of Sumner's tirades. 'Substantially, he has always had a large amount of sympathy with the United States much more than others whom you seem to dislike less.'

38. Wallace and Gillespie (eds.), *The Journal of Benjamin Moran*, vol. 2, p. 1421, 1 May 1865.

39. NARA, M.T-185, roll 8, vol. 8, Consul Zebina Eastman to Mr Hunter, Acting Secretary of State, 8 May 1865; Liverpool RO, Durning–Holt MSS, Diary of Emma Holt, 902 Dur 1/4, 8 May 1865.

40. William Forster insisted that American-style democracy was a force for good. But the House of Commons found Disraeli's arguments more persuasive – he articulated a fear shared by many MPs that the world they knew and understood

was under threat from Americanizing forces which, if transplanted to England, would be simply destructive rather than modernizing or redemptive. Hansard, 3rd ser., vol. 178, cols. 1613–1710, 8 May 1865.

41. MHS, Adams MSS, Diary of Charles Francis Adams, 1 May 1865. Adams's image of Lincoln remained frozen in time, however. His last memory of the slain President was of a political novice whose rough manners had caused such merriment in Washington.

42. Virginia Mason, *The Public Life and Diplomatic Correspondence of James M. Mason* (New York, 1906), p. 562.

43. Library of Congress, Mason Papers, private letterbook, Mason to Wood, 21 April 1865.

44. Louis Martin Sears, 'A Confederate Diplomat at the Court of Napoleon III', *American Historical Review*, 26/2 (Jan. 1921), p. 278, Slidell to Mason, 26 April 1865.

45. Robert Underwood Johnson and Clarence Clough Buel (eds.), *Battles and Leaders of the Civil War*, 4 vols. (Secaucus, NJ, 1985), vol. 3, p. 764.

46. James M. Morgan, *Recollections of a Rebel Reefer* (Boston, 1917), p. 238.

47. Frank E. Vandiver (ed.), *The Civil War Diary of General Josiah Gorgas* (Tuscaloosa, Ala., 1947), p. 184, 4 May 1865.

48. The money was taken from Davis when he was captured. A typical rate on the Inman line between New York and London was £5 per adult.

49. ORN, ser. 1, vol. 16, p. 333, report of Commander Reynolds, 16 May 1865.

50. James J. Barnes and Patience P. Barnes (eds.), *The American Civil War through British Eyes*, vol. 3 (Kent, Ohio, 2005), p. 302, Bruce to Russell, 16 May 1865.

51. William Watson, *The Civil War Adventures of a Blockade Runner* (College Station, Tex., 2001), p. 823.

52. Margaret Leach, *Reveille in Washington* (Alexandria, Va., 1962; repr. 1980), p. 379.

53. News and letters were trickling in from the South. Consul Arthur Lynn was finally rescued from his Crusoe-like existence in Galveston. He had continued to send his dispatches, never knowing if they reached their destination. Miraculously, a few did eventually arrive. The Foreign Office, on the other hand, had written him off as lost until further notice more than a year earlier. Lynn now learned that his sister had been trying to contact him for the past eighteen months with questions arising from their late father's estate. PRO FO5/976, draft, Foreign Office to Messrs Brown and Dunlop, Glasgow, Solicitors, 4 January 1865.

54. Edward Waldo Emerson, *The Early Years of the Saturday Club* (New York, 1918), p. 405.

55. PRO 30/22/38, ff. 186–9, Bruce to Russell, 20 April 1865.

56. PRO 30/22/38, ff. 198–9, Bruce to Russell, 27 April 1865.

57. James J. Barnes and Patience P. Barnes (eds.), *Private and Confidential: Letters from British Ministers to the Foreign Secretaries* (Selinsgrove, Pa., 1993), p. 362, Bruce to Russell, 22 May 1865.

58. South Carolina Historical Society, Feilden–Smythe MSS (49), Feilden to Julia, 30 May 1865.

59. Columbia University, Blackwell MSS, Blackwell to Bodichon, 25 May 1865.

EPILOGUE

1. The second largest army, the Prussian, was roughly half the size at 484,000; the French had about 343,000; and the British army no more than 220,000 regulars plus 370,000 volunteer and militia soldiers.

2. Allan Nevins, *The War for the Union*, 4 vols., vol. 4: *The Organized War to Victory 1864–1865* (New York, 1971), pp. 367–8.

3. Craig L. Symonds and William J. Clipson, *The Naval Institute Historical Atlas of the U.S. Navy* (Annapolis, Md., 1995), p. 105.

4. The reopening of communications with the South meant release for the many families in Britain held fast in the agony of limbo. Joseph Burnley received definite proof of Frederick Farr's death. He also began fresh enquiries after Robert Livingstone and Stephen Smelt, the Manchester boy who had run away with his best friend in 1863. Nothing was forthcoming with regards to Robert; Dr Livingstone had been so optimistic that he had visited the American legation on 11 March to make sure Charles Francis Adams had not forgotten his son. But there was positive news in Stephen's case. Burnley learned that the boy had been wounded at the Battle of Olustee and captured by the Confederates. The Federal authorities thought he was still alive. Mr Smelt, the father of Stephen Smelt, learned that his son had been found but was not coming home after all. Stephen had discovered a taste for army life. 'I have the honor to state that I have no desire to leave the US service as I wish to serve out my term of enlistment and become a citizen of the US since I joined from a Prisoner of War my health was never better, as the surgeon's certificate will show.' NARA, Stephen Smelt, in camp in Raleigh, NC, 9 July 1865, to Lieutenant J. O'Connel, Adjutant, 47th New York State Volunteers. I am grateful to Mike Musick for bringing these letters to my attention.

5. Drew Gilpin Faust, *This Republic of Suffering* (Cambridge, Mass., 2008), pp. 211–13.

6. Colonel Currie had married an American wife in 1864, Harriet Caroll Jackson, a granddaughter of one of the signers of the Declaration of Independence. After the war he became a special agent for the Post Office, overseeing the delivery of diplomatic mail en route between San Francisco and Hong Kong. On his retirement, the couple moved to Britain to live on the Isle of Wight.

7. A. S. Lewis (ed.), *My Dear Parents* (New York, 1982), pp. 159, 169.

8. *Isle of Man Examiner*, 2 October 1897.

9. The total cost of the war could have bought the freedom of every slave, given each one 40 acres and a mule and provided a bounty for a hundred years of lost

earnings. See E. B. Long with Barbara Long, *The Civil War Day by Day: An Almanac 1861–1865* (New York, 1971; repr. New York, 1985), appendix.

10. Frances Leigh Butler, *Ten Years on a Georgia Plantation since the War* (London, 1883), pp. 52–3.

11. The Consular records show that there were 352 British residents still living in Charleston in May 1865. Some of them were blockade-runners who had no means of getting home.

12. South Carolina Historical Society, Feilden–Smythe MSS, Trevor-Battye MSS, n.d.

13. Robert Summers, *The Fall and Redemption of Dr. Samuel A. Mudd* (n.p., 2008), p. 56.

14. Sir Frederick Bruce was relieved that the amnesty included the discharge of all military prisoners still awaiting trial. But there was a catch for foreign prisoners of war. Henry O'Brien sent a plaintive letter to the legation, asking for help because he did not want to swear allegiance to the United States, since 'by doing so I expatriate myself. . . . I am aware that I did wrong in joining a foreign army without Her Majesty's Licences and consequently have born humiliation and insult without any hope of redress, but now as the war is over and all the prisoners of war being released and as I only ask to be allowed to leave the US, I hope you will at least obtain for me some decision by the Washington Military Authorities.' PRO FO115/448, f. 402, Henry O'Brien to legation, 14 June 1865.

15. Lonnie A. Burnett, *Henry Hotze, Confederate Propagandist* (Tuscaloosa, Ala., 2008), p. 30.

16. *New York Times*, 26 June 1878.

17. James T. Hubbell and James Geary (eds.), *Biographical Dictionary of the Union* (Westport, Conn., 1995), p. 360.

18. Jay Luvaas, *The Military Legacy of the Civil War* (Lawrence, Kans., 1988), p. 122.

19. *Letters of Queen Victoria*, ed. George E. Buckle, 3 vols. (London, 1930–32), vol. 1, p. 594, Lord Clarendon to Queen Victoria, 1 May 1869.

20. Bancroft was so gratuitously rude about Lord Palmerston, who had been dead for less than four months, that an official protest was lodged by the Foreign Office with the American legation: 'Lincoln took to heart the eternal truths of liberty . . . Palmerston did nothing that will endure; Lincoln finished a work which all time cannot overthrow . . . Palmerston . . . was attended by the British aristocracy to his grave, which, after a few years, will hardly be noticed . . . Lincoln [will] . . . be remembered through all time by his countrymen, and by all the peoples of the world.'

21. MHS, Argyll letters, p. 86, Duchess of Argyll to Charles Sumner, 4 July 1865.

22. See Adrian Cook, *The Alabama Claims: American Politics and Anglo-American Relations, 1865–1872* (Ithaca, NY, 1975).

23. The easiest route to winning Seward's trust to behave towards him as if he were still the most powerful politician in Washington. 'He is vain,' wrote the British Minister, Frederick Bruce, on 2 May; 'to show deference to his judgment . . . is a species of subtle flattery which is not without weight.' James J. Barnes and

Patience P. Barnes (eds)., *Private and Confidential: Letters from British Ministers to the Foreign Secretaries* (Selinsgrove, Pa., 1993), p. 378.

24. *PRFA*, 1 (1868), p. 83, Charles Francis Adams to Seward, 2 May 1867.

25. Frederick Bancroft, *The Life of William H. Seward*, 2 vols. (Gloucester, Mass., 1967), vol. 2, p. 494.

26. The Dominion of Canada was a semi-autonomous state under the sovereignty of the Crown. In theory, its parliament was answerable to the imperial Parliament in London, but in practice the Canadians were left to govern their internal affairs, though not their external relationships with foreign countries, including America.

27. MHS, Adams MSS, Diary of Charles Francis Adams, 25 April 1867.

28. *Correspondence Concerning Claims against Great Britain*, vol. 3 (Washington, 1869), p. 674, Seward to Adams, 2 May 1867.

29. Wendell Philips Garrison, *William Lloyd Garrison: The Story of his life*, 4 vols. (New York, 1889), vol. 4, pp. 205–9.

30. *Correspondence Concerning Claims against Great Britain*, vol. 3, p. 683, Seward to Adams, 16 November 1867.

31. *Letters of Henry Adams*, ed. Jacob Clavner Levenson (Cambridge, Mass., 1988), vol. 1, p. 498, Henry Adams to Charles Francis Adams Jr., 14 July 1865. He remained the same stiff and isolated figure who had arrived in 1861. 'I am continually puzzled to know how we get along together,' complained his son Henry. 'I find the Chief rather harder, less a creature of our time than ever. It pains me absolutely . . . to see him so separate from the human race. I crave for what is new . . . He cares nothing for it, and a new discovery in physics or in chemistry, or a new development in geology never seems to touch any chord in him.'

32. Martin Duberman, *Charles Francis Adams* (New York, 1961), pp. 330–31.

33. MHS, Adams MSS, Diary of Charles Francis Adams, 26 March 1868.

34. Frederick W. Seward (ed.), *Seward at Washington* (New York, 1891), p. 538.

35. Henry Adams, *The Education of Henry Adams*, ed. Ernest Samuels (repr. Boston, 1973), p. 246.

36. New York *Nation*, 3 (1866), p. 234.

37. Calculations based on http://www.measuringworth.com.

38. Doris Kearns Goodwin, *Team of Rivals* (New York, 2005), p. 711.

39. Jay Sexton, *Debtor Diplomacy* (Oxford, 2005), p. 207. This pioneering study takes a close look at the relationship between diplomatic rapprochement and the realities of the Anglo-US financial markets. After Sumner's speech was known in England, John Bright wrote on 9 May: 'The American question gives much uneasiness. The rejection of the "Claims Convention" by the Senate is a great misfortune, and Charles Sumner's speech, so hostile and vindictive, has caused me much pain and disappointment.' R. A. J. Walling (ed.), *The Diaries of John Bright* (New York, 1931), p. 340.

40. David Herbert Donald, *Charles Sumner and the Rights of Man* (New York, 1970), p. 413.

41. James Phinney Baxter, 'June Meeting: The British High Commissioners at

Washington in 1871', *Proceedings of the Massachusetts Historical Society*, 3rd ser., vol. 65 (Oct. 1932), p. 344.

42. Maureen Robson, 'The *Alabama* Claims and the Anglo-American Reconciliation', *Canadian Historical Review*, 42/1 (1961), p. 22.

43. Baxter, 'June Meeting: The British High Commissioners at Washington in 1871', p. 350.

44. Mary Sophia Hill, *A British Subject's Recollections of the Confederacy* (Baltimore, 1975), p. 66.

45. Lord Edmund Fitzmaurice, *The Life of the Second Earl Granville*, 2 vols. (London, 1905), vol. 2, p. 100.

46. Richard Shannon, *Gladstone: Heroic Minister 1865–1898* (London, 1999), p. 114.

47. *Bruce Herald*, 28 March 1873.

48. Ulysses S. Grant, *Personal Memoirs of Ulysses S. Grant* (New York, 2003), p. 640.

49. William Michael Rossetti, 'English Opinion on the American War', *Atlantic Monthly*, 17 (Feb. 1866), p. 129.

50. H.W. Brands, *The Selected Letters of Theodore Roosevelt* (New York, 2001), p. 54.

51. Ella Lonn's magisterial studies of foreign volunteers (published between 1940 and 1951) shed much-needed light on their numbers, but placing the volunteers alongside the other aspects of Britain's role in the war was outside the scope of her work.

52. An essential reading list for the Civil War and Anglo-American diplomacy would include: Ephraim D. Adams, H. C. Allen, Richard J. M. Blackett, Kinley Brauer, Duncan Andrew Campbell, Adrian Cook, D. P. Crook, Hugh Dubrulle, Norman B. Ferris, Charles M. Hubbard, Brian Jenkins, Howard Jones, Dean B. Mahin, Robert E. May, Frank Merli, Phillip Myers, Frank Owsley, Jay Sexton, Warren F. Spencer, Brian Holden Reid, Philip Van Doren Stern and Robin Winks.

53. Gladstone, for example, later blamed his support for the South on his inability to see the issue in its entirety: 'That my opinion was founded upon a false estimate of the facts was the very least part of my fault. I did not perceive the gross impropriety of such an utterance from a cabinet minister, of a power allied in blood and language, and bound to loyal neutrality; the case being further exaggerated by the fact that we already, so to speak, under indictment before the world for not (as was alleged) having strictly enforced the laws of neutrality in the matter of the cruiser. My offence ... illustrates vividly ... an incapacity of viewing subjects all round, in their extraneous as well as in their internal properties.' John Morley, *The Life of William Ewart Gladstone 1809–1872*, 2 vols. (London, 1908), vol. 2, p. 82.

54. Rossetti, 'English Opinion on the American War', p. 149.

Glossary

adjutant A staff officer assigned to handle administrative duties for a commanding officer.

battery A Union battery had six cannons with more than 100 men; Confederate batteries usually had four; a position where cannons were mounted.

blockade-runner A swift vessel used by Confederates to evade the Federal naval blockade of Southern ports; the captain of a blockade-runner.

bombproof A shelter from artillery attack, often built with timber and packed earth.

bounty A cash bonus paid to entice men into the army.

breastwork A chest-high barricade built to shield defenders from enemy fire.

canister A tin can containing 27 iron balls packed in sawdust; when fired from a cannon, the can ripped open and showered the balls at the enemy.

contraband A term popularized by General Butler in 1861 for fugitive slaves who crossed into Northern lines.

corduroy road A road constructed with logs, often in otherwise impassable muddy areas.

crimping The forced enlistment of soldiers or sailors by trickery or coercion.

division A force of approximately 12,000 soldiers or three/four brigades. A brigade generally consisted of four to six regiments. A regiment was composed of 1,100 officers and men divided into 10 companies.

drill Formal training received by a recruit, including how to march in formation.

gunboat A shallow watercraft designed to carry one or more guns, usually used on rivers.

hardtack A flour-and-water wafer, usually three inches square; cheap and durable, it was a staple of military campaigns.

housewife A sewing kit that also contained toiletries and personal items.

Howitzer A short-barrelled artillery piece designed to propel projectiles at relatively high trajectories.

ironclad A warship clad with iron or steel plates to protect the wooden vessel from explosive or incendiary shells.

mess A group of soldiers who cooked and ate together; the place where food is prepared and eaten.

Minié ball A conical bullet whose hollow base expanded when fired, forcing its sides into the rifling and making it spin, assuring greater accuracy.

monitor A Federal ironclad warship with revolving gun turrets, named after the design of the USS *Monitor,* launched in 1862.

mortar Heavy artillery designed to fire projectiles, usually bails, with a high angle of fire into enemy positions. Mostly used in siege, garrison and coastal warfare.

musket A muzzle-loading shoulder gun with a long barrel.

parole The pledge of a US or Confederate soldier released from captivity not to take up arms until formally exchanged for an enemy prisoner of equal rank.

Parrott gun A muzzle-loading rifled artillery weapon patented by Union officer Robert Parrott.

percussion cap A small copper cylinder containing shock-sensitive explosive; the cap was placed over the hollow metal 'nipple' at the rear end of a gun barrel. Pulling the trigger released the hammer, which struck and ignited the cap. The flame passed through the nipple to ignite the main powder charge. Caps enabled muzzle-loading guns to fire reliably in any weather.

picket Soldiers on guard to protect a larger military unit from enemy attack.

pontoon bridge A portable bridge supported by floating pontoons.

provost guard Soldiers acting as military police under the authority of a provost marshal.

quartermaster An officer in charge of procuring food, equipment and clothing for troops.

ram A ship built with an iron prow designed to pierce and sink enemy vessels.

rifle pit A shallow trench dug to protect soldiers from enemy fire while shooting weapons.

round shot A solid spherical projectile fired from artillery.

shrapnel A hollow cast-iron projectile filled with metal balls packed around an explosive charge, designed to explode in mid-air, showering the enemy with smaller projectiles.

smoothbore A firearm or canon with an unrifled barrel.

solid shot A solid projectile with no explosive, designed to be used against cavalry, buildings or troops in a column.

Springfield rifle An American-made rifle; the most prevalent in the war. The second most popular was the Enfield, which was manufactured in England and exported by the hundreds of thousands. Both were single shot muzzle-loading rifles with an accuracy range that was excellent at 300 yards and passable at 500. Compared to the maximum range of 200 yards for a Napoleonic-era rifle, Civil War rifles were killing-machines.

sutler A merchant licensed to sell provisions to troops in an army camp or on the field.

torpedo A stationary underwater mine that exploded upon contact with a ship. Some torpedoes could be detonated electronically from the shore.

Zouaves Northern or Confederate regiments that modelled themselves on the original elite North African corps in the French army.

Acknowledgements

I would like to thank the following for sending me their ancestors' papers: John Knight, Derrick Mayhew and Mrs Iris Diggle; as well as John Hailey, Bill Torrens and Mrs Beata Duncan for their help.

I have been greatly helped by my assistants over the years, who have done everything from photocopying archives to picking up the children from school: Heather Nedwell, Jay Knowlton, Lorena Crackett, Christina Galbraith, Elizabeth Uzelac and Olivia Taylor. I would also like to thank all those at Penguin and Random House who have worked on the book.

The following individuals and libraries provided invaluable material: Library of Congress, National Archives US, National Archives UK, Massachusetts Historical Society, South Carolina Historical Society, Museum of the Confederacy, British Library, British Newspaper Library, The Royal Museum of Central Africa, Ms Sam Collenette – Bolton Archives and Local Studies, Roger Bettridge, Sally Mason, Linda Haynes – Buckinghamshire Record Office, Kate Fellows – Birmingham City Archives Assistant, Rachel MacGregor – Birmingham City Archives Assistant, John Hopkins – Cheshire County Council Archivist, Esther Williams – Cheshire County Council Archivist, David Thomas – Cornwall Record Office, Susan Worrall – City Archivist, City of Coventry, Rachel M. Rowe – Smuts Librarian in South Asian and Commonwealth Studies, University of Cambridge, Miss Diana Chardin – Assistant Manuscript Cataloguer, Trinity College Library, Cambridge University, Martin Beckett – State Library of New South Wales, David M. Bowcock – County Archivist, Cumbria Record Office, Tim Wormleighton, Janice Wood, Susan Laithwaite, John Brunton – Archivists, Devon County Council, Jennifer Gill, Elizabeth Rainey, Jane Hogan – County Archivist, Durham County Archives, Hugh Jaques, Deborah Stevenson –

County Archivist, Dorset County Archives, Sarah Chubb – Dundee University Library, Archives and Manuscripts Department, Ian Flett – Dundee City Archives, Michael Read – Head of Academic Studies, Welsh College of Music and Drama, Marion M. Stewart – Archivist and Records Management Officer, Dumfries and Galloway Archives, Robert Craig, Philip Bye – Senior Archivist, East Sussex Records Office, Dr Annette Hagan – Special Collections, Edinburgh University Library, Hazel Robertson – Thesis Librarian, Special Collections, Edinburgh University Library, Elizabeth Pettitt – Senior Archivist, Flintshire Records Office, Mr P. R. Evans – Gloucestershire County Record Office, Pauline Kane – Glasgow Public Library, Lynne Dent, Elizabeth Ball, Moira Rankin – Special Collections Department, Glasgow University, Steffan ab Owain, J. Dilwyn Williams – Caernarfon Record Office, Martin Taylor – City Archivist, Kingston upon Hull, Local Studies, Central Library, Department of Manuscripts, National Library of Ireland, Helen Burton – Special Collections and Archives, Keele University, Lancashire County Records Office, Dr Margaret Bonnet – Leicestershire Records Office, Adrian Wilkinson – Archivist, Lincolnshire County Council, Mr Roger Hull, Mrs Liz Williams – Liverpool Record Office, Stephen Freeth, James R. Sewell – Corporation of London, Guildhall Library, Susan Steed – Special Collections, University College London, Mr Paul Howell, Malcom Davis, Ms Gillian Moran – Special Collections, Leeds University Library, Dr Maureen M. Watry, Ms Gwen McGinty – Head of Special Collections and Archives, Sydney Jones Library, University of Liverpool, John Nicholls – London City Mission, William T. La Moy, Roderick MacDonald, Alec Hasenson, Mr R. Gerrelli, Stephen M. Dixon – Borough Archivist, Medway Archives and Local Studies Centre, Dawn Littler – Curator of Archives, Merseyside Maritime Museum, Mr Peter McNiven, John Hodgson – John Rylands University Library, Edith Phillip – National War Museum of Scotland, Public Record Office of Northern Ireland, Helen Sellars – Florence Nightingale Museum Trust, Ms Helen Wakely, Mr Douglas Knock, Mr Richard Aspin, Nyree Morrison – Wellcome Library for the History and Understanding of Medicine, Helen Arkwright – Manuscripts and Archives Librarian, Special Collections, Robinson Library, University of Newcastle, Miss Elizabeth Tebbutt, Mrs Caroline Kelly – Department of Manuscripts and Special Collections, Hallward Library, University of Nottingham, Jill Davies, Kiri Ross-Jones – Manuscripts Department,

National Maritime Museum, Tim Hughes, Mrs S. Wood – Record Office, Northumberland County Council, Mr A. J. M. Henstock – Nottinghamshire Archives, Caroline Dalton – New College Library, Oxford, Mrs Clare Brown – Department of Special Collections and Western Manuscripts, Bodleian Library, Oxford, Ms Marie Lewis – Pembrokeshire Record Office, Mr Steve Connelly – Perth and Kinross Council Archive, Josef Keith – Library, Friends House, London, Susan McGann, Barbara Mortimer – Royal College of Nursing Archives and UK Centre for History of Nursing, Alan Readman – West Sussex Record Office, Brian Smith, Mrs M. J. Meterscough – Stockport Central Library, Ms Di Tapley – Surrey County Council, Len Reilly – Local Studies Librarian, Southwark Leisure, John C. Balfour, Robert Fotheringham, John McLintock, Dr Alison Rosie – National Archives of Scotland, Ms Daniella Shippey, Dr Iain G. Brown – National Library of Scotland, Mrs Alison Healey – Shropshire Records and Research Centre, Christopher Lloyd – Tower Hamlets Local History, Bancroft Library, Rhys M. Jones, Ms Meriel Ralphs – National Library of Wales, Steve Hobbs – Wiltshire and Swindon Record Office, Ms Jeannette Griswold – Warwickshire County Record Office, Dr David Wykes – Dr Williams's Library, Elen Wyn Hughes – University of Wales Bangor, Bob Hale – Archivist, Sheffield Archives and Conservation Unit, North Yorkshire County Council County Record Office, Mrs R. Harris, Barbara Hick, Paul Harris – West Yorkshire Police, Mrs C. Boddington – East Riding of Yorkshire Archive Office, Andrew George, Roy Rawlinson, Mike Kanazawich, Elizabeth Briggs – West Yorkshire Archive Service. Lyons Papers, courtesy of His Grace the Duke of Norfolk, Arundel Castle, Mary Jo Fairchild – South Carolina Historical Society, Pat Boulos – Boston Atheneum, Ann Drury Wellford – Museum of the Confederacy, Mitch Frass – Duke University Library, Faye Haskins – Washingtoniana Division of the DC Public Library, Amy Elizabeth Burton – United States Senate Office.

Index

Page references in *italic* indicate illustrations. Footnotes are indicated by the letter n following a page number. Endnotes are indicated in a similar way, but with an additional number following the letter n, designating the note number, e.g. 917n2. Military ranks, shown in parentheses after names, refer only to the highest rank applicable in the discussions of that person throughout the book, and not necessarily to the rank held at the time of a particular discussion.

PENGUIN HISTORY

THE PENGUIN HISTORY OF THE UNITED STATES OF AMERICA
HUGH BROGAN

This celebrated one-volume history has established itself as the definitive and most readable work available on America, brilliantly capturing the dynamic events and personalities that shaped the nation's triumphant progress – from its earliest colonization up to the fall of President Nixon. Now, in this new edition, Hugh Brogan continues the story through to the close of the Reagan era and the end of the cold war, a time of radical change which has made America the global superpower of today: in his words, 'for good and evil, a power and civilization that surpasses...all the empires of the past'. There are also numerous revisions to previous chapters, taking into account the most up-to-date research into American history.

'[A] lively and wide ranging introduction to America's past ... Fresh, engaging, amusing, anecdotal and analytical in turn ... It deserves a large audience'
New Statesman

'Compelling reading ... Hugh Brogan's work will delight the general reader as much as the student' *The Times Educational Supplement*

Brogan has both a real gift for narrative and the ability to deal succinctly and tellingly with the individual and his contribution' Lord Beloff, *Daily Telegraph*

PENGUIN HISTORY

CRIMEA: THE LAST CRUSADE
ORLANDO FIGES

The terrible conflict that dominated the mid nineteenth century, the Crimean War killed at least 800,000 men and pitted Russia against a formidable coalition of Britain, France and the Ottoman Empire. It was a war for territory, provoked by fear that if the Ottoman Empire were to collapse then Russia could control a huge swathe of land from the Balkans to the Persian Gulf. But it was also a war of religion, driven by a fervent, populist and ever more ferocious belief by the Tsar and his ministers that it was Russia's task to rule all Orthodox Christians and control the Holy Land.

Orlando Figes' major new book re-imagines this extraordinary war, in which the stakes could not have been higher and which was fought with a terrible mixture of ferocity and incompetence. The iconic moments of the are all here, but there is also a rich sense of the Crimea itself and the culture that was destroyed by the fighting.

Drawing on a huge range of fascinating sources, Figes also gives the lived experience of the war, from that of the ordinary British soldier in his snow-filled trench, to the haunted, gloomy, narrow figure of Tsar Nicholas himself as he vows to take on the whole world in his hunt for religious salvation.

PENGUIN HISTORY

UNDERTONES OF WAR
EDMUND BLUNDEN

'An established classic … accurate and detailed in observation of the war scene and its human figures' D J Enright

In one of the finest autobiographies to come out of the First World War, the poet Edmund Blunden records his devastating experiences in France and Flanders. Enlisting at the age of twenty, he took part in the disastrous battles of the Somme, Ypres and Passchendaele, describing the latter as 'murder, not only to the troops but to their singing faiths and hopes'. In his compassionate yet unsentimental prose, he tells of the endurance, heroism – and despair – among the men of his battalion.

This volume, which contains a selection of Blunden's war poems, also reveals his close affinity with the natural world: the 'shepherd in a soldier's coat' whose love of the rural landscape gives him some refuge from the terrible betrayal enacted in Flanders' fields.

PENGUIN HISTORY

AMERICA, EMPIRE OF LIBERTY: A NEW HISTORY
DAVID REYNOLDS

'An enthralling tale' *Daily Telegraph*

It was Thomas Jefferson who envisioned the United States as a great 'empire of liberty.' David Reynolds takes Jefferson's phrase as a key to the saga of America, bringing to life presidents from Washington to Obama, whilst also drawing on the voices of settlers and immigrants, factory workers and suburban housewives. He examines how the anti-empire of 1776 became the greatest superpower the world has seen, how the country that offered liberty and opportunity on a scale unmatched in Europe nevertheless founded its prosperity on the labour of black slaves and the dispossession of the Native Americans.

Written with verve and insight, this extraordinary history reveals the grandeur and paradoxes of the world's great superpower.

'Readable, full of anecdotes, mini-biographies and arresting juxtapositions. Reynolds sprinkles his text with humour' *Independent*

'Let us not mince words. This is the best one-volume history of the United States ever written' *The National Interest*

PENGUIN HISTORY

THE STORM OF WAR:
A NEW HISTORY OF THE SECOND WORLD WAR
ANDREW ROBERTS

Why did the Axis lose the Second World War? Andrew Roberts's previous book, *Masters and Commanders*, studied the creation of Allied grand strategy; the central theme of *The Storm of War* is how Axis strategy evolved. Examining the Second World War on every front, Roberts asks whether, with a different decision-making process and a different strategy, the Axis might even have won. Were those German generals who blamed everything on Hitler after the war correct, or were they merely scapegoating their former Führer once they could criticism him with impunity?

In researching this uniquely vivid history, Roberts has walked many of the key battlefield and wartime sites of Russia, France, Italy, Germany and the Far East. The book also employs a number of important yet hitherto unpublished documents, such as the letter from Hitler's director of military operations explaining what the Führer was hoping for when he gave the order to halt the Panzers outside Dunkirk. It is full of illuminating sidelights on the principal actors on both sides that bring their characters and the ways in which they reached decisions into fresh focus, and it presents the tales of many little-known individuals whose experiences make up the panoply of extraordinary courage, self-sacrifice but also terrible depravity and cruelty that was the Second World War.

'Britain's finest contemporary military historian' *Economist*

'Andrew Roberts is a superb historian' Jonathan Dimbleby, *Mail on Sunday*